NO MORE HEROES

First published in Great Britain in 2006 by
Cherry Red Books (a division of Cherry Red Records Ltd.),
3a Long Island House, Warple Way, London W3 ORG.

ISBN: 978-1-901447-65-1

Design: Dave Johnson
Printing: Biddles

NO MORE HEROES

A Complete History of UK Punk from 1976 to 1980

– From The Anal Fleas To Zyklon B –

Alex Ogg

contents

Acknowledgements & Interviewees

Iain McNay, Adam Velasco and Matt Bristow (Cherry Red), Gareth Holder (Shapes), Iain Shedden (Jolt/Saints), Keith Gotheridge (Plummet Airlines), Paul (Punk77.com), Joe MacCall (The Now), Stewart Osborne (Grinding Halt fanzine, all-round helper), Leo Baxendale (comic artist and Damned inspiration), Edwin Pouncey (Art Attacks), Richard Smith (Stortbeat matters), Rocky Rhythm (Revillos), Ashley Cadell (Red Lights), Graham Sclater (Martin And The Brownshirts' manager), Dee Generate (Eater), Mick Rossi (Slaughter And The Dogs), Arturo Bassick (Lurkers), Dave McMaster (Protex), Peter Don't Care (Nihilism On The Prowl website), Daniel Seltzer (Acute website), John Esplen (Overground Records), Professor D.K.Smythe and Eugene Reynolds (Rezillos), Joseph Donnelly (all matters Northern Ireland punk), Steve Brotherdale (Warsaw, Panik, V2), Mike Gibson (Jermz), Callum McNair (Bee Bee Cee), Harry (Intestines), Neil O'Connor (Flys), Steve Phypers (Ordinarys), Jello Biafra (Dead Kennedys), Steve Diggle and Pete Shelley (Buzzcocks), Blank Frank (Blitzkrieg Bop), Pete Cole (Aldershot promoter), Paul Denison (sundry Hertfordshire bands), Brian Devoil and Mick Brophy (Trash), Howard Finkel (Cherry Vanilla), Paul Research (Scars), Ian Canty (the excellent Part Time Punks fanzine), Guy Trelford (Northern Ireland punk), Gerry Lambe and JJ Johnson (Skunks), Leigh Smith, Lol Hammond (Revenge, Spizz), Steve Eagles (Satan's Rats), Andy Johnson (Victimize), Fabhean Kwest (Raped), Martin Gordon (Radio Stars), Nick Tesco (Members), Rob Banks (Tights), Paul Aitken (Banned), Riff Regan (London), Ian Rankin (Dancing Pigs), Elli (Stinky Toys), George Maddison (Carpettes), Steve Pegrum (Southend punk), Jack Rabid (Big Takeover magazine), Sharon Elliott, Neil of the Alison Moyet Forums (for help on the Vicars entry), Brian (Grand Theft Audio), Ezri Carlbache (Plague), Dizzy (Detour/Bin Liner), Miles Tredinnick (London), Marlene (Kleenez/Lilliput), Doug Potter and Paul Birchall (Dodgems), Jon Dead Fish (Johnnie And The Lubes), Nick Dwyer (Nicky And The Dots), David Fitzgerald (Southend punk scene), Simon (Heartbeat Records), Steve Pegrum (Cut Throat and the Razors), Ezri Carlebach (Brighton Plague), John Crampton (Woody And The Splinters), Paul and Gary Robins (Perfectors), Matthew Berlyant (Big Takeover list, Undertones fan), Mark Lane (DJ of One Chord Wonders in Seattle, check it out), Helen McCookeryBook (Chefs), David Jaymes (Leyton Buzzards), Ozzie Osborn and Neil Hay (Billy Karloff), Lol and Simon Coxhill (ACME Sewage Co), Dave Berk (Johnny Moped, King), Noel and Charlie (Menace), Roy Jones (Red Beat), Tex Axile (Outpatients, Peroxide Romance, Moors Murderers), Mensi (Angelic Upstarts), Jeremy Valentine, Danny Swann (Cortinas), Rob Peters (Dangerous Girls), Greg Muden (K9s), John (Bleach Boys), Steve Mitchell (Low Down Kids), Pervez (Alien Kulture), Madoc (Tunnelrunners), Tim Williams (editor of Bristol fanzine Loaded), Howard Ingram (Tearjerkers, Detonators), Dave Philp (Automatics), Spizz (erm, Spizz), Pinky (Newcastle-area punk), Mike Clarke (They Must Be Russians), Doug Potter, Paul Birchall, Sean Hocking, Charles Zuber (Dodgems), John Crampton (Woody And The Splinters), CP Lee (Albertos), Gaz aka Jack Frost (Pathetix, Notsensibles), Andrew Nicholson (Pathetix), Keith Newman (Newcastle punk), Nadi Jahangiri and Kevin Perry (Das Schnitz), Harlan Cockburn (Those Helicopters), Kevin Wilkinson (Those Naughty Lumps), Chuck Warner (Hyped2Death), Trevor Tanner (Moskow), Dave Stinson (Twisted Nervez), Simon Hinkler (TV Product), Jeff Parsons (Dead Fingers Talk), George Borowski (the Out), Gary Pritchard (Ralph And The Ponytails), Ian 'Emu' Neeve (Dole), Ozzy Ego (ACME Sewage Co), Gordon Wilkins (Stortbeat compilation and lifts home), Richard Battye (Thrust), Stuart Murray (Fast Cars), Steve Hoggart (Amazing Space Frogs), Pete Monk (Spasms), Declan Barron (Rabbits), Bill Meadows (Gangsters), Jim Bennett (Dick Dripping), Mick Mercer (journo type, all-round nice guy), Diccon Hubbard (Salford Jets), Sean Burke (Open Sore), Paul and Ty Heyward (Molesters), Ian Roberts (Adrenalin), Melvyn (Amps & Bits Brighton), Leigh Kendall (Last Words), Bob Simmons (XL5), Melvyn Taylor (Brighton scenester), TV Smith (Adverts), Allen Adams (Blanks), Richard Dudanski (101ers/Bank Of Dresden), Ed (Hometown Atrocities), Mike Todd (Bacszax), Robert Sandall (Blunt Instrument), Big John Duncan (Axidents-related abuse), Paul Panic (Accused), Steve (Boys' website), Tot Taylor (Advertising), Andrew Jackson (Blanks), Scott at Fodderstompf (PiL website), Steve Shy and brother Pete (Shytalk/Worst), Tino Palmer (Negatives), Kevin Harrison (Urge), George Decsy (Stoat), Nicky Garratt (UK Subs), Jimmy Edwards (Public Piss-Take, Masterswtich, Sham 69), Charlie Harper (UK Subs), Alvin Gibbs (UK Subs), Dave Parsons (Sham 69), Kevin Eden (Slight Seconds), John Bennett (Reacto, Television Personalities), Steve Grimmond (Scrotum Poles), Andy Colquhoun (Rockets, Warsaw Pakt, Zips), Igor and Simon Paris (Take It, Blue Screaming), Gus Chambers (Squad), Paul Gilbert (Jerks), Grant Boult (NFI), Linder Sterling (Ludus), Mark Lancaster (Instant Automatons), Pete Gleadall (Verticle Strokers), Mike and Anja (Ugly Things magazine), Bruno (Rejects/Homosexuals), Faz (The Now), Poly Styrene (X-Ray Spex), Roddy Moreno (Section 20), Paul Tully (Autographs), Phil Hendriks (Stiffs), Col Bennett (UXB), Charles Reid (Blak Flag), Danny Drummond and Tony Barber (Headache), Jim Morrison (Ken Turner Set), Bradders (numerous contacts), Andy Gill (Gang Of Four), Greg Horton (Plague), Knox (Vibrators), Keith Shadwick (Zero Zero), Derwood (Generation X), Mark Laff (Subway Sect/Generation X), Paul Metcalf (Psykik Volts), James Dutton (Interrogators, Subway Sect), Mark Sweeney (Knife Edge), Mark Ormord (Zyklon B), Olli Wisdom (Unwanted), Julian (VDUs), Jeff (Stormtrooper), Patrik Fitzgerald *(his good self), Dave Cheesybits (Smeggy & The Cheesybits), Gerry (Fire Exit), Chris Anderson (Smeggy & The Cheesybits, Midnight And The Lemon Boys), Tony Grayson (Fatal Dose/Looney Toons), Poss (Prisoners), Marco Pirroni (Models), Clive (X-Certs), Gary Willcock (Disturbed), Josi (Disturbed), Mick Mada (affairs d'Liverpool), Paul Codman (Mutants), Chris Anderson (Midnight & The Lemon Boys), Bert Biscoe (Brainiac 5), Pete Lewis (Rats), Andy Pascoe (Cornish music), Lee Trewhela (Cornish music journalist), Mick Stewart (Cyanide), Kevin Wilson (Proles), GTs (Tony Berrington), Josi Munns (Disturbed), Paul Fairey (Amber Squad), Hillary Morrison (Flowers), Pete Eason (Negatives Sheffield), Andy Blade (Eater),.Robert Emms (Rowdies), Clive Arnold (X-Certs), Dave Reeves (Straps), Paul Leinster (Rivals), Poss (Prisoners), Martin Lilleker (author Beats Working For A Living), Jaki Florek (author Bridge Over Muddied Waters and also a member of Shattered Dolls), Doug P (Crisis), Colin Hall (Dansette Damage), Kevin Law (Sussed), Jon Buxton (Misspent Youth), Reg Renshaw & bandmates (Stunt Kites), Andy McLachlan (Social Dogs), Patrick Cunningham (Scabs), Huw Meads (Helpless Hew), Rick Goldstraw (John Cooper Clarke), Tony Gregson (Fatal Dose), Jay Derrick (of the Parrots, for info on the Atrix), Will Coon and Pete Jennings (Beaver), Gav Scollen (Crime), Stephen Gawtry (Excel), Alex Fergusson (ATV, Cash Pussies), Kathy Freeman (Accelerators), Tony McGartland (Control Zone), Andy Arthurs (Andy Arthurs!), Tam Dean Burn and Russell Burn (Dirty Reds), Johnny Brown (Speed), John Fuller (Ack Ack/Adrenalin/Cane), Russell Webb (Skids, Zones), Kev Hunter (Darlex, Epileptics), Terry Hurley (with gratitude for photograph of the Drug Addix/Kirsty MacColl), Nik and Chris Wade (Demon Preacher), Mark Reeder (Frantic Elevators), Jaki Florek (Shattered Dolls), Chris Lloyd (Manufactured Romance website), Paul Martin (Fan Club), Gordon Sharp (Freeze), Adrian York (AD 1984), Paul Sneap (Zoot Alors), Shane Roe (Sods), James Davis (Moral Support), Rob Chapman (Glaxo Babies), Alan Fearn (Zoot Alors), Ross Galloway (Axidents), Gail (for remembrances of Manchester music scene and amusing off-subject interludes), Nick Burt (Outpatients), Steve Nichol (Snivelling Shits), Long Phil (Blitz), Dave Newton (Oxford), Robert Worby (Distributors), Paul Betts (Favourites), Steve Gibson (Sema 4), Lu Edmonds (Edge, Damned), Jim Chapman (Edge, sundry other matters), Darryl Hunt (Favourites), Scott (Fatal Microbes), Roger Semon (and his secretary Falguni) (Horrorcomic), Geoff Veasey (Black Parrot Seaside), Chris Skornia (Cane), Adam York (AD 1984), Micky Beaufoy (Cock Sparrer), Ross Landau (Lightning Records), Andy Higgins (Rox, Blackpool stuff), Kevin Thorpe (Zoot Alors), Julian Isaacs (Auntie Pus), Rob Tynan (Reducers), David Viner (Toads, Norwich punk scene), Pork Dukes (the lot of them, rude bunch, but nice fellas), Anthony Rollinson (Portsmouth punk scene), Alan Griffiths (Apartment), Steve Kennedy (Boy etc), Nick Medlin (Fourth Reich), Palmolive (Slits), Gina Birch (Raincoats), Damon Shulman (Chaos), Cllr Vic Williams (for help in tracing Varicose Veins), John Entrails (Bears), Max Splodge (Doll), Dick Lucas (Mental), Glyn (Kickstarts), Keith Rimell and Bob Peach (Killjoys), Big George (Blitz), Gary Beard (Llygod Ffyrnig), Jim Simpson (Big Bear Records), Mick Dove (Rezistors), Robin Saunders (Axidents etc and camaraderie extraordinaire), Mitchell (DC10s), Phil Perfect (Lillettes, Flesh), Justin Banville (Jets), Barry Clifton (Laughing Gass), June Miles-Kingston (Modettes), Jesse Lynn-Dean (Wasps), Heathcote Williams (Nazis Against Fascism), Gerry (Moondogs), Mike Richardson (Deadkatz), Geoff Shannon (Ask Mother), Captain Sensible (Damned), Henry Badowski (Chelsea, Damned, King etc), Rob Lloyd (Prefects), Matthew Wells (Screen Gemz/Underworld), Howard Devoto (Magazine), John Farrer (Murder The Disturbed), Sue Gogan (pragVEC), Gavin King, Paul Guiver, Sybs (Private Dicks), Gail Egan (matters Manc and sustained encouragement), Billy Childish (Pop Rivets) Ian Damaged Goods, Severin (Banshees), Shane Roe (Sods), Mark Siddy (Pseudo Existors), Matt McArdle (What Of The Night), Roger C Rawlinson (Notsensibles), Mark Standley (V2), Colin Gourlay (Trax photo and band info), Mario Panciera (author of 45 Revolutions and a huge help in fact-checking and proof-reading), John Helmer and Bob Grover (Piranhas), Mark Brennan and Jon (Captain Oi!), Brett Ascott (Meat), Mike Richardson (Dedkatz and Potteries punk), John Clay (Classics), Charlie Higson (Right Hand Lovers), Graham Fellows (Jilted John), David Marx (Aggravators), Steve Harvey (Medium Medium), Denise Duffy (Quark Xpress PR), The Next Big Thing NUJ posse and the good lads and lasses of the Betfair Chit Chat forum, and anyone I've forgotten who agreed to answer questions.*

Thank you also to Michael Heatley for copy-editing and project co-ordination and David Johnson for design and layout.

Photographers:
I would like to express my gratitude to the following photographers who gave permission for their material to be used in this book.
Per-Åke Wärn provided original photographs of the following artists – Vibrators, Clash, Damned, John Cooper Clarke, UK Subs, Lurkers, Chelsea. You can see more of Per's work at http://medlem.spray.se/monokrom
Allan Adams provided live photographs of the Slits, Killjoys, Molesters, Prefects, Damned (original line-up), Generation X, Lurkers, Rezillos, Wire, Cortinas, Eater, Tanya Hyde etc.
Pete Thewlis provided the photos of V2.
Steve Metcalfe of the Boys website provided the photographs of the Boys and the Yobs.
Dozens of other individual band members provided photographs and scans.
My gratitude to all.

Author's Introduction

The original intention was to write a reference work that documented everything that moved in the punk era, and talk to as many original sources as I could, particularly those from neglected bands. In the end I found myself with far too much material, comfortably more than double what you will read here, and the editing process was sadly very harsh. In being forced to curtail the length of the project, I have abandoned any claims to equivalence or balance, and simply gone with the most interesting stories, and the freshest insights, that I could find.

Although I've covered the main stories, I hope my interest in exploring some of the roads less travelled, the DIY cassette bands, the art-pop bands, and some of those who were swept up in the movement from completely different musical traditions, is shared by the reader. As well as telling their stories, there has been an effort to measure such bands on their music rather than their historical reputation. I apologise to those bands that didn't make the cut, but something had to give. I hope that my enthusiasm for one of the greatest, most creative periods in music has survived the surgery.

My sincere thanks to all those who submitted to interviews and questions.

My greatest thanks, as always, go to Dawn Wrench, my wonderful partner, for all her strength and love over a strained couple of years. And to my beautiful children, Hugh and Laurence, of whom I am very proud indeed.

Special thanks also to Iain McNay for his faith in this project, and to my steadfast, loving parents Bill and Marion Ogg. Sue Pipe, Sharon Elliott and Ian Wills have also, in their own ways, helped this book come to fruition. Bless you all.

Alex Ogg

Foreword One

David Marx of the Aggravators

The musical/ideological revolt that was punk changed (most) things within the culture of popular persuasion forever: from identity to fashion to attitude to subject matter to song construction; from hair to language to live performance to production to making it totally acceptable – if not the norm – to have a go yourself. Which explains why teenage kicks, between punk's core years of 1976 and 1978, were indeed, incredibly hard to beat.

Throughout the UK, literally thousands of young bands emerged from an inner-sanctum of former musical disability, only to reign supreme amid a climate of absolute musical nihilism (not to mention free fall abandon). Admittedly, not all made it onto the infamous Bill Grundy Show (or Top Of The Pops for that matter), but whether it was the Clash of London's Westway or the Buzzcocks of Bolton's Institute of Technology or the countless garage bands contained within these pages (my own included), all adhered to the rallying call of "we're not into music, we're into chaos."

An amphetamine fuelled, delirious dogma if ever there was one – and one that remains as equally incendiary as it does oddly innocent and incoherent as it does icosahedronic.

And necessary.

For without said dictum, which (in some form or another) influenced much of the nation's youth – with the possible exception of the ghastly Bee Gees brigade – punk might not have evolved into the quasi-revolutionary movement that it was to become.

Stasis might have prevailed. Emerson Lake and Tosspot might have continued to churn out their turgid brain salad bollocks. And low-and-befuckin-hold, men might still be wearing purple infested loons – for whom the word shag was nothing but a distant ideal...

So God bless Johnny Rotten's territorial pissing(s), even if, as John Lydon, his current-day property philandering(s), are a tad deviant to his questionably regal rhetoric of yore.

But,

What a pose.

What a stance.

What a glare.

What a noise.

What a fuckin' great guitar sound Steve Jones squeezed out of his mighty white Gibson Les Paul (replete with pink jacket) which to these ears (and eyes), was/is as good as it gets.

As influential and important as Elvis, The Beatles and Dylan before them, The Sex Pistols are quintessential to their era.

That said, punk wasn't just about a guitar, three chords and the truth (if ever it was thus). Punk was surely about so much more. Punk was so radical and so cynical and (purists might argue) so ethical and (initially, non) musical – that it suggested and nigh substantiated that all things were possible. Regardless of Class. Regardless of ability. Regardless of divorced parents. Regardless of soul destroying (un)employment. Regardless of the then Prime Minister, Jim Callaghan (RIP), not quite seeing eye to eye with the miners. Regardless of the looming Winter of Discontent (1978/9).

Punk, first and foremost, said yes.

You too can participate. You too can belong.

And we did. And we still do.

Foreword Two

CAPTAIN SENSIBLE OF THE DAMNED

*__PUNK__... what the f**k was THAT all about? Don't ask me ladies and gents. I'm no intellectual, just a humble guitarist trying to get through my funny old life on this daft old planet with some semblance of dignity, and frequently failing on even THAT level as numerous attendees of my dubious concert performances will testify. And what WERE all those bananas doing in the dressing room anyway?*

No, punk rock, like most intangibles can mean whatever you want it to, I'm afraid, a bit like the numerous religious texts and bibles available at all good book shops as we speak. Some interpret the omnipotent one's words as preaching love and tolerance – others that they say gays are evil, wars are justified and women should be chained to the kitchen sink. Actually I can't think of one religion that isn't saying pretty much all those kinda things on a daily basis!

So, are there equivalent differences in the jolly old punk analysis industry? You bet your life there are – depends where you're coming from though. For posh toffs like the Jon Savages of this world, it was all about educated arty types like Malcolm McLaren leading the troops (cannon fodder in Sid's case) into battle to make some big anti-fashion fashion statement and a few bob for the manager along the way.

All of which is a little insulting to the bands and audiences involved who had never even heard of the likes of Vivienne Westwood, McLaren or Bernie Rhodes at the time punk started. Bands like the Saints in Australia, who formed their self-styled most primitive band in the world way back in '74 and the Ramones doing that glorious three-chord thrash thing down in New York's seedy Bowery, well before the London lot had got anything going. And loads of other bands (Buzzcocks, Damned, Stranglers, Skids, etc) who managed to get themselves together quite nicely thank you, without the help of a certain Mr "I invented everything" McLaren.

And you've also got to make your OWN mind up whether it was a) a glorious moment for working class youth in the UK who were bored to tears with a class ridden country and its dead end jobs who wanted to do something for themselves or b) a vehicle for some Bowie fans from Bromley to get all made up and behave outrageous. The truth is that it's a bit of both probably.

For myself, as a music fan in the early to mid 70s, there was precious little to identify with at the time. All that overblown dinosaur stadium rock with those appalling coke fuelled rock stars singing songs about Merlin and Pixies and Henry the 8th's wives and the like – what did THAT have to do with a bloke on the dole in Croydon? Bugger all! So the result was you had a whole bunch of people around the UK jamming away in the garage making some kick ass music mainly for themselves. Little did I know at the time when making that rancid noise with my fellow members of the Johnny Moped group that we would ever make a record – let alone be successful and be bunched together with all these other liked minded lo-fi merchants under the label of punk! I'd never heard of that word until some music journo grouped us all together and yes, it did seem there was quite a lot in common, now they came to mention it. Difficulty getting gigs in the first place being one of them.

No, you had to tell the venues lotsa porkies to get a booking in those days. You'd look down the list of forthcoming dates on the wall behind the owner and spot a theme going on, and tell them anything but the horrible truth "er, we're a blues band" or "we do mainly dub reggae"... "definitely country rock, no mistake!" Whatever it took to get the blasted gig. And THEN, they'd pull the bloody curtain on you while you were playing when they inevitably found out what particular type of band you REALLY were. That did indeed actually happen to the Damned on more than one occasion!

And I lost count of the times I got involved in some argy bargy or other in the street just cos of the clothes you happened to be wearing. Yes, we fought in the Punk Wars for the likes of Green Day and Blink 182. And I reckon the class of '76 probably all deserve medals for bravery in the face of an angry sheep-like public whipped up into an anti-punk frenzy by Britain's appalling tabloid 'newspapers' who dished out the same treatment to the Rolling Stones and rave music in their time.

So, 1976 and all that – was it glamorous? No – scuzzy sums it up better. Did we all get stinking rich? Unfortunately not. Would we do it all over again? Probably, cos at the end of the day it was just so much fun getting up everybody's noses like that, – and the music was pretty good too. I mean – I got to work with some talented so and so's like Joey Ramone, Johnny Thunders and Wayne Kramer, and that can't be bad, can it playmates?

Plus, when you are living under a dodgy so called democratic system like ours, where the individual is more or less powerless and, apart from at election times, pretty much considered a nuisance by our lords and masters in the political elite, surely we need a protest movement now more than ever.

The poll tax riots – now THAT was Punk!

Cheers
Captain Sensible, 2006.

Accelerators

Chris Martin (vocals, harmonica), Graham Marsh (bass; quickly replaced by Tony Doyle), Martin 'Yarker' Smith (guitar), Kathy Freeman (guitar, keyboards), Brian 'Damage' Harcombe (drums)

Formed in 1977, Liverpool's ACCELERATORS operated on the periphery of the punk explosion, expelled from being core constituents as much by the fact that they were way too together and prolific than their contemporaries – playing over 400 gigs in their five-year existence – than by any musical separation.

Marsh was with the band only for its first three months, after which Tony Doyle replaced him. Harcombe was a veteran of the Liverpool music scene, having played with numerous bands including Shop Soiled, who appeared at the Cavern in the 60s. The band grew out of the Biggles Blues Band, which Freeman formed on finishing at art school in Liverpool with her boyfriend Martin Yarker. "We both played guitar and we recruited this dreadful hippy bass player," she recalled to Fancymag. "My boyfriend ran a small second-hand shop in Liverpool 8. One day this guy walked in and bought a massive Chinese gong. Turned out he was a drummer, so we invited him to join (not realising the gong would be going to all of our gigs for the next four years). I think we found a singer in a pub." Shortly thereafter, punk hit Liverpool. "We found our rambling blues jams turning into fierce, sharp, two-minute blasts of hot punk rock. My boyfriend shaved off his beard and I started wearing panda eye make-up.

"We instantly changed our name to the Accelerators and were soon offered our first gig. The hippy got a cold and refused to get off his sick bed so we did it without a bass player. Brian Damage (our drummer's punk name, I was Kathy Apathy) had one of the few double bass drum sets in the country at that time. I just took all the treble off my rhythm guitar and turned it up higher. I guess that gig was my baptism into whatever it was I've been trying to achieve ever since, maximum adrenaline. We played like magic. The audience went crazy. That show as a four-piece was a one-off and we shortly found our first punk bassist, Miles From Nowhere (later replaced by Tony Monotony)."

Alongside Those Naughty Lumps the Accelerators set up their own club night at the Havanna (sic) in 1978, and played dozens of supports to XTC, the Rich Kids, Buzzcocks, OMD, TRB etc. They also headlined above Siouxsie And The Banshees on one of that band's first forays north. "They were still relatively unknown and wanted to get the last train back to London that night." Despite this, the Accelerators only made two vinyl appearances. The first came on the 1979 Liverpool compilation Street To Street, the second their official

Liverpool's Accelerators: "Possessed of a contemptuous and subordinating attitude to women"?

debut, headed by the track 'Pop Guns And Green Lanterns', was a self-titled six-track 12-inch on their own Spiv Records.

While they were regular attendees at Eric's, Roger Eagle's legendary Liverpool punk venue, they were, alongside their close friends the Mutants, one of the bands who never gigged there. "For some reason Roger Eagle never gave us a show. He came across as a hard-nosed business type who refused to help us out. Yet I remember once he invited me to his flat – no ulterior motive – and played me all his favourite 50s obscurities and gave me a cassette, I think it was called Basement At Eric's or something. It included some wild instrumentals." As for the local competition: "The Mutants were our buddies, but we had no time for the rest of them. I remember Brian planning to de-magnetise the backing tapes of Orchestral Manoeuvres in the Dark when we supported them at the Uni. We had nothing but contempt for a band that wasn't really playing everything live."

But for a band that was one of the hardest-gigging punk bands in the north west, why so few releases? Freeman: "Our whole focus was on gigging. I think we had little trust in record labels and didn't devote any energy to pursuing a deal. We did actually release a DIY cassette in 1979 called Have You Been Accelerated? It was available by mail order. Seems like nothing in these days of instant download, but at the time it was quite groundbreaking to sell a four-track self-produced cassette."

It's about this time that good form should require appropriate and tidily observed questions about being a lady and a punk guitarist for a possible new thesis about the role of women in rock'n'roll. Cos there are less than 400 out there already. However, the Accelerators were punk rock, and that should, and did, fly in the face of conformity, even if it was a new and marginally more temperate conformity. Kathy was kind enough to send me a cutting from Spare Rib about one of the Accelerators gigs.

"Our experience of punk has been really bad. A local punk band, the Accelerators, offered to play at a benefit for two people who'd been busted, one of whom was in the women's movement, so a lot of movement women were there. One of the band was wearing a patch on his clothes saying 'All women's libbers are cunts'. The volume of the music was so loud that there was no possibility of talking together. One of us went and tipped a pint of beer over the player's head. She was attacked by the singer, as a result of which she had to have 20 stitches in her face. The band carried on playing and their music became even more aggressive. The other women from the movement left."

The writer then notes, "We don't think that a band with such an anti-women attitude should be playing at alternative or left-wing events." But the absolute killer paragraph follows. "It seems difficult to discuss the relationship between direct sexism and the way the music is performed. Still, we don't think the volume at which the music is played, the aggressiveness of the sound and rhythm and the violence in the gestures of the lead singer are separable from a contemptuous and subordinating attitude to women."

The letter, which concluded that "the sounds and mannerisms of punk rock are an expression of fascism in music and we want nothing whatever to do with it," was signed, "in sisterhood", by Anne Cunningham and Carol Riddell, Liverpool 8. Riddell subsequently became part of the Findhorn community in Scotland, and has written several children's books.

Kathy herself used the magazine's pages to respond, pointing out that the 'Cunts' slogan was scrawled on the night in question, as a result of Brian getting pissed off with his girlfriend getting grief for wearing "sexy" clothes by the local Women's Action Group (WAG). "In the middle of our first number, one of the WAG, Ms Tasker, walked onto the stage and poured a pint of beer over Brian, his drums, and a plugboard. He hit her once and Chris, the singer, bundled her offstage. Some of her friends rushed forward, some of them wielding a mikestand. In the brief fracas, Ms Tasker's face was cut, either by the glass she was originally holding, or by one held by one of her friends. No-one in the band was holding a glass. We later learned that she had to have 20 stitches."

As a direct result of this incident, WAG attempted to have the Accelerators banned from student gigs, and organised a picket line at a Rock Against Racism gig they were scheduled to play at, urging people not to see "the sexist Accelerators". "It is sad that the WAG's campaign has totally ignored the music itself. My political stand is to play a dirty, noisy, rock'n'roll guitar. But the WAG wants to silence the band I play in. What a great step forward for women's

liberation." Funny to think that the term WAG would come to symbolise an altogether different branch of female endeavour in the 21st century.

After the band folded in 1981, Chris Martin, Smith (who had been replaced by Leigh Marles during their final year), Doyle and Harcombe, alongside keyboard player Tommy Moss, formed the Hellhounds, who played intermittent gigs in the city, including a support to Dr Feelgood. Doyle has also played with Lawnmower, again alongside Smith, the Adams Family and Cat Scratch Fever, while Freeman returned to her native London and became involved with sundry musical projects including Birdhouse and Joyride. Eventually she would form psychobilly Kathy X, one of several music projects she runs concurrently from her new base in Berlin. Now, if only she'd taken heed of the advice of Anne and Carole from Liverpool 8, she could be knitting jumpers for her nephews.

DISCOGRAPHY:

Have You Been Accelerated? Cassette (1979)
Hype Machine/Western Counties/Surf Patrol/Broken Promises
The Accelerators 12-inch EP (Spiv ACCEL 1980)
Popguns And Green Lantern/Liberate The Night/Broken Promises/Reason For Treason/Telepathic Romance/This Is Your Life
COMPILATION:
Street To Street (Open Eye OE LP 501 1979; 'Radio Blues')

Accident On The East Lancs

Andy Sharrocks (vocals), Nor Pilling (guitar), Andy Schemmet (bass), Phil O'Dell (drums)

Formed as Rochdale's first punk band in late 1978, ACCIDENT ON THE EAST LANCS went through numerous personnel changes over their career, failing to make the most of their potential because, in leader Andy Sharrocks' succinct words, they were "a bunch of lazy wankers. I kept the band together, all the songs were essentially mine, although I did give credits to other band members, and I also fronted the cash for the singles." The project started out as a covers band, peddling standards by the Stones, Faces, New York Dolls and Velvet Underground. "Then I started to write my own stuff, and the 'musicians' decided they didn't want to be associated with the band. So Kieran Miskella came on board, who was a totally outstanding guitarist, but a complete liability as a person.

"Then Dave Addison joined, who used to play in Tractor on bass. The drummer was called Pete Kenning, who was excellent in the Keith Moon tradition. Kieran and I were really into the punk ethic. Kieran was a biker, so already had a leather jacket and ripped jeans. The other two were just there for the sake of doing something. I really regret sacking Kieran, but I even had to sort out his amps for gigs as he only had a guitar, and that was on a good day. There were a couple of other bands around but not really doing what we were doing. They were either self-indulgent hippies or covers bands. The only other Rochdale band who played punk were Wilful Damage, from whom I nicked the drummer and bass player, Phil O'Dell and Andy Schemmet, respectively."

"Nobody is really sure where the name came from. It was actually used for any line-up of people in Rochdale who wanted to play a gig. As I played more than anybody else in the line-up, the name became associated with me. I think at the time it was believed that Eddie Cochran had died on the East Lancs, which is a road between Manchester and Liverpool, but obviously later it was clear he didn't."

Accident On The East Lancs were permanently cash-strapped. Therefore their debut single was recorded in a single day and released without the benefit of a picture sleeve. They also lacked a drummer until the week before recording 'We Want It Legalised'. The source of their heroic levels of lethargy was inspired, naturally, by their high-volume employment of marijuana. This fact was celebrated in their debut single's title, as well as the name of the label invoked by Sharrocks, Roach. "All my friends were being busted for smoking dope and put in prison for very small amounts. It was a lot different in those days to how it is now. I got a criminal record for 375mg of charred cannabis found in a roach, just as an example, so I felt really angry about it and wrote a song saying how I felt.

"I guess if I hadn't been angry about that, I would have found something else, but I did feel strongly about it, and still do actually, although I don't really smoke any more. But I don't think people should end up criminals because of an outdated law. The other side, 'Tell Me What You Mean', was a Bo Diddley-type riff that I came up with and built some words around, which is the only time I have ever done that. I always start with the words, but that was about young and reckless love, about a girl finishing with her boy because he has been having a good time, but she has too. He doesn't understand how she can say that's the reason. Most of my songs have some sort of personal experience behind them, but I would not say this was my greatest lyric."

Some measure of stability had been secured by the time they recorded their second single, 'The Back End Of Nowhere'. "That song came about because Rochdale used to close at 10.30. There were no clubs there, well, none that would let the likes of my crowd in, anyway. And if you wanted to stay up late getting fucked up, you had to go to Manchester. But the public transport stopped at some ridiculous hour, so you either had to get someone with a car, sleep on the streets or not go in the first place. The song was born out of frustration at this situation. I felt that a lot of kids in out of the way places would be able to relate to this. 'Rat Race' was just how it sounds – frustration at living in a money-orientated society and the pressures which go along with it."

After concluding their career with a cassette-only debut album, they did indeed disappear to the back end of nowhere, almost literally. Sharrocks: "I had a seriously debilitating heroin habit, and I could not keep myself together, never mind a band. So I took off to sort myself out, meaning to return, but never did." In 2004 Last Year's Youth reissued the band's debut album, after repressing the group's debut single in 2001. "Shotguns And Hotshots was actually an album which we recorded in four days. It was recorded while we were gigging every night, which is why it probably sounds like a demo. But it was only released on cassette, which was quite in vogue at the time."

Sharrocks is still involved in the music business in London. "I work as production manager for a promoter in London. After spending 15 years on the road as a tour manager, we have two large West End shows as well as promoting 60s tours. We have done people like John Mayall's Bluesbreakers, Tony Hadley, Go West, etc." He is also making music again. "I have just released a solo album of self-penned Americana featuring ex-Rolling Stones guitarist Mick Taylor, Paul Jones from the Manfreds and Jeff and Tommy Vee, Bobby Vee's sons." Walking In Familiar Footsteps, described as a cross between "Dylan and Beefheart", was released on Lanta Records in 2005 and should be available online.

DISCOGRAPHY:

We Want It Legalised/Tell Me What Ya Mean 7-inch (Roach Records SPLIFF 001 1979) (1,000 copies. Re-released by Last Year's Youth in 2001 with a picture sleeve. 500 copies)
The Back End Of Nowhere/Rat Race 7-inch (Roach Records RR1 1980) (1,000 copies)
Shotguns And Hotshots cassette album (Cargo 1981) (reissued on vinyl on Last Year's Youth 2004)

Accused

Paul Panic (aka Paul Florence; vocals), Martin Hopeless (bass), Dave Browne (guitar), Simon 'Cockroach' Baker (drums)

Formed in Solihull, Birmingham, from the ashes of the Zits, who recorded a single three-track live demo, the ACCUSED played regularly in the Midlands in the late-70s with other first generation pioneers such as the Killjoys, the Suburban Studs and the Prefects. They were members of the local Musicians' Collective alongside the latter's Robert Lloyd and Florence was in the same class at school as later GBH frontman Colin Abrahall. As indicated by the fact that one of their set highlights was a song entitled 'We're Crap', they were not as full of 'it' as some of their immediate Brum brethren.

"'We're Crap' was written," Florence told me, "not as a novelty song, but simply as a statement of fact – we couldn't play properly." They also produced their own fanzine, Stop, Look, Listen, and sold copies of a demo at local gigs while trying to build up their finances for a proper release. One of the songs on that cassette, 'W.M.P.T.E.', was dedicated to their local

bus service, West Midlands Passenger Transport Executive, in the unlikely event that you were wondering.

In 1979 they set up their own record label, No Rip Off, to record the Mell Square Musick EP. This consisted of three tracks from the Accused, 'Solihull'; 'Arrested' and 'Generation Gap', plus contributions from three other local bands, 021, the Undertakers and the Cracked Actors. Peel played the EP a couple of times, though a copy mailed to Prince Andrew, in case he'd caught the punk bug, was returned. They did get a nice letter from the palace, however. It pointed out that "Prince Andrew is unable to comment on the quality of the record...the danger always exists of such opinions of members of the Royal Family being used for commercial purposes."

However, the lyrics to 'Solihull' prompted a ban from the local council, who were still a little uptight about this punk thing. That made further live progress difficult, though they did support the UK Subs at Barbarella's. Their final show, by which time Ed Eccles has supplanted Dave Browne as guitarist, came as support to the Cockney Rejects, at the Exit Club in Birmingham, a show organised by Dexy's management. In the event, the Rejects didn't turn up because they were recording 'Bubbles' for a Top Of The Pops appearance. The band ended in 1980. Martin Hopeless and Paul would carry on with the Damned-influenced Bride Just Died. Browne works in a casino in Miami and Barker is a fireman, apparently. There was a one-off reunion show in 1993. Florence: "I am still well into punk and I am an avid collector of all things from 77-81." He's also behind a new DVD movie documenting the musical history of the Solihull and Birmingham punk scenes and the legend of Barbarella's – From The Home Of The Shirley Temple – The Accused/Square Musick Story.

DISCOGRAPHY:

Demo cassette (no label: 1978) Solihull/We're Crap/W.M.P.T.E./Police State/I'm Arrested
Mell Square Musick 7-inch EP (No Rip Off YAW 1 1979) (Solihull/Arrested/Generation Gap + tracks by 021 – 'Don't Wanna Be A Robot', Undertakers – 'Illusions' and Cracked Actors – 'Disco, Oh No')

Acme Sewage Co.

Ozzy Ego (vocals, guitar), Simon Sewage (aka Simon Coxhill; drums), Pete Barber (bass)

Welwyn Garden City-based band who contributed one track to the Farewell To The Roxy album, and a couple to the Raw Records compilation Raw Deal. When Damaged Goods collected a few retrospective Raw cuts together they also unearthed a fourth ACME SEWAGE CO track, 'I Wish You Dead'. Rumours had persisted that the band was the Users in disguise but these were unfounded. Simon Sewage takes up the story: "I met Ozzy back in December 1975, then I joined his band in January 1976. They were called Bullfrog originally. The original drum and bass player left, and Ozz tried out a bass player called Pete Barber, then I went for an audition."

With a gig booked but still without a name, Simon and Ozzy were returning on the train to Welwyn Garden City from London when Ozzy noted a haulage yard with the legend Acme Trucking Company emblazoned on their trucks. They thus became Acme Sewerage, although that was soon abbreviated to Acme Sewage and then Acme Sewage Company. Thereafter they played regularly at the Roxy and supported Johnny Thunders among others.

Lee Wood included them on his Raw Deal compilation (it's been pointed out that 'I Don't Need You' owes a debt to Hawkwind's 'Lord Of Light' riff but Ozzy insists that this is coincidental and has never really listened to the acid rockers). "Originally we did a four-track session for Lee Wood at Spaceward," Ozzy recalls. "This was for a single but we decided to use them on the Raw Deal album and record more for the single, but this never came about.

Lee came across as a likeable guy, but a lot of bands, especially the Soft Boys, had problems getting money from him. I spoke to Robyn Hitchcock at a gig and we were discussing a demo outside of Raw with all the Raw bands – but it never came off."

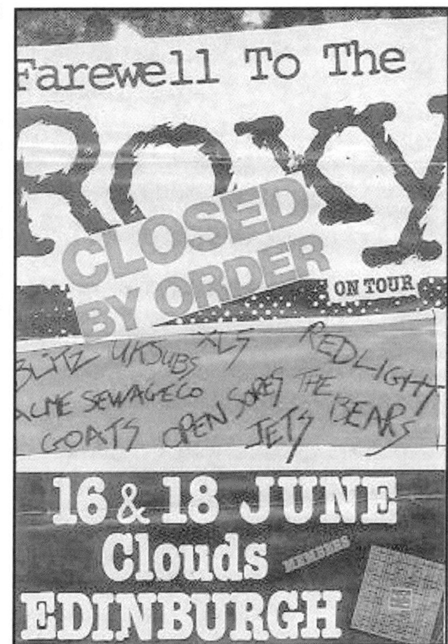

Simon Sewage was actually Simon Coxhill – son of jazz saxophonist Lol Coxhill. The latter was "persuaded" to join them on stage at various points, or "whenever I couldn't get out of it", he told me. They practised in the run-down cellars of Digswell House, a local commune celebrated in Lol's 1979 album, Digswell Duets, and often played alongside Veryon Weston's jazz-punk hybrid group, Stinky Winkles. Digswell House was a decayed Regency mansion and cottage complex which the Welwyn Garden City Development Corporation restored as a base for artists and studios, which were leased to a trust.

Six artists moved in during 1957 and, until 1980, several famous artists would be based there. "My recollections of Digswell are that it was a big house of flats with some nice people," recalls Ozzy. "It was an arts centre full of artists," Coxhill elaborates, "doing stained glass, guitar makers, potters, musicians, painters, all sorts of different people there. I lived there with my dad. He was doing art in music at the time."

And what of Ozz's memories of the punk movement? "I'm not sure if my punk recollections will be that valid, as I did media studies at university and I have different memories/thoughts to the academics! But basically I was a big fan of Lou, Iggy and the Dolls, etc, and wanted to play music in a similar vein. To me punk was a typical teenage thing of dressing different to the previous generation and having an excuse to get up the noses of older people. Bands like the Clash gave it a political focus and meaning, but then the hippies (Crass etc) moved in and destroyed its credibility. From being a way of showing teenage anger/boredom/frustration etc it went to being a peace and love/no nukes and vegetarian hotch potch."

As for Simon's memories: "We basically gigged for free, there was never any money in it. We would play the Roxy and get a tenner. And maybe that would cover the petrol. We played with Eater in Amsterdam and supported Johnny Thunders in London, and Scritti Politti at Hitchin College. We did gigs in Oxford, Brighton, Kettering, London etc. We never made money but that wasn't really the point."

"Pete (Barber) left the band in 1978, I think," Ozzy recalls. "We went for a period using stand-ins and even did a gig in Brighton supporting Throbbing Gristle with just me and Simon. The final line-up saw Simon moving to bass and Paul Walker on drums. We tried a keyboard player for a while, Simon Turner, but it didn't sound right." That meant they left unreleased such nuggets as 'Freedom (Revisited)', 'Car Ride (With My Friends)', 'The Mercenary', 'Everyone', 'I'll Be Your Stranger' and others. Much of these were recorded in the Digswell House cellar and also at various studios including the Edgar Broughton Band's studio in Barnet, at which Lol added saxophone. Their most popular live number was 'Freedom (Revisited)', which, as Simon pointed out to me, is actually only three notes, "but the way it was structured, going from simple to chaotic, was very much what we were about."

COMPILATIONS:

Raw Deal LP (Raw Records RAWL-1 December 1977; 'I Don't Need You', 'I Can See You') (reissued on CD by Damaged Goods, DAMGOOD209, February 2003)

Farewell To The Roxy (Lightning LIP 2 1978; 'Smile And Wave Goodbye')

Raw Records Collection CD (Damaged Goods FNARR 9 1991; 'I Wish You Dead')

Raw Records – The Punk Singles Collection CD (Anagram CDPUNK 14 September 1993; 'I Wish You Dead', 'I Don't Need You', 'I Can See You')

Adam And The Ants

Adam Ant (aka Stuart Goddard; vocals), Andy Ant (aka Andy Warren; bass), Paul Flanagan (drums), Lester Square (guitar)

Of course, we will not concern ourselves (too much) with the Adam who became the great pantomime dame of the new romantic era, nor the unfortunate soul who became so troubled in his dotage. But that still leaves us plenty of ground to cover in looking at the early career of ADAM AND THE ANTS, one of the most dangerous, exciting, daring, and, sadly on reflection, genuinely unhinged bands of the 70s.

Born into a working class north London family, albeit with gypsy blood on his grandfather's side, Goddard's father was a chauffeur while his mother cleaned house for Paul McCartney. He attended Hornsey School Of Art and was hugely influenced by lecturers Peter Webb and Allen Jones, both of whom were experts in 'erotic art'. The latter, in particular, had a peccadillo about sado-masochistic paintings and drawings, imagery which would inform much of Goddard's later songwriting.

It was at Hornsey that he met illustrator Danny Kleinman, who had his own group, Bazooka Joe. Goddard joined them as bass player. Bazooka Joe, led by Kleinman through some 25 personnel changes, included Robin Chapekar (later to join the Stukas, but not the Stukas of 'Klean Livin Kids' fame), Rick Wernham (Motors), Mark Tanner (Havana Let's Go!) and Vibrators Pat Collier and John Ellis. It was typical knockabout art school stuff, lacking any kind of unifying vision with the contributors contenting themselves with pulling stunts and clowning about on stage. They wrote lots of original material but none of it was serious, while covers of the likes of 'Teenager In Love' were rendered in mocking rather than affectionate tones. Frustrated by Bazooka Joe's indolence, Goddard left the band shortly after their show at St Martin's School Of Art in November 1975, which witnessed the debut performance of the Sex Pistols. It was his introduction to a whole new world.

As a result he set up the B-sides at the start of 1976, ostensibly so that he could be the frontman and write the songs. His partner in crime was Lester Square, a fellow Hornsey student. They recruited Andy Warren after posting an advert in the Melody Maker for someone to "beat on a bass with the B-sides." But they never found a suitable drummer or progressed beyond the rehearsal stage (though they did, for a while, feature future Monochrome Set singer Bid after Goddard threw in the towel).

Goddard had by now taken the name Adam, because of its biblical echoes, and even persuaded his wife, Carol Mills, whom he'd married in the summer of 1975, to change her name to Eve. However, there were profound psychiatric problems exacerbated by his inability to reconcile domestic life with his yearning to become part of the emergent punk scene. So he stopped going to college and effectively ended his marriage, though he continued to live in Mills's mother's house in Muswell Hill for some time.

By April 1977 he'd managed to put together the first line-up of the Ants, with Andy Warren, Paul Flanagan and Lester Square. While they worked on a series of songs, this line-up played no shows, principally because Lester quit two days before their debut at the ICA Cafeteria on 10 May 1977. Mark Gaumont, aka Mark 'Kid' Ryan, got the gig and learned the set as quickly as he could.

After that show Adam asked Jordan, whom he'd met at Malcolm McLaren's Sex shop, to come and watch him play at the Man In The Moon, at which he wore an S&M leather face mask. It proved, initially at least, to be an enduring alliance. Jordan would manage the band, and collaborated with Adam on their visuals and artwork, as well as adding vocals to songs such as 'Lou'. They were at the right place at the right time and Adam's schtick, sleazy art-rock with confrontational lyrics and music, was perfect. Stage shows involved Adam rolling around and writhing on the stage, taking a series of blows and kicks while alternately fending off his assailants and attempting to kiss them. Violence was endemic at all their early shows, probably more so than any other band in their peer group.

Jordan secured Adam a leading role, as the Kid, in Derek Jarman's Jubilee, the Ants contributing two songs to the soundtrack (they would also feature as the Maneaters on the Nine To Five soundtrack). Filming was completed with the help of Banshees' drummer Kenny

Poster for the Ants show at the 100 Club in January 1978.

Morris after Flanagan opted to take a day job. His permanent replacement was Dave Barbe, formerly a member of Desolation Angels, who'd played at Hornsea with the Ants. He was in place for the opening of the Vortex on July 11th, where the Ants joined the Banshees and the Slits. His first job was to cut a version of 'Plastic Surgery' for the Jubilee soundtrack.

By October 1977, with Beaumont moving on to form his own band, Johnny Bivouac had stepped in on guitar. He was quickly remodelled and given a haircut by Jordan. "When I joined the Ants I had to be given a stage name – John Beckett simply wouldn't do." There were headlining appearances around the major London venues, and they cut a second track for Jubilee, 'Deutscher Girls'. Jordan managed to get them the first of three sessions for John Peel, who was an immediate convert. But he was in the minority. In a manner that mirrored the Banshees struggle to gain a foothold in the record industry, nobody was interested. The Ants' blend of tribalism, fetishism and a growing reputation for violence seemed to be beyond the marketing ken of the majors. Their May 14th gig at the Roundhouse was the last to feature either Jordan or Bivouac, who left (or rather was pushed by Adam in one of his "spectacularly megalomaniac phases") to work with first Lastarza then Swim.

A comparatively permanent line-up coalesced by June 1978, with Ant, Warren and Barbe joined by Matthew Ashman, formerly of the Kameras, on guitar and vocals. A succession of shows around London, especially the Marquee, saw them build a hugely committed fanbase, though those outside the Ants' immediate circle were more hostile. Certain elements of the music press openly despised them (the pop-period Ants' song 'Press Darlings' singled out Garry Bushell and Nick Kent for particular criticism). A second Peel session was broadcast in July 1978. They finally signed with Decca, resulting in their much delayed vinyl debut, December 1978's 'Young Parisians'. This was promoted by their first headlining national tour in January and February of 1979.

But the move to Decca was not all they'd hoped for. The record label was in dire straits and it quickly became apparent that the band's future, if there was to be one, lay elsewhere. So they moved instead to independent Do It. A second UK tour commenced to promote their debut for the label, 'Zerox', backed by 'Whip In My Valise'. By now the group had established boltholes of support across the UK. Among their hardcore fans were Ralph Mitchard and Susan Wells of Frome's Animals And Men, who established a musical and personal relationship after meeting at an Ants show, and became committed fans, naming their band after their favourite Ants song. "We always got right up front leaning on the stage – usually at the feet of Andy Warren the bass player who was fascinating to watch – behind us mayhem erupted in the audience but our focus was on the stage. The Zerox tour was for us the best – the first time we heard 'Cartrouble' and unveiled the new look was great."

Sessions for their debut album began in August 1978. By October they'd been joined by Leigh Gorman on bass, as Warren committed himself to the Monochrome Set. Live, Adam And The Ants remained a peerless phenomenon, a fact attested to by dozens of bootlegs that continue to circulate 20 years after the fact (see Mick Mercer's comments later). Melding Gary Glitter rhythms with potent imagery about sex, deviance and across the board non-conformity, set opener 'Physical' was rendered deliberately taut and droning, paving the way for the feral impact of songs such as 'Zerox', 'Cartrouble', 'Press Darlings', 'Cleopatra' and the controversial 'Puerta Rican'. Not to mention the anthemic 'Beat My Guest'. A bootleg of their show at the Electric Ballroom on New Year's Eve 1979 witnesses Adam in full flight, encouraging his audience to get animated. "I dedicate this gig to the UK Subs, who will probably retire hurt after this gig (well, did he ever get THAT wrong). And if you like the Skids or Ruts there's the door. Don't come back…Have I made myself clear? They all want to do it like this. They fucking can't…" It was the last time the Ants Mark I line-up would play together.

In an effort to give the Ants a leg up, Jordan asked Malcolm McLaren to offer some guidance. For a fee of £1,000, he suggested introducing Burundi drumming to the group. He also thought hamming up the Indian warrior imagery might be an idea. After a couple of weeks, he decided that Adam was too old, couldn't dance, and had no future. However, he did like the rest of the band and took them to form Bow Wow Wow. Over whom the Ants would have the last laugh, but it must have shaken him to the boots at the time. Apart from anything else, Matthew Ashman was one of the best guitarists in town.

That would seem to be the consensual view of events, but James Dutton, aka Frank Discussion, suggests that the split might have been fuelled by a growing disenchantment with the violence at shows. "I roadied for the Black Arabs when they supported Adam and the Ants at that (aforementioned) Electric Ballroom show on New Year's Eve 1979. They got bottled off the stage by NF skins (the place seemed to be full of them, very scary). Most were aimed at me as the only white face on, or just off, the stage. We barricaded ourselves in the dressing room – there was no way out as the rear exit was locked and we thought our time was up! I remember Dave Barbarossa saying it was the final straw. I remember two of them being in tears at that gig after the Arabs were bottled off."

So just two months after the release of their debut album Dirk Wears White Sox, titled in appreciation of Adam's hero Dirk Bogarde, in December 1979, which in any case singularly failed to capture the fire of the band's apocalyptic live shows, Adam stood alone. By the end of the month he'd started talking to Marco Pirroni (formerly of the Models etc) about putting a new version of the band together, retaining the Burundi format and concentrating on branding a new style of 'Antmusic'. And the rest is pop history. But we shouldn't ignore their final 'punk' single, 'Cartrouble'. Recorded at Rockfield and featuring Pirroni as well as Merrick (aka Chris Hughes), plus veteran drummer Jon Moss on the B-side, it was a fine farewell to the old Ants.

Throughout their chart tenure former fans fell largely into two camps. Many loathed Adam's submission to the pop machine. Others simply yearned for the Goddard of old, dominating the stage, inciting his audience to question, rather than advocate meek consumption. As famous London tattoo artist Lal Hardy remembered in a piece for the Guardian: "When they were doing Dirk Wears White Sox the punks were well into them, and a lot came in to get Ants tattoos. Then the next thing you knew he was prancing around as Prince Charming, and everyone was coming back, saying: 'Can you cover this up? I'm no fucking dandy highwayman!'"

Adam ended up getting seriously burned by the flame. He fancied himself as an actor, and turned up in the Equaliser and Northern Exposure, but his pop icon status was slipping away. He would subsequently be charged with threatening the clientele at the Prince Of Wales in Kentish Town with a fake gun. He'd already been diagnosed with clinical depression in 1994. Things were getting worse. All that was left to him were a series of 80s revival tours, and a bizarre publicity stunt in which he promised to play music outside David Blaine's Tower Bridge endurance marathon (Blaine is a man who truly knows that ridicule is nothing to be scared of). It produced an interview with Lucy Cavendish which, in retrospect, is disturbing. He talks about his leather jacket as some kind of guardian angel. Said jacket contains: "Everything I love," he says, pointing to a key ring of Kurt Cobain, a painted-on Union Jack and a picture of Princess Diana. "This jacket has saved my life. I've been knifed in it, kicked in it, beaten up in it, but when I wear it, I know I will survive anything. I'm like an ant. Ants can survive a nuclear war."

But there are certain things ants can't survive. Like believing their own publicity. That's terminal. Even for termites.

DISCOGRAPHY:

Young Parisians/Lady 7-inch (Decca IF 13803 October 1978)

Zerox/Whip In My Valise 7-inch (Do It DUN 8 June 1979) (there was a 'mis-pressing' of 'Physical (You're So)' on some copies as the B-side)

Dirk Wears White Sox LP (Do It RIDE 3 November 1979) (reissued in January 1981. Remixed and reissued in April 1983 on CBS, CBS/40 25361 with 'Day I Met God' replaced

by 'Zerox', plus 'Kick!/Whip In My Valise. Reissued on CD in July 1995 by Columbia. Reissued once again by Sony in 2004, this time remastered with a 12-page booklet, plus bonus tracks: Physical/Cartrouble Pts 1 & 2 (Chris Hughes mix)/Friends/Cartrouble (single version)/Kick! (single version))

Cartrouble/Kick! 7-inch (Do It DUN 10 February 1980)

ARCHIVE RELEASES:

Deutscher Girls/Plastic Surgery 7-inch (EG EGO 5 February 1982)

The B-sides 7-inch EP (Do It DUN/X 20 March 1982)

Friends/Kick!/Physical (You're So) (also available as a picture-disc)

The Peel Sessions LP (Strange Fruit SFALP 115 1991) (reissued on CD, Strange Fruit SFRCD 115, June 2001)

(A 3-CD box set, working title Young Man Rocking, containing widely bootlegged and also wholly unreleased demos from the 1977-1979 period, has apparently been given the green light by Sony. It will contain sessions from their Decca days, as well as recordings made in Putney, Chelsea, Muswell Hill and Virtual Earth studios)

Bootlegs:

(I'm very grateful to Mick Mercer for the following section. Mercer, one of the finest and most accommodating authorities in this area, came up with a selection of Ants' bootlegs, at my request).

Mick: One point to make clear is that there are many, many Ants bootlegs because the Ants were the first band in the Punk era to have a huge network of supporters. With a long delay in actual vinyl appearing between the Decca and Do It phase, then between Do It and CBS, the swapping of live tapes really took off, and band members clearly made demos available to fans too. Other bands didn't have even a fraction of this trading activity going on.

As we know how powerful and commercially vibrant the Ants had become by the time of 'Dog Eat Dog'/'Kings Of The Wild Frontier', the best bootlegs predate that and provide the historical purpose of showing how they became what they did.

Electric Ballroom 31.12.79 captures them at their glorious best before McLaren ripped them apart to form Bow Wow Wow. Yet only five months later they would come back even stronger to the same venue on 22.5.80, which also exists on a bootleg, showing them to be very close to the CBS sound. The New Year's Eve gig represents better than anything how Punk's power took root in this underground act and propelled them forward. It is raw, pounding and riddled with an angry character all its own.

Chancellor Hall, Chelmsford 4.2.79 shows why the band has grown with no press support to being capable of selling out more large venues than any other band in Britain (often several times a year). It isn't the best sound quality of the boots available but the vibrancy of the songs and the remarkable variety is testament to Adam's ideas. It also contains the best version available of the passionate, grinding classic 'Nietzsche Baby'.

Home Demos 1977 is rubbish, which is what makes it so charming. It's just Adam and longtime stalwart, drummer Dave Barbe, experimenting with chirpy nonsense, and yet you can glean many threads of salacious, often comedic, thought which would then crop up in a meatier fashion later. Contains some absolute, tuneless dross ('Sex Rumples The Clothing', 'Ooh That Max' and 'Sally Is A Brat') but also basic beauties that became standards – 'Young Parisians', 'Cleopatra', 'Physical', 'Zerox' and 'Ruth Ellis'.

Addiction

Beva (aka Andy Bevan; vocals, who replaced original vocalist Steven Pittman early on), Willy Scream (aka Ashley Evans; bass), Blob (aka Robert Leader; guitar), Nicky Rees (drums)

A Cardiff punk band whose only vinyl output came via the Z-Block Records compilation Is The War Over, which also introduced the world to the Young Marble Giants. "This was our first real band," Beva told me. "The first version of ADDICTION featured a different singer, Steven Pittman, who had an unfortunate penchant towards Evo-stik at the time, which rendered him incapable of fulfilling his band commitments, luckily for me! I was recruited as the band was still writing a set of songs. We were all from the Pontypridd area, which lies between the Rhondda valleys and Cardiff and went to Hawthorn Comprehensive School.

There was a very healthy punk scene in the area from early 1977, driven mainly by our exposure to very early local punk bands like the Tax Exiles, who were a bit older than us, in their late teens, early 20s. The main meeting point for punks in the Pontypridd area was the Llanover Arms, which was also where all other musical types went; we all got on very well though!"

Andy Bevan playing with his post-Addiction band Campaign 1

They played their first show at the Drill Hall, Treforest, in Pontypridd. "The day had finally come for four punks aged between 15 and 16, our first gig! We'd rehearsed for at least two weeks and we were ready! Addiction was going to hit the South Wales valleys big time! We had a set of ten songs, which took about 20 minutes to play. The venue was a large Territorial Army drill hall. It was an afternoon gig arranged for us by one of the band's mothers. We should have been suspicious from the outset! Well, you've guessed it, we turned up, pumped up ready to really give the big one and it was a kid's party! The majority of the audience were younger than ten and the rest were mums in their 20s and 30s. Hardly the Roxy or the 100 Club!

"Anyway, we decided to give it a go, at least there was a stage and some lights. By then some of our mates had turned up with a few flagons of cider, it all seemed a lot better after a few swigs of that. We took the stage and ripped through the first five numbers at breakneck pace. I noticed one of the mums at the side of the stage trying to get my attention. I tried to crouch down to speak to her, trying to keep my cool. 'Will you announce after the next song, Happy tenth birthday to Johnny? And now we have the balloon drop?' Of course, I did this, and the room was covered with hundreds of coloured balloons, with loads of little kids running around bursting them, totally oblivious to the noise we were making on stage. A far cry from our dreams of playing gigs in underground punk rock clubs. Oh yes, and we stopped using any of our mams as an agent!"

Things did get better, however. "Due to our age a lot of our early gigs were in places like community centres, YMCA's, drill halls, schools and colleges etc. But, with there being a very active punk scene of our age group, this didn't matter. We soon made the transition to playing clubs. This was sometimes very strange as we would play a 'real club' venue in Cardiff on one day, then a social club or labour club in the valleys the next, which was quite a contrast. I think, looking back on Addiction, we were the real essence of what punk set out to be. A bunch of working class kids, picking up our instruments and doing it on our terms, in the main, having a lot of fun. The unfortunate thing being that it was very short lived. I think in its entirety the band may have lasted about 18 months, although these were very fast moving times and there seems to be a lot of memories from such a short space of time."

He was good enough to tell me about some of those, most amusingly, a 'typical' show. "When venues were difficult to find we even resorted to breaking into clubs to be able to play! Well, not quite. As far as we knew we had been booked, even if it was a vague booking, to play at the Trelewis Legion club. We arrived to find the venue in total darkness, which did seem a bit unusual, but we hung around. We were particularly keen to get in and set up, as it was the first gig after a line-up change, new bass player and guitarist, so nerves were high. After a while we thought, let's go and see if we can get in, it was getting on and we needed to get set up before the punters started to arrive. As luck would have it one of the rear windows was slightly ajar so one of our crew climbed through and walked around to open the side door for us. I kid you not, but within minutes police cars surrounded the place!

"Apparently the club had been broken into a lot lately and the slot machines were being broken into etc so, the club committee had invested in a new security system, which linked direct to the local plods! As you can imagine, they weren't overly impressed and accused us of stealing all our own gear, the majority of which was still in our van. As luck would have it, after a few minutes, a little bloke in his 70s trundled up. Apparently he was the entertainment secretary and OK'd it all with the police and apologised to us for not being there earlier as he had fallen asleep on the settee after his dinner! He was quite a cool bloke because he managed to swing a free bar for us as well because of the hassle."

Other memories included their sole vinyl appearance. "At the time of recording (Is The War Over?) the oldest member of Addiction was 17, with myself being 15 for the first two tracks and 16 when I recorded the third! So we were quite a young band. We received quite a bit of airplay with the songs, on radio shows like John Peel. The track 'Violence' was also used on television programme Something Else when it was broadcast from Cardiff. The track was played as the presenters walked down Charles Street, which was then the sort of centre for punk venues in the Cardiff, with Club Montmerence being the main one. Montmerence was also the first venue Addiction played in the city. Charles Street also later housed the Grass Roots coffee bar, which was a great venue to play and also where Is The War Over? was recorded, on a very basic eight-track set-up. Recorded live, plus one guitar and one vocal overdub.

"There was a very healthy scene in South Wales at the time, led by a number of guys who were in art school in London who were bringing the look and music home with them and forming bands like the Tax Exiles. There were many bands and modern day musicians spawned by these early days, but it's a shame there was no real support for the bands in Wales at this time."

By mid-1979 the original line-up became defunct, "basically due to musical/girlfriend differences". Original guitarist Rob Leader was replaced by Carl Hopkins and bass player Ashley Evans by Sian Williams. Ashley, along with Addiction drummer Nicky Rees, formed local 'dirt punk' three-piece the Intruders, who played locally. Ashley continues to perform as a "one man band" musician/comedian, still with his trademark peroxide white hair, as well as running a pub in Blackpool.

The second incarnation of Addiction played just one show mixing older material with a handful of new compositions. Afterwards, it was decided to make the transformation "into a totally different band". At this time Nicky Rees left to join Ashley Evans in the Intruders. "We then recruited Nicholas Horton on drums and changed our name to Campaign 1 around late 1980 or early 1981." However, Campaign 1 endured a series of line-up changes and, with interest in punk waning, found it difficult to get gigs, although Beva and Sian Williams, who later married, ran a successful punk/alternative night in Pontypridd.

The pair then moved to London in 1983 where Beva joined "Goth no-hopers" Temple Slang as singer. When this didn't work out he formed Flare Up, whose first demo featured Nick Burton and Bob Brimson, both former members of Temple Slang. Burton and Brimson subsequently joined Westworld, Derwood of Generation X's 'pop project'. Brimson subsequently pursued an acting career, notably playing 'Grey' in the Krays. Flare Up continued until 1986. When Flare Up collapsed Beva and Williams recorded the single 'Baby's Blue' as Southerndown, before they moved back to Wales with new daughter Rhiannon in 1990. They have continued to record and play together under various guises, including Cree (with DJ Boz), the duo Salvador and the 'art project' The Williams Syndrome.

COMPILATION:
Is The War Over? LP (Z-Block ZA-1 1979; 'Violence', 'Stampede', 'Seek And Search')
Archive Release:
The Tonypandy Tapes 1978 CDR (self-released 2004) (Andy Bevan: "The bulk of the tape is

just a copy of a cassette recording that we used as a 'demo' and something to sell at gigs. We were only kids and didn't really understand what a demo tape should be, would never have been able to afford one anyway! We also used the tape to send to Z Block Records.")

Adrenalin

Ian Roberts (vocals, guitar), Adrian Stephens (bass, vocals), Mike Farrow (drums), John Fuller (guitar)

Torquay's ADRENALIN originally formed in 1975 while founder members Roberts and Farrow were still at school. They were always the core duo of the band, with various other generally disinterested parties drifting in and out until they arrived at the above formation towards the end of 1976. The name Adrenalin was used throughout these early incarnations. Roberts: "Me and Mike lived opposite each other as kids, and we were into Bowie, Roxy Music, Lou Reed, the Velvet Underground. We then began to like things like Dr Feelgood. I loved Wilko Johnson and that's what inspired me to buy a Telecaster."

"When we started we were pretty primitive. Back in 1975, it was difficult to find people with the same frame of mind, especially musicians. Guys who wanted to play in bands wanted to play Status Quo and Black Sabbath. And where we lived Wishbone Ash were the big heroes. But we were just not interested in that." John Fuller remembers "answering an ad which read something like, 'Guitarist wanted; influences the Stooges, MC5, Velvet Underground, early Stones'. Ian's claim that Adrenalin were the original south west punk band has credibility. He definitely was checking out the emerging London scene back then."

The band's first gig had previously come in 1975, when they opened with a cover of 'Waiting For The Man'. However, Roberts managed to catch the Sex Pistols on one of their rare completed Anarchy In The UK shows at Plymouth's Woods Centre on 21 December 1976. "Me and my girlfriend Wendy went there. It was a miserable night and we were absolutely broke. But we thought, we've got to see this. So we got the train down to Plymouth. It was a life-changing event. The Clash were bottom of the bill, the Heartbreakers second on, then the Pistols. The Pistols were astonishing, but I was more blown away by the Clash really."

A review of the Pistols in the NME had convinced him that the Sex Pistols sounded like the missing link he was looking for. "My head was already there! I was wearing the straight trousers and had short hair. When I saw that review, I thought, fucking hell! This band is doing the same thing as we're doing here, stuck in Newton Abbot in Devon. I was doing an art foundation course and I'd already been up to London tracking down records, Bizarre Records in Paddington, trying to track down copies of Nuggets and 60s garage stuff. And we also went to Sex in the King's Road. The Pistols were all hanging round, or lying on the floor. When you walked round the clothes it was quite narrow and I remember stepping over Steve Jones' legs. They were all like, 'Who the fuck are these kids?' I might have been wearing some uncool trousers. But I did have a Metallic KO badge on, so they were eyeing that up. The other thing was hearing 'Spiral Scratch' on the John Peel show. The Sex Pistols were definitely the catalyst, but they weren't the only ones thinking that way."

Part of Roberts' musical education came from working part-time in Newton Abbott's only independent record shop, Zounds. "That probably saved me from getting beaten up. When the punk scene was going, in the provinces it was murder. The Ted scene was really big, and down in Devon, the grubbies – the rockers or greasers – they were about. But in the record shop I was the guy who used to order all their records and rock'n'roll stuff. They knew I knew my stuff so I got left alone." As he had to order stock for the shop, he was able to fill the racks with more interesting records. "The old lady who used to work there, she was a disco queen. Steve, who plays in the Weathermongers (his current band) with me, is five years younger than me. When I was working in Zounds, he was one of the kids who'd come in with their school satchels. I had 'Ian's punk box' written on the counter. And he and his friends would slip the records out and drop them in their satchel. The shop was the place to hang out on a Saturday. At the time, everyone seemed so focused on moving forward, and this was the way, that everything else seemed like old hat. I just felt as though I knew everything in that brief moment."

"We were definitely the first punk band in the area. It seems silly now, but back then, having short hair and not wearing denim trousers really marked you out. And because there were so few punks, you made an instant connection with anyone else that dressed that way." Within months they'd hooked up with Step Forward Records and entered the studio in the spring of 1977. Kim Turner, later manager of the Police, was nominated as the producer, after he came to one of their Newton Abbot shows. "We did this gig at a sports club, a recreational trust centre, in Newton Abbot, and the punk thing was all over the place. I put all these posters around the town and promoted it really well. I was at college doing my foundation course and one of the lecturers was a blues fan, an ex-communist, who loved the whole punk thing even though he was 20 years older. And he put it on through the cricket club or something, because you couldn't get gigs anywhere. Some of the places we used to play before the Pistols hit the headlines wouldn't have us any more. We got one of our gigs cancelled. 'What's going on? We've played here before?' 'Oh, I know what you guys are playing now! We've got enough swearing down our youth club as it is!'"

The sports centre show was a success and well attended. "Kim Turner turned up with his brothers from Wishbone Ash. He'd also brought along a chap called Lionel Digby, a local entrepreneur. They instantly said, let's record something. We'll take you down to Swan Street studio in Torquay. We'd never been in a studio before. We were up for it." Three tracks were recorded – 'TV Violence', 'No Love (In The Modern World)' and 'Don't Tell Your Parents'. However, the planned release never went ahead. Stephens left to move to London and was briefly replaced by Kirk Brandon, who had been in a pre-Adrenalin school band with Fuller, who recalls: "Kirk had a very obvious original talent that was evident right back to when I first met him at school. Kirk and I were at school with Steve Guthrie who was the original guitarist with Theatre of Hate. So we developed as players together. When Adrian Stephens left Adrenalin I introduced Kirk to the band – but it was soon evident that the band wasn't big enough for Kirk and Ian. Ian split the band and went to art school in London."

Roberts was happy to leave. "We didn't actually do that many local gigs. I just had to get away." While in London he became the singer for Rat Scabies' White Cats, but left before any recordings. Both Brandon and Fuller would briefly join Chris Skornia's band the Kane before regrouping as Pack Of Lies. They then too made the trek to London, abbreviating the group's name to the Pack.

Fuller would later play in the embryonic Culture Club under the pseudonym 'Suede', and is now back in Devon and playing live music again. Roberts returned to music in the 90s as part of the blues band the Nightporters from 1997 to 2002. He also had led another R&B combo, the Crowmen, prior to this. His current blues project is the Weathermongers. As such, he's one of myriad former punk rockers to convert, or revert, to the blues. "It has a similar attitude. With the Nightporters, we were a professional band playing something like 20 countries in just five years. But this time I'd doing all my own songs."

Adverts

TV Smith (aka Timothy Smith, vocals, guitar), Gaye Advert (aka Gaye Black, bass), Howard Pickup (aka Howard Boak, guitar), Laurie Driver (aka Laurie Muscat, drums)

TV Smith had been writing songs in his bedroom since the early-70s, putting on lunchtime shows at school. His first proper band, Sleaze, was formed after he moved to Torquay art school. They pressed up 50 copies of an album of original material to help secure gigs, but Smith was eventually slung out of the band when his compatriots decided they wanted to concentrate on cover versions. "I'd already had the experience of going out there to present my work to the great British public – and discovering that they weren't interested in listening to some teenager banging on about his problems," he told Steven Wells later. "I mean, one time I actually did look up and the audience had gone." Or, as he would later reflect to Big Takeover's Jack Rabid, "It was rubbish, quite honestly. We did our best. We were 17 or 18."

For all that, they did write their own material, though Smith would be ejected from the band when he wouldn't countenance the guitarist's idea of covering Jimi Hendrix's 'Red House'. Still, at least he got to meet lifetime companion and fellow art student Gaye while at Torquay, who was a regular at the handful of gigs Sleaze completed.

The pair relocated to London in the summer of 1976, having mused over the idea for a couple of years, and took a flat in Clapham in West London. "We'd sit in our flat going through the songs," Smith later recalled to Jack Rabid. "She couldn't actually play bass guitar – she had never played it before, and I couldn't play it, but I tried to transpose what I did on the guitar on to the bass. And we didn't have any other musicians for this sort of band, so first we looked for a guitarist and found Howard (Pickup). He was working at a music rehearsal kind of complex. So that was pretty handy, because that meant we could get free rehearsal time. So he was obviously the right guy for the job, and also he seemed to know chords. When I showed him to do something, he could play it straight away. That was a big bonus."

"So we rehearsed, the three of us, for a couple of months, before we could find a drummer. And we were getting absolutely desperate by then, because it was pretty obvious there were now gigs happening. There were a few bands playing around. There was the Stranglers, the Sex Pistols were doing an occasional gig. There was a festival in the 100 Club, in the summer. We were there, and we were going on about how we needed a drummer in order to do a gig, so when Laurie (Driver) came along, we said alright, you'll do!...He's in the dressing room, he's the only one who's got a kit. Alright, we'll have him!"

Thus did the **ADVERTS** make their debut at the Roxy in January 1977. Immediately they attracted the services of publisher Michael Dempsey, who became their manager. Events now moved at a head-spinning rate. Their second show was recorded for the Live At The Roxy compilation. On their third appearance at the Roxy, they impressed Damned guitarist Brian James sufficiently that he persuaded Jake Riviera and Nick Lowe at Stiff Records to catch the group at the venue and sign them for a one-off single. In the meantime, they were featured in issue seven of Sniffin' Glue, whose Mark Perry had briefly discussed the possibility of signing them to his Step Forward label.

'One Chord Wonders', its title originally envisioned as the band's name, followed in April 1977. "By the time I wrote the song I'd been to some Sex Pistols gigs," Smith recalled. "There was that feeling in the air that something was happening. Total joy and excitement. A band could get on stage and say – well, we like what we're doing and we don't care what you think. That was the difference between going on stage in 1975 and going on stage in 1977. In 1977 you went on stage and said – well, I like what I'm doing, fuck you! 'One Chord Wonders' was about what it was like being in a punk band. The sheer thrill of this music going on that wasn't under the grip of the music business. Just creativity and self-expression and just going out and doing it!"

A bruising statement of intent, the song birthed one of the enduring mottos of the punk era for their subsequent tour with the Damned: "The Adverts can play one chord, the Damned can play two. Come and hear all three at..." The Damned, particularly via Sensible and Smith, would form an enduring friendship as they were attacked by vicious 'straights' at such unlikely venues as Lincoln Drill Hall. In its own way the 1+2 tour was a more fun-based and less self-reverential answer to either the Anarchy and White Riot alternatives that preceded it.

Stiff cheekily switched the group photograph to the back of 'One Chord Wonders', which was promptly awarded single of the week status in the New Musical Express, and used a blown-up picture of Gaye on the front instead. The grainy black and white portrait became an enduring image for the band, but ultimately alienated its subject. She, in turn, was subject to a media pincer movement. Elevated on one hand to the slightly silly status of female icon and punk pin-up, at the other end of the scale there was some equally pathetic sniping at her abilities as a musician. However, she would later admit that other band members on the emergent punk scene were generally supportive. There's no questioning the fact that she served as an inspiration to others, and she and TV also took their blows for the cause. Smith was beaten up in Hammersmith by Teddy Boys on 21 June 1977. "Gaye was shouting at them trying to get them to stop," he told me. "We went up to the hospital in an ambulance together, and when we got there I was told, 'what do you expect if you go around dressing like that.'"

The timing of "One Chord Wonders', produced by former Pink Fairy Larry Wallis (credited as Larry Wallace on the sleeve), was perfect – Smith's recitation of "We don't give a damn" underlining the sense of disenchantment and apathy that had brought about punk's genesis. The B-side 'Quickstep' stood as a further testament to that spirit – at the fade out Driver can be heard complaining that his cymbal has just fallen off. The reason, apparently, that its time was credited as '2 Hours 49 Seconds' was due to Riviera's concern that it was "too long" for a punk song.

It was also an early indication that while the Adverts seemed to have captured punk's spirit brilliantly, they were more adventurous than some adherents of the format were prepared to stomach. Lyrically, as well, their debut established a reflective, discerning view of the punk movement that would be sustained throughout their career – TV Smith was certainly fired with enthusiasm by punk, but like a new parent, he was concerned about its development. He wanted it to eat its greens and not get lost on the way home from school. A week after 'One Chord Wonders' the group entered the BBC's Maida Vale studios to record the first of four radio sessions for John Peel.

After signing to Anchor on their manager's recommendation that a bigger label would be able to do more for them, a second single emerged in July 1977. 'Gary Gilmore's Eyes' was first aired as part of the aforementioned Peel debut session. Based on the wishes of executed murderer Gary Gilmore that his body be donated to medical science, it underscored Smith's ability to frame such concepts by using a steely literalism to pull off the gag ("Gary don't need his eyes to see, Gary and his eyes have parted company"). "I didn't know that much about Gary Gilmore," explained Smith later, "he was just in the news. What I wanted to write was this little Gothic horror story where Gilmore's retina gets transplanted into somebody and the guy who gets it reads the newspaper and realises it could be him." Anchor sent them down to Pebble Beach Studios in Worthing for the sessions, as Smith revealed to Record Collector, "probably because it was cheap".

"We thought about getting in ex-Pink Fairy Larry Wallis to produce it, because we liked what he'd done with 'One Chord Wonders'. But we finally decided on the way down to the studio and had to call him from a phone box on the outskirts of London to see if he was free. He wasn't sure if he could make it, but a few hours later, after we'd arrived at the studio and had finished setting up the gear, he walked in with a big smile and a crate of beer. We recorded and mixed the whole thing in a weekend, and stayed the Saturday night in a guest house above a pub, across the road from the studio, where they held a rock'n'roll disco in the evening, so the whole place was filled with Teddy Boys, sworn enemies of the punks."

Top Of The Pops beckoned, an experience that Smith would later analogise as finding out that Father Christmas and the Tooth Fairy don't exist at the same time. The B-side, 'Bored Teenagers', incidentally Boy George's favourite record of the period, was another memorable slice of generational entropy. It should really have been their third single, instead of the mildly disappointing 'Safety In Numbers' (another of Smith's songs to express doubts over the integrity of the burgeoning punk movement), which failed to chart. It was again recorded on the south coast at Pebble Beach studios in Worthing, this time with Miles ('because he'd once sat in on the recordings for Sergeant Pepper"). Gaye exacted her revenge for the 'One Chord Wonders' cover by leaving her bass to stand in for her on the group picture on the reverse of the sleeve. 'No Time To Be 21', the Adverts' fourth single, saw them return to Top Of The Pops, though it soon crashed back out of the charts again.

Crossing The Red Sea With The Adverts was the band's debut album. Produced by John Leckie at Abbey Road, it only scraped into the Top 40, but remains one of the quintessential punk albums – an engaging snapshot of an exciting time. Smith was flourishing as a songwriter, and the songs – effectively everything they had written to this point – expand on that giddy strain of pure energy without resorting to dumbed-down sentiments. In fact, a number of the lyrics were tempered with cynicism ('The Great British Mistake', 'Newboys' and 'Safety In Numbers') but Smith's delivery, and the band's appropriation of a pop rather than rock dynamic, mitigated any sense of world-weariness. The extracted single 'No Time To Be 21', backed by sessions outtake 'New Day Dawning', brought them back to Top Of The Pops. It was partially Leckie's production of 'Red Sea' that encouraged the Stone Roses to use him for their debut album a decade or so later.

Thereafter the Adverts entered a progressively downward spiral. 'Dustbin lid drummer' Driver quit the band, apparently in response to complaints by Gaye that he'd taken 27 takes to get a part right on the sessions for Red Sea. By the end of one tour, according to Smith, they were barely able to bear being in the same room together. His new band the Drivers were not to be a punk band, because "that's all finished!" he told the press. Driver's replacement was John Towe (ex-Chelsea/Generation X), who helped them complete their British and European tour dates. He was, in turn, succeeded by the Maniacs' Rod Latter.

The loss of Driver was bad enough, but the Adverts were handicapped more than anything by the fact that their original punk audience cared little for the group's newer, less hidebound material. Their career thus far had hardly been the most structured. For 'Television's Over' the Adverts switched to RCA, their fourth label, Anchor having collapsed. The release of the brilliant but determinedly odd 'My Place' in June 1979 did little to appease the band's detractors. I asked TV if, in retrospect, leaving the independent scene so early had been costly. "No, it was a vital move to getting the Adverts better known. Stiff was a great label to put out our first single, but we were always also-rans to the Damned, who'd been with them much longer. Anchor really wanted to have us on the label and worked hard to get us some exposure. The result was that we had a hit single with 'Gary Gilmore's Eyes', whereas 'One Chord Wonders' on Stiff had a great reputation but didn't really sell many copies. The only problems with Anchor came when parent company ABC decided to pull out and shut the label down. That left us with the in-house publisher at Anchor forming his own label, Bright, to release the album, which we'd already recorded. When that had only limited success, it prompted the move to another major, RCA, who promptly buried us."

Cast Of Thousands, the group's second album, eventually emerged in October 1979. After blowing the original budget, they were forced to record it on the houseboat of producer Tom Newman, who had previously worked with Mike Oldfield on Tubular Bells. And at times the reduced circumstances show through in the production. So whose idea was Newman? "Also a suggestion from Dempsey. I don't really know how they knew each other back then, but I guess they were probably drinking pals. He was one of a number of names that came up when we were looking around for someone new to work with, among them Blondie producer Richard Gottehrer. The situation was that we wanted to move on from what we'd achieved with Red Sea, and Tom was also looking for a new challenge. We met with him and liked his attitude. Although he'd been working with people like Mike Oldfield, he was actually a real maverick. The idea of working together was exciting – neither of us knew where it would lead."

Sadly, there was also immediate interference from their new label, as TV told Jean Ecoule. "It was our first record with a major label, and they wouldn't let me use the cover picture I originally wanted (the burning war protester that many years later ended up as the front cover of a Rage Against The Machine album). Instead they set up a photo shoot with the band which they explained would be in the dark, beams of light picking out our faces making us look 'mean and moody'. But of course, they shafted us and delivered a cover which made us look like some cheap shit pop band."

A quixotic effort, while it lacked the immediacy of its predecessor there was a huge amount to admire in some of Smith's more expansive moments, particularly the title-track. If anything, he had refined his talents as a lyricist, especially on the touching admission of defeat that was 'I Surrender'. In a few short months, however, he'd also outgrown his audience, and the critics considered the band some kind of unappetising leftover: "Look, we didn't know that punk rock meant having to make the same record over and over again. We wanted to do more, try new things, break out of the formula...We could hardly hear ourselves recording Cast Of Thousands over the sound of the critics sharpening their knives, but it still felt the right direction to go in." The critical dismissal of the record was such that, unlike the band's debut album, which has been reissued at least six times in the same period, it wasn't until almost 10 years later that it got an airing on CD.

Another Oldfield veteran, Tim Cross, joined the band on keyboards for their autumn dates, but Latter and Pickup, who died in 1997 from a brain tumour, had both quit in the run-up to Cast Of Thousands' eventual release. The Martinez brothers Paul (guitar) and Rick (drums) temporarily filled in on that final tour, with their last performance taking place at Slough College Of Art on 27 October 1979. Gaye subsequently went into video before working for her local council. Latter joined Alan Lee Shaw and Brian James in the short-lived Severed Dwarves, then formed the Loan Sharks. TV formed new bands the Explorers and subsequently Cheap before going solo. The Explorers line-up featured Dave Sinclair (drums), Mel Wesson (keyboards), Eric Russell (guitar) and bass player Colin Stoner of Doctors Of Madness (Smith had previously collaborated with Doctors' front man Richard Strange on 'Back From The Dead', the B-side of 'Television's Over'). Tim Cross and John Towe were also members of the Explorers in its rehearsal stages.

Smith's solo work, which it would be inappropriate to discuss further here, continues to be as heartfelt, intelligent and questioning as you would hope to expect. Where others have tired of the sheer personal labour that sustaining a career as a DIY musician requires, he's still out there, bashing away with a joy of performance and communication that is totally undimmed and just a might inspirational. And those original Adverts tunes fit into his acoustic set snugly. "I've always written the songs on acoustic guitar, from 'One Chord Wonders' right up to what I'm writing these days, so it feels right to deliver them up on stage that way. You see a lot of bands using the electric format to paste over weaknesses in what they're doing, but getting up there with an acoustic guitar feels more "punk" than ever to me – it's direct, it's honest, it's high energy, there's no spin, there's no distraction from the message. If that isn't punk, what is?"

He may have learned a few more chords over the years, but he remains a punk rocker at heart.

Discography:

(Buyer's Guide: The Devil's Jukebox reissues of Crossing The Red Sea and Cast Of Thousands are all you'll need)

One Chord Wonders/Quickstep 7-inch (Stiff BUY 13 April 1977)

Gary Gilmore's Eyes/Bored Teenagers 7-inch (Anchor ANC 1043 August 1977)

Safety In Numbers/We Who Wait 7-inch (Anchor ANC 1047 October 1977)

No Time To Be 21/New Day Dawning 7-inch (Bright-CBS BR1 January 1978)

Crossing The Red Sea With The Adverts LP (Bright-CBS BRL 2001 February 1978) (initial quantities in red vinyl. Reissued in October 1981, Butt ALSO 002, and September 1983 with the same catalogue number but in red vinyl. Reissued on LP and CD for the first time in December 1988 on Bright BUL 2/CD BUL 2. Next time round it was Link Classics , CLINK 001CD 1990, and Essential EMSCD 451 in 1992. However, the one to get is the Devil's Jukebox release: SDEVIL 901CD from March 2002. This features great sound, great notes, and a bonus CD of live material)

Television's Over/Back From The Dead 7-inch (RCA PB 5128 November 1978)

My Place/New Church (live) 7-inch (RCA PB 5166 June 1979)

Cast Of Thousands/I Will Walk You Home 7-inch (RCA PB 5191 September 1979)

Cast Of Thousands LP (RCA PL 25246 October 1979) (reissued on CD in February 1988 on Anagram, CDPUNK 102. The re-release on Devil's Jukebox – Cast Of Thousands, the Ultimate Edition, SDEVIL 905, 2004, is a model exercise in revamping a good artist's back catalogue. With a sticker boasting 'As It Was Meant to Sound', it features a booklet with notes by TV, as well as contributions from Henry Rollins, as well as a bonus disc featuring the Adverts' entire radio sessions (well worth hearing), which is effectively the same album as The Wonders Don't Care. And the remastering by Michel Schwabe adds a whole new depth to the sound)

ARCHIVE RELEASES:

Gary Gilmore's Eyes/We Who Wait/New Day Dawning 7-inch EP (Bright-CBS BULB 1 May 1983)

The Peel Sessions (25.4.77) 12-inch EP (Strange Fruit SFPS 034 October 1987)
Quickstep/Gary Gilmore's Eyes/Bored Teenagers/New Boys/One Chord Wonders
Live At The Roxy LP & CD (Receiver RR CD/LP 136 November 1990) (actually a great record. But, naughty old Receiver, this has nothing to do with the Roxy. The recordings are from Nottingham and Birmingham)
Live And Loud CD (Link LINK CD 159 1992) (later reissued on Harry May, MAYO CD 563, in September 2005. This was originally a bootleg. It was also reissued as part of a double set with the Ruts' Live And Loud! Tracks on Step 1, STEPCD 044, July 2002. In whatever version you find it, it's a ramshackle recording, and it's interesting to note how reliant the band were on TV's voice to pull the material through)
The Adverts Punk Singles Collection CD (Anagram CD PUNK 95 1997) (also issued on vinyl by Get Back, GET 30, 1998)
The Wonders Don't Care: The Complete Radio Recordings CD (New Millennium PILOT 3 1997) (now supplanted by the Cast Of Thousands reissue on Devil's Jukebox)
The Best Of The Adverts CD (Anagram CD PUNK 107 2001)
Anthology double CD (Devil's Jukebox SDEVIL 904CD March 2003) (a useful one-stop shop for Adverts fans. Sound quality is great, as is the annotation. The bonus CD is Live At The Roxy – which, of course, was not Live At The Roxy at all. Together with the reissues by the same label of Crossing The Red Sea and Cast of Thousands, this is all the Adverts anyone could want. And if you want more than this, check out TV's solo work instead)

Again Again

Rob Hutchings (vocals), Jeff Pountain (rhythm guitar), Mark Mason (lead guitar), Roger Payne (bass), Mark Broad (drums)

AGAIN AGAIN are one of the less celebrated of the south coast's first generation punk bands, but they did record a session for John Peel in December 1978. They played gigs at venues including South Downes College and practised in a down at heel backroom at Portsmouth's Museum Gardens. However, though generally considered part of the Portsmouth scene, Pountain notes that "We were really very much a Havant band. We had our own clubs, notably the Rugby Club. We supported (if that's the right word!) Boomtown Rats at the Locarno, and Sham 69 at the Pier, but otherwise Havant, believe it or not, had a very lively scene of its own."

Mark Mason was a bank clerk at the time of the band's existence, while Pountain, as he confirmed to me in 2006, was actually a college lecturer. "In 1977 I was a part-time art lecturer at Havant College. One of my major functions was to book out the college record player so students could play records while 'creating'. One day a student booked it. I can't remember his name, unfortunately, he was plump and a bit nerdy, but always first with interesting sounds. This day it was the Pistol's 'Anarchy in the UK'. We played it several times. At first, it reminded me of early Who, but with an added snottiness that impressed.

"A couple of students, Roger Payne and Mark Broad, knew I had been in bands, and shortly afterwards came to the staff room door and asked if I could give advice on forming a band. I replied, jokingly, 'Only if I can be in it'. Fateful words! We used Havant Scout Hut to rehearse and audition singers. After a couple of unsuccessful try-outs a notoriously taciturn, quietly aggressive and loftily uncommunicative student, Rob Hutchings, turned up. Our audition tune was the Velvets' 'There She Goes'. Rob tore the arse out of it and I said something crappy, like, 'Gentlemen, I believe we have a band!'"

Their first gig was at Havant Sixth Form College. "We had about eight songs, mostly original. These we tore through in about as many minutes. Total adrenaline rush, made the Ramones sound like Slade. We left the stage to complete mayhem. We went to a pub about 10 minutes' walk away. Drinks were had! Then the landlord noticed a mate of ours was wearing a 'fuck' badge and threw us out! Havant's first punk 'outrage'! Walking back we could hear this strange noise which got louder as we approached the school. As we got closer it became obvious that the noise was that of a hysterical mob, baying for more. This had been going on since we left half an hour earlier!

"The headline band was the Squeeze Levers who specialised in Stevie Wonder and prog rock covers. They abandoned the stage after 20 minutes of heckling. Shortly afterwards their guitarist Mark Mason (not Mabon as the BBC would have it) joined us. This opened chapter two. Mark could play everything from jazz to bluegrass. Phenomenal technique, looking for something REAL to play. At the first rehearsal it was a matter of telling him what NOT to play. So we became a 'punk' band with limitless aural horizons. It was like a Salvation Army band recruiting Albert Ayler. The sounds you hear on the Peel session are typical, but a bit restrained. The producers hadn't got a fucking clue what we were about, but seemed to enjoy it anyway."

Their 12-inch was released on the Ants' label, Do It. How did that come about? "I don't know how we came to Do It. I guess they asked us. We'd been talking to a few people, just a blur of ageing hippies or Thatcherite tossers, in my failing memory. Since you're interested, Adam (Ant) used to sit cross-legged on the table in Do It, shouting into the phone, "No toilets, I ain't playin' no more fuckin' toilets!' Which was odd, 'cause he was a quite well-spoken geezer. Bit of a 'thesp', as his subsequent incarnations proved. Still, his transfer to CBS paid for our 12-inch."

Several unissued recordings were made at Andy Czezowski's studio in Covent Garden. But for Pountain, it was all about the gigs, even if these were sporadic. "You HAD to see us live. We were either shit or transcendentally OUT THERE, sometimes a bit of both. There are rehearsal tapes of our 'mature' (ha-ha) style, straight from the desk, but they only give an inkling of the awesome anarchy of a gig. To cut an increasingly long story short, we kind of imploded after eight years together, during which time we'd notched up the staggering total of, roughly, 44 gigs! Work was not our middle name. Out of those gigs we perhaps did 15 or so that were staggering! That's what kept us going so long.

"As a footnote, I was in the Moonlight Club in London watching some shite band when I noticed a geezer eyeballing me. After the set he suddenly appeared in front of me. Big fucker. Sod this! Then he said, 'I'm sorry to disturb you, but weren't you in Again Again? I grunt, 'Maybe.' 'Well,' he said, 'I broke up with my girlfriend one night and was contemplating suicide. I wandered into this club and your music just seemed to reflect, totally, the way I felt. But it made me feel that life was worth going on with.' He apologised again and drifted off. I was in between filling up and thinking 'what a twat', but it stayed with me."

After Again Again split, and a few years of drifting including driving a fork lift truck in Acton for five years, Pountain is now back to his first love, art, and he has his own studio in Finland. There are some rather fine examples of the latter at his website, www.jspountain.com.

DISCOGRAPHY:

The Way We Were 12-inch EP (Do It DUN 7 1979)
Beached/Scarred For Life/Self-Employed/Next To Nothing/Co-Optimist

Aggravators

Steve Baker (vocals), Nick Brooker (drums), Ian Doeser (bass), Glen Doughty (rhythm guitar), David Marx (lead guitar, vocals)

Formed in March 1977, the AGGRAVATORS were Swindon's first punk band, the line-up finalised with the addition of David Marx, joining his 15-year-old schoolmates Doeser and Brooker. They rehearsed at the Doeser family home in the Park North council estate. The first original, Marx providing a riff to Baker's lyrics, was 'Easy Lay' (which is apparently still covered to this day by Swindon punk band the Charred Hearts, whose debut album Marx would produce). The collaborations continued as the boys made the age-old transition from fifth form to the dole, taking the name the Aggravators and securing their first gig at Swindon's The Affair nightclub on April 20 1977.

The show was due to be headlined by the Adverts before they withdrew, and they got their place on the recommendation of XTC's Barry Andrews, who had caught them rehearsing. Doeser got himself a scary fly-type skinhead haircut for the occasion, and Doughty gave the band a flying start with the media by punching out the local rock correspondent downstairs. Their influences were a broad church, the Velvets, Dolls and Springsteen on one hand, the new UK punk bands and tough R&B merchants the Feelgoods on the other. Marx was also a committed Beatles and Hendrix fan.

Alongside Subway Sect, the Aggravators supported the Clash on the Swindon leg of their spring 1977 tour. It wasn't meant to happen that way. The Clash were due to play The Central

The Aggravators: Swindon's finest.

Hall, the Cortinas and Aggravators across the road at The Affair. It was XTC manager Ian Reid's intention that they would play early enough so that the audience could cross the road to catch the Clash. But when the Central burned down on the day of the gig, for unconfirmed reasons, they all shared the bill at The Affair, which was understandably packed. They performed before an ecstatic local crowd, in what was to be the highlight of their short career. An impressed Joe Strummer dedicated 'Garage Band' to them at the close of their set. Marx: "The Clash were most gracious to all of us – got all their autographs, and Mick Jones was so taken with my guitar playing, that he signed his as: To David – Hendrix Lives."

There were a few more gigs, before the group's diverse musical influences led to a schism and Doeser was ejected from the band. Meanwhile XTC manager Ian Reid booked them their first, and only, London gig, at the Roxy on 25 May 1977. In an unconscious imitation of the Buzzcocks, Doughty brought along a crappy Woolworth's guitar to destroy on stage. It preceded a five-song televised appearance on local TV show Swindon Viewpoint. Sadly, the tape no longer exists, meaning there is no extant recording of originals such as 'Rock'n'roll Bitch', 'Easy Lay', 'Dole House Blues', 'Hey Jimi', 'Back In The Night', 'Suicide' and 'Tonight'. Andy Partridge of XTC was a fan of the band, and had offered to produce 'Rock'n'roll Bitch', but it never came to pass.

After a handful more gigs, the group's divergent musical influences surfaced again. Doughty and Brooker reunited in the Purges, who featured local Iggy clone Frank Famous on vocals. Ian Doeser put his surname to good punning effect in Ian Doeser And The Posers. Baker and Marx formed the Humans, alongside local blues guitarist Jim Luszcz (formerly of Candid Blue) who converted to bass, and a succession of drummers. Alongside the Jellytots, that meant quite a thriving punk scene had developed in Swindon by around 1978. The Purges, the Humans and the Jellytots would all play together at a Virgin showcase arranged after XTC made it big, but this came after Brooker had died in a motorbike smash, aged 18.

The Humans recorded 10 demo tracks in August 1978 before splitting. Marx moved on to join the Barry Andrews Band (which also featured Dexter Darwood of the Cortinas and who undertook a UK tour supported by Ian Doeser and the Posers, for whom Marx would also drum) and various solo projects. He also soiled his hands with a spot of music journalism while living in New York. He is now in Brighton, and there's talk of him actually recording some material with ex-Aggravators/Humans singer Baker at some point in the future.

Alberto Y Lost Trio Paranoias

Chris 'C.P.' Lee (vocals, guitar), Bruce Mitchell (drums), Les Prior (vocals), Jimmy Hibbert (vocals, bass), Bob Harding (guitar, bass), Simon White (steel guitar, guitar), Ray 'Mighty Mongo Hughes (second drummer), Tony Bowers (bass, guitar)

Long before it became a self-perpetuating picture postcard cliché for the benefit of tourists, punk was ripe for satire. None managed it better than this Mancunian comedy troupe with their 'Snuff Rock' EP, which many at the time believed to be an authentic punk record. But while that EP was themed on transient fame and death, the group behind it actually boasted an extensive pre-punk history. Heavily indebted to the Bonzo Dog Doo-Dah Band, they were formed in 1973 by Lee, a self-confessed "leftover 60s radical", and Mitchell, both formerly of Greasy Bear, Manchester's underachieving answer to the Grateful Dead.

They were part of the collective known as Music Force – which also included Tosh Ryan of Rabid Records – and took their name when Lee, tripping, misread a concert poster for Albertos Y Los Trios Paraguayas. They began by essaying parodies of rock acts such as the Velvet Underground, 'Anadin' lampooning Lou Reed's 'Heroin'. 'Dread Jaws', their first single, focused on the imaginary meeting point between Bob Marley and Steven Spielberg. Rather than submit demo tapes, they would pack Prior in a cardboard box, push it past bemused record company secretaries, and have him sing a few lines. Unsurprisingly, they weren't snapped up, though through connections with Pete Jenner they did get to record at Abbey Road Studios on the day Syd Barrett came in to hear 'Shine On You Crazy Diamond'.

They finally tied up a deal with Transatlantic. Their self-titled debut album was a cult hit with the cognoscenti, but didn't replicate that success in sales volumes. A second followed in 1977, Italians From Outer Space, by which time the new wave had presented a new target – the album's 'Teenager In Schtuck' points the way to their later punk pastiches. The Berts, as Mancunians knew them, had already devised a rock play, Sleak, written by Lee and staged at the Royal Court Theatre, where it broke box office records. Prior acted as a kind of DJ-cum-narrator (he was also master of ceremonies for the 1977 Live Stiffs tour).

Its central plot concerned Norman Sleak, who commits suicide live on stage after falling prey to record company machinations. It featured Gorden Kaye of Allo Allo as one of the roadies. "It had attracted so much media attention as being the next thing after punk," Lee recalled to Heartbeat, "and we played it up for all it was worth. We'd say, 'Oh, yes, there are kids in the north-west who've asked if they can sign up to die' and they believed it! Dave Vanian came every night for three weeks to see it and Stiff had a row booked at the Royal Court for visiting dignitaries."

It was the play that inspired the Snuff Rock EP, released on Stiff Records after their Transatlantic deal had expired (Lee actually came up with the label's immortal slogan, "If it ain't Stiff, it ain't worth a fuck"). Produced and mastered by Nick Lowe in 12 hours, the contents mugged the name punk bands of the day. The lead track, 'Kill', was an inspired take on the Damned's 'New Rose', copping its 'Is She Really Going Out With Him?' intro. The Damned would also, in a wonderful example of life imitating art imitating life, cover 'Kill'. 'Gobbing On Life' spoofed the Sex Pistols tabloid caricatures (they even managed some pretend vomiting on The Old Grey Whistle Test), while 'Snuffin' Like That' clearly drew on the Clash's canon. A fourth track, 'Snuffin' In A Babylon', took the rise out of punk's flirtation with reggae. It was a one-off, but a masterstroke. They even produced their own fanzine, Kill It, a parody of Sniffin' Glue.

Although a follow-up single, featuring the Status Quo tribute 'Heads Down No Nonsense Mindless Boogie' reached the top 50, they then moved on to other targets. The ensuing album, Skite, from the olde English word for 'shit', had some inspired moments, including a version of 'Anarchy In The UK' that was arguably better than the original, and featured the assistance of both Chas Jankel and Roger Ruskin Spear of the Bonzos.

Things could have gone better. As Lee admitted to Heartbeat, "Jake Riviera, when he was at Stiff, took me aside one day and said, 'I think you're hilarious but you're not going to get anywhere because you're making jokes about jokes which about eight people might have heard of.' I could see his point." The truth was they were a highly profitable live attraction, but that never transferred to record sales. They also had the Police support them in late 1978 just prior to that band's commercial breakthrough.

Prior succumbed to the leukaemia he'd been fighting for several years in January 1980. "Les Prior was great, unfortunately he died, but he was quite a star," notes Tosh Ryan. "I thought that stage show was quite good. The whole idea that music becomes theatre becomes quite exciting, that they'd taken it to that level. And the more people push those boundaries, the more I'm interested in them. The fact that you're either pushing a musical or performance boundary, or you're using mixed media, I find that interesting, making it a fuller experience for people, other than just watching a band play their repertoire."

Thereafter the Albertos took Sleak off-Broadway (disastrously – they opened on the night after Lennon was shot, and Lee received death threats for daring to stage a show about a dead rock star in that climate. Lee replied by recording a radio spot in a Scouse accent – "My name's John Lennon, and if I was alive today, I'd go and see Sleak.") A second punk-themed production, Never Mind The Bullocks, was less successful. There was also a TV show, Teach Yourself Gibberish, but the group splintered in different directions.

They temporarily picked up ex-Invisible Girls guitarist John Scott, who would also work with Lee in Gerry And The Holograms and was a member of Bet Lynch's Legs, before grinding to a close, finally, in 1982. Hibbert formed the rock band Heavy Duty before becoming the voice behind children's cartoon Count Duckula. Lee continued to work as a music journalist, writing a stage play about US comedian Lord Buckley. He recorded music as C.P. Lee Mystery Guild and numerous other aliases, worked in alternative cabaret with Josie Lawrence before winding up at a Tibetan monastery in Scotland following a drug-induced breakdown. He latterly became one of Britain's most respected Dylanologists (his Like The Night chronicled Dylan's famous 'Judas' gig). He's currently a lecturer in cultural studies at the University of Salford and wrote an acclaimed memoir of the Manchester music scene, Shake, Rattle And Rain.

Bowers moved on to the Durutti Column, and, shockingly, Simply Red. Mitchell also had a spell with Durutti Column while running a lighting and production company and writing music for Last Of The Summer Wine. White also became a production manager. Harding and Bowers also reunited briefly as the Mothmen.

Though their dalliance with punk may not have been conventional, 'Kill' at least has become something of a genre classic. It's been covered by Chaos UK, GBH and Scottish band the Real Mackenzies, who are wont to change the title to 'Kilt'. I'm not sure a couple of those bands are necessarily in on the joke...

DISCOGRAPHY:

Dread Jaws/De Version 7-inch (Transatlantic BIG 541 April 1976)
Alberto Y Lost Trios Paranoias LP (Transatlantic TRA 316 May 1976) (reissued on CD by D-Line 9.00554)
Italians From Outer Space LP (Transatlantic TRA 349 July 1977) (reissued on CD by D-Line 9.00776)
Snuff Rock 7-inch EP (Stiff LAST 2 September 1977)
Kill/Snuffin' In A Babylon/Gobbin' On Life/Snuffin' Like That (also released as a 100-copy promo 12-inch, DJ 1 EP, in handmade sleeve with invitation to Sleak)
Old Trust/Neville/Teenager In Schtuck 7-inch (Logo GO 106 November 1977)
Heads Down No Nonsense Mindless Boogie/Thank You (Logo GO 323 September 1978) (with free single, Fk You/Dead Meat Part II, Logo GO 335)**
Skite LP (Logo 1009 September 1978) (reissued on CD by D-Line 9.00779)
*****k You/Dead Meat Part 2 7-inch (Logo GO 335 November 1978)**
Juan Lopez/Teenage Paradise/Dead Meat Part 3 7-inch (Logo GO GO 340 December 1978)
Cruising With Santa 7-inch (New Hormones ORG 30 December 1982)
ARCHIVE RELEASES:
Worst Of The Berts LP (Logo MOGO 4008 July 1980)
Death Of Rock'n'roll LP (Mocambo, Canada, 1980) (obscure Canadian release)
Snuff Rock: The Best Of The Albertos (Mau Mau/Demon 1991) (31-track career summary)
Radio Sweat CD (Overground OVER56 CD February 1997)
Mandrax Sunset Variations dbl CD (Sanctuary Records CMDDD115 January 2001) (the three studio albums spread over two CDs. A helluva lorra laughs for about a tenner)

Alien Kulture

Pervez (vocals), Zaf (bass), Jonesy (guitar), Azhar (drums)

The way in which Asians were 'excluded' from punk, while the black community was ostensibly celebrated, was the subject of recent discussions in both the So What? academic compendium and the book Disorientating Rhythms. As a band featuring three Indians and a Welshman – or the token white bloke as he became known – ALIEN KULTURE stood pretty much alone in offering an Asian insight into the growth of the punk phenomenon.

As Pervez confirmed to me, the reasons for Alien Kulture's formation were explicitly political and directly addressed the visibility of Asians within the punk movement. "The germ of the 'idea' of Alien Kulture began in a coffee house in Wimbledon where the band members were bemoaning the lack of British Asians at gigs, the lack of involvement in politics and the general introspection of British Asians. The time was the height of the Thatcher goverment, the rise of the National Front, the killing of British Asians on British streets, riots in Southall (the main Asian immigrant area in Greater London) and the rise of anti-racist organisations such as Rock Against Racism and the Anti-Nazi League. We, along with friends, had picketed National Front election meetings at times outside London. We had also attended and organised numerous Rock Against Racism gigs and throughout this period saw very few Asian faces. We felt, as Asians, that more could be done by ourselves, for ourselves."

The idea evolved quickly. "During our chat at the coffee shop we initially decided to organise some sort of Asian political organisation for Asian youth, but this idea was quickly shelved as there needed to be something to make the idea more attractive to get people involved. The second and better idea was to start up a group. The idea was good. However, it was impractical, as we did not really know how to play instruments or to write songs. We decided to employ the Desperate Bicycles approach – "it was easy, it was quick, go and do it." We did not realise at the time we would be the first group of this kind and the impact this would have."

"The idea of Alien Kulture would be two-fold – firstly, to attract more Asian kids to gigs/politics and secondly to inform the general white population throughout the country that, as second generation Asians, we 'had arrived', and for them to learn something about us through our songs." 'Ratskank' attacked the Conservative Party, 'Airport Arrest' was about the problems of entering the country and 'Heavy Burden' concerned the supposed benefits of colonialism. 'Behind The Mask', discussed issues around the veil and 'Arranged Marriage' was self-explanatory. 'Siege And Turmoil' was a prescient examination of the rise of Muslim fundamentalism while 'Culture Crossover' was about the problems of "living within two cultures". 'Heavy Manners', meanwhile, was a love song.

These were issues that were simply not being addressed in music elsewhere. "At the time, there was only one prominent Asian musician in this country and he was producing disco music for the masses. We wanted our music to be agit prop and aggressive front-line punk – an image one did not associate with 'mild-mannered' and respectful Asians who only knew how to be subservient and run corner shops. We wanted to be right in people's faces. We wanted/needed to prove that essentially there was no difference between white, black or Asian youth in the England of 1979. However, there was the added pressure of being what our parents wanted us to be, marry who they wanted us to marry etc."

Audiences picked up on what they were trying to get across quickly. "Due to our connections through the anti-racist network, the news of Alien Kulture forming spread very quickly and we had got our fist gig (in Oxford) before we had written any songs. By the time of the gig we had managed to write several songs and practice some covers (e.g. the Clash's 'Garageland'). At the gig we were well received, and it gave us the confidence to go on. Within two months we had secured a spot on television for the BBC. In addition to the normal gigs we also played at the head of a demonstration (attended by 80,000) against the Immigration Bill being pushed through Parliament that year, in addition to other unusual gigs. Six months after forming, two band members had been elected on the National Central Committee of Rock Against Racism and one member was on the committee of Youth Against Nazis (the junior association of the Anti-Nazi League)."

The group's only vinyl release was the double a-side, 'Asian Youth'/'Culture Crossover' for Rock Against Racism in 1980. John Peel spent a full minute introducing the group and record before playing it. But with that release the band had effectively achieved everything it had set out to. "We finally called it a day a year and a half after forming, having achieved our aims. Asians had started turning up to our gigs, we had got our message across (about Asians) to the home population via national radio and television. We had even managed to get noticed by the fascist parties who had written about us in their newspapers and even trashed one of our gigs. Our following was a complete cross-section of society from Asians to punks, skinheads, anarchists and even converts from the ranks of the fascist organisations. The final postscript was that by the time we had broken up, we heard about Asian punk groups in Luton, Birmingham and Bradford."

DISCOGRAPHY:

Asian Youth/Culture Crossover 7-inch (London Rock Against Racism LRAR1 1980)

Alternative TV

Mark Perry (vocals), Alex Fergusson (guitar), Tyrone Thomas (bass), John Towe (drums)

Perry, Deptford's most influential but wayward son, was a music and football obsessive as a boy, but decided against pursuing a career in the former sphere due to 'dodgy ankles'. With a frankness that would typify his later adventures, and no hint of revisionism, he doesn't mind admitting that in the mid-70s his boat was rocked by ELP and AC/DC. However, after he'd seen the Ramones on the advice of Nick Kent, he subsequently fully immersed himself in the early punk scene via his editorship of Sniffin' Glue, launched in July 1976.

Sniffin' Glue was the most important independent source of news and opinion on the rapidly developing London scene. Enthused, he didn't remain long in his post as a bank clerk, and did his best to help his fellow travellers gain a foothold in the industry. Had he ever had the desire to put a band together, enquired Tony Parsons in February 1977. "Yeah, but it's too much trouble rehearsing and practising and all that shit..." However, he was quicker than most to sense that the vibrant punk scene of 1976 was beginning to turn inwards, and attract the sort of people who lacked the creative vision of its originators. So he did, in the end, elect to start his own band.

His first attempt to do so was, quite gallantly, entitled the New Beatles. It was late 1976 and his initial compatriots were fellow writer Steve Walsh, who'd been a fleeting member of Flowers Of Romance and would later form Manicured Noise, and Tyrone Thomas, a guitarist from south London. They specialised in "a version of 'Roadrunner' as played by

Alternative TV live on stage with punk's first media voice Mark Perry

Blue Oyster Cult." It lasted a couple of weeks and a similar number of rehearsals.

Thereafter he met Alex Fergusson after he'd travelled down from Glasgow to check out the emerging punk scene. He was introduced to Perry at the Roxy in February by his former Nobodies bandmate Sandy Robertson, soon to become a Sounds stringer. They began rehearsing a clutch of songs they'd written together, alongside Genesis P-Orridge of Throbbing Gristle. "We rehearsed at Genesis P-Orridge's studio (in Martello Street, Hackney)," Perry later told Jason Gross, "did a lot of work with him and he helped us. Once we saw we could do this, we did our first gig in May 1976 (at a punk festival in Nottingham). We did a couple of Roxy dates. By that time, I thought 'Oh, that's what I want to do.' It was just coming up to the 12th issue (of Sniffin' Glue)." Those rehearsals in TG's Industrial Studios would be posthumously released as the Industrial Sessions 1977.

The line-up for the band's inaugural gig in Nottingham featured the sole appearance by bass player Micky Smith, as well as Chelsea/Generation X drummer John Towe. **ALTERNATIVE TV**'s first 'proper' line-up saw Perry, Fergusson and Towe joined by bass player Tyrone Thomas in the summer of 1977. They cut a demo featuring four of Perry's most enduring compositions, 'How Much Longer', 'You Bastard', 'Love Lies Limp' and 'Life', after interest was expressed by EMI, though they rejected the results as too political and non-commercial.

Later, Perry would recall that it was Miles Copeland who had pushed the EMI interest, and that he and the rest of the band had simply indulged in making the best use of the major's high-tech studios and largesse. "We're all cocky," Perry recalled to Jack Rabid, "having a great time, hanging around Manchester Square, hanging off the balcony trying to be the Beatles." In fact, Perry was having such fun he insisted on inserting swear words on three of the four recordings just to make sure that EMI weren't actually going to bite. But EMI let them keep the tapes, which provided the basis for the first two ATV singles. Towe left shortly after the EMI sessions to form Strategem, a precursor to Rage, with Chris Bennett taking his place.

Instead of EMI Perry would launch Alternative TV on Deptford Fun City Records, a quasi-subsidiary of Step Forward. Deptford Fun City had originally been inaugurated for Squeeze to A&R before they jumped ship to A&M. ATV made its debut when 'Love Lies Limp' was attached to an August 1977 issue of Sniffin' Glue. A typically frank exposition on the sex wars, with its protagonist the eternal loser lolled into submission by a reggae backbeat, it established Perry's conversational, emotionally unfiltered vocal style. "I don't care who I go to bed with/Male or female, there's never any incentive." This was John Lydon's dismissal of lovemaking as 'three minutes of squelching' underscored.

Henry Badowski, then playing bass for Chelsea, saw all this unfold. "Chelsea were managed by Miles Copeland who had hired Mark Perry as his 'punk guru'. Mark had a free hand in signing bands and was also running Sniffin' Glue operations from Miles' office. We seemed to spend a lot of time in the office. Mark was a true inspiration and I found his 'here's a chord…' Sniffin' Glue summed up the spirit of the time for me. I'd always been intrigued by the role of the non-musician in music and Mark fascinated me. The combination of the ordinary geezer combined with inspired visionary was very appealing. I wanted to be in ATV like mad!" He would much later get his wish, in part, by playing drums for Mark Perry's Good Missionaries for a UK tour.

After the group's debut single proper, 'How Much Longer', Perry's prescient, bleak critique of the punk explosion, he parted company with Fergusson and Thomas, who quit after rows with Perry following their 1977 tour with John Cale (set up because Copeland was the latter's booking agent). Dennis Burns arrived on bass while Perry handled guitar himself. "I chucked Alex Fergusson out of the band," Perry later explained in the sleevenotes to the band's Best Of CD, "a move which shocked a lot of people at the time because he contributed most of the music. It was a difficult period but I felt that I knew enough about music to be able to write my own with the help of the other lads in the band. Although I respected Alex's musical prowess, I found him very difficult to work with at the time, which was as much my fault as it was his." Fergusson would go on to the Cash Pussies and Psychic TV, as well as production for everyone from the Go-Betweens and Orange Juice to Gaye Bykers On Acid, but would also crop up periodically in the ATV story.

'Life After Life' featured Jools Holland on the ivories with additional guitar from the late Kim Turner. Later the Police's road manager and producer to Menace and the Wasps among

others, he had originally made the Copeland connection as tour manager of the Cortinas, and before that had played in Andy Fraser (of Free)'s solo band. 'Action Time Vision' was another quintessential ATV moment, restating the 'one chord wonders' mantra of the Adverts – "chords and notes don't mean a thing".

ATV's debut album was a fascinating document of punk at its 1978 crossroads. Recorded in early 1978, it mixed studio material with snippets of broadcasts about the punk phenomenon and live excerpts from a show at the 100 Club in February. The idea of mixing live and studio tracks came from Perry's love of Frank Zappa. Many of the lyrics explored the divide between the optimism and reality of what had unfolded. It was intelligent, untutored but extremely engaging. And, as with every successive ATV release, profoundly humane and unapologetically emotional.

The album opened with 'Alternatives', in which Perry invited his audience to join him on stage and have their say. Typically of Perry and ATV, it's the kind of a bold experiment that only succeeds as a covenant of failure. It would have been easy for a band to commit such an exercise to vinyl had it been an obvious success. It wasn't, it was a glorious failure. Yet ATV still used it to introduce their debut album. Perry's earnestness is painful at times. But there were also purely musical successes. The guitar sound on the album closer 'Splitting In Two' is one of the most startling things I've heard both within and without punk.

Thereafter ATV embarked on a series of free concerts alongside hippy stalwarts Here And Now, with guitarist Mark Lineham joining the line-up. What You See Is What You Are was issued as a budget document of events, which were specifically intended to try to unite hippies and punks. It was a confusing and messy thing to do – though Perry's disillusioment with the status quo is made clear by the rewritten 'Action Time Lemon'. It upset purists. And it was very much in keeping with Perry's modus operandi, as he confirmed to Jason Gross. "When we played with Here and Now later on, it was almost like the most obvious thing to do. Why nobody did it before, God knows. The fact that these hippies were playing free gigs, that was totally punk, isn't it? Playing for the people, you know? That's what it was about. A punk was someone who said 'I don't want to be the same as everyone else. I want to make my own statement, I want to ask questions.'"

The tour was certainly an enriching experience, despite Miles Copeland being mortified by it, as Perry confirmed to Big Takeover. "We got on their (Here And Now's) big tour bus, which was a big coach converted with all these beds. It was fucking wild. It was incense everywhere and fucking and Indian rugs, Saris as curtains. All these hippie girls pissing in the street and breastfeeding their babies. And there were us punks in there. We got to play Stonehenge festival when it was like just a field, a generator, and a stage. No rip-off burger joints. No packaged New Age culture. None of that bollocks! Just good British hippydom. Which means a bunch of scruffy, dirty, bean-burger-eating, spliff-making hippies, and, in the middle, a bunch of Hell's Angels. It was great for us. It was a real eye-opener." Thereafter Perry and Bennett fell out over musical direction, Bennett still being welded to the idea of a more conventional rock aesthetic, resulting in the cancellation of an American tour that Miles Copeland had booked.

If Perry was aghast at the way punk was mutating, punk audiences were growing suspicious of ATV's development, as he told Tony Fletcher of Jamming, in 2001. "I always remember our bassist Dennis Burns, backstage after a gig. All through the set they were shouting for the old songs, and we were about not playing the old songs. We were going to move on, so we would play a song like 'Fellow Sufferer 'or 'Vibing Up The Senile Man', or 'Nasty Little Lonely' even, and people were just calling for 'You Bastard'. I remember our bassist getting off the stage and saying, 'Mark, I don't think I can do this any more, I just hate our audience.' And it's horrible for a band to feel that."

Continuing as a trio, ATV's next release was the perplexing Vibing Up The Senile Man, on which the perpetually restless Perry started to incorporate African influences, notably on 'The Good Missionary'. Though Perry's attitude and spirit of adventure is beyond question, the contents were just a little too aimless this time. Certainly those clinging to the idea that ATV could continue as a straightahead punk band were in for a big shock. But that was it – after Perry was bottled off stage at a show in Derby, he decided to draw a line under ATV and instead played the remaining live commitments as the Good Missionaries. "I felt betrayed when they all had a go at me," he later told Andrew Cowen. "It became a bad scene. I was touring with the Pop Group in early 1979 and at a gig in Derby, half the audience were punks and half were skinheads. A battle started and that was the end of it for me." ATV's final single for Deptford Fun City, 'The Force Is Blind', made clear his dissatisfaction with the turn of events.

He recorded a solo album, Snappy Turns, in 1980 and also worked with the Lemon Kittens and his pet side project, the Door And The Window. However, ATV reunited in 1981 at the suggestion of Miles Copeland, with Perry and Burns, and a reconciled Fergusson, joined by Alan Gruner on keyboards and Ray Weston on drums. Miles Copeland, legendarily, had become frustrated by Perry's indulgences and excesses and wanted a pop album. "He thought I'd flipped," Perry later recalled. Strange Kicks, as long-term Perry watchers may have predicted, explored an entirely different musical vista. Most of the songs, produced by Richard Mazda, were built around solid pop foundations, and there were recreations of several former ATV favourites.

However forced this album may have been due to Copeland's intervention, it still stands up well. Perry will never be a conventional pop singer. But he didn't sound completely lost in this environment, in which, he would later admit, he basically only provided lyrics and vocals and didn't involve himself in any musical aspects of the songwriting. However, the reunion was not permanent. Perry and Fergusson fell out again, nixing yet another proposed US tour. Miles Copeland was in clover due to the breakthrough of the Police and had lost interest in Perry, once the apple of his eye.

"By 1981, I was finished," Perry told Tony Fletcher. "I thought I would never play music again. I was happy it was over. I was going to become a nurse. I got together with someone who wasn't particularly interested in music. We bought a flat in Blackheath. I was doing an English Literature A-Level at night school." Perry has, nevertheless, reactivated the band on numerous occasions since. The second reunion came in 1984, though no recordings emerged, and then again two years later, with Allison Phillips and Steve Cannell on board. This line-up produced two 12-inch singles and an album, Peep Show. Probably the band's second most accessible LP, Perry's declamatory style is sweetened to a large extent by extensive use of horns and keyboards. Naturally, it doesn't sound like anything else in his canon, but you had to expect that by now.

My Life As A Child Star, released in 1994 but originally recorded in 1991, was effectively a Mark Perry solo detour using the ATV marque. It's one of his most personal collections, a fact driven home by the fact that daughter Laura appears on 'Reunion'. ATV returned in 1995 to play a punk festival in Bath and began to restore some of their more traditional punk choons to the set. A year later Perry provided the text for Erica Echenberg's photographic book, And God Created Punk, before Sanctuary released the full reprint of Sniffin' Glue in 2000. In the meantime he released Punk Life for Overground in 1997. While it suffered slightly, as do many ATV albums, from an irreconcilable smorgasbord of styles, there was plenty here to be welcomed, including the trip-hoppy 'Guntai Wa Moumoku'.

Apollo, released on Overground in 1999, built on ATV's resurgence. In interviews Perry described it as his most cohesive album since The Image Has Cracked, but to be fair, ATV has never been much about cohesion. Standouts included 'Politics In Every Sausage', while the band was filled out with the addition of Luci Bacchino on guitar and Rob Ugly on bass. Longstanding fan Roddy Frame of Aztec Camera also made a guest appearance on the title-track and 'Propaganda'. That first trip to America finally arrived in January 2001, set up by Tony Barber of the Buzzcocks who also played bass, including an appearance at Punk Magazine's anniversary party at CBGB's (original bass player Tyrone Thomas switched to guitar). It resulted in yet another live CD and some rave notices for long-standing American fans of the band who had been deprived of seeing Perry live for two and a half decades.

DISCOGRAPHY:

(Buyer's Guide: ATV's discography is a complex one. But you won't go too far wrong by starting with The Image Has Cracked or the Action Time Vision career summary. Strange Kicks has aged well and the youngster of the litter, Apollo, looks like it may do so in time. Some of the more esoteric archive releases in the late 90s are for hardcore fans only, but Radio Sessions is a must)

Love Lies Limp 7-inch flexidisc (Sniffin' Glue SG 12 September 1977)
(free with Sniffin' Glue 12)

How Much Longer/You Bastard 7-inch (Deptford Fun City DFC 002 November 1977) (issued in two versions. The second issue as 'alternative versions' on the labels. These versions feature more prominent, overdubbed guitar)

Life After Life/Life After Dub 7-inch (Deptford Fun City DFC 04 May 1978)

The Image Has Cracked LP (Deptford Fun City DLP 01 May 1978) (reissued on CD by Anagram, CDPUNK 24 in February 1994 as The Image Has Cracked – The Alternative TV Collection, with bonus tracks: Love Lies Limp/Life/How Much Longer?/You Bastard/Another Coke/Life After Life/Life After Dub/The Force Is Blind/Lost In A Room/How Much Longer (Different Version)/You Bastard (Different Version). A stunning collection)

Action Time Vision/Another Coke 7-inch (Deptford Fun City DFC 07 June 1978)

Life/Love Lies Limp 7-inch (Deptford Fun City DFC 06 November 1978)

What You See Is What You Are LP (Deptford Fun City DLP 02 December 1978) (shared with Here And Now. First three tracks by the latter)

Vibing Up The Senile Man (Part 1) LP (Deptford Fun City DLP 03 December 1978) (reissued on CD by Anagram, CDMGRAM 102, as Vibing Up The Senile Man – The Second ATV Collection in 1996, with bonus tracks: Vibing Up The Senile Man/Action Time Lemon/Going Round In Circles/Fellow Sufferer/Splitting In Two/Another Coke/The Body/The Force Is Blind/Fellow Sufferer In Dub). Has the huge advantage of letting you hear the tracks from the What You See LP with no risk of bumping into Here And Now on your travels)

The Force Is Blind/Lost In Room 7-inch (Deptford Fun City DFC 10 May 1979)

Knights Of the Future/Alternatives/Deluxe Green 7-inch (Nice 1980) (free single with Italian fanzine, Bazar)

Ancient Rebels/Dub In Bed 7-inch (IRS PFP 1006 June 1981)

Strange Kicks LP (IRS SO 70023 July 1981) (reissued by Overground, Overground OVER101VPCD in May 2004, with bonus tracks: Dub In Bed/Obsession/Mirror Boy/Pick It Up/Can You Feel The Heat?/Love Lies Limp. This is the usual quality Overground reissue, with extensive notes from Perry and lots of photographs)

Communicate/Obsession 7-inch (IRS PFP 1009 October 1981)

Welcome To the End Of Fun/Death Time/Anti 12-inch (Noiseville VOO 1T February 1986)

Love/Sex 12-inch EP (Noiseville VOO 27 July 1986)

Victory/Repulsion/You Never Know

My Baby's Laughing/Look At Her Eyes/I Had Love In My Hands 12-inch EP (Anagram ANA 36 August 1987)

Peep Show LP (Anagram LP GRAM 32 November 1987) (reissued on CD by Overground, OVER54CD, in 1996, with bonus tracks from the Noiseville EPs: Victory/Repulsion/ Welcome To The End Of Fun/Death Time/Anti/You Never Know, albeit with a changed running order)

The Sol EP 12-inch (Chapter 22 12CHAP 46 April 1990)

Everyday/The Word/Affecting People/Pain Barrier

Dragon Love LP (Chapter 22 CHAPLP 51 November 1990)

Best Wishes/Western World 7-inch (Feel Good All Over FGOV 6 1993)

Purpose In My Life/Company Of Lies 7-inch (Feel Good All Over FGOV 22 1993)

My Life As A Child Star CD (Overground OVER39 CD 1994)

Punk Life CD (Overground OVER70 CD January 1998)

Unlikely Star/Vertigo/Stockhausen In Space 7-inch (Sorted 1999)

Apollo CD (Overground OVER82CD 1999)

Revolution CD (Public Domain August 2001)

ARCHIVE RELEASES:

Live At the Rat Club 1977 LP (Crystal CLP1 December 1979) (re-released on CD in 1993 by Obsession)

Action Time Vision LP (Deptford Fun City DLP 05 March 1980)

Splitting In Two – Selected Viewing LP (Anagram GRAM 40 February 1989)

Live 1978 LP (Feel Good All Over/Overground OVER 29 May 1993) (now out of print. See Overground OVER98VPCD re-release for details)

The Radio Sessions CD (Overground OVER 44CD October 1995) (includes both the 1977 and 1978 John Peel sessions)

The Industrial Sessions 1977 CD (Overground OVER 49CD April 1996) (document of those early, pre-first album rehearsals, with sleeve notes by Genesis P. Orridge)

Punk Life CD (Overground 1998) ('odds and sods' selection that includes tracks recorded with Steve Albini in Chicago)

Action Time Vision – The Very Best Of Mark Perry And ATV 1977-1999 CD (Cherry Red CDMRED 163 1999) (a personal selection. Interestingly, it omits any tracks from Vibing Up

The Senile Man as Perry still maintains that album is a standalone project that doesn't work except in isolation)

25 Years of ATV – Live At CBGB's CD (Dressed To Kill 2002) (aka Love Lies Limp on Devil's Own Jukebox – recorded live April 2001)

Live 1978 (Remastered) CD (Overground OVER98VPCD May 2003) (Re-release of the 1993 CD version of ATV's Meanwhile Gardens Free Festival in August 1978. The original tapes were rediscovered by Italian journalist Red Ronnie (who'd issued three of the tracks with his fanzine Bazar in 1980), the tapes were cleaned up and notes added. John Esplen at Overground: "The original version had sold out many years prior, then Ronnie made contact with Mark. We got the original tape and decided to remaster it (sounds way better) add extra tracks and re-do the booklet.")

Now I Wanna Sniff Some Glue CD single (Public Domain DOMGLUE 010 2004)

Now I Wanna Sniff Some Glue/Total Switch Off (live at CBGBs)/Nasty Little Remix Viva La Rock'n'roll CD (Public Domain DOMCD010 2004) (20 tracks drawn from live recordings in England, France, Germany and the US. Includes ATV's take on Zappa's 'Why Don't You Do Me Right')

Amazing Space Frogs

Vocalist Bugsy (aka David Bryan) with a revolving cast of musicians including Sav, Paul Gardner, Geoff Fogerty, Pete Collins, Alan Cornforth, Peat Farrell etc.

The AMAZING SPACE FROGS were perennial support artistes around the Cleveland area in the late-70s, frequently playing alongside more celebrated acts at venues such as the Rock Garden. They were formed in 1977 and after their debut at the Wellington would share bills with the Cure, the Fall, the Angelic Upstarts and the Rezillos. And by all accounts give them a run for their money, backed as they were by ferocious local support.

By the time they got round to organising their debut EP the ever-fluid membership incorporated moonlighting members of Nicky Beat And The Beatniks, the Flaming Mussolinis, Basczax and No Way. The 500 copies they pressed of 'Dirty Habits' sold out in three weeks, mainly to their extended Middlesbrough musical family. It was aired by John Peel, only for the BBC to subsequently ban it. Any of the three tracks might have been responsible for causing offence; it's hard to narrow it down.

But it never happened for the Frogs, despite a nice write-up in Smash Hits, of all places. Diminutive loon about town Bugsy began to lose interest in the early-80s. He returned to the stage in 1993 after pestering local band Riot Act to serve as a new incarnation of the Amazing Space Frogs for a show he was putting together as a tribute to Dave 'Barbarian' Johns, mainstay of the Teesside punk scene. The revamped Space Frogs (featuring Riot Act members Steve Hoggart on bass, Boza on drums and Paul Tattersall on guitar, with Riot Act singer Marc Anthony playing additional guitar) made their debut in 1994 at the Sunn Inn. The subsequent benefit for Johns was such a success that Bugsy elected to resurrect the band with Hoggart "giving him a hand till it was sorted".

A year later, with Hoggart still with the band, and numerous changes in line-up, the band gigged with John Cooper Clarke and Hugh Cornwell. The line-up settled on Bugsy, Hoggart, Dave Gregory from local noise merchants Ardkore on bass and Craig Lester on drums. Porl Tattersall joined the band in 1997, at which time they recorded their debut album, on cassette only, Don't Tell Me Mam.

A year after its release Gregory left to join P.I.G. allowing Hoggart to move to bass. By the advent of the group's next recording, 1999's 'Talk Show' EP, Jonno had stepped in for the temporarily absent Lester. The inspiration behind the title-track, incidentally, was Jerry Springer. The inspiration behind 'I Should Be So Lucky' appears to have been Kylie's rear end. The band has kept going ever since. There was a live album recorded at the Studio, Hartlepool, in 2001. "It doesn't look like we're in a hurry to slow down," Hoggart noted to me. You've got to love a band that provisionally entitled its 2005 release Better Dead Than Wed, then reconsidered when they remembered that three-quarters of the band are actually married and it might not go down too well.

"People are always asking Bugsy to put all his exploits in one place," Hoggart tells me, "and it's looking like it might be a book. We had some young journo bird threatening to do one about the Frogs but I think she was only interested to get in gigs for nowt. I wouldn't mind but she was a smashing young lady and I think she had designs on Bugsy but as she was a total lightweight drinker, he lost interest. She joined the legion of punters who reckon that, as he has infected that many bands big and small, a book would be a good idea. No doubt it will be down to me and I'm buggered if I know where to start. Keeping him out of the pub for gigs is a nightmare, drunken little sod, and getting him to talk any kind of sense will be the hardest part."

DISCOGRAPHY:

Dirty Habits 7-inch EP (Ribbett Records RIB 1 1979)
Nuns Of Destruction/(I'm Into) Necrophilia/Norman And Jeremy (500 copies)
Don't Tell Me Mam cassette album (BOGSNORKELLER 120857 August 1997) (now available on CD from the band's website)
Talk Show CD EP (1999)
Mr Thumbprint Head/I Should Be So Lucky/Come On Feel The Noize/Talk Show
I'm Into Necrophilia/Popcorn And Bubblegum 7-inch (Bin Liner RUBBISH7002 August 1999) (300 copies only. Features new recording of 'Necrophilia' plus a new B-side track featuring Bugsy's four-year-old nephew on vocals)
Teesiders CD single (Bogsnorkeller 2003) ("A song for the mighty 'Boro that propelled them into Europe for the first time. Not many bands can do that...")
Balls To Christmas CD single (Bogsnorkeller 2003) ("Written, recorded and manufactured in a week")
24 Hours From Ulcers CD (Ribbett Records RIB 666 2004) (22-track release recorded live in Hartlepool)

Amber Squad

Richard Beechey (vocals), Paul Fairey (guitar, vocals), Robert Miller (guitar), Stephen 'Dubber' Rawlings (bass), Graham 'Tuzzy' Tyers (drums).

Formed in Rutland from the ashes of schoolboy aspirants Reflex and Blueprint, AMBER SQUAD released a debut single whose high-energy R&B neatly traversed punk/mod boundaries, in February 1980. The group hit its stride playing shows throughout Leicestershire and the Midlands and eventually London, including the Nashville Rooms and the Bridge House, after support from John Peel and an appearance on Kid Jensen's Round Table. Mike Read also played '(I Can't) Put My Finger On You' a couple of times.

"People talk about how much John Peel cared about music," Paul Fairey remembers. "Before we made a record, in 1978 – you can imagine how many thousands of cassettes he received each week – I sent him a rough demo of what became our first single. We got a hand-written slip back saying, 'This is really good, boys, you ought to be making a record. I assume you are already.' We were really knocked out about that. Someone then said, 'Oh, he writes that about everybody.' So I sent him another cassette just to check. And he wrote me another hand-written letter, saying, 'I've already heard this, boys. Are you making a record yet?' I was amazed. He really did listen to everything he got sent. Incredible man."

Mike Read was a little less incredible. "We were at the Nashville watching the Starjets, supported by the Original Mirrors, Ian Broudie's band, who we'd gone to see. And Mike Read was in the audience. He was quite hip – well, if he was ever hip at all, that's when he was hip. And he'd played our record so we said, let's go say hello and thank him. He was doing Pop Quiz at the time. I said, 'Mike, I'm from Amber Squad, you probably don't remember, but you played our record.' 'Oh, yeah? I remember, guys. Good little record.' And then Robert Miller says, 'Yeah. I always thought you were a bit of a puff. But now you've done Pop Quiz, I reckon you're all right.' Mike Read looked at him as if to say, 'Don't bother sending me any more records.'"

As for the mod/punk crossover: "Our drummer and bass guitarist were very much into R&B – in the old-fashioned sense – Dr Feelgood, the Pirates, etc. We were all into the Feelgoods, and that's the sort of band we wanted to be. Cos I was the principle songwriter, I was heavily into the Beatles, I was more pop than straight R&B, so it was a good blend. Then we got the record deal from S&T. They wanted to get into the mod thing, which was exploding then. So they put their mod logo on the middle of the record, totally unbeknownst to us. So were unwittingly caught up in the mod thing. At the time, we weren't really very happy about it, but we were grateful enough to have a record out. But we weren't part of that scene with Secret Affair and Squire, but caught up in it purely because of the logo on the record."

A second single followed for Lincoln's Dead Good Records, with the B-side an ebullient ode to masturbation ("I didn't write that one!" notes Fairey), by which time the group had lost Miller to become a quartet. "By the second single, we'd become ourselves again, and we got back into being presented as what we were meant to be. In our live set, we used to do a lot of covers of Motown stuff really fast, like 'In The Midnight Hour' and 'Mustang Sally', really fast. That was our live thing, fast R&B with thrashy guitars. We were obviously heavily influenced by the Jam too. They were kind of the band we wanted to be at one stage, because they were so complete, they had everything."

But not every gig was a screaming success and, especially towards the end, they were forced to wonder whether or not the effort was justified. "We played a Nottingham pub called the Hearty Goodfellow, on a nondescript midweek night around about 1982. One guy turned up. Just one guy. And he couldn't clap because he had a broken arm. Hilarious, not least because we were on door money, too. And we ended up giving him his money back."

The group sundered when its participants realised that day jobs and proper grown-up relationships beckoned. Amber Squad have just released a new CD via Detour Records, comprising everything they committed to vinyl, plus unrecorded stuff. "We got together and re-recorded three tracks that were 'lost'. It starts at our first demo and goes right up to that. It was interesting. I write music for TV and radio, so I'm still a songwriter and I have the studio (He has just produced, among other acts, Cardboard Box and Overdrive, and written songs for artists including Smokie). So it made sense that the lost songs we just re-recorded again. It was just the four of us, Dubber didn't want to join in. But yes, it was fun after all this time"

DISCOGRAPHY:

(I Can't) Put My Finger On You/Tell You A Lie 7-inch (S&T SAT1 1980)
Can We Do Dancing/You Should See (What I Do To You In My Dreams) 7-inch (Dead Good Dead 17 1980)
ARCHIVE RELEASE:
Arewehavinganotheroneinhereorwhat? CD (Detour DRCD 043 April 2006)

Amsterdam

Steve Allan Jones (keyboards/vocals), Dave Parry (guitar), Gary Jones (drums)

Formed in 1977 after the dissolution of Stripey, this Rhyl trio was active until 1979. As Allan Jones told me, it all began with the Sex Pistols. "Mike Peters (later Alarm singer), Steff Holt (brother of guitarist Andy) and I used to frequent a great club called Quaintways in Chester. They used to put bands on such as the Groundhogs, Pat Travers Band, rocky stuff. We noticed as we were leaving a poster advertising 'The notorious Sex Pistols' at Quaintways the next week. We had read of some of their early gigs (100 Club etc) and decided to see the show.

The very next week, we found ourselves in a packed club surrounded by 250 long haired rockers. The Pistols were great, really meaty sound, great attitude. I remember all their amps had other bands' names on them – we were told by someone close to the band that they were all nicked!"

"The three of us stood for the whole show open mouthed. Mike and I still talk of that night – we knew that whatever we had been doing wasn't right. We realised that you didn't need loads of gear and we also now knew that we could write our own songs not just cover others. Sadly Mike and I both knew that we couldn't be in the same band for a while. His ideas had guitars only in them, mine were more trad but with the attitude. Mike and I decided to go and speak to the band, we correctly guessed that they would be at the bar. For a few horrible moments we just stood in front of them. Finally, with a push in the back from Mike, I stepped forward.

'Hi lads. Really enjoyed the show' (uninterested looks from band) 'Errrr...' (another push from Mike) 'How do you write your songs? Do you just get in a rehearsal room or, erm, or...' Mr Lydon looked me up and down with the most disdainful sneer and said 'Get the beers in, Glen.' Mike and I walked away, very excited, it was a sort of conversation. Mike told me many years later that he always vowed that if he ever became famous, he would always take time to talk to the fans as a result of this encounter."

AMSTERDAM looked to take a more cerebral path than much of the class of 1977 and were occasionally compared to the Stranglers, predominantly because of the use of keyboards, and Elvis Costello. "About right," states Allan Jones. "I still loved Alex Harvey and some prog bands, Bowie and glam. I really like the idea of using echo effects on vocals and we used to carry our own light show, all home-made of course! I suppose looking back we had a strange space rock vibe as well, ala Hawkwind." Steve Oldfield (bass, later of Misery Brothers) and Eddie McDonald (guitar) bolstered the line-up shortly after their inception. McDonald would leave, however, after disagreements over songwriting. He teamed up with Mike Peters (another previous member of Stripey) in Seventeen. Dave Parry was replaced on guitar thereafter by Andy Holt.

In their various formations Amsterdam played dozens of shows throughout Wales and the north west, and a tape of their 'Nights On The Street' track got lots of airplay on the local Radio City, though it was never officially released. "Mike Peters sometimes plays the riff from the song when I am within earshot," Allan Jones recalls. "He said he loved it and remembers it better than me! Amsterdam did quite a lot of recording for the time and there are tapes out there."

Their two biggest shows were at Liverpool University at the Radio City battle of the bands, and as support to Siouxsie and the Banshees at Colwyn Bay pier. "The Liverpool gig was one of our biggest. I remember we didn't play so good and the crowd were still rockers at heart. I can remember that the winners of the comp were an Austrian band called Stonehenge! One of the judges was Mike Rutherford from Genesis. Really odd night, I think we realised that these comps were ultimately not for us." A better fit was the Banshees' support slot. "The Banshees gig was incredible. The Banshees (original line-up) turned up with a PA about an hour before the show was due to start. They had no bass or amp so they used ours. We went on, did OK. We were in our dressing room when we heard a yell from the only toilet backstage. We all rushed out. Siouxsie had managed to lock herself in. The doors were solid cast iron (it was a pier) and it took Steff and a screwdriver about ten minutes to release her. She emerged in full war paint, thanked us all and ran on to stage!"

Amsterdam broke up in 1979, Allan Jones going on to form the X-Men with Gary Jones, who also featured Glyn Crossley (bass; ex-Pax) and Dave Bradbury (guitar) and Pete Picton (keyboards) of the Units. They played just two shows, but did record two tracks, 'Drive' and 'Go Away', for the Systems Of Attraction compilation cassette. "The plan was for us all to move to London but only myself and Pete made it down. Almost immediately, Pete and I split the band and I joined the (Berlin) Blondes." Allan Jones moved on to progressively greater success with the Alarm and Spear Of Destiny. Gary Jones is still drumming with local bands and became manager of the Scala cinema in Prestatyn. He also does magic shows in his spare time. Dave Parry works as a telephone engineer. Steve Oldfield has an insurance business in Holywell. Andy Holt is a social worker in the Channel Islands and Eddie McDonald is a photographer.

Allan Jones is a successful theatre and TV composer (his credits including three series of

Gamepad and the Crow Show). Does punk rock, at least as an ethos rather than musical form, continue to inspire him? "Always and still. The idea that it doesn't matter that you can't play so good, it's your ideas and the will to carry them out that is important."

Anal Fleas

Dave 'Charisma' Cook (vocals), Simon 'Sensible' Walton (drums), Neil 'Yank Marvin' Carson (guitar), Jon 'Two Pints' Bloom (bass)

The ANAL FLEAS formed at Southampton University in 1980. They put in a series of appearances at local parties, most of which resulted in a visit from the police. As Neil Carson points out, this was largely attributable to the fact that the gigs "never started until way after the pubs had closed".

They became regulars at local punk haunt the Joiner's Arms, though they also wormed their way on to university bills as support to visiting headliners including the Thompson Twins and Higsons. It wasn't until the spring of 1982 that they managed to record, however, cutting four tracks at Toucan Studio at Hayling Island.

500 copies were pressed up and sold to friends and via Rough Trade, with another 50 circulated to the media which drew practically no response whatsoever. But it cemented their reputation as local legends for all of five or six minutes. Jon Bloom: I remember giving a copy of our record to John Peel in the Union Bar. He looked at the cover and the pictures and said, 'Which one's you?' I pointed to my picture and the great man said, 'Oh, you've got breasts!' Fortunately, before I could die of embarrassment, he then said 'So have I'. I don't remember him playing the record, but he did mention us once, saying 'What a pretty name'."

DISCOGRAPHY:

Anal Fleas 7-inch EP (Rectal Records FLEA 45 1982)
Landlord/Go Down/Psycho/Over The Edge (500 copies)

Androids

Joe Zero (aka Joe Moody; vocals), Aza (aka Andrew Middleton; bass), Steve AKA (aka (!) Steve Rainey; guitar), Billy Britt (aka Billy McIlwaine; drums)

Belfast punk band the ANDROIDS formed in December 1977. Joe Moody was watching the Outcasts rehearse in their attic when he announced his intention to form his own band (he'd actually had a go at doing so in London but it never got off the ground). Moody remembers Greg Cowan putting him in touch with a guitarist of his acquaintance, Aza Middleton: "I was at school with Greg," Middleton remembers, "but I don't think I had much to do with him. Possibly terrified of him! I don't think he knew I was interested in being in a band and I think I only realised he was in the Outcasts when I turned up to a gig at the Pound in 1977 and saw him on stage."

Moody and Middleton became fast friends. "Joe and I were like chalk and cheese in terms of our backgrounds. He was from the Shankill Road and lived in a dreadful flat. I was basically an English public school boy who had hit hard times (just like my hero Joe Strummer!) and I was living in the cosy environs of the university. What the hell the other punks in Belfast made of me, I don't know. Well, actually I do. A handful didn't like me, but most people didn't see me as anything odd – we were all odd and proud of it. Besides, I was one of the first punks in Belfast and we respected each other. Joe and I were really committed to each other and what we were doing. I was giving him his break and he was giving me mine, not that we saw it like that then."

"Joe and a student, I think called Sean, replied to an advert I put up, probably in Caroline Music in 1977. The three of us were all guitarists and I was the worst of the three so I think I ended up being 'manager' for a couple of rehearsals before Joe and I decided we didn't want to be in a band with a student! I remember Joe introducing me to Lou Reed and the Velvet Underground at the first rehearsal where the two guitarists basically spent the whole time playing 'Sweet Jane'. Shortly afterwards we advertised again and Steve Rainey, who was working at the Co-Op, replied. Basically, anyone who replied to an advert was in back then. I think that applied to all bands. Steve also was a guitarist! So, somehow I agreed to be the bass

player. Joe had a load of songs (I remember one called 'Cheap Thrills') and I had a load of songs. I can't remember too much about them. 'Wilma Is A Transvestite Now' was one of mine I'm ashamed to say! I had quite a lot of songs with meaningless lyrics about subjects I knew very little about."

All they needed now was a drummer. "I was involved with a community arts project (the Art & Research Exchange) based at 22 Lombard Street in the city centre. We got our first gig through that on 10th February 1978 at the Arts Council Gallery on Bedford Street. Steve knew Billy McIlwaine who worked in Texas Homecare in Holywood and persuaded him to be our drummer. I think Billy had been a drummer in an Orange band or something – he'd seen a snare drum, but never a full kit. Anyway, we played this gig and I think we did OK. Bands like the Outcasts and Rudi had set some standards for us to aspire to."

"I think we were one of the first Belfast punk bands to play live. Rudi and Stiff Little Fingers were playing gigs but they both had a background in glam rock bands. They knew how to play, if you like. For us we were driven by the punk ethic of picking up a guitar and getting out there – anyone can do it! I had been running a fanzine (9 to 5) and inspired by Sniffin' Glue, I included chord diagrams and told my readers to 'get yourself a guitar'. I've got a feeling all the chord diagrams were the wrong way round in hindsight, so I probably did a lot of damage musically!"

"I remember rehearsing two or three times a week. Because I was involved in the Art and Research Exchange, we managed to use Lombard Street. This was inside the barriers, and I remember the ritual of getting my mother to give us a lift down to Baird's Electrical Hire every Saturday morning so we could hire some AC30 amps. We would put them on the roof rack, and then wait an age as we tried to get cleared to drive in through the barriers into the ring of steel. I am English, so I used to do all the talking with the soldiers at the checkpoint to convince them we were just honest, friendly, harmless punks – not terrorists!"

They were also among the city's more confrontational bands. Sometimes you have to judge the importance of 'getting a reaction' in context. In London that could mean getting a write-up in the NME. In Northern Ireland it could potentially mean an obituary column. At a subsequent show at the Harp Bar, Joe Zero had a gun pointed at him by local paramilitaries. Middleton remembers that night all too well. "The great thing about Belfast punk, that I didn't fully understand at the time, was how for a lot of people, including Joe, it was a way of breaking down, or side-stepping, the sectarian barriers. Actually there were a hell of a lot of young, vulnerable people, including me, taking some very big risks."

"Most of the gigs we played were in the Harp Bar, which I think was a Republican bar. A majority of punks were from Protestant homes, I would say, but there was a very healthy mix a couple of times every week in the Harp Bar. The only time I remember any trouble was one night when we were playing and Joe who, like us, was always ready to be controversial, pulled out a Paratrooper's beret and put it on mid-song. Someone (not one of us punks) pulled a gun on him. This was one of the defining moments of that era. The whole audience of punks became an instant human shield and smuggled Joe out of the Harp. Then life went on as usual the next week without the blink of any eye."

The band also became involved in the campaign to free Noreen Winchester. "Noreen had killed her father by stabbing him 17 times when he eventually turned from repeatedly raping her to raping her sister as well. I wrote a song called 'Free Noreen'. I was on the front cover of some Socialist magazine waving a placard. I spray-painted 'Free Noreen' graffiti around Stranmillis where I was living. We did benefits and a couple of TV programmes paid us a small fee (Panorama and World In Action I think) to play the song for the documentaries they were making at the time, but were never actually shown. The campaign was successful and Noreen was released from Armagh prison where I had visited her. She came to live with us after she was released and then disappeared."

By the summer they'd cut their first demo at Downtown Radio, funded by the money from the documentaries, including originals 'Terminal Breakout' and a New York Dolls tribute, 'Lipstick Traces', featuring lyrics by manager Alwyn Greer, a local fanzine editor. The other three tracks were 'Suggestions', 'Nine To Five' and 'Terminal Breakout'. Another song, 'Inside The Barriers', inspired by the band's rehearsal location, missed the cut. "I have listened to this a few times over the years and it's a great shame it never got put on vinyl because it was fairly classic stuff. It was tight, fast, and Joe was a brilliant lead singer. He had a great voice and a great personality."

The songs were shipped to record labels in London, to little encouragement, though through their association with the Rock Against Racism movement, they ended up playing a gig in Uxbridge. "We really thought we'd made it! Playing in England where the real punk scene, as reported in the press, was happening." But any optimism was gradually dispelled. "I think the Androids started to get a bit pissed off when local filmmaker John Davis started to make Shell Shock Rock, the documentary about the scene. It seemed everyone apart from us was going to be in it. We were good, we had a following and were central to everything that was happening and we wanted to be in the film. For some reason, we weren't. John worked with Terri Hooley quite a lot on planning that and though Terri had been promising to release an Androids single on Good Vibes he never got round to it."

Disenchanted, Zero and Aza decided to join the reformed Victim, whose own original line-up had broken up weeks earlier. Middleton: "The band was always Joe and me and Steve and Billy. Steve and Billy were not really on the same wavelength as us two. They were into being in a band for the usual things, girls and booze, but weren't driven in the same way." Britt and AKA found three new members in Jim Megarry (vocals), Robin Holmes (bass; formerly of early Belfast punk band Chaos) and Jeremy Nicholl (keyboards; a photographer for Alternative Ulster fanzine). The Androids persevered through a series of local gigs, with Holmes famously resembling Frankenstein to add to their visual appeal, before entering the studio in December 1978 to record 'News Of The World' and 'Bondage In Belfast' for a projected new compilation album for Good Vibrations. However, Ulster On A Thin Wire was eventually shelved, and the Androids ceased to be.

Middleton, meanwhile, would play with the Sinister Cleaners. He also worked with Leeds band the Wedding Present. "I played on an early Radio One session with them and was in various musical collaborations with members of the Wedding Present, whom I toured with as a friend as they were making it." Middleton is about to release two new albums, the first with his solo project, the Tripping Cherubs, the second as part of the aforementioned Sinister Cleaners, a band he has worked with on and off with for nearly two decades.

COMPILATIONS:
Ulster On A Wire LP (Good Vibrations 1979; 'News Of The World', 'Bondage In Belfast') (unreleased)
Bloodstains Across Northern Ireland Vol. 1 LP (1998; 'Bondage In Belfast') (bootleg)
Northern Xposure Vol. 2 cassette (2002; 'Bondage In Belfast')
Good Vibrations – The Punk Singles Collection CD (Anagram CDPUNK 36 1994; 'Bondage In Belfast')

Angelic Upstarts

Thomas 'Mensi' Mensforth (vocals), Raymond 'Mond' Cowie (guitar), Steve Forsten (bass), Decca Wade (drums)

Though they made more of a connection with the second generation, 78-79 punk scene, the ANGELIC UPSTARTS' origins in the working class estate of Brockley Whins, South Shields, in 1977, make them original protagonists. Often bracketed alongside Sham 69 as punk's working class insurgents, though useful, there are times when that comparison is deceptive. The Upstarts' early career was certainly marked by similarly simplistic sloganeering, but there are moments of poignancy in their later canon and at times Mensi was able to articulate the reality of life on the breadline better than most.

While Jimmy Pursey could often be justifiably criticised for 'playing at it', former apprentice miner Mensi was the real McCoy – genuinely and unapologetically working class. Here was a man who could teach many a punk rock icon about sincerity and authenticity, even if he couldn't offer them singing lessons.

Hope Colliery miner Mensi and shipyard electrician Mond had first met while both attended Stanhope Road Secondary Modern, after Mensi been expelled from the local grammar school. The Angelic Upstarts "begged, borrowed or stole" enough equipment to get going after being energised by the Clash's White Riot tour, Mensi having seen them at their Newcastle

University date in May 1977. He formed the band the day after the Clash show, determined that he could do better than support acts the Slits and Subway Sect, though as he told John Robb, "I could never aspire to being as good as the Clash."

The Upstarts played their first show at the Percy Hudson Youth Club in South Shields, where they rehearsed, running through their six-song set a good three times to an appreciative reaction. The song cycle included 'Police Oppression' and 'Leave Me Alone' as well as covers such as Chris Montez's 'Let's Dance'. The original bass player Micky quit after violent altercations at their first show in Jarrow (his mother banned him from playing) and in came Forsten, a bricklayer. Very quickly they acquired an audience of what Mensi describes as "football hooligans and criminals".

The Upstarts were initially managed by Keith Bell, a fearsome former light-middleweight boxer, and self-confessed gangster. Their first release was an independently recorded 500-strong DIY pressing of 'The Murder Of Liddle Towers' in 1978, cut at the local Impulse Studios in Wallsend. An indictment of a particularly nasty case of police brutality (Towers was a rogue arrested for being drunk and disorderly, and later died in a police cell), it was sold in local shops and at shows until Small Wonder Records stepped in to give it a national release. "It was a song of protest 23 years ago," stated Mensi in 2001, "and it's still relevant today." Mensi asked guitarist Mond to get a similar sound to the Who's 'Won't Get Fooled Again'.

In an era when major labels were still desperate to climb aboard the punk bandwagon, Warner Brothers became their next suitors. Initially they'd been courted by Polydor, with whom Jimmy Pursey had set up a subsidiary JP Records, but Mensi scuppered any possibility of a deal after getting into a scuffle with one of the label's doormen. Or that was the reason stated. I asked Mensi what was behind that story. "He was not a doorman, he was head of Polydor security. Stix (Keith 'Stix' Warrington, who'd replaced Wade who'd left due to difficulties with the band's management) and the lads were just larking about, throwing snowballs. He was with another bloke and two girls, and a snowball went astray. It went near the girls but didn't hit them.

The bloke then asked Stix if he wanted trouble. He was a big bloke and Stix was only little, so I intervened and told him we didn't want trouble. He then turned on me and said, 'So, you're the one with the mouth?' He then took his coat off, removed his watch and rings, so I knew he didn't want to dance with me. The rest is history." So they were off Polydor and Mensi thought he'd blown any chance he might have had of a career in the music industry. Instead, they ended up signed to Warners the very next day.

They also secured a John Peel session, aired on 30 October 1978, which saw Stix make his debut. Ensconced in Maida Vale Studios, neither he nor Mensi could resist the temptation to walk through a door marked 'Do Not Enter', and promptly disrupted a Radio 3 orchestral performance.

The police harassment was constant, with venues challenged over their alcohol licence if they booked the band. I asked Mensi if the problems predated the release of 'Liddle'. "I wasn't exactly Mr Popular with the police, but my problems increased a hundred-fold after the single. In one incident I was physically attacked and was subjected to constant abuse from individual officers." A bit of a revenge mission was mounted in April 1979 when the band convinced the chaplain at Northumbria's Acklington Prison to let them play there. It was hardly Johnny Cash at Folsom Prison, but the band did entertain 150 convicts (many of whom remembered their manager Keith Bell from his 'holidays' there) by erecting a banner stating 'Smash Law and Order' and parading a pig in a helmet with the legend PC Fuck Pig emblazoned on it. They closed out the set with their traditional cover of 'Borstal Breakout' amended to 'Acklington

Breakout'. It brought them headlines in the Daily Mirror ('Punks rock a Jailhouse') and ratcheted up tensions with the local constabulary just a little bit further.

Debut album Teenage Warning, produced by Pursey, offered persuasive, gloriously unsophisticated rapid-fire punk. The extracted singles 'I'm An Upstart' (with its 'Tommy Gun' inspired intro) and 'Teenage Warning' ("Is my image right/For your fashion parade?") both reached the charts – the latter even leading to an appearance on Top Of The Pops. The album was actually recorded for free. Pursey, having half-inched the keys to Polydor's studio, snuck the band in overnight when it wasn't being used.

There are some clunkers – 'Student Power' ("What a shower") is painful to listen to, and while it's fine to be class-conscious, there's something to be said for hitting the right targets. In particular, I thought it was a misfire in an era when more and more working class kids were getting to college for the first time. Mensi: "Unfortunately, I stand by the sentiments. The song was written about an experience I had with students, we went to see the Clash at Newcastle University and they wouldn't let us in. I pleaded and pleaded our case. We were all told if we didn't have a student union card, we could not get in. After much deliberation I threw a bin through the window and we all clambered through. And we saw the band. At that time, I thought the students were quite elitist. Although you must remember in the early days, we didn't take no prisoners." My only other objection is to an ill-judged reggae break on 'Never Again' that simply doesn't work – though this served as a useful portent of directions to come. More fun is the snotty (pre-Ben Elton) rip-through of Cliff's 'The Young Ones' and the raucous 'Leave Me Alone', with its gratuitous swearing and teenage isolation schtick.

Yet (relative) success was already wearing thin on Mensi. "I hate it when you go down the Marquee and kids come up to you to buy them a drink and when you tell them you ain't go no money they don't believe you. Sometimes I get very cynical with the kids." The truth was that, despite signing to Warners, each member of the band was on a retainer of just £25 a week, less than unemployment benefit at the time. And resentment was growing with the antics of Keith Bell, who wasn't afraid to cuff his charges about if he thought they weren't on the ball. When they sacked him, things turned ugly. As well as intimidating the band's fans, he threatened Mensi's mother and had her windows kicked out. Reprisals followed, resulting in a raid by Mensi's brother-in-law Billy Wardropper and Decca Wade's father, comedian Derek Wade, on Bell's house. One of Bell's henchman was shot in the leg. Bell responded with an arson attack on property belonging to Mensi's sister. In the end both Bell and Wardropper served time, the judge admitting that the Upstarts' camp had faced "severe provocation", but he was unable to overlook the use of a sawn-off shotgun in exacting revenge.

'Never 'ad Nothing', in common with several of the Upstarts' broadsides, let its title say everything, replete with double/treble negatives. But no-one was in any doubt as to his meaning when Mensi launched into the strident chorus based on the story of an 18-year-old youth in Essex who took a hostage in a local pub and was shot dead by the police. Fourth single 'Out Of Control' saw Ronnie 'Wooden' Warrington (ex-Tom And The Hot Rocks) replace Forsten on bass, whom they claimed "left them for a woman". But Warrington didn't last long, with Glynn Warren stepping in by the time their last Warners single, a cover of the Animals' 'We Gotta Get Out Of This Place', had been released. It was a strange choice, in part a tribute to their regional debt to the aforementioned band, in part an acknowledgement that their own material simply wasn't yet of the same calibre. The accompanying album did feature a little piano on the R&B-styled 'Ronnie Is A Rocker', while 'King Coal' again acknowledged their debt to the Clash. The Keith Bell tale is recounted in graphic detail in 'Shotgun Solution' ("Look at your legs, they're full of lead/It's such a shame it wasn't your head"). In many ways, sonically, it's a better album than their debut, but some of the other tracks lacked grit.

Dropped by Warners in the summer of 1980, they moved to EMI's newly relaunched Zonophone label. By now the relationship with Pursey had soured – Mensi was particularly astonished that when Pursey had hooked up with Cook and Jones to explore the possibility of launching the Sham Pistols, he had casually informed Mensi that he was now going to be the lead singer of Sham 69.

'Last Night Another Soldier' was not, as many presumed, a 'troops out' statement over the Northern Ireland conflict (about which Mensi pondered, reasonably enough, that he did not have the answers), but about the lack of interest in the young, working class soldiers being killed on the streets of Belfast and Armagh. It won the band a Sounds single of the week award ("Guts. Tune. Drive. Something To Say...perfect punk") but stalled outside the top 50. Incidentally, B-side 'The Man Who Came In From The Beano' was a joke at the expense of Garry Bushell – the man who gave it single of the week status. Bushell also placed 'Last Night Another Soldier' and 'Guns For The Afghan Rebels' on his Oi! The Album compilation, meaning the Upstarts would forever be associated with that movement, though Mensi remained dubious about its merits.

After its release Warrington joined labelmates the Cockney Rejects, allegedly because the band sold his drum kit for £20 without his permission, and was replaced by former Roxy Music drummer Paul Thompson, who played on the subsequent singles 'England' and 'Kids On The Street'. 'England' was Mensi's heartfelt attempt to repatriate the Union flag from fascists. He has been unrelenting in his disdain for the far right, members of whom constantly tried to disrupt their shows. Yet he remained a fierce patriot, albeit one who envisioned the UK as a home for men and women of all colours. However, he admitted to the common working class lionisation of Enoch Powell in an interview with Rising Free fanzine in 1981. "I'll tell you who I thought was a really good politician who got slagged down, and that was Enoch Powell. I don't think he was a racialist at all, he just predicted things that DID happen. He was probably the most under-estimated politician of all time, until he was exiled in some remote Irish constituency. The papers branded HIM as a racist. If the NME get hold of this fanzine and read this interview they'll brand ME as a racist. I think he should have been Prime Minister, there you are."

I asked Mensi about these remarks. "In the early days I used to say a lot of things for a shock reaction. I had a certain amount of respect for Enoch Powell when he turned against the whole Tory party and told the people of Wolverhampton to vote Labour, which they did. I never set out to be political or anti-fascist. I evolved into a staunch, active anti-fascist, which I am still today and will be till the day I die. But I hasten to add that I had the same grudging respect for Thatcher, as she never hid her hatred of the working class, so in a way she also had a degree of honesty." In fact, questioned on what he believes the Upstarts most important legacy is, Mensi concludes: "If we can be remembered for one thing and one thing only, then let it be our unswerving and staunch anti-fascist stand."

2,000,000 Voices was titled after the number of unemployed in the UK at the time, though by the time the album was released, the figure was creeping up by another million. At that stage, it's important to remember, it seemed entirely conceivable that it may treble, such was the anxiety caused in traditional working class communities by Thatcherism's belligerent assault on manufacturing industries. It contained another anti-police song, 'You're Nicked' (taken from direct experience of an incident Mensi had witnessed at an Arsenal-Sunderland game), leavened by the use of brass, and 'Guns For The Afghan Rebels', which would probably not play as well in the current world climate as it did in the early-80s.

What was so admirable about 2,000,000 Voices was its guts in striking out for new territory without diluting the fire which has always been the pivotal element of the band's sound. Alongside the hard-boiled pop of tracks like 'Mr Politician' nestled the spoken word 'Heath's Lament', while closer 'I Wish' saw him joined by Honey Bane on violin. And 'Mensi's Marauders' is a diverting Geordie hoe-down. I asked Mensi if he thought the album stands as the Upstarts greatest achievement. "I think 2,000,000 Voices was done at a time when the band really gelled, and like anything it was a place of right time, right elements, and it all fell into place."

Alongside Sham 69 and the Rejects, the Upstarts were now considered godfathers to Oi!, though to Mensi's credit, he never had any truck with the right wing elements that later infiltrated the scene. Mensi's attitude initially was to invite them to the shows, to try to win them over – actions he later stated to be naïve in his communiques for Anti-Fascist Action, reiterating that bullies need to be faced down with physical action rather than words. He claims to have administered at least one good kicking to Skrewedriver's Ian Stuart. "It was in the 100 Club," he told Riot 77 fanzine, "and he was saying he was just proud of Britain and England and I said, 'Alright! I'll listen to anyone'. I'll listen to anybody if you've got something to say, you know? Anyway, he asked if I'd come down to the show and I'd see what they were like.

So I walked into the 100 Club with my cousin and took one look and they were walking around with German helmets on and all that (laughs). I said, "Let's get out of here" (laughs). After that we had various street confrontations and this is the god's honest truth – he always ran."

Of the Oi! connection, Mensi states: "I'm in a punk band. I have always been in a punk band. The punk movement was rebellious, not frightened to speak out against injustice, regardless of colour, creed or religion. To me the Oi! movement is a white, right wing movement. When you speak to some of them, they are the epitome of Thatcher's children." Yet while the Upstarts were being acknowledged as precursors to a brutal, simplistic working class punk ethic, Mensi, to his credit, was trying to stretch himself. Indeed, he contributed cello to some tracks on 2,000,000 Voices, which saw Decca Wade return to the fold. Even the NME, naturally resistant to any notion of working class 'street music', was impressed. "Musically, they've moved away from the iron spikes and black spaces of punk and back to cultural roots," the paper noted, "which are English, specifically Geordie... It should enlarge their following from politically minded punks to politically minded English youth in general."

But realistically, Mensi's concerns, and his constituency, remained the same. The group returned to the subject of deaths in police custody with the release of the reggae-tinged 'I Understand', this time concerning the case of Rastafarian Richard Campbell, who died while on remand in Ashford Remand Centre. "He was a Rastafrian," Mensi recalled to Wake Up. "He died for his beliefs when he was in prison. They're not allowed to eat certain types of food, and he wouldn't conform to the prison diet. But the prison authorities wouldn't accept his religion and they started giving him drugs to calm him down and they ended up giving him an overdose and killing him. I recorded a song 'Different Strokes' with Dennis Bovell, who was a member of Matumbi, and I went down the pub with another one of them, Bevan. We were talking in the pub, I said I'd wrote this song about this guy, and he said, 'That's my cousin!' It was really weird."

The song was originally titled 'White Nigger, Black Nigger', but Mensi changed it "Because I didn't want to be offensive to anybody. I thought it was a very sensitive period and it was a word that I used in the early days (frequently, in fact, in fanzine interviews) and I didn't understand how derogatory it was. I didn't want to cause any more offence, because it was about a kid who I thought was brilliant and I didn't want to offend his family." They kept the reggae theme with subsequent single 'Different Strokes', featuring Roy Young on vocals. It may have been subconscious, but the efforts to distance themselves from the model of working class white boys playing hard and fast with guitars was telling. But less palatable compromises lay ahead.

Warren had departed, warned by his doctor that if he didn't he risked going deaf, to be replaced by Tony Feedback (ex-Long Tall Shorty) for Still From The Heart, which saw them demur to EMI's request to make their sound more amenable. Although the lyrics maintained their bite, the musical compromise was an unhappy one. Bushell was unrelenting in his condemnation: "This isn't from the heart, it's rubbish, a pathetic, calculated shot at playlists and coffee-table credibility." We could truncate the quote here, but the rest is, again, illuminating. "'Action Man' is Depeche Mode on morphine, flabby futurism fighting to keep its eyes open, while 'Wasted' sounds more like Brotherhood Of Man being brassy Euro Song Contest style pop pap delivered with about as much clout as a sleepwalking Marc Almond." Ah, what a prose stylist that man was. However, on this occasion, he was correct. There are times when it's excruciating. Later Mensi would admit that he deeply regretted bowing to record company pressure. As he admitted to me, "Still From The Heart had some good songs, but the whole album was vastly over produced and it was me who objected to the production. And it was me who received all the criticism. But at the end of the day, there is nothing wrong with failure. The only thing wrong is if you don't try." Dispiriting dates in America followed, including sets at trendy new wave venue The Peppermint Lounge. God only knows what they made of them there.

The band padded out with the addition of Bryan Hayes on rhythm guitar and the return of Paul Thompson on drums for 'Woman In Disguise', an all-out attack on Lady Thatcher, who had inspired, and would continue to inspire, several Angelic Upstarts' tunes. Following 'Soldiarity', Mensi's tribute to the titular union movement in Poland, Mond stepped off the bus, later to work with New Model Army, and some assumed the band had broken up, not for the last time in the band's history. "Mond had just had enough," Mensi told Wake Up fanzine. "He was pissed off – we weren't making any money, you know. We wanted to be Bruce Springsteen. Mond was like the other side of the band and I was very unsure whether I could carry things on. I got a job as a taxi driver for a few months, but I really missed it, being on stage and everything."

With major label interest long behind them (and what an ill-starred marriage that was, yet so emblematic of the majors' confusion and desperation in the wake of punk), they returned to their independent roots with a succession of albums, Reason Why? (featuring the superb a cappella folk lament, 'Geordie's Wife' and 'Loneliness Of The Long-Distance Runner', inspired by Alan Sillitoe's book), Last Tango In Paris (with another 'borrow' from working class folk music, 'Blackleg Miner', featuring another new line-up of Derwent Jaconelli on drums, Ronnie Rocka on guitar and Max Splodge on drums) and Blood On The Terraces, for three different labels. The latter managed to cause something of a stir with what the media saw as its advocacy of terrace violence. Yet the militant reggae of 'It's Your Life' and the Mel Tillis cover version, 'Ruby', confirm once and for all that the Upstarts were more than one-trick ponies.

1986 brought Power Of The Press, which contained the controversial 'Brighton Bomb' single, the sleeve for which was withdrawn. The song lamented the IRA's bombing of the Tory party conference on the basis that it failed to take out Margaret Thatcher (the album was also titled Brighton Bomb for American release). Other tracks of interest were a cover of Eric Bogle's 'Green Fields Of France', and the Clash eulogy, 'Joe, Where Are You Now?'

They were quiet until 1992 when they reunited for Bombed Out. But the title could have served as an epithet for their critical reputation. A decade later a new line-up – featuring Mensi backed by Lainey (of Leatherface) on drums, Tony Von Frater (Red Alert) on guitar and Gaz Stoker (Red London) on bass, recorded Sons Of Spartacus, which included a version of the old Italian workers' anthem 'Bandiera Rossa'. With the guitar mixed much higher, this was a totally remodelled Upstarts, but it had its moments. Not least 'Action Man', re-recorded from the abysmal Still From The Heart, at the specific request of record label boss Mark Brennan, as an example of just how strong that material could have been with a different production. Meanwhile 'Don't Get Old (In Tony's Britain)' was a stinging rebuke to the halibut smile of Tony Blair, which had supplanted the Thatcher sneer but changed little else. "New Labour seemed to have captured the middle ground and moved further to the right on a weekly basis. I love the Spartacus album. If it wasn't for my voice there would have been five hit singles on that, but never mind, you can't have everything. I've always got my good looks to fall back on."

What place is there for the Angelic Upstarts in the new millennium? Like many who fought against Thatcherism, Mensi feels equally disenfranchised with New Labour and the false dawn. "He's a better capitalist than Thatcher," he says of Tony Blair, "at least Thatcher was more honest. You knew where you stood, at least Thatcher didn't pretend to be working class." He remains as political as ever (see 'Anti-Nazi' on the recent studio album), pulling out of Holidays In The Sun because he refused to share a stage with Condemned 84 and Section 5 unless they renounced their fascist connections.

DISCOGRAPHY:

(Buyers Guide: As ever, the Captain Oi! reissues of the studio albums are lovingly compiled. Teenage Warning can't really be topped for its sheer stripped-down punch, but 2,000,000 Voices is arguably the band's coming of age. We Gotta Get Out Of This Place is a keeper as is the far more recent Sons Of Spartacus, of which Mensi is justifiably proud)

The Murder of Liddle Towers/Police Oppression 7-inch (Dead Records IS/AU 1024 May 1978)

The Murder of Liddle Towers/Police Oppression 7-inch reissue (Small Wonder SW-001 September 1978)

I'm an Upstart/Leave Me Alone 7-inch (Warner Bros K-17354 March 1979) (initial copies in green vinyl. Also issued as a 12-inch, K-17354T)

Teenage Warning LP (Warner Bros K-56717 June 1979) (reissued on CD by Warners VACD1, and finally, after "seven years of bartering with Warners", according to Mark Brennan, by Captain Oi!, AHOY CD 227, 2002. Additionally features the single versions of 'The Murder Of Liddle Towers' and 'Police Oppression' as bonus tracks)

Teenage Warning/The Young Ones 7-inch (Warner Bros K-17426 July 1979) (initial copies in red vinyl)

Never 'ad Nothing/Nowhere Left to Hide 7-inch (Warner Bros K-17476 November 1979)

Out of Control/Shotgun Solution 7-inch (Warner Bros K-17558 January 1980)

We Got To Get Out of this Place/Unsung Heroes II 7-inch (Warner Bros K-17586 March 1980)

We Got To Get Out of This Place LP (WEA K-56806 April 1980)

(reissued on CD by Captain Oi!, AHOYD CD 228, in 2003, with bonus tracks 'Nowhere Left To Hide' and 'Unsung Heroes II')

Last Night Another Soldier/The Man Who Came In From The Beano 7-inch (Zonophone/EMI Z-7 July 1980)

England/Sticks' Diary 7-inch (Zonophone/EMI Z-12 November 1980)

Kids on the Street/The Sun Never Shines (Zonophone/EMI Z-16 January 1981)

I Understand/Never Come Back 7-inch (Zonophone/EMI Z-22 June 1981) (also issued as 12-inch single, 12Z-22, plus 'Heath's Lament')

2,000,000 Voices LP (Zonophone/EMI ZONO-104 June 1981) (reissued on CD, Dojo CD 81, with four B-sides, 'The Man Who Came In From The Beano', 'Sticks' Diary', 'The Sun Never Shines', 'Never Come Back', in May 1993, then on Captain Oi!, AHOY CD 158, in 1998, with those tracks plus 'I Understand (Single Version)' and Mark Brennan's sleevenotes)

Live LP (Zonophone/EMI ZEM-102 September 1981) (with free live flexi adding 'The Young Ones', 'Whit Riot', 'We're Gonna Take The World' and 'Leave Me Alone'. Reissued on Dojo, DOJOCD 169, February 1994)

Different Strokes/Different Dub 7-inch (Zonophone/EMI Z-25 October 1981)

Never Say Die/We Defy You 7-inch (Zonophone/EMI Z-28 March 1982)

Still From The Heart LP (Zonophone/EMI ZONO-106 April 1982) (reissued on CD, Dojo DOJOCD 144, November 1993, and on Captain Oi! AHOY CD224, 2002, with seven bonus tracks – 'Different Strokes', 'Different Dub', 'We Defy You', 'Action Man (demo)', 'Cry Wolf (demo)', Soldier (demo)', 'Gonna Be A Star (demo)'. The latter four tracks are especially interesting as they were from the tape the band submitted to EMI before the label, in their wisdom, opted to put them in harness with producer Steve Levene and attempt to turn them into a pop band)

Woman in Disguise/Lust for Glory 7-inch (Anagram/Cherry Red ANA-3 November 1982) (also issued as a 12-inch single, 12-ANA-3, with bonus track '42nd Street')

Solidarity/Five Flew Over 7-inch (Anagram/Cherry Red ANA-7 May 1983) (also issued as a 12-inch single, 12-ANA-7, with bonus tracks 'Dollars & Pounds' and 'Don't Stop')

The Burglar 7-inch (Anagram/Cherry Red ANA-12 July 1983; withdrawn)

Not Just a Name/The Leech 7-inch (Anagram/Cherry Red ANA-13 September 1983) (featuring Max Splodge on vocals; also issued as a 12-inch single with bonus tracks 'Leave Me Alone', 'Liddle Towers' and 'White Riot', 12-ANA-13)

Reason Why LP (Anagram/Cherry Red GRAM-004 December 1983) (reissued on CD as CDPUNK 17, November 1992, with the bonus tracks 'Lust For Glory', 'Five Flew Over The Cuckoo's Nest', 'Dollars And Pounds', 'Don't Stop', Not Just A Name', 'The Leech', 'Leave Me Alone (live)', 'Liddle Towers (live)' and 'White Riot (live)'.

Last Tango In Moscow LP (Picasso PIK-004 August 1984) (often listed as a live album, but in fact this is the Upstarts' seventh studio album. Reissued in February 1988 on Razor, RAZ 004, and on CD November 1993 by Great Expectations, PPCD 047, and May 1998 by Captain Oi!, AHOY CD87. The latter is the one to get – as it features the bonus tracks 'Paint It In Red/There's A Drink In It/Listen To The Silence/She Don't Cry Anymore/I Won't Pay For Liberty/Never Return To Hell/When Will They Learn/No Nukes)

Machine Gun Kelly/Paint It In Red 7-inch (Picasso PIK-001 October 1984) (also released as 12-inch, PIKT 001 with bonus track 'There's A Drink In It')

Brighton Bomb/Thin Red Line/Soldier 12-inch (Gas GM 3010 June 1985)

Live In Yugoslavia LP (Picasso HCLP 002M September 1985) (reissued February 1988 on Razar, RAZM 32, CD reissued August 1993 on Great Expectations, PIPCD 048, and again on Punx, PUNXCD2, October 1995. Finally reissued by Harry May, MAYO CD 504, in 2000)

The Power Of The Press LP (Gas GAS 4012 January 1986) (reissued June 1990 on Streetlink, CLINK 006. Note this was released in America as Brigton Bomb by Chameleon Records)

Blood On The Terraces LP (Link LINKLP 019 December 1987) (reissued on CD by Captain Oi! AHOYCD 116 with seven live tracks, Never 'ad Nothing', 'Leave Me Alone', 'Teenage Warning', 'Last Night Another Soldier', 'Guns For The Afghan Rebels', 'One More Day', 'Two Million Voices', taken from the band's Main Event show in 1988 – which did, indeed, result in blood on the terraces, or at least the dancefloor).

Bombed Out LP (Roadrunner May 1992) (reissued on Dojo, DOJOCD 198, August 1994)
Sons Of Spartacus CD (Captain Oi! AHOY CD 190 2002)
ARCHIVE RELEASES:
I'm An Upstart/Never 'ad Nothing CD-single (Warners SPZ2 April 1991)
Angel Dust (The Collected Highs) LP (Anagram GRAM 07 September 1983) (also issued as a cassette with extra tracks. CD resissue on Anagram, CDMGRAM 7, October 1988)
Bootlegs And Rarities LP (Dojo LP 7 March 1986) (reissued on CD on Great Expectations, PIPCD 049, November 1993. Pick up the Captain Oi! Rarities reissue instead)
Live And Loud LP (Link LINK LP 040 1988) (reissued on CD by Harry May, MAYO CD 560, in 2005. The set was recorded in Nijmegan, Holland, and produced by Dutch punk legends Brock and Gerrit from the Squats and the Magnificent)
Lost And Found LP (Link LINK LP 140 1988) (studio tracks recorded between their EMI and Anagram deals, alongside five live tracks from the band's Main Event gig at London's Astoria. Re-released by Harry May, MAYO CD 505, 2000)
England's Alive 12-inch EP (Skunx MENSIX 1 July 1988)
England/We're Gonna Take The World/Liddle Towers/The Young Ones
Alternative Chartbusters CD (Streetlink AOK 102 January 1992)
Greatest Hits Live CD (Streetlink STRCD 027 July 1992) (reissued on CD, Dojo DOJO CD 127, March 1993, then by Harry May, MAYO CD 512, in 2002. Recordings are drawn from 1982 shows.)
Kids On The Street CD (Cleopatra 1993) (American greatest hits package – only featuring dreadful sound quality and non-existent sleevenotes. To be avoided.)
The Independent Punk Singles Collection CD (Anagram CD PUNK 59 June 1995)
(all the Anagram/Cherry Red stuff)
Rarities CD (Captain Oi! AHOY CD80 December 1997)
(similar to the material on previous Dojo LP Bootlegs and Rarities, featuring 10 unreleased demos, including the original version of 'England', 'Spirit Of St. George', and 'Good Boy', which emerged on 2,000,000 Voices as 'Jimmy'. You can also hear Mond perform guide vocals on three demo tracks – which was the band's general approach in the studio at the time. Other cuts include their Wargasm contribution 'Victory In Poland' but the real stunner is the original version of 'Solidarity'. With excellent liner notes by Garry Fielding)
Who Killed Liddle double CD (Recall November SMDCD205 1998)
(less than essential double CD round-up of previously released material. Sleevenotes written by a complete ninny)
The EMI Punk Years (Captain Oi! AHOY CD 121 1999)
(nothing you won't have already if you have the EMI singles and studio albums, but decent sleevenotes)
The BBC Punk Sessions (Captain Oi! AHOY CD 138 2000)
(12 tracks from between 1978 and 1981, with spirited liner notes from Mensi. On the third session 'Liddle Towers' was broadcast as 'New Values' due to heightened police disapproval of the song causing the band all sorts of problems)
Never 'Ad Nothing CD (Harry May MAYO CD 106 2000) (pointless and redundant bits and pieces compilation featuring a smattering of live tracks)
Anthems Against Scum CD (Insurgence 2001) (recorded live in Hamburg, Germany, May 1999)
Live From The Justice League (TKO 2001)
The Punk Singles Collection CD (Captain Oi! AHOY CD 237 2005) (obviously this stuff is freely available elsewhere, but the liner notes and line-up annotation is useful)

Animals And Men

Ralph Mitchard (guitar, vocals, harmonica), Susan Wells (vocals), Nigel House (bass), Geoffrey Norcott (drums)

ANIMALS AND MEN were formed in Frome, Somerset, in 1977. Mitchard had been part of R&B/pub band the Bad Detectives, who built their repertoire around the 60s beat boom as well as newer acts such as Doctor Feelgood. But like so many they adapted, both musically and visually, as punk reached the provinces. Mitchard met Susan Wells outside a Wire and Adam And The Ants show in Bristol at the start

of 1978 and discovered that they both lived in the same town and had shared interests – notably the Ants. Mitchard quit the Bad Detectives to form Frome's first legitimate punk band, Psychotic Reaction, alongside schoolfriends Geoff Norcott and Nigel House, and practised on a nearby farm in Nunney.

Mitchard quickly decided that they needed a new singer, and thought immediately of Wells, as the band took its name from one of their favourite Ants songs. They would organise expeditions to London to check out the emerging punk scene. Chastened by his experiences with the Bad Detectives, Mitchard had no intention of slogging his way through local bars again, so they decided to try to make a record straight away. They sent a demo to John Peel who suggested they record a single. However, they were determined not to move to London full-time, despite House already having accommodation there. As Mitchard conceded in the sleevenotes to the Hyped2Death reissue of their collected works, "I suppose the inspiration was bands like the 13th Floor Elevators – we wanted to be mavericks out in the sticks, practising in a farmyard occasionally releasing brilliant singles. We got part of our wish..."

I asked Mitchard if Frome became one of those local scenes that developed like a microcosm of London. "Not really Frome, but towns like Warminster, Trowbridge – similar small towns. But there weren't many venues to play at that time and a lot of jealousies ruined any possibilities of a scene. Punk was for us an empowering thing, suddenly you could do things and be in bands and stuff. You kind of took on board a philosophy."

The only other copy of their first demo was sent to Allan Partner in Trowbridge, who was working with Moskow and was in the process of setting up his own TW Records. He immediately offered to release 'Don't Misbehave In The New Age'. Recorded in two hours on a four-track, it strutted somewhere between the Au Pairs and the Ants, with Mitchard's harmonica break, a hangover from his R&B days, offering an unexpected sonic contrast. John Peel's sponsorship – his playing of the single was the highpoint of the band's 'career' – and several good reviews resulted in interest from EMI and Sire, but Partner was unwilling to release them without getting a deal for his other TW bands. At the same time Norcott was posted to Gibraltar by the Royal Navy. Paul 'Puddle' Collyer, formerly of Stalag 44, stepped in. The band elected to break from Partner and establish their own label, Strange Days, which housed follow-up single 'Terraplane Fixation' (original title 'Car Crash Blues'). The B-side, 'Shell Shock', got most of the attention, stylistically mirroring Joy Division's innovations. "We were big fans from the beginning – we travelled to London to see their first London gig at the Hope and Anchor."

Finances were tight, and House was spending more time in London preventing them from practising. Collyer suggested drafting in former Moskow guitarist Dave Cole as replacement but when the band declined, he left too, joining Silent Guests. Was it frustrating not to be able to release more material? "It was pretty frustrating but we weren't really people that thought about albums really – we were 45rpm people – by the time bands did albums they often seemed to overdo it... we had loads of singles but the albums didn't ever make so much of an impact. Take the Subway Sect – 'Nobodys Scared' – we played that to death – but the LP? Who cared about that?"

In the meantime Partner had reissued 'Don't Misbehave'. But Mitchard and Wells, who remain a couple to this day, decided to change tack and renamed themselves the Terraplanes with the addition of local teenagers Dave Mackay and Andy Payne. Norcott also rejoined on his return from Gibraltar, while Brenda Austin became a second vocalist. They released one single, 'Evil Going On' (later covered by New York's Yo La Tengo) before being taken under old friend Adam Ant's wing as part of his new label deal, and tentatively renamed El Dorado. However, when Ant's career was suddenly revived with the success of 'Goody Two Shoes', the Terraplanes/El Dorado were left in limbo. At which point, the plug was pulled.

However, there's been enduring interest in the various incarnations of the band which eventually led to a reissue of their entire recorded output on Hyped2Death. The interest's seen the members tentatively inch back from retirement and cut some new songs, including a cover of 'Nag Nag Nag' for the Rebuilding The Bridge compilation in 2003.

DISCOGRAPHY:

Don't Misbehave In The New Age/Machines 7-inch (TW HIT01 1980) (1,000 pressed. Re-released a year later with a new sleeve)

Terraplane Fixation/Shell Shock (Cause/Effect) 7-inch (Strange Days SDAYS 1 1980) (1,000 pressed)
ARCHIVE RELEASE:
Revel In The Static CD (Messthetics 201 2005) (includes a four-song Animals & Men demo that survived only because they'd sent a copy to Zig Zag writer Mick Mercer. Plus a 1981 video of 'Evil Going On', etc)

Anorexia

Andrew Leigh (bass), Peter Leigh (guitar), Kevin Leigh (guitar), Nick Page (vocals), Kim Glenister (vocals), Graham Snell (drums)

ANOREXIA were teenagers from Hertfordshire, their personnel drawn from a council estate in North Watford, the Harebreaks. Kevin Leigh: "Anorexia were formed back in 1977 after being totally blown away by the emergence of punk in England, with the Sex Pistols being the number one influence in all our lives at the time. It felt so good to cut off all that heavy metal hair, spike it up, and then walk down the street scaring the crap out of old ladies.." The band was named "after an anorexic girl we saw at our local swimming pool. We thought it sounded fairly offensive, so we used it."

The band's ages ranged from 14 to 18. "None of us had any money, so all the band's gear was borrowed or made. The local wood yard would always smile as we turned up on a regular basis with a set of measurements for our next chipboard speaker cabinet which was gonna house any old 12-inch speaker we could get." They quickly became 'local heroes' around the Watford area. "The band's live image was pretty manic and well suited to the mood at the time, more fun than aggressive though, and we were not into all the spitting and gobbing crap that was going around at the time."

They put out one great little DIY single in 1980, 'Rapist In The Park', a feisty little self-financed artefact reminiscent of X-Ray Spex, not least due to the guest saxophone of Lisa Sinclair, which John Peel played repeatedly. "He had raved about it for a solid month, and in a matter of days we'd sold all our records to Rough Trade who made a tidy little profit on the lot. Unfortunately, with no management, we were too naive to quickly follow up our success with more pressings, and missed the biggest opportunity to make a national name for ourselves. Ah well, shit happens."

Anorexia nevertheless continued for some time. "We did some great London gigs at the Marquee, Dingwalls, Moonlight Club etc. The band stayed together for a further ten years, but with a couple of member and name changes." There was a second single in 1982, 'Steven', which featured Julie Hadwin on vocals (later the vocalist for Big Sound Authority). Kevin Leigh would subsequently open the rehearsal space Slim Studios a play on the band's name). His most famous client was George Michael's first band the Executive, who would also support Anorexia. "We're all still alive, in our 40s and teaching our kids guitar – but not to spit."

DISCOGRAPHY:

Rapist In The Park/I'm A Square/Pets 7-inch (Slim Records SJP812 1980) (the cheap sleeve – only printed on one side with a white paper bag glued to the reverse, demonstrates the budgetary constraints. This has subsequently been bootlegged)
Steven/Marching Songs 7-inch (Slim 1982)
COMPILATION:
Messthetics Vol. 5 ('I'm A Square') (the same track reappears on Messthetics Greatest Hits, The Sounds Of DIY 1977-80, 2006)

Apartment

Alan Griffiths (vocals, guitar), Richard White (bass), Emil (drums)

One of the best tracks on the much-admired Bristol area compilation Avon Calling of 1979 was APARTMENT's succinct 'The Alternative'. That same band's debut single, 'The Car', is even better, an urgent but playful slice of pop-punk that manages to sustain remarkable intensity over its two-minute duration. The influences were clear – the CBGB's set such as Talking Heads and Television, especially the latter on the single's B-side, 'Winter'.

Bristol's Apartment perfect their dazed and confused poses.

"I was playing guitar in a Bristol college rock band," Griffiths recalls. "Mostly covers with a few original songs thrown in. I was writing loads of songs experimenting and developing ideas with my trusty reel to reel tape recorder at home. College ended and so did that band. But punk had just arrived. Totally energised with what was happening around me, I decided it was time to form my own band with a lot of these new songs I had written." In April 1978 he put up adverts in local music stores for a bass player and drummer. "This led to finding Richard White, who had moved down to Bristol from Ross-On-Wye in search of a band and glory. By a stroke of good luck, he also knew of a great drummer in Bristol named Emil. So very quickly, Apartment just fell in to place."

They decided to keep to a three-piece line-up initially, and spent time rehearsing while checking out prospective venues. "We hired a room at the back of the Stonehouse pub in Bristol (sadly now replaced by an office block) for a fiver, and started playing gigs there regularly. After a short period of playing there we got more and more people turning up, and developed quite a following. Other bands started playing at the Stonehouse and for a while it was quite a thriving scene, like our own mini-CBGB's. We also sent a demo cassette to Simon Edwards of Bristol's Heartbeat Records. He loved it and kindly offered us the chance to record a track for his new Bristol compilation album – Avon Calling."

I asked Griffiths about the extraordinary variety of sounds on that album. "When Avon Calling came out in late October 1979 the punk thing had been going some two or more years, the explosion had happened, but by then had probably peaked. Certainly in Bristol there were many bands fusing the energy and excitement of punk, but coming up with a different blend. But the diversity of these different flavours is captured perfectly on Avon Calling – it's a snapshot of what was going on. Bristol at that time was a real melting pot of creative musical people. You then had new emerging bands like the Pop Group and the early formation of The Wild Bunch, which led on to Massive Attack."

Following the release of Avon Calling, Heartbeat were keen to work on a single. "We recorded 'The Car' and 'Winter' at Crescent Studios in Bath in December 1979, in between a flurry of gigs. 'The Car' gained a fair amount of radio play. We were playing quite a few gigs in London at the Marquee, 100 Club and the Moonlight. We were also supporting bands like the Cure and Gang Of Four locally. Around this time we added Steve Street of the Europeans on bass, as Richard wanted to switch to guitar.

But we got to a point where in retrospect, we should have released another single, but it didn't happen. In fact 'Poison' (the demo of which is on the re-release of Avon Calling) was to be the next candidate. By the mid-summer of 1980 we had decided to split after not getting to the next level."

Of the four Apartment tracks officially released, Griffiths is happiest with 'Winter'. "I still think it hits the right nerve. It seems to have held up quite well musically. We also recorded a four-track BBC Radio One Session for Mike Read in early 1980, that could be unearthed. Plus I still have various Apartment tracks on tape that have never been released." Well, my favourite is 'The Car', which has an incredible guitar sound, which I assumed involved overdubs. "No, no real multi-track layering or stacking up of guitar chords going on here. Just three different guitar parts, coming in and out at different times."

When Apartment stalled Griffiths and Emil put together the Escape, a Goth-aligned band who appeared on the BBC's Oxford Road Show and signed to Phonogram, at which time he

became friends with label-mates Tears For Fears. He continued to work with that band's Roland Orzabal. "I played guitar with Tears For Fears on their world tour in 1985. I did session work with Vitamin Z and Talk Talk between 1985 and 1986. I worked with Roland, co-writing and producing, between 1990 and 2000, including TFF's albums Elemental (1993) and Raoul And The Kings Of Spain (1995)." He also worked on Orzabal's 2001 solo album Tom Cats Screaming Outside, collaborated with Emiliana Torrini (on her 2000 album Love In The Time Of Science) and appeared on Seal's IV album, on which he co-wrote one track. Since 2002 he had been composing 'additional music' for US shows including CSI, CSI Miami and CSI New York. "And that's what I'm still doing at the moment."

Discography:

The Car/Winter 7-inch (Heartbeat PULSE 7 April 1980) (double a-side)
COMPILATIONS:
Avon Calling – The Bristol Compilation LP (Heartbeat HB 1 1979; 'The Alternative') (reissued on CD in October 2005 on Heartbeat/Cherry Red CDMRED 292 with additional track 'Poison' plus 'The Car' and 'Winter' on bonus CD The Heartbeat Singles Collection)

Art Attacks

Edwin 'Savage Pencil' Pouncey (vocals), J.D. Haney (drums), Rob Smith (bass), Steve Spear (guitar)

A great example of art school aesthetics mobilised by punk irreverence/get-up-and-go, the ART ATTACKS were formed in early 1977 by Pouncey and Spear at the London Royal College Of Art. Over a career that lasted just 18 months, they were good value for what amounted to footnote status in punk's timeline. Spear had been advised by a contemporary that he ought to hook up with Pouncey, so he walked up and asked him if he wanted to be a singer. "The ICA had a talent night," Pouncey told me in 2003, "and we thought we'd be a punk band. Instead of taking it as a joke, we took it seriously, they reacted as if we were a deadly serious punk band. Then after that we got invited to do stuff." Their two songs were 'Rat City' and 'Subway Train', which, according to Spear, just got faster and faster until the band collapsed at the end. Rick Slaughter, later of the Motors, played drums, with Rob Smith of the Snakes on bass.

The Art Attacks' first demos were cut with Rob Gotobed, formerly of the Snakes and later of Wire, on drums, comprising 'Rat City' and the (unreleased until much later) 'Chicken In Funland' at Pathway in Stoke Newington. 'Chicken In Funland' was titled after a Sun headline. JD Haney then took up the post of drummer permanently, though Pouncey recalls him being "involved" from the band's first sessions. Marion Fudger took over bass, by which time Albatross Records, run from a basement in Kensington Market, offered them a contract. A smattering of shows at the RCA and Wimbledon Art School ensued. The venues were not coincidental. "We were always more of an art school band than a punk band." They were also very much a fourth estate band, Pouncey was well known as Savage Pencil for his Sounds artwork, while Fudger wrote for feminist publication Spare Rib. She also authored Is This Your Life? Images Of Women In The Media for Virago along with Terri Goodard and Jan Pollock. She'd previously played in the Derelicts, who included Barbara Gogan (later of the Passions) and Sue Gogan (later Prag Vec). By February 1977 Pouncey was illustrating Rock'n'roll Zoo for Sounds, which was good for a few plugs.

The Art Attacks' first releases came via compilations. Arguably their best-remembered song, 'Arabs In 'Arrads', was included on Streets: Select Highlights From Independent British Labels, released through the band's connection with Beggars Banquet act the Lurkers. As well as Streets, Pouncey also provided the artwork for the Lurkers' 'Freak Show', the Fall's 'Lie Dream Of A Casino Soul', and later covers for Big Black, Sonic Youth and myriad others. 'Frankenstein's Heartbeat' and 'Animal Bondage' were also appended to Live At The Vortex.

The Art Attacks' debut single, 'I Am A Dalek', later became a collectible punk oddity owing to its tentative connection to the Dr Who TV series. Amusingly, some Doctor Who fans objected to 'I Am A Dalek's authenticity: "It's not a great song (three chords in quick succession, repeated ad infinitum) and the vocals can hardly be heard anyway," sniffed one

Time Lord-adoring website. "It would be wrong to associate this with the eloquence of the TV programme we love." Perhaps it was the guitar sound that deterred our sci-fi friends. Pouncey: "Steve used to make aluminium guitars at art school – cast aluminium, really unique sound that no-one else had. He made them in the furniture department." Although some critics compared it to the Buzzcocks' 'What Do I Get?', Pouncey claims he was inspired more by American no wave than Brit punk rock. "I didn't really like English punk much, it was lame, I liked the Ramones and Patti Smith."

But they were influenced by the Pistols. "The Pistols were amazing – we saw them at the 100 Club, where they played one evening a week. There'd be nobody there. They'd do their thing and were fantastic. It was a regular thing, then the press caught up with them. I used to chat to Glen, who was very friendly. I was at the ICA, trying to get them to perform there. When they blew up, the Royal College said there's been too much publicity, so we had to pull out. But we nearly had them at the ICA." However, like many others, Pouncey felt disappointed with their debut release. "We thought 'Anarchy' was absurd when it came out, we felt betrayed. Those two Damned singles ('New Rose', 'Neat Neat Neat') were fantastic. In comparison, the Sex Pistols were like the Shadows. I'll give them that 'God Save The Queen' is magnificent, though."

Their own shows attempted to capture the same confrontational approach of the Pistols. "We were very experimental, we wanted songs to go on for 15 minutes. I'd walk on stage and give the microphone to the tramp. I wanted to freak the audience out. What it would take to see how fragile their uniform was. I'd wear Jehtro Tull t-shirts. People would go insane. I really don't think we were a punk band. A lot of those bands weren't punk. They were rock'n'roll bands. We were into rock n' roll – the crudity of it makes it work as outsider art." Pouncey would suffer from stage nerves, however, and often put in, by his own admission, erratic performances. However, not everyone was comfortable with the circus aspects of punk. Fudger was hugely embarrassed by her association with the band when the girlfriend of the owner of Albatross Records, a stripper, undressed at the Marquee – some writers even mistook Fudger for the stripper in press reports.

"We would never, ever have allowed that to happen," Pouncey complains. "We were feminists. We were anti-racist, anti-sexist, everything, without having a big flag about it. I don't know what on earth they were trying to do. We were mystified by it. Marion was mad, not upset, but we were all a bit mad. We didn't think it was funny." So what actually happened? "I just carried on and tried to ignore her – the picture appeared in Sounds later on. My mother rang up and said, 'what are you doing?' She was really embarrassed. I had to explain it all truthfully, that it was nothing to do with us. When I did, she accepted it."

Subsequently, Pouncey tells me, Steve had 'words' with their erstwhile label manager. "People would do that a lot, people who ran labels thought they had a vision of what punks should be. We went to Keithley for a show. This guy asked, you're punks? He had a beautiful suit, he went and got changed into a tailcoat he'd ripped up the seam and stuck together with safety pins. This was the uniform he thought he should wear. We were in ordinary clothes."

As for the songs? "'Rat City' was about some city gent who did that every day. I wrote most of the songs. 'I Am A Dalek' is totally autobiographical (about his job in a department store, he actually had to dress as one) and my view on how I think everyone at the time was becoming a Dalek, wearing the same Dalek costume, doing what the press wanted them to do. 'Punk Rock Stars' was a big dig at bands who'd made it. I don't want to mention any of them."

But it effectively all ended when Pouncey elected to concentrate on passing his finals. "I was at art school to get a degree. When the band started getting in the way of my art and degree, I wasn't going to blow it. So that's why I left. They understood. But I'm still Savage Pencil, all these years later." The Art Attacks played their final set at the Vortex on 16 January 1978, playfully announcing that ex-members would keep the name for their own band, to be numbered Art Attacks #2 through Art Attacks #5. Naturally this never happened, though the members did record a further single as the Tagmemics in 1980 ('Chimneys'), supporting the Monochrome Set, with whom Haney was now installed, on one occasion. Fudger went on to teach at The Deptford Academy Of Music.

A second, posthumous single, comprised further meditations on the transitory nature of punk rock and living in the city. 'Rat City', in particular, is a neglected classic, invoking sundry depressive 70s images such as repeats of Police Woman, doner kebabs, fish fingers and secretaries' legs – "the only pleasure I get". It's a shame there wasn't more of either the Art Attacks or the Tagmemics, but no album ever emerged until the 1996 CD compilation Outrage And Horror, which collated everything the band recorded plus live tracks. Other songs which were considered for the first single, 'Monkeys In Cars' and 'Mutant Madonna', have disappeared from sight completely. Luckily the CD has now been reissued after selling out of its initial pressing.

Pouncey subsequently returned to journalism, most recently for Wire magazine. However, there have been some low-key solo releases, including a soundtrack for the Bikers movie, Angel Dust, and two singles with the Kray Cherubs.

DISCOGRAPHY:

I Am A Dalek/Neutron Bomb 7-inch (Albatross TIT1 March 1978)
First And Last/Punk Rock Stars/Rat City 7-inch (Fresh FRESH 3 1979)
ARCHIVE RELEASES:
Outrage And Horror CD (Overground OVER58 CD November 1996)
SELECTED COMPILATIONS:
Streets: Select Highlights From Independent British Labels (Beggars Banquet BEGA 1 November 1977; 'Arabs In 'Arrads')
Live At The Vortex (NEMS NEL 6013 December 1977; 'Frankenstein's Heartbeat', 'Animal Bondage')

Arthur 2 Stroke

Arthur 2 Stroke (aka Phil Branston; guitar, vocals), WM7 (aka Steve Nash; guitar), Naughty Norman (aka Norman Hobbs; drums)

Specialising in a mix of originals and skewed cover versions, ARTHUR 2 STROKE, the son of BBC wildlife filmmaker Brian Branston, made his name playing at the Anti-Pop nights organised on Monday nights at the Gosforth Hotel in Newcastle. Tim Readman: "In 1979 Anti Pop (aka Andy Inman) and Phil Branston started a regular punk night at the Gosforth Hotel. This was before punk became the leather/studs/tartan uniform and was more about nobody giving a toss what they wore. Some of the lasses turned up in black bin liners. Some of the lads ended up in them too. Most of the bands were beginners. They were hilarious. "

Local heroes of the time were the Noise Toys, the Scottish Polis Inspectors, 29 Steps, Parting Shots and the Rhythm Method. Arthur 2 Stroke started here. Songs were stuff like 'The

Arthur 2 Stroke live on stage at the Gosforth Hotel.

Wundersea World Of Jacques Cousteau', 'Navy Manners', 'Consumer' and covers of 'Wild Thing' and 'Midnight Hour'. As well as Arthur 2 Stroke, the Noise Toys and Dementia Praecox, each Monday would feature two or three guest bands, resulting in a broad-based community that was connected to punk in spirit if not attire or musical style.

Steve Nash: "I first started going to the Gosforth Hotel in the autumn of 1978. I was at that point a fan. I had met Martin Stevens and Rupert (of the Noise Toys) over the previous summer, when we and various other young reprobates and local notables had all been extras on a Walt Disney film that was shot at Alnwick Castle, The Spaceman and King Arthur. I was drawn to Arthur 2 Stroke much more so than the Noise Toys or the other bands. This was because he had a spontaneity and sense of humour that elevated him above the other bands on the scene. Also he did not have a regular line-up. Most the time he did not have a bassist, and often he played without a drummer. It was mainly churning guitars and showmanship. After seeing him two or three times I told him I could play guitar and that I wanted to be in his band. We did a couple of rehearsals and really hit it off. He found Norman and then he gave us our new stage names. WM7 was derived from an OMO campaign from some years before, with WM7 being the special added ingredient that produces extra brightness."

"Around about the summer of 1978 three young lads came into my office after having seen myself on a regional TV programme aimed at the local youth culture, Check It Out," Arthur recalls. "The three lads introduced themselves, and then produced a two-page comic with the title The Daily Pie, asking if I would be interested in funding a print run of a proposed future comic. I was genuinely impressed with what they had shown me and told them I would indeed support their enterprise, adding that if they could make it more of a fanzine-type format we could sell it at our gigs. Christmas 1979 spawned Viz's first issue, an Anti-Pop special, and those three lads – Chris Donald, Simon Donald and Jim Brownlow – all became millionaires. Except not really Jim Brownlow, he left quite early on and became a drunk."

Readman: "Viz used to sell their early comics at the Gosforth (the first issue came out in December 1979). They presented Phil with a 'Camouflage Record' 'cos his single 'went camouflage' in the charts. Yes, no wonder no-one spotted it! It was a joint single with the Noise Toys, now worth its weight in polystyrene. After that Arthur 2 Stroke was inspired by Dexy's Midnight Runners to turn to soul music and the bastard punk twin of the Commitments. Arthur 2 Stroke and the Chart Commandos (in which he played bass) was born. The rest is history."

"They became The Chart Commandos when another former Newcastle pub band called The Young Bucks split, circa 1980," Viz founder Chris Donald remembers." Seb Shelton, their drummer, went on to join Secret Affair then Dexys Mk II. The Young Bucks guitarist Tony Wadsworth went into A&R and ended up as CEO of EMI. Young Bucks keyboard player Pat Rafferty returned to Newcastle and joined up with Arthur 2 Stroke to form the Chart Commandos, recruiting a bass guitarist, brass players etc." Nash: "Our first show at a working men's club was a gig in Hartlepool and we were so worried about the reputation of that fair town that we changed the words of our Toots and the Maytals cover to 'Funky Man' – so as to avoid provoking any monkeyish sensibilities." The Chart Commandos rather divided the punters. "Never mind Tim's 'Inspired by Dexy's", notes Chris Donald. "Take my word for it, they were a poor man's Bad Manners.* However, Chris Waddle was a big fan of theirs and often turned up to see them." Such a ringing endorsement by the mullet-maned minstrel of 'Diamond Lights' fame might be viewed with suspicion.

The Chart Commandos issued two singles – for Satellite in 1980 and Logo in 1981. There was also a live LP. Chris Donald: "The Chart Commandos sacked Arthur 2 Stroke and became Watt Government, in a military coup orchestrated by Tim Readman. Red Wedge-style Watt Government politely requested that Margaret Thatcher stand down, in a musical fashion. She didn't, so Tim emigrated to Canada. Around 1988 I recruited a manufactured part-time pub band Top Group Fantastic, with Arthur 2 Stroke (calling himself Tony O'Diamond) on vocals, Pat Rafferty on keyboards, Ian Thompson on bass, and Archie Brown on guitar and saxophone."

Naughty Norman would go on to join the Spares. After Top Group Fantastic, Branston went on to collaborate with Viz contributors Simon Donald (brother of Chris) and Alex Collier on their short-lived TV series the Regionairres. As for Naughty Norman? "He went on to become a drum technician and roadie for the Who and various others," remembers Chris Donald, "and still plays with Wild Willy Barrett. Him and his wife Christine won the pub quiz at my local last Thursday. They win it every Thursday."

DISCOGRAPHY:

The Wundersea World Of Jacques Cousteau 7-inch (Anti-Pop EntertaiNMEntarama AP 1 1979 (split single with the Noise Toys, whose 'Pocket Money' is on the flip)

***Chris Donald: "I only made the Bad Manners comparison (which was a little bit harsh) with the benefit of hindsight. At the time I worshipped Arthur 2 Stroke and the Chart Commandos."**

****A last word from Mr Arthur 2 Stroke himself: "You've just about got it, apart from all the top birds I got to shag, for research purposes only – writing love songs, etc. The last one being 'Oh, Joan, How Doth She Moan', an account of a night spent with Joan Collins some ten years or so ago in Barbados."**

The Astronauts

Mark Wilkins (vocals) and a cast of thousands – original members Max (bass, guitar) and Roy (guitar) were joined by upwards of 30 others down the years.

The ASTRONAUTS were formed in Welwyn Garden City, Hertfordshire, in 1978. They were a punk band, but one in tune with the roots of English music, including both popular and traditional variants. It lent them a musicality that has resulted in a loyal, if limited, international following throughout the ensuing two decades.

"I started (the Astronauts) to do a one-off gig," Wilkins later told UK Resist fanzine. "I didn't even think I'd have a record out. It struck me as extremely bizarre when someone asked me if I'd do one. I said, 'What, really?' My attitude to things changed over the years. It was initially a bit of fun with a few mates. There was a gig and I thought I'd write a song and articulate the things I was feeling on a lyrical basis as opposed to just saying it. I suppose, over the years, I've become more involved with the craftsmanship of songs and atmosphere, as opposed to blatantly writing verse and chorus. I still enjoy a good two-minute pop song. I can still relate to the feeling that made me feel like that in the original days. My roots were in Merseybeat, so I'd never slag off innocent pop music, but I think I've moved a little from that." Or, as he now reflects, "I'd always liked music that, retrospectively, could be said to have a 'punk attitude' in various musical settings. I saw the Sex Pistols in a very early form, after being party to booking them at a local college. After this, several of my friends started to form bands, and at the time punk rock seemed a diversion from the usual music and it was possible for musical incompetents like me to play gigs."

The Astronauts' first show paired them with Johnny Curious & The Strangers, "which ended with 50 people being hospitalised due to an invasion of local idiots". Follow-up shows saw them support Alan Clayson & The Argonauts and Dire Straits, which left "80% of their audience mystified". The Astronauts' debut EP, produced by Argonauts' mainman Alan Clayson, is retrospectively considered a lo-fi classic, the lead track appearing on several compilations. "We were very naive about the whole process (I still am, incidentally), so we followed Alan Clayson's direction and did the best we could. Even as we recorded it, I was aware it was going to be difficult to pigeonhole. But I looked on that as a strength rather than a weakness. Initially, the single sold slowly, and mainly in our local area, but after a couple of plays on the John Peel Show, it sold out within a day."

After temporarily using the name Restricted Hour ("The label was part of a large network of anti-racist organisations, as the National Front were becoming worryingly visible at the time"), Wilkins revived the Astronauts name for the Pranksters In Revolt EP. The line-up now featured two members from Johnny Curious and the Strangers. It was followed by an album, Peter Pan Hits The Suburbs, for the Genius record label. "Genius was a label started by ex-NME journalist Jonathan Barnett, a friend of Gong and ATV. He saw us on one of the Here And Now tours, where we were supporting. We got to know each other, discovered a shared love of Van Der Graaf Generator, and he suggested to Bugle to do a joint release, as neither of them had sufficient funding to do it alone." As for its contents: "It was interesting, as we were working with Grant Showbiz (who later went on to produce The Fall, Morrissey and Billy

Bragg) and Jonathan Barnett, which in itself ensured an atmosphere of creative chaos. Many ideas were formed in the studio. I still like the album – I think it has a sort of simplicity that I could never reproduce, having learned too much."

As the band's career progressed, they moved through a number of labels, including several associated with the nascent anarcho punk phenomenon, with whom the Astronauts, whose founding principles included autonomy and self-reliance, made an easy fit thematically, if not necessarily musically. Releases on Annares, All The Madmen and Acid Stings continued to see Wilkins grow as a writer, with the personal always at least of equal importance to the political. He was and is, simply, a gifted pop songwriter working in territory where those values were, if not alien, certainly downplayed.

Bringing the story up to date, the Astronauts have continued performing through the late 90s and into the 21st century. Live work has been concentrated in London and the south east, and there has also been room for a resurrected Restricted Hours and a brand new outlet for Wilkins, the Otters.

So how does Wilkins reflect on the large body of work that the Astronauts have amassed? "I lay back with my pipe and slippers and tell the young scamps heroic tales of how it was in the old days. No seriously, I've enjoyed the majority of times and I think we created a niche – admittedly a very small one – for ourselves, and, on a musical level, we've never been afraid to experiment or change direction."

Discography:

Astronauts 7-inch EP (Bugle Records, Blast 1 1979)
All Night Party/Survivors/Back Soon/Everything Stops The Baby
As Restricted Hours:
Stevenage Rock Against Racism EP (RAR 1979)
Getting Things Done/Still Living Out The Car Crash (plus two B-side tracks by the Syndicate) (Fund-raiser for Stevenage Rock Against Racism with the Astronauts appearing as Restricted Hours).
Pranksters In Revolt EP (Bugle Records, Blast 5, 1980)
Young Man's World/Moderation Is Boring/We Were Talking/Big Ben.
Peter Pan Hits The Suburbs LP (Bugle Genius 001 1981) (re-released on CD by Lazy Dog in 1994 with extra tracks 'Everything Stops For Baby' and 'Back Soon', single versions)
Only Fools And Optimists Cassette (Anarres ASC 001 1982) (Songs on side one went on to become It's All Done By Mirrors)
It's All Done By Mirrors LP (All The Madmen MAD5 1983) (re-released on CD by Lazy Dog in 1995 with extra tracks, 'Big Ben', 'Moderation Is Boring' and 'Getting Things Done' from early singles)
Soon LP (All The Madmen MAD11 1986)
The Seedy Side Of... mini-LP (All The Madmen MAD LP 005 1987)
Peter Pan Hits The Suburbs/It's All Done By Mirrors cassette (Acid Stings ASR 5 1989) (combined re-release)
In Defence Of Compassion LP (Acid Stings ASR 15 1989)
Constitution/Please Don't Come 'Round Tonight 45 (Acid Stings ASR16 1990)
Up Front And Sideways Cassette (Dizzy Positivity BG1 1995) (originally intended as a vinyl release on Acid Stings)
You're All Weird CD (Irregular Records IRR 041 1999)
Baby Sings Folksongs 7-inch (Farce Stark 31 1999) (one-sided German single) (The entire back catalogue is due for re-release on CD in 2006, with the single and EP material included as bonus tracks. Details will appear in due course on http://www.astronauts.org.uk. News of The Otters can be found at http://www.myspace.com/cillablack)

Atoms

Keith Allen (vocals, piano), Keith James (guitar), Photios Demtriov (guitar), John Studholme (guitar, bass, synthesiser), Sue Gogan (synthesiser), Roy Dodds (drums)

The ATOMS' story features some notable personalities taking their first baby steps in the punk rock firmament. Principal among the principals was Keith Allen, not wholly coincidentally touted as 'the punk comic' for his stand-up routines. After the Atoms he went on to start his own cult TV series, appeared in Trainspotting and

became singer with Fat Les. In between he also served as a kind of beery mascot to Blur during their Cool Britannia zenith, and New Order, with whom he composed 'World In Motion', the 1990 England World Cup song.

Prior to all that, Allen, who'd spent time in borstal as a child, silk-screened posters for the likes of the Buzzcocks and Clash, was a temporary member of the Tesco Bombers. His former colleagues in the brief 1979 apparition that was the Atoms also moved on to, or continued with, better remembered projects, albeit still within the musical sphere. John Studholme and Sue Gogan concurrently worked in pragVec with Jim Thirlwell (aka Foetus), who shared a flat with Allen. Roy Dodds subsequently played in Weekend, Fantastic Something and Fairground Attraction.

So how did the Atoms come about? "My angle was, I just got fed up with doing theatre," Allen tells me. "I thought it would be much better to get to an audience without them knowing what you were doing, and the best way to do that was in a talent contest, cos there were no rules, no-one expected anything and it was free. We just used to make up tunes as we went along." Indeed, the Atoms three recorded gigs, or at least the only three Allen can remember doing, were all part of a talent competition being run at the North Pole pub in North Kensington, sponsored by the brewery. "For some reason, we won the rounds and got into the final. And we came third. I'm pretty sure there was an agreement on behalf of the brewers that no way could this band win. I think even they knew we weren't serious about it, whereas a lot of other kids really wanted to be singers, or comedians. But we came third, which prompted a riot." Indeed, one of the reasons Allen elected not to continue with the band was that, while performing at the talent shows, they'd picked up an audience of right-wing QPR-supporting skinheads. How on earth did that happen? "I think just the fact that we were singing a song called 'Max Bygraves Killed My Mother' was pretty on the nose. I think 'Beatle Jacket' really got them going, that was improvised, and sometimes we played it for about eight minutes. And they were very good musicians, believe it or not, they were a good band."

Well, they were mostly good musicians. With one exception. Was Photios Demtriov a real person? "Yes, he was a Greek guy. I met him in the Windsor Castle, a very good punk venue. Everyone was forming a band. And I met him, this kid who just wanted to be in a band, and I loved his enthusiasm. I said, OK, let's be in a band. And it was me and him, he was the first one, we were the Atoms. Then I got proper people in. But I couldn't get rid of Photios, it just seemed too unfair. And he couldn't play a fucking note. He was the worst guitarist EVER! On the PLANET! He was meant to be a 'rhythm guitarist' and one of those words, possibly both, was just not applicable to him! But he was so proud to be in that band, it made his youth."

The idea came about in 1979, and within a few months, a single had been recorded, and released. "I sorted all that. I got a bloke in Swansea who owned a restaurant to loan me £500. And I paid him back! I pressed 2,000. I printed all the inserts and cover myself, hand-printed everything. Did 2,000 of them and sold them all through Rough Trade. It was brilliant. When I heard it played on John Peel, it was one of the greatest moments of my life, and Photios was crying, because he'd been on the radio. John Peel played it three times. And twice, he segued at the end Max Bygraves's 'You're A Pink Toothbrush' – absolutely brilliant. I clearly remember us being in a squat off the Harrow Road, all listening to John Peel. It was fucking mind-blowing to be on John Peel."

DISCOGRAPHY:

Max Bygraves Killed My Mother/Beatle Jacket 7-inch (Rink R-23 1979)

Attrix

Rick Blair (vocals, guitar, keyboards), Chris Towsey (drums), Mark Duxbury (bass, vocals)

Unrelated to their Irish counterparts the Atrix, this Brighton-based group – originally Gerry And The Attrix – were a huge influence on the burgeoning local punk scene for a variety of reasons. Combining a punk attitude with the musical chops of the Dolls and Velvet Underground, plus excursions into dub and reggae, they were led by Rick Blair. Alongside wife Julie, he ran the famed Attrix record shop in Sydney Street. A meeting place for likeminded outcasts, it also gave birth

to a record label of the same name which would document so much of the early Brighton punk scene via the Vaultage compilations.

ATTRIX themselves would christen the label with the release of 'Lost Leonore' in 1978, the catalogue number, RB 01, coming from Rick's initials. After the Attrix dissolved, he would form the Parrots, who featured on the Vaultage 78 album. Blair died in May 1999. A lot of people who love music, and not just from the south coast, owe him a great deal.

Jay Derrick, organ player of the Parrots, was kind enough to send me an ancient taped recording of the Attrix playing 'Cold Day In Hell', from a pub gig in Brighton in 1977. "It's interesting because it must be one of the earliest reggae songs written and performed by a band in Brighton. It's got Paul Clarke on keyboards, later of the Dots, Piranhas, Pookiensnackenburger etc, and Colin Murray on bass, who a few months later formed the Parrots with Rick."

DISCOGRAPHY:

Lost Leonore/Hard Times 7-inch (Attrix RB 01 1978)

Auntie Pus

Auntie Pus (aka Julian Isaacs; vocals, hectoring, lunacy), Robin Bibi (guitar), Jim Payne (bass), Chris Millar (aka Rat Scabies; drums)

Who is the most idiotic, deranged fellow on the Damned tour bus? No contest, surely? Well, for a short period there was genuine competition, what with the Damned dragging the one-man support act AUNTIE PUS around on tour. Among other things, Pus was known for being the most efficient thief anyone had ever seen, and would regularly relieve the local branch of Woolies of sundry electrical items as the band criss-crossed the country. He would then walk down the line of punters queuing up for Damned gigs selling them discounted toasters. His live appearances were something else again, as Mick Mercer recalled. "He used to support the Damned, just a git with a guitar. He was absolutely covered in gob, like really steaming. I was down the front, retching."

Punk gave Julian Isaacs, as was, the opportunity to realise his musical dreams. "I always loved rock'n'roll. But I don't really sing in tune. I can sing rock'n'roll in key nowadays after years of practice. I always loved Syd Barrett and all the English mavericks. I never really got accepted at school. All my friends had bands doing Cream covers, and I couldn't play lead guitar like Clapton. But then people said, oh, your songs are great. Punk broke down the barriers, like the barriers of singing in tune. People weren't bothered about it."

The Damned link came about after two strands came together. He was managed by Brighton-based David Scott, "a gangster come antique dealer come second hand car dealer come rock'n'roll guitarist, singer and producer. I'm from South West London, that's how I used to know Rat. He used to knock around Kingston all the time and I'm from Wimbledon. The two brothers who were in Rat's first band are two of my best friends, and we all keep in touch. I entered the Melody Maker Folk Rock Contest in 1977. Because I entered it on my own they put me in a folk heat, though I played rock'n'roll guitar and my own tunes. So the whole heat was havoc. I would have won but the judges were laughing so much they couldn't mark the papers. And all my mates were creating havoc and yelling abuse at the folk acts, who were there to do it for real. A few months after that, Dave Scott was promoting the Hastings Pier Ballroom. I used to keep in touch with Rat, and I knew the Damned had made it big. David came up from Brighton to see me in Wimbledon, and he said, we had the Damned on at the

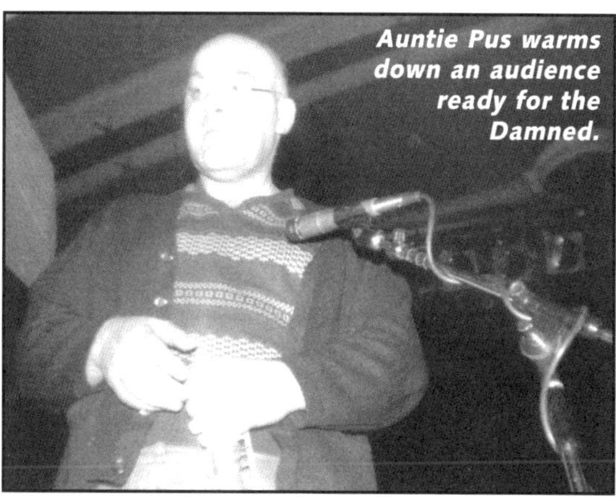

Auntie Pus warms down an audience ready for the Damned.

Hastings Pier Ballroom last week. I was chatting to the drummer backstage, he was a mate of yours. Yeah, I know! So he said, the next time the Damned play Hastings, we're going to have you on as a compere and first act. And that's how it all started."

Auntie Pus's famed sartorial elan arrived completely by accident. "I didn't have a clue what to wear. I saw a picture of Captain wearing an old school blazer. So I dug up my old public school uniform, with a rock'n'roll quiff and sideburns, and I wore the school blazer and cap. And it really took off. I had this review for it and that's how I became the 'public school punk balladeer'. But it was all by chance. I just thought this was a good thing to wear on stage for the first gig I'd ever done with the Damned." From then on he became a fixture at Damned shows. "The first Damned tour I went on was 1978, with Algy from the Saints on bass, when they went to France on their 'reunion' tour without Brian, and Captain playing guitar. And we got thrown out of five hotels in four days."

He eventually roped in Rat to drum on 'Half Way To Venezuela', recorded in 1978, produced by Dick Taylor of the Pretty Things. It was cut at Pathway "because I did it with Rat and that's where the Damned made their first single, and it was still dirt cheap and the engineer was good. The guy who played bass, Jim Payne of the Stukas, was a dear friend of mine and Robin's who died, tragically, in a hang-gliding accident aged 25. He was a real shining light – an up and coming guitarist. But I think 'Halfway To Venezuela' is the only thing that he actually recorded that got released."

So what caused the delay between recording and release? "Well, I recorded it, and nothing much happened. At the time I had a parallel career in shoplifting and drug addiction which interfered with things slightly. David Scott paid for it in the beginning. Then through the Damned I started touring with the Ruts as well. I really got on with the Ruts. And I ended up being managed by their manager, Andy Dayman, who got them their deal with Virgin. He got me a deal with Spartan Records. He heard the single and thought it was great. I said – it's there, ready to go. If you can get me a distribution deal you can be my manager, 20 per cent. That'd be great. And we got Single of the Week in Sounds."

Nowadays Isaacs is retraining to be a youth support worker and adult literacy officer. "I'm trying to get my foot in a few doors. It's that corny thing of putting something back and trying to do something useful." And yes, he still believes in the redemptive power of rock'n'roll, and the way it finds space for outsiders like him. "I like any English mavericks, whether it's Lol Coxhill playing jazz saxophone or John Otway. I may not be big fans of their music to take home and play, but I'm fans of them for what they do, because it's all part of that same tradition, both pre and post punk, being English and eccentric and a maverick and doing whatever you want to do."

DISCOGRAPHY:

Half Way To Venezuela/Marmalade Freak 7-inch (Septic AUNT 1 1980) (originally recorded in 1978. There was a 1999 CD reissue with four tracks. "I rewrote the words of the verses, re-recorded it with Robin Bibi, another fantastic drummer called Hans Ferrau, from Robin's band, and Segsy from the Ruts on bass. The idea was that it was a 20 years on version of 'Venezuela'. And it was rocked up a bit, with new drums, a weird trancey remix of it with a friend of mine called Ashley Wales, who's in a duo called Spring Heeled Jack who were a big drum 'n' bass act and now do free jazz. Also, for about ten years on and off, I had a punk rock'n'roll band called the Black Devils. We recorded one track only, which featured Arthur (Arturo Bassick) on backing vocals, and also little Helen, aka Helen Of Troy. She's also a dear friend. And that never came out and that's on there. And then there's the original too. It's got a whole new cover done by Rachel Howard – Dave Ruffy's ex-partner for many years, who designed the original logo for the first cover, whose father John designed the Grin 'n' Bear It sleeve for the Ruts.")

The Automatics, one of the great lost punk bands of the 1977 West London punk rock scene.

Automatics

David Philp (vocals), Walter 'Wally' Hacon (guitar), Rick Goldstein (drums), Bobbie Collins (bass)

Not to be confused with the Coventry Automatics, whose name change they eventually forced, the AUTOMATICS are principally remembered for their single 'When The Tanks Roll Over Poland Again'. A John Peel favourite, it topped the alternative charts in 1978, though such alternative charts were quite subjective affairs, not necessarily relating to sales. What should have been lift-off turned into a damp squib. "Like most punk groups we didn't last long," Philp recounted. "We played too fast, stayed up too late, and burned out quick. We came up through a time when you were more likely to get beaten up than paid every time you played."

Confrontational and opinionated, the Automatics cut their teeth by playing what they termed "guerrilla gigs" at major venues – pulling up on a flatbed truck outside shows by Queen (as recorded in the Evening Standard) or the Runaways. They would get through as much of their set as possible before the police intervened. They regularly headlined the Marquee, played the Reading Festival, and shared bills with X-Ray Spex, the Members and Eddie and the Hot Rods, whose Barrie Masters also helped out as an ad hoc roadie. They also befriended Johnny Thunders, who hung out with Philp and played on the band's 'Wild One' and 'Moth Into The Flame' album cuts (Philp would return the compliment by adding vocals, uncredited, to So Alone's 'He Was A Wizzard').

The band was formed after Philp had briefly rehearsed with the Boys in 1976, its operations centred around his flat in Comeragh Road. The early line-up featured Gary Tibbs, later of the Vibrators, Adam And The Ants and Roxy Music, on bass, alongside Hacon and Goldstein, before Collins replaced Tibbs. The Comeragh Road scene began "when my girlfriend got busted for smuggling heroin in Greece," Philp explained. He'd met Steve Lillywhite while working with the Boys, who moved into his flat in Comeragh Road. "Meanwhile, we had hooked up with Lady X and her pal Angie, who became de facto managers for the Automatics. Lady X was a really interesting woman. She had been blind and her sight was restored by an operation and she had this wonderful thing about her – like everything was new and innocent, even though she blew everybody shamelessly (something little English girls generally didn't know how to do in those days). They were always the first ones on the dance floor at the first Automatics gigs. Shortly after we met they moved in around the corner at Vereker Rd. Angie started banging Steve right around the same time that I started with Caroline White who briefly became my first wife. The marriage lasted a big 90 days. When eventually Caroline moved in with me Steve moved in at Vereker Road and then later I found a flat for him and Angie in the basement of 73 Comeragh Road."

"Michael Beal (who also lived in Vereker Road and helped design the Only Ones' sleeves) was, and is, a great guy. He really helped get that scene organised. He did artwork for small labels, and through him, Thunders came into the scene. The Comeragh Road deal was really me and the Autos, Steve Lillywhite, Eddie and the Hot Rods, Ultravox! and various Members (Steve's brother was the drummer), Thunders and X-Ray Spex guys like BP Hurding and to a lesser extent the Sham guys. After about 18 months the scene moved to Vereker Road when Steve did, although there were still parties at No. 73 but Caroline and I rarely got out of bed long enough to be social! There were no sofas for Thunders to nod out on though, mostly he was locked in the bathroom or playing my old Gibson in my bedroom. – just mattresses on the floor. Steve was working at Phonogram on that first Ultravox! album. Later we all moved to Island (after interest was shown from future Robbie Williams' manager Tim Clark) – The Rods, the Autos and Ultravox! – where a lot of stuff we had recorded at Phonogram was credited to Island for obvious reasons!" Philp managed to squeeze a quote out of Lillywhite for me about those times. "I think the Comeragh road scene is a bit stretched – but I suppose the facts do indicate a certain something in the water!"

The party wasn't over, however. "A lot of the scene transferred to Island. All the Island hangers-on were helping themselves to all the beers in the refrigerator and they were all getting charged to our account. Hordes of Jamaicans smoking ganja (the Wailers used to get all their grass sent to them in cowboy boots sent from Jamaica). Marley was recording Kaya at the next studio for some of the time. The recording continued and Steve and I were staying up all night doing coke and obsessing and wondering why things weren't going faster than they were. Island suggested we switch producers to the guy who had just done the Clash album, Guy Stevens. He came down to the studio and we talked but I couldn't bring myself to fire Steve. Compounding the problems was the fact that the management team we had hired was getting divorced and the one that stayed with us was falling apart, so no decisions were made. The singles contenders were 'Walking with the Radio', 'Run Forever' and 'Tanks'. We decided on 'Tanks'. The ads went out in the papers but the damned silver paper sleeves wouldn't dry – they took a month to complete the order by which time the marketing budget was consumed but nothing was available at the shops. So basically at no point when it was advertised was it available and at no point when it was available was it advertised."

Despite the single's 'success', Island were justifiably unhappy with the expenses the band rang up, as well as misplaced accusations of racism (despite the presence of a West Indian keyboard player, Phil Ramacon, at live shows). They even had the Jewish League attend one performance to clear them of Nazi sympathies. Nevertheless Island got cold feet and, according to the band, gave "our studio time, producer and equipment" to U2. They'd actually recorded nine other tracks with Lillywhite, but they were never released until many years later (the Walking With The Radio On LP). There was also disharmony from within – the band and singer disagreed over writing royalties.

They did regroup a year later in 1979 to record 'British Beat', but by that time Philp had signed his own solo songwriting deal, Hacon was on tour with Wreckless Eric and Goldstein had joined Sham 69. "The band had broken up after Island dropped us and Wally was off on the Stiffs World tour but when he came back we got together and recorded it ourselves without Steve (Lillywhite). Rick was out with Sham so he missed that session too. It was just kind of, 'I've got this new song – let's have a bash at it'. The Automatics really needed someone who could manage them- who could take what we did to the marketplace and we never really found them."

Finding a copy of 'Poland' on eBay in 2001 selling for an extortionate amount, Philp decided, with the help of Japanese independent Base Records, to see if there was still mileage in his songwriting. He toured Japan backed by local musicians, and set about rescuing the "lost album", Walking With The Radio On, as well as a collection of new songs, while old Sex Pistol mainstay Steve Jones was even encouraged to come along and play a hand, as only he can, on Forty Virgins In The Afterlife.

From then on the band have continued to pick up momentum. They're recording a new CD, Britannia, featuring Ian McCallum of Stiff Little Fingers on guitar, Rick Goldstein on drums, and backing vocals by Michael Des Barres, Mick Rossi of Slaughter And The Dogs and Phil Hendricks of the Stiffs. For a band whose moment passed very quickly back in the late-70s, the Automatics have done more than most to make up for lost ground. "I don't really have any bitches. I am appalled at the bullshit the big companies have jammed into the market place. I wish I had had a bigger career but I see a lot of people that did who are miserable and destroyed by it. Hunter Thompson said: 'The music industry is a cruel and shallow money trench, a long plastic hallway where thieves and pimps run free and good men die like dogs.' I guess I died like a dog. Those weasels took away the music from me for 20 years but now I have it back and I am loving doing it more than I ever have and I'll just keep on doing it so long as I can keep that gift. And let the chips fall where they may."

DISCOGRAPHY:

When The Tanks Roll Over Poland Again/Watch Her Now 7-inch (Island WIP6439 1978)
Walking With The Radio On LP & CD (Base Records 2000; Japan, Angel Air 2003; UK) (UK edition, CD only)
Automatics 2 LP (Base Records 2002; Japan)
Forty Virgins In The Afterlife CD (Base Records; 2002; Japan, Trash 2001 2004; Germany)

Axidents (And The Battle Of Forfar)

Arthur Axident (aka Ross Galloway; bass), Grum Accident (vocals and "denim jacket"), Shugg (drums) and five million guitarists.

Edinburgh band who flirted with a smattering of soon-to-be-famous types in their ranks. But there was no record deal, meaning that originals such as 'Plastic Worship', 'Youth Assault' and 'Soho', and their cover of the Neon Hearts' 'Regulations', are lost to the ether. Galloway picks up the story. "The AXIDENTS (then spelt Accidents) idea came about when me and my friends, the small group of kids who were the punk contingent at our high school, decided we could do that 'form a band' thing. This came after many nights spent watching the likes of the Damned, the Dead Boys, and many Edinburgh local heroes of the time, the Freeze, the Scars etc, that played the capital late 77 through to 79."

The band was active from 1978 onwards, "albeit just practising using shit amps with speaker cabs the size of a fag packet, and being kept neatly in time with the drummer's mum's upturned washing basket and anything else that made a noise." By early 1979 the band was on a slightly more professional footing. "We supported the fledgling Exploited, who were not yet a tartan bondage Mohawk band, at the Edinburgh YMCA. We rounded off our short set with a cover version of 'Somewhere Over The Rainbow', definitely not in the style of Judy Garland."

The band's three mainstays were Galloway, Grum and Shugg. "It was always guitarists that we seemed to piss off for some reason, the first being Graham McDonald, who was nicknamed Kid Curry due to the fact his cheapo, out of tune guitar sounded more like an Indian sitar. Among our guitarists was Derek Reid, who blazed a trail with his Gibson Les Paul and Mick Jones poses, and gave the Axidents that cutting edge and a wee bit more professionalism. We managed to record a demo with this line-up, from which one track was played on Uncle John Peel's show. Derek moved on and it was rumoured that he was going to work with the Associates (indeed he did). Who knows? Who cares? Next up was a very short stint with a certain Big John Duncan. We managed one hastily arranged gig with John and before we knew it the big man had been poached by the Exploited (now a tartan bondage Mohawk band)."

I asked the John Candy of punk rock about this, and, like a good 'un, he denied everything. "As far as I remember, I was never in the Axidents. I think I may have punched one of them in the face once. Or twice." So I sent him a picture and a link to convince him. "I just looked at the link you sent and the memories came flooding back. The tall guy was the singer, he was a twat, and the drummer was a midget, and still is probably. I knew the guys in the band, but I didn't really like the music. And I never had fuck all to do with them apart from we all rehearsed down Blair Street at the time." Thanks for clearing that up, John. Robin Saunders, who would later join the Axidents, ironically during Big John's tenure with the band, believes that he's suffering from a case of mistaken identity. "The band that Big John is thinking about

is clearly Twisted Nerve or Sceptix, not the Axidents. 'Wee Jeff' who was, and is, not the loftiest of blokes (agreed wording between cited source, who "does not fancy a ride cymbal winging its way towards me in the manner of a Ninja death star" and editor), played drums successively for the first two, never for the latter."

After that, "we really just faded into even more obscurity," remembers Galloway. "Probably our moment of glory came the evening we managed to piss off and cause what seemed like a whole town to erupt and drive us out of town. The Axidents and a few other local Edinburgh bands hired a bus and took a big crowd of punk types to play a gig in the hillbilly town of Forfar at the prestigious Reid Hall (the author would like to apologise at this point to the good townspeople of Forfar). The result was a full-scale riot, bands being smuggled out of the venue and a police escort out of town in a bus that had any windows left. I guess the good folks of Forfar just didn't quite get the punk thing, although I hear that the Clash is acceptable nowadays."

Robin Saunders, himself a veteran of early Edinburgh punk band Badweeks/Burning Flags, remembers the Forfar gig only too well. "The day the music died? Certainly the end of our youthful naivete and enthusiasm – a cynicism set in after the dust had settled and the end of our little 'happening scene' followed in short order." Oh, come on, you can't leave it like THAT. What really happened that night? "Forfar or 'the F-Word', as we veterans refer to it, whenever anyone breeches the unspoken taboo about not mentioning it at all! The bus that took us to our doom that day might very loosely be described as having been hired by 'the Axidents and a few other local bands'. However, the contract was in my name. It was actually arranged by a bloke who was briefly Burning Flags' manager, until we sacked him after an Edinburgh gig for cosying up to The Exploited. It was me that the coach company came to with their threats of broken legs unless I coughed up to replace their broken windows – which I naturally did, in very short order indeed. I was left seriously out of pocket on that one! A few (but by no means all) of the guys from the bands chipped in to bail me out. Arthur and his cohorts were among the good guys in that respect. As regards the debacle itself – with hindsight it was a serious mistake for us to take a load of spiky-topped urchins along with us. Seemed like a cunning plan at the time – get the camp followers to buy tickets for the bus to help cover the coach hire. What they got up to when turned loose, hours before the gig (whilst we musos did the soundcheck thing inside the hall), in the streets of a sleepy rural town in Angus – I dread to think. Which does not excuse what followed but perhaps goes some way to explaining it."

A snifter of brandy here, I think, before the reposed Saunders gathers his thoughts. "The local populace was aroused to repel invaders as their Pictish ancestors had done before them. Which is as fair as I am prepared to be to 'the good townspeople', as, at that time, they included amongst their number the kind of savages who were prepared to hit young girls on the head with iron bars. A beefy chapter could be written (well Robin, it's kind of on the way...) about the actual battle. Too much of it is etched forever in my memory (share! share!). Other details have faded, thankfully, with the passage of time. Suffice to say it was truly horrible. Our side won by the way! It's no consolation but the scruffs from the big city proved a match that day for the burly rednecks. I myself, being of the cowardly life-preserving persuasion, was on 'gear-saving' duty behind the front-line defences. The local constabulary (who could only have been aware of events from kick-off as their station was a few yards down the street) finally turned up to put a stop to proceedings after about an hour and a half. The only action they took was to arrest and charge Brian, the Sceptix singer, with breach of the peace, although he was guilty of nothing more than questioning their late arrival on the scene. No locals were detained. All of us were kept in the hall until the police could figure out what to do with us. We patched wounds and tried to calm everyone down – there were some very young kids with us that day and many were in shock – they, and others, were in real need of medical treatment which was, needless to say, not forthcoming."

Enough drama for one evening you would think? "There was more to come! A column of Hells Angels from Dundee, doubtless summoned by a local member, were on their way to finish us off. We prepared our defences, uncoiling fire hoses from the walls, gathering makeshift weaponry. Things get hazy for me at that point. You will agree it's all a bit surreal (granted). Rumours were flying that they were outside sawing through the bars on the windows to get at us. At some point Plod obviously decided to wash their hands of us, summoned our coach from the car park and sent us homeward with a blue-light escort all the way to the Tay Bridge. We were shivering from the cold in the windowless bus, dazed and injured, having been forced to leave a comrade alone in a cell in enemy territory. We arrived back in the comparative safety of our home city, where only a small (but considerable) minority of the population wanted to kill you for the way you dressed and/or the music you favoured. That's why I think of it as 'The Day The Music Died' – things changed. What had been a tight-knit collective spirit among the bands faded, friendships and priorities changed. All we wanted to do was make a bit of music, express how we felt about things – it's not easy to do! A completed song is a miracle of a kind when produced by untutored, undisciplined youngsters like we were. You go through all that hard work – and people want to hurt you for it."

According to Saunders, Derek Reid left the Axidents in short order and was replaced by, yes indeed, Big John Duncan. "He did one gig with them at Old St Paul's Church just off Edinburgh's Royal Mile. I know, cos I was there! By that time drummer Shugg had quit the Axidents and Craig 'Mole' Harrower was lured away from Burning Flags to replace him. Burning Flags effectively ceased to exist at that point and I found myself recruited to the Axidents, still playing bass at the time – Arthur having decided to form a band with two bass players! Of course, that enterprise was doomed to failure and Arthur disembarked to form his dub reggae/jazz-fusion flavoured outfit 4 Minute Warning. This latter version of the Axidents played only one gig, at a Scout Hall in Gorebridge – the line-up then featured Mole and me as rhythm section, former singer Grum on guitar and a young lady by the name of Elspeth Pleb as singer."

It was this line-up of the Axidents that attempted a second proper demo recording. "It seemed at times like fate was taking a hand in consigning us to the dustbin of history," notes Saunders. "We recorded a three-track demo intended for release as a split EP with three tracks by the Sceptix. The master tape was entrusted to one of our young camp followers (I believe, at the time, the only one among us who was not basically homeless!) with solemn instructions that it be kept somewhere cool. Naturally, the scamp took it home and left it on a radiator, with terminal consequences. Each of us had a cassette copy, all of which disappeared or were destroyed in short order – mine was reluctantly loaned to a friend, after much begging on his part, and finally returned with a Rush album copied over it, courtesy of his little brother." Shortly thereafter, Saunders and 'Moley' went off to join the Sceptix.

In the early 21st century, the Axidents are back to reclaim their legacy, with Galloway joined by Deek, Flembo and Baz Count. "We gig regularly in and around Edinburgh and have just recorded a nice wee demo and are doing very nicely in an obscure sort of way, just like the old days. It was just like a million and one other bands back then a bunch of young guys ready to change the world. But Shelley and Devoto's lyrics in 'Boredom' sum it up quite nicely: "I've taken this extravagant journey, so it seems to me/I've just came up from nowhere, but I'm going straight back there."

(Robin Saunders asked me to dedicate this piece to the memory of Glenn Campbell (aka Dru Stix of the Exploited) and Kenny Young. "They survived Forfar only to end up losing more personal battles. Rest In Peace.")

Badweeks (And The Story of Blair Street, Edinburgh) By Robin Saunders

If the Edinburgh punk scene could be said to have a heart then that heart would have to be the Blair Street practice rooms. Not a healthy heart by any means, its arteries clogged with the grime of centuries and the accumulated sinking damp of the city's spectacular rainfall. To spend time there was to guarantee a respiratory complaint and, for the hypochondriacs among us, fear of the onset of bubonic plague.*

In any other location Blair Street would have been long since torn down and redeveloped as plush executive flats but the street has a little secret that ensures its long-term survival. Glance upwards from the foot of the street and you will note the South Bridge directly overhead and realise that where you are standing is the prop that holds up half of Edinburgh. Any developer eyeing this prime piece of real estate would have to factor in the cost of cutting the city in two for perhaps years on end.

So, you are the leaseholder of the last building on the left, where planning regulations forbid any kind of structural alterations, where only a couple of measly windows admit any daylight and where most of your floor space is sited underground. What do you do with it? You rent it out for band practice space, fill the place with scruffy rockers unlikely to raise any objections to the squalid conditions, grateful for somewhere, anywhere, where they can crank it up without any neighbours to annoy. Then along comes punk and suddenly every kid and his dog wants to be in a band and you find yourself sitting on a goldmine and you milk it for all its worth.

It was here one evening in early 1978 that a band calling themselves **BADWEEKS** could be found lugging gear into what was to be their new home in the bowels of the earth. They arrived with the in-built inferiority complex of small-town boys taking on the Big City but, as it turned out, they needn't have worried. Punk in Edinburgh was a 'slow burn'. Pioneers like the Rezillos and the Valves with record releases under their belts and thus elevated into the Major League had taken the high road to London and were absent from the scene. Badweeks found that months spent 'honing their chops' out in the West Lothian sticks had put them a few steps ahead of emerging 'second wave' local bands like Twisted Nerve and the Axidents. These two caught up fast and all three would form a minor 'scene' of their own. There was no rivalry and no pecking order. Whoever arranged a gig got the headline slot, the others supported.

Personally, I was blissfully unaware that any of this was going on. I had heard that some old schoolmates had formed a band but, frankly, by 1978 I was already bored with punk. Like so many others I had reason to be grateful to the Ramones for demystifying the business of being a musician. Once the exclusive province of puffed-up prog elitists, it was now an open

The fabled Blair Street rehearsal rooms in Edinburgh.

democracy for anyone who wanted to give it a bash. What that meant for me was Saturday nights in a garage, in the company of friends who made up in enthusiasm for what they lacked in talent, hammering out Monkees and Troggs songs on my junk-shop bass, until the finger blisters threatened to burst, the beer cans were empty, and it was time to go to the pub. No ambition, just a hobby, a nice release from the nine to five grind. Until, that is, the phone rang one evening and on the other end was Alan (aka Coby), Badweeks singer, with a tale of bass players stormed out, an impending gig and booked studio time. Would I like to fill in? Why not! It's in banal little moments like that when life changes forever.

So it was that I found myself sentenced to be detained, several evenings per week, in a Blair Street cell, until such time as punk should disappear up its own asshole. How to describe my first encounter with the place? A maze of subterranean tunnels peppered with little square caves – from each issued forth an ear-splitting "rammy" that bled one into another as you passed. I'm fighting the urge to turn and flee into the night. In the Lord of the Rings Trilogy we are never shown the dwelling places of the Orcs. If I ever feel the need to fill in that particular gap I have a bank of mental images to draw on. And many of the denizens of Blair Street could be very Orc-like. Now I'm in Badweeks' personal space. It smells bad. I plug in, feeling like a fish out of water even among familiar faces, now grown more fearsome in appearance than I remembered from school days and, despite the laddish banter, clearly very serious indeed about what they were doing. We falter through 'No Fun', 'I Wanna Be Your Dog'. It starts to gel. Time to begin getting to grips with the 'originals', good ones with titles like 'Boredom Town' and 'Don't Trust'. Guess I'm in!

On band nights I am usually the first to arrive. Solitary in the cell, munching chips, seated atop my bass combo, listening to the latest tractor production figures from Minsk.** The room had shared occupancy in the evenings between Badweeks and Twisted Nerve and during the day with a good-natured rat. I often caught sight of his tail disappearing as I switched on the light. Sling a chip into the corner with the hole in it. It was always gone by the next evening. Electrical power was metered so, maintaining a continuous supply required careful forward planning. Needless to say, we were regularly plunged into pitch darkness and silence necessitating a frantic fumble for coins and much stumbling around with cigarette-lighter torches. When the supply of coins ran out you could always repair to a communal area where there was a drinks machine supplying water – just not quite hot enough to soften a pot noodle, but we ate them anyway. There was also a jukebox, surprisingly lacking in punk records and on which we often took great delight in pissing off the 'serious' types (Joy Division fans mostly) by playing 'Captain Beaky' over and over again. There was a less friendly rodent population too. After a night on the town, too drunk or too lazy to struggle home you could spend the night in Blair Street, if you were feeling brave. Try to claim the pool table. They can't climb up the legs, or can they? Try to drift off to sleep accompanied by the patter of tiny feet.

I still have a CDR of the demo tape Badweeks recorded shortly after I joined. It's fourth or fifth generation, so the hiss is as loud as any of the instruments but it still sounds pretty damn good. Gigs; good, bad, awful, indifferent, came and went. The times changed. Fascism was on the march again, the dread shadow of Thatcher loomed on the horizon and, oh yes, following the Soviet invasion of Afghanistan, we all confidently expected to be vapourised at any moment in a nuclear war. New songs shifted in focus from sarcastic social comment and teenage angst to political rhetoric. 'Which side are you on, boy? Where Pistols-brand yobbish anarchy had once been our touchstone, the spirited agit-prop of Crass, Crisis and Flux of Pink Indians began to hold sway. Not everyone was swallowed up by the desperately naïve idealism but the rest of us fell hook, line and sinker. Badweeks changed name to Burning Flags, a 'collective' was formed called 'Capital Chaos', which also included Axidents, Twisted Nerve and Sceptix – the latter being the serious revolutionaries in the pack. Burning Flags soldiered on for a while, even escaped Blair Street briefly, then fell apart. The other bands held their ground with ever-fluctuating lineups. Commitment was in and fun was out. Drummer Craig (aka Mole) and me went on to feature in an enfeebled version of the Axidents and finally Sceptix, then in the throes of drifting away from three-chord thrash towards the wider spaces being opened up by the likes of Killing Joke and PiL. The music drowned in politics, we lost the art of conversation, replacing it with speech making and heckling. We trailed behind banners on protest marches and cost ourselves a small fortune playing benefit gigs. It's no easy task to set about changing the world, but change it we did – even if only to the extent of making it a slightly more miserable and uncomfortable place for ourselves than it strictly needed to be. Then we fizzled out like a damp squib.

You're thinking "So what?" Half the people reading this will have a similar story to tell. So, go write it! This is mine. It's true that if success for a 70s band is measured in vinyl (and it is) then the various outfits I was in were utter failures – indeed, so long after the fact can barely be proved to have existed at all. No recording contracts were ever offered. Any label scout approaching Blair Street would very likely have taken one look, turned tail and run off to the nearest wine bar. To be schmoozed and boozed by the local music biz mafia who held (and still hold) the gig circuit in a death grip, and who dispensed their favours only to those 'other' bands – the ones willing to bow and scrape before them – the kind of bands who had 'rehearsal studios'. The kind who jumped aboard every passing Next Big Thing bandwagon as it rolled by and were used up and spat out in their turn by those same moguls, even then with a glint in their steely eyes about the age of stadium rock to come.

Other bands released their own records, why not us? A band called Desperate Bicycles put out a couple of EPs in 1977, the sleeves of which painstakingly detailed what they had cost to make. "It was easy, it was cheap, go and do it!" Seems you could make a record for as little as £500. Cue hollow laughter for those of us kids in dead-end jobs or on the dole, struggling to come up with the next hire purchase payment on guitars or amps. Hoping for a couple of quid left over at the end of the week to go and catch a band, have a couple of drinks. Me, I always suspected that behind all those 'own label' releases their lurked the patronage of someone's rich daddy. None of us had wealthy parents. I suppose we could always have applied for a bank loan?

For all those reasons Blair Street was never going to be any kind of Fame Academy. There were those who went on to bigger things, like the Exploited...and better things – our next-door neighbour Mike Scott of Another Pretty Face, soon to be Waterboy-in-chief. Then there were The Freeze, responsible for a couple of classic early punk singles of the kind which now fetch funny money on E-Bay from deranged Japanese collectors. Singer Gordon Sharp's haunting voice would later grace the first This Mortal Coil album, preceding his rise to international sub-cultural celebrity of sorts under the name Cindytalk, sadly still without honour in his own country. Late arrivals on the scene were an outfit by the name of Blak Flag (note the missing 'c', so, nothing to do with Henry's Hardcore Heroes). You would recognise the guitarist and drummer as those bespectacled twins who went on to unlikely stardom as music-hall act, the Proclaimers. OK, that's not a lot but it's better than nothing.

Edinburgh in 2006 is a very different place than it was in the late 70s. Turn left at the foot of Blair Street and your nostrils are no longer assailed by the emissions from the old brewery, pleasantly fragrant or sickeningly pungent, depending on which way the wind was blowing. That location is now occupied by the so-called Scottish Parliament, a carbuncle and a money pit down which has been flushed millions upon millions of pounds. All in the name of devolution, i.e. the addition of yet another layer of parasitical bureaucracy, which is supposed to make us Scots feel good about ourselves. Turn right and you find yourself in an area both desirable and gentrified, where once were the hostels that housed the city's derelicts. No more swerving to avoid the flailing fists of the punch-drunk (or just drunk) shadow-boxers. The air is no longer rent by the gnomic utterances of the Tourette's sufferers. Puce-faced bag ladies no longer offer al-fresco personal services for the price of a can of Special Brew (and one can only hope that there never was anyone so demented or desperate to take them up on it!) The city has lost a lot of its character and its characters along the way. However, that building at the centre of my story is still there, sullen, sooty and unchanged, still carrying Edinburgh on its shoulders. The practice rooms are long gone. There's no need for them to a generation which prefers to spectate rather than participate. So the inner space plays host to a bar/music venue constantly shifting its name and style in any direction considered likely to be conducive in parting passing trade from a portion of their student loans. Oh, and there's a sauna there too.

Take a wander around of an evening and you will find yourself dodging crocodiles of happily snapping tourists each led by an actor, earning a crust before his Big Break arrives, be-cloaked and white of face. Ghost tours are big business in Edinburgh these days. God knows, the place has the goods. Grizzly murders, body snatchers, spectral manifestations in abundance. I try to avoid the place myself. There are real ghosts down there. Some of them are me and my old mates – our younger, awkward, misfit selves. Whenever any of us meet these days there's a certain something that passes between us. The back-slapping bonhomie might seem just a little too hearty to an outsider. If strong drink has been taken we have even been known to hug (a practice otherwise unknown to Scottish men). Maybe it's that we remember a time that was a wee bit special, when we were Insiders Looking Out, a time that can never happen again. Then again, on the negative side, a whole lot of dangerous and unpleasant shit went down too and we lived to tell the tale. Which is as good a place as any to end mine.

* *(Not such a far-fetched notion as it might appear. A few hundred yards away down the Royal Mile lies Mary King's Close, in the late Middle Ages a teeming warren of slums ravaged by the Black Death, buried, built over and forgotten. In recent years the close has been disinterred and, despite medical experts not being certain quite how long plague viruses can lie 'dormant', has become a popular tourist attraction. I haven't been myself!)*

** *(In those far off Cold War days the English Service of Radio Moscow played out its propaganda at mega-wattage. You could pick it up on anything electrical, even dental fillings if you were very unlucky. For some reason that wee bass amp seemed to be precisely tuned to the voice of the 'Red Menace'.)*

(My thanks to Robin Saunders for writing this piece and throwing my own prose, my objectives with this book and any veneer of first-hand authenticity into hilariously sharp relief. Bastard.)

Bank Of Dresden

Dave Scott (guitar, vocals, trumpet, various arrangements and lyrics), Duart MacLean (keyboards, lyrics, vocals and arrangements), Richard Dudanski (drums, seniority, arrangements, and a very old, even then, Morris Oxford with leather seats and a fucked gearbox), Jane Crockford (bass, vocals and arrangements, and the odd argument) Line-up annotated for me by Dave Scott himself…

A hard-gigging London band formed in 1979, BANK OF DRESDEN featured a clutch of punk notables, but their sole single disappeared without trace and they have therefore seen their place in history pass largely unrecorded. Regulars in their audience included Jackie Leven of Doll By Doll and various Clash members. Dudanski was formerly a colleague of Joe Strummer's in the 101ers, and tried out for the Clash but turned it down due to worries about Bernie Rhodes' machinations. Richard Dudanski: "I was playing with Tymon Dogg and the Fools, an old mate of ours who later played with Joe in the Mescaleros and was on Sandinista! After the 101ers, I worked with him for about a year. After that I joined the Raincoats. They'd lost their drummer so I did a few gigs with them. We're talking spring of 1978. I was just filling in for them and wanted to get a band together."

His friend Neal Brown of the Vincent Units and Tesco Bombers introduced him to Duart. "Neil used to live in my street, Monmouth Road, off Westbourne Grove. He knew Duart and we set up a meeting. Duart wanted to get a band together. He played keyboards. I met Dave Scott through another mutual friend. Dave was a painter, quite famous – relatively – he had this exhibition in Hornsea Town Hall. He had this picture of the Queen on the toilet and someone masturbating. He was quite a character, Dave. And he played guitar and had never been a front man before, but I persuaded him to do that." All they needed was a bass player. "We met Jane Crockford. Jane hadn't played bass before but she was pretty damn quick."

After a month's rehearsal they had a set together, and made their debut upstairs at the British Oak on Westbourne Park Road. Dudanski: "Another friend recommended John Glynn (who'd replaced Lora Logic in X-Ray Spex) to play saxophone. He did a few gigs with us including the one at the Africa Centre, which I organised." As for the repertoire, the tunes came mainly from original ideas that Dave or Duart would suggest. "Then we'd knock them about and put a structure to them. We used to do a cover of 'Mack The Knife', the Brecht thing, a heavy, dub reggae version which was pretty good. I used to sing a Bo Diddley song too, 'I'm Going Home'." Among their originals was 'I Want To Play Your Drums Tonight'. "It was a homage to Palmolive of the Slits, my wife's sister. But I didn't write it!" As Scott recalls,

"Other stuff featured in the set was Duart's and a few covers. I thought Duart had a good ear for melody, but was a little, er, highbrow when it came to lyrics. One particular line I recall vividly went: 'A Dante is leading a Beatrice through to a Petrarch Park.' Now, I think that's pretty good, very literate, if you've ever been to Arezzo. But where did it fit?"

There was one recording session at an eight-track studio in Hornsea where four songs were cut in an afternoon. Dudanski still has a copy, but thinks the quality is too poor, and the tape too badly deteriorated, to make it serviceable. Scott has no memory of these sessions at all. The intention was to use it to get gigs and secure an album deal, for which they now had enough material. Sadly, the band didn't hang round long enough to sustain any interest there might have been. Dudanski: "It was very short-lived. We started in the summer of 1978. By April I was in PiL. That was three weeks after we'd decided to knock Bank Of Dresden on the head. We had the normal type of problems. We got a manager in who was someone I know. The normal kind of stuff, things started going wrong, he wanted to take more of a role in deciding on the songs, etc. It split the band really." Shades of Bernie Rhodes again? "Well, I'm not stupid. Maybe I don't get on with managers who start coming in and telling you what should be done. That's what happened there."

"It's one of those periods where there were so many different gigs," Dudanski recalls. "The Africa Centre was one of the better gigs." Scott: "I do remember a gig in Guildford which was set up by the 'manager', John Parker. A small pub in the middle of fucking nowhere, frequented by a fairly hostile crowd, it should be said. I was having a hose down in the cubicles at half time, and a very large bloke with strange tattoos, who looked to weigh about 25 stone, threatened me with severe violence if we didn't leave immediately." Scott also recalls playing "a few times in a really sleazy basement with the Furs. It was run by a Swiss bloke called Mr Sweety."

After the band broke up, Jane Crockford joined the Modettes and Dave Scott worked with Spizz Energi. As Scott recalls, "I really liked Jane, and we played some good stuff together, but she was a bit bonkers at the time. We later toured Germany together when she joined the Modettes and I joined Spizz Energi in 1980. All of us in a 12-seater minibus for two weeks. Not the sort of trip you'd enter a competition for." Scott recorded four singles with Spizz Energi and appeared on their A&M album Do A Runner, before leaving in October 1980. "I buggered off to Corsica for three months with a lovely German girl till the money ran out." Various musical endeavours followed upon his re-entry to the UK, including Baby Lotion, which featured Darryl Hunt of the Pogues, and later Pride of the Cross, also with Hunt, and Cait O'Riordan, later also of the Pogues.

Dudanski teamed up with Jim (aka Amos) of the Homosexuals in a project entitled the Noname Band in 1980. That evolved into the Decomposers by 1986, at which point he was reunited with John Glynn. In between, Dudanski played on PiL's groundbreaking Metal Box before joining Basement Five in 1980, touring the UK as support to Ian Dury and the Blockheads. He also rejoined the Raincoats for their Moving LP and US tour before reacquainting himself with Tymon Dogg.

In 1988 he moved to Granada, Spain, with his Spanish wife, recording an album with Por Si Las that was mixed by Strummer. His current project is The Dog House, with features singer/guitarist Tom Lardner and his son, Maki. Check out their garage punk take on Dylan's 'It's Alright Ma', aptly titled 'Ridiculous', available via their website. Their new record should be out now, released on the Andalucia label Dudanski and Joe Strummer first set up in 1981 to bring out the first version of the 101ers' Elgin Avenue Breakdown. Is the music in the same spirit as his punk roots? "Have a listen to the MP3s. It's difficult for me to say. You don't purposely make any relations." Dudanski was a key mover behind the tribute concerts when Joe Strummer passed away, helping organise both the London event, which saw the 101ers reform for the first time in 30 years at the Tabernacle, an old haunt, and the companion show in Granada.

Dave Scott, meanwhile, started a chain of bicycle shops called Yellow Jersey. "It started, survived, grew, lurched prosperously through the 1980s and plunged into the recession of 1992, emerging much smaller later on. I eventually sold it in 1998, and spent some of the money scratching my arse and funding my way through an MBA at Imperial College. Don't ever do this, especially if you're moving house and expecting your first child all at the same time." After various "strange business ideas", and a year spent "attempting to teach Business Studies to the recalcitrant students of Edmonton in North London", he is now running a business that installs garden offices, soho2go.co.uk, "for people who should know better".

DISCOGRAPHY:

Motorbike/Frederika 7-inch (Dresden DR1 1980)

Banned

Pete Fresh (guitar vocals), Rick Mansworth (aka Richard Harvey; guitar, vocals), Paul Sordid (aka Paul Aitken, drums, vocals), John Thomas (aka Jonathan Davie; bass). Also involved were Ben Dover (aka Ben Grove; guitar) and Tommy Steal (bass, vocals)

Widely considered to be one of the more outrageous efforts at punk bandwagon-jumping, Croydon's BANNED chanced upon a hit single with their version of obscure San Jose garage band Syndicate Of Sound's 'Little Girl'. This was initially self-released in a pressing of 1,000 with a few hand-made sleeves as well as handwritten white labels on Can't Eat Records. It was re-released by EMI on Harvest and became an unlikely chart hit in December 1976, reaching 36 in the Music Week chart, 26 in the NME and going all the way to number 1 in Time Out's Other singles chart. In total it would spend six weeks in the main chart. "EMI were going to put their machine on it," Aitken recalled to MOJO's Kieron Tyler. "I remember getting a bit confused by it all. I was playing with Mandy Morton in Spriguns, and then I'd turn on the radio and hear 'Little Girl'." Indeed, they even managed an appearance on Top Of The Pops and Get it Together on ITV.

The truth was that behind the sharp haircuts and skinny ties the Banned were a hybrid born of 1970s "medieval rockers" Gryphon, who frequently supported Yes. However, for Aitken the Banned sessions were merely a continuation, or an incarnation, of long-since established musical partnerships. And he's a mite suspicious about the prog-rock tag. "It was straightforward beat group stuff (that we were playing), mainly," he told me. "With the guys we always wanted to play what stirred us as kids, mainly classic 1960s and 1970s original stuff. We did some soul stuff, and some Searchers, Billy Kramer, Grateful Dead, etc. The interesting thing at that time was that we weren't averse to playing old 78 jazz pop, like 'Wake Up Children', the sort of thing that Paul McCartney did with 'Till There Was You'. We just wanted to copy and re-vamp good songs – we weren't snobbish about the tracks." He believes that this gave them a similar ethos to others in the punk movement. "The grip the large companies had on marketing meant it was controlled and lacking in spirit and enthusiasm. They saw buckets of money, not music. It's that passion for it that arouses you, and music of all kinds stirs people in the way few other things can. The joy of it was the fire in your belly."

Having just issued their final album for Harvest, the foremost harbour for mid-70s progressive rock, the assorted members of Gryphon were convinced by their A&R man that an uptempo cover of 'Little Girl', recorded at Riverside, might get some attention. The sessions featured Richard Harvey and Jonathan Davie of Gryphon, while Aitken was a bandmate of former Gryphon guitarist Graeme Taylor in Precious Little.

"Richard (Harvey) asked me to come to a session organised by Mark Rye, his A&R guy, and Willie Williamson, the roadie for Gryphon. He and Mark had gone to college together. They wanted to work a scam to do this punk thing. Mark was passionate about music, and it was a great track selection." Aitken had formerly worked on jingles with Harvey, including the Findus Double-Deckers theme, and even featured on a Gillette advert with (former Manchester United manager) Tommy Docherty.

The Sex Pistols were recording their original demos at Riverside at the time, and had impressed Aitken despite the scratch musicianship. "Punk gave vent to passion. Though the kids didn't necessarily play all that well, even Weller and people like that early on, even Townshend was playing a kind of punk in the 60s, developing his craft. A lot of punk was patently driven by that kind of energy. I recorded a lot at Riverside with Richard, and the Pistols were full of intensity. The demos were brilliant, much better than the released versions".

There was a follow-up single, a cover of Paul Revere And The Raiders' 'Him Or Me', but when that failed because EMI withdrew it from the shops, the members wandered off to other pursuits. "We fell out with Rye when he wouldn't pay us enough, we'd have had another hit, but I said we're going somewhere else. We did some demos for Chrysalis and was offered a deal by Ann Munday (then Head of A&R)." Some of these are featured on the compilation album Cherry Red recently released. Aitken can still be found playing classic 60s and 70s material in the Retros, who have recently issued a CD called "Undercover" and also contributed two tracks to the Banned compilation. He is still in contact, both musically and professionally, with the former members. Ben Grove and he still play together in the Retros .

DISCOGRAPHY:

Little Girl/CPGJ's 7-inch (Can't Eat EAT 1 UP September 1977) (1,000 copies, some in homemade sleeves)
Little Girl/CPGJ's 7-inch (Harvest HAR 5145 November 1977)
Him Or Me/You Dirty Rat 7-inch (Harvest HAR 5145 1978)
Little Girl: The Best Of CD (Cherry Red CDMRED 254 2004)
Precious Little: Clean Livin' Boy/Give It To Me Now 7-inch (Rock on Records)
Retros: (the Retros have released three CDs, Strings And Skins, Undercover and Captain Zed)
ARCHIVE RELEASE:
Business Unusual LP (Cherry Red ARED 2 1979; 'Little Girl', 'CPGJ's', 'Him Or Me', 'You Dirty Rat')

Basczax

Alan Savage (guitar, vocals), Mike Todd (bass), Alan Cornforth (drums), Geoff Foggarty (saxophone), John Hodgson (keyboards)

Cleveland's BASCZAX – pronounced Bahss-Axe – were formed in August 1978 by Mike Todd, a fixture on the local rock scene. "After trying out various people for the group," Tood told me, "I recorded a rough demo of 'Karleearn Photography' and Jeff Foggarty and Alan Savage got to hear it and they joined. Alan Savage quickly became the main songwriter. We played a few local gigs with Nigel Trenchard on keyboards and a lad called Cog on drums. John Hodgson, the lead singer of Blitzkrieg Bop, loved us and he wanted to join us, so he replaced Nige on the keyboards. After the Bop split John was able to get Alan Cornforth to join the band and that was our stable line up for two years."

'Karleearn Photography' came about because "I must have had some weird cheese before I went to sleep as the song was about a dream I had: 'Polar bears in a deep blue sea, waiting to tear out your eyes'. Crazy stuff. I'd also just read an article about this new type of

photography that was being developed that would mean a huge advance in medicine." It became their debut release on the Earcom 2 compilation of October 1979. "Our first ever gig was supporting the Rezillos at Middlesbrough Rock Garden, and they had good connections with Bob Last from the Fast Product label. We got in touch with him and he asked for a demo, which we duly recorded. We took it up to Edinburgh to see him in person but it took us an age to find his place. Thankfully, Alan Savage and myself finally found it and he gave it a listen and put us up for the night. We hitch hiked back to Teesside the day after but it was worth it as we landed a deal." It also brought the band some good press. "If I were an A&R person," ran Ian Birch's review in the Melody Maker, "I'd get up to Cleveland and start checking out Basczax." By this time, they'd already recorded their debut single, 'Madison Fallout', which appeared on Pipeline later that year.

Beloved of John Peel, while allied to the punk movement, they were a long way from some of its more rote adherents. "We loved The Clash and The Pistols , we were lucky enough to be around during this great period and we saw all the major punk groups play live, mostly at The Rock Garden. We played a few gigs with the likes of the Damned and Gang Of Four etc." They would also pick up a major support tour with OMD. "OMD were massive so every venue was packed, we went down really well. I remember one day in Wolverhampton we took them on at footie and they thrashed us. Sav (Alan Savage) was crap, couldn't kick a ball for peanuts, everyone just fell about laughing at his efforts. During the soundcheck we thrashed them at darts though."

After Hodgson left the band in 1980 they would persevere in various forms until they evolved into the Flaming Mussolinis in 1984. The Mussolinis recorded two albums for Epic and got plenty of airplay from Mike Read and Janice Long, for whom they completed two sessions, for their anti-Thatcher tract, 'Swallow Glass', while their drummer Craig McClune went on to become David Gray's percussionist and co-writer. Todd would later form Toddler Records. Grand Theft Audio is putting together an archive release of the band's unreleased recordings.

DISCOGRAPHY:

Madison Fallout/Auto Mekanik Destruktor 7-inch (Pipeline Product 1980)

COMPILATION:

Earcom 2 7-inch EP (Fast 1979: 'Celluloid Love', 'Karleearn Photography')

Bears

George Gill (guitar), Mick North (vocals), Ron West (bass), Cally Cameron (drums), Chris Kershaw (saxophone)

The BEARS (originally Smarter And The Average Bears) were put together in Watford by Gill, a founder member of Wire, in 1977. He formed them after he'd been dismissed for "one blues solo too many", a heinous crime in year zero, or even year zero plus one. He took sometime Wire saxophone player Chris Kershaw with him. The songs they subsequently wrote were, in many ways, the polar opposite of Wire's more earnest and arty pieces, glorying in profanity and a sense of humour that was both surreal and childlike.

By the time the Bears made their recorded debut on the Farewell To The Roxy compilation, North had been killed in a motorbike accident in September 1977, while travelling pillion with friend Pete Perspex (aka Pete Dallimore) of the Paper Dollies, who also died. The Bears continued as a four-piece while trying to audition a new singer, the role eventually fell to John Entrails (aka John Earthrowl, another former member of the Paper Dollies) in mid-1978, by which time Kershaw had departed. Earthrowl picked up the story for me. "Pete Dallimore was our guitarist in the Paper Dollies. He was riding the bike, and took Mick North back to Hemel, I think, to sign on. On the way back a lorry hit them. It went over both of them. Mick died instantly and Pete died basically of shock, cos it crushed his legs. It was pretty traumatic."

The singer got his new nickname from Gill. "It was his little joke, because he called me a gutsy singer." The revamped quartet recorded their debut single for Waldo's shortly thereafter. 'On Me', featuring surreal lyrics about cheese and mustard sandwiches, was immediately given Single of the Week status, the reviewer admitting it "really gets the ol' gonads going." The band initially kept to the basic set they'd developed with North, who wrote the lyrics for both sides of the single. "Originally, there were a couple of tracks that we were doing that they hadn't done. And we stuck in a couple of things from rehearsal, covers and fillers at the end, then we started doing our own material after that." Chris Kershaw (mistakenly referred to as 'Sissy' in some press reports) returned to add saxophone to the B-side. "Chris Kershaw's nickname was actually Icky, cos he worked for an undertaker's. And while he was playing with us he was doing an embalming course!"

The band's 'split' was prematurely announced in Sounds in August 1978, with Cameron and West said to be joining The Screaming Ad Dabs, though eventually they would form the Tea Set ('Cops And Saucers' EP etc). After initially stating in the same report that Gill was "unlikely to continue playing music", the Bears replaced their rhythm section. Earthrowl: "When I started it was me, George Gill, Ron and Cally. Then there was a bit of a row with them. In fact there was a bit of a scrap in the rehearsal room, and the band peeled off into me and George, and Ron and Cally. Then we got Richie the hippy on drums. He was a good lad. He came from Hayes originally, a good bloke but a bit of a nutter – all drummers are nutters aren't they? But he was an exceptionally good nutter. And Tim Brocket on bass was a great bloke. Unfortunately Tim is dead now, drugs victim type of thing. Very talented bloke."

They then hooked up with Terri Hooley's Good Vibrations International, a foiled attempt for the Belfast entrepreneur to expand his franchise across the water. Nevertheless, both tracks are excellent, especially 'Decisions', with its echoes of the Pistols' 'No Fun' – an influence Earthrowl acknowledges but states wasn't conscious. "We went over to Belfast via a bloke called Pugwash, who was a hell's angel. He was at college with Terri Hooley, the Good Vibrations bloke. What a brilliant scene! Great kids, we had a fantastic time. We were drinking in the Europa hotel, and at the time it was meant to be the most bombed hotel in Europe, and it had really tight security. But one of the security guys was a punk in one of the bands to do with Terri, so we got through all the security checks and were drinking there in the bar. We had an amazing time. We played at the Harp bar. Hookers hanging around in the bar downstairs, and goodness knows what. It was brilliant. There were loads of kids saying, God, if my parents knew I'd been here, they'd kill me. Fantastic, really crazy fans."

But it never happened for the Bears, doubtless due to the continued instability in the band. "Tim left, and it was in flux. We had a bloke called Phil Hootham drumming for us. John Peel wanted us to do a session. We went up and met him at Broadcasting House and went for a drink with him. We had a good chat about football. He said I've just got to agree it with Walters, his mate. What happened in the meantime was that Phil was a Geordie, and his old man was moving back up north. And he decided to go with him. So we missed our chance at the Peel session."

The band did not so much break up as drift apart. "Couldn't be bothered, really – one of those things. I suppose I should have kept it going. But it was great while it lasted, 100mph, a real good crack and I had a fantastic time. I wouldn't change it for anything But we were just having fun. Instead of going to see a stadium rock band, suddenly, four blokes off a council estate could play their local pub."

Tigerbeat issued a live retrospective in 1986 of a show recorded at Waldo's Jazz Club in 1977. Ah, Waldo's Jazz Club. Don't try to find it. "Waldo's didn't exist. To get on the London pub circuit and get gigs, it was Catch 22, you had to be gigging to get the gigs. So we invented Waldo's Jazz Club, and we put down that we had a residency there. So we played around Hemel, St Albans, Watford, Stevenage, all the local stuff. Then we threw this in. And when pubs asked us where we'd been playing recently, oh, we had a residency at Waldo's. And then you'd get a break at one of the pubs, like the Rochester Castle in Stoke Newington, places like the Pegasus. So we invented those gigs so we could say we're playing here or there, and eventually we replaced the fake ones with real ones we were playing."

The 'album' was actually the Bears' first proper demo. "A bloke called Phil Smee got us that. It was just a demo. Long after we'd parted it suddenly appeared as an album. It's quite ironic, because my oldest daughter is 16 and they're into the music scene and they're checking the catalogue, picking up on the old bands. They came across the first Roxy album being sold on the internet. They bought it for me for my birthday, cos I had it and it got broken at a party. That was strange! Ironically, I think our best material was just as we finally split up, a demo tape of us edging off in a slightly different direction. Never saw the light of day!"

B

DISCOGRAPHY:

On Me/Wot's Up Mate 7-inch (Waldo's Jazz Series 001 June 1978)
Insane/Decisions 7-inch "no a-side" (Good Vibrations International GOT1 November 1978)
Spain/Artist 7-inch (Release RL 970 1979)
Insane LP (Tigerbeat Records GROWL 001 1986)
COMPILATIONS:
Farewell To The Roxy LP (Lightning LIP 2 1978; 'Fun Fun Fun') (reissued on CD, Captain Oi! AHOY CD 86, 1996)
Good Vibrations: The Punk Singles Collection CD (Anagram CD PUNK 36 1994; 'Decisions')
Punk Rock Rarities CD (Anagram CD PUNK 63 1995; 'On Me')

Beaver

Dave Yelland (lead guitar, backing vocals), Will Coon (lead vocals, rhythm guitar), Paul Jennings (piano), Reg Hancock (bass, backing vocals), Nick Watts (guitar), Clive Jury (drums)

One of the bands to appear on the regional Double Booked compilation released in 1977, BEAVER could trace their origins back to Safron, winners of an annual Battle of the Bands contest in Truro in 1970. Their prize was a 'live' appearance at the Radio One Club with DJ Emperor Rosko, before line-up changes left founders Colin Hannah (guitar) and Clive Jury (drums) looking for new recruits. In came Mike Grose, original bass player with Queen (yes, that Queen), who introduced his friend Will Coon, a veteran of R&B bands such as The Soul Society. Eventually Grose too left, leaving Safron to add Reg Hancock on bass and Will's brother Dave as joint vocalists.

After triumphing in the south west heats, they reached the final of the 1975 Melody Maker Rock contest in London. RCA briefly considered offering the band a contract, only to switch allegiance to Limey, whose one album sunk without trace. "It was a bitter disappointment," notes Will Coon. Undeterred, Safron broadened the sound further by introducing piano player Paul Jennings. "He dazzled the band by auditioning with a faultless rendition of Rick Wakeman's entire suite, 'The Six Wives of Henry VIII', and of course he was snapped up immediately."

They successfully auditioned for Alan 'Fluff' Freeman's Quiz Kid for BBC Manchester, for which they cut five tracks at the BBC's Bristol Studios. Safron were voted second by the combined listener's and panel vote. But afterwards, frustration set in. "We felt that the emergence of punk, which by then was approaching its zenith, was undoubtedly one reason for our failure to break through." When founder Colin Hannah left the band in the spring of 1977, Safron was laid to rest. The remaining members auditioned new musicians, eventually bringing in Dave Yelland on guitar, while Nick Watts would cover when Yelland was unavailable due to college commitments. The enlarged ensemble, which would also occasionally feature guitar player and flautist Mike Guy, chose Beaver as their new name.

Beaver built their reputation playing at the Cornwall Coliseum, before being invited to contribute to the Double Booked LP. They were already a popular draw at the William IV pub in Truro that was financing the album as a showcase for local talent. Beaver contributed three songs, including the title-track, written at the request of pub landlord Alan, 'Ellis Island' and 'Third Time Lucky'. The latter pair had featured on the Quiz Kid programme, and were re-recorded in Roche, Cornwall, with Martin Griffin engineering and Simon Fraser producing. However, any chance of building on their vinyl debut was lost when Paul Jennings and Nick Watts left the band in the spring of 1978. Beaver broke up a few months later.

Earlier, in Coon's words, they had "come face to face with our demons", when they opened at the Coliseum for the Lurkers. "We suffered the humiliation of being pelted with fruit and veg by the large contingent of punk fans that had come to Cornwall for the gig. The Lurkers tried to humour us by saying that if punks didn't like you, they would have thrown bottles and bricks instead. That was small comfort, and was another factor that led to the band's demise."

Beaver was revived in 1982 when Yelland returned to Cornwall, and they continued to play until the end of 1993, with various line-up changes, most notably the addition of keyboard player Tony Cousins. Where are they now? Paul Jennings took a degree in music and has since become Programme Manager for the Foundation Degree in Music at Truro College and now plays bass guitar in his band Rocket Dog. Dave Yelland became a science teacher and still plays in a band with bass player Reg Hancock, called Re-Run. Guitarist Nick Watts returned to his native Scilly Isles and Mike Guy works in the Middle East. The band's sound mixer, Phil Wilton, took a job with Sony and worked with artists including Paul McCartney, while Will Coon reformed The Soul Society and formed a duo with brother Dave until injury forced him to give up music in 1998. Clive Jury died after a long illness on New Year's Eve 1999, aged just 46. The group reformed to play a tribute show to their old friend and colleague in November 2003 at the Band Club in St Austell. ***(the former members of Beaver requested that I dedicate this piece to their former drummer Clive Jury)***

DISCOGRAPHY:

Doubled Booked LP (W4 W4001 December 1977; 'Double Booked', 'Ellis Island', 'Third Time Lucky')

Bee Bee Cee

Blackie (keyboards), Bob Gilhooley (bass), Dave Gilhooley (vocals), Callum McNair (guitar), Zokko (drums)

Released on REL Records, BEE BEE CEE's 1977 single 'You Gotta Know Girl' was one of Edinburgh's first punk efforts, and, in common with so many such indie one-offs, it's become a very collectable artefact, reaching prices of up to £75. You're probably better getting the Raw and Rare British Punk (Volume 1) compilation or Overground's more legitimate offering, though that has since been deleted.

Callum McNair filled me in on the story behind the single. "Bee Bee Cee were formed at the end of 1976 when punk was just starting to bite. The band would meet up with lots of other kindred spirits outside Hot Licks, a record shop in Edinburgh's Cockburn Street (also home to a pub called The Wig and Pen, which was a local gig). We were managed by Clouds Entertainment who were essentially a nightclub and venue. We were very fortunate to be able to support many famous names (Generation X, the Damned, the Ramones, the Jam, the Jolt, Siouxsie and the Banshees). Almost too many nights to remember!"

The single came about after the group was signed to REL, or Radio Edinburgh Limited. "It was the obvious choice as there were not too many options at the time and we must have struck some kind of financial agreement with them. I think Dave the singer had got some girlie pregnant, that was the truthful influence behind the single. We had a great time recording those songs – I think the B-side was one take – in and out the studio in a very long day. We pressed up a couple of thousand copies and sold them at gigs and through local shops as we developed a following."

McNair's memories of the local scene are that it was both friendly and supportive. In particular he remembers "the Unclean, The Dirty Reds (who became the Fire Engines), the Flowers, the Scars and lots of others whose names seem to escape me right now. All the bands knew each other and got on well, even swapping personnel when things got messy." The band split up in 1978 and McNair has lost touch with the former members. He would later join the Syndicate, the Apples and then the Bathers in 1997. "I couldn't lose the punk ethos although I have been involved in some very diverse music since the old days."

DISCOGRAPHY:

You Gotta Know Girl/We Ain't Listening 7-inch (REL RE 48-S November 1977)
COMPILATION:
Raw and Rare British Punk Vol. 1 (Raw Sounds 1977; 'You Gotta Know Girl')
Short Sharp Shock – Independent Recordings UK 1977 CD (Overground OVER47 CD 1996; 'You Gotta Know Girl', 'We Ain't Listening')

Big In Japan

Phil Allen (drums), Bill Drummond (vocals, guitar), Kevin Ward (vocals, bass)

Formed in Liverpool in May 1977, the original trio of Allen, Drummond and Ward were all converted to the punk cause by the Clash's legendary gig at Eric's. The other catalyst, however, was Ken Campbell's 24-hour event Illuminatus, staged at the

Liverpool School Of Music, Dream, Art And Pun. Drummond was set designer, while Ian Broudie played guitar and 'Peter 'Budgie' Clark appeared on drums. Broudie had first encountered Drummond when he'd approached him in the café and asked if he could try his Telecaster, and promptly broke two strings.

Jayne Casey was one of the cast. The original trio played a handful of shows – the first two days after that Clash show – before Broudie came on board on guitar and Casey joined on vocals. Deaf School's Clive Langer would also play at several dates partially as a pretext to allow them to use Deaf School's equipment. As Broudie recalled to Pete Frame, "When I joined they played two songs in rotation – '**BIG IN JAPAN**' and 'Snow Monkeys', but we introduced a third one – 'God Readin' The Charts', which was Jayne reading the top 20 over a discordant musical backing."

Langer also appeared on their debut single for local venue/label Eric's, which featured the Chuddy Nuddies, or the Yachts under a pseudonym, on the flipside. But it suffered from terrible production, rendering the lyrics almost indecipherable. Ward and Allen left the band shortly after its release. As Ward conceded to Q in 1992, "Ian Broudie started turning our simple stuff into real songs and I was defunct." Allen, for his part, reckoned "The whole idea was to be a caricature of punk rather than the real thing." He subsequently worked with bands including the Egyptians, Moderates and Hunters, before becoming a session musician.

Their replacements were Holly Johnson on bass (after Ambrose Reynolds joined for a while before moving on to the Walkie Talkies) and old acquaintance Budgie on drums. The latter had spent a few weeks rehearsing with Julian Cope's Nova Mob before joining the Spitfire Boys. Budgie remembered Drummond as "one of the craziest, fiercest, most passionate and, at the same time, gentlest, men I have ever met. He'd rage, then cry, only minutes later – emotions that none of the rest of us could come even close to. We'd all sit around watching him while secretly nursing our own deep scars."

Over the next six months they gigged heavily, developing a theatrical slant that mixed cabaret with an art-school grasp of punk. They were confined to appearances in the north west (supporting the Buzzcocks, Warsaw, Wire, X-Ray Spex etc) as Drummond was the only one who could drive. Luckily, the music remained the focus rather than a trapping of their stage show. By this stage they were all but the house band at Eric's, whose Roger Eagle would insist on grooming interested parties in musical taste, loaning out his reggae, Nuggets and New York Dolls records on a rotational basis.

However, Johnson would leave after being 'voted out'. "Someone said," he told Q, "we don't want to work with you any more, though they didn't give me a reason. I know I wasn't the greatest bass player, because I wasn't that interested. I was 16 whereas the others were in their twenties, and some of them were taking themselves seriously, like it was their last chance to be in a pop group. But it was something to do, and meant I got into the Eric's club for free and my picture in the NME. I also remember some jealousy because Jayne and I got offered a record deal by Stiff as our sideline, the Sausages From Mars, while the band were desperate to get one. I always thought the rest had no talent whatsoever, although I liked working with Budgie. I thought I was destined for better things."

His departure allowed David Balfe of Dalek I Love You to join, although Steve Lindsay, again formerly of Deaf School, filled in for a while. After a couple of solo singles, Johnson was joined for a while by another Deaf School alumnus, Ambrose Reynolds, in the first incarnation of Frankie Goes To Hollywood. Lindsay would also appear in the Secrets and the Planets. Other temporary members of Big In Japan included Paul Rutherford and Pete Burns, later of Dead Or Alive. "Every member had really strong ideas," Casey later recalled to Q. "Holly and I were into the whole Warhol superstar, plasticky mentality, Ian was the proficient musician, while Bill was just off his head – and remains so." There was, at various points, major label interest in the band. They were 'on a promise' with Jet Records when the latter suddenly changed their minds and took the wind out of their sails. Big In Japan played their farewell show at Eric's on 26 August 1978, a date Drummond would commemorate, cryptically, in the notes to the compilation LP To The Shores Of Lake Placid. This amid rumours that the final straw had something to do with Drummond pressing up an extra 500 copies of the single, flogging them and keeping the profits.

The activities of the former members reads like a who's who of popular music in the 80s.

Bill Drummond formed his own label, Zoo Records, and marked its investiture with a second Big In Japan release, the 'From Y To Z And Never Again' EP, comprising four previously unaired songs. From there, alongside Balfe, he formed Lori And The Chameleons before they concentrated on backstage chores. Drummond subsequently managed the Teardrop Explodes and Echo And The Bunnymen, did some solo work and then founded the KLF. Balfe joined the Teardrop Explodes before setting up Food Records (home of Blur, etc). Broudie's bands included the Original Mirrors and Care before the more enduring Lightning Seeds, though he still found time to be one of the industry's busiest producers, beginning with Echo's 'Rescue'. Budgie would go on to the Slits, Siouxsie And The Banshees and the Creatures, and before that, alongside Broudie and Lindsay, the Secrets. Jayne Casey put together the critically revered Pink Industry/Pink Military before moving away from music to directing the Liverpool Festival of Comedy, the Bluecoat Gallery and broadcast media. And Holly Johnson became frontman for the aforementioned Frankie Goes To Hollywood. Ward retired from music to make models for the petro-chemical industry.

Holly Johnson was recently asked on his thoughts about the band for an interview with an 80s website. "Big In Japan were an interesting group of people, rather more than an interesting group. I was never that into being a bass player in a group. I did it for the experience, and was more interested in writing the lyrics for that band – although there were different writers vying for that role. I met up with Budgie recently. I did a club P.A. on Valentine's night and he came along. He is a very sweet person. I don't count many heterosexual men as friends but I love Budgie. I haven't seen Bill Drummond for a while. We met up a few years back after the KLF had decided to call it a day for a while. I loved those records. I talk to and see the band's singer, Jayne Casey, a lot. We have been through a lot together over the years."

Jayne Casey also passed on her own thoughts in an interview with Caught In Flux magazine that was not published at the time. "It's quite funny now, because everyone has gone on to do other things and it's given Big in Japan a prestige it didn't have at the time. Like there was no way we could get a record deal at the time. Nobody wanted us. We were all a bit too eccentric at a time when punk was quite macho and clear cut; to have a guitarist in a kilt, Bill Drummond, and a gay boy with a shaved head, Holly Johnson, and a mental girl with a shaved head, guess who – it was a bit too much for people to handle. We always wanted to be like The Monkees or something. We wanted to be a cartoon, and that's how we tried to sell ourselves to the record companies: there's some good characters here, and it would make a really good cartoon."

DISCOGRAPHY:

Big In Japan 7-inch (Eric's 0001 November 1977) (B-side by Chuddy Nuddies)
From A To Z And Never Again 7-inch EP (Zoo CAGE 001 November 1978)
Nothing Special/Cindy And The Barbi Dolls/Suicide A-Go-Go/Taxi

Blak Flag

Stuart Ross (bass), Dean Nicolson (vocals), Charlie Reid (guitar), Craig Reid (drums)

It's hard to imagine a greater contrast between the sinewed uber-machismo of Henry Rollins and the bespectacled, supposedly meek twins that were the Proclaimers – but they both started out in a band called Black Flag. Or near enough. The removal of the 'c' in their name was way punker.

The Scottish **BLAK FLAG** were founded in 1979. Charlie Reid: "We were all 16 or 17. Dean was still at school. We were influenced mainly by the Pistols, Clash, Buzzcocks, Damned etc, and then later Joy Division. We rehearsed in a bedroom at our house in Macduff Place, Auchtermuchty. Practice amps, crappy drum kit etc. Great fun! Most rehearsals involved the consumption of snakebite, and then trying to play 'Police and Thieves' with feeling."

Eventually they moved to Edinburgh in an effort to secure more gigs, arriving at the infamous Blair Street rehearsal rooms. Inmate, for that would be the appropriate term, Robin Saunders watched their arrival. "Blak Flag arrived at a unique moment in Blair Street history. The proprietor finally stirred from his apathy and decided that the place needed tarting up. Minions were dispatched to whitewash over the filthy walls festooned with layer upon layer of multi-coloured graffiti. A strict embargo was imposed against any future impromptu artwork, upon pain of immediate eviction. Enter Blak Flag, all unknowing and unbelieving of their luck in being presented with a blank canvas on such a scale. They set to work with spray can and stencil to advertise their presence for all to see."

However, they never actually joined the Blair Street circus. "They were just down on a scouting mission. Sceptix singer Tam bumped into them that very day and invited them along to their room. This was by no means the friendly, hospitable gesture it might appear! The now omnipresent Blak Flag band logo featured the anarchist 'Circled A' and Sceptix had already laid claim to being the big cheeses in that particular sub-cult locally. The boys from Auchtermuchty were being put on trial! I don't think they expected every member of the 'Capital Chaos' bands to be squeezed into that room, together with a good number of camp followers. The poor guys were visibly a-quiver. However, they picked up the borrowed gear and they were quite blindingly good. I can even recall a standout song with the name 'Bombsite'. They did their whole set, finishing up with 'Tomorrow Belongs To Me', which might have been the song from Cabaret by way of Alex Harvey's version, if memory serves. The twins seemed very quiet and serious and, ironically, given what happened later on, it was the other two, Stuart and Dean, who looked to have the star potential. We didn't see much of them after that and I don't think they played any gigs locally – we would have turned up for that. Stuart and Dean became 'faces' around the Edinburgh punk clubs and I believe that the latter succumbed to some of the more dangerous temptations on offer. I last saw him in the toilets at a venue called the Nite Club, very out of it indeed. Not long afterwards I always seemed to be either immediately in front of or behind one of them in the Castle Terrace dole queue and would nod an acknowledgement but, never knowing which twin it was, I never risked striking up a conversation."

Blak Flag fell apart soon after their Edinburgh adventure. "All good memories, though," reflects Charlie. In one of the most bizarre news stories of 2005, the Reid boys' punk rock history came back not so much to haunt them, but certainly to ambush them. The scene? The American Embassy in London, and Jimmy Pursey and John Lydon queuing up to sort their visas. Lydon rejects Pursey's proffered hand and instead throws coffee over him. Pursey is then pinned to the wall by an armed guard holding a sub-machine gun, who tells him not to move, and actually, he's got all Sham's singles. At this exact point the Reid brothers walk past, not today looking for a letter to America, simply a visa.

Blanks

Neil Singleton (vocals), Andrew Jackson (guitar), Andrew Butler (drums), Allen Adams (bass)

The BLANKS, whose history criss-crosses with that of the Destructors, were originally formed in 1978 in Market Deeping near Peterborough. Jackson had just left the Dole, and met Allen Adams later that year. Jackson: "He really was the only punk in Peterborough at the time. He was the one going to see all the gigs, managing the Now etc. He was Peterborough's punk constituent. He was also writing a lot of songs and had his own band. They were a shambles though. They relied on Joe (Macoll) from the Now drumming for them. But the rehearsals were terrible, you'd never get everyone turning up at the same time. That was the Destructors, or 666 (pronounced Sick Sick Sick), as they were sometimes called."

Jackson was working in Andy's Records at the time. "Allen used to come in and we got on really well. He said, 'Why not join the band?' I had half a dozen rehearsals and in the meantime they played a few gigs I saw. The gigs were chaos, but they were so well received. I saw them at the Key Theatre in Peterborough, and there were about 200 people. They were appalling, they would start a song about four times in a row, but all the bikers and hippies that were there went wild. They finished the set with a song called 'Thalidomide'. You'd never get away with that now. It would go on for about 15 minutes, and people were screaming and raving, it got a great reaction. So I joined the band. One of my friends at school was Andrew Butler, so he joined as well and gave them a permanent drummer."

There were problems with organisation and logistics, though, as Jackson remembers. "There would be gigs arranged, but the dates were wrong, or not everyone would turn up, that sort of thing happened all the time. So by mid-78 I'd left and then I formed the Blanks. The name was taken from the Pistols' bootleg – the reason being that we thought we might get some people to turn up for gigs thinking we were the Pistols in disguise. Cynical, isn't it? I went to school with Neil Singleton. He was the person who got into things before everyone else. He was into early Adam And The Ants, into Crass really early on, etc. He was into all that before it became popular. We had another guy from Andy's Records, Colin Maxey, on bass. And then the Destructors imploded, basically. Andrew Butler left and joined the Blanks with us. We did some gigs with the Only Ones. Then we started to get more like a hardcore punk band, and Colin wasn't into that, he was more into Television, Springsteen, etc. We were stumped. And we asked Allen to join."

"The only reason they asked me was because I had a bass guitar and amp at the time," reckons Adams. "Actually," says Jackson, "there were two main reasons – he was up for doing anything, God bless him, and, to be honest, he seemed to have more money than we did." The Blanks were therefore complete. They already had a set list, and later Adams would bring his own songs to the band, such as 'Northern Ripper', Son Of Sam', 'Understand' and 'Police State', which he'd played with the Destructors. But it was a two-way street. When Adams later reformed the Destructors, their first album would feature songs Jackson had written for the Blanks, including 'Born Too Late', 'Overdose' and 'Breakdown'.

In the meantime the Blanks had a support booked with the Damned at the Wirrina in Peterborough, and Adams had only a few days to learn the bass. Jackson: "He learned the set very quickly, he was really up for it. We would learn three or four songs a week to start off with, and when he turned up for the next practice, he would have them note-perfect. He worked his nuts off to get it done." Adams: "My memory of the Damned gig was that for some bizarre reason Captain Sensible kicked me in the bollocks for no reason – perhaps this was his usual greeting."

The Blanks began to draw reasonable audiences, and had a little interest from Sounds and NME. They had about 20 to 30 original songs once Adams' originals had been accommodated. Jackson: "We were a full-flight punk band, but the problem was we were now chasing everyone else's coat-tails. It had taken us too long to get to this stage. I arranged the gigs. I phoned up the Music Machine in Camden in about mid-78. Can we get a gig? Yeah. I played them the stuff and the woman said, 'Love, we were doing that 18 months ago. You're too late.' It had already moved on."

Their lone single, a real collector's item, used a tape of the famed hoax caller who claimed to be the Yorkshire Ripper (before Peter Sutcliffe was arrested). Adams: "It was recorded in a barn around the back of the Three Tuns pub in Market Deeping (where Jackson lived) on an ex-BBC two-track tape recorder operated by a biker called Henny. I remember accompanying Andrew to Rough Trade to sell the singles and I think we dropped one off at the BBC for John Peel." Jackson: "We had two mics, one that Neil sang directly into, the other one, the band were in a crescent, and the mic was pointing up to the roof in the middle of that. And Elaine (Neil Singleton's girlfriend) did a live scream for it, stood across the other side. We did it once, and you couldn't hear Elaine the first time, so we did it again. It went straight into a tape deck and it was all recorded in maybe three-quarters of an hour. We didn't even use a new tape. It was an old crinkly tape on it. But I liked all that."

However, given the subject matter, it was always going to be of greater appeal to the tabloids. "The News of the World took Neil Singleton and me out for a drink at the Bull in Market Deeping to muckrake about us," remembers Adams. "The intro with the alleged Ripper voice was recorded off the help line the police had set up. The front cover has the drummer, Andy Butler, as the Ripper and Andrew's girlfriend as the prostitute. The angle the reporter was looking for was that Neil's dad was a headmaster ('Headmaster's son in Ripper Glorification'). To cut a long story short, I was later sick on the reporter (punk rock or what?)." The single was subsequently sold for 50p at Destructors' gigs as a souvenir. Adams: "I think the single originally sold less than 100 copies and now goes for up to £120 a pop."

However, that wasn't the end of it. Adams: "I was interviewed about being the Northern Ripper," he claims. "I matched 13 of the 16 things (such as do you possess a copy of Mein Kampf? Do you possess a pair of jackboots?) they were looking for. I had to write out some letters the police had. Unfortunately, I could not drive a lorry. The reason they interviewed me was that I had been interested in the case and had thought I'd spotted a pattern. I predicted a date I thought he would strike and unluckily was correct. I had mentioned this to a few people and one of them phoned the police hotline. There were two policemen, one obviously a graduate, the other up from the ranks. The ranker interviewed me while the graduate had to make the tea. The ranker had a look at my book collection (the occult, concentration camps, serial killers – I was into Throbbing Gristle) and told me if it was up to him, he'd have me locked up. And he was going to keep an eye on me."

For a while the single gave them a little credibility. They again supported both the UK Subs and the Damned, whose Captain Sensible was kind enough to tell Sounds that if he was going to start a band again, he would want to sound like the Blanks. Jackson: "In the Blanks we perfected our own wall of sound. Allen had this massive bass combo with an 18-inch speaker in a Reflex cabinet. That gave us a really booming drone sound on the bass. That combined with Butler being a really good drummer, live we sounded as professional as the bands we were supporting. We didn't have a weak sound. Allen would for the most part play these bass root notes and little runs around the chorus, but it meant the guitar and bass were flat out and even if we weren't allowed to use the PA or got a bad mix, we were really, really loud. With Butler drumming, he filled in the spaces, what in a rock band the guitarist would do, and that gave us our sound."

Sadly, it never progressed from there. Jackson: "We were miles down from anywhere, we never had an agent or manager. We only got gigs by seeing who was touring, and phoning up the promoter, and turning up with a bottle of Scotch to get on the bill. But when Butler left, that knackered everything. Neil had a friend, Andrew McDonald that he brought in, and it was awful. After two years of building the sound up so we could fill the sound on stage, we were suddenly back down to sounding like 16-year-olds practising in the garage again."

The Blanks managed a handful more gigs concluding with a support slot to Discharge at Cottesmore Village Hall on 17 May 1980. The headliners' penchant for throwing bovine parts at their audience was only one of the problems. Jackson: "That was a complete disaster for two reasons. First, Discharge played the way we used to – and we couldn't play like that any more. That really pissed me off. Every single song we did now had the same tempo and same drum sound. A drum break would be Andy hitting a cymbal. Then the hall got trashed at the Cottesmore. Fine. Except we had a bond of £150, which in 1980 was a lot of money. When you've got part of your entourage ripping holes in the ceiling and laughing, then one of Neil's mates stole my amp – it was like, for fuck's sake. At the time I was really into the Banshees, Cure, Killing Joke. The Clash had moved on. I'd had a couple of years of playing music, had some brilliant laughs, loads of women. But everyone else was taking it a lot further."

Various members of the Blanks would, of course, reconvene in a new model of the Destructors in the 80s (Jackson would video several of the band's shows). They would also continue to play 'Northern Ripper' at shows – check out 1983 live album Armageddon In Action (a studio version was also included on their Exercise The Demons Of Youth LP). The Destructors in various forms are now active again and putting together new releases and lining up shows, with two retrospective CDs on Captain Oi!

DISCOGRAPHY:

Northern Ripper/Understand/Break Down 7-inch (Void Void 1 1979)
COMPILATION:
Messthetics #6 ('Northern Ripper')

Bleach Boys

Mr Frankenstein (vocals), Mr Rocket (guitar), Mr Phnuff (aka John B; bass and guitar), Mr Nuke (drums), plus Rocket (guitar), Max Profit (roadie/Mr Fixit), Jimmy Jesus (bass)

The BLEACH BOYS formed in Hitchin in 1977, originally as the (ahem) Fur Coughs. They were noisy, loudmouthed, obstreperous urchins and perfect for punk rock. Brought up on Slade and the Stooges, they were hot-wired by their first exposure to the Ramones. They were the first punk band in Hitchin, way predating the town's more famous residents, Chron Gen. "Our first gig was supporting

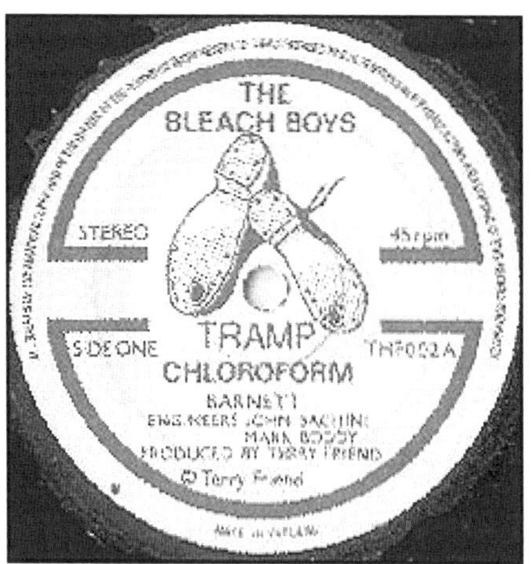

Ultravox!," Phnuff told me, "who were the first semi-punk thing to hit our area. A degree of bravado was involved as we had the gig before we had a band. It was wild, in a hall of 400 people, with a home-made PA complete with still drying paint on the speakers and a microphone made out of a bog roll and a telephone receiver. We went down very well, and a few weeks later our second and third gigs took place in local pubs: both venues totally packed. The initial response was amusement. However, because of overcrowding at gig three, damage occurred to the pub and we hit trouble and ended up banned from five venues after three gigs."

Their debut single was released on Tramp Records in 1978. "Terri Friend was a local gravedigger who had a small label mostly releasing folk music. Terri saw us on a sober night on about gig seven and called me up the next day asking if we wanted to release a record. We said yes and the whole thing was done pretty informally, no contracts or advances, etc. We wrote the two songs in a day and set about recording it over at Piper Sound Studio's in Luton (it's now gone). It was pressed by Linguaphone and appeared about six weeks after recording it. Wonderful! The A-side was written about a local heavy metal guitarist who worked in a lab and got through the days by sniffing chloroform." Sadly Friend's finances didn't stretch to a picture sleeve. Adverts were placed in the NME to sell it via mail order.

A second 12-inch was recorded and released on their own Zombie International Records. The title "came out of a review of a computer game in which the phrase 'Stocking Clad Nazi Death Squad Bitches' featured. We were rehearsing in a studio and a bloke who worked there bet us we couldn't get the words 'Stocking Clad Nazi Death Squad Bitches' into a song, so we did, about 38 times. We created an image of a 'Stocking Clad Nazi Death Squad Bitch', called her Foo Foo, and started to think of what she would be into. I have a vague recollection that Mel Brookes' film The Producers had been on TV a few days before. There are lots of SCNDSBs in that!"

The group bumped into several of the prominent bands of the day on their travels, including the Banshees, XTC, Radio Birdman and ATV, while a gig at the 100 Club saw the stage invaded by Captain Sensible. "I met Sid Vicious at the Ramones gig that was recorded for It's Alive and managed to have a piss on the shoes of the Pretenders drummer at the Marquee. In terms of favourite gigs, the first three were pretty memorable at Hitchin College, the George and the Red Hart. They really were packed solid and Hitchin had never seen anything like it. The George gig had about 130 people in an upstairs room licensed for 60, all pogoing away. The landlady kept coming up and asking us to stop the dancing because it's an old building, and apparently, the ceiling below was cracking and the internal beams could be felt moving. At the Hart it was even more crowded, although it was at ground level. There were people hanging off of windows inside and out and climbing on tables, a significant number of which were broken."

Bizarrely enough, though they seem to have crept under the radar of most punk histories, the Bleach Boys have continued to survive, if not prosper. To the extent that in 2004 they finally released a full-length CD, full of uncompromising rudeness and anti-social tracts. Well, someone has to keep the flame burning. Though they still won't tell me their real names.

DISCOGRAPHY:

Chloroform/You've Got Nothing 7-inch (Tramp THF 002 1978) (1,000 only)
Stocking Clad Nazi Death Squad Bitches/Death B4 Techno/Nuclear War 12-inch (Zombie International ZOMBO 103010 1981)
Children Of Wallyword Go Wild For Kicks 4-track cassette (Zombie International)
Let's Dance/Psycho Semtex Sex/She's Not My Wife, She's My Slapper/Cliff
4 Cyclists Of The Apocalypse CD (Zombie International/Damage)

The Bicycle Song/Weirdo 7-inch single (Zombie International)
Taking The 'O' Out Of Country CD EP (Zombie International December 2002)
Stealth Bomber/Free Fi Fo Fon/We're All Fucked/I Married (A Lesbian Sex Commando)/Jesus Stole My Fridge
Brain Plugins Spaghetti CD (Fragile November 2004; Germany) (16 tracks, including a video of 'Nuclear War' at the Club 85 in Hitchin in a 7-inch single CD bag)

Blitzkrieg Bop

Nicky Knoxx (aka Alan Cornforth; drums), Telly Sett (aka Damien 'Dimmer' Blackwell; guitar), Mick Sick (aka Mick Hylton; bass), Gloria (aka Ann Hodgson; guitar), Blank Frank (aka John Hodgson; vocals).

Formed in Cleveland in 1977, the origins of BLITZKRIEG BOP can be traced back to Adamanta Chubb, which began life three years earlier. Alan Cornforth (drums), Kevin McMaster (vocals, rhythm guitar), Stephen Sharratt (lead guitar), and Mike 'Duck' McDonald (bass) were the original participants, with McDonald replaced by Damien 'Dimmer' Blackwell, whose parents owned a farm where, handily enough, they could practice.

They played their first show at St Mary's youth club in Stockton in November 1974. This, by all accounts, was a disaster, and John Hodgson, formerly of schoolboy band Purity, was recruited on the basis that they needed a songwriter. Thereafter Sharratt left the band to go on to a career in set design for EastEnders and other programmes. Dimmer took over guitar and McMaster doubled on bass and vocals. They also gradually moved away from the stilted hard rock that had been their province to more pop-orientated material. Going nowhere fast, the band had drifted apart in May 1976 when Hodgson joined soul band Contrast, who became the unfortunately titled Erection.

Dimmer kept Adamanta Chubb active, and bumped into Hodgson on New Year's Eve in 1976, who rejoined. In February they introduced 'Now I Wanna Sniff Some Glue' by the Ramones into the set, with the line-up settling on John Hodgson (vocals/keyboards), Dimmer Blackwell (guitar), Mick Hylton (bass), Alan Lawrence (drums), the latter soon to be replaced by Alan Cornforth. Their slide towards punk rock was confirmed by watching the Stranglers appear at Middlesbrough Rock Garden. Soon after they demo'd their first 'punk' song, 'Bugger Off'. "It is an example of anti-art," Blank Frank later explained, "the three lines were written only to rhyme with each other – 'You think I'm a bloody fool, You laugh at me, You think it's cool, You wanna throw me in a muddy pool, well bugger off!'"

With John Hodgson taking on more of the vocals and less keyboards, Dimmer brought along friend Ann Hodgson (no relation) to provide rhythm guitar. At which time they all adopted new, punky pseudonyms, and became Blitzkrieg Bop in May 1977. New material in keeping with their transmutation flowed, including 'Police State', 9 'Til 5' and the hastily written 'Let's Go'.

The band cut a demo at Dimmer's farm on May 20th, featuring cover versions but also '9 Till 5' and 'Bugger Off'. Five days later they attempted to record again, this time with the intention of cutting their first single. All they needed now was a label. "Mortonsound wasn't really a proper record company," stated Frank Blank in his history of the band. "Most of its clients actually paid them for pressing records, and it was this method that Blitzkrieg Bop used to release their first single. They could have sent copies of the tape to labels in the hope of getting a contract, but the atmosphere in mid-77 was hostile to large record companies, and the onus was on self promotion and independence." He took out a loan to pay for 500 copies of the record (£275, including 5p for each sleeve) and a picture sleeve that consisted of passport photos taken in Newcastle shopping centre. Meanwhile, their Sunday night residency at the Speedway Hotel was becoming something of a focal point for Middlesbrough's punks, inspiring fellow travellers Bladze and Dangerbird, though they were still playing two sets, one of 'straight' material, the second 'punk'. However, Dimmer was dismissed from the band due to the length of his hair, which hadn't noticeably shortened (he would later be assassinated in song by the band in 'Mental Case'). In the meantime the band started their own fanzine, titled Gabba Gabba Hey, while making unsuccessful attempts to secure the interest of Raw and Stiff Records.

The single was eventually released on 14 July 1977. "Pretty awful, actually, but fun," noted Sounds. Tony Parsons was more enthusiastic: "I wanna see this mob live because nobody – well almost nobody – has heard of them and they're good enough for six-figure recording contracts at the current rate of inflation." It resulted in a letter from Keith Yershon of Lightning Records who offered to distribute the single, while Larry Ottaway took over as band manager.

In September they travelled to Berry Street Studios in London, at the behest of Lightning's Roger St Pierre, to re-record 'Let's Go'. Three others tracks were run through for the B-side, 'Get Out Of My Way', which was never finished, 'Life Is Just A So-So' and 'Mental Case'. Despite the ostensibly luxurious 16-track environment, time constraints meant the band were unhappy with the final mixes produced by Alan Davison and Bill Farley.

After support shows to Ultravox! and Radio Stars, Ann Hodgson elected to leave. Via word of mouth, former Erection guitarist Ray Radford (soon to be christened Ray Gunn) was drafted in time for a support slot to the Saints at Middlesbrough Rock Garden. They were trying to convince Lightning, who kept postponing the release of the single, to fund an album, but with little success, so they recorded a cassette of live rehearsals at Whinney Banks Youth Club to sell in the Teesside area. They were beginning to attract a little national press too. Phil Sutcliffe, writing for Sounds, reviewed a subsequent show thus: "It seems to come down to freshness and inspiration. Their best moments were when they followed their first ever song 'Bugger Off' (a one-minute 'up yours' to the National Front) with their latest, 'Prostitution'. The original excitement was there in both of them, sheer momentum and intensity. Regroup around that kind of energy and they'll lift themselves from acceptability to compulsiveness."

The re-recorded 'Let's Go' finally appeared in January 1978, but, unlike other records on the Lightning label, it did not have the distribution weight of Warners behind it, even though Alan 'Fluff' Freeman gave it a spin on Radio 1. It was followed by a second session at Berry Street studios for the follow-up single for Lightning. '(You're Like A) U.F.O.' was backed by the 'white reggae' of 'Viva Bobby Joe'.

They were confirmed as support to Slaughter And The Dogs on their Do It Dog Style national tour, having already supported them on one riotous occasion in Newcastle. This didn't provide the breakthrough the band expected, but it was at least eventful – Wayne Barrett disappeared halfway through, and when Slaughter drummer Mad Muffett doused everyone in water during a hotel stay in Manchester, Blitzkrieg Bop's guitars were held until the bill was paid. Several shows were cancelled, and then the transit, which they still hadn't paid for, broke down. Around this time they also sussed that they weren't going to be paid. That was enough to see off Ray, who was replaced by Micky Dunn, aka Bert Presley, guitarist with local punk act the Lice.

The band entered the studio for the final time in August 1978 at Impulse Studios in Wallsend, cutting 'Radio' and 'West Side Story'. Lightning finally released '(You're Like A) U.F.O.' on 31 August, featuring a picture of John's future wife Denise Liddell on the sleeve ("she's regretted it ever since"). 50 copies included free 'hairy' bags made from mohair. Melody Maker called it "cruddy", but John Peel played it at the top of his show on 15th September, which revived spirits. Afterwards, Mick Hylton was replaced by another former member of Lice, Graham 'Kid' Moses.

John poured his energy into a new fanzine venture, Teesside Smells. Meanwhile Dimmer Blackwell's new band, Nicky Beat & The Beatniks, released their single, '(I Can Hear) Voices'. Their drummer, Pete Collins, was drafted in for a show supporting Penetration in Redcar when Cornforth was injured in a bizarre accident while attempting to take a leak on the way home from a show in Chester. Five days later Blitzkrieg Bop appeared at the Hope & Anchor in London, where RCA and Satril were due to check out the band. RCA never turned up, and Satril passed. With the band stuck in neutral, Hodgson received a phone call from Alan Savage asking if he wanted to join Basczax. Moses joined Cleveland punks No Way and formed his own band Private Eye. Dimmer would set up Teesbeat studio and help record local bands, including his own group, Commercial Acrobats.

Blitzkrieg Bop reunited (with Blank Frank and Moses joined by members of Viva La Diva) in 1994 for a benefit show for the family of Dave Johns, former guitarist of the Barbarians, who was terminally ill with cancer. The gig, which was videotaped, was a great success, raising over £2,000 for Johns, who died four days later. Another show with the reformed line-up was held seven days later. It was Blitzkrieg Bop's final bow.

In 1998 John Esplen of Overground Records got in touch about the possibility of a compilation album. From John's enormous cassette collection he sent about 60 prospective tracks to Overground. Many of those that did not make the cut were later released on Bottom Of The Barrel. One result of the Overground compilation, apart from arousing international interest, was that Blank Frank was able to locate his former bandmates. Dimmer, Moses and Ann Hodgson remain in the Teesside area, but Mick Hylton lives in Calgary, Canada and Ray Radford in Folkestone. Micky Dunn teaches psychology at Derby University and plays part-time in the Blues Basement.

DISCOGRAPHY:

Let's Go/Nine Till Five/Bugger Off 7-inch (Mortonsound MTN3172-3 July 1977)
Let's Go (version 2)/Life Is Just a So-So/Mental Case 7-inch (Lighting GTL-504 December 1977)
(You're Like A) U.F.O./Viva Bobby Joe 7-inch (Lightning GTL-543 August 1978)
Scum 78 cassette (Animated Tapes HUMAN-7 October 1978) (unofficial, though band-authorised bootleg, released due to frustration with Lightning, featuring various studio and rehearsal versions)
Scum 78 cassette (version 2) (1979)
ARCHIVE RELEASES:
Top of the Bops CD (Overground Records OVERCD 69 February 1998)
Bottom Of The Barrel CD (Opportunes BOTCD1 August 1998)

Blue Screaming

Simon Pearce (vocals, guitar), Igor (aka Steven Wright; vocals, keyboards), Godfrey Old (bass), Chris Nikolov (drums)

BLUE SCREAMING were formed in early 1977 after Pearce placed an advert in the Melody Maker. Igor was the first respondent. "There were a lot of responses, as I worded the ad quite differently to the 'bass player wanted for rock band' type of thing. Despite it being 1977, most of the ads still sounded like it was 1974. Eventually the band became four of us."

Blue Screaming were up and running quickly. "We played our first dates six weeks after birth, a four-week residency at the Duke of Lancaster pub in Barnet. Igor blagged it on his past reputation with other bands. We put enough stuff together to make a set and by the end of the dates we had written a lot more stuff and had learnt to play better with each other. Other dates followed including the Roxy, the Pegasus, the Marquee and Upstairs at Ronnie Scott's."

One of their more memorable reviews followed a support slot to the Monochrome Set, "which referred to us as sounding 'like a fairground in a cement mixer', which was, unbeknownst to the reviewer, a fabulous compliment". As for the Roxy, which they played on 6 September 1977, "I remember Igor having beer tipped over his keyboard electrics from a balcony – probably a compliment. We had long hair and were 'old' at 21 or 22, or so it seemed. A much weirder gig than the Roxy was being on the same bill as Moorgate And The Tube Disasters and the Door And The Window in some dark corner of Barnet. That was the gig where we had to high-tail it out of the place as Moorgate And The Tube Disasters, embracing the true anarchic flavour of the time, took to mashing up the place and kicking a dead pig's head around the stage (John Cale eat your heart out). We had done our soundcheck, but decided that was probably it if we wanted any of our gear or limbs to survive the attention of 20 or 30 young offenders on a night out, apparently being supervised by some social worker who had lost the plot."

Psi-d-Real (aka Gordon Mitchell) joined the band in 1978 as an extra guitarist (he also played the oscillator and contributed vocals on the later Maida Vale sessions). "He added another guitar dimension to the band. I was still banging away on the chords, he could play a bit more fancy stuff." Their debut single, 'Bland Hotel', eventually emerged on Albatross Records. This earned some degree of notoriety for its artwork, which parodied the sleeve of CBS pomp rockers Grand Hotel's single 'Secret Life'. CBS responded by refusing to distribute the single, ensuring it disappeared from the shops. Sounds' Dave McCullough (who mistakenly presumed they were using the Art Attacks' former drummer) caught their Marquee show and noted the influence of early Pink Floyd. He lambasted their more 'long-winded dross' but pointed out that 'Bland Hotel' was "truly catchy and if the name of the band wasn't so incredibly bad I'd wager it'll get some airplay." "How can you resist the thought of psychedelic punk?" noted another of the inkies. They also recorded five songs at the BBC's Maida Vale Studios in 1978, produced by Neal Burn, which they had intended to make into an EP. Thereafter Pearce and Igor moved off to form Take It.

DISCOGRAPHY:

Bland Hotel/Thin-x-Cinema 7-inch (Albatross TIT 2 1978)

Blunt Instrument

Robert Sandall (guitar, vocals), Bill Benfield (guitar), Ed Shaw (bass), David Sinclair (drums)

A London-based punk outfit, in the loosest terms, who provided a musical outlet for prolific rock writers Dave Sinclair, originally from Griffnock in Scotland, and Robert Sandall. Sinclair has described BLUNT INSTRUMENT as a 'pseudo punk band', but his former band leader isn't so sure. "We weren't a lot more pseudo than many of the other middle class blokes playing punk – and there were plenty. David was very sceptical about the style of the music and the attitude, but it felt serious to me, anyway."

They managed to play a series of shows around London, including a support to Metal Urbain at the Roxy and a show with Wire at Imperial College, before releasing 'No Excuse'. It was "Immensely derivative" noted Sounds, whilst also clocking the MC5 influence. That's a little uncharitable, as it's one of the better-sounding obscurities from the period. The sleeve suggests that the band members had made the transition from the hippy era with a fair degree of sartorial reluctance, though the stencilled lettering was more contemporaneous. Blunt Instrument's quick demise was recounted in Sinclair's Love Is The Drug. Sinclair broke his wrist falling off his drum kit, "caused by a flying bottle, thrown by a drunk at an open-air courtyard gig outside a squat in King's Cross," notes Sandall. During the hiatus Benfield elected to return to his former post as an English teacher following Blunt Instrument's final show on 3 July 1978. Although Nick Aldridge replaced him, by now any chance of seizing the moment had passed.

After renaming themselves London Zoo they signed to Zoom to release 'Receiving End', as part of Bruce Findlay's attempt to build a roster of acts around Simple Minds after he'd taken Zoom to Arista. A further single for Gramaphone, 1980's 'Who's Driving This Car', backed by 'You And Your Big Ideas', followed in 1980. Sinclair worked briefly with TV Smith's Explorers before concentrating on writing. As did, eventually, Sandall. "I subsequently fell into journalism at Dave Sinclair's suggestion, five years after we stopped playing together. During the intervening period I played with an Edinburgh based band called Epsilon – a casualty of the city's 1982/3 heroin epidemic – then devised music for radio plays, became a ski bum etc." He eventually became the rock critic for the Sunday Times. "Punk was the moment that made me realise I had to put up or shut up as far as music was concerned. It was a call to arms, an end of mildly stoned inertia, and I can't imagine I would still be caught up in writing or anything music related if punk hadn't happened."

DISCOGRAPHY:

No Excuse/Interrogation 7-inch (Diesel DCL 01 March 1978)

Bondage Boys

Con O'Donaghue (vocals), Dan O'Donaghue (bass), Steve Fowler (guitar), Simon Randall (drums; though at times Alan 'Polo' Pollard was borrowed from the Toads)

Variously known as the BONDAGE BOYS, the Turkey Molesters, Relish And The Perverts and Rasputin And His Mad Monks, this little bunch was, after the Toads, probably the first punk band on the Norwich scene in 1977. It all grew out of a fanzine, Vomit, produced by the O'Donaghue brothers at school, the publication of which promptly saw them expelled.

One of the first bands they included in their fanzine were the Toads, and, in sympathy, they invented their own band, Electric Orgasm, to give themselves more than just the one band to write about. In fact, the myriad name changes came about because they had so little confidence in their abilities that they didn't want anyone remembering who they were before they played their next gig. But then as David Viner of the Toads, who once remembered them turning up for a gig with their 'equipment' shoved in a shopping trolley, would point out, "We tended to use them as support in order to make the Toads sound far better."

Eventually, after adding Steve Fowler on guitar, they played their first gig, after three days' rehearsal, at the 3C's (which subsequently became the Charing Cross Centre). They turned up without a drummer, but managed to persuade Pollard to deputise. Although the set mainly consisted of covers, they did play their first original composition, 'Betsy The Cow', a dig at their local folk club at the Cambridge Arms. Eventually they found a more permanent drummer in the form of Simon Randall.

Incredibly, the band did actually make a studio tape of seven songs, which Viner committed to posterity at a rehearsal (and has made available for download at his website www.davidviner.com).

Boys

Jack Black (aka Jacek Lempicki; drums), Matt Dangerfield (aka Matt Walker; vocals/guitar), Honest John Plain (aka John Splain; vocals/guitar), Duncan 'Kid' Reid (vocals, bass), Casino Steel (aka Stein Groven; vocals/keyboards)

The BOYS were not of punk rock's making, though they did make something of punk rock. Throw your preconceptions aside for a while, and view the Boys as they actually were – superb songsmiths, as innately musical as any of the bands of 1977. They were a cracking live act, chiselled three excellent albums and one good one, and wrote half a dozen singles that filleted the new wave of its energy and garnished it with 60s pop suss. It's a mystery to me why they attract so many naysayers.

But if we need to cling to punk's entirely imagined grand scheme of things, and pretend that Joe 'Woody' Strummer hadn't played in a succession of hippy bands, ignore the fact that Cook and Jones had been at it since 1974, etc, then the Boys are guilty as charged. Casino Steel had been a member of the Hollywood Brats as far back as 1972. Alongside vocalist Andrew Matheson, he co-opted the New York Dolls' aesthetic of wasted glamour and trash shock values. Originally called The Queen until Freddie Mercury's elite soft rock corps collared the name, they played regular shows at the Café Des Artistes and Speakeasy to spread the word, which found an early convert in Keith Moon of the Who. But by the advent of their debut album, Grown Up Wrong, which was only released in Scandinavia in 1974 and credited to Andrew Matheson And The Brats, they had broken up.

In the meantime Matt Dangerfield had converted his basement in Maida Vale to a recording studio with friend and fellow songwriter Barry Jones. A who's who of punk passed through its portals, including Mick Jones, Tony James, Bryan James, Rat Scabies, Gene October and Billy Idol. Sid and Nancy were also regular visitors, as Dangerfield recalled, with some horror, to Phil Hanson. "They were always arguing and she was always locking herself in my bathroom. Once Sid thought she was committing suicide, so we broke down the door to my bathroom, and she was just sitting there on the toilet saying, 'Can't a girl have a shit in peace?' That doesn't endear you to people who are house guests!"

Among those who made their first recordings in the ad hoc studio were the Sex Pistols, the

The Boys tear it up on stage.

Damned, the Clash, Generation X etc. 47A Warrington Crescent was the maternity ward for so much that came thereafter, but it was inevitable that its owner would tire of his role as midwife. Among the most notable visitors were the embryonic London SS, the capital's great underachievers, with whom both Dangerfield and Steel were involved. When this adventure collapsed, or rather never got to the extent where it was capable of collapse, Steel and Dangerfield hooked up with vocalist Andrew Matheson and bass player Wayne Manor. Geir Waade (a veteran of several bands involving Mick Jones) and Honest John Plain, who had been at art school in Leeds with Dangerfield, completed the line-up. Honest John Plain: "I met Matt Dangerfield and Barry Jones at art school and I quickly realised that they were the sort of people I wanted to hang around. After I had known Matt and Barry for a year or so they decided to move to London with some other friends. Back in the early 1970s it was very different from today in that if you wanted to do anything at all you had to go to London because everywhere else was so far behind. Leeds was just not the place to be. And I was becoming sick and tired of going to the local chip shop and almost getting into fights because I was so different from everyone else. In those days you'd get attacked just because of the clothes you wore. Matt and Barry had become my best mates and everyone I was knocking around with, including my future girlfriend Karen, had decided to move to London together."

After a few rehearsals Matheson, Manor and Waade moved on to other ventures. Plain, concurrently a foreman in a T-shirt factory, recruited two fellow employees, Duncan 'Kid' Reid (bass) and Jack Black (drums) in June 1976. Honest John Plain: "They were both very young at the time and I was a complete bastard to them! It was the first bit of 'power' I'd been given. When I first started at Gaz T-Shirts, I was younger than everyone else and given all the donkey work. So when Jack and Duncan started I was made the foreman of the print works and I took it out on them, especially Duncan, because he was so skinny and small. I gave Duncan all the big boxes to move and chuckled to myself at the way he struggled! I should have picked on the drummer really, but Jack was so cool in those days and as Duncan hated it so much, I enjoyed picking on him even more. I was a horrible boss!"

They tried out a number of vocalists, including Mick Jones' old sparring partner Kelvin Blacklock, before they decided they'd be better off sharing vocal duties between Dangerfield and Reid. "To start with we covered a few Brats songs as a starting point," Dangerfield told Phil Hanson, "the ones that survived, 'Sick On You' and 'Tumble With Me'. We did a few more Brats songs, but then the Boys songs started coming and we gradually dropped the Brats stuff bit by bit." This new line-up played its first gig at the Hope & Anchor in September 1976, with several old friends from 47A present. These included Live Wire fanzine writer Alan Anger, who became their road manager after manager Ken Mewis, who'd previously steered the Hollywood Brats before taking over the reins with the Boys, promised him a life of rock'n'roll and huge sums of money, which of course never appeared. Anger: "I really liked them because they had a pop feel and their music was very exciting. Most bands were trying to copy the Ramones or the Pistols but The Boys always had their own ideas and their own unique sound, they really were very good and it was great to see a band who were playing short, catchy songs." However, he entered Boys' folklore by writing in his fanzine that Casino was "unnecessary". The next occasion he bumped into the band, Casino had designed his own button badge, "I am unnecessary".

"There were still no rules about punk," reckoned Dangerfield, "so we started picking 60's records that had been picked up at the market for 10p. We plundered a lot of that for ideas. Tried songs out, songs to fill out our first few gigs, do a few covers, 'cause we hadn't written many songs by then... We were looking for obscure B-sides like 'Take A Heart'... 'You're My World' which was by Cilla Black, the Searchers' 'Walk In The Room'. But again, as our songs were coming through we were gradually dropping the covers."

I asked Dangerfield about the Boys uneasy fit with punk. "I think it was just because we were a bit too melodic! We had a bit of harmony and things, which none of the other bands were really trying to do that much." It was noticeable, however, that the Boys never sought to bury that. "No. We didn't believe in playing 'beneath' ourselves, as I suspect bands like the Police were, for example." But would the band have sounded like it did without the advent of punk? "There were definitely influences there. But it was such a small scene, and we all knew each other and what each other was doing. It was very much a small movement that snowballed. We were all influenced by each other and bands like the Velvet Underground and the Ramones – the Ramones were a big influence." And did they, as so many bands now admit, 'speed up' in keeping with the zeitgeist? "Yeah, sure. It was a case where you'd do a rehearsal for a live gig, to play for an hour. You'd end up doing it live and be finished in 40 minutes, wondering where we'd lost the songs." Jack Black: "We were a beat band till punk came along. Then in about two weeks we had to speed up our songs to 100mph. That's what happened. We had to do it. Otherwise, nobody would have written anything about us. We had to speed up to 100mph then we could join the punk set." Ah, but as drummer, didn't he have responsibility for the tempos? "Yeah, but I was TOLD what to do! It just became faster and heavier. But the whole scene was sensational. Absolutely fantastic."

Subsequent gigs at the Brecknock and Rochester Castle ensued before a show supporting Babe Ruth at Dingwalls where they impressed the A&R staff of NEMS Records. Which was odd, given that they were stupid-drunk at the time. "We'd been hanging around drinking in the pub, so we were "relaxed", and by the time we came to play, there were quite a few of our mates there, just laughing and joking, and we were drunk, sloppy and not your typical band. I remember the DJ there saying we were the worst band he'd ever seen on stage. The same night we were signed by NEMS and got a rave review in the NME."

The result was a five-year deal with NEMS, the first British punk band to sign such an extended contract. The euphoria of the times resulted in a counter-offer from Polydor to buy out their contract, but NEMS declined. In retrospect, signing with NEMS was the wrong decision. Dangerfield: "Totally the wrong thing to do. But we were a bit desperate. In those days, all you could do was the pub circuit – that was the whole scene. Every gig we played, we had the venue manager grudgingly paying us and telling us we were the worst band to ever set foot on that stage, and never darken their doorstep again. So we were burning our bridges as we went. When NEMS turn up offering us a recording contract – we'd never really heard of them as a recording company but they were quite big on live stuff – we thought, well, at least we'd get some gigs. Nobody else had been signed at the time. The Pistols were out of contract or been dumped by EMI, the Damned had a singles deal, so to be offered an album deal..." And did that engender any jealousy in such a small scene? "Definitely. We signed for bugger all basically, but everybody thought we were super-rich because we'd signed a record deal. The only difference is, we weren't on the dole. But we were on more or less the same money from the record company, so not much difference!"

The first result of this misbegotten marriage was 'I Don't Care', backed by 'Soda Pressing', the first of several songs to parody the emerging po-faced nature of punk rebellion, recorded in February 1977 following a recording session in Ecclestone Street, Victoria. It perfectly echoed the sentiments of the day, though in retrospect it's the one Boys' single that sounds a bit forced. Released in April, the Boys set out on a national tour supporting John Cale of the Velvet Underground

As soon as the tour was completed they returned to the studio, recording a total of 16 tracks in two days for their debut album in early May, with Pete Gage as producer. But the band were unhappy with Gage's interventions, insisting that the extraneous Hammond organ frills and vocals were either limited or negated. It took until September for the record to be released, in an era when speed, in so many senses, was the order of the day. The album does, however, still stand up. You can't argue with the first-rate proto-punk of 'Sick On You', which is great fun, even if it doesn't match the brilliant Hollywood Brats' version. 'Tumble With Me' and 'No Money' still sound good too, betraying the band's indebtedness to the Rolling Stones more than the Clash.

The album really should have taken off. The Boys were popular both in the press and with their peers, musicians ranging from Steve Jones to Bruce Foxton to Johnny Thunders and Marianne Faithful (also on NEMS) volunteering their services for encores. But they never got the breaks. The delay of their debut album was just the first instance of dreadful timing. Just as significant was the death of Marc Bolan just before he was about to put the band on his TV show.

The group's second single was Plain's 'The First Time', a touching and remarkably candid retelling of the loss of his virginity, released on 30 July 1977. Recorded alongside the other debut album tracks in May 1977, both the single and album versions of the song were edited down with the removal of the original's third verse. Plain: "It was partly based on when I lost my virginity at 15, although it's actually turned round. I went with this girl behind the youth club I attended, and she actually did say those words, which made me feel more relaxed and confident as I thought that she also didn't know what she was doing. I found out later that she was the local 'bike' and she used to say that to all the boys! Ironically it was my first time but I had suspicions about her being a virgin when I had to visit the clap clinic a few days later. I wrote the song in early 1977 as I was trying to break through the Steel/Dangerfield songwriting stranglehold. Matt was convinced that I couldn't write, and I was determined to prove him wrong. 'First Time' was a punk love story based loosely on my first time and written in a 'Ramones' style. For ages afterwards Matt refused to believe that I had actually written the song!"

It got a single of the week plaudit in Sounds, and the band were invited to record their first Peel session for broadcast on 8 August, the DJ having given the single lots of airtime. However, its ultimate chart placing, at 77, was disappointing. It didn't help that shortly after its release Elvis Presley expired, meaning all the energies of RCA, who were NEMS' distributors, were expended serving the huge demand for reissues.

By Christmas, the ever-prolific membership of the band settled on reinventing themselves as the Yobs for a light-hearted Christmas album (see Yobs entry). Meanwhile the mother project ensconced themselves at Rockfield Studios in Wales in November 1978 to record 'Brickfield Nights', Dangerfield's nostalgic eulogy of his lost youth – 'Late nights spent kicking round a football/We carved our initials on the school wall.' It was a great pop song, simple, effective, charming.

Their second album, Alternative Chartbusters, was released a month later in March, but once again distribution problems at NEMS meant they failed to get sufficient quantities into record shops to help promote the accompanying tour, though that again was well attended. You could criticise Alternative Chartbusters for its punky affectations, but you really couldn't argue with the songwriting, the production, or the sheer enthusiasm behind the presentation.

Following a second Peel session they returned to Rockfield in the summer of 1978 to work on a follow-up set, under the provisional title Junk. However, relations with NEMS, already on a delicate footing, deteriorated further when they refused to pick up the tab for the sessions. Rockfield, incensed, wouldn't surrender the master tapes for the 15 songs they'd recorded. They never were released, though examples of the material, saved by Dangerfield from monitor mixes, were salvaged years later for the Odds And Sods and Punk Rock Rarities compilations.

The Boys' relationship with NEMS collapsed as a result of the impasse. But they were still under contract. So the band went on strike until NEMS agreed to release them. "It was a good story going on strike," Reid later admitted on the band's website. "I suppose literally that's what we did, we just decided we'd do nothing until they gave up. Again it was the incredible self-belief we had at the time, but we probably lost a lot of momentum, although eventually when we came back and played again there was still a big following there. With hindsight, by then our time had probably passed and that was that. There wasn't any point struggling on with NEMS really."

An 18-month hiatus ensued, which doubtless wrecked the band's momentum. When they finally negotiated themselves away from NEMS they signed to Safari and returned with a fresh album recorded in Trondheim, Norway, released in November 1979. Ostensibly it was recorded there because Casino's friend Bjorn Nessjoe had just started a new studio and wanted to raise its profile and was offering free session time. To Hell With The Boys picked up from its predecessor but added a tad more sheen to proceedings, though Nessjoe barged Kid Reid out of the picture, believing his vocals weren't doing the songs justice. But the songs survived the interventions, especially a scintillating cover of 'Sabre Dance'. Extracted from the album, 'Kamikaze', featuring a rare vocal outing for Plain, was released as a single. The band then joined the Ramones on their extensive UK End Of The Century tour. Reid and Steele joined the brudders on stage for their live rendition of 'Baby I Love You', with the rest of the Boys helping out with the harmonies from behind the curtain. As Duncan Reid recalled to me: "I think the Ramones found it hard to accept other musicians being on stage with them, but they knew they needed help to play the song. Therefore Cas's organ was put right at the side of the stage, practically behind the curtain. We both sang into the same mic." As a direct result of this, Casino was actually invited back to New York to join the Ramones, but declined.

During that tour they released 'Terminal Love', Plain's paean to doomed romance, which saw them finally throwing off their punk shackles, and sounding all the better for it – power pop meets 'Love Will Tear Us Apart' in tragic embrace. Dangerfield: "We developed quite naturally. We were always quite tuneful. You can't carry on being an angry young man forever. Not that we were, really, we enjoyed it. We didn't have anything to be angry about!" The production was almost Spector-esque. "Sure. The other thing, we got into production, or I did anyway. After the first album, which was pretty raw and basic. I had a studio and was interested in that kind of thing. Whereas at first we were almost playing live with overdubs. We got more into recording technique."

But by now the Boys had disappeared off the critical radar. After further BBC Radio sessions they readied a follow-up single, Steel's 'Jimmy Brown', a memoir of his 'troubled' childhood ("I wish I could play like Johnny Ramone/I wouldn't have to sit in corner of the pub alone"). However, this was ultimately rejected, though Pojat would take their version of the song to number 1 in the Finnish charts. Instead, they elected to go with a version of the Rolling Stones' 'You'd Better Move On'. Afterwards Steel returned to Norway to work with Gary Holton after experiencing some personal problems and illness (due to his drink-fuelled diet, and lack of vitamins, he actually contracted scurvy). Rudi Thompson of X-Ray Spex stepped in to fulfil dates on their French tour.

Their first release post-Steel came in October 1980. 'Weekend' was another great slice of catchy power pop, produced by Nick Tauber, and was even aired on Noel Edmonds' Multi-Coloured Swapshop, but it again failed to make any impression on the charts. After a further festive outing as the Yobs, January 1981 brought both their final single 'Let It Rain' and album, Boys Only. Plain was taking an increasing role as songwriter, partially because others weren't contributing. Boys Only lacked the fire and verve of earlier releases, and 'Let It Rain' (a revamped remnant of the Junk sessions written by Dangerfield and former colleague Casino) passed everyone by when released on single. The critical reaction was more supportive than might have been expected, Melody Maker saluting the group as a "veritable delight" with the capacity to "demand a smile from a corpse, a dance from a paraplegic". Nevertheless, they were subsequently dropped by Safari. For a short time Howard Wall of the Lurkers deputised on vocals for Kid Reid and they did fulfil some contractual obligations in the form of dates in New York and Italy.

Plain then hooked up with Pete Stride of the Lurkers to recorded the Faces-inspired album New Guitar In Town, and Dangerfield recorded an album in Norway in 1983 with the Single Mirrors, did some production for Toyah and ran the Werewolf In London radio show. Jack Black started designing board games. Anger, meanwhile, ended up working as a traffic warden and made the front pages of the tabloids when he gave Chris Evans a parking ticket ("Punk Rocker Nicks Chris Evans"). However, to comprehensively list the extracurricular activities of just one core member of the Boys since the band's demise would require a book in its own right. Your best bet is to check out the Boys' homepages, probably the most comprehensive and lovingly crafted single-artist punk website I've come across, for details.

A variety of CD reissues kept interest in the band alive, notably in Japan, where Michelle Gun Elephant scored a major hit in 1998 with covers of 'Soda Pressing' and 'Sick On You'. There was also the constant championing of the band by Germany's Die Toten Hosen, and two tribute CDs released by Vinyl Japan and an Italian label, though this has yet to be released officially. All of which helped drag the band out of retirement. Four original members, plus Steve 'Vom' Ritchie (a veteran of numerous bands including Jackel, Miracle Babies, Plus Support, Doctor and the Medics, Brotherland, Stiv Bators etc, as well as Plain's Crybabys) in the place of Jack Black on drums, played their first reformation shows in Japan in the summer of 1999. This was followed by an appearance at the Holidays In The Sun festival in Bergara, Spain, in 2000, where Black made a guest appearance, reuniting the original line-up for the first time in 20 years. They also played the UK Holidays In The Sun at Morecambe in 2001 and further German shows with Die Toten Hosen. Grudgingly, it seems, the Boys are finally beginning to gain recognition for their excellence.

Which is a point I put, again, to Jack Black, after informing him that, whenever any friends suggest that 'punk' bands couldn't play, I put on the Boys' 'Sabre Dance'. "That's great. Thank you very much. Obviously, I take that as a compliment. I think you're right. I love it as well. I used to go see Gary Holton at the Marquee when I was 14. I never knew we'd be on the Marquee stage five years later. I never knew he'd come on tour with us. I never knew he'd go to do an album with Cas in Norway. I never knew he'd kill himself with heroin. But all of THAT – I used to go and see him play and think, FUCKING HELL! But then I was on at the Marquee. And we used to pack the Marquee. Absolutely brilliant. But we never quite made it." But then, that doesn't really matter. You made some great records. "I think so," he reflects. I know so, says I.

DISCOGRAPHY:

(NOTE: Everything you need by the Boys is now available, well packaged and with exemplary sound quality, via Captain Oi! These replace the original Link two-for-one reissues which, as Matt Dangerfield notes, sold the band short. "Some of the Link stuff was badly mastered. All they had to do was call me up and I would have happily gone down and overseen it. They just shoved it through the mill and the sound was compressed, all the dynamics was squashed out of it. It annoys me that that stuff is still out there." If you want a buyer's guide, tackle all four studio albums, and then try the BBC Sessions and Punk Rock Rarities CDs. The latter is especially worthwhile as many would say the versions of the songs that ended up on To Hell With are superior here. Avoid Live At The Roxy)

I Don't Care/Soda Pressing 7-inch (NEMS NES 102 April 1977)

First Time/Turning Grey/Whatcha Gonna Do 7-inch (NEMS NES 111 July 1977)

The Boys LP (NEMS NEL 600 September 1977) (reissued in 1989, Link CLINK2. Reissued on Captain Oi! AHOY LP/CD 519/CD101, 1999, with CD featuring bonus tracks: Watcha Gonna Do/Turning Grey/The First Time (Long Version)/Lonely Schooldays (Demo)/I Don't Care (Alternate Version)/Take A Heart (Demo)/Run Rudolph Run (The Yobs)/The Worm Song (The Yobs)

Brickfield Nights/Teacher's Pet 7-inch (NEMS NES 116 February 1978)

Alternative Chartbusters LP (NEMS NEL 6015 March 1978) (reissued in 1989, Link CLINK3. Reissued on Captain Oi!, AHOY LP/CD 520/CD 104, 1999, CD featuring bonus tracks: Teachers Pet/Schooldays/Lies/She's No Angel/You're The Other man/Silent Night (The Yobs)

Kamikaze/Bad Day 7-inch (Safari SAFE 21 November 1979)

To Hell With The Boys LP (Safari 1-2 BOYS November 1979) (reissued on CD by Captain Oi!, AHOYCD 113 in 1999 with bonus tracks: I Love Me/You Better Move On/Schoolgirls/Rub A Dum Dum (The Yobs)/Another Christmas (The Yobs)

Terminal Love/I Love Me 7-inch (Safari SAFE 23 February 1980)

You Better Move On/Schoolgirls 7-inch (Safari SAFE 27 May 1980)

Weekend/Cool 7-inch (Safari SAFE 31 October 1980)

Boys Only LP (Safari BOYS 4 January 1981) (reissued on CD by Captain Oi!, AHOYCD 117, in 1999 with bonus tracks: Cool/Lucy/Terminal Love (Single Version). The latter is way better than the To Hell With The Boys version. But it only got tacked on here because the band forgot to add it to To Hell With The Boys)

Let It Rain/Lucy 7-inch (Safari SAFE 33 January 1981)

Svengerland/Only A Game/Svengerland (Karaoke Mix) CD single (Captain Oi! AHOY SVEN1 CD 2002)

ARCHIVE RELEASES:

The Boys/Alternative Chartbusters CD (Street Link STRCD12 1989) (reissued on Dojo LOMACD 12 1993)

To Hell With With The Boys – The Original Mix LP/CD (Revolution CS CD 003 1989) (issued on Casino's own label, this featured alternative, more 'raw' recordings of the eventual To Hell With The Boys album, featuring Dangerfield instead of Kid Reid on vocals on 'Terminal Love' and 'Rue Morgue'. These are not the same as the 'Junk' recordings issued elsewhere)

Odds & Sods – Out-takes And Rarities LP/CD (Totenkopf TOT/RTD 910 1990) (Band supporter Campino of Die Toten Hosen compiles 13 unreleased Boys tracks recorded between 1977 and 1981)

Live At The Roxy LP/CD (Receiver RRLP/CD 135 1990) (of course, it's not Live At The Roxy at all. It's recorded on the French tour with Rudi Thompson deputising for Casino)

Live At The BBC LP/CD (Windsong INTLP/CD 036 1993) (also featuring the Vibrators)

To Hell With The Boys/Boys Only CD (Dojo LOMA CD 20 1994)

The Best Of The Boys CD (Dojo DOJO 137 1995)

Complete Boys Punk Singles Collection CD (Anagram CD PUNK 85 1996)

Powercut – Unplugged CD (Revolution REX 013 1996) (also issued on EastWest, 0630-18041-2, and Anagram, CDMGRAM119, in 1997)

Sick On You/Soda Pressing 7-inch (Vinyl Japan PAD 63 1999)

BBC Sessions CD (Vinyl Japan ASK CD 88 1999)

The Peel Sessions LP (Vinyl Japan ASK LP 89 1999)

BBC In Concert LP (Vinyl Japan ASK LP 1999)

Sick On You CD (Harry May MAYO 113 1999)

The Very Best Of The Boys CD (Anagram CD PUNK 112 1999)

Punk Rock Rarities CD (Captain Oi! AHOY CD 120 1999) (a real treasure trove, including the original, full-length version of 'The First Time', plus monitor mixes of the abandoned 'Junk' album tracks that later made it in reshaped form on to To Hell With The Boys, etc)

To Original Hell With/Odds N Sods CD (Captain Oi! AHOY CD 144 2000) (compiles the two foreign releases of out-takes previously available on Revolution and Totenkopf)

Brainiac 5

Charlie Nothing (aka Charlie Taylor; guitar, vocals), Bert Biscoe (vocals, guitar), John 'Woody' Wood (bass, harmonica), Steve Hudson (drums)

Penzance band formed in 1975. Biscoe takes up the story: "Woody owned a house in Penzance to which I moved in about 1974/5. I'd met Charlie (Taylor) through a friend from Truro, Vanessa Johnson, when he travelled from North Wales to visit her at Oxford." Johnson herself would later be a member of Biscoe's Metro Glider band, and married American pianist and composer Pete Williams. Biscoe had served an apprenticeship on the highly active Cornish folk scene at venues like the Folk Cottage in Mitchell and Piper's in Buryan, while Taylor had been a member of Oxford college group The Half Human Band. Woody, for his part, ran Jacey's Blues Bar from his own house.

A session was convened in a garage at Pendeen, in which Taylor and Woody took one of Biscoe's songs, 'Marilyn Monroe', and radically altered its folksy feel to that of "a driving boogie". Thereafter the band line-up was cemented with the addition of Steve Hudson.

From the start the band's repertoire included original material – much of it from Biscoe, whose folk background often produced quite startling results when pulled apart and reassembled by the band. Taylor was the band's other major songwriter. There was also a smattering of covers including Elvis standards such as 'Blue Suede Shoes' and 'Heartbreak Hotel'. However, these were later the subject of complaints from would-be rock'n'roll purists, "who would complain so loudly to landlords that the band, which usually whipped up a storm, sold loads of beer, and sent everybody off happy, was banned from venues for not playing rock 'n roll properly!"

The **BRAINIACS** had a galvanising effect on the local music scene, especially as Biscoe and Woody ran the local Gulval Mead club, which helped groom "fine combos such as Body In The Library and Septic And The Sceptics". Biscoe thinks that the hardest gig in Cornwall was the London Inn at Redruth. "It was populated by R&B-propelled bikers, miners and manic engineering apprentices – a hard school, tough to please. Things weren't helped by the route to the mens' toilet, which lay at the back of the stage – meaning that any male seeking relief had to walk through the band to find the porcelain!" But the Brainiacs were well received, and for subsequent rebookings added a touch of theatricality to their stage act. "At the end of our second set, we would move from 'Marilyn Monroe' into a wah-wah version of 'God Save The Queen'. The pub would halt in its tracks. Charlie would hold a long note and then Steve, screaming 1-2-3-4, would kick off the crazed 'Natty Punko' gallop. The instrumental would be extended – this allowed me to slip out of the toilet door, run down the road beside the pub, come in through the front door and wait. Charlie would wind up the solo – the band would stop – Steve would cry 1-2-3-4, and then... silence. I would then run towards the band, screaming, barging and shoving my way through. Eye contact with Steve heralded the count and the last verse!"

Martin Griffin, who had been a member of the Half Human Band with Taylor at college in Oxford, eventually took over Roche Studios, originally set up by famed local musician/hippie Gerry Gill. It was inevitable, therefore, that the Brainiacs would berth at Roche. "Thus began a long, happy and fruitful association – never profitable – between band and studio. Somewhere is miles of tape filled with Brainiac experimentation and demos." Eventually, the band produced 'Mushy Doubt' – an EP of "innovative white reggae" that John Peel approved of.

Roche would also produce the sessions that resulted in the Double Booked album. "The pub music scene was exploding in Cornwall. One of the most sought-after gigs was William IV in Truro. An agent, one Barrie Bethel, had suddenly arrived and set up office. He was from London and a showbiz man – he persuaded the William to put out an album featuring its best bands." Double Booked was recorded at Roche with Martin Griffin engineering and Bethel producing. The Brainiacs contributed two tracks – 'Marilyn Monroe' (mis-spelt Munroe on the sleeve) and 'Natty Punko'. "We even got the reserved Bethel pogo-ing before midnight!" Both tracks were recorded in a single day. 'Natty Punko' was their regular show finale. Its hook, a silence followed by the spoken question, 'Why, Bert?', he now describes as "a deeply metaphysical moment in an urban snapshot".

There was interest in the Brainiacs from Virgin after the release of 'Mushy Doubt', who were lined up to finance a second pressing of the EP. There was talk of a move to London but Biscoe, to this day a stout-hearted, proud Cornishman, refused to leave. The band continued from its new London base with the addition of rhythm guitarist Richard Booth, originally recruited to allow Biscoe to concentrate on vocals. Biscoe subsequently formed Lipservice, soon to be renamed Metro Glider, with guitarist and sculptor Chris Price, working with a variety of collaborators. Meanwhile, the Brainiacs were encouraged to put an album together by Martin Griffin, as they played around the capital including several shows at Dingwalls. The World Inside album was drawn from recordings in 1979, but was released posthumously in 1988 on Reckless, a label co-owned by Charlie Taylor. It additionally featured Duncan Kerr on keyboards, who, alongside Hudson, served time as a member of Plummet Airlines.

The Brainiacs became lost to history thereafter. But Biscoe is convinced that, for a time, there was a magic to the band. "Too many people remember us fondly and enthusiastically for that to be just an old man's fancy! They touched a nerve, they touched hearts, and they lifted audiences." As for the participants, Biscoe is a member of Cornwall Council and an advocate of devolution to a Cornish assembly. He continues to write poetry, perform music, and has published several books. Woody joined the Avant Gardeners as did Hudson, and is now a conservation architect in London and occasionally plays harmonica in his son's band. Taylor is a successful businessman.

There is continued interest in the band in Germany due to a single released there in the mid-90s, 'Monkeys And Degenerates'. Biscoe: "The Brainiacs were never number one, never earned anything other than petrol money, never won an award. But the band did play good music, sparked interest from a large number of small audiences, alerted younger musicians to new possibilities, and left its members with a human experience which has affected the ways in which each of their lives has subsequently evolved."

DISCOGRAPHY:

Mushy Doubt 7-inch 33rpm EP (Roach/Roche RREP-5001 May 1978)
(I Was A) Vegetable/Endless River/Move Up Trotsky/Waiting For The Woman
Working/Feel 7-inch (Roche RR-5002 January 1980) (labels state 1979. 1,000 copies)
ARCHIVE RELEASES:
Monkeys & Degenerates/Time 7-inch (Roadrunner August 1986; Germany only)
World Inside LP (Reckless RECK-1 LP 1988) (recorded, for the most part, in 1979)
COMPILATION:
Doubled Booked LP (W4 W4001 December 1977; 'Marilyn Munroe', 'Natty Punko')

Brakes

Phil 'Moriarty' Pentecost (vocals), Pete Damo (aka Pete Smythe; guitar), Kenny Brooks (aka Kevin Brooks; bass), Sid Slater (drums)

The first punk band to evolve in Exeter, the BRAKES' roots go back to the Catharsis Club in Clifton, hosted by DJ Len Gammon, who imported a series of New York records when there were few domestic records that fitted the bill. "Everything at that time revolved around him," Brooks told me. "He was The Man. I'd been friends with Phil Pentecost (Moriarty) for a few years before we both got together with Pete Smythe (Damo) and Phil Salter (Sid Slater) and formed a band. Phil and me were into stuff like Eddie and the Hot Rods, The Sensational Alex Harvey Band, Cockney Rebel, Bowie and Bolan. We were also pretty keen on all the Beat guys – Kerouac, Burroughs, etc."

The group's origins dated back to school covers band Harry's Meathouse, which operated between 1975 and the summer of 1977, when they left school. Brooks: "We didn't write our own songs then, we just played the usual rock'n'roll cover stuff – Stones, the Who, whatever. I played rhythm guitar. We played school dances and local clubs and stuff. The change to punk came with the Ramones' first album. Pete brought it into school one day – it must have been 76 or 77 – and we played it REALLY loud, over and over again, and that was it for us. That was music. And that's what we wanted to do. The bass player got kicked out for not being punky enough. I bought a cheap bass, we all cut our hair, changed our name to the Brakes, and started playing LOUD and FAST. I'd always loved basic rock'n'roll music – Elvis, Wild Angels, T. Rex – and punk music for me was just really good, really fast rock'n'roll. I never really bought into the whole cultural revolution thing. I don't think any of us did really. It wasn't about politics or fashion or attitude or protest – none of us gave a shit about that. We didn't have anything to rebel against. It was just a music thing. We liked the Clash, Buzzcocks, Pistols, Ramones etc because they played good music. We hated the Jam and Police because they were shit. I remember buying 'Spiral Scratch' by the Buzzcocks and listening to it continuously at home, not quite believing how good it was. Same thing for the Damned's 'Neat Neat Neat' and the first Clash album. I loved it. I can still remember the shiver that hit me when I first heard 'White Riot' – I was in a barn somewhere, some kind of party, and I just stopped doing whatever I was doing and listened in awe."

That awe was filtered into the Brakes. "We started off doing Ramones and Damned stuff, but pretty soon gave that up and began writing our own material. Pete and Phil did most of the writing. Within a few weeks we had a whole new set, about 12 or so brand new songs, and we started playing them at gigs. Song titles I remember include 'Shut Up', 'Plastic Doll', 'Sunday Papers', 'I'm Bored', 'Son of Sam', 'Computer Breakdown', 'So What?' etc. We also did a punk/reggae cover of 'Sweet Jane' and a very fast version of '1970' by The Stooges."

Len Gammon was at one of their first gigs. "He was a few years older than us, a stalwart of the Exeter music scene, and despite our initial faux-punky hostility towards him, he really liked us and helped us a lot with gigs and equipment and stuff. He also introduced us to John Jacques and Dick Gerrish, who produced magazines and DJed around the area – all very helpful and supportive. John Jacques kind of managed us for a while."

The band became a popular local attraction. "By 1977 we were quite well known, playing gigs all over the West Country, and also getting chased and beaten up all over the West Country. Everyone hated punks, and my abiding memories of the time are of bottles flying through the air, getting chased (by car, on foot), friends getting glassed and stabbed. Pete and Phil seemed to love all this, and they'd actually go out of their way to find it – looking for danger, intentionally provoking bikers and skins, looking to shock and insult everyone else. Being pretty weedy myself, I hated it. I loved the music and the excitement of playing loud and fast, the thrill of being part of something, but I hated all the rest of it."

"I can't remember when I decided to leave the band, but I suppose it must have been sometime in 1978. I just couldn't stand all the shit that went with it any more. So I said I was leaving, and I left, and I started doing quieter, kind of Hunky Dory-ish stuff – just me and an acoustic guitar. I played a few gigs, but didn't like performing solo very much, then concentrated on writing and recording with Len Gammon." "Kevin and I did some stuff after the Brakes," Gammon recalls, "with me recording his solo stuff, of which there is tons somewhere. That's what we used (local rehearsal space) The Building for, as a little four-track studio."

The Brakes fell apart shortly after Brooks left. "I kind of lost touch with Pete and Phil for a while after that. I think they did some stuff with Len and John Tye (from a band called XS), and Pete played with Avant Gardners, then Missing Chemicals." Shortly afterwards, Phil Pentecost died from leukaemia. His condition was allegedly attributable to a beating he received at the hands of travelling Wolves' supporters following an Exeter City game. Brooks: "Pete moved to London, Phil got beaten up badly and was very ill, then died. I don't know what happened to Sid. I moved to London for a while, then Birmingham, then back to Exeter. All the time I was writing my own stuff. Then I moved to London and ended up in the same squat as Pete. He was still with Missing Chemicals then. I was recording my own stuff, getting a few tracks on compilation albums, offered a few dodgy management contracts. I also did some recording in the early-80s (as Halloween) with another Exeter escapee called Mike Coulthard, aka comic book artist Shaky Kane/Shaky 2000." He subsisted by working variously as a petrol pump attendant, a crematorium handyman, a civil service officer, a vendor at London Zoo, a post office counter clerk and a railway ticket salesperson, while nursing his ambitions. "Then I got too old for rock'n'roll, so I bought myself a pipe and a tweed suit and became a writer." Martyn Pig, his first book, was short-listed for the Carnegie Medal and won the Branford Boase Award. A second novel, Lucas, featured on the long-list (they like these lists, don't they, literary types?) for the Guardian's Children's Book Award. Most recently, he published Kissing The Rain, in 2004.

If you want to have a peek at the legend that was the Brakes, our heroes grace the cover of Year Zero, the Exeter punk compilation. The band, sadly, don't appear on the CD. Les Gammon, who helped bring that project to fruition, would have loved to include them, "but they just didn't have any good tapes". The picture was taken at The Building. "Kevin is playing through my Orange bass amp on that picture," he points out. As for his punk rock past, Brooks notes that: "People tend to forget that it wasn't all about postcard punks on the King's Road – the heart of it all was scruffy little shits in small towns getting beaten up by bikers and skinheads all the time. Ah, good times..."

Buzzcocks

Pete Shelley (aka Peter McNeish; guitar, vocals), Howard Devoto (aka Howard Trafford; vocals), Steve Diggle (bass; later guitar), John Maher (drums)

BUZZCOCKS (the band hate being called the Buzzcocks) are many people's idea of the finest punk band of them all. Devotees prefer the Mancunians' dizzying, razor sharp pop tunes to the shattering musical jihad of the Pistols, or the studied rhetoric and rock'n'roll mannerisms of the Clash. Certainly there's an argument for the Buzzcocks' catalogue being the strongest in the genre. And those records, in their sheer vivacity, musical cunning and emotional colour, constitute one of the greatest songbooks in popular music. Shelley's unrequited and gender-unspecific romanticism, admirably supported by Diggle's brickie-with-a-broken-

heart interludes, produced something Tony Wilson would memorably contrast with the surface nihilism of the Pistols. "Real punk was saying 'fuck you'. With all the simplicity, energy, delight and youthfulness of punk, Pete Shelley was saying, 'I love you'."

Pete McNeish, who had buried his head in Beatles sheet music and songbooks from an early age, wrote his first song in 1971, at the age of 16. He formed his first band, the Jets of Air, two years later. By 1974 he'd recorded a set of self-written, electronic-based songs, essentially musical doodles, which he'd later release on his own Groovy label in 1980 as Sky Yen (don't bother, it's practically unlistenable). Other tracks from this period would eventually emerge on his Homosapien solo album, while the Jets Of Air's set list included such later Buzzcocks' staples as 'Love You More' (about a girl who worked at the Bolton branch of Woolworth's), 'Nostalgia' and 'Sixteen Again'.

McNeish and Howard Trafford first met in January 1974 at the Bolton Institute of Technology. Both had attended a meeting of the wonderfully titled Bolton Institute Sexual Liberation Society, presumably in pursuit of more than intellectual discourse on the subject. "This consisted of about six people meeting in someone's room – six emotionally disaffected souls whingeing about how lonely they were," Devoto later recalled. McNeish was vice-president of the student's union and served on the National Committee Of Part-Time Students. He was about to become even more part-time. Prior to this, Trafford and future Buzzcocks' manager Richard Boon had put together a five-strong comedy ensemble, the Ernest Band, whilst at Leeds Grammar School. Trafford was working on a video project and required some incidental electronic music, having abandoned his original psychology course in favour of the humanities. But it was only when Trafford, who'd by now acquired the Stooges' back catalogue, placed an advert: "Wanted: musicians, euphonium players, both sexes, to do cover of 'Sister Ray'" – that McNeish re-established contact. "I thought I knew the chords but wasn't too sure," Shelley later told Q. There was no phone number on the advert. Instead, willing partners were asked to meet by the notice at the appointed time. Shelley was the only respondent.

They did indeed play through a handful of Velvet Underground and Stooges covers, including 'Your Pretty Face Has Gone To Hell' as well as Eno's 'The True Wheel' and various Rolling Stones tracks, with a variety of musicians. "I met Howard and we started trying to write some songs," Shelley later told Q. "At college, Wednesday afternoon was free for sports – completely free if you didn't do sports. And, of course, me and Howard didn't want to do sports. We had in our mind what music we wanted to do. It was the Stooges, wasn't it? We wanted people to say it was rubbish and walk away – all that sort of stuff. We were also thinking about the early Kinks and the Troggs – all nice fast songs." However, the liaison came to nothing, mainly due to the fact that McNeish was living in Leigh and Trafford was based in Salford, and they were only able to meet up during college hours.

Later, in October 1975, Trafford introduced McNeish to Richard Boon, who would become the Buzzcocks' manager and occasional co-lyricist. But the band, such as it was, was going nowhere. "It really was not happening," Devoto told David Nolan in I Swear I Was There. "So by February 1976, I don't think we really knew where any of this was going, except that we were vaguely still trying to get a band together."

It was at this point that they read Neil Spencer's review of the Sex Pistols' support to Eddie And The Hot Rods at the Marquee in February 1976. Sniffing the winds of change, and noting the review's reference to Iggy Pop's 'No Fun', they arranged to borrow a car to see the Pistols play in London. "I didn't have a car," Devoto told David Nolan, "but someone in the house I was living in at that time had asked me to pick up their car and said, 'You can borrow it for the weekend.' I don't think they meant 'You can drive to London for the weekend,' but, anyway, that's what Pete and I ended up doing. Just on the basis of reading this review and the fact that I could borrow this car. It was the weekend that changed our lives." Accommodation would be provided by Boon, who'd started his studies at Reading University, while the finances were helped by the fact that McNeish had been given the train fare for a student committee meeting. It was spent on petrol.

Drawing inspiration from the Pistols' chaos theory (literally 'we're not into music, we're into chaos' – "Well, it clicked with me," Devoto recalled) they decided to put their own band on

The reformed Buzzcocks in the late 90s.

a more formal footing. The name was taken from a Time Out headline quoting dialogue from TV series Rock Follies – "It's the Buzz, cock!"). Of course, cock was a well-worn northern idiom for 'mate' or 'fella', but was also a nicely suggestive double entendre, a lyrical quirk that Shelley, in particular, was to prove partial to. On the same day this momentous decision was made, they traced Malcolm McLaren to his Sex boutique, after first contacting Neil Spencer at the NME to ask where all these Sex Pistols gigs were actually taking place, and walking by foot from Sloane Square. Impressed by their pluck, McLaren invited them to forthcoming Pistols shows at High Wycombe (supporting Screaming Lord Sutch) and Welwyn Garden City (supporting Mr Big) on the 20th and 21st of February. Which rounded out their away day weekend nicely. "We liked them," Devoto admitted, in that kind of bored but succinct tone he has mastered when dealing with tiresome questions about his past, to Q, "they were good. We saw them and were duly enlightened."

Both Trafford and McNeish experienced epiphanies watching the Sex Pistols, recognising them as immediately special, a band to be treasured and a gospel to be spread. Their conversion complete, they swapped their given names to become Pete Shelley and Howard Devoto. Shelley because it was the name McNeish would have been given had he been born a girl, and Devoto after a bus driver named in a story he'd been told by a favoured philosophy tutor.

Returning to Manchester, Shelley contacted his old Jets Of Air bass player Garth Davies, inviting him to rehearsals for their scheduled debut at the Bolton Institute of Technology on the 1st of April. It was advertised thus: "Textile Students Social Evening Present Buzzcocks, B.I.T., Thursday 1 April 1976." Garth turned up in a tuxedo. They still hadn't found a drummer but in the event they borrowed one, Dennis, from local band Black Cat Bone. The organisers pulled the plug after two numbers, Bowie's 'Diamond Dogs' and the Stones' 'Come On', though they did still pay the band the £5 they'd promised. In other accounts, Devoto speculates that they were due to play originals such as 'Oh Shit!' or 'No Reply'. The set was also scheduled to include putative covers of the Kinks, Who and selections from Brian Eno's Here Come The Warm Jets. But they never got that far. As Shelley later recalled to Q: "We started off and, immediately, 'Diamond Dogs' was half the speed it was supposed to be and we got the plug pulled."

May saw an urgent search for a sticksman, with an advert placed in the New Manchester Review. The urgency was increased by the fact that they'd now booked the Sex Pistols at the Lesser Free Trade Hall for the 4th June for £32, after Devoto offered the group its first northern show. Shelley had failed to persuade the Bolton Institute's students union of the merits of the Sex Pistols, the executive having never heard of them. Devoto, using his contacts as a rock reviewer for the New Manchester Review, had similarly tried but failed to fix a date at the Commercial Hotel in Stalybridge.

The gig, and Buzzcocks' debut, was advertised in the Manchester Evening News. Two potential drummers bottled out, and they also lacked a bass player, meaning they had to cancel with a week to go. Their place was taken by Solstice, a member of whom Devoto knew through his work at a mail order company (though several histories, including the sleevenotes to Product, erroneously finger Blackburn's Mandela Band as the replacements). McLaren also forwarded posters for the show, as well as a demo tape, which Devoto copied on to reel to reel, sending a copy to TV presenter Tony Wilson, thereby sowing the seeds for yet another Pistols-related epiphany.

Despite their non-appearance, the night had good portents for Buzzcocks. Steve Diggle was on his way to meet a friend at Cox's Bar, in the hope of forming a Who-styled rock band, when he was ushered in by the circus barker skills of Talcy Malcy. McLaren had overheard an earlier telephone message for Devoto from someone wishing to audition for the Buzzcocks as a bass player. When McLaren realised Diggle played bass, he conned him into believing his friend was inside the hall, though doubtless he was more interested in the gate receipts than his hosts' career prospects. Shelley, working the door, then struck up conversation, and voila, the Buzzcocks had half of the required rhythm section.

The circumstances surrounding drummer John Maher's recruitment were even more bizarre. He replied to a Melody Maker advert, "Girl, looking for musicians to get together and form a band," only to find out that the advertiser too was a drummer. Devoto was another to respond to the advert, thinking a Moe Tucker-esque female percussionist would be quite the thing, and was pointed in Maher's direction. Devoto immediately invited him to join the Buzzcocks, ringing him up one lunchtime before he was due back at school to do his chemistry O-level, as they moved from Lower Broughton Road to regular rehearsals at St Boniface's Church Hall in Salford.

The inaugural line-up made its debut on 20th July, this time completing their engagement as support to the Pistols at the Lesser Free Trade Hall. The set included rough versions of 'Breakdown' (which is still a regular 25 years later), 'Time's Up' and Captain Beefheart's 'I Love You, You Big Dummy'. Shelley had purchased a Wooloworth's 'Audition' guitar especially for the occasion, so it could be destroyed at the show's close, with Devoto ripping out the strings. "We were out there for 20 minutes and we got away with it," Devoto recalled, "and people clapped and we were in the music papers the following week." The Pistols' Glen Matlock approved too. "I thought the Buzzcocks were wonderful. In fact, I preferred them to the Clash at that stage because, whereas the Clash, it seemed to me, were trying to do the same as we were doing, only not as well. The Buzzcocks were doing something entirely different, with a totally different attitude. There was something funny about them. They were provincial and very sweet, although I'm sure they'd hate me saying that." I'm sure they would, Glen.

Shelley felt compelled to purchase three copies of the NME after Jonh Ingham gave them an enthusiastic review. Important attendees included Boon, his friend Sue Cooper, later of the Poison Girls, who would help him set up New Hormones, Linder Sterling ("When the Buzzcocks appeared they were furious, shambolic and unlike anything I'd ever seen"), who would design the group's early artwork and become Devoto's girlfriend after that night, and designer Malcolm Garrett. With Boon this team would establish a visual signature to the band's releases and promotional materials that drew heavily on Andy Warhol's pop art and the geometric abstract paintings of Kasimir Malevich and Piet Mondrian. The Buzzcocks would on no account be photographed in murky black and white with their backs against graffiti-strewn brickwork.

A couple of weeks later they played for the second time at The Ranch, the former gay club in Manchester, before being asked to leave after three numbers because the noise was seeping into drag act Foo Foo Lemarr's show in an adjacent room. There was another show at the

Stalybridge Commercial Hotel before an audience that Devoto estimated at eight people, before they became the Sex Pistols' support at their Screen On The Green show in Islington. The Clash were also making their first public performance, though any sense of punk unity was eclipsed by their entourage's attitude to the Buzzcocks, whose own performance was described as "rougher than a bear's arse" by Giovanni Dadamo of Sounds (a bootleg of the show confirms the analysis). However, McLaren was encouraging, telling Devoto that he admired the Buzzcocks' 'content'.

On the 21st of September they closed the second night of the 100 Club Punk Festival, establishing once and for all that punk was no longer a function or expression of the capital. Sex Pistols apart, they were streets ahead of the opposition on that bill. "That was a good night," notes Mancunian fanzine legend Steve Shy. "There were about 15 of us that went in a small coach. Paul Morley was there with us. And Ian Hodge (of the Worst). He was all in leather and had a big red swastika on his back. We were walking down the King's Road on the Sunday afternoon. There were loads of Japanese tourists, and everybody wanted to take photographs. Paul Morley was going up asking for people to pay for the photographs. I think we got enough money for the beer all night." However, the infamous Sid glass-throwing incident meant that many in the audience left before the Buzzcocks took to the stage, despite Siouxsie doing her best to remonstrate with them to stay. They were certainly almost universally popular with their punk peers. "Out of all the English groups," Vic Godard of Subway Sect later told 3am magazine, "they were the ones we felt closest to." Although there was friction in their native Manchester with Slaughter And The Dogs and their enclave, elsewhere the Buzzcocks were well liked, even admired, amid the bitchiness that consumed many of the London groups.

In mid-October they entered Stockport's Revolution studios for a single afternoon, committing their live set to posterity with the help of engineer Andy MacPherson. The goal was sheer "vanity", Shelley later told Q, and not part of a record company persuasion campaign. "We didn't know about things like that. We weren't sophisticated enough. We were from Manchester." The cost was £45, and the recordings would later be aired as the Time's Up bootleg in 1977, including covers of 'Dummy' and the Troggs' 'I Can't Control Myself'. 'Lester Sands' aka 'Drop In The Ocean', not released officially until 2003 when it was re-recorded for a new studio album, highlighted Devoto's ability to offer withering cynicism, his innate capacity for sarcasm rivalling Lydon's, albeit from a more bookish perspective. The reason for the legendary status of Time's Up can be attributed to the fact that it was the only document outside of 'Spiral Scratch' to capture the Devoto-led incarnation of the band, including radically different takes on later staples such as 'Love Battery' and 'Orgasm Addict'.

A further engagement with the Pistols followed, replacing the Damned after they were controversially excised from the Anarchy tour. However, their appearance on 9 December at the Electric Circus proved to be Devoto's final outing with the band, though neither he nor they knew it at the time. Instead they democratically decided on which four tracks from the Time's Up sessions they should include on their debut EP, then recorded the selections on 28 December 1976 at Indigo Studios with booking agent and local legend Martin 'Zero' Hannett. "We believed him that he was a record producer," Shelley told David Nolan. "We were just as gullible as everyone else."

In the meantime, Boon was finding it difficult to secure a record deal, and prompted by Hannett's promise of free studio time, which never materialised, resolved to organise it himself. He borrowed £250 from Shelley's dad, as well as £100 from Sue Cooper (her university grant) and tapped up a teaching friend of Boon's from London, Dave Snowden. Devoto solicited some advice on self-releasing a record from Stiff's Dave Robinson, who offered vague encouragement. With the finances in place, they formed New Hormones Records, with a deal arranged through Phonogram to press the record. Boon used a Polaroid Instamatic – both perfect medium and metaphor for the moment – to photograph the band beside the Robert Peel statue in Manchester's Piccadilly Gardens in grainy black and white. Having scraped the readies together from parents and friends, they inserted each copy into sleeves by hand – practically defining the independent ethos in the process. Over four kinetic tracks, 'Spiral Scratch' became the calling card and the template for rock's next, perversely anti-rock, generation.

It was finally released on 29th January 1977, and its effect on the course of popular music was as dramatic as its origins were humble. As Shelley told Jon Savage in the sleevenotes to Product: "We had 1,000 done, and we checked each and every one for scratches and stuff. The day they arrived we bought two bottles of Spanish wine and drank a toast to it, and the toast was that we'd sell half of them, so we'd get the money back." Shelley remembers "going round the Ranch, selling them out of this handbag I'd made from some string and one of the cardboard boxes that the records arrived in. I mean, £1 was the same price as a bottle of Special Brew." That recollection is shared by then girlfriend, Gail Egan, enlisted as his co-vendor at the Ranch. "People were waiting to buy Spiral Scratch! And I do not remember any returns!"

Within four days the first pressing of 1,000 had sold out. Within six months, it had moved 16,000 copies. While the historical impact is key, it's often easy to overlook the bright-eyed punch of the music – the rudimentary two-note Shelley guitar solo on 'Boredom', which he retained after its use in rehearsals caused widespread hilarity. Or Devoto's vocals, part high priest of punk camp, part ruthless cynicism. Yet for all that, Martin Hannett insisted in an interview with John Tobler that the record was 'unfinished'. "When we went back to the studio to remix, we found that the 16-track master tape had been wiped. It's the sort of thing that happens when you get a cheap recording deal, but we felt that they'd reused the tape rather more quickly than normal, because they thought it just contained a horrible noise." The lyrics for the EP were written while Devoto worked a nightshift in a tile factory. They fitted perfectly. And Morrissey wrote a typically eulogising letter in the NME, expressing his support for the band, in that missionary tone he is wont to adopt.

Yet after a total of just 11 shows and the EP behind him, Devoto decided he wanted to leave. His reasons were complicated. He indicated he was tired with the punk bandwagon, but he also wanted to complete his degree, though he eventually failed his finals. "By that time there were hundreds of other bands with a similar sound, which didn't make it very interesting for me," he later told Jon Young in Trouser Press. "I didn't feel committed in any way to that sort of music. I would have pulled the group back because my heart wasn't in it." He elaborated further in I Swear I Was There, confirming that he really didn't want to "bugger up" his degree for a second time, but also acknowledged his frustration with what punk had become. "I was not fantastically taken, I suppose, with the aesthetic of it all. I wasn't that wild about the vibe and ambience of it in a way – it didn't feel exactly musically right for me at the end of January 1977."

"Howard said, 'I've done what I wanted to achieve with 'Spiral Scratch', that's it,'" Diggle told Uncut in 2003. "At first, me and Pete thought, 'Fucking hell!' I can remember it now. The two of us were sat in Howard's house on the couch. We just looked at each other, shocked for about maybe two seconds. Then we said, 'Right, we'll carry on anyway.'" Diggle went into further detail in a 1987 Big Takeover interview. "We were really sorry he left at the time. We thought, this is the end of the band. It was like Devoto was the biggest star in the band. He was the big thing. But the best thing was, I really developed the guitar (after switching from bass) and Pete developed his voice, and I think he was even better to take it to the next stage... We wouldn't have been so successful if he'd stayed in the band. But for the early days he was perfect. We found ourselves through him, and we found ourselves after him as well, so it was a good agreement really."

Robert Lloyd of the Prefects was touted as a possible replacement, while Bernie Rhodes invited Shelley to join Keith Levene in a new band. Both options were declined, and Shelley took over vocals. Devoto's defection also left Shelley as principal songwriter, as the group's axis shifted from the established punk métier of generational angst to a unit profiling romantic tensions. Shelley steered the band through lyrical waters that were just as neurotic and self-searching as they were idealistic, though the narratives were offered over stop-dead chord progressions, and the spirit of effervescent, perpetual adolescence was never far removed. After Devoto left, the initial intention was that he'd share management with Boon, and Shelley and Devoto remained good friends, Shelley often crashing at Devoto's house (indeed, he wrote 'Sixteen', a take-off of Ravel's 'Bolero', one night there after seeing Star Wars with Jon Savage).

The decision was taken to switch Diggle from bass to second guitar, with old friend Garth

Davies rejoining on bass following an advert placed in Manchester's Virgin record store, reading: "Leading North-West beat combo require bass player who is pretty or competent, or pretty competent!" Davies would never quite fit in with the group's ethos or aesthetic, though. As Diggle recorded in the sleevenotes to Chronology: "Garth's dress sense wasn't that tasty, so we were looking around for something for him to wear, and we found this boiler suit. We put him in that and for some reason it seemed to work perfectly, it fitted in exactly with the kind of group look. It seemed to be the only workable thing because it covered his huge body and put him more into perspective with the rest of us." Their first show with the new line-up came at Harlesden Coliseum as support to the Clash, their second London date, with the Slits making their debut. Their first TV appearance, on Tony Wilson's So It Goes, followed on the 7th of April. Not coincidentally, Shelley had his dole money stopped shortly thereafter.

They then joined the Clash's White Riot tour, alongside Subway Sect and the Slits. It ended at the California Ballroom, Dunstable, on the 30th May, and was widely judged a success by all concerned, incorporating greater camaraderie and less bitchiness than the Pistols' Anarchy forerunner. In between, the Buzzcocks headlined the Electric Circus with Penetration in support, as well as Warsaw, playing their first show. It was on this night that Andrew Lauder of United Artists, who wasn't endeared to the testing social environs of Collyhurst at all, resolved to sign the band, not put off for a moment by Shelley's leopardskin top, or the death of his amp during the encore.

After talks with several labels, included a counter-offer from Maurice Oberstein of CBS, the Buzzcocks completed the deal with Lauder, signing a contract offering an advance of £75,000 on the bar of the Electric Circus on 16th of May, a show filmed for another airing on So It Goes. Diggle bought a Gibson Les Paul Junior in celebration. Davies celebrated by purchasing a new £500 Thunderbird Gibson bass. But already the 'man mountain' or 'punk monster' was proving problematic. At one infamous show in Leeds he attacked the audience, admittedly after Shelley had inflamed them by wearing a Manchester United football shirt. The confrontation is recalled in the bootleg Razor Cut, on which Davies can be heard to threaten to take on the entire audience, single-handed. Though they didn't know it, their future bass player, young Prestwich punk Steve Garvey, having seen the band for the second time at Rafters on the 1st of September, had already decided he was going to join up.

The early weeks of September saw them record their first John Peel session (broadcast on the 19th September) and sessions at T.W. Studios in Fulham for their debut single with Martin Rushent. 'Orgasm Addict' and 'Whatever Happened To?' were eventually chosen (other options included 'What Do I Get' and 'Oh Shit!'). The session took place on the day that Marc Bolan died – whose 'Electric Warrior' Rushent had formerly engineered. Further sessions at Olympic Studios in Barnes were interrupted by an argument between Shelley and Davies, which resulted in the latter throwing his expensive new bass guitar down the stairs. Mutual loathing escalated over subsequent gigs until breaking point was reached after playing St George's in Coventry, at which the already brutalised Thunderbird took another bashing, this time splintering against the backline, with Davies walking off leaving the remaining members to finish the show. Despite the looming prospect of their first headlining tour, the decision was taken to sack Davies. It meant the release date of their first single, and their 'Tour No. 1', was put back while auditions were held. In the end Garvey got the gig after being recommended to Boon by Martin Bramah of the Fall. He was handsome, which would help get girls to the gigs, and he'd bought John Maher a Mars bar, so it was a fair cop.

'Orgasm Addict' finally became their debut single for UA on the 28th of October. Lauded in the music press, it gained absolutely no radio coverage because of the subject matter. Even 25 years down the line, it's hard to imagine the lyrical titbit "a habit that sticks", from the opening lines written by Shelley, ever gracing the Radio 1 airwaves. The line about robins placed by hand on Crimbo cakes, incidentally, is an image sourced to Devoto's Christmas job at a bakery in Leeds, for it was he who wrote the bulk of the lyric. The words on the flip, 'Whatever Happened To'. came from manager Richard Boon, credited as Alan Dial. Notable too was the sleeve, a collage by Linder Sterling featuring a naked female torso with mouths on her breasts and a steam iron for a head. It would prompt industrial action at the pressing plant. "I suppose what I like about it now is that it's a refreshing take on dada," art critic Matthew Collings later reflected. "It's silly and clever. It doesn't matter if you don't know about Dada."

Although Garvey was in place, he wasn't yet ready to perform on the group's Tour No. 1, and was replaced by Barry Adamson, later of Devoto's Magazine. Garvey eventually joined the rest of the band for their seventh show at Nottingham Sandpiper. In between, Shelley wrote 'Ever Fallen In Love (With Someone You Shouldn't've)' while in Edinburgh, the line taken from dialogue in Guys And Dolls and applied to his friend, Francis. Following another protracted UK tour, 'Tour No. 2', they embarked on sessions for the debut album, again with Rushent, on 28th December.

Their second UA single, 'What Do I Get?', was delayed, after female staff at EMI refused to press copies due to its B-side, 'Oh Shit'. No true punk band ever prospered without a little controversy over the use of Anglo-Saxon. When it did emerge two weeks later, it brought them to the Top 40 for the first time. Their debut album followed in March, to universally rapturous reviews, with the 12 tracks on Another Music In A Different Kitchen placed in the order that the band wrote and played them. The album closed with a sustained return to Shelley's 'Boredom' guitar solo. There was a sense of adventure and daring-do here that no-one, with the possible exception of Wire and the certain inclusion of the Pistols and Clash, had tried before. "We were working without limitations," Diggle told Uncut later. "We'd never been in pub bands or anything, we were learning it as we went and it was that thing of the less you know, the braver you can be."

Among the highlights was 'Fast Cars', a Diggle song that he lost the lyrics to, before Shelley and Devoto came up with a new set. Diggle was also responsible for 'Autonomy', jointly sung with Shelley, and inspired by listening to Can. "I thought they sounded like a German band trying to be English, so that was us being an English band trying to be German. Those were the kind of ideas we had for songs." '16', which berated the stupor of modern pop music, featured a freestyle section in which each member recorded their part in isolation – Diggle intended it to sound like lasers firing. By the end of the month they were back in the studio, this time Abbey Road, to cut their third UA single. 'Love You More' was lionised as "the most realistic, sentimental love song every written" by the NME.

By July the band were back in the studio to work on their second album, in the interim returning to the Lesser Free Trade Hall, a concert filmed by Granada and later used in a documentary on the band, B'dum B'dum, wherein they were interviewed by Tony Wilson. The show saw Devoto rejoin to sing vocals on 'I Can't Control Myself'. Love Bites, released in the autumn of 1978, married the group's eternal pop suss to some more esoteric efforts, notably Steve Garvey's attempt to emulate jazz bass player Stan Clarke on the instrumental 'Walking Distance' – the only song he wrote with the band. Diggle's 'Love Is Lies' and Shelley's 'Operator's Manual' were untypical of the Buzzcocks in their romantic cynicism, but still boasted exquisite melodies. The album sessions also yielded Diggle's superb 'Promises'. It was initially written as a 'political' song, but Diggle left the lyrics at home when they came to record it so Shelley filled in the blanks. He was then dismayed when he realised it had turned into 'yet another love song'.

They travelled to Europe for the first time thereafter, joining Blondie on their Parallel Lines tour, before the release of 'Ever Fallen In Love' (With Someone You Shouldn't've)'. It would become the group's biggest success, reaching number 12 in the charts and later being voted the NME's single of the year. In later years it provided Shelley with a much-needed financial fillip when the Fine Young Cannibals piloted a new version, to accompany Jonathan Demme's Something Wild, into the UK Top 10. Approximately 15 years later, the pension fund was boosted again when it was re-recorded by Peter Yorn for the soundtrack of Shrek 2. The flipside, 'Just Lust', was credited to Boon (again under the pseudonym Alan Dial). It was one of several songs where Shelley passed him a title and Boon came back with lyrics.

They toured to support Love Bites but Shelley, in particular, was tiring of the treadmill, and frequently had to be persuaded by Boon to complete the dates. "Around the time of the Love Bites tour I'd become very disillusioned," Shelley later confirmed. "I thought we had become entertainers, separated from our audience. We had attracted a teenybopper audience made up of lots of screaming young girls and I hated it. I wanted to pack it all in during that tour." He completed the tour, exhausted, but it was clear that nerves were becoming frayed.

Some of the tensions within the band were tempered by a series of solo projects, with Garvey playing with members of the Fall in the Teardrops, and Maher working with Patrik

Fitzgerald and later the Things, and Pauline Murray as one of the Invisible Girls. Shelley produced Albertos Y Lost Paranoias and worked solo. Naturally, they rejected press assertions that these solo activities meant the group itself was on a rocky footing. Shelley's mood wasn't helped by being burgled while the band were away in Europe. The band regrouped to record 'Everybody's Happy Nowadays', the group's most whimsical single thus far, preceding their first European headlining dates. The B-side was equally striking – 'Why Can't I Touch It? – a lascivious plea later recorded by both Ian McCulloch and the Christians. Both tracks were described by Shelley as efforts to write more 'philosophically', though it probably had as much to do with the band's acid intake. It brought about a memorable Top Of The Pops appearance, with Shelley using a handkerchief woven from sterling notes.

The next single, cut at Eden Studios in Acton, was, to some minds, their finest work to date – Diggle's rhapsodic 'Harmony In My Head', "my James Joyce thing", backed by Shelley's kitchen sink drama 'Something's Gone Wrong Again'. They would also record demos for their third album (originally to have been titled Don't Worry, It's Only The Third Album) at Eden, through July and August of 1979. On the last day of August they finally made their American debut at the Boston Paradise Club, with dates in New York, Long Island and Washington, before the release of their first US single, 'Everybody's Happy Nowadays'. Luckily their large and stoic US fanbase was prepared to survive the indignity of being starved for so long of either domestic releases or appearances.

The group's third album, entitled A Different Kind Of Tension, followed in September 1979. Although reviews were supportive, the contents were a little spotty, with Shelley withdrawing as a writer. The second half of the album in particular provided a terse listening experience. The rejoinder to 'I Believe' – "there is no love in this world any more", serves as a piquant bookend to the existentialist soul-cry former colleague Devoto had achieved with Magazine on 'Song From Under The Floorboards'. But it could just as well have served as a metaphor for the band's decline. That's not to dismiss what was still a solid piece of work, Shelley's 'I Don't Know What To Do With My Life', inspired by watching Superman, in particular.

The appearance of a band in decline was confirmed by the subsequent tour, a huge, demoralising tranche of dates through to the 10th of November, followed two weeks later by an American trek. When Shelley's 'You Say You Don't Love Me' emerged as a single, more blue-eyed Beatles than punk rock hellfire, it broke the band's impressive run of hit singles, characterised by Mark Paytress as "one of the best since the days of Bolan, even the Beatles and Stones". By now Shelley, who was always a "last minute" composer in contrast to Diggle's more methodical approach, had almost stopped writing entirely, and spoke openly of his weariness, despite spending some time in Italy to recuperate. Then it was back to the studio and demos with Martin Hannett, mainly around Diggle's new compositions. But inside the band drug consumption was escalating to unsupportable volumes, now embracing cocaine, heroin and acid. As Diggle elaborated later to Uncut: "We'd gone a bit crazy. We'd be listening to playbacks walking round the studio in circles, letting off fire extinguishers, off our heads. We just lost the plot. After five years recording and touring, we were getting sick of seeing each other every day. Plus we were getting heavy on the coke. We used to have van-loads of women backstage, you know. We were partying big time. Not a lot of people know that about Buzzcocks. We could give Guns N'fucking Roses a run for their money. Our road crew were like bloody Vikings. I remember reading the Led Zep book Hammer Of The Gods and thinking, 'That seems pretty mild'. It was a great time, but it all started to catch up with us."

A one-off show at Manchester Polytechnic on 22th May was their first for five months, with Shelley dedicating 'Strange Thing', a new song about depression, to Ian Curtis, who had been found dead four days previously. The quality control in terms of songwriting, nevertheless, remained staunch, as the Buzzcocks entered a third phase of single releases – from punk-pop epistles to energetic psychedelia to a more earthy, garage-influenced sound. 'Why She's The Girl From The Chainstore' was strident, defiant pop inspired by Henry Miller's Black Spring, with a great major/minor flick, released as a double A-side with 'Are Everything', a kind of post-modern cut-up performed while Shelley and Hannett were both tripping. Such behaviour was enough to see Garvey bugger off to pursue his horse racing interest (including ownership of Regent's Boy). Linder played the checkout girl in the accompanying video, in which Shelley's parents also appeared.

'Strange Thing' c/w 'Airwaves Dream' was again a double A-side, but suddenly the Buzzcocks seemed like yesterday's men – the pervading sense of lethargy informed partially by the fact that Shelley recorded it while on anti-depressants. Matters were made worse by EMI, who had taken over United Artists, withholding further advances due to the non-delivery of a fourth album. Their long-time ally Andrew Lauder had left to form Radar, so their A&R rep became Tim Chacksfield. This potential ally then subsequently left to pursue his own music as a saxophonist, leaving the band totally alienated from their label. So they did what they'd always done and toured again, only this time the Tour By Instalments was poorly attended and the band was visibly ill at ease with one another on stage. The third single in the trilogy, 'What Do You Know?'/'Running Free', the former featuring a nod to the Northern Soul scene, appeared to absolute apathy. A rash of gig cancellations in December 1980 added fuel to doubts now being openly expressed about the group's long-term viability. Their final concert came in January 1981 at the Markethalle in Hamburg. A planned 'Part 4' single, 'I Look Alone', was given to the NME's C81 cassette instead.

They were also broke. Worse, Shelley was all but out of songs. What he did write was being rejected by the band, in favour of compositions by Diggle and Garvey. The group did, however, embark on a fourth album, and Martin Rushent was hired to oversee sessions at Pluto Studios in Manchester. When Shelley left for Martin Rushent's country studio, ostensibly to record Buzzcocks songs, it was the space he needed. On the 4th of March he instructed his solicitor to write to Boon informing him of his intention to quit the band. The story hit the music papers on Saturday, 28th March.

"Pete had a couple of acoustic songs and he went back with Rushent to Genetic," Diggle recalled in Chronology. "He was there for about four weeks, as they'd got all this new stuff which Rushent had used on the Human League album, and he wanted to use it again. We were just waiting around to see what would happen. The first call I got was that it was all going well, but when I phoned a bit later on it was all a bit vague. That was when I had this notion that something wasn't right. I went back to Pluto to finish off the tracks we'd started, but by then it was all over, 'cos eventually we got this letter saying the band was finished. I didn't want it to happen, but it kind of felt like a release." The fact that Diggle had found out about Shelley's defection via the post created a huge emotional fissure between the two that would not heal for years.

That left Shelley to release his solo recordings, Garvey to form Motivation, who lost members and also a potential contract with CBS, leaving behind just a six-track demo. There's a rumour that one of these tracks, 'Heart Under Cover', was considered for Michael Jackson's Thriller. Boy, could Garvey have used the money. Instead, he went back to work on the docks. Diggle recorded the solo single 'Fifty Years Of Comparative Wealth' before forming Flag Of Convenience. Shelley signed a solo deal with Island, immediately scoring a minor hit with 'Homosapien', which was banned by the BBC for its 'gay overtones'. He toured, with Garvey as his bass player, but the follow-up album, XL1, which contained a unique computer game, wasn't nearly as strong. Three years passed before he signed a new contract with Phonogram and released Heaven And The Sea.

O World! O Life! O Time!
On whose last steps I climb
Trembling at that where I had stood before
When will return the glory of your prime?
No more – oh, never more!

(Shelley – the other Shelley – from A Lament, reflecting on that old second-time around feeling)

The Buzzcocks' legacy thereafter entered semi-mythic proportions. During the mid to late-80s they became acknowledged as the people's punk band, championed by everyone from the Wedding Present to Alice Donut in their absence. Bob Mould of Husker Du was only one of a clutch of American indie-rock stars to salute them. Others just robbed them. They were particularly influential on the bleeding heart guitar semantics of the C86 indie movement (sample band name: Razorcuts, from the closing line in 'Love You More'), as well as earlier incarnations of the same spirit, Orange Juice, who quoted directly from 'Boredom' on 'Rip It Up'. The Smiths, obviously, were hugely indebted. Morrissey "liked their intellectual edge. I really despised the idea that in order to be in a group and to play hard music you had to be covered in your own vomit."

Creation Records' founder Alan McGee "once offered to buy me a drink," Shelley told Uncut, "because he'd said he'd made a million out of me. I graciously accepted." Very few bands can boast of having an influence on quite so many different spheres of music – running the gamut of indie, alternative and grunge, from inner-M25 bedsit land to Seattle and all points in between. And then there was Volkswagen's use of 'What Do I Get?', ironic given the band's previous epistle on the subject in 'Fast Cars' (not that they knew much about the song's commercial appropriation). 'What Do I Get?' ended up on a cat food commercial.

And then the inevitable happened. A French promoter started billing Diggle's Flag Of Convenience as Buzzcocks FOC, which was appreciated least of all by Diggle. Then Flag Of Convenience imploded, with most of the members going on to form the High. Eventually an offer of an American tour proved too financially inviting to resist, and the 1981 line-up of Shelley, Diggle, Garvey and Maher agreed to reconvene. "When we had our first rehearsals back together, most of the time was spent in the pub laughing at each other," Shelley told Andy Peart. "It was like when you meet old school friends and you remember the same little in-jokes." The dates were wonderful, celebratory affairs, but Maher subsequently departed to concentrate on his still-successful Volkswagen drag racing business, to be replaced by Mike Joyce of the Smiths, a lifelong Buzzcocks fan. "The two Steves were auditioning people down in London and not getting very far when one day they met Johnny Marr in the canteen and asked him for Mike's telephone number." Joyce was only too happy to join the ship. As he'd pointed out in a Smiths interview for Record Mirror in 1984, "John Maher used to be my favourite drummer, and maybe I borrowed some of his style. The Buzzcocks were triumphant, they used to make me cry."

A series of demos were recorded at Drone Studios in Manchester, funded by Shelley's Fine Young Cannibals royalties, but there were no takers. One A&R executive returned a note citing the Buzzcocks as one of his biggest influences, and expressing regret that they were now getting back together, forcing Shelley to tell Mark Paytress "He can piss off as far as I'm concerned." The major label reluctance forced them to release them on their own Planet Pacific label as the 'Alive Tonight' EP. Nobody really noticed, and plans to release the best cut, 'Last To Know', were shelved. The songs were fine, but the production left a lot to be desired (especially in the Buzzcocks' cornerstone tradition of dovetailing guitars). "We did have lots of problems with the studio and production," Shelley admitted. "We didn't have the money to go into a big studio and also since we've been doing all the new songs live they've improved greatly." It seemed at this stage entirely probable that Buzzcocks might remain a viable live act, but not a recording one – a fact not helped by manager Paul O'Reilly's suicide after the 1989 reunion tour. They did attempt to record a new album in 1991 with Bill Laswell, but these recordings were shelved and the results effectively used as a demo recording. A shame, as that was a lost opportunity to document this impressive line-up – thereafter Joyce decided to hook up with PiL, leaving Maher to help out temporarily until former Icicle Works' drummer Steve Gibson was recruited (Maher, Joyce, Gibson – the Buzzcocks only ever used the very, very finest percussionists).

By 1992 Garvey had decided that commuting between his family in New York and London was proving too much. Auditions saw him replaced by old friend and superfan Tony Barber. "I've got scrapbooks at home full of Buzzcocks stuff," Barber told Mark Paytress. "I'm the oddball who's got all the one-sided 12-inch test pressings!" He also had the added advantage of knowing the group's back catalogue by heart, to the extent he has been able to remind his grizzled chums of the chords to some of their more obscure songs. Previously Barber had recorded for the Crass-affiliated Lack Of Knowledge, as well as Rubella Ballet, Daniel Drummond, Slaughter Joe, Ear Trumpet and Boys Wonder/Corduroy. His friend Phil Barker, also formerly of Lack Of Knowledge, took over on drums, as the band completed 18 months worth of solid touring commitments. The first new album finally came with 1993's Trade Test Transmissions, which was good enough to force even the NME and Melody Maker to suspend their cynicism at the motives behind the reunion. Diggle described it as "a sort of reintroduction". It proved Buzzcocks could still write intuitive, energised pop songs with the best of them – notable examples included 'Unthinkable', said to concern child killers, though the intro owed more than a small debt to the Clash's 'Tommy Gun', and Shelley's 'Crystal Night'.

A world tour and support slots to Nirvana in 1994 helped bring the Buzzcocks back to the mainstream. As Diggle explained to me in an interview in 1993: "We can really put on a live gig. And that's one of the reasons why people have stayed with us. It's a good exchange between the two parties, not a marketing man's dream. We've tried to maintain a bit of personal credibility." In the meantime, the band was able to witness the Nirvana phenomenon at first hand. "They came to see us play in Boston first," Diggle told Uncut. "Our stage show at the time involved smashing up about 50 second-hand TVs every night. I remember teaching Kurt how to smash a telly properly with a mic stand, because there's an art to it, you've got to be careful not to electrocute yourself – like I nearly did once. So he liked that, and I slowly got to know him. I'd read about Nirvana, and at first I just thought he was going to be an American brat – but he was quite intense, a phenomenal guy really. Which reminds me, I still owe him a few lines of coke..."

All Set, released in 1996, featured more great songwriting, notably Diggle's 'Back With You' and Shelley's 'Totally From The Heart'. There were strong echoes of past glories – 'Your Love' was indebted to the chord sequence from 'Love You More', while the similarities between 'Pariah' and 'Moving Away From The Pulsebeat' were self-evident. However, some reviewers queried Neil King's lacklustre production, particularly the lack of bottom end in the mix. There was a historical precedent for the choice of producer. The band had first encountered King, engineer for Rancid and Green Day, when he was Rushent's assistant at Eden Studios during sessions for A Different Kind Of Tension. The fact that IRS folded about a month after All Set's release did little to help the cause. In the meantime, the Buzzcocks supported the Pistols at their June 1996 Finsbury Park comeback shows – this time in front of 40,000 punters rather than the 400 or so who caught the billing first time round at the Lesser Free Trade Hall.

Modern, released in 1999, solved the production problems, thanks to bass player Tony Barber's efforts. However, the record company insisted on packaging it with a greatest hits set, which served first to demonstrate their lack of faith in the band and secondly to contrast the new songs with established back catalogue booty. In the circumstances, the comparison was not too unkind to the newer material, which made a conscious effort to break new ground, incorporating elements of funk and even techno – in a manner that partially recalled the sonic adventurism of their EP collection. "We're trying not to make a rock album," Shelley conceded to Ear Candy website. "So instead of trying to make it sound like we were a rock band, we tried a more studio-based approach. And more control over what was going on. Also, we felt uncomfortable with trying to be a rock band, when everybody's trying to be one." The single, 'Thunder Of Hearts', meanwhile, was inspired by Shelley's reading of Japanese literature, specifically Even Monkeys Fall From Trees.

In 2002 Shelley reunited with Howard Devoto ("as mad as a brush") for the Buzzkunst album, credited to ShelleyDevoto. Though not bereft of riff and melody, a large portion of the contents were angular and keyboard-driven, representing a kind of intellectual digital pop filtered through Kraut Rock and Eno. And, as ever, Devoto's lyrics were remarkable, especially on 'Deeper' and the bleak 'Self-Destruction', bizarrely inspired by seeing the same song title on a Johnny Winter Blues Band album. Elsewhere, on notes on the songs printed on the Buzzcocks' website, he confessed that 'Can You See Me Shining' was "Robbie Williams at his most arch having a stab at 'The Light Pours Out Of Me'. Okay, maybe not." All of which meant that Devoto was dragged out of the library for his views on life and music, and he was as entertaining as ever in print, especially about his career trajectory in the 90s. "I don't mind having a job," he told PopMatters. "People don't really believe me, I think, but it's okay. In myself, when I took that decision in 1990, I actually became a far happier person. On that basis, I feel I'm entitled to be a bit cynical about a world that seems to put such a high premium on creativity. I think such a lot of bollocks is talked about how wonderful creativity is. So that's kind of how I am sometimes." There are times when yer man Devoto just can't help but talk absolute, unyielding sense.

2003 brought the Buzzcocks. Or the album with no title, if you prefer. "It isn't self-titled," Shelley insisted to Rolling Stone. "People think that because it doesn't have a title, the title must be Buzzcocks. But it's not. It doesn't have a title – it's not eponymous." Again produced by Barber, its release was delayed after Diggle crashed his motor scooter in Greece, breaking his wrist. The album included two Shelley/Devoto compositions, 'Stars' and 'Lester Sands', the latter a 'proper' recording of the old Time's Up tune, the former having appeared on the Buzzkunst album in different form (and title – 'Til The Stars In His Eyes Are Dead'). Devoto later confessed the lyric was the first one he had ever written, aged 14.

Another 'old' song was 'Jerk', written in the late-80s, but the group had never previously managed to attain the right 'feel' for it (it was drummer Barker who thought they should persevere with it). The inspiration behind 'Morning After', however, was pure Shelley. "We had two days in the studio and Phil came in and he brought some cans of lager," he told Rolling Stone. "The inspiration got further and further away as the alcohol consumption increased, so I ended up not doing anything that day. Early the next morning, I had to go to a hairdressers' appointment to bleach my hair, and I was sitting in the salon waiting for the bleach to take effect with the worst hangover I've had in a long time. And as soon as I was finished I had to go straight to the studio, because it was the final day. So I thought, 'What can I write?' Oooh, my head! And I thought: 'There it is.'"

Of all the heroes of 1977 to reform for a paying audience in the late-80s, the Buzzcocks, who framed the terms of reference for a thousand subsequent bands, are among the few to do so with an eye no anything other than the cheque stubs. They probably needed to pay their mortgages as much as anyone else does. But rather than recycle their greatest hits, the Buzzcocks have now recorded five genuinely good to great LPs, Trade Test Transmissions (1993), All Set (1996), Modern (1999), whatever posterity chooses to title their 2003 missive and the new Flat Pack Philosophy (2006). The latter, as Diggle revealed, related to the fact that "You get a lot of instructions in life. But you have to put it all together yourself."

DISCOGRAPHY:

(Buyer's Guide: Singles Going Steady is one of the great rock'n'roll primers of any period, ever. Really, for anything more than a passing glance, Product is essential. After that, pick up the Time's Up CD reissue for all the Devoto-period tracks. Of the post-reformation albums, Buzzcocks aka self-titled probably just shades it over Trade Test Transmissions and Modern, with All Set probably the weakest of the four. But then I'm just listening to Flat Pack Philosophy and jeepers, that's excellent too)

Spiral Scratch 7-inch EP (New Hormones ORG 1 January 1977)

Breakdown/Time's Up/Boredom/Friends Of Mind (re-issued in August 1979 with 'With Howard Devoto' on sleeve. Reissued on CD by Document in 1991, then again by Mute in February 2000)

Orgasm Addict/Whatever Happened To? 7-inch (United Artists UP 36316 November 1977) (The French version of 'Orgasm Addict' is a collector's item; UA sent the wrong master to France, and it therefore features a different take)

What Do I Get?/Oh Shit! 7-inch (United Artists UP 36348 February 1978)

Another Music In A Different Kitchen LP (United Artists UAG 30159 March 1978) (initially with carrier bag)

I Don't Mind/Autonomy 7-inch (United Artists UP 36386 April 1978)

Love You More/Noise Annoys 7-inch (United Artists UP 36433 July 1978)

Ever Fallen In Love (With Someone You Shouldn't've)/Just Lust 7-inch (United Artists UP 36455 September 1978) (some mis-pressings featured a Gerry Rafferty song on the B-side)

Love Bites LP (United Artists UAG 30197 September 1978)

Promises/Lipstick 7-inch (United Artists UP 36455 November 1978)

Everybody's Happy Nowadays/Why Can't I Touch It? 7-inch (United Artists UP 36499 March 1979) (three different sleeves)

Harmony In My Head/Something's Gone Wrong Again 7-inch (United Artists UP 36541 July 1979) (two different sleeves)

You Say You Don't Love Me/Raison D'etre 7-inch (United Artists BP 316 September 1979)

A Different Kind Of Tension LP (United Artists UAG 30260 September 1979) (with free limited single: You Say You Don't Love Me/Raison D'etre 7-inch (United Artists BP 316 September 1979)

Why She's A Girl From The Chainstore/Are Everything (Part 1) 7-inch (United Artists BP 365 August 1980)

Strange Thing/Airwaves Dream (Part 2) 7-inch (United Artists BP 371 October 1980)

Running Free/What Do You Know? (Part 3) 7-inch (United Artists BP 392 December 1980)

Alive Tonight 7-inch EP (Planet Pacific April 1991)

Alive Tonight/Successful Street/Serious Crime/Last To Know

(also available as a 12-inch, cassette and CD EP) Innocent/Who'll Help Me To Forget/Inside 7-inch EP (Essential ESSX 2025 May 1993) (also available on 12-inch and CD single)

Trade Test Transmissions LP/CD (ESM 389 June 1993) (reissued on CD July 1996. Remastered and reissued by Sanctuary in January 2005 with new booklet written by Tony Barber, plus bonus tracks 'Do It (single version)', 'Libertine Angel', 'Roll It Over' and 'Excerpt From Prison Riot Hostage')

Do It/Trash Away/All Over You 12-inch EP (Essential August 1993) (also available as a CD single)

Libertine Angel/Roll It Over/Excerpt From Prison Riot Hostage CD single (Essential ESSX2038 April 1994) (also available as a 12-inch, ESST2038)

All Set CD (IRS EIRSCD 1078 April 1996)

Modern CD (Go Kart 58 September 1999) (released as a double CD with greatest hits package)

Jerk/Don't Come Back/Oh Shit! (live) 7-inch (Damaged Goods DAMGOOD 214 2003) (pink vinyl, 'Oh Shit!' recorded live in 2000)

www.buzzcocks.com CD (Buzzcocks 2002) (downloadable live album available from the band's website. Features 21 songs from throughout the Mark II version of the band's career spanning seven or eight years. Taped at various locations, including America, France, Dublin, Brazil etc. Also released as a double vinyl LP, Secret Public's Best In Good Food, via Damaged Goods, DAMGOOD 254, 2005, in multicoloured vinyl)

The Buzzcocks CD (Merge 2003)

Sick City Sometimes/Never Believe It/Paradise (live) 7-inch & CDS (Damaged Goods DAMGOOD 219 2005) (vinyl version in red vinyl)

Wish I Never Loved You CDS (Cooking Vinyl FRYCD261 February 2006)

Wish I Never Loved You/Don't Matter What You Say/Orion

Flat-Pack Philosophy CD (Cooking Vinyl COOKCD370 March 2006) (also available in four different colour vinyl versions, grey, orange, dark red and yellow, via Damaged Goods, DAMGOOD 262)

ARCHIVE RELEASES:

Singles Going Steady LP (Liberty LBR 1043 November 1981) (essentially an attempt to corner the American market, but subsequently one of the best loved compilations of all time)

Peel Sessions 12-inch EP (Strange Fruit SFPS044 1987)

Fast Cars/Moving Away From The Pulsebeat/What Do I Get

Peel Sessions LP (Strange Fruit SFRLP 104 1989) (also released on CD, SFRCD104, and reissued on DE181062. Interesting, especially for the final May 1979 session and a great version of 'E.S.P.', though it does remind you how integral Martin Rushent had become to Buzzcocks' best work, as you miss his presence here. There are a number of 76-79 era bands whose recordings for Peel are totally essential – the Buzzcocks are not one of them)

Product 4xLP Box Set (EMI LPPRDT1 1989) (also released as 3-CD package, EMI CDPRDT1. All the post-Spiral Scratch, pre-reformation Buzzcocks you need. In addition to their three studio albums, plus those parts of Singles Going Steady not reprised elsewhere, it includes their final three singles (plus unreleased 'seventh' cut from the same sessions, 'I Look Alone') and a terrific recording of their Friday 10th March 1978 show at London's Lyceum, broadcast by Capital Radio)

Live At The Roxy Club LP (Absolutely Free FREELP002 1989) (also on CD, FREECD002, with extra track, 'Love Battery'. Reissued in December 1991 on Receiver, RRCD131, with new sleevenotes by John Tobler, who draws a hitherto unacknowledged, and wholly inaccurate, parallel to New York's Television. The sound has no wallop, sadly. 'This is a love song. Can't be bad, can it?" Shelley states from the stage as the band are barracked, before launching into 'What Do I Get?')

The Fab Four 12-inch EP (EMI 12EM 104 October 1989)

Ever Fallen In Love (With Someone You Shouldn't've)/Promises/Everybody's Happy Nowadays/Harmony In My Head (also issued on CD, EMI CDEM 104)

The Early Years 12-inch EP (Receiver REPLAY3013 1990)

Orgasm Addict/No Reply/Boredom/Love Battery (all live)

Time's Up LP (Document DLP2 1991) (also released on CD, DCD2, vinyl issue includes interview flexi with Devoto, FDLP2. This is the first 'legit' version of the famed 1977 bootleg on Voto Records (LYN5333) with Devoto on vocals, and different versions of the Spiral Scratch songs, including alternate lyrics on 'Time's Up' and 'Friends Of Mine'. The interview is with Q's Dave Henderson. Re-released by Mute, The Grey Area, SCRATCH2CD, in March 2000, with new artwork drawn from Devoto's photo archives – including one that nails his Brian Eno fixation. There's also a Greil Marcus sleevenote and period ephemera. It's worth noting that neither reissue was drawn directly from the original 'masters' which results in slightly different mixes)

Operator's Manual dbl LP (EMI EMI1421 November 1991) (also released as CD,

CDEMI1421; cover designed by original collaborator Malcolm Garrett)

Entertaining Friends CD (EMI Gold CDGOLD 1029 May 1992) (taken from a set at the Hammersmith Odeon in March 1979)

Lest We Forget CD (ROIR Dancetaria RE158CD April 1993) (All tracks are live and taken from shows in Boston (1980), Chicago (1979), Minnesota (1979) Birmingham (1980), New Jersey (1980), Providence (1980) and New York (1979). Also released as a cassette, ROIR A158, with slightly different artwork and sleeve notes including Harmony In My Head newsletter writer Joan McNulty's comments)

French CD (Dojo DOJO CD 237 November 1996) (recorded at L'Arapaho Club, Paris, France 12 April 1995. Reissued on Snapper, SMMCD 541, in 1998, with new sleevenotes by yours truly. Great sound quality and a rousing version of 'Boredom', including 'rockist' ending...)

Chronology CD (EMI GOLD 7243 8 57026 2 4 June 1997) (a varied trawl through the band's backpages, and Shelley's loft, from 1977 to 1981. Demos, out-takes, alternative versions. Most notable are the Devoto-less version of 'Boredom' featuring Garth on his first session (August 1977), the previously unavailable (for good reason) 'Mother Of Turds', which haplessly recalls Chas 'n' Dave, and the first recorded version of 'Promises', with the hilarious lyrics made up by Diggle as he went along. Iso features the unheard Garvey composition 'Run Away From Home' which was reactivated for their 1991 reformation, and Diggle's 'Drive System'. Good first-hand sleevenotes but not essential unless you're a complete devotee)

BBC SESSIONS: The Archive Series (BBC/EMI 7243 4 97771 2 5 1998) (there were other BBC DJs apart from Peel, of course. This entertaining scrapbook – though disappointingly bereft of anecdotage or anything beyond basic biographical and chronological data – not only documents tracks recorded for Kid Jensen, Mike Read, Johnny Walker, Jackie Brambles, Mark Radcliffe, Robert Elms and Phil Jupitus, but the group's 1978 appearance on the Old Grey Whistle Test. A 1993 version of 'Ever Fallen In Love (With Someone You Shouldn't've)' demonstrates how far Phil Barker has come in emulating Maher's drumming, while the two Johnny Walker tracks were never originally broadcast. Entertainingly, it includes many of the spoken introductions and jingles)

Beating Hearts dbl CD (Burning Airlines Pilot 78 May 2000) (featuring scorching shows from the Manchester Apollo on 27/10/1978 and London Rainbow on 9/11/1979. And some nice asides from Shelley to his unruly home audience. Easily the best live recordings available of the Buzzcocks' circa 1978-1979 when hardly anyone could touch them live)

Another Music In A Different Kitchen/Love Bites dbl CD (EMI 2000) (for those of you who don't own Product, presumably)

Driving You Insane dbl CD (Snapper/Recall SMDCD544 2005) (recorded live at the Shepherd's Bush Empire 27 April 2003. A fair to good performance well recorded, notable for Shelley's dedication to Joe Strummer before 'Autonomy')

C

Cancelled

Paul Denison (drums), Dave Hawley (guitar), Steve (bass, vocals)

Formed in 1979, the CANCELLED was essentially a garage-only band, but they did provide the foundations for several later punk groups in the Aldershot area. Other local bands of the time included Deadlock, Hiroshima's Heroes, the Innocents, the Zymotics and Farnborough's Lethal Dose. All of their members would intermingle, but none of these managed to release any vinyl. Two of the main movers in this scene would fall victim to drug-related deaths. Lethal Dose's singer Martin Dyson died in the early-80s from a heroin overdose, while Dave Robinson, drummer with Hiroshima's Heroes, fatally jumped from an eighth-storey window whilst tripping on LSD.

I asked Denison about his memories of the Aldershot punk scene of the late 70s. "I have many fond memories of the punk scene in Aldershot, the best of which lay in the local band scene during the golden years of punk. Most of the punk bands in Aldershot came from a large group of teenagers that used to assemble every night at the Heroes Shrine in Manor Park just to be together socially and have a bit of a laugh. Those days were great, we were all mates and most of us had an appreciation for punk and new wave music. Many relationships and friendships began in Manor Park, and many still remain today. Many of us from the Manor Park crowd would meet up and go to punk gigs to see the well established punk bands. I can remember as punks, often being hassled by Squaddies on the trains and in the train stations on the way home, Aldershot being an army town of course. So one would go out with an air of caution at times. Sometimes we would have to run for our lives to escape large gangs of skinheads and local hoodlums in London and various towns and cities. But all in all, and especially when young, problems like this were put aside and didn't spoil the enjoyment of being a punk and going to gigs. Punk also enabled me to get into bands as a musician without too much talent or a degree in music."

Cane

Kip (guitar, vocals), Dave 'Pixie' Parker (drums), Steve Jefford (bass), Chris Battersby (guitar)

Another of those Lightning Records' artistes who rarely merit even a passing nod in discussion of the 70s punk scene, CANE were one of the more interesting of the roster's acts, though the competition wasn't fierce. They are best known for their contribution to the Streets compilation, 'College Girls'. It was written after a show at Cassio College in Watford, with Kip writing the music to Parker's alcohol-inspired words. Its risqué lyrics ("Everyone knows how juicy they are – college girls' clits") were hardly Voltaire, but managed to successfully offend a few moral arbiters, which was certainly the intention. However, 'Dice' was appalling soft rock, having more in common with Sad Café than the Sex Pistols, though 'D.K. Dance' saved the day somewhat. The suspicion remained, however, that this was another example of Lightning trying to reinvent what was basically a trad rock band.

Cane was originally formed in 1975, at which point they were essentially a Mott The Hoople/Bowie tribute band. But Kip was converted to punk in 1976, when they started to pen more originals such as 'College Girls'. Kip made the contact with Lightning, representatives of whom came to watch them rehearse and were convinced enough to put them into Berry Street studios to record demos. It was from these sessions that 'College Girls' originated, which Lightning managed to place on Streets. Thereafter Battersby left the band, leaving them as a trio by the time the single was recorded.

There were subsequent shows with the Raincoats and others, but the single disappeared without trace. Cane followed it shortly thereafter. Kip would go on to join the Vibrators in 1979 and subsequently the Chords after a further, abandoned studio session at which they recorded the unreleased 'Wormwood Scrubber'.

DISCOGRAPHY:

Dice/Suburban Guerilla/D.K.Dance 7-inch (Lightning GIL531 78 25 1978)

COMPILATION:

Streets LP (Beggars Banquet BEGA 1 November 1977; 'College Girls')

The Cane

Chris Skornia (lead vocals, guitar), Kirk Brandon (bass, vocals), John Fuller (lead guitar, vocals), Simon Wright (drums, vocals)

THE CANE, or initially The Kayo Punks, came into being when Devon promoter Lionel Digby booked the Sex Pistols for a show at the 400 Club in Torquay on 28 September 1976. However, the Pistols were not exactly flavour of the month in conservative south coast holiday resorts, and the gig was pulled, just like the preceding event at the Scunthorpe Priory and the subsequent dates in Plymouth, Penzance and Wolverhampton.

With interest growing in his much vaunted punk night, and no band to fill the bill, Digby asked local musicians Chris Skornia and Simon Wright if they could help him out. They put together a quintet drawn from local musicians who quickly learned a basic set of covers using recently issued 45s as the template. Despite these inauspicious beginnings, the Kayo Punks proved a success and that convinced the main participants that they were on to something. They duo was joined by Jerry Iles on bass, and changed their name to The Cane, unaware of the existence of a similarly titled outfit who'd contributed to the Streets compilation. Nevertheless support slots with Chelsea, Sham 69 and the Cortinas ensued.

By 1978 Iles had bowed out and was replaced by future Pack, Theatre of Hate and Spear Of Destiny mainstay Kirk Brandon, with John Fuller also joining on lead guitar. Simon Wright left and was replaced by Mike Farrow, like Fuller formerly of Adrenalin. They decided to make the move to London, armed with demos they'd recorded in a Torquay studio, and set themselves up in a house near Heathrow, with Rab Fae Beith taking over drums. The songs they wrote there (though none were actually recorded) are lost to posterity. Skornia: "It was much harder to get recordings made cheaply in those days compared to now, and we were all broke at the time!" Despite stout-hearted efforts at blagging their way into the London punk community, they never quite made it, despite changing their name to The Pack Of Lies. "On reflection, our 'bright lights, big city' move to London may not have been the wisest thing to do," notes Skornia, "as we ended up competing with so many other bands who had the advantage of being on their home turf. We may have done better by staying in Devon, continuing with the local support tours etc. and making a good name for ourselves there first. What a wonderful thing hindsight is!"

We all know what Brandon did next, but Skornia joined the Boyfriends with Pat Collier of the Vibrators then formed the Truth with Dennis Greaves (ex-Nine Below Zero). Fuller, who joined Ack Ack, had a band in California and was in an early version of Culture Club on his return. Wright still performs in and around Torquay. In the summer of 2006 Skornia's new play Vincent – Prisoner Of A Dream, a dramatisation of the life of Van Gogh co-written with Neil Keveren, began its run in London's West End.

Carpettes

Neil Thompson (vocals, guitar), George Maddison (vocals, bass), Kevin Heard (drums)

The CARPETTES were, with hindsight, an under-rated bunch, bestowed with a surfeit of catchy pop-punk tunes that were the equal of some of the heavyweight bands of the period. There was nothing especially revelatory about the County Durham band's formula, which moved closer to conventional pop dynamics as their career progressed. But they did it all with a bit of panache and a sense of fun and optimism that was sorely lacking in the circles they moved in. In some ways it's possible to speculate that it was only their timeframe that separated them from the mod revival movement. Maddison doesn't entirely dispute this, but believes that, especially live, they had a 'harder' sound than the Mod bands.

As long-term fan Mick Mercer noted: "The Carpettes were hamstrung by not having an image, or a scene into which they might fit... they were really firing on all cylinders when they were expected to fit into the birth of indie scenes everywhere, and it wasn't easy for them. The songs can't be faulted... "

They were formed in April 1977 in Newcastle as a progression from the trio's earlier school band, Brown Sugar. The transforming moment came, as with so many bands, when they first heard the Ramones. Their earliest rehearsals, in fact, comprised a mixture of Ramones and Gene Vincent covers. Having played just two shows in their new incarnation, they replied to an advert placed in Sounds by Small Wonder, forwarding a five-strong demo tape and waiting for the phone to ring. Happily, it did. "It may be hard to believe now," Maddison told me, "but not only did we not have mobile phones in those days, we didn't have a phone in the house. So I communicated with Pete Stennet, who ran Small Wonder Records, in a public phone box, with the 10p coins rapidly disappearing into the slot." The result was a recording contract with the Walthamstow shop-cum-label and the release of their debut EP, 'Radio Wunderbar', in December 1977. The tracks were all re-recorded from that original demo tape.

Jim Devlin of the Carpettes at the 2005 Wasted Festival.

Reviews were good, and the group built on their breakthrough with a series of support slots in the north east. Their second appearance with Penetration, at Middlesbrough Rock Garden, was particularly memorable. "This was a real steamy, raucous night," Maddison recalls. "The place was packed and it was pretty wild. I ended the set with just two strings on my bass. Excellent gig, though this was in the period when it was still the thing to spit at the band to show your appreciation."

They made their London debut supporting fellow Small Wonder interns the Leyton Buzzards in March 1978 and were booked for a summer session with John Peel (recording 'Reach The Bottom', 'I Don't Mean It', 'Away From It All' and one of Maddison's best songs, 'Indo China'). This was aired as their second single, 'Small Wonder', was released. In the light of the generally positive reaction everything they'd done had received thus far, it was decided to relocate to London to establish themselves at the heart of the beast. Heard wasn't prepared to make the trip, so they recruited former Young Bucks drummer Tim Wilder in his stead.

Wilder was immediately set to work on a second John Peel session broadcast in December 1978, featuring 'Cruel Honesty', 'What Can I Do', 'It Don't Make Sense' and 'Routine'. "The decision (to move to London) wasn't too hard," reckons Maddison. "The only problem was lack of money. It was definitely the right decision, as far as the Carpettes were concerned. There was no chance that we would have been signed up and had the chance to record the two albums if we'd stayed in the north east." They'd previously stayed above the Small Wonder shop when they'd come down to cut the singles. "After we moved to London we lived in a number of dodgy flats in Clapton Pond, Woodford, Kensal Rise and Finsbury Park. In the years we lived there we didn't really socialise with other bands. We knew the Lurkers, from Beggars Banquet, and played an excellent series of gigs with them at The Marquee, but we were never part of any scene, although we went to hundreds of gigs during this time."

Thereafter they transferred to Beggars Banquet, a label who had coveted their services but lacked the finances to entice them to their roster until Gary Numan finally hit the big time with 'Are Friends Electric?' "After I'd visited the Beggars Banquet headquarters touting our demos we were contacted by Beggars' A&R man Mike Stone. Mike was keen to sign us for Beggars, but shortly after this he decided to break away and form his own label, so he asked us if we wanted to sign with him. However, Beggars Banquet still wanted to sign us, so we had to make a choice. All of this took quite a few months (which, looking back, could have harmed us as times change in music quickly). Eventually we decided to go with Beggars, as they were having a lot of success by then with Gary Numan and had signed a deal with Warner Brothers."

By October 1979 their debut album Frustration Paradise, produced by fellow Geordie Bob Sargeant, who'd overseen the Peel sessions, was in the shops. One of the better tracks, the Nuggety 'Lost Love', also gained some valuable exposure via its inclusion on the second volume of Polydor's 20 Of Another Kind compilation series. The album's title-track, meanwhile, with its crescendos of rhythm and echo, is arguably the band's finest two and a half minutes.

A second single, 'Johnny Won't Hurt You', was extracted from the album in December, along with a free live single featuring 'Total Insecurity' and 'Keys To Your Heart'. These originated from a show at the University of London after an earlier attempt to record them at the Windsor Castle was abandoned – the landlord refused them entry to the premises. There were other hitches. There was reluctance from the bigger agencies, due to their unfashionable lack of image, to offer them suitable support slots and projected national tours with Stiff Little Fingers, the Pretenders, UB40 and others never came to pass. And Beggars weren't prepared to stump up the cash for 'buy-ons'. Wishbone Ash was suggested at one point as an alternative but the band, understandably, wouldn't hear of it. Nor were they overjoyed at the idea of being promoted as a "slightly edgier Police". They eventually set up an 11-date jaunt with the Inmates, who'd just had a hit with 'Dirty Water' ("a great bunch of lads and some good gigs") and appeared on the Old Grey Whistle Test performing 'Johnny Won't Hurt You' and 'Indo China'.

After two Italian tours, including one supported by the Merton Parkas at the start of 1980, they recorded a further single, 'Nothing Ever Changes' in June. A second album for Beggars, Fight Amongst Yourselves, produced by Colin Thurston, who would later enjoy success with Duran Duran, the Thompson Twins et al, failed to ignite much interest. Generally considered inferior to its predecessor, it's still a fine collection of chirrupy pop-punk bereft of preciousness or pretence. The songwriting had progressed but there wasn't the same rhythmic crunch of old. The title-track and boisterous 'Saturday Night Sunday Morning', with its cutesy vocal inflections, part-Weller, part-Les Gray of Mud ("Les Gray?" opines Maddison. "I'm flattered"), are notable exceptions.

The accompanying single, the reggae-inflected 'The Last Lone Ranger', the band having already experimented with ska-like rhythms on 'Johnny Won't Hurt You', closed their account. After their release Wilder left and Maddison and Thompson, who were always the songwriting axis anyway, picked up Simon Smith of the Merton Parkas. A four-track demo was recorded but interest in the band had dwindled, not least at Beggars Banquet who had bigger fish to fry. Smith could see the writing on the wall and moved on to psychedelic revival act Mood Six, with Wilder returning to play their remaining live commitments ending with a show at the Clarendon Hotel in Hammersmith on 4 June 1981.

The Carpettes reformed following an invitation to play the 1996 Holidays In The Sun festival at Blackpool. And from then on the band has been kept going on and off, touring the UK, Germany and Japan, where their stature is greater than many of their more celebrated UK peers. The first of two tours to the latter territory resulted in their Fair Play To 'Em album of 2002, with drums provided by Neil's brother Paul Thompson.

In 2005 the Carpettes, now featuring Maddison, long-time Carpettes' fan Jimmy D on guitar and drummer Jim Cosgrove, recorded a new album for Texas label NDN (which additionally featured Paul Thompson drumming on the first few tracks). They appeared at the Wasted Festival before a 2006 tour of Germany and Austria. According to Maddison, there are "new tracks in the pipeline."

C

DISCOGRAPHY:

The Carpettes 7-inch EP (Small Wonder SMALL 3 December 1977)
How About Me And You/Help I'm Trapped/Radio Wunderbar/Cream Of Youth (also known as 'The Wunderbar' EP, simply because John Peel played that track so much)
Small Wonder/2 Ne 1 7-inch single (Small Wonder SMALL 9 July 1978)
I Don't Mean It/Easy Way Out 7-inch single (Beggars Banquet BEG 27 October 1979)
Frustration Paradise LP (Beggars Banquet BEGA 14 November 1979) (reissued in 1988. Reissued on CD, Captain Oi! AHOY CD 65, alongside Fight Amongst Yourselves, in 1996)
Johnny Won't Hurt You/Frustration Paradise 7-inch (Beggars Banquet BEG 32 March 1980) (came with free 7-inch, Total Insecurity c/w Keys To Your Heart, SAM 119)
Nothing Ever Changes 7-inch EP (Beggars Banquet BEG 47 August 1980)
Nothing Ever Changes/You Never Realise/Frustration Paradise (live)
Fight Amongst Yourselves LP (Beggars Banquet BEGA 21 October 1980) (reissued on CD, Captain Oi! AHOY CD 65, alongside Frustration Paradise in 1996)
The Last Lone Ranger/Love So Strong/Fan Club 7-inch EP (Beggars Banquet BEG 49 December 1980)
It Doesn't Matter/No Chance 7-inch (Waveform WAVE 5 2002)
Fair Play To 'Em CD (Waveform WAVE 6 2002)
I Just Called To Say I Love You 1-sided 7-inch single (Waveform 2003) (the Stevie Wonder song annihilated at the sessions which produced Fair Play To 'Em. Also released in Japan as a 1-track CD to coincide with their 2003 tour there)
ARCHIVE RELEASES:
The Best Of The Carpettes CD (Anagram CD PUNK 80 1996) (liner notes from Mark Brennan)
Frustration Paradise/Fight Amongst Yourselves CD (Captain Oi! AHOY CD 65 1996) (2 for 1 reissue of the band's studio albums with extensive liner notes by Neil Thompson)
The Early Years CD (Overground OVER 68 CD 1997) (comprises two unreleased John Peel sessions, seven previously unreleased tracks and alternate versions of their early Small Wonder efforts. Reissued in 2003 as The Early Years 1977-1978 with a new cover and booklet annotated by Neil Thompson)
Small Wonders – The Singles 1977- 1980 LP (Last Year's Youth Records LAST BIG 6 2003) (for the vinyl loyalists out there)

Chaos

Calvin Shulman (lead vocals), Damon Shulman (bass), Adrian Strokes (guitar), Simon Lindsey (keyboards), Mike Lindsey (drums)

At the last census there were 643 punk bands named CHAOS. This version, from Portsmouth, secure minor footnote status by dint of employing an eleven-year-old bass player, Damon Shulman, who later formed The Working Stiffs. Chaos, who played in and around the Portsmouth punk scene of the late-70s whenever they could cadge a spot on the bill, also featured his elder brother Calvin, now a sub-editor at the Times.

Chaos was very much a family affair – the Shulman brothers' father was one Phil Shulman of Gentle Giant fame. "I was a child," Damon confirmed to me. "I'd been learning how to play instruments from a very early age, but that isn't so surprising given my family history. Punk music or playing in a band would have completely passed me by if it hadn't been for my brother, Calvin. He is six years my senior and had already formed a band with his friends at Portsmouth Grammar. They were called the Sticky Fingers and contained the members of Chaos plus one more guitarist. Their set was chiefly Rolling Stones and Who covers. I am told that their sound was unwittingly punk anyway. When I was about ten I did actually see them playing at a place called the Drayton Institute, which ran various events like youth discos.

"Though punk hadn't really hit Portsmouth at that time, my brother and his mates were aware of it through magazines, TV and radio, and were palpably influenced. They were pretty sharp kids and soon adopted a completely punk approach, kicking out two square bears and renaming their band Chaos. To be honest, I really don't know why they thought of getting me into the band. It must have been simply because I knew how to play the bass. There must have been a shortage of grown up bass players at the time. There was certainly no premeditated commercial plan behind it. I can remember Calvin and Mike Lindsey auditioned me at home. I was asked to play 'Live With Me' by the Rolling Stones. I played it, and my

PUNX GET YOUNGER EVERYDAY

KIDDIES LIBERATION strikes again. Calvin Shulman is 11 years old. He also happens to play bass in a Portsmouth punk rock band called Chaos . . .

It's a family trade: his 17-year-old brother Damon is the group's singer, and dad Phil, now a teacher, is a former member of Gentle Giant. In fact, two of Calvin's uncles still are.

Apparently Damon and Calvin write their own material. Damon reckons he's in the business for a giggle, but Calvin says he's looking for a career.

Better getchaself a good manager, Calvin, and remember — don't trust anyone over 15 . . .

JAMIE MANDELKAU

The precocious Calvin Shulman (above, onstage and left with his dad and bruvver), captured by the camera of JOHN ANDOW

Chaos on stage with 11-year-old bass player Damon Shulman.

performance was greeted with approving nods. I was pretty chuffed, though it is weird. I mean, it sounds so uncool having a junior school kid in a hard-hitting punk band. As I said, the rest of the lads were genuinely 'on the money' original punks, possibly some of the first punks in Portsmouth. I would've been privileged to speak to them let alone be in their band."

Nevertheless, Damon's enthusiasm got the better of him at his first gig. "We were booked to play at Waterlooville golf club. It turned out to be a club presentation. The audience was full of suited wide boys and clown-faced disco girls. There a few local dignitaries dotted about as well. The set started without too much controversy, as we did a few uptempo Who covers. Then we did one of our own songs and I think the moment must have got the better of me – I gobbed in a girl's face. If I'd have been a few years older and slightly bigger, I'm sure someone would have filled me in. There was a bit of a commotion but we continued to play. However, by the end of the next song the whole audience had taken exception to our aggressive demeanour. We were dispatched by the wide boys with a chorus of 'Off, off, off' etc. They carried on for ages after we'd left the stage. To be fair they were probably expecting something a little nearer to Donna Summer and certainly wouldn't have wanted to be spat at."

A more suitable and appreciative audience was to be found at Portsmouth's first punk venue, the Rotary Club. "We had our first 'real' gig there. It was a three-band line-up. There was us, a band called Alice and Staa Marx. That gig was packed, bursting at the seams. There was a small dressing room for the bands. Alice had a woman lead singer. I recall she looked a little like a cross between Janis Joplin and Tin Tin. She certainly gained my immediate attention and respect in the dressing room as she stripped naked in order to don her stage garb. It was disarming to say the least, bearing in mind I was only eleven. The gig itself was great. My brother opened by shouting, 'Hello we're Chaos, we're from Portsmouth and this is 'Life Today', then I'd steam in with a bass riff. Four bars later the whole band smashed in. The whole place lurched forward. The lighting rig fell on us and we were pushed back as people jumped on to the stage. The gig had to be stopped. The lighting rig was broken so a group of skinheads held the lights up for us until the rig was fixed. It was a great night."

Not all the established bands were as welcoming as Staa Marx. "We played with the Lurkers at Waterlooville Community Centre. They wouldn't let us set up our gear on the stage, so we had to push together about a dozen tables and set up on the dance floor. Actually, I went out to get some sweets with my brother's girlfriend and our keyboard player before the gig and on the way back we were chased down the road by some old twat dressed in teddy boy gear. He must have felt really hard chasing two teenagers and a boy down the road. But there you go, antipathy towards punks (whatever their age) was palpable even in Waterlooville."

Then there was their nationally covered support to Sham 69. "We played with Sham 69 at Clarence Pier. The voice of youth, Jimmy Pursey, barely acknowledged our presence. Still, Pompey did us proud and gave us a rousing reception. We had established a loyal, loud and large following by then. I think someone threw a beer glass at Sham 69. The NME did an article on us after that – something about 'kiddies liberation' and 'punks getting younger every day'. Of course, they focused on me being only eleven, but got mine and my brother's name the wrong way round, calling me 'precocious Calvin'."

They also managed a few out of town shows. "We were supporting a band called Sore

Throat at the Camden Palace. We had our own dressing room. Sore Throat's lead singer came in and offered us some drugs. I think it was some kind of cannabis resin. Obviously, we were horrified and turned the offer down. However, Mike our drummer, not wishing to appear aloof, reciprocated by offering a line of Cadbury's Fruit 'n' Nut. I don't think he got a response."

Sadly, there isn't much formally recorded, though there are some practice tapes. "I think we genuinely had a few good-ish songs. Calvin used to write most of the lyrics while I wrote most of the music, believe it or not."

Chefs

Helen McCookerybook (aka Helen McCallum; vocals, bass), Jim 'Bruv' McCallum (guitar), Russ Greenwood (drums), Carl Evans (guitar, vocals)

Cute but gritty at the same time, the CHEFS were a Brighton outfit formed at the end of 1978. Their modus operandi may have been distinctly poppy, but for McCookerybook they were definitely an extension of the original punk ethos. "I'd started off playing bass in a punk band called Joby and the Hooligans and was literally still learning on stage in The Chefs. We also liked being loud and noisy, although our songs were really tuneful and poppy."

Much beloved of Uncle John Peel and most everyone that caught them live or on record, the Chefs delivered choppy pop-punk with sweet melodies but occasionally brutal lyrics. Their subject matter included venereal disease, sexual politics and the glories of food. About all of which, they were unremittingly direct. Probably their most famous lyric came from 'Thrush'. "I was just a bunk-up for you to get your spunk up." Rendered against the sweetpea rush of pristine pop music, it was some contrast.

I asked McCookerybook what it was about the Brighton punk scene that produced such maverick and disparate bands. "We were all following the true spirit of anarchy – which is all about being individual, not following things other people do. All of us listened to loads of music, all different, including punk stuff, and each band picked up on different influences and developed it in the Brighton scene. We all went to watch each other play constantly too, and I think this may have encouraged us to develop really strong musical styles of our own."

Songs grounded in domesticity and everyday observation were key to the Chefs' dynamic. "They were based on personal experience, whichever member of the band was writing them. Right from the very first EP, with songs co-written by the original drummer, Rod Bloor, while 'Lets Make Up' was co-written with a girl called Tracy Preston who sang with the Molesters and was in a pre-Chefs band called the Smartees."

They contributed two of their earliest recordings, 'Food' and 'You Get Everywhere' to the Vaultage 1979 compilation, before the aforementioned four-track EP. In an attempt to build on the popularity of the EP they moved up to London. The subsequent '24 Hours' remains a defining moment, a joyous, charming ode to obsessional love. "I know if I catch you it might turn out/That it's not as much fun as I'd hoped that it would be/'Cos wishing and waiting is what it's all about/And dreams are worth ten times more than reality." Buddy Holly meets Billie Holliday. So who was the subject of '24 Hours'? "The subject of 24 Hours existed," McCookerybook confirms. "There is a clue as to who he is in the sleevenotes of the Helen and the Horns album, but you might have had to be around at the time to pick up on it."

'24 Hours' became a John Peel favourite, but not without some strategic intervention by the band. McCookerybook: "We had been having photos done by a food photographer, strangely enough, and another band had told us you could meet John Peel by going along to the BBC at 9.45 just before he did his show. So our manager (Jonathan Chrisp) and myself stood outside waiting, and sure enough he came along and invited us up into the studio with him, took the record and played it on his show live, there and then. I was so embarrassed I talked all over it but he told me to be quiet because he really liked it – and played it every night after that for weeks. What a gem."

But despite a fair slab of critical admiration, the Chefs never did make it. Bad luck, or bad decisions? "Bad luck and too much alcohol. We signed to Graduate for a ridiculously small advance and they didn't know what to do with us. At one stage one of their guys helpfully suggested that I should wear make-up all the time. We had a lot of interest from Pete

Waterman but he wanted us to sack Bruv (my brother) and Carl (brilliant songwriter) so that just didn't happen. What was I going to do with just a drummer and no guitarists? We met up with all sorts of glamorous producers too but nothing came of that."

The highlight of their misadventure with Graduate came shortly before they signed, and they would have done well to take it as an omen. "Graduate had come to see us play in a draughty church hall before signing us. They had a brand new BMW bought with the profits from their success with UB40. They came to our horrible house for a chat after the gig, giving me a lift, and parked outside; meanwhile the rest of the band had all piled into our van with my friends from home sitting in the back peering out of the back windows. As we sat in their car, the cruddy old Chefs van started reversing towards us at high speed – the Graduate people started yelling. At which point Jonathan fell out of the van, he'd been leaning out of it to see as he reversed, and the van ran over him, backwards! It stopped millimetres away from the brand new BMW with my friend's faces frozen in shock in the back window. Russell had fallen on the brake and stopped the van just seconds before it crashed into the BMW and before the second wheel could run over Jonathan (he'd had the steering wheel at full lock). Jonathan was fine – I went and sat in hospital with him but his ribs had just 'bent' a bit. I suppose we might have wanted to have some sort of cool image before we signed our deal, but there was no chance. I just wonder if anyone else has ever managed to run themselves over!"

After changing their name to Skat in 1982 ("which was suicide") they recorded a third and final session for John Peel. A cover of the Velvet Underground's 'Femme Fatale' for Graduate followed, but they then broke up. McCallum formed Helen and the Horns, featuring Dave Jago, Marc Jordan and Paul Davey, who cut records for RCA, Thin Sliced and Rockin' Ray. After that finished she released a 12-inch EP, 'Leaving You Baby', on Pure Trash Records. Evans put together Yip Yip Coyote (again loved by Peel). He would later marry Michelle Archer of Brigandage fame. Greenwood spent some time with the Parrots and then joined the Popticians. He died in 2003 from a brain haemorrhage.

Helen Reddington, as she is now known, has been a regular turn at the Edinburgh Festival for several years, writing the music and libretto and playing in the band for a pantomime version of Titus Andronicus that played "to two nuns and a Scotsman reviewer". Her most recent production was Voxpop Puella, a multi-media show that looked at the 'seven ages of women' and she's just completed a thesis detailing, in academic terms, some of those formative experiences in Brighton. She also returned to live performance for a series of shows beginning in September 2004 and announced plans for a Chefs/Helen and the Horns compilation CD. I asked her if, like so many of her peers, she remains indelibly altered by her experiences in the punk wars. "Yes, yes, yes. I have never changed from that and never will. What a liberating thing to just be able to get up on stage and do it all without stupid music teachers getting in the way with their rules, and without record companies excluding you before you'd even played a note! Makes you feel you can try anything at any time, and makes you want to encourage other people to be like that too."

DISCOGRAPHY:

Sweetie/Thrush/Records And Tea/Someone I Know 7-inch EP (Attrix RB 10 1980)
24 Hours/Thrush 7-inch (Graduate GRAD 11 1980)
24 Hours/Let's Make Up/Someone I Know 7-inch (Attrix RB 13 1981)
COMPILATIONS:
Vaultage 1979 (Another Two Sides Of Brighton) LP (Attrix RB 08 1979; 'You Get Everywhere', ' Food')
Vaultage Punk Collection CD (Anagram CDPUNK 101 1997; 'Sweetie', 'Thrush', '24 Hours', 'Let's Make Up')

Chelsea

Gene October (aka John O'Hara; vocals), Billy Idol (guitar), Tony James (bass), John Towe (drums)

It is ironic, is it not, that the Premiership's most upwardly mobile and filthy rich football club, and one of the most exclusive areas of West London, should share their name with one of punk's most terminally unfashionable brands. To admit to a scintilla of respect for the lifetime achievements of Gene October and co is to

Gene October of Chelsea, live at the Marquee.

commit heresy. Even the UK Subs are routinely afforded greater respect. Of course, it's easy to dislike a guy who is as mouthy and opinionated as Gene, but his band's recordings are not without merit.

Although **CHELSEA** were and are October's baby, the story overlaps with that of Generation X in their early days. Billy Idol had quit Sussex University in 1976. In Brighton he'd been a member of the Rockettes, a garage band that also featured Rob Harper on drums (he'd later play on the Anarchy tour with the Clash). The Rockettes gave Malcolm McLaren a demo tape, which he dismissed, but a relationship was established between Idol, still travelling under the name Billy Broad, and the Sex Pistols' camp.

The Clash link was important too. It was Mick Jones who suggested to his erstwhile London SS partner Tony James he should hook up with Idol. Gene October, already a fabled figure on the emerging punk scene, and drummer John Towe, also formerly of London SS, would complete the initial line-up. October had been trying to get a band together for some time, and had tapped up Marco Pirroni about becoming his musical collaborator, before placing the advert in the Melody Maker ("Musicians Wanted, Into Television and Rock'n'roll") which Broad replied to. Auditions took place somewhere under a railway arch in South London and when Broad had secured the gig, he suggested Tony James as the band's bass player (other versions suggest that both Broad and James applied for the Chelsea job independently). At the time, neither had met October.

Informally managed by John Krivine and his assistant Steph Raynor, who ran ACME Attractions on the King's Road in competition to McLaren's Sex boutique, the name Chelsea was adopted in reference to the area's role in the Swinging Sixties. Or so they said at the time. Later, speaking to American magazine Flipside, October would state that "Chelsea sums up that concept (of punk), the spirit of the beginning of the whole thing, where it was born, the fashion thing and everything, it was born in Chelsea. That's where Seditionaries is, where Malcolm McLaren first got the Pistols together, where I met my first manager, where the Damned met up, and the Clash. That's where all the little shops sprang up. It's like there's a Greenwich Village where everyone hangs out, that's Chelsea." James maintains that the band was Krivine's direct attempt to keep pace with McLaren's manoeuvres with the Pistols. James and Broad began to write songs together, practising in one of the workrooms on Portobello Road where Krivine had clothes made for Acme Attractions. However, most of the songs they came up with, including 'Ready Steady Go' and 'This Heat', would be taken with them when they split camp to form Generation X.

The fact is that October was a bag of contradictions and remains so, arguably not helped by the number of hallucinogenics he'd taken in the early-70s. In a fanzine interview with New Wave News printed in 1977, he would posit that the band were champions of "the poor, the underdog and the loner". His songs, meanwhile, were intended to "convey the anger, frustration and struggle of his colourful life". At times like this he came across like Jimmy Pursey's less media-savvy younger brother. Totally committed to the cause, of course, but you just knew that he'd happily swap that cause for another one without a second thought if it offered a better chance of substantiating his ego. For all that, he was a great live performer, with a distinctive vocal style, even if his appearances over recent years have become increasingly erratic. Encouraging your audience to smash the hall to pieces, and then bemoaning the lack of venues for punk bands, was not a particularly smart move in 1976. Doing the same 25 years later is decidedly dumb.

Chelsea's 'official' live debut came at the end of 1976 when they served as support act to Coum Transmissions famed Prostitution exhibition at the ICA on 18 October, though October maintains that they'd earlier played sets, primarily of Stones' covers, at the Chelsea Potter pub on the King's Road. Genesis P-Orridge, the leader of Throbbing Gristle (aka Coum Transmissions) and also managed by Krivine, booked them under the name LSD on the basis that "everybody hated hippies then". It ended up with questions in the house when the event descended into violence and recrimination – the loveable Cosi tearing up pictures from porn mags she'd appeared in and throwing them from the stage, much to the self-flagellating ire of a Conservative MP who'd got wind of events. The prototype line-up of Chelsea managed just two further gigs, supporting the Buzzcocks at Manchester's Electric Circus and backing the Stranglers at the Nashville on 21 November, at which October and his band "had a little tiff". Both Broad and James had grown uncomfortable around October, so when they encored they told him they were playing a new song they'd written, 'Prove It', and that he was surplus to requirements.

Broad had grown resentful of his role as second fiddle to October. Well, that's one theory. Another has it that a writing team had sprung up which their lead vocalist was separate to and envious of, and he wanted rid of anyone who was going to interfere with his ascent to stardom. So the trio upped and left their vocalist as sole proprietor of Chelsea, and to his credit he took the mass exit on the chin.

But October wasn't about to give up, despite the head start he'd conceded. He switched manager to Andy Czezowski and a new line-up of Chelsea was assembled featuring former Stranglers' roadie Carey Fortune on drums, with Martin Stacey, who would stay long enough to write 'Hi-Rise Living', and Bob Jessie joining briefly on guitar and bass. This incarnation of the band played support to the Clash at the Roxy but managed little else. When it became clear that it wasn't working out, October and Stacey brought in James Stevenson (ex-Inner City) on guitar. He'd been hanging around the Roxy while doing his A-levels and was already a fan of the band. Henry Badowski (aka Henry Daze) also joined on bass to cement Chelsea's first stable line-up in March 1977. Badowski: "My friend James Stevenson had joined Chelsea and I asked him if they needed a bass player. He had a tape and I learned the bass lines. I'd barely picked up a bass guitar in my life, so it was truly incredible to be thrown into the punk thing at its height."

They set about building a reputation as a live band and they initially attracted some admiring glances, playing alongside the Boys, Cortinas, Sham 69 and others. Mark Perry, who had set up Step Forward Records in consort with Miles Copeland, offered them some studio time. Indeed, Chelsea would become, by some considerable margin, Step Forward's most prolific act. The firstborn of this new coalition was 'Right To Work', one of the most widely misconstrued records in punk history. It was initially assumed by many that the song signalled October's indignation at rising unemployment. Then it became apparent that there was a strong anti-union thrust to the lyric. The truth behind its inspiration, however, was that Gene October, bless him, was venting his spleen at being denied an Equity Card. After all, he'd put in the hard slog. He'd appeared in a raft of low-budget gay porn films. There are hundreds of stories about October. I got a couple of good ones from Faebhean Kwest of Raped. "One time we were in a bar, and Gene says, 'If you let me touch you while I have a wank, I'll give you a fiver.' He still owes me that fiver." Or the time that some of his friends found some publicity materials relating to a porn flick that October had appeared in. So they photocopied them and plastered them all over the venue that Chelsea were appearing at that night, the Chelsea Potter. Only for the promoter to come out and plead with them to take them down before his dad, who owned the venue, saw them.

However, Faebhean also points out that at one stage, Chelsea really were thought of as being on the same level as the Pistols and the Clash, and were hugely important to the punk scene that sprang up around the King's Road. Yet, as Badowski points out, 'Right To Work' was a song that was recorded prior to he or James' involvement in the band. "I was involved in two recorded versions of 'Right To Work' – the version recorded for Derek Jarman's Jubilee film, plus the John Peel session version from July 1977. Neither James nor I played on the single version although we are credited as having done so. It had been recorded by the previous line-up before we arrived. I was never that keen on 'Right To Work' as I actually enjoyed being on the dole – plus I preferred the more arty/outrageous/irreverent aspects of the punk thing to the serious political side. My favourite Chelsea song was 'Curfew' (never released at the time) as it pounded along relentlessly. I remember being impressed by it when James first played me the tape. It was based on a four-chord loop, which gave it a hypnotic, pulverising effect. It was dead easy to play as well. 'Right To Work' was a dreary lump in comparison."

Badowski was present at the band's 'farewell' gig in October 1977. "I remember Chelsea being supported by a group called the Makers, who apparently turned out to be an early incarnation of Spandau Ballet! I sat on my amp for that one. James and I weren't told that after our brief set a new, more exuberant version of Chelsea, still with Gene on vocals, would storm the stage with lots of glammy hair and pouting power pop. James and I sloped off to continue the Mysterons project, which lasted one gig at the 100 Club supporting Alternative TV after which our bass player left to become a ballet student. James then rejoined Chelsea so it wasn't really a 'farewell' gig, more an excuse to showcase the new line-up." He was only with Chelsea for a short time, but Badowski maintains that "I've never had so many life-changing experiences in such a short space of time. It seemed as though each day provided another piece of popular music history taking shape around me. There are several key moments which will stay with me for ever: Shortly after joining Chelsea I ended up living in a squat in the New King's Road with a girl from New York and her Stooges LPs, which enhanced my whole 'punk' experience. I remember walking into the Man in the Moon pub and experiencing an unsigned X-Ray Spex in full screech – incredible. Or supporting Wayne County on my first gig. A glorious baptism – outrageous!"

Badowski, who would join first Wreckless Eric, playing saxophone, King and then the reformed Damned, was replaced by Simon Vitesse, who was in place for their second single, the competent if unexceptional tower block rock of 'Hi-Rise Living'. The 'glam' apparition of Chelsea was part of October's plans to put together "the ultimate teeny-bop band", which also travelled under the name Love And Kisses. But this misbegotten project came to nothing and he and Stevenson instigated a new line-up of Chelsea, featuring Geoff Myles, formerly of Stromtrooper, on bass, Dave Martin (briefly of Glen Matlock's Rich Kids and Peroxide Romance) on guitar. The new drummer was Stevenson's former Inner City Unit colleague Steve J Jones. This line-up gigged heavily in the early months of 1978, including dates at the Marquee, Roundhouse and the 100 Club. There was a succession of dates with the Clash and the Specials, and a second Peel session, recorded in July 1978, as well as the Kit Lambert-produced single 'Urban Kids', written for them by Mark Perry. After which Chris Bashford (ex-Swank and the Bazoomis) replaced Jones on drums.

It was 1979 by the time their self-titled debut album was released, and most of their peers were long since up to their second or even third efforts. Miles Copeland's energies were focused on the increasingly successful Police and poor old Chelsea had ground to make up. Reviews were tempered with a growing cynicism about the way punk had evolved. Which is possibly why what is essentially a solid effort is routinely overlooked. 'I'm On Fire' is particularly worthy of note in this regard, but the album houses at least four first-rate punkers, and the cover of Jimmy Cliff's 'Many Rivers To Cross' isn't quite as excruciating as it looks on paper. Incidentally, if you look closely at the cover, there's a tyre track mark across Dave Martin's face. The courier delivering the artwork had run over it by mistake but hadn't told his bosses, or client, for fear of being sacked.

A second album, again produced by Who veteran Kit Lambert, Alternative Hits (titled No Escape for its American release), failed to readdress Chelsea's standing with critics. In essence it was more or less a collection of previously released singles, including both sides of their first 45, which had escaped inclusion on their debut album. 'I'm On Fire'/'Decide' was issued in the US to try to drum up interest (I'm On Fire' was a song originally recorded by Myles, aka Jeff Piccinni, and his former band Stormtrooper in 1978), while 'No One's Coming Outside' and 'Look At The Outside' were issued in Britain. The latter was promoted by a show at the Notre Dame Hall in London where Sting guested on bass for a couple of songs.

But by now the critics were really on their case, as Stevenson recalled to punk77. "We never got the credit we deserved. I'll stand by any of the records we made and I don't think they have dated that badly. The music papers at that time gave us an absolute hammering and we had few allies. I can remember when we were going up to a gig in Leeds and the hotel was raided and (we were) pulled out of our beds at six in the morning. We thought we'd mention it to the NME to get a bit in the gossip column. They wrote instead that the police were probably trying to stop us playing! It's funny now but back then we were getting it all the time. Really nasty."

In the aftermath of Alternative Hits' commercial failure and the critical barbs that accompanied any mention of their name in the press, Chelsea disbanded again. Martin departed to play with Pink Military while Stevenson kept the band's historical traditions consistent by moving over to Generation X. Subsequent to which he's played with everyone from Kim Wilde to Tricky and Jimmy Nail. Dave Martin and Geoff Myles put together the Smart, who issued one single, 'This Time' for Complex Records, and toured the US twice as support to Orchestral Manoeuvres In The Dark and Iggy Pop.

Chris Bashford was initially retained as October fulfilled commitments including London shows, as well as a brief US tour filmed for Ugh! A Music War, before he too bailed in December. He eventually became a graphic designer (having put together the sleeve for Alternative Hits). October brought in Nic Austin, who'd been a long-term fan of the band through their embryonic years, on guitar, alongside a second guitarist Stephen Corfield, bass player Sol Mintz (aka Malcolm Aisling) and bass player Tim Griffin. The new line-up made its debut at London's Gossips on 7 January 1981 before hitting the road again. This line-up were responsible for a couple of so-so singles, 'Rockin' Horse' and the singularly odd 'Freeman's'. After which Griffin bowed out. With a show booked at the Fulham Greyhound, Sting helped out, before a permanent replacement was found in Paul 'Linc'.

The fiery 'Evacuate', based around the then endemic anxiety about prospective nuclear war, saw Linc make his debut. It was a great little number, not that October wholly endorsed the sentiments, famously deriding the anti-war movement at, of all things, a CND benefit in Brixton in the early-80s. Somewhere along the line he'd misread the script and decided being contrarian about everything was a substitute for taking a view. By the time of the band's subsequent tour with Southern Death Cult, Corfield too had departed.

On 'War Across The Nation' and the band's third album, also titled Evacuate, the main songwriter and arranger was Austin. The album is for the most part a success, bolstered by clearer production than many of their other records were afforded. It should have restored them at least to parity with the younger upstarts, with whom they were now frequently touring, but by now the punk scene had fractured into three separate splinter groups – new punk, as exemplified by the Exploited and GBH, Oi! bands such as the 4-Skins and the anarcho movement led by Crass. Chelsea failed to fit into any of these categories, yet they shared billing with members of each faction as they stubbornly refused to face their mortality. By the time of the album's release, Aisling had hooked up with the UK Subs and Geoff Sewell was their bass player, as they joined the Anti-Nowhere League, Defects and Chron Gen on the So What UK package tour.

After a final single for Step Forward, 'Stand Out', the line-up disintegrated again as Austin moved over to Bandits At 4 O'Clock and Linc joined Beki Bondage in Ligotage. October responded by issuing a couple of truly unremarkable solo singles ('Suffering In The Land' and 'Don't Quit') before trawling around London for yet another line-up. This time the lucky incumbents were Davey Jones on guitar, Pete Dimmock (ex-Chron Gen; bass) and a returning Geoff Sewell on drums. That line-up lasted long enough to cut a live album Live And Well before Tim Briffa replaced Davey on guitar.

The mid-80s produced three more singles, the most notable of which was 'Valium

Mother', and an album for Jungle Records, Rocks Off, which is notable for the ambitious 'Fool's Paradise', but is a failure in every other respect. Amazingly enough, they washed up back with Miles Copeland and IRS for their 1989 collection Underwraps, which featured the Clash's Topper Headon on two tracks. One of those was 'Let The Good Times Roll', which also featured former Police guitarist Henry Padovani. There's a cover of the Clash's 'Someone Got Murdered' which isn't too bad. But this was essentially a retread of their (limited) former glories.

Surprisingly, 1993's The Alternative was a vast improvement, primarily due to the fact that Austin was back on board and piloting a ship which October was doing his best to run aground. However, you can safely ignore most of their subsequent recordings without fear of compromising your standard of cultural life. And on they went, inexorably, veterans and inveterates of the punk rehabilitation circuit.

There was an ill-fated Social Chaos tour of America in 1999 featuring first-album principals Stevenson, Myles, Martin and Bashford. It was a good opportunity to ditch their day jobs. October had been working behind a bar in the West Country, Myles was a video cameraman, Martin had worked as a courier (oh, the irony!) before sadly developing Multiple Sclerosis, which saw the tour curtailed. More recently October has been sighted working the bins. As Stevenson later recalled, "in spite of the fiasco that was Social Chaos, we had a good time. We enjoyed playing together again and started talking then about making a new studio album. But we needed songs, time and money." As he suggested, it would take a while for those plans to come to fruition.

As it happened, Chelsea did make a comeback with a good album, 2005's Faster, Cheaper And Better Looking. OK, so only the middle part of that title may have stood up to scrutiny, but a revamped line-up, featuring Stevenson, Bashford and the Buzzcocks' Tony Barber, who since 1999 had been playing as stand-in bass player for Myles who'd returned to San Francisco, sounded great. Perhaps the lyrics hadn't improved dramatically, although Bashford's 'Cosy Family Way' is pretty funny, and there's some affecting nostalgia in '45 RPM' and 'If We Knew Then'. But the sound was pretty pumping, especially Stevenson's elephant stampede chord work, which never did get the credit it deserved.

DISCOGRAPHY:

(Buyer's Guide: The band's self-titled debut is the place to start. Alternative Hits was essentially a collection of singles, so try Evacuate next and pick up one of the more comprehensive anthologies, probably Captain Oi!'s Punk Singles Collection, if you want to cover that angle. The BBC Punk Sessions offers an alternative insight, and if you want a one-stop introduction, try Sanctuary's Anthology. Faster, Cheaper And Better Looking isn't going to change anyone's opinion about the band, but it far outstrips anything post-Evacuate in their catalogue)

Right To Work/The Loner 7-inch (Step Forward SF 2 June 1977)

High Rise Living/No Admission 7-inch (Step Forward SF 5 December 1977)

Urban Kids/No Flowers 7-inch (Step Forward SF 8 August 1978)

Chelsea LP (Step Forward SFLP 5 November 1980) (reissued on Captain Oi!, AHOY CD 91, 1998, featuring bonus tracks: Urban Kids (demo), No Escape (demo), Twelve Men (demo), All The Downs (demo))

No-One's Coming Outside/What Would You Do? 7-inch (Step Forward SF 14 February 1980)

I'm On Fire/Decide 7-inch (IRS 9004 February 1980; US only)

Look At The Outside/Don't Get Me Wrong 7-inch (Step Forward SF 15 April 1980)

No Escape/Decide 7-inch (Step Forward SF 16 July 1980)

Alternative Hits LP (Step Forward SFLP 5 November 1980) (retitled No Escape in America. Reissued on Captain Oi!, AHOY CD 92, 1998, featuring bonus tracks: High Rise Living and No Admission, plus sleevenotes compiled by Mark Brennan with the help of James Stevenson)

Rockin' Horse/Tears Away 7-inch (Step Forward SF 17 April 1981)

Freeman's/ID Parade/How Do You Know? 7-inch (Step Forward SF 18 August 1981)

Evacuate/New Era 7-inch (Step Forward SF 20 November 1981)

War Across The Nation/High Rise Living (remix) 7-inch (Step Forward SF 21 March 1982)

Evacuate LP (Step Forward SFLP 7 April 1982) (reissued on Captain Oi!, AHOY CD 94, 1998, featuring bonus tracks: Rockin' Horse/Years Away /Freemans/I.D.Parade/How Do You Know (Single Version)/New Era/ War Across The Nation (Single Version) /Stand Out. This time Nic Austin helps Monsieur Brennan out on the sleevenotes).

Stand Out/Last Drink 7-inch (Step Forward SF 22 October 1982)
Live And Well LP (Picasso PIK 003 May 1984) (reissued on CD in November 1993 by Great Expectations, PIP CD 056, and also Punx, PUNXCD 1, in October 1995. And what the hell, one more time in 2001, on Rhythm Vicar PREACH 003)
Valium Mother/Monica, Monica 7-inch (Communique LITTLE 1 June 1985) (also released as a 12-inch, 12 LITTLE 1, with bonus track 'Break This Town')
Original Sinners LP (Communique LARGE 1August 1985)
Shine The Light/Believe Me 7-inch (Communique LITTLE 2 March 1986)
Rocks Off LP (Jungle FREUD November 1986) (reissued on CD, apparently in Japan only, in 1994, Jimco JICK-89357)
Give Me More/Sympathy For The Devil 7-inch (Chelsea CH 001 May 1988)
Underwraps LP & CD (IRS EIRSA CD 1011 June 1989) (also issued on cassette. Reissued on CD in October 1994 on Weser, WL 24662)
The Alternative CD (Alter-Ego ALTGO CD 002) (also issued in Germany in digpack, Weser, 2466-2)
Traitors Gate CD (Weser WL 2480-2 August 1994)
We Dare 7-inch (Weser WL 2482-7 May 1995) (some copies in white vinyl)
Faster, Cheaper And Better Looking CD (Captain Oi! September 2005)
ARCHIVE RELEASES:
Chelsea Live cassette (Chaos Cassettes Live 005 1982)
Side A: Live At The Marquee Side B: Live In Norwich 22/10/81 (a dodgy, pseudo "bootleg the bootleggers" type effort supposedly limited to 3,000 copies. Yeah...)
Just For The Record LP (Step Forward SFLP 10 May 1985)
Backtrax LP (Illegal ILP 024 September 1988)
Unreleased Stuff CD (Clay CLAY LP 101 1989) (reissued on CD, CLAY CD 101 in May 1993 and July 1994)
Live At The Music Machine 1978 CD (Released Emotions REM 016 CD March 1992) (Recorded live in 1978. Limited edition of 1,000 copies. Later reissued, as Live And Loud!, by Harry May, MAYO CD 558, in 2004)
Fools And Soldiers CD (Receiver RRCD 242 July 1997) (a typical Receiver release, in that some of it is useless and replicates better versions of songs freely available elsewhere, while this is a unique hiding place for covers of 'Route 66', which also featured on an October solo album, and the Animals' 'Bring It On Home To Me'. Whether the fact that these recordings are unique makes them in any other way meaningful is another issue entirely)
Punk Singles Collection 1977-82 CD (Captain Oi! AHOY CD 98 1998) (pretty straightforward introduction, but it does include full line-up details, which is handy given Chelsea's propensity for 'losing' their musicians)
Punk Rock Rarities CD (Captain Oi! AHOY CD 106 1999) (put together with the co-operation of Chelsea guitarist James Stevenson, this features 19 studio tracks the band cut between 1977 and 1980, including their first ever demo)
The BBC Punk Sessions 1977-1979 CD (Captain Oi! AHOY CD 159 2002) (handy package contained both Peel sessions, plus a 1978 session for Kid Jensen and a 1979 session for Mike Read. The final nine tracks come from a September 1979 BBC In Concert broadcast from the Paris Theatre in Regent Street. James Stevenson provides the sleevenotes, and apologises for his bum notes during 'Twelve Men', but the sound is excellent)
Metallic F.O. CD (Red Steel RMC PG 9224 2002)
Urban Kids – A Punk Rock Anthology double CD (Sanctuary CMEDD1027 January 2005) (OK, but you're probably better off with the singles collection)

Chimes

Ade Oakley (vocals, guitar), Daryn Price (drums), Mick Jefferys (bass), Peter Taylor (guitar)

Portsmouth band the CHIMES were formed in 1979 by lifelong friends Oakley and Price. Mick Jefferys, another school pal, and mutual friend Peter Taylor subsequently joined on bass and guitar respectively. By their own admission, they were not the most accomplished of musicians initially, with Taylor learning to play lead guitar on the hoof while Oakley concentrated on rhythm. Prior to this, Oakley had been a member of proto Portsmouth punks the Boasters and the Precautions. The latter had recorded a demo tape, but Oakley became frustrated with the lack of commitment to a DIY ideal shown by the other members. Hence the Chimes, the name adapted from a Portsmouth FC terrace chant.

By 1980 the Chimes had three tracks included on the South Specific compilation of

Portsmouth bands issued on local independent, Brain Boosters Records, alongside Attic, the Frames, Dance Attack (X), Nice Boys and oddball duo Renaldo And The Loaf, who later collaborated extensively with the Residents. This was quite an idealistic effort, featuring a sleeve note acknowledging the Desperate Bicycles' dictum "If you can understand, form a band." Six of the eight bands shared the costs, with invitations extended to two others who simply did not have the finances to pay their share, after they submitted demo tapes. It was to be the Chimes' only official vinyl release, although between 1979 and 1983 several DIY cassettes were recorded. These may eventually see release on the Hyped 2 Death label, or they may not. It just depends. Time, money, those sorts of things.

Taylor was replaced on guitar by Barry Hepple in 1981 and Jeffreys by Nic Allen in 1982. "I can't remember how we got in touch with Barry," Oakley tells me, "but he was an accomplished guitar player who totally changed the band's sound and gave us a more commercial direction." The Chimes' last performance was at Leigh Park Community Centre, a punk festival, at the start of 1983. Oakley notes that they never played outside of Portsmouth in their four-year life span, but he and Daryn would make amends for that in his subsequent long-running venture Red Letter Day, one of the hardest gigging bands on the south coast. Or anywhere really. Two Chimes songs, 'Pictures' and 'Triangle', would survive the transition to Red Letter Day, with the former included on their 1986 John Peel session.

COMPILATION:

South Specific LP (Brain Boosters Lobotomy 01 August 1980; 'Through To You', 'I Can't Smile', 'Who Do I Believe')
Pictures In The Snow cassette (Brain Boosters 1982)

Clash

Joe Strummer (aka John Mellor; vocals, guitar), Mick Jones (vocals, guitar), Paul Simonon (bass, vocals), Terry Chimes (drums), Keith Levene (guitar)

It's way past the point where anything worthwhile to be said about the CLASH has already been aired, alongside a fair amount that isn't. There are over a dozen books on the subject and it seems to be a growing literary genre. In the wake of Joe Strummer's death, it's apparent that there was a huge reservoir of affection for the band that was just simmering away while its participants got on with their lives, post-Clash.

Rather than the traditional drugs or ego fuelled personality disorders, Strummer's demons came in the form of record companies and the music business. He did indeed hold legitimate gripes, though some of the perceived wounds were self-inflicted. It's obvious that some form of musical accommodation between Strummer and Jones was on the cards when he died, unexpectedly, in 2002. But we'll never know for sure. In any case, the canonisation of Saint Joe continues apace, much of it a little icky. It's all very well the likes of Bono paying tribute, but when Elton John starts talking about the "huge importance" of your work in Interview magazine, sorry, but having the Pinner pianist wank on your bones means you're in deep do-do. Joe Strummer as the Lady Di of punk? Poor bugger doesn't need that.

The Clash was very much more than one man, though. Indeed, they positively revelled in a gang ethos and much has been made of the fraternal bonds at the heart of the Clash. As Martin James, who attended their early shows behind his parents' back, wrote for the Independent, "They made us – their hormonally challenged disciples – feel like we were also part of the same gang. They were, they argued, the same as us and everything about them portrayed an us-against-them attitude." The family vibe was important to the band itself. Both Jones and Simonon saw their parents divorce, while Strummer was packed off to boarding school and hated almost every moment of it. When they worked as a unit they were near untouchable. When that chemistry and ethos broke down, they were very mortal indeed.

After years of knocking at the door, and having his door knocked upon, it gradually dawned upon Mick Jones that London SS, managed by the combative idealogue Bernie Rhodes, were treading water. His travails in that band are explored elsewhere in this book. Although ostensibly a waste of everyone's time, their rehearsals did enable Jones to make the acquaintance of Keith Levene, and later, Paul Simonon, who'd just dropped out of his course at the Byam Shaw School of Drawing and Painting. He'd tagged along to a London SS audition with friend Roland Hot and tried, unsuccessfully, to sing 'Roadrunner'. "But what's really strange," Simonon later recalled to Scott Rowley, "is that there was a guy in the corner, who was Bernie Rhodes, and my first words to him were, 'Are you their manager?' And he was like: 'Why? What's it to you?' So I was like (shrugs) 'Fair enough'. And then a couple of days later he told Mick to sack his group and get a group together with me."

Jones and Levene, a former Yes roadie, became friends and musical collaborators. "Mick had about five songs at that time," the forthright Levene would later tell Sean Egan, "but until I came along and added my bit to it, and added my sound to it, they sounded like shit." Jones proposed Simonon, the guy he'd met at that London SS rehearsals. He looked the part, even if he wasn't much of a musician. Later, Jones would tell Clash magazine that "I was very keen on, as an idea, Stuart Sutcliffe (of the Beatles). He didn't even know how to play very well, but he was a fantastic painter and he brought something else to the band as well. I was aware of that... (but) I don't think we'd have done very good if none of us could have played nothing – it would have been awful!"

Initially Jones attempted to teach Simonon some guitar chords at his nan's flat in a tower block off Harrow Road, but it proved painfully obvious that Simonon was not divinely encumbered with musical talent. So Jones bought him a bass guitar instead, and invited him to move in to the group's adopted Davis Street squat. Initially they tried out a singer named Billy Watts, remembered by those around as a "Mick Jagger wannabe", and took the name Young Colts. There was also talk of NME writer Chrissie Hynde fronting the band. At one point in time, there was talk of Chrissie Hynde fronting every band in London.

Meanwhile John 'Woody' Mellor was beginning to make some headway with the 101ers. He's already played in bands as long ago as 1972, when he was a member of the Vultures in Newport. "Noisy, brash and fun," long-time friend and Newport art school student Allan Jones recalled. In fact, a tape of pre-Vultures 1973 recordings was unearthed in 2004, which included 'Bumble Bee Blues', and Mellor attempting to play slide guitar.

The 101ers, their name taken from their squat at 101 Walterton Road in Maida Hill, featured guitarist Clive Timperley, bass player Dan Kelleher and drummer Richard Dudanski. Their first gigs came at the Charlie Pigdog Club, upstairs at W9 pub The Chippenham. They'd begun to write their own material but still relied heavily on R&B standards, as they tried to work their ticket alongside other pub rock vouchsafes such as Dr Feelgood and Eddie And The Hot Rods. He acquired his Telecaster via the largesse of a South American woman, Pam, whose visa had expired and needed to marry a Briton to stay in the country (she eventually came forward to confirm the story when it was reported in a British newspaper). Other funds were sourced from the dole and a part-time job emptying the rubbish at the Royal Opera House.

Feelgoods' producer Vic Maile looked them up in November 1975 to offer them a demo session. Bolstered by the partisan reporting of Mellor's old friend Allan Jones, who'd landed a job at the Melody Maker, the 101ers were eventually offered a record contract with Chiswick. It resulted in the release of 'Keys To Your Heart', backed by 'Five Star Rock'n'roll'. But by the time it actually reached the shops, the 101ers were no more.

Strummer attributed the transformation of his musical horizons to the 101ers playing two shows supported by the Sex Pistols at West Kensington's Nashville Rooms. As he recalled to Sean Egan: "Suddenly, the boot was on the other foot. A cog in the universe had shifted there. They were the only new thing that had been seen in London within living memory." Reviewing the first of those shows in the Melody Maker, Allan Jones called Strummer "one of the most vivid and exciting figures currently treading the boards," but dismissed the Pistols. The embryonic Clash, meanwhile, had caught the 101ers at the Red Cow in early 1976. The next day Jones and Simonon, and Jones's then girlfriend Viv Albertine, with whom he was sharing the Davis Road squat between stints at his gran's, were waiting to sign on at Lisson Grove when they saw the singer in the queue next to them. They didn't speak. Glen Matlock has also claimed that Jones first met Strummer when he bumped into a bunch of soon to be famous punks and got them in to see Tom Waits at Ronnie Scott's.

Bernie Rhodes had checked Mellor out too and approached him at a Pistols show at the 100 Club, asking for his phone number. He wanted him to meet Jones, Levene and Simonon. However, when he rang his Orsett Terrace squat, where Mickey Foote had managed to install

a telephone, 101ers bass player Dan Kelleher answered. He pretended to be Mellor in order to discover what was afoot, so Mellor's subsequent defection could hardly have been a surprise. Rhodes and Levene then took in a 101ers show at the Golden Lion in Fulham. After Levene convinced Rhodes that this was their man, Rhodes took Mellor outside and asked him to join the embryonic Clash.

Mellor was invited round to the band's rehearsal place at Davis Road, where the somewhat awed Mick Jones and Paul Simonon were waiting. "We were sitting in the living room area, me and Mick," Simonon later recalled, "then Keith turns up with Joe. So we go into the rehearsal room, which is a box, about five foot by five foot, it was cramped. We wasn't exactly jumping around in there… Mick played a couple of songs and then Joe played one, we alternated back and forth… The fact that he'd turned up, that made a statement, well, this is it, we're going from here onwards together. That was the first day of the Clash." "They were kind of already doing it," Strummer recalled to Egan, "Simmo, Keith Levene and Mick Jones, and what they really lacked was someone to give it a front. A front guy or a lyric writer. They were a jigsaw waiting for the piece to fall in." Bernie Rhodes asked his friend Glen Matlock what he thought of his new recruit. "'He's alright,' I said, 'but he's a bit old.' 'Don't you worry about that,' said Bernie. 'I'll have 10 years off him.' And he was right, he did. Next time I saw Joe he looked maybe not 10 years younger, but certainly a totally different man and ready to rock."

Mellor returned to tell his former bandmates that the 101ers were no more. And he was taking their soundman Mickey Foote with him. He invited Dudanski to join the new band, but there was no way Dudanski could put up with Bernie Rhodes' patter – which included a tentative idea for the band to mount a fake armed robbery in pursuit of publicity. He would not be the last potential Clash drummer to find Rhodes' blowtorch rhetoric discomforting. As Dudanski sagely pointed out to Uncut, while promoting the re-release of the 101ers Elgin Avenue Breakdown Revisited, for which he did the sleevenotes: "The point where the 101ers were when we split was very close to where the Clash got to." There is some truth in that.

Thereafter Strummer eschewed any involvement with his former pub rock brethren. In what would become a familiar Clash 'dusting' operation, the chapter was closed. In his new band he would wear a T-shirt with the legend "Chuck Berry Is Dead", when a few months earlier he'd been ripping through covers of 'Maybelline'. The 101ers set list also included Beatles and Elvis standbys ('Back In The USSR' and 'Heartbreak Hotel'), in contrast to the infamous year zero lyrics of '1977'. There were some other important throwbacks to the 101ers. 'White Riot' partially updated the 'Keys To Your Heart' riff'. 'Jail Guitar Doors' owed its genesis to a former 101ers number, 'Lonely Mother's Son'. Sandinista's 'Junco Partner' also dated back to the 101ers set, while 'Know Your Rights' would feature an intro once used on the 101ers' ode to venereal disease, 'Rabies (From The Dogs Of Love)'. And by the end of the 70s, 'Keys To Your Heart' had been welcomed into the Clash live set, long after the necessity for any punk revisionism had been eclipsed by the band's success.

Strummer, as now was, Jones, Simonon, Levene and Foote decamped to an empty warehouse that Rhodes had found near the railway lines of Camden Town. They renamed it Rehearsal Rehearsals and set about redecorating it and auditioning drummers. A succession came and went. Among those to clock in was Paul Buck, later Pablo LaBritain of 999 fame, who had been at boarding school with Mellor and remained a close friend. But by June 1976 Terry Chimes, known to the band through his brief London SS liaison, was in situ.

They lived hand to mouth. Paul Simonon did his best to learn the bass, practising to reggae records on the jukebox they'd installed, while Mick and Joe wrote songs, both at Rehearsals and their respective squats. Rhodes lectured them on writing something that "means something", of the importance of drawing upon their own experiences. His dictum was that soppy love songs (for example 'She's Sitting At The Party', part of their early live repertoire) were redundant in the new climate. Strummer would revise that impression later, whilst crediting Rhodes for the design and look of the band. "Bernie's been maybe over-praised for saying 'Write about things that affect you.' We've been careful to give him his due but as far as the actual songs, it was strictly down to me and Mick." Or more humorously, as he recalled to Gavin Martin, Rhodes was right to insist on the change because "we couldn't have written about Mick's girlfriends forever." Jones had already come up with 'Protex Blue', which Chrissie Hynde once claimed to have co-written, and 'Deny', shortly to be joined by 'Complete Control'. Strummer wrote 'London's Burning' inspired by a day spent overlooking the Westway at Jones's nan's flat. The first song they collaborated on together was 'I'm So Bored With The USA'. It was the start of one of the truly great songwriting partnerships. "Later, he (Joe) used to sit at the typrewriter at one end of the table," Jones told Clash magazine, "and I'd sit and wait, and he'd just bang it out straight, and he'd pass it over the table and then I'd put in my bit – it was that good."

They threw around about half a dozen potential names, including the Mirrors, the Weak Heart Drops (after the song 'Lightning Flash (Weak Heart Drops)' on Big Youth's Dread Locks Dread LP), the Outsiders and Psycho Negatives. Ultimately, Simonon thought that 'The Clash' sounded nicely tabloid-esque after thumbing through a copy of the Evening Standard.

Two months later, the Clash played their first gig in public as support to the Sex Pistols at the Black Swan in Sheffield on July 4 1976, on the same night the Ramones made their UK debut at the Roundhouse. On the journey north they dangled their footwear by its laces out of the back of the van to amuse themselves. "It was great," Strummer later recalled to MOJO. "At least I think it was good, I'm not sure... We made a few screw-ups. It was the first time Paul Simonon was on stage and so forth (Simonon managed to cock up the instrumental opener, 'Listen'). We actually managed to play the tunes. It was highly entertaining. There were punks even in Sheffield at that moment. It was a Sunday and 200 people turned up. They were very receptive." The show prompted a hostile review in the letter columns of the NME's 17 July issue, claiming the band were "just a cacophonous barrage of noise. Their bass guitarist had no idea how to play the instrument and even had to get another member of the band to tune it for him. They tried to play early Sixties R&B, and failed dismally... it's enough to turn you on to Demis Roussos."

The following night there was an altercation between the Stranglers and the Clash/Pistols camp at the Dingwalls bar following the second Ramones show. Jean-Jacques Burnel, having consumed a large quantity of red wine, and not being the stoutest of drinkers at the best of times, decided that Simonon had deliberately spat in his direction and thumped him. As a result of the impact he fell into Cook and Jones of the Pistols, and all three attempted to retaliate against Burnel until the bouncers intervened. The fight continued outside. Burnel faced off against Simonon, while Cook and Jones, and Chrissie Hynde, eyed up the Stranglers associates, Garry Coward-Williams and 'Dagenham' Dave, in a quasi-Mexican stand off. Neither Strummer nor Hugh Cornwell could be bothered to join the ruck, but when John Lydon made a smart remark, he was thrown against the wall by Dagenham Dave. Thereafter the tension dissipated. As a result the Stranglers were further excised from the growing punk subculture, and the bonds deepened between the Pistols and the Clash.

After their first interview with Caroline Coon in the Melody Maker (which had been agreed with Strummer originally to promote 'Keys To Your Heart') the Clash continued to write songs through the summer of 1976, building up a 14-song cycle. Several of these would be gradually weaned out of their set, including 'How Can I Understand The Flies?' aka 'For The Flies', 'Deadly Serious' and 'I Know What To Think Of You'. However, sections would be recycled into other songs, notably the latter, which would eventually transmute into 'Clash City Rockers', though its chord progression could also be traced to the Who's 'I Can't Explain'. Levene also poured his growing alienation about his role within the band into 'What's My Name', although Strummer would later contest his assertion that the song was primarily his creation. Specifically, that Jones wrote the third verse, which directly referred to his father losing money in a bookmaker's.

The group's second show was an invite-only occasion for their journalist friends (Caroline Coon, Jonh Ingham, Giovanni Dadomo) and music industry figures on Friday 13 August at Rehearsal Rehearsals. By all accounts they put in a fantastic set, leading Dadomo to conclude that they'd "frighten the Sex Pistols shitless". A more formal coming out gig followed on 29 August at the Screen On The Green in Islington, again supporting the Pistols, with the Buzzcocks along for the ride. They spent the whole day building the set, at McLaren's insistence, then guarding it. When they did play the sound was murky. And Charles Shaar Murray committed to posterity his immortal put-down: "They are the kind of garage band who should be speedily returned to their garage, preferably with the motor running." The criticism clearly hurt. In fact, it burned. "At least it was clear cut," Strummer later reflected to Gavin Martin. "There was no fucking around with poncey intellectual bollocks. He said what he meant. But so did we. We knocked one back on him."

The next day Strummer, Simonon and Bernie Rhodes attended the Notting Hill Carnival and became immersed in the riot that ensued. It was an enlightening moment, especially for Strummer, who would write both 'White Riot' and '1977' in its aftermath and attempted, but failed miserably, to set a car alight in an act of solidarity. However, the stoical Chimes rather dampened the revolutionary frisson the Clash attached to these events. "I just felt that when you have a carnival you sometimes have a bit of aggro and it's no big deal. They were talking about it like it's some major event in world history. In fact, it was just a few punch-ups at a festival, which happens all the time." Certainly, the early Clash could be criticised for romanticising violence. "You have to be prepared to punch, that's all,"

Afterwards a support slot to the Kursaal Flyers at the Roundhouse in September, a band meeting was convened. It was felt that Levene, who'd become moody and precious, wasn't working out. "It's always said: 'Keith got thrown out of the Clash 'cause of drugs!'" Levene later told Jason Gross. "That's bollocks! The reason I left the Clash was because I was too depressed being in the band. They were embarrassing. They were just too lame for me. I'd start turning up at rehearsals and I was really being a miserable git. I wasn't saying anything, just playing the numbers fine. Things would happen when Mick wasn't there where we'd work out something of mine. Then the next rehearsal, we'd get there and it would be a completely different version. That different version could have been another song. We could have kept the idea I worked on, kept what they worked on and called it something else. There seemed to be a my way/your way of doing things. At the same time, they suddenly came up with this idea for 'White Riot'. I said, 'I'm not fucking singing 'White Riot' – you're joking!' That 'No Elvis, Beatles or the Rolling Stones' in '1977' was bad enough for me. We were just about to make the first record. By the way, I wrote on all the tunes, not just one-third of one tune ('What's My Name') like it says on the disc." Strummer gave his side of the exit to Sean Egan. "I thought Keith was brilliant, but I realised Keith had other eggs to fry, so we just got on with it." Although the band was heavily influenced by Bernie Rhodes, he wasn't consulted about the exit, possibly due to the fact that Levene had been his 'find'. Levene, who would go on to work with old friend John Lydon in PiL, has also stated that both Rhodes and Strummer tried to invite him back into the group.

The group's first post-Levene show was at the 100 Club Punk Festival in September 1976, set up by McLaren and Rhodes. The Clash and Pistols were set to play the first night, the 20th. It was significant, in addition to its historical import, for the new songs the Clash unveiled. Primary among these was 'White Riot', Strummer's response to the Notting Hill riots, as well as 'Janie Jones' and 'I'm So Bored With The USA', in essence Jones's old London SS song 'I'm So Bored With You' changed at Strummer's suggestion after a serendipitous mishearing of the title. Later they would open all their February 1978 American dates with it. Recalling the 100 Club Festival, "The Clash were in the middle of this ludicrous Stalinist vibe," Strummer later told Johnny Black, "where we decided it was uncool to talk to the audience. Inevitably we broke a string, so suddenly there's no music. Luckily, I always used to have a transistor radio with me because there were those cool pirate radio stations. We didn't have spare guitars, so I just switched on the radio and held it up to the mic. At the mixing desk, Dave Goodman was hip enough to put a delay on it and it happened to be a discussion about the bombs in Northern Ireland. It was pure luck, but it sounded absolutely brilliant. Apocalyptic."

The 100 Club Festival also resulted in an interview conducted by Steve Walsh for Mark Perry's new punk fanzine, Sniffin' Glue. But the early part of the interview was given to Strummer pontificating on the political implications of Hot Rod Dave Higgs' trousers. More helpfully, Mick Jones would try to crystalise the band's ethos. "Rock'n'roll is about rebellion. I had this out with Bryan James of the Damned: he stands for enjoying himself and I stand for change and creativity. Groups like the Hot Rods are bozos. They've got a great thing going for themselves, but it's not to do with change, it's just keeping people as they are. The important thing is to encourage people to do things for themselves, think for themselves and stand up for their rights. I hate apathy."

A more incongruous booking followed supporting Shakin' Stevens at the ULU on 15 October, which brought the punk movement into direct confrontation with the Teds. Only a handful of the Clash's inner circle attended the show, including Perry and Sebastian Conran. There were scuffles, but the Teds didn't, in the end, get to lynch the punk rockers, something that had looked on the cards. But after a further show at the Royal College Of Art, at which Sid Vicious joined the band in a ruck with hecklers, Terry Chimes decided he wanted to bow out. He agreed to fulfil further dates in November and their first demo sessions at Marble Arch studios before leaving.

The Clash were angered and rounded on him, putting out a fictitious story that he'd decided to leave after a wine bottle broke on one of his cymbals. In truth he'd started playing the drums because he wanted to be in a rock'n'roll band and make good money. The prospect of running with a hunted, anti-authoritarian pack like the Clash, at that stage constantly on edge and with a permanent spectre of violence surrounding them, had considerably less appeal.

And Chimes never liked the politics. Without ever saying it as such, it's clear he considered the Clash to be a little fraudulent in this regard. And, frankly, they were. In an interview with

Richard Cromelin in the LA Times in 1988, Strummer would try to rationalise the political aspects of the band. "I used to say to journalists – 'Hang on, don't get the wrong idea that we're carrying around Das Kapital and loads of pamphlets. We had Mott the Hoople records and reefer, you know?' I often felt that all got a bit unbalanced. I kept trying to stress that – 'Hang on, we're be-bop guys, we're down in the alley on 57th Street. We're not in there with John Reed and Ten Days That Shook the World.' We'd be in the alley with (Charlie) Parker shooting up junk. That's where we were at really. I mean not shooting up junk, but if you had to say which camp are you in, I'd have to say hey, we were up Bop Alley. I often felt worried that people thought we were Che Guevara." Despite such statements, as heartwarming as they are clumsy, the band were certainly riding the revolutionary wagon for all its worth, egged on by Rhodes, who admired the 'low overheads' that punk provided in terms of getting the message across. And for a time the band served as a blank canvas for his ideas, intellectual and sartorial. Yet they always harboured the secret ambition of being the biggest band in the world. And they would be, helped in no small part by their appropriation of the left's inconography.

The sessions at Marble Arch were paid for by Polydor, via A&R man Chris Parry, while Rhodes drafted in Guy Stevens as producer, an old acquaintance but also the man who had sacked Mick Jones from his pre-London SS band Little Queenie. Vic Coppersmith-Heaven was the engineer. Always a maverick, Stevens was by now some way advanced in his alcoholism. Five songs were recorded, 'Career Opportunities', 'White Riot', 'Janie Jones', 'London's Burning' and '1977'. But everyone was disappointed with the flat-sounding results, and Stevens also allegedly clashed with Strummer over his 'diction'. "We picked Guy Stevens," Rhodes told the press, "because we wanted a nutcase to produce the band, because that's what our music is all about. But there are different kinds of nutcases, and it didn't work out with him." Stevens' 'moment' with the band would have to wait a few years.

Their first major music press interview, again with early advocate Caroline Coon who would become romantically engaged with Simonon, followed on 13 November 1976. She would also take the photo that adorned the cover of 'White Riot'. A second interview followed with Miles for the NME, at which Strummer outlined the Clash philosophy of being anti-Fascist, anti-racist, pro-creative and anti-violence, while spending the entire interview toying with a flick-knife and making veiled threats to the journalist. He was also indignant at the same journalist's attempt to point out the potential pitfalls of making racially stereotyped generalisations a la 'White Riot'.

The group started rehearsals for their upcoming tour with the Pistols, bringing in Billy Idol's friend from Sussex University, Rob Harper-Milne (aka Rob Harper) as their drummer, after he replied to a Melody Maker advert. Dates were scheduled with the Clash bottom of the bill to Johnny Thunders Heartbreakers, the Damned and the Pistols. But after Steve Jones indulged himself at Bill Grundy's expense, the Clash were caught up in the resulting hullabaloo.

Only seven out of 21 dates were completed. Confusion and copious drinking reigned, although Jones did manage to utilise the time off to write a new song about their adventures, 'Remote Control'. "It was exciting for us," Strummer recalled to Gavin Martin. "Suddenly, there was mad hacks from the tabloids motor-rallying their cars around the coach, racing people to the hotel. There was people singing religious songs when we got off the bus in some Godforsaken place in Wales, about 100 of them singing holy songs against our evil presence. It was quite a kick. You should have seen our faces. We were stunned. It was like something from a surreal movie."

There was even talk of a transfer between the bands (Matlock for Simonon) instigated by McLaren and Rhodes. And the student union at Lanchester Polytechnic voted to ban 'White Riot' because it was 'racist'. But things were still hand to mouth, and on their return the Clash ended up eating a turkey cooked by Caroline Coon on Christmas day. On New Year's Day the Clash performed at the Roxy. It was Rob Harper's last show with the band after he bowed out by mutual consent – despite Rhodes telling the press he'd been sacked for ideological reasons. For an upcoming round of demo recordings, Terry Chimes was asked to help out.

Polydor was still interested in the band, or at least Chris Parry was. But his boss Jim Crook was unconvinced. Parry, having failed to land the Pistols, was getting desperate. Rhodes was trying to get the best deal, at times working alongside Malcolm McLaren following the Pistols departure from EMI. A tentative deal was agreed with Polydor after Parry finally managed to secure a £40,000 advance. Suddenly, this was countered by a far larger advance, £100,000, offered by CBS. Rhodes tabled those offers to the band at Rehearsals, and Mick Jones immediately informed him that they should take the bigger advance. Rhodes, just like McLaren before him, neglected to tell Parry that the deal was off. The CBS contract was signed on 27 January 1977 and the band were put on £25 weekly retainers, while Mark Perry at Sniffing Glue made his famous pronouncement that "punk died the day the Clash signed to CBS".

They set to work immediately on album sessions. They'd already started demo-ing material that January at the National Film and Television School in Beaconsfield, through the auspices of ex-student Julien Temple. Live soundman Mickey Foote was overseeing affairs. Foote proved himself sufficiently adept to be asked to produce the full CBS sessions, which began at the end of the month at Whitfield Street's Studio 3. Much of the technical side was overseen by staff engineer Simon Humphrey, who was more used to working with Gary Glitter, Smokie and Hot Chocolate. "We were all in love with the Beatles, and I'd grown up with progressive rock, Yes and Led Zeppelin" Humphrey later told Marcus Gray. "We weren't prepared for punk, and we didn't particularly fancy having it thrust at us head on. None of us knew what to expect, whether the band were going to burn the studio down…" Or, as disc mastering head Beryl Ritchie remembers, "The second floor was gutted because there'd been a fire. We had a receptionist downstairs, an Irish guy, and when the Clash came in, dressed in all their tatty gear, he thought they were workmen. He said, 'The fire's up on the second floor,' and they said, 'Nah, we're 'ere to record.'"

Accounts of these sessions, as recounted by Pat Gilbert in Passion Is A Fashion, picture Humphrey as the beleagured ex-hippy trying to rally the troops into observing some of the basic protocols of record production. Meanwhile the central trio (minus the quiet, time-serving Chimes, but plus the interfering Rhodes, whose suggestions routinely received short shrift from Strummer and Jones) looked on suspiciously at anything that could possibly be perceived as intrusion or artistic compromise. This was a budget studio – the lowest of the low in CBS's terms – and the band rattled through the sessions. As Mick Jones would later tell Danny Baker, "We worked really hard! We used to rehearse like this; we'd do a number really fast, and then, when it came to a halt, have ten seconds' break where we all shouted our heads off at each other. Whoever shouted loudest got heard. And then, about ten seconds later, we'd do the number again, then shout again."

Humphrey's main problems were getting all parties to converge on the studio at the same time, and also resolving a disagreement between Simonon and Jones about the bass sound. Simonon favoured a syrupy, lugubrious, reggae-styled tone, Jones thought the songs required a harder edge. It was resolved when Humphrey invited them to record in both styles and then choose the superior mix. It's indicative of the fact that, although Simonon was very much the junior member in terms of musical technique, his voice carried equal weight in discussions. "I think me and Joe decided that there was a line," Simonon later recalled to Clash magazine, "and that on one side was Mick and Topper – they were the musicians – and me and Joe were on the other side, and we were the performers. That's how we saw it." Strummer certainly didn't concern himself with the minor details, leaving the arranging to Jones and Foote. But he insisted on doing his vocal takes while playing guitar, as it felt unnatural to him to do otherwise.

Pretty soon they had documented their live set, but it only amounted to half an hour's worth of material. So they decided to record their version of Junior Murvin's 'Police And Thieves', having toyed with the idea of mixing reggae into their sets for some time. It was, in its own way, an epochal decision. Legendarily, Bob Marley and Lee Scratch Perry – the song's original co-author – were so impressed, they wrote 'Punky Reggae Party' in tribute.

The album was completed and delivered on 3 March 1977. It was premiered at the Harlesden Coliseum, by which time they'd dropped their Pollock-esque, stencilled slogan look for military fatigues, though their former stylistic incarnation was still apparent on the cover of 'White Riot', released in mid-March. The Clash, predominantly thanks to Simonon and Rhodes, knew how important it was to look good. And, as Pennie Smith once observed, "They made good shapes, and they were into the romance of the thing." 'White Riot' briefly flickered in the Top 40 while the group's album sessions were ongoing.

The group's eponymous debut album was released on 8 April 1977 with a sleeve using a Kate Simon photograph doctored into a line print by Rhodes. Terry Chimes was credited as Tory Crimes, which didn't much please him, while the back sleeve featured a baton charge from the Notting Hill riots from a photo taken by band friend Rocco Macauley. When reviewers 'got' it, they really got it. Tony Parsons at the NME described it as "some of the most exciting rock'n'roll in contemporary music" while Mark Perry, forgiving them the switch to CBS on this evidence, called it "the most important album ever released". Only Melody Maker's Mike Oldfield complained of the headache its unrelenting bluster and velocity gave him.

For many the Clash's debut has taken on mythic properties. It would be sacrilege to criticise any moment of it. But there are weaknesses. 'Hate And War', its verses sung by Jones, is just a ready slogan with a plodding chord progression. The band's subsequent attitude to both '48 Hours', written in haste for their second gig, and the heavily phased 'Cheat', never before performed live, that they were effectively filler, is pretty accurate. 'White Riot' doesn't convince, especially in this form (they decided to remix the Beaconsfield recording rather than the superior single version) and, with the gift of hindsight, is embarrassingly patronising. And without the insertion of 'Police And Thieves', there would have been a real lack of sonic variety. That aside, its life-affirming qualities haven't dimmed down the years. 'Janie Jones' demonstrates just how sweet the Clash's hoarse vocals could sound in melodic syncopation. Mick Jones' guitar solo on 'Remote Control' is perfectly brittle. 'I'm So Bored With The USA' sounds valedictory, 'London's Burning' romps along and perfectly frames one of Strummer's most persuasive vocals. 'Career Opportunities', inspired by Jones's experiences with the GPO during the IRA letter bombing campaign, and owing an obvious debt to the 101ers' 'Motor Boys Motor', is priceless, sardonic Clash. 'Deny', allegedly written about Levene's drug use, with its improvised vocal section by Strummer, came out better than anyone expected. 'Garageland', which kicked back at Shaar Murray's famed condemnation, was both self-knowing and defiant. And the aforementioned 'Police And Thieves' successfully mined the sonic hinterland of punk and reggae without diluting either of the traditions. The band was immediately excited by it. "It wasn't like a slavish white man's Zerox of some riff," Strummer later told Sean Egan. "It was like, 'give us your riff and we'll drive it around London.'" The production is only just about par, at best, and CBS's indifference to the band, measured in the production budget, was further confirmed when they neglected to release it in America for two and a half years.

Much of the myth of the Clash was attributable to the subsequent Tony Parsons NME cover story, based on interviews conducted on the Circle Line and back at Rehearsals. As a journalistic exercise it had little to do with relating the truth, instead painting its subjects as tearaways who not only advocated but relished violence, street toughs presiding over the collapse of urban society, etc. It was disingenuous to a fault. Strummer was ex-boarding school, but when pushed on the matter claimed his father was a diplomat rather than a minor civil servant (he later claimed this was essentially because he wanted to please his father rather than devalue him). And he was significantly older and more experienced than some of his peers in the punk movement. Regardless, the Parsons piece did the trick, and it's not hard to picture Bernie Rhodes rubbing his hands over the resultant copy. The NME and the Clash were in the business of joint promotion. The first 10,000 copies of The Clash contained a sticker, which, if attached to a coupon printed in the NME, could be sent off to receive a free 'Capital Radio' EP.

Meantime the Clash were still without a permanent drummer. An advert in the Melody Maker insisted that there should be 'no jazz, no funk, no laid back' in the successful applicant's kit bag. Several punk drumming notables tried their hand, including later Chelsea man Chris Bashford. Jon Moss was offered the spot, but instead chose to throw his lot in with London, chiefly because he found Bernie Rhodes so grating. It was only when Mick Jones went to see the Kinks play at the Rainbow and bumped into former shipping clerk and headmaster's son Nick 'Topper' Headon, whom he'd known from the London SS days, that they found their man. Headon, who had been briefly employed by the Pat Travers Band before being sacked for 'not hitting the drums hard enough', and also worked on the construction of the Channel Tunnel, was invited to Rehearsals the following day. He wasn't going to make the same mistake twice though, ironically given the aforementioned advert, he was a jazz fan.

Headon played his first show with the band at the Roundhouse on 10 April, prior to rehearsing for their White Riot tour, beginning on 1 May 1977 at the Guildford Civic Hall, on a package featuring the Buzzcocks, Subway Sect and the Slits. It was also planned that the Jam, whom Chris Parry had finally nailed as his 'punk' act, should play on the bill. But after the Rainbow gig a rumbling argument between Rhodes and Jam manager John Weller saw them take their leave. The tour has passed into UK punk lore, not least for the coach driver Norman, who was driven slowly but surely insane by the visual appearance and habits of his entourage. The highpoint, though not for the venue's janitors, was the show at the Rainbow, where 200 seats were ripped out. There was also a huge mound of punk fashion detritus, including combat boots and ammunition belts, left outside the auditorium at the insistence of security. "The Rainbow's foyer looked like a ten-foot high, third world munitions dump," Rick Buckler told me. As to the show itself: "Absolutely epoch-making," Strummer recalled to Gavin Martin. "I went to bed obscure and woke up famous, a three-page spread in the Evening Standard."

However, the tremendous impetus felt by everyone involved with the tour was quashed when they realised that, in their absence, CBS had readied a new single for release without their permission. 'Remote Control' featured a sleeve lazily copied from the debut album. The band's preferred choice had been 'Janie Jones', which wasn't as 'soft'. Strummer was not just tabloid-surfing on the latter song. He'd befriended Janie Jones, a former singer and cabaret artist, after she was released from prison in 1977 for controlling call girls, and would later write 'House Of The Ju Ju Queen' for her, on which she was backed by the Lash (the Clash under a pseudonym). Both the Clash and Rhodes were mortified by the release of 'Remote Control'. It was the beginning of their realisation, confirmed when they sussed just how binding their contract with CBS actually was – they thought they'd signed for five albums, but hadn't checked the small print – that it was going to be a stormy relationship.

The group's third single was written by Strummer and Jones in the latter's gran's flat. 'Complete Control' lashed back at CBS. But the title actually came from one of Bernie Rhodes' rousing, if frequently ignored, pub lectures about the way forward for the group. A press statement was issued to coincide with its release. "'Complete Control' tells the story of conflict between two opposing camps. One side sees change as an opportunity to channel the enthusiasm of a raw and dangerous culture in a direction where energy is made safe and predictable. The other is dealing with change as a freedom to be experienced so as to understand one's true capabilities, allowing a creative social situation to emerge." Not everyone was convinced. As John Peel later told Jack Rabid, "You thought, either you're being amazingly stupid or you're being dishonest, because they must have known when they signed to CBS that it's not a charity." It's a point that, Strummer at least, would take on board 20 years down the line, after he'd spent almost the entirety of his adult life battling music industry corporations. "We should have gone independent," he told the Big Takeover. "But we didn't know any better. We were too stupid." But in the same interview, he cloaked that opinion somewhat. "But also, it was probably worth it, because we took it to the world."

It was also during June 1977 that Joe Strummer and Roadent attended the reggae all-nighter at the Hammersmith Palais that would provide them with the inspiration for '(White Man) In Hammersmith Palais'. Thereafter the Clash ended up forming a mutual admiration society with legendary Jamaican producer Lee Perry, who was actually the co-author of 'Police And Thieves'. They recorded 'Complete Control' together in the Sarm East studio in Whitechapel after Rhodes tracked him down. It came out in October, after Mickey Foote had remixed it. The band were unanimous that they loved what Perry had done, in the 15 odd minutes Strummer remembers him remaining in the studio, in which time he nearly blew up the studio trying to get Simonon a good bass sound. But they were conscious that his subsonic layering might confuse their growing audience.

The group then embarked on its Get Out Of Control tour in Belfast on 20 October 1977, or would have done, had insurers not withdrawn their cover. Their withdrawal caused the 'Bedford Street riot', as disgruntled punk fans clashed with the RUC. Events also inspired several songs by Belfast's upcoming punk generation, including Protex's 'Black Riot' and Rudi's 'Cops'. It wasn't really a riot, of course, but it was quite exciting. Still, there was nothing wrong with getting some photographs taken against the backdrop of armed soldiers at checkpoints, was there? Well, yes, there was. It caused a lot of ill feeling. But they returned to Belfast two months later, so at least they'd made good on their word. However, the original headlines that greeted the trip to Northern Ireland, "The Clash united Protestant and Catholic youth with punk rock", later paled when Strummer made an NME statement advocating support of the H-block prisoners and the withdrawal of troops from the province. The Belfast punk scene, uniquely, had managed to unite young men from two, otherwise strictly segregated, and warring communities. Now Strummer was deemed to have taken sides. As Guy Trelford succinctly states in his book 'It Makes You Want To Spit,' "we didn't need that crap". Strummer's comments would come back to haunt him when he had to pull out of a gig with the Undertones in Derry after he received a death threat from the loyalist Red Hand Commando.

They were accompanied on the tour by the ever petulant Television, Tom Verlaine telling all and sundry that their natural status as inculcators of the punk movement had been usurped by the London upstarts, as the tour continued in Dublin. It was again pretty riotous stuff, with Strummer contracting glandular fever after a fan gobbed directly in his mouth. Hotel rooms, one of which Paul Simonon shot up with an air rifle, became makeshift refugee centres for the Clash flock, with fans invited to share the available bed space. All of this was documented by Lester Bangs, over from the States, as well as camp followers Kris Needs and Robin 'Banks' Crocker for Zig Zag.

Preparations for a second album were partially informed by the fact that the American record company had passed on releasing their debut. In an attempt to solve this, CBS in England demanded a 'name' producer. From a shortlist prepared by CBS, Blue Oyster Cult veteran Sandy Pearlman was selected and flown over to see their show at Manchester's Elizabethan Ballroom. He was taunted from the stage by Strummer who then launched into an uncompromisingly savage 'I'm So Bored With The USA'.

If was all very well for CBS to keep demanding a new album, but the Clash didn't have any new songs. So Rhodes set up a writing trip to Jamaica in January 1978 for Jones and Strummer, which hugely annoyed reggae aficionado Paul Simonon, who wasn't invited and got a conciliatory trip to Russia with Caroline Coon instead. "Yeah, I was a bit pissed off. To say the least," Simonon would later state. Topper kicked his heels and scored some drugs. The songwriting duo arrived at the Pegasus hotel in Kingston, where the aftermath of political violence was still brewing, and practically became prisoners there, at least during nightfall. The experience was faithfully and wistfully recalled in one of the songs that emerged, 'Safe European Home'.

The group's new single was the self-eulogising 'Clash City Rockers', produced by Mickey Foote during sessions between September and December 1977 at Whitfield Street studios. The B-side, 'Jail Guitar Doors', featured references to three of the band's rock'n'roll influences and their drug/mental health problems – Wayne (Kramer, of the MC5), Peter (Green, of Fleetwood Mac) and Keith (Richards, of the Stones). The A-side contained some typically Strummer-esque career advice: "So don't complain about your useless employment, Jack it in forever tonight." But when they got the promo copies, it became obvious that someone had interfered with the masters, speeding them up. According to Pat Gilbert's detailed assessment of what happened, Foote had asked Rhodes for more time to re-record the song, but was told that the deadline held. So Foote doctored the masters and, for his sins, was subsequently ostracised from the Clash fold.

Demos with Pearlman began in January 1978 at Whitfield Street, after Simonon's return, though these were further inconvenienced by the fact that Strummer had now contracted hepatitis from the flying spittle which accompanied Clash live shows. In the meantime Pearlman attended another show at Lanchester Polytechnic in Coventry where, on trying to gain entrance to the dressing room without fully disclosing his credentials, he was thumped by Robin Banks. The producer took it in good part, after he'd regained consciousness, but it was an unconventional way to make friends and influence people in the music industry.

While Pearlman was back in America, Mick Jones oversaw production of further sessions for '1-2 Crush On You'. When it was suggested the track could benefit from a saxophone break, Simonon suggested his old friend Gary Barnacle. He duly arrived at Rehearsals with his brothers, one of whom had an air rifle. In the evening, the Barnacles, Robin Banks, Headon and Simonon got out on the roof and Topper started taking aim at pigeons over-flying the railway tracks. It subsequently transpired that these were actually racing pigeons owned by a yard mechanic below, George Dole. Within a few seconds flashing lights were everywhere, and a helicopter wheeled above them. One of the mechanics suspected the band were terrorists and had raised the alarm. The entire party were thrown into police cells and charged with criminal damage. On hearing the news, Bernie Rhodes refused to come up with the bail, doubtless thinking that it would be good publicity. It was left to Simonon's girlfriend, Caroline Coon, with all her experience dealing with authority as the head of Relate, who persuaded CBS to advance the bail money.

Meanwhile the group recorded new sessions in Marquee Studios in Richmond Mews with engineer Simon Humphrey and Jones producing. From these came '(White Man) In Hammersmith Palais', judged by many to be the finest song the Clash ever recorded, or "punk's Gettysburg Address", according to Danny Baker. Instead of the amphetamine-fuelled, finger-bleeding, finger-pointing exercises they'd put on the form book earlier, there is a warmth and playfulness in Strummer's voice as he effectively sends himself up. The moment when he can't help snickering while denouncing the Jam for their Burton suits, is pure schoolboy mirth. Just as importantly, the presentation of this rock-reggae hybrid, sweetened by harmonies and mouth organ, sounded very little like punk.

The Clash loved their chic affiliation with the black community, though there were reports that band members and their entourage verbally attacked Tom Robinson backstage over his homosexuality during their appearance at the Anti-Nazi League rally in Hackney at the end of April. Strummer would also wear shirts bearing the insignia of the Red Brigade. Alongside previous comments about Northern Ireland which had incensed a punk community desperately trying to work together under the shroud of sectarianism, it shows Strummer was still a youngish man making mistakes, especially when he tried to play with symbols.

The much-delayed sessions for second album Give Em Enough Rope began in earnest in April 1978. Demos were recorded with Pearlman at Utopia Studios in Primrose Hill, but after a few discipline problems (Simonon and Headon constructing a motorbike dirt track out of the contents of upturned plant pots) they moved off to Basing Street Studios near Westbourne Grove.

Pearlman and the Clash were born of very different rock cultures, and the Clash didn't find it easy to adapt to his meticulous precision, especially Strummer, who had little patience for endless studio doodling, and Simonon, whose technical deficiencies were more under the microscope than ever. Simonon responded by treating the fish-out-of-water Pearlman with disdain. There was talk of CBS being unimpressed by the initial demos. So Pearlman suggested they travel to San Francisco to record at Automatt Studios. Well, Mick and Joe at least. They flew out in August and spent three weeks performing overdubs and adding vocals while Pearlman multi-tracked the guitars for all they were worth, then brought in session musicians like Al Lanier of Blue Oyster Cult and John Lennon session man Stan Bronstein. The Clash's songwriting core then travelled separately before pitching up in New York. A few days later, Topper and Simonon were flown over to New York to hear the final mixes of the album.

Meanwhile Rhodes, critical in the press of the band's 'rock star indulgences', scheduled two shows in Harlesden at the end of September. But the group stuck to their guns and rescheduled the dates for October. Rhodes was losing his hold. It was Paul Simonon who eventually gave public vent to these feelings in an interview with the NME. "Bernie Rhodes makes us look daft and it gets our fuckin' backs up the way he assumed he can just speak away for the four of us. He can't. No one person can really speak for us, especially him." Eventually, Rhodes was fired, against Strummer's wishes, and Caroline Coon temporarily took the management role after Chris Salewicz and Pennie Smith were both considered. But Rhodes wasn't going to take that lying down. He immediately obtained a court order meaning all the band's income would be, temporarily, paid directly to him. The Clash toured through November and December as Give Em Enough Rope was finally released.

It was a transitional album, and critics who'd invested so much in the Clash were quick to point out its flaws. "So do they squander their greatness," lamented Jon Savage in Sounds. Nick Kent accused them of proffering a "totally facile concept of shock-politics". The Jam had just released their first classic album, All Mod Cons, a month previously, and comparisons were inevitable, given the ongoing rivalry between the camps. The general consensus was that 'Rope was overproduced, 'Cheapskates' in particular. Its elasticated power chords and sentiments sounded positively Mid-Atlantic, despite the London references in the lyric. 'Last Gang In Town' was a celebration of the myriad musical tribes around the capital, but the prominence of the rawkish guitar made it sound perversely monocultural. The laborious production process had certainly squeezed some of the group's natural juice, but it isn't nearly as bad an album as some have painted it – in fact, you could make a pretty good case for it featuring at least three to four of the Clash's greatest songs. It charged all the way to number two in the British charts while it was greeted with the utmost reverence in the States, where Greil Marcus compared it to the Rolling Stones' Let It Bleed. 'Safe European Home' was brutally honest and arguably the finest song the band had written to date, 'White Man' aside. 'English Civil War', Strummer's rewrite of 'When Johnny Comes Marching Home' with its non-explicit subject matter the rise of the National Front, was a stunning slice of Orwellian folk-punk. 'Julie's Been Working For The Drug Squad' recalled the British goverment's ill-fated Operation Julie attempt of 1977 to break up an LSD ring – including a clever reference to the Beatles' 'Lucy In The Sky With Diamonds' with all that song's historic baggage. Other highlights included Jones's 'Stay Free', a memoir of he and Robin Banks' south London youth, and the knowing 'All The Young Punks (New Boots And Contracts)' – "Of course we got a manager, Though he ain't the mafia, A contract is a contract, When they get 'em out on yer." This time, the album did get immediate release in America, though the Chinese lettering was considered too redolent of left wing politics, and changed. A few swift phone calls ensured that this error was rectified quickly.

In January 1979 the group entered Wessex Studios in Highbury Park to record their version of Sonny Curtis's 'I Fought The Law', best known for the version by the Bobby Fuller Four. It would become the band's first US single, and was added to the running order of the American release of their debut album, where it made an ugly fit. Bill Price, who had helped on the Pistols' Never Mind The Bollocks, was the engineer. The additional tracks were a reworking of 'Capital Radio', 'Gates Of The West' (formerly 'Ooh Baby Ooh, It's All Over', from Mick Jones' pre-Clash days) and 'Groovy Times'.

The Clash duly set off for America in January 1979, after spending some time convincing their record label that the expense of underwriting the tour was justified. Caroline Coon, who fronted up £3,000 of her own money, also managed to secure the services of Bo Diddley as support act, which thrilled the band, even if he was paid more than the headliners. "That was great," Jones later told Jack Rabid, "because people here don't seem to even know they have this enormous wealth of really fantastic stuff that was looked up to... And it took an English band to come and get those people to play with them, to expose them." But despite her best efforts, Coon was expelled, ostensibly over an alleged incident when friends of the band were banned from their dressing room at the Santa Monica Civic. Coon insists she was acting under orders, but that didn't save her and they separated at the end of the tour.

On the day of the May 1979 election which swept Margaret Thatcher to power, the Clash, still manager-less and unsure whether or not CBS were going to renew their contract, released 'The Cost Of Living' EP. It featured four tracks recorded at Wessex Studios in January including their homage to The Bobby Fuller Four's 'I Fought The Law', probably the most straightforward commercial rock'n'roll song they'd committed to vinyl to this point. They were about to nail their colours to the mast.

The group finally found a new base at Vanilla in April 1979, a rehearsal space at Causton Street in Pimlico, above a car repair shop. They would practice there for eight hours a day, punctuated by stops at the local café and games of football with their entourage on a concrete playground opposite. Slowly they began to build the song pool that would birth London Callling. Initial results were taped by Who engineer Bob Pridden and were enough to convince CBS to pick up their option. The Vanilla Tapes, which included several songs that didn't make London Calling, would eventually be released in 2004, after Mick Jones discovered the tapes while moving house.

Discussions as to a suitable producer came round to Guy Stevens. Although they'd had an unfortunate experience recording the Polydor demos together, they thought his spontaneity would best capture the meld of musical styles the band were now embracing. The band, with

Sid Vicious in tow, went to visit Stevens at his unkempt flat in Swiss Cottage to sound him out. Stevens was having a fit about Led Zeppelin's new film and flung a record across the room, hitting Strummer in the eye. While the band rooted around for something to treat his injury, Sid Vicious helped himself to Stevens' extensive medical cabinet.

Sessions were booked at Wessex Studios in Highbury New Park. Stevens gladly played the maverick. His behaviour included wanton destruction of property, barking orders and making unreasonable demands, such as attempting to improve the sound of a new Bosendorfer piano by pouring red wine into it. But somehow it all gelled. Stevens was determined to vibe up the atmosphere so that it was edgy. His technique for pushing the musicians generally revolved around sneaking up on them and shouting in their ear the name of a musician he thought they should be emulating. With Strummer, it was Jerry Lee Lewis. Or he would (almost) belt Jones with a ladder.

Towards the end of the sessions, his behaviour would become so destructive and erratic that the band would lie to him and tell him they weren't working that day to keep him out of the way, but he certainly gave the whole project much of its initial momentum. And legendarily, by lying in front of Maurice Oberstein's Rolls-Royce and refusing to move, he persuaded the visiting mogul to loosen the purse strings and back the band's demands to release a double album. Or at least to admit he had a brilliant record on his hands, depending on which version you believe. The stories are legion, including his attempts to insert commentary from a game between Leeds United and his beloved Arsenal halfway through 'Death Or Glory', an idea which, strangely enough, got vetoed.

Stevens' antics had a galvanising effect, not least on Paul Simonon, who plucked up the courage to deliver a song and lyric, 'Guns Of Brixton', which the others convinced him to sing himself. "Previous to doing London Calling," Simonon recalled to Clash magazine, "we had Sandy Pearlman, who was trying to achieve this supersonic sound of rock'n'roll or whatever. I suppose he sort of achieved it in some ways, but the procedure of making the record was very tedious in so far as it was down to every centimetre had to be exactly so. It took the life out of the thing, I thought, to a point. Whereas with London Calling, Guy Stevens' method was just to charge in the room and smash chairs up while the group's playing and keep everybody on their toes. You feel like the group is actually in the room playing live, which they are."

Band confidante Kosmo Vinyl led them to their next managers, Blackhill Enterprises's Pete Jenner and Andrew King, who'd originally looked after the early Pink Floyd. The Clash, still in hock to CBS for a considerable sum, lined up an autumn tour of the US. The 24 dates, with support variously from Bo Diddley, Sam And Dave, Screamin' Jay Hawkins and the Undertones, was completed on a bus formerly owned by Dolly Parton. By now the Clash were a huge deal, and a major inspiration to the second coming of the US punk scene. Brett Gurevitz of Bad Religion saw them at the Hollywood Palladium in October 1979 and became a lifelong fan – and would eventually help rescue Strummer from his post-Clash CBS/Sony blues by signing him to his Epitaph label.

The tour was documented in film by Pennie Smith, and in cartoon form by the NME's Ray Lowry. These two would actually combine to produce the artwork for London Calling. Smith had taken a startling image of Simonon destroying his bass at the second New York Palladium show on 21 September, due to frustration at the sound and the band's distance from their fans. When it was suggested it could be a cover shot, she protested vigorously that it was out of focus. Strummer was adamant that it was 'the' shot and won the argument. It was embroidered by Lowry's pink/green typography, a tribute to Elvis Presley's 1956 debut album that they'd picked up in Chicago's Wax Trax record store.

Released in December 1979, London Calling did eventually emerge as a double set, at the budget price of £5. This took a little bit of engineering. CBS had denied permission for a double. So Strummer asked if they could include a free single? Sure. 12-inch single? No problem. And could it be a 33rpm 12-inch single? Why not. CBS would discover their mistake too late to do anything about it. It was a nice payback for the 'Remote Control' farrago.

London Calling featured a succession of splendid musical tangents linked by more urbane, satisfying lyrics. References are split between London and America, though rather than the revolutionary froth of old, there's a distinct progression. From 'Clampdown', with its echoes of Battista as well as Orwell, through the retaliatory, vigilante terseness of 'Guns Of Brixton' to 'Spanish Bombs', a more logical and problematic outcome of urban struggle that the band had been guilty of romanticising. The urgency of old is transposed into a looser dynamic that retains an edgy tension and a powerful sense of menace, but the majority of songs chew the groove they hit rather than reel around looking for the next shotgun riff. A sense of ambivalence rather than certainty pervades the whole album. Strummer, in particular, was no longer seeing things in wholly black and white terms.

It felt current as well as urgent, thanks to songs like 'Rudie Can't Fail', the Clash's tribute to the then burgeoning 2-Tone movement started by Clash fan Jerry Dammers. 'Hateful', Strummer's take on the Velvet Underground's 'Waiting For The Man', lamented the recent death of old punk comrade Sid. The more personal songs such as 'I'm Not Down', allegedly written by Jones about his on-off girlfriend Viv Albertine of the Slits, sounded considerably less forced than on previous Clash records. It made for great pop music. That was very much the case with the unashamedly sentimental, quietly heartbreaking 'Lost In The Supermarket', written by Strummer as an imaginary depiction of Mick Jones' youth.

There are so many highlights and few lows, with the possible exception of the misfiring 'Lover's Rock'. Their irresistible rockabilly cover of Vince Taylor's 'Brand New Cadillac', that Stevens had earlier insisted on including, powerfully resuscitates a bygone musical era, but was undoubtedly influenced by the Cramps, who'd supported them in the States. 'The Card Cheat' is Jones's doo wop soundtrack to an imagined spaghetti western with everything double-tracked for extra punch. And Headon's relish in finally attacking some be-bop on 'Jimmy Jazz' is tangible. The title-track, which reached number 11 in the UK charts and featured Don Letts' rain-soaked video, was another trump card, marrying familiar images of London, the BBC World Service call signal and 'phoney Beatlemania' to the prospect of coming Armageddon, inspired by the March 1979 Three Mile Island nuclear scare. Simonon's ominous bass intro invites echoed werewolf howls as Strummer etched the most adept encapsulation of Cold War paranoia and resignation ever recorded. The author's visualisation of the Thames River bursting its banks is genius.

On release, their old adversary Charles Shaar Murray had changed his mind emphatically. In Rolling Stone, Tom Carson dubbed the Clash the greatest rock'n'roll band in the world. The same magazine would later famously describe it as the greatest rock album of the 80s, neatly side-stepping its December 1979 release date. Shaar Murray was also commissioned to review the 25th anniversary reissue in 2004 for MOJO. With the benefit of hindsight, he noted that London Calling "arrived at precisely the moment when the Thatcher/Reagan era was kicking off, and the title song caught the mood of that moment like lightning in a bottle".

The album was promoted via the 35-date 16 Tons tour, with reggae DJ Mikey Dread supporting, between January and February 1980. At their Brighton date Pete Townshend joined them on stage and clumsily encored on three songs. And on the Sheffield date, meanwhile, Strummer decked Jones backstage following his blunt refusal to return to encore with 'White Riot', a song Jones was never especially fond of.

At the start of February the Clash poured their new-found confidence into a single, 'Bankrobber'. Mikey Dread masterfully layered the sound, while the band replicated the JA harmonies like old hands – name-checking 'Satta Massa Gana' in song was one thing, pulling off a record that could stand up to it quite another. But CBS passed on releasing it. They simply didn't understand it. A stand-off occurred. In March Rude Boy was released, Ray Mingay's film of the band's embryonic years focusing on star-struck fan Ray Gange. The group had long since become ambivalent about the whole venture, initiated by Rhodes, especially after they were forced to repeat their performances to live footage to improve the sound quality.

Subsequent dates in America followed that month, where 'Train In Vain' had reached the Top 30 when pulled as a single, with support provided by Dread and Lee Dorsey. Dread then accompanied them on a trip to Kingston to record in the Channel One Studios. But CBS, still at loggerheads with the group over 'Bankrobber', refused to foot the bill. They tried to record 'Junco Partner' but were subject to the unwanted attentions of would-be interlopers looking for the pockets stuffed full of money. Of which there were none. According to Strummer, Dread had advised them that they had to stump up an 'honour tithe' to the local drug barons. They didn't have it. So they piled into a Renault station wagon and headed for the airport, reconvening at New York's Iroquois Hotel. They then checked into the Power Station in

Manhattan with the intention of recording a follow-up to London Calling.

Sharing a studio with Chic and Diana Ross, they retained Mikey Dread, ostensibly as producer, but also engineer Bill Price. However, they were forced to relocate to Jimi Hendrix's Electric Lady studio after Oberstein and CBS started to quibble about the money burn. Richard Hell's guitarist Ivan Julian was invited to the ensuing sessions, as were Blockheads Micky Gallagher and Norman Watt-Roy. With each member of the band subject to their own private distractions, Headon's increasing dalliance with heroin, Strummer luxuriating in the New York vibe and Mick Jones' relationship with Ellen Foley, the sessions were fragmented. After Simonon returned to the fold for a couple of low-key gigs they returned to Europe for the rest of the 16 Tons European tour, which would conclude at the Hammersmith Palais. In the summer sessions for the forthcoming album were resumed at Wessex Studios.. Meanwhile, CBS had finally relented and 'Bankrobber' emerged as a single.

The sessions saw songs spill out, with little in the way of editing. Everything was poured in; brass, steel drums, piano, saxophone, with contributions from Headon's dog Battersea and Simonon's new girlfriend Pearl Harbor (Simonon would return the compliment on her album Don't Follow Me, I'm Lost Too). But as the sessions wore on, the sheer weight of songs amassed generated the curious idea of releasing a triple album, at the same price as a single LP. Their management were horrified by the idea but were told to 'fuck off'. Jenner: "I felt Sandinista! negated what punk was about. Punk was supposed to be about cutting the bullshit. I told them it would make a great single album, a good double album but a waffly triple album. That didn't make me very popular." Maurice Oberstein at CBS was persuaded by Kosmo Vinyl to issue the triple set at a reduced price of £5.99 on condition the band waived performance royalties on the first 200,000 copies.

Sandinista! was a sprawling, incoherent album with fantastic strands of pure innovation, but hugely annoying losing streaks in between. Strummer later insisted he wanted it to be seen as a 'snapshot' rather than an album in its own right, but always maintained that he was as deeply proud of it as any of his Clash records. Its references to the Nicaraguan rebellion were inspired by political radical Moe Armstrong, whom Strummer had met in San Francisco, but also knew through his membership of late 60s band Daddy Longlegs.

After the success of 'Guns Of Brixton', Simonon came up with another, though less compulsive reggae effort, 'The Crooked Beat'. There's a cover of Mose Allison's 'Look Here' and a new strain of militancy explored in 'The Call Up', though it seemed odd to hear West Londoners decrying the Vietnam draft rather than bitching about their giros. 'Junco Partner' is the album's most effective stab at reggae, and 'Hitsville UK', a duet between Jones and Foley using the 'You Can't Hurry Love' bass lick, the album's most intelligent, literate pop song. Others you need never hear more than once. The nadir is 'Mensforth Hill', using a tape of 'Something About England' played backwards. 'Silicone On Sapphire' sounds like something the BBC Radiophonic Orchestra would have taped over. Or perhaps the lowpoint is the kiddie chorus versions of 'Career Opportunities' and 'Guns Of Brixton'. But returning to the album bereft of the expectations and assumptions, it's a treasure trove of outstanding music. Check Topper Headon's frenetic percussion on 'Midnight Log', the gospel-punk of 'Police On My Back', or 'Rebel Waltz', the Clash's 'Golden Brown'. But it's true. There's an awful lot of frogs to be kissed before you get to the princes.

The record was released on 12 December and tapes were hand-delivered to Nick Kent at the NME, who tore into its perceived sloppiness. The Clash approached editor Neil Spencer and asked him to get the record re-reviewed. He refused. Other reviews were tepid. The Clash suddenly woke up to the fact that they had a critical disaster on their hands. The album sold relatively poorly, alongside the accompanying singles 'The Call Up' and 'Hitsville UK'. Rolling Stone gave it five stars, but criticism closer to home stung.

Partially as a result, the Clash split with Blackhill Management, despite both Jenner and King having argued so vociferously that the project was misguided. Instead, Bernie Rhodes, who'd been concurrently managing Vic Godard and running Club Left, came back into the fold, working hand in hand with Kosmo Vinyl, who'd stuck with the band. Rhodes was acknowledged officially as manager in February 1982, despite Mick Jones's protests. The others thought that it might be the way to make the good times roll again, and Rhodes immediately set about rekindling the group's original 'Wild Bunch' ethos. He instigated a switch from the standard tour itinerary in favour of weekly residencies in New York, Paris and London. The band also returned to Vanilla in the hope of finding the spark that had existed there prior to London Calling.

In April they recorded 'Radio Clash', themed on a pirate radio broadcast with lines inspired by Strummer's reading of Michael Herr's Despatches book of frontline reports from Vietnam. Then they flew over to America to play a residency at Bond's in New York. Rick Rubin and the Beastie Boys were transfixed by the performances, which featured Grandmaster Flash And The Furious Five as support, though they were bottled off the stage. "You really mean well sometimes," Jones later reflected, on giving the new hip hop pioneers such a platform, "and then other people are not ready for it. It pissed us off, I remember." Jones, in particular, had been obsessed with hip hop since encountering it on trips to New York to see girlfriend Foley. Graffiti artist Futura 2000 would decorate backdrops during the Clash set, which meant he at least escaped the missiles.

The first show was a triumph, but thereafter the venue was forced to limit entrance and disgruntled, ticket-holding punters were turned away. Then came a court ruling that the building was a fire hazard. The only way out was to agree to play 14 shows to a reduced capacity audience. News of the ticketing dilemma spread quickly and was flashed across the American news media. The Clash suddenly acquired some celebrity fans such as Robert De Niro and Martin Scorsese, who invited the band to appear as extras in his film King Of Comedy. Strummer would invite various spokespersons to join him and speak from the stage, including Allen Ginsberg.

The group was energised by the trip and the manner in which they had been clasped to Manhattan's bosom, and reconvened at their latest rehearsal space on Freston Road. A seven-night stand at the Theatre Mogador in Paris was followed by a further seven nights at the London Lyceum, as part of a short tour that concluded in Glasgow. In between they would start further recording sessions using the Rolling Stones mobile studios, including their tribute to the recently departed Guy Stevens, 'Midnight To Sevens'. However, Jones, missing Foley, persuaded his colleagues to relocate back to Electric Ladyland, where Jones would produce, working alongside engineer Jeremy Green and a returning Micky Foote.

The most conspicuous early song to take shape was 'Rock The Casbah', its title coming from Tymon Dogg, while he was performing some eastern scales. With Rhodes apparently complaining that the band was just recording 'ragas', that gave Strummer the inspiration for the song's opening lines. Headon developed the musical framework using a keyboard riff he's been playing around with, but also adding bass and drum parts. He wrote some lyrics for it that were instantly rejected by Strummer, who promptly disappeared to the toilet for 20 minutes and came up with the song's verses and chorus. But the band still credited Headon as the principal songwriter for the publishing, which would help him out considerably further down the line.

Combat Rock, initially known as Rat Patrol From Fort Bragg, was noticeably more self-contained than its forebear. The narratives were overwhelmingly about America. 'Sean Flynn' was inspired by Errol Flynn's son's service in Vietnam. Similar territory was explored in 'Straight To Hell'. 'Ghetto Defendant' saw Ginsberg repeat his spoken word recitation from Bond's, at Strummer's invitation. 'Charlie Don't Surf' was influenced by Charlie Sheen's line in Apocalypse Now – further evidence of how deep an impression the film had made on the Clash's psyche.

However, when they flew back to England for Christmas, customs discovered a small quantity of heroin on Headon's person. The cat was out of the bag. With Combat Rock unfinished and Far East tour dates pending, Headon's counsel prevailed upon the judge to let him off with a £500 fine and a promise that he'd undergo addiction treatment. The judge advised Headon not to be the 'best drummer in the graveyard' and consented. Headon was immediately packaged off to the Priory in Roehampton before returning for the dates in Japan and Australia.

There were disputes again, though, this time over the length of the tracks, with Jones preferring more extended, dance-based mixes. His compatriots were unconvinced. Rhodes suggested bringing in Gus Dudgeon before it was decided that Glyn Johns, who'd sorted out Let It Be for the Beatles as well as working with the Who, Stones and Small Faces, was the man for the job. He would remix the album at his home studio in Warnford, West Sussex, where the Clash reconvened, after a fashion. Jones hated what was being done and played the truculent, aggrieved artist for all he was worth, leaving the producer to threaten to walk out. Jones eventually relented after a few panicky phone calls. Johns' intervention meant that several songs were scrapped or trimmed back, so that the contents would be more focused and fill a single album. CBS were unlikely, after all, to be persuaded of the benefits of another multiple-album release. Strummer would later credit Johns with an "11th hour" rescue of the contents.

For all its difficult germination, Combat Rock revealed a rejuvenated Clash. Futura 200 reappeared on 'Overpowered By Funk', while 'Red Angel Dragnet' was jointly inspired by the death of Guardian Angel Frankie Melvin and De Niro's Travis Bickle character (the Bickle dialogue sourced with permission from Scorsese). If anything, it was even more fixated on America than its predecessor, but had the benefit of a trilogy of extraordinary songs in Strummer's fatalistic 'Straight To Hell', the exquisite but often-misunderstood 'Rock The Casbah' and 'Should I Stay Or Should I Go'. The latter was Jones' creation, and has historically been fingered as an expression of his growing discontent with the Clash. He's never confirmed or denied that reading.

The single, 'Know Your Rights', backed by 'First Night Back In London', trailed the album in April, with Combat Rock coming out the following month. However, before that happened, Strummer went AWOL. Bernie Rhodes had initiated the idea as a ruse to maximise expectation for the album and accelerate ticket sales for their tour. But Strummer had been down about the group for a long time, and not only ran with Rhodes' idea, but ran away with it. By the advent of a scheduled gig in Aberdeen, of all places (Aberdeen seems to be the preferred location for first generation punk bands to lose personnel) Strummer still hadn't shown up. The group was still totally unaware of his whereabouts until word got back he'd been spotted in Paris. Kosmo Vinyl was despatched to track him down, with a full UK tour and European dates scheduled and the risk of huge financial penalties if these shows were cancelled. Strummer was found, complete with beard. He'd even run the Paris Marathon incognito.

The band members were staggered when they found out that this had started out as a Rhodes wheeze. They fulfilled a planned festival appearance at Lochern, but it was Headon's last show with the band. His heroin addiction had been a concern for some time, but it had become increasingly obvious that it was now affecting his drumming. At the urging of Rhodes, he was told at a band meeting on the return from Lochern that he'd been 'suspended' from the American tour. He would never play with the band again. "That was very hard," Jones later conceded. "I was extremely reticent. I didn't want to do it, actually. But when you are like that, you don't have no time for reflection or analysis... you're just going that fast. So I reluctantly went along with it and it was very hard. Joe actually said that probably that was the start of the end for us as well, and that could have been so. We were very sorry to let Topper go, but if you can't work you can't work and it got like that. We felt like we didn't have any option at the time."

Though shocked, Headon has since become philosophical and accepted that he left his bandmates little alternative. "The band had no choice in the end but to get rid of me because I was out there and I didn't even think that I had a problem myself." His departure was reported as being due to "a difference of opinion over the political direction the band will be taking". It was black propaganda and an off-white lie. His next years were lost to the narcotic. Mick Jones later would invite him to join an early version of Big Audio Dynamite but he blew that, as well as various advances for a solo deal and ended up driving a cab to support his habit. Terry Chimes re-entered the fold for the upcoming US dates. Strummer would maintain that the Clash only ever played one good gig (in New Jersey) after Headon left, though several fans would dispute that.

The band played some rescheduled gigs in Britain that had been cancelled due to Strummer's disappearance, and then returned to America. They were then approached to support the Who on their farewell tour of 1982, having turned down the opportunity to back the Rolling Stones a year earlier. The shows culminated in two sets at Shea Stadium, though they got a mixed reception, and at an earlier arena show at the Detroit Silverdome they were bottled off stage.

Pete Howard, formerly of Bath's Cold Fish, eventually won through the drummer's auditions, which additionally involved playing a footie game for the Clash XI against the Damned XI. He was in place for the band's warm-up American shows leading to their appearance at the Us Festival in Los Angeles, organised by Steve Wozniak of Apple Computers. The band appeared in front of 150,000 people but spent the whole day wrangling with the organiser about donating profits to good causes, culminating in an on-stage fist fight at the end of their set.

Tensions between Jones and the rest of the band, which had been exacerbated over the previous gruelling months of touring and the decision to remix Combat Rock, were still evident when the band reconvened in June at Ear Studios. His appearances were irregular, his timekeeping lax. "I arrived in the studio and Topper, who'd already left the group, was there for some reason with Paul and Joe," Jones later told Danny Baker. "There was a really different atmosphere from usual, more intense. Joe just said, 'Mick, we've decided we don't want to play with you any more.' I asked Paul what he thought, but he didn't really say anything. So I put my guitar back in the case and stormed out. Bernie came running out – he wasn't in the studio, he was in one of the other rooms – and he gave me a cheque. 'What's happened?' sort of thing. I told him and he said, 'Well, have this, it'll be alright.' A gold watch! Oh, I was devastated." The crucial songwriting axis at the heart of the Clash was over. By the end of the same afternoon, Jones had started putting together what would eventually become Big Audio Dynamite – an extension of his interest in the hip hop phenomenon he'd caught first-hand in New York.

Strummer later intimated that it was Rhodes who pushed the decision. But being Strummer, he made no attempt to excuse himself. "I did him wrong. I stabbed him in the back. Really, it's through his good grace we got back together (as friends). That's a good thing, a rare thing." Simonon told Clash magazine: "I suppose Mick got carried away with things for himself in so far as he didn't wanna go on tour, and I suppose me and Joe felt like, 'Sod it. Let's chop our arm off and let's just keep going anyway because we wanna go at 100mph and maybe Mick just wants to go at 80mph at the moment. Who knows? It's just one of those instinctive things that we just reacted to and kicked him out." Jones was philosophical. Eventually. "These things happen after a while, and they're supposed to happen sometimes. We were really fed up with each other. If we'd have had a holiday maybe it would have been different, but we didn't have holidays in those days. We never stopped… I was hurt, obviously, as you would be… especially if you formed the band. But these things happen and then we made it up."

A statement was issued to the NME, stating that "Jones had drifted away from the original idea of the Clash". The same edition carried a denial by Jones that the statement was true. Musicians wanted adverts subsequently appeared in Melody Maker and auditions at the Electric Ballroom in London saw two aspirants taken on board. Nick Sheppard, formerly of the Cortinas, and Greg White, a science student from Southampton, who would be renamed Vince White. Bernie Rhodes took advantage of troubled minds to reassert his control of the group and decreed an end to the gratuitous rock star behavior that had overtaken them. The new line-up played its first shows together on a six-date tour of California in January 1984, then returned to England for a show at the Brixton Academy in March, before setting out on the extensive Out Of Control tour which amounted to some 80-odd shows. Meanwhile, Strummer became a father.

CBS were still waiting for a new album, and by early 1985 were pressing the case. With Jones, the group's musical compass, cast adrift, Strummer hit on the idea of using programmed drums and synthesizers and Rhodes, trying to ape his old friend/nemesis Malcolm McLaren's success as an artist, got himself involved in the musical orchestration under the pseudonym Joe Unidos. At this point, we can assume, Strummer's eye was not on the ball any more. Both Sheppard and White worked on chord arrangements, though the album's signature song, and arguably the only one worth hearing, 'This Is England', arrived readymade by Strummer, composed on a single string of a ukulele.

On release, Cut The Crap took a hammering in all but one of the main British journals. Its title, also suggested by Rhodes, was an open goal for critics. Never the thickest-skinned of artists, Strummer admitted he'd been remiss in handing over so much musical control to Rhodes and practically disowned the album. He took a month off in Spain, but then told fellow band members Sheppard and White, that he considered the band finished. "When the Clash collapsed," he later reflected, "we were tired. There had been a lot of intense activity in five years. Secondly, I felt we'd run out of idea gasoline. And thirdly, I wanted to shut up and let someone else have a go at it." For a brief time Simonon and Rhodes auditioned for new singers, before hatching a new project, Havana 3AM. The Clash split was finally announced at the end of 1985.

After Havana 3AM Simonon reacquainted himself with his first love, and became a successful full-time artist. Despite sticking in there the longest, he was the member of the band who remained most resistant to any notion of a reformation. Mick Jones enjoyed sustained success, alongside Don Letts, with Big Audio Dynamite, also working with the Farm and others, before forming Carbon-Silicon with his best friend Tony James. He also produced Theatre Of Hate, the Libertines and Babyshambles.

Strummer's post-Clash career was hindered by his strained relationship with CBS. He never really forgave them. As he would tell Big Takeover's Jack Rabid, "What day is it? Monday? Then the record company must be pissing on me." In the end, the only way he could escape his CBS/Sony contract was to "bore them" into submission in 2000 by refusing to record. There was soundtrack and acting work, and collaborations with the Pogues, Levellers, Happy Mondays and Latin Rockabilly War. Shortly before his death, he had been clearly rejuvenated leading the Mescaleros. He had long since patched up his relationship with Mick Jones, for personal rather than professional reasons. The reunion stories had been doing the rounds for years, though Strummer would retaliate that the band only considered such a move in moments of "the bitterest financial gloom". One such moment occurred when they were offered big bucks to headline Lollapalooza. They declined. Strummer, typically honest, would admit that he was the one most open to such an idea, but understood his former colleagues' reticence.

It didn't matter, and perhaps it was for the best that Strummer's knocked up Telecaster and Jones's flashy Gibson Les Paul only danced together one more time, at a Fire Brigade Union benefit in 2002. The first time the entire band had been together in the same room in 16 years came when they went up to accept an Ivor Novello Award. "We spent the first 10 minutes apologising to each other," Headon recalled to Clash magazine, "and then we all just laughed and realised that we were young men. We were young men with the world at our feet and we all dealt with it in different ways."

Strummer and the Clash were riddled with contradictions. They were happy to lie to their record company but mortified when they received the same treatment in return. They opted for a major label and then were surprised when chosen major label behaved in a manner that every major label has done, since time immemorial. When the tributes to Strummer flowed in, probably the least hysterical and most accurate came from former manager Pete Jenner. "Joe was always the most articulate man. But he wasn't constantly rational, which I found difficult on a business level... one minute he'd be perfectly rational and the next it would go into rock'n'roll irrationality. For example, there was no way he was going to go on Top Of The Pops and mime. So we ended up with Pan's People dancing to 'Bankrobber' or something. Frankly, they'd have been better off miming... They also said they weren't gong to do big gigs, only theatre-sized gigs. But then after they left us they promptly went and toured with the Who. And they only wanted to charge £3 at gigs, but they wouldn't cut the production costs in the way that a pricing policy like that dictated. The result was we were always in debt to CBS because we had to ask the record company for tour support. Then they always had to have top-class hotel rooms, but they'd want to take all the kids back after a gig, and that caused problems. My view was that if you wanted to be down with the kids, then you stayed somewhere cheaper in the first place."

But contradictions aside, you can't argue with someone who had to be nightly covered in gaffer tape to try to prevent him mutilating the Strummer strumming hand, so hard did he play. A commitment that was matched by the rest of his band, and yes, for a long time the Clash truly were the most exciting group in rock music.

DISCOGRAPHY:

(Buyer's Guide: It's relatively straightforward. Begin with The Clash, Give Em Enough Rope and London Calling (the reissue is sumptuous), then Sandanista! and Combat Rock. Give Cut The Crap a wide berth. Of the various compilations, The Clash On Broadway is

excellent, with great sleevenotes and (in some cases superior) alternative takes. The live album, From Here To Eternity, is well worth checking out, but there are many excellent bootlegs, especially of the Bond's material)

White Riot/1977 7-inch (CBS 5058 March 1977)

The Clash LP (CBS 82000 April 1977) (released, nearly 18 months too late, in the US with a totally revised track-listing – with the singles 'Clash City Rockers', 'Complete Control', 'White Man In Hammersmith Palais' and 'I Fought The Law' added at the expense of 'Deny' and 'Protex Blue'. Until October 2000 the various CD reissues in America never attended to this folly. And even then, instead of issuing the UK version with the tracks added to the original US issue of the album as bonus tracks, they decided to issue The Clash in separate UK (4953442) and US (4953452) versions. You can't beat a multinational record company for Olympic standard stupidity, can you? Or perhaps just good old-fashioned profiteering. The original CD reissue, Columbia CD32232, in April 1989, featured the US track-listing too)

Capital Radio/Interview/Listen 7-inch (NME CL 1 April 1977) (free single given away to those who sent in stickers attached to the album and NME voucher)

Remote Control/London's Burning 7-inch (CBS 5293 May 1977)

Complete Control/City Of The Dead 7-inch (CBS 5664 September 1977)

Clash City Rockers/Jail Guitar Doors 7-inch (CBS 5834 February 1978)

White Man In Hammersmith Palais/The Prisoner 7-inch (CBS 6383 June 1978)

Give 'Em Enough Rope LP (CBS 82431 November 1978) (reissued in 1984 on vinyl and cassette, CBS/50 32444, and on CD in January 1991, Columbia CD 32444, and again, in remastered form, in October 1999 on Columbia 4953462)

Tommy Gun/1-2 Crush On You 7-inch (CBS 6788 November 1978)

English Civil War/Pressure Drop 7-inch (CBS 7082 February 1979)

Cost Of Living 7-inch EP (CBS 7324 May 1979)

I Fought The Law/Groovy Times/Gates Of The West/Capital Radio

London Calling/Armagideon Time 7-inch (CBS 8087 December 1979) (also issued as a 12-inch, 12 8087, in January 1980, with bonus tracks 'Justice Tonight' and 'Kick It Over')

London Calling dbl LP (CBS Clash 3 December 1979) (reissued on double album/cassette in February 1988, Columbia 460114-1/3 and on CD in April 1989 on Columbia 460114-2, then again on 4953272 in 2004. See archive releases for details of fuller 25th Anniversary re-release that year)

Bankrobber/Rocker's Galore... UK Tour 7-inch (CBS 8323 August 1980) (B-side by Mikey Dread)

The Call Up/Stop The World 7-inch (CBS 9339 November 1980)

Sandanista triple LP (CBS FSLN 1 December 1980) (reissued on double CD in April 1989 on Columbia, 463364-2, and again, in remastered form, in October 1999, on Columbia 4953482)

Hitsville UK/Radio One 7-inch (CBS 9480 January 1981) (B-side by Mikey Dread)

The Magnificent Seven/Magnificent Dance 7-inch (CBS A1133 May 1981) (also issued on 12-inch, A12 1133, with stickers)

This Is Radio Clash/Radio Clash 7-inch (CBS A131797 November 1981) (also issued on 12-inch, A13 1797, with bonus tracks 'Outside Broadcast' and 'Radio 5')

Know Your Rights/First Night Back In London 7-inch (CBS A2309 April 1982)

Combat Rock LP (CBS FMLN 2 May 1982) (reissued on vinyl and cassette in November 1986, CBS/4032787, and on CD in January 1991 on Columbia, 32787, and again, in remastered form, on Columbia, 4953493, in October 1999)

Rock The Casbah/Long Time Jerk 7-inch CBS A 2479 June 1982) (also issued on 12-inch, A13 2479, with the B-side 'Mustapha Dance', and 7-inch picture disc, A11 2479)

Should I Stay Or Should I Go?/Straight To Hell 7-inch (CBS A 2646) (also issued on 12-inch, A13 2646, with free stencil, and on 7-inch picture disc, S CBS A11 2646)

This Is England/Do It Now 7-inch (CBS A 6122 September 1985) (initial copies in poster sleeve, also issued on 12-inch, TA 6122, with bonus track 'Sex Mad War')

Cut The Crap LP (CBS 26601 November 1985) (reissued on CD, Columbia 465110-2, in April 1989, and again in July 2000 on Columbia 4953502)

POSTHUMOUS/ARCHIVE RELEASES:

The Story Of The Clash dbl LP (CBS 460244 March 1988) (Also issued on cassette and CD. Re-released in October 1995 as The Story Of The Clash Volume 1 on Columbia, 460244-2, then again in March 2004 on Columbia, 4953512. Unfortunately, nobody thought to blow up the sleevenotes for the CD release, so you'll need a microscope)

Black Market Clash 10-inch mini-LP (CBS 36846 November 1980) (at the time this was a useful release to round up odds and ends. It's now been reissued on CD as Super Black Market Clash, Columbia 474546 in November 1993, and again in October 1999 on Columbia 4953522. Both the latter releases comprise a revised and expanded tracklisting)

The Singles CD (Columbia 4953532 November 1991) (if convenience is death, this is a pleasant way to go for those who want the Clash-lite experience)

The Clash On Broadway triple CD box set (Epic/Legacy 46991 November 1991) (a nice collection, with some great alternate versions and some stomping live takes, plus a great little booklet drawing on first-hand quotes)

From Here To Eternity CD (Columbia 4961832 October 1999) (also available as a double vinyl album. One of the world's greatest live bands never released a live album in their lifetime. Purists might have opted for a single-concert option, but this collection of superb recordings is still welcome, and not just for the already initiated. The band themselves oversaw the selection of tracks, settling on 17 tracks spanning 1978 to 1982, with Jonesy working on the mixing and Simonon designing the accompanying booklet. The latter features an oral history of the band's gigs from fans which rather gets lost in each person saying how great they were, or, as a spectacular nadir, thanking them for "having the balls to rock.")

The Essential Clash dbl CD (Columbia 5109982 March 2003)

London Calling 25th Anniversary Edition CD (Sony 517928-3 September 2004)

CD1: Standard version of London Calling. CD2: The Vanilla Sessions. CD3: The Last Testament – The Making Of London Calling DVD (Vanilla sees the rehearsal tapes prior to London Calling released officially for the first time, and a fascinating insight it is. It had long been thought that the originals were lost when roadie Johnny Green left them on a tube train by mistake. However, the quality is pretty rank and you're not likely to want to play it more than once. The DVD is OK, but you're far better off with Letts' earlier Clash-themed work, Westway To The World. Not as deluxe a package as you might think, and pretty expensive. Funny to think, the Clash used to outrage their record company by issuing triple albums at the price of a single disc. Now they, effectively, release single albums at triple-album price. Maybe the marketing men won after all)

The Classics

John Clay (vocals, guitar), Ash Aisthorpe (bass, backing vocals), Mick Freer (drums)

Following the fragmentation of their previous band, in 1977 John Clay, Keith Newby and Rob Hampson brought in Ash Aisthorpe to play bass in a new venture, to be called THE CLASSICS. Based in Lincolnshire and South Humberside – specifically Scunthorpe and Grimsby – the first few months of 1978 were "pretty tempestuous", according to Clay. "It became apparent after a fair number of gigs that Keith and Rob were not entirely committed to things, so Ash and I split and found a new drummer in Mick Freer from Grimsby, whilst retaining the name." At the same time Steve Robinson, also from Scunthorpe, joined on guitar and vocals for a brief period. "But his time was short-lived due to a preoccupation with all things American or the Rolling Stones – hardly credible leanings for a budding punk/new wave band."

They continued as a trio for a short period after Robinson's departure, until Shaun Ashworth of Doncaster joined on keyboards. Clay sees this period – between 1978 and 1980 – as the band's most creative. They toured regularly around the east of England: Yorkshire, Lincolnshire, Humberside and Nottinghamshire, while breaking in a set of originals. These included 'Zero Ambition', 'Check Her Alibi', 'New Generation', 'Backseat Romeo', 'Hello World', 'Sign Of The Times', 'The Cull', 'Legends Of The Greeks', etc. The golden period ended in 1980 when Ashworth left and they became a three-piece once again.

A three-song demo was recorded at Fairview Studios in Hull, comprising 'Check Her Alibi', 'New Generation' and 'Zero Ambition'. It resulted in a deal for a single with Future Earth Records in Doncaster, and saw them return to Fairview to record 'Zero Ambition' and 'In The Night' (featuring Terry Wincott from Scunthorpe prog rock band Amazing Blondel on keyboards). However, by the time it was released on 18 October 1980, the band had elected to change its name to Back Street Romeos, having been alerted to the presence of another Classics with a prior claim.

That Christmas, John Clay had two lengthy auditions in London to join Magazine. But, when asked to spend a week with the band with a view to joining full-time, he had to pull out because of work commitments (Magazine split anyway a few months later). The Backseat Romeos, too, never got that much further. Freer left the band, to be replaced by Trevor Fearnley (who'd served in Clay's old band the Seagulls in the early-70s). "This led to a rockier sound," reckons Clay, "but whilst this line-up was potentially the strongest the band had, things were getting tired and by late 1981 we decided to split."

C

Of the former members, Ashworth would go on to tour the world as part of Edwin Starr's band. Aisthorpe and Freer both live in Grimsby. Aisthorpe still 'dabbles' in bands. Freer moved away from music, but was drawn back for a series of concerts in 2001 when the Classics reformed for his 40th birthday. Clay continued to play in bands to the present day, and now runs Stunted Records. In 1999 he compiled a CD of demos and out-takes of Classics/Backstreet Romeos material, which may see the light of day at some point.

Cock Sparrer

Micky Beaufoy (guitar), Steve Bruce (drums), Steve Burgess (bass), Colin McFaull (vocals)

COCK SPARRER, oft-cited as progenitors of the Oi! movement, actually existed in a time-frame long distant from the skinhead scene of the early-80s. They formed as school friends in the East End of London in 1974, the original quartet having known each other from the age of eleven. They took their inspiration from the Rolling Stones and, in particular, the Small Faces. Theirs was a naturally aggressive, hyperactive form of R&B, their resolve further hardened when bands such as Dr Feelgood and Eddie And The Hot Rods began to energise the pub rock scene. They quickly picked up support slots to the then rampant Slade, and were regulars at Terry Murphy's Bridgehouse venue in Canning Town. They were grateful for the exposure at a time when others were reluctant to give them gigs. They eventually built up such a following that their shows there became, according to Sparrer mythology, akin to "home games".

With the advent of punk, Cock Sparrer were quick to sniff the winds of change, and two members of the band approached Malcolm McLaren in his Sex boutique at 430 King's Road after he'd placed an advert in Melody Maker. McLaren, after playing their demo tape, was intrigued enough to go and watch them upstairs at their local, the Roding in East Ham, in 1976. However, legend has it the band resisted his approaches when he blatantly refused to get a round in. History might, indeed, have been a little different had Talcy not been such a thoroughgoing tightwad.

Despite being passed over by McLaren, the group was soon embroiled in the nascent punk scene, playing regular shows at the Roxy. However, their 'boisterous' following, the Poplar Boys, similar to the Finchley Boys but with tattoos and West Ham scarves, would get them barred from the Nashville and Vortex. Decca made them one third of a roster of punk bands, alongside Slaughter And The Dogs and Adam And The Ants, who were all heavily associated with violent followings. Two singles ensued. 'Runnin' Riot', produced in Hampstead by Thin Lizzy collaborator Nick Tauber, allowed them to half-inch a barrowload of studio gear, but was more enduringly a template for much of the Oi! movement that would follow in their wake. It was arguably the first time a link was cemented between aggressive R&B and the football terraces, violence at which was entering one of its cyclic peaks. A demo version came in a picture cover featuring a West Ham pitch invasion. The B-side, 'Sister Suzie', was pure hand-me-down Slade, however.

If battle lines had been drawn between art-punk and prole-punk, though perhaps not as clinically as Jon Savage would later suggest, there was little doubt about which side of the fence Cock Sparrer chose. More pertinently they'd have been quite happy to nick the fence and sell it as firewood at the first opportunity.

The follow-up single was a thumping cover of the Rolling Stones' 'We Love You', which begs the question, why did so many hard-arse skinhead bands hold the Stones in such esteem (for example, Skrewdriver) when Jagger was surely the most fey vocalist on the planet? Even the band members, who now included Burgess's cousin Garrie Lammin on rhythm guitar (from late 1976 to mid-1978), are a little perplexed as to why they entertained the idea. Following the single's commercial disappearing act, they were left in no man's land by Decca's escalating financial difficulties. They were so aggrieved at various absurd marketing suggestions that 'We Love You' was released in a blank sleeve at their insistence. They also managed to fall out with manager Cliff Cooper and ended up booking their own shows. Which wasn't easy, given the reputation of their fans, who liked to emulate their heroes by nicking anything that wasn't physically nailed down. In truth, neither single had sold at all well, and the band, with e-bay still just a twinkle in Pierre Omidyar's eye, were reduced to shooting unused crates of both in the garden of their communal house in Dagenham to appease their boredom.

A 1978 review in Sounds confirmed that the media, when it paid any attention whatsoever, maintained a patronising view of Cock Sparrer. "Musically and visually, the Cock Sparrer crew are just about as motley and uncouth as it's possible for a band to project," it began. "Imagine five collectively imageless Cockneys with hair length varying from skinhead to Woody Roller, wearing clothes that look like they pool from jumble sales, and singing about how East End life is tough but fun." This is the only occasion I can ever remember when a rock magazine criticised a band for being uncouth. In an interview in the NME published that same February, they made no pretence about their preference for football over fashion, reasoning that there was nothing in the King's Road they could afford to buy, even if they wanted to. But they talked with optimism about their debut album, on which Steve Marriott was slotted to guest after they managed to secure a support slot to the Small Faces.

The album would, ultimately, remain in the can, as Decca collapsed. The band didn't so much break up – after all, they remained the best of friends – as stop playing. Lammin departed to become an actor while his former colleagues financed a trip to the US by selling their PA. It wasn't theirs anyway. Eventually Cock Sparrer transmuted into the Little Roosters, wearing their Stones influences on their sleeves again, and were better able to secure gigs. Their 'I Need A Witness' single was produced by Joe Strummer.

With the advent of Oi! in the early-80s, Cock Sparrer's legacy was unearthed and celebrated by almost all of the principal participants, partly due to the fact that Garry Bushell included 'Sunday Stripper' on the first Oi! compilation, and both 'Runnin' Riot' and 'Taken For A Ride' on 1981's Strength Thru Oi! As a result they reformed the band and released a series of albums throughout the decade, but only the one single, 'England Belongs To Me', later covered by Roger Miret's Agnostic Front.

We needn't concern ourselves unduly with this second incarnation, apart from noting, firstly, that comeback album Shock Troops, which distilled all their frustration with being messed about by Decca, is actually pretty engrossing, if a little short on subtlety. Sadly, 'England Belongs To Me' was mindlessly co-opted by a host of right wing skinhead groups as some kind of anthem. Which didn't appeal to Cock Sparrer at all, especially given that the original title was 'London Belongs To Me', which was ultimately rejected because it didn't scan. It is not, as has been reported, based on Elgar's 'Land Of Hope And Glory', it merely includes an excerpt as the guitar solo. In any case, Eglar's family refused them permission to use it, so Beaufoy composed an alternative guitar solo, using the same basic chords. 'Watch Your Back', a succinct statement about their distrust of politicos, more adequately stated their distrust of factions.

Thereafter Beaufoy decided on a career break – he needed to earn some real money – though he would guest at several future dates, including the Gibus Club in Paris, Bushell's Birthday Bash at the Bridgehouse and the show that produced the Live And Loud album. Brazilian Chris Skepis was recruited as rhythm guitarist while Shug O'Neil temporarily took over on lead guitar. Both of them are pictured on the sleeve to Shock Troops when it was finally released, though Shug didn't actually play a note on it. Skepis did provide rhythm guitar on a few of the tracks.

The two new recruits were both present for the Runnin' Riot In 1984 LP, notable for the inclusion of 'The Sun Says' and a more sophisticated approach to songwriting – 'Think Again' sounds like the Skids composing a theme for a 50s TV show. Indeed, several of the tracks are far more 'poppy' than the band's reputation might suggest. Afterwards they slunk back to their day jobs, until Bruce, landlord of the Stick Of Rock in Bethnal Green, was approached with a view to putting the band back together. The original quartet, plus rhythm guitarist Daryl Smith, reconvened for a sold-out show at the Astoria. And they have been playing together on and off ever since, cutting two new studio albums in the form of Guilty As Charged and Two Monkeys. By a bizarre quirk of fate, Daryl Smith, who has also played with the Crack, Argy Bargy and the Mistakes, is the son of Mike Smith, who first signed Cock Sparrer to Decca in 1977. Since he bowed out of live performance in 2004, Beaufoy has also covered for the Crack as a means of staying in touch with the scene and keeping his fingers supple.

Beaufoy points out that, as far as the band is concerned, they have never been more successful. "For us, it is a period where we have moved from being just an influential band (many top US 'street punk' bands have cited us as a major influence) to being one that most promoters really want to headline their festivals. We now have a reputation for putting bums of seats." In addition, he points to their headlining performances at the 2003 Wasted Festival, recorded for DVD release, as evidence of the band's popularity and still current appeal. "The key point is that this band is more than just a band – it is first and foremost a group of mates, who really like and respect each other, and somehow the fans have latched onto this and want to come and see us perform. Which they do in their thousands."

For anyone who wants to check out the history of Cock Sparrer, I'll point you in the direction of their What You See Is What You Get DVD. As well as footage of their headlining performance at Holidays In The Sun in 2003, it also includes the documentary Memory Lane, which is an excellent primer on their 30-odd year career.

Discography:

Runnin' Riot/Sister Suzie 7-inch (Decca FR 13710 July 1977)

We Love You/Chip On My Shoulder 7-inch (Decca FR 13722 November 1977) (also issued as a 12-inch single with picture sleeve, unlike either of their first two 7-inches)

England Belongs To Me/Argy Bargy 7-inch (Carrerre CAR 225 1982)

Shock Troops LP (Razor RAZ 9 1983) (reissued by Link in 1991 with extra track 'England Belongs To Me' and on CD by Captain Oi! AHOY CD 004, in 1997, with bonus tracks 'Argy Bargy' and 'Colonel Bogey', plus lyrics)

Runnin' Riot In '84 LP (Syndicate SYNLP 7 1984) (reissued on CD, along with Shock Troops, by Step-1 STEP CD 028 in 1998. Also re-released as Runnin' Riot by Link in 1988. Reissued by Bitzcore, LP 01724-RED and then by Captain Oi!, AHOY CD 57, with bonus track 'The Sun Says' (Oi! LP version' and lyrics)

True Grit LP (Razor RAZ 26 1986) (this includes the Decca material and a number of demos recorded at that juncture for a proposed album that was shelved)

Live And Loud LP (Link LINK LP 05 1987) (reissued by Harry May, MAYO CD 507, in 2001)

Guilty As Charged LP & CD (Bitzcore LP/CD 01692-1-2 1994) (amusing footnote. The original working title was 'Smells Like Metholated Spirit')

Run Away CD (Bitzcore 1995) (also released on 7-inch and 10-inch vinyl)

Two Monkeys CD (Bitzcore 1997) (yup, it's the same 'Back Home' as that once sung by the England World Cup Squad for the 1970 Mexico World Cup. Yikes).

ARCHIVE RELEASES:

Runnin' Riot/Live And Loud CD (Link 1991) (two for one re-release)

Shock Troops/Runnin' Riot In 84 CD (Slogan 1992) (ditto)

Rarities CD (Link 1992) (16 tracks compiling both early and later material, including their three contributions to the Oi! compilations. Re-released by Captain Oi! AHOYCD 36 1994 with bonus tracks: What's It Like To Be Old (Oi! LP Version)/Teenage Heart (Oi! Chartbuster Version)/Run For Cover (Oi! Chartbuster Version)

The Best Of Cock Sparrer CD (Step-1 STEP CD 014 1993)

England Belongs To Me CD (Can Can CANCAN 007CD 1997) (also released by Harry May Recordings, MAYO CD 130)

Bloody Minded (The Best Of Cock Sparrer) CD (Dr Strange DSR 73 1997)

Live And Loud (with the Business) CD (Step-1 STEP CD 004 1998)

Chip On My Shoulder CD (Harry May MAYO CD 112 1998) (inessential career retrospective which also includes four live selections drawn from Live And Loud!)

Diamonds And Pearls (DDS DDS 003 2000) (though the sleeve won't tell you, this is actually the same material compiled on True Grit, albeit without the bonus tracks and decent packaging)

Runnin' Riot Across The USA dbl LP/CD (TKO Records 2001) (drawn from February 2000 shows at the Great American Music Hall in San Francisco and CBGB's in New York)

Back Home CD (Captain Oi! AHOY CD 231 2003)

The Decca Years CD (Captain Oi! AHOY CD 279 May 2006) (this is the first official CD release of the band's original Decca recordings with familiar Captain Oi! attention to detail in packaging, illustration of foreign sleeves, etc)

Control Zone

Barry Sweeney (guitar, vocals), Mushy McGuigan (bass, vocals), Aidy Connolly (drums)

Omagh's CONTROL ZONE formed in 1978, the original trio later joined by Tony McGartland (aka Ernie Badness). McGartland, later a journalist and biographer of

Control Zone playing on the steps of Omagh Courthouse in July 1981. Tony McGartland is on the left, Barry Sweeney on the right.

the Buzzcocks, convinced them that they needed someone with the "influence and the maturity that would get them recognised." The name, incidentally, came from "the circumstances of the Troubles. All of the town centres in the North were 'Control Zones', as a result of restricted parking and the possibility of car bombs. The name came from the street signs that were posted over the security barriers. We tried to take one of the signs down one night, to use as a backdrop for our gigs, only to be chased by an army foot patrol."

Within weeks of Badness joining, the band had written several numbers and managed to talk BBC producer Don Cootes into featuring them on BBC2's Grapevine community programme. Through their acquaintance with Cootes they also featured in the BBC Northern Ireland short series, 'Bout You (recorded in February 1981, screened in April). For the latter they were commissioned to record six songs in the BBC's Belfast studios. McGartland: "On the way to the studio we used our expenses for the day to buy enough cider and Guinness from an off-licence in the city. By the end of the mammoth ten-hour session," notes McGartland, "we fell out with each other and left the engineers to do the final mix and production while the band found their separate ways back to Omagh."

They struggled to make much headway, usually begging support slots with Outcasts, Rudi, the Moondogs and visiting bands from either Derry or Belfast. However, they did win a local Battle Of the Bands competition, got their four-track demo tape, featuring 'Left Right March', 'Johnny Johnny', 'So Complete' and 'Borstal' played by Davy Sims on Downtown Radio, and recorded six songs for the BBC. The idea, bizarrely, was to cut tracks representing each county in the North (for example, 'Lovely Derry On The Banks Of The Foyle') in punk rock fashion. McGartland: "We signed the rights to the recordings over to the BBC for £175 and bought our first PA system. As a result of the TV exposure, gigs were more frequent and we managed to talk a local man, Pete McLaughlin, into organising gigs and doing the talking. He had a bit of style about him, he dressed well and had no problem asking for the money." The band stayed loyal to their following by playing frequently at their local youth club, using a boxing ring as a stage. Sweeney was writing at "an incredible rate", songs which were crafted from "experiences of the things that affected us socially".

In 1983 they contributed two tracks to the United Skins compilation album, after being sent a £275 advance by Mickey French of the Last Resort for recording costs, and appeared alongside several other lesser lights of the Oi! movement, as well as Skrewdriver. McGartland:

"I recorded one of our rehearsals at a local youth club and sent the demo to Micky French in London. He rang me to say that he'd been playing the demos in his East London shop and that all the skins from the East End were in the shop and were asking who the band was. He thought we were great, so asked us to go into the studio and record three songs. We did, but it turned out that he dropped 'Left Right March' because I told him it was about the H-Block campaign." It wasn't the only song prompting controversy. "I wrote 'Bloody Bouncers' after being barred from a local night club, the bouncers there were notorious for their heavy handed behaviour on the door. We played the song at a local open-air festival in town and were threatened never to play it again in public or they would 'sort us out'."

Following United Skins' release, the band was invited to tour the UK with the other featured artists, but rejected the idea when they realised Skrewdriver would be part of the bill (Skrewdriver had been renamed Freedom Of Speech for subsequent CD reissues of the record). "Micky French called me to say they had a tour of the UK lined up to promote the album and was keen to get us over. When I put it to the rest of the band they were not impressed. We were told by French that we would see a draft of the album sleeve before it was finalised. He didn't keep to his word and as a result we were on an album which basically was adorned by union jack flags. We were worried about the response on the street here so we quickly withdrew from any further contact. The band asked me to contact him and make it known that we were unhappy, which I did, and that was our last contact with the label."

McGartland: "After the album was released, I just lost interest in the way things went. The Lady of the Lake festival outdoor gig was August 1982. One week later I remember playing a local gig, I broke a string halfway through the set, threw my guitar on the stage floor and walked off. It was my last gig with them. I felt that I had fulfilled a lifelong ambition to make a record and now with it done, I suppose the band had no purpose for me." Control Zone split up without recording anything else, though apparently good live recordings do exist.

COMPILATION:
United Skins LP (Boots & Braces SKREW LP 1 1983; 'Bloody Bouncers', 'Johnny Johnny') (later bootlegged by Pure Impact on CD)

John Cooper Clarke

The Salford Bard, JOHN COOPER CLARKE pepped up many a dreary punk rock gig with his droll, drawled snapshots of internecine cultural warfare, decaying Britain and the follies and foibles of the age. Visually, he was a cross between Bob Dylan, Bob Willis and a coathanger, a besuited beanpole with shocked locks and a scything tongue that was every bit the equal of his Mancunian compatriots Mark E Smith and Morrissey. Clarke was, like them, of Irish Catholic descent and working class background.

The double-barrelled name (Cooper is his middle name) only arose because there was another poet working the circuit called John Clarke when he first started out. His first poem was inspired when the local priest farted during a service, and while familiar with all the great literary figures and the many facades of high art, he never forgot the importance of toilet humour.

Permanently wearing darkened glasses due to his long-sightedness, Clarke left school at 15 to go on to a succession of menial jobs, including stints as a window cleaner, dishwasher, mortician and apprentice mechanic. These culminated in two years as a lab technician at Salford Tech College. "I've had a few jobs, but if you want to be a writer, you're better off getting a job that doesn't require that you do anything," he later confessed to the Idler. "There used to be a lot of these jobs around. The best one I had was as a firewatcher on Plymouth docks. I had to be there, but once I was there, there was nothing to do. It's ideal because you're not surrounded by distractions of your own choice. You're doing the Graham Greene thing – you're going in at nine and coming back at five and that's a long time to write. Some of it's good, some of it's shite. It's a lot easier to write under those circumstances than it is when you're a completely free man. You can always find something better to do than writing when you're at home."

In the meantime he'd immersed himself in music, playing bass in a series of obscure psychedelic bands from the late 60s onwards, while nicking 'pep pills' from his mum that soon led to an "amphetamine psychosis" diagnosis from his GP. "I gave it to the foreman, Mr Jeffries. He looked at it and said, 'amphetamine psychosis, eh? My wife had that. She were right poorly with it'." Thereafter he became a fully-fledged mod, checking out the latest soul imports at the Twisted Wheel club (Manchester's Northern Soul venue which was revived in 1999). He began to concentrate on performance poetry in the early-70s, using machine-gun puns that recalled the Mersey poets like Roger McGough. However, his stated influences were Woody Allen, Lord Buckley, Lenny Bruce, Beaudelaire and the futurist school of poets as well as painters such as Magritte. He was also as fond of Ian Dury as Salvador Dali (indeed, he was subsequently asked, but wisely declined, an offer of leading the post-Dury Blockheads).

Having already experimented with combining music with poetry with local band the Ferrets, led by Rick Goldstraw, he performed readings in folk clubs around the Manchester area. But his main income was from nightclubs. "There was a thriving club circuit. I did manage to get a residency at this club called Mr Smith's. They'd have Shirley Bassey, Matt Munro – top acts. I got £30 for a twenty-minute set – that was an engineer's wage. Then I met Howard Devoto and Pete Shelley. And punk didn't look that outrageous to me. I slotted in – I was wearing three-button suits with narrow skinny trousers, skinny tie and Perry Como haircut. At the time it came across as quite unusual, because then middle management were wearing mustard-coloured flares. Howard said, 'You should do some of these punk rock gigs, John.' I'd heard the term but equated it more with the American side of things. He said come to the Free Trade Hall and play with the Sex Pistols. I did a couple of support slots for the Buzzcocks, and it got me out of Manchester, and then around the world. So, great, thanks Howard, thanks Pete. It was right place, right time, I looked right, my face fitted."

Clarke was impressed with punk because, as he told the NME, "It's the nearest thing that there's ever been to the working classes going into areas like surrealism and Dada. Until now they've been the domain of the middle classes... I don't think I've ever seen a punk rock group that didn't have something very imaginative about it. It's not being a traitor to your class to go into those areas. It only widens your perspective. I think the New Wave has revived an interest in words. Initially, because you couldn't hear them. You're always interested to find out words you can't hear. You get odd words jumping out of the mish-mash. If those odd words that jump out are potent, it gives you the impetus to find out what the rest of them are. I like punk rock because it allows the softness to come through. It's not like hard rock – throwing somebody's crotch in your face. They're human beings singing about being human beings."

Long before the emaciated apparition became beatnik stooge to the Honey Monster in Sugar Puffs TV adverts, he was dodging spittle at some of Manchester's celebrated but insalubrious punk clubs. He was support to the Buzzcocks at the opening night of the Vortex in July 1977 and got a hostile reception for his troubles, including a dismissive shout of 'intellectual' from the audience (perish the thought). He was also the support act for the Buzzcocks' show at the Electric Circus recorded for later release on Virgin's Short Circuit compilation. It became his vinyl debut via the inclusion of 'You Never See A Nipple In The Daily Express' and 'I Married A Monster From Outer Space', which attacked racism by abstracting the theme to a space age turf war.

Thereafter he hooked up with Tosh Ryan's Rabid Records. "Tosh found him walking down Barnall Road, dressed as a rabbit," Martin Hannett later told Jon Savage. "He'd been around for years. I'd heard stuff he'd done for Radio Manchester. He'd been doing it in pubs since 1967 at least, but he'd split up with the Monster From Outer Space (aka his wife) and moved into a cupboard on Barnall Road. We stuck him in the basement of Tosh's house with various people and he came out with the 'Psycle Sluts' EP." More accurately titled the 'Innocents' EP, the track(s) to which Hannett alludes were a reference to the Los Angeles erotic/sex revue, the Cycle Sluts. Only given a north of England twist. Martin Hannett was on board to produce alongside keyboard player Steve Hopkins, who would become Clarke's regular collaborators. Lester Bangs reckoned it proved that punks were the true heirs of the beat poets. Tosh Ryan isn't so sure, when I asked him about the leap in the dark that putting a poet on vinyl might have seemed to some. "There were precedents. It wasn't such a strange thing to do, but it was strange because he was very much of a type, John. He was a performing poet and a bit of a ranter. Even though John's got a hell of a lot of talent in his writing, his performances were getting to be quite boring, I thought, repetitious." Which was why the decision was made, with Hannett's urgings, to provide him with musical accompaniment.

Ou Est La Maison De Fromage? followed, the title adapted from one of JCC's ad libs. A rough collection of rehearsals and demos with only limited musical accompaniment on 'Split Beans' and 'Gimmix', allegedly drawn from recordings thrown into a cupboard at Rabid. "It was a fucking bootleg," reckons Rick Goldstraw. "That was fucking Tosh Ryah. He was John's manager! And John never got a penny out of it, and it's meant to have sold 20,000 copies on mail order." Most of the tracks would end up better recorded elsewhere. Notably after he moved to Epic Records, via Hannett's intervention. "I met a CBS stringer, Jeremy Ensor, and sent him a copy of the film soundtrack and some pieces... I sent it (Psycle Sluts) to Oberstein and he came up, and we went for a cheap kebab. He signed John on the understanding that Steve (Hopkins) and I would do the tracks." Fans of 'Psycle Sluts' included Frank Zappa, who played it as a guest DJ on Radio One in 1980 and commended Clarke on his "exquisite diction".

Disguise In Love was released after Clarke signed to CBS/Epic for a five-figure sum, and it still holds up years after the event. There are contributions from both Bill Nelson of Be Bop Deluxe and Pete Shelley of the Buzzcocks in the first incarnation of Cooper Clarke's ad hoc backing band the Invisible Girls. It opened with 'I Don't Want To Be Nice', which neatly encapsulated all those snotty sentiments of the punk era (it could almost have been an Eater lyric). 'Reader's Wives' was reprised from Fromage and doffed its cap to "Wives from Inverness to inner London/Prettiness and pimples co-exist/Pictorially wife-swapping with someone/Who's happily married to his wrist." His adenoidal, dispassionate delivery underscored the loneliness of his subjects in 'Post-War Glamour Girls' with their 'Mau Mau lovers', while 'Valley Of The Lost Women' conveyed the grinding levels of poverty and disappointment which would later inform his epic 'Beasley Street'.

A live 10-inch album, Walking Back To Happiness, followed, alongside the splendid Gimmix, released as a triangular 10-inch single. He subsequently represented Britain at the first World Poetry Olympics at Westminster Abbey's Poet's Corner. 'Twat', a double-tracked single, was his eloquent and wholly laudable assault on the reputation of Conservative politician Michael Heseltine.

All of which heralded Clarke's landmark recording, Snap, Crackle & Bop – a celebration of sarcasm as the highest form of wit, heavy on alliteration, but beyond anything else savagely comic and breathlessly urgent. He was helped by some fantastically inventive work from the Invisible Girls (Hannett and Hopkins as the core with a cast of thousands). But as Tosh Ryan recalls, it is Hannett who deserves much of the credit, even if he drove him up the wall at the time. "The production on those records is remarkable. At the time they were being produced, I was really opposed to what Martin was doing. He was spending fortunes in the studio. By today's standards, it was a very small amount of money, but at that time it was a lot of money. We were spending between 15 and 30 grand on an album, which was a lot of money in 1979 or whenever." The CBS advances were gone in a flash. "You only get so much up front. You don't get the whole amount. We'd get our percentage up front and that would immediately go, and you'd have to wait for your sales to get your payment periods throughout the year. But of course, John Cooper Clarke, he never recouped. We never got any more money out of CBS, because we were still paying back the advances. A lot of the advances Martin spent on new technology, like digital delay lines and harmonisers, the very first CD player that I ever saw, I was amazed. He bought a CD player and it cost us £800 – what the hell are we doing spending £800 on a weird piece of technology! It didn't even record, it was only a player." According to Rick Goldstraw, Hannett "spent all the money buying mics and headphones and shipped them over to Strawberry Studios, then charged bands to record there".

'Evidently Chickentown', a pacey expletive-fest, set the album's tone, which was most fully realised in the album's centrepiece, 'Beasley Street'. It laid bare the kind of squalor and hopelessness that Jim Cartwright so perfectly framed in Road, "a Lancastrian Under Milk Wood for the 80s." Indeed, a later theatrical production of Road employed 'Evidently Chickentown' as its intro, and Clarke would also appear in a stage version. If punk was tower block rock, rummaging around for slogans to articulate the grating misery of so many people's existence in the late-70s, Clarke's superior vocabulary elevated the dialogue from prose to poetry. Some were kind enough to call 'Beasley Street' his version of Dylan's 'Desolation Row', and it's a feasible comparison. Elsewhere the nightmare of family get-togethers is laid bare in 'A Distant Relation', 'It Man' derided the 'solid dirt heart' of the swinger about town, 'Conditional Discharge' was an extended pun on venereal disease and '36 Hours' discussed incarceration.

By the advent of Zip Style Method in 1982 his worldview was not quite so bleak. In fact, judging by some of the contents, he was a man in love ('I Wanna Be Yours' especially). The music this time took a more central role, the tracks standing as 'songs' in their own right. Inevitably, however, this dimmed the intensity and natural imprint of Clarke's verbiage, though the single, 'The Day My Pad Went Mad', was one of his better domestic disaster as shopping list efforts – "The kitchen has been ransacked/Ski trails in the hall/A chicken has been dansaked/And thrown against the wall." The humour is less cutting, less encumbered by a sense of injustice, and more purely observational, notably on the lyrically inert '90 Degrees In My Shades'.

The single 'Night People', however, was to be his last release for Epic. He continued to work sporadically throughout the 80s and 90s, but never did secure a new recording contract (partially because CBS still held a nominal 'option' on him). Nor did he expend much energy, if any, looking for one. Much of his time was spent in his best recreation of the contemporary opium den, sharing a flat with partner Nico until her death.

There was a Channel 4 documentary, Ten Years In An Open-Necked Shirt, also the title of his first anthology. 'Evidently Chickentown' was included, alongside works by Yeats and Milton in the Faber Book Of Political Verse, selected by Tom Paulin. Throughout he subsisted on a steady diet of pub dates, which paid the bills, and the dealers, but did little to see him expand as an artist. There was a bit of myth-making involved, reckons his ad hoc manager, Rick Goldstraw. "He was a rubbish junkie too, a lot of that was him playing up to the image. He's just a lazy bastard. He's completely soft. My daughters used to beat him up." However, there were times when he did push the envelope. "When we were both junkies, they brought out this new medicine to stop cramps. The first place that had it was the Betty Ford clinic in Chelsea. So CBS paid for him to go there. And he couldn't even get enough blood pressure up for them to do the injection. It cost them £70,000 to get the stuff, and they couldn't get it in him because he was so laid back."

There must be more stories? "At the Betty Ford clinic, he goes in there the first night. He leans out the window and a kid is passing. 'Excuse me,' he says. 'You wouldn't know where I could get some heroin?' 'Yeah, all right.' Clarke gives him £20. He comes back with a quarter gramme. Peter Cook was in when we were there. Well, I say we. Clarke gets the Betty Ford clinic. I was in fucking Clouds charity clinic."

It was only in the early 90s that he finally junked the junk and began to get his act together, relocating to Colchester from Salford after he became a father. "He's a right soft cunt," notes Goldstraw. Clarke's life was later turned into the Studio Salford play 36 Hours in 2004, which was nominated for several awards. "Without him there would not have been punk poetry and therefore no alternative comedy and therefore no me," Jenny Eclair enthused, without fully thinking through the impact of that statement, before dubbing him a "Dorian Gray in winklepickers, a national treasure." Other grown up fans included Christopher Eccleston, who recited 'Evidently Chickentown' in Danny Boyle's film Strumpet.

In 2006 news broke of a projected new album with Goldstraw and Joe Strummer associate Tymon Dogg in Blueprint Studios in Manchester. Hooray! Also, the news of his upcoming appearance in the Big Brother house. He rung up Rick Goldstraw for advice. "How much?" 150 grand." "Pack your suitcase." As Goldstraw points out, he's perfect. "He can sit in that house and agree with everyone. Sit down, and do nothing. He could do that on his fucking head, John. He just agrees with everyone, he'll do anything anyone says. It's just what he does, sit there doing fuck all. That's what he does all day anyway. He'll live till he's 150."

Discography:

Innocents 7-inch EP (Rabid TOSH 103 October 1977)

Suspended Sentence/Innocents/Psycle Sluts Pts 1 and 2 (available in both blue and blue/orange sleeves with different labels. Re-released in 1978 with different black and white sleeve design. Credited to John Cooper Clarke and the Curious Yellows, because his backing band, rejoicing in the anonymity of names such as Eric Ferret and Joe Vitality, all had hepatitis at the time. Apparently)

Ou Est La Maison De Fromage LP (Rabid NOZE 1 1978) (reissued on Receiver RRLP 110 in

March 1989 and on CD on RRCD 110 in November 1996 with bonus tracks: Ten Years In An Open Necked Shirt (Part Three)/Salome Malone/Psycle Sluts (Part 1 & 2). Reissued on Castle, CMOCD 1234, in 2005 with Receiver bonus tracks, plus Bronze Adonis, I Married A Monster From Outer Space (live), Reader's Wives (live), Health Fanatic (live), Split Beans (live), Suspended Sentence (live), You've Never Seen A Nipple In The Daily Express (live), I Married A Monster From Outer Space vers 2 (live), Day My Pad Went Mad. Those bonus tracks neatly round up JCC's early recordings, with all three Innocents tracks, his contribution to the NME's C-81 cassette and to the Short Circuit compilation as well as Peel sessions)

Post War Glamour Girl/Kung Fu International (live) 7-inch (Epic EPC 6541 August 1978)

Disguise In Love LP (Epic EPC 83132 October 1978) (reissued on CD in June 1995 on Rewind, 480530-2)

Gimmix (Play Loud)/I Married A Monster From Outer Space 10-inch shaped orange vinyl (Epic 12-7009 February 1979) (also released as a 7-inch promo single. 'Monster' is a re-recorded version of the Disguise In Love song)

Walking Back To Happiness 10-inch mini-LP (Epic JCC1 June 1979) (essentially an unaccompanied live album, aside from a studio version of 'Gimmix'. 'Who Stole The Marble Index' is JCC's rant when he discovers that someone has stolen one of his notebooks)

Splat/Twat/Sleepwalk 7-inch (Epic EPC 7982 October 1979) (a twin-grooved record, which meant that the A-side played alternate versions)

Snap, Crackle & Bop LP (April 1980 EPC 84083 April 1980) (originally released with a sleeve pocket containing the album's lyrics. Reissued on CD by Rewind, 477380-2, in September 1994)

The It Man/36 Hours 7-inch (Epic EPC 8655 May 1980)

The Day My Pad Went Mad/A Distant Relation 7-inch (Epic EPC 2077 April 1982)

Zip Style Method LP (Epic EPC 85667 May 1982)

Night People/Face Behind The Scream 7-inch (Epic EPC 2521 June 1982)

ARCHIVE RELEASES/COMPILATIONS:

Me And My Big Mouth LP (Epic EPC 84979 May 1981) (pointless exercise. Everything's available elsewhere)

Word Of Mouth – The Very Best Of John Cooper Clarke CD (Epic 506343 2 August 2002)

Cortinas

Dexter Dalwood (bass), Mike Fewings (guitar), Nick Sheppard (guitar), Daniel Swan (drums), Jeremy Valentine (vocals)

Bristol's CORTINAS started life as a garage R&B band, average age 15, in 1975. The story goes that they were bitten by the punk bug after seeing the Ramones play at the Roundhouse, and began to introduce sharper original material to their sets thereafter. Well, that's kind of the truth, though there was never any formalised conversion, as Valentine elaborated to me. "Punk existed as some live reviews of the Pistols and Clash etc in London and Patti Smith and the Ramones and Television etc in New York, in the NME and Melody Maker and Sounds, before anyone who was not at those gigs had heard any music. It is unlikely that anyone at the gigs thought they were listening to something called punk.

The reviews worked because the music was described in terms of Stooges, Velvets, garage bands, New York Dolls, etc, just things that made it sound exciting against what was then currently passing for rock'n'roll music. So if you picked up on that, and those references, then you were pretty predisposed to liking it unheard. It made sense in that place and time and at that age. You queued up for the first Patti Smith album, the Television 7 inch, the Ramones album, all of which came out long before any of the UK bands."

Valentine: "At that time the Cortinas (the name chosen because it symbolised the 'cheap and nasty' end of the automobile spectrum) was basically an R&B covers band in the style of Dr Feelgood etc. The transition to punk was quite easy – just play it faster with less notes and make up your own words. You didn't have to hear it to work it out – but the Ramones showed the way. So all over the UK bored, alienated, sexually frustrated suburban teenagers like me did the same thing. It's well known the Ramones freaked out at the response, but for me a more important gig was Patti Smith supported by the Stranglers at the Roundhouse and then the Clash at the ICA afterwards. The Clash were good because Strummer's guitar broke so

The Cortinas, live at the Leicester Punk Festival.

C

Jones played rhythm. It was a bit disappointing to hear the album with all those Mott the Hoople guitar solos on." Nick Sheppard adds a small postscript to this. "The Ramones gig was a turning point in that it forced us into writing our own songs; up until then we had only written one, and it was still an R&B thing. We came away from that gig going, 'right, this is it, no time to lose, let's get on with it'."

The Cortinas made their London debut as support to the Stranglers at the Roxy and thereafter signed to Miles Copeland/Mark Perry's Step Forward label. I asked Valentine what he thought of the deadly duo. "At the time he (Copeland) wasn't popular on the scene, although he did give a lot of help to McLaren. So his unpopularity made him popular with me. He was basically a business man who would have made even more money if he hadn't had the silly idea that he could make money out of rock'n'roll. But he had also lost a lot of money in the early-70s and was a bit down on his uppers when we met him, at the Roxy. But the fact that he was American and his dad ran the CIA was exciting to us. He had enormous energy and drive. Mind you, we thought his brother's band were a bunch of wankers, like trendy teachers. Miles didn't really understand 'the creative process' and liked simple solutions. Usually he was hands-off, but when he interfered it was bit depressing. Mark Perry was and is an angel but he allowed wankers like Danny Baker to get in on his act, although now I quite like Danny Baker. But you can see the same pattern in his relationship with Chris Evans whom I definitely don't like."

Their first two Cortinas' singles are essential slices of snotty 77/78-era punk. These sandwiched a session for John Peel which is also worth tracking down. There was some misguided conjecture about the band being some kind of right wing apologists because of 'Fascist Dictator', the point originally brought up by Carol Clerk then resurrected in an essay by Robert Christgau. But that is and was just arrant nonsense. The song was, however, dropped from their set. "The two events weren't related," reckons Valentine. "Caroline Coon reviewed it in Melody Maker and said it was 'very irresponsible' which we thought was very funny. The idea of responsible rock'n'roll music didn't make much sense – this was years before U2 and Coldplay etc. But I do remember getting worrying fan letters from Italy. We didn't get any of that NF punk stuff at our gigs. If we had I think we would have been forced to do something about the song, but the reason we dropped it was that we got tired of it and 'it wasn't working creatively'. I always preferred 'Television Families'."

However, thereafter, after a run of gigs supporting the likes of Blondie and Chelsea they signed to CBS and lost their way. The resulting album was mild-mannered R&B/pop lacking the cut or dash of their opening salvos. There was an unhappy overhaul of 'Further Education', references to The Man From U.N.C.L.E. and Blue Peter presenter Valerie Singleton, a sleeve designed by hippy icons Hipgnosis (although they'd also done the fetching/retching cover of 'Defiant Pose') and the over-riding feeling that this was a band who should never have 'grown up'. It received lukewarm reviews in the press and the Cortinas disappeared in September 1978.

"The reaction to the album wasn't entirely negative," Valentine reflects. "John Peel played it approvingly. Basically I realised that, OK, you've made a big decision at 17 so you need to think medium to long term. Even shorter than medium term, you knew that this punk thing wasn't going to be around much longer, and if it was, you didn't want to be around with it. Gigs at the Vortex told you that. We could see things coming up. For example, we played a gig at the Marquee with our great Bristol mates the Pop Group (several of whom had attended the same school in Bristol as the Cortinas) as support, and blew us off stage. There wasn't much point going on after that. For me, they totally opened up a way to listening, thinking about and playing music which I thought was brilliant, but which I knew wasn't for me to do.

"Similarly, we played a gig at Acklam Hall supported by Sham 69. They blew us off stage too, but from a completely different direction, and one we could have quite easily gone down but it would have meant becoming a cartoon and I didn't have Jimmy Pursey's looks and huge gay skinhead following. So I thought the direction to go was basically writing pop songs and that's what we tried to develop. We all liked pop, but classic pop, Motown, Spector, Abba too. Not the Beatles, for some reason. So the album is basically a series of technical exercises in writing pop songs. It's not a bad attempt but what we didn't know about was production. There is no production on the album. We didn't know what to do and how to do it and neither did the producer. Later we recorded a bit with Will Birch who was the drummer and songwriter in the Kursaal Flyers and who had written a very enthusiastic review of us in Sounds. We had always liked the Kursaals and actually went on tour with them in order to mark our distance from punk. The recording was much more like what we were after, but by then we had got bored of the whole thing."

Sheppard played with the Cut The Crap-era Clash when that band was in its post-Mick Jones death throes. He went on to form trip-hop forerunners Head with Gareth Sager (ex-Pop Group, Rip, Rip & Panic) and most recently worked as the arranger on the Ramones' musical, Gabba Gabba Hey! Fewings hooked up with Essential Bop while Swan joined California's Sneetches (several albums for various labels). Later he ended up working with Green Day's management team, which gave him an interesting perspective on the dismissive view that some wizened punks held about that band. "I can assure you that Green Day took a lot of flak from the local scene when they first got successful," he told me. "I am pleased for them that they have maintained their success and more importantly their creative success."

Valentine collaborated with members of the Glaxo Babies and Maximum Joy before taking a teaching post at Queen Margaret University College in Edinburgh. Dalwood toured with Barry Andrews of XTC then became a world renowned, Tate-exhibited painter of the wonderfully titled "neurotic realist" school.. One of his most famous paintings depicts the Chelsea Hotel bedroom where Sid 'done for' Nancy, among several other 'popular culture' subjects.

I pointed out that, for a bunch of teenagers swept up by the punk movement, and then spat out by the record industry, the former members of the Cortinas seem to be doing pretty well. Valentine reckons he hasn't "done very well for myself" at all. "I think it's pretty much impossible to get back on the straight and narrow, to work for 'the man' as Jack Black says. I think that it's probably explained by our ordinariness and cowardice and good intuition to quit while you're ahead. The punk rock wars were an enormous laugh and then all of a sudden they weren't. It did a job then it wasn't necessary. I think more important are the vastly more talented and interesting people than us who haven't been able to keep their heads above water. That's why everyone salutes Mark E Smith. He did everything right."

DISCOGRAPHY:

Fascist Dictator/Television Families 7-inch (Step Forward SF 1 June 1977)
Defiant Pose/Independence 7-inch (Step Forward SF 6 December 1977) (also issued as a 12-inch single, without a picture sleeve)
Heartache/Ask Mr Waverly 7-inch (CBS CBS 6759 1978)
True Romances LP (CBS 828331 1978)

The Crime

Pete Howard (vocals), Gav Scollen (drums), Rance Og (bass), John McCabe (guitar)

THE CRIME formed in 1979 in Seaham, County Durham, a small mining town about 20 miles from Newcastle. The seeds were sewn in the ashes of an earlier Seaham band, the Epileptic Fitz, whose members had included both Howard and Scollen. The Fits formed in 1978, originally performing punk covers before writing their own material such as 'Test Tube Babies' and 'I Wanna Be A Miner.' Your assumption might be that the latter was an ironic title, given that two of the band members worked for the local colliery. You would be wrong. Scollen: "I was still at school and Pete was unemployed, desperate to be a miner, as it was the only work available, hence the song title."

The Fitz gained a degree of notoriety. "We had a huge local following, regularly playing gigs to 100 – 500 people in our home town. However, our first gig outside of Seaham ended in a riot, with a policeman being knocked unconscious. As a result we were headline news in the local press and punk heroes overnight. Unfortunately, there was a lot of infighting in the band, and we split up just when we were ready to take off." Scollen and Howard recruited Og and McCabe in 1979 to form The Crime, quickly building a healthy following through frequent gigs in the north east. One of their finest shows was at the Continental in Sunderland, alongside Remnants Of Warsaw, who included Frankie Stubbs of Leatherface fame. "The venue was packed and we went down a storm," reckons Scollen.

The band's debut single, 'Johnny Come Home, was recorded in 1979 and released in 1980. Only 500 copies were produced, which sold out almost immediately. It has since become one of those punk ultra-rarities demanding prices upwards of £200 to people with more money than sense, and a hell of a lot more than the people in the band ever did. "The front cover originally had a picture of Margaret Thatcher lying dead, as she summed up everything that we thought was wrong with Britain. However, we finally settled on a cover which summed up our feelings about urban decay and destruction." The band's only other release in their lifetime was 'R.A.F.', for the Sunderland Musicians Collective LP.

Initially influenced by the Clash, SLF and the Ruts, the band also became attuned to the emerging ska scene, but split up at the end of 1980 before they could properly incorporate those elements. They continued as Breakout, named after the SLF song, with the exception of Howard.

Breakout released one single, 'Wall Of Solitude', and 'Get Out, Fight Back', for Guardian Records. "'Get Out' was very SLF-influenced. However, 'Wall of Solitude' was over produced and by the time we came out of the studio it was unrecognisable as the song we went in with, for all the wrong reasons?" News of the single reached Jake Burns, who agreed to produce a follow-up, but the subsequent termination of SLF meant he was unable to finalise arrangements, despite a couple of meetings. Eventually Scollen would move on to join Uproar "who had a good vibe and were really getting things together" in 1983.

DISCOGRAPHY:

Johnny Come Home/Generation Gap 7-inch (Punk Product PP1 1980) (500 copies; two separate bootleg versions exist, and it has also showed up on the 'Wasted Youth' compilation)
COMPILATION:
N.E.1 – The Sunderland Musicians' Collective LP (Durham Book Centre Label 1980; 'R.A.F.')

Crisis

Rob Ledger aka The Cleaner/Insect Robin (drums), Douglas 'P' Pearce (rhythm guitar), Lester 'Picket' Jones (guitar), Frazer 'Phrazer' Towman (vocals), Tony Wakeford (bass, vocals)

As punk began to develop a more realistic dialogue with anarchist philosophies in the late-70s, beyond McLaren's shop-front tokenism, CRISIS stood out for espousing a more orthodox, hard left ideology. While their music similarly borrowed from The Clash, lyrics were inspired by opinion leaders in the Socialist Workers Party and International Marxist Group such as Paul Foot and Tariq Ali. As well as being wholeheartedly serious about their political concerns and aspirations, the band maintained a sense of theatre, too – Frazer would sometimes employ a rapist's mask for gigs. There was certainly no shortage of drama at their live shows. While much of their lyrical focus was on anti-Nazi rhetoric, their gigs progressively provided a platform for clashes between right wing skinheads and the group's followers.

They set about their task in the spring of 1977 with touching enthusiasm. "We're going to get people annoyed, and we'll shock people in Surrey with some of our songs!" Wakeford told the local press. But, according to Pearce, Crisis were not primarily interested in shock tactics. "No. The idea Tony and I had was that Crisis would be deadly serious and that our politics were to be taken seriously. That, in itself, turned out to be shocking enough for some people, so inevitably we did get up some people's noses – especially in the mass media. But, that wasn't our raison d'être." Wakeford was formerly a member of Status Quo cover band Backwater before he put together his new, punk-fired project, alongside postman Pearce, the group's principal songwriting axis. Lead singer Frazer Towman was a hairdresser, while Ledger, who somewhat incongruously for a punk band operating in those times, occasionally sported a full-grown beard, was at art school in London. Wakeford worked at Chertsey hospital. Jones was permanently unemployed.

They made their debut at a Rock Against Racism gig at Guildford's Surrey University, before 300 people, having only had the line-up formalised for two weeks, while rehearsing at the Canlo Club in Chertsey. Pearce: "The Canlo Club was a sort of youth/community/sports centre that was about two miles from where Tony Wakeford lived. Tony had somehow managed to get the hire of it when it was closed on Sundays for next to nothing, so the rest of us travelled there and we rehearsed and wrote most of our early songs there. Weirdly enough in late 1986, after I had split from my long-term relationship which had started in 1976, just before I got involved in the punk thing, I ended up living within spitting distance of the club for a few months. That was always a bit like a constant reminder of what had been!"

They subsequently picked up shows at The Roxy, whose Kevin St John started to book their shows. "Kevin St John was also the booking manager for Sham 69 at the time and liked us – especially Phrazer our lead singer. And for the grand price of a tequila sunrise each, we agreed to him being our booking agent. I didn't stand in the way of that at all as it guaranteed us getting gigs at The Roxy on a regular basis and even one with Sham 69 and Menace in our hometown of Woking. He was basically one of London's gay gangsters and because of his underworld connections we were always wary but, in retrospect, we did OK from our relationship with him. Years later I saw a photo of Kevin St John on the front cover of London's leading newspaper – he'd been found floating face down in the Thames, probably as a result of a gangland hit. He had a criminal record as long as your arm. I was surprised when I read about all his convictions etc. He was far worse than we'd imagined!"

As for the Roxy: "In comparison to some of the clubs I've been in over the years the Roxy wasn't so bad and definitely had its moments. I always liked the way the clientele mixed up the restrooms, so you'd often see girls peeing in the men's urinals in a completely unabashed way. I also have fond memories of turning up way too early on a Sunday evening and Crisis walking into an upstairs packed with elderly gay gangsters dancing and partying together. There were pink shirts and leather Trilbys everywhere! It was a great gay gangster party! But our presence was definitely not appreciated and before we got to see too much, one of their minders quickly escorted us downstairs where we were told to 'fucking stay 'ere.' He even slammed his revolver on the bar as if to emphasise the point! My partner Jack and I talking to Captain Sensible about Marc Bolan having been killed in a car crash earlier that same day also is a poignant memory of the Roxy. He later got up with Dave Vanian and did an impromptu Damned set which was brilliant."

Beyond the gay mafia, the Socialist Workers Party would play a big role in supporting the band and getting them gigs as part of the Rock Against Racism network. There were constant questions about their affiliations, though they were unafraid about declaring their allegiances. As Pearce protested to Search And Destroy magazine when asked if they were members of the Communist Party (he was actually in America in December 1977 at the invitation of Slash magazine with his 59-year-old male partner): "No way would we be members of the CP – Stalinists! We're split between two Trotskyite groupings, the SWP and the IMG (International Marxist Group)" Ironically, they earned early rave notices from, of all people, Sounds journalist Garry Bushell, who wrote in September 1978 that Crisis reminded him "of Sham a couple of months back, musically simple and muscular". For a while, members of the group were indeed friendly with the Hersham fraternity via not only their connection with St John and Bushell, but also because of their proximity in Surrey.

Gigs continued to be shambolic, not least a second Anti-Nazi League Carnival at which Pearce managed to electrocute himself. "I touched a live mic at this huge Anti-Nazi Rally open air music festival in London where the Clash were headlining and I got electrocuted! I remember all my muscles tensing, only seeing blackness with kaleidoscopic colours mixed in, a noise like a jack hammer going mad inside me and realising that my heart was beating so fast it couldn't keep up that pace for very long. Luckily I fell back into the drum kit which knocked the microphone out of my hands and I survived. Loads of people clapped because they thought it was all part of the act but the two or three First Aid guys around me knew better. I felt as high as a kite and brilliant for the rest of the day, although I was told to take it easy and I couldn't walk very well after. My legs were like jelly."

Douglas Pearce of Crisis attended to by medics after electrocuting himself at an Anti-Nazi Rally.

There was further violence in 1979 at the Acklam Hall in Notting Hill which, as recounted by Stewart Home in Cranked Up Really High, resulted in a full-scale riot as the band and its supporters took on locals and Nazi skinheads. I asked Pearce if there was any element of 'getting off' on the continued clashes, and whether he thought confronting the NF physically was as important as it was politically. "At that moment in time we did think it was important to stand up to the NF on all fronts but we certainly never got off on the violence that was involved with being a punk rocker, regardless of whether or not it was 'politically' inspired. In truth, that violence wore us down and it was another good reason for abandoning punk in 1980. Acklam Hall was something else. That whole riot might have had elements of the NF thrown in – on both sides of the conflict – but it was probably mainly lads who wanted a fight with punks that night which was a problem everywhere you went in the UK."

The band had other targets beyond the far right, however. Songs such as the unreleased 'Search And Destroy' celebrated union militancy (though Pearce had actually felt alienated by the Post Office unions whilst he was a shop steward) and blasted the National Front. 'Militant' openly supported the flying pickets of the late-70s that Thatcher later set out to crush. Other songs saw Crisis refine their own political thoughts by attacking selected targets on the left, i.e. 'Back In The U.S.S.R.' – 'Don't rebel, you won't get thanked/You'll just get run over by a tank/Don't wanna buy the Morning Star/Just be a boss in your big black car."

The band's first recordings took place "in a terrible studio somewhere in South Wimbledon", with three tracks, 'Militant', 'Kill Kill Kill' and 'PC 1984' recorded. "The engineers were the bog-standard hippies associated with the music 'biz' at the time and hated us." They continued to play live constantly and it is this, Pearce thinks, that led to the opportunity to utilise a free day's recording at Surrey University Music Department's recording studios in Guildford. Among those the tapes were circulated to were Nic Jones of Step Forward Records. He arranged for a further day's free recording time at Surrey Sound Studios in Leatherhead. Although Step Forward eventually passed on Crisis, they allowed them to keep the master tapes. "We immediately sent them to John Peel. There was a lot of material on these but neither Tony nor I kept any copies, wrongly assuming they'd be handed straight back. However, on the strength of those particular tapes, we did get the very important Peel session broadcast in 1978."

Their debut single came about after one Peter Bibby had seen the band play on the back of a truck at a Right To Work demonstration. Inspired by these gigs and the DIY mantra expressed on Scritti Politti's 'Skank Bloc Bologna', he was emboldened to approach the band to record a single for a specific cause – to stop the destruction of the existing Southwark Town Hall to make way for a new building. "At first we didn't think he was serious but after his continued persistence we agreed, seeing it as our chance to finally release something. Tony wrote the song 'No Town Hall' specifically for this but, due to one screw up after another, including the awful sleeve which was printed back to front, it eventually came out on Bibby's Action Group Records." 'P.C. 1984, or 'P.C. One Nine Eight Four' as the sleeve preferred, was written about an incident experienced by Wakeford and Pearce at the inception of the band's formation (the Lewisham riot between the National Front and various anti-fascist groups, which also inspired 'Search And Destroy').

'UK 79'/'White Youth' became their second single, offering a halfway house between the Clash's 'White Riot' and 'White Man In Hammersmith Palais', including dub reggae effects. The lyrics, "We are black, we are white, together we are dynamite", whilst a little cloying, left no-one in any doubt as to their intentions. Pearce: "It was originally titled 'UK 77' but as we didn't get around to recording it for the John Peel radio show until 1978, we decided to call it 'UK 78' for the BBC. The session was broadcast three times in quick succession (the norm was evidently twice and then a long wait before a possible third play). But Peel loved Crisis and even invited us up to Broadcasting House onto the show after the first broadcast to grunt 'Hullo!' in the background, which at that time only the Fall had managed to do – albeit with Mancunian accents. The arrangement with the BBC was that we could then buy the tracks from them for £100 each. This was an incredibly good deal so we bought that track and 'White Youth' and issued them as a 7-inch in 1979 and re-titled the track to fit the year." (the original recording title was used for the Holocaust Hymns compilation however)

Their only LP, as such, was Hymns Of Faith, but by the time of its release there was already discord within the band. Dexter had come in on vocals and Luke Rendall was the latest in a long line of drummers. They also played on a Rock Against Racism tour of Norway. But continued violence, notably at a set in Guildford at the Wooden Bridge pub in February 1980, began to grind the band down. They played their final gig in May 1980 as support to Magazine and Bauhaus at Surrey University where it had begun in 1977. Pearce: "A review of one of the shows we did at Surrey University with The Ruts read; 'Crisis blew the Ruts off stage and the Flys (the other support group) off the face of the earth' has never left me. Norway seemed to be a month of one fight after another with drunk Norwegians who wanted to have a go at the English punk rockers. Luckily we all had over two years of street fighting experience and luckily most of these guys were completely pissed out of their minds, so we returned to England relatively unscathed. But it's the only time I have ever been homesick as I was so tired of it all. However, it was in Norway I read about Joy Division and when we returned in September 1979, they were the first group I made sure I saw performing in London. I knew it was only a question of time for Crisis to be over."

'Alienation' and 'Bruckwood Hospital' were released, combining the final two John Peel session tracks, some 16 months after the band had ended (the run-off groove contains the message "And now for Death In June"). For final emphasis, the cover featured the Berlin Wall and an unsuccessful would-be escapee being dragged away. Despite a 1997 double CD compilation, several songs the band played live, including 'SPG', 'Waiting For Reaction', 'Garbage', 'With Everyone I Disagree' (which traditionally opened their set) 'Assault' and, criminally, 'Search And Destroy' ('We saw you kneelin', praying to heaven, remember Lewisham 1977'), were never released. Pearce: "'SPG' (aka Special Patrol Group) and 'Search And Destroy' were certainly on the tapes we sent to John Peel that secured a session with him in 1978, and some of the others were probably as well, but that tape was never returned and I don't know of any copies. Those tracks are almost certainly lost forever unless someone finds them in his famous barn where he kept his thousands of demos etc."

Luke Rendall subsequently joined Theatre of Hate. Lester Jones helped form Carcrash International and worked widely with Andi Sex Gang. Tony Wakeford and Douglas Pearce formed industrial/neo folk pioneers Death In June, whose 'All Alone In Her Nirvana' was originally a Crisis number. Death In June, despite its founders' roots in the avowedly anti-fascist Crisis, would become embroiled in accusations that they, and Wakeford's subsequent band, arch-paganists Sol Invictus, romanticised Teutonic and fascist imagery. They were widely criticised in the music press – one journalist doing so by pointing to alleged fascist connotations stemming back to the Crisis song 'White Youth', which made it obvious the writer concerned had never heard the song or known of Crisis's history.

So I gave Pearce the opportunity to react to these accusations, most of which have arisen from the quasi-academic work of Stewart Home, and whether or not he and Wakeford 'crossed the floor' politically by exploiting Nazi imagery in their subsequent work. "After punk there was no floor to cross as far as Tony and I were concerned. The floor had been shit on and destroyed. We were both sick of our very real involvement with far-left politics and realised that established politics no matter if they were from the left, right or centre, did not work. And, that's what I still believe in. Home makes an attempt at a career from his memories as a 15-year-old following Crisis around and seeing some early Death In June shows. His experiences around us obviously had a huge impact on his life and he's gone on to write ad nauseam about them in one way or another whether it be in so-called critiques on the internet or his books. I have to say I've never yet read one all the way through but the overall tone I understand from them is that he resents me/us. But, in truth without those experiences he wouldn't have anything to write about. At all! We gave him source material to last his lunchtime. Thankfully, in one way or another, our experiences – both good and bad in Crisis – gave Tony and I a lot more!"

Discography:

No Town Hall (Southwark)/Holocaust/P.C. One Nine Eight Four (Peckham Action Group NOTH 1 1979)

White Youth/UK 1979 7-inch (Ardkor CRI 002 1979)

Hymns Of Faith mini-LP (Ardkor CRI 003 1980) (Pearce: "Within the space of three days, Rough Trade distribution had sold nearly 5,000 copies. On the verge of a commercial breakthrough...we then split up!")

ARCHIVE RELEASES:

Alienation/Bruckwood Hospital (Ardkor CRI 004 1981)

Holocaust-UK 12-inch (Crisis NOTH 1/CRI 002 1982)

No Town Hall/Holocaust/P.C. One Nine Eight Four/White Youth/UK 1979 (comprises the deleted first two singles and released primarily in Europe and not widely available in the UK)

We Are All Jews and Germans double CD (CRI6 CD 1997) (Pearce: "The title was inspired by a 1968 French situationist poster featuring the German Jew student leader Danny Cohn-Bendit. He's now a member for The Greens in the German Parliament and evidently, according to Stern & Spiegel magazines, a Death In June fan. He was a contemporary of Tariq Ali of the IMG etc. Due to my legal dispute with this CD's distributor in 1999, it was then deleted")

Holocaust Hymns CD (Apop CRI007 January 2006) (effectively replacing the We Are All Jews And Germans double CD, this features the first three singles (1-7), tracks from the Hymns Of Faith LP (8-14), plus the band's first studio demos and alternative takes (15-19) and live material (20-23) recorded in 1979. Available through www.deathinjune.net)

C

Cult Figures

Gary Jones (lead vocals), Jonnie (aka Jonathon Hodgson; guitar, vocals), Howie (guitar, bass, vocals), Joe (vocals, guitar), Barry (bass), Marv (drums)

The CULT FIGURES lived up to their billing, its membership being shrouded in minor-league mystery which they were glad to perpetuate for the duration of their short career, which saw them leave behind one classic 7-inch record, with an equally cool action figure cover. Part of its charm was the fact that it featured one of the most chaotic arrangements you are ever likely to encounter, with a stop-start riff, and frankly bewildering vocal interjections. Zip Nolan, depicted on said sleeve with his head carefully transplanted on to Ersel Hickey's body, was a character from Lion & Thunder comic. This weekly strip detailed the strange tale of a Yankee Highway Cop relocated to Middle England.

The foldout cover additionally featured the following cryptic message: "This wonderful record was recorded at WMRS studio, Leamington Spa on the 29th December 1978. It was produced by the very gear Swell Maps without whom this disc would never have been possible. Any rumours that Marv, Joe, Barry & Howie (the names credited on the sleeve as musicians) are in fact Swell Maps are vicious and slanderous." The truth? Well, the disclaimer didn't work because everyone presumed it was the Swell Maps anyway. But no, the Cult Figures were their own men, if not their own 'band'.

Jones and Hodgson first met in 1976 at Solihull College of Technology on an art foundation course, which was also attended by later Swell Maps members Epic Soundtracks and Richard Earl. Hodgson was the first to get a band together, the Scent Organs, who actually reached the semi-finals of the preposterously titled Melody Maker Rock, Pop And Folk Awards regional heats. Jones "jumped on the bandwagon" and formed Cult Figures, initially using college pal Tim Wilday as drummer, with Jones playing guitar. Of course, neither of them could actually converse with their instruments in anything other than the most rudimentary fashion, though Wilday's claim to fame is that he managed to blag some drumsticks from Rick Buckler after the Jam played Barbarella's. For his part, Jones acquired a Kay guitar and amp and they started to write songs, among the earliest of which was 'Zip Nolan'. At which point Hodgson became involved, contributing bass, guitar and even violin. He continued with Scent Organs, meanwhile, and doubled up with both bands when the Cult Figures made their debut at Jones's old youth club, supporting Scent Organs.

Jones and Hodgson thereafter forged ahead as a songwriting partnership while Wilday slowly removed himself from the band. Epic Soundtracks, meanwhile, remained a staunch supporter, and when Swell Maps got Rough Trade's backing to start their own label, Rather Records, he offered the Cult Figures the chance to release 'Zip Nolan'. Which is where the confusion began. The Cult Figures were a duo rather than a band. So it was suggested that the Swell Maps, who really were an actual functioning group, should 'impersonate' them – indeed, Epic actually played drums on the single. It was the fourth release on Rather, following two Maps' singles and an EP by Steve Treatment, and many would argue it was the best of the lot.

They were now "a real gigging band", according to Jones, with additional members Martin Hughes on bass and Jock on drums, A second single arrived in 1980, the 'In Love' EP, which featured both Nikki Sudden and Epic on backing vocals, with Sudden producing. After allegations of sexism from some quarters, notably Epic himself, about the lyrics, 'Clambake', a "typical Cult Figures bit of fun", was dropped from the EP. The song, written by Hodgson, featured lyrics such as: "At the Clambake I went and grabbed you by the hand, and we danced to the sound of a rock'n'roll band/Juicy sweetcorn, I'm thinking soft porn in my head/And I'm dreaming of acting dirty in your bed/You're the sort of girl I'd like to eat, I can hardly wait/Cover you in something sweet and use you as a plate..." The song, notes Jones with hindsight, was probably not in keeping with the Rough Trade ethos of the time, "but you have to understand, we took the piss out of everything back then. In fact a friend's band played us a song which included the lyrics 'Gary and Jon, Gary and Jon/They take the piss out of everyone.'" The instrumental B-side, 'Laura Kate', incidentally, was named in tribute to Hodgson's stepsister, who had just been born.

But it was to be the last release by the Cult Figures, with the exception of a 2004 retrospective live CD. Hodgson would go on to collaborate widely with Nikki Sudden, former Barracuda Jeremy Gluck and Cottonmouth, and also had a brief spell as rhythm guitarist of Pete Wylie's Wah! Heat. He is currently an award winning animator. Jones is an exhibiting artist living in Brighton. There was a brief reformation of the principals in 1988, when Jones and Hodgson started a new band, The Iron Fish, who recorded one session with Nick Cave engineer Tony Cohen. Max Decharne of Gallon Drunk sang lead vocals on two self-penned numbers, and also played drums and keyboards. But as Jones says, "we were ahead of our time", and nought came of it.

DISCOGRAPHY:

Zip Nolan (Highway Patrolman)/Playing With Toys/Zip Dub (Rather GEAR 4/Rough Trade RT 020 1979)

In Love 7-inch EP (Rather GEAR 8 1980)

I Remember/Laura Kate/Almost A Love Song

ARCHIVE RELEASE:

Live At The Cedar Club 6/4/80 (Topplers November 2004) (A great historical curio, but don't expect any PR guff from the Cult Figures. The gig was "awful" according to Jones. As he says in the amusing sleevenotes, "It could serve as a 'don't do this kids' lesson to up and coming bands!" The show, at the Cedar Club, was an ill-advised double bill with hardcore punks GBH, whose guitar and bass they had to borrow. The following incident said much about the clash between two generations of punk rockers. "When I handed the guitar back to Jock of GBH after our set, I was asked, 'What have you done to my guitar?' 'I've tuned it,' said I. 'What? I usually just tighten em all up.'")

Cut Throat and The Razors

Chris Davies (vocals), Graham 'Gobo' Godfrey (guitar), Steve 'Cut Throat' Pegrum (drums)

Southend-On-Sea, 30 miles from London and known euphemistically as the "Thames Delta" had always enjoyed a flourishing music scene, from the Paramounts and Procal Harum in the 60s to pub rockers the Kursaal Flyers and Dr Feelgood in the mid-70s.

It was the latter, according to Cut Throat drummer Steve Pegrum, that provided the link with Southend's subsequent punk tradition, bringing rock music back to its basics. "However, for myself, and many other punks in the area, it was the Vandals/Vicars (featuring Alf Moyet) and The Machines who really ignited the punk flame for us... after the initial flowering and for the altogether too-brief period that these bands lasted, approximately 1977 to 1979, a slew of new bands carried the torch. In 1978 you had Idiot (latterly Speedball, who recorded the excellent 'No Survivors' single) who can be heard, along with the Vicars, on the 1979 Compilation LP 'Southend Rock'. Then unrecorded but no less legendary local acts like the Psychopaths, the Deciballs, the Nomads and my own outfit, **CUT THROAT AND THE RAZORS**."

The punk scene in Southend centred around 'Dave's', a rehearsal room used by most of the bands. There was a local fanzine, Strange Stories, put together by one of the Machines' co-managers, while punk-tolerant shops included Nasty's, Graffiti and Projection Records.

Inspired by seeing the Sex Pistols perform on So It Goes, Pegrum and Godfrey embarked on a pilgrimage to the King's Road in 1978 to purchase bondage trousers and other tribal apparel. By this time Pegrum had started his fanzine Protégé (later Slaughter). Cut Throat and the Razors were formed while all three members were classmates. "Being from the punk DIY school, we saw no need to spend hours learning musical theory etc, so immediately we started to play." Their 'glorious racket' encompassed originals such as 'G.B.H.' and 'Saliva', with some primitive recording taking place at Pegrum's parents' house. The backdrop to these musical excursions was a deal of territorial conflict. "There was the omnipresent threat of being chased along the seafront by the Neanderthal teddy boys who still seemed to be around – thankfully come bank holiday Mondays, they would soon be routed by the visiting punks and skins. 1978 and 1979 were notably anarchic years, making the front page of many tabloids and Southend was literally over-run with punks. Stiff Little Fingers, the Damned and the Ruts played notable local gigs and inspired us n the process, making us feel we weren't the only ones who felt like we did."

Sadly Cut Throat and the Razors never did make a record. However, both Pegrum and Godfrey would re-emerge in 1980 with the Bleeding Pyles. That's the band rather than the medical affliction.

Cyanide

Bob De Vries (vocals), Dave Stewart (guitar), Mike Stewart (drums), Jock Marston (bass)

CYANIDE were formed in York in the mid-70s, originally as a trio with De Vries also playing bass, before Marston was added to the line-up. They were gigging around the York and Leeds area from the start of 1976 and cut a demo tape of two tracks, 'Mac The Flash' and 'No Progress', in August of that year. The former song, including a suitably lascivious voiceover, was a tribute to an imaginary local exhibitionist. Both these rudimentary but tuneful first stabs were later packaged on the band's 1998 CD compilation and neither sounds radically different to the later studio versions.

After catching the Sex Pistols on the Anarchy tour, the band found themselves with an instant peer group. Suddenly it was easier to get gigs, and Cyanide were not a band to turn down any opportunity to play live. They made it down to the Roxy, and were part of a smattering of local bands including the Jermz that flourished during the period. As a result Cyanide, alongside Hull's Dead Fingers Talk, were snapped up by Pye, home of the Muppets, Des O'Connor and sundry disco acts. It was the perfect example of a major coming to the punk party late, and Pye were never able to reconcile themselves with the new acts they signed.

The option of turning professional didn't appeal to Marston, however, who left, later to return to the fray with Sema 4. Dave Thompson was his replacement, just as sessions were booked for their debut single, an arguably ill-advised cover of the Who's 'I'm A Boy', which boasted an unscreened video directed by Mike Mansfield. The single and a self-titled album both emerged in February 1978, as Cyanide embarked on a 60-date UK tour to promote them. Mike Stewart: "When recording the album at Pye's Edgeware Road studios, the Muppet people were recording in the studio next door. And Des O'Connor was hiding in the toilet when we went to pick up our gear the morning after we had finished – had we signed to the wrong company, or what?"

By the advent of second single 'Mac The Flash', re-recorded from their original demo in June 1978, their relationship with Pye was deteriorating fast. Poor management didn't help. "Cyanide's management were crap – probably the one thing that held the band back," notes Mike Stewart, succinctly. They made an effort to overcome the management/record company hassles by playing a series of headlining shows at London venues such as the Nashville and Marquee, and for a while RCA were interested, "but weren't sure about the singer". They also embarked on further recording sessions, including what would have been the band's second album. But in frustration at the lack of a breakthrough, Mike Stewart left at the start of 1979. His replacement was Steve Roberts, who up to that point had been playing in a funk band. He played on the group's third and final single, 'Fireball', released on independent label Pinnacle. Shortly thereafter, Cyanide broke up.

Dave and Mike Stewart would subsequently form the Pullovers with original Cyanide bass player Jock Marston, guitarist Paul Carroll and vocalist Dave Astley, who legendarily had a day job as a taxidermist. He also auditioned for the post-Lydon Pistols and had a brief walk-on part in the Great Rock'n'roll Swindle. The Pullovers managed one release, 'Peter Pan Pill', backed by 'Spare Part Surgery', for Supermusic. This enjoyed a small amount of notoriety when it was packaged with a kidney donor card.

Dave Stewart would subsequently join cult New Wave Of British Heavy Metal band Maineaxe over the course of two albums. Brother Mike played with the Incinerators before going into tour management. Bob De Vries attempted a short-lived solo career before putting together DV & The Clients. Steve Roberts would go on to join the UK Subs in June 1980, partially at the prompting of Subs tour manager, and fellow York native, Chutch. "We (Cyanide) did a really big tour supporting the Subs, see," Roberts later explained to Sounds. "And me and Nick (Garratt) got really friendly, I suppose you could say I wormed my way in." He later played briefly in the Exploited and the Damned. Tragically, Marston died in a car smash with his wife and baby daughter at the turn of the 1980s. Bob De Vries has now also passed on, dying of a heart attack in November 2005 at the age of 48.

On a brighter note, the Cyanide story has come almost full circle. Dave Astley and Mike Stewart have set up Metro Music Management, looking after artists including Steve Ze Suicide (aka Steve Roberts of the Subs). The Ze Suicide album, which features Trevor Bolder of the Spiders of Mars/Uriah Heep on bass, was released in May 2006 by ZSM Records, distributed by Cargo and online via iTunes etc. Former Cyanide stalwart Dave Stewart has just joined the band on guitar.

Completists can pick up Cyanide's entire discography, plus some unreleased tracks, on the 1998 Captain Oi! retrospective. The production values of the original album still sound horribly weedy, but the later tracks such as 'Your Old Man' have a bit more punch. Mike Stewart: "Pye didn't have a clue what to do with us. They took the songs we had, without any interference in terms of arrangements etc. But, in terms of the 'horribly weedy' sound – Dave laid down six guitar parts for each song, which took ages – everything from low register to high – so the 'producer' would have plenty to work with. Around that time the dreaded 'power pop' movement was raising its lightweight head and guess what? Someone at Pye thought it would be a brilliant idea to just use Dave's higher register stuff. This – coupled with our spineless management – well, you've heard the vinyl album. How they thought they could tie in our image with that style of music still evades me to this day. I must say Mark Brennan did improve the sound somewhat when mastering the CD."

The album, to some extent, soured the whole experience for Mike. "All in all, it wasn't that happy an experience. Sure, belting up and down the country playing gigs had its usual (as in every band, ever) shenanigans and highpoints. We used to stay at a 'rock'n'roll' hotel in Sussex Gardens when playing London, where Wayne County used to live. One night, we got back late after a gig at Ronnie Scott's Upstairs in Frith Street in London's Soho (full of the joys of lager and smart-arse jazz arseholes!). A soul act called Heatwave was also in the hotel. They had just headlined at the Hammersmith Odeon. We received a call from hotel management saying that they had complained about the racket we were making and were trying to sleep. We thought, jeez, if we had just headlined there, all of London would be kept awake!"

DISCOGRAPHY:

I'm A Boy/Do It 7-inch (Pye 7N 46048 February 1978) (also released in France with a completely different picture sleeve)

Mac The Flash/Hate The State 7-inch (Pye 7N 46094 June 1978)

Cyanide LP (Pye NSPL 18554 February 1978) (Mick Stewart: "We did our own artwork for the album, which was put together by Dave Astley's brother Nev, who now runs his own animation company and has produced Big Knights for the BBC, Peppa Pig for Channel 5 etc")

Fireball/Your Old Man 7-inch (Pinnacle PIN 23 1979)

The Punk Rock Collection CD (Captain Oi! AHOY CD 64 1998)

Damned

Dave Vanian (aka David Letts; vocals), Brian James (aka Brian Robertson; guitar), Captain Sensible (aka Ray Burns; bass), Rat Scabies (aka Chris Millar; drums)

Popular clichés abound in popular music. Some of them are truisms born of considered sifting of the evidence. Others are fomented by repetition of isolated facts in support of specious received wisdom. It is the latter school that informs us that the DAMNED were merely decorative and amusing adjuncts to punk's existential discourse. Hugely entertaining clown princes of punk they surely were, but like Feste or other Shakespearean jesters, there was more to their art than diverting spectacle.

Perhaps the enduring motif might better be analogised as speed. Though that drug was synonymous with London's punk scene, and Brian James admits their early forays were motivated by "a honkful of toot", only the Damned truly distilled its essence into song, without compromising an innate musicality. And there were the Damned's famous firsts -in the first 18 months of their existence, they were the first punks to release a single, the first to appear on daytime TV, the first to record an album, the first to tour America and the first to split up, and then reform again. One final point: most of punk's big players had major corporations supporting them, for all their political gravitas. The Damned subsisted on a series of low-budget indies well into their first decade.

The origins of the Damned lay way back at the turn of the 1970s, when brothers Ray and Dave Burns played keyboards, alongside drummer Dave Berk and guitarist Fred Mills, in Paul Halford's Black Witch Climax Blues Band. When Ray Burns, later Captain Sensible, took over as guitarist they had become Genetic Breakdown. He played his first show with them in 1973, a talent contest at Thornton Heath pub the Brigstock Arms. "We were allowed two songs and we only got through about one and a half. As they pulled the plugs on us because we were so loud, so obnoxious and so awful. But we had loads of spirit. I remember I was shitting myself before we went on but afterwards I felt so good that I thought, blimey, I'll have to do this again. 'Cause you know it's fun showing off and I've never grown tired of it."

By the time Halford was reborn as Johnny Moped in 1974, Phil Burns was about to leave and this embryonic troupe was christened Five Arrogant Superstars, then Assault & Buggery – evidence already of their commercial disinclination. At the same time Bryan (later Brian) James was writing songs drawing on his MC5/Stooges influences for a band of similarly inflammatory title, Bastard, who were founded in Crawley but eventually relocated to Belgium for live work.

By March 1975 James had moved from Bastard to London SS with future Clash founder Mick Jones, embarking on a series of rehearsals with a variety of ill-fitting personnel. Among these would be drummer Chris Millar, formerly of Tor (aka Rot), "awful, rotten, horrible, the pits," he reckons, though they did get a residency at a 'loony bin', St Lawrence's in Caterham. But he never forgave them for making him put towels over his drums because he was too loud. He phoned in following the famous Melody Maker advert looking for Stooges, MC5 and New York Dolls-influenced musicians. There followed a brief argument on the phone with Bernie Rhodes when Millar admitted he didn't know anything about the MC5 or New York Dolls, but that if they wanted to miss out on one of the world's greatest drummers, that was up to them. He was subsequently invited to a café in Praed Street and then auditioned in the group's rehearsal studio below.

Rat Scabies became his new punk sobriquet after he turned up suffering from said affliction and his startled potential employers were forced to put newspapers down wherever he'd been. His new identity was finalised at Tony James's suggestion. Later that evening, he noted a rodent sat by the drum kit Millar had used. This was executed with a brick, before they decided that it reminded them of the infested young drummer. (Other versions of this story, including Scabies's own, have the rat running past him as he played and Mick Jones coming up with the name) According to Scabies, he never got the gig because "Mick Jones didn't think I was pretty enough." Brian James had no such misgivings. "It was a case of boys versus girls really," he elaborated. "Mick and Tony are basically girls, and Rat and I wanted to play man's music." Duly acquainted, James and Rat would quit London SS and agree to stay in touch and work together.

At this stage Malcolm McLaren introduced himself to Rat, through whom he met Chrissie Hynde, then a shop assistant at Sex, and journalist Nick Kent, her then boyfriend. They talked about forming a band but nothing came of it. However, Rat was eventually inducted into McLaren's latest project. Masters Of The Backside (aka Mike Hunt's Honourable Discharge) was to feature Hynde dressed as a boy and wielding a cane. She would then 'whip' her musicians during the songs – usually run-throughs of standards such as 'I Can't Control Myself' and 'Gimme Some Lovin''. Scabies thought Hynde merely "a loud-mouthed American boiler", but was quite impressed by McLaren.

Hynde was accompanied by two male singers, the blond Dave White, and the dark-haired Dave Zero. Dave White was apparently an effeminate hairdresser from Bromley. That left them short of a bass player, so Rat called up his old friend Ray Burns, literally picking him up en route to a rehearsal. He'd originally tried to rope in Tor's bass player Phil Mitchell but he was completely disinterested.

Burns had first met Scabies when both were porters at Fairfield Hall in Croydon, where Sensible, then a member of Assault & Buggery, instructed him in the best locations to skive and have a sleep. They set up a makeshift bed in the basement for the purpose, and generally ran riot until they were sacked – although Sensible reckons he has a standing offer of his old job back if "this showbiz thing" doesn't work out. And yes, they did clean toilets. For his part, Burns had gone on to various permutations of what was always, effectively, the Johnny Moped Band – travelling under guises such as the Commercial Band. They were also intermittently known as Oasis in their 'cabaret' period, where Burns would sing 'Tie A Yellow Ribbon' for a fiver a night. "I remember telling these people, change the fucking name," he later told Free Radical Sounds. "No band's ever gonna get anywhere with a name like Oasis."

Masters Of The Backside died after a few rehearsals. Rat would also briefly play with Big Girl's Underwear, which Hynde formed with fellow London SS-er Mick Jones. The next development was Kent asking Rat to put together a backing band after he secured two well paid shows at Cardiff Art College for the band he was to call the Subterraneans. As well as Burns, he also got James involved. James immediately insisted he give Burns a hair cut, played him MC5, Stooges and Ramones records non-stop, while letting him kip in the corridor outside his basement flat in Kilburn. Kent then returned to journalism, though the Subterraneans did set in place the connections that would allow the Damned to form. Indeed, 'New Rose' was given its first public airing by the Subterraneans.

By early 1976 a fundamental cast of characters was solidifying. All James, Rat and Burns (now switching to bass) required was a vocalist. Dave Vanian, aka Masters Of The Backside's Dave Zero, aka David Letts, aka Dave Vanium when the press got it wrong, as they frequently did, and aka the 'singing gravedigger' from Heath Lane cemetery in Hemel Hempstead, was perfect. They did toy with the idea of using a pre-Pistols Sid Vicious, whom they'd approached on the same night they spotted Vanian at the Nashville, but he never turned up for auditions at their Lisson Grove rehearsal space, a gay club in a church hall. So they went for Vanian, whom Scabies falsely claimed he met at the funeral of his sister and whom he'd overheard singing 'I Love The Dead'. Vanian went "berserk" and stated smashing things up around him at his audition. They also liked his Johnny Thunders-esque clothes. "Always a good dresser," recalled Scabies. Vanian, for his part, legendarily delighted in singing Alice Cooper's 'Dead Babies' in the execution of his work. He was somewhat loathe to give it up considering he had a decent wage and company car, plus the run of three cemeteries if he'd stayed with his employers – which is a pretty attractive perk for any would-be vampire. Not only did he look the part, customising his stage apparel to reflect his interest in vampirism and horror movie schtick, he could also sing. Again, it's an often overlooked fact that Vanian was possibly the best 'conventional' singer in any of the major punk bands, his authoritative baritone lending the Damned, as they were now named by James after the 1969 Visconti film, part of its melodic bite.

They had to wait for Rat to complete his professional posting as percussionist in the pit orchestra for the Yorkshire Theatre Company's Puss In Boots. By now they were also rehearsing at a Bermondsey warehouse run by John Krivine, owner of King's Road clothes shop ACME Attractions, where Don Letts worked. He also briefly operated as the group's manager. Being in direct competition with McLaren, as soon as he heard about the Pistols he knew he wanted his own band too. But eventually they became clients of future Roxy and Vortex promoter Andy Czezowski, who did the books for both Krivine and Vivienne Westwood. Scabies claimed Czezowski talked them into it, Czezowki claims it was the band's idea. Regardless, by 6 July they were playing support to the Sex Pistols at the 100 Club, their first gig proper after four consecutive Saturday open rehearsals at Lisson Grove in June. They received £5 in recompense while McLaren tried to sting them for £50 for use of the PA.

The Damned had arrived at exactly the right time and place. "It had to happen," noted Rat of punk's development. "The music scene just became so stagnant that it had to change." Which made them, alongside the headliners and the Clash, figureheads of the punk movement. Not that they would ever attain the same level of respect – Lydon later dismissing them as "a glossy Eddie And The Hot Rods". Their public pronouncements also distinguished them. Rat, for one, made no bones about wanting to have "a big house, a big car, and a big colour TV. And so does everyone else, if they're honest." But then, he reasoned, "I've been poor all my life." And some of the in-crowd treated them with suspicion, notably Siouxsie. "It was when everyone started lauding the Damned – that was the beginning of the end as far as I'm concerned; the start of the rot setting in and they all got the wool pulled over their eyes and Rat Scabies started making spitting on stage trendy. That was all his doing."

But the Damned were perfect for punk, and punk, largely, returned the compliment. While James's Gibson SG-guitar playing owed a debt to the MC5 and Dolls that he could hardly have acknowledged more fully, Scabies's astonishing 16 to the bar drumming, accurately described by John Hamblett as "like a man trying to pin down a ground sheet in a hurricane," reeked of Keith Moon. Burns was a loon of the finest vintage, an undoubted idiot savant but a gentleman first and an eccentric second. And Vanian, whom Mick Farren noted "could have been designed by Fritz Lang", completed the most memorable sweep of personae in any punk band ever. As Burns later noted, "There were a lot of volatile characters in the Damned. We were all trying to elbow each other out of the way to get our share of the limelight."

Their second gig was booked by Shanne Bradley (later of the Nipple Erectors) at St Albans Art College. She'd met Rat when he'd 'roadied' for the Pistols, and offered the band £100 for their appearance – a fortune at the time. They ended up back at Shanne's mum's that night and completely drained the drinks cabinet, the cads. Their third show was at the Nashville, supporting Salt. Unsurprisingly, they were roundly booed. However, in the audience that night was Elvis Costello, Jake Riviera, Ted Carroll and Roger Armstrong, with whom the Damned would become much better acquainted. "We nearly signed the Damned the first time out after seeing them at the Nashville Rooms, but Stiff got in first," remembers Armstrong, who actually paid for the band's first demos. "The tables at the front of the stage were occupied by cider drinking long hairs who did not like the Damned. "You expect hippies to be friendly people, but..." Scabies noted, ruefully, to Sniffin' Glue. "Regardless, the Damned played on and on and on. Eventually someone pulled the curtains over at which point all hell broke loose culminating in a bass drum careering through said curtains and sending the pints of cider all over the poor hippies at the front." Which set a nice precedent for both punk and the Damned.

They cemented their position by travelling to the Mont de Marsan festival in the south of France on 21 August 1976. Organised by Marc Zermati and Larry Dubais (who also ran Praed Street's Bizarre Records) of SkyDog Records, it saw a clutch of French rockers appearing alongside Nick Lowe, the Count Bishops, Eddie And The Hot Rods and the Pink Fairies. It was Sean Tyla who gave Captain Sensible his new nom de plume after he advised Burns to rinse the stale eggs that he had somehow accumulated in his hair in a toilet bowl before they reached customs on their return journey. Other versions of this story cite Larry Wallis of the Pink Fairies as the culprit. Tragically, Burns had actually wanted to be called Duane Zenith. On the same journey, Scabies took umbrage at Nick Lowe's Eddie Cochran T-shirt and attempted to rip it off him mid-conversation with Caroline Coon. It was the beginning of a beautiful friendship.

The Sex Pistols had originally been approached but were thrown off the bill after Sid Vicious attacked Nick Kent at the 100 Club. The Clash pulled out in solidarity. The Damned got the gig through Scabies' friendship with Dubais – because Bizarre was situated just round the corner from where the band collected its dole money in Lisson Grove, it was a frequent haunt on giro day. Czezowski has also claimed credit for getting the Damned on

D

The Damned: Scabies, Sensible, James and Vanian.

the bill. "When it came to doing the Mont de Marsan thing," Scabies told Will Birch, "we travelled in a St Trinian's school bus that Jake had hired from somewhere (This was the first time they'd encountered Jake Riviera). We were quite appalled by our fellow travellers. I was expecting it to be punk, but there was nobody under 35 except for us." Although the money was useful, the Damned may as well have not bothered. They'd partied till 8am and were on stage at midday. "They did their barnstorming to about 50 people and a chicken," reckoned Czezowski. They headlined the second night at a more agreeable hour. Yet the Damned represented "an authentic expression of a new lifestyle," according to Mont de Marsan reviewer, Caroline Coon, who was among their staunchest early champions. More importantly, Riviera, having seen their performance, offered them a chance to record a single for Stiff. Czezowski, having seen their personal behaviour at close range, decided that managing them might be the end of him.

By September things were moving apace. They played on the second night of the 100 Club's punk rock festival alongside the Vibrators and the Buzzcocks. But when Sid Vicious threw a bottle during their set an innocent girl lost an eye and made the group's name synonymous with carnage. The incident was prompted by tensions between the Pistols and Damned camps, though at the time Sid's friends kept him out of the frame. The Damned visited the victim in hospital, and tried to organise a benefit at the Nashville, but after their previous show there, they'd been banned – Eddie And The Hot Rods played instead. It gave them a reputation, not helped by the Evening Standard headline "Is this the most nasty, vicious band ever?" that wasn't wholly deserved. James preferred to liken their gigs to 'kindergarten chaos', what with Sensible's nurse's costumes prompting the regulation chant of "Sensible's a wanker". The abuse was often orchestrated by Rat, who loved nothing more than setting his drum kits ablaze, or covering them with talcum powder. Then there were the Hammer Horror vocals of Vanian, who by now "hated people getting too close in case they smudged his make-up," according to Keith Gotheridge of friends Plummet Airlines, and James himself, all studied Keith Richards shapes in black leather.

They signed with Stiff Records and Jake Riviera, following a brief period when their affairs were guided by 100 Club punk promoter Ron Watts. At the time Riviera (formerly Andrew Jakeman) was considered "The only happening man in London" because of his entrepreneurship – setting up your own label was pretty much "unknown". He would turn out to be one of the most brilliant managers in British music history – by turns creative, volatile and authoritarian. "We liked the idea of Stiff because it was an independent," Scabies told Will Birch. "We felt that signing to a major wasn't very punk. Also, Jake knew who the MC5 were. You could talk to him about music. He was a bit older and a hustler and he knew his way around. He also had a good pedigree from working with the Feelgoods, who were a cool band."

Their debut single, 'New Rose', featuring the spoken intro "Is she really going out with him?" co-opted from the Shangri-La's 'Give Him A Great Big Kiss', was written by James in 15 minutes in his flat in Kilburn. It was backed by a whizzy update of the Beatles' 'Help!' on the B-side when released on 22 October. The single was produced by Nick Lowe, on a budget of £50 at Pathway Studios, where only one band member at a time could fit into the control room, and recorded "purely on cider and speed", according to Sensible. The session lasted from morning to lunchtime, and even used borrowed tape. It earned single of the week status in Sounds thanks to Jonh Ingham, but more importantly became the definitive first-mover British punk rock artefact. When Scabies took a wrecking ball to his cymbals at its close, just two minutes had elapsed, but a new musical generation had been born. The band was flushed with pride. Sensible remembers touting its brilliance to anyone who would listen. It's interesting to note in retrospect that it was only selected ahead of 'I Fall' as the first single by a majority vote. After selling 4,000 copies through mail order, at the princely sum of 70p ("with free poster"), its distribution was picked up by United Artists. The attendant press release talked about the "Punk Rock Breakout".

The single was publicised by support slots with the Flamin' Groovies, who self-evidently did not 'get' punk rock judging by their dismissive comments about the Damned, who were quickly dropped from the remaining tour dates, "because we blew 'em out," insists Sensible. They also played beneath the Troggs when the Groovies failed to appear for their Roundhouse show. They cut their first John Peel session at Maida Vale on 30 November. Producer Jeff Griffin was nervous before his first encounter with a punk band. "In fact, when we got to the studio, I'm not sure who was more apprehensive, them, about being in a BBC studio, or me about working with them. The amusing thing was quite a few other people had heard that the Damned were in, and every now and again we got people creeping in through the door, looking in through the window to see if they were being sick all over the place or spitting at us. Which they weren't at all, of course: they were four of the nicest blokes I ever got to work with."

Their momentum seemed to be assured when it was announced they were to join the Pistols' Anarchy In The UK tour. It seemed the dream ticket, with the Pistols headlining over the Clash and Johnny Thunders and the Heartbreakers. However, before the tour started, the Sex Pistols elected to respond to Bill Grundy's urgings to reveal themselves as the subhumans they obviously were and delivered their Pavlovian obscenities to the TV nation. Punk bands were now briefly the source of moral panic, folk devils in bad clothes. The enemy.

Out of the proposed 19 dates only three were played, the Damned appeared at only two, Leeds and Manchester. They were thrown off the tour after Riviera clashed with Malcolm McLaren. Prior to the first date, a proposed show at Derby's King's Hall was cancelled when the Pistols were told to play an afternoon audition so that local councillor Leslie Shipley could decide if the show should go ahead. The Pistols didn't show and so were banned by the council by default. The Damned's tour manager, Rick Rogers, volunteered their services so the gig could go ahead. For some, this brought about a question of punk ethics, exacerbated by the fact that the Damned were travelling separately in a transit van – although that was simply because they didn't have the same budget as the headliners. "Our tour manager said we'd play if the Pistols couldn't," Sensible told me. "Meanwhile, the Damned were stewing in a dodgy B&B. We couldn't afford to stay in the flash hotels the Pistols' record labels were stumping up for. We knew nothing of this shady dealing. We'd never have played." McLaren jumped in, sensing a publicity coup, and told the press: "The Clash and the Heartbreakers are behind us, but we are not in sympathy with the Damned and we will ask them to leave the tour after the show at Leeds Poly." The truth was the Damned had been caught up in a little power struggle between McLaren, Rhodes and Riviera.

Much of January 1977 was spent on their debut album, released on 18 February after 30 hours of studio time – including mixing. Aside from the originals, Damned Damned Damned contained 'Fish', a Brian James/Tony James composition from their days in London SS when it was known as 'Portobello Reds'. There was also another leftover from his past, Bastard's '1 Of The Two', their Jonathan Richman tribute 'Feel The Pain' and 'I Feel Alright', their rewrite of the Stooges' '1970'. Incidentally, the 'Hey Keith!' remark that prefaces the latter was a pastiche of Johnny Thunders' behaviour when the Heartbreakers toured the UK on the Anarchy tour. Keith was Thunders' gofer, and was summoned in such curt fashion, apparently, every five minutes.

The cover depicted the band in a custard pie fight, emphasising their playful reputation. It was again 'produced' by Nick Lowe, though he later admitted to doing little more than pressing the record button as the band rammed through their live set. But he did achieve a fantastically 'clean' guitar sound. Sensible constructed a handmade bass cabinet with plywood barely housing an 18-inch speaker, which resulted in the distinctive 'squelch' of the bottom end. Lowe purloined a series of old Costello demo tapes for the purpose of the recording, and set up the eight-track mixing desk by tying lolly-sticks to the levers so that he could manoeuvre four at a time.

The first definitive long-playing UK punk record, although it stayed in the charts for 10 weeks, Damned Damned Damned only reached 36 – evidence of the fact that while the British public's appetite for punk had been whetted, we were a long way from commercial appropriation of the mainstream. But what still makes the band spit is the rumour that the tapes were speeded up. They were not. But the inference can be traced to John Collis in Time Out and Mac Garry in Zigzag, two of the few dissenting voices in a wave of praise. The latter claimed to have heard ice cream vans with a better sense of melody. Other reviews were ecstatic. In the NME Tony Parsons declared that the Damned "have delivered the goods". "These boys have got all the residual skills needed for the actual performance of exhausting modern music," declared Melody Maker. Old stalwart Giovanni Dadomo in Sounds announced that the band "stand sturdily on its eight cleft feet with precious few regrets and a great deal of very splendid rock'n'roll brimstone."

After Sensible played a smattering of shows with Johnny Moped, the Damned embarked on a March UK tour (nine dates between the 10th and 20th) in support of faded pop icon Marc Bolan. At the time being dismissed as overweight and out of touch, he befriended the band at Hammersmith's Red Cow because "one of them had the good taste to wear a Marc Bolan T-shirt". "I've always been a big fan of Bolan," Sensible admitted. "But I'm a much better performer than he is." Bolan, for his part, had compared 'New Rose' to the Stones' 'I Wanna Be Your Man'. In fact, Sensible had watched Bolan play Croydon's Fairfield Hall when he was ostensibly meant to be on duty and decided that pop stars got the girls whereas toilet cleaners, on the whole, didn't – a pretty big inspiration to a man like Sensible.

The dates were a resounding success, with the Damned happy to provide "next best thing" sexual relations with doting Bolan fans who would get backstage only to be confronted by the midget minstrel's wife. However, the Damned still faced censure in a music press dominated by ludicrous notions of musical authenticity. "The Damned produced their usual tedious brand of badly played, over-loud songs," complained Robin Smith in one review. This was typical of the snobbery which greeted punk bands in general, but the Damned in particular. "Good musicians?" queried Ian Cranna of their Glasgow show. "How can anyone tell at that speed?"

Their second single, 'Neat Neat Neat', was released at the end of February to accompany the dates. Another 'rolling thunder' production courtesy of Scabies' drumming and fantastically nonsensical lyrics, and if anything even swifter than 'New Rose', it was backed by 'Stab Your Back' and 'Singalonga-Scabies' – 'Stab Your Back' played backwards. Vanian was spitting entire verses in the space of time Johnny Rotten was twisting a single syllable of 'Anarchy'.

The tour was then extended to encompass a few tentative dates in America in April 1977. The Dead Boys supported them for their first two shows at CBGBs, which were marred by equipment troubles, mainly exacerbated by Sensible getting carried away. Although the nurse costume was diverting, his inability to negotiate the stage while maintaining pinpoint knowledge of the whereabouts of his bass lead left the band a mess of badly mixed treble. The final night they played support to an uppity Patti Smith, who made some disdainful comments about this "new British music" she'd helped inspire and had them thrown out of her dressing room ("What a bunch of redundant old rock shit they were, the Patti Smith Group," noted Sensible later). The tour was completed with shows in Philadelphia, Long Island and Cleveland.

They then flew out to LA for a show backing Television at the Whiskey only to be dismissed by Verlaine's image-conscious no-wavers because they were too "amateurish". The band took its revenge by attending the gig with the legend "Television are cunts" on their T-shirts, and, later, writing 'Idiot Box'. Years later, Captain Sensible's legendarily protective Aunt Sadie would confront Verlaine at a solo show in London to personally berate him for his ill-treatment of her nephew. Tomato Du Plenty of the Screamers ended up putting them up on his floor and fixing up gigs at the Starwood and Mabuhay Gardens as compensation. In the audience at the latter venue on 21 April was Jimmy Wilsey, aka Jimmy Blaze of the Avengers. "The Damned's show at the Mab had everybody from around here who was in a band. They played everything, and everybody was sort of looking at each other with their mouths open, and after that I think the bands started changing a little more. Songs got faster, set lists got shorter." The Starwood gigs saw every would-be guest-lister turned away by Jake Riviera, who put up a sign: "Everyone has to pay, so the Damned can go home, otherwise we'll be stuck with them forever."

On their return they embarked on another UK tour, with friends the Adverts as support. This was billed, famously, as 'The Damned can now play three chords, the Adverts can play one (relating to their single 'One Chord Wonders') – hear all four of them on tour." The Damned's backdrop presented themselves as "The Tax Exiles Return", a self-mocking reference to their US jaunt. Johnny Moped introduced them at the Roundhouse, by which time Sensible was getting the hang of his ballerina's tutu, they were roping in Gaye Advert for the 'Neat Neat Neat' encore and Jon Savage was forced to concede they'd "reached the crest of their first wave". Even for the Damned, the speed of their ascent was dizzying. "It's amazing, really amazing," Vanian confessed. "It's happened so quickly. In the past, bands have taken years to get anywhere. For us, everything's been so fast. But I love it because the pressure is on and I work much better like that. It's better to have it rush at you like this."

But outside London, local authorities still viewed punk gigs as crucibles of potential insurrection. The date at Southampton University was called off when staff refused to serve the Damned's audience. The show at Lincoln Drill Hall saw massed ranks of punk-haters attempt to lynch the Damned, as Sensible recalled. "We were attacked by a whole bunch of blokes, about 30 or 40 of them, all with iron bars and bricks and stuff. We actually had to fight our way out of that one. They'd smashed all the windows of our van, out the back. We had to get the mic stands back out and get stuck in, which was not really my cup of tea after a hot sweaty gig just spreading peace and joy throughout the world, ya know?" The Mecca Organisation pulled a gig at Newcastle-Under-Lyme, and shows at Cromer, Cheltenham Town Hall and Southend's Kursaal were also aborted. Then Vanian dislocated a shoulder in a dressing room incident, again after they were attacked, forcing the cancellation of their show at Wigan Casino.

Twelve months on the road was celebrated by four dates at the Marquee, a year to the date after supporting the Sex Pistols at the 100 Club – playing an identical set. For the occasion they recorded a give-away single. 'Sick Of Being Sick' was backed by 'Stretcher Case Baby' (with lyrics from Rat), produced by Shel Talmy and limited to 5,000 copies. There was a near riot on the Sunday night caused by fans trying to grab extra copies. However, the final two dates, including the anniversary bash, were pulled when Jake Riviera fell out with the Marquee's management over, of all things, their insistence on using their own backdrop on stage which obscured the Marquee logo. As a result, the Marquee's management also pulled them from the Reading Festival, which they organised.

At this stage they rescued second guitarist Robert 'Lu' Edmunds from the dole queue to bolster their sound after placing ads in the Melody Maker: "Wanted: dynamite guitarist into

Iggy, the Beatles and the Damned." Edmunds passed the final audition while the rest of the band stood naked in front of him and gobbed on him, en masse. Edmunds was the only one who didn't bottle it, so they christened him 'Lu', as in 'Lunatic', and called him back. But Sensible was displeased at James's decision and refused to talk to either guitarist: "If ever there was a guitarist who didn't need a second guitarist," Sensible later told Carol Clerk, "it was Brian." Thereafter Sensible mellowed a little, to the extent that he enjoyed tripping Edmunds up on stage by carefully walking round him with his bass lead.

Following further European dates the band embarked on sessions for their second album. Stiff were keen for new product – according to the band, because they weren't at all sure this punk thing was built to last and wanted to maximise the Damned's potential while it did. The original intention was to try to rope in Pink Floyd eccentric Syd Barrett (the Damned always shared Pink Floyd's publishers, and this was their attempt to try to lure the reclusive one back into the fray). Marc Bolan was approached but declined, while Jimmy Page, a huge fan of the Damned's first album, was tentatively interested at one point. These discussions followed abortive sessions with Talmy – who, being nearly blind, could only work at certain studios. They also worked on some of the songs with Nick Lowe, but in the end they hooked up with Floyd's Nick Mason. James wanted a more 'psychedelic' record. Captain was not impressed, not even a little bit. Mason was "a bit flash" and would turn up at the studio in his Ferrari, while the Damned got there by bunking the tube.

They invited jazz saxophonist Lol Coxhill, who'd played with them at a show in Dunstable in June, to join them in the studio. It seemed they were not going to be content to stick to basic punk rock mechanics. But the sessions were fraught and unsatisfactory – though they all liked Coxhill, who, having a regular teaching job, would mark papers in his downtime at gigs. The rest of the group were growing resentful of James's autocratic methods, however, his refusal to listen to their material, and also the intrusion into their affairs of photographer Erica Echenberg, his girlfriend. They'd failed to secure a recording contract while on tour in America, which was at least half the purpose of that jaunt (Sire and CBS were both at the CBGB's shows, but passed), and they were still depressed at the lack of respect afforded them back home. And Mason seemed, to the band, to be more interested in his cars and motorbikes than their music.

Disillusioned, Rat decided to jump ship as the group toured Europe. He bailed after the French National Front attacked the band at a show in Nancy. There was talk of an opportunity to join the Heartbreakers, but the reality was he'd simply burned out, and hated the new album. Press reports of him trying to chuck himself out of a hotel window basically boiled down to the effects of alcohol-induced psychosis. He almost persuaded Sensible to join him in retreat, but Sensible, by his own admission, "bottled it". Dave Berk from Johnny Moped stood in for the remaining dates. In return, Rat crashed in Berk's house and became Jake Riviera's man with a van. "The punk thing has become the quickest sell-out I've ever seen," Scabies complained to Melody Maker. "Now it's completely run by businessmen. It's just a trend to make money out of. That was one of the main things getting me down. Instead of boring old farts, we had boring young farts. We were all getting fat, especially me and the Captain. Suddenly we were on £50 a week when we were used to a tenner on the dole. We had it easier than we'd ever had it in our life and with that the desperation went." The rest of the European tour was a disaster, notwithstanding shows playing to ex-pat Paras, a gig at a cattle market in Rennes and generally behaving in a manner which meant Stiff had to send out a deputation to "tell them off". But this time the chaos was underpinned by genuine antipathies rather than communal clowning.

Scabies' contributions were still evident with the release later that month of Music For Pleasure. The reviews weren't kind, the Melody Maker dubbing it "damned feeble". It comprised 11 originals, including a re-recorded (and inferior) 'Stretcher Case', two moderate singles, Scabies and James' 'Problem Child' (released in October) and 'Don't Cry Wolf' – which owed a big debt to Eddie And The Hot Rods' 'Do Anything You Wanna Do'. The best song was arguably the Rat and Sensible composition 'Idiot Box', which James now concedes is the highpoint of the album. Music For Pleasure caught the Damned straddled between two stools – lacking the raw energy of its predecessor just as it was bereft of the spirit of adventure that would distinguish later albums. Nobody was happy with the finished result, especially Sensible.

"Absolute crap! Don't be afraid of saying it. It was rubbish." But as Joe Foster later noted in an article for MOJO, perhaps received wisdom has undersold the goods. "The sound of a band over-reaching and being punished for it? Maybe. Place Music For Pleasure next to the hundreds of mediocre 'punk' albums that have appeared since 1977, though, and it sounds like a full-blown masterpiece."

The critical admonishment was partially deserved. The album simply lacked the guts of its predecessor, though how the album might have sounded with a more sympathetic producer is a moot point. The Damned were also always better working within a really tight budget. Give them any leeway and they'd piss it up against the wall. The fall from grace was spectacular. Captain complained to Pete Silverton that "the Damned are in the dumpers. Everyone knows that. No-one wants to know us." Jake Riviera, the one person the Damned had total respect for at the time, left Stiff to set up Radar to work with Nick Lowe and Elvis Costello, which meant sole managership of the band fell to Dave Robinson. They lost momentum, not to mention inner cohesion, despite recruiting former London and future Culture Club drummer Jon Moss for a November tour to thinning audiences. By December Robinson, also head of Stiff, could take no more of his unruly charges. "Jake just walked out," reckoned Scabies. "He went off with Elvis Costello. We didn't even know he had gone. Dave Robinson said 'Jake's fucked off I'm managing you now.' Without Jake there, it wasn't the same for us. It was, 'We ain't signed to you, we signed to him.' And that was it. They were pleased to see the back of us, it was back to their good old pub rock boys." Perhaps anticipating the end, Stiff pulled the plug on the band at the start of 1978. A Stiff spokesperson told the press: "This is a record company, not a museum." Charming.

The truth was, the Damned were never the easiest band to oversee. "This is the problem of being the most raucous punk rock band in the world," Scabies later stated. "You get your accounts and it says – miscellaneous damages, £28,000." That was a big problem for a low-budget label like Stiff. Several times Robinson, and others, tried to mediate. But the band was overtaken with their own internal wrangles and were, by their very nature, reluctant to genuflect to any authority figures. "I had a real affection for them," Robinson told Carol Clerk, "but to deal with them in business was really impossible."

There was also plenty of discord from within. When Moss was involved in a serious car crash, no-one from the band bothered to visit him in hospital. "The band as it stood was incapable of change," James told the press. "It had grown into such a mess that we'd gained the reputation as a vaudeville act. The fact remained that some of us wanted to play music, and some of us preferred to mess around with custard pies." The split was officially announced in March 1978, amid rumours that Sensible had been sounded out about replacing Sid Vicious in the Sex Pistols. The truth was that Sensible was devastated by the end of his beloved Damned.

From there the Damned scattered to far-flung corners. In January 1978 Scabies formed the White Cats, who only lasted just over eight months, but played frequently ("every toilet in London") and cut a session for John Peel. Later Scabies would also drum at Sid Vicious's last British gig at the Electric Ballroom, as well as organising the 'Greedy Bastards' collaboration with members of the Pistols and Thin Lizzy. Lu Edmunds and Jon Moss formed the Edge, who cut three singles and an album in their two-year tenure, before producer Liam Sternberg used them as Jane Aire's Belvederes and as the musicians on Kirsty MacColl's 'They Don't Know'. Moss, pre-Culture Club, also worked with the Nips. Edmunds later worked with Athletico Spizz 80, Shriekback, Thomas Mapfumo, the Waterboys, the Mekons and PiL. Brian James put together Tanz Der Youth with Andy Colquhoun (ex-Warsaw Pakt, Deviants), Alan Powell (Hawkwind) and Tony Moor. James also managed a couple of solo singles before more permanently finding a home alongside Dead Boys' vocalist Stiv Bators and Sham 69 bass player Dave Treganna in Lords Of The New Church.

Vanian joined his best man Kid Strange's Doctors Of Madness and helped promote their Sons Of Survival album. Captain, inevitably, rejoined Johnny Moped. After suffering a nervous breakdown in Holland he put together the Softies with former paratrooper and ex-Damned roadie Big Mick, who cut one memorable single, 'Jet Boy Jet Girl' – a very rough translation of the Plastic Bertrand hit 'Ca Plane Pour Moi'. Later still he would form King in June 1978, who recorded a solitary, but excellent, John Peel session, and played a grand total of five shows, with Henry Badowski (ex-Chelsea and Wreckless Eric) and Kym Bradshaw (ex-Saints). Sadly, he was never able to persuade Vanian to join him in the venture.

As a farewell gesture the Damned played a final show on 8 April 1978 at the Rainbow, after weeks searching for a suitable venue. It was a classic performance in the best traditions of the band. Sensible walked off stage halfway through. There was some serious counter-aggression from the audience, sniffing the mood. Then Rat climbed up from the audience, pushed Moss away from the drum kit and proceeded to play a solo. After playing their final song, 'I Feel Alright', the stage was smashed to matchwood.

It was only August before rumours of the Damned's imminent resurrection began to take shape. Fact was, they were skint. One drunken night, Scabies and Sensible got together over a drink in Croydon and decided to ring Vanian – convincing him of the promise of non-existent major contracts in the offing. By 5 September, operating under the guise of Les Punks, Scabies, Sensible, Vanian and Motorhead's Lemmy on bass played the Electric Ballroom. They were re-christened the Doomed due to James's refusal to relinquish rights to the name. Badowski, whom Scabies didn't get on with and picked on relentlessly, briefly helped out. Badowski: "Rat must have been aware that King was the best of the ex-Damned members' solo efforts and he even auditioned as drummer and didn't get the job. He then persuaded Captain to reform the Damned and I joined on bass for a short UK tour. Rat would constantly complain that he wanted Paul Gray on bass and never gave the impression that I was a member of the group. Having been physically and mentally abused by him throughout the tour we ended up having a serious fight on the M4 motorway after he'd started punching me in the car. I needed to be dragged away from him by the others. I was told my services were no longer required soon after that. This was a great shame as I'd genuinely loved the Damned and it should have felt like a true privilege to be actually playing with them. Rat has lived near to me for several years now and we meet occasionally and get on very well." His replacement was Algy Ward of the Saints.

Their first show as the Damned, following Mr Millar Senior's intervention over rights to the name, came in January 1979 at the Croydon Greyhound. They cut six new songs and placed two of them, 'Love Song' backed by Scabies' vocal showcase 'Burglar', on a freebie single given away at a Christmas show at the Electric Ballroom (the 'Dodgy Demo' single) while they were still billed as the Doomed.

The Damned's latest manager Rick Rogers also worked for Chiswick Records, so that became the obvious next port of call, after he persuaded Roger Armstrong to attend their gig at the Lyceum. "They were playing the Lyceum one night and it was packed," remembers Armstrong. "The third business partner in the company Trevor came along out of curiosity – he certainly was not a punk fan. He encouraged us to sign them on the basis that they were drawing crowds who bought records – pretty straightforward." The Damned were the least hot property on the market, but Armstrong, a fan since their third gig, couldn't resist giving them another shot. But he was cautious enough to sign them for just one single, with an option on an album. The Damned, desperate for cash and living in reduced circumstances, were in no position to decline.

In April 1979 the band reintroduced themselves with the release proper of 'Love Song', the perfect marriage of Vanian's towering stentorian phrasing and Sensible's plunging guitar lines. The acerbic lyric was essentially by Scabies, the music came from Sensible. They toured extensively to promote the single with the Ruts and seasoned warm-up act Auntie Pus, attempting to wean the public from the view that they were a band prone to both violence and cancellations. To their surprise, it crashed into the Top 20 and took them to Top Of The Pops. At one point sales were so strong the pressing company had to suspend manufacturing of the current Wings single to meet demand. A fantastic double whammy for music fans, in short.

The Ruts and the Damned proved a good match. There were constant efforts at outdoing each other. As Vanian recalled, "They came running onstage during our set (while they were doing an encore of 'Burglar') dragging sackfulls of horse shit they got after visiting a farm. We all had a fight with them and were rolling about in a pile of putrid dung. After a few minutes of that we convulsed with laughter as we remembered there was an audience watching... it was a university and the students sure looked clean, but not for long (laughter)... you should have seen the mad rush for the exits!" Except for Sensible, who rolled about, naked, in the manure, happy as a pig in the literal. Tour manager Tommy Crossan was physically sick. The next night, Scabies perforated Ruffy's drums. And Malcolm Owen was hospitalised after headbutting cymbals, etc, etc.

Following a brief European tour, the Damned cut 'Smash It Up' as further evidence of their rejuvenation. Arguably the Captain's finest moment, he'd envisaged the song in four parts. The single itself was part two – part one had been written in the direct aftermath of Marc Bolan's death in September 1977. Part three was never written, at least not at the time, though part four he would cut solo in 1990. Evidence of the band's progression was confirmed with the November 1979 release of 'I Just Can't Be Happy Today', with 'Ballroom Blitz', featuring Lemmy, on the flipside. The A-side was sumptuous pop, a neo-orchestral piece built on Scabies' bass drum and cymbal crescendos. It featured an exhilarating organ solo (the same one he had tried out for King's Peel session track 'Baby Sign Here With Me') which sounds like Sensible is physically breaking the keyboard at one point. Vanian's biblical declamation came courtesy of punk writer and occasional Snivelling Shits' singer Giovanni Dadomo, because they were "struggling" with lyrics. It was conclusive proof, also, that the Damned could prosper without Brian James, the dominant songwriter on their early releases who had frustrated Sensible's, and to a less extent Scabies', ambitions to contribute songs.

Machine Gun Etiquette is often considered the album that Music For Pleasure should have been – but there are a few caveats to that conclusion. First, without James, the songwriting was more equally shared and, rather than decline because of that, it improved. Secondly, Sensible's guitar playing was a revelation. Despite James' reservations about the 'custard pie' image he'd lent the band, Sensible was turning out to be a real find. And Vanian had never sounded better.

The title track, a re-write of Scabies's White Cats vintage song 'Second Time Around', featured Joe Strummer and Paul Simonon of the Clash on handclaps. But there wasn't a misplaced note on any of the 11 tracks, many of which were emboldened by Sensible's keyboards, as well as violin on 'These Hands'. 'Anti-Pope' announced Sensible's still fervent distrust of organised religion, while, more playfully, 'Melody Lee' was written about a character from the Bunty comic – rather anticipating the Human League's 'Don't You Want Me', the dialogue was lifted straight from speech bubbles. It still seems absurd in retrospect that Chiswick never saw fit to issue the exquisite 'Plan 9 Channel 7', Vanian's tribute to James Dean which featured arguably his greatest ever vocal, as a single. The overdubs were completed at Wessex Studios at the same time as the Clash were recording London Calling, and it's an album that deserves to be mentioned in the same breath. Not that reverence is ever an option for the Captain. "Entering their studio was like walking into a London pea-souper smog of the 60s – billowing clouds of dope smoke so that you couldn't see from the sofa to the mixing desk. Nice enough blokes, though. They saw the funny side when some wag sent a helium balloon to the rather high (converted church) ceiling with a cartoon of Mick with a vulgar slogan. He wouldn't play another note until it was removed. Ha!"

Touring continued with support from New York's Misfits, who would later only half-jokingly accuse the headliners of accosting their girlfriends on the tour bus, after Sensible had invited his friends Bad Brains over only to see them turned back at the airport due to a lack of work permits. With the Damned at the height of their pre-'Eloise' popularity, it would have been nice if they'd been able to keep the ship steady. But instead Algy Ward departed, with Sensible covering for some of his bass parts. Ward and Scabies had become increasingly intolerant of each other, a situation that ended in fisticuffs on the set for the video of 'Smash It Up'.

After he was sacked, Ward formed Tank in February 1980, a metal trio wholly indebted to Motörhead's influence, and actually jointly managed by that band's Eddie Clarke. The new bass player was Paul Gray, formerly of Eddie And The Hot Rods and well known to the band – who liked his musical approach. He was not officially inducted until June 1979 – mainly because his fellow Hot Rods were utterly cheesed off with his defection. "They kept sending these messages," remembers Gray, "'Join our band, you bastard, we'll double your wages.' They never did." Roger Armstrong arranged for a week on a barge in which time Gray would be taught the material by Scabies and Sensible. They did no such thing, preferring instead to explore the farthest reaches of a Good Pub Guide and improvise some impromptu clay pigeon shooting via the use of the galley's plates and a borrowed air rifle. Gray's first memory of waking up on the boat was seeing his shoe float past him, set ablaze, in the opposite direction.

Evidently his induction into punk's craziest band played on his nerves. The group arranged a week-long tour during sessions for The Black Album, and invited Billy Karloff's band to support. Neil Hay: "The first gig Captain was arguing about having the wrong beer in the dressing room. Dave Vanian accused him of not taking his songs seriously, they were playing 'Dr Jeckyll and My Hyde', and Captain was rolling around on the ground. Vanian threw the Hammond organ into the audience, and then it all kicked off backstage. Paul Gray escaped to our dressing room and was virtually in tears. 'What am I gonna do? If this band splits up, I haven't got a job.' The second night in Derby, things were kicking off between Captain and Dave again. One guy at the front vomited into the monitor while we were playing. The smell was awful. There were bikers at the side, ripping up parts of the stage so they'd have some weapons. We thought this wasn't the warm, friendly family environment we were used to. We knocked it on the head after two days, we'd had enough."

The new Damned line-up, now handled by Motörhead manager Doug Smith, intended to release a cover version of Jefferson Airplane's psychedelic chestnut 'White Rabbit', cut at Wessex Studios, but Chiswick confined its release to Europe in preference for original material. The Damned were not amused, their original choice of '(Rabid) Over You' having been rejected. "These stinking Frogs deserve it but our loyal British fans don't," Rat sniffed to the press. They made amends in September with 'History Of The World Part 1', a song matching 'I Just Can't Be Happy Today's dark melodrama while denouncing Crossroads character Adam Faith and Zorro as false Gods, instead deifying the mishap-prone Dandy comic strip character Corporal Clott. It was recorded over the space of two weeks with producer Hans Zimmer.

The Black Album, spread over four sides of vinyl and produced by the band with Hugh Jones as engineer, continued the dark but rich melodic persuasion of the singles. As Paul Gray told the Second Time Around website, Jones had his work cut out. "Me and Rat would be knocking at his door at midday raring to go, Captain would surface about six, and Vanian would be ready after his bottle of red wine at about midnight. Me and Rat would cut out about 3am leaving the others to it. The poor sod never got much sleep for over a month." Scabies was also incapacitated for much of the sessions with an injured hand, meaning the cymbals had to be overdubbed. The third side of the double LP was taken up by a 17-minute version of 'Curtain Call', originally written by Vanian on a Sames Harmonium. Sensible encouraged him to expand the song while adding the guitar parts. Vanian would hum the tune and Sensible transpose it to chords.

Other highlights including the roustabout 'Hit Or Miss', which Gray had originally road-tested with the Hot Rods, and Sensible's 'Silly Kids Games' (later he'd use part of the melody for his solo single, 'Come On Down'). There was also a fourth side featuring a show recorded live at Shepperton in front of the group's fan club, though the band were dubious about this detracting from the studio work. They also hated the mix. Lifted from the sessions, but not included on the album, came 'There Ain't No Sanity Clause', based on an old Marx Brothers' joke lifted from A Night At The Opera. Giovanni Dadomo once again co-wrote the lyric. But Chiswick were concerned that, despite their high profile, the Damned were still losing more money for the label than they were bringing in. It was mutually agreed that they would leave Chiswick, but the label were still owed £40,000 in unrecouped advances (which, when Scabies's father checked out the accounts, turned out to be true). Chiswick said they'd write that off in return for another album, but the band were aggrieved, especially Sensible, who was angered by the label's determination to release further singles.

When they finally signed to NEMS Records on a one-off deal, Chiswick sold their copyrights and master tapes to another indie, Big Beat, which would lead to a good deal of confusion over new Damned material (much of it unreleased). But it wasn't only Chiswick and Big Beat who were cashing in, Stiff also released their first four singles in a wallet. Their sole release for NEMS was the 'Friday The 13th' EP, released on that date in November 1981. The four tracks offered a nice bridge to their forthcoming album. 'Billy Bad Breaks', in particular, featured a phenomenal performance from Gray, who wrote the song about an unfortunate cocaine smuggler in the book Snowblind. During the sessions the band recruited Roman Jugg (ex-Victimize) to provide additional organ. With a single day's notice Jugg made his way to Newcastle for the first date of the Damned's new tour with their ultimate touring partners, the Anti-Nowhere League.

NEMS closed down within a few short months of signing the Damned, leaving them still in hock to Chiswick. However, John Millar, with the help of Paul Gray's girlfriend Lynne, managed to negotiate a new contract with Bronze before stepping down. Most of the new album had already been recorded in demo form at Rockfield studios. Their relationship with Bronze, their fourth label in as many years, began with the release of 'Lovely Money'. Featuring a guest appearance from Vivian Stanshall of the Bonzo Dog Band, this was a lovely piece of English whimsy but nothing that the Damned's core fan base were ever going to get their heads around.

Conversely, Sensible had been approached by A&M to arrange a solo deal. Among the songs he worked on was a version of 'Happy Talk' from Rodgers & Hammerstein's South Pacific musical, despite producer Mike Mansfield's misgivings. In June 1980 it was released as a single and vaulted to the top of the charts. Sensible mailed copies to Reagan and Brezhnev in an effort at single-handedly ending the cold war. Suddenly Sensible was framed as the perfect children's entertainer, garishly visible on a succession of children's TV programmes. Only he wasn't the perfect children's entertainer, loathed being set up as one, and self-medicated by trying to take as much alcohol and drugs before each appearance as his constitution would sustain.

If Sensible's solo success was a spur to the Damned themselves, it would also invoke a deal of personal envy and enmity, but for now the Captain returned to sessions for their Bronze debut, scheduled for October release. For now, the rest of the band were content to abuse his new-found wealth by making him get all the drinks in. Strawberries was a delightful selection of Nuggets and Left Banke-inspired psych-pop and beat, containing Vanian's Interview With A Vampire tribute 'The Dog' and his epic 'Stranger On The Town', though he would struggle to hit the high notes on it live, as he'd always done with 'History Of The World'. There was also another strong single, 'Dozen Girls'. Sensible indulged his passion for unadorned, wistful English pop in the shape of 'Life Goes On', its intro later pinched by Killing Joke for 'Eighties' and then Nirvana for 'Come As You Are', and the throwaway 'Don't Bother Me'. He also, in a feat of sonic one-upmanship in a wager with Rabies, managed to bury the sound of flushing toilets in the mix. It's a superb suite, existing fans swerved it, though among the critics, Sounds attested to the Damned's power of melody and subversion. The NME, typically, noted that it scored "fewer goals than Hereford United". However, with Captain's star still rising it was levered into the Top 20, while early purchasers were rewarded with a strawberry scented lyric sheet. 'Generals' was taken as the third single for the album, though perhaps the band may have been better served employing the storming 'Ignite' or effervescent 'Bad Time For Bonzo'. Yet tensions once again re-emerged. This time Scabies was unhappy with Gray, and, in particular, his girlfriend. It ended up with Scabies punching Gray unconscious over a disagreement about Gray's 'Pleasure And The Pain'. It was at this point that Sensible's relationship with Scabies began to cool.

In February 1982, Rat, while working with his friend Paul Fox from the Ruts on the side project Foxes And Rats, handed the Damned's stewardship to Sensible's manager Andrew Miller, in the hope that having joint management might help the logistics of live shows while Sensible undertook ever more arduous promotional opportunities. Sensible himself scored a second hit single in September with the improbable 'Wot', which reached number one in France for seven weeks.

Which provided a stark contrast with the Damned's fortunes, who were back on tour in September and October supported by Charge, playing in front of Vanian's gothic film set cum stage design, and with three girl fans dressed as nuns. But the tour, otherwise successful, marked the departure of Gray, who had left by February 1983 to take up an engagement with UFO, with whom he stayed until 1987. He subsequently become part of Andrew Ridgeley's touring band before forming Mischief with Alan Lee Shaw, though Gray's subsequent activities have been limited by the onset of tinnitus.

The Damned still had a small club tour booked, so by March 1983 they recruited Roman Jugg's former Victimize bass player, Bryn Merrick. But despite Captain's self-evident commitment to the band, having Miller as a manager started to store up further tensions, exacerbated by a miserable, impoverished tour of America. Thereafter Scabies took over their business affairs. Bronze, too, had rapidly tired of the group's behaviour, particular Scabies', and were prepared to release them. The Damned were free agents. Again.

By the start of 1984, things were looking perilous for the Damned. Months were wasted over band wrangles as their publisher, Peter Barnes, tried to help steady the ship, as well as Andy McQueen, who signed on as manager. A possible major label deal with CBS seemed to be in the offing. But the distance between the Captain's successful solo career (sitting at number six with 'Glad It's All Over') and the Damned's indolence was marked. According to Scabies, Captain was down to write "a hit single" to make the mother group a marketable commodity once more, but had come up with nothing. So instead they returned to a demo, 'Thanks For The Night', that they'd cut during the Strawberries sessions. It had then turned up on Sensible's solo album.

The new single emerged on Plus One Records. 'Thanks For The Night' was the Damned by numbers. But the B-side, 'Nasty', recalled their heyday and was given good exposure by its insertion into an episode of The Young Ones, at the suggestion of Alexei Sayle. It was but a temporary fillip, however. The single didn't chart as highly as they'd hoped, and CBS decided to pass on them. MCA were interested, old fan Steve Kutner having moved there from RCA. But simmering tensions between McQueen and Scabies, who'd also had a fight with McQueen's wife, seemed to see any potential deal unravel. On 4 August, Sensible played his last gig with the band. He was unhappy with Scabies' decision to get rid of McQueen, whom he liked enormously, and was prepared to end his involvement with the Damned if the others did not relent. They did not.

Instead, Roman Jugg moved to guitar, his place behind the keyboards temporarily filled by Steve McGuire of Doctor And The Medics. Thereafter they tentatively decided to work up some new demos to see what would happen. By October they'd found a new manager, Andy Cheeseman, and the deal with MCA was back on, thanks mainly to Kutner's nudgings and a demo of Roman's new composition, 'Grimly Fiendish' – a song inspired equally by vaudeville and the Who's 'A Quick One, While He's Away'.

It would be released as their first single for MCA in March 1985 produced by Bob Sergeant, announcing a new 'Edwardian' image. It made 21 in the charts but the band were disappointed that it didn't do better. It also saw the Damned return to comic books for inspiration, Grimly Fiendish was drawn by Leo Baxendale. "It didn't surprise me when the Damned brought out a single about my creation, Grimly Feendish," Baxendale told me, "because the timing made sense – the right amount of time had passed for readers of my Wham! comic in the 1960s to become adults and make careers of their own." Thanks to the Damned, Baxendale would later be accused by a fundamentalist religious site of being part of a "web of Satanic intrigue". "Just who is 'Grimly Fiendish' in this rock song by The Damned?" raged Eric Holmberg of Gainesville, Florida's Reel To Real Ministries. "He wears a coat that is black and long and is a deceptive liar. Some may say that this is an isolated case of occult imagery in rock music by a heavy metal band known for promoting sadomasochistic sex, suicide, and murder in its songs..." Go look up his website. It's full of this shit.

'Grimly Fiendish' itself was excellent, but it was from here that more discerning fans felt the band lost its sure-footedness. The singles on Phantasmagoria, their debut for MCA, were all serviceable and workmanlike, but lacked the sparkle and mischief of the Damned's classic repertoire. Both 'Shadow Of Love' and 'Is It A Dream', the latter an older piece co-written by Sensible, exhibited a good grasp of mechanics but were bereft of magic (the BBC version of 'Is It A Dream' is also vastly superior). The sessions saw Merrick contribute his first song, 'Trojans', while Paul 'Shirley' Shepley, whom the band knew from his contributions to the Anti-Nowhere League, and had already contributed to the studio version of 'There'll Come A Day', was recruited to fulfil Roman's keyboard role. But producer Jon Kelly was forced to work to a murderous schedule imposed by MCA, leaving some of those involved to consider Phantasmagoria an 'unfinished' record.

Subsequently the Damned enjoyed the briefest of clutch-embraces with mainstream pop success when their cover of the Paul and Barry Ryan oldie 'Eloise' reached number three in the British charts. Vanian had long been planning to release it as a solo single. For a brief few weeks the Damned clowned around on TV programmes, Vanian looking a little uncomfortable being grilled about whether or not he slept in a coffin on the couch with Anne and Nick on TVAM. Their biggest US tour yet followed in March.

By the summer of 1986 a second album was in preparation for MCA, recorded in Denmark with Kelly once again handling production. By now Jugg had emerged as the band's main songwriter, which was beginning to frustrate Scabies. In the end the material was recorded in a piecemeal fashion, with one or two members in situ at any given point to record their parts.

Anything, finally released in December 1986, was a poor effort by anyone's standards, a reluctant nod to the title-track aside, released as a single a month previously. Vanian still defends the period, however. "Some of those songs were just as heartfelt as anything that had gone before, despite the frills and ruffles.." The singles that followed were much of a mushness, in truth. 'Gigolo' was awful. Their version of Love's mighty 'Alone Again Or' added nothing to the original. Its B-side, 'In Dulce Decorum' was then issued in the vain hope of capitalising on its inclusion on the soundtrack to an episode of Miami Vice. But when the BBC failed to show it, the single bombed.

That left them to tour behind the November release of the double retrospective Light At The End Of The Tunnel, which was badly sequenced and nowhere near as concise and hard-hitting as the original Best Of The Damned compilation released by Big Beat six years previously. It was also accompanied by a biography from Carol Clerk that some members were less than pleased with. "All I can say is that Rat must have been a better shag than I was," reckoned Captain. "That's all I'm saying and you can draw whatever you want from that." Vanian's criticisms that the subject matter should have concentrated a little more on the music and less on the beery, leery anecdotes is somewhat moderated by the fact that he missed all his interview appointments.

The Damned had pretty much broken up again. From then on it's a case of charting the Damned reformations. Some reunion shows in 1988 were eventually released as Final Damnation on Essential Records. The first 'original' line-up effort came in July 1989 at the Brixton Academy as Sensible, Scabies, Vanian and James regrouped, touring under the banner "We really must be going". But the shows, which included a huge Amnesty International benefit at the Milton Keynes Bowl, were so successful they ended up doing nothing of the sort, scheduling an American tour instead. Afterwards, Captain carried on with his solo work with collaborations with various Damned personnel en route. Vanian formed the Phantom Chords alongside Roman and Bryn, touring with the Cramps and releasing a version of 'Johnny Remember Me'.

The first 'authentic' Damned release post-MCA came when a few unreleased tracks slipped out of Captain's new but ill-fated Deltic record label (which would basically cost him most of his 'Happy Talk' loot). 'Fun Factory', featuring King Crimson guitarist Robert Fripp, whom the band had met through Coxhill, was drawn from a lost studio tape from the group's Bronze days. There were a few more 'farewell' Damned shows in the UK and America in 1991, prompted, as Sensible admitted to Jack Rabid, solely by money. "We're not doing it for the kids, we're doing it for our own pockets. We need the dosh." There were also a few college dates at the end of 1992 and they opened up on the Ramones UK tour.

In 1993, with Sensible releasing his Geoffrey Brown album, Rat and Vanian got together with Rings/Maniacs veteran Alan Lee Shaw, Jason 'Moose' Harris of New Model Army and Kris Dollimore of the Godfathers, to play shows as the Damagement in November. By December a new eight-date tour had been announced, before travelling to America to partake of the CBGB's anniversary concert. But a vaunted original line-up reunion was nixed while, on tour in Washington, Sensible and James once again fell out. The 1995 Damned touring party again featured Dollimore and Moose. They were welcomed back, but Scabies brushed aside questions about Sensible's non-presence. "Everyone keeps saying 'get the Captain' and do this and do that, and it's like, they don't have to sit in a van with him for 10 hours." This line-up was also documented on a live album taken from their final European show in France, entitled Looking At You.

By 1996 the Damned had also released a 'studio' album for America's Cleopatra Records, Not Of This Earth, titled I'm Alright Jack And The Beanstalk for UK consumption. However, though it also featured Vanian, Scabies, James, Moose, Dollimore and Sex Pistol Glen Matlock, this was essentially an Alan Lee Shaw project. He wrote all the songs, though Scabies helped with the arrangements, before rough demos were sent over to Vanian to record vocals. And there it gets a little murky, as Vanian later explained to Flipside. "In a nutshell, I did work with him, expecting us to then do a rough demo version of an album and then improve on it and actually have Captain. I wanted to have Captain write a few songs on it, and I was going to contribute to it... and then we were going to get some more writers together on it – even have Brian (James) write one song... What happened is that he (Rat) managed to obtain a release without my signature and I've never got paid, I never got anything from it. I did all this work for it and it ended up in a bitter, horrible, twisted end to our friendship." The album itself is worth a listen, and there are a couple of good tracks ('Testify' and 'Need A Life' for two). But is this a 'real' Damned album?

Let's get a sideways view on this whole unhappy chapter from Alan Lee Shaw: "At the start I had got to know Rat quite closely through rehearsing with him and Brian around 1990-1992, although I had known Rat on and off since 1977. After the Damned original line-up's last US reunion tour, the idea was mooted to do a new album – three songs from each founder member. Demos were done but they just sounded like individual's contributions, as you can imagine (Rat's account). I have listened to some of the stuff and I also agree. So Rat blocked the idea, which I guess did not go down very well. Rat still wanted to put a new Damned together and rowed in Kris and Moose. They did some song demos up in Scotland but it sounded at bit 'rock-heavy' and not really focused. I had a few raw demos I had recently made, which I played to Rat. Rat to his credit saw the potential and focus and I was in, so to speak, as rhythm guitarist/songwriter. We then made proper demos of five songs. Rat got Dave to come down to the studio and he really liked the songs. I think he could see the band and songs had legs and he was in from that point. We spent three years, me writing some 30 songs or so which we got down to eleven, to play live and record, and were set to gig worldwide. At all times Dave seemed to be a willing and enthusiastic group member. I think the crunch came when he found he was not going to get a writing credit – i.e. Rat and I would not give him one. On the principle that he had contributed zero to the writing. But had every opportunity to do so and had been encouraged to do so.

"I wanted us to do another album straight away because we seemed to be on a roll and others could bring things to the table including Dave, but alas etc. Dave then cited this nonsense about it was not a real Damned album and going back to the old idea of all the founder members contributing tracks. Which, as you can see, was muddled thinking and somewhat naive, considering he had just spent three years with us making the album and not saying a word. Sadly, I think it was Dave's only way to get back at Rat and get rid of his bitterness of the break up with Rat. Which of course left me, Chris and Moose as piggies in the middle, with a load of split Damned fans over the album. Dave's continuing position to diss the album and not to play any of the songs live is just plain silly, I think. Dave is a great singer and talent and it was a great pleasure and privilege to have worked with him. I think the words 'life's too short' should come to mind here!"

By 1996, Scabies finally relinquished his tenure of the Damned's affairs after he claimed he couldn't work with Vanian any more following his non-committal efforts on I'm Alright Jack. "We eventually fell out over writer credits," he told Summer Of Hate webzine. "His heart just wasn't in it. He never managed to contribute so much as a single word... I'd had enough of DV and the machinations around him. After a lot of reflection, I decided that it was time to move on."

Sensible, however, was prepared to lay down the reason for his dispute with Scabies in explicit terms. "It's very tedious but I'll encapsulate it in the shortest possible time. Stiff Records released the first two studio albums and a live album called Not The Captain's Birthday Party. Now, when Stiff went bust Rat bought the rights to these three albums. He licenses these albums to other record labels around the world and I don't receive any royalties. You have to pay the people who played on the records the royalties. But Rat doesn't seem to think that he needs to pay me. I can't work with someone who's done that to me... I know exactly what his angle is – 'Get yourself a good lawyer Captain, cause I've got the best in the business.' That's the attitude."

Scabies remained active on a variety of fronts, hosting sessions for a proposed second La's album, working with Joe Strummer on film soundtrack Grosse Point Blank, and forming bands including the Beats Of Bourbon and the Germans. He also published Rat Scabies & The Holy Grail in 2005, through Sceptre Books.

Then, by happy coincidence, the Captain and Vanian bumped into each other again – while Sensible was playing with his Punk Floyd project, and ended up on the same bill as Vanian's Phantom Chords. They started chatting, and when a mutual acquaintance offered them a series of European shows they decided to go for it. They were joined by Vanian's new wife Patricia Morrison (ex-Bags, Gun Club and Sisters Of Mercy) on bass after a brief try-out with Paul Gray stumbled. Monty Oxy Moron (aka Laurence Burrow; a veteran of Sensible's Punk Floyd) joined on keyboards and there were various drummers; ex-boxer Pinch, aka Andrew Pinching, formerly of the English Dogs and Janus Stark, took over in 2000. At that time they washed up on Nitro, run by Damned fan Dexter Holland of the Offspring (who'd previously covered 'Smash It Up' for the Batman Forever soundtrack), and sounded almost as good second time around.

The Damned finally cut a new studio album, Grave Disorder, in August 2001, their ninth studio album, but the first for 12 years, with David Bianco (Tom Petty, Teenage Fanclub, Afghan Whigs etc) producing. The packaging was luxurious, although that came at the insistence of the band. Undoubtedly their finest work since Strawberries, it reminded everyone of what the Damned minus Sensible lacked – a playful pop sensibility. He also had an aspiring young co-writer in Pinch, who contributed 'W', 'Amen' – a kind of update on 'Anti-Pope', and, with Sensible, 'Thrill Kill'. Sensible himself contributed the – say it quietly – political treatise, 'Democracy', which wasn't as big a departure as some assumed. 'Looking For Action' could have happily found a home on side two of Damned Damned Damned, but arguably the best song was 'She', up there with the band's finest vintages.

The Damned celebrated its release by squeezing 750 fans into Dingwalls (capacity, 500) on a hot night in the summer of 2001, without air conditioning. Returning heroes? Yup. But what about those pensionable punk rocker jibes? "I tend to like people who go on forever," responded Vanian, "like John Lee Hooker, who died recently but whom I saw a little while back and was brilliant. Or Iggy Pop, who is still as good as ever. I don't think we've lost our fire. We were always on the outside, the outsiders. At the time, a lot of people would have preferred that we weren't so popular. I'm not sure what they're thinking now, but here we are."

"It's a glorious noise the Damned make," Sensible confirmed for Q. "And Vanian's voice is better than ever. He's developed into a fine crooner over the years. You see, we were slagging off the old farts of the 70s because of their appalling rock star behaviour and 'up yer own bum' twiddly-diddly musical self-indulgence. I honestly believe the Damned still have more raw passion and sheer musical verve than pretty much anyone on the scene today, so continue we will. Plus, it's bloody good fun and the beer's free."

DISCOGRAPHY:

New Rose/Help 7-inch (Stiff BUY 6 October 1976) (reissued as limited edition white vinyl double pack with 'I'm Bored' BUY 6/DJ 6 1986 and in red vinyl in 1988 and at various other times with other combinations of the Stiff singles)

Neat Neat Neat/Stab Your Back/Singalonga-Scabies 7-inch (Stiff BUY 10 February 1977)

Damned Damned Damned LP (Stiff SEEZ 1 February 1977) (first 2,000 copies 'mistakenly' had picture of Eddie And The Hot Rods on rear cover. Reissued on CD by Demon, FIEND CD 91, in March 1987, then as a limited edition picture CD in 1991, then by Edsel, EDCD 6700, in 2000, and Essential, CMFCD505 in June 2002. The latter is notable for not only being digitally remastered, but also including the 'mistake' Eddie And The Hot Rods rear cover).

Stretcher Case Baby/Sick Of Being Sick 7-inch (Stiff DAMNED 1 April 1977) (5,000 copies given away at Marquee shows on 14, 15 and 16 April)

Problem Child/You Take My Money 7-inch (Stiff BUY 18 September 1977)

Music For Pleasure LP (Stiff Seez 5 November 1977) (originally with 3D inner sleeve. Reissued on CD by Demon, FIEND CD 108, in March 1987, and, remastered, by Essential, CMFCD506, in June 2002)

Don't Cry Wolf/One Way Love 7-inch (Stiff BUY 24 December 1977) (500 in pink vinyl)

Love Song/Burglar 7-inch (Dodgey Demo SGS 105 1978)

Love Song/Noise Noise Noise/Suicide 7-inch (Chiswick CHIS 112 April 1979) (red vinyl, 5,000 copies come in alternate Vanian/Scabies/Sensible/Ward p/s. Later reissued on Big Beat NS 75 1982 in blue vinyl: 2,000 copies each with Vanian/Sensible/Scabies p/s)

Smash It Up/Burglar 7-inch (Chiswick CHIS 116 October 1979) (reissued on Big Beat NS 76 1982 with 5,000 copies in red vinyl)

Machine Gun Etiquette LP (Chiswick CWK 3011 November 1979) (reissued on CD by Big

Beat, CDWIK 905, July 1985. The US reissue on Emergo/Roadrunner in 1989 features excellent sleevenotes from Jack Rabid of Big Takeover)

I Just Can't Be Happy Today/Ballroom Blitz/Turkey Song (Chiswick CHIS 120 December 1979)

History Of The World Part 1/I Believe The Impossible/Sugar And Spite (Chiswick CHIS 135 August 1980) (12-inch version, CHIS 12 135, includes 'I Believe The Impossible (extended)

The Black Album LP (Chiswick CWK 3015 October 1980) (Originally released as a double album, with side four recorded live at Shepperton. Reissued on CD in July 1986, Big Beat CDWIK 906, without live tracks but with 'Curtain Call'. However, the version of 'The History Of The World Pt 1' is from the 7-inch single, not the original album version. In 2005 Chiswick released the 25th double-CD anniversary edition of the album, CDWKM2 275, with the second CD featuring all the live tracks plus White Rabbit, (Rabid) Over You, Seagulls, The History Of The World (Part 1), I Believe The Impossible, Sugar And Spite, There Ain't No Sanity Clause, Looking At You (live), White Rabbit (extended version))

There Ain't No Sanity Clause/Hit Or Miss/Looking At You (live) (Chiswick CHIS 139 December 1980)

Stiff Four Pack (Stiff GRAB 2 1981) (First four Damned Stiff singles – BUY 6/10/18/24 – in plastic wallet)

Friday The 13th EP (NEMS TRY 1 November 1981) (Disco Man/The Limit Club/Billy Bad Breaks/Citadel)

Wait For The Blackout/Jet Boy, Jet Girl 7-inch (Big Beat NS 77 May 1982) (limited edition picture disc; B-side credited to Captain Sensible and the Softies)

Lovely Money/I Think I'm Wonderful/Lovely Money (disco mix) 7-inch (Bronze BRO 149 June 1982) (limited edition picture disc)

Dozen Girls/Take That/Mine's A Large One Landlord 7-inch (Bronze BRO 156 September 1982) (different vocal on lead track to Strawberries version)

Lively Arts/Teenage Dream 7-inch (Big Beat NS 80 1982) (2,000 copies in green vinyl; 10-inch NST 80 adds 'I'm So Bored')

Strawberries LP (Bronze BRON 542 October 1982) (with a strawberry-smelling lyric sheet – the best thing about it, according to one idiotic punk commentator. Reissued on CD by Castle/Dojo, DOJO CD46, October 1986, Essential ESMCD473, February 1997, Castle, CMRCD 246, June 2001).

Generals/Disguise/Citadel Zombies 7-inch (Bronze BRO 159 November 1982)

White Rabbit/Rabid (Over You)/Seagulls 7-inch (Big Beat NS85 1983) (12-inch, NST85, features 'White Rabbit (extended)'

There Ain't No Sanity Clause (remix)/Looking At You (live) 7-inch (Big Beat NS 92 1983) (12-inch, NST92, features 'Anti Pope')

Thanks For The Night/'Nasty (Plus One DAMNED 1 May 1984) (limited edition picture disc: DAMNED 1P, plus reissue in white, red, blue vinyl. 12-inch version, DAMNED 1T, 1,000 pressed in marble vinyl, adds 'Do The Blitz')

Grimly Fiendish/Edward The Bear 7-inch (MCA GRIM 1 March 1985) (1,000 copies with autographed gatefold sleeve, 10,000 copies with gatefold sleeve, limited edition picture disc: GRIMP 1; 12-inch, GRIM T1, limited edition 1,000 autographed copies, adds 'Grimly Fiendish (Spic N Span Mix)'. 12-inch, GRIMX 1, limited edition white vinyl, adds 'Grimly Fiendish (Bad Trip Mix)')

The Shadow Of Love/Nightshift 7-inch (MCA GRIM 2 June 1985) (limited edition gatefold sleeve, also limited edition double single, GRIMY 2, with Rat Scabies solo single Let There Be Rats/Wiped Out. 12-inch, GRIM T2, adds 'Shadow Of Love (Pressue Mix)'. Limited edition 12-inch, GRIMX 2, adds The Shadow Of Love (Hell Mix)/Would You)

Phantasmagoria LP (MCA MCF 3275 July 1985) (In keeping with the rest of their MCA releases, Phantasmagoria was also available in different formats – including a white vinyl issue, a picture disc, while later versions incorporated a free 12-inch version of 'Eloise'. It was reissued on CD by MCA, MCA DMCF 3275, in September 1985, then in July 1987, MCA DMCL 1887, on mid-price, reversing the order of the last two songs, and finally as part of the MCA Masters series, MCA MCLD 19069, in 1993)

Is It A Dream/Street Of Dreams 7-inch (MCA GRIM 3 September 1985) (with five Damned badges. 12-inch, GRIM T3, adds 'Is It A Dream (Wild West Mix)/Street Of Dream (live)/Curtain Call (live)/Pretty Vacant (live)/Wild Thing (live))

Eloise/Temptation 7-inch (MCA GRIM 4 January 1986) (12-inch, GRIM T4, adds 'Eloise (Extended Mix)' and 'Beat Girl' with 2,000 copies in blue vinyl. Limited edition 12-inch, GRIM X4, adds 'Eloise (Extravagant Mix) (2,000 copies). Further limited edition 12-inch, also GRIM X4, adds 'Eloise (No Sleep Mix)')

Anything/The Year Of The Jackal 7-inch (MCA GRIM 5 November 1986) (blue and yellow vinyl 10-inch MCA GRIMX 5 adds Anything (Mix)/Anything (Instrumentle)/Anything (Another Mix). 12-inch, GRIM T5, adds 'Thanks For The Night (Rat Mix)')

The Peel Sessions 10/5/77 12-inch (Strange Fruit SFPS 002 1986)

Sick Of Being Sick/Stretcher Case/Fan Club/Feel The Pain (Also issued on CD, SFPS CD002 in 1988, and cassette single, SFPS C002)

Anything LP (MCA MCG 6015 December 1986) (also issued on CD MCA DMCG 6015, with lyric booklet. Not reissued since. Not that anyone much wants a copy).

Gigolo/The Portrait 7-inch (MCA GRIM 6 January 1987) (10,000 copies in red, green, blue and yellow vinyl; poster sleeve. 12-inch in limited clear vinyl)

Alone Again Or/In Dulce Decorum 7-inch (MCA GRIM 7 April 1987) (12-inch, GRIM T7, adds 'Psychomania'. CD single, DGRIM 7, adds 'Eloise' and 'Psychomania')

In Dulce Decorum/Psychomania 7-inch (MCA GRIM 8 November 1987) (12-inch, GRIM T8, adds 'In Dulce Decorum (Mix)')

The Peel Sessions 30/11/76 12-inch (Strange Fruit SFPS 040 1987)

Stab Your Back/Neat Neat Neat/New Rose/So Messed Up/I Fall (Also issued on CD, SFPS CD040 in 1989)

Fun Factory/A Riot On Eastbourne Pier 7-inch (Deltic DELT 7 1990) (12-inch, DELT 7T, adds 'Freedom' and 'Pasties': 500 copies in blue vinyl. Same tracks on CD single, DELT 7CD) (only 'Fun Factory' features Vanian. Scabies and Gray play on 'A Riot On Eastbourne Pier')

Prokofiev/Prokofiev (Instrumental) 7-inch (Skinnies Cut AVL 1077 1991) (independent single released in US in November and sold at gigs. Written by Rat, also featured Vanian and James)

Shut It/Shut It (Die Krupps mix) 7-inch (Cleopatra CLP 9998 1996) (limited edition of 1,000 singles on red vinyl. CD single adds 'The Shadow Of Love (Live)')

Not Of This Earth CD (EMI/Toshiba TOCP8593 1995)

Aka I'm Alright Jack And The Beans Talk CD (reissued on Castle CMRCD 543 in September 2002 with four extra tracks, 'Testify', 'I Need A Life', 'Never Could Believe' and 'Neat Neat Neat', taken from a Mark Radcliffe session in November 1993)

Disco Man (live)/Pretty Vacant 7-inch (eMpTy MT 418 March 1998: Germany) (Also issued in Canada on Sudden Death Records)

Democracy CD single (Nitro CD5 2001; US promo)

Grave Disorder CD (Nitro 15844-2 August 2001)

ARCHIVE RELEASES:

Best Of The Damned (Big Beat DAM 1 November 1981) (this WAS a great place to start in the early-80s. However, beware of import CD copies, which, for licensing reasons, substitute live versions of several songs. Various other reissues on CD have also messed with the tracklisting, while the version of 'New Rose' here is from a demo – while US variations issued on Emergo feature a live Shepperton 1980 recording rather than the original studio version)

Damned Damned Damned/Music For Pleasure double LP (Stiff MAIL 2 February 1983) (mail-order only double album package, 5,000 copies, reissue in yellow vinyl, 4,000 copies, exactly five years later. Track-listing as per original albums)

Live In Newcastle – This One's For The Fans (Damned DAMU 2 November 1983) (recorded at Newcastle Mayfair on 14 October 1982. "Awful": the Captain. reissued on CD on Receiver RRCD 181 January 1994 with different sleeve as Live At Newcastle)

Damned But Not Forgotten LP (Dojo DOJOLP 21 December 1985) (demos from Strawberries/Bronze recording sessions, including the original version of 'Dozen Girls' and 'Disco Man'. Reissued on CD by Castle/Dojo, DOJOCD 21, in January 1986, Essential, ESMCD472, in February 1997, and Castle, CMRCD 245, in June 2001).

The Captain's Birthday Party – Live At The Roundhouse LP (Stiff Get 4 June 1986) (recorded at The Roundhouse, London, on 27 November 1977, with Jon Moss drumming. Reissued on CD by Demon VEX CD7 October 1991 as Not The Captain's Birthday Party with the addition of 'I'm Bored (I Fall') between 'Problem Child' and 'So Messed Up'. Then reissued again on Castle Music CMRCD 542 in August 2002 with the title reverting to The Captain's Birthday Party Live At The Roundhouse. The title suggested the show actually took place on 24 April 1977. It didn't, as the improved sleevenotes attest. "Why the peculiar title? The Damned had first headlined the Roundhouse on the Sunday after their debut American tour. Behind the drum riser at that show was a banner emblazoned: 'Tax exiles return, Hooray for the Captain's birthday'... when Stiff first issued the album, they thought it was recorded at the April show. Pretty slack considering that later songs like 'Problem Child', issued as a single by Stiff in October 1977, were included. So when the Demon reissue came around, the title was cunningly altered to Not The Captain's Birthday")

Mindless Directionless Energy LP (ID CDNOSE 18 November 1987) (recorded at the Lyceum, London, on 12 July 1981. Only CD version has 'New Rose'. A second issue, CDNOSE 18X, has a different sleeve. Also released, with extra tracks, as Ballroom Blitz. If you want to hear the Vanian/Sensible/Scabies/Gray line-up in full-flight, however, you're better off sticking with the Live At Shepperton album that originally comprised side four of The Black Album)

The Light At The End Of The Tunnel double LP (MCA MCSP 312 November 1987) (nice packaging, including nice Pete Frame family tree, but the track-listing/running order is not what it should have been. This is also a different version of 'Rabid'. CD version, DMCSP 312, then reissued at mid-price, and then as part of the MCA Masters series, both MCLDD 19007)

Live Shepperton 80 CD (Big Beat CDWIKM 27 June 1988) (recorded at a fan club gig at Shepperton on 29 July 1980, and originally part of The Black Album's fourth side. Excellent sound quality and the pick of the half dozen or so 80-82 Damned live albums out there)

Best Of Vol. 1/1/2 Long Lost Weekend LP (Big Beat WIK 80 June 1988) (contains both tracks from Motordamned session)

Final Damnation LP/CD (Castle ESSLP/CD 008 August 1989) (recorded at The Town & Country Club, London on 13 June 1988, a "naff" performance, according to Sensible. He and James helped mix the tracks – James insisted on keeping it 'real'. Sensible preferred to throw flangers, reverbs and effects at his side, for all he was worth. The cheeky scamp. Reissued by Castle, CLA 338, in 1994, and Castle again, CMRCD 247, in 2001)

The Collection LP/CD (Castle CCSLP/CD 278 December 1990) (live tracks from Help! onwards, recorded at Town & Country Club 1988)

The Damned Live LP (Pickwick Pwk 3105/Marble Arch CMA CD 124 July 1991) (recorded at The Town & Country Club, London on 13 June 1988)

Alternative Chartbusters CD (AC AOK 101 December 1991) (live tracks recorded at London Town & Country Club, 13 June 1988. Reissued by Streetlink STRCD 034 in October 1992 as Damned Busters)

Totally Damned CD (Dojo DOJOCD 65 January 1992) (limited edition picture disc CD. Live tracks, from 'Born To Kill' onwards, recorded at London Town & Country Club, 13 June 1988)

Ballroom Blitz CD (Receiver RRCD 159 June 1992) (recorded at the London Lyceum on 12 July 1981 – the same gig as Mindless, Directionless Energy, but with extra tracks)

The Damned Singles – The MCA Singles A's + B's CD/Cassette (MCA VSOPCD 174 August 1992) (originally included an impress booklet with sleevenotes by Lee Connolly)

Skip Off School To See The Damned CD (Demon VEXCD 12 October 1992) (compilation of all the Stiff a-sides and B-sides. First CD appearance for the Talmy version of 'Stretcher Case')

Damned Busters LP (Link STRCD 034 October 1992) (effectively a reissue of Alternative Chartbusters)

The School Bullies CD (Receiver RRCD 179 August 1993) (recorded at the Moonlight Club, West Hampstead in April 1979, when the Damned played as the School Bullies. Interview with Scabies by Mark Brennan)

Tales From The Damned LP (Cleopatra CLEO 71392 1993) (originally issued as a CD homage to the Damned's overlooked non-LP material recorded between their third and fourth studio albums, including the Friday The 13th EP as well as sundry a- and B-sides and the Motordamned recordings)

Sessions Of The Damned CD (Strange Fruit SFRCD 121 November 1993) (reissued in 1998, SFRSCD070. With the tapes of their 1978 session having gone walkabout, this was partly mastered from the tapes Scabies made of the original broadcasts. This is absolutely scintillating stuff, and there's a good case for suggesting that the first, November 1976 session, completely outstrips the original eight-track recordings by Nick Lowe for their debut album of the same material. But the real joys are the January 1979 session featuring Algy Ward on early versions of the material that would form Machine Gun Etiquette. There's also a previously unreleased cover of the Rolling Stones' 'We Love You' and Phantasmagoria-era material recorded while Sensible was still in the band – he greatly improves the familiar 'Is It A Dream'. The lyrics to 'Burglar', incidentally, are revised by Scabies to take account of him thieving old blues records from John Peel's record collection).

Eternally Damned – The Very Best Of The Damned CD (MCI MUSCD 017 June 1994) (a good potted history, though why it kicks off with 'Neat Neat Neat' instead of 'New Rose' is anyone's guess)

Noise – The Best Of The Damned Live LP (Emporio EMPRCD 592 1995) (compilation of previously issued live recordings from Live In Newcastle, School Bullies and Ballroom Blitz. All of them edited into each other. The definition of pointless?)

From The Beginning CD (Karussell 550747-2 1995) (Hmm. From The Beginning? The earliest tracks here date from Strawberries. Live tracks recorded at Town & Country Club, 13 June 1988)

Neat Neat Neat 3-CD Box Set (Demon FBOOK 14 1996) (the first and second discs feature Damned Damned Damned, Music For Pleasure and Not The Captain's Birthday Party in their entirety. For what it's worth, the version of 'Stretcher Case Baby' is taken from the Shel Talmy-produced single, not the album)

The Radio 1 Sessions (Night Tracks CDNT 011 June 1996) (reissued on Strange Fruit SFRSCD014 in 1997. Note this is an accompaniment to Sessions Of The Damned and doesn't replicate the 17 songs included on that release, but instead mines the 1979 to

1984 era of the band and their recordings for Peel, Mike Read and Janice Long. Sensible, who wrote the liner notes alongside Alan Harwood, concedes that he prefers several of the takes here to the eventual album versions, and with good reason. The more primal versions of the Black Album material in particular are essential listening)

Fiendish Shadows Live LP (Cleopatra CLP 9804-2 December 1996) (recorded at the Woolwich Coronet, London on 11/7/85. The live version of 'Street Of Dreams' was previously issued as the B-side to 'Is It A Dream?')

Testify (Cleopatra CLP 9899 January 1997) (Rat discovers a sequencer, in other words)

The Chaos Years (Cleopatra CLP 9960 March 1997)

Born To Kill double CD (Snapper SMDCD 143 May 1997) (tracks above from 'Neat Neat Neat' onwards all live. Absolutely nothing here that isn't available elsewhere)

Eternal Damnation LP (Big Ear Music EAZ 4019 1999) (recorded at the London Lyceum on 12/07/1981 and the Moonlight Club, West Hampstead, in April 1979)

The Damned Boxed 3-CD box set (Cleopatra CLP O542-2 1999) (contains three CDs, Not Of This Earth, Chaos Years, Testify. Just how much of Rat's tinkering can you take?)

Marvellous CD (Chiswick CDWIKK 198 December 1999) (the version of 'I Just Can't Be Happy Today' is from a DJ promo version released in 1979)

The Pleasure And The Pain: Selected Highlights 1982-1991 CD (Castle ESACD 901 June 2000) (live tracks, inevitably, recorded at Town And Country Club, 13 July 1988).

Sham 69 Vs The Damned: Punch-up Of The Punks CD (Castle CMDDD 284 July 2001) (oh, what a tremendous idea. Nice to see those Town & Country Club recordings given another outing. Well done to all involved. Fabulous)

Live Anthology double CD (Castle Music CMDDD 357 October 2001) (or why not make your own compilation of the highlights from Ballroom Blitz, Live At Newcastle and School Bullies? You probably couldn't do a worse job. The Silverline CD reissue in May 2002 is in "surroundsound" but features the first disc only)

Smash It Up – Anthology 76-87 CD (Castle CMEPR 476 May 2002) (A really good intro to the band – not least because it has only four MCA-period cuts. The sleevenotes are OK with some fresh quotes from James, Sensible and Scabies, though there will come a point in time when Rat will get so fed up with seeing his surname mis-spelled that he'll change it by deed poll. Mind you, he always hated being called Chris so…)

The Stiff Singles 1976-1977 CD Single Box Set (Castle CMHBX 644 January 2003) (cool repros of the Stiff singles, though it sounds like 'Stretcher Case Baby' may not have been reproduced from the original masters)

Play It At Your Sister: The Stiff Years 3-CD Box Set (Castle CMXBX1128 August 2005) (the Stiff material again – this time all the studio recordings over the first two CDs, as well as the band's June 1976 demos, the original two Peel sessions and their May 1977 BBC In Concert broadcast. The third CD is a lo-fi recording of their fifth ever concert, at August 1976's Mont De Marson Punk Festival (widely bootlegged previously). There's an error-strewn 130-page booklet, introduced by old man Peel himself. Damned fans will have much of this, of course, though even they will be knocked out by the 1976 demo version of 'Feel The Pain'. There is a downside though. Someone forgot to include the single version of 'Stretcher Case Baby' for the completists, while many would take issue with interspersing the Peel sessions chronologically, so they often buttress against more familiar, and generally superior, studio versions. More, ahem, damningly, the mastering just doesn't work. Some of this stuff sounded far better when it existed on bootlegs, and some of the familiar studio recordings have lost all their punch. I'm no hi-fi snob but even I noticed the disappointing sound quality)

Dancing Pigs

The DANCING PIGS witnessed the musical birth of renowned author Ian Rankin, of Inspector Rebus fame. He also worked in a chicken factory, as an alcohol researcher, the latter being a particularly plumb gig one would have thought, trod grapes and herded pigs. The latter employment may well have influenced the name of his punk band, who played around Edinburgh between 1978 and 1979. He once described them as "Fife's second greatest punk ensemble". This was specifically in reference to the Skids, who were the only other punk ensemble in Fife. "Artistic differences closed us down after our drummer left to become a quantity surveyor," he would add. "Very punk, that."

Or, as he confessed to Bookpage, "We weren't very good. I was on vocals (under the pseudonym Ian Kaput); singing would be putting it too strongly." They did not otherwise register on the radar, however, so he did a PhD before embarking on a literary career. However, he would revive the Dancing Pigs in his novel Black And Blue as a kind of mega-successful U2-ish supergroup. "The boys in the band would enjoy that," he later told Optusnet. His literary colleague Peter Robinson also mentions the Dancing Pigs in his novel In A Dry Season. This, we can be sure, is some kind of inside joke.

Ian Rankin is a very busy man. But he did manage to issue me with this communique about his punk band's glorious career. "Nothing to say about the Dancing Pigs. Played about five gigs (in Cowdenbeath, Dunfermline, Kinghorn). Never put out a record. Folded...."

Dangerous Girls

Mykocupa (aka Michael Robert Cooper; vocals), Chris Ames (guitar; replaced by Baron Beetmoll Troy before first single), Rob Rampton (bass), Rob Peters (drums)

Post-punk, partly-punk, party-punk group who released a succession of independent recordings which were cherished by John Peel (although their only Radio 1 session was for Mike Read) and a handful of more enlightened souls. From Birmingham and formed in 1978, they suffered from the same fate that would befall countless generations of Brum musicians. In so much that, despite having their own vibrant punk/post-punk community, their contributions tend to be overlooked in the rush to garland less image-shafted city scenes. "Yes," Rob Peters confirmed to me, "and it's still extremely prevalent. I'm currently playing with a young Birmingham band called The INKlings. The same attitudes as 25 years ago are still there. However, some really great bands did emerge from Brum. It was a privilege to be in some way part of a 'scene' that included amongst our friends people who made up UB40, the Beat and the Au Pairs, to name a few."

Yet, in many ways, the **DANGEROUS GIRLS** belonged almost as much to Exeter as Birmingham, where Rob Peters had studied and formed the band Apathy Society. Exeter's Len Gammon remembers Peters attending a Bob Marley gig there in 1975, before booking Apathy Society to play at his Catharsis 'punk night'. Gammon: "It was a bit like a university band coming down to the town, bridging the town versus gown thing. They were a lot like Manchester's Alberto Y Lost Trio Paranoias. They went over really well. I was still playing bass in an R&B band, Junkyard Angels – perversely, they're still going – and we asked Rob to play with us, which he did."

"Our first recordings (thankfully few ever released) were quite punky, but I think that was purely by accident," Peters reckons. "We were originally called In The Jungle With No Guns and were extremely influenced by what you might call the first wave of new punk, Public Image Ltd and Alternative TV. But we soon found ourselves in a cul de sac. So we went back to the punk ethos and wrote an entire album of songs in just two weeks and recorded them in two days and changed our name to the much punkier Dangerous Girls (despite being all blokes). It then took us a couple of years to redevelop as musicians so that we were writing more challenging material and thus became 'new wave'." Among the band's most memorable efforts was 'MO7S'. Mis-spelt on the sleeve, it was later compiled on the Messthetics compilation, and drew on the band's experiences driving back to Brum from a show playing 'I Spy' (there was also a reference to trade unionist Moss Evans, general secretary of the TGWU, in there).

There's been something of a renaissance in interest in those bands who ploughed their own furrow during the late-70s and early-80s, and the Dangerous Girls are among many enjoying a critical reappraisal. "Our early singles were particularly good. I think we lost our way in the recording studio and never really captured the band on vinyl, but we were an incredibly good live band, which is where our reputation truly lies. Yes, any band from that period had the potential to achieve greater success, but it's not something I dwell on as I've been very fortunate to have worked and still am working with some brilliant bands and artists. It is truly gratifying to know that lots of other people have fond memories of our band though, something that has been brought home to me very strongly since the advent of the internet." Rob Peters would later go on to work extensively with Boo Hewerdine, erstwhile Bible vocalist, and Everything But The Girl. In 1999 he released his first solo album Zinc, later followed by a second set, Flatiron.

Three whole albums of Dangerous Girls material have finally been made available through Peters' Wafer Thin Records.

DISCOGRAPHY:

Dangerous Girls/I Don't Want To Eat (With The Family) 7-inch (Happy Face MM115 1979)
Taaga 7-inch EP (Happy Face MM116 1979)
Safety In Numbers/Jump Up And Down/Down On The File/Sex
Man In The Glass/MO75 7-inch (Human HUM 1)
Step Out/Sidekick Phenomena/Men In Suits 7-inch (Human HUM 6)
ARCHIVE RELEASES:
The Dangerous Girls CDR (Wafer Thin Records WAFT 022 2001)
Never Ends CDR (Wafer Thin Records WAFT 023 2001)
Dangerous Girls Live! CDR (Wafer Thin Records WAFT 027 2002) (taken from their North Staffs Poly set, plus tracks for their final ever live appearance)

Dansette Damage

Eddie Blower (vocals), Colin Hall (vocals, guitar), Jeff Collins (bass), John Kavanagh (guitar), Les Salcombe (drums)

Birmingham's DANSETTE DAMAGE released a classic debut single in May 1978, with production mysteriously credited to the 'Wolverhampton Wanderer', more of whom later. In addition to the band's regular line-up, it featured Alan Pegg and Steve Kinloch on backing vocals. Hall: "There was seven of us and we all bunged £40 each to pay for the recording. Alan Pegg and Steve Kinloch made up the numbers – their cash was very welcome and cheap at half the price to get your pic on the cover." As for the songs: "'The Only Sound' and 'N.M.E.' were written in a couple of days – listening to them you would have thought it would have taken a lot less! 'The Only Sound' was a collaboration between myself, Eddie and John, a mish-mash of ideas on the injustice of working for sod all. 'N.M.E.' was written as a tribute to the New Musical Express. Eddie had a room full of back copies and he wanted to pay salute to the paper, so the lyrics came from Eddie. I wrote the tune and sang the vocal on it. We did in fact get record of the week in the NME, for obvious reasons."

In fact, they had neither played a gig nor named the band at the time of the recording. Hall: "Listening to the playback of 'The Only Sound', Robert commented on the power of the track, saying 'Fuck Me, this would DAMAGE MY DANSETTE!' So we now had a name as well as a couple of OK tracks. The problem we had then was which track to have as the A-side. Both tracks were a bit ropey and everyone was doing double A-sides. So, of course, we decide to release (possibly the first ever) double B-side, and we had the labels printed on the wrong sides just to confuse everyone further." It was only when the band released a compilation album some 16 years later that it became apparent that the Wolverhampton Wanderer was, in fact, Robert Plant of Led Zeppelin, who can actually be heard low in the mix on 'N.M.E.' contributing backing vocals.

The single was released on Shoestring Records, formed for the purpose, which would later also house the sole release by their friends from Bearwood, the Sussed. 'The Only Sound' sold 2,500 copies, was much beloved of John Peel and his producer John Walters, and latterly featured in the TV documentary about him.

Thereafter the group continued as a quartet with Blower moving to keyboards and Steve Hall joining on guitar and vocals. There was a second single, recorded in June 1978, but it was only released in 1980. So why the long delay? Hall: "With the money we made from the single we went out and purchased some keyboards and recorded the second single. We asked Robert if he would like to join us in the studio again but he declined because Led Zep had got back together after a long break and they were rehearsing. So me and Eddie produced it. We ran out of money, so we couldn't at that time release it on Shoestring, so we sent a couple of tapes to people in the biz. We were gigging and had built up a fair reputation as one of the better bands around, but we had a few disagreements and split. A few months later Eddie called us all together and told us Pinnacle Records had got hold of the tape and liked it so we reformed."

By the time the second single came out they'd all but abandoned punk for a more synth-pop sound, changing their name to Swing Music early in 1981 to try to catch a bit of the prevailing New Romantic action. By July of that year they'd split up.

DISCOGRAPHY:

The Only Sound/N.M.E. 7-inch (Shoestring LACE-001 May 1978) (copies were deliberately mis-labelled)

2001¾ Approximately/Must Be Love 7-inch (Pinnacle PIN-30 March 1980)

ARCHIVE RELEASES:

Sold As Seen LP (Shoestring BL-002 1994) (complete discography, and then some)

Darlex

Kev 'Hunter' Biscoe (guitar, backing vocals), Paul Robbins (vocals), Mick Galvin (bass) and a series of drummers, the first one being a Moody Blues fan from college. "You make do," reckons Hunter.

Distinct from the South London Daleks, Bishop Stortford's DARLEX were formed by Kev Hunter. "I'd been toying with the idea of forming a band during the summer of 1976, but more in a sort of basic rock style. I'd had a guitar for a few years but never really thought I was proficient enough on it. Me and a few of my mates used to watch So It Goes on TV, and we were lucky enough to catch the Pistols doing 'Anarchy'. I'd read one or two reviews about the band in the NME prior to this, but I hadn't been particularly interested in them, but after seeing them on TV, it changed everything. Me and one mate, in particular, thought they were amazing, but the rest of our crowd hated them! Punk really did split people like that."

Hunter read up some more about the Pistols, the Damned and the Clash. But it was seeing Janet Street-Porter's LWT documentary on punk that really persuaded him that "this was it, I have to do this". Thereafter he managed to obtain a couple of C90s of recordings from the 100 Club punk festival. "I got them through an ad in ZigZag magazine. They were pretty poor quality, sound-wise, but what I could hear was enough to make me realise that this is what I wanted to do musically. My mates and I decided to form a band, so he bought a bass and the other guy thought he could sing (or shout) and that was that basically. We were originally called the Antichrist, which seems a terrible, metal-type band name now, but we got the idea from the first line of 'Anarchy In The UK'. Within a few months we'd had a few name changes including Dead City, the Urban SS (yeah, I know! terrible idea, and such a rip!), the Dentists and finally the Darlex." Hunter also confesses that the Moody Blues fan, who was the only person they knew with a drum kit, couldn't play as fast as the songs required. "The poor lad was trying his best. We liked him so much, when we realised we needed a different drummer,

The only known photograph of Bishop Stortford's Darlex.

we told him we'd split." Then the band reformed. "It was a horrible, cowardly thing to do, but we couldn't bear to hurt his feelings!"

The band rehearsed "every other Sunday afternoon", and quickly built a set. "Our first gig wasn't until August 1977 though, when we supported a male/female outfit called Babylon (who included Teresa D'Abreu, previously of the Sadista Sisters) in Saffron Walden, Essex." That led to the offer of a support slot to the Tom Robinson Band the following week. "But we decided against it for some reason. It must have seemed like a good idea at the time." There were several line-up changes. "I had originally taken over on vocals, and let my mate play guitar, and the singer switched to bass. That wasn't working, so we changed back to how we'd begun, and that got better. We did a series of gigs in Bishops Stortford during late 1977 to spring 1978, including a support slot to the Jolt. Originally the gig was to have had Generation X headlining, then the Jolt, and local Harlow band the Sods third. But the week before this Derwood had been bottled offstage at some Uni gig, so the Jolt took the headline place. Then the Sods moved into second slot and asked us if we wanted to open, so we did."

The band played its last gig around May 1978. "We didn't actually split, it was just that we never got around to rehearsing or playing any more gigs after that for some reason. Then, in early August, I got to hear about the Epileptics, saw their name sprayed around the town, and decided that I wanted to be in that band. I hadn't heard what they sounded like, but I was intrigued, and they'd already been banned from the Triad for booting a monitor offstage. I introduced myself to Col and Rich, and said, 'If you're ever looking for a guitarist…' And it just so happened that they were, because their guitarist was leaving to go to college. Col and Rich had seen the Darlex play, so they asked me to go along to one of their practices in Clive's bedroom the next week, and I was in. During this time we'd seen Crass at Triad, and had been blown away by them, got talking to them, and the rest just fell into place."

Das Schnitz

Tim Dodge (vocals), Kevin Perry (drums), Stuart Gordon (bass), Nadi Jahangiri (guitar). (Gordon was later replaced by Tony Morrell, mainly because he owned a delivery van)

DAS SCHNITZ's sole single is currently rated at a whopping £150 in some price guides. Which is crazy. The first 100 sleeves were all custom made – the band couldn't afford to have any proper ones done, so they bought a load of unused sleeves from a market stall that sold, well, unused picture sleeves. These were assembled in Perry's bedroom, the de facto HQ of Operation Das Schnitz.

They thought that as well as cost-cutting this might have the additional advantage of engendering a bit of press coverage. Which it surely did, especially when someone from "a major record company" expressed their displeasure over their hijacking of the illustrious cover art of the likes of Chaka Khan's 'I'm Every Woman'. Others to be 'customised' included Darts and the Tavares. It might actually be fun, if a little expensive, trying to track down further copies to see what else they used.

Speaking of tracking down, I managed to trace the band's drummer, Kevin Perry, through the local paper. "You're writing a book on the less celebrated bands of the era, hey? I think there was a huge celebration when we finally jacked it in and went our separate ways to see what life was really about, rather than sneering and moaning about how difficult life was for four comfortable middle-class 'punks'. Cynical? Me? But of course. Maybe things haven't changed that much through the years. Maybe we were right after all. The government always breaks its promises; jobs never satisfy or pay you enough; girlfriends leave you and now my progeny are rebelling. Just as well I'm still writing songs about it or I'd implode."

Thanks for sharing! He also filled me in some of the band's history. They were formed at Torquay Boys Grammar School, but did manage to play a 15-minute lunchtime set at the neighbouring Torquay Girls Grammar School as their first gig. "Although it was a strictly girls-only affair," noted the very same local newspaper, "the numbers were swelled rather by a 'road crew' from the group which would have put the numbers of roadies used by groups like the Rolling Stones or Emerson Lake And Palmer to shame." In similar vein to Mrs Merton's query to Debbie McGee about what originally attracted her to the millionaire Paul Daniels, one can only speculate as to the true motivation for this mass incursion to an all-female school.

Das Schnitz had quite a local following, and would organise coach trips to larger venues such as Exeter or Plymouth to catch touring bands. They themselves would support visiting bands like the Lurkers and Vibrators. Meanwhile they wrote a set of original songs back in Perry's bedroom, "where we used to do most of our full-volume rehearsal or in the assembly hall of the tiny little junior school opposite our house in the quiet, leafy suburbs where my mum was the dinner lady. Christ, I don't know how the neighbours put up with the noise. We never got one complaint."

The single was recorded at the end of 1978 at Swan Street Studios, the only such local facility, on an eight-track. The recording budget was £12, so at £8 an hour that meant a full 90 minutes of studio time. Ellie Jay, the London-based company who pressed singles on a contract-basis, delivered records in early 1979 at a pre-arranged meeting at a pub in Barnet. It was only sold via record shops in the Torquay area but did get them a bit of local notoriety, only being held off the top of the local charts by 'Bright Eyes'. They'd already got into the local news by attempting to convince everyone that they'd signed with Raw Records. Which they hadn't. But it got them in the papers. Again.

The group also helped organise a 1979 punk rock benefit for MENCAP at the Torquay Victoria Hotel, alongside other local legends Critical Press, Hedge & The Hogs, Systum and the Gatecrashers. But at the dawn of the 80s college careers beckoned. When Jahangiri left Perry and Gordon continued for a while with a band called Rhythm On Two, "later joined by Dodge on vocals. Midge Ure even asked the guys to join them for the rest of the 1980 Ultravox tour, but this had to be their last gig before splitting to go to various far-flung colleges. What a story that never was."

DISCOGRAPHY:

4am/Getting Nowhere/My House 7-inch (Ellie Jay DJSP9249 1979) (533 copies pressed)

DC10s

Andrew Reader (guitar, backing vocals), Mitchell Edmond (vocals), John 'Cab' Phillips (bass), Steve Hyett (drums)

Swansea punk band formed in 1978, originally featuring drummer Jeremy Ratcliffe and with Reader handling both guitar and vocals, under the name Johnny & The Nuforms. After the line-up shifted with Edmond arriving on vocals and new drummer Steve Hyett joining, they continued to gig in and around Swansea until August 1980, playing alongside local friends the Dodos, the Standards and the Tunnelrunners.

In June they recorded their sole single, 'Bermuda', at Spaceward Studios in Cambridge. Edmond: "We recorded it in one day, then drove to London the next day to get it mastered and leave it at a pressing plant. We had 1,000 made – all in picture sleeves, but 500 went in glossy card sleeves and the other 500 were printed on ordinary paper. That was the only recording of the band. It was self-financed through our own cash and money borrowed from friends."

John Peel liked the single and played it, and it was also reviewed in the NME (who subsequently called it one of the best independent singles of 1980). Soon they found themselves pursued by WEA, and Greg Shaw of Bomp! Records. But any promise was forfeited when, in the autumn of 1980, Reader elected to take up a place at Cambridge University, while Hylett joined the RAF. John 'Cab' Phillips also set sail for college, but after a long intervening period returned to music with his Johnny Jet project.

DISCOGRAPHY:

Bermuda/I Can See Through Walls 7-inch (ACE ACE451 1980)

Dead Fingers Talk

Tony Carter (drums), Andy Linklater (bass), Jeff Parsons (guitar), Bobo Phoenix (aka Robert Eunson; vocals)

Though they grew out of the local band scene and only had punk status thrust upon them by default, Hull's DEAD FINGERS TALK are historically significant. Not least to Tom Robinson, who took up Bobo Phoenix's mantle of open homosexuality and

spread the gospel of tolerance, though it's arguable as to whether or not he managed to improve on Eunson's genuinely funny lyrics in doing so. Parsons; "We didn't so much have punk status thrust upon us as actually go out and claim it. We were always musically quite punky, with a big influence from Lou Reed, also the Who, Stones, New York Dolls, MC5, Stooges, but we still had the hair and beards! (Apart from Rob, who still looks like he did when I first met him in 1969 and has never looked any different). So the rest of us merely shaved our beards and cut our hair, and shamelessly jumped on the punk bandwagon. We also ditched the platform boots, cheesecloth shirts and loon pants, and Rob dragged us all into the charity shops!"

The group grew out of late 60s band Bone, which featured the Dead Fingers Talk line-up with the exception of Rocky Norton on bass. Bone broke up in 1971 but various permutations of the line-up continued. The above quartet reconvened in 1975 as Dead Fingers Talk, and a year later brought in Linklater on bass, formerly of Beverly hard rockers Bogey and concurrently a member of Snake Eye, in place of Norton. They were pretty popular around the Humberside area, managing to sell out venues such as the New Theatre. "We moved to London in July 1977, having been playing down there on and off since late 75, and during the first six months of 77 we played a lot in the working men's clubs in County Durham, where we became very popular (and tight!)."

They released two singles and an album that was produced by Mick Ronson, which included the standout 'Nobody Loves You When You're Old And Gay' as well as the more strident 'Fight Our Way Out Of Here'. In truth, they had as much in common with Hendrix and Page as the new wave, and supporting Whitesnake does nothing for your credibility. Parsons: "Supporting Whitesnake was something we did to get in the good books of Straight Music, who had been reluctant to give us their gigs, such as the Nashville, Red Cow and Golden Lion. We wanted those gigs badly, and doing the Whitesnake gig was part of the price of getting them."

The lyrics lifted the album beyond the predictable, and Ronson does a solid job. "Working with Mick Ronson was good and bad; we got on really well – too well, really. We spent too much time having a laugh, and not enough getting the work done. One Friday we decided to lay four new songs down on two track at the end of a day's recording, so we could take them home and think about doing them properly the next week. But the record company decided that we'd had enough time. So the four rough tracks (with some hastily added overdubs) became the first four tracks on the album. We always felt that these tracks were unfinished, and we later re-recorded 'Old And Gay' at the Kinks' Konk Studio, with Rod Houison producing. We also did several tracks with Steve Lillywhite at RAK Studios (including the second single) which never saw the light of day. When Sanctuary decided they were going to re-release the album on CD they told me they had lots of tapes. I offered to go to London to sort through them, but they declined. Consequently, some of the 'bonus' tracks are spurious; two are wrongly named, and one is simply an instrumental version of 'Everyday' from the album. There are several dynamite tracks still lying in boxes (hopefully!) somewhere. I can't help feeling that the price of a return ticket to London would have been a good investment, but there you go."

Parsons is still active in the music industry as leader of Access To Music courses at East Riding College in Yorkshire. Phoenix would go on to briefly work in the Monsters with Slaughter And The Dogs' Mick Rossi.

DISCOGRAPHY:

Can't Think Straight/Hold On To Rock'n'roll 7-inch (Pye 7N 46069 1978)
This Crazy World/The Boyfriend 7-inch (Pye 7N 46156 1978)
Storm The Reality Studios LP (Pye NSPH 24 1978) (reissued on CD, Storm The Reality Studios Plus, on Essential ESMCD 929 in June 2002, with eight bonus tracks)

Dedkatz (& Potteries Punk)

Mick Richardson (vocals), Steve 'Coug' Colclough (rhythm guitar), Steve Eyre (lead guitar), Mark 'Dim' Dimmelow (bass), Gary Chell (drums)

From Trent Vale in the Potteries, the delightfully titled DEDKATZ formed at the start of 1978 under the name The Graves. After a handful of gigs they collapsed in January 1979, though in the interim they did record a two-song demo at Bumble

Studios in Penkhull in the winter of 1978. Live, there was a mix of originals and a reggae version of 'New York' by the Sex Pistols, which did at least show a depth of imagination.

The band reformed in the summer of 1979, with Richardson, Colclough and Dimmelow joined by session drummer John Crowe to record the single 'Day Of The Dogs' c/w 'Living Is A Nightmare'. A proposed release on Market Drayton's Redball Records never happened, however. Colclough subsequently joined fellow Potteries punks Beyond The Wall. Richardson, who had also contributed keyboards to 'Living Is A Nightmare', would go on to play synthesizer in All The Madmen, Decades By Night, Elegant Unease and the Cone, as well as bass for The Friendly Campaign (featuring several ex-members of Beyond The Wall).

I asked Mike Richardson for his memories of punk in the area. "Stoke On Trent was a backwater city that wasn't; six towns grouped together – not sure whether it was in the Midlands or the North, and like most provincial towns and cities, a bit late coming to punk. By mid-1977, as 'God Save The Queen' was (almost) topping the charts, only one band had actually got up off their arses to get a set together and play live – the Verdicts. They were fronted by twenty-something Mark Renaudon, a Jagger wannabe and John Martyn fan. Hardly the ideal credentials to be the area's answer to John Lydon. Indeed, part of their set consisted of Stones and Beatles covers. And the rest of the band were veterans of the city's rock scene, just with shorter haircuts than the previous years. But the local kids, having listened to the first Clash album, and the Pistols singles, could smell anarchy in the air. Soon, word got round of some new kids on the block. The Veins, six or seven leather-clad fans of the New York punk scene would emerge, supporting the Verdicts, and going on to play gigs on their own."

"Un-named support bands would appear for one gig, play, then disappear without trace. By 1978 The Veins were recording and releasing their own singles, selling well locally but failing to break nationally, even though they gigged outside the city. By the summer of 1978, The Verdicts were no more, Renaudon signing with Decca as a soloist. A cassette of their final gig sold well locally. The Veins went through a number of line-up changes before splitting up in 1979. Two bands from the south of the city started to break through towards the end of 78 – Dedkatz and Discharge. Both were influenced by the mainstream punk of the day, Dedkatz's sound being reminiscent of Buzzcocks, Ruts, Stiff Little Fingers; Discharge was slightly more hardcore, though nothing like the sound they would eventually end up with. As punk died out and evolved into new wave, these two bands did a number of gigs in the area, and also recorded demos. Dedkatz split in 1979, Discharge changed their front man, discovered Crass, and went on to be the most successful act the Potteries ever produced – until Robbie Williams appeared."

Demon Preacher

Nik Fiend (aka Nik Wade; vocals), Camilla Branson (bass), Joe Schmo (guitar), Gerry Healy (drums) (Nik's note: "This is probably the longest serving line-up, and essentially the one that recorded 'Little Miss Perfect' – probably the most famous Preacher record, though the drummer differed")

Prior to becoming Alien Sex Fiend, the most lovably deranged slice of zombie carrion in the underworld of Gothic rock, Nik Wade piloted London-based punk band DEMON PREACHER who, with the exception of Wade himself, never boasted a stable line-up. But they did have a lot of fun. The band was formed in 1975 by Wade and guitarist Tony Gialanze, initially as little more than a bedroom project. They were eventually joined by Gialanze's friends Tony Ward (guitar), Geoff Bedz (guitar), Gerry Healy (drums) and Gialanze's girlfriend, Sharon Mac (bass). Picking up on the emerging punk buzz, they spent most weekends working on putative punk rock songs, eventually finding proper rehearsal space in the crypt of a Roman Catholic Church on Holloway Road – somewhat ironic, given the church's subsequent views of Alien Sex Fiend's no-holds barred live shows. Nik Wade: "All the other lads were choirboys when they were younger. So it was OK for them to rehearse in the crypt of Our Sacred Lady Roman Catholic Church, off Holloway Road.

Ciggie break time for London's Demon Preacher.

Tony Gialanze introduced me to Tony Ward, Gerry and Geoff, and they would let me have ten minutes at the end of their 5 hour and 50 minute rehearsals, to do 'Dead End Kids'. Eventually, cos they'd had such a buzz from doing one of my songs, they dropped the other band and joined Demon Preacher. After some time the church found out that Demon Preacher were 'at it' in their crypt. We were then banished."

Demon Preacher played their first show at the end of 1977 with Lydon, Cook and Jones from the Sex Pistols all attending. They began to pick up regular work at venues such as the Roxy and the Hope & Anchor. This led to their first studio session and debut EP. The lead track pilloried the Royal Northern Hospital in London, generating a good deal of local press. Wade: "I saw a piece in the Islington Gazette about porters having to help out on operations – I thought, fuck me!" However, like the other three tracks, the sound betrayed the financial strictures the band faced. With money tight, it took a loan from Wade's boss to finance the venture. But he was reimbursed quickly as the single, whose cover Nik had photocopied and sellotaped, and individually numbered himself, flew off the shelves. John Peel liked it, played it, and even suggested that Wade sounded like a young Mick Jagger. The line-up now featured Wade, Camilla Branson (bass), Healy and Ward with additional guitar from Kevin Armstrong. Armstrong, who would later produce Alien Sex Fiend's Acid Bath album, played lead on the EP's fourth track, 'Dead End Kidz'. But the line-up always remained fluid, with Wade talking up his band to get gigs and then worrying about covering the musical bases as an afterthought.

The tracks were cut at IPS Studios in Shepherd's Bush, though their original intention of having everything completed in two hours proved unrealistic. Luckily studio owner Pete McGhee was sympathetic enough to allow them a further two hours to get everything straight. Tony Ward and Gerry Healy departed after the EP's release because they weren't prepared to give up well-paid jobs and make a go of the band full time. Concurrently the EP had caught the ear of Pete Stennet of Small Wonder. He'd sold numerous copies of it through his shop and offered the band the chance to do a follow-up. The result was 'Little Miss Perfect', the story of Joyce McKinney. McKinney was the crackpot former beauty queen accused of kidnapping and sexually assaulting a "manacled Mormon missionary", who regaled the newspapers at her committal hearing with lurid details, milked the publicity, and then jumped bail and fled to Canada. The single had elements of the signature aural chaos that would denote Alien Sex Fiend recordings, and a suitably lascivious spoken introduction, as well as a dub version on the flip.

By the time of the single's release photographer Joe Schmo, whom Wade had met at the

Roxy, had joined as guitarist. Camilla Branson and Kevin Armstrong (as producer) were still aboard, and the new drummer was Paul Wilson, later of the Psychedelic Furs. However, after he'd completed a show at the Stoke Newington Open Air Festival he disappeared, so for the recording session sticksman about town Max Splodge (aka Martyn Everist) pounded the toms.

After the single's release the band shuffled personnel as they continued to play regularly around London venues such as the Music Machine, the Old Queen's Head in Stockwell and the Islington Pied Bull (later to become the Powerhaus). After contracting their name to the Demons, they released a third and final single, 'Action By Example', featuring later Belle Star Claire Hirst on saxophone. The B-side, 'Wish I Woz A Dog', would later re-appear on Alien Sex Fiend's Who's Been Sleeping In My Brain? album though with a completely revised musical backing.

Thereafter they reverted to the full billing as Demon Preacher again, with the late Hanoi Rocks drummer Razzle on drums, Jim and Boo later of the Babysitters on guitar and bass, with Piece Thompson on lead guitar. This line-up headlined a festival on the Isle Of Wight, but it was to be the group's final performance. Fuelled by a session of magic mushrooms, Wade and Piece decided to create a new experimental venture, No Longer Umpire, which was a short-lived precursor to Alien Sex Fiend. When Piece left to join Turkey Bones & The Wild Dogs, after a momentary spell as The Boneshakers, Alien Sex Fiend began.

DISCOGRAPHY:

Royal Northern 7-inch EP (Illegal SRTS 78110 1978)
Royal Northern/Laughing At Me/Steal Your Love/Dead End Kidz
Little Miss Perfect/Perfect Dub 7-inch (Small Wonder SMALL 10 1978)
As The Demons:
Action By Example/I Wish I Woz A Dog 7-inch (Crypt Music DEM1 1980)
COMPILATIONS:
Small Wonder Punk Singles Collection Vol. 1 CD (Anagram CDPUNK 29 1994; 'Little Miss Perfect')

The Depressions

Dave Barnard (vocals, bass), Ozzy 'Crowbar' Garvey (drums), Frank 'Hammer' Smith (guitar), Eric 'Rico The Knife' Wright (guitar, vocals)

Authenticity is a big issue in punk rock, and THE DEPRESSIONS suffered more than most. Despite putting out at least three great singles, and an accomplished album, the snipers were never far away. Barnard, Wright and Smith, all grew up in the same street and had been messing about with bands for several years. The most successful was the pub rock-influenced Tonge, whose repertoire consisted principally of Who and Small Faces covers, who also intermittently featured local music shop owner Melvyn Taylor. In this formation they managed to get banned from practically every local venue. With the arrival of punk they not only changed name, but also image, all four members dying their hair blonde. Ozzy Garvey took to wearing an eyepatch while his colleagues indulged in hysterical punk pseudonyms.

Though they certainly switched tempos, the musical bedrock remained beefed-up, Stones-influenced pub rock, though their songwriting now reflected the changing times by focusing on squarely punk themes of alienation, boredom and poverty. And Barnard's raspy vocals were initially all Steve Marriott but ended up reminiscent of the bark and growl of Jean-Jacques Burnel.

The band hooked up with East Sussex's Pebble Beach Production company, in the hands of future Bad Manners' manager Andy Cowan Martin. As well as securing gigs, he brought them to the attention of former Hendrix and Slade manager Chas Chandler. Chandler signed them to his Barn label after catching one of their Brighton shows. It brought about immediate publicity in the Daily Mirror when it reported in July 1977 that "Two punk rockers were each fined £100 at Brighton yesterday for daubing walls with the name of their group, the Depressions, after signing their first record contract." They made their debut with 'Living On Dreams', which had the distinction of being named Sounds 'joint single of the week' alongside the Sex Pistols' 'Holidays In The Sun'. "How can they fail?" was the question posed. Well...

On the week the single appeared, they received a more caustic review of their gig at the Speakeasy by Barry Cain of the Record Mirror. "Listen, these boys have had it really rough. They've all been brought up on council estates in Brighton. Wow! My heart bleeds. Must be hard, paddling in the winter." Barnard is reported to have replied to his accusations: "Honestly, everything I sing about actually happened to me. I ain't gonna try and change your views about us, but we ain't shamming." Cain was unimpressed. Looking back, 'Living On Dreams' sounds astonishingly like West Coast soft rock.

Their singles, 'Can't Stop Messing With Your Heart' and 'Get Out Of This Town', both showed up on the indie charts, leading to a debut album, which opened with the wonderfully crass 'Screw Ya'. It may have been punk by numbers, but it sounded great. After its release the group reverted to billing themselves as the DPs, moving in an overt power pop direction. Smith left following an incident at a Vibrators show when a fan was beaten to death at Preston Polytechnic during a fight between rival football supporters. As Bob Simmons of XL5 remembers: "Frank just got into drugs and took too many and went mad and never really came back. He was only 16 or 17, but in the end he just couldn't handle it." Tony Maybury came in from local band Midnight And The Lemon Boys, who'd just completed a tour with U2. He was also ex-Joe Cool And The Killers. By now their collective peroxide bill had eased slightly. But when there were few takers for a proposed second album, produced by Motors associate Pete Keru, they split up at the end of 1979.

Subsequently Barnard formed the more mod-inspired band Vandells (who featured on the Vaultage 79 compilation) and toured with Steve Ellis's Love Affair. He still plays around the Brighton area, notably at the Portland's jam sessions. He currently tours and records with Terry Callier and is a music tutor for the Prince's Trust. Ozzy Garvey passed away in 2005.

DISCOGRAPHY:

Living On Dreams/Family Planning 7-inch (Barn 2014 112 October 1977)
Can't Stop Messing With Your Heart/Street Kid 7-inch (Barn 2014 119 February 1978)
Get Out Of This Town/Basement Daze 7-inch (Barn 2014 122 April 1978)
The Depressions LP (Barn 2314 105 1978)
As the DPs
If You Know What I Mean/Running Away 7-inch (Barn 2014 126 1978)
If You Know What I Mean LP (Barn 2314 107 1978)
Television Romeo/Born To Win 7-inch (Barn 2014 129 1978)
ARCHIVE RELEASES:
The Punk Rock Collection CD (Captain Oi! AHOY CD 66 1997) (contains the first album, first three singles and unreleased demos)

Desperate Bicycles

Danny Wigley (vocals), Dave Papworth (drums), Nicky Stevens (guitar), Roger Stevens (bass)

Arguably responsible for a whole sub-section of music, not least the determinedly DIY vinyl and subsequent tape-trading scene of the early-80s, the DESPERATE BICYCLES' myth continues to grow. Not least because those involved refuse to come forward to take their moment in the limelight. Which is kind of admirable. So much credibility-grasping rock music constitutes pounding self-interest masquerading as principle. Not so the Bicycles, who have shunned publicity with JD Saalinger-like commitment.

Formed in London early in 1977, they took their name from J.B. Priestley's Angel Pavement, and threw elements of Syd Barrett-esque psychedelia and garage rock into the mix, alongside primal, kitchen sink punk. The sound was reminiscent of the Fall strained of literary pretensions and Krautrock influences. Long since the idea of concept albums had become a filthy term, the Bicycles inaugurated the masterstroke of a concept single. The idea was to establish how much it would cost to record and distribute. To this end they formed their own label, Refill, and issued 'Smokescreen' in 1977. It remains one of the most singular and important artefacts bridging the gap between the punk movement and the later independent scene. Musically, it was bracing stuff, Wigley doing all he could to squash a surfeit of verbiage into the compressed musical narrative, ending up breathless as a result. Which provided its own stylistic metaphor about escaping the confines of the art form in which they found themselves.

THE DESPERATE BICYCLES

The medium was tedium Don't back the Front

Danny Wigley (voice) Roger Stephens (bass) Dave Papworth (drums)
Nicky Stephens (organ)
© Office Music Refill records RR2 SLIGHTLY STEREO

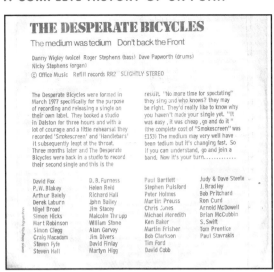

The Desperate Bicycles were formed in March 1977 specifically for the purpose of recording and releasing a single on their own label. They booked a studio in Dalston for three hours and with a lot of courage and a little rehearsal they recorded 'Smokescreen' and 'Handlebars' It subsequently leapt at the throat. Three months later and The Desperate Bicycles were back in a studio to record their second single and this is the result. "No more time for spectating" they sing and who knows? they may be right. They'd really like to know why you haven't made your single yet. "It was easy, it was cheap, go and do it" (the complete cost of "Smokescreen" was £153) The medium may very well have been tedium but it's changing fast. So if you can understand, go and join a band. Now it's your turn............

David Fox, P.W. Blakey, Arthur Baiely, Derek Laburn, Nigel Broad, Simon Hicks, Mart Robinson, Simon Clegg, Craig Macadam, Steven Fyfe, Steven Hall, D.B. Furness, Helen Reid, Richard Hall, John Bailey, Jim Stacey, Malcolm Thrupp, William Stone, Alan Garvey, Jim Divers, David Finlay, Martyn Higg, Paul Bartlett, Stephen Pulsford, Peter Holmes, Martin Preuss, Chris Jones, Michael Meredith, Ken Baker, Martin Frisher, Bob Clarkson, Tim Ford, David Cobb, Judy & Dave Steele, J. Bradley, Bob Pritchard, Ron Curd, Arnold McDowell, Brian McCubbin, S. Swift, Tom Prentice, Paul Stavrakis

sleeve design by Ingram Pinn

500 copies of the debut were pressed, at a cost of £153, inspiring the likes of Scritti Politti to list the costs of recording, pressing and distributing their own debut single on its cover. Others then copied Scritti Politti. It advanced the idea of aesthetic integrity being worthless without economic visibility. The process of demystifying the production of art was underway. By the advent of a second single, they'd decided they could push the boat out and pressed 1,000 copies. Again, both songs were featured on either side of the vinyl. Within a fortnight they'd sold the lot. And they carried through on the promise/threat of their debut. The rear cover of the single harangued "They'd really like to know why you haven't made your single yet." 'The Medium Was Tedium', meanwhile, repeated their famed mantra "It was easy, it was cheap, go and do it" from 'Smokescreen'. These bon mots made flesh of punk's more vague commandments.

A six-track EP and further single ensued, the latter notable for its B-side, 'Skill'. "You don't need skill, but the desire/The interest and desire to do what you believe in." Plain speaking, honest, direct. It preceded a full-length album, by which time both Papworth and Roger Stevens had left the band. Their replacements were Dan 'Electro' Driscoll (guitar) and Jeff Titley on drums. There were also two John Peel sessions which again, have never been officially released.

There was one further single before the band disintegrated, leaving behind a template that thousands of others would adopt or assimilate. And yet they still have not made it to (official) CD. It's certainly not due to lack of offers. Dozens of record labels have approached them. They remain steadfastly opposed to any 'compilation'. Any attempt to subordinate their efforts to 'catalogue'. You've got to admire that. Even if you just want to listen to the music and you're irritated by their truculence, it's a hell of a line in the sand.

As Roger Stevens once wrote in a letter to a fan/collector: "One thing that would sway us would be the thought that we could still have a positive influence; maybe encourage someone to take control of some part of their life – by musical means perhaps, but not necessarily." They continue to exert that control. The heroes of 1977 have long since cleared their attics of every conceivable half-assed demo while the Bicycles have steadfastly refused to make their recordings available.

The Stevens quote was nicked from a site in which the great Desperate Bicycles debate rages. Someone had decided to make MP3s of the stuff available for ready download. The ensuing discussion evolved around the legitimacy of these actions. Well, I downloaded them, in the absence of a decent CD reissue. And I'm sorry, but... It was easy, it was cheap (in fact, it was free), so I went and did it. I did ask Roger Stevens if he wished to contribute to this book, querying the Bicycles' media silence, but he very politely declined. "Media silence makes us sound very big time. I think I speak for the others when I say that our records say it all."

Discography:

Smokescreen/Handlebars 7-inch (Refill RR 1 April 1977) (both songs appeared on each side of the single)
The Medium Was Tedium/Don't Back The Front 7-inch (Refill RR 2 July 1977) (ditto)
New Cross New Cross EP (Refill RR 3 May 1978)
Product/Paradise Lost/Advice On Arrest/Holidays/The Housewife Song/Cars)
Occupied Territory/Skill 7-inch (Refill RR 4 July 1978)
Remorse Code LP (Refill RR 6 February 1980)
Grief Is Very Private/Obstructive/Conundrum 7-inch (Refill RR7 March 1980)

Detonators

Howard Ingram (vocals, guitar), Alan Gourley (vocals, guitar), Ali McMordie (bass, vocals), Rod Murray (drums)

D

Belfast's DETONATORS originally formed in 1976 under the name Roche 4 and played at early punk venue the Glenmachan Stables. For the occasion they employed the name Skull after another band of that title who were billed to play broke up on the day of the concert. Earlier, Ingram had been in the school band Essence with Barry McIlhenny, who would later form Shock Treatment. The group was schooled on a tape of the Ramones debut album that McMordie provided as part of his initiation into the group.

However, after McMordie was poached by Highway Star (soon to become Stiff Little Fingers) after a show at the Glenmachan, Ingram switched to bass and Paul MacIlwaine was added on vocals and guitar, and they became the Detonators. The new line-up played together for the first time on Jubilee Day 1977, and tried to secure as many gigs as they could. There was a tentative deal with Terri Hooley's Good Vibrations, but the studio session he booked for them was aborted when the producer declined to put in an appearance. Their first recordings proper were undertaken shortly later at Hydepart Studios for George Doherty's Rip-Off imprint. 'Cruisin'' and 'Light At Your Window' were thereafter included on the Belfast Rock compilation.

They were part of the Battle Of The Bands competition in June 1978 alongside Rudi, the Undertones and the Outcasts, before supporting the Buzzcocks at the Ulster Hall. By this time Murray had left for university and was replaced by Steve Mulree, while MacIlwaine was splitting his time with the Tearjerkers, to whom he would eventually pledge himself full time. That led to the premature end of the band. Mulree went into cabaret and Ingram started the Violence Brothers' project, wherein Everly Brothers' harmonies were deconstructed in punk rock style. Eventually he would rejoin MacIlwaine in the Tearjerkers.

The Detonators got back together in 1990 for their 13th anniversary, as Howard Ingram recalls. "We did some recording together. We did the same in 2002, this time in Sheffield, where Rod Murray has his own studio. We got a long weekend for the Queen's Golden Jubilee, remember? So Paul (MacIlwaine) and I flew over and Alan Gourley drove up from Cardiff. We did about ten tracks, if I remember rightly, although I can say with absolute certainty that none have ever gone into circulation, since that wasn't really the point. Some turned out OK. The reason for that particular weekend was that Paul replaced Ali (McMordie) and our first rehearsal with the Paul MacIlwaine line-up was on the day of the Silver Jubilee. So 25 years on, we got together!"

COMPILATION:
Belfast Rock LP (Rip-Off ROLP1 1978; 'Cruisin'', 'Light At Your Window')
ARCHIVE RELEASE:
Now And Then CD (CDBRA 1001 2000) (live recording of their 1990 reunion show)

Dirty Reds

Dave Henderson (guitar, vocals), Graham Main (bass), Russell Burn (drums), Tam Dean Burn (vocals)

Just as Glasgow's Orange Juice grew out of punk forerunners the Nu-Sonics, so too did Edinburgh's much admired agit-poppers the Fire Engines. Similarly the DIRTY REDS never released any records, but they did provide base camp for three later members of the Engines, as well as actor Tam Dean Burn.

There were effectively two versions of the Dirty Reds, as Tam Burn elaborated. "There was a Dirty Reds Mark I, which was myself and Russell, my brother, and Andy Copeland on guitar, and Dave Carson on bass, who went on to join Boots For Dancing. We only played one gig, supporting the Revillos, then we folded and Russell and Andy joined Hillary (Morrison) in the Flowers. My wee brother Russell was only 16 at the time, still at school, and she didn't really look after him very well. I raised this at one point with her, and I was forever branded as a misogynist thereafter by Hillary. So there was a bit of friction there. Our first gig as Dirty Reds Mk II, which was myself and Russell, and Davey Henderson on guitar and Graham Main on bass, was for the Edinburgh University Communist Society. When I saw Hillary was in the audience, I went, 'Where have all the flowers gone?' She jumped on stage and tried to grab the microphone off me. There was a fair bit of hoo-hah then. After the altercation with Hillary, I pointed at the banners of Marx and Lenin draping the walls and said, 'Fuck all that old-fashioned shite, we are anarchists!' That prompted the crowd to pull them down which resulted in the freaked students pulling the plugs on us. Then I saw Russell's cymbal come flying past me and clattering off the wall, fortunately not taking anyone's head off! That gig set the tone for the Dirty Reds. It was ironic that in the 1992 General Election I was the Communist Party candidate in Glasgow Central. I didn't tell my comrades about my sacrilegious punk days!"

The lyrics were written by Tam Burn, with Henderson and the others providing the music. Russell Burn: "I can remember Mike Scott of Another Pretty Face, later the Waterboys, saying we were 'the worst band ever'. I thought likewise. I also remember Graham Main smashing Davy's guitar to bits after a gig and me slashing my arms in the YMCA toilet with a broken tile – we used to take Mandys and Do-Do's and smoke hefty 'Black' before and during gigs. The outcome always ended in tears. We played a gig at a hall in Cramond. We'd been up for a few days on Black Bombers, and Graham fell asleep on stage while leaning on a pillar, wearing black leather police gloves. The acid in the Dirty Reds days was called 'The Force' – it was little paper blotters with a picture of Darth Vader printed on it. You got 50 blotters on one, the size of a Polaroid picture, for £30". The band's other claim to fame, according to Tam, "is that we came second to the Exploited in a punk rock talent contest on Leith Links!"

The Dirty Reds never did record, despite an offer from Alan Horne of Postcard Records to release one of their songs, 'Dine On My Mind'. Tam Burn: "'Dine On My Mind' was our angst-ridden epic that we'd always finish the sets with, about having to go into the world of work, really. It was a sub-Dylanesque thing with lots of symbolic figures in it." His brother Russell remembers "I always had problems playing it, because it made me start greetin' with angst. Probably too many downers in hindsight." Other songs included 'Bad Sex', of which video footage survives. The lyrics probably didn't do much to dispel Hillary's jibes. "It sounds a lot worse than it is," confesses Tam, "'Please go away fat whore... Leave me to my animalistic heresy, fat whore!' I would always introduce 'Bad Sex' as a 'defensive song'. But I have to accept, it was what it was... " The Dirty Reds appear as a trio in the footage. "Graham, the bass player, he was away roadying for Tangerine Dream when we did the video at Stevenson College. I just held on to the bass, I didn't actually play it. It was taped at rehearsals, so we're actually miming on there. You can probably tell. We used to open with the Velvets 'We're Gonna Have A Good Time Together'. We did Stooges covers with the Dirty Reds Mk I, 'Not Right' and 'I Wanna Be Your Dog'. But we were mainly doing original numbers with Mk II."

But by the end of 1979, the Dirty Reds had evolved into the Fire Engines. Tam Burn: "I was at drama college at the time, and it was getting a bit tough to keep both things going. Things were just a bit too mad, each gig seemed to bring out the craziness in us. I think I knew that Davey was going to be a better singer than me, so I stuck with drama college and became an actor. Murray Slade joined and they became the Fire Engines." Tam became an actor, his TV credits including Taggart and Hamish MacBeth, as well as several films and dozens of theatre shows. If you buy the talking book cassette or CD adaptation of any of Irvine Welsh's novels, there's a good chance the former vocalist of the Dirty Reds will be reading it to you.

The Dirty Reds did actually reunite in 1996 after Tam appeared in the play Two Sevens Clash, which celebrated the year 1977 and took a Scottish view of both the punk movement and Scotland's famous victory over England at Wembley ('the crossbar game'). They ran through a short set that climaxed, in keeping with history, with 'Dine On My Mind'. And somewhere in Russell Burn's possession, apparently, is a cassette of unreleased material.

Disorder

Mark 'Roughy' Rough (vocals), Steve 'Holly' Halstead' (guitar), David 'Leroy' O'Leary (bass), Malcolm 'Coomby' Comb (drums)

Not to be confused with the second-generation cider-punks from Bristol, DISORDER formed in Sunderland in late 1978 as Cranium Disorder, and began rehearsing in the hall of their local school, progressing from a set of covers to their

own original material. Gigs were hit and miss affairs, largely due to their ingestion of quantities of alcohol that would have impressed their titular cousins in the west. There was a support slot to the Revillos but the band were subsequently banned from colleges throughout the north east when bass player O'Leary left Fay Fife a love token in her dressing room sink.

They put two singles out, the first on Ace, 'Air Raid', written by Halstead, is something of a minor classic. Finances were provided by O'Leary after he was awarded compensation from the Criminal Injuries Board after a pellet became lodged in his right eye during a game of cowboys and indians. Only being Sunderland, they were using air rifles. The single was recorded in February 1980 with Michael Sweeney as producer and released in April. All 750 copies sold out quickly, with 100 coming in an improvised 'picture sleeve', which Comb manufactured using a page photocopied out of a page ripped from his grandad's World War II reference book, who was predictably displeased by both the record and the act of vandalism.

A second single followed on the bracingly provincial Durham Book Centre label, by which time Paul Coates had replaced O'Leary. It was recorded in August 1980 in Newcastle, and engineered by Conrad, aka Cronos of local death metal legends Venom. Halstead had left by September 1980, replaced by Jim McCulloch, and three months later the group disbanded after a farewell show in Newcastle. Rough later went on to work as a stand-up comic.

DISCOGRAPHY:

Air-Raid/Law And Disorder 7-inch (Ace 012 April 1980; 750 copies only, 100 with sleeve)
Reality Crisis/1984 7-inch (Durham Book Centre DUMBLE-1 October 1980)
COMPILATION:
Bored Teenagers Vol. 2 CD (Bin Liner CD003 March 2001; 'Air Raid', 'Identity Parade')

The Distributors

Mick Switzerland/Robert Worby (guitar, keyboards, tapes, vocals), Keith James (guitar, vocals), Enzo Raphael/Jeremy Welsh (bass, vocals), Dave Holmes (drums)

An experimental post-punk outfit from Wakefield and London, formed in 1978. In addition to three singles, THE DISTRIBUTORS recorded two sessions for John Peel, in June 1979 and December 1981. By the advent of the second of these, the line-up consisted of James, Holmes and Worby/Switzerland with Jes Snow (bass). 'Get Rid Of These Things' earned a positive notice in the NME, who described it as "a screaming demand to clear the decks that threatens, but never quite manages, to break its bonds." The Distributors' live shows were frequently given approving notices in the UK music press, where their sound was described as, among other things, "shattered metallic dub-funk".

Robert Worby, who also worked extensively with the Mekons in the mid-80s, later wrote about music for the Guardian, the Independent and the Sunday Times, among others, while working as a composer in film, contemporary dance and performance art. He also worked with John Cage in 1989 at the Huddersfield Contemporary Music Festival and assisted Michael Nyman on the scores of films directed by Peter Greenaway, Michael Winterbottom and Neil Jordan. He currently (2006) presents Hear And Now, the main contemporary music programme on BBC Radio 3.

Jeremy Welsh (Enzo Raphael) subsequently worked at the artists' media centre London Video Arts during the 80s, and is currently (2006) a professor of Fine Art at the Academy of Arts in Bergen, Norway. Jeremy Welsh and Robert Worby have continued to collaborate and in recent years have produced several video/sound installations together which have been shown in galleries and museums in Europe. Keith James has lived and worked in New York since (1984), where he was a member of 80s electronic duo The Picassos, with Mike Nolan. After The Distributors, drummer David Holmes returned to the field of improvised music and, for some time, played with Kahondo Style.

DISCOGRAPHY:

TV Me/Wireless 7-inch (Tap TAP 1 1980)

Lean On Me/Never Never 7-inch (Red Rhino RED 5 1981)
Get Rid Of These Things/Hold/Wages For Lovers 12-inch (Red Rhino RED 9 1981)
COMPILATION:
Hicks From The Sticks LP (Rockburgh ROC 111 1980; 'TV Me')

Disturbed

Josi Munns (vocals), Ian Willcock (guitar), Steve Strand (bass), Trevor Warburton (drums)

London DIY punk band the DISTURBED formed at the end of 1977, in the sixth form of their local school in East Grinstead. Munns: "After Marc Bolan died in September 1977 I was a devastated fan. We met Raped and became friends and started to hang out in London." They subsequently signed to Raped's short-lived Parole label and in March 1979 entered Riverside Studios to record the two Willcock compositions that comprised their debut and sole release, 'I Don't Believe'/'Betrayed'. The latter is a belter, a little like an Anglicised version of the Waitresses. They'd started life as a more conventional punk band, developing an affinity to bands like the Au Pairs or pragVEC, as they progressed. Of the reviews of the single, Paul Morley's in the NME's was by far the kindest, noting it resembled a "more grown-up Honey Bane".

They played extensively on the south coast, their live sets including Patti Smith's 'Pissing In A River'. "Punk was a revolution for women," Munns notes, "an opening in an otherwise male-dominated music industry. It was the first time women felt that they could have a go and get themselves in bands. Before this it was a closed shop unless you wanted to be Mary Hopkin. It was an extremely innovative and exciting time." The Disturbed split up in 1980 when Willcock elected to go to university and Munns went on to study drama. Willcock would become quite a name in 'new music' and composition, with several of his electronic/multimedia scores reaching the stage or celluloid.

It's been reported elsewhere that Munns went on to appear as an actress in several Radio One plays. "I don't know where that came from! I did do backing vocals on Cuddly Toys and Swell Maps Radio 1 sessions though." She subsequently formed Josi Without Colours, a self-confessed Goth band. They supported Fields Of The Nephilim and Voice Of The Beehive on tour and cut the singles 'Heroes', 'Tell Me A Story', 'Hear The Animals Cry' and the T-Rex cover, 'Children Of The Revolution' as well as probably their best known song, 'Treasure'. She subsequently recorded solo, taking the name Josephine Lascaux, purely because "I wanted something French sounding", enjoying minor success with the single 'All This And Heaven Too?'

DISCOGRAPHY:

I Don't Believe/Betrayed 7-inch (Parole PURL 3 June 1979)
COMPILATION:
Messthetics #8 ('Betrayed')

Dodgems

Doug Potter (guitar, vocals), Gary Turner (bass, lead vocals), Charlie Zuber (drums), Paul Birchall (keyboards)

The DODGEMS were formed in Brighton at the start of 1978 by Potter, Turner and Zuber. "We were fired up by the exciting and creative Brighton music scene and wanted to seize the opportunity to do our own thing," Potter notes. "I had not felt such a vibe since the early 60s, when I was lucky enough to be a teenager in North

West London, as the whole R&B/mod scene exploded. Seeing the High Numbers/Who every Sunday at the Railway, Wealdstone; Clapton with Mayall's Bluesbreakers at Klooks Kleek, West Hampstead, Tuesday night, and the Graham Bond Organisation with Jack Bruce and Ginger Baker at the Fender Club, Kenton, on a Friday."

The intention was to write and perform original material with a "trash-pop" mentality, incorporating the vibe and energy of punk with heaps of self-deprecation and left field subject matter. Happily this coincided with the founding of The Resource Centre, whose basement became popular local venue the Vault, and Attrix Records. Suddenly other venues like the Alhambra, Richmond, Buccaneer, Concord and others opened their doors to Brighton's burgeoning punk scene.

"The gigs were FANTASTIC," recalls Potter. "So many great nights seeing The Piranhas and (Nicky And The) Dots, especially at the Alhambra. It was like those early High Numbers/Who gigs at The Railway Hotel when you felt something special and unique was jumping off. We formed the Dodgems because we wanted to be a part of that." They never saw themselves as a 'punk' band in the accepted sense. If there were in any doubts about that, a later support slot to the UK Subs, at which they were greeted with a hail of beer cans, put them straight. "In the face of a gale of missiles and abuse we decided to move 'Lucan' up the set list in a futile attempt to win over the baying, gobbing mob. As I sang the song, I realised the drums had stopped. I then saw Charlie at the front of the stage flailing the crowd with his hi-hat stand. He told me later that he had been upset by being hit by a full can of lager." They got paid £5 extra that night for "all the grief".

Undoubtedly their best known song was the aforementioned 'Lord Lucan Is Missing', which was aired on the Vaultage 1978 compilation. Potter: "We had just started The Dodgems and were still writing and rehearsing our first songs when the Vaultage 78 project came along and we were invited to submit some tracks for consideration. This was our first recording experience, and we spent a day recording in Paul Milo's very lo-fi DIY studio (a front room of his house in Brighton). This resulted in 'Lord Lucan Is Missing', 'I Don't Care', 'National Front' and 'You're Just A Habit'. The first two songs went onto the Vaultage 78 LP. The Dodgems had gigged very little or not at all at that stage, hence the 'pleasingly shambolic' ambience you observed."

By the advent of their singles and John Peel session, Paul Birchall had been installed as keyboard player. "I think I was brought in to fill out the sound a bit," Birchall told me. "The sound certainly changed a little as we became a little more pop and very much tighter as a band. Doug Potter was the musical inspiration behind the band and had very definite ideas of the direction the band took musically. Every one had their input but Doug was definitely a driving force."

Further sessions were recorded for Criminal Records. They were "an interesting company who could provide anything," notes Potter, "use of state of the art 24-track studios (Trident etc), Jonathan King to produce a re-recording of 'Lucan' as a chart-aimed single, and later Charley Charles of the Blockheads on drums for a weekend recording session after Charlie Zuber had left for Fiji. Anything, that is, except money." 'Lucan' reached number two in the NME alternative charts and was only kept off the top by Joy Division's 'Love Will Tear Us Apart'. Meanwhile John Peel introduced the band on Radio 1 thus: '(Here is) their classic 'Lord Lucan Is Missing'. This version is even better than their admittedly excellent version on Vaultage 1978'." 'Lord Lucan' finished, he offered these bon mots. "It's very easy, you know, when you're a Radio 1 DJ, to start imagining from time to time that you're actually quite an important and significant person. Whenever I feel this creeping over me I always remind myself that in aeons of droning away on Radio 1 I have created precisely nothing. The Dodgems, even if they do nothing else beyond that, are at least one up on me, if not more, with that excellent piece."

The sessions with Charles took place over the summer of 1981 just as the rioting season started. "I recall driving across London to pick up Charley as shopkeepers boarded up their windows, with the Specials' 'Ghost Town' providing the soundtrack on the van radio. We were excited with the results from those sessions and were looking forward to Criminal putting another Dodgems record out. Two weeks later, they went belly up." The band fell apart

Brighton's Dodgems performing live.

shortly after, meaning gems like the fiscal love letter 'Will You Be My Cohabitee' and especially the Members-esque arrested development of 'Throw A Wobbly' remain unreleased. Turner would join a reconstituted version of the Piranhas before becoming a digital artist.

"All in all I think the Dodgems died young," reflects Birchall. "Looking back and listening to what we did I think we could have made some really great stuff, given time. The Brighton scene was a fun place to be at that time and I played around with a few bands from that time. Most of the bands had some interconnections and there was communal appreciation of what others were doing. At a time when all our equipment was stolen the other bands got together and did a benefit gig. Which shows something of the community spirit born out of the Vaultage 78 album and Attrix records." I asked Potter about the legacy that punk left with them, or the legacy they bequeathed punk, if you'd rather. "For me it was the 'do it' attitude, which I found inspiring. And a spur, to, well, do it!"

Interest in the group was revived when Luke Haines' Black Box Recorder covered 'Lord Lucan' on the US version of their England Made Me album.

DISCOGRAPHY:

Science Fiction/Hard Shoulder 7-inch (Attrix RB 7 1980)
Lord Lucan Is Missing/Gotta Give It Up 7-inch (Criminal SWAG 12 1980)
ARCHIVE RELEASE:
Lord Lucan Is Still Missing 12-inch (12 Apostles 2005) (a limited edition remix 12-inch featuring new interpretations of 'Lucan' by DSICO (Australia), Ollo (Australia), Stefen Robinson (USA), DJ Foundation (UK) and Hamster Dragster (UK))
COMPILATIONS:
Vaultage 1978 (Two Sides Of Brighton) LP (Attrix RB 03 1978; 'I Don't Care', 'Lord Lucan Is Missing')
Vaultage Punk Collection CD (Anagram CDPUNK 101 1997; 'Lord Lucan Is Missing')

The Dole

Ian 'Emu' Neeve (vocals), Pete Howsam (keyboards), Matthew Gillat (bass), Simon Page (guitar), Paul Vjestica (drums)

Formed in 1977 while their drummer was still at school and with an average age of 17, THE DOLE became Peterborough's second serious punk band after the Now, with whom their story entwines. However, there was an earlier incarnation of the band that originally featured Page on vocals, as well as Andrew Jackson on guitar. Neeve arrived on vocals after co-founder Jackson departed, to join the Destructors

and subsequently formed the Blanks. "The gigs were really poor," Jackson recalls of this first version of the Dole, "and it wasn't really punk music, it was pretend punk, I suppose."

D

The Dole secured local support shows to visiting bands including the Radiators and 999 and quickly found a sympathetic home at local imprint Ultimate Records, who'd released the first Now recordings. 'New Wave Love', its subject a local girl who followed the band around, was surprisingly deftly executed, and earned a place on Cherry Red's popular Business Unusual compilation in 1979. It was based on a riff that Jackson had contributed to the band early on. Jackson: "The riff from 'New Wave Love' is the same one as used in the Destructors' song 'What's In Your Life'." However, by year's end the Dole had broken up. Howsam joined Dancing Mirage, Page joined the Point and Neeve formed mod revival band the Name with former Now drummer Joe Macoll before leaving after a few weeks.

In 1978, Howsam was featured in a News of the World scoop about a punk and a vicar's daughter after it was revealed he was getting up close and personal to the offspring of a local cleric. Ah, those were the days. This was actually also the source of the song 'New Wave Love', as Neeve elaborates. "The title of the News of the World piece was 'Punk Rock Boss Plays Hell With Vicar's Daughter!' It concerned the fact that Jo Edwards, our manager at the time, was pissed with Belinda Cawood, who was seeing Heron (Pete Howsam), but whom I'd also shagged. She told Pete about our quickie, and after I made it clear that that's all it was, she gave him an ultimatum – her or the band! Pete chose her. A sad loss as he was our best songwriter. He wrote 'New Wave Love' about her and on its release was featured in one rag giving her a six-foot Valentine's card."

DISCOGRAPHY:

New Wave Love/Hungry Men No Longer Steal Sheep But Are There Hanging Judges? 7-inch (Ultimate ULT 402 1978)
COMPILATIONS:
Business Unusual LP (Cherry Red ARED 2 1979; 'New Wave Love')
Punk Rock Rarities Vol 2 CD (Anagram CDPUNK 83 1996; 'New Wave Love')

Dole Q

Gerry Lambe (guitar), Franco Cornelli (guitar), Hugh Ashton (bass), Pete Sturgeon (drums)

DOLE Q played a few shows at the Roxy in late 1977 and early 1977, supporting the Buzzcocks and others, before reforming the line-up as Skunks and taking in supports to XTC at the 100 Club, the Police at the Vortex and Buzzcocks again at Manchester's Free Trade Hall. The reason for the name change? A Siouxsie and the Banshees interview with Jane Suck in Sounds. Asked about the punk scene, Siouxsie sniffed, "It has all gone very stale," before Severin chipped in with, "There's even a band called Dole Queue – the pits."

Cornelli and Lambe met Hugh Ashton, heir of the Ashton's funeral parlour business, after his dad had kicked him out. Ashton, who was a member of Specta with later Skunks and future Electric Chairs drummer JJ Johnson, went on to build a four-track recording studio in Brixton Hill with his pay-off. Dozens of bands would use his four-track Revox equipped basement for rehearsal and recording, including Aswad. As Lambe told me, "The band (then) consisted of Steve Poggio (bass; a friend of Elton John), myself (vocals and guitars), Dave Munns (drums; classmate at Clapham College and now an actor and London taxi driver) and Franco Cornelli (vocals and lead guitars). We played at the Two Brewers, Clapham High Street, in 1976. (Previously) we were good Catholic boys and attended St Mary's Church and the Junior School prior to Clapham College 1972/1973. The set on the night featured 'Brown Sugar' and 'Roll It'. Frank had a mate who played on Jesus Christ Superstar in the West End. We went along to see it. And really the band was formed from that as a major influence." They also befriended Two Taverns regulars the Merton Parkas. "In fact we nearly nicked their drummer, but he saw sense and stayed with them. Their keyboard player was a mate called Mick Talbot. The last time I saw him on Clapham underground circa 1978 he said, 'I'm getting into soul music,' to which I bah-bah'd, I never saw him again, but I believe he bumped in to Paul Weller at the other end of the line!"

They went through several names, including the Murderers and the Anarchists, before settling on Dole Q, inspired by the fact that their then lead singer Ward was unemployed, and had written 'On The Dole' about his non-existent lifestyle. "They were very young at the time," JJ Johnson told me. "I think Gerry was about 14 or 15, and they wanted to form a punk band, and they were still learning how to play, but at that point they didn't have a drummer. So, over the following weeks, I did a short tour with Specta at various venues around the country, and by now Dole Q felt that they were ready and wanted to play some punk venues, but they still didn't have a drummer. From what I remember, they asked me to play with them. I wasn't sure about joining them but I said I would 'sit in' with them until they found a permanent drummer. One of the first gigs was at the Roxy Club in Covent Garden, probably as Dole Q, I can't honestly remember, but I remember it was a laugh. Then I think at some point later they auditioned drummers, and Pete Sturgeon joined."

Ward didn't survive the transition to the Skunks (see separate entry), and left to join the Parachute Regiment as it became apparent his fellow bandmates were beginning to take everything more seriously, with Lambe taking over vocals. He was last seen working as a scaffolder.

The Doll

Marion 'Baby Doll' Valentine (aka Marion Suava; vocals, guitar), Christos 'Whizz Kid' Yianni (bass), Adonis Yianni (keyboards), Mario Watts (drums; replacing Max Splodge)

THE DOLL, formed in late 1976, were very much a family affair. Valentine was the group's chief songwriter while her husband, known only as Black Lou, handled vocals. Alongside bass player Christos, they started advertising for a drummer, which is where Max Splodge enters the story. "I saw an advert in Melody Maker, when I was working as a tape operator, for a new band. I thought it was for the Banshees. I called and went to a rehearsal in Pimlico. There was a bass player called Chris, Marion was on guitar, and the singer was her husband Black Lou. They were quite spooky. I was 16 at the time. They were more gothic looking than anything, black leather and shades. There were about three other drummers auditioning. They said, 'I hope you can play fast'. We got halfway through the first song and they said – not that fast!"

"They whittled us down to the last two and they said I could have the job if I cut my hair. So we rehearsed under Beggars Banquet record shop three times a week for nearly a year. One night a mate was playing at the Speakeasy, so I got them to play three songs live and they were chased out at knife point cos they were so scary. After that Lou said he wasn't going to be the singer anymore, which was a touch as he was shit. Then Marion was going to front it. At another rehearsal Adonis appeared, some cousin or something, and he played keyboards. So they rehearsed again and recorded two demos, 'Trash' and 'Don't Tango On My Heart.' Then I was offered another job and moved on to play with the Mistakes."

The Doll's first vinyl appearance, with Mario Watts joining on drums, came on Beggars Banquet's inaugural Streets compilation, to which they contributed 'Trash', produced by Ed Hollis and Steve Lillywhite. Streets was ecstatically reviewed by John Peel for Sounds, who advised punters to: "Steal the Pistols album, buy this one" and awarded the compilation five stars. The Doll also joined the Streets promotional tour, headlined by the Lurkers, during December 1977.

Thereafter they signed a full deal with Beggars. The debut single, 'Don't Tango On My Heart', and the aforementioned 'Trash' are the tunes a punk rock fan will want to hear – essentially the Tubes meet the Ramones in over-revved and high-pitched sonic mini-dramas. Splodge: "They got another drummer for 'Don't Tango' and 'Trash', then they called and said they had a gig and the new drummer couldn't play. So I played with them at a gig in Stoke Newington. They asked me to rejoin, but I didn't. The last thing I saw was a tour with the Lurkers and a support with the Jam in Croydon, but it was a family outfit and I didn't want to play with them any more. Just after that they had their hit with 'Desire Me', but I'd gone off to do Splodge by then."

'Desire Me' actually pushed them into the Top 30, which was a bit of a shock for all concerned. Thereafter Valentine shuffled the line-up, with Denis Haines replacing Adonis, Paul Turner taking over on drums and additional guitarist James West Oram, later of the Fixx and Rupert Hines' Thinkman, coming in.

By 'Cinderella With A Husky Voice' and 'You Used To Be My Hero' the synths are starting to dominate, the pace is dropped, and Marion Valentine comes off like a proto-Hazel O'Connor. Beggars Banquet could potentially have had a pin-up pop star on their hands, but lacked the marketing muscle to pull it off. The album Listen To The Silence is actually more listenable than silence, even if the touchstone influences are no longer the Ramones but Abba and fellow Beggars Banquet labelmate Gary Numan, whose success they spectacularly failed to replicate.

DISCOGRAPHY:

Don't Tango On My Heart/Trash 7-inch (Beggars Banquet BEG 4 January 1978)
Desire Me/TV Addict/Burning Up Like A Fire/Desire Me (extended version) double 7-inch (Beggars Banquet BEG 11 + SAM 93 December 1978) (also available as a 12-inch single, BEG 11T, with tracks 'Desire Me' (extended) and 'TV Addict')
Cinderella With A Husky Voice/Because Now 7-inch (Beggars Banquet BEG 26 October 1979)
Listen To The Silence LP (Beggars Banquet BEGA 12 October 1979)
You Used To Be My Hero/Zero Heroes 7-inch (Beggars Banquet BEG 31 January 1980)
Burning Up Like A Fire/Frozen Fire 7-inch (BEG 38 April 1980)
COMPILATIONS:
Streets LP (Beggars Banquet BEGA 1 November 1977; 'Trash')
Beggars Banquet – The Punk Singles Collection CD (Anagram CD PUNK 73 1996; 'Don't Tango On My Heart', 'Trash', 'Desire Me', Cinderella With A Husky Voice', 'You Used To Be My Hero')

The Doubt

John 'Rat' Clarke (bass), Hugh 'Chad' Cairns (vocals), Paul Corken (guitar), Steven Clarke

Formed in Bangor in 1978 from the ashes of the town's first punk band, the Standards, whose best-known song, or possibly the only song anybody remembers them playing, was 'Don't Just Watch'. 'You can't say no when they search you in the Co (Op)/And Belfast is a no-go' is a sample lyric from the latter. However, the only remnant of that group, John Clarke, was soon replaced on bass by Robert Scott, formerly of the Skis, after he started to display 'muso' aspirations.

Rehearsals took place in the singer's bedroom. Gigs took place wherever and whenever they could get them, at birthday parties, at pubs where they had to bluff their age to get in, even on the beach. Robert Scott: "I remember several live occasions when the guitarist had to rouse the permanently-inebriated drummer and tap out the relevant beat for him to cotton on to before the song could begin properly. The drummer passed out over the drums in the middle of a gig with one of his equally pissed mates trying to cover for him (very unconvincingly)." Comfortably their most successful gig was a support to visiting Belfast bands the Androids and Ruefrex at St Columbanus Church in Ballyholme in April 1978. Otherwise it was shambolic, it was utterly non-careerist and it great fun while it lasted, but it didn't last for long. By 1979 the band was all over.

However, Corken and Scott decided to fulfil a commitment to record an EP and used Adrian Maddox (guitar player with Fifth Column and future partner of Scott in Palace Of Variety) to provide drums, with Corken as vocalist. Maddox managed to break his snare drum, which accounts for the rather unusual percussion sound. The results were eventually released on Solo Records in early 1980. The EP, of which only a few hundred were pressed, has subsequently been widely bootlegged on the Bloodstains and Powerpearls compilations. Eventually this led to the release of a compilation of the band's material in November 2002 on Italian label Rave Up, featuring the EP plus 10 demo recordings.

Robert Scott: "A while after the **DOUBT** called it a day, I teamed up with Adrian Maddox in a band called Palace of Variety. At the time Adrian was working for Melody Maker, I was stringing for NME and our drummer Bill Aiken was doing bits and pieces for Sounds. Unfortunately, none of this helped us get anywhere. After Bill left we played on with two drum machines (as this was pre-midi – well, for us anyway – you can imagine the results live). We did some recording and a bit of local TV but eventually petered out."

DISCOGRAPHY:

The Doubt 7-inch EP (Solo CUS 750 1980)
Contrast DIsorder/Time Out/Look Away/Fringes
Contrast Disorder CD (Rave Up Records Italy SSR 01 November 2002) (the EP tracks plus 10 1978 demo recordings) (Scott is still recording, and you can find some of his work as dirtbird on myspace)

The Drive

Gus McKenzie (vocals), Ron Neish (lead guitar), Bob Phillips (slide guitar), Roger Patterson (bass), Ron Jack (drums)

One of Dundee's pioneering punk bands, their N-R-G label competed with Sensible and Zoom for the honour of being the nation's first new wave label. THE DRIVE opened their account with their ode to masturbation, 'Jerkin". Unusually for the time, it was issued without a picture sleeve, which was a testament to the financial strictures at work. The presence of slide guitar was equally at odds with prevailing trends.

A projected second single, 'Blow Job', backed by 'Gonorrhoea A Go Go', was never released. Which is probably a very good thing. As Jock Ferguson of Dundee fanzine Cranked Up notes, "Gus's band put out probably Dundee's first punk single, on NRG Records. The local press didn't realise what it was about and gave it good coverage! When the People's Journal reviewed 'Jerkin'", the reporter missed the point, believing it to be about a garment. With 'The filth and the fury' in the press, Gus's boss in the bank where he worked called him into the office; 'Now, I've nothing against homosexuals...' he began."

But then McDonald suddenly lowers his tone: "Gus then wrote the Dundee United official song, the swine. It plays when Dundee United run out on match days – 'It's United, they're my own team, It's United, Black and Tangerine...' Terrible."

DISCOGRAPHY:

Jerkin'/Push 'n' Shove 7-inch (N-R-G RE-46 August 1977)
COMPILATION:
Streets: Select Highlights From Independent British Labels (Beggars Banquet BEGA 1 1977; 'Jerkin")

Drones

M.J. Drone (aka Mike Howells, vocals), Gus 'Gangrene' Callendar (guitar), Pete 'Purrfect' Lambert aka Pete Howells (drums), 'Red Arse Whisper' Steve Cundell (bass)

Never the most fashionable of Manchester's punk set, the DRONES grew out of a straight R&B group, Rockslide, "Middleton's answer to Slik," according to Mick Middles. They released one single, 'Roller Coaster', before they, like Slaughter And The Dogs, Ed Banger And The Nosebleeds and countless others before them, were transformed by the Sex Pistols' second show at the Lesser Free Trade Hall in Manchester. Callendar, who joined the band in October 1976, was in attendance that evening. "That was it," according to leader singer Howells. "We got our name out of the dictionary – we liked its meaning, a low humming noise. It also mentioned bees, which appealed." Many were left totally unconvinced, especially Middles, who dismissed them as "pushy bandwagoners". Pete Silverton saw them at the end of 1977 and was just as cutting. "The Drones didn't do nothin' worth venturing out of the bar for. They were like most of the bands on the abysmal Streets album that Peel perversely drooled over the other week: clones bereft of either inspiration or thought. They should have had the conviction of their opinions and stuck to being a glitter band."

After a few further gigs, the Drones made their first foray into London and were befriended by the Stranglers' Jean-Jacques Burnel. He got them a support slot on their Rats On The Road tour. There was a shared sense of machismo, as Steve Shy of Manchester fanzine Shy Talk told me. "The Drones used to have a minder. He was the leader of an ex-Hell's Angels chapter, called Sarge. I think he works for Harvey Goldsmith now. He was the head doorman at the Apollo. The Drones played the Roxy one night and we'd gone down there. There were a few drunks getting out of hand. Sarge just picked two of them up off the ground and smashed their heads together. So the Drones could get away with what they wanted because they always had him to back them up."

They then shared a tour with Slaughter And The Dogs, though they complained that they were underplayed on the billing for the tour. By this time their debut EP, 'Temptations Of A White Collar Worker', had been released on their own OHM Records in July 1977. Featuring one 'Joan Juice' on the handmade cover, and produced by Paul Morley, journalist and sometime band manager, it sold over 12,000 copies. Recorded in 10 hours on 7 April 1977, Sounds noted that it boasted "awful playing and sound quality", but that the lyrics were "powerful and direct". As Mick Middles later recalled in Muze, after watching Ed Banger of the Nosebleeds attempt to attack Morley at the Electric Circus, "Morley's writing doesn't deserve the threat of physical violence. His managing and subsequent producing of the Drones, however, probably does." Despite the muddled sound, the standout was clearly 'Lookalikes', which would also be their contribution to the Electric Circus compilation LP.

They were an increasingly popular draw at Manchester venues such as Rafters and the aforementioned Electric Circus, where Morley advertised them as "Manchester's number one punk band". In London they played venues including the Red Cow, and were warned by the man from the GLC about their noise levels, as well as the Roxy. There they were support to XTC, whose audience started a mini-riot during the set, aided by Tony Parsons who was so disgusted with their set he "smashed a chair". For their second single they moved to Valer Records, the signing broadcast live on Piccadilly Radio's Reflextions programme. A 12-inch version of their update of the Ronettes' standard 'Be My Baby' was due to be backed by 'Lift Off The Bans'. The latter was their protest at the closure of the Electric Circus due to the refusal of a food licence, which also inspired them to dress up as chefs for the day. "I like girl groups and soul music," Howells later told Q, "and mentioned to our producer Simon I'd like to do 'Be My Baby'. He was a classically trained pianist, so he added the piano and he took scratches off old records and added them on electronically, so it had a 'back to the 60s' feel." However, in the end, the disc was withdrawn (don't go believing the porkies around about the discovery of a few hundred rogue copies). Instead 'Bone Idol' preceded their debut album, selling a highly respectable 20,000 copies,

Released in November 1977, Further Temptations contained re-recorded versions of two songs off the debut EP, plus the 'Bone Idol' single and its B-side. It's an appealing blend of nouveau glam, hammed up Dolls-like rock'n'roll with a punky veneer. Hugely derivative, but fun. Copies were given out with free dog collars (mimicking M.J.'s dress sense) at a press launch, while the model featured on the cover was a masseur at the parlour the record label booked for the purpose. It's rumoured she was 'close' to several band members. All four of them, apparently. They also found time to record a complete set of Clash parodies while messing about in the studio, playing them to an amused Joe Strummer and Mick Jones, who were in the same CBS complex.

The album was followed by the group's first John Peel session in December 1977, rounding out a busy and productive 12 months. But things quickly went awry. Before the album's release the group fell out with Morley, who was touting local rivals Stiff Kittens/Warsaw, later to become Joy Division, who were a more earnest proposition than the notoriously prank-loving Drones, even though they continually pestered the better known band for support slots. Morley then wrote a scathing review of his former charges' debut album to get his own back, leaving Callendar to exact physical revenge. There was also a late night confrontation with Wayne Barrett of Slaughter And The Dogs on a night bus. Valer went down the tubes, and the reviews of the album did not spare the band. Alan Lewis at Sounds was at least even-handed: "If there's no place for the Drones (or the Lurkers, or the Zeros, or any of the average, enjoyable but non-significant young bands) then the new wave is going to wind up every bit as boring as the old wave."

A keyboard player joined the band, and they temporarily recruited female backing vocalists, but the move was greeted with widespread cynicism, not least in a cutting review from Sounds in February 1978 ("... a pathetic failure... back to rock cabaret") The Drones signed a deal with Island offshoot Fabulous, but these 1979 sessions were never released, with the exception of a final single, 'Can't See', which featured John Ellis of the Vibrators on guitar. They were still active in 1982, by which time they'd clocked a TV appearance on Brass Tacks, but their moment had long since passed.

Eventually the band, who had remained friends and drinking buddies, reunited in 1996, apart from Cundell, who was busy working as a house-builder and raising a family. They met up with old friends V2 at the 1996 Holidays In The Sun festival in Blackpool, which resulted in Mark Standley joining the Drones on a full-time basis. An album of new material on Captain Oi! Records, Sorted, followed three years later. It included the title-track, released as a single in Finland, and their tribute to local Mancunian punk legend, 'Jon The Postman'. There were also covers of the Marvin Gaye soul classic 'Heard It Through The Grapevine' which sounded more Gary Glitter than Whitfield/Strong, and a punked up 'American Pie', with slightly ruder lyrics, which was at least a little more palatable. Of the originals, 'Phones' didn't sound altogether unlike a Mancunian 'Pills', while 'Dirty Bastards' is a winning, if simplistic, 'snotty like the old days' effort.

DISCOGRAPHY:

Temptations Of A White Collar Worker 7-inch EP (OHMS Good Mix 1 July 1977) Lookalikes/Corgi Crap/Hand On Me/You'll Lose

Bone Idol/I Just Wanna Be Myself double A-side 7-inch (Valer VRS 1 October 1977) (also issued as a cassette, in cigarette box packaging, as Fifth Avenue CAS 107)

Further Temptations LP (Valer VLRP 1 November 1977) (reissued in October 1993 on CD, Anagram CD PUNK 20, with seven bonus tracks –'Lookalike (single version)', 'Corgi Crap (single version)', 'Hard On Me', 'You'll Lose', 'Just Wanna Be Myself (single version)', 'Bone Idol (single version)', 'Can't See', 'Fooled Today')

Can't See/Fooled Today 7-inch (Fabulous JC4 1980)

Sorted 7-inch (Alternative Action AA 034 1999; Finland)

Sorted CD (Captain Oi! AHOY CD 111 1999) (the cover is a nice pastiche of the familiar Further Temptations image)

ARCHIVE RELEASES:

The Attic Tapes LP (Get Back GET 25) (rarities, unreleased action, and alternate versions)

Expectations – Tapes From The Attic CD (Overground OVER 60 CD 1997) (unreleased and alternate material, including a cover of Iggy's 'Search And Destroy', retitled 'Expectations', dating from November 1975. There are also two songs from their final recording session in May 1979, another take from their Live At The Electric Circus set, and six songs from their first reunion, that took place in 1996)

Further Temptations dbl LP (Get Back Get 6) (A complete vinyl retrospective of the band's 70s and 80s work)

Be My Baby/Lift Off The Bans 12-inch (Valer VRSP 1 1977; withdrawn) (Interesting story behind this one. Purportedly copies were finally unearthed of this one, and it was advertised as a stunningly scarce collector's item. Until collector guru Mario from Venice got hold of a copy and had it carbon-dated for chronological accuracy. Turns out it was manufactured in the 21st century. Hmmmmm.)

COMPILATIONS:

Streets: Select Highlights From Independent British Labels (Beggars Banquet BEGA 1 1977; 'Lookalikes')

Short Circuit (Live At The Electric Circus) 10-inch LP (Virgin VCL-5003 June 1978; 'Persecution Complex')

1-2-3-4 A History Of Punk And New Wave 1976-1979 5-CD box set (MCA/Universal MCD 60066 1999; 'Bone Idol')

Drug Addix

Ron Griffin (drums), Mandy Doubt (aka Kirsty MacColl; vocals), Art Nouveau (aka George Lloyd; vocals, guitar), Alan Offer (bass), Sterling Silver (aka Rick Smith; vocals)

Croydon's DRUG ADDIX, originally entitled the Tooting Fruities, were the first musical shelter for that inimitable firebrand Kirsty MacColl, releasing their sole EP in 1978 when she was just 18. They'd put together a four-track demo, taken it to Chiswick, who considered it strong enough to release immediately as an EP. Given the subject matter of the lead track, it predictably generated a few column inches. 'Gay Boys In Bondage' was intended to be a homage to Lou Reed's New

York sleaze period, "a piece of camp corn that lent itself to stage dynamics," Lloyd later told Record Collector.

"All I did on the record was backing vocals," MacColl revealed. "You can barely hear me. We weren't actually a punk band, but at the time punk was king and we called ourselves that just to get some gigs. Everyone expected an outrageous, Sex Pistols type of band but we weren't. We were all slide guitar and R&B. I was just the token boiler on backup vocals. Of course that annoyed me but you've got to start somewhere. If you can't really sing and you can't play anything, you can't argue about it."

Kirsty MacColl singing on stage with the Drug Addix at the Venue in 1978.

'Gay Boys' also appeared on The Chiswick Story compilation and as part of a Spanish release (billed as 'Los Gay Estan Escalvizados') where it was paired with Billy Bragg's Riff Raff and the Jook. There was a second record credited only to the Addix, under which guise the band supported the Vicious White Kids at the Electric Ballroom. MacColl was long gone, having been kicked out of the band. But on hearing this she was invited to a meeting at Stiff Records, who duly set her to work writing her first hit, 'They Don't Know'.

DISCOGRAPHY:

The Drug Addix Make A Record 7-inch EP (Chiswick SW 39 July 1978)
Gay Boys In Bondage/Addington Struggle/Special Clinic/Glutton For Punishment
As the Addix:
Too Blind To See/No Such Thing As A Bad Boy 7-inch (Zigzag 1979)
COMPILATIONS:
The Chiswick Story LP ('Gay Boys In Bondage')
Rock'n'roll Suburbano De London 7-inch EP ('Los Gay Estan Escalvizados') (also tracks by Riff Raff and Jook)

Eater

Andy Blade (aka Ashie Radwan; vocals), Brian Chevette (aka Brian Haddock; guitar), Social Demise (drums; soon replaced by Dee Generate, aka Roger Bullen), Ian Woodcock (bass)

Youth, according to Jon Savage, is, of itself, not enough. But it was plenty for many who were enchanted by EATER's inability to accept age as any form of constraint. There are those who view Eater as a joke band, the kind of artless school knockabouts – as opposed to art school knockabouts, presumably – that would never have been heard outside of lunchtime rehearsals were it not for the happy accident of timing and location. But Eater were better than that, and, musically and symbolically, came to define punk's internal dialogue and physical presence better than many of their more celebrated contemporaries.

The group began in Finchley in the summer of 1976. "Like most kids of our age (15)," Andy Blade related in the sleevenotes to Compleat Eater in 1993, "Brian Chevette and I wanted to be in a rock band. The fact that we couldn't play and didn't have any instruments never really bothered us. We decided to call ourselves Eater after a Marc Bolan line: 'Tyrannosaurus Rex, the eater of cars', and told all the girls in our school that we had this band. Girlfriends were suddenly easier to find. After about two months of writing our imaginary set lists and lyrics to songs that didn't exist, while informing all and sundry of a forthcoming imaginary gig, we decided we'd better get our act together. A lot of people wanted to see us play! We managed to 'obtain' the necessary guitars, learned a few chords and promptly set about writing tunes to our ever growing bundles of lyrics. All of them basically speeded up variations of Velvet Underground songs."

Producer Dave Goodman would later throw some light on what 'obtaining' those guitars amounted to. "They used to have regular gatherings, with friends, (including Brian) and called it the Bedroom Club. With an old Spanish guitar, a fake microphone and some pots and pans they started miming along to their favourite records. Word of their performances soon spread and they were contacted by the local paper, who arranged an interview and photo shoot. 'By the way, can you make sure you bring your guitars with you for the photo?' the man at the newspaper said, before hanging up. 'Shit, we've only got this poxy acoustic guitar and that won't look any good in the picture,' someone said. Not wanting to miss out on this golden opportunity for self-promotion, they hatched a plan to steal two guitars from the local music shop, which they passed every day en route to and from school." Erm, well, that's Goodman's take. "Rubbish," Blade told me. "We were forced into having to steal the guitars because we'd told all of our friends at school we had a band."

However, the rest of Goodman's story is, apparently, true. "They spent several days just looking in the window, observing the activities of the shopkeeper and noticed that just before he locked up each evening, he went out the back to get his coat. This would give them just enough time to run in, grab the guitars and leg it, before the shopkeeper returned. They planned to escape down a side alley and leave the guitars hidden in some bushes in a garden, until they could go back under cover of darkness and retrieve them. They did the dastardly deed and it worked a treat. They looked great in the photo, really professional, and the kids at school were mightily impressed. The photo appeared in the same edition as the news about the music shop robbery, but amazingly no one put two and two together. Armed with their three newly acquired axes, they soon found a drummer and bass player."

Social Demise, whose true identity remained uncovered until Blade revealed in his recent book that it was actually his little brother, was replaced by the diminutive Dee Generate (aka Roger Bullen), recommended to the band via journalist Jonh Ingham. Rat Scabies lived near Bullen and often popped in to see his mother to cadge a meal and get his washing done. In return Bullen got a few free lessons, a few of Scabies' old toms (at a price) and opted for the new 'punk' name Dee Generate before "someone called me Sid Short Arse". He'd also been to see the Damned at their 100 Club Punk Festival appearance. The new bass player was Ian Woodcock. Ron Watts agreed to let them make their debut at the 100 Club Punk Festival in September, but was knocked back by the council due to their age.

By November they were ready, and on the 26th played their first gig at the Holdsworth Hall, Manchester, with the Devoto-era Buzzcocks as support. The billing was legendarily decided by the toss of a coin – another myth. Blade: "We headlined cos we hired the hall." Blade had picked Manchester as the site of this momentous occasion and contacted the Buzzcocks on the advice of Martin Hannett. The gig was arranged at a Wimpey Bar in Manchester – Blade being informed that he'd spot Howard Devoto easily, as he'd be wearing a pink carnation. But following the Buzzcocks' set Eater would be furiously heckled by the home crowd, resulting in their stand-in bass player (Woodcock hadn't actually joined at this point) walking off after three numbers, leaving Eater to continue as a three-piece.

They quickly garnered quizzical notices, most of them focusing on the group's age, as Woodcock related to Sniffin' Glue in January 1977. "They (journalists) always ask stupid questions like: 'What does mummy think?' 'What about safety pins?' you know. They ask 'What's behind it?' Stupid. There's nothing significant or shocking about what we do. We just play for ourselves, to kids like ourselves." Meanwhile their connection with Rat Scabies led to them persuading the Damned to play a date at Eater's school in Finchley, where soft drinks were served, at least in public view. Presumably Andy Blade's comments to Sniffin' Glue: "I'd really like people to go and blow up schools. Turn on their parents and slash 'em up with razor blades," had not yet been related to their teachers. They also featured on the Roxy live album, contributing a version of Alice Cooper's 'Eighteen', amended to 'Fifteen' for the occasion, and 'I Don't Need It'.

By now the tabloids had discovered their ages and seized on the intrinsic novelty value of schoolboy punk rockers, particularly 13-year-old Dee Generate, who had the body of a stripling at least six years younger. He was singled out for an interview in an article in the Daily Mirror in December 1976. "Unfortunately his (Dee Generate's) voice has not yet broken so he sounds slightly incongruous when he is talking about his commitment to punk. 'Some bands might get accepted,' he piped, 'But WE will never be acceptable.' His mum, Mrs Helen Bullen is fully behind him. 'I was a bit frightened for him at first, but now I have seen the band play I can see what they are trying to do,' she said. 'I think it is great really. You should see him walking around – he looks like an old ragbag. It's so funny. Unfortunately we are having a bit of trouble with his school right now because he has taken so many days off. His headmaster doesn't seem to understand about punk rock.'" Ah, that's not an uncommon problem with headmasters.

Dee's tiny stature also led to an uncomfortable night at the Hope & Anchor when the police raided the venue looking for underage drinkers. He was grabbed and hidden in someone's coat during the raid. "Unbelievable," he recalled in an interview with June Bird in 2002, "two pairs of legs sticking out from under this huge old trenchcoat and they didn't see."

Dave Goodman, the late Pistols' soundman and top bootlegger of this parish, signed them to his The Label on a one-year contract that was later extended (Blade: "actually it was an 'eternal rip-off contract'). The band was originally told that this was to be a co-venture with Lydon of the Sex Pistols, under the title Rotten Records. "When I asked Rotten if it were true that he was setting up a label with Dave," Blade later told Record Collector, "he cackled sarcastically for a very long time in a 'You are fucking kidding, aren't you?' kind of way. I suddenly felt like a silly 15-year-old. Which I was."

Their debut single, 'Outside View', written in chemistry class by Blade and Chevette, had been recorded by Goodman in Decibel Studios in November 1976 when he had some downtime from mixing Pistols' tracks there. There were, at most, a couple of overdubs, while

Chevette completed the sessions using Steve Jones guitar – which he would eventually inherit – after dropping and breaking his own. The labels, when eventually printed up, stated 'arranged by Dave Goodman'. When Blade queried this, he was succinctly told "Well, he arranged the studio, didn't he?"

It was released in March 1977. "Crap," retorted Sniffin' Glue. "Not even good crap." Blade was amused to see it melted into a makeshift ashtray on a visit to Nora's, where John and Sid hung out. They hadn't actually sent them a copy. "Nora had bought a copy. They melted it because I had been found in bed with her."

Arguably Eater's finest moment, 'Thinking Of The USA', followed. The lyrics were an appealing mix of parochial naivety and ambition, reflecting on their own travails, and the pop culture dream that existed somewhere just over the water. "Walter Lure comes from the USA/Lou Reed comes from the USA/Richard Nixon comes from the USA/Gary Gilmore came from the USA."

As the song acknowledged, they had become regulars at the Roxy, as well as the Vortex and other punk haunts. But Dee Generate's whirlwind rise to celebrity was halted, much to his dismay, when Eater suddenly announced that Phil Rowland was to become their new drummer in June 1977. "They said I was always pissed and took too many drugs," Dee later recalled to punk77 of the crisis meeting that was held with Label financier Caruso and the band to discuss matters, at which he did indeed turn up drunk. "I left the meeting thinking that I'd sorted it all out, promised to behave, and practice more, and share my drugs, but the next day, I think, Andy phoned me and I said I was sacked."

Dee Generate, who went on to the barely visible Dirty Works (with a college friend of Lydon and Vicious), played on only one track on the subsequent album, 'No Brains', the song featured in the 'pig's head scene' on Don Letts' Punk Rock Movie. He claims he'd already been having second thoughts after a Roxy gig was destroyed by rampaging Millwall fans and his step-father was 'bottled' while trying to help the group escape. Thereafter he attended art school but became hooked on heroin, as did his sister, who was lost to an overdose in her early 20s. He is now manager of a social work department in Northampton. He's run the London marathon seven times and has just put another band together. And he's since made his peace both with Blade and his Eater legacy.

Rowland made his debut on 'Lock It Up', backed by a version of T-Rex's 'Jeepster' (like the Damned, Blade was a huge Marc Bolan fan). Their debut long-player, sarcastically entitled simply The Album, followed. Though it featured rather too many covers (the Velvet Underground, Bowie and Alice Cooper were all brushed down) there's an unmistakable sense of aural glee about the whole event. And while the playing had improved from basic to basic-plus, Andy Blade's songwriting is better than you may have been led to believe.

But from then on Eater began to stall. The Label issued a live EP, 'Get Your Yo Yo's Out', as a schoolboy take on the Rolling Stones' live album Get Your Ya Ya's Out, recorded at Dingwalls and featuring two new tracks. Chevette was then replaced by Gary Steadman on guitar after he took "a rest from the rigours of life on the road". Doubtless he had exams to attend to, as well. Steadman, who started playing with the band in June 1978, contributed to their final single, 'What She Wants She Needs'. By January 1979 the group was over completely.

Former members appeared in the Studio Sweethearts, Slaughter And The Dogs and, much later, the London Cowboys (Rowland), Dave Goodman & Friends' 'Justifiable Homicide', then the Vibrators (Woodcock), Classix Nouveaux, A Flock Of Seagulls and the Roytes (Steadman). Brian James of the Damned and Andy Blade joined forces on 'Lyin' To Me Again', which was never released though it was later given away free with an Eater compilation album. Blade also cut the solo single 'Break The News' (SMS SMS001 1980) and played on one song by the Musical Meames. In the mid-90s Blade restarted his solo career, releasing From The Planet Pop To The Mental Shop for Creative Man and a single, 'Junkie Shooting Star'. 2005 brought a new studio album for Cherry Red, Treasure Here.

Despite Blade eschewing any idea of a reunion, he was eventually prompted to do so via the offer (eventually not received) of a big pay cheque for appearing at the Holidays In The Sun festival in Blackpool in 1996. So Blade and Chevette were joined by Steve O'Shea on bass and Reg-Urgitate (aka Graham Best; drums), who were already members of Blade's own band. Two unreleased Blade compositions, 'Going Down' and 'Vegetable Girl', were unveiled at their practice, and at one point were considered for release as a single. They also re-recorded Eater's debut album on four-track (later released as the second CD with The Eater Chronicles). But after a few gigs Blade decided he didn't want to get locked into the nostalgia circuit and disbanded Eater again. Not before the band, who contributed a version of 'Thinking Of The USA' to the Holidays live album, did get to visit America at last – playing support shows to Fugazi, punk veterans almost as long in the tooth as Eater themselves.

Andy Blade has now committed to posterity his memories of Eater's two years in the limelight. The Secret Life Of A Teenage Punk Rocker is as entertaining and amusing a first-hand document of the period as any, the gravity of the occasion undercut by the author's bemused and amused nostalgia at his own growing pains.

DISCOGRAPHY:

Outside View/You 7-inch (The Label TLR001 March 1977)

Thinking of the USA/Space Dreaming/Michael's Monetary System 7-inch (The Label TLR003 May 1977)

Lock it Up/Jeepster (The Label TLR004 October 1977) (also on 12-inch, TLR004+12, which features the same songs on both sides in reverse order)

Eater – The Album LP (TLRLP001 January 1978)

Get Your Yo Yo's Out EP (The Label TLR007 September 1978)

Holland/Debutantes Ball/Thinking of The USA/No More (live 7-inch EP on white vinyl, also available on 12-inch TLR007+12)

What She Wants She Needs/Reach For The Sky (The Label TLR009 December 1978)

ARCHIVE RELEASES:

(Buyer's Guide: The Compleat Eater, also released in the US with a different sleeve as All Of Eater on Creative Man, for a long time constituted pretty much everything you needed. However, the more recent release of The Eater Chronicles, which also adds a CD of new recordings, unreleased stuff and a spoken word clip, is now the place to go – although you'll miss out on the more informative sleevenotes that came with Compleat. Live At Barbarella's is also worth checking out)

The History Of Eater Volume 1 LP (De Lorean EAT 1 February 1985) (there was no volume two, of course. Now long out of print, this was essentially The Album with bonus tracks drawn from the 7-inch singles, and free Brian James/Andy Blade 7-inch, EAT Freebie 1, erroneously credited to Eater. Due to the release of Eater Chronicles, this is no longer worth tracking down)

The Compleat Eater LP/CD (Anagram CD/LP PUNK 10 April 1993)

The Eater Chronicles 1976-2003 dbl CD (Anagram CD PUNK 133 September 2003) (the first CD replicates the existing Compleat Eater. The bonus CD features 1997 re-recordings of familiar Eater classics – now at last you can hear what 'Outside View' might have sounded like if you could hear the bass. There's an abandoned single from the same era – 'Going Down', 'Vegetable Girl' – a single Blade recorded with Brian James and Mark Laff in 1979 – Lyin' To Me Again', 'Death Awaits Me', as well as a near half-hour extract from Andy Blade's book)

Live At Barbarella's 1977 CD (Anagram CD PUNK 137 October 2004) (Decent live show from the Barbarella's punk festival of 1977. "You know this is being recorded, don't you?" comes the question from the stage at the outset of 'Bedroom Fits'. Not going on their reaction, it doesn't. Sleevenotes by Eater's biggest fan, Paul Marko from the fine punk77 website. The bonus 'No Brains' remix by Pojmasta is ruddy scary too)

IMPORTANT COMPILATIONS:

Live at the Roxy LP (Harvest/EMI SHSP-4069 April 1977; 'I Don't Need It', 'Fifteen')

The Album, The Label LP (Label TLR LP 002 November 1977; 'Outside View', 'Point Of View', 'Typewriter Babies')

Ed Banger And The Nosebleeds

Ed Banger (aka Ed Garrity; vocals), Peter Crookes (bass), Iain Grey (guitar), Toby 'Romanov' Tolman (drums)

Once feared on the Manchester punk scene because of their predilection for settling scores personally, in tandem with their vocalist's openly confrontational approach to audiences, nowadays the NOSEBLEEDS, where they do merit a mention, are acknowledged principally as a finishing school for later post-punk talents. Former students include Morrissey, employed briefly as their singer, Cult

guitarist and Morrissey sidekick Billy Duffy and the hugely talented but career-blighted Vini Reilly, later of Factory house band the Durutti Column. But it's important to remember that Ed Banger himself, Ed Garrity, was a star in his own right. He was one of the select few to attend the Sex Pistols' first Lesser Free Trade Hall show, dragged there by his NME-reading friend Iain Grey, having gravitated from a childhood love of Slade and Bowie.

Their origins lay in Wythenshawe's Wild Ram, a hard-rocking, hard-rucking R&B/pub rock band. They shared the same formative influences, and to an extent outlook, of fellow Wythenshawe hardcases Slaughter And The Dogs. They actually played at the Dogs' celebrated Wythenshawe Forum show, introduced by Tony Wilson, but like the headliners quickly realised that the times were changing, once Garrity, Tolman and Crookes attended the Pistols' first show. As a result, they were "desperate" to get on the bill of the second Pistols show. "There was talk about getting the Buzzcocks out of the way, trying to find their address to go down and beat them up so they couldn't play," Garrity later conceded to David Nolan. "We was even going to wait outside on the night and do it, but we got talked out of it." In the event Garrity ended up backstage, looking after the beer. Having ventured out of the dressing room to take in the Pistols, he was struck squarely on the forehead with a beer bottle. "All the lads were coming in," he related in I Swear I Was There, "so I didn't want to seem soft. I'm there with blood pouring down my head, my mate Pete had been punched on the nose. Someone says, 'You're a right bloody mob, aren't you? Headbanger here and him with a nose bleed.' And the name sort of came about that night."

They only got it together when they were joined by guitarist Vini Reilly, son of a piano playing father, from Wythenshawe. He'd previously studied judo and had trials for Manchester City. His first musical endeavours were around local clubs with the flautist Gamma, billed as Reilly/Gamma, playing standards such as 'Jumping Jack Flash'. Reilly then joined the mixed race Lady with Vinni and Mike Faal (who were also deeply involved with Slaughter) and Donald Johnson (later A Certain Ratio's drummer). When Vinni Faal ended up managing three lads out of school who needed a guitar player, Eddie Garrity, Toby Toman and Pete Crookes, he put them together. "They were punk, naturally punk," Reilly told Mick Middles, "before I had heard of punk. They really were the wildest lads I had ever come across. Completely, utterly mental."

Reilly was a strange recruit in many respects: amid the carnage of their performances, here was a shy, somewhat fey youth, stricken by illnesses throughout his career, customarily mistaken for a girl, who periodically brought doctors notes to sessions saying he wasn't able to practice that week. It was a bizarre contrast with Garrity, famous for leaving stages to pour beer over the girlfriend of anyone who looked at him strange, and on one occasion physically assaulting Paul Morley at an Electric Circus date, pinning him behind a fruit machine after denouncing him from the stage. "I'll attack anyone, me, anyone who slags us off," he told Mick Middles later. "I won't stand for it."

They toured in a ramshackle second hand ambulance, before Vinni Faal persuaded Tosh Ryan to put up the money for a single on Rabid. "We taught Factory everything they ever knew," he later recalled. "They managed

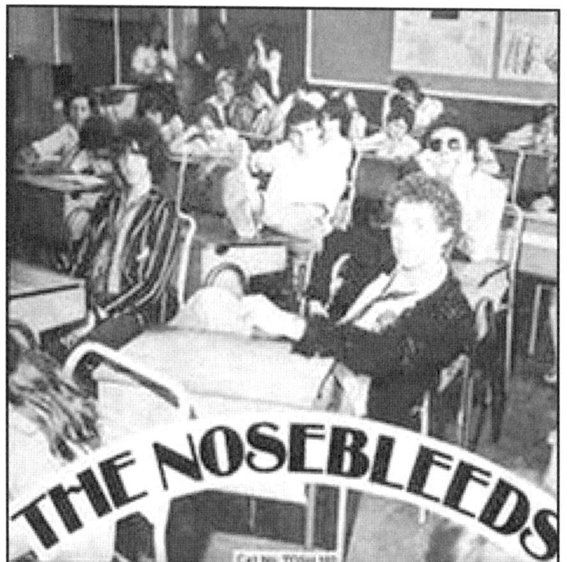

The sleeve of Ed Banger And The Nosebleeds' debut single, 'Ain't Bin To No Music School'.

the top five single, the marketing scams, the situationist enigma, the unplayable records, they even managed the ignominious bankruptcy!" They had half a day in a local eight-track and came up with 'Ain't Bin To No Music School', an agenda-setting piece of white collar rock'n'roll thuggery inspired by Sad Café's attitude to them when they played together at Chorlton's Oaks pub.

It should be pointed out that, despite the single's title, Reilly had taken two piano lessons a week for 14 years. A generally well liked single, albeit one not taken terribly seriously by the cognoscenti, it earned them a support to Sham 69 at the Roxy, at which Sid Vicious was in attendance. According to Mick Middles, both Rob Gretton and Vini Faal walked round the venue slapping people indiscriminately and telling them, "We're from Manchester. You take notice." Their set consisted of the two songs on the single played over and over again. As Vini Reilly later confirmed: "The audience went absolutely berserk, and consequently we were asked to play again and again, because that was what was required. But I would also do things like sit with my back to the audience and play a very melodic guitar piece, which was what I'd always been doing all my life anyway. And the punks were totally confused by this, and baffled and maybe hostile, but at least it was a reaction, and I thought that was valid."

After Garrity's departure the rest of the band continued as the Nosebleeds, recruiting future Cult guitarist Billy Duffy, who brought in local 'face' Morrissey, performing their first public show together on 15 April 1978 at Manchester Polytechnic. Duffy: "I went to see the Nosebleeds to ask if I could be their roadie… I went to their bassist's house and I played 'Ain't Been To No Music School' in the kitchen while this little Korgi dog ran around farting. He said, 'You're in', then asked me to recommend a singer, so I said Steven Morrissey. Morrissey and I used to buy New York Rocker and read about the Dolls and Ramones." But they only lasted a few weeks, playing a May support to Magazine at the Ritz, and a show headlining above Snyde, V2 and Joy Division, reviewed for the NME by Paul Morley, who was feeling more charitable now his nemesis had left the band. "The Nosebleeds re-surface boasting A Front Man With Charisma, always an advantage. Lead singer is now minor local legend Steve Morrisson (sic), who, in his own way, is at least aware that rock'n'roll is about magic, and inspiration."

By this time Duffy and Morrissey had collaborated on a number of new compositions, including 'I Get Nervous', 'Peppermint Heaven', 'The Living Jukebox', 'I Think I'm Ready For The Electric Chair'. There was also a cover of the Shangri-Las' 'Give Him A Great Big Kiss', further evidence of Morrissey's New York Dolls fixation. Yet none of these songs was ever recorded. The Nosebleeds fizzled out, with Tolman joining Ludus. Meanwhile, Ed Banger And His Group Therapy continued to tour, picking up the following review for their September 1978 show at Liverpool's Eric's: "Don't look now, but here comes old Ed Banger ("and his therapy group"), a slightly grizzled flower child who entertains with the same determination of Gary Glitter. Come what may, Ed's still game. You want industrial rock? Well, try 'I Like The Sound Of Breaking Bricks'… Actually I loved him."

Garrity's solo career started with the football-themed single, 'Kinnel Tommy', for Rabid in 1978, before a one-off single for Absurd Records under the name Eddie Fiction. By the end of 1979 he'd joined Slaughter And The Dogs in time for their Bite Back album. He then released another solo single, 'I've Just Had My Car Nicked', backed with 'Yer Sponge' and 'PC Plod', on his own Spiv Records in 1981. There was another single, 'Poor People' c/w 'Vicars In The Dark' for Cloud Nine in 1983. He disappeared without trace until 1991 and the Sound Of The Baskerville LP, combining new material with selections from his Nosebleeds/Slaughter days, and also did some stand-up comedy. He also recorded two sessions for Mark Radcliffe's Hit The North BBC Radio 5 Show. In 2000 he was reportedly working on new songs, as part of Leon, and reformed the Nosebleeds for a couple of one-off shows in 2001. He currently has another new group, a 70s glam band called Edwina's Rockschool, while in 2005 John Crumpton's 1977 documentary "The Rise And Fall Of The Nosebleeds" was re-released.

DISCOGRAPHY:

Ain't Bin to No Music School/Fascist Pigs 7-inch (Rabid Records TOSH 102 July 1977)
COMPILATIONS:
Streets LP (Beggars Banquet BEGA-1 1977; 'Ain't Bin To No Music School')
The Crap Stops Here LP (Rabid/Absurd LAST 1 1980; 'Ain't Bin To No Music School')

Rabid/TJM Punk Singles Collection CD (Receiver RRCD 227 1996; 'Ain't Bin To No Music School', 'Fascist Pigs')
1-2-3-4 A History Of Punk And New Wave 1976-1979 5-CD box set (MCA/Universal MCD 60066 1999; 'Ain't Bin To No Music School')

Epileptics

Colin Latter (vocals), Clive Griffiths (guitar), Derek Birkett (bass), Richard Coveney (drums)

E

The EPILEPTICS, who in their short life span managed to court controversy on an impressive scale, were formed in 1978 in Bishops Stortford, announcing themselves with a local graffiti campaign urging the youngsters of that parish to 'Smash Guitar Solos'. Steve Drewett, later of the Newtown Neurotics, actually played bass for them at their first show, at the local Triad venue in July, after Derek Birkett elected to go on holiday instead. It wasn't the first time they'd have to find a deputy. Stan Stammers, later of the Straps and Theatre Of Hate, would stand in for them at one point, before the band decided to retain Birkett out of loyalty. "Yeah, I do remember standing in for Derek at the first Epileptics show," Drewett remembers. "I think the Neurotics had done a couple of gigs by then, otherwise I wouldn't have had the nerve to stand on stage and play bass (I had never played bass before that night). That was what was so great about those days, the willingness to have a go at anything in front of an audience and see where it took you, a sort of punk jazz aesthetic."

The Epileptics grew to prominence by sharing a stage with Crass after they'd played the Triad on the 21 August 1978, and were immediately impressed by the group's unyielding political stance. A while later the bands played a show at the Basement in London's Covent Garden which only five people attended. So Crass played to an audience of the Epileptics and the Epileptics to an audience of Crass, thereby cementing the spirit of solidarity between the groups. Kev Biscoe (aka Kev Hunter), formerly of Darlex, replaced Griffiths as the band honed its set list and made his debut at the Railway Hotel in Bishops Stortford, which was coincidentally the first time they played their signature song 'Tube Disaster'.

The Epileptics were again billed to appear alongside Crass, as well as the Poison Girls, at a show at Bradford University on 18 January 1979. They didn't actually play, having broken down on the motorway ("that was the van breaking down," notes Hunter, "our own breakdowns came later"), though they did arrive at the venue after the show was finished. However, following a complaint by a member of the university's student union, the band was contacted by the British Epilepsy Association's senior regional officer. Take a bow, Miss A Aspinall. In comically pompous terms, she outlined her objections to the band's name. "It offends and labels thousands of your fellow countrymen when a group in the pop world assumes the title of 'the Epileptics', the implication being that this particular disability is something shallow, and one which lends itself to ill-considered jocularity. There would only be one justification for a pop group calling itself 'the Epileptics', and that would be if each member of that group did, in fact, have epilepsy." So the band, who had no intention of feigning disability, became Epi-X instead. In truth, their original name had been suggested, not by some barricade-storming anarchist, but by Colin Latter's mother.

In March 1979 they recorded their first demo at Romford's Speedway Studio, and even played a Melody Maker Rock Contest to much bemusement. "We'd never seen 'Tube Disaster' as anything other than an also-ran, we'd moved on," reckons Hunter. "It's funny that one of the earliest things that Colin and I put together somehow endured." The Epileptics and Flux's best remembered song "was just something I'd been pissing around with, that Colin said, 'that's good, I've got some lyrics for that.' But then years later, I heard the (pre-Joy Division) Warsaw demos, and it sounds very similar to a track of theirs called 'The Kill'. But I had no idea at the time, I'd never heard it! It was never a comment on 'vicarious living', as some people have said. Colin wrote it in the early days, just because he wanted to make something sound outrageous."

Local label Stortbeat then gave the group the chance to release their debut EP, recorded at Cambridge's Spaceward Studios in just eight hours. On the same day Crass offered them a deal to do a single. "What the hell Crass ever saw in the Epileptics, at first, we have absolutely no idea! The Epileptics were doing songs like 'I Wanna Give You A '69'. Crass obviously couldn't have heard the lyrics, but maybe they liked the attitude." (The Epileptics' problems with Stortbeat were subsequently recounted in detail on the sleeve of the re-release of the '1970s' EP, issued through Latter and Birkett's Spiderleg label. This featured re-recorded versions of the original EP with Penny Rimbaud of Crass sitting in on drums, due to the fact that Coveney "point-blank refused to do it", according to Hunter. "A day before we were due to record, he said he didn't want to do it. I was on the phone to him for half an hour, and no way could I change his mind. To this day, we don't know why. But we have our suspicions.")

The EP was eventually credited to the Licks, owing to pressure from Stortbeat. The decision to change name was made in a "moment of stupidity when we were just tossing names about the night before we had to sign the contract", according to Hunter. They were pressured into the switch due to Stortbeat's simmering doubts over the offence that Epileptics might cause. "We only did one gig as the Licks, before we thought, sod that for a name. I'd like to think we had better ideas during our career." As for the Stortbeat EP: "We didn't know what tracks we were going to do before we got there for the Stortbeat single. We ran through a set and they'd go, nah, not that one. We wanted to do one that we'd only ever played live once, called 'Can't Stand Sitting Down'. And it's bloody awful. It was our go at doing something funny. Thank Christ that never made the single, it would have been a nightmare. Yet Colin and I wanted to do it, so all credit to Stortbeat for getting us to do '1970's', which was always a bit of a crowd-pleaser."

The Epileptics also fell out with Derbyshire nouveau punks Anti-Pasti. The latter had heard one of the Epileptics' songs on a demo tape, and on hearing the band had broken up, decided to claim it as their own. Members of Anti-Pasti would later insist they had asked the group's 'manager' for permission so to do, in a letter to Sounds in January 1981. "Dear Spider Leghead, although Anti-Pasti have recorded the track two years too late, their ex-manager (Dave Direktor) gave our lead singer the lyrics and said it was alright to record it, as the Epi-X had split and would no longer be playing the number. All credit to Epi-X (Flux of Pink Indians) for writing a good number. Thanks for the photo and the publicity." Hunter remembers Dave Direktor – that was, unbelievably, his real name – very well. "He was brighter than all four of us put together, but we couldn't ever get him to shut up. One day, just for a laugh, to try to keep him occupied, I said, if I mixed up a pack of cards in a set order, how many variations would it take before you reassembled them in the correct original order. And about five minutes later he came back with a completely annotated formula."

But by December Hunter and Coveney had left permanently, leaving Birkett and Latter to persevere as Flux Of Pink Indians, one of the most inventive and enduring anarcho bands of the early-80s. A second Epileptics single, 'Last Bus To Debden', is a posthumous live recording from September 1979 which features one of the great songs of 80s anarcho punk, the aforementioned 'Tube Disaster', later re-recorded by Flux for their 'Neu Smell' EP.

Flux Of Pink Indians arose from Latter's interest in North American Indian culture (they were originally to be called Tribe Of Pink Indians, but Flux sounded "more exotic"). In an interview with Mick Sinclair in Sounds in 1981, they recalled their earlier incarnation: "The Epileptics were just four local people. When we started playing round London, we met people from there and later got a London-based drummer and two London guitarists." There was a summary of the situation with Stortbeat in that 1981 Sounds article. "Crass asked us to do a single or an album when we were still the Epileptics, back in September 1979. The first Epileptics single came out on the local Stortbeat label, with whom we had a two-year contract, and a letter saying we're free to do what we wanted to with Crass. The single went very well, the first local record to get anywhere and Stortbeat thought they were on to a good thing. It took two years to sort out the legal bits and in the end, Stortbeat went bankrupt and used us to pay off their debt to Spartan (a distribution company). We got our contract back then."

The whole episode caused divisions within the Epileptics camp over who was responsible for an illicit extended print run of the single on white labels, some of which came out on the Mirror Co imprint. A storm in a teacup? Nevertheless, it did create a bit of a furore and push the band's profile. "I'm amazed at the historical prominence the whole story has gained," notes Stortbeat expert Gordon Wilkins. But then, his experiences of the machinations of the music industry were evidently not lost on Birkett. He set up first Spiderleg with Latter to release Flux's records, then One Little Indian.

DISCOGRAPHY:

As the Licks:

1970s EP (Stortbeat Beat 8 1979)

1970s (Have Been Made In Hong Kong)/System Rejects/Hitler's Still A Nazi/War Crimes (re-recorded and reissued by Spiderleg as Spiderleg SDL 1 in 1981, credited to the Epileptics)

As the Epileptics:

Last Bus To Debden EP (Rough Trade/Spiderleg SDL 2 1981)

Target On My Back/What've You Got To Smile About/Tube Disaster/Two Years Too Late (features the legend "No thanx to Anti-Pasti" on the reverse...)

ARCHIVE RELEASES:

System Rejects CD (Overground OVER 57CD) (completist's dream, with liner notes.

Epileptics/Flux Of Pink Indians – Fits And Starts CD (Dr Strange 97 October 2003) (Remastered material featuring several demos, and the re-recorded version of their debut EP's '1970s', featuring Penny Rimbaud from Crass on drums)

COMPILATIONS:

Stortbeat: A Musical Collective double CD (Handsignal Recordings Handy 2 and Handy 2A 2004; '1970s', System Rejects/Hitler's Still A Nazi") (contrary to reports elsewhere, Colin Latter and Derek Birkett are not brothers. They have never been brothers, nor does either party, at this stage in their lives, anticipate becoming brothers in the future)

Excel

Stephen Smith (bass, lead vocals), Richard Taylor (lead guitar, keyboards, vocals), Alan Walsh (rhythm guitar, vocals), Stephen Gawtry (drums, vocals)

EXCEL was formed in 1976 when the two Stephens, along with keyboard player David Fahy and guitarist Paul Naylor, put the band together in their last year at Whitcliffe Mount Comprehensive in Cleckheaton, West Yorkshire. In 1977 Richard Taylor replaced Naylor, and when David Fahy bowed out the following year, in came Alan Walsh. The band played hundreds of gigs up and down the country, mostly doing covers, but gradually increasing the amount of original material, best described as 'pop-punk', as they progressed.

After many demos and residencies in Germany and the north of England, they eventually recorded and released an EP of four original tracks, under the title 'If It Rains'. Released on their own ARSS Records (an acronym for Alan, Richard, Stephen, Stephen), it prompted a fresh bout of gigs and interest from major labels including Polydor, Virgin, CBS and Arista. Eventually they opted to sign with Polydor, and moved down to London.

The result was a 45, 'What Went Wrong', backed by 'Junita'. There was a batch of gigs at London venues including the Windsor Castle and Hope And Anchor to promote it, and they also appeared on Granada's Get It Together, playing both sides of the single. However, as Gawtry acknowledges, "Moving to London was a bad move for the band – it was the beginning of the end. We should have stayed in Yorkshire and travelled down to London when we needed to."

Then there was the Pretenders tour that almost happened, at the end of 1979. "When 'Brass in Pocket' was number one in the charts, over 500 bands applied to be their support band. The final two bands in the running were Excel and UB40. Apparently, the idea was that the Pretenders would go see each band live and make a decision once they'd seen us both. However, while Pete Farndon came to check out one of our gigs at the Music Machine in Camden, the Campbell brothers from UB40 took Chrissie Hynde and James Honeyman-Scott out for dinner and came away with the tour. Of course, I'm not suggesting that Excel would have been as successful as UB40 had we got the tour, but it would have been a great experience to do a proper tour of major venues."

Later in 1980 they were invited to record four tracks for a Polydor compilation, Made In Britain, to promote the major's new signings, alongside the Invaders, Comsat Angels and

E

Early Polydor promotional photograph of Excel.

Protex. Excel's four tracks were produced by Pete Gage, of Vinegar Joe and Elkie Brooks fame, at Maison Rouge Studios in Fulham. "Looking back, that was the final nail in Excel's coffin," Gawtry concedes. "Pete was a good producer, but he didn't know what Excel were about. The raw energy that made the band exciting and great on stage was lost in over-production."

Before the album was released, a major falling-out resulted in Walsh, Taylor and Gawtry moving back to Yorkshire and replacing Smith with Tony Kelly on bass and vocals. The band returned to Germany for another residency and continued to gig prodigiously, but the contract with Polydor expired, they didn't take up their option, and eventually Excel ground to a halt. Stephen Smith continues to work in the music industry and has his own studio in Soho. Stephen Gawtry worked on Top Of The Pops as a camera assistant for many years, but now edits the magazine-catalogue for Watkins Books in London, the oldest and largest occult bookshop in the world. Sadly, Richard Taylor died in August 1999.

In 2002, a fan of the band, Steve Mitchell, contacted Gawtry and Smith and put together an Excel bootleg consisting of 12 tracks. Hopefully a more legitimate and comprehensive archive will be made available shortly.

DISCOGRAPHY:

If It Rains 7-inch EP (ARSS XL1 1979)
If It Rains/Rolling Home/She's One Of The Boys/Rock Show (1,000 copies)
What Went Wrong?/Junita 7-inch (Polydor POSP 110 1980)
IMPORTANT COMPILATION:
Made In Britain LP (Polydor 1980; 'Tonight In The Park', 'Rock Show', 'I Never Knew', 'Summer Of '42')
ARCHIVE RELEASES:
If It Rains LP (Low Down Kids LDK-LP3 2002) (vinyl only. aka the demos album)
Untitled LP (Low Down Kids LDK-LP3 2004) (vinyl only, same tracks both sides. Tracks taken from debut EP and Polydor single)

Exile

Stan Workman (guitar), Dougie Burns (drums), Robert Kirk (bass), Graham Scott (vocals, guitar)

One of the front-running Glaswegian punk outfits, formed in February 1977, EXILE was originally a straightforward rock band until the prevailing mood of punk insurgency swept them up. Indeed, they would later admit that they made their move because punk audiences "were the only ones interested in rock'n'roll". Scott had been a member of Free Flight, who began by tackling Rolling Stones covers

before gravitating to "Santana crap". It was disenchantment with his former band's direction that led to the formation of Exile. However, he had some task in persuading his new bandmates that "the new wave thing was where it was at", as he conceded in a later interview with Kingdom Come fanzine. If the transition was not an entirely natural one, you could 'see the join' on the cover of their debut EP, which revealed that half the band defiantly retained shoulder length hair.

Glasgow venues were wholly resistant to punk at this stage. Despite their best efforts, they managed only 14 gigs in the first nine months of their existence, including a support to Trapeze at Strathclyde University. Thereafter punk bands were banned from there too, though it didn't help that Scott slated the venue in an accompanying interview with a student documentary maker. Exile were also behind the Plain Sailing – A Boring Fanzine publication, and secured support slots to the Boomtown Rats, with whom they would establish something of a bond.

The Exiles made a national impact via their inclusion on Beggars' Streets compilation, shortly after releasing their debut four track EP on their own Boring Records. Recorded in just three hours and suffering awful sound balance, it nevertheless boasted a couple of notable early Glasgow punk nuggets. 'Jubilee 1977' was a self-evident attempt to write a Scottish version of 'God Save The Queen', while 'Fascist DJ' took as its specific target local DJ Tom Perrie. He'd done everything in his power to block punk and new wave reaching the airwaves and was similarly denounced in the Jolt's 'Mr Radio Man'.

There were offers of management and interest from Polydor and CBS but they declined these advances because "we were not ready". Instead they signed a deal with John Caulfield and Richard Jacabowski, who asked the band to give them a "commercial punk sound". The relationship ended in tears, and litigation. Caulfield helped them set up their own club, Gigi's, but then pulled the plug on the venture the day before its opening night. They were desperate to get down to London to air their wares but had to be happy with being the first new wave band to play Aberdeen. A second single, 'The Real People', followed for Charly in January 1978, following a one-off deal with the renowned blues imprint secured by Caulfield and Jacabowski. The three tracks, including their definitive 'Disaster Movie' previously extracted for the Streets compilation, had been recorded back in October 1977. But the single failed to up their profile and Exile were relegated to the status of Glasgow's forgotten men.

In May 1978 Kirk left the band, to be replaced, albeit briefly, by Paul Armour of the Cuban Heels, as the group began to write a new set of songs. By August he'd made way for Gavin Paterson, but the band was effectively over by the end of the year. Scott, Burns and Workman, alongside Frank Douglas on bass, regrouped briefly as Friction, recording one single, 'World In Crisis' c/w 'Hold On You' in 1980.

DISCOGRAPHY:

Don't Tax Me 7-inch EP (Boring BO1 August 1977)
Jubilee 1977/Hooked On You/Fascist DJ/Windmill (1,000 copies)
The Real People/Tomorrow Today/Disaster Movie 7-inch (Charly CYS 1033 January 1978)
COMPILATION:
Streets: Select Highlights From Independent British Labels LP (Beggars Banquet BEGA 1 November 1977; 'Disaster Movie')

Ex-Producers

Henry 'Sav' Savage (vocals), John Cullen (drums), Dee Moore (bass),
Tom 'TC' Condon (guitar)

The EX-PRODUCERS grew out of a band formed in 1978 by mates from the Twinbrook area of West Belfast. As former member Joe Donnelly remembers, "London seemed a million miles away and it might as well have been on another planet to a kid on the mean streets of 70s Belfast. But here we were at the start of something new, our time had come and for once we had our fingers on the pulse. So we dived in, determined to play our part and take our place in the Northern Ireland punk story and we started on the mission that would eventually become the Producers then the Ex-Producers.

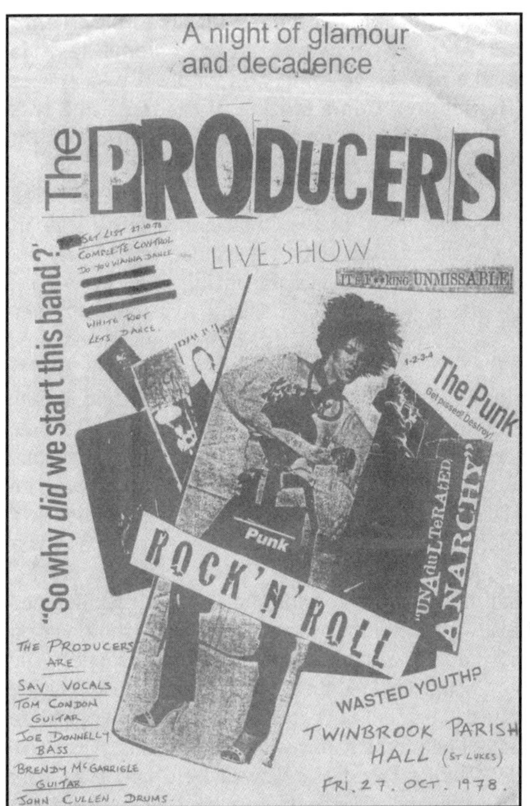

"In 1977 we put together our own strictly amateur version of a comedy punk band with crude humour called the Flamin' Dingleberries. There was nothing elitist, contrived or sophisticated about our vision of amateur punk. At that time we were fans and we had no message to preach, it was fun winding people up. We were armed with a set of near-the-knuckle self-penned classic tunes like 'Rats', 'Beat Me Daddy With The Shitehouse Door', 'Mammy I Don't Like My Meat'. There was also a reworked 'Is You Is Or Is You Ain't My Baby' from the Tom and Jerry cartoons, plus punked-up covers of 'Mull of Kintyre' and a lyrically risqué version of Ronnie Lane's 'How Come'."

Their limitations were obvious, yet a badge of honour. "We couldn't play well but some of us knew at least two of the required three chords and with the right attitude, enthusiasm and cheap guitars that was all you needed. The band was Joe Donnelly, John Cullen, Ray and Jim Maguire and Sandsy. We did a few impromptu acoustic appearances in the local youth club and al fresco on the club steps. In mid-1978, inspired by local heroes like Rudi (I had broken my wrist at a gig of theirs on 2 February 1978 going mental, they were brilliant live) we had dropped the now tiresome 'tee hee' comedy aspect. We managed to get a gig on a variety show in a local girls' secondary school in front of a bishop under our new moniker Blitz. How we got on the bill I don't know. We were a glorious shambles of noise and bad punk fashion sense, all badges, chains, rips, zips and graffiti. The crowd hated us as we butchered our way through a couple of Pistols songs ('Anarchy' and 'God Save The Queen') and managed to damage the newly laid stage floor and equipment belonging to the school in a frenzy of Who-like instrument destruction. It was hilarious. I was wearing my recently-purchased Destroy T-shirt which I had bought from Seditionaries on a trip to London with John Cullen back in late February to see a Sweet gig and we met the Damned who were chuffed to know they had fans in Belfast. It was my first and last time as a lead vocalist as I did my best Richard III back to the audience, crouching, Johnny Rotten impersonation. We had placed punk mates in the audience who threw stuff at us onstage. It was a great laugh, we trooped off to deafening silence. The Blitz logo was spray-painted by someone on the local school's rooftop water tank, where it was visible all over our estate. It lasted a hell of a lot longer than the band."

From this carnage evolved the Producers, titled after the Mel Brooks' film, which had been on the TV in the week of their first rehearsal. "We were still pretty basic musically, but much better than the Blitz era excuse for a group. But we had no idea what we were doing this was our first real attempt at playing in a band. We practised in a couple of halls around the Beechmount area of West Belfast and through time managed to get a set of rough and ready punk/new wave covers from the Clash, Ramones, Cars etc together. Our first gig was on 28th October 1978 in the Twinbrook parish hall playing during the intermission break for a C&W band, who didn't have a drum kit. We sent out for a loan of a kit from Seamy O'Neill (Bankrobbers) and set up the gear as the C&W band watched nervously as we had their amps at our mercy. Friends of ours brought along a reel to reel video camera, which was state of the art in 78 to film our debut performance. The gig went well and everyone in the hall had a good time and after seeing the video we were surprised how good we looked and sounded, we were on a real high. Unfortunately no-one had the foresight to buy the tape as home video was a thing of the future and we didn't have the cash to buy it anyway, it was very expensive. So the tape was wiped and reused, another bit of NI punk history gone for ever! A couple of months later I left the band as there weren't many gigs and I preferred to socialise with my punky pals rather than practise. My lack of commitment was causing friction so I went without being pushed and they hired and fired a couple of bass players to replace me before finally settling on Dee Moore a while later, though the band and I remained friends throughout. Brendy McGarrigal left the band shortly after me in mid-79."

The band improved and adopted the name the Ex-Producers, who made their recording debut by cutting tracks for a Downtown radio session in October 1979, featuring four originals – 'Loyalty', 'Newer Wave 1979', 'P-Check' and 'Hole In The Head'. The second of those was also recorded live for broadcast in a segment of the Something Else BBC programme broadcast in January 1980. Thereafter Savage split, and Cullen took over the vocals. They gigged regularly thereafter, cutting two songs, 'Behind The Door' and 'The System Is Here' for the Belfast compilation on Shock Rock Records, while Cullen would promote shows under the billing Future Legends alongside old friend Joe Donnelly. In 1981 they broadcast a live session for Radio Ulster but by 1982 the band had ground to a halt. It was the usual combination of bad luck and bad timing. They were due to be interviewed by the NME on the week the NUJ called a strike.

After leaving the Producers, Joe Donnelly initiated various bedroom practise bands and recorded a succession of demos. One of these, the Rays, also featuring Joe Carey (later of Stalag 17) have a number of very gritty, very basic raw demo tracks on the Northern Xposure 1, 2 and 3 bootleg compilations. He also promoted club nights in 1980/81 with Cullen (a throwback to their mid-70s youth club DJ days). He still writes for punk websites and zines etc. John Cullen is now better known as the local mid-morning radio and club DJ Johnny Hero and dabbles in artist management. He has also fronted his own glam rock tribute band Glam Slam/Ballroom Blitz for many years, which had Henry Cluney, post-SLF, as a member for a time. They released a single on Good Vibrations called 'The Leader' in the 90s. Brendy McGarrigal plays guitar in showbands. Dee Moore is a session bassist. Donnelly: "I'm not sure what Sav and the rest of the lads get up to in their spare time now, but we are all still punk fans and we all still show up at retro punk gigs every now and again." The Ex-Producers reunited in December 2004 for a few nostalgic comeback shows, supporting Shame Academy at the Belfast Empire.

COMPILATIONS:

Belfast LP (Shock Rock SLR 007 1980; 'The System Is Here', 'Behind The Door')

Fakes

Johnny McGuire (vocals), Marion 'Mairi' Ross (guitar), Jamzy (aka James McDonald; bass), Brian (drums)

Scotland's FAKES evolved out of the cheerily titled Cunts, who formed in Stirling in 1978. The latter managed to play one show before realising that their commercial prospects were likely to be somewhat constrained. The new line-up was cemented when Mairi, who was concurrently the girlfriend of Mike Scott of Another Pretty Face and later the Waterboys, arrived to replace their original lead guitarist (confusingly, also called Brian). Their early influences, according to ex-plumber Jamzy, were Skrewdriver, Johnny Moped, the Adverts and UK Subs.

F

The Fakes recorded their one and only single for Deep 2 in July 1979 at Cargo Studios in Rochdale. Johnny Briggs, aka Mike Baldwin of Coronation Street, had been in the studio just before them. The sessions came about after a recommendation to Deep 2 by Stuart Adamson, after the Fakes and Skids had played a show in Dunfermline together. Reviews were generally lukewarm, with Dave McCulloch noting the single's debt to Samuel Beckett and bemoaning its "naïve yowling of precocious nine-to-five grievances over a tin-bucket, would-be 'atmospheric' backing."

"For Scotland in the late-70s," reckons Jamzy, "the Fakes were a bit different, not out and out 1-2-3-4 – punk. There was a different sound and style, mostly because of Mairi's guitar style, and also the fact that we could not play that well anyway. It was 'get better as you go along' time. But for Stirling at that time, the Fakes started a lot off."

After the Fakes ended "We went in and out of other bands. Mairi moved to Edinburgh and got involved with one of the guys from the Waterboys. Brian was killed on his motorbike. I started a few guitar bands but then got into electronic music and now do Egebamyasi." The latter are staples of the old school acid house scene, having released over a dozen singles such as 'Pizzacid', 'Acidnation', 'Remont' and 'Store In A Cool Place' as well as a couple of albums.

DISCOGRAPHY:

Production/Look/Out 7-inch (Deep Cuts Deep 2 September 1979)

Fan Club

Dave MacDonald (vocals), Marc Storr-Hoggins (aka Mark Oggins; drums), Nick 'Sago' Sayer (guitar), Demetri Pete Smith (vocals, guitar), Paul Martin (bass)

Brighton punk 'n' roll group who never really capitalised on their strong local fanbase. They formed in 1978 after local legends Wrist Action and Hastings' Plastix collapsed. The first incarnation of FAN CLUB featured former Wrist Action interns Pete Smith, and two former members of Plastix, Hoggins and Sayer. McDonald was taken on as vocalist and Paul Martin took on bass duties. This line-up was responsible for Fan Club's sole release, the 'Avenue'/'Night Caller' 45 for M&S in 1978. Reviewing it, Danny Baker saluted it as "all round amateur dynamite".

Thereafter Sayer and Hoggins left to form the Kemptown Rockers. Paul Martin: "Essentially Fan Club was Dave McDonald and Pete Smith. Pete wrote good pop songs, some even great, some others were what would then have been called kitsch, perhaps. Dave as a singer could not hold a note, but he was a pretty good showman, and made a good front man in that capacity. He was originally Wrist Action's manager and that function suited him better, as he was an entrepreneur in the decade before that was fashionable. Although Nick Sayer and I were in Fan Club at the time the single was made, neither of us are on it. We were not allowed to be! Marc Storr-Hoggins played drums, only because Pete could not. He only did this reluctantly, as he wanted his friend Nick Sayer to play guitar as well. I think the reason for this was because Dave felt that if the record should become some kind of indie hit, then there would be no claims for royalties etc from anyone else but him and Pete. And to be fair, they did actually fund the recording and record pressing. That was the reason both Nick and Mark then went off to form the Kemptown Rockers. It reduced us to the level of hired hands, although we were not getting paid anything so were not even hired!"

Fan Club dabbled with other musicians but by the end of 1978 they had a settled line-up

Paul Martin's subsequent band the Molesters, live on stage at the Buccaneer in 1979. Paul is on the left

F

featuring Smith, Marc Passi (also formerly of Wrist Action and the Satellites), McDonald and new bass player Jon Sussams, formerly of Smeggy And The Cheesy Bits, who frequently supported Fan Club. Martin: "I played a few more gigs with them after Marc Passi joined on drums then left to form my own band Siren and then later in 1979 joined the revamped Molesters." Fan Club then arranged a Thursday night residency at the Alhambra, with the Chefs as their regular supports. These nights proved immensely popular and a focus for the emergent Brighton punk scene.

They set about recording demos of 'Cops & Crooks' and 'Moonbeam' in an effort to secure a new recording contract, but failed to attract any interest. Sadly, their most obvious route, hallowed Brighton punk label Attrix, was closed to them because of past differences between Attrix and their former label, M&S. They were also the source of some heated local controversy when newspaper writer John Wellington called them the "worst band in Brighton". A flurry of letters to the regional press ensued, including several allegedly written by band members under pseudonyms.

It all went pear shaped at a show at the Alhambra in April 1979, when Smith, having had his beloved guitar stolen a few days previously, refused to play with a substitute despite the venue being packed. Sussams quit in disgust. By the end of the summer the band was over. Passi, Smith and Turvey elected to continue working together again, briefly, as the Brite Tones. Martin: "Dave had the right business mind to have made something out of it in the 80s, he was definitely one of Thatcher's children, politically clueless but with a hungry business mind – and was ahead of the times then. Pete, I think, just went along with it. As a duo Smith and McDonald could, I am sure, have hustled something worthwhile for themselves eventually in music – a pity they didn't really." But Martin has reason to be grateful, too, to Dave McDonald. "One thing I should thank Dave McDonald for is that he signed the whole of Fan Club up to appear as extras in the Brighton filming of the film Quadrophenia. That was a great experience. If you watch the Brighton crowd scenes as the Mods swell up from the seafront, through Pool Valley towards Old Stein, chanting 'We are the Mods' – I can name nearly everyone in that crowd, as they were all Brighton musicians and band members."

Martin, who after the Molesters also played with Life Sized Models (who recorded "Have You Seen My Friend' for Vaultage 80) and Venus In Furs, wound up writing reviews for Shindig! magazine and the Sweet Floral Albion website. He contributed the following memories to the excellent Brighton Punk website. "I remember I was rehearsing in the Vault with Fan Club the first time the neo-Nazis tried to burn it down (unsuccessfully on that occasion!) So were Laughing Gass, if I remember rightly, and it was their singer who came along pounding on the door of our 'arch' shouting something we couldn't make out. We thought it was some yobs who'd got in and so armed ourselves with mic stands etc, gingerly opened the door and there was this guy yelling about a fire. We all got out and Nick Sayer wouldn't leave his amp behind. So having rescued our equipment from potentially burning to a frazzle, we watched rather alarmingly as a trickle of water turned into a small stream from the fireman's hose laying on the ground that was advancing towards our amplifiers!"

Having been 'there' from the outset, Martin seemed like a likely mark to dump a sweeping question on, especially given that he writes so widely (and eloquently) about other musical scenes. Was the Brighton punk scene of the late-70s really that special, or is it just a case of middle-aged nostalgics exaggerating the impact those days had? "I think Brighton was special at the time. In 1977 the main towns to the east and west of us, Eastbourne and Worthing, were still elephants' graveyards for the elderly. Everyone came to Brighton from the surrounding area (and beyond) to get something going. We have two universities, an art college and a bohemian kind of unemployed youth at the time. There is no way it could not have been a bit special. In 1978-9, pundits termed it the 'Brighton Beat'. This meant something and nothing. The Brighton groups tended towards a poppier sound than elsewhere perhaps. Probably only Wrist Action and Joby & The Hooligans really saw out the whole of 1977 as punk bands of any note locally. Most of the stuff on those Vaultage albums is pop and it has a local flavour to my ears. At the same time of course, we were all just trying to find our own voice in common with groups everywhere. We certainly had a lot of camaraderie in the beginning, sharing each other's equipment etc, then later on groups got more individualistic. You could go and see a live band seven nights a week somewhere in Brighton then, there were a lot of them and a lot of venues too."

As for punk's impending 30th anniversary: "Nostalgia and middle age are key elements of it, as they have been with every sub-cultural movement once its original exponents start to sag with age! It's strange when you think it was meant to be a slash and burn exercise, a scorched earth policy of taking no prisoners from the then complacent and jaded present. It wasn't meant to last, it was of its moment, a perfect situationist thing. No-one expected people on eBay to be offering hundreds of pounds for old ticket stubs of their favourite punk bands 30 years later or for middle aged ex-punkers to be playing on package tours out of season at Butlin's for Christ's sake! The problem today is that we live in a reinvented, highly stylised and fantasy version of the past. The present is so tackily furnished with Disney-esque versions of people's favourite past decades that you can't see the present properly. Of course, I write about the 60s and 70s music scenes myself, so I'm as guilty as anyone. But I like to think I do so as a form of public history and add more context to it at least. I'm now waiting for the 30th anniversary of the Oi! movement in a few years. That will be really sad!"

DISCOGRAPHY:

Avenue/Night Caller 7-inch (M&S SJP 791 1978) (500 copies) (Paul Martin: "There may be other recordings, we used to record rehearsals quite often in the Crypt, Dave had a suitcase full of cassette tapes at one time of various musical stuff, but who knows if they are still extant") (check out www.shindig-magazine.com and www.punkbrighton.co.uk for more on Fan Club/Paul Martin)

Fans

John Tye (vocals), Clive Smart (guitar, vocals), Len Gammon (bass, vocals), Steve Rickeby (drums)

Theatrical Exeter punk band who had origins in XS – both recorded studio sessions but neither managed to secure a vinyl release. Which is a shame, based on the evidence of the FANS' contribution to the 2002 Exeter compilation Year Zero. They were musically indebted to Television and the New York set, but lyrically, they seemed more concerned with science fiction and the fantastical. A fact, sage observers have noted, which is probably due to their large intake of local speciality, the magic mushroom.

Len Gammon: "XS was John Tye, Clive Smart and Steve Rickeby. Steve is about my age, about eight years older than the other two. I joined them and at that point we changed the name from XS to the Fans." Gammon was DJ at Exeter's first punk club, Catharsis at the

Labour Club in Clifton Road, alongside John Jacques, who "had a good reggae collection which we used as we took turns each week DJing." Gammon was also co-founder of Worthless Words (an alternative music fanzine) and a vital cog in Exeter's music community for several years. He subsequently established punk nights at Groucho's and Routes, also running The Building rehearsal space and arts co-op.

"The Fans really came from a desire to play original music," reckons Gammon. "However, because we played a lot in places like Cornwall, Plymouth, North Devon, Torquay and Somerset, we put a few other things in. We did a cover of Fats Domino's 'Ain't That A Shame', and a Yoko Ono song 'Move On Fast', and an Arthur Lee/Love cover, 'A House Is Not A Motel'. We didn't have enough material to play an hour and a half in a pub setting. The covers were very carefully picked, they were not standard punk covers. We weren't doing songs by the Clash or the Pistols, for example."

After the Fans broke up, Tye joined Pete Damo (aka Pete Smythe) of the Brakes in the Missing Chemicals. Tye and Smythe then formed the Music Of Life Orchestra after relocating to London, recording numerous ambient/trance singles, culminating in the release of the triple album Plastic Apple. Gammon too subsequently moved to London and worked with VOK (Voice Of Kenya). Recently, he discovered some old tapes. "We were doing these recordings as the Fans in early 79, at least a couple of years on from when we started. That was the other thing about us, by the time we had some money to do a single, we split up!"

COMPILATION:

Year Zero: The Exeter Punk Scene 1977-2000 CD (Boss Tuneage/Hometown Atrocities Home 08/Bostage 508 2003; 'Help Me To Think')

Fast Cars

Steve Murray (vocals), Tony Dyson (drums), Stuart Murray (bass), Craig Hilton (guitar)

The FAST CARS story is an illustrative one, because it says much about the contrast between musical quality and the perception of its value in a UK music industry still hidebound by fashion and credibility. While they get only the most fleeting mention in the annals of British punk rock and new wave history, if at all, they remain massively popular in other areas of the globe. Notably Japan, where they are routinely garlanded with billings such as 'Kings Of Powerpop' and 'The Best British Powerpop Band', which perhaps doesn't trip off the tongue quite as fluently. The plaudits eventually resulted in them playing Tokyo's Studio Jam Club in July 2001 and releasing a clutch of new records there, underwriting the resurrection of the band.

It's arguable that confusion over whether Fast Cars were mods, punks or, retrospectively, power-poppers, may have hindered their progress. "We seem to have been given all three labels," Stuart Murray confirmed to me. "This has happened over the last 25 years. At the time we were classed as a new wave band along with many others like the Undertones etc. I don't recall the term power pop back in the 70s although I do think it best describes our sound, as it is just that, powerful pop songs! As for the mod revivalists – that is probably because we played with the Jam, the Chords etc. We played with Dillinger, but we were never a reggae band! If you look at our old photos, we never had an image. We were just young lads that liked playing music, in particular our own songs, as we enjoyed being creative. I don't think looking back the Buzzcocks looked 'punk', but our ethos was the same, breaking away from the prog rock or manufactured pop that had gone before, and writing your own songs, not Chinn and Chapman etc. The deals were on small labels that cared about you as people and if they didn't make a lot of money, so what? It was all about having fun for us. Our early influences were the pop songs of the Who, the Beatles and Rolling Stones and latterly David Bowie, Marc Bolan, Slade etc, that's the era we grew up in."

They originally formed in Manchester in 1978 after Steve Murray had spent the previous year rehearsing with the Sirens. They played one show together at Pips in November before the other members of the band, Marc Riley, Craig Scanlon and Steve Hanley, elected to hook up with Mark E. Smith's Fall. Murray dusted himself down, and with his brother Stuart, drummer Tony Dyson and guitarist Haydn Jones, put together Fast Cars, titled after the

Buzzcocks song. The group made its debut, again at Pips, in February 1978. By the following month they had established a Saturday night residency at the Butcher's Arms in Pendlebury that lasted for seven months. By September another former school friend, Craig Hilton, had replaced Haydn Jones, meaning that the line-up was an almost exactly replica of their former school band, Piledriver.

They were one of the many bands of the time to rehearse at T J Davidson's, alongside Joy Division, the Buzzcocks, Fall and Slaughter And The Dogs, with whom they'd also gig regularly. There were also shows with the Rezillos, John Cooper Clarke and XTC, and they were supported by Mick Hucknall's Frantic Elevators at venues including the Band on the Wall. "Our favourites on the Manchester scene at the time were bands more like us, like the Smirks, the Freshies, the Distractions, etc. We never got the Fall or Joy Division etc, and we didn't get on with them also. As for the punk movement, the kids used to go to see live bands, it didn't really matter what you were as long as they liked the music. Punks, mods, and 'ordinary' teenagers came to our gigs, including the occasional biker. I don't recall any trouble." Their recorded debut came via the inclusion of two tracks on the 1979 A Manchester Collection album, which grew out of the Manchester Musicians Collective. "The collective was a good way of getting gigs, as they had bands on a regular basis and had a regular audience. People used to go there to see the latest up and coming bands. One of the organisers was Dick Witts. He got us a spot on Granada TV's What's On programme that he co-presented, so that alone was worth being in the collective for. Also, A Manchester Collection was put together by Steve Solomar, another one of the organisers of the collective, so it did have a bearing on our development."

Their appearance on What's On, hosted by Tony Wilson, saw them perform 'Images Of You'. They were due to release this as their debut single for TJM Records but fell out with owner Tony Davidson prior to its release. Shortly thereafter Steve Brotherdale (Warsaw, Panik, V2) stepped in to take over from Dyson on drums in May, but Dyson had returned by July. The following month they played Bury's Deeply Vale festival, a landmark event in the development of north west music which was later the subject of a major TV documentary.

Their debut single, 'The Kids Just Wanna Dance', which had been premiered at Deeply Vale, was recorded at Smiles Studios in Chorlton by owner and producer Steve Foley during August 1979. Released in October on Bob Jefferson's Streets Ahead Records, which grew out of his Altrincham record shop, it was played regularly by both John Peel and Peter Powell on his daytime Radio 1 show. They supported the Jam at Manchester's Apollo Theatre in November 1980 and were almost signed by their A&R man Dennis Munday, who had been impressed by the single. "Dennis Munday invited us down to London to make some demos. Paul Weller heard us and invited us to play a guest spot at the Apollo Theatre as they were playing there in a few weeks. But Tony (Dyson) refused to do it and left, that's when we got Pete Bates of the Two Tone Pinks. He played on the Polydor tapes. We did four songs over two days and Dennis was pleased with them, but the money men didn't want to spend any more on our type of band as they had the Chords and the Jam and the music scene was starting to change. It was now late 1980 and bands like Spandau Ballet and Duran Duran were starting on the London scene."

The Jam support turned out to be their penultimate show and they broke up when the record contracts failed to materialise. Their final stand came in November at the Portland when Hilton had his guitar stolen and Bates walked out of the band, according to Stuart Murray because he was "more interested in shagging than playing". Afterwards, "we couldn't be bothered auditioning more drummers," he admits. The band folded. "We had run out of time. New wave had really started in 1976 so it was time for a change. Although Buzzcocks made it at the time, Manchester was not really the place to be, that happened later with The Smiths et al. In hindsight we should have quit our jobs and gone to London, but we did have jobs, which was rare in those days, and none of us were prepared to take a chance."

That was it, until they reformed for a one-off show with the Salford Jets in 1996, with interest prompted by 'The Kids Just Wanna Dance's inclusion on the Back To Front 4 sampler two years previously. Shortly thereafter they became aware of the ridiculous prices being generated on auction sites for their debut single, and the rekindling of interest in the era. It led to them signing with Detour Records and releasing a single, 'Everyday I Make Another

Mistake', and album, Coming... Ready or Not! in August 2001. Two further singles were released in Japan in 2002 on 1977 Records, 'Here We Are Today' and 'Turn On The Radio', the former dating from 1980. They played the 2002 Holidays In The Sun festival and have remained active ever since.

DISCOGRAPHY:

The Kids Just Wanna Dance/You're So Funny 7-inch (Streets Ahead SA 3 October 1979) (re-released in 2002 on 1977 Records Japan, 500 copies, then again in 2004 on Last Year's Youth Records)

Everyday I Make Another Mistake/I'm All Right 7-inch (Detour DR075 June 2001) (1,000 copies only)

Coming... Ready Or Not LP (Detour DRLP034 August 2001) (sleevenotes by Mark 'Lard' Riley, former Silos/Fall member)

Turn On The Radio/Marching As To War 7-inch (1977 Records Japan 2002) (recorded live in Japan 2001)

Here We Are Today (2002 version)/Way Of The World 7-inch (1977 Records Japan 2002)

Best Friend/Here We Are Today (1980 version) 7-inch (Detour DR078 May 2004)

IMPORTANT COMPILATIONS:

A Manchester Collection LP (Object Records OBJ 003 1979; 'Why', 'What Can I Do?')

Fatal Dose

Tony Trouble (aka Tony Gregson; lead vocals and 'scratchy guitar'), Johnny Ace (aka John Rendle; lead guitar), Paul Weston (bass), Maggot (aka Maggie Simpson; drums), later joined by O.B. Lee (aka Owen Lee; alto saxophone)

Formed in the Isle of Wight in the spring of 1979, FATAL DOSE were a precursor to Looney Tunes, who took shape in 1982. "One of the band's major attractions," Gregson told me, "was Maggot, our 17-year-old female drummer. Lechers used to come to our gigs just to watch her not inconsiderable breasts bounce as she pounded the skins." In terms of music, "we were pretty dire," he admits. "But weren't most bands in those days? None of us had ever played in bands before. Bassist Paul was so nervous he tended to play with his back to the audience."

Their very first show came under the headline Rock Against Thatcher, which was reviewed in a local fanzine. "Fatal Dose played long pieces with frenzied tribal drumming. They played three encores and went well over their allotted time much to the annoyance of the other bands." And they would continue to annoy. "We played few paid gigs and when we did manage to get one they rarely invited us back, partially because we were too offensive and partially because they didn't like the crowd of weirdos that we attracted. But the local charities loved us because we'd do most benefit and charity gigs just to get a chance to play. Our performances often degenerated into a kind of free-form musical primal scream where it seemed that everyone was off on their own trip and it didn't matter too much if we were playing in the same key as long as the rhythm was there to keep the machine rolling along. And I'd be yelling and speaking in tongues and pouring beer on those punks who dared to gob on me and eventually the song would fall back into a recognisable form with verses and chorus. I think people liked to see if we could pull it together or if we would just fall apart completely, there was a kind of 'will they or won't they' thing going on... a bit of danger. Songs were rarely performed the same twice. That was boring, anyway, we weren't that good!"

Some of the local press of the time confirms Gregson's take on Fatal Dose's live appeal. "The onstage antics of Fatal Dose were a revelation, particularly the boundless energy and enthusiasm of lead vocalist Tony Trouble, complete with lurex tights. They seem to have the current following. The minute they stepped on to the stage, dozens of fans swarmed on to the floor in front of the band. Their 'electric cabaret' features all original numbers. The most popular being 'I'm Not Right In The Head' and 'I Just Wanna be Frank (Sinatra)'. Tony, who reminded me of a young man's Max Wall, told me 'Music is not the primary thing in this band. It's only a part of it. Entertaining is our main aim.'"

Gregson remembers the show well. "I was being interviewed by a middle-aged guy while eating handfuls of magic mushrooms. The boundless energy came from the amphetamine sulphate. We were a drug-fuelled bunch of wierdos that didn't really fit into the 'ever so serious' punk/thrash scene of the time. The music was kinda punky psychedelic reggaeish. I like to think that we had a lot to do with psychedelicizing the punks. We would hand out mushrooms at gigs, it was hilarious. I once watched a six-foot spikey-bleached haired guy dancing round and around a fixed point on the dance floor. When I asked him what he was doing, he told me that he didn't want to step on the tortoise. We found that we were more likely to get a positive audience reaction if we drugged them."

Sadly, Fatal Dose never got to commit any of their set to posterity, which included such epic songs as 'He Who Lives By The Train Will Die By The Train' (about commuting), 'The Ripper' (Peter Sutcliffe had recently been 'banged up' in an Isle Of Wight prison), 'Those Old Barbiturates', 'The Fallout Waltz', 'You're So Normal', 'Johnny (Wants to Be a Pop Star)', 'Bloody Mary' (about deviant sexual practices), 'The 1st Freedom' ("you better button your lip 'cos censorship is just the tip of control") etc. Gregson, Simpson and Lee would all regroup thereafter in Loony Tunes.

Fatal Microbes

Honey Bane (aka Donna Boylan; vocals), Pete Fender (guitar), Scotty Boy Barker (bass), Gem Stone (drums)

While Talcy Malcy was pimping 14-year-olds in various states of undress to the glossy pop mags with Bow Wow Wow – in a manner that, frankly, could kindly be described as ethically dubious – the emergence of the similarly aged Donna Boylan, then residing in a home for wayward teenagers, was a more authentic example of young women using punk to articulate their condition. But, as Scotty Barker points out, the story wasn't that straightforward.

"After years of playing and forming local one-off bands I heard from a mate that a real punk band had moved into Epping and went along to a big house on Bell Common called Burleigh House and introduced myself to the Poison Girls. The line-up was complete but Sue the bassist was in the process of leaving and I was asked if I would like to join. I did and had a lot of fun with these very creative people. At the same time I was jamming with Dan (Pete Fender) the son of Francis (aka Vi Subversa). His style was a lot more rock-inspired. Unlike the Poisons, who, being new to performing music, had more of a grounding in performance art and fringe theatre and had a more burlesque element to their music. Dan and I would jam for hours and even though he referred to me as a fucking 'rippy' (hippy) we messed about with my Gong, Jefferson Airplane, Doors and psychedelic-inspired shit and his raw garage punk shit. About this time a drinking buddy of mine, Dave Parsons, who worked for the probation service, told me of a girl in care at St Charles who was giving the staff there a hard time, cos she had a shitload of creativity and no outlet for it. So she was getting destructive to herself as well as others and he asked if we (the Poison Girls) would look at some lyrics she had written and put it to music. Myself with Dan and various Poisons got together one evening and bashed out a quick, uninspiring tune to her words and gave Dave a tape to try to placate his young charge."

However, an indication that they weren't dealing with some meek, diffident soul was confirmed by return of post. "Within days I had a letter from this young 'un with stinging criticism of our efforts. All that she said was true, the tune was crap, the singing (mine) was even worse and overall she said it was the worst piece of shit she had ever heard. However, she gave her own suggestions as to how best to do the song, and we then knew that we were dealing with someone who had a vision of what she wanted and how to do it, and we crawled away with our tails between our legs. Soon after Dave bowed to intense pressure and after a lot of dealings with the Home Office and the law was able to get a limited release of this bothersome girl to visit the band and speak to us face to face. Enter Honey Bane (aka Donna Harrison and other names; too many to list). She was young, pretty and very tough, but was so full of creative energy it seemed like a tornado had been let loose."

The meetings became more regular. "As time went on the authorities relaxed and we were able to get down to making some music for her words. The first song we did was 'Locked Up Life', basically what she felt about her situation in St Charles. She was not easily pleased, and Dan and myself worked very hard to try and get the sound she wanted. At this time Dan, Gary (Poison's drummer) and myself were just trying to interpret her stuff for her, with no idea or plan. Then Francis suggested we record some of this stuff as she thought it was worth others hearing it. We arranged an evening visit and hung a small cassette recorder in the middle of the room and made a very primitive demo. It sounded just as you would expect, muddy, cloudy, distant, distorted, shite, but we liked it, and so, it seems, did Small Wonder. They agreed to do a single in conjunction with the newly-formed Xntrix Records."

The news that a recording was in the offing helped create even more hurdles for the prospective collaboration. "After a lot of big hassles with Donna, St Charles, and it seemed the whole world, we finally got to Spaceward Studios in Cambridge and attempted to get some tracks down. We had decided to do a song called 'Violence Grows' that we thought was relevant both nationally and to our own situation, i.e. Donna was not adverse to a bit of strong arm tactics when it suited her. 'Beautiful Pictures' included the line Pepsi Cola (for some reason we decided not to sing Coca-Cola, the original words, cos we thought they would give us trouble) and 'Cry Baby', a song about softies. The line-up was now Honey Bane vocals, Pete Fender, guitar and backing vocals, Gem Stone (Dan's sister, Gemma) drums and myself on bass and 'cat strangling' backing vocals. I managed to sneak in a bit of a hippy Doors' influence into 'Violence Grows' (listen to 'When The Music's Over'). It was a lot of fun but nerve-wracking, as it was our first time in a studio and you must remember that apart from myself, an old fart of 23, the other members of the band were under 16 years old. If you listen to the end of 'Cry Baby', or it may be 'Beautiful Pictures', you can hear Dan start to have a go at his sister for changing the on beat to an off beat or something."

In the end, though, the band was pleased enough with the results, which were pressed on a 12-inch EP. "We got some very positive reviews including single of the week in one of the music papers. Then the trouble started. First the band split, then got back together again, and then split etc. Then the music press could not tear itself away from Donna's ample cleavage and a bunch of other musicians got interested in Donna i.e. Jimmy Pursey of Sham 69 then UK Subs singer Charlie Harper and the geezer from the Skids, Ricky Jobson."

That didn't escape the attention of the police and the authorities, either. "There was this cat and mouse game with Donna turning up at Burleigh House. After an hour or so of either pure sweetness and joy or a raging slagging off, she would disappear into the night and we were then treated to a visit from the police or other government heavy, demanding to know where Donna was. This was most unwelcome. As you know, even punks indulge in herbal and chemical recreation and having the fuzz call round was not conducive to a good time. So Donna became a bit persona non grata during this part of the story. In the meantime the record was doing well and the first pressing of 5,000 12-inchers sold out and was repressed in 7-inch format and certain people said that we should capitalise on all the press coverage and do some gigs. As you can imagine, this was easier said than done with Donna on the run and not a small amount of infighting going on within the band. Also, Burleigh House was basically supposed to be part of a London University course for Life Studies i.e. encounter groups, meditation, and a whole bunch of hippy type shit. It became important that Donna give herself up soon-ish. I am not sure what was done to placate the heavies, but suddenly the sky cleared and a gig was arranged at Epping Hall, supporting Black Uhuru, I think."

Scotty doesn't remember much about that gig, apart from it being a 'musical disaster'. "But this made it a punk triumph! I think about this time egos reared their head and that was basically the end of the Fatal Microbes. Dan and myself carried on with the Poisons. Gary continued as the Convulsions but this was just because we loved playing and was not part of any 'let's get famous' plan."

And that was the end of the Fatal Microbes story – almost. "Some time later I got a call from John Loder, the affable boss of Southern Studios. He said that Donna (who had been missing for some time by now and only turned up in the papers once in a while) wanted me to play bass on her solo single and I would even get some dosh for it. I duly turned up at the studio to be told that Donna would be late as she was in Scotland and would be flying down to London to do the session. This gave me some time to bullshit my way around the fact that this plodding bassist was totally out of his league amongst these studio pros. As it turned out, they were a great bunch of guys and gave me a lot of encouragement and probably re-recorded my bass bit as soon as I left, who knows? Anyway, Donna turned up and I could see straight away that she had been moving in different circles than before and had the air of a seasoned muso about her. We did the session without a lot of messing about. I got my dosh (not a lot) and left. I think the single got in the charts around the 50 mark. Apart from one night when a bedraggled and rather sick Donna turned up in Epping for a chat, that is the last I heard from her. I believe she finally got her rage out of her system and did some theatre and film work and is still in rock'n'roll and I wish her luck. As for the rest of the band, Gemma got on with her school, Dan kept in music (joining Rubella Ballet and Omega Tribe) and is still giving it some today, and I myself joined the Sods in Harlow for a while and am now playing bass for Corcobado. They're a Spanish band led by singer and writer Javier Cacobado." Donna spent some time as a member of rock band Dog's Tooth Violet in the 90s. When last sighted, the former Miss Honey Bane was thought to have settled down in America and married a pilot. No, she has not become a porn star, as some rumours have suggested. Although if you have evidence to the contrary, I'm quite prepared to spend a weekend or so sifting through the footage in the name of the bigger truth. Nah, lewdness aside, I can confirm that Ms Bane is recording again.

DISCOGRAPHY:

Fatal Microbes Meet The Poison Girls 12-inch EP (Small Wonder WEENY 3 1979)
Violence Grows/Beautiful Pictures
Violence Grows/Beautiful Pictures/Cry Baby 7-inch (Small Wonder SMALL 20 1979)
COMPILATIONS:
Small Wonder Punk Singles Collection Vol. 1 CD (Anagram CDPUNK 29 1994; 'Violence Grows')
Small Wonder Punk Singles Collection Vol. 2 CD (Anagram CDPUNK 29 1994; 'Beautiful Pictures')

Favourites

Darryl Hunt (vocals), Kevin Green (bass), Duncan Kerr (guitar), Keith Gotheridge (drums), Tony Berrington (guitar)

From Nottingham, the FAVOURITES recorded their debut single at Spaceward Studios in Cambridge on the night that Margaret Thatcher was elected. Yes, it is a cover of Abba's 'SOS', but it features some amazing textural guitar flushes, convincing you it's a lo-fi gem and then mixing in all the barre chord bluster that you'd associate with a band like the Boys, including a fabulous little Morse Code guitar run. Annie Nightingale made it her single of the week. The second single, a cover of the Wasps' 'Angelica', arrived in a cover that was a delightful pastiche of Blondie's Eat To The Beat album.

Hunt, Kerr and Gotheridge formed the Favourites after Plummet Airlines ceased operations at the start of 1978. "The band folded," Gotheridge told me, "which left Darryl, Duncan and myself band-less. Kevin and Tony were in a local band, called the G.T.'s. They had also folded, so the two bands joined. That's the line-up that recorded 'S.O.S.' and other stuff. However, Kevin and Tony wanted their old mate from the G.T.'s in on drums (Paul Betts) so I was ousted." "We maybe should have been stronger and stuck with Keith," reckons Hunt. "We felt uncomfortable about all that."

They played regularly at the Imperial on St James' Street in Nottingham before moving to London. But the move didn't work out. "It worked in Nottingham, but it didn't work in London. Once we came down, everybody got jobs, and it became a bit disparate. In Nottingham everyone stayed together. But you don't in London. When the second single didn't happen, we didn't really get the album going. We never got a buzz going from doing supports. Early on we played with the Rich Kids, several times with the Only Ones, and so on, but it didn't really do us any good. The second single should probably have been an original. With 'S.O.S.' nobody had done something like that. These were in the days when Abba was still unhip. And we did a nice version." Duncan Kerr considers it "an odd musical period, coming soon after punk had shaken things up. I think some of it sounds contrived but lively. Our two managers wanted to work on image/hype and style rather than any particular musical value (which was fine but superficial), although a few of the songs are OK."

Paul Betts would eventually join Alan Fearn of Zoot Alors in his band Blue Train, while Kevin Green played in a series of blues bands, notably Out Of The Blue. Hunt became part of the thriving King's Cross squat scene in London. He was a member of the 'doo wop punk band'

The Favourites attempt moody 'behind bars' promo shoot but the roundabout from a children's playground is clearly visible in the background.

the Lemons before hooking up once again with his art school pal Dave Scott (ex-Bank Of Dresden, Spizz Energi etc) to put together Baby Lotion. He and Scott then worked with Cait O'Riordan in Pride Of The Cross before eventually gravitating to the Pogues. He is now working on his solo project, Bish, and is still an active member of the Pogues. Gotheridge joined doo wop band Darts with whom he and Kerr occasionally play to this day (Kerr: "about once a year with as many of the original members as are still available or alive"). Gotheridge works in IT. Berrington went on to play with Bill Hurley (of the Inmates) and currently Damned support artistes Girls On Top. Kerr is currently the general manager of Reckless Records in Soho. After the Favourites he played with a number of bands, including rockabilly outfit Rob And The Rustlers, joining Darts in 1981. He worked with them through the 80s while concurrently performing with western swing band the Magnificent Seven, the jive/R&B band the Sitting Ducks and Latin jazz band Easy Money. He then reunited with Richard Booth of the Plummets at the end of the decade in honky-tonk band Audio Murphy. He now works with Nottingham singer-songwriter Michael Proudfoot and, again alongside Booth, performs in another band with Man bass player Ken Whaley.

DISCOGRAPHY:

SOS/Favourite Shoes 7-inch (4 Play FOUR-002 1979)
Angelica/Cold 7-inch (4 Play FOUR-003 1979)
ARCHIVE RELEASE:
The Favourites SOS LP (Low Down Kids LDK LP4 2002)

Fire Exit

Gerry Attrick (aka Gerry Rodden; vocals), Billy Holland (bass), Doggie Maxwell (drums), Brian Kerr (guitar)

Glasgow's FIRE EXIT released one of the great, lost punk singles of the late-70s, 'Timewall', before reactivating in the 21st Century and being one of the revelation acts at subsequent HITS and Wasted festivals.

Songwriters Rodden and Kerr formed the band in December 1977 following a hefty drinking session. The name was appropriated from the nearest visible sign, or at least the first one that they could focus on. Once the decision was made, Rodden was able to pull out a book of lyrics that he'd been working on and with Kerr adding his Telecaster to the mix, and

12 songs were written in a single night. Rodden was able to draw on his experience with the Invaders, the band he'd put together which had lasted about six months in 1976, and the Pencils. As leader of the latter he'd booked a gig at Paisley College Of Technology's Christmas Ball, alongside the Heavy Metal Kids. That led to him being invited to book further shows, and led to the famed gig where the Pencils appeared alongside the Nu-Sonics, the Subhumans and Rev Volting And The Backstabbers. The gig, which ended in a riot after Big Frank from Bearsden's The Shock destroyed the venue's piano and Rev Volting of the Backstabbers let off all the fire extinguishers, became the subject of a news item on local TV. However, eventually Rodden became frustrated with the Pencils' lack of ambition – he wanted to play further outside Glasgow – and he left the band. They did record one of his songs, 'Radio Mania', for a Paisley 7-inch EP later, under the name the Sneex, "but the fuckers didn't give me a mention".

With the addition of Billy Holland on bass and drummer Doggie Maxwell ("he looked like a poodle with his fuckin' permed hair") Fire Exit's initial line-up was set. Practice sessions were convened in Renfrewshire and Paisley, before gigs at all the major Glasgow venues (Burns Howff, Amphoria, the Mars Bar). The decision was taken to cut a single in London, as they couldn't find suitable premises in Glasgow. So, using their connections with capital-based ex-pat Glaswegians Alex Fergusson (who'd originally found the Invaders a rehearsal space) and Sandy Robertson, as well as Charlie Harper of the UK Subs, they travelled down to London. They got in touch with Scritti Politti who told them all about putting together a DIY single. "We went to see them and spent some time with the guys, they were great. They helped us shitloads." They then set about playing London dates with new drummer Andy ("We never did get his second name. We just called him "wee fuckin' Andy"), while spending nine months living in the back of their transit van. These included a date at the Ally Pally in London supporting the Angelic Upstarts and Rodden's all-time hero, Alex Harvey.

Eventually Pat Collier of the Vibrators got them in at his studio in Waterloo in August 1979 and helped them produce and engineer 'Timewall'. They released it on their own label, Timebomb Explosions Records, and saw it quickly sell out of its print run of 2,500 copies, principally due to support from John Peel. On the back of his support and good reviews they signed to Decca Records, which proved to be a disaster. The label was entering its death throes and precisely nothing happened. After a celebratory gig with the Poison Girls and Fatal Microbes at Stonehenge, Rodden then returned to Glasgow to set up a tour. When he retraced his steps back to London, the band's rhythm section had done a bunk. Fire Exit stuttered on but was effectively over from this point.

But both Kerr and Rodden stayed committed to music. In 1985 Kerr began working with Captain Sensible while Rodden formed Action Men and then The Serpents Of Love (one single, 'Sailors Cry' and an appearance on The Power Of Scotland LP) with his brother Billy and later UK Subs guitarist Alan Campbell. He also kept Fire Exit going as a live concern in some form or other during this period, though they didn't record. Eventually the two principals got back in touch and in 2001 reformed to play Holidays In The Sun at Morecambe. The band has kept going ever since. The line-up was augmented in 2004 with Doogie (ex-Bladdered and Clash tribute band Combat Rock) joining on bass in time for that year's Wasted Festival and Joe Jaconelli of the Zips joining on drums. They've now put together a new CD, We're Just Punks.

DISCOGRAPHY:

Timewall/Talkin' About Myself 7-inch (Timebomb Explosions TBE 1 September 1979) (the 'Timewall' single has been compiled on bootlegs several times, including Killed By Death 6 and 7, Bloodstains Over The UK 4 etc. Also reissued on CD, TBE CD 01, in 2001)

10 Wee Smashers From Fire Exit CD (Timebomb Explosions TBE CD 02 2001) (10 tracks, 100 copies. Full title: 10 Wee Smashers From Fire Exit Enjoy Its (sic) Your Fuckin Last (well maybe). This is a live rehearsal which the band admits is "very poor quality" that was given out free to punters at gigs in Glasgow and Morecambe in 2001)

We're Just Punks CD (Timebomb Explosions TBE CD 04 2004) (11 tracks, 5,000 copies. Recommended – includes covers of the Boys' 'First Time', the Vibrators' 'Whips 'n' Furs' and Del Shannon's 'Runaway', plus new versions of 'Timewall' and 'Talkin' About Myself' plus six other originals)

Live At Wasted 2004 CD (Timebomb Explosions 2005) (13 tracks documenting their appearance at the festival. There is also an accompanying DVD)

Patrik Fitzgerald

Naturally enough, John Cooper Clarke is considered the definitive punk versemeister, but acoustic troubadour PATRIK FITZGERALD deserves a little recognition too. He may not have had quite the mystique one assumes when you surround yourself with French existentialist poetry and class-A drugs, but occasionally Fitzgerald captured the whole ethos of punk. For evidence see his most enduring 'hit', 'Safety Pin Stuck In My Heart', or the more reflective 'Make It Safe' ('Come and buy your punk in Woolworth's, Bondage trousers £12...'). And with his distinctive appearance – badge-encrusted blazer and red drainpipes – he was visually as well as aesthetically diverting in an era of leather jackets and power chords. Fitzgerald: "My favourite story about not looking the part is when I was in Leytonstone, probably in about 1978 or 1979. A couple of 16-year-old guys were walking along behind me through a block of flats and they didn't know what to make of me, they were in the usual leather and bondage uniform. They came up and spoke to me and asked me if I liked Adam And The Ants, and I said no. They walked away and I heard one of them say to the other: 'See, I told you he wasn't a punk.'"

F

Fitzgerald was born in London in 1956 of Irish immigrant stock, and grew up in the East End. He shared his enthusiasm for music with his cousin Bobby and his sister. "Bobby liked American stuff. My sister liked the Beatles, the Monkees, Tamla Motown and the Herd. I liked people like the Animals, the Rolling Stones, the Zombies, the Yardbirds and the Kinks. My sister and I went to see the Beatles when we were nine. I impersonated Mick Jagger on trains and wrote my own versions of pop songs of the day when I was 11, and escaped into music from the age of about 15. My sister introduced me to reggae and my school friends and I collected elitist reggae stuff from the age of about 15 from market stalls in Petticoat Lane. By 16, I had arrived at people like the Doors, Roxy Music and David Bowie. Later I liked Cockney Rebel and Sparks."

After attending school in Forest Gate his six O-levels secured an office job while he continued to teach himself acoustic guitar. Self-compositions including 'Safety Pin' and 'Backstreet Boys' were busked in the local underpass. "They were not my first songs, but they were probably the first of my songs that I performed live. My songs prior to punk were in the same vein, however, examples would have been 'Amateur', which was in the same vein as 'One Chord Wonders' by the Adverts, and 'Don't Sit Down', which was about people planting bombs under cinema seats." He'd offered his services to David Bowie manager Ken Pitt in 1975, though understandably, Pitt insisted that Bowie remain his priority artist and declined the invitation to steer the cheeky mongrel's career. He did, however, put him in touch with Noel Gay of Noel Gay Music, though he too, bizarrely, passed on compositions such as 'No Fun Football'.

1976 brought an audition for London SS with Mick Jones and Tony James, but they too passed. Instead he did some acting for a community theatre group. "I joined the Soapbox Theatre in Stratford, which was where Benjamin Zephaniah and I later crossed paths. It was a commune and I acted and wrote songs and worked as a social worker in their advice centre." Later, he would co-write a play, Babytalk, with TV director Tim Fywell. "Tim often compared my stuff to Roy Harper. Not the obvious comparison but from the same lineage of – in which box does this one belong?" There were also myriad musical collaborations. "We had a knockabout group called the Failed Operations (by then, the third group that I had been involved in). We were terrible, but had fun. My other groups were the Redskins (not the same as Chris Dean's skinhead socialists) and a reggae band that I was the only white member of." Zephaniah was supportive of his efforts. "I was living in Handsworth when I first heard it, and at the time we were all angry with white people, we didn't have white friends, and all we listened to was reggae. Then I heard this guy talking about living on a council estate and saying that all he's got left is reggae. I thought, white people like reggae! I couldn't believe it. I moved to London two days after hearing that album."

Fitzgerald's link to the nascent punk scene was cemented by buying records at Pete Stennet's Small Wonder Records. After he'd started a record label Fitzgerald decided he'd push a demo tape through the Walthamstow shop door one evening. Stennet thought there was something there, and ended up putting out three EPs of varying quality. The first of which, 'Safety Pin', had to be re-recorded because Fitzgerald was so nervous in the studio. And he sounds it on 'Set We Free', an ambitious attempt to incorporate reggae. The second, 'Backstreet Boys', attacked street thuggery. The third contained two of his strongest efforts, 'The Paranoid Ward' and 'Irrelevant Battles'.

He played many of the regular punk haunts including the Roxy, Vortex and Marquee, but was often abused for his efforts, being a little too gentile for the tastes of the audience. Touring as support act to the Hawklords (aka Hawkwind) and Sham 69 took a fair amount of bottle. And Fitzgerald duly did, indeed, take quite a lot of bottle(s) in return. However, he did play major shows with the Jam on a national tour and the Clash's Rock Against Racism carnival at Victoria Park. Mick Jones was a big fan of Fitzgerald's 'Your Hero', while Paul Weller was another early advocate. "Paul Weller liked my stuff and watched me every night when I toured with the Jam. I later nearly got into a fight with him at the Music Machine, because I was quoted as saying that I thought he had sold out (some would say, hello Mr Kettle, this is Mr Black). The Hawklords tour was quite amusing. I got to the stage where I wouldn't even bother to sing and would just stand on stage and say: 'I don't care if you listen or not. I'm being paid to stand here for half an hour and you're paying for me to do so. Which one of us is the idiot?' The answer would probably be both of us."

"I always wanted to write different songs to other people," Fitzgerald notes, "and this was probably due to the different types of music that I listened to pre-punk – people like Sparks, Cockney Rebel, 10cc, Dr Feelgood, Alex Harvey, Bowie, the Doors, Randy Newman etc. And also the theatre connections I had also been exposed to – people like Brecht, Tom Lehrer and Jacques Brel, the inevitable theatre musicals and a bit of classical stuff. Plus, of course, pop, Motown and reggae. I was always more influenced by music outside of rock but learnt to play guitar on an electric guitar so also wanted to make a bit of noise preferably with a melodic and structural difference and originality."

Polydor came in to sign him in October 1978 and he put together a full backing band, featuring Penetration's Robert Blamire on bass, John Maher of the Buzzcocks on drums and Peter Wilson on guitar. But when two singles and an album, Grubby Stories, split between band workouts and solo acoustic performances, failed to provide any kind of breakthrough, he toured with a new line-up – Colin Peacock (guitar), Charlie Francis (bass; later Toyah) and Rab Fae Beith (drums; later the Wall, UK Subs etc). "The 'new line-up' angle hints at the idea of a master plan," Fitzgerald remonstrates. "My main problem with the music world was that I didn't have a master plan, and rather like in life, I had no real guidance either (I am certainly not going to say at this point that I have since found God)."

Thereafter, he once again became a solo artist and moved to Red Flame for a single and album, which aroused little media fanfare. Himalaya Records alongside Red Flame co-released the Drifting Towards Silence LP (it may as well have been released in the Himalayas for all the attention it got). By the April 1984 Tonight EP he was working with Peter McDonnell (keyboards), Alisdair Roberts (bass) and Jilly Jarman (drums).

By the mid-80s he'd retired from the music scene to work as a waiter in the House of Commons, before moving to Normandy, France, doing some acting work in the early 90s and touring and recording with Anne Clark. The reformed Wonder Stuff, meanwhile, recorded their version of 'Safety Pin' to keep his name alive.

His moment in the sun passed quickly, but he remains reflective, as he noted in the sleevenotes to the posthumous CD collection Safety Pin Stuck In My Heart. "Various rock-world adventures ensued – don't ask about the wild, torrid affairs with Soo Catwoman or Honey Bane, or the various love children. Punk died the day Patrik Fitzgerald signed to Polydor (fan letter – NME) so where did it all go wrong? Don't know. I've turned it over a thousand times – I could have been Billy Bragg, Tom Robinson, Joan Baez, Joan Armatrading or Tracy Chapman, but I never did get to the top of the pop tree... I've been averagely content, I've been to France, Holland, Belgium, Germany, Austria, Italy, Norway, Sweden, Denmark, Spain, Crete, Tunisia and Barbados – they always make me come back though." He now has an addendum. "The follow-up line to the NME fan letter would have been that I died the day I played at The Hammersmith Odeon with the Buzzcocks (and Hawkwind) and played the song 'Hammersmith Odeons', which criticised people for playing at the Hammersmith Odeon. Oh, and the relationships mentioned were probably somewhere between point one and point one two five in terms of significance in my life and were thrown in just to introduce a bit of fake music world involvement and credibility."

Fitzgerald is now resident in Christchurch, New Zealand. "I've never much cared for working and have done a variety of crap jobs. The working life side of my life is just too dull, mundane and uninteresting to talk about." But for the record, he is currently a postman after several years working as a tutor in community education and adult literacy programmes. But he's writing songs still and once again making them available, this time online.

DISCOGRAPHY:

Safety Pin 7-inch EP (Small Wonder Small 4 December 1977)
Safety Pin Stuck In My Heart/Banging And Shouting/Work, Rest, Play. Reggae/Set We Free/Optimism/Reject
Backstreet Boys 7-inch EP (Small Wonder Small 6 July 1978)
Buy Me Sell Me/The Little Dippers/Trendy/Backstreet Boys
The Paranoid Ward/The Bedroom Tapes 12-inch (Small Wonder Weeny 1 October 1978) (reissued in December 1978 as a 7–inch EP, 'The Paranoid Ward, first five tracks only)
All Sewn Up/Hammersmith Odeons 7-inch (Polydor 2059 091 March 1979)
Grubby Stories LP (Polydor 2383 533 April 1979)
Improve Myself/Bingo Crowd 7-inch Polydor 2059 135 June 1979)
Personal Loss/Straight Boy 7-inch (Red Flame RF 708 September 1982)
Gifts And Telegrams LP (Red Flame RF 8 November 1982)
Drifting Towards Violence LP (Red Flame 1983)
Drifting Into Silence LP (Himalaya HIM 009 February 1984)
Tonight 12-inch EP (Final Solution FSEP 001 April 1983)
Tonight/Mr And Mrs/Animal Mentality/A Superbeing/Waiting For The Final Cue
Tunisian Twist LP (Red Flame RF 48 June 1986)
Without Sex/Pop Star Pop Star (Ellie Jay AHPF 1) (as Josef Garrett)
Pillow Tension CD (Lazy Dog LZD-012 1995)
ARCHIVE RELEASES:
Treasures From The Wax Museum CD (Red Flame RFCD 7 1993)
Safety Pin Stuck In My Heart – The Very Best Of Patrik Fitzgerald CD (Anagram CDPUNK 31 April 1994) (no less than 31 tracks, plus sleevenotes from the man himself)

Flesh

Tony Morewood (vocals), Ken Phelps (drums), Dave Robson (bass), Phil Perfect (guitar). Later members included Mick Perrin (guitar, bass, accordion)

Alongside Wrist Action and the Depressions, with whom they frequently shared a stage, FLESH were one of the first punk bands to form in Brighton in 1977. They never did get round to recording, but they played regular gigs at the Vault, Resource Centre, Alhambra and Richmond Art College, setting the template for a later live punk scene in the city. "We took our name from an Andy Warhol movie," Phil Perfect recalls, "based around the artist's penchant for surrounding himself with junkies, transsexuals, experimentalists, freaks and other assorted oddballs. Which kind of fitted us lot and the people we hung out with."

All accounts suggest that the Sex Pistols' influence was incorporated unrepentantly, Morewood regularly haranguing audiences from the stage. Song titles included 'Apathy In The UK', which gives a clue as to their influences and aspirations. The band sundered when Morewood left. Robson, Perfect and Perrin went on to form the Lillettes, who were recorded on the Vaultage compilations, Perrin having also played with Laughing Gass.

Flowers Of Romance

Sid Vicious (vocals), Jo Faull (guitar), Sarah 'Rouge' Hall (bass), Viv Albertine (guitar), Palmolive (drums)

There were two semi-mythical pre-punk groups operating in London in the late-70s. Both saw myriad later stars of the movement pass through their ranks. Both never got past rehearsals, and neither released so much as a single. London SS were the

more celebrated contributors to the gene pool, but the FLOWERS OF ROMANCE played an almost equal role in birthing the new movement.

The band 'formed' as such in the summer of 1976 when a loose aggregation of squat-dwellers centred around noted Sex Pistols' camp follower Sid Vicious began to congregate. Sidney, having just had his first taste of stardom as drummer for the Banshees at the 100 Club, quite fancied the idea of leading an all-female backing group. Jo Faull and Sarah Hall were the girlfriends of Steve Jones and Paul Cook respectively, and the other participants were future Slits' founders, Chelsea Art School student Viv Albertine and Joe Strummer's girlfriend, Palmolive. The name Flowers of Romance was suggested by John Lydon, who would later nick it back again for Public Image Limited. "It was the name of a song we used to start with in the early days (of the Pistols)," he recalled to Giovanni Dadomo in 1977. "Just noise, no music – just to confuse the people who said we couldn't play."

F

The band were, by their own admission, some way short of competence, and would spend their days trying to play along to the Ramones. At some point Sid switched from vocals to playing rudimentary saxophone, but he wasn't much cop at that either. The drum kit had no cymbals. In most bands at least one person has some musical ability to sustain the less gifted. In this band everyone fell into the latter category. Marco Pirroni was invited to help out. "They never got together on any one occasion, ever. There were originally 15 people in this band, and I never actually met the others until years later. We never rehearsed. The idea of it became famous. I think I only knew two of the original members – Sid and Viv Albertine. Sid had some song ideas, 'Belsen Was A Gas' and 'Postcard From Auschwitz'. Then he got arrested after the 100 Club bottling incident. It was definitely Sid who threw the glass."

Despite being nothing more than a basement band, though they did occasionally use the Clash's Chalk Farm Studios, the group members were tackled by tabloid sensation hunters as well as the debut issue of early punk fanzine Skum at the start of 1977. Sid wrote some songs for the band, including 'Piece Of Garbage', 'Brains On Vacation' and the later Sex Pistols' song 'Belsen Is A Gas'. But before any recordings could take place Faull left the band, and then Sid unilaterally sacked Palmolive – allegedly because she wasn't interested in sleeping with him. "We didn't really play," Palmolive would later recount to punk77. "Nothing really happened. I don't think they even played. Sid Vicious wasn't very like into practising. He was really high on drugs. He couldn't stick to something in the same way that someone like Joe Strummer could, or even Johnny Rotten. He was a messed up kid. He became a puppet of the media and turned into what was expected of him. If you have no respect for anything, how will you respect yourself?"

Keith Levene, formerly of the Clash, joined alongside later ZigZag writer Steve Walsh (later Manicured Noise) towards the end of 1976, working alongside another, surname-less Steve. Viv then also got her marching orders from Sid. Which didn't really matter much anyway. The group was all over by February 1977 when Sid fulfilled his long-standing dream of joining the Sex Pistols.

Flys

Neil O'Connor (vocals, guitar), David Freeman (vocals, guitar), Joe Hughes (bass, vocals), Pete King (drums)

The FLYS began life as Midnight Circus in Coventry in the mid-70s (with Paul Angelopoulis on drums instead of King), and featured Hazel O'Connor's brother Neil as lead vocalist. Initially they were regarded as a trad rock band with hippy tendencies. "I guess I could have been described as a hippy," O'Connor admitted to me. "I had been one from '69 until 1972 or 1973, but I don't think Midnight Circus was a hippy band. The name, though, does come from a song from the album Parachute by the Pretty Things, who were a hippy band (it's still one of my favourite albums of the time). No, we wanted to play rock style, at the time pretty badly, and by the time we were getting the band together, most of the hippy-style bands had been getting more what we call prog rock – and nobody boogied, they just sat on the floor. We would have liked to have been glam, some of my favourites from 1970 onwards had been Alice Cooper, Iggy Pop, The Velvet Underground and eventually

Bowie, Lou Reed and Roxy Music. The rock style I wanted was more Dr Feelgood. I bought my first real good guitar, my Tele, having seen Wilko Johnson play his. David (Freeman) was a bit more into the Eagles, Santana and Joe Walsh, and wanted to be a furious and fast virtuoso."

The band originally came together – a trifle unconventional this – as a result of O'Connor dating Freeman's mother. "When I met David and Joe I was 21 and seeing David's mum, a beautiful 30-something. David was nearly 16 and Joe, his schoolmate, was 15. To try to get closer to David, I agreed to teach him to play guitar and his mate Joe was also interested to learn. So for the next two years while putting Midnight Circus together, I helped them start out on their individual roads to be musicians. We must have been pretty terrible and loud in those early days as at one time the neighbours circulated a petition to ask us to stop rehearsing in the house."

Like so many others, Midnight Circus were energised by punk and got their hair cut and streamlined their sound. This happily coincided with shifts in the Coventry music scene which were evident all around them. "I think the Wild Boys played their first gig opening for us in Birmingham. Their bass player, whose name I can't remember, had been a mate of ours and asked us to give them a spot. My first impression of Terry (Hall) was that he was very energetic but he had terrible pitch, thank God he learned his own style. When we were starting in the Midnight Circus days, we used to rehearse at a community centre in the centre of Coventry at least once a week. At this place there was a majority of West Indians who would hang out there, including those guys who would eventually make up the Specials. They would sometimes be rehearsing their reggae and we'd drop by each other's rooms to check each other out. As punk started coming in and likeminded souls were meeting up in clubs, we met with Jerry (Dammers). I already knew Rodney (Byers) and found out that they were playing with these same guys from the community centre. We would help each other out with loaning gear and being each other's opening act from time to time around Coventry. Eventually, Terry split from the Wild Boys and joined the Specials, as you know. My most recent memory of The Specials is from eight or nine years ago when they came here to Montreal for a show. At the time Hazel had come to spend some time with me and while looking through the local 'what's on' news I came across the announcement. Of course, we had to go. We went down to the place just after soundcheck time and knocked at the stage door and asked for Rodney or Linval or Horace without giving our names. You can imagine their shock – 'What the hell are you doing here?' Nobody knew I'd moved here or that Hazel might be visiting. Anyway, as you can also imagine, we spent our evening partying together."

As Midnight Circus transformed into the Flys, the group made a string of local appearances, the most memorable of which were as support to the Buzzcocks, which provided evidence of the turning tide. "We opened for the Buzzcocks at Mr George in Coventry and eventually opened for them on all their Midlands dates. We'd played twice before at this place and we'd never had a good reaction, evenings of dodging glasses and bottles, etc. When I phoned Pete to tell him of the gig offer, he said he'd quit if it should turn out like the other times. It went so well, we couldn't understand how this same crowd could be so different. It changed everything for us. We played more shows with the Buzzcocks, EMI came out to see us quite a few times and, voila, a deal." This came despite the fact that the label had rejected the band's demo in its previous incarnation just a few months earlier. At another early show they were supported by the Shapes, whose Gareth Holder was immediately impressed. "The Shapes played one of their first gigs as support to the Flys at the Leamington Spa Centre in 1977. We threw beans all over the audience and were promptly banned from the venue, not that it ever stopped us from playing there another three or four times. I was amazed by the Flys. We thought we were quite good in the Shapes, but the Flys were amazingly tight and professional, whilst still being nice blokes. They actually came up to us later and said how much they had enjoyed us, and would like to see us support them again. No other buggers ever did that."

The Flys' debut EP, released on their own Zama Records, contained O'Connor's finest moment, 'Love And A Molotov Cocktail' . Engineer Danny Perloff recalled "The Flys were definitely Neil and Dave's baby and 'Molotov' was kinda like their first. They were proud parents. All of us thought the song might take the band some place, like a cross between the

Damned and the Jam." O'Connor adds: "Zama was set up by our manager of the time, who was called Chris King, and he was the older brother of Pete. It was also Chris who had suggested inviting Pete to play with us. Chris had a little money to put behind it and our interest in going in that direction was more because we had seen the success of other independents at the time. We were especially impressed by the sound of Stiff Records roster of artists like the Damned, Elvis Costello and Wreckless Eric. We even went to the studio where most of the Stiff artists had recorded called Pathway in Islington, run by a guy called Mike Finesilver. We had a show to make in Brighton one Saturday in the autumn of 1977 and so we arranged to go into the studio on the Friday before, and to stay at Hazel's overnight. The studio went really well and we recorded 13 songs in one day. It was only eight-track, so in fact the set up was pretty simple – two tracks for drums, one for bass, one each for guitars, one for guitar solos, one for lead vocals and one for backing vocals. The studio was very small, about the size of a one-car garage, and there was room for two people in the control room, if they both breathed in. We came away with rough mixes of everything and during the next week decided on the five songs we would concentrate on to mix better for our debut release."

"As it happened, all this was taking place just as EMI were developing an interest in us but we decided to go ahead anyway. Eventually when we signed the contract, we were limited to a pressing of 2,500, which all went, as EMI wanted to take 'Love And A Molotov Cocktail' for the first EMI release. They also bought out all of the other recordings from the session. The other big memory from around that time is when we heard from EMI that probably John Peel was going to be playing our disc on his radio show. We had a rehearsal scheduled and we took a radio with us, so that when his show came on the air we could hear for ourselves. And, yes, he played 'Love And A Molotov Cocktail'. I guess that it's a bit like losing your virginity the first time you hear your own music on air? We were so euphoric."

The debut album that followed is really worth looking up, as there's a lot of songcraft that transcends the punk sphere and draws equally on the pop and R&B suss of their stated influences the Who, Dr Feelgood and the Creation. And in O'Connor and Freeman they boasted a dynamic twin guitar sound that gave real impetus to the songs, particularly O'Connor's 'I Don't Know' and 'We Don't Mind The Rave'. The high camp of subsequent single 'Name Dropping', written by Freeman, with its "Do you know who I was with last night?" coda, was a keeper too.

By the advent of their second album, Graham Deakin, formerly of John Entwistle's Ox, had replaced King on drums. He actually sang lead on one track, 'Freezing'. But the material lacked the punch of their debut, though '16 Down' and 'Living In The Sticks' were notable exceptions. But by now the writing was on the wall. Which is a shame, as they were musically far more interesting than some of the mod revival bands who scored chart success in the early-80s, not to mention their punk counterparts.

They had fallen apart by 1980. King joined After The Fire and briefly played with Emerson Lake and Palmer, before dying of cancer aged 26. Hughes and Freeman signed to A&M as The Lover Speaks, whose song 'No More I Love You's' was later a hit for Annie Lennox. "Both me and my accountant loved Annie's version," Freeman later noted, sagely. Freeman also worked on Alison Moyet's Raindancing album and played with Roddy Radiation and the Tearjerkers. He also penned songs for Kiki Dee and Tom Jones and picked up a BMI Award and three Ivor Novello nominations. O'Connor joined his sister Hazel's band, notably sorting out the arrangements and programming for her album Smile, co-produced by Martin Rushent. He continued to work alongside Rushent at Genetic studios for the next four or five years, learning 'the craft'. I mentioned that Rushent is my favourite producer of the period. "I learned a hell of a lot from Martin. He was my mentor and is still one of my best friends. He gave me belief in myself not because of anything he may have said to me, but more because here was this world famous producer who enjoyed working with little old me. He taught me how to produce discs and encouraged me to find my own direction. We had a lot of fun in those days in and out of the studio." Before Genetic closed its doors one of the last bands he worked with was Montreal's the Box. As a consequence, their manager Marc Durand invited him back to Quebec to help with other projects.

In 2004 Neil updated me on his activities. "For the last 14 years I've lived and worked in

Montreal, Quebec, Canada, where I'm still working in music, mainly recording and producing Canadian and especially Quebec Francophone artists. I love it here. Montreal has a very open and multicultural society, which has a very supportive atmosphere for artistic and creative endeavours. My French was only at the level of secondary education when I first arrived, but now and for a long time, I'm very comfortable communicating with none of the shyness to talk in French, with that big Brit accent, that I had in the early days. I'm married to my lovely French speaking wife, Kristeen, who, of course, has been my greatest teacher. Also I'm still playing live, from time to time, mainly with artists that I've produced." He often includes '16 Down' and 'Love And A Molotov Cocktail' in his set. "I still like those songs. 'Love And A Molotov Cocktail' was supposed to be about leaving home, and '16 Down' was supposed to be about living in a high rise. 'Molotov' was the fastest song I've ever written, it took me about 20 minutes and it was one of those rare times when you feel that something has taken you over when you write and that you are just a spectator to the whole affair."

So does Neil still clutch the punk ethos to his heart? The 'destroy everything' ethos? No, not really. The anarchist, get the government out my hair ethos, yes (though I can get very disturbed by the selfish right wing kind of anarchy). The Music… absolutely."

DISCOGRAPHY:

Bunch Of Five 7-inch EP (Zama ZA 10 EP November 1977)
Saturday Sunrise/Love And A Molotov Cocktail/Can I Crash You?/Me And My Buddies/Just For Your Sex
Love And A Molotov Cocktail/Can I Crash Here?/Civilization 7-inch (EMI EMI 2747 January 1978)
Fun City/E.C.4 7-inch (EMI EMI 2795 1978)
Waikiki Beach Refugees/We Don't Mind The Rave 7-inch (EMI 2867 1978) (yellow vinyl)
Waikiki Beach Refugees LP (EMI EMC 3249 November 1978) (reissued on Captain Oi!, AHOY CD 182, with bonus tracks Love And A Molotov Cocktail, Can I Crash Here?, Civilisation, Fun City (Single Version), E.C.4, Beverley (Single Version), Name Dropping, Fly V Fly)
Beverley/Don't Moonlight On Me 7-inch (EMI EMI 2907 1979)
Name Dropping/Fly v Fly 7-inch (EMI 2936 1979) (some copies in green vinyl)
Living In The Sticks/We Are The Lucky Ones 7-inch (EMI EMI 2979 1980)
What Will Mother Say?/Undercover Agent Zero 7-inch (Parlophone R 6036 1980)
Fly's Own LP (EMI EC 3316 1979) (reissued on CD by Captain Oi!, AHOY CD 183, with bonus tracks We Are The Lucky Ones, Living In The Sticks, Lois Lane, Today Belongs To Me, What Will Mother Say?, Undercover Agent Zero (Single Version))
Four From The Square 7-inch EP (Parlophone R 6063 1980)
Night Creatures/Lois Lane/16 Down
ARCHIVE RELEASES:
Flys Buzz Back CD (See For Miles 304 1990)

4th Reich

Nina Spencer (vocals), Mark 'Chips' Chapman (guitar), Nick Medlin (bass), John 'Abe' Lincoln (drums; replaced by Benny Di Massa)

4TH REICH were formed from a circle of friends who were either members, or fans, of all-female group Muvva's Pride. That band's drummer, and Fourth Reich's singer, was Nina Spencer, according to Melin "an original punk rocker from late 1976. She lived with her mum and younger brother in a top floor flat off Finchley Road. I was the first, and for a long time the only, punk rocker from Upminster in Essex. I was notorious for chasing down local dogs to relieve them of their collars if they had better ones than I did." He got hold of his first bass by stealing it backstage at the 100 Club in Oxford Street.

Medlin met Spencer while squatting at the derelict Elizabeth Garret Anderson Hospital building in Belsize Park. "I moved in with Nina and started writing material for 4th Reich." Chapman knew Spencer from her Muvva's Pride days. "He was one of the aptly named 'Muvver Fuckers' who followed the band." Chapman also wrote songs for them, including their signature tune, 'Brighton Rock'. "He lived with his family at the Prince Alfred pub in Warwick Avenue, which was frequented by members of the Clash, the Boys, Chelsea, the

Cure and Glen Matlock etc." John 'Abe' Lincoln also had a Muvver's Pride connection, being the long-term partner of singer Suby Barnes. "Lousy drummer but always wore natty threads," reckons Medlin. "Abe was in with Nina and I at the outset of 4th Reich and co-wrote the earliest material with us." After a few months Benny Di Massa replaced him, "once the band decided that tight rhythm was more important than tight-fitting leather jeans". Di Massa was an old friend. "Benny knew all the band members independently from the summer of 1977 and the King's Road battles against London's teddy boy community". In fact, Nina is pictured on the cover of the 'Clash City Rockers' 7-inch in a photograph of one such confrontation.

Medlin talked me through the band's early set list. 'Your Mistake' was a "lyrical kicking for all in authority," sentiments which also applied to 'Sweet Cyanide'. 'Normal Norma' was "Nina's take on the resistance thrown up by her parents to the punk movement". 'Who Needs Them Anyway' was "the band's testimony that we would remain punk rockers for ever". Related to that spirit was 'Flowa Power', a "warning to the punk movement to avoid the same mistakes that the hippies made". 'This Way Up' "extolled the virtues of the DIY attitude for bands, fashion, fanzines and record labels" as, in its own way, did 'Déjà Vu', a warning "not to be seduced by major record companies and big business". And then there was 'Piss In Your Ear' – 'I wouldn't piss in your ear if your brain was on fire/You become a punk with me and we can both retire'. "You work it out!" laughs Medlin. Manufactured Romance', meanwhile, was their sole attempt to write a love song. "In hindsight the songs seem very naïve, but were totally honest and passionate. In the true punk tradition they were short, spiky and we played them at 90 miles an hour."

The group played live for the first at the Marquee in Wardour Street. "Our biggest surprise was jumping off the stage after the soundcheck and being surrounded by dozens of young punks after our autographs. We sat on the stage to sign books/tickets etc and chat with them. At the back of this group was none other than John Peel. He waited till we had finished with the kids then sat down with us to say how much he was looking forward to hearing the whole set. He was so enthusiastic. We thought, this is easy! Less than one year ago we were leaping around in a grotty rehearsal room, learning how to play and writing our first songs. Now here we were about to play one of London's most famous music venues, signing autographs and chatting to a guy we had all listened to and respected for years. I think our next gig was at The Windsor Castle in Harrow Road, which we packed out. I don't know how it happened, but we had already picked up quite a healthy following, the Witton Mob. Forty or fifty of them would turn up to all our shows with the band's name painted on the back of their leather jackets. They even knew the words to some of songs already."

4th Reich were perennial support act to the UK Subs at venues such as the Marquee and the Lyceum, and also on the Subs' 1979 south coast tour, by which time Charlie Harper was talking them up to anyone who would listen. Which included Basingstoke punk Marc Maslin, who was arrested for wearing one of their t-shirts. Both Medlin and Spencer, incidentally, both appeared in The Great Rock'n'roll Swindle and Punk Can Take It.

Once promoters found out about the band's ready-made following, they were offered a series of headline slots at venues including the Fulham Greyhound, Acklam Hall and the Clarendon. "We did have a bit of a rough reputation though, and some nights at the Moonlight in West Hampstead descended into chaos, with mass brawls spilling out of the club and down to the Underground station. We managed to get a residency at the Music Machine on Sunday nights. It was prior to one of these shows that the music press carried a piece about Rock Against Racism's objection to the name 4th Reich. We pointed out that the name was meant to get a reaction but did not convey any political leanings and that Nina herself was half-Jewish. But threats of protests and boycotts persisted. We were advised to ditch the name if we wanted to get on. We agreed that we wanted to distance ourselves from the skinheads who were starting to appear at the live shows (we assumed for the fights), and thus ended the 4th Reich."

The participants would subsequently regroup as Manufactured Romance in July 1980, with the line-up expanded with the arrival of guitarist Bob Moore. Manufactured Romance managed to issue one single for Fresh and generated some reasonable press interest before becoming Foreign Flags between 1983 and 1985, then Blue In The Bush and the Bicycle

Thieves. Spencer is currently living in America after starting a family and is getting involved in music once again. Di Massa apparently went on to play sessions with the Cocteau Twins. Bob Moore, meanwhile, ended up doing sessions for Cliff Richard.

Fractures

Formed in and around Rhyl in 1977, the FRACTURES played a handful of shows, including the 1520 club (set up by Mike Peters of the Alarm), while vocalist Dimmo roadied for Peters' then band the Toilets. Drummer Sara Sugarman would go on to become a well-known film screenwriter and director, working on movies including Confessions Of A Teenage Drama Queen, Mad Cows and Very Annie Mary. She also featured in both Sid And Nancy and Alex Cox's Straight To Hell as an actress.

As Steve Allan Jones told me in 2005, "1976 and the surrounding years were an amazingly creative time along the North Wales Coast – but especially in Rhyl and Prestatyn. For example, I was in my school play with a young 14-year-old called Sara Sugarman. She also dabbled in the punk scene and tried a few things out. Sara went on to drama school and eventually began writing and directing. She now resides in Hollywood and her latest directing job Confessions of A Teenage Drama Queen (a Disney picture, no less!) was number one at the US box office earlier this year."

She wasn't the only prominent personality from that fissure in time and geography. "Around at the same time, obviously, were the Alarm crowd, including Redeye (now stage manager for Bob Dylan), Gareth 'Gaz Top' Jones and Pete Picton (now editor of the online Sun newspaper). Also around were Carol Vorderman and Karl Wallinger (of the Waterboys, World Party and writer of 'She's The One', a number one for Robbie Williams). Add to that numerous actors/opera singers and musicians all still in the biz. Many of us used to converge on the Bistro – the main pub/club in Rhyl at the same time. Every week we used to swap ideas, contacts etc. I don't know what was the springboard for all this – punk had to be one of the ingredients though."

Frantic Elevators

Mick Hucknall (vocals, guitar), Neil Moss (guitar), Brian Turner (bass, keyboards), Kev Williams (drums)

It took Mick Hucknall a fair while before he made the mainstream, and for his apprenticeship he led this frenetic punk-inspired band that released singles for a number of labels, but never truly rose beyond the status of Peel favourites. Obviously, most of the interest in the band comes from Simply Red fans trying to trace Hucknall's musical lineage, but the singles are worthwhile in their own right. The voice is there, although it's not allowed to gorge on its own importance to quite the same extent it would in later years, and the music is far more urgent and vital than the dinner party soul which would ensue. However, there were certainly indications of both inclinations. As well as hard-edged R&B and bug-eyed driving pop, the band would tackle soul classics like 'Hey Mama, Keep Your Big Mouth Shut'.

"I was one of the founder members of the **FRANTIC ELEVATORS**," recalls Mark Reeder, speaking from Germany in 2006. "Our drummer then was called Steve Tansley, and he and Mick had previously performed together in Joe Stalin's Red Star Radio Band, a short-lived blues-rock band of which I was also a founder member. But I left before we had a vocalist and any gigs. I always thought Mick had a really great voice and saw that from the early JSRSRB days (I introduced him to Barry Stopford, the band's guitarist). I was very pleased and proud to see him do so well."

According to Reeder, Hucknall left Joe Stalin's Red Star Radio Band due to musical differences. "He'd been bitten by the punk bug. Mick was one of the few people (along with Jon The Postman) whom I knew that had actually seen the Pistols play the Free Trade Hall. I had already heard of the Pistols and their new style of rock after reading about them in the Daily Mirror or Sun, and after seeing them live, his enthusiasm about their new sound was very contagious. When we bought their Anarchy' single on EMI, we were hooked. As the

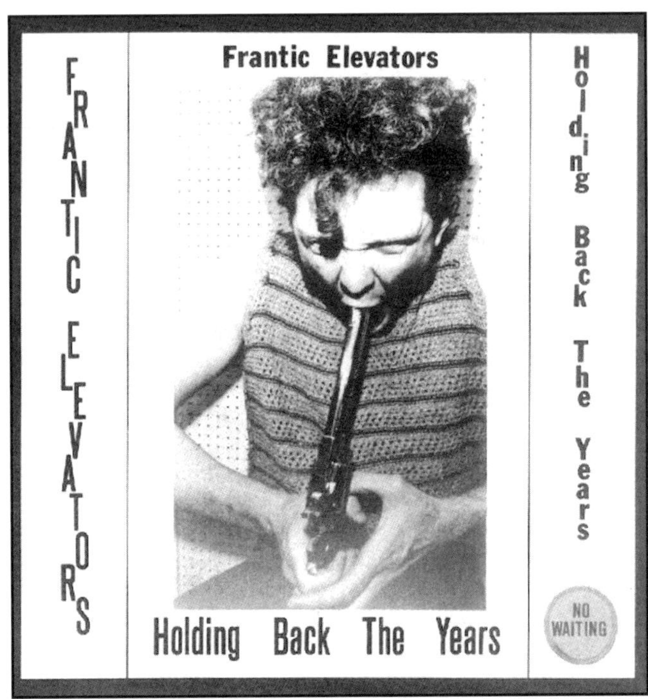

The cover of Frantic Elevators' pre-Simply Red version of 'Holding Back The Years'.

punk sound swiftly developed (and I had started to work full time at Virgin) I had access to all the latest punk records, and it was only a matter of time before Mick and his old friend Moey decided to form a punk band."

Moey became the band's guitarist. "Mick and Moey asked me if I was interested in joining them to form a new band and for weeks we sat in Mick's bedroom, listening to Bowie, Iggy, T-Bone Walker and 60s Rolling Stones records for inspiration, thinking of a name. I suggested a few daft names, but Mick really liked Elevation – inspired by the 13th Floor Elevators – and Moey liked the word frantic (but was against being just called "the Frantics"). And so we became The Frantic Elevators."

But this would not be the line-up that eventually released the singles. "Although I was dedicated to my position as the band's bassist, I had other plans, even at the beginning. I had told Mick and Moey that I would only play bass until a suitable replacement had been found, as I was already planning to leave the country. So when I felt the time had finally come to leave Virgin Records in Lever Street and to leave England, Moey and Mick appeared really surprised when they realised that I actually meant it. And they were not happy, as we were starting to get some decent gigs and they had to find a 'suitable replacement', ie Brian Turner. I only met Brian a few times to go through the set with him and I didn't know him at all." The mood of his stranded bandmates wasn't improved by the fact that Moey always used Reeder's guitar. "When I left, he had to go around to my parents to plead and beg for it, to play a gig with. Incidentally, although I was promoting Factory's records in Germany, I was never sent any of the Frantic Elevator singles, so I actually haven't heard any of them, believe it or not!"

Reeder's decision was made, but he retained his faith in the material. "Some of our songs, such as 'Production Prevention', I thought were very powerful and quite original and I really enjoyed playing them. I left for Germany before any Frantic Elevators recordings were made, but I do still have a reel-to-reel tape (somewhere) of one of our practice sessions from the Broomstairs working men's club in Denton."

"Mick has always sounded completely unique," George Borowski, of Manchester peers the Out, told me about watching the Frantic Elevators play at the 1978 Deeply Vale Festival. "Mick was very spiky and fiery. Very impressive. But I only met him to speak to properly in 1979 through TJM. They asked me if they should put 'Voice In The Dark Out'. I said yes, and they put a thank you on the back of the sleeve because of that." But at this stage, they seemed destined to be remembered as perpetual underachievers. The Frantic Elevators bowed out with an early version of 'Holding Back The Years', credited to Hucknall and bass player Brian Turner (Reeder: "The song was actually written by Mick and Neil 'Moey' Moss"). For an overview of the Frantic Elevators, we could always turn to the sage tongue of one of his fellow travellers, New Order's Peter Hook. "They were a punk band," he told

Dave Simpson. "He used to scream so much the blood vessels in his throat burst and the PA guys would beat him up for covering the microphones with blood. They were wild, but since then he's become the biggest cunt on earth."

Hucknall is not the only member of Frantic Elevators to graduate with honours. Before going on to helm Germany's "mfs – masterminded for success" label, one of the pioneering trance music labels, Mark Reeder released Tranceformed From Beyond, the first trance compilation. "Artists like Paul Van Dyk, Cosmic Baby, Mijk Van Dijk, ex-Clock DVA member Paul Browse and John Klimek, Ellen Alien, Dr Motte and many others made their debut on the label." He also has a second label in Berlin, Flesh, on which he releases 'Wet & Hard' sounds from the likes of Corvin Dalek, Eiven Major, Jan Kessler and Fidelity Kastrow.

DISCOGRAPHY:

Voice In The Dark/Passion/Every Day I Die 7-inch (TJM TJM 5 June 1979)

Hunchback Of Notre Dame/See Nothing And Everything/Judge Me 7-inch (TJM TJM 6 1980) (demo copies only)

You Know What You Told Me/Production Prevention 7-inch (Eric's Eric's 6 December 1980)

Searching For The Only One/Hunchback Of Notre Dame 7-inch (Crackin' Up CRACK 1 1981)

Holding Back The Years/Pistols In My Brain 7-inch (No Waiting WAIT 1 1982)

ARCHIVE RECORDINGS:

The Early Years mini-LP (TJM TJM 101 1987) (reissued on Receiver KNOB 2 – are you trying to get at Mick? – in 1988 with a new sleeve and an interview disc as Mick Hucknall And The Frantic Elevators)

Singles (Essential ESMCD 797 2000) (features six tracks from their TJM period and an interview with Mick Hucknall that doesn't even mention the Frantic Elevators)

COMPILATIONS:

Rabid/TJM Punk Singles Collection CD (Receiver RRCD 227 1996; 'Voice In The Dark')

Freeze

Gordon Sharp (vocals), David Clancy (guitar, keyboards), Keith Brant (bass), Graeme Radin (drums)

The FREEZE typified Edinburgh's more adventurous take on punk, injecting lots of art damage into their brief discography. They were fellow travellers with the Scars, with whom they enjoyed an intense local rivalry, in that their first full-bore punk thrashes soon expanded to accommodate an effective glam-punk hybrid. A cover of Eno's 'Baby's On Fire' was a staple of their live set and a clue as to where they were coming from, and they also covered Roxy's 'Virginia Plain' on a couple of occasions.

Prior to the move to Edinburgh, the group was formed at Linlithgow Academy in 1976, where English teacher Alistair Allison encouraged their early progress. He wrote some of their early lyrics including 'Paranoia' and set up and financed the A1 record label which would release both Freeze records. Sharp and Clancy were both only 15 when they formed the band. "I just volunteered to hold the microphone and shout in it, for a number of years," Sharp later admitted. "I was the local Linlithgow punk 'missionary'," he confirmed to me, "spreading the word as best I could." Freeze began to pick up local gigs, often playing alongside the Skids, another band that shared their arty leanings.

By the time the Freeze folded in 1982 Sharp and Clancy had come to the decision that they wanted to charter 'darker' territories, fully explored in their next incarnation, Cindytalk (there was also the fact that London-based funk band Freeez were getting lots of attention). However, in the interim they left behind an excellent debut EP, which included stage favourite 'Paranoia', a second single (featuring silent film goddess Louise Brooks as its cover star, to whom the A-side was dedicated) and two John Peel sessions. The first of these was broadcast in November 1980, featuring 'Quietly Burning', 'Sunday', 'And Then We Danced' and 'Lullaby In Black'. By the advent of their second booking for the DJ in August 1981, a new rhythm section had been recruited featuring Neil Braidwood (drums) and Mike Moran (bass). This time the selections were 'From The Bizarre', 'Building On Holes' and 'Location'.

As well as Cindytalk, Sharp sang on three songs on the first This Mortal Coil album It'll End In Tears; 'Kangaroo', 'Fond Affections' and 'A Single Wish'. "The first two were cover versions (Big Star and Rema Rema respectively) and 'A Single Wish' was co-written by myself, Simon Raymonde of the Cocteau Twins and Steven Young of Colourbox. I'd also been involved in the very first This Mortal Coil release, the 'Sixteen Days – Gathering Dust' 12-inch, singing alongside Elizabeth Fraser."

The collaboration led to rumours that he was about to join the Cocteau Twins. "That's more of an apocryphal story," Sharp thinks, "possibly one of my own, naïve, making. Around the time I was recording the 1983 John Peel session with them and singing at the occasional gig, Ivo Watts-Russell, head of 4AD, spoke to me about the possibility of joining up with the Cocteaus. He was musing over the possibility of adding new instrumentation, developing new ideas with their sound. He suggested that the combination of our voices (Elizabeth's and mine) might be a unique way for them to further that sound. I'm fairly sure he had not discussed this with any of the band and I'm even more convinced they would not have been interested in the idea. They quickly showed they had enough in their armoury to develop their sound without me. Anyway, I quickly passed over the subject with Ivo. Cindytalk was gearing up to record its first album Camouflage Heart, and that was my main concern."

However, there's more substance in the rumour that, much earlier, Sharp had been invited to join Duran Duran. "It's true that I was courted by Duran Duran back in 1980. They'd lost their singer Stephen Duffy. I'd met them at a Japan gig in London some months earlier and they'd recalled my gender-blurry look and the fact that I was a singer. I wasn't looking for another band but being hungry for experience(s) I went to Birmingham, hung out with them and auditioned. They offered me the "job" but I decided against it as it wasn't really my kind of music. I also felt that their headlong descent into pop stardom, pretty evident even then, was not for me. I was already following my own musical path."

DISCOGRAPHY:

In Colour 7-inch EP (A.1 A.1.1A1 1979)
Paranoia/For J.P.S. (With Love & Loathing)/Psychodalek Nightmares
Celebration/Cross-Over 7-inch (A.1 A.1.1.S.1 1980)

Friction

Cary Greaves (guitar), Roger Holdstock (vocals), Colin Salmon (drums), Mark White (bass)

FRICTION formed after the members left Ashcroft High School in Luton. Indeed, they'd talked about the idea of forming a punk band throughout the last year of their academic endeavours, which may account for the appalling exam results they achieved. Alongside sometime fifth member Daize Headbanger, they rehearsed in Greaves' garage, before arranging their debut gig in April 1979.

The venue was Luton Town Hall, on a bill also featuring UK Decay, the Statics, Pneumania the Cinematics and the Clips. The gig sold out, despite little advertising and the lack of a PA. The evening was a success, though minor damage to the toilets led to a ban on punk rock shows by the council. The second gig was, if anything, even more memorable – a show at the Richmond Hill School For The Mentally Handicapped in front of an audience of French exchange students (the line-up featuring Phil Imber of the Jets deputising on bass). In June 1979 the group made its first studio recording, 'Murder', for inclusion on a four-track EP issued as 'The Voxhall Tracks', now one of the rarest records in British punk.

Through 1980 they were regulars around Luton venues the Baron Of Beef, Christchurch, the Arts Centre and the Starlight Club. Their appearance at the Plastic Records audition night was taped, leading to the release of their Cocksure Punko Insanity cassette album. But the fact that Salmon and White were now squatting in London and Greaves had moved out to a local village but lost his driving licence, meant the group found it hard to attend rehearsals, and some gigs even took place with a tape recorder in place of Greaves' guitar. This occurred the night they played a Dunstable bikers' pub, under the stage name Anarchist Formation Dance Team. Salmon too had departed (he would work briefly with the Tee Vees) meaning that subsequent gigs featured not only the reel to reel but also a drum machine to keep it company. Nevertheless, the remaining duo did record a new demo tape. They bowed out with a final show at London's South Bank Polytechnic, with Salmon returning on drums and Tim Vaas of the Cinematics guesting on vocals.

The Herald & Post – Luton & Dunstable's biggest

adverts 01582 700601 news 01582 700666 web www.lutontoday.co.uk

Is he the first black James Bond?

by Jacqueline Dolan

HE went to Ashcroft High School in the 70s, got kicked out of Luton Sixth Form College and squatted in Camden with his friend Mark.

Now, Colin Salmon is tipped to make film history as the first black James Bond.

Colin, 42, was born in Luton in 1962, brought up on a Luton housing estate and played the drums in a local band called The Friction.

Colin, ranked in People's Magazine's 50 Most Beautiful People in the World, has already appeared in the last three 007 movies as agent Charles Robinson, M's chief of staff.

Pierce Brosnan, said recently when asked who should succeed him: "I find myself saying Colin Salmon. I think he's a great actor."

Brosnan is expected to continue playing Bond until 2005

LICENSED TO KILL: How Colin Salmon would look as 007.

Greaves is now in Australia, White suffered a stroke in the Far East and is now in a Surrey nursing home and Salmon is now a famous actor, having appeared in two recent James Bond films (he's also been tipped as 'the first black Bond')

DISCOGRAPHY:

The Voxhall Tracks 7-inch EP (Pink Records INK 1000 November 1979; 'Murder') (other tracks by TeeVees ('War Machine'), Paranoia ('Ever Been Conned'), Clips ('Ultimatum')

Cocksure Punko Insanity cassette (Friction Product FP001 1980) (recorded live at Plastic Records audition night in 1980. Reissued on CD in 2002 by Old Stock Records, OLDS1, with addition of original uncut studio version of 'Murder', remastered by Gary Olds)

Fear cassette (Friction Product FP002 1981) (reissued on CD in 2004 by Old Stock Records, OLDS2, remastered by Gary Olds)

ARCHIVE RELEASES:

Teenage Treats Volume 3 LP (Xerox MZE8603 1983; 'Murder')

Xmas 3-inch CD single (Old Stock Records TOCK 1 December 2003)

Christmas 1978/Poser Without U/Let's Dance

Gang Of Four

Andy Gill (guitar, vocals), Jon King (vocals, keyboards), Dave Allen (bass, vocals), Hugo Burnham (drums, vocals)

Leeds' left wing stalwarts GANG OF FOUR are, just possibly, the second most influential band of the late-70s. You can detect their influence everywhere you look in both mainstream and non-commercial American rock (whether you wish to term it post-punk, alt rock or whatever). Naked Raygun, Jane's Addiction, Helmet, and Big Black's Steve Albini number among their fans, while REM have covered both 'We Live As We Dream, Alone' and 'He'd Send In The Army'. As Michael Stipe confessed, "I stole a lot from them." Henry Rollins routinely name-checks Gang Of Four as if doing so was an Olympic sport, and his Infinite Zero label, set up with Rick Rubin, reissued the band's first three albums in 1995. More contemporary art-pop groups such as (most strikingly) Franz Ferdinand, the Rapture and Bloc Party are similarly indebted. Bono loved them ("... a corporation of common sense, a smart bomb of text that had me 'at home feeling like a typist'"). Even Michael Hutchence and the Red Hot Chili Peppers, both of whom Gill would later produce, bowed down before the Gang's anti-fascist groove thing.

They were "the first rock band I could really relate to," noted Flea of the Peppers, having originally made their acquaintance at the Los Angeles Palladium by jumping on stage naked and shaking his butt. Kurt Cobain was a noted fan, as was his friend Tad Doyle. Doyle even owned up to being in a Gang Of Four tribute band, Red Set, that played every track from Entertainment! Pick a chapter at random from Our Band Could Be Your Life, Michael Azerrad's excellent document of the development of an authentic alternative American music, and you'll doubtless be reading about a critically revered outfit in hock to Gang Of Four. They are referenced eight times in the index, only twice less than the Beatles. In fact, when Gang Of Four reformed in 2005, it had reached the stage where founder member Andy Gill (no relation to the MOJO journalist of the same name) had become bewildered by the avalanche of soundalikes doing the rounds.

But is it a case of oft-cited, rarely listened to? The stunning thing about going back to Entertainment! is that now, 25 years on and awash in punk nostalgia, in a world where Gap want to commission 'Holiday In Cambodia' to flog jeans and they sell toothpaste to the tune of the New York Dolls, Gang Of Four are the one group who still sound absolutely jarring, unprettied by the wash cycle of history. The further away from 1976 we get, the more the Sex Pistols sound like a pop band. Not so Gang Of Four. What is equally amazing is that a group so versed in the pitfalls and trappings of the music industry, so wary of the 'spectacle', could make music that was, in essence, so entertaining.

Their origins can be traced back to the friendship of Gill and King at school in Sevenoaks, Kent. There they formed a band, the Bourgeois Brothers, in 1973. Their songs included an embryonic version of 'Anthrax', one of Gang Of Four's signature tunes. They also hung about with future Mekons' members Tom Greenhalgh, Kevin Lycett and Mark White, practising in the art room where White's father taught. Gill made his stage bow at the Sevenoaks School Ball. "Just me and a couple of other guys, one of whom was called Mark Laver and the other I forget. One song was 'Sweet Jane', another was a Desmond Dekker track and also something original that I played congas on." Gill and King, both studying fine art, met Burnham, a self-imposed exile from the drama department, on campus at Leeds University. Kendal native Allen was recruited from an advert in the student union (becoming the band's "token working class member" – though unverified accounts suggest he'd already attended Lancaster & Morecambe College Of Art). The advert, penned by Burnham, read: "Fast rivvum & blues band requires a fast rivvum & blues player." They initially liaised while Gill and King were domiciled in New York, as part of their degree course. They'd managed to get Mary Harron (co-founder of Punk magazine and later director of American Psycho) to put them up at her flat in St Mark's Place and introduce them to the emergent CBGB's generation.

Their punk-funk hybrid was soon branded 'perverted disco', while an early critical notice offered the sobriquet 'neo-Marxist funk'. My favourite would be Van Gosse's observation in the Village Voice that they offered "a deeper aesthetic for pop". Their influences ranged from

Television and the Ramones, tutored by Gill and King's immersion in the New York scene, to the abrasive guitar of Wilko Johnson, Jimi Hendrix at his most free-flowing, Muddy Waters for his simplicity, and the spatial awareness of both Jamaican dub and George Clinton's funk. Gill, in particular, would specialise in 'non-solos', simply dropping out of the mix where more conventional song structures would demand some kind of showy intervention. The ideological debts were to writers such as feminist Griselda Pollock, Fred Orton and Situationist TJ Clark (the latter taught at Leeds). Other influences included Walter Benjamin, Gramsci, Althuser, Fellini and Godard as well as the impressionist school of painters. As for good ol' Uncle Karl Marx: "Neither Jon nor I read much of him," Gill notes.

There was an insistence that, while the Pistols may have lit the fuse, they wanted clear blue water in terms of style and approach. "If you think of the first crop of punk stuff," Gill later told Jason Gross, "it was all just tedious guitars cranked up through Marshalls. In the wake of the Damned and the Sex Pistols, it was heavy metal but faster and not as well played. Certainly Gang of Four, Television and Talking Heads weren't interested in going down that road at all. So there was a kind of sparseness about the guitar stuff, it was more staccato with space around it. That's something that those bands have in common. Where we diverge is (in) the funky side of things in the sense that Television and Talking Heads (early on) weren't in that area. Gang of Four was from the get-go." Gill maintains that these musical differences meant it was "definitely not punk music", though they were intrinsically linked, and codified, within that movement. And some critics would argue that they embraced its agenda better than most simply by having their own manifesto.

These ideas, musical and theoretical, a source of permanent inner contention, gelled over rehearsals upstairs at the Fenton, a haunt of Leeds punks and students which was regularly a flashpoint between anti-fascist and National Front supporters. In regular attendance would be Green Gartside, later of Scritti Politti, Marc Almond, Frank Tovey (aka Fad Gadget) and sundry members of the group's brothers-in-arms, the Mekons. It was Andy Corrigan of the latter who suggested a name for their fellow travellers when he spotted the headline "Gang Of Four On Trial' on a news-stand. They initially accepted it as a joke, but they also enjoyed the link with the Maoist faction, significantly one led by a woman, Mao's widow. But, as Burnham would point out to Martin Aston, "We were the most aptly named band.... One of our strengths is that we were four different people pulling in different directions." Gill thinks differently. "My feeling is that it is one of our fundamental weaknesses."

Formed in April 1977, the group played its first gig in May in the basement of Leeds Corn Exchange, but their most important early engagement came as support to the Buzzcocks at Ilkley College in November 1977, with sound man and collaborator Rob Warr acting as manager. They were already an arresting sight – King and Gill's 'wired' performances, wherein effecting the correct note took secondary status to the amount of kinetic tumult they could engender, existed in contrast to the disciplined, taut sound that would characterise them on record. By now their set had solidified around ideas of consumer alienation through the eyes of marginalised individuals. Or, as Greil Marcus would observe: "What was on their mind was the notion that everyday life-wage labour, official propaganda, the commodity system – but also the way you bought a shirt, how you made love, the feeling you had as you watched the nightly news or turned away from it – was not 'natural', but the product of an invisible hand." Gramsci on Gramophone records, no less.

Their first demos, which included 'Love Not Lust', which later became 'Damaged Goods', were recorded at the end of 1977. Looking for an outlet, they despatched a tape to Bob Last of Fast Records, which had just put out its first record, the Mekons' 'Never Been In A Riot'. Chivalrously, the Mekons had told Last all along that Gang Of Four predated them and were the better band. Fast duly released GO4's debut EP in 1978, comprising 'Damaged Goods', 'Love Like Anthrax' and 'Armalite Rifle'. The comic depiction of a conversation on the rear of the cover between a bull and a matador, the former lecturing his quarry that "we have to give the audience what they want", was prompted by the band sharing a bill with a stripper at the Pagoda Club in Carlisle. The same story has been attributed to a reactionary comedian, but Andy Gill is happy to quash that myth. "Our support act was a stripper. We were impressed by the stripper's analysis of the Entertainment industry. It was her words Jon and I placed coming from the mouth of the female matador as she addressed the bull."

With their explicit politicisation of the pop manifesto (though they would argue that it was other bands who were avowedly apolitical which heightened the contrast) and support of both the Rock Against Racism and Rock Against Sexism movements, and via a series of polemical interviews in the music press, the band were regarded by their detractors as dour worthies, or hidebound socialists. However, Allen, under direct questioning, would respond that "no-one's a member of anything", preferring to eschew straightforward affiliations to fringe organisations like the Socialist Workers' Party who would have dearly liked to claim them as their own. Or as King explained to Ross McGibbon: "We came in as part of the left and I'm very proud to be part of that new left. When you look at the oppression of Eastern European governments and Maoist governments, we didn't support that. I did an interview in America and a reporter said to me, 'How can you be a communist and make money from shows?' I said, 'Well, first of all I'm not a communist, but actually I think you've got your categories in a twist. Actually Marx would have said that money exchanges hands rightfully in a communist system. And the headline said 'Jon King denies he's a communist!'" Then there was the famed off-stage spat between Gill and Allen when the latter put his foot on a monitor and was berated for striking such a 'rockist' pose. Not by the press, but by his own band members.

Their exact position on the political compass mattered little to their enemies, however, who included students union members they'd previously enraged by disrupting a blandly consensual sit-in on campus. It was not unusual for local constabularies to take a dim view of punk, but with the Gang Of Four there was something darker at work. There was an incident after a show in Kendal where the police found, or according to the band, planted, a block of hashish in their van, resulting in a night in the cells. They were also arrested in Leeds and faced routine dust-ups with the National Front, who at that time regarded the Yorkshire city as something of a stronghold and even fomented plans to build themselves a platform by sponsoring a handful of far right bands.

With the success of their debut EP, Gang Of Four faced the eternal dilemma of any band critiquing contemporary capitalism when an offer from EMI, megalith of the music industry and major investor in the arms trade, arrived. Critics immediately pointed out the contradictions (David Fricke suggesting they "undoubtedly fancy themselves as cultural guerillas based in the heart of the beast"). But it wasn't as if the band members were unaware of the tightrope they were walking. The response was a familiar one, boiling down to the fact that it's harder to overthrow the state on an empty stomach, and that working musicians are just that, workers. "I don't know if anyone in the band said that," notes Gill. "But I would never have used such a weak argument." The band did, however, retain artistic freedom, in so much as that is a viable proposition in context, and operated as a semi-autonomous unit providing their backers with not just music, but a completed package of artwork, etc, effectively licensing the finished product. In any case, they didn't seem at all vexed by the compromise, eschewing notions that they should have remained with a small independent label as a nonsensical exercise in little-league capitalism. As Gill later explained to Jon Savage, "It was like a production deal, they gave us the money, we gave them the tapes. We had total control over the packaging and the production of the records. From the beginning, we picked EMI as being a perfect label for us to be on; one of the biggest industrial conglomerates in the UK – a huge multinational, trading in everything from arms to Entertainment. If we'd been on Rough Trade, it would have been a far less potent juxtaposition."

Their relationship with the 'beast' was consummated with the release of 'At Home He's A Tourist', drawing on classic Marxist texts about workplace conditioning and commodity fetishism, and the inability of drilled workers to reassimilate in their home environment. Greil Marcus, the group's most prominent supporter, references the lyrics in The Dustbin Of History. Just as stark was B-side 'It's Her Factory', on which Hugo Burnham recited a news story he'd encountered about 'heroines' in the kitchen. This would be a familiar facet of the band, recycling commonplace imagery without undue editorial tinkering, letting the meaningless internal rhetoric of the utterances articulate themselves.

Their chances of reading a wider demographic were stymied, however, when they were banned from appearing on Top Of The Pops to perform 'Tourist'. This was due to the song's reference to 'rubbers', or condoms. After entreaties were made to secure an amendment, they settled on 'packets', thinking that not to offer some compromise would be foolhardy. That didn't prove enough, the Beeb suggesting that 'rubbish' might make for a neat couplet. At which point the group walked away, mid-rehearsal, believing that the lyrics had been a ruse to get rid of them. Instead Dire Straits got to play 'Sultans Of Swing'.

Debut album Entertainment! dissected the impersonal nature of contemporary consumerism, albeit with more realpolitik than similar concerns advanced by, for example, X-Ray Spex. The lyrics, in isolation, ostensibly felt like a soundtrack to an agit-prop pamphlet, but the music was constantly inventive, questing, dissatisfied. Abetted by the discordant musical doctrine, the images evoked took on their own sinister nuances. The process was entirely deliberate. "For the songs on Entertainment!," Gill told Jason Gross, "we'd sit there and Jon would have a few lines and then I'd throw in a few lines, we'd argue about it. We were going for pithy lines that summed up certain images, structures and relationships that we saw around us. Because we took it seriously, which a lot of people don't do, the whole lyrical side of things was extremely important in the whole set up. 95% of bands don't place very much importance on lyrics. Usually, it's all left up to the singer, the guy who writes the songs. We took it seriously and we weren't trying to copy anybody else."

G

The parable of Lot's wife was revisited (as in the Stranglers' 'Choosey Suzie', but to rather different effect) in 'Natural's Not In It', in which the author is throttled by the transience and emptiness of his desires. Other punk bands talked openly about sex – herein the Gang Of Four preferred the term 'fornication', making the sense of discomfort formal, measured, impersonal and inescapable. 'Return The Gift' saw them implore the alienated to reject their life choices, but collapses into the heartbreaking emotional cul-de-sac that "evenings and weekends" are the only release life is likely to offer. And '5.45' emphasised the disparity between the pallid comforts of the home with the daily ritual of bloodletting exhibited on television news. Arguably the keynote remained 'Anthrax', its title shortened, in which the personal and the political counterbalance awkwardly, even tragically. "And I feel like a beetle on its back/And there's no way for me to get up/Love'll get you like a case of anthrax/And that's something I don't want to catch'.

They continued to tour, including two trips to America where the album hadn't yet been given a domestic release, whilst releasing the 1980 single, 'Outside The Trains Don't Run On Time'. Meanwhile, the group's internal dynamic was showing signs of wear and tear – there were constant arguments, according to Gill, right down to the price of a Mars bar. Or Gill would routinely clash with Burnham about expunging anything that sounded remotely like conventional rock drumming. The subsequent Solid Gold never garnered the critical plaudits afforded its forerunner, but it doesn't wholly deserve the neglect afforded it. "Is it neglected?" Gill asks. "I suppose everyone goes on about Entertainment! so much that it seems neglected." Certainly tracks such as 'Cheeseburger' ("the whole releationship between the USA and the old world, entrepreneurship and culture") and 'Outside The Trains Don't Run On Time', reminiscent of the comments made about that nice Benito Mussolini in Anglicised sections of Rome, and also mentioned in Rick Moody's short story collection Demonology, are up there with the band's best. 'Why Theory' is perfect Gang Of Four, proferring both defiance and resignation in the face of incalculable odds. And 'Paralysed', a despondent epistle from a used and discarded worker, is simply wonderful as a standalone music statement.

The group elected to concentrate building on the high-profile stature they were gaining in the US with a succession of tours throughout 1980 and 1981, often paired with fellow travellers Pere Ubu as part of an enthralling double bill. However, while on tour there in 1981 Allen quit and joined Shriekback. His temporary replacement was Busta Jones, a Talking Heads affiliate formerly of the Sharks.

Bass player and backing vocalist Sara Lee, formerly of Jane Aire and Robert Fripp's League Of Gentleman, joined during the recording of Songs Of The Free in 1982, with producer Mike Howlett. Extracted single 'I Love A Man In A Uniform', written by King and Gill, argued that you could dance to feminist dialectics, and was co-opted by gay clubs, but was banned by the BBC due to Falklands-era paranoia. 'We Live As We Dream, Alone', again featuring Joy Yates on backing vocals, is a keenly observed precursor to the synth pop of Heaven 17 or early Human League, only with far greater gravitas. The title and inspiration for the song were both taken by Gill from the line in Conrad's Heart Of Darkness. 'Everybody is in too many pieces..." Indeed. Burnham was sacked by Gill and King in April 1983, ostensibly because they considered themselves the writing force behind the group, with Burnham spending much of his time on management issues. But the way they conducted the ousting proved a major obstacle to the band working together again. "I don't regret it," Gill notes of the decision.

The remaining duo put together the disappointing Hard in 1983. Featuring a variety of backing vocalists, namely Jon Astrop, Chuck Kirkpatrick, Alfa Anderson, and Brenda White, with Astrop (bass) and Steve Goulding (drums; ex-Rumour, Elvis Costello) manning the rhythm section for live dates, the choice of Ron and Howard Albert (Crosby Stills And Nash etc) as producers raised eyebrows. It didn't work for several reasons. The songs shifted in focus and dropped some of the political observation that was the band's stock in trade, and the backing tracks lacked sparkle. In essence, they sounded like a totally different band, seemingly shooting for some form of commercial approbation and taking out the golden goose instead. The exception was Gill's 'Woman Town', which drew on the character of Natacha in Jean-Luc Godard's Alphaville in its depiction of sexuality and love as a threat. They split the following year after a farewell live album, recorded at the Hollywood Palace on their final tour.

G

In the wake of the band's demise Gill, having released one solo single, 'Dispossession' (August 1987) produced the Red Hot Chili Peppers, Killing Joke, the Futureheads and Michael Hutchence. In collaboration with King, who formed King Butcher, he also produced a track for the Karate Kid soundtrack, before the latter became an IT consultant. Gill also worked on the soundtrack to Derek Jarman's The Last Of England in 1988. They've also worked on instrumental music for TV, including – a nice touch this – Parliament Today and Westminster Live. Allen co-founded the much under-rated Shriekback with Barry Andrews, formerly of XTC, then Low Pop Suicide and cut two solo albums. He set up an online business after moving to Portland and ran World Domination Records and currently works in multimedia. He also plays in local band Menomena. Sara Lee continues to work as a musician in New York having worked extensively with the B-52s. Burnham joined Illustrated Man and did sessions for ABC before managing Shriekback – having turned down a similar offer from ABC. He also temporarily joined PiL, play-drumming Ginger Baker's contribution on 'Rise', on Top Of The Pops in 1986, before performing the chops for... Samantha Fox. Drummers. No principles. He is now a Boston-based lecturer (at the New England Institute Of Art) after a mixed career that included stints as a truck driver and work with Quincy Jones before becoming A&R director of publishing for EMI, the auld enemy. "You will change things more at the heart of the beast than you will banging your head on the wall outside," he reasoned in a 1997 interview with Q. Some battles are never won, nor lost, seemingly.

Gill and King would put the band back together in 1990 to record Mall and its two accompanying singles. Everyone seemed disappointed with the results, with both good and bad reason. This simply was never a band, rather like fellow travellers Wire, who were going to attempt to recreate former glories. The album certainly falls short of those. Having said that, I still like opening tracks 'Cadillac' and 'Motel' a fair bit, though the former recalls Big Audio Dynamite and both betray the fact that the band had spent an awful lot of time in America. There's a cover of Bob Marley's 'Soul Rebel' that doesn't work at all, while 'Satellite' is quietly affecting, but as with much of their later output the cooing backing vocals and filtered electronica often subtract rather than add. The band themselves, which in this incarnation featured later Bowie collaborator Gail Ann Dorsey on bass and vocals, have subsequently expressed dissatisfaction with the finished product. They also stepped out on an ill-fated 1991 package tour that ended after a few dates, though this did pair them with Public Enemy, a group whose resistance to harmony and fondness for the harsh and atonal mirrored theirs.

They had another crack in the mid-90s, or at least King and Gill did with new recruits Laurence O'Keefe on bass (ex-Curve) and former Levitation drummer Steve Monti after they were asked to score a Peter Hall film and realised they had the basis of an album. Shrinkwrapped was in many ways darker than the preceding Gang Of Four long-player, less optimistic, with strong hints of mental illness and fragility in tracks such as 'The Dark Ride'. 'I Parade Myself' and 'Better Him Than Me' are probably the only tracks here that would fit readily with the band's sonic history, but the rich textural depth of the accompanying tracks compensates. "I think that doesn't do it justice," reckons Gill. "The songs 'Showtime' and 'Shrinkwrapped' are weird and complex masterpieces in my book."

A full reunion of the original line-up was announced in 2005, prompted by the wave of posthumous adulation from a besotted new generation of bands. Artists such as Franz Ferdinand, Rapture, Radio 4, Futureheads (whom Gill had, as previously noted, produced) Bloc Party and Radio 4 all acknowledged their influence, adding to what Burnham later described as the "critical mass" behind the reformation. The other main motivating force, however, was Gill's manager, Jazz Summers. He organised a meeting in London in 2004, which saw Burnham fly over from Massachusetts and Allen from Oregon. It was the first time they'd all been in the same room for over two decades. They tentatively booked five shows, which immediately sold out, as well as a warm-up gig to see if it all hung together at the Montague Arms in Peckham in January. The decision was taken to stick almost exclusively to the first two albums and To Hell With Poverty EP, though later Shrinkwrapped's 'I Parade Myself' would be added to the set.

"The idea was to unpick new music," Gill told Uncut in 2005 in a neat summary of their history, "whether it was disco or funk, and put it back together in an original form, to consider every last drum beat. There was constant discussion." That rationale is something they rekindled wonderfully in a series of shows that demonstrated what a good live act they always were, and what an astonishing back catalogue they were now able to draw upon. Which was pretty much what Hugh Burnham confirmed to Rolling Stone. "We all agree(d) that it had to be fun, and that it had to work around our individual lives to make it worthwhile. We have a strong creative legacy, and the last thing we wanted to do is go out and fuck that up by doing a half-hearted job."

It didn't sound like that happened, as long-time fan Jack Rabid noted of their Irving Plaza shows in May 2005. "Once again, like ping pong balls in a lottery machine, Gill and Allen glanced off each other as they moved around, as if they were trying to play some hyper game of Twister. Meanwhile King hopped around and through them on his own personal frog-leap race. Behind, a much larger Burnham added a tribal element to his neo-funk rock beats, exhorting the visual mayhem in his sight. The last kicker was watching King smash the fuck out of a microwave each night with a baseball bat to the one in four beat of 'He'd Send In The Army'. Outrageously great!"

DISCOGRAPHY:

(Buyer's Guide: Entertainment! is a must (get the Rhino version if you can). After that, The Peel Sessions and A Brief History Of The 20th Century are the places to go next. If you have an open mind, the band really do nail it on the re-recorded Return The Gift, though the sound variance may blindside some long-term fans)

Damaged Goods 7-inch EP (Fast Products FAST 5 October 1978)

Damaged Goods/Love Like Anthrax/Armalite Rifle

At Home He's A Tourist/It's Her Factory 7-inch (EMI EMI 2956 March 1979)

Entertainment! LP (EMI EMC 3313 September 1979) (reissued on CD by EMI, CZ 541, in 1995 with additional tracks 'Outside The Trains Don't Run On Time', 'He'd Send In The Army' and 'It's Her Factory', with the surprising omission of 'Armalite Rifle' from the Yellow EP. The US reissue, with 'Armalite Rifle' present and correct, came out on Infinite Zero, 9 14502-2. However, the version to get is the Rhino/WEA release, 78428, released in May 2005. Completely remastered by Gill and King at Abbey Road, the sound knocks spots off previous CD versions. There's liner notes by Michael Azzerad with contributions from Flea of the Peppers, the Yellow EP tracks in full, plus four other bonus cuts – 'Guns Before Butter (alternate version)', 'Contract (alternate version)', 'Blood Free (Live From The Electric Ballroom)', 'Sweet Jane (Live From The American Indian Center)'. There is also a vinyl version available without the bonus tracks)

Outside The Trains Don't Run On Time/He'd Send In The Army 7-inch (EMI Zonophone Z1 April 1980) (aka The Yellow EP. Also released on 12-inch, EMI Zonophone MINI 3494, with additional tracks 'It's Her Factory' and 'Armalite Rifle')

What We All Want/History's Bunk 7-inch (EMI EMI 5146 March 1981) (also released as 12-inch)

Solid Gold LP (EMI EMC 3364 March 1981) (reissued on CD, Premier CZ 561, 1996)

Cheeseburger/Paralysed 7-inch (EMI EMI 5177 May 1981) (also released as 12-inch)

To Hell With Poverty/Capital (It Fails Us Now) 7-inch (EMI EMI 5193 July 1981) (also released as 12-inch)

Another Day, Another Dollar mini-LP (Warners MINI 3646 February 1982)

To Hell With Poverty/What We All Want/Cheeseburger/Capital (It Fails Us Now)/History's Bunk! (US only, recordings taken from Hammersmith Palais in 1981)

I Love A Man In A Uniform/World At Fault (EMI EMI 5299 April 1982) (also released as 12-inch)

Songs Of The Free LP (EMI EMC 3412 1982)
I Love A Man In A Uniform/I Will Be A Good Boy 12-inch (Warners 29921 June 1982) (US only, notable for 'extended' version of a-side)
Call Me Up (If I'm At Home)/I Will Be A Good Boy 7-inch (EMI EMI 5320 July 1982)
Is It Love/Man With A Good Car 7-inch (EMI EMI 5418 August 1983) (also released as 12-inch)
Hard LP (EMI 1652191 September 1983)
Silver Lining/Independence 7-inch (EMI EMI 5440 November 1983)
I Will Be A Good Boy (live)/Is It Love (live)/Call Me Up (If I'm At Home) (live) 12-inch (Mercury GANG 12 October 1984)
At The Palace (Live) LP (Mercury MERL 51 November 1984) (also issued on cassette with bonus tracks 'I Will Be A Good Boy', 'Call Me Up')
Money Talks (The Money Mix)/Use The Colour From The Tube 7-inch (Scarlett June 1990)
Mall LP & CD (Polydor 849 124 May 1991)
Cadillac/Motel/Favourites 12-inch (Polydor P2 152 DJ May 1991)
Tattoo/Banned Words/Cop Goes Home 7-inch and cassette single (When! WEN 71M 1002 August 1995) (also issued on CD single, with 'Tattoo (Quiet Guy mix)')
Shrinkwrapped CD (When! WEN CD/MC 003 September 1995)
ARCHIVE RELEASES:
The Peel Session 12-inch (Strange Fruit SFPSC 8 1986)
I Found That Essence Rare/Return The Gift/5-45/At Home He's A Tourist (rec. 18.1.79) (released on CD in 1990)
The Peel Sessions (Complete Sessions 1979-1981) LP (Strange Fruit SFRLP 107 1990) (also released on CD, SFRCD 107. Three good to excellent BBC sessions – particularly the first which had already been issued as a standalone)
A Brief History Of The 20th Century LP (Warner Brothers WB 26448 November 1990) (also released on CD, EMI CDEMO 3583. Features extensive sleevenotes by Greil Marxist. I mean Marcus. A very good starting point, though sadly there's no 'Armalite Rifle' or 'I Found That Essence Rare'. And by encompassing so much later period material, it highlights the band's artistic decline).
You Can Catch Up With History (1978-1983) LP/CD (Capitol Greenlight GO 2028 March 1990) (although this has been listed in numerous books, it seems that this was never released, and instead evolved into the 'Brief History' project)
To Hell With Poverty (The Loaded Edit)/To Hell With Poverty (original version)/Cheeseburger (live)/Call Me Up 7-inch EP (EMI EMS 172 January 1991) (also available as CD EP and 12-inch single)
Solid Gold/Another Day, Another Dollar CD (Warners 43935 October 1995) (album + mini-album package)
100 Flowers Bloom (Rare Tracks) double CD (Rhino R2 75479 November 1998) (live tracks recorded at the North American Indian Center, San Francisco, 22/5/80, apart from 'I I Could Keep It For Myself', live at the Apollo Theatre, Oxford, 29/3/81, 'What We All Want', live at the Hammersmith Palais, London, 30/3/81, and 1984 tracks recorded live at the Palace, Hollywood, May 1984. A completist's fantasy)
Return The Gift double CD (V2 October 2005) (the first disc features new studio versions of classic GO4 material. Second disc features guest remixes. Surprisingly, the re-recorded versions sound great, with the new studio technology available adding bite rather than burying the original songs. It takes a little getting used to. Those familiar with the skewed, zig-zagging cross-rhythms and minimalism of the originals may be taken aback by the sheer sonic force of the new versions. They make the pull-push of the Gang's inimitable original rhythm section more of an equal contest, with Burnham's drumming the most prominent beneficiary. Certainly worth hearing, though)
SELECTED COMPILATIONS:
Fast Product – The First Year Plan LP (Fast/EMI F11/EMC 3312 1979; 'Love Like Anthrax', 'Armalite Rifle', 'Damaged Goods')
Urgh! A Music War LP (A&M SP6019 1981; 'He'd Send In The Army', recorded live at the Rainbow Theatre, London, 18.9.80)

Gangsters

Bill Meadows (vocals, guitar), Richard Holgarth (vocals, guitar), Peter Capaldi (bass), Allan Meadows (drums)

Alongside the Sods, the **GANGSTERS**, formed in 1978, were Harlow's first band to release an independent single. They evolved out of the Oscars, who featured the Meadows brothers plus bass player Paul and guitarist Steve 'Wally' Walton, who also played with the Gangsters a couple of times. The Oscars played three shows,

one alongside Pete The Meat and the Rage at an Epping Centre Rock Against Racism show. They then, briefly, became the Incinerators in 1976. This was a rehearsal-only band wherein the Meadows were joined by vocalists Kevin Jones and Ivan Carpenter as well as guitarist Vince Skobal.

The Gangsters played regular local gigs including the Triad in Bishops Stortford. Bill Meadows: "The Triad all-dayers were the epitome of the local Stortford and Harlow/Epping music scene. They were great times – enthused young bands, receptive, appreciative audiences, guest bands from London and Brighton (such as the Passions and Piranhas). It was a really good atmosphere. There was an all-day bar as well! It was just a nice time, but it didn't last – people went their different ways." The B-side of their debut single immortalised those origins and their locale. The vocals are very reminiscent, or perhaps prescient, of later Harlow 'name' band the Newtown Neurotics. The A-side was a proud stab at independence: 'I don't want to be... in no record company." The songs were tightly played, energetic, somewhere in the vein of the Jam, although shorn of major label production values.

G

After the single's release, Allan Meadows was "given the elbow because he preferred the pub to playing impromptu gigs," according to his brother, Bill. Capaldi also departed for no stated reason. Their replacements were Terry Hardy on drums and Martin Holden on bass (Richard Holgarth, Terry Hardy and Martin Holden were also, concurrently, Pete The Meat And The Boys).

They began recording their debut album in Cambridge in March 1979, scraping together enough money to hire a basement studio. They cut the contents of the album in just one day, although Bill Meadows was almost sacked from his day job when, due to outright exhaustion, he turned up at midday the following afternoon. Eventually he jacked the job and instead he went on to helm Stortbeat Records (ironic, given the lyrics of their debut single). Stortbeat issued all the band's recordings, though Stortbeat was actually more of a bands' collective and an outlet for the local music scene, rather than a record label proper.

However, the debut album, which featured Steve Horton on keyboards, got minimal exposure, and there were further line-up problems. Hardy left the band under his girlfriend's influence and was replaced by Billy Jorden, who blew their showpiece gig at the Square in Harlow in 1980 when nerves got the better of him and he was rendered incapable due to alcohol consumption. Bill Meadows chose to end the band in disgust, though there was a farewell appearance as a three-piece after Martin Holden failed to turn up.

And that was that, until Gordon Wilkins organised his Stortbeat compilation. "A launch party was held at the Square Harlow on 4 November 2004, 25 years later! And that was a really fantastic night a great atmosphere, quite magical really – check the DVD! Peel was smiling down on events."

DISCOGRAPHY:

Record Company/Harlow Town 7-inch (Stortbeat BEAT 1 1979) (no picture sleeve)
The Gangsters LP (Stortbeat BEAT 2 1979)
Best Friend/Best Friend (dub) 7-inch (Stortbeat BEAT 3 1979) (whereas by now they could afford a picture sleeve, at least for a second pressing)
COMPILATION:
Stortbeat: A Musical Collective double CD (Handsignal Recordings Handy 2 and Handy 2A 2004; 'Record Company', 'Harlow Town', 'Best Friend', 'Trouble We Go Through', 'Weekend') (note: not the same as the ska band Gangsters who recorded for Big Bear)

Generation X

Billy Idol (aka William Broad; vocals), Tony James (bass), Bob 'Derwood' Andrews (guitar), John Towe (drums)

Flashy glam pusses, GENERATION X were among the most image-conscious of punk's first movers, especially in the person of William Broad, aka Billy Idol, a throwback to an earlier age of quiffed teen rebellion. The references to the 50s and 60s were echoed in their approximation of both the music and the vernacular of those times, notably in songs such as 'Ready, Steady Go' and 'Your Generation'. They mocked punk's anti-commercial instincts but they also produced one of the movement's most coherent and durable albums, and a number of great singles.

Their origins can be traced back to 1975 when James, who had already experimented with a Hawkwind/Pink Fairies-style band entitled Random Frog, answered an advert for a bass player in Melody Maker. That brought him to the attention of Kelvin Colney (later of Violent Luck, the Tools, Sister Ray, Tuff Darts, White Cats, etc). Colney thought the youthful applicant might work better with his flatmate, Mick Jones. And so began the long and ultimately fruitless adventure that was London SS, their Bernie Rhodes-sponsored Paddington rehearsal room and the conveyor belt of punk would-be's that passed through.

In 1976 Idol, having bored of his English Literature and Philosophy degree course in Brighton, returned to Bromley. He'd already adopted his new name. "Very early on a teacher in one of my school reports had written in gigantic letters 'William is I-d-l-e'. And then I thought, 'but it should be rock idol' – I-D-O-L." As his father confirmed in the VH1 series Before They Were Famous, "As far as I was concerned he was a normal, nice boy, and it was difficult for me when he began to show a lot more interest in music then he did in arithmetic." His parents, who had spent four years in America, were solidly middle class, and his youth was spent by turns in Bromley and bucolic Worthing. Later, scorned for his lack of working class punk credentials by the likes of Boy George, he would rail to ZigZag: "The insinuation is that middle class people can't sing or something. What is it, man?" By the mid-70s he was regularly attending gigs by Roxy Music and Kilburn and the High Roads, his constant travelling companion Steven Bailey, later the Banshees' Severin.

One story is that Idol met Tony James, himself soon to graduate from Brunel University with a maths degree, in a Soho pub. They allegedly, and amusingly, decided they looked cool together. A bit of myth-making would seem to be at play here. James had actually answered an advert placed by Idol in Melody Maker – "Wanted: guitarist into Small Faces, early Who, Rolling Stones, Velvet Underground." "I drove over to his parents' place one Saturday afternoon," James later told Pat Gilbert. Severin and Siouxsie were also at the meeting. Even though James was a bass player rather than a guitarist, he was in. "There was an instant bond. Billy and I sat and played some Lou Reed songs, the Stones' 'It's All Over Now'."

James had finally tired of London SS's inability to get their act together. Bernie Rhodes had bid him farewell with the pay-off, "James, you're too fucking soft. Tell your parents you're going to spend Christmas with a hooker." As James confirmed to Pat Gilbert, age and class were big issues at the time. "The problem was that Billy and I were clearly middle class in a movement created by Bernie and Malcolm McLaren, to look working class. We were the guys who had been to university. But Bernie had given me a vision. He'd toughened me up." Such was the power of perception within the embryonic punk scene that Idol later enlisted Derwood's sister to teach him to speak in a less plummy accent. Gor blimey.

Idol, by now a face on the scene as part of the Bromley Contingent of Pistols' camp followers, had turned down the offer to work as Siouxsie's guitarist after he'd found out that Sid Vicious was playing drums – Sid had recently whacked Idol, who was still fuming. Idol and James were then involved in an embryonic line-up of Gene October's Chelsea (earlier Love and Kisses and then, with Marco Pirroni on guitar, the Infants) after answering another Melody Maker advert, alongside drummer John Towe. They played three gigs, including a support to Throbbing Gristle under the name L.S.D (at which Towe was terrified, believing widespread rumours that Genesis P. Orridge was going to hang himself at the climax of the show). There was a second show supporting the Buzzcocks at Manchester's Electric Circus, culminating in a support slot to the Stranglers at the Nashville on 21 November. But the trio soon elected to start their own band, after Gene October failed to hit the right notes, both musically and thematically, while demo-ing material like 'Your Generation'.

They took their new name from a 1964 paperback, written by Charles Hamblett and Jane Deverson, found on Idol's mother's bookshelf. "It was about all the youth movements and calling it Generation X, saying that really our generation was searching for an identity," Idol later recalled. "(It) seemed like a perfect name and then we phoned all our friends up to tell them. They all said they hated it, so I knew it was right." Rather than some exploitation pulp classic as it has frequently been referred to, said tome is actually a series of transcripts of interviews with young Mods by a couple of journalists trying to find out what the new media folk devils really thought.

The rest of the band encountered Bob 'Derwood' Andrews while he was playing 'Smoke On

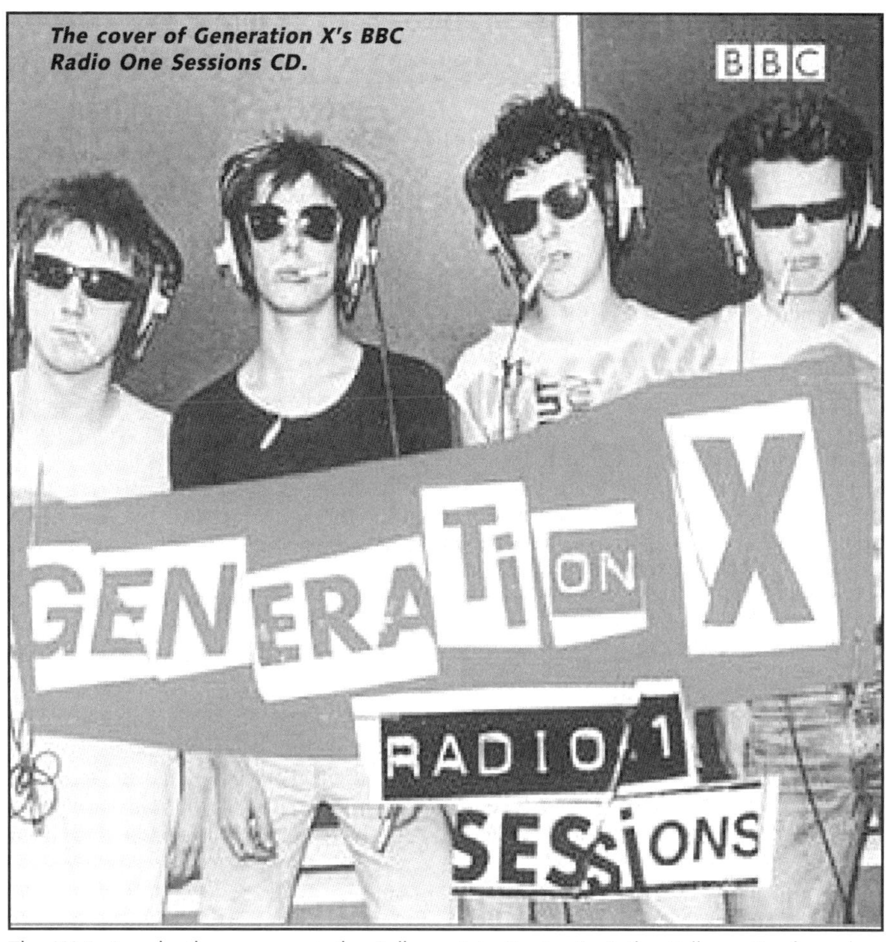

The cover of Generation X's BBC Radio One Sessions CD.

The Water' and other covers at the Fulham Arts Centre (not the Fulham Greyhound as erroneously reported) as part of youth club band Paradox on 4 December 1976. It was Paradox's only gig, Derwood, who was immediately told to get his hair cut, joined on guitar so that Idol could take over vocals. They'd already tried out a variety of guitarists who were either 'deaf or ugly'. He'd previously been a gardener on Princess Margaret's estate, "sunbathing and smoking dope in the royal tool shed." His nickname, incidentally, was drawn from the mispronunciation of Darren by his mother-in-law in the long-running US sitcom Bewitched. "I went along and was blown away with the power and the purity of the music and joined right away," Derwood later told The Big Takeover. "I probably should have been the singer from the start," Idol later admitted, "but it was a great kind of few months of playing the guitar and singing because then I learned how to be onstage." They immediately took Derwood to a Marc Bolan party to convince him they were going places, and got him to listen to James Williamson's playing with the Stooges. Derwood also looked 'right'. "We'd never have a fat person in the band," James pointed out.

10 December 1976 saw their live debut at the Central College Of Art and Design in London, their second appearance coming at the Roxy 11 days later – the first punk band to play the venue. They were the headliners of the first punk festival there, largely due to the fact that its owner, Andy Czezowski, had taken over their management. A series of shows followed through January, including supports with Squeeze and a show at Liverpool's Eric's. They also got their first press via a half page article written by Tony Barnes in the NME, and cut demos for Chiswick Records of 'Listen', 'New Order' and 'Ready Steady Go'. Meanwhile at their biggest show yet, playing with the Boys in March 1977, their set was stopped when Derwood was hit in the head with a glass beer mug and required stitches. The projectile was, as Derwood pointed out to me, not the reported 'can of beer'. "They don't hurt!"

Tony Parsons penned good reviews of these early shows, notably on 30 January 1977. "Generation X may well be the 'punk rock' group that many people have been waiting for; lyrics about change and revolution, but with melodies cute enough for 'boy meets girl'." But by the time he interviewed them in February for the NME he was having second thoughts. "Street soldiers fuelled on orange juice? Revolutionaries who don't give a shit about Bergen-Belsen? The orders-nouveau sung to pleasant pop melodies? If Generation X didn't hype themselves as being such a big deal then I would probably not be as turned off by the band as I am now." The 'Orange Juice Punks' stuff arose from his shock at their drinking said beverage in the pub. Idol stated unequivocally that the band didn't do drugs or alcohol: "The revolution can't happen if you're knackered tomorrow." The truth was that both Idol and James had contracted the clap after sleeping with the same woman and were on medication.

G

They were also under new management, Rough Trade employee Stuart Joseph and Sounds writer Jonh Ingham having replaced Czezowski in February. Czezowski did try to enlist them for his Live At The Roxy compilation. They refused, James claiming the Roxy had turned into a 'horror show'. Jonh Ingham was immediately impressed by James' ability to conceptualise the group and what he wanted to do, as he confirmed to Pat Gilbert. "We were sitting in this room I rented in Notting Hill, going through the whole thing, listening to Low and The Idiot, all focused on the same things that made them great. This was when I realised Tony had a skill – he was saying, 'Listen to the mix, listen to the kick drum, listen to what he's doing with it.' Really analysing the music to see what made it work. His understanding was very detailed." It was also James who would write the band's lyrics, with Idol annotating the musical structures.

A support slot to John Cale at the Roundhouse followed when the Clash pulled out, and they were filmed performing 'This Heat' and 'Kleenex' for Don Letts' film The Punk Rock Movie. The footage was memorable for James getting his member out and Idol observing that "I sounded a bit like Elvis there". Ingham managed to secure their debut (thrice broadcast and widely bootlegged, to the extent that there were rumours of an official BBC release) John Peel session in April 1977, comprising 'Day By Day', 'Listen', 'Youth Youth Youth' and 'Your Generation'. While they had numerous detractors, Peel would stick with the band, citing them as "perfect".

Thereafter Towe was ejected, leaving to join Mark Perry's Alternative TV (and later the Adverts) in April 1977. Replacement Mark Laff, aka Mark Laffoley, late of Subway Sect, who'd just lost the vacant Clash spot to Topper Headon, had been recommended to them by Mick Jones as consolation. The new line-up made their debut at Cardiff Top Rank on 14 June 1977.

By the advent of a second Peel session on 21 July they had declined several competing offers to throw in their lot with Chrysalis. It was widely reported at the time that the band received the biggest 'advance' of any of their peers, a sum now confirmed to be £75,000. By this time the band were pulling a regular audience but were systematically pummelled by a music press who were convinced that they were a bunch of clothes horses – a situation aggravated by Idol's pouty appearances in a number of teen rags. There was also deep suspicion of them from within the punk scene, as Gareth Holder of the Shapes noted: "Little William Broad was a big tosser even then, before he started calling himself Billy Idol. We used to call him the punk Cliff Richard, because that's what we thought he looked like. When Generation X were playing (in fact they were the first band to play the Roxy), we'd all be throwing shit at them, because even then, Billy Idol was a wanker." Ranking Roger, later of The Beat, was appalled by his attitude to the provinces on a northern excursion, and remembers severing his mic lead as a response. He was also knocked unconscious on stage at a show in December 1978 at Aston University by a hell's angel who was similarly displeased with his deportment. Poor old Billy hadn't yet sinned against the world of popular music – it was as if karma was getting a few kicks in early.

'Your Generation', produced by Sweet and Bay City Rollers' veteran Phil Wainman, was released in September. It reached 36 in the charts, selling 52,000 copies. Chrysalis had intended a big promotional push, but their plans were scuppered when a bootleg version featuring demos of 'Your Generation' and 'Listen' began to circulate. Worse, some of the music papers were reviewing the wrong version of the single. An answer record to the Who's epochal 'My Generation', it was nevertheless successful enough to see them become the first punk band to appear on Top Of The Pops. "That was a big deal in those days," James recalled to Q. "We went on Top Of The Pops and it was a dream to be on there because only proper groups went on that programme. We never had this problem about going on television because we wanted to be stars."

To promote the single, Generation X embarked on a national tour, then set up a weekly residency at the Marquee through September. They were also invited to play 'Your Generation' on old friend Marc Bolan's TV show. "Next on are a group whose lead singer is rumoured to be even prettier than me!" cooed Bolan. Billy presumably wet himself.

Their first foray abroad came with an engagement at the Gibus Club in Paris in October for a week of shows, before returning to London and further work on their debut album. A second single, 'Wild Youth', a perfunctory glam-mod effort apparently knocked together in five minutes after seeing some graffiti on a wall, and recorded at the same sessions with Phil Wainman as their debut single, failed to chart. It was notable for the dub rhythms of flipside 'Wild Dub', effectively a scuzzed up, reggae-tinged version of the a-side. James Dutton, whose band the Interrogators were one of the first to mix punk with reggae, recalls it as one of the better experiments. "I really liked it. Until you get to the end where Billy Idol shouts 'A heavy, heavy dub, punk rockers!' which was incredibly cringe-worthy and ruined the record."

Having been among the first to merge reggae with punk, could Generation X have pushed that side further? "What can I say?" Derwood responded when asked about this by Jean Encoule. "We should (have) pursued the 'Wild Dub' thing much more. It wasn't until the third album that we got back on track to try and solidify what Generation X music was to be. By then it was too late." They closed 1977 by supporting the Ramones on New Year's Eve at the Rainbow.

'Ready Steady Go', a thrilling, impassioned tribute to the 60s music show hosted by Cathy McGowan, was extracted as the lead single from their forthcoming album in February 1978. It was the first song that Idol and James had written together. The band's debut album, recorded over just seven days with Martin Rushent producing and Alan Winstanley engineering at TW Studios in Fulham, was released at the same time in March 1978. Phil Wainman was again slated for the job until he objected to Laff's drumming, claiming it was too wild and unsyncopated. When James refused to sack him, Wainman walked and aborted the sessions. So, much to Jonh Ingham's ire, Martin Rushent, who'd enjoyed success with both the Buzzcocks and Stranglers, was drafted. Idol later complained that the recordings were rushed because Rushent "was trying to mix us, mix the Stranglers, run the United Artists A&R department, and do 999 all at the same time."

The sleeve photos were taken by Gered Mankowitz, famed for his work with the Who. It's a great set, full of swagger without tipping over into arrogance. Derwood's slicing guitar is a revelation, and the handclaps on outsider anthem 'One Hundred Punks' don't even jar. There are a number of topical songs in keeping with the new punk ethos. 'Listen' implored its audience to get off their backsides and do something, while 'Kleenex' is one of many songs in the punk canon celebrating masturbation, though the Kleenex company unsurprisingly declined an invitation to provide sponsorship. 'Promises, Promises', meanwhile, sagely reflected on the increasing absurdities about authenticity in the punk revolution. The cornerstone of the album is 'Kiss Me Deadly', its finest approximation of kitsch and clout, pointing to the band's future direction. And if the 'I Never Want To Be An Adult' coda of 'Youth Youth Youth' brings the group close to repetitive self-parody, it's still a great set closer. It's also, again, a real showcase for Derwood, whom Rushent would later rate as the best of the punk/new wave guitarists he worked with (and he worked with some good ones).

The American version of the LP added covers of Lennon's 'Gimme Some Truth' and 'Wild Dub', as well as the two singles, forsaking three album cuts, 'Listen', 'The Invisible Man' and 'Too Personal'. Nowadays the British CD release also adds the two singles and 'Wild Dub' (while incongruously opting for the two B-side tracks to 'Friday's Angels'). The album was promoted with a full UK tour itinerary, dates accompanied by the familiar tales of rock'n'roll excess. Idol in particular was enjoying his popularity with the girls, despite the fact that he was meant to be enjoying domestic bliss with Des O'Connor's daughter in Notting Hill. But the album stubbornly refused to rise above its highest chart position of 29.

Disappointed by their failure to achieve a more significant commercial breakthrough, the group returned to the studio. Stuart Joseph was now in sole charge of the group, Ingham having fled to America after a stand-off with James because he backed Wainman's judgement that Laff couldn't play in time. James was becoming increasingly annoyed at Chrysalis's refusal to entertain the idea of a dub album (the tapes for this, tentatively entitled Generation Z, remain unreleased).

Having been turned down by Jimmy Page, sessions with Mott The Hoople's Ian Hunter at Wessex Studios ensued. Press criticism, meanwhile, centred on the fact that, in their perception, the band had 'gone metal'. There was some truth in that – their soundcheck favourites had long included Led Zeppelin's 'Rock'n'roll', Jimi Hendrix's 'Purple Haze' and Deep Purple's 'Highway Star'. But the music had become something of a side issue, masking the fact that the band was indulging in all manner of excessive behaviour, particularly James, who became seriously ill. Keith Moon had introduced him to the joys of valium. "I can't really remember making it (the album)," he confirmed to Kris Needs of ZigZag. "I remember doing the tracks, but I remember being very untogether – having to be taken home from the studio. It was a bit strange, and Hunter very much took control over it."

G

Valley Of The Dolls was finally released in January 1979, spearheaded by the profoundly silly 'King Rocker' aka 'King Kong', backed by an earlier Peel version of 'Gimme Some Truth'. Concerning an imagined boxing match between Elvis Presley and John Lennon, it was released in four separate editions of coloured vinyl, each featuring a different band member on the sleeve. It finally gave the band a substantial hit, peaking at number 11. Both 'Valley Of The Dolls' and 'Friday's Angels' were also released as singles, but these tracks, along with 'Running With The Boss Sound', are the only essential moments from a lacklustre album.

"It was interesting working with Hunter," Derwood recalled to Encoule, "but by that time we were all guilty of being blinded by ego. We took a wrong turn away from the first album, that was truly 'us', and began to emulate our heroes and so, to me, that album sounds like anyone else. Not Generation X music. Billy wanted to be Bruce Springsteen, I wanted to be Paul Kossoff/Mick Ronson, Mark wanted to be Keith Moon and I was never sure about Tony… But you have to realise how young and naive we all were. As soon as a taste of 'rock star' trappings came along, ethics went out of the window. Not just for Generation X. I don't mean money either, we never got more than about 30 quid a week, ever! Just the fact of being taken seriously and getting away with stuff."

The never camera-shy Idol was turning up in the pages of Smash Hits with alarming regularity. He would also begin to date Perri Lister, the Hot Gossip dancer. "I don't think it's bad that the group's in teenybopper papers," James responded to ZigZag, "as long as we don't do dopey things for 'em like kissing 'em under the Xmas tree and all that kind of bollocks. I'd rather young girls go and get into something a bit raunchier." I'm sure he would…

But the ensuing tour, which included another Radio 1 In Concert show at the Paris Theatre, ended in debacle. At the closing Lyceum date, over 1,000 punters were turned away and duly set upon by the following of support act the UK Subs. They spent the gig with chair legs, ashtrays and beer cans raining down on them. They also supported the Jam at Wembley Arena as part of the Capital Radio Music Festival and appeared on Top Of The Pops once more when 'Valley Of The Dolls' charted. However, 'Friday's Angels' was a disappointing single, despite being backed by two songs ('Trying For Kicks' and 'This Heat') from their first album sessions on the flip. Afterwards they flew to Japan for three shows in June.

The band, however, was on the verge of splintering. They were essentially two factions pulling in different directions, Idol and James in one corner, Derwood and Laff in the other. "That year, 1979, was really hard for me," Derwood later told The Big Takeover. "Billy and Tony wouldn't let me join the songwriting side of things and hated when I played too much guitar… Halfway through recording the third album (at Olympic Studios) and before we were due to tour Japan, I reached the end and quit the band. A meeting was called by the manager at the time (Stuart Joseph) and it was agreed to go to Japan and finish the album with all four of us splitting the songs. This was done, but by the end of 1979, I just didn't want to be around these two people anymore, and quit for good."

From Idol's point of view, as he confirmed to Jon Savage, "It was just as if things were out to destroy me. It was really heavy, there was a lot of betrayal when Generation X ended. It was all very weird. Now I understand a lot more about things, I realise life is just like that. But then it was a fight for survival: it was easy for Generation X to disappear, we'd been made into pop puppets. And if we disappeared, that would be it." Later, in their final interview with ZigZag, James pointed at Derwood's 'heavy metal' aspirations, ironic given Idol's subsequent solo career as a bubblegum hard rocker. But even James was forced to concede "Derwood is a fuckin' great player. He should do something good."

Idol has intimated he had already offered to leave: "I sat down and told them if they didn't do this 'Dancing With Myself'/'White Wedding' music, I was going to leave the group." But Derwood suggested it should be he who walked the plank and leave the others to decide their future. Laff was shown the door by James about six months later, going on to form 20 Flight Rockers. Later, Derwood and Laff would reunite in Empire. Their album, Expensive Sound, much praised by the likes of Henry Rollins, Ian MacKaye and the Dischord family, has now been re-released on CD by Poorly Packaged Products and is well worth checking out if you're a fan of the guitar sound on the first Generation X album. Empire also briefly included Ian Woodcock of Eater on bass. Derwood currently lives in America, having spent several years as leader of moderately successful 'pure pop' band Westworld and now plays in MoonDogg and the alt-country band SpeedTwinn while residing in the Mojave desert. Laff now runs a stress management company in Brighton.

The tapes of that aborted third album, the masters of which remained in Derwood's possession, would finally be released as Sweet Revenge in April 1998. They were later re-bootlegged by James to form part of Anthology. "For me, I felt we were finally making Generation X music," Derwood recalled of the sessions at Olympic Studios to The Big Takeover. "Just us, and an engineer/producer, Doug Bennett. But what was happening was, me and Doug would stay up all night making guitar tracks, only to be greeted in the morning with, 'That's too much,' which drove me nuts. So, like I said, I quit. But every night I took home quarter-inch tapes of the work and just put them in a box." Years later, he would take the tapes to Chrysalis to see if they had any interest in re-releasing them, but they didn't. "So it was actually me that made the 'bootleg' of the third album and went to various people to see if anyone would be interested in releasing it." Derwood felt justified in so doing because he was annoyed at the lack of credits he and Laff were given on subsequent Generation X reissues. Later the set was reissued as part of Anthology, though strangely this included a different version of 'Triumph' that James still had a cassette version of and a remix Derwood had done of one of the tracks, hilariously retitled 'Dancing With My Wealth'. It's not hard to work out who the subject of that one might have been.

The remaining members of Generation X took almost a year to extricate themselves from the management of Stuart Joseph, which ended up in a horrendous round of litigation, and saw them very nearly sign with Kiss manager Bill Aucoin, who would pilot Idol's subsequent solo career. It also left a huge amount of debt while Idol spent the impasse building up an impressive heroin habit. "I think they (previous management) wanted us to be a pop group," James told Zigzag, "and they also seemed to be becoming rich, and we weren't. Basically, it boils down to a lot of respect and we didn't respect them anymore, and you can't work in that sort of situation. Unfortunately, they have the contract on you, you don't have the contract on them. It's you that has to get out of it, so we spent a year in lawyers' offices, and were unable to release records during that time." Chrysalis, however, stuck by them, although James conceded that "We owe hundreds of thousands to the record company… It's a fuckin' trying time when you can't record, you know, it's like having your bollocks cut off, you don't know where to put it. You can't even have a wank when your bollocks have been cut off. But now they've sewn them back on again and we're wanking ourselves to death."

The remaining duo of Idol and James set up auditions for replacement members in the spring of 1980. Terry Chimes of the Clash became their new drummer, with Idol picking up the guitar again as they truncated their name to Gen-X. "Gen X had been the only group I'd ever been in," James later recalled on his website. "There was a time when we were recording the Kiss Me Deadly Album, when the band had been reduced to just me, Billy and drummer Terry Chimes, that we had this mad idea – to merge Gen-X and the Pistols. We even rehearsed one day that week in Air studios, two drummers, Chimes and Cook, me, Billy and Steve Jones. We played about 10 tracks, a mixture of Gen-X and Pistols songs, now that had a big beat. I guess it was one of those drink fuelled 'wouldn't it be great if' kinda moments. Imagine the ego nightmare! It was contractually impossible too, and everyone else involved from our record company to their manager freaked out, but it was a hell of a day."

Their first release as Gen-X was 'Dancing With Myself' in September 1980, written after the band had visited Japan and been entertained by the sight of Tokyo youth admiring themselves dancing. Derwood's original guitar parts were overdubbed by Steve New at Pete Townshend's Eel Pie studios, though New's drug problems over this two-month period drove producer Keith Forsey (a future Idol collaborator who had also worked with Giorgio Moroder) to despair. In the end New was asked to leave, with first Danny Kustow of the Spectres helping to finish 'Dancing With Myself', with Steve Jones of the Pistols completing the overdubs. The sessions were further supplemented by John McGeoch, as James attempted to explain to ZigZag. "McGeoch, who we played football with a bit, always says, 'Oh I'll come down and help you out.' He phoned up and said, 'I've got five weeks off'. And we were just going in to do the album wondering who the fuck we were going to use for a guitar player, and he rehearsed for three weeks and did the majority of the record with us. Jonesy came back from Thailand and supplied bollocks on five tracks – patented Jonesy bollocks, and he was real good on the raunchy stuff. Danny Kustow did a bit on the single. I think the album came out real good."

The band and Chrysalis were shattered when 'Dancing With Myself' only managed a paltry showing at 62 in the charts. As a sign of desperation, it was also released on 12-inch and then in reconstituted form as a clear-vinyl EP in December 1980. This featured one of their best Mark II songs, 'Untouchables', which was almost entirely an Idol solo creation.

Deciding they really did need a permanent guitarist for their upcoming Christmas tour, James Stevenson of Chelsea was recruited. Idol was all buff and bluff to the press. "It's like saying it's a new group but there are still seeds of the old style in it. Me and Tony are just carrying on from what we should have been doing before, so it's symbolic in a sense." Kiss Me Deadly was released in January 1981, delayed due to the need to re-shoot the cover artwork now that Stevenson had been recruited. 'Dancing With Myself' and the elegiac 'Untouchables', apart, it's a bit of a clunker, with producer Tony Forsey unable to save it. 'Heaven's Inside' was written about Steve New and his 'problems', while 'Stars Look Down' concerned their interminable period in litigation. But while the footnotes may be interesting, the body text is pot-boiler.

Time had run out on the band, and they'd broken up within a week of the album's release. So Billy launched his solo career, making that comic book rebel-lite sneer a fixture on MTV. "Billy Idol left the band to write his solo album in New York," James recounted on his website. "So I was faced with the emptiness, this awful feeling of loss, like losing someone so dear to you... the group had been my whole life for nearly four years and just like that it was over and I was completely alone, no manager or record company. Billy moved to New York and I didn't see him for more than a year till out of the blue he called me up and came round! He brought with him a white label 12-inch of a new track he'd just finished called 'White Wedding' which was so great I was completely thrown..."

Tony James hooked up with Terry Chimes in Lords Of The New Church, produced Sex Gang Children and others, toured with Johnny Thunders then gave us Sigue Sigue Sputnik. At the height of the latter's fame, he would tell Jon Savage: "Bill Aucoin was my idea; I met him and liked him. It was a very difficult time: Generation X were falling apart and needed marketing properly. Aucoin had the expertise through his Kiss days. Billy was becoming increasingly difficult and unreliable. His leaving was a scammy trick: he didn't have the guts to tell me. Although he writes terrific dance songs, what he's doing is basically Generation X with nothing new. What I'm doing with Sigue Sigue Sputnik is 10 years on..." After a spell with the Sisters Of Mercy, James has put a new band together with, fantastically, his old London SS mucker Mick Jones, Carbon/Silicon. Stevenson would work with Kim Wilde and Gene Loves Jezebel, among numerous others.

Generation X reformed for one night in September 1993 at the Astoria, 14 years after last playing together, for a one-off show paid for by MTV. The seven-song set, which was an encore to Idol's Cyberpunk show, enabled Mark Laff to buy his house in Brighton from the proceeds. But the engagement hasn't been repeated. As Derwood noted, "Billy was fatter, but still sang out of tune. Tony's head was bigger and with less hair on it."

DISCOGRAPHY:

Your Generation/Day By Day 7-inch (Chrysalis CHS 2165 September 1977) (also issued as a demo, GX 101, with 'Listen' on B-side)

Wild Youth/Wild Dub 7-inch (Chrysalis CHS 2189 November 1977) (some copies had a mis-pressed B-side, 'No No No')

Ready Steady Go/No No No 7-inch (Chrysalis CHS 2207 March 1978)

Generation X LP (Chrysalis CHR/ZCHR 1169 March 1978) (reissued on CD in January 1986, CCD 1169, and March 1995, CD25CR 14, and on EMI Gold, CDGOLD 1039 in July 1996. Note: the tracklisting of the US version of the LP is radically different. 'Listen', 'The Invisible Man' and 'Too Personal' get the heave-ho, in favour of the two singles, "Wild Youth' and 'Your Generation', plus 'Gimme Some Truth' and 'Wild Dub'. The most recent CD reissue, Chrysalis 7243 5 389 262, in April 2002, features bonus tracks 'Your Generation', 'Wild Youth', 'Wild Dub', 'Trying For Kicks' and 'This Heat', but again no sleevenotes)

King Rocker/Gimme Some Truth 7-inch (Chrysalis CHS 2261 January 1979) (in red, pink, orange and yellow versions. Overkill? Oh yes)

G

Valley Of The Dolls LP (Chrysalis CHR/ZCHR 1193 January 1979) (reissued on CD, CCD 1193, January 1986. The 2002 reissue on EMI Gold adds bonus tracks 'Gimme Some Truth' and 'Shaking All Over'.)

Valley Of The Dolls/Shaking' All Over 7-inch (Chrysalis CHS 2310 March 1979) (brown vinyl)

Friday's Angels/Trying For Kicks/This Heat 7-inch (Chrysalis CHS 2330 June 1979)

As Gen X:

Dancing With Myself/Ugly Rash 7-inch (Chrysalis CHS 2444 September 1980) (also issued as a 12-inch, CHS 12 2444, with additional tracks 'Loopy Dub', 'What Do You Want')

Kiss Me Deadly LP (Chrysalis CHR/ZCHR 1327 January 1981) (reissued on CD, CCD 1327, in January 1986)

Dancing With Myself 7-inch EP (Chrysalis CHS 2488 January 1981)

Dancing With Myself/Untouchables/King Rocker/Rock On (clear vinyl 7-inch, also issued as a 12-inch, CHS 12 2488)

ARCHIVE RELEASES:

The Best Of Generation X LP (Chrysalis CHM/ZCHM 1521 November 1985)

King Rocker/Valley Of The Dolls 7-inch (Old Gold OG 9693 February 1987)

The Original Generation X LP (MBC JOCKLP 9 June 1987)

Generation X Live LP (MBC JOCKLP 11 June 1988)

Perfect Hits (1975-1981) LP & CD (Chrysalis CCD/ZCHR/CHR 1854 October 1991) (has a nice fold-out sleeve and includes a twig from Pete Frame's family tree to explain their evolution, but no notes and the pics and items of memorabilia end up looking tiny when transposed to the CD booklet. And, well, this might seem an obvious thought and I may be missing something, but I wasn't aware they had any hits in 1975, as the notes suggest. They were still in school)

Sweet Revenge CD (Mutiny MUTINY 14 1998) (this is the unreleased third album in bootleg form)

Live At The Paris Theatre 1978 and '81 CD (EMI 7243 4 99402 2 1999) (the first show is from the Paris Theatre on 11 May 1979, the last eight tracks from the same venue on 7 January 1981. Features an otherwise unobtainable cover of Bowie's 'Andy Warhol'. The sound quality is excellent, even if Idol's voice, at least on the first eight tracks featuring the original line-up, is a tad croaky)

Radio 1 Sessions CD (Strange Fruit SFRSCD 105 July 2002) (At last, some decent sleevenotes, and an excellent collection with some noticeable differences to the released versions of familiar songs)

BBC Live In Concert – One Hundred Punks CD (Strange Fruit SFRSCD 107 November 2002) (this is essentially the Paris Theatre CD in new packaging)

Ready, Steady, Go! aka Anthology 3-CD Box Set (Chrysalis April 2003) (sloppily assembled box set with poor annotation, but the music is OK. Disc 1 is the singles collection with added B-sides and unreleased material from a planned covers album. Disc 2 is the unreleased Sweet Revenge album. Disc 3 is an unreleased live show from 1978, recorded in Osaka, Japan, recorded through the mixing desk)

Live At Hatfield Polytechnic 1980 CD (Chrysalis 09463 30245 2 6 July 2005) (snapshot of the brief Idol-James-Stevenson-Chimes line-up, although some of the songs are drawn from a show at Liverpool Eric's. A couple of interesting covers, though it should be noted that 'Vicious' is not an Idol/James original as the sleeve suggests, and so-so sound quality)

Glaxo Babies

Rob Chapman (vocals, rhythm guitar), Geoff Alsopp (drums), Dan Catsis (guitar, vocals), Tommy Nichols (bass, vocals)

It's a bit forced to try to pinpoint a prevailing ethos to punk's regional outgrowths, but if there was a defining characteristic of the Bristol and Avon bands in the late-70s, it seemed to be sonic bedlam. The Pop Group pioneered a new approach to songwriting that, in essence, ignored the central tenets of the form, preferring to pursue musical ideas without trying to frame them within any kind of conventional dynamic. That was an approach shared by GLAXO BABIES, who, if anything, deepened the post-punk voyage into wilful discord, while maintaining some thematic link with the anti-pop of Pere Ubu.

G

Chapman had originally placed adverts in both Sounds and the NME looking for musicians "to take over where the Velvet Underground left off" in the winter of 1977. Tom Nichols responded, and Chapman was invited to watch his 'band' rehearse in City Road in St Paul's. Catsis was there as his collaborator, though the drummer didn't show. Catsis already had a name, derived from adverts he'd Xeroxed for an art school project. One of these featured an infant and the caption "Smiling one-year-old Glaxo Baby."

Their first gig took place three weeks later at a Christmas party in the Docklands, playing eight rudimentary songs, originals and Beatles/Stones covers. The second show came at Bristol's hardcore punk venue, the BQ Club. The audience was bemused. The band was scared rigid. Their third gig, at Redlands Teacher Training College, was a support to the Only Ones, while Nichols found a cave in the Avon gorge where they began rehearsing thrice weekly.

They didn't play much out of town – only two gigs in London, one of which was a disastrous support to Resistance, and a show at Dingwalls – and they were never part of the Bristol music clique. But they did appear at the Ashton Court Free Festival in the summer of 1978. "I think the key to the whole (Bristol) set-up at the time," noted Gerard Langley in his sleevenotes to the reissue of Avon Calling, "is comprehending the importance of the Glaxo Babies. The Glaxo Babies' performance at the 1978 Ashton Court Festival has lived long in many people's memory. The intensity! The dyed-blond hair! The guitar played with a vibrator! Subsequent journalistic takes have seen the Pop Group placed at the centre of that era, but I remember it differently. For me, the Glaxos were the cornerstone of the whole Bristol scene. Both sophisticated and primitive, they were basically pre-post-punk. The Gang of Four didn't come as the shock of the new round here, mate. I had read that Iggy Pop cut himself with a glass, but it was different seeing Rob Chapman do it immediately in front of you at the Stonehouse pub. They were real, man, and I loved them."

Chapman's recollection of the Ashton Court festival is of playing to a bunch of "disinterested hippies". A more formidable memory actually occurred later that same evening. Their drummer Geoff Alsopp found them a gig in his native Kingswood, where, after indulging in mountainous quantities of psychedelics and sulphates, they were invited to distract an audience of Bristol Rovers hooligans by playing avant-garde noise.

Simon Edwards, of Heartbeat Records, invited them to record a demo in December 1978. Though the band, as ever, were unsure as to the efficacy of their performance, it led to the offer of an EP. 'This Is Your Life' was recorded early the following year at Crescent Studios, Bath and released as a 12-inch in March, featuring four of the five demo tracks. It was listed at the top of various permutations of the then unofficially recorded independent charts. The first of two John Peel sessions followed, alongside supports to the Human League and Adam And The Ants. There was even their one and only national music press feature, when Sounds came down to interview them on the day Airey Neave was assassinated by a car bomb.

Yet within a month of that feature running, the Glaxo Babies had broken up. They sacked Alsopp. He was a great drummer, but he had a beard and some terrible mates. Chapman was manoeuvred into making the phone call. A few weeks later, he felt the twang of karma's elastic band as exactly the same treatment was meted out to him. For a personal account of what occurred, again, check Chapman's sleevenotes to the recent Cherry Red compilation Dreams Interrupted. It's messy, complicated, and involves a deal of psychic pain. But for once, the expression 'musical differences' does actually cover most, if not all, the bases.

The denouement was played out over sessions for their debut album, Nine Months To The Disco, featuring Charlie Llewellyn of Gardez Darkx on drums and saxophone player Tony Wrafter, formerly of Peru. At their penultimate gig supporting the Cure, Chapman and Nichols clashed. Those tensions continued at Crescent Studios in June 1979. They did manage to record a new song, 'Christine Keeler', which they'd premiered in improvised form back at the John Peel Roadshow. "It's funny," recalls Gavin King of Bristol band the Private Dicks, "the Glaxo Babies were never part of that 'Clifton Trendies' art scene. They were totally apart from the Pop Group, etc. That's why we had a lot of time for them. I remember when 'Christine Keeler' came out and being amazed, we thought it was fantastic."

'Christine Keeler' would become Record Mirror's record of the week on release in August, but by then that version of the Glaxo Babies was no more. Hence the lack of vocals on Nine Months To The Disco when it eventually reached the shops. A subsequent album five months later, the archival exercise Put Me On The Guestlist, featured the original line-up on recordings made between 1978 and 1979. Chapman moved on to the Ealing-based Transmitters, arguably an even more esoteric and experimental outfit, often analogised as 'West London's Residents'. He later became a music journalist and author, his work including 1992's Selling The Sixties, The Pirates And Pop Music Radio.

Thereafter the Glaxo Babies, now featuring Tim Aylett on guitar and Allan Jones on various instruments, released a further single for Heartbeat and an EP for Y Records. But effectively this was a very different group. They were eventually forced to change their name after objections from the pharmaceutical giant. Catsis, Wrafter and Llewellyn reappeared in 1981 as Maximum Joy, a name invoking the Glaxo Babies' song 'Maximum Sexual Joy', alongside Janine Rainforth on clarinet and former Pop Group guitarist and vocalist John Waddington. Tom Nichols is now a professor of art at Aberdeen University and a world-renowned authority on Renaissance painting.

DISCOGRAPHY:

This Is Your Life 12-inch EP (Heartbeat 12PULSE 3March 1979)
This Is Your Life/Stay Away/Because Of You/Who Killed Bruce Lee
Christine Keeler/Nova Bossanova 7-inch (Heartbeat PULSE 5 August 1979)
Nine Months To The Disco LP (Heartbeat HB 2 April 1980)
Shake (The Foundations)/She Went To Pieces (live 28-3-79) 7-inch (Heartbeat PULSE 8 June 1980)
Put Me On The Guestlist LP (Heartbeat HB 3 September 1980) (a compilation of odds and sods including the original Heartbeat demos. The title came after a gig at Tiffany's in Bristol, where Chapman was so disgusted by the rush of liggers in the wake of their new-found suggest, that he changed the lyrics of 'Who Killed Bruce Lee?' from 'put me in the picture' to 'put me on the guest list')
Limited Entertainment 7-inch EP (Y Y6 December 1980)
There'll Be No Room For You In The Shelter/Permission To Be Wrong/Limited Entertainment/Dahij
COMPILATION:
Avon Calling – The Bristol Compilation LP (Heartbeat HB 1 1979; 'It's Irrational') (reissued on CD in October 2005 on Heartbeat/Cherry Red CDMRED 292 with additional tracks 'This Is Your Life', 'Who Killed Bruce Lee?', 'Christine Keeler', 'Nova Bossa Nova' and 'Shake' on bonus CD The Heartbeat Singles Collection)
ARCHIVE RELEASE:
Dreams Interrupted CD (Cherry Red 2006) (track listing to be determined at time of publication)

Golinski Brothers

Darris (aka Dave Harries; vocals), Bob Golinski (guitar), Will Gibbs (saxophone), Alan Bines (saxophone), Ollie Crook (bass), Tom Beattie (drums)

There is nothing more certain to endear a punk band to adolescent fans than copious swearing. Whilst 'Bloody' is far from the most offensive song in the punk canon, the use of an expletive (then still considered a fully-fledged naughty word) in such a repetitive nature as the Golinski's 'Bloody' did was guaranteed to impress. "What am I bloody well supposed to do," ran the chorus, "I've got my bloody well self bloody

stuck on you." Sheer poetry. John Peel played it repeatedly and a nation's fingers hovered over the record button. Sadly, they never bought the record.

Peel was still playing it as late as 1999. In fact, in one of his final written pieces, a review of Nick Hornby's 31 Songs for the Observer, he couldn't help returning to it. "Two of the records that would be under consideration for a place on any comparable list I might make would be the **GOLINSKI BROTHERS**' 'Bloody' and Roy Buchanan's version of 'Lonesome Fugitive', but I've never seriously attempted in-depth analysis of these songs as songs. For me, it is enough that the Golinski Brothers' obscure but, trust me, unforgettable record includes the lines: 'Still you gotta have a laugh (pause) ha ha ha ha' and: 'Send my Giro to Cairo'."

It's thought that Dave Harries entered the world of politics with the SDP, standing at Wandsworth, while Bines, who also played intermittently with the Piranhas, ran a North London gardening business.

G

DISCOGRAPHY:

Bloody/Toy 7-inch (Badger BAD 6 1980)

COMPILATION:

Vaultage 1979 Another Two Sides Of Brighton LP (Attrix RB 08 1979; 'Bloody', 'Too Scared')

Vaultage Punk Collection CD (Anagram CDPUNK 101 1997; 'Bloody')

Gonads

Garry Bushell (vocals), Al Strawn (bass), Pete Lunn (drums), Mark Gladding (guitar, mandolin), Chris Culmer (cowbells)

Although the GONADS became well known as journalist Bushell's musical alter-ego in the 80s, the first incarnation of the band was actually formed in the first flowering of punk. They came together at school in South East London, in 1976, evolving out of an earlier school band, the Monty Python and Dr Feelgood-influenced Pink Tent. Bizarrely, given Bushell's later proclamations, they were proud situationists.

Augmented by a second guitarist, Clyde Ward, they self-released a single, 'Stroke My Beachcomber Baby', on their own label in 1977. Recorded in a shed in Blackheath, and released on the band's own label (which featured two testicles as its visual motif), it was their sole release before splitting up in 1978. I've heard tell, by the way, that the single does not actually exist. But old Gal reckons it's kosher. In fact, Captain Oi! are about to include it in a rarities package for release some time in 2006, he tells me. Only I checked with Captain Oi! and it appears Gal is on the wind-up. It exists only in Bushell's imagination. Never trust a tabloid journalist where the truth is concerned.

Bushell, who formerly ran the fanzine Napalm, went on to join Sounds to champion the Oi! movement before reversing his politics and joining Fleet Street as the Sun's pre-Littlejohn knee-jerker and TV critic. "Yes I championed Punk, Oi!, 2-Tone, Mod, NWOBHM etc on Sounds," Bushell retorts. "And yes, I became disillusioned with Marxism, and more precisely idiot Marxists, but that was a gradual process not a 'reversal'. It was jump-started by the Falklands, but the seeds had been sewn when I was an active member of the SWP, pre-Sounds, and disagreed vehemently with their attitude to paedophiles and terrorists. I worked at the Mirror for months before I joined the Sun. Pre-Littlejohn knee-jerker? Priceless. This must be a reference to pro-capital punishment articles, an opinion shared by Parsons, Burchill, etc. The other stuff? I used to be a leftie but I'm all right now (1986?) was a wind-up, and you fell for it. Well done." I actually don't know what he's talking about here, never mind falling for it, but there you go.

The later inception of the Gonads featured Gazz's own inimitable music hall cockernee stylee japes – this being someone, after all, who thinks Jim Davidson is a funny man. "Chris Rock, Jerry Seinfeld, Jackie Mason and Robin Williams would be in my Top Ten favourite comics," Bushell retorts. "Cameron 'Jim' Davidson would not. But do you hate Davidson because of his politics or because of his class? Have you ever seen him live? Probably not." No, I haven't seen him live. I don't hate him because of his class origins, Gaz. I hate him because he's not funny. And I never swallowed that patronising bollocks that if you're working class you should walk around pretending you've never read a book and reducing everything to geezer vocabulary and lowest common denominator homilies.

Oops. We got quite a bit off subject there. Documenting the Gonads' subsequent career would be soul-destroying even for the most committed archivist so I won't bother. I'm sure there's a UK Subs live album I haven't written about yet. Last word Gaz? "The Gonads are more punk than you will ever be. And the delicious irony is that just by hating us, you validate us. The joke's on you, old son. Now gertcha."

DISCOGRAPHY:

Steal My Beachcomber Baby 7-inch EP (Scrotum Scrotum 1 1977)
Punk Rock Will Never Die/Got Any Wrigley's, John?/Sandra Bigg (Really Big)/I Lost My Love To A UK Sub/Annie's Song (destined to become a fixture on worldwide rarities lists. Only it doesn't actually exist)

GT's

Neil Downe (aka Tony Berrington; guitar, vocals), Kevin Green (bass, vocals), Paul Betts (drums)

The GT's sole vinyl appearance came on the Raw Records' compilation Raw Deal, issued in December 1977. Thereafter they vanished from the radar. Tony Berrington gave me the low-down. "We formed from the remnants of our school band, some of whom didn't get punk at all. Me and Kev were 'in like Flint' and we convinced the drummer that he liked punk. These were early days for punk in Nottingham, which can be a naughty place. It's true to say that we fought the punk wars and got a few beatings for our trouble. I remember fighting for my life with a load of bikers at a Johnny Thunders gig in Derby. Happy days!"

The GT's subsequently recorded a demo in a local church hall, which was despatched to Lee Wood of Raw Records. "We only had about six original songs and we used to cover 'Remember Walking In The Sand' by the Shangri-Las and 'Please Please Me'. Raw contacted us and put us in a studio in Cambridge to do two tracks. I remember taking a 24-can case of lager so it was a boozy session, but everything came together very quickly and sounded pretty good. So it was a very enjoyable session, unlike some I've done since. We went back to Nottingham and then Raw Deal came out."

But that was it for the GT's, after Berrington accepted an invitation to join Plummet Airlines, who subsequently transmuted into the Favourites. "They had a proper record deal with Stiff and management. I don't have many fond memories of playing with them (what was I thinking?). I later played with the Deadbeats who released one album on New Rose which is pretty damned good if I may say so myself. I also did some stuff with Bill Hurley, doing purely Elvis covers, which came out on Mute." Betts stayed in Nottinghamshire and played in local bands including the Eyes. Green joined Berrington in the Plummets when they moved to London, and also the Deadbeats, alongside Mark Robertson of the Meteors. Later he would play with Nigel Lewis in the Tall Boys. Green went on to work in studio installation and has done work for Vince Clarke, Flood and Depeche Mode. "Kev has done OK and lives in a big house in the country. Unsurprisingly, 'Millionaire' was his song."

COMPILATIONS:

Raw Deal LP (Raw RAWL 1 December 1977; 'Millionaire', 'Move On')

headache

Steve 'Headache' Lambert (guitar), Danny Drummond (vocals), Paul Cremona (bass), Colin Chew (drums).

East London punk band, formed in 1977, HEADACHE started out in the Barking area and were originally known as the Electrodes. Danny Drummond: "The Electrodes played a couple of gigs before I'd joined with another singer, a guy called Johnny Mills. They only had a couple of songs and played Rolling Stones and Who covers. They played at the Man in the Moon in King's Road, as support to the Unwanted. They were still the Electrodes when I joined, about a month later, after Johnny got the bullet for not getting on with Steve. I was a friend of Colin, the drummer, who was from North London like me." They subsequently gigged heavily around the capital's punk haunts, including the Vortex and Roxy through 1977.

"We played a really strange gig at the Vortex alongside Mean Street. It was a bizarro time when everyone was trying to jump on the punk bandwagon, and there were two Page 3 girls from the Sun, and for some reason they had a band that week that was going to be punk. It was completely surreal. Even though they were dressed 'punk', they looked utterly different to everyone else in the venue. But the Roxy gig I can't remember at all. I'd probably had a drink."

Other acts they shared a stage with included the Models, Raped, Bethnal and other lesser lights of the London punk fraternity. They also had a residency at the Greyhound in Chadwell Heath. "Steve, our guitarist, kind of ran that, in that he contacted a lot of the other bands that played. We played on a fortnightly basis. The punk night happened once a week and got other bands in for the other week. It went on for a few months. One of the bands who played there was the Sockets, who went on to become the Purple Hearts."

That led to the release of their solitary single in November 1977, 'I Can't Stand Still'. "We made the absolutely standard condenser-mic mono cassette recording of a rehearsal in a garage. We took it around – I've no idea why anyone would listen to it, but it was punk, and ridiculous record companies were falling over themselves to sign anything they thought might be punk. A few people were interested. We found these guys who ran a distribution company called Relay. They got it into their heads that they could do something like Lightning Records did, and have a hit single distributing one of their own singles – like Althea And Donna. They thought, if they could get a punk single out they could get it into the stores and do a similar thing. Steve really wanted to do the single, cos he thought that would help us get more gigs. I was a bit more dubious."

For once, this wasn't the small pressing obscurity so beloved of punk collectors. In fact so many copies remained unsold that 5,000 were apparently melted down within the year. By then the band had long gone, having disbanded only a couple of months after the single's release. And that was it, until Overground released the contents on its Punk Rock Rarities compilation in 1995. After Headache split, Drummond and Lambert continued to work together for several months, in the mod band Exit 22, but "nothing really worked out". Drummond then formed Crass-influenced second wavers Lack Of Knowledge in 1980 with latter day Buzzcocks' stalwart Tony Barber. He was also involved in the Crazy Pink Revolvers. Lack Of Knowledge's Americanized CD includes the unreleased Headache track, 'I Wanna Be On The Dole'.

DISCOGRAPHY:

I Can't Stand Still/No Reason For Your Call 7-inch (Lout Records LOUT 1 November 1977).

helpless huw

Huw Meads (vocals, guitar), Dave Sutherland (bass), Roger Cornish (guitar), Nick Hills (drums)

There were many vinyl tributes/cash-ins doing the rounds when Sid was banged up over that nasty business with Nancy – others included Cash Pussies, Nazis Against Fascism, the Surgeons etc. Huw Meads piloted one such artefact to minor notoriety before disappearing from view, only to reappear again at the 1992 General Election – standing against Sir Norman Fowler in the Sutton Coldfield ward.

Meads had actually recorded his first sessions several months earlier, an acoustic solo 'double B-side' recorded at Tamworth's Mind's Ear Studios. The resulting single was a heartfelt, enchantingly naïve effort that will appeal to fans of Patrik Fitzgerald or Jilted John. In keeping with the amateur tone of the recording, it was mistakenly credited to Helpless Hew due to a spelling mistake on the cover. That mistake was rectified on the better known 'Innocent' EP, which featured a full band as listed at the top of this entry. The title-track was a clear re-write of Bob Dylan's 'Hurricane'. "Yes, I admit that!" Huw told me. "The original song was 'Sid Vicious Is Innocent', then I changed the tense after he died, but everything else was the same. The inspiration came from when he was arrested. I was asked by a friend to write a song about this, and that's what we did. The other songs, I was listening to 60s pop, and that was the musical influence for those."

There were to be no more vinyl releases, though a cassette album, The Bedroom Tapes aka Bricks Hit Strangers, circulated in the 80s. "It was a collection of all the demos beyond the Sid single, which I took to record companies and publishing companies. There was some interest from three or four companies including EMI's publishing arm, but nothing concrete came of it in the end. I stuck at it for several years, and played gigs around the West Midlands area, up to about 1983. It became **HELPLESS HUW** and the Hesitations, then we became the Hesitations (with original Dexy's drummer John 'Jay' Bottrill). I was still recording demo tapes. Then other things in life took over, and I became a teacher of transcendental meditation in 1990."

H

He stood for the Natural Law Party again in the 1997 General Election in Selly Oak, Birmingham, as well as the European elections for Birmingham West in 1994 and 1999. "I've been doing transcendental meditation from the age of 18. It's basically a relaxation technique but you can take it further than that. The NLP was basically an attempt to take a short cut to make the world a better place. As an organisation, it's been trying for years. The NLP was an attempt to take it mainstream." As for his punk years: "I took a very strange musical journey. In 1977 I got into punk, saw the Clash, Jam, Stranglers, and was a regular at Barbarella's. I went there every weekend. Within six months I got fed up with the musical dead-end ness of punk and started getting work in pubs. So I got into more folk-influenced music. Then I went off to Kingston Poly and the friends I made there got me listening to the new wave stuff again, and I got into Talking Heads and the emerging power pop bands, and so I got back into it that way."

DISCOGRAPHY:

Still Love You (In My Heart)/Lisa Jane 7-inch (Universal Spirit US-001 February 1979) ('double B-side', no p/s)

Sid Vicious Was Innocent 7-inch EP (Universal Spirit US-002 September 1979)

Sid Vicious Was Innocent/Going Through The Motions/Baby We're Not In Love/When You're Weary (some with folded p/s, others with picture inserts in a polythene bag. "When I got a distribution deal, I got to do the picture sleeves")

homosexuals

Anton Hayman (lead guitar), Bruno Aleph Wizard (lead vocals), Jim Welton (bass) (all members sang and played various instruments, other members included Suzy, Davey Duff, etc)

Legendary London art punks, the HOMOSEXUALS epitomised the DIY ethos that percolated under the more mainstream punk constructs of the late-70s. They simply didn't give a shit about commerce, whereas some of their brother bands clearly did. Throughout their existence they never attempted to market their work by buying 'media space'. In fact, the only coverage they ever garnered came from Jamming! magazine, when a helpful relative of the band suggested to Tony Fletcher that he should write about the band. The Homosexuals were, apparently, none too pleased with this intervention, even if it did produce the only press notice in their entire existence. They didn't send out their records for review. They boast that they never got paid for a single show they performed at. Art for art's sake, to the nth.

The Homosexuals grew out of Bruno's previous band, the Rejects, who had been a perennial support act at the Roxy. Indeed, he continued to use the Rejects' tag for a couple of gigs before deciding on a new name. Prompted by a hostile review from Tony Parsons, which Bruno loved but the rest of the Rejects hated, he set about putting together a new line-up.

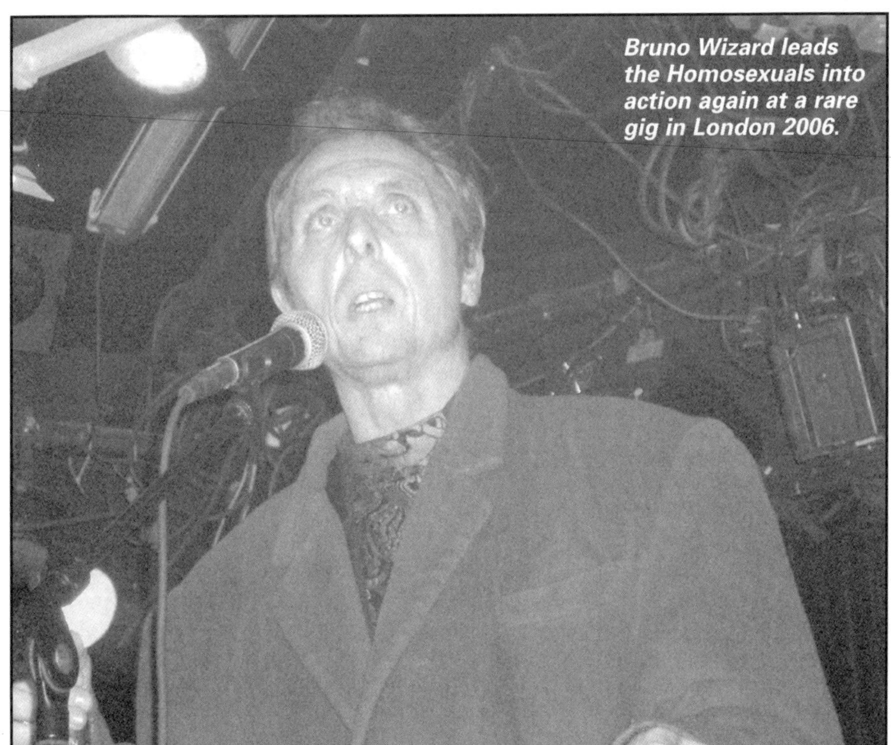
Bruno Wizard leads the Homosexuals into action again at a rare gig in London 2006.

Bruno: "I looked around and heard about this young kid in Speedwell House in Deptford, not far from where I was living, who was a shit hot bass player, Jim. I was told about him by his local drug dealer. I went to see him, and he was a great bass player. 'Do you want to play with the Rejects?' 'Cool.' 'Great.' So I drafted him into the band. Then he brought in some guitarist that he knew, a nice chap but a little too sensitive and frightened of his own shadow. We did one or two gigs with different people playing here and there. I thought, no, we've got to get a proper guitarist. I was up the King's Road one night, at a gig by X-Ray Spex. Poly Styrene had invited me down to see them play.

A week before, I saw this guy who I'd seen at the Roxy drumming for Wayne County and the Electric Chairs. Wayne County had come over from America, and I knew about her after reading about Andy Warhol and all that. When I saw Jayne County and the Electric Chairs at the Roxy, I thought, fucking hell, this is really good. And they had an ANIMAL of a drummer. I thought, wow, I might have to go to America to get a drummer if this is the way American rock drummers are. I didn't realise this guy wasn't American, he'd just been picked up by Wayne over here. So I saw this drummer at the X-Ray Spex gig at the Man in The Moon, in King's Road, just round the corner from Sex. He came up and said, 'Hi, you're the singer from the Rejects, great front man, what are you doing?' I said I'm getting a new band together. He said, let's do it together. 'Aren't you going back to America with Wayne?' 'No, I'm from Hungary, I was just playing with Wayne over here.' Fantastic."

Thus began the Homosexuals story. However, immediately there were problems. "Jim and Davey didn't get on, because Davey was a classic rock drummer with paradiddles, and he wanted Jim just to be tight on bass, to play as a rock rhythm section. They argued a bit. We put an advert in Melody Maker for a guitarist. I let Chrissie Hynde know we were looking for a guitarist and putting a band together, with a different name. Anton answered the ad, he was the third or fourth person, I heard him play and thought – this is the boy. Then Anton joined the band. We did two gigs as the Rejects tightening up before we decided on another name. We were living over in Battersea in this high-rise squat on the 18th floor, all falling asleep with our noses in this giant bowl of amyl nitrate, trying to think of a name for the band. I was reading about Ancient Greece at the time.

Once a month all the great thinkers, and philosophers and poets and mathematicians and scholars got together and had a symposium and told apocryphal tales about each other, and passed on wisdom. I thought, that's a good idea. We should have a band that reflects that kind of idea. You know what it's like when you're stoned, you have all these lofty ideas. At the same time I'd read that Homo, the Greek root of the word, meant men of the same idea. I don't know if it's actually the case. I thought, Homo, what a great idea. But we're a rock band so there's got to be some sex in there. So Homosexuals. It can be a modern day version of the Symposium. Jim was like – we can't call it that! Let's call it the Non-Homosexuals. Anton took a look at me with a glint in his eyes – Anton always had this thing about the Glimmer Twins, like Jagger and Richards. In his mind he had this vision of us being like the Rolling Stones, but on the astral plane! So Anton said, yeah, Homosexuals. So we became the Homosexuals. Jim started to fall out more and more with Davey Duff, the drummer. Davey couldn't handle it and left after an argument with Jim. We just got different drummers together when we played. That's how the Rejects become the Homosexuals."

One of the stories about the band is that they lost an Asian drummer, Nyrup, to National Front violence. "No, he wasn't in the Homosexuals. I met Nyrup through Jim. Nyrup's dad was Asian but his mum was English. He'd gone to Dulwich College. In terms of education and breeding he was more English than I was. He'd gone to public school, and he was a really, really nice guy. He played drums. There were a few bands at the time, a nucleus of musicians drifting in and out of bands based around New Cross. Jim knew Nyrup and when Anton first joined the Homosexuals, he had an album's worth of stuff from previous bands – real hard, driving, pounding rock music. He wanted to get the songs out of his system. So he rehearsed with Nyrup. Then they went to Spaceward Studios and Nyrup played on those recordings. Nyrup might have jammed with us a couple of times, but he was never in the Homosexuals as such. But he did get murdered by the National Front. He used to live where I was living in Deptford. There were a few of these kids walking past one of the blocks where Nyrup and his friends were having a party. They started throwing bottles up at the window. The students all went down there to confront them. There was a kerfuffle and everyone got a good kicking. The only one they really attacked severely was Nyrup. They put a broken bottle in his throat. He died the next day."

Despite that, the Homosexuals played in the midst of the Front's turf. "We did do a gig in Deptford at a National Front pub when we were the Homosexuals. That was my idea. I'd lived there for quite a few years. Most of the kids in the National Front in that area, I would play them at pool in pubs. I was living amongst them. They regarded me as some slightly brain damaged leftover hippy from the 60s who'd had too much LSD. I beat them at pool all the time. So when we played in that National Front pub, I knew once we started playing the music, we battened our ears back, because I knew the kind of stuff they liked. I wasn't bothered about keeping those people away. We never actually advertised gigs anyway. We only ever advertised one thing, when Susie joined the band in 1979, and we moved into a squat in Bloomsbury. She became the 'artist' in the band. She was a well-known performance artist in Israel. She'd come over here to do some things at Slade College of Art. I met her the day she moved into the squat and she joined the band and took charge of the performance side of things. She did amazing multi-media things with us."

Living in squats and co-opting studio downtime, the Homosexuals wrote songs that were too restless to settle into any kind of groove, that would disintegrate and become something new halfway through, whilst maintaining an ear and affection for pop music that permeates just about all their work. Their output between 1978 and 1982 comprised two singles, a 12-inch EP and two compilation tracks, but that hardly scratches the surface. There were other releases under different guises on their own Black Noise label. A further 12-inch emerged ('Ici La Bas') and a third single by Bruno, solo, and an album written and performed mostly by Anton, as well as a cassette release, Venceremos. It is only recently, with the release of the 3-CD set Astral Glamour, that the true extent and worth of the Homosexuals' archive is becoming clear and, more importantly perhaps, accessible. The music they recorded spanned almost every conceivable genre, but it wasn't mined in that kind of 'eclectic', totemic, musicianly way. It was just incorporated for convenience in pursuit of 'the idea'. Given this, it's amazing how fitfully engrossing the music they produced actually was, and how mesmerising some of the lyrics are.

In 2003 Chuck Warner, a long-time fan of the band, began gathering and remastering the material for Astral Glamour with extensive help from Bruno and his ex-wife Suzy (Susanna Vida). Coincidentally, experimental musician Chris Cutler decided to re-release The Homosexuals LP (the band's posthumous 1984 LP on Cutler's Recommended label). Cutler enlisted Bob Drake to remix the tracks from his old two-track LP masters – originally dubbed from cassettes – to ensure an accurate duplicate of the original release. Warner licensed the Recommended/Drake recordings for Astral Glamour but ended up using little of it because, as Warner notes, "better recordings surfaced at Suzy's place in France". She was a member of the band from 1979 to their 'last' gig in 1985. According to Warner, the "widely-varying sources and stages of decay/preservation I encountered required a more 'activist' approach to balancing and restoring the Homosexuals' recordings to present them in their best light on Astral Glamour." It's definitely the place to head for if you're interested in this most perverse and wilfully marginal of groups.

Bruno is an interesting character. Take my word for it. He's flogged upmarket clothes to the New York designer behind Sex And The City, managed Poly Styrene (helping put together Conscious Consumer) and promoted hip hop at old friend Andy Czezowski's Fridge venue long before it became the lingua franca of contemporary music. His Homosexuals remain a fine example of what a stubborn, inviolate assumption of music's free flowing potential can achieve. Watch out for his latest project, the Guru Dolls. "We're going to have Jesus on drums, Buddha on vocals, Krishna on bass, etc." Again, this could be interesting.

DISCOGRAPHY:

Hearts In Exile/Soft South Africans 7-inch (L'Orelei No. 1 1978)

Bigger Than The Number... Yet Missing The Dot 7-inch EP (Black Noise BN 1 1981.)

You're Not Moving The Way You're Supposed To Part 1/You're Not Moving The Way You're Supposed To Part 2/Prestel

The Homosexuals 12-inch EP (Black Noise No. 2 1979.)

Astral Glamour/Collected Of You/The Birds Have Risen (parts 1 & 2)/Divorce Proceedings/Mecho Madness (first edition in hand-painted sleeve. Second edition in purple sleeves with white sticker)

Ici La Bas/Les Incroyables 12-inch EP (Black Noise No. 4 1979)

Regard Omission/The Total Drop/Galore Galore/Nippon Airways/Flying/Cause A Commotion (though each track is credited to a different band, it's effectively Jim, Anton and Bruno at work again)

The Homosexuals Record LP (Recommended RR 18 1984)(reissued on CD in ReR, MEGACORP/Morphius Archive in January 2004 with additional tracks Collapsible You, Snapshots Of Nairobi, Soft South Americans (raw version), Walk Before Imitate and Still Living In My Car. Remastered by Bob Drake. 'Soft South Americans (raw version)' exists only as a typo on the CD packaging though – the song is, according to Chuck Warner, "the original 'rough mix' of 'Hearts In Exile', aka the 'Full Mix', because the vocals aren't faded in and out as on the 45.")

ARCHIVE RELEASES:

Astral Glamour 3-CD set (Hyped2Death/Messthetics #204 2004) (includes 81 songs plus a colour 32-page booklet)

horrorcomic

Frankie Dean (guitar), Roger Rep (aka Roger Semon; vocals), Ray Boghart (bass), Wally Bantam (drums)

In a classic "it's not who you know" scenario, HORRORCOMIC were supposedly all members of the Lightning Records label staff who decided they deserved vinyl glory in their own right. Another tale suggests they were a cabaret act who fancied trying their luck. Neither story is entirely true. But then neither is entirely incorrect.

Horrorcomic evolved out of rock band Crackers, who during the early-70s supported the Who, Move, Tremeloes, Small Faces, Brian Auger, the Herd, Julie Driscoll and many others. However, after a series of demos for major labels came to naught, Crackers resorted to playing covers of the day. By the mid-70s they were on the cabaret circuit, pushing out workmanlike covers of everything from Bowie and Hendrix to Cliff and Elvis. They even appeared on Opportunity Knocks in 1975, introduced thus by Hughie Green – "Crackers by name, crackers by nature!"

While punk killed off so many other bands of Crackers' ilk, in this case, it gave them a second stab at the big time. They'd always wanted to be a raw rock band. Now that was in vogue. Semon, working for RCA Records, found himself talking to the bosses of Lightning Records, the North London distributor, one day. At that point in time, anything remotely connected to punk (and some of Lightning's releases really were only remotely connected to punk) were selling out almost as quickly as they could press them. So the suggestion was made that Semon get in on the act. He persuaded his fellow band members it was worth a shot, and hey presto, Crackers became Horrorcomic, partially inspired by the recent release of The Exorcist.

Two singles resulted from the sessions, the best of which was their debut, 'I'm All Hung Up On Pierrepoint'. This was basic punk rock, ala the Upstarts, though the cover art rather bravely confirmed the band wasn't in its first flush of youth, and their trousers were definitely in the sphere of second flush of flaredom. The title, of course, was a play on the Pierrepoint family legacy – generations of whom held the post of Britain's chief executioner, or hangmen. And yet the foremost of them, Albert Pierrepoint, would later state that he did not believe the executions had "prevented a single murder."

The follow-up, 'I Don't Mind', was clearly an exercise in self-parody, but it's quite funny in its own way. However, John Peel, in his Sounds review, rumbled that all was not as it seemed with these debonair born again punk rockers. A third single was pencilled in for B&C Records, and a handful of copies pressed of 'Jesus Crisis' (value, £700+) but it was never officially released. They also entered Surrey Sound Studios to cut an album. The latter wrapped on 17 August 1977, the day Elvis Presley died.

In 2006 Sanctuary released a complete Horrorcomic archive, titled England 1977. The choice of record label was no surprise – Semon is now a Sanctuary Records executive and their official 'Elvis expert'.

DISCOGRAPHY:

I'm All Hung Up On Pierrepoint/The Exorcist/Sex In The Afternoon 7-inch EP (Lightning/B&C BCS 007 August 1977) (miss-spelt Pierrpoint on the label)
I Don't Mind/England 1977 7-inch (Lightning GIL-512 1978.)
Jesus Crisis/Cut Your Throat 7-inch (B&C BCS 17 1979; withdrawn)
ARCHIVE RELEASE:
England 77 CD (Sanctuary/Castle CMQCD1263 March 2006)

idiot

Rob Paveley (vocals, guitar), Barry Godwin (guitar), Paul 'Blue' Dunne (bass), Dave Dyke (drums)

LINDISFARNE CATHOLIC CENTRE
Valkyrie Road, Westcliff

DEENO'S MARVELS
IDIOT
VICARS
SNIPER

On TUESDAY, MAY 30th 1978
at 7.30 p.m.

Licensed Bar Tickets 60p

IDIOT formed in 1977 at Westcliff High School For Boys while the participants were studying for their A-levels. Initially there was a different lead singer, but Paveley would soon get the job, as he elaborated to Surrey Vomet fanzine: "It was at a Sunday School in front of these 10-11 years olds, y'know, little kids, and the singer, who I'd already figured out was a bit of a nutcase, was screaming into the mike and lashing out with his foot into the crowd! He had to go and I took over the singing!"

Idiot gigged around the Southend area, usually alongside local pub rockers Deeno's Marvels, whom Dyke would join in 1978. However, in order to finalise a planned demo recording session, as recalled to Steve Pegrum's Southend Punk website, John Dee of the Machines stepped into the breach. 'Ging Gang Gooley' was extracted from these sessions to mark the band's sole vinyl appearance, as part of Sonet's Southend Rock compilation in 1979.

The band then decided to chance their arm in the London music business. Things didn't work out though, and after living in squalor in flats in first Wood Green then Acton, through October and November 1978, and flirting with a new name, the Bright Boys, they were home in Southend for Christmas. Paveley then joined Deeno's Marvels on bass, where, reunited with Dyke, he decided to temporarily reform Idiot, before putting together Speedball (one Mod-ish single, 1979's 'No Survivors' for No Pap Records), whose live set included a number of unrecorded Idiot songs.

COMPILATION: Southend Rock LP (Sonet SNTF 806 1979; 'Ging Gang Gooely')

instant automatons

Mark Lancaster (vocals, saxophone, guitar), Protag (aka Martin Neish; various instruments) later joined by Mic Woods (guitar)

One of the most celebrated collectives from the crop of DIY musicians who flourished in the wake of the Desperate Bicycles and the cassette culture they helped spawn, the then nameless INSTANT AUTOMATONS were formed in the mid-70s near Scunthorpe in Lincolnshire. But this initial incarnation, largely informed by Krautrock, was more an imagined band than a real one.

When punk's crusading independent spirit scooped up a thousand bands' half-formed ideas and helped channel them into something more tangible, Mark and Protag were primed for the task. They later equated the sense of discovery and triumph engendered as being akin to the Berlin Wall coming down. By the time they'd left school, they'd amassed a home made synthesiser and a drum machine, alongside more conventional instruments. The core duo were joined in the still untitled band, intermittently, by friends including Vicky Lofas, Sally Norman and Mike Holmes. They eventually placed a series of unrelated words in a hat and settled on what was drawn out. Of course, the name should have been Instant Automata, but the linguistic travesty seemed entirely appropriate.

By now they had several hours of taped studio experiments. The best of these were culled for the 1978 cassette album Radio Silence – The Art Of Human Error. This was advertised in the music press with the express invitation that anyone who sent in a blank C-90 would have the album's contents dubbed on to it by return post. It was essentially a pragmatic way to allow people to access their songs, but it also signalled a sea change in music distribution. The methodology was soon copied by many DIY and bedroom bands, prompting an originally disinterested music press to run regular columns on the latest underground cassette releases.

As for the music, reference points included Krautrock and folk, as well as punk, as Protag told Wilson Neate in 2003. "I was influenced a lot by the records Mark had, and lent to me. I'm not sure where he found out about the Velvets, maybe it was reading the music press, or sixth formers on his bus journey home. My bus ride was a lot less informative and I've had a more or less lifelong boycott going on with the weekly music papers (with a few lapses). I can't remember what they did to upset me now. They did represent a tremendous bulk of conventional wisdom, a kind of unshiftable ballast holding a party line whereby Yes and Genesis were OK and Bob Calvert was quite crap. I did listen to John Peel a lot, but in between Loudon Wainwright and Neil Young I could not, at first, see what was good about the Ramones." In the same interview, Lancaster admitted that: "We were really just riding on the coat tails of punk, so when it appeared to be coming off the rails (to mix a metaphor) we weren't unduly bothered. Personally, I was far more offended when Bow Wow Wow brought out 'C30, C60, C90, Go!' – that marked the death of the cassette music scene for me!"

One of those who encountered Radio Silence was Here And Now drummer Keith Dobson (aka Kif Kif Le Batteur) who was involved with London studio, Street Level. He was organising a show featuring various stars of the cassette underground and persuaded the Instant Automatons to perform at the Acklam Hall, their first live appearance, as part of The Bad Music Festival. Although they were 'awful', it did lead to their inclusion on Street Level's Weird Noise 7-inch EP, released on the charmingly titled Fuck Off Records, which included fellow travellers Danny And The Dressmakers and 012.

The 'Peter Paints His Fence' EP was their inaugural own-name vinyl release on their own Deleted Records in 1980. John Peel played two of the tracks. The EP also included an advertisement for a 'helper/driver', and although Mic Woods didn't actually have any transport, he did have a guitar and was invited to join the band, which allowed Mark to concentrate on his singing. Woods, who remained based in Plumstead and would collaborate with his band mates via cassettes exchanged through the post, would also cut a few solo compositions for Deleted.

The trio continued to record on sundry cassettes over the next few years, as well as vinyl projects such as the 'Angst In My Pants' double EP, which featured various interconnected bands. They also gigged regularly with likeminded artists such as Zounds, but by 1982 Lancaster, their main lyricist, was drained of inspiration, his increasing alienation communicated in songs such as 'Worcester Avenue' and 'Violence'. After the band dispersed, Protag worked with Alternative TV, Blyth Power and Zounds. 20 years later Mark Lancaster began to issue solo recordings through his own Waterden empire. "The Waterden Studio is, in fact, my converted dining room," he told me in 2005, "and I assemble the CDs in my kitchen before sending them off around the world."

The enduring interest in the band is reflected in, and will hopefully be expanded by, the beautifully packaged Hyped2Death compilation Another Wasted Sunday Afternoon, released in 2005. Here you can experience for yourself one of the UK underground's most acute but unaffected lyricists. Subjects tackled are as diverse as being a lunatic for extreme music ("Why pay £6 for an album when you can listen to a weird noise band?" Mark Automaton notes in 'People Laugh At Me Coz I Like Weird Music'), hair length ('Short-Haired Man In A Long-Haired Town') and the dearth of opportunity ('Nice Job For The Lad'). There's also far more personal, less polemical efforts such as 'When The Pubs Close', as well as reflections on friends and colleagues ('Gillian Is Normal', 'Emma' etc) which read like Bontempi-powered Undertones missives. The sound is tremendously lo-fi, often like ultra-rugged Fall outtakes, especially vocally. But for all that the Instant Automatons know how to pin a chorus, with the songwriting somewhere between the TV Personalities and early Mekons.

Discography:

Radio Silence – The Art Of Human Error cassette (Deleted Records DEC 001 1978)
Eating People – Hints For The Housewife cassette (Deleted Records DEC 003 1979)
Peter Paints His Fence 7-inch EP (Deleted Records DEP 001 1980)
Nice Job For The Lad/Laburnum Walk/New Muzak/People Laugh At Me (Coz I Like Weird Music)/John's Vacuum Cleaner/Peter Paints His Fence
Blues Masters Of The Humber Delta cassette (Deleted Records DEC 010 1980)
Tape Transport cassette (Deleted Records DEC 011 1982)

ARCHIVE RELEASES:
Not So Deep As A Well CD (Waterden WDCD002)
Archaeology CD (Waterden WDCD010)
Last Train To Woolwich Arsenal double CD (Waterden WCDD015)
Disc 1 features Blues Masters Of The Humber Delta plus bonus tracks: Abstract Albert's Second Journey/The Dentist/Radio Silence/St. James Infirmary/Little Girl Disc 2 features Tape Transport plus bonus tracks: The Machine Takes Over/Nigel Wouldn't Approve/Underneath The Wardrobe/Eating People No. 2/Lost On The Way To Find Myself
Another Wasted Sunday Afternoon CD (Hyped2Death Messthetics 210 2005)
***Mark Automaton has released at least four solo CDs available via Waterden Music**

interrogators

Frank Interview (aka James Dutton; guitar, vocals), Andy Cameron (guitar, vocals), Kevin Latchford (bass), Janie Hagger (drums)

I

The INTERROGATORS were an urecorded London punk band from 1977 led by guitarist James Dutton, whose sets incorporated dub reggae, ably assisted by live mixer Dread Lepke (aka Leroy Anderson, Rita Marley's brother). Lepke would use tape loops and echo to add effect, and was also behind DBC, or Dread Broadcasting Corporation, London's first pirate reggae station. Through this Dutton was exposed to a coterie of reggae acts, including Dillinger and Tapper Zukie.

"I must just say that we were quite amateurish and haphazard. We also only played a couple of dub numbers. It's just that they could last for fifteen minutes whereas the 'punk' tunes would last about two. We only ever played at squat parties and then only three or four times. We weren't interested in pubs and stuff. I think people couldn't believe it when we played the dub stuff. Although we weren't great musicians it came alive, mainly because of Lepke's mixing." As for any historical significance of the era when two sevens clashed and the punky reggae party kicked off: "I think you had to be there to appreciate that there wasn't much else to listen to back then. The punk singles that were out were fine but you didn't want to play them when you got back from a night out. No-one would object if you put on some reggae, which was virtually all we played. I also had a few Motown singles and a Northern Soul tape and a James Brown album or two as well. I'm not sure that that many people were massively into reggae, maybe the few that were had control of the decks though. It was also fashionable with Rotten, McLaren and Rhodes and quite a few journalists, which might have made it seem bigger than it was."

The Interrogators formed after Dutton moved to London where he had obtained a job at ITN as a 'making-the-tea-type trainee'. "Do you wanna make tea at ITV?" he muses, as a twist on the familiar Clash lyric from 'Career Opportunities'. "I heard the Sex Pistols recording their video for 'Pretty Vacant' in Studio 3, but never saw them in the building. They got chucked out the first day for throwing beer cans at the mullet-haired cameramen and had to return the next day. Within a few weeks of joining there was a 12-week strike and I worked part time in Honest Jon's record shop (partly in the reggae shop in Covent Garden, near Seven Dials) to get by. I worked alongside Lepke, who used to muck about with a seriously pro-style EQ unit. He could do a sort of dub by mixing out the instruments and leaving the bass and drums. I was in the Interrogators by then. Some people in the shop thought Frank Interview was my real name. Bass player Kevin was a chef in Oxford when I lived there and we shared a taste in music, in particular reggae. He used to come down to London to rehearse. Lepke came along and immediately started to muck about with the sound. I bought a WEM Copycat, which was an analogue tape echo unit that gave the sound quite a nice dub feel. We were playing 80% punk but the more Lepke was involved, the more dubby the sound became, so it became more 50/50. He even used to dub the punk stuff whether we wanted him to or not."

Fame and riches were not the motivation, which is just as well. "I think we might have become quite an interesting band but Kevin got tired of coming down to London and I got mixed up with a three-quarters girl punk band called Defiant, and ended up forming a band with a couple of them (54-36 Travellers, later Bongo Express)." The Interrogators continued into the early-80s, often playing as support to Local Operator, and were frequently besieged by a young skinhead fan nicknamed Suggs to come and see his new band, Madness.

Dutton's musical adventures continued with a band called Self Control, before joining Subway Sect. "I replaced Rob Symmons when he was sacked by Bernie Rhodes, but never played any gigs. I only rehearsed with them and played on the B-side of 'Stop That Girl'. I got to know Vic Godard because we both used to rehearse at Rehearsal Rehearsals. Vic was a big fan of DJ rather than dub reggae – Bog Youth, U-Roy etc. Lepke was great cos he knew everyone in reggae. He recorded Bob Marley jamming in his hotel room. We went to see Dillinger at The Music Machine and ended up playing pinball with him."

Dutton would subsequently set up Motion Records, home to Godard's more recent works. It will, alas, not house the reissue of any Interrogators recordings, as I found out when I asked Dutton if any tapes still exist. "Only a rehearsal tape and a live tape which was quite good, but then the tape went mouldy – otherwise I might have put it out!"

intestines

Rob Banks (drums), John Baptiste (aka Dave John; guitar), Dale Clarke (bass), Harry Scrubber (vocals)

Bournemouth's INTESTINES were the town's first proper punk act. "Bournemouth was a pretty 'happening' place in the late-70s," Harry told me. "It had (and I believe still has) a thriving music culture. At the time it seemed like everybody was in a band and only natural that we took that direction to channel our teenage angst. Punk, though, had no real representation in the town at the time. There were several venues in the town which were of diverse quality from Capone's on the top floor of a disco complex, the Village Bowl, a full size venue to the Town Hall (great stage, no bar) and various pubs and clubs which all had regular live entertainment. I guess there was a hardcore of about 300 punks in the town whose appetite was satisfied by regular visits from most of the top punk outfits. It wasn't unusual to go to three gigs a week."

The Intestines were the first 'serious' punk band in town. "There had been a couple before us, the Drawbacks (populated by two of the town's first and most legendary punks, Nelly and Clive) and the Stains. It didn't take long for a whole host of local punk outfits to surface after we started. Most were young kids who just needed someone to give them a gig to get them started. The Illegitimate came from Poole and became our regular support. Rabies also came from Poole. The Housewives came from New Milton. Then came the likes of Porno Squad, U-Boats. That led to a host of 'new wave' groups along with The Martian Schoolgirls, the Clinic and the Tours (who became Da Biz with some chart success)."

The Intestines formed in July 1978 while the members were still at school. Harry wrote the lyrics and John Baptiste was able to play a few Beatles songs. They played their first show in August 1979 and immediately garnered interest from Leicester's Alternative Capitalists label, run by Dave Dixey. How did the connection come about? "I never knew," confesses Harry. "Rob Banks was a vinyl freak, he had the biggest vinyl collection I've ever seen. He owns a record shop now. He had contacts all over the country from his dealings and just announced one day that they were interested."

With Clarke, who left for a career in the RAF, replaced on bass by Sid Bladder in September, they set out on an ambitious 'Inept' tour, which lived up to its billing after collapsing after the first show. As for local venues: "We drank at The Gander on the Green, the Buccaneer (the pub attached to the Royal Bath Hotel, as long as we behaved they let us in. Most other places wouldn't). After the Buccaneer banned us we went to the Third Side Club (a gay club where we had a corner and no-one bothered us, there was an empathy between the two parties, we were all outcasts) and for a time at the Quaterdeck on the seafront. Eventually we moved to the rehearsal rooms below Comix in Norwich Road. The place stank and the floor was always covered in water."

They took part in the annual Beat Contest, ostensibly an entertainment for holidaymakers, at the Pleasure Gardens in August 1978. This caused something of a stir when the Generators, who played their one and only show there, were accused of swearing on stage. When the Intestines returned the following year, by invitation, they were told they were banned. "Still, it led to a manic day and created a storm of chaos on a sunny day in a docile seaside abode.

The headlines in the local paper the next day were great!" Displeasure at being locals in a town devoted to tourists was always evident in the band's make-up, as the lyrics to 'Living In Bournemouth' attest: "This is 1980/This is a seaside town/Where all the grockles congregate/To tan fat bellies brown."

Undeterred, they entered Studio 95 to cut three tracks, 'Life In A Cardboard Box', 'New Recruit' and 'Anyway'. Alternative Capitalists also issued a various artists cassette including three live Intestines' tracks. They also recorded their own 15-song cassette album, Borborygmus, titled after their collective euphemism for 'farting', of dubiously recorded live cuts.

By March 1980 Richard Jones had replaced Sid on bass. In July they promoted a show by Brighton's Piranhas, with themselves as support. When 'Tom Hark' shot to the top of the charts, they found themselves playing before an audience of over 1,500 in a venue designed for only 750. By October 'Life In A Cardboard Box' was finally released, and aired by John Peel, though Jones was concurrently sacked after disagreements with Harry. His replacement was Steve 'Snatch' Morgan, formerly of Rabies.

However, Snatch soon left. "About a week after we sacked Snatch we went in to record Borborygmus and 'Label Madman' at Studio 95. There were some test pressings done which I know Rob and John have. But I never got to see them or hear them myself. By then I was getting pretty sick of the whole thing." Instead of recruiting yet another bass player, the remaining trio elected to merge with their support band Illegitimate, bringing in 'Menace' on rhythm guitar, Paul Hurst on bass and Mike Shaw as a second vocalist. They persevered for a few months in this fashion before Hurst was replaced by Dave Flanagan of the U-Boats. Menace soon followed, meaning the effective dissolution of the group. Their final show came in 24 August 1981.

Rob Banks, John Baptiste and Snatch formed a new band, Butcher, who released two good-ish singles, though Snatch died in 1982 of a pills/alcohol overdose. Harry also played with Ten Tall Men in 1989, but not before the Intestines reunited in 1989 to record three songs, 'Lowdown', 'This England' and 'Western Divide'.

"I write and record for fun now," reflects Harry. "I have released three albums on Inept since 2003, as OFS (Our Fathers Sins). They are No Faith, For Whom The Bell Tolls and Shallow Heart. There's still a hefty thread of punk in them, old punks never die they just blend into the wallpaper and live amongst you as agent provocateurs. I'm a senior manager of a large national company now and the chief executive of my company still travels the country watching Stiff Little Fingers. Baptiste has done various projects over the years and has a string of credits as a session musician. He's a lecturer at Bournemouth University. He's a great guitar player. I feel guilty though when I think that he was only fifteen coming on sixteen at our height. We just took him for granted."

DISCOGRAPHY:

Life In A Cardboard Box/New Recruit/Anyway 7-inch (Alternative Capitalists AC01 October 1980)

Borborygmus cassette album (Inept Products 001 1981)

Borborygmus II double cassette album (Inept Products 002 1981.)
('What Ken Said' featured a taped argument with Ken Bailey (sponsor of the show) as to why the band was not allowed to play at the Beat Contest. 'The Man Speaks' was taped off the radio when Peel introduced 'Life in a Cardboard Box'. "The cassettes contained a mix of home recorded and live versions of the songs," says Harry. "The sound quality was fairly poor. We bought a job lot of unsold David Cassidy cassettes from Uptown Records and taped over them.")

Live At Poole Tech 15/5/81 cassette (Inept Products 004 1981)

Life In A Cardboard Box/New Recruit/Anyway 7-inch (Sorted SRS 013 2000) (reissue)

COMPILATIONS:

Illigitimi Non Carbonori cassette (Alternative Capitalists 1980; 'Life In A Cardboard Box', 'Rich', 'Family At War' (all live)

Second Alternative Capitalists cassette (Alternative Capitalists 1980; 'Wet Paint', 'Repressed', 'Alternative Capitalist')

Jam

Paul Weller (vocals, guitar), Bruce Foxton (bass), Rick Buckler (drums)

One of the great 'were they punk or not' knots to unpick for any survey of the era, the JAM provided several complications on musical, aesthetic, ideological and sartorial grounds. Even geographical, they were from Woking, after all, sleepy suburbsville rather than sexy urban Strummersville. Yet they have more in common with the punk upsurge than many credit them with. Energy levels on a par with anyone, generational conviction as well as genuine youth. And while they didn't necessarily have the same disregard for the old order, with Weller remaining a stoically unapologetic Beatles and soul fan, they similarly set their faces against rock's descent into musical indolence.

J

Paul Weller was born in Stanley Road, Woking, the son of featherweight champion John Weller, who earned a crust from building sites and taxi driving. Weller Jnr was an immediate Beatles convert and later adopted the Kinks and Small Faces, sharing his musical devotions with school friend Steve Brookes, with whom he soon started a duo. Weller and Brookes were inseparable and for a time, when the latter experienced difficulties at home, he was domiciled with the Wellers.

They made their debut at Sheerwater School, where teacher John Avory had offered early encouragement at lunchtime music room sessions, in the summer of 1972. Alongside 'Blue Suede Shoes' and 'Johnny B. Goode' were originals such as 'Crossroads', 'Together', 'Busted' and the hilariously titled 'Wicked Woman Blues'. Both participants noticed the galvanising effect on their romantic prospects being seen walking around with guitar cases provoked. Weller's father, taken with the idea of championing their cause, managed to bend the ear of Wally Dent, a local agent who had discovered Jim Davidson. Dent let them support one of his acts on a Sunday afternoon at the Albion pub in Woking. John Weller then booked them for a show at Woking Working Men's Club in November 1972. The latter saw them play Tom Jones and Donovan covers as part of a six-song set that again included a few tentative originals.

Fellow members of 'the Clan', Roger Pilling and Steve Baker, later of Squire, contributed to the embryonic band for a short time, before local beatnik Dave Waller became a more permanent addition. Weller opted to move to bass, partially in tribute to his hero Paul McCartney, with Waller encouraged to raise his competency to a level sufficient for him to become rhythm guitarist. Their first drummer was Neil 'Bomber' Harris, who'd previously been a member of a Shadows' cover band with one Bruce Foxton. As such the Jam, as they had called themselves, would face off against local heroes Rock Island Line (who had appeared in the David Essex film That'll Be The Day) in a rock open at Kingfield Community Centre in Old Woking. To their own amazement, their version of Chuck Berry's 'Reelin' And Rockin'' won the day, though having the cup engraved "Paul Weller and the Jam" caused a few raised eyelids.

When Harris had to miss a youth club show to go on holiday, he found his place had been taken by one Paul Buckler, another student at Sheerwater, albeit a couple of years older. As a prefect, he'd once caught Weller and his mate Roger Pilling smoking in the toilets, but let them off. Harris would go on to an engineering course before regular work in clubland with a dance band. Buckler, the son of a post office and telephone worker, had been working through a variety of jobs including stints in a drawing office, fish shop and as an electrical inspector. He was handed a bunch of Chuck Berry records by Brookes and Weller as study aids, while negotiating a drum kit he'd 'borrowed' from Guildford YMCA. Of course, there were now too many Pauls in the band, so Buckler became Rick, but not before Brookes had managed to foist the name 'Pube' on him, which Brookes had originally acquired when a friend had used it to describe his hairstyle. Brookes had been keen to divulge himself of it ever since, so Rick Buckler now became the aggrieved recipient.

The group persevered as the Jam. "There were lots of suggestions," Buckler later told me, "but they were all terrible. Even in the early days we thought, what a horrible name. But because we'd been using it, and couldn't think of anything better, it just stuck." Progress was slow. A show at Sheerwater Youth Club in the summer of 1973 misfired when the participants over-quelled nerves with alcohol, leading to a major rollicking from John Weller. At their very first demo session, at Eden Studios in Kingston, they recorded 'Taking My Love' and 'Blueberry Rock'.

But by the end of that summer it was mutually accepted that technically, Dave Waller wasn't the match of his compatriots, and he was asked to leave. Paul Weller would later publish his poetry volume Notes From Hostile Street on his Riot Stories imprint in 1979. He died three years later from a heroin overdose. In the meantime the Jam continued as a three-piece, with Weller reverting to guitar. A second studio session was booked in November 1973 at a studio in Swiss Cottage. Though the studio is remembered as being 'awful', not surprisingly given their £17 budget, they did cut originals 'Some Kinda Loving' and 'Making My Way Back Home', of which an acetate exists.

In January 1974 the band began a residency at Michael's, a club on Goldworth Road in Woking, which passed itself off as a disco in order to circumnavigate drinking laws, run by a Greek landlord known only as Hermes. After passing an audition they were offered a regular Friday night slot for £15 for two sets each evening. That was a fair sum of money at the time, and the outdoor staircase also offered the bonus of peering into the strippers' changing rooms.

It was May 1974 when printer's apprentice Bruce Foxton, formerly of progressive rock band Rita, was drafted in to replace Waller, having originally been put forward as a candidate by Neil Harris. At that time the Jam were still predominantly a covers band, so he was reluctant to join. He remained cautious however, and would see through all five years of his apprenticeship before committing to the band full-time. He made his debut at Michael's during their second set as the band's rhythm guitarist. Shortly thereafter he was asked to switch to bass, inheriting Weller's Hofner Violin bass in the process.

Brookes and Weller were writing together prolifically but they hadn't yet found a distinctive sound. But the endless round of youth club gigs and working men's clubs did allow them to gradually filter new material into the set, usually after playing an initial set of golden greats. As well as the residency at Michael's there was also regular work at the Tumbledown Dick in Farnborough, a hangout beloved of drunk squaddies. However, a prestigious gig scheduled for Bunters in Guildford was cancelled when the Horse & Groom was one of two pubs bombed by the IRA. Bruce Foxton escaped meeting friends at the pub by a matter of minutes. Other venues included a police ball (for the Twickenham CID), a show at HM Prison Coldingley where they shared a bill with a drag queen, a gig at Chelsea Football Club and sundry British Legion dates. And the notable occasion when they shared the back of a borrowed Luton van with the owner's 'tame' lion.

Eventually they began to pick up London shows, and played what was, for them, a major support to Thin Lizzy at the Croydon Greyhound in November 1974, booked through one of John Weller's boxing contacts. It was Bruce's first big show with the band, joining them for the second half of their set. They went down pretty well. Shortly thereafter they entered a competition held at the ABC cinema in Woking to appear in a film called, auspiciously, That's Entertainment, but didn't get the part. Their first recordings as a four-piece took place at TW Studios in Fulham. No-one was won over by the results, but not long after John Weller finally secured some record company interest. Terry Slater of EMI came to see them rehearse at Michael's, but decided to "let them down gently".

By mid-1975, when they supported Stackridge, again at the Greyhound, Brookes was having second thoughts. He didn't back the decision to move away from straight pop to a more rock-based sound after Paul Weller had been transformed by seeing Wilko Johnson play on TV. Brookes wanted to stay with the plan, and was particularly aggrieved when Paul persuaded Buckler and Foxton to join him in wearing black Burton suits. He quit, but was persuaded to give the band another chance over a pint with John Weller. But the Stackridge show didn't go well, and after seeing out other commitments, concluding with a show at Woking Football Club, Brookes left. He initially found work gigging as a solo guitarist before setting up his own shop, Abacorn Music, in Brookwood (the Jam helped him open it), before becoming a car dealer. The longstanding friendship, which Weller later recalled in 'Thick As Thieves', was over.

Paul Weller first encountered the Sex Pistols at the Lyceum in August 1976, followed a few months later by his first exposure to the Clash. The latter's Joe Strummer legendarily told him to "write about what you know". Which was, of course, a paraphrase of what Bernie Rhodes had been telling him. To that point, Weller had doted on the Motown and Beatles catalogues, with the Jam's set featuring covers of Martha And The Vandellas' 'Heatwave', Arthur Conley's 'Sweet Soul Music' and Lee Dorsey's 'Ride Your Pony'. But now, in Buckler's words, "we had to toughen up". Suddenly both the ante and the tempo had been upped, and Paul Weller was immediately galvanised into writing fresher material, reflecting the new energy being created in London. Yet the band would never renounce their links to the 60s. This was most obviously signified by the decision to continue playing in suits, purchased from Hepworth's in Woking. These would later be upgraded to the famed mohair threads they found in the Carnaby Cavern, not Burton's, as Strummer would lampoon on 'White Man In Hammersmith Palais'.

Their first real entrance into the punk milieu came when they played their ostensibly impromptu but actually meticulously planned gig at Soho Market in October 1976, under the sponsorship of Rock On Records. The plan was, of course, to stoke a little controversy. However, when the police kindly allowed them to play on, they realised that they'd have to play for considerably longer than planned. Mark Perry of Sniffin' Glue and members of the Clash dropped by, as did Caroline Coon, who wrote their first unfavourable review for the Melody Maker, accusing them of being 'revivalists'. This was later cut out and stuck to a piece of cardboard by Paul Weller, with the slightly illogical assertion "How can I be a fucking revivalist when I'm only 18", which he wore round his neck on stage. A copy of Sniffin' Glue was burnt on stage after Mark Perry dared to suggest they spent too long tuning up. Perry would later talk about the Jam being a fantastic band, but characterised Weller as "the easiest person to wind up in punk".

The Jam then got the chance to support the Pistols for their Dunstable show on 21 October, at which they planned to play with new recruit, keyboard player Bob Gray, who had already appeared with the band at the 100 Club. Eventually logistics – the fact that it's considerably harder to lug around a piano than it is guitar, bass and drums – saw to it that he left the band. He later moved to Canada, became a professional stage magician and now lectures on memory recall. Of greater import, however, was the Pistols' performance. "We'd read all these things in the press about them not being able to play a note," Foxton, who was encountering them for the first time, later told me, "that they were just a creation of Malcolm McLaren, and they didn't have any songs. Well, they did have some songs, and they were absolutely brilliant."

A residency at the Red Cow in Hammersmith helped them to build up their own fanbase. Among their most devoted fans was one Shane MacGowan, aka Shane O'Hooligan of the Nipple Erectors. It was MacGowan who convinced Chris Parry of Polydor to check the band out. Parry was interested, but for some reason thought Buckler's drumming was too 'showy'. There had already been a cut-price offer from Chiswick for three singles on the table, while Island had dismissed them for "not being punk enough". It wasn't the first time they'd face the charge.

Eventually, after their first demo session for the label had been blown out by an IRA bomb in Oxford Street, the Jam signed to Polydor via Parry for a £6,000 advance, for one single and an option on an album. This was, of course, a triumph for Parry, who'd seen both the Pistols and the Clash slip through his fingers. According to Parry, John Weller was so grateful to finally get his boys signed that he didn't bother reading through the contract. Had he done so, he might have queried the 6% royalty rate. Further, he wasn't able to cash the cheque. Neither he, nor his charges, actually had a bank account. Parry therefore transferred the money into his own account so he could produce the ready cash. Some of the phone calls, too, had to take place from kiosks during breaks at the building site John Weller was working at – the Wellers had been forced to skip paying their telephone bill so that they could purchase a new amp for Paul.

By the time they came to re-record a new version of 'In The City' from their original audition demo, Parry was able to confirm that Polydor was ready to action its album option. He was also self-evidently interested in managing the band, but their loyalty remained to John Weller. Parry brought in Vic Coppersmith-Heaven to see the band play the Half Moon in Putney, who would later become their established producer and studio foil.

The band was then invited to join the Clash on their White Riot tour. They accepted, but immediately there were problems. Bernie Rhodes wanted the signed acts, the Clash and the Jam, to subsidise the other groups on the package, the Buzzcocks, Subway Sect and the Slits. John Weller decided that this was unfair, not least because Subway Sect were also managed by Rhodes. A number of small arguments festered away until the tour reached the Rainbow. Angered by not being allowed to soundcheck and their resultant unbalanced sound, the Jam pulled out.

The feud with the Clash would escalate when Paul Weller made his famous "I'm going to vote Tory at the next election" quip to the press. This neatly played into the hands of a self-consciously uptight and pious music media. The Clash sent Paul Weller a nice telegram. "Congratulations on victory of Mersyside (sic) and Manchester. Maggie will be proud of you. See you in South Africa for gun practice." It's easy with hindsight, but who really was toeing the party line here? The fact that the Jam were no longer interested in running with the punk pack was emphasised by the fact that, in open defiance of the Pistols' hijacking of the Queen's 25th celebrations, the Jam were happy to appear at three Jubilee shows, in Chelsea, Tower Hamlets and Battersea.

'In The City', recorded at Bond Street, came out in April 1977. It perfectly encapsulated Weller's knack for capturing the optimism of youth that the whole mod movement was a celebration of, matched by a complementary surge of sound, which Weller would later credit to Vic Smith. "It was pretty much us doing what we did anyway, but the only difference was with overdubbing the guitars. At first I thought that was kind of cheating, because I thought we should just sound exactly like we do live, but on reflection Vic was probably right. Most of what people call 'the Jam sound' I'd put down to Vic Smith, or at least part of it, anyway." Weller had been toying with the idea for the lyric for a while, and had taken to wearing a button badge featuring the song's original title, 'In The City There's A Thousand Things I Want To Say To You'. The riff was a corker too. A fact that was clearly spotted by Steve Jones, who would lift it for the Pistols' 'Holidays In The Sun'.

Peaking at number 40 in the charts, it brought about a Top Of The Pops appearance and, finally, some respite from Buckler and Foxton's parents about when they were going to get a proper job. The B-side, 'Takin' My Love', incidentally, dated from as early as 1973 and had started out as a Brookes-Weller rewrite of the Beatles 'One After 909'.

Their debut album was hurriedly recorded in just 11 days, essentially a document of their live set. In retrospect, it highlights, a couple of tracks aside, a talent as yet not fully formed. Many of the lyrics are simplistic, pummelling obvious targets, though the overall sound and sizzling energy is engaging. The fact that traditional set-closers 'Slowdown' and 'The Batman Theme' make the cut reinforces that view. But certainly the title-track is one of the killer songs of the late-70s, and 'Away From The Numbers' ('Gonna break away and gain control') offers a further indication that Weller could, given time, grow in magnitude as a writer. 'I Got By In Time' sounds like pub rock, and it's interesting to note the Phil Lynott fixation in the vocals. In fact, compared to the more distinctive style he would have developed by the advent of All Mod Cons, there's a huge amount of stylistic variation in Weller's phrasing and delivery. 'Sounds From The Street' relates to that hardy perennial about Weller visiting London and being so excited he made tape recordings of the city's sounds. Elsewhere, he occasionally toned down the breast-beating and certainty that characterised these early lyrics, noting on 'I Got By In Time' that "I don't mean to fail anyone, but you know it's something that I do". And if those barbed comments about revivalism had stung, there was an unapologetic debt to the Who and Motown, especially on 'Non-Stop Dancing', which relocated the Northern soul tradition from Wigan to Woking.

Meantime, the debate raged over whether the Jam were a punk or a mod band. They denied both affiliations, but in many ways they were children of both traditions. They had already put clear water between themselves and the Clash. There was also antagonism with the Pistols' camp after Paul Weller struck Sid Vicious with a bottle one night at the Speakeasy. As for the Damned – there was a rumour that they were planning something 'special' for the Jam's debut album, having agreed to exchange copies of their first long-playing releases. Foxton: "We decided we shouldn't be outdone. So we took a copy of our album into the toilet, shat in it, and sealed it up in a parcel." When the Damned's album finally arrived, it was rather quaintly smeared in jam. A humorous aside, but the truth was that it suited the Jam to operate in effective isolation.

Reflecting in 2002, Paul Weller would explain to Simon Goddard, that "I fucking hated most other bands, really. I just had that feeling that what we were doing was right and everybody else was rubbish. That's the way I was – I'm still not that fucking far off it now, but I'm a bit more sociable. I don't know what it was, not even stand offish, but arrogant, I suppose. I had this absolute belief in what we were doing." Not everyone was wholly enamoured of Weller, either. Captain Sensible: "The trouble with Paul Weller is with all other musicians, you know that their parents have said to them, 'Fucking get rid of that guitar, turn the fucking noise down, get out there, fucking do your work at school and get a fucking job! Don't be a cunt all your life, you're never gonna make a fucking living out of music!' Now, there's one musician I can think of who's not like that. Whose Dad said to him, 'Right take that guitar, go down, 'ave the lessons, learn how to play and we might make a fucking packet of money.' Now I'm not going to tell you which musician that was, but his manager is called John Weller." Maybe the Captain was the one who opened that parcel.

The band's first national tour proper ran from 4 June to 24 July. However, the proposed tally of 40 dates had to be cut short. It was a grinding tour, but after it finished up at the Hammersmith Odeon, the Jam had decided to drop its Union Jack banner due to associations with the rise of the National Front – a point acutely made by Jon Savage in his Sounds review of the show. He also lamented the Jam's 'no risks' and 'deeply conservative' mentality.

The group's second single 'All Around The World' was released in July 1977. Lyrically, Weller's mood of optimism evinced in 'In The City' was dissipating quickly. The "what's the point in saying destroy" lyric was much quoted, and taken as a critique of the Pistols, which it undoubtedly was. Weller is self-diagnosed here as an idealist, never a nihilist, and there's a yearning for a 'youth explosion' that 'we can command'. If it reads a little clumsily in retrospect, its musical exposition meant you couldn't doubt the veracity of those sentiments.

The band's first major European date was scheduled for August when they appeared at the Mont De Marsan punk festival, after which they made their first trip to America. Chris Parry, on whose credit card much of this was being booked, also ended up in a stand-off with tour manager Dickie Bell when a show at San Francisco's Old Waldorf was pulled because of unhappiness over safety. Parry, having invited half of the west coast music industry to attend, was not best pleased. The beginning of a power struggle over the band's management was emerging. And Paul was especially unhappy, allegedly fuelled by homesickness having just met girlfriend Gill Price, variously making dismissive remarks about Americans and announcing on stage at CBGB's that the band was splitting. Still, just like the Damned before them, they were snubbed by Patti Smith, so they must have been doing something right.

The band was then rushed back into the studio to record a second album. In The City had been a success and Polydor were keen to capitalise. John Weller didn't mind, as it meant another £20,000 advance. Parry had come up with the idea of relocating them to the countryside to encourage Paul's songwriting. But all they did was sit listlessly in the pub or rehearsal room, like fish out of water, and their 'holiday' was truncated from two weeks to one. Instead sessions were rescheduled for Basing Street Studios in Notting Hill during August.

Six months after their debut, This Is The Modern World was released, its title-track having been issued as a single two weeks previously. Foxton contributed more to the songwriting, principally because Weller's head was elsewhere, though the critics ragged on both 'Don't Tell Them Your Sane' and 'London Traffic'. Of Weller's own compositions the most successful was 'Life From A Window', 'Tonight At Noon' (inspired by Adrian Henri's 'Mersey Sound' poetry from whence came its title) and 'I Need You (For Someone)', which, it was reasonable to conclude, might just have been inspired by his new relationship. As for the title-track, there was some controversy over the decision to censor the line "I don't give two fucks about your review" with the rather tame insertion of damns in place of the original expletive. And anyway, if you don't give a fuck (or even a damn) about something, it seems to be self-defeating to write a song around it, doesn't it?

The reviews were mixed – not the 'barrage of flak' that they've been likened to, with both Chas De Whalley and Record Mirror writer Barry Cain, who got an acknowledgement for his contribution of the word 'teenage blue' used in the lyric to 'Life From A Window', absolutely trilling with enthusiasm. One of the problems was that the songs hadn't been tested on the road. As Chris Parry would later confirm to John Reed, "The Modern World was rushed, and sounds it. Paul's songs were all right, but they weren't as well prepared, so the session wasn't as quick as In The City – and not as much fun either... Paul got caught up with everything-on-a-Rickenbacker. If he'd just been more open-minded, we could have moved the session on more fruitfully, with more time and care. It didn't achieve its full promise." Later, speaking to Uncut in 2006, Weller would reveal that he hasn't listened to the album in 25 years, and that Parry's decision to forge ahead with a second album so quickly left him wholly unprepared as a writer.

They embarked on a tour through November, the most notable incident occurring after their show at the Queen's Hall in Leeds, which resulted in a poorly advised confrontation with an Australian rugby squad after Paul Weller cut their manager with a glass after he'd knocked their drinks over. Weller was later arrested for his part in the affair, but it was Foxton who ended up with the cracked ribs after being cornered in the hotel. The band started 1978 with 'London Blitz' shows at the Marquee, 100 Club and Music Machine, well away from the Antipodean front row. At the same time, Foxton's 'News Of The World' became their third single, and received a critical pasting. That was a little harsh. The lyric is nowhere near as bad as some would leave you to believe, and it's a sprightly effort musically. In any case, Weller wasn't able to offer any alternatives, with new-found romantic satisfaction having quickly developed into writer's block. Looking back in 2006, he accepted that the early stages of his relationship with Gill became a "John and Yoko thing".

Their second tour of America, which turned out to be even more frustrating than the first, followed. Signed to a co-management deal with Eric Gardner, the Jam became support to his charges Blue Oyster Cult for three weeks in the spring of 1978. It was a soul-destroying and exhausting experience. In total contrast to the sweaty clubs they were packing in London, the Jam were now confronted with disinterested rawk fans in vast auditoriums. Paul's output as a writer had slowed to a trickle, and the quality was worsening. They booked Polydor's Stratford Place studio in April 1978 and set about recording a third album. But when they played the results to Parry, he was singularly unimpressed. A whole batch of songs were abandoned. Parry went round to Weller's flat that evening and told him to start again from scratch. So Weller returned to the family home in Woking, away from the temptations of London, to get back on track.

The band's next single would be a cover. John Weller had sought Mickie Most's advice after the Jam appeared on Revolver about which of their songs was most likely to crack the charts. He'd expressed his preference for their version of 'David Watts', a Kinks obscurity from their 1967 album Something Else. Paul had stumbled across it on the otherwise blighted American tour. Originally it was scheduled as a double A-side with a new Weller composition, "A' Bomb In Wardour Street', another contemplation on his frustration with the punk movement, prompted by an evening of bad vibes at the Vortex. "I mention the Vortex in that song," he told Uncut in 2006, "because that club had a particularly horrible, heavy atmosphere. In my mind, I thought punk was about bringing the kids together, man. I thought it was about uniting everybody and that it was our time for revolution. Not necessarily politically, but just culturally and as a generation. But that lot got it so fucking wrong. It wasn't about cheap speed and pints of cider and rucking. I thought punk was supposed to take us out of all that bollocks and lead us somewhere else. So that song came from my disappointment with it all, whereas I thought the Jam took good aspects of punk and used it positively for what we wanted to do."

'David Watts' brought them no less than three Top Of The Pops appearances. It was followed by a set at the rock-dominated Reading Festival, as the Jam moved in to Most's RAK studios to work on their third album. This time Parry was told he was surplus to requirements, which the band would later admit was genuinely the case, but they enjoyed dropping that little bombshell after he'd been the one to burst their bubble and tell them that the songs on the abandoned third album were "shit".

The sessions went well. Weller had immersed himself in old Kinks albums back in Woking, and the middling reviews of the previous album and the failure of 'News Of The World' had stung him. "There was a feeling we were being written off," he later told MOJO. "That pressured me into writing All Mod Cons. It was me proving myself." The songs, as he confirmed in an interview with the NME, were intended as a series of 'minute and a half, two-minute classics", while he also stated how he was thrilled at the idea of having "15 different tunes in one song". Much of that ambition can be sampled in the layering of sound throughout the album, its use of effects and the complexity of its arrangements.

The band felt confident that anything from it could be lifted as the next single. With the exception of 'Down In The Tube Station At Midnight', a snapshot of late night terror intruding on fragile domestic realities. It was therefore released as an act of perversity. Many still see it as Weller's finest moment – though it's also arguably Foxton's, whose bass runs carry the song (Buckler actually also contributes 'dead string' guitar). It was undoubtedly the moment when critics at last began to appraise Weller as a glaring new talent, the diamond in the rough they could pick out of the perceived collapse of the punk movement. Yet it was nearly stillborn, as Vic Coppersmith Heaven would tell Goddard. "I don't think Paul had the patience then that he has now. If something didn't work, his attitude was to discard it rather than work at it. He couldn't get 'Tube Station' to fit, but when I saw the lyrics they looked absolutely brilliant. I encouraged him to persevere with it and eventually it turned into a really great track. I recorded the underground noises myself down at St John's Wood underground station, just round the corner from Mickie Most's RAK Studios, where we were working."

J

All Mod Cons was and is a truly great album, with Weller's songwriting achieving a depth eclipsing their earlier efforts. While Buckler maintains that it was primarily based on reworked material from the abandoned sessions, it was clear that the two surviving songs, 'Billy Hunt' and "A' Bomb In Wardour Street', had undergone more than a mere tweak.

'To Be Someone (Didn't We Have A Nice Time)', with its fantasy of "being number one" provided a continuous thread with 'Away From The Numbers' as a diary entry, embracing both the possibility and reality of fame, was partially inspired by Weller's hatred of record companies. And the cartoon lyric of 'Billy Hunt', which was slated as a possible single instead of 'David Watts' and was one of the songs rescued from the 'abandoned' album, is captivating boyhood fantasy stuff. But really, there are no weak tracks, although 'It's Too Bad' is pretty much a straight rewrite of the Who's 'So Sad About Us', a song Weller liked so much they would cover it the B-side to 'Tube Station'.

Importantly, after a couple of earlier misfires (notably 'I Need You' on This Is The Modern World) Weller proved he had a big, romantic ballad in him, in the form of 'English Rose'. Pretty much Weller's bow as a solo artist, featuring only sound effects, acoustic guitar and a yearning, naked vocal, it was written about girlfriend Gill Price while stuck in a hotel room on the disastrous Blue Oyster Cult tour. Weller was so sceptical about the reaction it would receive, he had to be persuaded to include it by Coppersmith-Heaven, and the song was originally not credited on the album sleeve. The vicious put down of 'Mr Clean' was also partially inspired by Price, and a lecherous young businessman who had attempted to grope her at a hotel.

The album was plugged via the band's typically arduous live schedule, with their third major UK tour followed by dates in France and Germany and a third tilt at America, then back to the UK for the Jam 'Em In mini-tour. Meanwhile they continued their run of classic singles in the form of 'Strange Town'. A tale of alienation fuelled by feeling the capital's pull but never being completely at home with London, it was an astonishingly complex piece of music with a fantastic arrangement. It also featured one of the all-time great B-sides, 'Butterfly Collector', Weller's savage dismissal of punk super-groupie Soo Catwoman. Allegedly.

'When You're Young' became the second in what would be a straight run of stupendous singles. Weller's take on 'My Generation', it was partially inspired by the mod revival scene that had sprung up that summer and claimed the Jam as their figureheads. The release that year of the Quadrophenia movie also had a galvanising effect. But the Jam, having spent such a long time distancing themselves from one bandwagon, were not keen to hitch themselves to another, and Weller made a number of statements to that effect.

There was, conversely, a more seasoned, almost embittered coming of age tinge to the lyric of 'When You're Young', underscored by the crushing of dreams and aspirations enshrined in one of the most evocative lines Weller ever wrote, "But you find out life isn't like that." The B-side also featured by far the best song Foxton would contribute to the Jam, 'Smithers-Jones', a cautionary tale of the worthlessness of working for the boss.

The album was ready for release in October 1979, with the first gigs to promote it being the John's Boys secret shows at the Marquee and Nashville. Having proven themselves, to an extent, with All Mod Cons, Polydor were prepared to indulge the band a little, and rather than working in a blur and to a deadline, there was more of a workaday atmosphere at the studio. As Bruce noted, "Even the roadies were getting taxis home at the end of the day." Additionally, Weller was growing frustrated with Coppersmith-Heaven's diligence and preciousness, as the album sessions doubled the projected budget of £60,000.

Setting Sons' distinctive cover was taken from Benjamin Clemens' sculpture from the Imperial War Museum. It is often overlooked next to All Mod Cons, the established 'classic' Jam album. This may have been prompted to some extent by Weller's dismissal of his own writing style. At the time he was reading Alan Sillitoe and George Orwell and, inspired by a short story old friend Dave Waller had shown him, he intended that Setting Songs be a concept album about three distinct characters. In the end, only five of the completed songs were themed along these lines. Among them was the album's standout, 'Eton Rifles', which delightfully depicted the 'Citizen Smith' character of the triumvirate being distracted from the revolution by the prospect of beer, fags and posh totty, and the inalienable instinct for self-preservation. It was their first single to break the UK Top 10, peaking at number three. It had originally been inspired by news footage of an unemployment protest march that was jeered by Eton schoolboys. But Weller's class consciousness derived from a much earlier date. While he'd grown up in a tumbledown Victorian council house with an outside toilet, he'd sometimes accompany his mother while she cleaned houses for the rich. It made both a deep and lasting impression on him.

'Saturday's Kids' is a roll call of reference points for the working class at play, Babycham for the birds and full-trim Escorts for the boys. But what's interesting is that only occasionally does Weller flush out the frustrations, citing his fellow travellers (and yes, it does have the feel of shared experience rather than condemnation) as "the real creatures that time has forgot". Of the other songs, 'Private Hell' was influenced, it transpired, by Joy Division, though if Weller hadn't subsequently made this public you'd have been hard pressed to guess aside from Foxton's vaguely 'Hooky' bass line (Weller would also state that Joy Division's 'atonal' influence permeated 'Eton Rifles' too). But the inclusion of 'Heatwave' was wholly attributable to a lack of original material. And 'Little Boy Soldiers', with its self-conscious Kinks-like breakdowns (and Foxton on cello, of all things) doesn't convince.

1980 was destined to be the year when the Jam became the biggest band in Britain by a street, cultivating a cross-gender and cross-generational constituency unknown since the Beatles. 'Going Underground' was a thumping, if somewhat conventional Jam song, originally intended as a double A-side with 'Dreams Of Children'. The Jam were in America, en route from Houston to Austin when news came through that 'Going Underground' had debuted at number one, the first time that had happened since Slade's heyday. They celebrated on their return to the UK by playing two Easter gigs at the Rainbow over the bank holiday, riotous and triumphant shows that featured up to five encores. There were then tours to Spain, Holland and five dates in Japan, then Scandinavia. And a valedictory appearance on Top Of The Pops, in which Weller wore a back to front apron. "Fuck knows what I was doing," he would later recall.

'Start' promptly followed 'Underground' to the top of the charts, though the group had to dissuade Coppersmith-Heaven and Polydor, who went as far as pressing up sleeves, from issuing 'Pretty Green' instead. A lot of attention focused on the obvious steal of the bass riff from George Harrison's 'Taxman', which provided the popping, highly rhythmic undertow of the song, while Weller would subsequently admit to a "slight Gang Of Four influence". The lyric was written partly in tribute to George Orwell's Homage To Catalonia and his adventures fighting fascists in the Spanish Civil War in 1938. There were criticisms of the band's continual over-reliance on their influences with 'Start'. However, the B-side, 'Liza Radley', was arguably more derivative of 'Eleanor Rigby' and Revolver, which all three members of the band were listening to constantly on the tour bus, which now also berthed live keyboard player Mick Talbot.

Sessions for the band's fifth album, to be entitled Sound Affects, began at Townhouse Studios in Shepherd's Bush in July 1980 spanning three months. The band requested a break but Polydor wanted new product to promote for the autumn tour. In interviews Weller told critics that it would see an end to his "sitting on the fence" period as a lyricist. What resulted was the band's second, and last, great album. Only four of the songs had been written before Weller arrived at the studio.

'Man In The Corner Shop' was Paul Weller's balancing of class envy, said to be partially inspired by Geoffrey Ashe's Camelot And The Vision Of Albion. But if one author provided the keynote it was again Orwell. 'Music For The Last Couple', complete with trapped bluebottle recorded in the drum booth, saw the band branch out into shrill parade ground ska, while 'Dream Time' was prefaced by a backwards guitar interlude. But his finest imagining of the dull ache of English working class life was 'That's Entertainment', which he'd knocked off in a few minutes while on holiday in Bracklesham Bay. It was partially inspired by a poem written for his publishing imprint by Paul Drew. When released as a single (in Europe only, though it was heavily imported into Britain) it was accompanied by a live version of 'Down In The Tube Station At Midnight' – pairing together two songs that are routinely regarded as Weller's best, both of which nearly ended up in the trash.

Sound Affects works so well because the gravity of songs such as 'Corner Shop' and 'Entertainment' is leavened by the likes of 'Pretty Green', a joyous ode to the temporal liberty afforded by the arrival of the Friday pay packet, and unaffected love songs such as 'Monday'. In the NME end of year awards, the Jam won best group, male singer, guitarist, bass, drums, songwriter, single ('Going Underground'), album (Sound Affects) and Cover Art (Sound Affects). There was, definitively, no more popular group in Britain.

By 1981 they'd earned a break. It was decided there would be no new album, though the band did fit in tours of Europe and Japan, the "bucket and spade" tour of English coastal towns and CND benefits, as well as two singles. Both 'Funeral Pyre' and 'Absolute Beginners' stalled at number four in the charts. The former was by far the better, including a star turn by Buckler, while the latter was eclipsed by its B-side, 'Tales From The Riverbank'. 'Funeral Pyre', which grew out of a studio jam and thus earned a rare collaborative songwriting credit, was a thinly-masked swipe at the emergence of the new romantic culture and its embrace of wholesale hedonism while Thatcher wreaked havoc with a nation's social structures. It was an objection that Weller made clear in several pointed letters to the press. Many falsely presumed 'Absolute Beginners' was written as a tribute to the Colin MacInnes novel. It was the band's first attempt at funk, as a song concept rather than an adornment, with recording taking place on the day of Charles and Di's wedding.

Sessions for what would be, unbeknownst to at least two-thirds of the band, the last Jam album, began at the end of 1981, at Air Studios in Oxford Street. Its contents were premiered by 'A Town Called Malice', backed by 'Precious'. The two songs were a further conscious attempt to escape the strictures of rock music. It was ambitious stuff, but it was achieved almost effortlessly, despite reservations from Buckler in particular. Weller has maintained subsequently that the band was incapable of moving in the same direction as he was, but there's little evidence of that here. 'Malice' was particularly infectious, the band's attempt to stand their own identity on the framework of an old Motown classic, the Supremes' 'You Can't Hurry Love'. 'Precious', in its own way one of the fastest songs the band ever recorded, looked to a much more contemporary source, Pigbag's 'Papa's Got A Brand New Pig Bag'.

The double A-side again topped the British charts, with both tracks played back to back on Top Of The Pops, an achievement unprecedented since the Beatles were at the height of their powers 16 years earlier. Weller's increasing dissatisfaction with a conventional rock aesthetic and love of Motown was made even more obvious on the attendant album. With Vic Coppersmith-Heaven dispensed with, engineer Pete Wilson was promoted to full production duties. A brass section comprising Keith Thomas and Steve Nichol was added to live shows.

The Gift works, and it doesn't work. 'Happy Together' is an excellent pipe-opener, a great symphonic pop song. 'Just Who Is The 5 O'clock Hero', again intended as a European single release (in Holland) but eventually issued domestically by Polydor, featured one of Weller's most astute lyrics about the indignity of labour and sacrifice. But sometimes Weller overreached. The calypso section of 'The Planner's Dream Gone Wrong' was woeful, and 'Transglobal Express', which attempted to harness dub, electronica and Grandmaster Flash's cut and scratch techniques, was a mess, and sounded like a Sandinista out-take.

When Foxton and Buckler trooped along to Marcus Studios to record 'The Bitterest Pill (I Ever Had To Swallow)', they had no idea that Weller would be asking them to actually live out the sentiments of the title. While staying with his girlfriend in Italy for a fortnight, Paul Weller had decided to end the band (he's suggested that he came to the decision while physically on board the Orient Express). Foxton and Buckler had little inkling, and neither, apparently, did Paul's father, John, who was the most shocked by the decision. They carried on recording the single – an absolute howler with a deliberately corny lyric, featuring Jam PR Lee Kavanagh as the bride on the sleeve and the Belle Stars' Jennie McKeown on backing vocals – but the news was made official in a statement to the press on October 30 1982. That meant a final tour, with packed houses over five nights at Wembley and shows in Guildford and Brighton, beneath which tensions simmered. Foxton had to be talked into performing the final dates, as 'Beat Surrender' was readied as the farewell single.

'Beat Surrender' is Jam by numbers, but it readily overcame its orthodoxy. A thumping backline (Buckler and Foxton had been next to invisible on 'The Bitterest Pill') was a treat, while Weller retreated into his more familiar, declamatory writing style ("As it was in the beginning, So shall it be in the end" was mock-biblical). But the production is great, it sounds appropriately huge, and well, that was it, goodbye.

The last time the band was together was at their annual Christmas party at the Fulham Greyhound on 12th December 1982. Polydor thoughtfully rewarded them each with a Christmas gift. Previously, they had received Cartier watches and video players. This time round they each got a solid silver rhinoceros. Foxton and Buckler were more inclined to see these physically inserted up Weller's rectum than residing on their mantelpieces. Meanwhile, they got their contract-filling sixth album out of the way in the form of Dig The New Breed, which did a pretty poor job of capturing the band's mesmeric live power. Following the announcement of the split, Polydor also released all the band's singles in their original sleeves, which led to the Jam having 13 singles in the UK Top 100 at the same time.

That was it. It was the Style Council for Weller, daft clothes and haircuts, Red Wedge and the Cappuccino Kid. Thereafter he settled into a solo career which has seen him become one of the elder statesmen of British music, either the modfather to his fans, or the king of dad rock, to his detractors. For a long time he would barely acknowledge the existence of the Jam, but he's come to terms with his legacy, if not the blokes who helped him create it. In the course of a dozen or more interviews he's given, usually with Rick Buckler popping up as a sidebar, the non-existent Christmas cards from Paul to his ex-rhythm section have attained legendary status. They were never "big buddies" anyway, reckons Paul. "It's not fair," say Rick and Bruce, still recovering from the fact that they used to be in the biggest band in the country until someone decided to pull the rug from underneath their feet. Someone ought to write a book about this, get in a hapless, naïve ghost author and produce a literary classic. Or maybe not.

Buckler put together Time UK with Jimmy Edwards, but they never landed the major label deal they sought. Foxton was offered a solo deal via Jam publisher Brian Morrison, who hooked him up with Arista Records. But one Top 30 hit aside, 'Freak', it was to diminishing returns. He would also temporarily work with Buckler again in Sharp, who released one single. Foxton then spent four years as part of The One Hundred Men, again, to little fanfare. Buckler meanwhile ploughed his energies, and royalties, into running his own studio, which eventually collapsed, leading to the loss of his house. The rhythm duo again tried to work together in Built Like Stone, before knocking that on the head, leaving Foxton to hook up with Stiff Little Fingers, with whom he'd recorded demos prior to establishing his solo career. He'd stay with them right up to the start of 2006, while Buckler eventually set up his own Jam tribute band, the Gift. Cue gratuitous sniping from Weller.

Weller was awarded an Outstanding Contribution To Music gong at the February 2006 Brit Awards. He used the platform to graciously salute the contribution Buckler and Foxton had made to his career. Well no. Actually, he used it to tell reporters there was "no fucking way" he would reform the Jam. Still off the Christmas card list then, lads.

Discography:

(Buyer's Guide: Direction Reaction Creation is a pretty definitive box set, exhaustive and at times exhausting, and there's some great stuff on the Jam At The BBC release. But still the best way to catch up for new listeners is to work through the individual albums, all of which have been remastered with informative sleevenotes from John Reed. Hard to disagree with popular sentiment that All Mod Cons should be your starting point, followed by Sound Affects. I have a soft spot for Setting Sons, while, as an equally personal view, In The City and This Is The Modern World haven't aged terribly well)

In The City/Takin' My Love 7-inch (Polydor 2058 866 April 1977)

In The City LP (Polydor 2383 447 May 1977) (reissued on CD in July 1990, Polydor 817 124-2. Reissued again in August 1997 as part of the Jam Remasters series, Polydor 537 417-2, with sleevenotes by John Reed)

All Around The World/Carnaby Street 7-inch (Polydor 2058 903 July 1977)

The Modern World/Sweet Soul Music/Back In My Arms Again/Bricks And Mortar 7-inch (Polydor 2058 945 October 1977)

This Is The Modern World LP (Polydor 2383 475 November 1977) (reissued on CD in July 1990, Polydor 823 281-2. Reissued again in August 1997 as part of the Jam Remasters series, Polydor 537 418-2, with sleevenotes by John Reed)

News Of The World/Aunties And Uncles/Innocent Man 7-inch (Polydor 2058 995 February 1978)

David Watts/'A' Bomb In Wardour Street 7-inch (Polydor 2059 054 August 1978)

Down In The Tube Station At Midnight/So Sad About Us/The Night 7-inch (Polydor POSP 8 October 1978)

All Mod Cons LP (Polydor POLD 5008 November 1978) (reissued on CD in May 1987, Polydor 823 28202, and again in May 1997. Reissued again in August 1997 as part of the Jam Remasters series, Polydor 537 419-2, with sleevenotes by John Reed)

Strange Town/The Butterfly Collector 7-inch (Polydor POSP 34 March 1979)

When You're Young/Smithers-Jones 7-inch (Polydor POSP 69 August 1979)

Eton Rifles/See-Saw 7-inch (Polydor POSP 83 October 1979)

Setting Sons LP (Polydor POLD 5035 November 1979) (reissued on CD in March 1987, Polydor 831 314-2. Reissued again in August 1997 as part of the Jam Remasters series, Polydor 537 420-2, with sleevenotes by John Reed)

Going Underground/Dreams Of Children 7-inch (Polydor POSPJ 113 February 1980) (with free live EP featuring 'The Modern World', 'Away From The Numbers', 'Down In The Tube Station At Midnight' – Polydor 2816 024)

Start!/Liza Radley 7-inch (Polydor 2059 266 August 1980)

Sound Affects LP (Polydor POLD 5035 November 1980) (reissued on CD in April 1990, Polydor 823 284-2. Reissued again in August 1997 as part of the Jam Remasters series, Polydor 537 421-2, with sleevenotes by John Reed)

Funeral Pyre/Disguises 7-inch (Polydor POSP 257 May 1981)

Absolute Beginners/Tales From The Riverbank 7-inch (Polydor POSP 400 November 1981)

A Town Called Malice/Precious 7-inch (Polydor POSP 400 February 1982) (also issued as a 12-inch single, POSPX 400, with live version of A-side and extended version of B-side)

The Gift LP (Polydor POLD 055 February 1982) (reissued on CD in June 1990, Polydor 823 285-2. Reissued again in August 1997 as part of the Jam Remasters series, Polydor 537 422-2, with sleevenotes by John Reed)

The Bitterest Pill (I Ever Had To Swallow)/Pity Poor Alfie/Fever 7-inch (Polydor POSP 505 September 1982)

Beat Surrender/Shopping 7-inch (Polydor POSPJ 540 November 1982) (with free single featuring 'Move On Up' and 'Stoned Out Of My Mind'. Also issued as a 12-inch single with same tracks as double 7-inch)

Dig The New Breed LP (Polydor POLD 5075 December 1982) (reissued on CD in June 1990, Polydor 810 041-2. Reissued again in October 1999)

ARCHIVE RECORDINGS:

(the entire singles output of the Jam up to 'Going Underground' was reissued by Polydor in May 1980. Then in January 1983 all the Jam's singles were reissued once again. Obsessives can apparently tell these different versions apart, but I can't)

In The City/This Is The Modern World dbl LP (Polydor 2683 074 August 1980) (first two repackaged as a double)

Just Who Is The Five O'clock Hero?/The Great Depression 7-inch (Polydor 2059 504 January 1983) (UK reissue of heavily imported European single)

Snap! Dbl LP (Polydor SNAP 1 October 1983)
(a then state of the art best of package, originally released with a free 'Live At Wembley' EP, SNAP 45. Reissued, criminally to most fans' minds, as the single-CD Compact Snap! In September 1984, losing 'Away From The Numbers', 'Billy Hunt', 'English Rose', 'Mr Clean', 'The Butterfly Collector', 'Thick As Thieves', with several alternative versions of the remaining songs. It was also reissued again in June 1990. The tracklisting heresy was finally corrected by the recent full-blown re-release. Polydor 987 718-2 is the one to get, as it features a bonus third CD of the live tracks, in keeping with the original free EP – the standard double CD is catalogued as just 987 718-1).
The Peel Sessions 12-inch EP (Strange Fruit SFPS 080 July 1990)
In The City/Art School/I've Changed My Address/The Modern World
(recorded 26/4/77. You can make a good case for this containing more enduring recordings, particularly of 'I've Changed My Address', than the album versions)
In The City/This Is The Modern World CD (Polydor 847 730-2 January 1991) (reissue of first two albums on single CD)
That's Entertainment/Down In The Tube Station At Midnight (live) 7-inch (Polydor PO 155 June 1991) (released to coincide with Greatest Hits package)
Greatest Hits LP/CD (Polydor 849 554 June 1991) (given what's happened since, it seems amazing that Polydor released basically sod all from the archives between Snap and this, which was the first time most people got to hear the songs on CD. And a right pig's ear they made of it, too. See the incoherent sleevenotes)
The Dreams Of Children/Away From The Numbers (live)/The Modern World (live) 7-inch (Polydor PO 199 March 1992)
Extras dbl LP/CD (Polydor 513 722 May 1992) (demos and out-takes and odds and ends, but well sequenced, making for a good listen. Paulo Hewitt does the Paulo-like sleevenotes. The version of 'A Solid Bond In Your Heart' taped in Stanhope Place, gives an indication of Weller's future trajectory. Other highlights include the alternative version of 'Boy About Town' and 'Pop Art Poem', both originally issued as fan club flexidiscs. The unreleased 'No One In The World' is an affecting acoustic effort. At the time it was great to hear all those classic B-sides again too)
Wasteland cassette/CD (Pickwick 4129P October 1992) (the first of a shedload of iffy Jam CD compilations)
Beat Surrender CD (Karussel 550 006-2 June 1993)
Live Jam CD (Polydor 519 667-1 October 1993)
The Jam Collection CD (Polydor 531 493-1 July 1996) (well, as back catalogue raids go it has some kind of internal logic, avoiding the singles for a good selection of album tracks and B-sides)
The Very Best Of The Jam CD (Polydor 537 423-2 October 1997)
Direction Reaction Creation 5-CD box set (Polydor 531493-1 October 1997) (that's a hell of a lot of Jam for your money, though it ain't cheap. 117 tracks, effectively everything that's worth hearing by the band, and a lot that isn't – the demo tracks on the fifth CD offer some interesting working sketches, especially the first version the band recorded of 'The Bitterest Pill', but it's unlikely that you're going to return to it too often. But the rest is a treat, especially the unheard covers of the Beatles 'Rain' and the Kinks' 'Sunny Afternoon')
The Jam At The BBC (Polydor 589 938-2 November 2002) (excellent stuff, with good but, unfortunately, not really track-specific, sleevenotes by Adrian Thrills, the man who was there when the Jam cut 'In The City' and got them to staple his fanzine together)
Gold dbl CD (Polydor 9832572 September 2005) (oh, come on, you've ransacked the vaults enough already, surely. And as for the title? Gold? This wasn't fucking Spandau Ballet you know. The Jam meant something)
All Mod Cons Deluxe Edition dbl CD/DVD (Universal 9839238 June 2006) (this, however, is more like it. The album, plus all the attendant single versions, B-sides and a clutch of demo versions, of which 'Mr Clean' and 'Fly' have never been released before, plus a 'making of' DVD, filmed by Don Letts)

Jerks

Simon Snakke (vocals), Paul Gilbert (guitar), Mark Jackson (guitar), Charles Chaos (aka Charles Acid; aka Charles Menotti; bass), Andy Caves (drums; replacing original drummer Deadleg Dave)

The Jerks were born after five teenagers from Mirfield, near Dewsbury in West Yorkshire caught the Sex Pistols on their Anarchy tour in 1976. Duly enthused, they found themselves the nearest serviceable garage and embarked on recreating what they'd seen, initially under the rather unwieldy title Simon Snakke & The Amputated Leg Band. "I remember that Sex Pistols 1976 show as having really rough sound and Rotten making big holes in the ceiling with his microphone stand," Paul Gilbert

remembers. "It was at Leeds Polytechnic on 6 December, supported by the Clash, Damned and Johnny Thunders' Heartbreakers. Classic stuff? It certainly changed my life. I was also at the Pistols' last British gig (Ivanhoe's, Huddersfield) which was on Christmas Day 1977. Rotten was walking around with a Jerks sticker on his deerstalker hat and we had a long chat backstage – solid geezer. Sid Vicious was in a bad mood. He just sat there cradling Nancy. The live sound by then was brilliant. It was like listening to a live version of the Bollocks album, which I suppose it was."

The Jerks actually forsook the support slot for the show. "We were offered it by the Bankhouse Agency, but they wanted a £30 'bribe' to set it up. We thought it was too much – probably £150 at today's prices – so we told them to get lost."

The Yorkshire punk scene isn't one of the most celebrated, but the Jerks were arguably the biggest band produced by the white rose county. Gilbert: "Being a punk anywhere in 1977 brought attention and aggression, far more than it would these days when people are more familiar and tolerant of different cultures and appearances. We were involved in many punch-ups at a time when, thankfully, it was with fists rather than knives." Spotted by local entrepreneur Derek Deegan, in the summer of 1977 he signed them to a five-year deal with his Petal Records agency and put them to work in his attached studio facility, though the sessions were underwritten by Phonogram.

Their debut single, the cheery 'Get Your Woofin' Dog Off Me', was issued in November in a pressing of 5,000 copies, via Petal subsidiary Underground. The original title was 'Get Your Fucking Dog Off Me', but they wisely decided this may hamper the chances of any chart action. A great single, it's notable for peeling off into a version of Iggy's 'I Wanna Be Your Dog' at the end, which was always the song's underlying influence anyway. According to Gilbert, it was all a metaphor for "telling someone to back off and not invade your personal space". It actually broke the UK Top 100, and brought shows alongside the Adverts, Penetration, Generation X and Sham 69, as well as a tour with American band The Heat.

"It was definitely a disadvantage being based outside of London," Gilbert notes, "far more than it would have been these days with the improved mode of media. We made so many trips up and down the M1 for gigs/recording sessions. I now work for a charity just around the corner from Berry Street Studios (still there) where the second and third singles were recorded. Our main rivals in Yorkshire were SOS and the Killermeters." They certainly cultivated ferocious support, as Steve Eagles of Satan's Rats recalls, remembering being "blown off stage" for the first time at a show in Dewsbury. "The very partisan audience told us to fuck off, so we did and then the Jerks who were supporting us came back on and mimed, would you believe, to their latest record, 'Get Your Woofin' Dog Off Me'. We ran with our tails between our legs."

There was interest from several major labels but eventually the Jerks signed to Lightning, which may not have been the most sensible option in retrospect. "London was fun in those days so in that sense it was worthwhile. I can't remember it being particularly beneficial music career-wise, probably too late by then. Completely fed up with the place now and only stay for child contact reasons. Would happily move to Spain! Lightning Records were supportive but not effective promotion-wise, as we found out."

They released their second effort, 'Cool', in 1978, with Rolling Stones' production team Bill Farley and Dave Hunt helping out, and backing vocals provided by the amusingly titled Di Harde and Joy Holmes of the Straits. But Lightning was undergoing a difficult transitory period as it became Warners' subsidiary Laser (or 'Loser', as some wags noted). There were also numerous line-up changes. Jackson and Caves left, with Barry Firth on drums and keyboard players Veronica Newt and John Best joining. Firth and Best were replaced in turn by Pete Van Rental (guitar) and Kelvin Knight (drums), both formerly of The Issue. Knight subsequently joined Delta Five, while Pete Van Rental formed Road To Ruin. Knight was replaced by Phil Parkin (ex-Rudy And The Zips and Be Bop Deluxe). Thereafter there was a conveyor belt of drummers.

Despite the band moving down to London and releasing their third single, 'Come Back Bogart' at the start of 1980, their boat had sailed. When sales of 'Bogart' disappointed, despite good reviews, the band accepted the inevitable and broke up. Which is a shame, as the Jerks were both amusing and atypical of what other punk bands were doing at the time. In the end their career was symbolically tombstoned by the fade-out mantra on 'Bogart' – "A ton of bricks fell out of the tree, a ton of bricks fell on me."

There was a brief reunion in 1997 to promote the release of the Overground compilation Jerk Off, with Snakke, Gilbert, Menotti and Pete Van Rental joined by former Headbutt and Homage Freaks drummer Lewis Richardson, but "it was a pain, due to a car crash". Where are they now? "Other band members are musically inactive but I do dabble in some individual projects on my home 12-track recorder. Experimental, I suppose you could call it. I played in bands until about 1994. We have vague plans for a final, 30th anniversary reunion in 2007 if I can be bothered. Simon Snakke lives in the Canaries, Charles and me are in north London. No idea about the others."

DISCOGRAPHY:

Get Your Woofin' Dog Off Me/Hold My Hand 7-inch (Underground URA 1 November 1977) (re-released by Last Year's Youth, 2001, with bonus tracks 'Back To Berlin' and 'Dole Queue Boys')

Cool/Cruisin' (Again) 7-inch (Lightning GIL 549 November 1978)

Come Back Bogart/Are You Strong Enough?/The Strangest Man Of All 7-inch (Laser LAS 25 January 1980)

ARCHIVE RELEASES:

Jerk Off CD (Overground OVER 65 1997) (15-track career retrospective including unreleased demos, etc)

We Hate You CD (Overground OVER 91 2001) (tracks taken from three gigs, including support to Sham 69 at the Vortex in January 1978, the Marquee in January 1979 and their 20th anniversary reunion in Leeds in May 1977. Eight of these tracks were only ever performed live and are therefore exclusive to this package. Sleevenotes by Gilbert)

COMPILATIONS:

Lightning Records Punk Collection CD (Anagram CDPUNK 79 1996; 'Get Your Woofin' Dog Off Me')

Jermz

Mike Normal (aka Mike Gibson; guitar), Jacko Jerm (vocals), Kelvin Nite (aka Kelvin Knight; drums), Ozzie Spitfire (aka Aussie Spitfire; bass)

York's JERMZ released one killer single before disappearing into sundry other pursuits. These days they are chiefly recalled for being the original home of Mike Gibson, a fixture of the Godfathers line-up for several years, and the pseudonymous Jacko Boogie, then travelling under the name Jacko Jerm.

As he later recalled for the Glitter Suits website: "About the time of punk I felt confident enough to put an advert in the local 'paper asking for punk/new wave musicians to form a band, which got a few replies, one of which was from Mike Gibson. We did eventually put a record out as the Jermz, which is now a collectable punk single." He's right, with copies now fetching £80, as only 500 were ever pressed. "I guess it's bloody rare," Gibson explained to me, "because most of them got dumped." Gibson's recollection is that he met Jacko via Kelvin Knight at a Cyanide gig.

As for the local scene: "There were a good handful of bands in York and we all went to see each other regularly, swapping from audience to stage," Gibson continues. "It felt like the London thing was very trendy and removed, though we did occasionally go to see the bands at the Oval Ball or anywhere we could." In terms of securing gigs, manager Gordon Brown (aka Hugh Bernays) was the band's "very own Malcolm McLaren". The single came about because "We were offered the chance by a local record shop Feelgood Records who paid for the studio and pressing. We had to cut out and paste the sleeves ourselves by hand." Urban Blitz of Doctors Of Madness travelled up from London to produce it. It was recorded at Pollen Studios, where two further classic punk singles, by Sema 4 and Xpress, were also recorded. Afterwards Ozzie left to become an army medic and was replaced by Charlie Francis.

Sadly, they never got the exposure that a London band might have enjoyed, a question of wrong place, right time. "We decided to call it a day 'cos we were tired of each other, I guess," Gibson reckons. "Wanted to do other things." As for other recordings, Gibson reckons there's a tape somewhere of one of their shows, but that's about it. Jacko then started 70s revivalists The Eight Track Cartridge Family, who briefly appeared on the front cover of the NME and whose singer, Ciara, is now a Chi-Kung teacher. No, I know that's not relevant to anything. Kelvin Knight would subsequently join the Jerks, then Delta 5, and was recently spotted in the most recent reincarnation of the Chameleons. Jacko went on to found the STIM label (Terry Edwards, etc). Francis worked with both Patrik Fitzgerald and Toyah. Post-Godfathers, Gibson has just released his solo album City Farm. Once a punk, always a punk? "Dunno if it qualifies as punk in any way… I'm more proud of it in some ways than anything else I've done. I see it reaching people, making them think, relate to it, so although it's very different music I still get the same kind of kick from it."

DISCOGRAPHY:

Powercut/Me And My Baby 7-inch (One Way Records EFP1 1978)

Jet Bronx & The Forbidden

Yup, it's true. JET BRONX & THE FORBIDDEN, who briefly recorded for Lightning Records, was the home of Masterchef and Behind the Keyhole vowel-mangler and concurrent rock critic, Lloyd Grossman. Their single, 'Ain't Doin' Nothin', is the sort of prole-prose you'd hardly expect from sauce-boy, reminiscent of the Streetband pulling off a novelty hit with 'Toast'. The sleeve advertised the fact that the first 15,000 were on "terrific red vinyl" instead of "crummy black vinyl".

Whether any in black were actually pressed is another matter. It also brought them to the stage of Top Of The Pops, incredibly, though 'Ain't Doin' Nothin" is pretty basic stuff. It lacks spice. Even a little garnish would not have gone amiss. But enough of the crass-culinary conceits already.

Afterwards Grossman would front the Commercials, who released a listenable album in 1980 for Eat Records (Compare And Decide). Yes, Eat Records. Nurse, the screens!

DISCOGRAPHY:

Ain't Doin' Nothin'/I Can't Stand It 7-inch (Lightning LIG 501 December 1977) (first 15,000 copies in red vinyl)
As Jet Bronx:
Rock & Roll Romance/On The Wall 7-inch (Lightning LIG 525 1978)
COMPILATIONS:
Lightning Records Punk Collection CD (Anagram CDPUNK 79 1996; 'Ain't Doin' Nothin")
Cool Punk CD (Newsound NST015 2000; 'Ain't Doin' Nothing")

The Jets

Gerry (vocals), Reggie (bass), Phil Imber (guitar), Joe (guitar), Justin Banville (drums) (line-up at the time of recording Farewell To The Roxy)

Aside from appearing on Farewell To The Roxy, this Luton quintet, who went through numerous line-ups, played support to Steel Pulse at the Vortex and a few other dates around the capital without ever making a breakthrough, though they did leave behind one cracking single for Good Vibrations. The fact that similarly titled outfits were also recording at the same time for labels including EMI probably did them few favours.

But **THE JETS** were the first punk band in Luton, and enormously important to that scene, as Roger Holdstock of Friction recalled. "The Jets, and Phil Imber in particular, were initially responsible for what happened in Luton in the late 70s/early 80s. They organised gigs, did a fanzine, set up a label. They were there. And then they weren't… An inspiration."

The band started life in a terraced house in Hibbert Street, Luton, initially taking the name BB Exiles, then simply the Exiles. Justin Banville: "With the front room decked out in egg boxes to help suppress the sound, we were soon driving the neighbours to a point where they were likely to commit multiple homicides. We then moved operations to the relative safety of a scout hut (or whatever it was) which was sited at the edge of the Marsh Farm Estate, now known more famously for the large scale riots that took place in the summer of 1995."

They made their debut at Dunstable College and were booed off stage after a couple of songs, not that the hostility caused them to rethink their career path. Rather, it spurred them on. Still under the name the Exiles, they recorded their first demo at Strawberry Studios in

Stockport. "We arrived just one day after the Bay City Rollers had vacated the premises. With many of their young (female) fans still milling about outside, we could easily be forgiven in those days of extreme naivety, for thinking we were already halfway there."

The line-up evolved over the ensuing years as they became the Jets. On the 7 December 1977, they took part in an audition night at the Roxy – events organised principally as it meant proprietor Kevin St John wouldn't have to pay the bands. There were subsequent appearances including the Christmas 1977 extended bill, and again the following Boxing Day. The Jets would later appear on the Farewell To The Roxy album. They actually contributed two songs, because no-one noticed how quickly the first, 'TV Drink', actually was – it ends one minute and nine seconds in, before they launch into 'Dreg Town'. They were also part of the ill-fated Farwell To The Roxy tour of Scotland.

The band's subsequent career was aided by Terri Hooley. The head of Belfast's Good Vibrations label not only showed the band his 'glass eye in pint' trick, he sorted them out with some Northern Ireland dates and put them up in his own house. He was, in short, "a man of great character and sincerity," according to Banville. "I remember the general sense of disquiet as our trip up there began," he continues, "like we were embarking upon some precarious, almost unheard-of, but undoubtedly little travelled musical pathway to God knows what. It was after all, that Ulster, globally infamous for its hoards of balaclava-clad paramilitaries, for bombs, bullets and an apparently insatiable lust for sectarian bloodletting at every opportunity. Normally these things were only ever observed through the bubble-like safety of television glass. However, there was also much excitement too and in equal measure, for myself especially, as we were also seemingly following in the footsteps of such then contemporary greats as the Clash."

J

The Jets ended up releasing two singles for Good Vibrations, the first, 'Original Terminal', shows rapid development, with a sound more akin to post-punk. By the advent of a second the band had changed names to the Tee-Vees for the more reggae-influenced 'Doctor Headlove'. Afterwards Banville stepped aside to be replaced by Colin Salmon, late of Friction, who would go on to be a highly successful actor. The band continued for a while before petering out.

DISCOGRAPHY:

Original Terminal 7-inch (Good Vibrations International GVI 2 1979)
Block 4/The Iceburn (recorded September 1978)
As the Tee-Vees
Doctor Headlove 7-inch (Good Vibrations GOT 11 1979)
COMPILATION:
Farewell To The Roxy (Lightning LIP 2 1978; 'TV Drink') (at least, 'TV Drink' is the only song credited, but it's actually TWO songs, 'TV Drink' and 'Dreg Town' aka 'Dreg')

Jilted John

It's hard to underestimate the psychic role the chip shop played in 1970s Britain. As one astute writer noted, it was "the amphitheatre of dreams and the romantic crucible for urban youth". It was also the setting used by Manchester faux-punks Jilted John, who were, of course, not punk rock at all, to mount an unlikely raid on the charts and Top Of The Pops. The creation of Graham Fellows, and an early production by Martin Hannett, 'JILTED JOHN' addressed the emotional heartbreak of being dumped in favour of someone cooler. Fellows recorded it then went off to a Christian youth camp, using the religious pretext as a cover for the fact that lots of girls were attending.

To the shock of everyone concerned, it reached number four in August 1978, and spent 12 weeks in the charts. Bernard Kelly, a Mancunian Fellows met on a weekend drama course, was given the part of Gordon for Top Of The Pops. That was fun, but then for the last 20 years he's had to put up with people shouting "Oi! Gordon. You're a moron!" at him, despite a long and successful subsequent career as a TV writer. Fellows was delighted to bump into Blondie on the set, though the song he composed in tribute, 'Debbie Debbie', with lyrics including 'Every time I see your face, I get an erection,' failed to impress. On the same set Renaissance's Annie Haslam launched a tirade at him for being "musically insulting".

Fellows was a Yorkshireman studying drama at Manchester when the plot was hatched with Tosh Ryan at Rabid – there's been some suggestion from Ed Banger of the Nosebleeds that he was briefly pencilled in for the job but declined due to inter-band rivalry. I cannot confirm or deny this because Tosh Ryan is so bored at being asked about 'crap records' that he insisted on talking to me about Marcus Stockhausen instead. "It's a new one on me," notes Fellows. Alternatively, as Fellows states in the sleevenotes to the Castle reissue of True Love Stories, "I'd written a couple of songs and I wanted to record them. So I went into a local record shop and asked if they knew any indie or punk labels. They said they knew of two; Stiff in London and Rabid just down the road. So I phoned Rabid up and they told me to send in a demo." The idea was to offer a punky update on John Otway's 'Really Free', and the original demo was recorded with the late Colin Goddard of Walter And The Softies on guitar and the rhythm section of local band the Smirks. Rabid were won over and Martin Hannett produced a new version at Pennine Studios with John Scott on guitar.

Originally, however, 'Going Steady' was intended as the A-side, until John Peel and then Piccadilly Radio started playing 'Jilted John', which also became Fellows' new sobriquet. "John Peel must take credit for being the one who played 'Jilted John' repeatedly," notes Fellows, "prompting the decision to switch, probably before Piccadilly. And 'Jilted John Thomas' was a half-serious contender as a name for a while." Tony Parsons made it single of the week, and Paul Morley managed to quote Shelley in his fawning tribute to its greatness (that's poet Shelley rather than Buzzcock Shelley, incidentally). Once it started to do well, and given the vocal support of Barry Lazell of Record Business and Peel, it was licensed to EMI International, a decision queried by Tony Wilson in a Granada Reports feature on indie labels. The streetwise Ryan accused him of living in the past. A couple of follow-ups failed to repeat the formula, consigning Jilted John to perennial one-hit wonder status. However, the album True Love Stories announced a serious, albeit quirky, songwriter, schooled in a love of 60s pop and open-hearted confession. As Sounds wrote, "Don't get the impression that the mind behind the hit has suddenly turned into a wimp, meaningful songster. Believe me – that would be criminal. The album reveals perhaps one of the most original and important rock'n'roll sensibilities to emerge in the Seventies." Indeed, if there's a song more evocative of callow youth grappling with teenage-hood than 'I Was A Pre-Pubescent' I haven't heard it. Especially the bit where he sums up the courage to say the word 'masturbation' and the whole song collapses in embarrassment. However, as again revealed in the sleevenotes to the reissue, Fellows remains ambivalent about Hannett's decision to give keyboards prominence over John Scott's guitar on the finished mixes. "It all sounds so over-arranged and over-produced. Not punk at all."

There were a couple of follow-up singles pulled from the album, but by the time they were released Fellows had gone back to drama school. In January 1979, when he should have been promoting the first of them, 'True Love', he appeared in Coronation Street, where he attempted to pick up Gail Tilsley. In a bizarre parallel to the True Love Stories concept, he eventually did get the girl (Gail) when he took the fuller role of Les Charlton in the serial, but only for a few weeks in the summer of 1982. Gail would return to the none too loving arms of Brian, murdered in 1989 outside a nightclub when he was on the razzle, and then married Martin Platt, the dullest character in Soapland. Later she dated homicidal maniac Richard Hillman and a gruff Scottish chiropodist who is approximately three times her own height, so perhaps Les Charlton might not have been such a bad call. The eternally jilted Fellows transformed himself into comic and music hall throwback John Shuttleworth, with his own radio and TV shows. He also attempted a Eurovision Song Contest coup in 1997 with 'Europigeon', and developed a second alter ego, musicologist and media studies lecturer Brian Appleton. "I'm currently resting Brian, but about to unleash concreter from Goole and aspiring after-dinner speaker Dave Tordoff at the Edinburgh Fringe in Dave's first full-length show, Neighbours From Hull."

DISCOGRAPHY:

Going Steady/Jilted John 7-inch (Rabid TOSH 105 July 1978) (reissue EMI INT 567 August 1978, with A and B-sides flipped over)

True Love Stories LP (EMI International INS 3024 December 1978) (CD reissue Castle ESMCD 771 1999, with addition of 'Jilted John (2)', 'Gordon's Not A Moron', 'I'm Just Happy To Know You')

True Love/I Was A Pre-Pubescent 7-inch (EMI INT 577 January 1979)

The Birthday Kiss/Baz's Party 7-inch (EMI INT 587 April 1979)

NOTE: Julie And Gordon's 'answer' records, 'Gordon's Not A Moron/I'm So Happy To Know You (POGO 03) and J-J-Julie (Yippie Yula)/Gettin' It Tighter (POGO 04) are nothing to do with Fellows, but merely cheap novelty cash-ins (of a cheap novelty cash-in?) Not that Rabid was impressed, with talk of legal action at one stage. Bernard Kelly's alter ego Gordon The Moron released two singles, 'De Do Dough Don't Be Dough (TOSH 107) and 'Fit For Nothing' (TOSH 111) after he and Fellows had fallen out. Life mirroring art mirroring life etc)

COMPILATION:

The Crap Stops Here LP (Rabid LAST 1 1980; 'Mrs Pickering') (reissued by Receiver Records on CD)

Joby And The Hooligans

Joby Visigoth (vocals), Helen McCookerybook (bass, vocals), Steve Beardsley (guitar), Tracey Preston (vocals), Carol Reed (vocals)

Early Brighton punk band who played regularly at the Vault, the city's first punk venue. McCookerybook would later join the Chefs, but it was lead singer Joby, who was also involved with the Pic Of The Poseurs fanzine, who got all the attention for his textbook punk sneer and novel costumes.

J

Songs such as 'A Vandal Ain't No Scandal', 'Sex Motor Flash Attack Repeat Last Time', 'Seeboard Gas' and the Adverts' pastiche 'Looking Through Gary Glitter's Eyes' (which was actually written by founding member Nick Dwyer who would subsequently form Nicky And The Dots) never did make it to the studio. Perhaps the greatest loss, though, was 'Mary Bell', about the child-killer's incarceration. "One day I'm gonna bust her out/And take her for my wife/Cos she's good with kids."

"**JOBY AND THE HOOLIGANS** was conceived within a week, Monday to Friday," Joby told me. "We got the set together in the squat we shared with Helen, Beardsley and another geezer. Personal reasons for the band were #1 ego, #2 political and #3 wot the fuck! The BTN Resource Centre was a vibrant facility staffed by social workers, liberal wankers and diesel-dikes, but gave an opportunity for degenerates to use the Vault as a music venue. Helen remains a great friend and was my best man/woman when I married but that is another story. Joby & the Hooligans came about because I knew how to use serigrafix for Attila the Stockbroker, then known as Brighton Riot Squad, for posters, and they needed a support band. The rest is history. I recall we had approximately four numbers that we could repeat at will for however long the audience would tolerate it. 'A Vandal Ain't No Scandal' was a particularly significant angst-ridden polemic, but I consider my best work was 'Kiss Your Feet', an obvious take on 'I Wanna Hold Your Hand'. The lyric went thus – I suppose I should have known/Second night that I walked you home/Night was dark and the moon was black/Raindrops glistened on your plastic mac/I wanna kiss your feet, lick your meat/I wanna poop your hop, lollipop/And kiss your feet, kiss your feet."

On reflection, Joby thinks the lyrics may have been inspired by a chemistry student at Sussex University. "He seemed to spend his academic time developing MDMA and distributing it to lab rats like me. The last I heard of him was he was arrested on the M4 in a transit van full of E's en route to Glastonbury. Shit happens, but why the fuck are they proposing to close the chemistry department when it may have produced some of the best synthesized drugs ever?" Erm, not qualified to answer that one, Joby lad. Back to the matter at hand. "We blew Riot Squad off stage (Attila admits this), some of us never looked backed i.e. Helen. Some had to move to other things. I chose fishing and moved to Penzance. Beardsley chose loony nursing (erm, I think the proper term is 'mental health'). Fuck knows what happened to the drummers? Perhaps they exploded ala Spinal Tap?"

These days Joby describes himself as a "Tao Socialist." His manifesto? "Achieve one's gratification, intellectual, community and social enhancement, with no cost or less to the people or environment, then die." And there's more. "Like the 60s, if you can remember the late 70s then you weren't there! Waking up next to some dodgy tart and making excuses to leave certainly developed my artistic creativity. Better than waking up in a jail cell, but I still do both." I'll bet he does, too.

Johnny & The Self-Abusers

Jim Kerr (vocals), Charlie Burchill (guitar), Ali Mackenzie (guitar), John Milarky (guitar), Tony Donald (bass), Brian McGee (drums), Alan McNeil (guitar)

The gene pool that produced Jim Kerr, aka the Laird of Ardchullaire, for better or for worse. But, as Dave Thompson once wrote for British Punk Collector: "There are many people who, as they spin New Gold Dream further into soporific oblivion, still doubt whether a band so elegant as the Minds eventually became, could ever have been spawned by something so clattering, so raucous, so downright AWFUL as the Self-Abusers."

In February 1977 Jim Kerr and Charlie Burchill were drinking in Glasgow's Doune Castle when a local punk, Alan Cairnduff, approached them and asked them if they'd heard of his band – **JOHNNY & THE SELF-ABUSERS**. They hadn't. He then admitted he'd made it up. But it might be an idea to form such a band, as he had already convinced the landlord to book them. He was going to the singer. Only he wasn't. He just drifted away (in various alternative versions of this story it is Milarky that initiates the formation of the band). The next day Kerr and Burchill wheeled an amplifier down to John Milarky's house whose occupier had hung a microphone from the ceiling. He regaled them with a version of his first composition, 'Pablo Picasso'. They decided to book the Doune Castle for no other reason than to make absolutely sure they maintained their impetus. Burchill later stated that "We decided, if we were going to do anything, we should do it, sort of, full-heartedly." The line-up was fleshed out with the addition of McGee and Donald, who'd been involved in Kerr and Burchill's school band.

Given that it was rare to find a venue willing to put a punk show on, when they did turn up to play at the Doune Castle, armed with one original song and a week's rehearsal, they found a queue down the block. They managed to pull the event off reasonably well, with their three-guitar line-up and hurriedly enlisted female dancers masking some of the deficiencies in their musicianship. "Charlie and I only had to do it once to realise that this was what we wanted," Kerr later recalled. "It was all lots of fun. Charlie had a violin, I played the few chords Charlie taught me on the keyboards, and we also had a few girls who had made themselves up like Indians out for war, at our request. There was a touch of glamour there. Even then it wasn't punk. No spitting or anything, more like kitsch."

Two weeks later they played support to Generation X in Edinburgh and then took up a residency at the Mars Bar. Kerr set about mouthing his intention to channel "the blackness and negativity" of the period. But everyone seemed to agree that the Self Abusers were shite. They kept practising and writing, but a schism quickly opened up. Milarky's songs were weeded out (in particular, his 'Toss Yourself Off' anthem was deemed a no-no) with Kerr and Burchill taking on more of the songwriting.

They reached the attention of Chiswick Records after journalist and former Zoom Records' press officer Brian Hogg sent down a demo tape, recorded after Milarky's parents fronted the money. Chiswick made a good number of pre-sales on the strength of their name alone. The band then thought twice and asked to change the name – only for Ted Carroll to tell them it was too late, it had gone to the printers. "This was maybe not completely accurate," Roger Armstrong told Punk77.com, "but we were determined not to blow the good pre-sales." Yet the intended name change was symptomatic of problems within the group.

They split amidst growing tensions, which escalated when McGee threw a Wellington boot through Milarky's front window. Only the promise of the upcoming single release on Chiswick held them together. They even tried to move into a flat together in October, but that only cemented existing divisions and jealousies.

So on the very day that their debut single was issued, they broke up. Which may have made a round of dreadful reviews from the inkies easier to take, not least the NME's assertion that: "...the song is a drab parade of new wave that jerks off aimlessly into the void". Goodness knows what the reviewer would have made of Simple Minds – though Kerr did mail a tape of their first demos to Chiswick. Milarky subsequently formed the less successful, but far more interesting, Cuban Heels. McGee, in addition to playing on five Simple Minds albums between 1979 and 1981, worked with Glasgow's Endgames, Germany's Propaganda, Cyndi Lauper and Cheap Trick's Robin Zander's solo work.

"When the Self Abusers split," Armstrong recalled to Spiral Scratch, "we did get the demos of the two bands they split up into, Simple Minds and Cuban Heels. At the time I quite liked the Simple Minds demos, they sounded a bit like the Sweet, oddly enough. I remember discussing it with Ted and saying, 'Yeah, it's pretty good stuff, maybe we should look at them, it's a shame they've got such a dreadful name'. It was like, 'Oh, they'll never get anywhere with a name like Simple Minds.'"

DISCOGRAPHY:

Saints And Sinners/Dead Vandals 7-inch (Chiswick October 1977)

COMPILATIONS:

Punk Lost And Found LP (Shanachie SH 5705 1996; 'Saints And Sinners')

The Chiswick Sampler (Good Clean Fun) LP (Chiswick CDWIKX162; 'Dead Vandals')

(There's also a CDR of the band's first 'Demos' kicking around. It features 18-18, Tonight, Little Bitch, Pablo Picasso, Subway Sex, Lies, Wasteland, Act Of Love, European Son, Cocteau Twins, Chelsea Girl, Did You Ever? and Pleasantly Disturbed. Sadly, Toss Yourself Off doesn't seem to have survived)

Johnny Moped

Dave Berk (drums), Fred Berk (bass), Ray Burns (guitar), Johnny Moped (aka Paul Halford; vocals), Xerxes (vocals), Phil Burns (keyboards)

The labyrinth of pre-Damned groups Captain Sensible was involved in should interest no-one but the Captain himself. However, when you reach JOHNNY MOPED, in which he hooked up with the incomparable Moped, his former colleague in Genetic Breakdown and all sorts of other underachieving bands, you really have to pay attention.

Mr Moped, aka Paul Halford, is something of an oddity. No, he's more than that. He's like a cross between a less savvy Homer Simpson and Wesley Willis, imbued by the spirit of Elvis and with a voice that sounds like a cement mixer on its last legs. He is not of this planet. He was a big fan of motorbikes as a young man and wanted to be the leader of a rock band called something like 'Johnny Harley'. In the first of a long series of indignities visited upon him, the good Captain started to call him 'Johnny Moped' instead.

The myth of Johnny Moped is, I can confirm, entirely true. He is indeed bossed around by Brenda, his long-suffering wife, who attempts to stop him appearing as a top flight box office draw. Or at least his mother-in-law does. The latter hates Johnny and the feeling is mutual. So his bandmates have to kidnap him from work. Elaborate ruses are hatched by his band in order to keep the legend alive, and Brenda isn't getting any less ferocious about it as the years pass. And Moped isn't getting any less confused. She apparently attacks Sensible on sight, knowing full well his 'agenda', to the extent that he once ran into a police station to escape her. Legendarily, Brenda is just as eccentric as Johnny. Roger Armstrong recalls her coming to see Johnny play at the Marquee and insisting on placing a wooden chair on the dance floor. Each time she was knocked off her perch by pogoing punks, she got up, put the chair back and sat down again. This happened about 20 times. It must have been love at first sight.

Sensible, then still simply Ray Burns, was a member of the team when Genetic Breakdown evolved into Johnny Moped's Assault And Buggery, and would pop in to contribute from time to time thereafter. His brother Phil Burns was also on board at various points. I once saw a Pete Frame-like family tree that Slimey Toad or Dave Berk had come up with, but jeepers, it didn't make things that much clearer. Captain first met Johnny through a mutual friend. Johnny had befriended a group of hell's angels. The deal was that they'd take him for a spin of about 50 yards on the back of one of their bikes. In response to which Johnny would give them his week's wages. It all evolved out of that, as Xerxes would tell me. "Someone once said if you put John Arlott in a field, eventually a test match would grow around it. Well it was a bit like that with Johnny, cos it was obvious that the man had so much talent. And although people didn't have that much idea about forming a hand at that stage, it was obvious that Johnny was the catalyst for it. And it sort of grew from that. It was never a question of rehearsing or anything like that, it was just a question of letting him loose in front of a microphone, and us doing the rest of it behind him, and just letting it grow organically. And it was really strange cos this must have been around 1971 and people used to say we really sounded like the Velvet Underground. And we didn't even know what the Velvet Underground sounded like. I suppose over the years it grew out of that."

Dave Berk takes up the Johnny Moped story in the sleevenotes to Basically... "We were a strange band, rehearsing/jamming in Phil's bedroom or my garage, and tape recording everything during the day so that we could have a few beers in the evening and listen to it back. We always refused to play the same thing twice and this put quite a demand on Johnny and Xerxes to ad-lib new vocals and make up new songs every week. We tried to find bizarre venues for listening to the tapes – the Gas Works, on top of multi-storey car parks, Gatwick Airport. And I remember on one occasion we decided to simply go to the local park armed with a gas stove and some grub, but we attracted too much attention (particularly when Captain set fire to the place) and the police arrived just as we were vaulting over the fence. I was asked, 'what are you doing with that saucepan of beans?'"

When Captain tied his colours to the Damned mast, the group needed another guitarist. So they put an advert out: "A big funky mundane band looking for a local way-out rock group for some work!!! Johnny Moped is looking for a way-out funky bass guitarist into moronic rock'n'roll & pip-squeak progressive stints (Male or Female) sex not import, must have own bass guitar and sound system – strictly amateur band. Interesting. Phone Dave, etc" Who could resist such a summons, apart from possibly someone with a love of the English language? The applicants turned out to be Chrissie Hynde and Slimey Toad. Dave Berk already knew Slimey from Tor, where he'd replaced Rat Scabies. Both got the gig and they started to play at the Roxy, until Slimey came up with a "it's me or her" ultimatum and Hynde was sacrificed and faced financial penury as singer with the world conquering Pretenders. Them's the breaks.

The Moped band made its debut on the landmark Live At The Roxy compilation, contributing a version of 'Hard Lovin' Man' that set the group's agenda for hard rocking nonsense. This was moron boogie of a fine vintage. Thereafter they issued the famed 'Official Johnny Moped Bootleg'. Chiswick decided to give the band a recording contract when anyone more sensible would have kept their distance and not returned phone calls. "Moped was and probably still is eccentric to the point of being legendary," Roger Armstrong later admitted to punk77. It was the good Captain who brought them to his attention. His later band mate Henry Badowski remembers playing only his second ever show with Chelsea and seeing "Captain Sensible arrive at the Railway Hotel, Putney with Johnny Moped in an orange boiler suit asking Gene (October) if they could support us. They were stunningly amazing. Dave Berk drummed like a machine. Mad, mesmerising, funny, weird and dangerous."

The first result of the liaison with Chiswick was 'No One', backed by 'Incendiary Device'. The latter was the pick (it was meant to be the a-side, until Radio 1 apparently objected to the line "Stick it in her lughole") and though it's difficult to make out what passes for a lyric, we can assume lascivious intent is at the forefront of young Johnny's "mind". The follow-up was the tender 'Darling, Let's Have Another Baby'. Only any sensible woman would run a country mile from Johnny intoning "I'll be quite happy/To wash and change his nappy." Yet it picked up at least three single of the week awards and was later covered by Kirsty MacColl, a member of the Moped band's extended family. And then came the immortal Cycledelic, which elegantly represented a whole different side to the punk explosion. The one where dirt poor working class chaps with borderline mental health problems made a stand for their right of expression. And do it better than the art school set.

The album "was a nightmare," according to Dave Berk, "because Johnny was virtually under lock and key by this time and we only had a few days to get the vocals finished. We had to drive to where he worked, spin a story about some emergency that we needed to see him about (I think it was that we'd run his mother over by accident), explain that really we just wanted a chat in the café about the future of the band, and once he was in the car drive non-stop to the studio. 'How far is this café?' Johnny asked."

Cycledelic became a cult hit the world over, or at least in Croydon. However, there were continual problems getting Johnny to the stage. On one memorable occasion for a showcase at the Roundhouse, eventually released as part of the Basically... CD package, they couldn't find him all night before bumping into him in the queue, on his to way to pay to enter the venue, presumably to watch himself. At least fame hadn't gone to his head, although, as Captain would later point out to me, some of the industrial fumes he would routinely inhale in his various horrific factory jobs probably had. And when he did appear he could be quite cantankerous, berating those members of his audience he suspected of being students, or giving some rudimentary observations on the development of his favoured mode of transport, the moped. And then sometimes he would take to the stage on a Raleigh Runabout. You never quite knew. They were once booked to support Motorhead and left 7,000 hard rock fans at the Hammersmith Odeon baying for their blood.

But the band fizzled out after the album's release. Fred Berk was sinking into a progressively worse depressive state, and at the end of 1978 the group called it a day. Dave Berk joined the Damned for a few weeks and also worked with Sensible for a few months as drummer for King. Sadly, Fred would eventually commit suicide by jumping under a train at Thorpe Mead station.

There was a reunion show in 1991 at the Marquee, which this writer attended, with all sorts of faces coming out of the woodwork. Kirsty MacColl asked me who I was and what I was doing there. "You don't work for the Melody Maker then?" 'Certainly not.' "Better not be the NME, cos I'll fucking headbutt you now, y'bastard." Captain, in his wisdom, had elected to put out lots of unrecorded songs from the 1978 period as The Search For Xerxes. No wonder his record label went bust. He was on top form, however, having bought the biggest cigar I've ever seen to present to Johnny to celebrate him coming out of retirement. I remember Xerxes quizzing him on his current domestic circumstances, and the exact aspect of his personality his mother-in-law was not enamoured of.

Johnny: She thinks I'm a slob. She thinks I can't provide for Brenda, cos we haven't got our own place yet.

Xerxes: How is Brenda, is she still working?

Johnny: She's not working. She hasn't worked for the last seven or eight bloody years.

Xerxes: Are you getting a lift home tonight? How did they get you up here? They didn't have to kidnap you did they? That was always the bit about the band that I remembered with most affection. Putting dark crepe paper round the car, putting baraclavas on and going in to kitchens with dark glasses on and stealing their favourite kitchen porter.

Apparently the gig was organised in some haste because Johnny had fallen out with his mother-in-law. Again. When they took him back to Croydon after the gig they asked him where he was living now. "Yeah, just stop here, lads," was the response. "I'm in the third bush on the left." Xerxes, who resolutely refused to tell me his real name, was present for the evening and now works for the council. Slimey is a truck driver, Dave Berk works for the gas board and Johnny makes beer pumps.

As spiritual fellow traveller Billy Childish has pointed out, "Johnny Moped had all three ingredients necessary for maximum rock'n'roll: amateurism, mayhem and humour." That contrasts just slightly with Xerxes' take on things. "It's strange because a friend was telling me that a lot of bands who came over from the US, like Dinosaur Jnr, and even The Ramones in the 70s, were big fans of Moped. Why? How they ever heard him, we have absolutely no idea. It is odd, that such an untalented bunch of people are still held in such affection."

DISCOGRAPHY:

No One/Incendiary Device 7-inch (Chiswick 515 July 1977) (two versions of the label credit S. Toad/Lancaster)
Darling, Let's Have Another Baby/Something Else/It Really Digs 7-inch (Chiswick NS 27 January 1978)
Cycledelic LP (Chiswick WIK 8 April 1978) (initial copies came with free 7-inch single, below)
Basically The Original Johnny Moped Tape 7-inch (Chiswick PROMO 3 April 1978)
Starting A Moped/Groovy Ruby (vinyl reissue of the 'Starting A Moped' tape)
Little Queenie/Hard Lovin' Man (live) 7-inch (Chiswick NS 41 June 1978)
The Search For Xerxes LP (Deltic DELTLP 6 May 1991)
ARCHIVE RECORDINGS:
Basically (The Best Of Johnny Moped) CD (Chiswick CDWIKD144 September 1995) (all

studio recordings and live tracks from the Roundhouse 19th February 1978, with affectionate sleevenotes from Dave Berk)
IMPORTANT COMPILATIONS:
Live At The Roxy WC2 LP (Harvest SHSP 4069 June 1977; 'Hard Lovin' Man (live)')
Long Shots Dead Certs And Odds On Favourites LP (Chiswick CH 5 1978; 'No One')

Jolt

Robert Collins (guitar, vocals), Jim Doak (bass), Iain Shedden (drums)

Before they were absorbed into the mod revival, probably a couple of years too early to secure any fiscal return, and despite a reliance on R&B standards such as 'Route 66' from early in their development, the JOLT, from Wishaw, 15 miles outside of Glasgow, were definitively part of Scotland's late-70s punk movement. Shedden, a local newspaper journalist for the Wishaw Press, whom he'd joined after leaving school, was the founding force behind the Jolt, linking with Collins and Doak after both had dropped out of university.

"We were most definitely in tune to the punk thing," Shedden told me in 2003. "When we first got together we were into the Feelgoods, the Stones, Them, even AC/DC, but latched onto the Damned, Pistols and Clash as soon as they first appeared in Sounds and NME. We were of like mind even before they even had records released, writing our own primitive, punky songs. When the whole thing exploded it seemed meant just for us. Throughout the rapid rise in Scotland from local punks to national contenders, we were essentially a punk band with a punk following."

Or, as Robert Collins noted in 1977, "The new wave came along at the right time for us, because it made us feel that we weren't alone in what we are trying to do and helped us move our ideas into the 1970s."

But by the time they played their debut Glasgow show in March 1977 at the Burns' Howff, steady gigging was made more difficult by a media convinced punk rock was a perilous half-step up in the evolutionary chain from eating your own children. But they also played on this, such as this newspaper advert in April 1977. "Punks – they stopped The Pistols! No one can stop the Jolt. See them tomorrow at the Burns' Howff in Glasgow." Partially because of this resistance to punk, the Jolt took an early decision to relocate to London – one that may have seemed adventurous at the time, but probably lost them some development time afforded Scotland's other name punk group of the time, the Rezillos. "We were all desperate to get out," Shedden told me. "Go to Wishaw, I dare you. I know there was a school of thought at the time (particularly with Simple Minds, I recall) that you didn't have to move to London, that in fact you were selling out if you did. I'd only ever been to Wembley for the football and I don't think Jim and Robert had been at all. Reading every week about the Marquee, the Hope and Anchor, the Nashville, the Music Machine, all the places we ended up playing, gave us a romantic notion of the place, which was, of course, in sharp contrast to sharing a house in Golders Green and living on 10 quid a week." At the time, the Jolt were considered a seriously hot property. Polydor demonstrated their belief by offering £90,000 for a four-year contract. Shedden remembers having "every label in the country after us". Indeed, he thinks they may not have ended up so hopelessly pigeonholed as a Tartan Jam had they accepted a counter-offer from CBS. "Although I may not have had tea at Mr and Mrs Weller's," he concedes.

The group locked horns with the London punk scene by supporting Generation X, X-Ray Spex and, of course, the Jam. They'd first played on the Jam's bill in Glasgow, and at a subsequent Falkirk gig finally agreed to sign with Polydor. "It was also the night when we adjourned to the pub with the Jam to watch them, the Sex Pistols and the Saints on Top Of The Pops," recalls Shedden. "I think we knew then the Jam would be big, but if we didn't, 70-odd gigs with them over the next year convinced us." Debut single 'You're Cold' was unspectacular but solid, somewhat derivative of the Damned's 'New Rose', though its urgency was emblematic of the times. Thereafter the Jolt streamlined their approach, and began composing music with a steadily more obvious debt to the band's heroes – the Who, Kinks, Faces and Rolling Stones. That conversion was signified by their subsequent cover of the Small Faces' 'Whatcha Gonna Do About It' as they picked up further supports to the Motors and, inevitably, the Jam. However, the decision to pursue the Mod fanbase wasn't altogether an organic one. "It was only when we signed to Polydor, and in particular with the Jam's producer Chris Parry," Shedden tells me, "that we were talked into the whole Mod thing. Considering the label already had a three-piece Mod outfit on the books, it was an incredibly dumb move. But we were young and, of course, in the music business you learn by your mistakes."

Here was a three-piece, bedecked in sharp suits playing high-velocity R&B with punk attitude – a market which Weller's mob had effectively cornered. Indeed, they penned an open letter to the Record Mirror insisting: "We would like to say we do not rip off the Jam. But if you just glanced at us, it might appear that way." 'I Can't Wait' preceded an eponymous debut album, produced by Jam production team Chris Parry and Vic Coppersmith-Heaven, and a Radio 1 In Concert recording, after which they extended their line-up by adding second guitarist, Glaswegian Kevin Key. The new line-up made its debut on 30 September 1978 at London's Marquee. But by now interest was cooling, even though they remained a decent live draw. The Jolt's final release came in 1979. The 'Maybe Tonight' EP featured a then unreleased song written by Paul Weller, 'See Saw'. Soon drummer Shedden had left for the Small Hours, another mod revival band, before joining the Saints and helping them cut 1982's Casablanca. He recorded and toured with the Saints for most of the 80s, with spells in the drum stool for UK bands the Snakes of Shake, Summerhill and 13 Frightened Girls and Arizona rock band Giant Sand. He relocated to Australia in 1992 where he now works as music critic for The Australian newspaper. He rejoined the Saints for an Australian tour in 2002 and is currently playing with Belfast (now Melbourne-based) singer/songwriter Andy White. Neither Collins nor Doak pursued music after the Jolt – "I think they were disillusioned," reckons Shedden. Collins now works with the handicapped in Cornwall. Doak moved back to Scotland and lives with his family in Lanarkshire while working for Sky.

DISCOGRAPHY:

You're Cold/All I Can Do 7-inch (Polydor 2058-936 October 1977)
Whatcha Gonna Do About It/Again And Again 7-inch (Polydor 2059-008 April 1978)
I Can't Wait/Route 66 7-inch (Polydor 2059-039 June 1978)
The Jolt LP (Polydor SUPER 2383 504 July 1978) (reissued on CD on Captain Mod, MODSKA CD21, in 2002 with the following bonus tracks – thereby encompassing the band's entire discography – 'You're Cold', 'Again And Again', 'Route 66', 'Maybe Tonight', 'I'm In Tears', 'See Saw', 'Stop Look')
Maybe Tonight/I'm In Tears/See Saw/Stop Look 7-inch EP (Polydor 2229-215 June 1979)

Jon The Postman

JON THE POSTMAN, aka Jon Ormrod, was the type of character that punk, and Manchester in particular, seemed to throw up at will. His modus operandi was to lurk at gigs, before grabbing the microphone of the headline act after they'd completed their set, and occasionally before, before treating the venue's astonished clientele to completely overpowering, ribald takes on rock'n'roll classics. It happened for the first time on 2 May at the Band On The Wall, as he told Dave Haslam in Manchester, England. "I think the Buzzcocks left the stage and the microphone was there and a little voice must have been calling 'This is your moment, Jon.' I've no idea to this day why I sang 'Louie Louie', the ultimate garage anthem from the 60s. And why I did it a cappella and changed all the lyrics apart from the actual chorus, I have no idea. I suppose it was my bid for immortality, one of those great bolts of inspiration. And I was drunk, of course, I never performed sober."

This earned him a cult following and minor celebrity throughout Manchester. His first 'official' gig – i.e. he had permission to be on the stage – came on Sunday 29 May 1977, as support to Warsaw, their first gig, the Buzzcocks and Penetration. He would routinely stay up all night taking in the punk action, only to go straight back to his late night shift at the sorting office, which was meant to finish at 10pm but from which he always sneaked out. Eventually he formed a band entitled Puerile, with unidentified members of the local music scene who had by now embraced him. Fans included Mark E Smith, with whom he struck up an enviable camaraderie after Smith saw him heckle the Jam for being "Tory cunts", and the Buzzcocks, whom he joined for their final Electric Circus encore. But as Mick Middles remembers, his act had a 'unifying' effect on the whole scene. "Those not accustomed to the strange vision of him, straddling the stage, beer bottle clutched tightly in one hand, microphone in the other, would simply stare, aghast. Those 'in the know' whooped and clapped joyously. It was an 'in' joke." Be that as is may, there was no doubting the postie's considerable dedication to Manchester's live music scene – he has documentary evidence of seeing the Fall 160 times. Such was his infamy that, at the final night of the Electric Circus, Pete Shelley introduced him thus – "That's it from us, but the favourite of all Manchester, the one guy who never appears on the bill but is always there – Jon The Postman, step forward, this is your life!" As Kevin Cummins told me: "He'd just turn up at gigs pissed and on speed. He'd occasionally jump up with the band. The Buzzcocks thought that was great and used to let him do it. It ended up getting completely out of hand. They'd take him on tour with them. He'd jump up at the end and do 'Louie Louie' and piss the audience off, I suppose." As Gail Egan, Pete Shelley's then girlfriend recalls, "A gig was not a gig without Jon The Postman. He would get a huge cheer every time."

Drones' manager Dave Bentley invited him to make a record. Puerile was cut over a single Sunday after the pubs shut. Which meant no rehearsals, and the sessions were concluded in a single take. The album revealed there was more to him than a drunken pre-karaoke shambles, taking in krautrock, electronica, freeform jazz and psychedelia. As long as the version of 'Louie Louie' was, it only ended when it did because the engineers ran out of tape. Five Skinners included a neo-waltz in 'I Woke Up In Scunthorpe', which utilised the John Peel radio theme, and is one of only two songs I know about that benighted 'industrial garden town' in which I personally woke up for all of my young life. The rest was just as varied and unexpected, fingering world music and folk on 'Senegal', while the extended 'Gloria' (and boy, I mean extended) is a natural follow-up to 'Louie Louie'.

But afterwards he lost his job with the GPO and set to travelling around Europe, before spending five years in San Francisco. He returned to Salford to read history and politics, before running the Fall's fan club. He was also scheduled to appear, backed by members of V2, at the 1996 Holidays In The Sun festival, but eventually declined. Thereafter he drew an income from selling second hand vinyl, until an accident with a water pipe reduced his collection to pulp. Eventually with the release of Michael Winterbottom's Factory docudrama, 24 Hour Party People, those outside Manchester got their chance to see a facsimile of the Postman experience, as depicted by Dave Gorman (though he did not perform at the Pistols' Lesser Free Trade Hall gig as was implied). The latest news is that he's rejoined the Postal Service.

DISCOGRAPHY:

Jon the Postman's Puerile LP (Bent Records 1976) (came in a brown paper bag with white labels, one side, with six tracks, plays at 45rpm, the other, including his definitive version of 'Louie Louie' and its reprise, plays at 33rpm)

Jon the Postman's Psychedelic Rock'n'roll Five Skinners Steppin' Out (Of Holts' Brewery) 7-inch EP (Bent Records 1977)

Gloria/Senegal/I Woke Up In Scunthorpe/Mahatma Ghandi's Heartbreakers

ARCHIVE RELEASES:

John The Postman's Puerile CD (Overground Records 1999) (reissue of both albums)

COMPILATIONS:

Disparate Cognoscenti (Cog Sinister 1988) (features two tracks from the "lost sessions" by Jon The Postman, drawn from the 80s when he was very much an ex-postman, and are billed as Jon The Postman's Legendary Lost, alongside the Hamsters, ObiMen and others. Apparently a bootleg CDR now exists of the 'lost' sessions, which is just as well, as Mark E Smith is said to have lost the masters)

J

Billy Karloff & The Goats

John 'Billy Karloff' Osborn (vocals, guitar), Chris Pye (guitar), Pedro Ortiz (drums), Ed Duane (bass)

By the start of 1977, Osborn, a native of Orpington, had already had extensive experience of outfits including Slippery Sam, the Punks (such irony!), Scum of the Earth and Streamliner. The latter were a fixture of the London pub scene in the mid-70s. Duane was just one of a series of bass players who passed through as they set about establishing their reputation, becoming fixtures at the Roxy, and appearing on the Farewell To The Roxy compilation, recorded over three nights in January 1978. By the time they released their debut single they were merely the Billy Karloff Band – a deeply unfashionable billing that may have contributed to the low profile Karloff's efforts achieved at the time, but more particularly since.

Augmented by second guitarist Ivan Julian, they cut their debut album in 1978. Thereafter they changed name to Billy Karloff and the Supremes. The line-up now included Karloff as well as Neil Hay (guitar; ex-Somme), Paul Jelliman (guitar; ex-Somme), Glen Buglass (bass) and Gus Boyd (drums). They secured a weekly spot at the Newlands Tavern and, a few months later, under the stewardship of former Marc Bolan manager Tony Howard, they undertook a national tour with Hawkwind. They were then signed by Bob Krasnow, vice president of A&R at Warner Brothers America, after a show at the Fulham Greyhound in January 1979. However, their new paymasters stipulated a name change, due to fears of law suits from the American soul band the Supremes, so they started a competition, documented in the pages of the NME and Evening Standard, for fans to suggest a new name. They eventually settled on Billy Karloff and the Extremes and the competition winners walked away £100 richer.

K

Further shows ensued with the Damned (Hay: "We used to wear raincoats to avoid all the spit") and ZZ Top, while they were themselves supported by U2 at Dingwalls. They also toured with Hawkwind at short notice at the end of 1979. "We were all phoned by the management and told we had to go off and do a two-week tour. We all had day jobs, so they said, just ring in sick. The funniest bit was that Gus worked as a lorry driver, and managed to get a Harley Street certificate. Which was a bit of an odd thing to take to your depot in Catford."

Laurie Latham came to a London show and wanted to produce the Extremes' debut album. However, there was management pressure to ditch Boyd in favour of Brian 'Dolphin' Taylor, who was now between stints with the Tom Robinson Band and his future employers, Stiff Little Fingers. Reluctantly they agreed, but the new line-up never gelled properly and this was not to be the only compromise forced upon them. Warners had decided that the album should be recorded in America with Allman Brothers producer Johnny Sandlin instead of Latham.

No-one was particularly happy with the finished album, Let Your Fingers Do The Talking, feeling that Sandlin had imposed an AOR gloss to the production which didn't suit the material. It was all a tad incongruous, as Neil Hay told me. "I remember being in the studio in America, amid all the noise, in a luxurious studio where Eddie Kendricks had just finished recording. Billy was sat there with his socks off snoring under the air conditioner. We were just five working class blokes from south London who got very lucky very quickly... Musically we weren't allowed to go into the direction we wanted. We ended up sounding like a Transatlantic rock band, when we were aiming for more Joe Jackson, Elvis Costello, the writers we admired."

The London Warners office was also unhappy that they'd signed directly to the US office, and refused to release it, meaning the album was only available on import. All that the UK office would agree to was the release of a single, 'Headbangers'. So the band were in a position where they had demand for the record in the UK but couldn't get it into the shops, while there was a demand for live shows in the States but their label wouldn't pay for them to tour behind it.

The next management intrusion was to ask the band to cut a version of Cliff's 'Summer Holiday', a live favourite, recorded at Ringo Starr's house (formerly owned by John Lennon, where he filmed the 'Imagine' video). Dolphin was on tour so session drummer Charlie Morgan stepped in. Once again, the single stiffed, and with their relationship with both management and record label increasingly hostile, the band folded. Despite this, a second album was recorded over Christmas 1981 with Squeeze producer John Wood, dominated by cover versions, simply to fulfil their contract with Warners. It was never released.

Ortiz later played with David Bowie at Live Aid, and Pye recorded with the Books. Karloff himself released a 'Stars On 45'-styled Bob Dylan medley under the name Frankie Lee ('It Ain't Him, Babe', ZIM 001). Afterwards he became better known as a songwriter, his credits including the Damned's 'Wait For The Blackout', while the Business covered his 'Back Street Billy' (he would also write 'Anywhere But Here' for the latter). Via his friendship with Rat Scabies, he also sang Strawberries out-take 'Take Me Away'. The connection came, according to Hay, because "Peter Barnes, their publisher, was in the same building as our management. Rat knew our manager because they'd supported Marc Bolan on his last tour, and Tony Howard was managing Marc Bolan. Rat produced some of our demos. From then on, they liked what we did. Billy wrote the lyrics and melody for 'Wait For The Blackout' for them and they used to soundcheck to a song of ours called 'Here'."

In the 80s Karloff concentrated on songwriting while working for his local newspaper. Buglass studied drama and is now a local authority arts manager. Jelliman became a London cabbie and now works in insurance. Hay worked with Q-Tips, Steve Gibbons and Ruby Turner among others, using the name Wango Wiggins, and is now a music teacher. Boyd briefly played with Abba Gold.

In 2002 the original members of Karloff's band hatched a plot to organise a one-off reunion show in May 2003 at the Newlands Tavern (now the Ivy House). Sadly, it never happened. Having fought cancer since the late-80s, in 2003 Billy Karloff was diagnosed with throat cancer. He underwent several operations but died in hospital on 16 July. He was buried at All Saints' Church in Orpington on 1 August.

DISCOGRAPHY:

As The Billy Karloff Band
Crazy Paving/Back Street Billy 7-inch (Wanted Records, CULT 45-001 April 1978)
The Maniac LP (Jupiter SOS LP 2 1978; Germany)
Back Street Billy/Crazy Paving 7-inch (Jupiter 1978; reversing A-side/B-side combination)
As Billy Karloff & The Extremes
Headbangers/Don't Keep Me Down 7-inch (EMI K17753 1981)
Let Your Fingers Do The Talking LP (EMI K5694 1981) (US only)
Summer Holiday/It's Too Hot 7-inch (EMI K17818 1981)
The Vinyl Solution LP (EMI America) (never released)
COMPILATIONS:
As Billy Karloff & The Goats
Farewell To The Roxy (Lightning LIP 2 1978; 'Relics From The Past')

Kenneth Turner Set/Hatchets

Chris Cummings (guitar), Jim Morrison (vocals), Mark Nodder (guitar), Anthony 'Spud' Herrington (bass), Nicholas 'Gick' Hardiker (drums)

The KENNETH TURNER SET grew out of the Hatchets, who'd formed in 1977 and featured Nodder, Hardiker and Morrison, who recalls: "I played bass then and we were influenced by The Stooges, NY Dolls, MC5 and Ramones, then the early English punk bands also. We played our first gig at the Anchorage in Lytham in January 1978, which I believe was the first punk gig in Lytham St Anne's. I think it inspired some local musicians to go on and do the same, a bit like the Pistols did in Manchester, cos everyone you talk to from Lytham says they were there! We only did a handful of gigs as the Hatchets in and around St Anne's and Blackpool but they were quite memorable. I only had three strings on my bass 'cos the machine head was broken."

Morrison met Chris Cummings in 1979, who would later form the Riverside Trio. Morrison: "Chris Cummings had already been in Skrewdriver and quite a few other Blackpool bands when he joined and was quite experienced and a very good guitarist. In fact I used to have to coax bad taste out of him as he was too modest to go overboard in the way I wanted." Cummings and Herrington were drafted into the trio as the Hatchets evolved into the Kenneth Turner Set, with Morrison taking over on vocals. It sounds like they should have been playing

Ronnie Scott's, but Morrison chose the name because "it sounded like a middle of the road name for a punk band". He would bill himself as THE Kenneth Turner, or perhaps Trevor Whiteside. "In fact I used to make names up at every gig to sound quite dull in contrast to the music." They would play regular Monday night sets at Jenk's bar in Blackpool alongside a revolving cast of local punk bands including the Fits, Membranes, Section 25, Herman's Effey and Syntax, as well as playing in Preston and the surrounding Lancashire area.

The band's only release was a one-track contribution to the Blackpool Rox 7-inch EP on Vinyl Drip Records, cut at Cargo Studios in Rochdale. Morrison: "We gave The Membranes a lift to Rochdale Cargo studios and did an all night session recording 'Overload' and they did 'Ice Man'. The 'Blackpool Rox' EP was a collaboration between all four bands and John Robb (of the Membranes) carried on using the name Vinyl Drip later on."

By 1982 they'd changed their name to the Velvasheens, with the addition of a new drummer, Kev Ploughs. Thereafter Morrison played bass for the Zanti Misfitz for a short time while their bass player was in prison and through that was invited to join the Turnpike Cruisers in 1984, with him he played until 1989. He is currently a breakbeat DJ, operating under the name Jim 'Crimson' Morrison. Herrington now edits The Wire but no longer answers to the nickname Spud. Probably.

COMPILATIONS:

Blackpool Rox 7-inch EP (Vinyl Drip 1 1980) Includes the Ken Turner Set's 'Overload', plus tracks from Syntax, Section 25 and the Membranes

The Ugly Truth Volume 1 CD (Just Say No To Government Music JSNTGM 018 August 2005; 'Overload')

K

Killjoys

Kevin Rowland (vocals), Gil Weston (aka Gem, aka Ghislaine Weston; bass), Mark Phillips (guitar), Heather Tonge (backing vocals), Joe 90 (aka Lee Burton; drums)

The KILLJOYS were a rum Brum bunch, spearheaded by a front man of great personal drive and ambition in one Kevin Rowland. He would, of course, subsequently become a figurehead of the 80s when he donned his dungarees and too-rye-ay'd his way to the top of the charts with Dexy's Midnight Runners.

The origins of the Killjoys can be traced to the embryonic Lucy & The Lovers, formed in Birmingham as a kind of Roxy Music-orientated club act, featuring saxophone and girl singers, as well as Rowland, Weston and Phillips. But Rowland sensed straight away that his best shot lay in updating the band's sound to something more in step with the contemporary, and set about doing something about it.

New songs were written and by 1977 they had perfected a live show that drew some admiring glances, not least from that old skullduggerer and bootleg king Lee Wood of Raw Records. "There were eight people in the audience (including us) and on came The Killjoys," he told punk77. "It soon became clear from the jeering that the other five people were soul music lovers. Kevin Rowland gave as good as he got and for their entire set the band gave it everything they had. This impressed me most. We chatted afterwards and I agreed to meet them in London and watch them rehearse. A few days later, I met them near Euston. I found they came from Birmingham, but were staying in London. Five members were sleeping IN the van. The drummer slept either on top of, or underneath, depending on the weather." They did indeed move to London, where they eventually took up lodgings in a disused Barclays Bank.

Gareth Holder of the Shapes remembers playing their first gig as support to the Killjoys at Warwick University. "The headline act are Raw Records favourites the Killjoys. Their singer is notable for two things. Firstly, he is Kevin Rowland, soon to trade in his punk rock credentials for the more lucrative position of mastermind of Dexy's Midnight Runners, and from thence to dress up as a woman in a rather alarming attempt to curry public favour. The second notable thing about him is the level of hatred that the rest of the Killjoys appear to have for him. The Killjoys also have a rather fine female bass player in Gil Scott Weston. She is remarkable for two things also. Firstly, that she goes on to better things with the all-female heavy metal combo Girlschool, and secondly, that she rather quite bafflingly refuses an offer of sexual congress from yours truly. Bugger. She'll come around though, they always do. Mind

you, as of this writing in January 2002, she has yet to call." They were managed by Barbarella's proprietor John Tully, in partnership with Dave Corke, who would also help pilot Dexy's Midnight Runners before Bernie Rhodes arrived on the scene.

The result of the liaison with Raw was the single 'Johnny Won't Go To Heaven', backed by 'Naïve', both recorded at Spaceward Studios in Cambridge, with the band camping out in their van the night before – an impressive 18,000 sales resulted. There was also a cut, 'At Night', included on the compilation album Raw Deal, and a fourth track, 'Recognition', that was eventually unearthed by Damaged Goods in 1991. The first of two John Peel sessions was recorded in October 1977. By the advent of a second, the following February, the group's line-up had switched. Keith Rimell (guitar) and Bob Peach (drums) auditioned following an advert in a Midlands paper, and were given a slot in the band. Also at the audition was bass player Kevin Mangan, who had been a part of Supanova with Rimell and Peach, but was not offered the job, with Weston continuing on bass and Heather moving off but remaining Rowland's girlfriend. Rowland, a trained hairdresser, immediately ensured their locks were shorn. But this hardly improved matters. Rimell maintains to this day that an "us against him" ethos prevailed, and that the rest of the band never saw a penny for their efforts. The new line-up lasted for 18 months as sessions began for a debut album, including stints at Riverside. Recordings included the unreleased 'Definitely Down On The Farm', which was later re-recorded by Dexy's as 'Definitely Not Down On The Farm'. Lee Wood, bless him, apparently lost the master.

Rimell departed after a spat with Rowland before a UK tour (he offered to complete the dates but Rowland took umbrage at his insubordination). Bob Peach: "Keith (Rimell) left the band about 12 months before me, so we recruited Kevin Archer, who became Al Archer as Rowland would not have two Kevins in the band!" Finally the group's already tempestuous internal politics – notably Rowland's enforced eight-hour practice sessions – reached a head and they collapsed, just as a £20,000 contract with Bronze appeared on the table, which Rowland apparently rejected because it was only a singles deal. Peach: "That was the last straw and me, Mark Phillips and Gil left to form a band that was first called Out Of Nowhere, then Alternating, before we finally settled on the name Luxound Deluxe. We recruited a sax player called Aiden, a keyboard player called Pete Lee, and vocalist Dave Plested. We did quite a few gigs around the country but mainly London, and split in the early 80s." Weston then became part of Girlschool on Lemmy's recommendation. Phillips later picked up a job with Her Majesty's Treasury. Rowland, well, you know what he did.

The best way by far to sample the Killjoys is to access their two John Peel sessions, especially the second one, which sees the band in transition. Notable are 'Ghislaine' with Weston on vocals, singing in French, and 'Smoke Your Own', which features the opening for later Dexy's song 'Liars A to E'.

DISCOGRAPHY:

Johnny Won't Get To Heaven/Naïve 7-inch (Raw RAW3 July 1977) (four different label designs, some of which miss-spelt Rowland as "Roland." Reissued by Raw in 1978. Reissued by Damaged Goods, DAMGOOD 165, in a new sleeve)
Naïve LP (Damaged Goods FNARR 10 1991) (issued in purple (500) and green (1,500) editions)
Studio Demos 18/10/1977 7-inch (Last Year's Youth)
Recognition/Back To Front/At Night/Naive
A Million Songs CD (Mushroom D 30930 1993)
IMPORTANT COMPILATIONS:
Raw Deal LP (Raw 1977; 'At Night')

King

Captain Sensible (vocals, guitar), Kym Bradshaw (bass), Henry Badowski (keyboards, vocals), Dave Berk (drums)

On his exit from the Damned the good Captain at first hooked up with Dutch band the Softies, who featured Damned roadie Big Mick on vocals and guitar as well as a drummer known only as Big Thumper. They recorded the rip-roaring version of Elton Motello's 'Jet Boy Jet Girl' that eventually turned up on several Damned compilations, notably the first version of their Best Of The Damned. He then put together KING, featuring some of his favourite musicians and sparring partners. Henry Badowski, previously with Chelsea, was invited aboard by Sensible while he was touring Amsterdam with Wreckless Eric. Berk was an old friend from the Johnny Moped days, while Kym Bradshaw of the Saints was recruited as bass player.

K

The group only lasted between June and August 1978 and played just five shows together, at the Gibus Club in Paris, but they did cut one excellent John Peel session broadcast on 20 July 1978. It featured the aforementioned 'Jet Boy Jet Girl', 'My Baby Don't Care' and 'Baby Sign Here With Me', as well as 'Anti-Pope', which would be revived on the Captain's return to the Damned, where he took Badowski with him for a short time.

King could have been great, especially if they'd succeeded in Captain's stated ambition to recruit Dave Vanian as their singer. But it didn't happen and finances dictated a reformation of the Damned, or Doomed, because Brian James wouldn't relinquish the rights to the name, in August 1978. "The most disappointing thing about King," reflects Badowski, "was the fact that Paul 'MTV' King pinched the name, which I'd come up with originally. He apparently asked Captain if he minded, but never asked me. I would have minded. Perhaps he bought Captain a drink. King was fun. It would have been great to take things further as Captain and I worked very well together. I was aware that the Peel session went down well. I was sent a contract from Strange Fruit in 1984 asking me to allow them to release it, but never signed it. Not sure why I didn't!"

Badowski, whom Captain remembers as being a "genius", and "as difficult to work with as geniuses tend to be", released the fine, but distinctly un-punk Life Is A Grand album for A&M in 1981. He released his version of 'Baby Sign Here With Me', a staple of King's live set, as the B-side to his debut single 'Making Love With My Wife' in 1979. "Mark Perry had heard it, and he eventually took me into Pathway Studios a year later to record it, so there was a happy ending after all!"

Knife Edge

Mark Sweeney (vocals), Tim Knowles (guitar), Charly Peace (bass) and a small army of drummers until Martin 'Edge' Edgerton (drums) finally took over permanently.

Prior to the Mekons, Gang of Four, Delta 5 and the campus-based bands that shaped Leeds' punk identity, there was KNIFE EDGE. Despite never gaining access to the kind of label backing that would have ensured their stature as the city's punk forefathers, they did play a huge amount of shows in the Yorkshire area, supporting 999, Penetration, the Only Ones and others throughout the late-70s.

Their influences were framed around American garage bands like the Stooges. Vocalist Sweeney's penchant for singing naked from the waist up certainly owed a debt to Iggy. In fact, a specially lengthened vocal lead allowed him to wander from the stage and establish his eyrie at various positions in the audience in an effort to engender some spectacle and theatricality. Sweeney: "The first punk gig I went to in Leeds was the infamous first Pistols, Damned, Heartbreakers and Clash tour, as Leeds was one of the very few places to not cancel given the notoriety of punk at the time. Of course I formed Knife Edge not long afterwards – didn't everybody form a band at that time?"

The group's local popularity was confirmed by a March 1978 article in Melody Maker by Nigel Kine (aka Des Moines when he wrote for Sounds), which looked at the music scenes of Edinburgh, Bristol, Dublin and Leeds. "The most encouraging developments in Leeds over the past few weeks have been the re-opening of promoter John Keenan's F Club and the rising stature of local band Knife Edge. Keenan, having lost his old venue through 'unsympathetic management', only recently found an alternative venue – in Chapeltown's Roots Club. While this was the only venue able to meet Keenan's requirements, it's not without interest that the club is in the heart of Leeds' immigrant area, and (if Marley and Rotten can find their hearts in the same places) the new location has potential to break some cultural barriers." That same No Dice show also gained a glowing review in Melody Maker. As for the drummer situation: Sweeney: "We went though nine drummers in our heyday as none of them could quite keep up with the pace of our live sets, apart from John Shepherd (the best drummer in Leeds at the time) and our final mainstay, Edge."

I asked Mark if there was any division between the arty, campus bands in Leeds like the Gang Of Four and Mekons, and the more, ahem, indigenous punk bands. "There was a bit of town versus uni bands atmosphere – maybe just a class thing. But we tended to keep ourselves to ourselves. It didn't stop us getting some great supports to 'hot' bands of the time (at the Uni/Met/F Club venues) such as 999, Penetration, Wreckless Eric, Only Ones, etc. My memories of these gigs are of our fantastic following – it must have been the most vocal set of fans ever. They made an enormous racket between songs and especially during our singalong numbers. 'I'm A Believer' was one of these which always went down a storm – albeit it was a cover version of the Monkees song played with venom yet also with a great 'take it down to the drums' Stooges-type middle bit with shout-response bit, ultra quiet bit then explosive finale…"

They finally entered the studio in 1980 to cut the double A-side 'Favourite Girl'/'Say You Will'. It sold well locally and got some support from John Peel, but the band were unhappy with the production. It was rather optimistically advertised as "the first in a long line of hit singles". The label name they chose, incidentally, referred to their manager's home in Hessle Terrace. There was also a six-track demo tape, recorded in 1981, that the band would sell at shows (one track from which was included on Bored Teenagers Vol. 2). A further two tracks, 'Bombing Pearl Harbour' and 'Me And My Girl', were recorded but "we split before we could release these on another double A-side single". All ten studio tracks feature on a CD that Sweeney now sells direct to the public, entitled Street Credibility – one of the songs that the band would always start their sets with in their later days. "On request I sent hundreds of copies of this CD (along with many vinyl copies of the single) to Nat Records in Tokyo, Japan, where there is a real cult following for UK punk of the late 70s."

The band's final show came on 1 August 1981 (a CD of which is also available), with Sweeney subsequently forming the occasionally captivating Red Lorry Yellow Lorry. Ten years after their break-up, in 1991, he reformed Knife Edge for a one-off reunion show with proceeds going to charity. This was followed by a 21-year anniversary gig in Leeds in 2002, and a show at the Garage in London later that year, alongside three other bands also featured on the Bored Teenagers Volume 2 compilation.

DISCOGRAPHY:

Favourite Girl/Say You Will 7-inch (No Hessle Records F001 1980) (2,000 copies)

COMPILATIONS:

Rock On – Battle Of The Bands LP (EMI 1981; 'Street Credibility') (Knife Edge came second out of 400 bands. The competition was sponsored by Tetley!)

Bored Teenagers Vol. 2 LP/CD (Bin Liner RUBBISHLP/CD003 March 2001; 'Fighting In The Chapel', 'Say You Will')

K

Last Words

Original line-up: Malcolm Baxter (vocals, drums), Andy Groome (guitars, bass)

The output of Australian imports LAST WORDS, so far unavailable digitally, unless you can contact band members individually in which case they'll be happy to put it on a CDR for you, points to an unjustly overlooked legacy. There are many who rate 'Animal World', a rollicking Saints-like effort, as one of the undiscovered gems of the period, and they were by all accounts an excellent live band.

By the time 'Animal World' was released on Rough Trade, which is why the band is included here, it had already been issued in two separate versions in Australia. The first was recorded in Baxter's house in Sydney. He also played drums, with Groome providing the guitar and bass parts. It was originally issued in a consignment of 500 copies on the band's own Remand label.

The second version on Wizard featured drummer Derik Wapillspoon, aka Ken Doyle, as well as bass player Ricky Leigh Kendall. It was re-recorded, with a different B-side, at United Sound Studios in Sydney in 1978. Rough Trade used this more professional-sounding, though structurally similar version, to introduce them to UK audiences. The link came about, according to Kendall, because "We approached them with the Wizard label 'Animal World' from whom we got permission to release on our own Remand label distributed by Rough Trade. Rough Trade organised our tour with the UK Subs as well as with The Pack and Killing Joke. Curiously, I'd met the drummer from the Pack in Canada when he played in an outfit called Dee Dee and the Dishrags."

In fact, the incoming bass player Kendall was something of a global punk veteran. Before starting the Thought Criminals (of 'Hilton Bomber' fame) in Sydney, he had been the singer for pre-DOA Joey Shithead's Canadian punk band the Skulls. "I lived in Canada for six years. My family emigrated there after the teachers strike (my dad was on the organising committee and the strike was lost). I actually went to school with Brian, the bass player of the Skulls, although I didn't know that when I answered the ad. Joey Shithead took a dislike to me when I took an interest in a girl he was keen on, next thing you know I'm out of the band. No worries! I met him again at a DOA gig and he pretended he couldn't remember me. His problem. The Skulls were fun but I really wanted to play guitar."

Following the single's release, Ken Doyle would transfer to the Thought Criminals in mock retaliation for Kendall's desertion. Jeff Wegener, the Saints' original sticksman, filled in for a while with the Last Words, and appeared in the video clip that was filmed for 'Animal World'. A more permanent replacement was then found in the shape of Johnny Gunn. The Last Words went on to cut two further singles and an album, the latter recorded in Berry Street, London, featuring additional accompaniment from Steve Beresford on keyboards and Dick Nightdoctor on saxophone. So what was it like relocating to London? "Whilst we were from Sydney, none of us were born there. Johnny Gunn was born in Hammersmith but emigrated as a child. Andy was born in Dublin but had a Nottingham accent as he spent a bit of time there before emigrating. Malcolm was born in Dundee. I think there was a perception that because we were Australian we were culturally backward. I personally never got shit for being an Aussie outside of London. I always gave as good as I got. As for the band, I don't think it made that much difference. I remember Ivor Hay from the Saints complaining about some attitude the Saints got when they got to London – but then they did look like clueless boguns from Brisbane." I don't know what a 'bogun' is, but I suspect it is unflattering.

The music was certainly punk-influenced, but Kendall reckons that at heart it was 'power pop'. "Malcolm was very keen on 60s Brit pop, particularly the Beatles. To me, we were like the Beatles with distortion pedals. I personally preferred it harder like the Ramones or the Pistols and I tried to play the bass that way, using a plectrum with either up and down stokes or steady down strokes." The album was notable for the inclusion of Jefferson Airplane's 'White Rabbit'. "After we laid down all the tracks, we had some time left so I suggested we do a cover of 'White Rabbit'. Andy and I used to jam a lot doing versions of different songs we liked. The tapes were rolling and Johnny said, 'How does it go?' I said, 'Like this' and Johnny came in after one bar and that's how it was recorded. Andy put the guitar track down after that and the next day Malcolm did the vocals as he had to learn the words. This was the only spontaneous recording we ever did as we rehearsed everything until we could play it in our sleep. In Sydney, we were known for our tightness, after we signed with Wizard we rehearsed eight hours a day, five days a week for six months before we played our first gig. I also think 'White Rabbit' was the only track where Adrian Sherwood's production worked. Andy regrets the album strayed from our earlier sound." The band broke up shortly after its release. "Right after the album was recorded, there was a band meeting where Malcolm announced that I was out of the band. Andy told Malcolm if I was out so was he and that was that. All of us eventually ended up back in Oz. We had over 40 songs so a second album would have happened, no worries.

"As far as what it would have sounded like, fuck knows. For a while in the early-80s Andy and I played in a ten-piece reggae band. After that, Andy never played again. Malcolm had a ska band going for a while called Tenement Dance. I got more into reggae and recorded some tracks on my own and later with a band called the Sabcats. I last played live in 1991 at a pub in North Melbourne. Johnny Gunn recorded 'Gunn Sound', a dub-style effort. Malcolm found God and is heavily involved in his church. Andy teaches graphic arts at New South Wales TAFE (Technical and Further Education). John works at Australia Post and I am currently an unemployed labourer."

DISCOGRAPHY:

Animal World/Wondering Why 7-inch (Remand RRCS 2439 March 1978; Australia only, 500 copies)
Animal World/Every Schoolboy's Dream 7-inch (Wizard ZS-196 February 1979; Australia only; blue vinyl)
Animal World/No Music In The World Today 7-inch (Rough Trade RT 022 October 1979)
Today's Kidz/There's Something Wrong 7-inch Remand REMAND 2 January 1980)
The Last Words LP (Armageddon ARM 2 August 1980)
Top Secret/Walk Away 7-inch (Armageddon A-S-002 August 1980)

L

Laughing Gass

Paul Amey (vocals), other personnel included Steve Wilkes, Dave Bainbridge, Barry Clifton, Mick Perrin (guitars), Steve Bray, Gez Griffin, Phil 'Captain Scud' Nash, Den Woolmer (bass), Rob Wilkes (drums)

LAUGHING GASS were among the first Brighton punk bands to form in 1976, and became regulars at local practice hall/venue the Vault. The members were drawn from the Hollingbury estate in north Brighton "with no art students or graduates in sight", according to Barry Clifton. In an e-mail to the punkbrighton site he recalled: "We all had drug problems, allegedly, and our gigs were a carnival of pushers and burglars and prostitutes and robbers of all descriptions." The band was managed, after a fashion, by 'bong shop' owner Neal Dean, and the best musical description might be 'proto-punk'.

Or, as Clifton himself recalls: "Punk became something that was quite different to its beginnings. For young musicians in the early-70s, emulating the bands such as Yes, ELP, Pink Floyd etc was all but impossible due to the technical aspect, so we looked at songs by bands such as the Stooges, Velvet Underground, early Stones and Who stuff. Van Morrison's 'Gloria' was a staple of many bands, as it only had three chords repeated over, and could be played after five minutes rehearsal. We didn't dress up, glam up or even wash, but played in our ordinary scruffy clothes that we had probably slept in and the audience could either take it or leave it, we played for ourselves. We soon realised that if we could play three-chord songs then we could write three-chord songs. This to me was punk. It was an attitude. When the media got hold of it and bin liners and safety pins became the order of the day, Laughing Gass just didn't buy into it."

They got themselves together long enough to release one record, 'New Tart', which was sponsored by both John Peel and his Radio 1 comrade Annie Nightingale. However, the band was undone by a disastrous tour of Amsterdam where there were simply too many temptations. Clifton: "All our gigs were fun but playing the Paradiso in Amsterdam on the same bill as the Knack and Marmalade was just bizarre and fantastic. The Alhambra and the Belvedere were good regular gigs for us, and I remember playing outside the Heart and Hand pub on the Queen's Jubilee."

Following the band's break-up Woolmer formed the more pop-orientated Mockingbirds, who also featured Julie Blair, co-owner of Attrix Records. Amey now manages the Tin Lids – a band featuring his own son Dylan and daughter Emma, alongside the offspring of other Brighton-based bands the Depressions (Dave Barnard's son Jamie and Ozzy Garvey's son Spencer). After a few line-up changes they became Special Patrol Group and were signed for a time to Martin Rushent's Gush Records before breaking up. It's a small world, etc. Rob Wilkes died in 2004 after a long battle with heroin addiction while Dave Bainbridge had previously died after suffering a heart attack in Greece.

DISCOGRAPHY:

New Tart/Bandito 7-inch (Wessex WEX264 1979) (hand-painted numbered sleeves. Barry Clifton: "The single sleeve for 'New Tart' – I hated that title and much preferred the B-side 'Bandito' – was originally painted by Mick Hill, now a top antique restorer. We copied his design for the first 500 by silk-screen printing, as we knew a guy who printed T-shirts. That design was then cut out and stuck on each single sleeve by hand.")

Leyton Buzzards

Geoffrey Deane (vocals), David Jaymes (bass), Dave Monk (guitar), Kevin Steptoe (drums)

The LEYTON BUZZARDS were one of those bands who picked up speed, figuratively rather than physically, as punk hit at the apposite time. They hopped the bandwagon, rode it for all it was worth, then buggered off as soon as it appeared convenient to do so. "That's how we were judged," James reflects, "probably rightly, but we weren't getting anywhere." However, in common with many other faux-punk bands, it's better to judge the music on its merits, and the Buzzards had their moments.

L

The group's dynamic had much to do with the childhood friendship of Deane and Jaymes in Waltham Forest, East London. The name was a pun on the Bedfordshire town of Leighton Buzzard, adapted to reflect their own locale. They became attuned to the punk movement after visits to the Roxy and the purchase of the first punk singles. "As far as I remember," Jaymes recalled to me, "it was actually Geoff (Deane) bringing in 'New Rose' and 'Anarchy' on 7-inch to the clothes shop I worked in at the Bakers Arms, Kooks, where he also worked. I don't remember the band that supposedly changed it all (at the Roxy) but I saw many, many bands there."

This gave Deane and Jaymes the impetus to construct a new set of originals. Regular venues included the college bar at the North East London Poly, upstairs at the Red Lion in Leytonstone, and the Bridge House in Canning Town, in addition to the central London circuit. Practices were conducted in Deanne and Jaymes' flat above an optician's, again in the Baker's Arms region.

Demo tapes were duly despatched and they found a willing backer in Small Wonder, literally a five-minute car drive up the road in Walthamstow. "Pete Stennet was not an easy man," Jaymes recalls, "but I liked him a lot. He could be very encouraging but also very damning. I used to love going into the shop though. A fine and inspired old hippy!" Andrew Jacquemin was brought in to oversee the production of their debut single, though opinions differ as to how well he managed the job – there's a lack of definition in the sound. Yet '19 And Mad' is a great little punk snorter. The band had decided to take new identities in keeping with the change of image. Deane was now Nick Nayme, Jaymes was Dave DePrave, Steptoe became Gray Mare and Monk was now… Chip Munk. The first of four John Peel sessions ensued.

Sales of 10,000 for the single were encouraging but nothing abnormal for the time, though Monk was then ditched after his bandmates decided his escalating interest in pet fish outweighed his commitment to the band. Which makes a change from musical differences. I'd always thought that using such a bizarre cover story was surely a scam. "Actually this is true, sort of. Dave Monk sadly left the band because his job – working in a tropical fish farm – was suffering. He had to choose the band or the fish." Vernon Austin was drafted in to replace him on guitar.

The new line-up entered the Band Of Hope And Glory Contest, an event open to unsigned bands with sponsorship from the Sun and Radio 1. The prize, a contract with Chrysalis Records and a Radio 1 session with Kid Jensen, was duly secured. Steve Lillywhite was brought in as producer for their major label debut, 'Saturday Night (Beneath The Plastic Palm Trees)', released in February 1979.

A nicely observed lyric on the 'skinhead stomp' at the Royal pub in Tottenham in 1969, it drew on Deane's own experiences as a former skinhead and the universal currency that is underage drinking and rejection by the opposite sex. Aided by a pop-reggae undertow and a namecheck for 'Guns Of Navarone', expectations were high for its success. Although both John Peel and Jensen played it repeatedly, they were the only Radio 1 DJs to do so – others fearing that the station might be accused of favouritism due to their sponsorship of the competition. The record, voted single of the week by Tony Parsons in the NME, stalled at 53 in the charts, though they did get the chance to appear on Top Of The Pops, the stage, memorably, decked out in plastic palm trees. "I was very drunk that day," Jaymes recalls. "We were drinking with Lemmy and Whitesnake. Inner Circle and Dennis Brown were on too. We tried but failed to make a gig in Sheffield after, which had been booked months earlier."

They continued to play around London, often on Rock Against Racism bills, and recorded a second John Peel session prior to 'I'm Hanging Around'. Again produced by Lillywhite, it was released in green vinyl and backed by two new songs. 'I Don't Want To Go To Art School' was an expression of defiant class-consciousness, a recurring theme for the group, though, of course, it was somewhat tongue in cheek. "Er, we went to Waltham Forest College, which incorporated an art school which Ian Dury went to years earlier!" 'No Dry Ice Or Flying Pigs' related to their unpretentious live show while poking fun at the likes of Pink Floyd. The A-side was pretty much straightahead pop, though its bleak view of romantic expectation was charming in its own right.

Thereafter they shortened their name to the Buzzards and had another crack at the charts with 'We Make A Noise'. This was notable for the exploding Enoch Powell on the cover, designed by Terry Gilliam of Monty Python. "Our first manager was a sound engineer in a studio owned by Michael Palin. We did most of our recordings there. We got to know Terry and all the rest of the Pythons there. Terry had a studio upstairs." Distinctly more abrupt than the singles which had preceded it, with Chas Chandler serving as producer, it too stiffed. A fate the lyrics almost predicted – "The music climate's turned against us it seems/We're full of East End promise but we've lost our dreams/Now everybody says we're a noisy band/We've got a one-way ticket back to garageland."

Chrysalis was evidently keen to rid itself of these under-performers, yet their contract stipulated an album release. The result was the mid-price compilation From Jellied Eels To Records Deals, released in October 1979. As well as the Buzzards' entire canon for the label to date, it added selections from the Jensen and Peel sessions as well as demos. Some of the contents hold up well. Although there are weak links, tracks such as 'British Justice' showed the band beginning to find their pitch.

They did manage one further single for WEA, a cover of Andy Williams' 'Can't Get Used To Losing You', but that closed their account. However, Deane and Jaymes had one more trick up their sleeve. A change in musical direction had been sign-posted on the sleevenotes to the Jellied Eels album, but few could have predicted the severity of that about face. In 1980 the duo, together with David's brother Robbie Jaymes, John Du Prez, Paul Gendiler and Andy Kyriacou, formed Modern Romance, though there were earlier formative line-ups. The music was based on Latin American salsa. "We read all the publicity around Blue Rondo A La Turk," Deane later confessed to Q, "stole the idea and made obviously crass, commercial records with the minimum of effort." While this would work eventually, the first exemplar of their new style, 'Tonight', issued on WEA where they still had a contract, was widely ignored.

Modern Romance finally made the big time with 'Everybody Salsa', one of the most inane songs of all time, which reduced a complex musical form to the sort of banal revisionism that would make the Police or UB40 cringe. Peaking at number 12 in the UK charts, they followed it with an even bigger hit, 'Ay Ay Ay Ay Moosey'. It sounded like exactly the same song. It was actually written to settle a £10 bet Deane had with a local Turkish cab driver, named Moosey, that he couldn't write a hit with his name in the title. I put it to Jaymes that, while people have said lots of rude things about Modern Romance, no-one has been nearly as rude as the participants themselves. "Yes, I guess."

However, the success drove Deane and Jaymes apart, and in order to preserve their friendship, Deane left the band late in 1982 for a solo career. He did not fare well, despite setting up his own record label, ironically entitled 'Plastic Palm Tree'. Meanwhile Modern Romance continued to prosper, former fireman Michael Mullins replacing Deane on 'Best Years Of Our Lives' and a cover of Eddie Calvert's 'Cherry Pink And Apple Blossom White'. When the hits dried up the band sundered at the end of 1984, though it is surprising to learn that they were actually hugely popular in South America from whence salsa originated, and scored a succession of number ones in Venezuela. Go figure.

Subsequently Deane wrote 'You Think You're A Man' for Divine, co-authored a book with Ronnie Biggs ('Biggsy's Bible') and wrote comedy scripts for the likes of Smith And Jones and Keith Allen. In common with another old punk sweat, Riff Regan of London, he's also written for Birds Of A Feather. Jaymes moved into publishing then management, handling Jah Wobble, Republica, Mike Scott, Beth Orton, Damien Dempsey, Sinead O'Connor, Rialto, Drum Club and Miles Hunt (ex-Wonderstuff) among others. He also runs IRL Records.

DISCOGRAPHY:

19 and Mad/Villain/Youthanasia 7-inch (Small Wonder SMALL 7 July 1978)
Saturday Night (Beneath The Plastic Palm Trees)/Through With You 7-inch (Chrysalis CHS 2288 February 1979)
I'm Hanging Around/I Don't Want To Go To Art School/No Dry Ice Or Flying Pigs 7-inch (Chrysalis CHS 2328 May 1979) (green vinyl)
As the Buzzards:
We Make A Noise/Disco Romeo 7-inch (Chrysalis CHS 2360 August 1979)
Jellied Eels To Record Deals LP (Chrysalis CHR 1213 October 1979)
Back as the Leyton Buzzards:
Can't Get Used To Losing You/Weird Frenz (WEA K18284 July 1980)
ARCHIVE RELEASES:
The Punk Collection CD (Captain Oi! AHOY CD 225 2000)

L

Lillettes

Tim 'Vicious' Falla (drums), Dave Robson (guitar, bass), Mick 'Reggie' Perrin (vocals, guitar, bass, accordion), Phil Perfect (aka Phil McCavity; vocals, lead guitar), Barb Dwyer (vocals, keyboards), Robin Banks (keyboards)

The LILLETTES were formed in Brighton in January 1979 as an outgrowth of Flesh, one of the city's earliest punk bands, of whom Perrin, Perfect and Robson were all prior members. Vicious, despite his punky sobriquet, had been drawn from local folk band Biggles and 'corrupted'. Their songs were "about life in the 70s" and among their lyric writers was the thrillingly named Barb Dwyer, as well as Perfect and Perrin. The music was written collaboratively.

Their only vinyl appearance came on the second Vaultage compilation, Vaultage 1979. Both their tracks made the leap to Cherry Red's CD compilation of Vaultage tracks released in 1997. And both are snazzy efforts in an uncomplicated melodic punk vein, although 'Nervous Wreck', with its south coast spaghetti western guitar, probably takes the honours. "The Lillettes stayed true to the spirit of punk by failing to have any hit records or make it into the charts," reflects Phil Perfect. "Though we did attract a significant following and featured on various albums, which can be found if you look hard enough in second hand record stores."

Mick Perrin went on to be road manager for comedians including Eddie Izzard, Ardal O'Hanlon and Julian Clary, and currently runs Mick Perrin Productions. He was able to confirm that the song he wrote for the Lillettes which appeared on the Vaultage 1979 LP, 'Hey Operator', "has since been played in auditoriums and stadiums across the globe as part of the build-up to Izzard's live shows".

Falla played briefly with Reward System, who appeared on Vaultage '80, and works at Sussex University. Phil Perfect now does graphics and web design, including the fantastic punkbrighton website, and in 2006 released his first solo album. Robin Banks is keyboard player with the Provocateurs. Robson works in social services, Barb Dwyer runs a Fair Trade group.

COMPILATIONS:

Vaultage 1979 (Another Two Sides To Brighton) LP (Attrix RB 08 1979; 'Hey Operator', 'Nervous Wreck')
Vaultage Punk Collection (Anagram CDPUNK 101 1997; 'Hey Operator', 'Nervous Wreck')

Lockjaw

Bo Zo (aka Gary Bowe; vocals), Micky Morbid (aka Stuart Hinton; guitar), Andy Septic (aka Simon Gallup; bass), Oddy Ordish (aka Martin Ordish; drums)

One of the less celebrated bands to feature on Lee Wood's' Raw Records, Crawley's LOCKJAW did achieve footnote status in the subsequent history of the Cure when their bass player Simon Gallup joined Robert Smith's goth-poppers. Gallup's brother, Dave, also served as Lockjaw's manager.

The band was originally known as the Guernsey Flowers, though the name came about entirely by accident. They'd managed to secure a gig at St Francis Church Hall in Horley, and placed a box of confetti at the front of the stage to be kicked over into the audience for dramatic effect during the show. No-one in the band clocked it at the time, but the cardboard box they used for the purpose was labelled Guernsey Flowers because of its previous contents and everyone in the audience assumed this to be their name. Via an understandably brief period as the Amazing Doctor Octopuss they eventually became Lockjaw.

Lee Wood picked up the band after what he describes as a "great" demo tape. But the two singles they released are nothing to write home about, and even their cover of Cliff Richard's 'The Young Ones' is unappetising. 'Radio Call Sign' was written by Dave Gallup, though the credit to D. Gallot on the label was due to a misprint rather than a bid for anonymity. 'Journalist Jive' crops up from time to time on lists of songs berating the music press. But that's about it, apart from noting that the Cure connection ensures both singles reach ridiculous prices at auction. Apparently several other tracks were recorded, but these have all disappeared and even the band members don't have a clue where.

Their regular haunt was The Rocket, where, in February 1978, Lockjaw supported the Easy Cure, though Simon Gallup and Robert Smith were already good friends. "They (Lockjaw) were really hardcore," Smith recalled in 10 Imaginary Years, "really like the Clash, whereas we had more melody, like the Buzzcocks. All their songs were really fast and it was the only time they ever played the Rocket because the place was torn apart. They only got to play there in the first place because they had a record out and we said they were a big group!"

In the same book Simon Gallup appraised his first forays into punk rock thus: "Putting that record out was a big mistake. We sent a tape to a record company called Raw Records and they thought we were this really good suburban punk band, but we were actually shit. They signed us and put out this record (Radio Call Sign)… If I see any around today, I break them."

The Easy Cure and Lockjaw played together several times, often under the billing 'I Know an Easycure for Lockjaw'. But eventually Lockjaw would transmute into The Magazine Spies, and then Mag/Spys. They released one single, but when the Cure signed to Fiction Records and began to pick up momentum, it was an easy decision for Gallup and (and also keyboard player Matthieu Hartley of the Mag/Spys) to accept an invitation to join them.

DISCOGRAPHY:

Radio Call Sign/The Young Ones 7-inch (Raw RAW 8 November 1977)
Journalist Jive/I'm A Virgin/A Doonga Doonga 7-inch (Raw RAW 19 1978) (reissued by Damaged Goods, DAMGOOD 204)

London

Riff Regan (aka Miles Tredinnick; vocals), Jon Moss (drums), Colin Wight (guitar), Steve Voice (bass)

LONDON were hardly trailblazers of the capital's 1977 punk scene, but they were in there scrapping, releasing two singles, an EP and an album for MCA before the energy dissipated. It was a classic case of a quasi punk band being signed up with impunity by a major label instinctively at odds with the prevailing climate. London were certainly competent, but their connection to punk was tenuous, and the music press tended to disregard them entirely. There was some cultured musicianship in there though. Moss was always a high quality sticksman and even, lordy, turned down a chance to play with the Clash to join them.

Some kind of distillation of Mott the Hoople, Roxy, Bowie and punk seemed to be the modus operandi, and they didn't take themselves too seriously. Witness the guitar break on 'Summer Of Love' as an example, or their supposed tribute to punk goddess Siouxsie Sue. This went down like a lead balloon when the two acts bumped into each at a motorway service station. Voice's song was originally titled simply 'Susie Sue' and had nothing to do with her Bromley Contingent-ness. It was changed at the suggestion of Moss, who always had an eye for a good promotional angle.

It was Riff Regan, his 'punk rock' name derived from a character in West Side Story and John Thaw's character in the Sweeney, who was the driving force behind the band. He'd previously worked as an assistant to Robert Stigwood and had written a musical, Doomsday Genesis, with composer Keith Kerslake before place a musician's wanted advert. The first respondent was Steve Voice, with whom he would form a writing partnership. Moss was next aboard, as Regan recalled to punk77. "He was being tried out as a drummer for the Clash at the time and wasn't happy. I seem to remember that he didn't really hit it off, with Joe Strummer accusing him of crappy pseudo-revolutionary rhetoric!" Regan still rates Moss as the biggest nutter he ever met during the punk years. "He chose us over the Clash! To this day I don't know why for sure. I mean, who would do that! It was like the Beatles/Pete Best story in reverse! It was an extraordinary act of faith. When Jon joined, the band was just Steve Voice and me, practising in our front rooms. We had no equipment, had hardly written any songs and didn't even have a guitarist. Jon was great at propelling the band forward and without him London might never have been heard of. So thanks, Jon!"

London's line-up was complete at the end of 1976 after Lincoln-based Wight joined. He applied under his own name and was told that his influences, Hendrix, Motown, blues etc, were not compatible. But he was sharp enough to take note of the trio's musical inclinations and rang up a few hours later using the name 'Dave Wight' to secure an audition. "I had no idea that this happened until I read about it in an interview that Colin gave," Regan told me. "It made me laugh when I heard about it. It could well have happened. The only vaguely well-known person I can remember coming along for an audition was Henri Padovani, Sting's first guitarist in the Police. He was a nice guy, bit serious, but we passed on him. Most of the people who turned up to audition were pretty talentless actually. When Colin arrived he impressed us no end and we wasted no time in getting him on board."

London played their first gig at the Rochester Castle in Stoke Newington. Present that evening was Danny Morgan, assistant to veteran manager Simon Napier-Bell (Marc Bolan,

Yardbirds etc), who subsequently checked them out at the Roxy. He booked them into the IBC Studios in London in the dark of night, and had 15 cassettes of the results sent by courier across the capital. Several labels were taken by this novel concept, before the band signed with MCA. Napier-Bell immediately booked them further gigs at the Roxy and Dingwalls, as well as a three-month UK support tour with the Stranglers.

"We got on pretty well with The Stranglers," Regan recalls. "Musically they were streets ahead of every other band at that time and that alone impressed us. When we were being considered as their support band, Hugh and Jean had heard about us and came down to listen to us play in our rehearsal room, which was a lock-up garage in Kilburn that we shared with David Sylvain and Japan. We were shitting ourselves but managed to nervously knock out our set of about ten songs. Hugh and Jean sat on the floor listening and when we finished, offered us the support slot. We couldn't believe it. We'd only played about five gigs at this time so it was a huge deal. The tour itself was very long and covered the entire country, right through the spring and summer of 1977. There was the usual backstage stuff with girls and stuff and we thoroughly enjoyed the life. It was exactly what we always thought it would be! The Stranglers album Rattus Norvegicus was selling well and the audiences were big. It was very good exposure for us and we released our first single 'Everyone's A Winner' halfway through it, which was very exciting. I remember Jon, Steve, Colin and I being in a music shop in Newcastle when it got its first play on Radio 1 on the Dave Lee Travis show. It was one of those moments, you know, that you wait for all your life. Your record actually on the radio!"

There was some attempt to market them as snarling punk rockers by Napier-Bell. But these were essentially nice boys in love with playing their music and attempts to project them as rabble-rousers made a poor fit with their natures. "We never set out to be a punk band," Regan told me, "and I think if you were to speak to the other three members of London today they would agree with me that we never really were a punk band. Not in the sense of the Pistols and the Clash anyway. The point was we were all living in central London and just wanted to be in a band, full stop. We were all going to different gigs every single night of the week in 1976 and a lot of them weren't what you would call punk. Graham Parker and the Rumour, the Jam, Eddie and the Hot Rods, Squeeze, the Stranglers, Dr Feelgood etc. Then punk bands like the Damned, the Clash, Generation X and the Adverts started playing and really gave the scene some excitement and colour. MCA and Simon Napier-Bell, of course, pushed us... nasty, oikish ill-mannered, street urchins. He still does, if you read his books, but it never worked. Nobody bought it. It was a joke. I remember that there was a TV producer that he invited along to our recording studios and Simon told us to be rude to her and shock her by swearing etc. We wouldn't do it and his plan completely backfired... The best thing about London was our live show. It was exciting and loud and gained us a loyal following. Unfortunately that never converted into huge record sales."

'Everyone's A Winner' was heavily promoted by MCA, but despite this there was no commercial breakthrough. It wasn't as if they weren't trying. Napier-Bell had to open an account with the Ann Summers sex shop chain in order to keep the band supplied with the blow up dolls (or 'Randy Mandys') that they would routinely dispense to their audience. They became regulars at the Nashville and Hope And Anchor, as well as undertaking their own headlining UK tour in September 1977 to support their 'Summer Of Love' EP. This contained both 'Siouxsie Sue' and a cover of the Easybeats' 'Friday On My Mind'. It reached 52 in the charts and the band was placed on standby for Top Of The Pops. However, the BBC were concerned about the swearing on the EP, so they dutifully wrote out in longhand the lyrics to 'Summer Of Love' to prove that the nation's morals were not under direct threat. A motorcycle courier was despatched with said document but in the end these frantic efforts proved to be in vain. Their shot at the title may have ended right there.

Despite this, the tour went well. Heather McCartney was impressed enough to tell the tabloids that London were one of her favourite bands. The group's final single, 'Animal Games', got an airing on Tony Wilson's So It Goes, on the same edition that featured the Sex Pistols. Ever one for frankly irrational acts of pretension, he introduced the band with this topical nugget: "If Sadat can get into Jerusalem, you can get into London." Thanks, Tony.

The band's debut album, like the singles, was completed at IBC Studios. By now the band were all involved in the writing, while Napier-Bell conducted from the producer's chair. In retrospect there's nothing wrong at all with cuts like 'No Time' and 'Us Kids Cold', and the entire contents are easy on the ear, albeit most of the material passes by in a blur of speed. "I think the London album is pretty good too," Regan expands. "Especially 'No Time' and 'Summer of Love'. 'No Time' is still the London song that people say they like the most. The album was of its time, obviously, but many of the songs have a nice melodic edge to them in the same way that the Clash's first album did. The one thing that I regret is that the songs are too fast! I remember Paul Cook saying that he deliberately held the beat back on the Sex Pistols' songs because he knew they were being delivered too fast. I only wish Jon had done that with London. Having said that, some of Jon's drumming is brilliant – up there with Keith Moon in my opinion! Listen to 'Friday On My Mind' and 'Summer Of Love'. The only song I'm not mad about is 'Reaction' which was me raving against the hippies who'd come to some of the gigs on the Stranglers tour and sit cross-legged on the floor just staring at us."

But the band were unable to transfer their live popularity to sales, and Jon Moss, concerned about the lack of hits, was about to be poached by the Damned. London's final show turned out to be their set at the Marquee just before Christmas 1977, with Regan dressed as Santa Claus, dispensing sweets and other goodies from the stage. Dressing up was nothing new; Regan frequently took the stage wielding an umbrella to protect himself from the volleys of gobbing the band had to endure.

After the band dissolved Riff Regan cut a succession of solo singles for MCA and Epic, all of them self-penned. He also co-wrote a single for the Hard, featuring Bernie Tormé, 'The Hottest Woman In Town'. When it became evident that his music career was stalling he quit the business and started to write comedy, beginning with Because Of Mr Darrow and Laugh? I Nearly Went To Miami. His credits include scripts for Frankie Howerd, the self-created BBC series Wyatt's Watchdogs and Birds Of A Feather, and he's written comic strips for Walt Disney. There's also a comedy novel Fripp and the play Topless. Voice went on to form two punk bands, Original Vampires and Blind Yeo. Wight's now a lecturer in international politics (most recent academic article is listed as 'theorising the mechanisms of semiotic and conceptual space'). Simon Napier-Bell, of course, piloted the career of Wham! and George Michael (who would also write notable academic texts including 'Club Tropicana'). Moss joined the Damned, then the Edge with fellow Damned evacuee Lu Edmonds, before hitting paydirt with Culture Club. Wight almost joined them too, though in the event he signed on with Holly and the Italians for a US tour. Apparently Moss once played his old mucker Regan an acetate of 'Do You Really Want To Hurt Me' at his house in Hampstead. Regan told him it was 'crap' and wouldn't get anywhere.

So, does the number of writers, academics and media wallahs who have gone on to 'great things' tell us that punk was a uniquely empowering phenomenon which allowed creative people to tap into new possibilities? Is playing fast songs with sarky lyrics amid a hail of gob essentially character building? "Punk was just a time of people being given the opportunity to express themselves in an almost DIY way that is now taken for granted because of websites and the internet. But then it was new and exciting and liberating. I don't think there were necessarily any more creative people around then than there are now. The difference then is everyone was into writing songs and making great records and now they're into making dreadful TV reality shows! Nothing character building about walking out on stage and being spat at! The reason why most punk bands moved around on stage was to avoid the gob."

DISCOGRAPHY:

Everyone's A Winner/Handcuffed 7-inch (MCA MCA 305 June 1977)

Summer Of Love 7-inch EP (MCA MCA 319 September 1977)

Summer Of Love/Friday On My Mind/No Time/Siouxsie Sue (also available as a 12-inch, MCA 12 319)

Animal Games/Us Kids Cold 7-inch (MCA MCA 336 November 1977)

Animals Games LP (MCA MCF 2823 January 1978) (reissued on CD in November 1997 as Punk Rock Collection on Captain Oi! AHOYCD 77 with bonus tracks Everyone's A Winner (single version), Handcuffed, Friday On My Mind, Siouxsie Sue)

London SS

Mick Jones (guitar), Tony James (bass) plus a cast of thousands

One of the great mythical groups of our times, LONDON SS was the finishing school for a cluster of musicians who would fire the capital's punk revolution. Their origins can be linked directly to future Clash guitarist Mick Jones' tribulations in his avowed ambition to make it as a rock star. He'd started out early with Schoolgirl, formed at the Strand comprehensive. By 1973 he was plotting the rise of the Delinquents, originally the Juvenile Delinquents, who also featured another member of Schoolgirl, John Brown. Primarily driven by Mick Jones' first efforts at songwriting, they cut an acetate in September 1974 comprising 'You Know It Ain't Easy' and 'Hurry', but these were respectively Brown and guitarist Paul Wayman's compositions.

The Delinquents had largely abandoned that name by the time they finally hired a singer after a series of Melody Maker adverts. With interest from Pye Records' Tony Gordon (later manager of Sham 69 and Culture Club), who'd attended an earlier rehearsal in abeyance until they found a vocalist, Jones reluctantly accepted his colleagues' overtures to recruit Kelvin Blacklock. He worried that the former singer with Schoolgirl, then performing with Overtown, would be a divisive element in the band. They subsequently adopted the name Little Queenie, after the Chuck Berry song, at the suggestion of Gordon after he'd attended a further rehearsal in April 1975.

However, dissatisfied with demo versions of the two songs they cut at their first studio session in May, Blacklock decided to ring notorious alcoholic (and ironically, future Clash producer) Guy Stevens and bludgeoned Tony Gordon into ripping up their management contract. Stevens convinced them to change their name to Violent Luck, but also persuaded them to axe Jones in favour of a keyboard player. Jones was informed of his departure from the band he'd formed, and for whom he wrote most of the songs, at a band practice on 5 June. Stevens' reasons for doing so are obscured in the mists of time and the day-long drinking sessions that were by now his custom. But the result was that Violent Luck got nowhere, while Mick Jones, though he ostensibly took the news well, was left to nurse his pride and redouble his efforts to make it in the music industry. The fact that he was still living in the same house as Blacklock on Gladsmuir Road, North London probably didn't help.

By happy coincidence one of Blacklock's associates was Tony James, whom he'd met through a musician wanted advert while still singing with Overtown. Like Jones, Tony James was a huge fan of the New York Dolls and Mott The Hoople (though Jones' former bandmates in Little Queenie insisted to Marcus Gray that, when they first encountered him, the Brunel mathematics student was a Blue Oyster Cult fan with a greatcoat and "a little wanker"). James subsequently attended that fateful Little Queenie practice session at which Jones was ousted. The two shared the tube journey home together to Jones's gran's flat and resolved to work together. Chastened by the criticism that he wasn't a good enough rhythm guitar player, Jones committed himself to marathon practice sessions while taking a job at a Camden bookshop to put by enough money to purchase a Les Paul from a guitar shop in Denmark Street. The name London SS was revived after originally being considered for Little Queenie, where it had been dreamt up but subsequently rejected by one or all of John Brown, Geir Waade and Jones.

On 15 July, Jones and James put an advert in Melody Maker. "Lead guitarist and drums to join bass player and guitarist/singer, influenced by Stones, NY Dolls, Mott etc. Must have great rock'n'roll image." Nothing came of it, but between the first advert and a second one placed on 9 August, the pair had a fateful meeting on the 2nd, when they both attended a Deaf School show at the Nashville Rooms. When Jones introduced himself to a figure at the bar, thinking he may have been a like-minded musician, it turned out to be Bernie Rhodes. Rhodes informed him that he was wearing one of his T-shirt designs – 'One day you'll wake up and know what side of the bed you've been lying on'. Rhodes had enjoyed a rich history as an associate of the Who, T-Rex and the Stones, and had studied as closely as he could various youth culture movements – not just the Paris Revolts and the Situationists, but also the American Yippies, White Panthers etc. When the duo told them about their band, he immediately offered his services as manager, though they would have to overcome his objections to the choice of name (Rhodes was Jewish, although Jones himself was half-Jewish). The band insisted that SS stood for social security rather than any allusion to Hitler's notorious death's head legion, but it seems rather unlikely that they would have been unaware of its more sinister connotations. "It was deliberately provocative," Jones conceded to Danny Baker over 25 years later, "but in retrospect pathetic. I'm not proud of it in any way."

Meanwhile one Brian James felt he fitted the 'great rock'n'roll image' part of the MM advert perfectly, although he was at that time still playing in Bastard, an MC5-influenced rock band based in Belgium. The duo liked Bastard's demo tape, and agreed to work with James pending his return to Brussels to finalise his affairs over there. In the interim they also tried out a line-up including Matt Dangerfield, singer Andrew Matheson of the Hollywood Brats and keyboard player Casino Steel. These rehearsals took place at Dangerfield's squat at 47A Warrington Crescent, a kind of living space cum rehearsal room cum social venue. Another one to try out was Geir Waade, the drummer who'd exited Little Queenie just prior to Jones' departure. But realistically there was no settled line-up, just a lot of "fucking around".

Another involved in these early efforts was Honest John Plain, later of the Boys. "I don't know whether it was actually as London SS but it was certainly the same line-up," he later recalled about his induction, and his subsequent appearance at the band's only live performance. "There was Mick Jones, Kelvin Blacklock, Matt, Tony James and I was on the drums. We played near Turnham Green station at an Art College and it was the first big stage I'd ever been on. I'm pretty sure it was London SS but you'd need to check that with Matt. It wasn't punk; we were very glam and very New York Dolls-ish." I asked Matt Dangerfield if he could confirm, once and for all, whether tapes of the London SS were ever made. "The tapes definitely exist, the trouble is, knowing where they've gone. So many people moved in and out of that flat after I moved out. Things just went missing. Maybe Mick Jones stole them because he was embarrassed! It was his first attempt at singing!" Later Tony James would confirm the existence of a dated cassette demo recording to John Robb. But then admitted he'd lost it. It apparently was recorded in front of McLaren and Rhodes and included versions of 'Ramblin' Rose', 'Roadrunner' and Jones's 'Protex Blue', as well as an unidentified Nuggets and Rolling Stones' cover.

James and Jones responded to another Melody Maker advert placed in October citing Johnny Thunders as an influence, placed by Sex Pistols' manager Malcolm McLaren, who wanted to expand his coterie of groups. A meeting was convened, attended by Jones, James, Matheson and Steel. But, as Glen Matlock revealed to Pat Gilbert, at that stage they were still very much into sneering at aspirant musicians, especially if they hadn't got their hair cut. Then again, it would seem that the further the years roll on, the more Matlock seeks to distance himself from the nice grammar school lad image and invent a persona more in keeping with the era's zeitgeist. In the meantime, Dangerfield bowed out. "The basic line-up I knew was me, Mick Jones, Tony James and a drummer called Geir Waade. From that I hooked up with Cas and Andrew from the (Hollywood) Brats. I weighed up the options, and thought, 'Well, they've made an album', which I thought was a brilliant album, so that was the way to go."

Meanwhile Rhodes kept exhorting his remaining charges to stand out, to be radical, to make their mark, as he pursued his ongoing rivalry with McLaren, who'd knocked him back in his claims to half of the Pistols' management. To this end the band members would be issued with ideological dictums and book lists. They were pointed towards texts on anarchy, Dada et al. Tony James received hour-long phone calls to his parent's home in Twickenham imploring him to subvert his middle-class existence, to go out and buy a copy of Gay News from the local newsagent, or to read French existentialist literature or check out a new modern art exhibition. James did as he was told.

The duo conducted further auditions in November 1975 at a café in Praed Street. Tony James and Mick Jones had decided they'd like something similar to the Two I's coffee bar from the 60s, a central base. So they set up shop there while Rhodes persuaded the owner to let him restock the jukebox with classic rock'n'roll records. Aspirant musicians endured grilling by greasy spoon, with both Jones and James admitting they were "truly horrible" to applicants.

Later, Rhodes informed them that he'd acquired the basement of the café as their rehearsal space. They moved in shortly thereafter. Rhodes decided to decorate it with pictures of Nazi war atrocities. It was his way of trying to persuade them that the name was a bad idea. Much of the musical equipment was borrowed from Steve Jones, who had purloined it from David Bowie's Hammersmith Odeon show. Aspirant vocalists and drummers would be interviewed in the café before they were allowed downstairs, where they would attempt to play along to the Dolls' 'Personality Crisis', the MC5's 'Sister Anne' or the Flamin' Groovies' 'Slow Death'. The only originals the band were trying out were two songs written by Jones, 'Protex Blue' and 'Ooh Baby Ooh', plus his collaboration with James, 'Portobello Reds' (later recorded as 'Fish' by the Damned). When Brian James returned from his stint with Bastard in Belgium, he immediately joined the sessions as the 'third' member of London SS.

The auditioning process lasted between November 1975 and January 1976. Musicians passing through included Chris Millar, nicknamed Rat Scabies by Tony James due to his disgusting appearance and the fact that a rat suddenly appeared in the vicinity of his drum kit when he played. Well, that's one story. For alternate versions see Damned entry, though it seems likely that the rat may have been eliminated before its soon-to-be namesake's arrival. Millar, who really did have scabies at the time, was auditioned in December. He remembers noting how bored with the process Jones and James had become, indicated by the fact that they were sat watching a war film on the telly while he auditioned – which encouraged Brian James to impersonate the sound of the plane engines as they dived from the sky. Scabies didn't get the gig, despite playing with them over Christmas, due to the fact that his image didn't fit. But in that moment of dovetailing with James to the sound of duelling Messerschmitts and Spitfires, a chemistry developed which would have much to do with the subsequent formation of the Damned.

At various stages two future Clash drummers tried out. Topper Headon stayed around for a couple of rehearsals but was then drawn away by the offer of a lucrative tour with a soul band. Terry Chimes was around for a while, alongside future Clash guitarist Keith Levene. Even Morrissey sent in a letter and apparently entered into some correspondence with Mick Jones. Martin Newell, later of the Cleaners From Venus, had a go, as he revealed to Richie Unterberger. He got a grilling from what he later presumed was either Mick Jones or Brian James. "At the end of it, after a half an hour conversation about clothes and the rest of it and attitudes, I said, 'What kind of music are you going to do?' And the guy said, 'Oh, just a kind of Keith Richards voice – just a kind of rock'n'roll thing.' And I thought, that's a shame, that. 'Cause that sounds really boring. I wanted to go in the space age. And in the end, it was a toss of a coin whether I went down to do this audition or not. And I didn't do it."

Drummer Roland Hot auditioned in January 1976. He'd brought along his friend Paul Simonon, who was coaxed into trying out for vocals on a version of 'Roadrunner', but he didn't know the lyrics. With the sessions stalling, a different approach was taken. Members of the group started sizing up vocalists in other bands playing around the London scene. And the obvious candidate, almost immediately, was Joe Strummer, lead vocalist and rhythm guitarist in pub rockers the 101ers, who were playing regularly at the nearby Windsor Castle. Fired with Rhodes' missionary zeal, Jones and the two James didn't think much of the material the 101ers were playing. But they were awfully taken with Strummer. So they took him. Eventually.

The three main members had all been taken to see the Pistols play at Andrew Logan's party in February 1976 at the behest of Bernie Rhodes. Rhodes brought McLaren along to one London SS rehearsal towards the end of this period, along with Sex shop assistant Chrissie Hynde (with whom Mick Jones would begin to write songs, until news of this prompted Rhodes' disapproval). McLaren immediately pronounced them unworthy of competing with the Pistols.

Thereafter London SS just fizzled out. James and Scabies went off to form the Damned. Months later Jones would bump into Paul Simonon in the Portobello Road, and mentioned the meeting to Bernie Rhodes. Allegedly, Rhodes responded that he should forget all about any further efforts at making it alongside Tony James and hook up with the better-looking non-musician instead. So that was the Clash sorted. James formed Generation X after briefly linking with Billy Idol as part of Chelsea.

London SS played, perhaps, one gig. They recorded three or four cover versions and perhaps one or two original songs. No photographs were taken of them. And apparently, everyone who heard them reckoned they were awful. Still, as a result of the networking that took place in the basement of that café in Praed Street, lives were about to be changed.

Ludus

Linder Sterling (vocals), Arthur Kadmon (aka Peter Sadler; guitar), Phil 'Toby' Tolman (drums), Willie Trotter (bass)

Formed in August 1978 in Manchester, LUDUS were led by ex-Polytechnic art student Linder, famously cited as Morrissey's muse. Linder Sterling: "I was the first member of my family to attend full time education beyond the age of 14. I was born in Liverpool and my parents moved to a small village near Wigan when I was nine years of age. I exchanged the remnants of the Merseybeat sound for northern soul, folk music and prog rock. When at the age of 18 I decided to prolong my education further, I left the mining village and enrolled at Manchester Polytechnic to study graphic design." Punk saw her change both her identity and her outlook. "The advent of punk in the UK in 1976 simultaneously saved and severed my life line. I edited myself down to one name, Linder. I have a sketchbook still from 1977, and there I describe myself as a 'monteur'. I am following faithfully in the footsteps of George Grosz and John Heartfield et al, who renounced the title of artist and preferred to describe themselves as assemblers and engineers. They anglicised their names and I adopted a European spelling for mine. No signatures, just a stamp."

While living in Salford she had been in a relationship with Howard Devoto that ended around the time of the first Magazine concerts, though she continued to work with Magazine on flyer and T-shirt designs, as well as the sleeve of Real Life. She'd already published a pamphlet of collages (Secret Public) alongside later punk writer Jon Savage as the second 'release' on the New Hormones label (ORG 2). The Buzzcocks had also used one of her photomontages for the sleeve to 'Orgasm Addict'. "I remember seeing that image pasted all over the streets of northern towns and it suddenly became a pin up for a generation, some glorious, elegant transgression of female sexuality, a new breed. United Artists paid me £75 for the use of the image and I could then finally afford a pair of Vivienne Westwood's equally elegant and subversive bondage trousers." She was legendarily also the subject of the Buzzcocks' 'What Do I Get?' She was, in author Mick Middles' words, "the most potent post-punk sexual figure in Manchester." Others, such as Steve Shy, simply remember her as being "a really lovely person".

Ludus were heavy on metaphors about sexuality and commodification, but didn't entirely dispense with pop music in this pursuit. Whilst trenchant they were never hectoring, and Linder herself was playful with the medium, exploiting preconceptions and challenging her audience. Arthur Kadmon of Manicured Noise, Toby Tolman of Ed Banger And The Nosebleeds and Willie Trotter were recruited to back her while management was provided by Buzzcocks' supremo Richard Boon. Two studio demos were recorded by the quartet in October 1978 and February 1979, produced by Devoto. They got a clutch of strong reviews for their support slot to the Pop Group at the Factory Club in October 1978, which preceded four shows in London at the Venue, alongside Magazine. It was quite a billing, Magazine at the height of their powers, Ludus brewing up something quite distinctive themselves. And Linder was a natural on stage. Morrissey would review a later show for Record Mirror and praised her for "a wide melange of ill-disciplined and extraneous vocal movements, apparently without effort." In January they returned to the Factory and this time had Paul Morley in raptures. "A rich, bewitching quartet, led by the enigmatic Linder, whose maturing, enchanting voice adds layers of mystery, fragility and haunting strength to the esoteric music."

They supported the Buzzcocks through March 1979 before Kadmon quit, leading them to recruit Cardiff-based Ian Devine (aka Ian Pincombe) through an NME advert. He made his debut in July as the band played alongside Joy Division and the Fall at the Funhouse in Manchester, and quickly became Linder's principal co-writer. Factory were keen to release something by the band, but a verbal agreement already existed with Richard Boon to release their records on New Hormones. Linder did still manage to get on the Factory release schedule, however, when her menstrual egg timer, part of a range of 'mad jewellery' she designed, was given a catalogue number, Fac 8. "I made sketches and small bloody beads that would be used to show menstruation – I have them still; ironically they look like medieval relics. I showed my designs to Tony Wilson who loved the whole idea. I have a sketch of the original, it's interesting – on one side of the paper are Tony's budgets for the next Factory single and then on the other, is a drawing of the egg timer, except that that title is crossed out and Tony has written 'The Factory Egg Timer'. It was never made."

In the event, Ludus did not make their recorded debut until March 1980 with 'The Visit (4 Compositions)' 12-inch EP. Recorded by Linder, Devine and Toby, it was pretty caustic stuff lyrically, positing ideas about sexual identity and conformity, while the musical backdrop was a kind of jazz-inflected agit-funk. Linder: "There was rivalry everywhere then, between the north and south, between Factory and New Hormones, between every band. Like trying to put your finger on mercury, the post punk period endlessly divides and sub divides, escaping easy classification and display. Even whilst singing, I still made mono prints, took photographs and was being photographed. I also collaborated on a short film 'Red Dress' – a rare New Hormones and Factory project. I still have the signed contract for this, it has a very good clause – 'all parties are agreed that this is a very nice film'. Those were unique years within culture and arguably, we were participating in the last of the days of a British underground before the late 80s malaise."

The band continued to play live supports to acts such as the Psychedelic Furs and Monochrome Set, including the ICA Rock Week in July, before Toby left the band at the end of the year. His replacement was Graham 'Dids' Dowdell, while Magazine's Barry Adamson would also help out for live shows. The follow-up single 'My Cherry Is In Sherry', returning to one of Linder's favourite themes, menstruation, was released in October. In light of which, it's interesting to note that the tentative name for the band had originally been Bloodsport. The following spring they toured Belgium and Holland as part of a New Hormones package with Eric Random. Their show at the Free University in Brussels brought them to the attention of future benefactor Benoit Hennebert of Les Disques Du Crepuscule. In the meantime they released a six-track cassette in April 1981, followed by their third and greatest single, 'Mother's Hour', in June. It was unyielding, powerful stuff, awarded single of the week in Sounds. Thereafter the group took a sabbatical.

When they re-emerged in 1982, former Magazine keyboard player Dave Formula having joined in the interim, it was with a total of three separate albums. The first, The Seduction, was a double 12-inch package released in February. It came with a picture of a woman in fishnet stockings and 'sanitary belt', an archaic menstrual device, as the cover. Danger Came Smiling in September featured 18 short, jagged tracks, Linder's attempt to escape the orthodoxy of rock lyrics, using screams, yells and psychiatric tape recordings. The third album was an Italian compilation, Riding The Rag, which incorporated many of the tracks from the Pickpocket cassette with new recordings.

They were then approached again by Hennebert who asked Ludus to cover Brigitte Bardot's 'Nue Au Soleil'. This was recorded in Manchester with additional help from bass player Paul Cavanagh, drummer Roy O'Shea and saxophone players Lee Buick and Graham Revell. However, the record was continually delayed and eventually only emerged in Italy on Base Records. The band's management was now being handled by a new generation of female Mancunian shit-kickers, Cath Carroll (later Miaow and solo) and Liz Naylor (later manager of Riot Grrrl act Huggy Bear), who were previously behind the notoriously bitchy City Life fanzine.

Following a Peel session in August 1982, Ludus played its legendary show at the Hacienda on 5 November 1982. As a surreal take on the ra-ra skirt exhibitionism of Bucks Fizz the previous year, Linder performed in a dress consisting of chicken meat and fishnet. "The Hacienda immediately withdrew the 'Bloody Linder' cocktail from the 'Gay Traitor' bar and huffed and puffed. I carried on singing regardless and triumphantly removed my skirt for the last song. I'd found my own vocabulary of protest in the form of a black dildo that I had strapped on under my skirt. It was my retort to the Hacienda's casual and interminable showing of porn films. I finished singing the last song to absolute silence from the audience." That audience was satisfyingly horrified. There was also the small matter of table decoration. Naylor and Carroll, aka the Crones, had placed a paper plate on each containing a stubbed cigarette and a tampon, coloured red at one end. Tony Wilson was mortified. Mortifying Tony Wilson is a favoured pastime of all Mancunians.

That was it, pretty much, statement made. "There was a sense of having ventured as far as we could go within that world, at that time." Their final show came at Islington Town Hall in

December. There was one further recording, for French label Sordide Sentimental in Mach 1983, which paired 'Breaking The Rules' with 'Little Girls'. There was also a Janice Long session but by now there were divisions between Linder and Devine. Though they returned to Belgium the following year to work with Hennebert, once again things didn't work out. The pair fell out completely and didn't speak to each other for a decade.

Toby later joined Primal Scream, Formula continued to work with Devoto solo and teaches musicology. Devine first formed Heb Gariad then teamed up with Alison Statton (formerly of the Young Marble Giants) to form Devine and Statton. He joined the Low Gods in 1992. Eventually he reunited with Linder in 2000 to work on the soundtrack to The Return Of Linderland as well as her 'requiem', the 2001 performance piece Clint Eastwood, Clare Offreduccio And Me, staged at the derelict Gorton Monastery. She would also feature images of Eastwood in her multi-media presentation The Working Class Goes To Paradise. A CD was released on Welfare State. Linder had spent much of the intervening years working in art, publishing a book of photos about Morrissey and also shot two of his album covers. She convened What Did You Do In The Punk War Mummy? at the Cleveland Gallery in London in 1997 and then constructed 'the salt shrine', wherein she gutted a room in a disused school in Widnes and filled it with 42 tonnes of industrial salt. A book of her artwork was published in 2002.

In June 2004 Ludus, or at least Devine and Linder, reformed to play two shows at the Royal Festival Hall in London as part of Morrissey's Meltdown Festival. Morrissey as well as Nancy Sinatra joined them on stage. Bringing us up to date Linder told me: "The monograph about my work was finally published in March 2006 – by JRP Ringier – a Swiss fine art company (maybe the Crepescule of the book world)." She was also invited to take 'The Working Class Goes to Paradise' to Tate Britain as part of the Triennial. "It's an exciting time. I'm working with Barry Adamson on a version of 'You Open My Legs Like A Book'. I think it was the god Janus who had to look backwards and forwards at the same time – I know how he felt!"

DISCOGRAPHY:

The Visit (4 Compositions) 12-inch EP (New Hormones ORG 4 March 1980)
Lullaby Cheat/Unveil/Sightseeing/I Can't Swim, I Have Nightmares
My Cherry Is In Sherry/Anatomy Is Not Destiny 7-inch (New Hormones ORG 8 August 1980)
Pickpocket cassette (New Hormones CAT 1 May 1981)
Mutilate/Box/Mouthpiece/Patient/The Fool/Hugo Blanco
Mother's Hour/Patient 7inch (New Hormones ORG 12 July 1981)
The Seduction 2x12-inch EP (New Hormones ORG 16 December 1981)
Seduction (Unveiled)/A Woman's Travelogue/My Cherry Is In My Sherry/See The Keyhole/Her Story
Danger Came Smiling mini-LP (New Hormones ORG 20 September 1982)
Linder Sings Bardot cassette (1983)
Nue Au Soleil LP (Interior IM 013 January 1988) (aka Let Me Go Where The Pictures Go, which was slated for release by Les Discques Du Crepescule in 1985 but never appeared)
ARCHIVE RELEASES:
The Damage CD (LTM LTMCD 2328 2002) (Start here if you're interested. Studio material between 1980 and 1983, with live cuts – appropriate term, perhaps – from the legendary Hacienda show. Artwork by Linder, photography by Hennebert, liner notes by Morrissey)
Pickpocket/Danger Came Smiling CD (LTM LTMCD 2338 2002) (Remastered compilation of the group's two "albums")
The Visit/The Seduction CD (LTM LTMCD 2333 2002) (Remastered selection of the group's New Hormones material)

Lurkers

Pete Stride (guitar), Nigel Moore (bass), Pete 'Plug' Edwards (vocals), Manic Esso (Peter Haynes; drums)

A band for whom the prefix second division punk band seems to be compulsory, the LURKERS never got taken terribly seriously but managed to eke out an existence on the margins of the UK punk scene as a kind of unpretentious, domestic Ramones. For some, their reputation will always be enshrined in that cheeky Television Personalities' single, 'Part Time Punks' – "They'd like to buy the O Level

single/Or 'Read About Seymour'/But they're not pressed in red/So they buy the Lurkers instead." Others just get plain sniffy. Paul Davies' Q review of their Beggars Banquet Singles Collection, "one-dimensional bludgerama (which) represented punk's dreary foot soldiers at their most mundane," is about par for the course.

But while it would be a stretch to advance a case for the Lurkers as world-beaters, there's much that appeals about both their music and fortitude. And volume. They were the first band DJ Steve Lamacq saw live. "My ears rang for three days afterwards," he later confessed.

The initial line-up had known each other from school in Ickenham, Middlesex, from the early-70s, and decided to form a band together over a few drinks (it's a common misconception that they were from Fulham, though certainly many of their fans were). Given that three of the original cast were named Peter, Edwards became Plug and Haynes, who had formerly worked on a garage forecourt, became Manic Esso. Howard Wall subsequently became their singer, though the ousted Edwards stayed on as roadie and harmonica player. After two gigs, however, Moore had departed to form Swank, with Arturo Bassick (aka Peter Arthur Billingsley) taking over on bass in May.

Rehearsing in the small but functional basement of their local Fulham record shop, Beggars Banquet, they played a handful of pub dates, making their debut at Uxbridge Technical College supporting Screaming Lord Sutch, before supporting Generation X at their party to celebrate signing to Chrysalis on 20 July. Their debut single, the endearingly shallow, dumb-as-a-doughboy 'Shadow', backed by 'Love Story', both written by Stride, followed in August. It was the first release on Beggars Banquet Records, formed after employee Mike Stone convinced his boss, Martin Mills, to invest in the band. "Underneath our Fulham shop we had a basement which we turned into a rehearsal room where punk bands like Generation X went to rehearse," Mills recalls. "One of the bands who rehearsed down there was a band called the Lurkers who were one of the great three chord punk bands. The manager of the shop (Stone) started to manage the band because they needed help. Then he needed help so we started managing them and we started trying to get them a deal but we couldn't. This was 1976 and at that point there weren't very many labels, and each one had already signed their one punk band – and that was it. So we set about doing the record ourselves in a way that is now second nature to almost anyone in a band. But then it was such an unusual thing to do. Then there was no roadmap. There were no small independent record companies. So we worked out how to put a record out ourselves. We pressed it and got a very old fashioned distributor called President." It went on to sell over 10,000 copies.

Arturo has mixed memories of Stone. "He was OK but he didn't take any notice of anything other than what Pete Stride had to say... he used to call Pete Stride the new Pete Townshend. He loved Stridey... He thought Esso was a lunatic, which he still is, but a smarter lunatic you will never meet. Mike did all he could for us, but I got lots of the early gigs through knowing the Albion agency who ran the Red Cow, the Hope and Anchor and the Nashville rooms, so that's how we got all the gigs supporting the Stranglers, the Jam and 999. But Mike drove that old Bedford van that I get out of in Punk In London, all of us on the gear, going from London to Barrow-in-Furness and Accrington for £50 a night. Mike was good like that."

The blind date-themed 'Freak Show' followed in November, backed by 'Mass Media Believer', the first song Bassick had written for the band. It sounded a lot more professional, the result of bringing producers Ed Hollis (of Eddie And The Hot Rods) and Steve Lillywhite on board. "When we recorded with Ed Hollis and Steve Lillywhite," Bassick recalls, "I remember Ed trying to give us speed – he was doing a lot at that session. But we were boozers and not into drugs at all. Steve was really the engineer and I don't recall him saying much at all, but they did a good job on that 'Freak Show' single." The sleeve was better too, featuring a Savage Pencil design. The band was slowly building a rep – mainly as London's answer to the Ramones. "A lot of people say that," admits Bassick, "but I don't think they're absolutely right, because the Lurkers put a lot of different tones in the songs, different chord sequences from the Ramones. I think the Lurkers leaned more towards dirty rock'n'roll, a bit more like the New York Dolls than the Ramones. But there was an influence there, of course. I saw the Ramones in 1977, many times. I saw them every year they came." At this juncture the Lurkers featured heavily in the hysterically funny Punk In London movie. A gaggle of German art students (if that is the correct collective noun) had

L

The Lurkers on stage at the Y Club in Chelmsford.

been told to come to London and document the new wave. They settled on interviewing Bassick because they wanted a punk rocker who lived in a tower block. So they asked their questions with his quizzical parents looking on in one of the great non-event set pieces of the punk era. "My mum and dad were OK after the film students left, just bemused by it all. You see, I didn't live at home at the time, I was in a squat in Twickenham with Dave Treganna of Sham 69. Those students wanted a big celebrity from the punk scene to do the high rise living thing. But they ended up with me, 'cos that's where I really was brought up, not like some of those arty farty King's Road bands who would have sold their grandmothers for fame, and tried to make out they were working class, bunch of phonies."

However, Bassick would only contribute to one more release, 'Be My Prisoner', recorded at the same session as 'Freak Show' and 'Mass Media Believer', which was included on Beggars Banquet's Streets compilation, before leaving to form Pinpoint in November 1977. He felt his songwriting didn't fit in with what the Lurkers were doing, and Pinpoint had a deal with Albion Management, who also had the Stranglers and 999 on their books. Pinpoint released three singles (the first of which, 'In Richmond', would later be covered by Die Toten Hosen) and an album, Third State, which fared poorly, despite supports to the likes of Adam And The Ants, Generation X, 999 and – ironically – the Lurkers. He then formed the Lucky Saddles, who released a single for Albion, before putting together the Blubberry Hellbellies, from 1983 to 1988, a country-punk band distinguished by the size of their girths.

The Lurkers continued, recruiting Kym Bradshaw from the Saints, who stuck it for a year before Nigel Moore, the band's original bassist, returned. He was in place by the time they cut 'Ain't Got A Clue', probably the band's touchstone single, which came with a free gold flexidisc of the none-too-serious 'Fulham Fallout Firty Free', aka 'We Are The Chaos Brothers'. Selling over 15,000 copies, it rose to number 45 in the UK charts, but with solid airplay from Mike Read and John Peel, who always adored the Lurkers, it could have done much better. "'Ain't Got A Clue' was like a Lurkers tragedy," Stride later told Record Collector. "Because we were meant to be on Top Of The Pops, and it had gone in the chart, and we would have been on TOTP, but the show was cancelled that week because of the World Cup or something like that. So it might have done a lot better, or like a lot of things these days, gone straight out again. But in those days there was a bit of a bandwagon going on and I think we would have gone up if we had gone on and been fantastic, ha ha!"

Their debut album Fulham Fallout was produced and engineered by Mick Glossop and arrived in April 1978. This was principally a collection of Stride originals, alongside Bradshaw's 'Hey You', Moore's 'Go, Go, Go', a cover of 'Then I Kissed Her' retitled 'Then I Kicked Her', a band composition 'Gerald 'and the Stride/Esso collaboration 'It's Quiet Here'. 'Total War' itself was one of the few semi-political tunes the band wrote, though its assertions are based on class-consciousness rather than revolutionary fervour. This time the artwork was provided by Chuck Loyola. It went on to reach the Top 20.

The next single was 'I Don't Need To Tell Her', sticking closely to the Ramones template but adding a distinctively Brit-brat vocal, backed by their cover of 'Pills', the Bo Diddley via New York Dolls chestnut. It finally brought the Lurkers to the stage of Top Of The Pops. Pre-dating Chiswick's marketing of the Damned, it was released in four different picture sleeves – one each of the band members. "We wanted it to be a bit more over the top than it turned out," Stride reckoned in 1978. "It sounds sophisticated to us. The idea that we're going for is layers and layers of rhythm guitar over a good heavy drum sound." It was promoted via a gig with Adam And The Ants as support. January 1989 brought 'Just Thirteen' backed with 'Countdown'.

However, there were a few ominous developments. Violence was creeping into their shows, with members of the British Movement and National Front seeking, and failing, to claim the band as their own. The worst moment came when a celebratory gig at the Lyceum was ruined by a series of scuffles and fights in the audience. In March 1979 they travelled to Muscle Shoals, Alabama, to work on a second album with esteemed Motown producer Phillip Jarrell. However, the sessions ended in acrimony – especially once the band discovered that Alabama was a dry state and necessitated a three-hour trip across the state line in order to purchase alcohol. They played several shows on a subsequent American tour but their problems escalated after their van collided with a brick truck and exploded. In the meantime Beggars pushed out 'Out In The Dark'. One of the three B-side tracks, 'Cyanide', which recalls the Ramones' 'Pinhead', featured Plug on harmonica, and is one of Henry Rollins' favourite punk songs. "Could I be the biggest Lurkers fan there is?" he would reflect. "I may very well be. I don't think anyone can be bothered to contest that one so it's a hollow victory, but a victory nonetheless." God's Lonely Men, released in June 1979, was comfortably the band's most accomplished album. The highlights included another Stride/Esso collaboration, 'Whatever Happened To Mary' and Moore's 'She Knows'.

By the end of 1979 Boys' guitarist Honest John Plain had joined, and appeared on their final single, 'New Guitar In Town', which he co-wrote with Stride, as well as their Killer tour of the UK. The Lurkers broke up soon after four final shows at the Marquee. As Moore confirmed to Trees and Flowers fanzine: "We split up originally because of Beggars Banquet's financial problems after God's Lonely Men. And our parents were hassling us cos we were only 19 at the time."

"Beggar's Banquet decided to give us another chance," Stride told HitList in 1999. "But since Esso and Nigel had been fired at John Plain's insistence, we decided to change the name of the band to the New Guitars." Sessions for a new album under this guise took place at three separate studios, including Rockfield under Pat Moran, with the album, released in June 1980, credited to Pete Stride and John Plain. Tony Bateman played bass and sang backing vocals, Jack Black played drums, Mick Talbot added keyboards. Howard Wall and Plug shared the vocals. It included covers of R&B standards like 'You Better Move On', famously covered by the Rolling Stones, and 'He'll Have To Go', best known in the UK through Jim Reeves' sentimental treatment. A further cover, Sonny Bono's 'Laugh At Me', was excerpted from it and released as a single. Shortly thereafter, Beggars released Last Will And Testament, a Lurkers greatest hits collection.

By 1982 the Lurkers decided to give it another crack. Wall wasn't interested, so via the Melody Maker, Stride, Moore and Esso recruited Mark Fincham as vocalist. They also signed to Mike Stone's new project, the Clay label. Which meant the old punks rubbing shoulders with the new – notably Discharge and GBH. The second version of the Lurkers made their debut at West Hampstead's Moonlight Club in 1982. Their first new release was 'This Dirty Town', then 'Drag You Out'. The latter's 'Heroin (It's All Over)' B-side was notable for its anti-drug message – earlier 'Pinhead' had delighted in announcing "I've had enough of whisky and gin/I can't afford hero-in." In February 1983 'Frankenstein Again' continued the run of credible singles for Clay, though little attention was paid to them.

But they'd split again by 1984. "Musical differences" resurfaced during album sessions – Clay took the five songs they had completed and released them as the 'Final Vinyl' EP in March 1984. The next reunion took three years to get together. This time Arturo helmed it, having been contacted by one of the band's old fans. That fan was Campino, the lead singer of Die Toten Hosen of Germany, who also offered to finance any comeback LP. Bassick had spent the wilderness years as a spectacularly unsuccessful furniture remover, his misdemeanours including dropping a piano and scratching antique tables. Later he would act as a one-man home for abandoned whippets. But he'd met Campino in 1985 while touring with the Blubberry Hellbellies, who was keen to get the band together. Their resurgence began with a sell-out show in Dusseldorf. "We enjoyed playing so much," Bassick told Hitlist, "that we haven't stopped again." However, this time he took over on lead vocals, because Stride didn't want to work with Wall or Fincham again. With Esso and Moore back as the rhythm section, they recorded Wild Times Again for the German Weserlabel in 1988, co-produced with ex-Vibrator Pat Collier and Campino of Die Toten Hosen at Greenhouse Studios. Bassick's 'Miss World' and Stride's 'Fanatical Heart' were the 'keepers' here.

However, by the time it came to tour to promote the album, Esso had decided to concentrate on his career as a playwright (he currently works in mental health). Dan Tozer joined them to help out on their Link mini-LP, King Of The Mountain. It was these dates that also produced their Live And Loud! album for the same label. Bassick briefly toured as The Tower Block Rockers with John Plain and Darryl Bath, and also helped organise Die Toten Hosen's anglophile punk tribute, Learning English (after all, he had the contacts). Meanwhile the Lurkers washed up at Released Emotions, for whom they recorded Powerjive, one of their finest latter-day collections, produced by Lee Heighwood. The same label also issued a further concert album, Live In Berlin, but its release coincided with the defection of Moore, leaving the Lurkers as a three-piece, with Bassick handling bass and vocals. Another German release followed, Nonstop Nitropop, but its (relative) success in Germany was not replicated elsewhere.

L

Bassick also started playing with 999, with whom he'd been friends since 1977. Nick Cash was having "problems" with 999 bassist Danny Palmer. "I'd always liked 999 and jumped at the chance." He combined the two for many years, starting with 999's 1993 Anagram studio album You Us It! He has also played with the Business from time to time, the old tart.

After a long European tour in 1992, Stride dropped out of the Lurkers, hoping to concentrate on songwriting, and recording his own compositions at home. Bassick still invited him to contribute songs to the Lurkers, but he's expressed some displeasure at the fact that the band's name is still in use. Which left Bassick and Tozer in charge. They used former UK Subs guitarist Alan Lee for a while, then Gabba of Chaos UK (third generation UK punks who had earlier covered 'Ain't Got A Clue'). However, Bassick's attention was taken with 999 so the band played infrequently. That didn't prevent them from releasing 1995's Ripped 'n' Torn for Step One Records. This introduced new guitarist Tom Spencer, who joined them for a European tour, and also dates in Argentina and Brazil (Bassick performing with both the Lurkers and 999). "You never know what's around the corner with music," Bassick told Die Toten Hosen's fan site. "And you get a call and someone says he wants to take you to South America, and you think, 'Great! Absolutely wonderful!' And then you find out that he's an old fan and he's made money or something, and he flies you there and you play some concerts." The current line-up also features Nelly (ex-Fiend and Hang-Ups) on drums and Bill Gilbert (ex-16 Forever, Chelsea, Hang-Ups) on guitar.

So would Bassick have had it any different? "I wouldn't change much, maybe just try not to get ripped off. When I left the Lurkers in 1977 I got £70 and a Peavey bass amp. I was never accounted to at all and still haven't been. Also Punk In London has been released about eight times, it's now on DVD and I've never seen a penny out of that, either. I'm not surprised punk has lasted, it's just as relevant as any other music that's been around for years as Charlie Harper said back in 1977, it's another kind of blues."

Discography:

(Buyer's Guide: Start off with the Captain Oi! Punk Singles Collection. From there, pick up the Fulham Fallout and God's Lonely Men reissues. The BBC Punk Sessions is well worth hearing, and as for later material, Powerjive, handily repackaged with King Of The Mountain, is recommended)

Shadow/Love Story 7-inch (Beggars Banquet BEG-1 August 1977) (1978 reissues in limited edition, 1,000 each, in red, white and blue vinyl. Widely known as the 'free admission' single)

Freak Show/Mass Media Believer 7-inch (Beggars Banquet BEG-2 November 1977)

Ain't Got a Clue/Ooh Ooh I Love You 7-inch (Beggars Banquet BEG-6 May 1978) (first 10,000 with free gold flexidisc single of The Chaos Brothers performing 'Fulham Fallout Firty Free'. A December reissue featured a different picture sleeve plus 'picture disc' flexi)

Fulham Fallout LP (Beggars Banquet BEGA-2 June 1978) (1997 Captain Oi! CD Ahoy CD 73 re-release adds 'Shadow', 'Love Story', 'Freak Show', 'Mass Media Believer', 'Be My Prisoner' from the Streets compilation, an unreleased song, 'I Love The Dark', and demos of two of the LP songs 'Total War' and 'Then I Kissed Her')

I Don't Need to Tell Her/Pills 7-inch (Beggars Banquet BEG-9 August 1978) (issued in four different picture sleeves; one of each band member)

Just Thirteen/Countdown 7-inch (Beggars Banquet BEG-14 November 1978)

Out in the Dark 7-inch EP (Beggars Banquet BEG-19 May 1979)

Out In The Dark/Cyanide/Suzie is a Floozie/Cyanide (pub version)

God's Lonely Men LP (Beggars Banquet BEGA-8 June 1979) (1997 Captain Oi! CD Ahoy 74 re-release adds, wait for it, 'Just Thirteen', 'Countdown', 'Suzie Is A Floozie', 'Cyanide (pub version)', 'New Guitar In Town', 'Little Ole Wine Drinker Me', 'Cold Old Night (demo)', 'Pick Me Up (demo)', 'Mary's Coming Home (demo)', 'New Guitar In Town (demo)', 'Little Ole Wine Drinker Me (demo)')

New Guitar In Town/Little Ole Wine Drinker Me 7-inch (Beggars Banquet BEG-28 November 1979)

This Dirty Town/Wolf at the Door 7-inch (Clay CLAY 12 July 1982)

Drag You Out/Heroin (It's All Over) 7-inch (Clay CLAY 17 October 1982) (also issued as a limited edition picture disc, CLAY 17P)

Frankenstein Again/One Man's Meat 7-inch (Clay CLAY 21 February 1983)

Let's Dance Now/Midnight Hour 7-inch (Clay CLAY 32 May 1984)

The Final Vinyl 12-inch EP (Clay PLATE 1 March 1984)

Let's Dance Now/Midnight Hour/By The Heart/Shut Out The Light/Frankenstein Again (also available as a picture disc)

Wild Times Again LP (Weserlabel EFA 2433 February 1989) (reissued on CD in November 1994 as WL 024332CD)

King Of The Mountain mini-LP (Link 1989)

Barbara/Never Had A Beach Head/Unfinished Business/Going Monkee Again/King Of The Mountain (part 1)/Lucky John/King Of The Mountain (part 2)

Powerjive LP (Released Emotions REM 008 1990)

Live and Loud! LP (Link November 1989)

Nonstop Nitropop CD (Weserlabel 1992)

Ripped 'n' Torn CD (Step One STEPCD 075 1995) (contains Arturo's favourite Lurkers' song, the Stride composition, 'Don't Seem Right To Me'. However, it's currently not available on CD after an American corporation bought out the Receiver back catalogue)

Go Ahead Punk Make My Day/Lucky John 7-inch (Empty MT 481 November 1999) (first 125 copies in 'glow vinyl')

26 Years CD (Captain Oi! AHOY CD 229 October 2003) (the group's most recent studio album. 'Go Sane' features lyrics by old pal Manic Esso)

ARCHIVE RELEASES:

Shadow/Love Story/Freak Show/Mass Media Believer 7-inch EP (Beggars Banquet BACK-1 August 1979) (reissue of the first two singles as a double-pack)

I Don't Need to Tell Her/Pills/Just Thirteen/Countdown 7-inch EP (Beggars Banquet BACK-3 1979) (reissue of singles three and four as a double-pack)

Greatest Hit: Last Will And Testament LP (Beggars Banquet BOPA-2 November 1980) (a reasonable introduction losing some of the stodge from the studio albums. Reissued on LP/CD by Beggars subsidiary Lowdown BBL2/BBL2CD in 1988)

This Dirty Town LP (Clay CLAY 104 July 1982) (rounds up all the band's Clay material. Reissued in December 1989 with same catalogue number. Reissued on CD, CLAY CD 104, in April 1993)

PowerJive/King Of The Mountain CD (Anagram Records CDPUNK 69 November 1995)

Live in Berlin CD (Released Emotions REM-015CD 1991)

Totally Lurkered CD (Dojo CD74 December 1992)

Greatest Hits Live CD (Street Link STRCD-009 1992)

Take Me Back To Babylon CD (Receiver RRCD 243 December 1997) (though it features pictures of the Wall/Stride/Esso/Moore line-up, the first 10 songs of this CD are taken from This Dirty Town, though they've lost something in the mastering, while the other 13 feature Bassick on vocals on re-recordings of the originals)

Beggars Banquet Singles Collection CD (Anagram CD PUNK 94 May 1997)

The BBC Punk Sessions CD (Captain Oi! AHOY CD 137) (All the group's John Peel sessions, including one for the BBC that was never broadcast, but did provide songs for the New Guitars In Town album, with sleevenotes from Pete Stride, and featuring five otherwise unavailable songs)

Wild Times Again/Non-Stop Nitro Pop CD (Captain Oi! AHOY CD 178 2002) (first UK release for their two German-only studio albums, with sleevenotes by Arturo Bassick)

Punk Singles Collection CD (Captain Oi! AHOY CD 188 June 2002) (a good starting point as the Lurkers were a fine singles band and the package reprints all the sleeves etc)

Lurkin' About CD (Bassick Productions BP CD 01 2004) (recorded live at the Newcastle Punk Fest 16 August 2003)

Live Freak Show CD (Kotumba Records K105 2005) (recorded live in Berlin).

Machines

Nick Paul (vocals, guitar), Duff (bass), John Dee (aka John Dearlove; drums)

Southend's MACHINES were put together by Nick Paul, who sat in his freezing seaside bedsit writing a set of about 16 originals, before placing adverts in the local music press to find some accomplices. The line-up was complete by the summer of 1977.

However, there's a much more interesting evolutionary tale than the bare facts above suggest, as Nick Paul told me in 2005 when I asked him about being the first punk band from a town that was then synonymous with the pub rock explosion. "Yes, Southend was firmly in the grip of R&B and pub rock because of the Feelgoods, Hot Rods and Kursaal Flyers. Whilst I often went to see those bands in the early-70s I had no real interest in what I saw as their retrograde 'travelling jukebox' mixture of old covers and 12-bar blues. From about 1971 onwards I was much more interested in American rock (or pre-punk as it's probably called now). Bands like the Velvets, the Stooges, MC5 and then the NY Dolls and this is what influenced me. In 1974, I formed a group called Raw Power, named after our favourite Stooges album of course, with bass beast Steve Reddihough. We peddled our own brand of pre-punk in the Southend area, mixing covers like the Who and the Stones with Dolls and Lou Reed songs, plus our own originals. We had a great time but just couldn't break out of the local gig scene and the band lasted about a year and we split up in the summer of 1975. As Steve said at the time, if we had been born 35 miles up the road we would have been there at the beginning with the Clash and Pistols."

Nick Paul then headed for London. "In July 1976 I moved to London for the first time. It was incredible luck, as it was just as punk was starting to take off. I think I must have seen about every punk band going several times and was lucky enough to be at the 100 Club Punk Festival in September 1976. It was the buzz of all this that drove me on to form the Machines. I had been listening and playing punk-type music for four years by then, and I knew that at last it was finally HAPPENING – whooppeeee!"

Four months after the 100 Club Festival, he returned to Southend to form the Machines. "I'd tried in London but endless Melody Maker ads led to nothing except a strange day in the studio playing guitar with Billy Idol and Tony James in Generation X, a ghastly experience. I'd never met two men so ego-driven and in love with themselves. So it was back home for me to search for local likelies. My thinking was that at least I knew the local music scene and where to get gigs etc."

They played a handful of local dates, but never got sucked into the local scene as such. Nick Paul: "Once formed we never really had anything to do with the local R&B bands, we didn't talk to them, they didn't talk to us. It was a happy compromise that worked well enough." They also secured London shows at venues including the Roxy and Vortex, as well as the City Of London Polytechnic where they were asked back for six encores. They were jointly managed by an "on the run from his wife" hairdresser, Dave, and Richard, an "18-stone, pogo-ing civil servant with a leg iron", who also produced an in-house fanzine, Strange Stories, from Dave's bedroom. Naturally enough, it featured the Machines as cover stars.

The Machines recorded their sole record in 1978 in Spectrum Studios, Westcliff On Sea, Essex, after their managers introduced them to a local would-be entrepreneur who wanted to form a record company. The 30-minute session cost exactly £4 and the results were well received by John Peel and the music press. This despite the fact that Nick Paul howled in protest at the poor sound quality of the finished vinyl and, unbeknownst to him, his managers and the label owner actually cut a second version of the single at Tape One Studios, with much clearer sound, for their own undisclosed purposes.

The single made a couple of 'alternative' charts and all boded well. And it did lead to the NME citing Nick Paul's guitar playing as "so beautifully crazed that John Lennon himself would be proud to achieve this sound". However, as satisfying as the comparison was, Nick Paul was restless and wanted to take the band in a different direction. He and Duff decided that Dearlove was no longer suitable and he was axed. They auditioned for replacements through the summer of 1978 but were unable to find the right blend. So Nick Paul chucked in the towel and moved to London, where he would eventually form the Collectors, and release a further 7-inch single, 'Different World', on Central Collection Records in 1980.

Much of the group's live set, including 'Parent's Zone', 'Weird Phone Calls' and the stop-start set closer 'Head On Crash', remain unreleased. However, two tracks, an early version of 'You Better Hear' and the unreleased 'Racing' are set for inclusion on a new Bored Teenagers release. Dearlove's drumming skills are still spoken of with great reverence by fellow Southend musicians such as Steve Pegrum, who remembers the Machines as being 'fantastic'. Dearlove later joined the Electric Shocks, who then truncated their name to the Shocks. "They were a straightforward Ramones-style punk band, but very powerful." Duff subsequently became a printer and Dearlove also played in the reggae band Wild Fire.

But that's not all folks. Nick Paul: "Strangely, I have recently been back in the studios with bass man Steve Reddihough from Raw Power and Ade Powell, the drummer from the Collectors. That provides a continuous musical link stretching from 1974 to 2005. God, that's almost as bad as Quo!"

DISCOGRAPHY:

True Life/Everything's Technical/You Better Hear/Evening Radio 7-inch EP (Wax EAR 1 March 1978) (1,000 copies. Later released on CD by Gecko Records in 1995. The tracks have also featured on several semi-legal compilations including Killed By Death 2, Bloodstains Across the UK, Break The Rules 7, Everyone A Classic! Vol 6, etc)

Magazine

Howard Devoto (vocals), John McGeoch (guitar), Barry Adamson (bass), Martin Jackson (drums), Bob Dickinson (keyboards)

Having left the Buzzcocks just as commercial comforts beckoned, celebrated egghead Devoto, taciturn intellectual of the post-punk parish, had outed himself as a clairvoyant, in the words of Simon Reynolds, for abandoning the good ship punk rock "long before it started to sink". In fact, he was overboard before it had even left the quayside. He was an enthusiast rather than a sceptic, but a supremely analytical one. Such was the inherent distrust he bore in relation to punk's funnelling of creative energy, the advert he placed in Manchester's Virgin Records concluded with the telling post-script "Punk mentality not essential".

He hooked up with John McGeoch, whom he'd met in April 1977 after the guitarist had moved to Manchester to study art and ended up sharing a flat with Malcolm Garrett. Recruiting Bob Dickinson on keyboards, Barry Adamson on bass and Martin Jackson on drums, they formed **MAGAZINE**. Devoto had stated on his exit from the Buzzcocks that he'd wanted to concentrate on his academic studies. Having been the promoter behind the Sex Pistols' legendary Lesser Free Trade Hall shows, he'd also quickly tired of what he saw as punk's artistic collapse, a point alluded to directly in the statement he issued to the press on his exit from the Buzzcocks. College attendance aside, he was keen to regain a free hand, to explore less conventional forms of rock music and, specifically according to his first interview with the NME, to expand into areas that would allow him space to 'breathe'. "There was something very limiting about punk," he later told Michael Bracewell of the Guardian. "And in the early days that was punk's strength. You knew your themes, you knew how to look and you knew your musical style. And there you were, for a while. But I'd loved all kinds of other music up to that point. There was some big elemental thing that happened with the Sex Pistols, but in terms of music there was a whole gamut of other stuff which I had liked, and which, in the realm of ideas, was not a totally different tin of biscuits – Leonard Cohen, Dylan, David Bowie. With the Pistols and Iggy Pop, it was the anger and poetry which hooked me in, really." The Buzzcocks, ultimately, were a pop group. Devoto's instincts were, ostensibly, anti-pop. His former co-writer, Pete Shelley, wanted to write songs about unrequited love. Devoto wanted to write songs with lines like "I will drug you and fuck you on the permafrost".

Magazine made their first appearance, playing 'The Light Pours Out Of Me', 'Shot By Both Sides' and Captain Beefheart's 'I Love You, You Big Dummy', using equipment borrowed from the Buzzcocks, as guests on the closing night of the Electric Circus on 2 October 1977. Memorably, Devoto would cavort with a doll during the finale. "It was not a 'blow-up doll'," Devote points out. It was "a life-size punk doll (female) made of various fabrics. It had been made by my then girlfriend, Linder Sterling." Jon Savage reviewed the show for Sounds and was instinctively drawn to the possibilities. "Immediately, they're more musician than the other bands (Warsaw, Negatives, Prefects, Worst, Fall) so far, capable of different textures – the sound isn't as clear or as confident as on the demo tapes, but this is understandable, and more than complemented by the visual presence of the band. Still the centre of attention is Devoto; on stage he's a curious, compelling performer, awkward yet graceful, commanding yet ambiguous."

The initial press buzz around the band, and Devoto in particular, was massive, as McGeoch recalled to Paul O'Reilly. "Well, I was still at college and it was during the holidays and I was working in an electrical shop selling TV's. It was ridiculous – I'd got this job and it was the sort where you had to wear a suit. I had to borrow one of my dad's and anyway, one day I'm walking from work to the bus stop and there's an NME lying on the floor. I picked it up to have a read and there's Howard staring up at me from the cover." This was, of course, the "most important man in rock" cover.

Within four months Dickinson, also half of the bizarre Bob And His Dick, had left, after only two further gigs. He did, however, contribute to the band's original demo recordings (which included the unreleased, Samuel Beckett-indebted 'Suddenly We Are Eating Sandwiches'. Parts of the music of which were cannibalised for 'My Mind Ain't So Open', the flipside of 'Shot By Both Sides', and provided the structure of 'Motorcade' and the keyboard embellishments to 'The Light Pours Out Of Me'.) He would later reflect that it may have been Virgin A&R man Simon Draper who was responsible for his outing, especially after Devoto made him an offer of continuing with the band as a songwriting/live collaborator, which he rejected. In later life as a prominent rock climber, with partner Gary Gibson, he regularly names climbing routes after old Magazine or Stranglers songs.

Magazine signed with Virgin in October 1977, though the announcement was delayed until January of the following year. The deal attracted a great deal of media hoopla – Paul Morley leading that particular congregation in eulogy, while Melody Maker put Devoto on their front cover and proclaimed him "the man for 1978" before his band had released any material. Their debut release was the sublime 'Shot By Both Sides', a showcase for John McGeoch's guitar, though its original author was actually Pete Shelley (who would later employ the same riff for the Buzzcocks' 'Lipstick'). McGeoch, alongside Stuart Adamson of the Skids and Andy Gill of Gang Of Four, all but defined the sound of a mini-era. And was this the same Devoto who had languidly extolled the virtues of 'Boredom' with the Buzzcocks, belting out the feverish, semi-operatic lead vocal? The lyric neatly staked out Devoto's ground – restlessness, isolation, and the aesthetic triumphs and tragedies of the self being submerged. There's a line of continuity with the Buzzcocks' 'Breakdown' in the way Devoto celebrates the instances when certainties disappear as the most creative moment for any individual, crisis as rebirth. Speaking of which, that spitting thing was a no-no. Gail Egan watched them play at the Russell Club in Manchester in July. "I remember Howard coming on and everyone started gobbing and he threatened to walk off if they did not stop, and he promptly did when they continued! He would only go on with the gig, which was great in the end, when they stopped."

As Devoto recalled in 1979, punk was "a new version of trouble-shooting modern forms of unhappiness". But it wasn't all po-faced. "I wormed my way into the heart of the crowd," the lyric expanded, adding the coy, Joe Orton-esque pay-off: "I was shocked to find what was allowed." In Rip It Up And Start Again Simon Reynolds cites this same lyrical section as Devoto's pointed rebuttal of the entrenched political readings and sloganeering of the less intellectually gifted adherents of the punk rock generation. But it can equally be taken as the singer being at his most playful, amusement rather than disdain. The single peaked at number 41 in the charts, and after turning down the chance to appear on Top Of The Pops to promote it for a week, Devoto was eventually persuaded to appear by Virgin the next. But he resolutely refused to participate in the ritual, standing stock still for the entire performance, partially a result of discomfort, partially stage fright. A beautiful televisual moment born of truculence and single-mindedness, though sales may have been 'dented'. Indeed, some still point to this as the point at which Magazine started its decline as a commercial proposition.

After recording the first of four sessions for John Peel, they released second single 'Touch And Go'. It discussed prostitution in vernacular lifted directly from Shakespeare, backed by their flamboyant cover version of John Barry's James Bond theme, 'Goldfinger', which few other bands would have contemplated, let alone pulled off. Prior to the release of their debut album, Real Life, Dave Formula (aka Dave Tomlinson) swelled the ranks as additional keyboard player. In recruiting him Devoto had successfully assembled one of the most profoundly and unapologetically musical franchises of the era. Real Life, produced by John Leckie, was greeted with some of the most effusive praise ever visited on a debut album. And it's an entirely deserving recipient of that acclaim. The music had a quality of frigidity and brittleness, as though things might snap apart at any moment, resulting in tiny explosions of melodrama before settling back into a push-pull of tension and restraint. It was, and is, a unique accommodation, perfectly framing Devoto's beautifully layered, and rendered, lyrics.

'Motorcade' was not, as many including this writer assumed, Devoto's oblique take on the Kennedy assassination. Devoto: "I've rebutted this many times. Some of the idea for the song came from reading an article about a South American dictator who drove around throwing money out of the window of his limousine. Kennedy was never in my mind. The combination of the words 'motorcade' and 'into the null and void he shoots' leads people to think this. It's supposed to be the man at the centre of the motorcade who is doing the shooting – in his car – into the 'null and void'. Blame the lyricist, I say." 'Definitive Gaze', original title 'Real Life', was radically extemporised compared to the Peel session version that had aired six months previously. 'Recoil' saw McGeoch dispense shards of trebly riffage all over the shop, while Adamson was beginning to emerge from the shadows as a significant talent in his own right. It is his chugging undertow, which the Stone Roses would remould for 'I Am The Resurrection', that provides a spine for the vivid surround-sound of 'The Light Pours Out Of Me' (although the latter was rather unkindly retitled 'The Light Pours Out Of Me Arse' by some of Devoto's critics in Manchester). Meanwhile the group picked up the services of long-term manager Raf, who remained with the band until its demise and is still involved with Devoto to this day.

By the end of 1978 John Doyle had joined as drummer, with Jackson going on to the Chameleons and later Swing Out Sister. Devoto was hoping to embark on sessions for a follow-up album with John Barry, who eventually declined. Next on the wants list was Tony Visconti. When he proved unavailable, the band opted to use his former engineer Colin Thurston, who'd worked with Visconti on Bowie's Heroes, as well as Iggy Pop's Lust For Life. Iggy and Bowie remained Devoto's touchstone influences throughout the punk years, especially Bowie's 'Berlin' output of 1977. Later Thurston would recall his first meeting with the band to Dave Simpson. "It was In Manchester. I drove up there in a blizzard – snow flying everywhere – saw them go through about ten or twelve songs in a little basement place that they rehearsed in and came back to London. I think they were a bit nervous and so I didn't tell them it was my first production. We sort of talked generally about music. Barry Adamson, the bass player, was the most open guy. He would say, 'So what's you favourite kind of music?' I mentioned Abba and he nearly freaked! Or was it Cliff Richard? I did it as a joke, but I think they all took it terribly seriously."

Serious they indeed were. Devoto, newly christened the Orson Welles of punk, was at the height of his powers as a writer and was keen to press on. Sessions began in Good Earth studios but they ran out of time because the Moody Blues had block booked it. So they repaired to the Farmyard where the Manor Mobile captured their efforts, with everyone involved frozen to the bone. Those conditions audibly informed the atmospherics of Secondhand Daylight, most self-evidently on McGeoch's instrumental 'The Thin Air', which was only instrumental because Devoto couldn't come up with a fitting lyric. See also the vicious monologue of 'Permafrost', the vocals partially informed by the fact that Devoto had a horrible cold (Devoto can't actually remember having a cold at the time and believes this may be Colin Thurston's own interpretation), and album opener 'Feed The Enemy'. Little wonder that it fared so well in Q's 'Winter Albums' poll. "We were moving away from punk and into the idea of soundscapes," Adamson later told Toby Manning, "music that was both emotional and descriptive." The best example might well have been 'Cut-Out Shapes', which included a beautiful keyboard arrangement from Dave Formula, while the lyric offered up the album's title. Extracted from the album, and re-recorded, 'Rhythm Of Cruelty', the most upbeat of a decidedly downbeat bunch, on an album where McGeoch's role was notably downplayed, was released as a single.

In contrast to the frothy reviews granted its predecessor, Secondhand Daylight was rubbished by critics, notably Garry Bushell, with the exception of Allan Jones and Nick Kent. Some of this may have been due to Devoto's sudden reluctance to grant interviews, and the consequent perception that he was becoming way too big for his boots. There was some surprise in the camp, and concern from Virgin, who had to this point been sure of the commercial momentum of the group. That meant expectations were heaped on third album The Correct Use Of Soap to deliver on Devoto's man most likely to status.

The wonder of Soap lies as much in its conception as its execution. The group brought in the inimitable, and unstable, Martin Hannett as producer. Though Devoto would end up fighting him over almost everything, especially his unquenchable thirst for reverb, Hannett would subsequently refer to the album as "professionally my best". There was clearly an attempt to reconcile the group's more obtuse inclinations with the commercial climate. For some, including Adamson, that was a compromise. For others, it proved that Devoto was more than a tone-deaf art-pop recalcitrant. In retrospect, Soap is actually stuffed to the gills with pop songs. Arty, self-effacing, self-obsessed pop songs, but pop songs nevertheless. And greatest of these was, of course, the Dostoevsky-thieving 'A Song From Under The Floorboards'. It synthesized, in four unutterably perfect minutes, everything Magazine stood for, and almost everything that Devoto was reaching for. And to pick just one line, "My irritability keeps me alive and kicking", it offered arguably the most accurate self-examination ever enunciated by any singer of the generation. A simply phenomenal piece of work, and while it's the crux of the album, and in some ways stands in its own universe, it doesn't totally overpower the remainder of the contents. 'Because You're Frightened' has one of those great spider-effect riffs from McGeoch, but it's side two that's the real killer. 'I Want To Burn Again' is one of Devoto's more absorbing lyrics, beautifully emphasised by the rhythmic accompaniment. The soul-y backing vocals, anticipated in the previous album's 'Feed The Enemy', that accompany Devoto's defeated "And I still turn to love", are totally unexpected but wonderfully fitting. The sentiment is so exquisitely expressed it anticipates Morrissey's finest tragicomedies about his painful inability to achieve emotional congress. 'Thank You (Falettinme Be Mice Elf Again) cements the thematic link with Sly And The Family Stone. And 'Sweetheart Contract' is the most embittered and cynical song about romance – documenting each incidence in the birth of a relationship like a shopping list, or more acutely, like a private eye documenting guilt – you are ever likely to encounter.

In a perfect world Soap should have been ripped from the shelves and devoured by a spellbound populace. In reality, it sat like a deserted vol-au-vont long after the trestle tables had been folded away, and quickly became the preserve of bookish students and self-regarding rock critics. It sold diddlysquit, and its commercial failure effectively signalled Magazine's demise, a failure emphasised by the concurrent rise of city neighbours Joy Division. Shortly after its release, McGeoch left the band to join the Banshees and took much of its musical soul with it. Magazine had moved down to London and that put them in contact with a new social circle of fellow musicians. Devoto would later admit that he was very withdrawn at this time, mainly due to the death of his father. One theory suggests that McGeoch took this as a sign of faltering commitment to the band. He was also concerned about the way in which his role was being slowly reduced. However, McGeoch was already moonlighting from Magazine with Steve Strange in Visage and filling in on Generation X's third album. And when he got the phone call from manager Nils Stevenson to come along for an audition for the Banshees, met them and liked them, the decision became an obvious one. However, he would not immediately relinquish his place in Magazine, and after recording and performing with the Banshees he would complete their spring tour promoting Soap before finally quitting in the summer.

Magic, Murder And The Weather saw Ben Mandelson, formerly of Amazorblades, fail to fill McGeoch's shoes. For a brief spell Robin Simon of Ultravox! joined and appeared on live album Play! He could do a reasonable impersonation of McGeoch's sound, but the fabric of the group was torched by the fact that, creatively, it was no longer a five-cornered fight. Mandelson was a friend of Devoto's from Bolton College, but their familiarity on personal terms didn't necessarily make the transition to the studio. That left a huge hole in the group, and the fact that the original John Brand mix of the sessions was rejected and Martin Hannett brought back in, speaks of the anxiety and frustration within the band.

John Clay, formerly of Scunthorpe bands the Classics/Back Seat Romeos, undertook two auditions with the band and was offered a week's try-out, which he declined. "I did the Magazine auditions at a time when Robin Simon had left and just before Magic, Murder And The Weather was released. I still have some demos of new material they gave me that Robin Simon was playing on. One of the reasons I didn't push the boat out for the band was that Howard actually seemed like he'd had enough. It was Dave Formula who was pushing things along at that stage, but my gut instinct (that the band was in terminal decline) proved correct."

The resulting album was simply inferior in almost every regard to its predecessors. In particular, where Devoto's lyrics had previously been playful, now they just sounded tired and sarcastic. "A lot of the driving anger which had been where I was coming from was evaporating under pressure," he later told the Independent. It still has its moments, especially what Dave Quantick noted was "the bizarre insect Motown" of 'About The Weather', which is so much lighter in mood it practically levitates above the other contents. But you would be hard pressed to, one suspects, find a Magazine fan who plays it anywhere near as much as its three forerunners. The band had broken up by the time it eventually came out. Which prompts the question, why bother recording it in the first place? It seems, as Devoto confirmed to Melody Maker, that there was a certain amount of indecision and self-doubt about actually closing the door, as if to do so would be to admit, rather than musically eulogise, defeat. "There was always the chance that it (making the album) would have made a difference because I love writing so much. I thought I might feel substantially changed after the album – but I didn't."

Devoto, "unwisely" in his own words, recorded the solo album Jerky Versions Of The Dream in 1983 before putting together a duo, Luxuria, who recorded Unanswerable Lust in 1988, followed by Beast Box in 1990. When that got a deal of negative press, Devoto simply elected to withdraw from music and took a job in a photo library, though he did bring out a book of lyrics, It Only Looks As If It Hurts. The late, great John McGeoch went on to work with the Banshees, PiL and others, while Adamson embarked on a very successful solo path, particularly in the realm of film soundtracks. Dave Formula teaches keyboards in South Humberside/Lincolnshire, while Mandelson would work with Billy Bragg and 3 Mustaphas 3 – who would play at Devoto's wedding.

Devoto has occasionally been lured out of retirement, notably to work with Pete Shelley again on the Buzzkunst album, which didn't undermine either participant's pedigree, and also worked with Mansun ("because they asked"). There may yet be plenty left in the locker.

DISCOGRAPHY:

Shot By Both Sides/My Mind Ain't So Open 7-inch (Virgin VS 200 January 1978)
Touch And Go/Goldfinger 7-inch (Virgin VS 207 April 1978)
Real Life LP (Virgin V 2100 June 1978) (reissued on CD in October 1988, CDV 2100)
Give Me Everything/I Love You, You Big Dummy 7-inch (Virgin VS 237 November 1978)
Rhythm Of Cruelty/TV Baby 7-inch (Virgin VS 251 February 1979)
Secondhand Daylight LP (Virgin V 2121 March 1979) (reissued on CD in October 1988, CDV 2121)

A Song From Under The Floorboards/Twenty Years Ago 7-inch (Virgin VS 321 1980)
Thank You (Falettinme Be Mice Elf Again)/The Book 7-inch (Virgin VS 328 1980)
Upside Down/The Light Pours Out Of Me 7-inch (Virgin VS 334 1980)
The Correct Use Of Soap LP (Virgin V 2156 May 1980) (reissued on CD in October 1988, CDV 2156)
Sweetheart Contract/Feed The Enemy/Twenty Years Ago/Shot By Both Sides (all live) dbl 7-inch single (Virgin VS 368 1980)
Play (Live At Melbourne Festival Hall) LP (Virgin V 2184 November 1980) (reissued on CD in October 1988, CDV 2184. Recorded at the Melbourne Festival Hall on 6 September 1980. This is that rarity – an absolutely worthwhile live album, with some splendid renditions and good sound quality, both on the original vinyl and the reissued CD. 'Parade' is wonderfully atmospheric in this setting. No 'Shot By Both Sides', and you kind of wished that McGeoch was still marshalling the riffs instead of Robin Simon, but otherwise a fantastic souvenir)
About The Weather/In The Dark 7-inch (Virgin VS 412 1981) (also released as 12-inch, VS 412-12, with extra track 'The Operative')
Magic, Murder And The Weather LP (Virgin V 2200 June 1981) (reissued on CD in October 1988, CDV 2200)
ARCHIVE RELEASES
After The Fact (Best Of) LP (Virgin VM1 May 1982)
Shot By Both Sides 12-inch EP (Virgin VS 592-12 May 1983)
Shot By Both Sides/Goldfinger/Give Me Everything/Song From Under The Floorboards
Rays And Hail 1978-81 CD (Virgin COMCD 5 May 1987) (reissued on CD in July 1993, CDVM 9020)
Scree CD (Virgin CDOVD 312 July 1990)
BBC 1 Radio Live In Concert CD (Windsong WINCD 040 August 1993)
(good, but not as good as Play)
Maybe It's Right To Be Nervous Now 3-CD Box Set (Virgin MAGBOX 1 September 2000) (A well put-together effort, though the 'booklet' is essentially image-based. The third CD almost entirely comprises Peel session tracks, while there are live cuts drawn from Play and just about everything from the old odds and ends compilation Scree. But be warned, as an introduction to the band this is exhaustive rather than precise, and some of the better versions of the songs are to be found on the original CD reissues).
Where The Power Is (A Definitive Guide To Magazine) CD (Virgin CDV 2924 September 2000) (a useful accompaniment to the box set in that encompasses the album versions of those tracks featured in live versions on the latter. The exception is 'Model Worker', replaced by 'You Never Knew Me')
Real Life/Secondhand Daylight dbl CD (EMI 58173782 March 2003) (sure, they're great albums, and you should own them. But the copy protection, for those who would like to listen to them on their computer, let alone turn them into MP3s – and it's not as if it's a struggle to get hold of MP3s of any of these – is bloody annoying)

Maniacs

Alan Lee Shaw (vocals, guitar), Rod Latter (drums), Rob Crash (bass)

One near-hit wonders the MANIACS were formed in June 1977 when Latter and Shaw ejected Twink from the Rings and, via a Melody Maker advert, added Rob Crash, formerly a member of both Cold Fever and Kamikaze, to become the Maniacs. Hijacking songs written in their previous incarnation, they took the stage at the Mont De Marsan festival, with Johnny Thunders' associate Henri Paul guesting on guitar, as replacements for the Rings. Unbeknownst to them, Twink had upped the ante by putting together a new version of the band, who also played on the bill. Manager Ian Dickson later admitted that it was his involvement with the Rings that may have triggered Twink's departure – apparently he was unable to sate the great man's extreme financial demands.

On their return from France they auditioned for a bass player to allow Crash to move to second guitar, while Henri Paul would continue to accompany them at live shows. However, there were no suitable candidates so they persevered as a trio for the remainder of their brief career, which encompassed residencies at the Red Cow in Hammersmith and the Vortex, often supported by the Nipple Erectors.

After recording a five-song demo tape, recorded at Pathway under the tutelage of Dave Goodman, they secured a one-off single deal with United Artists through Andrew Lauder. It resulted in the entirely splendid 'Chelsea 1977' single, and they later contributed two tracks to the Live At The Vortex album. There was talk of an album but when Lauder fled the label to form Radar with Jake Riviera the interest disappeared. "We appeared in a short film made by film students at the London film school about punk, called Punk Kebab," notes Shaw. "We did one track live in the film entitled 'I Don't Wanna Go To Work'. The Nipple Erectors also appeared including Shane MacGowan. I have a DVD of this, it has not yet been on general release."

After the band's dissolution in January 1978 (after a final show at the Paris Gibus Club) Shaw moved on to the Physicals, then, via Brian James and the Brains, the Damned. He is currently a member of Mischief with former Damned bass player Paul Gray. Latter joined the Monotones then the Adverts and Crash resurfaced in the Psychotic Tanks, before becoming a producer whose credits included the Eurythmics and collaborations with Jah Wobble. He also produced and co-wrote the Robert Plant album Now And Zen.

There was a brief reformation in 1991 at which time they handed over enough out-takes and demos, plus the released material, for Released Emotions to put out an album. Long deleted, these tracks were eventually repressed as part of the So Far So Loud CD in 2002.

DISCOGRAPHY:

Chelsea 1977/Ain't No Legend 7-inch (United Artists UP 36327 November 1977) (a demo version of the single, with the misleading declaration 'Release date 28-10-77', includes the original mixes of the songs which were rejected by the band)

IMPORTANT COMPILATION:

Live At The Vortex LP (NEMS 6013 December 1978; 'You Don't Break My Heart', 'I Ain't Gonna Be History') (reissued on CD in 1995 by Anagram)

ARCHIVE RELEASES:

Ain't No Legend LP (Released Emotions REM 006 1991) (contains the single, the Vortex tracks, plus unreleased studio recordings with Dave Goodman. Later reissued by Get Buent So Far So Loud CD reissue)

So Far So Loud CD (Overground OVER77CD October 1998) (comes with a 12-page booklet and liner notes from Shaw)

Martin And The Brownshirts

Norman Graveney (vocals), Paul Urmston (guitar), Addy Adams (bass), Willie 'Wet Eye' Williams (drums)

Chester's MARTIN AND THE BROWNSHIRTS were part of a Lightning Records roster that were but a blip on the punk radar screen – but of those acts the Brownshirts did manage one fantastic punk 45, 'Taxi Driver'. "We saw the film together the week it came out. Next day we wrote the song in about 10 minutes," Williams told MOJO in 2001, who placed it in its 100 Punk Scorchers list. Music publisher and producer Graham Sclater, an organist who toured Germany in the 60s and jammed with Hendrix, managed them. In his role as publisher he'd turned down 'The Birdie Song' – as did just about everyone else – as well as Daniel Miller's first, pre-Mute project, The Normal. He ran Tabitha Music, which issued 'Taxi Driver' in Belgium.

They'd hooked up via Graveney's girlfriend, who designed the single's sleeve. Sclater put them up while they were in Exeter, cutting demos in his studio. He also arranged an audition in Warrington to get the band a tour of Scandinavia – and although they impressed the promoters, "they were rebels" and never took it seriously. Nevertheless, Sclater confirms that they were model houseguests – "a nice bunch of lads".

Their first foray into a proper recording environment was in London to record a song that had been passed around several bands, 'Hey Punk, Punk Off'. But when the producers failed to get a deal for the release of the single, the taste of a "pro" studio encouraged them to write and record their own, "real" songs. Sclater took them into the studio to record the first of these, 'Taxi Driver' and the B-side 'Boring' – deliberately leaving their guitars un-tuned as a punk rock statement of intent. Both were recorded in one session at Gooseberry Studios in Gerard Street, Chinatown, not KPM Studios as has been suggested. On completion they returned to Chester where they made use of the spare time to work on more of their own material. The closed groove 'gong' effect, actually a sustained guitar note, at the end of 'Taxi Driver' was Sclater's idea, which the CD format isn't able to replicate. Sadly, John Lydon, whom they'd met in a café during a break in the session, could not be encouraged to take part in the recording. A tribute to De Niro's dialogue in the film of the same name, 'Taxi Driver' was a little gem, not that it did the group a smidgeon of good. As Williams confirmed to MOJO: "I left school at 16 – two months later I was in London making a record, and two months after that we split up."

They also faced problems because of their name, which attracted the interest of the National Front, particularly at one gig at Liverpool's Swinging Apple, and another at Exeter, where members of the band were beaten up. "They did have problems," Sclater told me. "To be honest, I didn't know what the Brownshirts name signified until I was involved in an attack when I was with the band." Happier times came at the Vortex on New Year's Eve 1978, where Marianne Faithfull popped into their dressing room to express her admiration.

The group decided they'd had it with punk and became Co-Starz, a more power-pop based assemblage. They recorded 12 new tracks at Decibel Studios in Tottenham at a session originally scheduled when they were the Brownshirts. "Norman was always ahead of trends," reckons Sclater, "he just wanted to move on from punk." Graveney and Williams went on to form the Montellas, touring America with Was (Not Was) and recording an album for Arista in 1988.

Discography:

Taxi Driver/Boring 7-inch (Lightning GIL 507 March 1978) (also issued in Belgium on Tabitha, 160.3-180)

COMPILATION:

Lightning Records Punk Collection CD (Anagram CDPUNK 79 1996; 'Taxi Driver')

Masterswitch

M

Jimmy Edwards (vocals), Stephen Wilkin (guitar), Mark Steed (bass), Martin Lee (drums)

MASTERSWITCH were a vehicle for the talents of Jimmy Edwards, a veteran of the music industry who had been in numerous bands since the late 60s. At the age of 16 he was the leader of one of the first mod/skinhead bands, the Neat Change, who were regulars at the Marquee. However, they were pressured into releasing an uncharacteristic single, a psychedelic version of a Peter Frampton song, 'I Lied To Aunty May'. "It will cost you a fortune to find that record now," Edwards notes. "But I think it's shit!"

After the Neat Change, he worked on the soundtrack to the 1970 film Groupie Girl. Again, a copy of the soundtrack album is impossibly rare. He then came under Robert Stigwood's management. "Then one of our managers got shot dead, Rik Gunnell. The Gunnell brothers were big club owners, the Bag Of Nails, the Ricky-Tick, all the big R&B clubs. They looked after Georgie Fame. They amalgamated with the Stigwoods but then Rik Gunnell got shot. I didn't want to stay with them any more...."

Instead he and partner Linton Guest joined ATV as writers, producers and A&R staff. It was actually Guest and Edwards who discovered Carl Douglas's 'Kung Fu Fighting' and persuaded the powers that be that it could be a huge hit. "The label I looked after with Linton was called Dawn, where the Washington Flyers and Stumpy came out. The Washington Flyers single was nearly a hit. It's a bit Roxy Music-like. I was always a bit punky before punk. When punk came along it was great, because I was always out on a limb. I liked listening to the Eagles and stuff but I never liked playing that stuff. Stumpy were a little group that came from somewhere in Devon. Nothing to do with us, the signing of the group. But when we got them in there, they couldn't play! So Linton and I just made the record, wrote it, produced and played it. Along with a guy called Steve Holly who was later in Wings. This is all pre-new wave." Edwards was also involved in signing Ian Dury's Kilburn And The High Roads to Pye Records.

As for Masterswtich, "It was very short-lived. It shouldn't have been. We got a £1 million deal with Epic, but the whole thing got so fucked up. We did a couple of gigs at the Marquee, supporting the Boys and a few other people. We had a girl manager, called Louise, who was a page three pin-up, more of a friend than a manager. Then Keith West, of Teenage Opera took over. He'd had a band called Tomorrow, who had a hit with 'My White Bicycle'. He'd been a friend of mine for years and started to manage us. I was at the Vortex one night with my mate Mark Laff of Generation X. There was a CBS convention going on and we were looking for a deal. We were going to sign with Don Arden, Sharon Osbourne's dad. I met this guy called Bruce, he had a big cowboy hat on. He said, what do you do? I said I write songs, I'm in a group. He said sing me some of the songs now! And I did, I sung 'Action Replay' and some other songs, thinking this has be some kind of joke." This is beginning to sound like Pop Idol. "He gave me a hotel number, and said ring me tomorrow. I want to hear more about what you're doing. I thought, fuck, this is stupid. But I rang him the next morning. He said I'd really like to give you a deal on what I heard last night. He organised a deal and we signed to CBS America, to Epic, and got a massive deal. I don't think it was a great idea – we were playing new wave clubs and we were English. To cut a long story short, we got Vic Maile, who did Live At Leeds for the Who. He produced 'Action Replay'.

"The whole thing went to the group's heads really quickly," explains Edwards. There were shows at the Roxy, Vortex, regular slots at the Marquee and a last stand at the Music Machine, but in the end, only one single ever emerged, and it didn't even have the benefit of a picture sleeve. Wilkin later summed up the Masterswitch story for his website. "Unfortunately we had been signed to the UK office under pressure from a New York A&R man who recognised our stadium potential for the USA; not an ideal situation politically and by June we ran out of steam and broke up." As Edwards remembers: "We just put that one single out and the group got so big for their boots that they'd got such a big deal that I sacked them, basically."

He did contemplate a new line-up, but only briefly. "I was going to do it with Terry Chimes of the Clash. But it was very half-hearted. I'll tell you why. I was absolutely skint. The girl I was living with had two kids and I was really skint. I was doing work with a pop group all the way through this called Flintlock – the biggest group that never was! The band used to write all the songs, and I used to fucking hate the songs. But they could have been good. I used to basically produce them and try to knock the songs into some sort of shape. They just kept offering me work all the time. I remember speaking to Jimmy Pursey saying, what the fuck should I do? I needed the money so I went for the cash and worked with Flintlock for a while. Flintlock bought me out of my contract with CBS. I was really pissed off, because Masterswitch could have gone a long way and should have. It was just one of those things. It all became very calamitous."

Edwards released a succession of solo singles for Warners and Polydor, working as leader of the Profile, including the Jimmy Pursey-produced 'Nora's Diary' which was played regularly by Mike Read. In 1983 he formed Time UK alongside Jam drummer Rick Buckler and Ray Simone on guitar, who had also served time in an earlier incarnation of Masterswitch, before putting together Sharp. Both Steed and Wilkin would work together again in Neo. Edwards was additionally largely responsible for discovering, and tutoring, Sham 69. He played on many of their studio recordings, and helped write some of their early material. He was also married to Honey Bane for a while.

Discography:

Action Replay/Mass Media Meditation 7-inch (Epic EPC 6259 February 1978)

Mean Street

Kenny 'Animal' Bishop (drums), Chris Gorgier (aka French Chris; guitar), Jeremy Harrington (vocals), Gary Webb (aka Gary Valerium, aka Gary Numan; bass)

The first proper band formed by 'Biggles' Numan, MEAN STREET were actually a regular fixture on the punk merry-go-round of the late-70s, playing most of the major venues, notably the Roxy over a dozen times and the Vortex. The latter venue included their 'Bunch Of Stiffs' on its 1978 compilation album. However, by this time Numan had left, the other three having kicked him out. He would later claim that this was due to jealousy caused by his creative stature. Hmmm. After his departure Harrington moved to bass and vocals, and 'Essex Chris' took over on guitar and vocals.

Mean Street was "an uplifting experience for me," notes Harrington. "It was so sincere – the flat we shared, the chords, the riffs – and also so pure – pre-drug youthful energy – lyrics that were naive but relevant, en fin; a really good time." Mean Street continued as a trio until they broke up in April 1978. There was a brief reformation in 1980, but this again came to nothing. "The time I spent with Mean Street was a wonderful time," reflects Harrington, "but the collective manifestation present at the Roxy and Vortex (just over a year before) was gone. There was some extremely interesting music being made, played and recorded at the time, but those furious months between 1976-1977, I think were a return of the early 60s beat/R'n'B club culture. With the benefit of hindsight I can see now that at the time when Wire were recording Pink Flag, Britain was still in post war reconstruction."

The split came about because "basically, Chris got married, and we all felt that the punk scene (as per Live At the Roxy) was over. 'Kev San Juan' (Kevin St John) was no Andy Czezowski, who had made the difference in the first place, and who was in charge when I started going there. Anyway, I remember French Chris and Kenny coming to see me at the Music Machine and telling me that they were still playing. They may have been saying that Mean Street had been revived, but on that particular occasion, we were supporting Jayne County and the dressing room was full of her, the Electric Chairs, sundry hangers-on, etc. That was the last time I saw Chris and Kenny."

After the band's demise Bishop and Gorgier would both join Action Replay, presumably titled in tribute to Masterswitch's sole single, while Harrington moved on to briefly join Gloria Mundi before taking up a more permanent position with Monochrome Set. The boy Webb would go on to perfect his lifelong imitation of David Bowie.

Tubeway Army, Numan's subsequent band, played the Roxy at least four times, twice under misnomers (Two Way Army and Tubala Army). However, Tubeway Army Live At The Roxy, a longstanding bootleg added to the reissue of their eponymous debut, should actually read, Tubeway Army, Live At The Rock Garden 1st February 1978. Bless, they probably couldn't fit all that on the sleeve...

DISCOGRAPHY:

Bunch Of Stiffs 7-inch split single (NEMS NES 115 December 1977) (B-side by the Wasps)

COMPILATION:

Live At The Vortex LP (NEMS NEL 6013 1978; 'Bunch Of Stiffs') (re-released on CD, Anagram CDPUNK 68, in 1995)

The Meat

Mick Wayland (vocals), Brian Early (bass), Mick English (guitar, backing vocals), Brett 'Buddy' Ascott (drums)

From Orpington in Kent, THE MEAT were playing live by the summer of 1977. "We were definitely a punk band from day one," notes Ascott. "I'd only played in a band with people from school before that, doing things like Mountain or Peter Frampton. This was a complete change of direction. I remember what did it for me was watching the Pistols on the London Weekend Show, one Sunday lunchtime. It was the first time since I'd seen footage of the Who in the 60s that I'd seen such aggression. The whole thing had a threatening atmosphere, and it just appealed to me. The first punk band I would have gone to see was the Jam at Bromley College, then the May 1977 Rainbow gig, with the Clash, Jam, Buzzcocks, Subway Sect and Prefects." Ah, the famous gig where all the seats were ripped out? "I was upstairs and I was responsible for a whole row of those seats going over! I think it was shortly after that I joined the Meat."

As the most popular local band alongside the Mistakes, they played several shows at the Orpington Civic Hall, including a support to Penetration. "Which was memorable," reckons Ascott, "because we all had the hots for Pauline Murray, as you do. But we played the Civic Hall twice or three times. There was nearly always a fight. But then there was at most gigs then." There were further shows at the Roxy, where they managed to get banned, though a quarter of a century on, through the haze of drugs and drink, for what reasons Ascott cannot remember, plus another support slot to Penetration at the Vortex. By that time the Meat had written an extensive set of originals, including 'Sulphate City', 'Meet The Meat', 'Sunday Papers' and 'One Alternative'. "The only two covers we used to do were 'All Day And All Of

The Night', and I think we tried to do 'I Gotta Move', the Kinks song. But we couldn't do that cos it was too difficult. Like I say, we weren't very accomplished musicians! Mick Wayland wrote the lyrics, and Mick English wrote most of the music if I remember. All we've got is two four-song demos. One was recorded in a crappy little eight-track studio in Crystal Palace, the other one I can't remember. But I've got copies of those. They are very rough and ready!"

However, by the summer of 1978, with the addition of Kevin Peters of the Heroes, the Meat transmuted into Nada, who ended up marooned in Paris that June. "We put all our stuff into the back of a van, went across the Channel, and were on our way to Hamburg. We did one gig at the Gibus Club in Paris. And the first night, there was a riot, Mick jumped into the crowd, someone pulled a knife, they destroyed all the equipment, and Lenny our manager – who is now dead, and he was one evil bastard, nasty piece of work – he reckoned he'd had his passport stolen that night. So we couldn't go any further. So we did a three-night residency at the Gibus Club, and got stranded in Paris for six weeks with no money or food. We were going to a baker's, running in and stuffing our coats with bread and chocolate and running out again. It was a terrible time. I got caught stealing from a supermarket." Mais non! La French police cells are not noted for being very alluring places, n'est-ce pas? "The good thing was I was rescued by this old boy, he was in the French Resistance. He managed to talk the manager out of calling the police. Otherwise I might still be banged up!"

Stuck in Paris, they also took part in a huge open-air festival in front of 15,000 people. "We got booked on this festival, run by Liberation, the left-wing newspaper. We were supposed to go on about two in the afternoon. But they delayed it. We'd taken some speed, so we took some more speed. We were supposed to go on at six, then they delayed it again, so we took some more speed. We ended up going on about midnight." By which time they must have been like clockwork mice. "Absolutely! Frothing at the mouth! The stage was surrounded by Hell's Angels and Teddy Boys. Someone threw a bottle, and Mick made the mistake of throwing it back. Within five minutes, the whole stage was covered in people fighting, and I was hitting people with cymbals etc. And this hand appeared through the crowd holding a spray and I got tear-gassed."

The Paris debacle came about because their manager was more interested in splitting the band up than keeping it on track. "It was all done on the hoof. He was trying to pry Mick Wayland away. I don't think he liked the rest of us, I think we were too much of a handful for him. So he wanted to concentrate on Mick Wayland as a solo punk star!" Eventually Mick English moved on. "He joined Splogenessabounds (Max Splodge is from Orpington too). I remember seeing him on Top Of The Pops wearing tights!" The remaining quartet resumed as the Bombshells, and found themselves supporting Wayne County in October and the Tourists at the Music Machine. But again, it didn't happen. Ascott would go on to join the Chords. "I'd had enough. It was a bit shambolic and amateur. So I saw an advert for the Chords in January 1979 in Melody Maker, and that's where I went."

As for the other members: "I haven't seen Mick English for 15 years. Brian joined another band that I saw at Dartford Zen's. Nice bloke, Brian, always reminded me of Brian Glover. When he played the character in Porridge who says, 'I read a book once. It had a green cover!' A gentle soul."

Medium Medium

John Rees Lewis (vocals, saxophone), Neil Campsie (guitar), Alan Turton (bass, backing vocals), Nigel Stone (percussion). Campsie left in March 1979, with Andy Ryder joining on guitar and vocals in February 1979. Graham Spink responsible for 'special sounds' between February and July 1979

MEDIUM MEDIUM occupied similar post-punk territory to the Pop Group, Gang Of Four, etc, though operating out of Nottingham meant they never quite registered on the post-punk radar to the same extent as those peers. This fact has not been rectified in either Simon Reynolds' Rip It Up And Start Again or genre surveys such as In The Beginning There Was Rhythm. Yet their 'extreme dance music' (or 'free-blown dubbed-up white funk' according to the NME) shared similar punk roots, was aimed similarly at the dancefloor as well as the intellect, and produced one bona fide

era classic, 'Hungry, So Angry'. Converts to the latter included writer Robert Christgau and Coldcut, who included the single on a CD of their formative influences.

The band formed out of the remnants of the Press, active since 1976, who specialised in a blend of punk and rhythm and blues. But with the possibilities opened up by first the advent of punk, and then the black hole of its subsequent artistic collapse, Medium Medium was formed. They dedicated themselves to the art of making a noise that was at once both alarming and seductive, notably in extended instrumental passages featuring multi-layered rhythms, careering saxophone and treated electronica.

They made their debut in 1979 with 'Them Or Me' on the London independent Apt Records, a song which later transferred to the hip (not least with Mr Peel) regional compilation Hicks From The Sticks. From there they branched out from local venues the Sandpiper and Hearty Goodfellow to shows around London, including the Nashville, Hope 'n' Anchor and Rock Garden. They also immersed themselves in the Rock Against Racism movement and appeared as support to reggae acts including Aswad, Prince Far I, Creation Rebel, etc. They were support to U2 at two of their earliest London shows, the Moonlight Club and Clarendon. The latter provided a night that "... urged you to observe that these bands were not ordinary," noted Phil Sutcliffe, reviewing the show for Sounds. Medium Medium would also subsequently support U2 on the English leg of their Boy tour.

As the band developed, they incorporated soul influences (Chairmen Of The Board, Ashford And Simpson) while lyrics steered clear of contemporary polemic and focused instead on personal and emotional conflicts, indecision, apprehension and individuality. All of which was perfectly condensed into its February 1981 debut for Cherry Red, 'Hungry, So Angry'. This immediately took off in America, where its 'popping' bass sound was widely admired and duplicated, and it made the top fifty of the Billboard Disco chart.

Debut album The Glitterhouse followed in October 1981, by which time Steve Harvey had replaced Stone. "Sour morality tales from grubby emotional backstreets," noted Dave Hill of the NME in his review of the album, while Phil Sutcliffe praised the "savage" and "scalding" nature of its sonic constitution in Sounds. Touring the album in America that December, Lewis announced his intention to leave on the band's return, going on to explore world music with fellow departee Nigel Stone in C Cat Trance.

M

The remaining members persevered for several European and American tours before recruiting Les Barrett on guitar and keyboards, in April 1982, who appeared on their next release, 'If You Touched Her She'd Smear' for Sound Products. This came about during a break

in a Dutch tour, from which the posthumous live album, Live In Holland, was culled in 1988. Barrett was replaced on keyboards by Julie Wood prior to their 1982 tour of America. As Turton recalled, "Our first tour after John left was America in early 1982. We had to start the tour sharing backline equipment with our support band, Ministry, after our manager and tour manager crashed the van carrying our rented gear while driving from New York to meet us in Chicago. It was on that same tour that John Cale befriended us. He invited us to a very late-night recording session at Sky Line Studios in Manhattan. As far as anyone knows, the recordings never made it onto his next release, Music For A New Society."

There were management shuffles and sessions for a prospective second album but by the summer of 1983, the group had sundered. Barrett and former manager Chris Garland formed U-Bahn X, a project to which various former members of Medium Medium would contribute, as well as former Slits and Pop Group manager Dick O'Dell. Ryder worked with the Scarehunters and then became Wycliffe's musical director, and is currently a composer for film and TV. Harvey joined former compatriots in C Cat Trance before relocating to Los Angeles and working with the Mirrors. Lewis took a PhD in social psychology in 2002. Stone eventually left C Cat Trance to bring up a family and plays in local country bands.

In 2004 Medium Medium, comprising Lewis, Turton, Ryder and Harvey, discussed the idea of a reunion. The result was a series of shows on both the east and west coasts of America, before, in mid-2006, they entered the studio to record a planned year's end release.

DISCOGRAPHY:

Them Or Me/Freeze 7-inch (Apt SAP 01 1979)

Hungry, So Angry/Nadsat Dream 7-inch (Cherry Red CHERRY 18 1981) (also released by Cachalot, USA, as a four-track 12-inch in 1981. Re-released in 2004 by Punk Disco Beat with B-side by the Monks – 'I Can Do Anything')

The Glitterhouse LP (Cherry Red BRED 19 1981)

If You Touched Her She'd Smear/Splendid Isolation 7-inch (Sound Products; Hol; Intercord; Ger; 1982) (also released as a 12-inch single with additional track '7th Floor')

Archive Releases:

Live In Holland LP and CD (Trance/Line; Ger; 1988)

The Glitterhouse & Plus LP and CD (Trance/LINE; Ger; 1988)

Hungry, So Angry CD (Cherry Red CDMRED 182 2001) (a pretty much ideal 15-track compilation that covers just about everything you need)

IMPORTANT COMPILATION:

Hicks From The Sticks LP (Rockburgh ROC 11 1980; 'Them Or Me')

Mekons

Jon Langford (drums, vocals), Tom Greenhalgh (guitar, vocals), and a cast of thousands

"The MEKONS are the most revolutionary group in the history of rock'n'roll. They are also the finest artists ever to have graced this admittedly somewhat degenerate form with the grace of their aesthetic sensibilities, rarefied as a glimpse through a butterfly's wing. The muses gobbled cantharides for these fellows. Collectively they compromise a kind of Sistine Chapel ceiling neath which the pathetic mess of pottage which is commonly snickered off as the 'rock scene'. from PiL to Black Oak Arkansas, can but swash buboed forearms cross their offal-crusted snouts and recommence to grovel together in the La Brea-trackless depths of corporate swill." (Lester Bangs)

Well, there you go. The most celebrated (and to many, over-rated) journo in the history of rock'n'roll deifies the most outlandish but stubborn band of non-conformists in rock'n'roll and the world pays little heed but dedicated cultists, and culturalists, drool. And I go to the trouble of looking up cantharides in a dictionary and still have no clue whatsoever as to what he's talking about. But that shouldn't put you off the Mekons, their name taken from the dreaded foe of British comic book hero Dan Dare. "He was like a Nazi-stroke-Communist bogeyman," Langford later recalled to Option. "And Dan Dare was like a Battle Of Britain fighter pilot who somehow got into outer space – sort of a British imperialist fantasy." Here were punk's playful purists, musical and sociological scholars who turned out, of all the bands of 1977, to be the ones to keep the flame burning, close on three decades after their inception. In that time they have veered far away from their original thrashy agit pop incarnation, and now are more likely to be found caressing a ukulele or banjo than slashing away at a Woolworth's guitar. History is habitually written by the victors, but perhaps not in this case.

The Mekons were formed in Leeds in 1977 by art students Tom Greenhalgh and Jon Langford as part of a punk scene forming around the local university campus, which also birthed the Gang Of Four and Delta Five. Langford, as well as putative Mekons Mark White and Andy Corrigan, was in the fine art department alongside Andy Gill and Jon King of Gang Of Four. "Basically, we didn't do any art, we just formed a band," Langford later conceded to Perfect Sound Forever. The original inspiration can be traced back to the Sex Pistols' Anarchy tour. "It was like a package," Greenhalgh recalled to Option, "and it came around to Leeds in about December of 1976 and it was the first punk thing – and then about May of 1977 we had a band. Suddenly it seemed possible." Later member Kevin Lycett also attended that Pistols show, wearing a tampon earring for effect. For his part, Langford had moved to Leeds on the Sunday following the Grundy story breaking in the national press.

Their formation came about, bass player and concurrent Delta Five vocalist Ros Allen later recalled, because the Mekons had "been to see a band at the F Club, which was a popular punk venue, and had managed to get themselves on the bill the following week supporting the Rezillos. They had to get a set together really quickly and as they didn't have a bass player they asked me; they knew I used to play the cello. That gig went surprisingly well. Bob Last, who was the Rezillos' tour manager, was about to start his own label, Fast Product, and approached the Mekons that night." The Mekons quickly reassessed their stated manifesto that they would never release a record and only exist as a support band. However, Jon Langford, in response to Bryan Swirksy's questioning for the Big Takeover, reckons that this was at least their second performance, following an opening show at the Ace Of Clubs, also run by F Club promoter John Keenan. "It was fantastic! We told him that we were the only punk band that played slow songs. He was like, 'You can't play then. You can only play fast'. So we went and rehearsed all the songs fast. We danced on the stage and this bloke Simon Snake and his two handmaidens – who were called Rats and Delicious – hopped on. They had the whole punk thing down. They dressed the part. It was great."

Their debut was the first single on Last's influential but short-lived Fast Product. "I still like the record," Last later recalled to Brian Hogg, "but we did meet resistance. Geoff Travis says he absolutely cannot remember this but when my partner, Hillary Morrison, took a suitcase full to Rough Trade, he said 'These people can't play. I'm not going to stock this, it's terrible.' That was a shock because we thought that if you had some kind of attitude and wanted to communicate it, that was it. You could get all the musical element together later. However, in some ways it helped us focus on what we did because we now knew we couldn't rely on these people down there."

Rough and ready, and lo-fi before that description begat a genre, the standout was '32 Weeks', which detailed the exact levels of labour time required to purchase different consumer durables. 'Never Been In A Riot' was a sublime response to the Clash's 'White Riot'. "Different people in the Mekons liked different bands," Greenhalgh later confirmed to Pioneer Press. "I really liked the Buzzcocks. It was a very fluid, creative time. Alliances shifted subtly all the time, but basically punk meant just doing your thing, so it wasn't really about having to fit in with anything." Many thought that the rudimentary nature of the songs, recorded over a weekend, was some sort of art school joke. But as Langford would later confirm, no, they were playing as best they could.

Following a further single, 'Where Were You', they signed to Virgin and expanded the band to include Andy Carrigan on vocals, Kevin Lycett on guitar, alongside Allen on bass. Their relationship with Virgin was only ever going to be temporary, but it did span two singles and their debut album, The Quality Of Mercy Is Not Strnen, its title a play on the old adage about a room full of monkeys eventually coming up with the works of Shakespeare given infinite time (or the entire works of Sham 69 given five minutes). The songs retained the group's sense of musical abandon, unregulated by such throwbacks as song structure. And while they didn't duplicate the overtly political line taken by the Gang Of Four, they shared many of the same sentiments and also took inspiration from their peers' choppy, harsh funk. And, of course, the Gang Of Four were also pictured on the back cover. "People always thought that was us,"

Langford later told Option. "Virgin obviously did when they put that record out without even talking to us about it." Listening now, it's a messy affair, with lashings of self-deprecation, but at heart this was a band trying to escape their shackles rather than have them gold-plated. It was recorded, at great expense, at Richard Branson's Manor Studio. Which was "pointless", according to Langford, though the band did have fun killing time driving go-karts between takes. "Virgin had no idea what was going on," he told Bryan Swirsky. "We never really liked the sound of it. We thought it sounded bad. And now if I listen to it, it sounds even worse. But I liked the songs."

It seemed to all concerned that the end was nigh, and their disenchantment with the path punk had taken underscored their decision to put the band on hold. Or it would have done, had not Andy Gill's girlfriend booked them on two tours of Europe in 1980. Then Gang Of Four themselves took them to New York to play at Hurrah's on a bill that also featured the Au Pairs on New Year's Eve 1980, their performance caught by Jerry Wexler as well as soon-to-be superfan Lester Bangs. And from then on the wagon kept a rolling, or at least stuttering. Langford, Greenhalgh and Lycett would continue to work with a bewildering variety of accomplices, not to mention record labels ("We look for honesty, but have yet to find it..."). Despite some excellent releases and a fanbase including the likes of Village Voice critic Robert Christgau, when most acknowledged their continued existence it was with a degree of surprise. However, from the mid-80s onwards this most idiosyncratic of fringe bands gravitated towards mainstream acceptance not by choice, but because of the incremental increase in quality of their recordings.

The subsequent Mekons oeuvre is largely fantastic, but it veers so far away from the punk idiom that it would be inappropriate to discuss it further here. Well, I'd love to. But it's a word count thing.

SELECT DISCOGRAPHY:

(Buyer's Guide: If you're not familiar with the Mekons, their albums visit such disparate points musically that the best plan is to get the sampler Heaven And Hell and take it from there. Having said that, Fear And Whiskey should win over even the hardest of heart and hearing, while Punk Rock does do a good job of placing the band's punk rock past in context)

M

Never Been In A Riot/32 Weeks/Heart and Soul 7-inch (Fast Product FAST 1 January 1978)

Where Were You/I'll Have To Dance Then On My Own 7-inch (Fast Product FAST 7 December 1978)

Work All Week/Unknown Wrecks 7-inch (Virgin VS 300 September 1979)

The Quality Of Mercy Is Not Strnen LP (Virgin V 2143 February 1980)

Relevant Archive Releases:

Punk Rock CD (Quarterstick QS82CD January 2004) ("The Mekons were very interested in punk rock and punk rock was very interested in them for a few glistening months back in the white powdery heat of late 1970s anarchy UK... The Mekons wrote these songs THEN and recorded them NOW." So say the sleevenotes)

Heaven & Hell – The Very Best Of The Mekons double CD (Cooking Vinyl COOKCD 315 December 2004) (pretty much the definitive intro to a band with an output surpassed only by the Fall, though fans will argue long and hard around the track selection and the sleevenotes could have been meatier. Still, at less than a tenner, a bargain)

Members

Nicky Tesco (vocals), Jean-Marie Carroll (guitar), Nigel Bennett (replacing Gary Baker who left before 'Solitary Confinement'; guitar), Adrian Lillywhite (drums), Chris Payne (bass)

The MEMBERS belong in that dodgy dossier marked "Were they or weren't they?" with regard to punk. But they had closer associations to the movement than say, the Boomtown Rats or Elvis Costello. And if we were to judge punk credentials (what a concept) by inclusion on best-of-punk-rock compilations, 'Sound Of The Suburbs' would get them there in a jiffy. In actual fact, it's been used as the title of at least two such artefacts as well as a radio show and a TV programme presented by John Peel. "I feel we were a punk band," Tesco told me. "I define that as a UK band of that time who still saw the potential of the changes going down and not the second wave of lumpen punks who boiled it down to sub-Pistols riffing, Mohicans and studded leathers."

OK boys, you're in. Who's behind this operation? I'll tell you what I know. The Members were formed in Camberley, Surrey in the summer of 1977 as part of the ripple effect of punk's first wave, though the band were a little older, and more cerebral, than some of the upstarts doing the rounds. As Nicky Tesco, a political science graduate working as an insurance salesman, would admit: "I used to look at groups and things and think, 'I want to do it.' I'd have daydreams of me being onstage doing it and enjoying it. And I did it and I haven't any real talent, except I blag well." He certainly did – the Members came about because he'd started telling everyone he'd formed a band and eventually had to get round to proving it. He'd been approached by one Mike Kingsley while sat at a typewriter at a rehearsal studio and asked what he was doing. He replied that he was writing lyrics, and was duly invited to audition the following week. So he set about bringing together a band that encompassed his central influences, the Stranglers and Jamaican DJs Big Youth and U-Roy.

He linked with bass player Steve Morley and a drummer, Clive Parker. "Clive Parker was a cunt," Tesco informed me, delicately, "and was kicked out of the band soon after. Steve Morley introduced me to Adrian Lillywhite (brother of producer Steve) who didn't hesitate to join the band. We'd turned up at his parents' house quite late at night and his mum had invited us in as Adrian was out; she was very thrilled at the idea that we'd come round to invite her son to join a band and plied us with drinks and snacks. I always liked his mum. JC joined the band on my instigation. (Bank clerk Jean-Marie Carroll, who was born in England the son of an expatriate Belgian who'd come to Britain to fly Spitfires, had formerly recorded demos with Graham Parker) I'd always seen him around at parties and heard him playing his wild songs and he'd always had a lot of style. The fact that he couldn't play guitar was not a problem for me, though it was for Gary Baker." Within a short space of time BA technician Chris Payne had taken over on bass and Nigel Bennett had taken over from Baker.

Their first show came at the Roxy in July 1977. Punk mecca or toilet? "It was a toilet," admits Tesco, "though it had romance. I drank a huge amount of beer and it was the last time I ever went on stage in that state. It was also the night I got the name 'Tesco' – a supermarket chain in the UK – after blagging drinks all night in a place where the bands never got free drinks." Their recorded debut followed with the anti-National Front tract, 'Fear On The Streets', on Beggars Banquet's legendary Streets compilation (several discographies mistakenly list 'Fear On The Streets' as an abandoned debut single on Ed Hollis's XS label). Stiff Records were impressed enough with their goofy punk-pop-reggae to offer them a one-off single deal in early 1978. Although they could boast a strong live following, the majors had repeatedly passed on the Members, being a little bemused as to what they actually represented. The result was the splendid 'Solitary Confinement', produced by former Pink Fairy Larry Wallis, a bleak narrative of bedsit land laid bare, with some deft observations about moving to London but not getting invited to the party. Any party. It was written by Carroll and Tesco, who confessed to Noise For Heroes that the song was indeed "about my experiences coming to live in a bedsit in London at the age of 18. The boss of Stiff at the time was a guy called Dave Robinson, a tough Irishman who according to legend had started as a roadie for Jimi Hendrix and then rose to the height of barman at a famous music pub called the Hope And Anchor. Eventually he got into music management and managed my old mate Graham Parker. It was Graham who, I believe, persuaded Dave to give us a break – £150 to record a single... the original version is scratchy but has charm. We were overjoyed to have a single out on Stiff. They were the place to be." However, it was not to be a lasting relationship. Although they were now done with Stiff, Payne and Carroll would also contribute to the Stiff project Children Of 7 (one single, 'Solidarity').

Virgin picked up the band for their second single, the enduring 'Sound Of The Suburbs', which could have been a horrible cliché save for the group's rousing delivery and lyrics which perfectly encapsulated the perma-gloom surrounding weekdays in commuter land. The Broadmoor reference was drawn from the fact that every time there was an escape from the local high security mental institution, a siren would sound, and this was tested at 10am every Monday morning. In many ways it could have been Surrey's national anthem. It was only when they played it live at the Marquee that they realised its hit potential. It shot into the Top 20, peaking at number 12 after a nine-week stay, selling 250,000 copies in the process.

Their debut album, At The Chelsea Nightclub, was produced by Adrian's brother Steve

Lillywhite, long before he would hit paydirt with U2 et al. It is, in many ways compelling, not least on 'Sally', written by departed guitarist Baker about a young girl's dream gone sour, and a new version of 'Solitary Confinement', featuring sax player Rudi Thompson from X-Ray Spex. There was further pleasing variety in dub rocker 'Electricity' and the class-conscious 'Don't Push'. The album's title-track was recorded live while the band toured with Devo. "It was an insane set closer," Tesco confirmed to Noise For Heroes. "In fact so insane that on one occasion at a gig in Edinburgh, where we had the Skids on stage with us, JC threw his guitar in the air where it tangled in some netting and came down on my head. My head opened like a ripe peach and Huwie, our road manager, had to rush me to hospital. As I was being taken out there was a whole bunch of young kids who couldn't get into the gig who asked me to bleed on their posters." In the meantime their run of three John Peel sessions began in January 1979, followed shortly by a session for Andy Peebles (there were later ones, too, for Mike Read and two for Richard Skinner).

But their momentum was derailed by the follow-up. 'Offshore Banking Business' was their attempt at a straight reggae song with complex harmonies and lyrics detailing tax fraud and corruption. Virgin hated the idea. Bahrain banned the single (which must have really hit sales figures...) It was brave. It was ambitious. It was influential, as acknowledged by Jerry Dammers and others in the nascent 2-Tone movement. It was the closest thing in the punk canon to 10cc's 'Dreadlock Holiday'. And it bombed, effectively, failing to breach the Top 30, making it one of punk's most glorious failures. It was the start of their problems with Virgin, who refused to release their choice of follow-up single, 'Goodbye To The Job'. "There was a lot of shit around that time with everyone wanting to keep this so-called cred and not rip off 'the kids'," Tesco told me. "The fact is we should have followed up 'Suburbs' with the re-recorded 'Solitary Confinement' and then maybe another track off the album before going to 'Offshore'. The fact is we had more faith in 'the kids' than they did in us!" A headlining show at the Lyceum was poorly attended and Chris Payne dropped out of their UK tour due to nervous exhaustion. Paul Gray of Eddie And The Hot Rods and JC's brother Paddy, who also played with the Outpatients, who could have been massive according to Tesco had not their drummer got wrecked with nerves and blown their showcase gig, stood in for him to complete the dates.

Two further singles, 'Killing Time', produced by Jam producer Vic Coppersmith-Heaven, and the skewed, ska-influenced 'Romance', prefaced a second album, The Choice Is Yours, in April 1980. The band had wanted to stick with Vic Coppersmith-Heaven but he'd been booked to record a live album for the Jam, so Virgin, rather than waiting, pushed them into the studio with Rupert Hine. Nick Tesco had desperately wanted to go with the legendary Jamaican producer Niney the Observer, as the two of them had been hanging out together. Virgin "were worried at the idea of the notorious weed smoking Members being left to their own devices with one of JA's finest." The resulting album was slightly thinner gruel than their ebullient debut, though there are still some fine moments of comedy and bathos. The opening instrumental, 'The Ayatollah Harmony', sets a light-hearted tone, while 'Brian Was' beautifully encapsulated the humdrum existence of the drone worker ("He had got a memo. He would obey") which culminated in said bank clerk jumping out of a window. This was written from Carroll's own bitter experience. A version of producer Larry Wallis's wonderful 'Police Car' provided another highlight, and there was also a guest appearance from Joe Jackson. The album came with a free 'Members' tie. Tesco suggested they give away a Specials' tie instead, as an ironic comment on marketing excess. But of more import was the fact that the band were unhappy with the final production. "Steve (Lillywhite) was living the life and walking the walk," Tesco lamented to Noise For Heroes. "He was immersed in the whole scene, was hungry for it and knew what we were like. The second album we did was with Rupert Hine and it was sonically a fucking disaster. He's a very nice guy but didn't have a clue what we were about. In fact it wasn't until after the album was in the can that he saw us live. He came up to me after the gig and apologised. 'If I'd seen you live before we went into the studio I would have made a completely different record' were his exact words." Tesco told me his principal objections were that "It lacked life, it lacked spirit, it sounded polite, restrained and had nothing of us, in terms of attitude, in it anywhere."

There was a last double-pack single for Virgin, headed by the album's 'Flying Again', plus remakes of 'Rat Up A Drainpipe' and 'Love In A Lift'. The disco pastiche 'Disco Oui Oui' actually featured the sound of a band member urinating into a dustbin, such was their inclination to see how far they could push things. They then toured America to excellent reviews, but they were dropped by Virgin after they'd informed them they were looking for new management. "For 18 months the band lived hand-to-mouth, earning a good living through gigging," Tesco told me, "and in between they disappeared down into a basement under a friend's clothes shop on Portobello Road and wrote a new set and a new direction." Their next single 'Working Girl' came out on Albion in 1981, produced by Steve Lillywhite, who had stepped into the breach as a favour to the band. A re-recorded version, produced by Martin Rushent, became a US hit on its re-release in 1983, and was one of the most played videos on the new MTV channel. Martin Rushent then signed them to his Genetic label, via the Members' new manager Ian Grant, and the band were able to prosper on the back of their own tours and help from Virgin Publishing that financed a series of European dates.

Rushent's label released what was to be the band's last album through Arista in America, Uprhythm, Downbeat, which featured horns and synth-dance trimmings; it was eventually released in Britain as Going West, but not before all momentum had been spurned. In essence it was a Martin Rushent record, his attempt to repeat the formula with which he'd enjoyed huge success with the Human League. It wasn't an easy fit for the Members who were always at their most captivating as a result of their rough edges and sonic informality, and the band's core fans hated it. The critics weren't too kind either, including the NME's Mat Snow. "Once upon a time I thought the Members fell between the stools of the Clash and the Boomtown Rats. Little has changed, except you might throw in the Barron Knights for good measure... The Members could once have been contenders, but now they're well on their way to Palookaville. It's usually a one-way trip." Just as 'Working Girl' was becoming a hit in the US any chance of the band capitalising on its success was scuppered by Arista's distribution problems. However, by now the writing was not so much on the wall as tattooed inside their eyelids and the group broke up shortly after its release. As the candid Tesco pointed out to Q, "We split up due to lack of success."

On their return from their last American tour a shell-shocked Tesco walked away and disappeared. There had been "enough drinking, whoring and drug taking" and he wanted to "refocus". It took some time. Carroll briefly formed JC's Mainmen, recorded with Johnny Thunders, Glen Matlock, Transvision Vamp and Frank Tovey, then formed Cajun band the Wise Monkeys as a multi-instrumentalist. He also worked as accordionist on the soundtrack to movies including Loch Ness and Don Juan De Marco. Meanwhile he set up business running The Dispensary boutiques in London and travelled the world as an international fashion buyer.

Tesco had cut a single with New York rapper J Walter Negro, 'Cost Of Living', prior to leaving for the Members' last tour. The track came out with no fanfare and it looked promising until he discovered J Walter in bed with his then girlfriend. Thereafter he wrote and produced with the Leningrad Cowboys, acted with Finnish auteur and Cannes prize winner, Aki Kaurismaki (Leningrad Cowboys Go America and I Hired A Contract Killer), did some work with Spizz, Glenn Gregory of Heaven 17 and Harriet Roberts. He also wrote and produced material for internationally renowned artists like Ute Lemper and Udo Lindenberg. In 1999 he took up a job with Music Week, where he continues to this day. Nigel Bennett did studio sessions with Hugh Cornwell, Joan Armatrading, Stephen Duffy, Julian Lennon and Tom Robinson as well as joining the Vibrators for a while. Adrian Lillywhite also worked with Julian Lennon as well as appearing on Bruce Foxton's solo releases and then joined King. He would subsequently work in A&R for Chrysalis before setting up management company Hit The Beat. Payne formed the short-lived The Men Who Came In From The Cold in 1986 (alongside Carroll) before returning to work as an electrician and opening a jewellery business.

The Members were one of those bands that used humour to make their point. Does Tesco think that because they did so, critics and audiences somehow got the impression that you weren't serious about what you were doing? "Yeah, but that was mainly JC's thing, to be honest. He had a thing that we ought to have humour in everything while I wanted to be a bit more serious. I don't know who was right." So would they ever consider reuniting for a wee comeback? There's money in them thar nostalgia hills. "Never. I remember when we were first starting and I saw this billboard outside one of those sad venues that advertised a 60s Night starring The Swinging Blue Jeans and I swore I'd never, ever, do anything like that. The idea of a bunch of overweight middle-aged blokes running around playing songs that were relevant in their twenties fills me with horror."

DISCOGRAPHY:

M

Solitary Confinement/Rat Up A Drainpipe 7-inch (Stiff ONE 3 May 1978)

The Sound Of The Suburbs/Handling The Big Jets 7-inch (Virgin VS 242 January 1979)

Offshore Banking Business/Solitary Confinement 7-inch (Virgin VS 248 March 1979) (also released on 12-inch, Virgin VS 248 12, with extended dub mix)

At The Chelsea Nightclub LP (Virgin V 2120 April 1979) (note: US track listing is different. Reissued in 1980 and again in 1984, Virgin OVED 44, 1990. Reissued on CD in September 2005 by Captain Oi!, AHOY CD 271, with bonus tracks 'Fear On The Streets', 'Solitary Confinement (Stiff single version)', Rat Up A Drainpipe (Stiff single version)', 'The Sound Of The Suburbs (single version)', 'Handling The Big Jets (live)', 'Offshore Banking Business (7-inch single version)', 'Solitary Confinement (new 7-inch version)', Offshore Banking Business – Pennies In The Pound (12-inch version)'. Sleevenotes written by moi in collaboration with Nicky Tesco)

Killing Time/G.L.C. 7-inch (Virgin VS 292 September 1979)

Romance/Ballad Of John And Martin 7-inch (Virgin VS 333 March 1980)

1980 – The Choice Is Yours LP (Virgin V 2153 April 1980) (Initial copies came with a Members' tie. Reissued in 1991 on CD. CDPVD 310. Reissued again on CD in September 2005 by Captain Oi!, AHOY CD 273, with bonus tracks 'GLC', 'Killing Time', 'Ballad Of John & Martin', 'Disco Oui Oui', 'Love In A Lift (Soul Version)', 'Rat Up A Drainpipe (new version)'. Sleevenotes written by the author, this time with JC)

Flying Again/Disco Oui Oui/Love In A Lift/Rat Up A Drainpipe double 7-inch (Virgin VS 352 May 1980)

Working Girl/Holiday In Tanganika 7-inch (Albion ION 1012 May 1981) (also issued as a 12-inch single, Albion 12 1012, with extra track 'Everybody's A Holiday')

Radio/If You Can't Stand Up 7-inch (Island WIP 6773 April 1982)

Working Girl/The Family 7-inch (Albion ION 1050 July 1983) (new version. Also released as 12-inch single, 12ION 1050, with bonus track 'The Arcade')

Going West/Membership 7-inch (Albion 1ON 153 August 1983) (also released as a 12-inch, 12ION 153)

Going West LP (Albion ALB 115 August 1983) (released in the US as Uprhythm Downbeat. Reissued on CD in February 2006 by Captain Oi!, AHOY CD 280, with bonus tracks 'Working Girl (original single version)', 'Holiday In Tanganika', 'Every Day Is Just A Holiday', 'If You Can't Stand Up', 'At The Arcade', 'Membership'. This time, as it was the third in the trilogy, we got both Nicky and JC involved in the sleevenotes)

ARCHIVE RELEASES:

At The Chelsea Nightclub/1980 – The Choice Is Yours CD (Virgin CDOVD 310 February 1991) (compiles both Virgin albums, now deleted)

Sound Of The Suburbs – A Collection Of The Members' Finest Moments CD (Virgin CDOVD 455 1995)
Res-Erected CD (EMI 5906592 February 2005) (It took a while but at last a serviceable Members compilation, notably because it's the first time the single version of 'Sound Of The Suburbs' actually appeared – all those compilation versions are taken from the album track. Also includes the overlong 12-inch take on 'Offshore Banking Business'. Who came up with that title, though?)
IMPORTANT COMPILATIONS:
Streets LP (Beggars Banquet BEGA 1 1977; 'Fear On The Streets')

Membranes

John Robb (vocals, bass), Mark Tilton (guitar), Martin Critchley (vocals), Martin Kelly (drums)

The idea for the MEMBRANES germinated as early as 1977, but John Robb had neither the band mates, musical instruments or social cache to do much about it. Eventually he persuaded his mate Mark Tilton, who lived a few doors down Anchorsholme Lane in Blackpool, that he should be the guitarist. Further inspiration came from watching the Stranglers, or "the fat men in black", play Lancaster University. In an ensuing biology lesson the term Membranes was seized upon, as were classmates Martin Critchley and Martin Kelly, who took on vocals and drums respectively. Their first show was on 13 June 1979 at Kirkham Palms. They played a few haphazard gigs in this formation but Critchley was neither a particularly confident nor able vocalist, and Kelly soon switched to cheapo synthesizer. So 13-year-old Coofy Sid (nee Andrew Coulthart) manned the drumkit.

Robb marshalled the troops into recording a demo of 'Ice Age', a "doom ridden thing with a semi-funk bass line". Displaying the up and at 'em vigour which would distinguish his multifarious subsequent careers, he immediately sought to get it released. The idea of a compilation EP dawned. Local acts Syntax, newly formed from original 'Pool punk band Zyklon B, came on board, as did the pre-Factory Section 25 and Ken Turner Set. Meanwhile Robb started Blackpool Rox fanzine, one of the most messy, fun, bitchy, halfway-legible zines of the punk-indie era. All of which served as a springboard for Robb's subsequent career as blitzkrieging pop journo.

M

The Membranes' debut own-name release was a flexidisc comprising 'Fashionable Junkies' and 'Almost China'. Meanwhile they continued gigging and rehearsing in Tilton's dad's garage, and soon had a set of originals together. The subsequent 'Muscles', released again on the local Vinyl Drip imprint, not only got a single of the week award from Dave McCullough in Sounds, but repeated John Peel sponsorship. At this stage Kelly left to design shoes and concentrate on his academic career, while Steve Farmery came in to play additional guitar. Rondolet Records signed them and reissued 'Muscles' as both a 7-inch and 12-inch. 1982's 'Pin Stripe Hype' EP was well-reviewed, with Robb's 'High Street Yanks' garnering most of the attention. But Rondolet's inept distribution and publicity failed to give the record the requisite nudge.

Farmery's tenure was a brief one as the band was moving away from their original messy pop aesthetic to a more discordant sonic base – Captain Beefheart as a soundtrack to Blackpool's seaside chintz, or the north west's very own Zen Penny Arcade. They moved to another ill-fated indie, Criminal Damage. Their experiences there, notwithstanding dodgy accounting, poor production and non-existent distribution and promotion, made their stay at Rondolet seem like a holiday in the sun. The Crack House mini-LP, a collection of spiky, almost jazz-flavoured punk songs, recorded at the label's suggestion, was lost in the shuffle.

Their finest moment followed in June 1984. 'Spike Milligan's Tape Recorder' was a screeching, feedback-saturated, unhinged effort with a great, hunking central riff. Peel loved it, the press notices were hugely favourable, and yet the label only pressed up 1,500 copies. Criminal Damage were living up to their name, at least in terms of its effect on the Membranes' standing. Nevertheless, there was the mini-album Death To Trad Rock before they could sever links. This built on the single's sonic clatter and added a few barbed lyrics about anything that crossed Robb's mind, and a penchant for swathes of all-out noise that would echo the emergence of US art-fuck bands like the Swans, Sonic Youth, Big Black etc.

But mention this to Robb and he'll get a cob on if you don't point out that the Membranes were doing this earlier than any of those bands. However, Criminal Damage collapsed with a thud shortly after the record was released. Which meant, again, that interest from all the positive press and TV appearances, including the Tube, were largely dissipated. Fed up, Tilton walked, later to join Marc Riley's Creepers, leaving Robb and Coofy Sid to recruit Stan, a Blackpool bass player, to complete the line-up.

By Robb's own admission, Gift Of Life, released on Creation, lacked the adrenaline-surge of their previous album and was less coherent, despite a starring role for Jon Langford on the title-track. And the production was "really crap", to the extent that when German label Constrictor offered to release it as Giant with a slightly different running order, they re-recorded the album tracks. The Membranes bounced back to Manchester to work with the city's In Tape imprint. It resulted in their second finest moment, the elegant 'Everything's Brilliant', which was irresponsibly catchy.

European dates proved too much for Blackpool Stan, who retreated to the comfort of the hearthside, so Wallace Tadpole stepped up. Phillip Boa produced Songs Of Love And Fury, but again it failed to return the band to the peaks of their debut album. But it did get an international release, meaning the band were able to tour the States for the first time in 1987, at which time Nick Brown augmented the line-up alongside Keith Curtis, both providing additional guitar.

After a further single, the acid-folky 'Time Warp 1991', the Membranes set to work with fan and friend Steve Albini of Big Black on Kiss Ass... Godhead. It was the album that Robb remains most pleased with, the band retaining its lyrical and musical idiosyncrasies despite the backdraft of layered guitars and a typically bullying Albini production.

Thereafter Tadpole left and Paul Morley, formerly of the Slum Turkeys, got the call. The ensuing To Slay The Rock Pig, produced by That Petrol Emotion's Steve Mack, was not the album they wanted to make, however. Thereafter even Robb's world-renowned enthusiasm was on the wane, and he elected to spend most of the 90s putting together a new band, first Sensurround and currently Gold Blade. He's a regular on TV too these days, replete with splendid flat-top circa mid-80s, offering his punk rock-filtered insights on the issues of the day, and he's finally finished his great punk rock tome (an oral history to my anal history?) Obviously, he's not cowed by competing literary talents, however huge. So let's ask the man who put together the first oral history of British punk for his bon mots on the phenomenon. "Punk saved us from the boredom of the late 70s. Growing up in a tatty seaside town we felt a million miles away from the action. The great thing about punk rock and DIY was that YOU were the action. Anyone could get involved was the message. So we did!"

DISCOGRAPHY:

Blackpool Rox 7-inch EP (Vinyl Drip 1 1980) Includes the Membranes' 'Ice Age', plus tracks from Syntax, Section 25, Ken Turner Set

Fashionable Junkies/Almost China 7-inch flexi (Vinyl Drip VD 005 December 1980)

Muscles/All Roads Lead To Norway 7-inch (Vinyl Drip VD 007 January 1982)

Muscles 7-inch EP (Rondelet ROUND 19 May 1982)

Muscles/All Roads Lead To Norway/Great Mistake/Entertaining Friends (also released as a 12-inch, 12 ROUND 19)

Pin Stripe Hype 7-ich EP (Rondelet ROUND 28 November 1982)

High Street Yanks/Funny Old World/The Hitch/Man From Moscow (also released as a 12-inch, 12 ROUND 28)

Crack House mini-LP (Criminal Damage CRIMLP 105 December 1983) (reissued June 1985)

Spike Milligan's Tape Recorder/Kennedy '63 7-inch (Criminal Damage CRI 115 June 1984) (reissued with Phillip Boa on Constrictor, CON 9)

Death To Trad Rock 12-inch EP (Criminal Damage CRI 12-125)

The Gift Of Life LP (Creation CRELP 006 August 1986)

Everything's Brilliant/Cleansed Again 7-inch (In Tape IT 029 March 1986) (also issued on 12-inch, ITT 029, with extended mix of a-side, plus bonus tracks 'New Blood For Young Skulls', 'King Cotton Whiplash')

Giant LP (Constrictor CON 00004 June 1986) (half a compilation, half a studio album proper)

Songs Of Love And Fury LP (In Tape 038 IT 038 October 1986) (also released on Constrictor, CON 00010)

Time Warp 1991/Too Fast To Love, Too Fast To Die 7-inch (Glass GLASS 052 August 1997) (also issued on 12-inch, GLASS12 052, with remix of a-side, plus extra tracks 'Groovy Fuckers' and 'Dragon Fly')

Kiss Ass... Godhead LP (Glass GLALP 028 April 1988) (also released on Constrictor, CON 00034)

Euro Pig Vs Auto Flesh 12-inch EP (Vinyl Drip SUK 8 July 1989)

Voodoo Chile/Tatty Seaside Town II/Auto Flesh/Hey Bryn Mawr* (*'Tatty Seaside Town' sung in Welsh)

To Slay The Rock Pig LP/CD (Vinyl Drip SUK LP/CD 9 November 1989) (also released on Constrictor, CON 00041)

ARCHIVE RELEASES

Pulp Beating And All That LP (Criminal Damage CRIMLP 130 April 1986)

The Virgin Mary Versus Petter Sellers – Back Catalogue (Vinyl Drip DRIPLP 1 June 1987) (15 songs of early Membranes' vintage, subsequently made redundant by the Best Of on Anagram)

Wrong Place At The Wrong Time CD (Constrictor CCON 001CD July 1993)

The Best Of The Membranes CD (Anagram CDMGRAM 112 June 1997) (start here for an introduction to the band)

Menace

Morgan Webster (vocals), Steve Tannett (guitar), Charlie Casey (bass), Noel Martin (drums)

MENACE were London's first generation no-nonsense prole punks, pre-dating Sham 69, who overtook them in terms of mass popularity, and the Cockney Rejects. They formed in 1976 at the Hope And Anchor in Islington when Webster met the other three members and were soon playing the Roxy. Their high-energy, unpretentious sets won them few admirers in the inkies, but they swiftly built a strong following that brought together both punks and skinheads. They're often cited as the first to unite this potentially volatile mix. However, there was nothing premeditated about the audience they attracted. "Sham were more overt in their leanings towards skinheads," Noel Martin told me. "We had that crossover thing. We liked that idea."

M

Partly that was because most of the band themselves were skinheads in their youth. However, they had no truck whatsoever with the far-right boneheads who would attach themselves to Sham's rising star. For a start, half of the band were themselves first generation

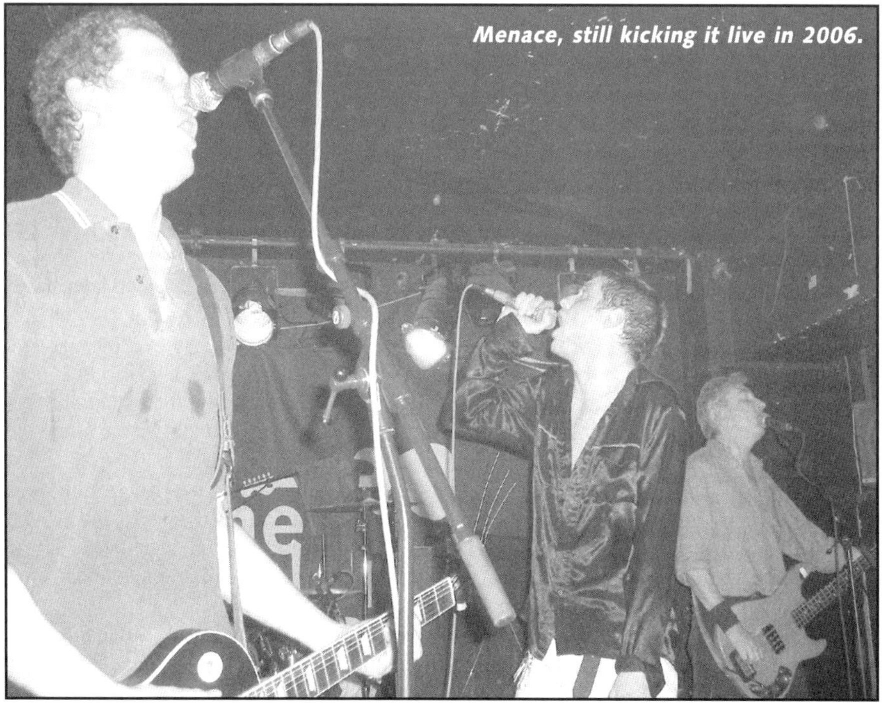

Menace, still kicking it live in 2006.

Irish immigrants. "We were working class lads from around King's Cross. Charlie and me came over from Ireland when we were about 14. We were both from the Galway area, but we didn't actually know each other until we met in England. We were in the same class together, at St William Of York school, and being Irish, there was obviously an immediate connection. Steve Tannett was in the year below us. St William Of York was also John Lydon's school. When we saw him on TV, when the punk thing got going, we thought – it can't be that wanker we knew at school! He was a bit of a nancy boy. He didn't stand out. He wasn't good at football and he wasn't one of the tough kids." Neither Casey nor Martin belonged in the 'most likely to achieve' category either. "You automatically became prefects in the fifth form at our school, and we were the only two that didn't. Charlie lived round the corner from the school, so every time we'd go to his house and make lunch and play our guitars. I started off playing guitar (in pub rock band Stonehenge). The drums came later. We hooked up with Steve Tannett after leaving school."

Martin also believes that a lot of the violence that attended those Sham 69 shows was related to the age-old phenomenon of working class kids having a punch up over the football. "There was a lot of football related stuff. Millwall used to chant against Chelsea fans when they found out they were in the venue, and vice versa. In fact, Millwall fans would base one of their chants on 'GLC'. We wouldn't allow it to grow. We wanted to talk about the music. It was music first, football afterwards with us. Some of that element tagged on to us, but when they saw they wouldn't get anywhere, they ended up tagging on to someone like Skrewdriver."

Menace were initially signed to Miles Copeland's Illegal Records and made their debut in August 1977 with 'Screwed Up' backed by 'Insane Society'. Charlie Harper of the UK Subs bought the very first copy when he bumped into Martin picking up the first box of singles from Copeland's office. It was good, honest, working class sloganeering ("If we're the working class/Why ain't we got jobs?") and more musically adept than you might imagine. Sniffing Glue trumpeted that they "are the best punk band in England today!" after witnessing some highly charged early shows at venues such as the Vortex and Hope And Anchor.

M

However, a projected second single, produced by the Velvet Underground's John Cale, was shelved until 1979. Instead the band switched to Walthamstow's Small Wonder Records for their enduring, 'GLC', which attacked the Tory Greater London Council's vindictive and restrictive attitude towards live punk shows.

It's a song that has become synonymous with Menace, which perplexes the band a little bit. "When you put a song down, you don't imagine you're going to be marked by it for ever," explains Martin. "It was a song that people like Jayne County told us to record," he explains, "because it was so popular live. Then John Cale came in to produce it. Cale sang on it. Miles Copeland, Kim Turner, the police manager, they all sang on that four-track session. It was the first time we'd done that sing-a-long thing. We had a repertoire of 11 songs, and that's what we stuck with for our live set. We did write other songs, but we usually rejected them as substandard, and all eleven of those songs were released on singles. There were a couple of others that slipped into the set. One was 'I Like Chips', which was about having a chip on your shoulder. That never got recorded until it came out on a live album much, much later. Most of the eleven songs that people know, they're accessible and you can sing along to them."

What was working with the legendary Miles Copeland like? "Well, Steve Tannett worked for him anyway. It's only recently that Steve has broken away from him. He lives in a big house in St John's Wood because of all the money he made! Which is one reason he wouldn't rejoin Menace later on. From our point of view, we were young guys, we thought he's a funny old American bloke, but he's putting our records out. So fair enough. He said, at one point, that we should wear crash helmets on stage, and bash ourselves about with baseball bats. Maybe that would have done the trick. We could have been huge." They weren't, and Martin reminds me that, even with Menace a very successful gigging band at their peak, all the members had to hold down day jobs, often returning straight to gainful employment after driving through the night back from a far-flung concert.

After two more singles in 1979, the best of which was 'Last Year's Youth', the band hung up its boots, just as the Oi! movement was beginning to salute them as founding fathers (indeed their roadie, Roi Pearce, would later be the vocalist with Last Resort and the 4-Skins).

In 1980 Tannett, Casey and Martin formed the Aces (who would back Vermilion). Thereafter Tannett would concentrate on running I.R.S. Records and Casey joined the Dark. Morgan Webster died in 1991.

And that was that, although 'GLC' continued to show up on a million punk compilation albums. The former members stayed in touch, however, and started rehearsing together again as the Collection in the mid-90s. They then appeared, billed as Jennifer Blue, supporting Alternative TV at Chat's Palace in Hackney in 1997. "We played a set of Collection songs, apart from 'GLC'. We figured some punks might remember 'GLC'. We did it, and people rushed up to us and said, that's the best Menace cover we've ever heard. Then they realised it was us. We then got a call from Darren Russell, the organiser of Holidays In The Sun. We weren't planning that, we were looking at taking a band out under the name Last Year's Youth, playing a combination of songs by Menace and the Collection. But we agreed to do it, and played a warm-up show at the Dublin Castle, then did Holidays In The Sun."

Menace Mark II was up and running, in which Casey and Martin were joined by Andrew Tweedie on guitar and John Lacey as singer. At which point songs Casey and Martin had written for the Collection were reworked to suit Menace. There was a 12-inch EP for Vinyl Japan which featured a new song, 'Society Still Insane', and a four-track EP for Knockout which featured the most promising of their new compositions, 'C&A' and 'Punk Rocker'. A 'live' album followed for Vinyl Japan, taped before a select audience at Rogue Studios in Bermondsey. The label had asked them to re-record their studio originals, but they baulked at the idea. Finally they asked Mark Brennan of Captain Oi! if he'd be interested in an album. He gave them a budget of £2,500 and the result was Crisis, released in 2000, their first studio album, 24 years after their inception.

It may have been a new line-up, but as Martin explains, the methodology was the same. "We've got a basic formula that comes from the Irish tradition, subconsciously probably, so the songs usually have three parts. A reel or jig tends to be one piece of music twice, then another piece twice, then another twice, then it repeats. We don't quite do that, but it's similar. We do the first part of the song, take a step up, and then do the chorus over a step up again. 99% of the time we have the lead break in a different place. It's a graduated way of songwriting which means the momentum of the song continues without taking a break." As he further points out, those who would assume that Menace songs are in any way simplistic should have a go at playing them.

The album attracted some glowing reviews, and songs such as 'C&A', 'Punk Rocker' and 'Rocks And Dust' more than measure up their existing canon. I was particularly swayed by 'Suburban Queen', an opposites attract epistle that read like a DH Lawrence narrative in an urban setting, or Pulp's 'Common People' with bovver boots on.

2004 brought a second comeback album, Rogue's Gallery, by which time Casey and Martin had been joined by new singer Oddy and guitarist Paul, aka Uncle Albert. It's actually a very convincing set, with great production, and lyrics that are more thoughtful and evolved than many would associate with the band. But once again, they had to overcome allegations of being career punk rockers. Not only that, but the recruitment of Oddy (concurrently of Resistance 77) meant that a central element of their sound had changed. "People would say, they've lost the singer and guitarist, how can they continue with two new guys? Charlie and I said, shall we just go out to pasture? No. We want to play so we'll keep going. I think the songs are similar. There are good songs on that album. 'Test Of Time' (an affectionate tribute to the early punk era that forged the band's identity), 'Lottery', that's a classic Menace-styled song. 'Oliver Reed', I'm proud of all of those. The main difficulty is because we've got a different vocalist. John (Lacey) was very London and Oddy is a northerner." In the end, Oddy's stay was a brief one. He left the band at the end of 2005 due to work commitments, though he did play at that December's Wasted shows. The band's new vocalist is Jasper.

DISCOGRAPHY:

Screwed Up/Insane Society 7-inch (Illegal IL 004 August 1977) (also released on 12-inch with same cat. Number)

GLC/I'm Civilised 7-inch (Small Wonder SMALL 5 March 1978)

I Need Nuthing/Electrocutioner 7-inch (Illegal IL 008 March 1979) (recorded by John Cale in June 1977 but not released until March 1979)

M

Final Vinyl 7-inch (Small Wonder SMALL 16 June 1979)
Last Year's Youth/Carry No Banners
The Young Ones/Live For Today/Tomorrow's World 7-inch (Fresh FRESH 14 September 1980)
Society Still Insane/GLC/Insane Society/The Young Ones 12-inch EP (Vinyl Japan TASK62 February 1999)
C & A/Punk Rocker/It's Not Unusual/Last Year's Youth (Knockout Records KOEP 101 October 1999)
Menace Live In Bermondsey CD/LP (Vinyl Japan ASK CD/LP 108 2000) (recorded 'live' at Rogue Studios in Bermondsey in front of a select audience. Not both the Ruts cover and an update of their debut single, 'Society Still Insane')
Crisis CD (Captain Oi! AHOY CD 171 2000) (fantastic cover, looks like a scene from Nil By Mouth)
Oi That's Yer Lot/ Bad Cards (Menace)/C&A/ Good Old Rich Kids Bashing Day (Loikaemie) (Knockout Records KOEP 139 October 2001) (split EP with German band Loikamie)
Rogue's Gallery CD (Captain Oi! AHOY CD 248 2004)
ARCHIVE RELEASES:
GLC – R.I.P. Best Of CD (Captain Oi! AHOY CD 63 1996) (also released on vinyl in a limited edition of 1,000 copies, AHOY LP 17)
Alive Alive O! CD (R27) (released on R27, Menace's own label, and available at gigs and via the band's website. This features all three different line-ups of Menace, as well as the previously unrecorded 'I Like Chips', recorded at an early show at the Lord Raglan in Wolverhampton. Menace fans will note that part of the riff from the former is revisited in 'Rocks And Dust')
Punk Singles Collection CD (Captain Oi! AHOY CD 264 2005) (both the last two-named tracks taken from US compilation Screwed Up. 'C&A (U.S.A. Version)' taken from Scene Killer Vol. 2 CD)

The Mental

Dick Lucas (vocals), SiKick (aka Simon Walters; guitar), Steve Collapsible (aka Steve Lucas; bass), Tony (drums)

M

Before he went off to lead the Subhumans, where anarcho punk enjoyed probably its sole flirtation with Led Zeppelin guitar licks, Dick Lucas led this more conventional late-70s punk band (though the label design and handwriting on the single offers a clear pointer to Lucas's later artwork). Formed in Wiltshire, their sole release was self-financed and issued on their own Kamikaze Pig imprint in 1979. Shortly thereafter THE MENTAL broke up, with Lucas forming the Subhumans with ex-members of another Wiltshire band, the Stupid Humans.

OK, Mr Lucas, so whose identities were being protected by the pseudonyms? "SiKick is Si Walters, Steve Lucas is my brother, and Tony is… oh! If I ever knew it, I've forgotten it. Last names used to be accorded to Adults and Sensible People. I was over 30 before people started using my last name in zines (how did they find out?) and I tell you it felt like I'd had Normality slightly forced upon me! The whole punk identity deconstruction (all the nicknames) was a way to reinvent ourselves, say bollocks to family values and, er, start the destruction of the patriarchal naming system!"

The Mental was the first band any of the participants had been involved in. So what provided the impetus to be a punk band – the words, the music, the art, the ethos? "The whole lot? Punk was such a massive invitation to join in, make as much noise as you liked, make an impression of any kind, even if you couldn't play, it didn't matter. Anyone with any of the following – practice space, any instrument, any words that rhymed, could form a band as fast as asking 'who wants to be in a band?' Which is why punk at first was SO musically varied. As for groups, well it sounds a cliché by now, but the Sex Pistols really did it first and foremost; then other faves were the Adverts, Clash, Vibrators, Menace, Ramones and so on."

As for the songs on the EP, 'Kill The Bill' is pretty self-explanatory. "Yes, subtlety and shades of meaning were a way off at that point! Kill the pigs, go insane, being 18 is shit, that sort of thing." As for the ease of getting the single out. "As easy as taking all my meagre wages from a crap job I had, and borrowing from Si's parents." The Mental played ten gigs in total. "Mostly awkward chaotic (read 'terrible' from a more objective angle!) – abrasive, uncoordinated, the list goes on. But then most small bands were doing similarly messy gigs at the time, and being Good didn't matter as much as Doing It, and a few of the ten were totally excellent fun! One of which was with the Stupid Humans (and Vice Squad, in Warminster). I'd met Ju and Bruce (of Stupid Humans) at an Angelic Upstarts gig, and saw them practice and do gigs. When we split up it was partly cos I wanted to sing with Bruce in the new band he was forming in the wake of the Stupid Humans breaking up (summer 1980). And partly cos the Mental were geographically held together by the fact that we were all at the same (cred drop coming up!) boarding school. So when we all left that, it was an insane travel distance to keep practising, so we called it a day (much to Si's annoyance). Steve formed Wild Youth, and I joined Bruce in his new band Subhumans."

While the Subhumans had a quite distinct set of socio-political viewpoints, according to Dick, that philosophy came later. "Very few of the songs the Mental had were socially aware to the point of any profundity, and those that were, were written by Si. Our later songs were written after we'd heard Crass. I think that helped our attitude expansion a lot!"

As for other abiding memories of that time, that place, that band, etc: "Having our EP played by John Peel, the engineer getting drunk midway into recording the EP, getting drunk on 2 cans of anything, sniffing Zoff! Oh my God! Being stranded in King's Cross all night with some London punks. Going to Stonehenge festival. Us four taking turns to doodle until the EP cover was full up. Playing the EP to our parents (my Dad's never listened to anything I've done since, I think he thinks it still sounds like that). Being so embarrassed by the chaotic performance in Basingstoke I sang from the side of the stage. Steve dyeing 'UK Subs' into his hair. Shouting at the sky. Playing records with the speakers hanging out of the window. Getting the Buzzcocks' first LP. Realising that work was an extension of school i.e. full of wankers!"

DISCOGRAPHY:

Extended Play 7-inch EP (Kamikaze Pig Records RAM 1 1979)
God For A Day/18/Kill The Bill/Off The Rails (500 copies)
The Mental/Stupid Humans split CDR (Bluurg)

Midnight And The Lemon Boys

M

Marcus Myers (vocals, rhythm guitar) Nick Sayer (aka Nick Sago; guitar), Marcus (vocals), Ogs (aka Mrs Hoggins; drums), Chris Anderson (bass)

Brighton's MIDNIGHT AND THE LEMON BOYS were formed in 1978 by Fan Club's Nick Sayer and Marcus Myers, who'd previously played in Urban Delights. They played a fairly accomplished pop and punk hybrid, and were popular enough locally to pick up support tours with the Lambrettas, the Photos and U2. Indeed, Bono once sang one of their songs, 'Strange Love', at a local venue called Jenkinson's. "I was at the Lemons Boys/U2 gig at Jenkinson's," Grant Boult of the Vitamins told me. "and Bono changed the words on the night as they were devoted Christians at the time!" Chris Anderson: "Grant is right about Bono changing the words to 'Strange Love' – the song is about drug use, which he didn't approve of. The first line of the song is 'I love taking drugs', which God's representative on earth chose to alter to 'I love wearing gloves', which served to make the song sound even trippier!"

However, despite numerous demo recordings and the best efforts of manager Simon Watson, they never secured a recording contract. Any chance that they may have eventually done so was scuppered in 1981 when Sayer had to retire hurt with a back injury. Which caused some amusement to Ty Heyward, brother of Paul of the Molesters, who was living in the same building in Sillwood Terrace. "I always used to hear him coming down the stairs and I'd race to get him with a bucket of water as he left the communal front door to the house (a landing window conveniently overlooked the front door). Very juvenile, but fun at the time."

They continued for several months with the late Tony Maybury on guitar. The group finally splintered in 1981. Sayer eventually turned up in Transvision Vamp, while Ogs became Peter And The Test Tube Babies' full time drummer. Myers moved to London to form Brilliant with Youth (ex-Killing Joke) and then Hard Rain. He too would play with the Test Tube Babies (as Marcus Mystery) for three years and then, by way of some small contrast, joined Then Jerico. He's now a session musician with credits including Alisha's Attic and Belinda Carlisle (the latter, let it not be forgotten, had served her time in the punk trenches). He now lives in Spain. Chris Anderson subsequently worked for a management company handling Siouxsie And The Banshees and the Pogues. "They finished me off." Meanwhile, former manager Simon Watson is rumoured to be hoarding a box of old demo tapes that remain unreleased.

Misspent Youth

Jon Buxton (guitar, vocals), Tony McIlwain (drums), Steve Cull (vocals, bass)

MISSPENT YOUTH, who formed in 1975, were one of the more popular underachieving punk bands of the era, their name to be found immortalised on many walls and underpasses in the Midlands. The graffiti became so widespread that the band was forced to write to the Birmingham Evening Mail to disassociate themselves from the ongoing campaign to publicise their name. Yeah, right.

The group's initial line-up featured Buxton alongside Ian Hewitt on bass and Terry Boazman on drums. They made their debut in early 1976 as support to Birmingham heavy metal non-legends Supernova (whose guitarist Keith Rimell would later join the Killjoys) at the Golden Eagle. The band's initial influences were the familiar ones for upstart aspirants of the era – the New York Dolls, Stooges, etc, and there was a self-evident indebtedness to the glam era. They were already writing original material, including 'The Smoker', 'Machine Gun' and 'Midland Red Bus', eventually adding vocalist Dave Banks as they secured a residency at the Barrel Organ.

However, there were a few hitches along the way. Boazman would leave to be replaced by an old school friend, Tony McIlwain, with whom the band recorded its first demos at the city's Nest Studios. Buxton: "The master tape of the three songs, 'School Report', 'Misspent Youth' and 'Suzie's Shinin', either still resides in the EMI vaults (to where it was sent) or most likely ended up in the bin." Shortly thereafter they also lost their singer, Dave Banks. "Dave was known to like a drink or two. He took to offering out most of the other local bands/promoters/landlords single handed." That was all very well, but his band drew the line when one day he turned on them. Hewitt was sacked shortly afterwards for lack of commitment after his girlfriend banned him from turning up to a practice when they were auditioning new singers.

Undaunted by these knockbacks, while still ducking and diving to avoid the threat of redemptive violence that resulted from their legacy of working with Banks, McIllwain and Buxton set about writing a new set, one which would deliberately stoke controversy. 'Powder Room Obsession' was themed on lesbianism, 'Goodbye Baby Doll Blue' on rape, and 'Plaything' on underage sex. At the same time they added Steve Cull on bass. Not only did he fill out the sound, he also added another visual dimension on stage – a leopard cat suit-like dimension. Dozens of gigs followed, before they recorded a second round of four-track demos at Outlaw Studios in Birmingham – 'Nightclub', 'It's A Raid' and 'Birmingham Boys'.

After support from local radio station BMRB, which was sustained throughout their career, further sessions were convened at Horizon Studios in Coventry. The idea was to get a fuller sound, and thus they committed to 16-track their most commercial song, 'Betcha Won't Dance'. There are some who say the latter had a direct bearing on Duran Duran's subsequent hit 'Planet Earth'. Certainly, future Duran Duran members (then performing in TV Eye) were present at Misspent Youth gigs, as were Martin Degville (Sigue Sigue Sputnik), Boy George and the hapless Kevin Rowland. Speaking of whom, as Buxton recalls: "I was making an impromptu appearance at a Sussed gig and borrowed Kevin Law's guitar. 'Careful with that,' he said, 'it's Kevin Rowland's. He's just bought it from a catalogue.' I couldn't resist. I smashed it up and rubbed it against the microphone stand so hard that the top frets all came out. This might not seem hugely funny to you, but I can assure you to all those who knew Kevin Rowland, this was a scream."

Eventually they found someone to release 'Betcha Won't Dance', local entrepreneur Jim Simpson, head of Big Bear Records. The single is now a huge collectors' item, largely due to the problems the band experienced with Simpson. He'd given the single a provisional catalogue number of BB20, but its release was continually delayed, resulting in a major falling out. The band, after being told to take time out and chill, drove to the pressing plant in

Dagenham and disposed of 950 copies of the 1,000 pressings by throwing most of them in a dump. Buxton: "The next and last time I met Jim Simpson was when I was running Flick Recording Studios and we used his local paper, Brum Beat, for advertising. There was that real movie moment when our eyes met, each waiting for a comment. Nothing was said, just negotiation over the advert."

The gigs continued but were becoming more fractious all the time. At Martin Degville's private party at Barbarella's, they ended up in a pitched fight with skinheads after making some disrespectful remark about Sid Vicious. On another occasion 'Plaything' was deemed a little beyond the pale by some of the same venue's audience (especially when its subject matter was spelt out by Buxton's on-stage introduction) and resulted in a hail of pint glasses arcing towards them. Buxton concedes that, with one glass breaking over his arm, "we realised that maybe things were getting a little out of hand."

By now they were able to sell out Barbarella's Friday night Spectrum club and pull over 1,000 people through the door. It was heady stuff, and a little too heady for Cull. At the start of 1979, he left to form his own band, but became hooked on narcotics and, suffering from depression, committed suicide in 1984. The band had already written a song based loosely on his life, 'Cry Tonight', which he'd come along to hear them play on an emotional night at the Barrel Organ in 1980. He was replaced by science graduate Peter Chapman.

But handicapped by the limited distribution of their grand opus 'Betcha Won't Dance', Misspent Youth began to flounder, despite a two-song appearance on the BBC's Look Hear TV programme as support to the Specials. This was broadcast in January 1980 after 1,000 local signatories had petitioned the BBC to get the band this media exposure, a campaign instigated by McIlwaine's girlfriend Twig.

The BBC appearance was somewhat surreal. "We are sitting on the edge of the stage waiting for a rehearsal, heads bowed. Up comes the TV make up lady. 'OK, guys, time to make up.' As we lift our heads, faces already caked in the stuff, she exclaims: 'Oh, my God! Roger (Castles), who are these people?' Then she turns to us. 'I think you're done!' Later, we're running through our opening song, the cameramen are practising angles/positions etc, but there is a fault in the studio wiring and all the producer's confidential comments are heard loud and clear through my Marshall amplification. 'OK, camera two – George, move in on the great big poof playing the bass'. At which point Peter (our great big puff playing the bass) pouts his lips, rests his hands on his hip, exclaims: 'Who's he calling a poof?' And he flounces off."

But the piece de resistance came when the show started. "The music comes on and at this point each week, Toyah Willcox rides into the studio on a different form of transport. This week, it's on the back of a motor scooter. Chris Phipps, the other presenter, is driving. Chris has forgotten to tell the producer that he has never ridden a motorcycle before. He cocks the throttle and rides the motor scooter straight into the audience, flattening half of them and sending Toyah skidding across the studio." Carnage ensues. "Needless to say, Toyah storms off and the show is put on hold for 20 minutes while the show's staff persuade her to do the professional thing and return. It also took that long to stop laughing."

However, despite a further studio session at Outlaw where six new tracks were recorded, the cracks were beginning to show, exacerbated by the band failing to secure any interest from the majors on a trip down to London. Buxton wanted the band to take a more melodic pop direction, while McIlwaine favoured a rockier approach. When later that year it emerged another Misspent Youth was operational in London, Brum's finest live band of the punk generation, according to many who saw them, collapsed.

Buxton would later work in the Jet Set with former members of local punks the Sussed, and then the Broadway Rebels, before setting up The Attic and then Flick International recording studios, working with bands ranging from the Sweet to Felt and Napalm Death. McIlwaine joined metal band Steel and then The Boy, before obtaining a publishing deal with Warners and writing hit records for artists including Jane Wiedlin, Debbie Harry and Tevin Campbell, eventually settling in Los Angeles.

Misspent Youth finally realised silver surfer certitude over two decades later when Garden Records released Misspent Youth – The Punk Years 1976-1980.

That would have been that, only I nudged Jon for some anecdotes about their errant erstwhile lead singer, Dave Banks. He surpassed himself. Here are some of the, gruesome, edited highlights.

"Dave was raised in a house where his father came home drunk and for recreation he would remove his jacket and beat Dave to a pulp. One day our van driver Laurence was there and because he was 'in the way' he was thrown through the front door window, head first, by father and son, so they could get on and finish the family business. That window was boarded up for about five years after that and was a constant reminder to us all, you don't visit Dave's house on a Friday.

"One time we played an Irish pub called The Bull's Head in Small Heath, Birmingham (now knocked down thank goodness). After the show the landlord refused payment, Dave in his usual fashion invited him to fisticuffs. The landlord went downstairs and came back up with eight or nine Irish friends. Dave said great, we'll take you all on. 'Err, Dave, let's just go home,' we exclaimed. Too late. He dived into them fists flying. It was all over in 30 seconds and I can still see Dave sat on the floor beaten and bleeding, smiling, saying, 'Well, we're not going to play here again'.

"One day we went to see local rock band Cryer, and afterwards we went into the dressing room to say hello. The rather posh keyboard player asked Dave what he was doing in the band's dressing room, and we are shaking our heads and mouthing to Mister Keyboard man – 'Nooooo.' But too late, he was on the deck, floored by Dave's famous headbutt.

"One memorable incident was when the Damned played Rebecca's night club in Severn Street, Birmingham. After the gig, Captain Sensible was returning from the toilet and Dave invited him to sit with us for a drink. Again, we are thinking: please, Dave, no… 'How much did you get for this gig?' asks Dave. '£250' replies the Captain. 'We had 300 people in here last week,' replies Dave, 'and they only paid us £20. You get 150 punters and get paid £300, you bleep…bleep… London Softie bleep, bleep, etc.' At which point we are thinking, please, Captain, leave now (which he did) with the brilliant retort: 'You better take it up with the management lads, they've ripped you off.' They don't call him Sensible for nothing! So Dave heads toward the door manager, who happens to be a major league gangster, and puts his complaint to him. He pulls out a baseball bat from under the counter, and we drag Dave away quickly to fight another day."

DISCOGRAPHY:

Betcha Won't Dance/Birmingham Boys 7-inch (Big Bear BB20 1979)

ARCHIVE RELEASES

Misspent Youth – The Punk Years 1976-1980 CD (Garden November 2002) (the single plus radio and TV appearances)

Models

Cliff Fox (guitar, vocals) Marco Pirroni (guitar), Mick Allen (bass), Terry Day (aka Terry Lee Miall; drums)

Pirroni had played briefly with Siouxsie and the Banshees as roped-in guitarist for their debut 100 Club show, and was already one of the punk 'faces' that would hang around McLaren and Westwood's S.E.X. store – though he never did score the job there that he secretly yearned for. He would, of course, subsequently discover fame and fortune with the dandy highwaymen version of Adam And The Ants, alongside drummer Terry Lee Miall, the MODELS having supported the Ants in their 1977 incarnation, but it started here.

The Models' sole release was the one-off single, 'Freeze', backed by 'Man Of The Year', one of the initial batch of singles released on Mark Perry's Step Forward label. The above average production values can be traced to the fact that his partner, Miles Copeland, had done a deal with Polydor to allow his acts access to their distribution and studio, as well as later Jam engineer Pete Wilson. But the Models just managed to miss the boat in terms of punk chronology.

Originally known as the Beastly Cads, the band was thrown off stage at their first show after forming in October 1976. The most notable of their original compositions was 'I Wanna Form My Own Nazi Party'. While they claimed it was a "cynical look at all the silly punks who wear

Nazi armbands", not everyone got the joke, including Sounds' Viv Goldman, who reckoned that the irony was going to be lost on audiences of impressionable punks who would only hear the chorus. They were a popular live band for a while, playing venues including the Vortex and appearing third on the bill to the Heartbreakers and Banshees at the Rainbow, before joining them on tour in October 1977.

Aside from the single there was an excellent John Peel session from July 1977 that included versions of 'Man Of The Year', 'Censorship', 'Brainwash' and 'Freeze'. Following the single Pironni and Allen would form Rema Rema after the Models were laid to rest in April 1978. Thereafter Pirroni would become an Ant and Allen would join Mass and then Wolfgang Press. Pirroni's recent activities centre around the Wolfmen, who in 2006 provided the soundtrack to a series of fetish films for the Fashion In Film Festival.

DISCOGRAPHY:

Freeze/Man Of The Year 7-inch (Step Forward SF3 June 1977) (They are not the same Models that recorded for A&M in the early-80s)

Modettes

June Miles-Kingston (drums), Ramona Carlier (vocals), Kate Korus (aka Katherine Corris; guitar), Jane Crockford (bass)

The MODETTES tend to get brushed under the carpet in discussions of punk in the late-70s, their music, when it's referenced at all, usually categorised as mod-influenced pop (it didn't help that they underscored that influence in naming the band) or proto 2-Tone. However, in so many ways the Modettes were intrinsic to the fabric of the punk story, their members connecting with the main participants both on personal and professional levels, while the attitude they brought to the project, as well as elements of the music, were authentically punk.

Kate Korus, formerly of all-female precursors the Castrators and the Slits, had arrived in England from her native America in 1974. She was also involved in a formative line-up of the Raincoats. Ramona Carlier was a former ballet student from Geneva, Switzerland, who'd come to England to involve herself in the emergent punk culture. However, she was not, as some histories suggest, part of her nation's finest punk band, Kleenex, though she had done some backing vocals and played a one-off show as a member of the Bomberettes. Jane Crockford was a regular face seen around the squats of west London she shared with Rotten and Vicious of the Sex Pistols, among others, and had previously played in Bank Of Dresden. It was she who'd drawn the blood of Shane MacGowan by biting his ear at a Clash gig, resulting in one of punk's most celebrated tabloid scare stories. June Miles-Kingston joined them after meeting Korus on the set of the Great Rock'n'roll Swindle. Miles-Kingston: "Kate and I were production assistants on the Swindle. We started playing music together after, when I bought a drum kit from Paul (Cook), who also first put us in the studio to record 'White Mice'".

Their first gig came at the Acklam Hall as support to the Vincent Units. They made their recorded debut with the dapper 'White Mice' in 1979, released on their own Mode label and distributed by Rough Trade. A succession of singles for Decca subsidiary Deram followed, including a cover of the Stones' 'Paint It Black', which reached 42 in the charts, preceding their full-length debut, The Story So Far. Sadly, the album's clever, bristling pop dynamic was neutered by poor production. They released their final single, 'Tonight', in June 1981. Thereafter several demos were recorded. A second guitarist, 17-year-old Melissa Ritter, joined the group and within four days had learned the set for her stage debut at the Venue. Bob Kingston of Tenpole Tudor, Miles-Kingston's brother, introduced her to the band. Ramona departed in February 1982, and was eventually replaced by Sue Slack in May. Before her arrival June handled vocals from behind her drum kit. Then Korus too walked, again citing problems with the record label and management. Further recording sessions took place under the tutelage of Chris Neil (Sheena Easton's producer, who had also worked on 'Tonight') in an attempt to mine a more commercial direction, but the group eventually sundered in November 1982.

Of the former members June went on to drum with the Communards and worked with Fun Boy Three and Everything But The Girl. She also released a solo single for Go! Discs. Ritter collaborated with Jennie McKeown of the Belle Stars and would marry Stray Cats' producer Hein Hoven. Jane Crockford, who subsequently married Woody of Madness, meanwhile, is apparently the subject of the Dolly Mixtures' song 'How Come You're Such A Hit With The Boys, Jane?'

DISCOGRAPHY:

White Mice/Masochistic Opposite 7-inch (Mode/Rough Trade MODE 1 December 1979)
Paint It Black/Bitta Truth 7-inch (Deram DET-R-1 June 1980) (with free 7-inch flexidisc, 'Twist And Shout')
The Story So Far LP (Deram SML 1120 October 1980)
Dark Park Creeping/Two Can Play 7-inch (Deram DET 2 October 1980)
Tonight/Waltz In Blue Minor 7-inch (Deram DET 3 June 1981)
White Mice/The Kray Twins (live) 7-inch (Human HUM 10 July 1981)

Molesters

John Ellis (vocals), Paul Hayward (guitar), Andy Parks (bass), Derek Bunf (drums)

One of the less celebrated bands to appear on Walthamstow's Small Wonder imprint, the MOLESTERS featured John Ellis, though this was not the John Ellis of Vibrators/Stranglers etc renown. "Molesters started when I met John Ellis in a pub in Brighton," Paul Hayward told me. "He said: 'I've never sung in my life before but I've written these lyrics and I really would like to have a crack getting them put to music and singing.' I liked the political and social messages in his songs and so that was it, we worked for a few weeks, John the lyrics and me the music, and ended up with about eight tracks. I was squatting at the time in a big house in Lansdowne Place with a mate of mine, Andy Parks, who was a pretty able bass player, and Derek 'Bunf', a drummer. They started to play with us, and then we were four. After playing a couple of gigs as a four-piece we came across a couple of crazy girls from Coventry, Lesley and Blimp, who like John had no previous singing experience but wanted to get involved. They added lots of visuals to the line-up, now we are six."

The Molesters were featured in a Southern Television documentary on punk in Brighton, as they were auditioning female singers. There was footage of the band rehearsing in the gents' toilet by the Clock Tower in Brighton, and living in their communal squat. As Paul Martin of Fan Club, and a later Molesters member, recalls: "Both The Molesters and (Fan Club singer) Dave McDonald appeared in the Clock Tower 'loos' footage. I remember the filming for some of that programme. The UK Subs were playing at the Buccaneer which the TV crew wanted to film, but being a 'real' punk band, the audience went along knowing the film crew would be there and were resolved to shower them in as much 'gob' as possible! The crew whilst filming on the tiny stage were all wearing full length Macintoshes and Souwester hats to protect themselves! They knew what to expect!"

Paul Hayward: "Within a few months, John I had decided we wanted to get serious about the band and sought the same commitment from the other guys. As a result Andy, Bunf and the girls went their own way. We replaced Andy and Bunf with Mark (Grestly; bass) and Wayne (Calcutt; drums) whose musical abilities and commitment gave us the jump-start we needed. Leonie (Nichol) and Stella

(Anscombe) also gave us some real backing vocals." The Molesters went on to appear as support act to artists including the Cure, the Ants, the Damned, Here and Now, UK Subs and ATV.

The first John Peel session in October 1978, which featured all four of the songs released on Small Wonder, followed a show at the Marquee where the band supported Annie Lennox's Tourists. "Bob Sergeant was checking them out for a session, but didn't like them. So he came into the dressing room after and offered us the session. We got on with Peel (Uncle John) who invited us to play at a number of his road shows. He even stayed overnight with us in the famous Sillwood Terrace band house."

There was also an offer to work with John Cale's Spy Records. "It was completely one-sided and at the same time, Small Wonder offered us a couple of singles. It was a done deal." The result was 'Disco Love' and 'End Of Civilisation', the latter featuring a fetching Crucifixion painting. By the time of the second Peel session, in February 1979, Anscombe and Nichol had been replaced by Carole Brooks, Ellis's then girlfriend, and Tracy Spencer. The latter would later marry Paul Hayward "in Brighton's first punk wedding, which made the front page of the Argus," according to Grant Boult of the Vitamins. "Her real name was Tracy Preston, and her dad Dennis was a big name in the music business and owned Landsdowne Studios, where the Pistols did some early recordings." Vocalist Tom Maltby and ex-Fan Club and Siren bass player Paul Martin also appeared with the band in its later stages, before Martin was replaced by 'Francois', another intern of Paul Hayward's 'famous band house'. Paul Martin: "Interestingly, after I left them, singer Tom Maltby only did one more gig with them (in Salisbury, I think). The gig after this was at the Buccaneer, which I was at to watch. Tom Maltby did the sound check, and John Ellis, who was also there, called from the floor to Paul Hayward something like, 'What's happening with this gig then Paul, am I doing it or not?' Evidently he did, as although Tom did the soundcheck, John did the actual gig! The quickest singer turnaround ever perhaps! That was the final line-up of the Molesters as far as I know." The changes were symptomatic of the band's decline. Hayward: "Soon after differences appeared about the future direction of the band and that was the beginning of the end."

Anagram's reissue campaign has rounded up their entire output with the re-release of the Small Wonder catalogue on CD. But the Peel sessions remain unreleased.

DISCOGRAPHY:

Disco Love/Commuter Man 7-inch (Small Wonder SMALL 14 1978)
End Of Civilisation/Girl Behind The Curtain 7-inch (Small Wonder SMALL 18 1979)
COMPILATIONS:
Small Wonder Punk Singles Collection CD Vol. 1 (Anagram CDPUNK 29 1994; 'Disco Love', 'End Of Civilisation')
Small Wonder Punk Singles Collection CD Vol. 2 (Anagram CDPUNK 70 1996; 'Commuter Man', 'Girl Behind The Curtain')

Moondogs

Gerry McCandless (vocals, guitar), Jackie Hamilton (bass, vocals), Austin Barrett (drums)

Perennial Undertones support act, the MOONDOGS, named after an early incarnation of the Beatles, hailed from the same city, Derry, and had a similar knack for infusing punk with pop melodies. They actually featured Vinny O'Neill, brother of the Undertones guitar twosome, in their first incarnation, formed in September 1977, before Hamilton was drafted in from Ventura Highway. He'd never actually touched a musical instrument at this point, but was happy to buy a bass guitar and start to get his head around it. The other genetic connection to the Undertones came in the form of Barrett, who was a cousin of Billy Doherty.

Initial rehearsals took place at the Bogside Inn, soon after which the Undertones invited them to support them when they played a celebratory show from the back of a coal lorry in Bull Park after signing with Sire. They also regularly supported the Undertones at the Casbah, Their first studio demo in November at Magee University (featuring 'My New Girl', 'Jenny', 'Hey Joanna' and Two-Timed') was followed by a session for Downtown Radio. Their debut show in England, as part of the 'A Sense Of Ireland' festival, followed.

They signed to Good Vibrations in April 1979, resulting in debut 45 'She's 19', backed by

'Ya Don't Do Ya'. Mainland UK support tours with the Undertones followed, and the latter's handlers, Sire, professed interest in the band. They recorded their first session for John Peel, who'd played their debut single, in April 1980, and signed to Sire subsidiary Real in June. That resulted in a move to London, where the label put them up in a flat on the King's Road while they were ushered into the studio.

The first single for Real, 'Who's Gonna Tell Mary', was co-produced by Pete Waterman (alongside Pete Collins). But then the increasingly unstable Andrew 'Loog' Oldham took a hand. Convinced that the band had the potential to conquer America, he stole the master tapes from the studio. Which resulted in all sorts of shenanigans.

However, the Moondogs' closest shave with pop stardom followed in 1981. Granada hit upon the idea of turning them into a teatime TV show. They were despatched to Rockfield Studios in Wales to come up with a couple of dozen songs to accompany the series. Everything, it seemed, was in place. The first show was broadcast in April 1981, after which they set off to New York to record a debut album with producer Todd Rundgren. In the interim two singles surfaced for Real. The first, 'Talking In The Canteen', was produced by Nick Garvey of the Motors. The second, 'Imposter', had Ray Davies of the Kinks at the controls, which was a thrill for all concerned.

However, Rundgren was a different kettle of fish. They arrived at his studio in May 1981, but broke up halfway through the sessions for That's What Friends Are For. They were confused about both their music and their direction, unsure whether or not to accommodate elements of the New Romantic thread. In the end, they were scuppered by their own indolence. And Rundgren didn't really know what to do with them either; he was still busy working on the backing tracks.

So they made a decision. They returned home, and went to the bank, withdrawing all the advances for both signing and publishing, paid the VAT required, and declared themselves bankrupt. Then they signed on. Radical circumstances sometimes suggest radical solutions. Rundgren eventually completed work on the album and it was released in Germany later in 1981. The band never saw a copy.

Later McCandless began a solo career and in September 2002 added keyboards to several Undertones tracks. Hamilton and McCandless then formed the Hickeys with Billy Doherty of the Undertones for a short time, before the former became a TV presenter and producer (for the Patrick Kielty Show) while the latter became a software whizz. Barrett drums for blues cover band, Double Trouble, and runs a dog training school in Derry. Apparently. So the canine connection endures.

The Moondogs returned in 1990 for a 10th anniversary show, then 1996 to support the Saw Doctors in Galway, and again in the 21st Century for a benefit for Derry City FC. Eventually the group's Peel Sessions were released by Detour as well as the Red Fish album of new studio recordings for Reekus in 2003. However, several Moondogs recordings remain unreleased, including 'TV Girl', 'Boy's Stories', 'Jenny', 'Tell Tail', 'I Am Trembling' and early favourites 'Two Timed' and 'Hey Joanna'.

The band are currently active again, working on a new album, and in 2006 had four songs from the Red Fish CD included on the film soundtrack to Dead Long Enough.

DISCOGRAPHY:

She's 19/Ya Don't Do Ya? 7-inch (Good Vibrations GOT 10 November 1979)
Who's Gonna Tell Mary?/Over-Caring Parents 7-inch (Real ARE 13 1980)
Talking In The Canteen/Maker Her Love Me/You Said 7-inch (Real ARE 14 1981) (with free 'neckerchief')
Imposter/Babysnatcher 7-inch (Real ARE 16 1981)
That's What Friends Are For LP (Sire SIRE 204061 1981; Germany only)
Getting Off In Amsterdam/Everyday Things CD single (Reekus RKCDS12 2003) (200 copies only)
Red Fish CD (Reekus RKCD11 2003)
ARCHIVE RELEASES:
The Peel Sessions CD (Detour DRCD040 2003)
COMPILATIONS:
Good Vibrations – The Punk Singles Collection CD (Anagram CD PUNK 36 1994; 'Ya Don't Do Ya')

Moskow

David Ashmore (vocals), David Cole (guitar), Trevor Flynn (bass), Jan Kalicki (drums), Michael Matthews (keyboards)

Based in Trowbridge in the West Country, MOSKOW were managed by local impresario Allan Partner, a carpenter by trade. He'd taken up the band's reigns after they'd released their debut DIY single in 1978, 'Man From U.N.C.L.E.', its connection to the famed 60s cult TV series ensuring good sales and a modicum of interest. As a result, the band moved to Rialto and re-recorded the song with a new B-side, 'Too Much Commotion' (which was also compiled on Heartbeat's Bristol compilation, Avon Calling). Thereafter the single was re-released for the second time on Partner's own TW label, which would also be home to the first releases by Frome's Animals And Men.

Trevor Flynn is, in fact, Trevor Tanner. "I changed to my mother's maiden name (Flynn) for about a year, because I was fighting with my father at the time due to the fact that my parents had recently got divorced." Via his friend, Kalicki, he would roadie for Moskow "to get free beer" and replaced their original bass player when he became ill. "This was obviously before I started to get very serious about playing guitar and singing, etc." Ralph Mitchard of Animals And Men has several amusing memories of Partner's business acumen. "Moskow were asked to play Blitz by Rusty Egan, who played their single a lot. They were just right for that scene but Allan Partner wouldn't let them play 'to a club load of shirt-lifters'." 'Man From U.N.C.L.E.' was later reprised on volume one of the Teenage Treats series, earning this glowing review from Gullbuy: "A punk song almost as crucial as The Times' mod classic 'I Helped Patrick McGoohan Escape'."

Former members of the band continued to work with Partner after Moskow's dissolution. The Silent Guests featured Dave Cole, as well as later-period Moskow member Boris, in addition to Paul 'Puddle' Collyer of Animals And Men. Crazy House, who briefly recorded for a major, featured Dave Lockhurst. He also wrote a column for the Bath Chronicle and had a slot on local TV. Jan Kalicki and Trevor Tanner, who were much younger than the other members of Moskow, subsequently moved to London and formed late-80s indie stalwarts the Bolshoi, by far one of the most literate and engaging acts to be tarred with the Goth brush. It's also worth pointing out that two years below them at school was one Mike Edwards of Jesus Jones, who was a big fan of both Moskow and the Bolshoi.

Tanner has now signed to Emperor Penguin Recordings and recently released a 3-CD set, Bullish, Bellyache & Belch (from three alternatives offered by a spellcheck that couldn't get to grips with 'Bolshoi'). The 46 songs were edited down from over 100 he's written following the demise of the Bolshoi. His new solo set, Eaten By The Sea, will be released by the same record label in 2006, and he is also part of the production team working with new act Mysterious Creature.

DISCOGRAPHY

Man From U.N.C.L.E./White Black 7-inch (Moskow SRS 2103 1978) (re-released three times; first in 1979 on Rialto, TREB 107, with 'Too Much Commotion on the B-side, then reverting to 'White Black' as B-side on T.W. HIT 103 in 1981, and Moskow SRT 3 in 1982)

COMPILATION:

Avon Calling – The Bristol Compilation LP (Heartbeat HB 1 1979; 'Too Much Commotion') (reissued on CD in October 2005 on Heartbeat/Cherry Red CDMRED 292)

MPs

Mark Read (vocals), Tim Read (guitar), John Evans (bass; replacing earlier bass player Wallace), Ian Tully (drums; later replaced by Tommy Watson), Rob Anderson (rhythm guitar)

The MPs were one of the de facto first wave Newcastle punk bands, formed at the end of 1976. Mark Read: "I lived in Newcastle city centre, and my brother and most of the others lived in Washington new town." They were vaguely aware of Penetration, but although they became fast friends with Speed, they were unaware of any other punk bands in the vicinity.

Their inspirations were the usual suspects, "the Pistols, Velvets, Gil Scott Heron,

the Dolls, Wire, Augustus Pablo, Bunny Wailer, Clash, Buzzcocks etc." The rest of the band, however, was significantly younger than Mark Read. "I was 21, they were much younger, 16 and 17. My brother heard Hendrix, picked up a guitar, and a couple of years later came out of his bedroom playing blues, As soon as he heard punk, he was into that, which isn't that massive a leap from the basics. I'd grown up with the Tamla, Bowie thing. The rest of the band grew up in the punk thing. I was five years older. I was writing lyrics just for the hell of it. Then my brother put a band together that was playing at school in Washington. Then they suggested I sing the lyrics I'd written. That's how it is in my memory. Others were reading from their own scripts and may have been watching a completely different movie."

The band rehearsed at Mark Read's hairdresser's. "I was running a salon in Newcastle at the time called Capo. Quite a few bands would come down and rehearse on a Sunday morning. Penetration came down once or twice, and Murder The Disturbed, the Proles, Speed, the Angelic Upstarts; several bands. It became like a public rehearsal spot. For the first few months, it was just us down there, then gradually it built up. Towards the end, some Sunday lunchtimes, there would be maybe 20 or 30 people there, most of whom were musicians. Eventually, we got a tag, because a lot of young, spiky-haired people came in, we got the image of being a punk hairdresser's. Which we weren't, particularly."

As for their early songs: "One of the first ones was 'Left, Right, Black, White', which was just a bit of a chant. I remember words like 'exploitation' and 'humiliation' rhyming easily! I was probably a little more political. I was into what was going on in South Africa and the political and racism things going on at the time. We were involved with people like the Anti-Nazi League. But partly because we got the gigs – it was gig first, politics second – but I definitely moved the lyric that way."

Mark Read remembers gigs at the Bridge Hotel, Gatsby's on the Whitley Bay coast, Gosforth pub the Bridge, where the bands played upstairs, etc. The MPs supported Sham 69 at Sunderland Poly ("Jimmy Pursey was a bit of a grumpy twat, the Sham Army were good, though"), and backing the Lurkers at Middlesbrough Rock Garden. "Really good blokes," he remembers, "and they encouraged us." The latter gig provides Mark Read's favourite memory of his time with the MPs. "We always used to think, if we cause a fuss, it doesn't matter if it's good or bad. We caused a bit of chaos at the Lurkers gig. Afterwards, I got up on a table so I could see the Lurkers play. I was watching the Lurkers, and people were still throwing bottles and glasses at me. I was going, 'Howay! I'm finished now, lads! I'm part of the audience now!"

However, he'd departed by the advent of the MPs sole EP, 'Toytown Living'. "The lyrics to 'Toytown Living' were written by my brother. It was based on Washington, a new town, and the monotony." Other songs included the quasi-romantic 'Hot Line to Your Heart'. "There was also a song we did about (execution victim and would be medical donor) Gary Gilmore's eyes, but we thought it was a bit too obvious and tabloidy, a bit too obvious. We were amazed when the Adverts had a hit single with that! We were always quite right on about the 'principle' of punk, we didn't want to get involved with the corporate side of things. We wanted to keep it rough and ready, we wanted it to be a revolution, a glimmer of hope and anarchy against the dull backdrop that was the depression of the impending years of Tory clampdown. You could see and feel it coming. Of course, we also wanted it to be fun and not a job."

The EP came out in 1978. "By that time I'd left and Brian Nylon (Roberts), a fan of the band who wrote a fanzine, had come in as singer. A local character called Professor Fate helped them get the record out. He was famous for writing a couple of the NME letters of the year. At the start of 1977 he wrote them a letter saying just "You'll all be sorry." Then at the end of the year he wrote another letter, saying "I told you so."

Mark Read had, meantime, departed for London. "We'd done as much as I was interested in. It was only ever for fun for me. I never had any big plans. I had my own business. I moved down to London. In Newcastle I was running around with a lot of daft characters, not living a very healthy lifestyle, and I disappeared down to London, rehabbed on a council estate in Bethnal Green, and chilled out down there." The band continued until the end of 1978, before the members moved on to other projects. Ian Tully became a props buyer for the BBC, working on the League Of Gentlemen, etc.

Mark Read now manages hot Newcastle hip hop crew Dialect. Sadly, Rob Anderson died in London. "He always had a struggle with smack, and even if he wasn't dead, I would say he was a great bloke with a natural joy for music which made me smile. He has two kids (now adults) Jude and Rachel. She is now bringing up his grandchildren."

DISCOGRAPHY:

MPs 7-inch EP (Acid Nose 1978)
Toytown Living/Hot Line To Your Heart/Bombs (Death Make Money)/Betray

Mud Hutters

The origins of DIY-punk legends the MUD HUTTERS go back as far as 1971, when Dick (Richard Harrison) and Moon began playing together in North Cheshire. By 1976 the founding duo were joined by others in the form of Benny, Malc and Pete Collier, although by the time they became the Mud Hutters at the end of 1978, Collier had departed. As for influences: "Before punk came along, Kraut rockers Can, Faust and Neu were important to us," notes Harrison. "After 1976, the Buzzcocks and the Fall, for starters. Moon and I were into anarchism from an early age, spurred on by a distaste for the education system. I would guess that Pete and Malc would drink to that too, literally!" Their debut EP was followed by a second effort, 'Declaration', recorded in the summer of 1979 with guest guitar by Mike Hinds. It was judged by Johan Kugelberg to be one of the 100 greatest DIY efforts ever in his landmark article for Ugly Things magazine.

As the band gigged throughout Cheshire and Lancashire, a meeting with Paul Emmerson of Dislocation Dance at the Band On The Wall led to the Mud Hutters throwing in their lot with the Manchester Musicians Collective. Collier then returned on bass while Benny left to attend university, and the band joined the I Like Shopping tour alongside the Diagram Brothers, Dislocation Dance, Decorators, Ludus and Eric Random. Eventually they released a full studio album and contributed four tracks to the Four Ways Out compilation, before entering semi-retirement. However, there have continued to be outbreaks of activity since, and several unreleased sessions have also seen daylight, if not official release. Harrison continues to form half of Spaceheads alongside Andy Diagram, who joined the Mud Hutters in 1984. They also espouse the same values they've always advocated. "During the 'Reagan years', we were involved in CND marches, standing on picket lines during the miners strike. Moon and Malc were arrested for dancing in the road in front of Ronald Reagan's motorcade in London. We daubed anti-nuclear messages on many motorway signs. I'm very proud of our peace sign we planted over 20 years ago, it still blooms every spring. One of Moon's classic lines that sums up the Mud Hutters: I used to believe in the power of love, now I believe in the strength of lager."

M

DISCOGRAPHY:

Information 7-inch EP (Defensive NATO-1 1978)
No God/Nice Guy/Left Right/All About/Neolithic Dub
Declaration 7-inch EP (Defensive NATO-2 1979)
Water Torture/Chances/Stabbings/Fragments/Danger/It Doesn't Seem To Help Now
Factory Farming LP (NATO-3 1981)
COMPILATION:
4-Ways Out 12-inch (PACT 1 1980; 'Vision On', 'Rire To Laugh')

Mutants

Sweet William (vocals), Roddie Rodent (aka Rod Gilliard; guitar), Al Sation (bass), Keith 'Kid' Steele (aka Keith Wilson; guitar), Paul Pleasant (aka Paul Codman; drums)

One of the few punk bands to emerge from Merseyside in the 70s, alongside the Spitfire Boys and the more arty Big In Japan. The MUTANTS, from Birkenhead, actually played a more MC5/Dead Boys-derived version of punk. I remember picking up their second single (I'm a sucker for red vinyl) in the early-80s, by which time Keith 'Kid' Steele had left, and being convinced it was an American band I was

listening to. Which could have been confusing, being that at least two American bands entitled the Mutants were extant at the time.

Codman: "You're right, we were a bit of a hybrid of MC5/Pink Fairies type rock with a dash of Bowie/Lou Reed thrown in, rather than the Pistols or Clash. In fact, when we supported the Police at the Roxy in Covent Garden, Miles Copeland said: 'Get those two to cut their hair or get the other three to grow it and smell and then we'll talk....' Who said punk was anti-image? I think we were the first Liverpool 'punk' band to play the Roxy. When we came off stage, Sting said, 'You can't go in the dressing room just yet.' A short time later a sexy girl in a pencil skirt emerged followed by a sweaty Stewart Copeland. Well, he was already a pop star with Curved Air! I remember the Police brought their gear in a small Bedford van and a taxi and Sting asking if he could share our bottle of cider."

They were also the first punk band to play the Isle Of Man, in this case the Lido. "We got ourselves on the front page of the Echo because Sweet William took his own birch, which was confiscated when we disembarked in Douglas. We were supported by two out-and-out rock bands, whose fans didn't take kindly to us. Me and Roddie were at the bar as two groovy young chicks approached us: 'Are you the Mutants?' I replied yes, in my best rock star pose. (It was the first time we'd had carpet and a phone in the dressing room, so I can be forgiven) 'Well, why don't you fuck off back to Liverpool and leave the real music to Debris and Exile!'"

One of the Mutants' other claims to fame was that they never played Eric's. "Roger Eagle wouldn't have us after we fly posted his club. We thought, 'All his bands do it everywhere else, why don't we do it to him?' He wasn't too pleased. Anyway, Joe Strummer got wind of the story and announced in NME that, 'Liverpool's Mutants may well be the next new wave band to enjoy mass market breakthrough...' Lovely! I actually got to thank him personally in Eric's dressing room. That is a great memory, along with meeting Jane County in the same tiny, squalid room."

Prior to the Mutants Gilliard had been a member of the Bugs and Mother's Ruin. After the Mutants dissolved, Codman, Wilson and Gilliard would then regroup as the Geisha Girls. Gilliard also played in the Gypsy Blues, the Press, Afraid Of Mice, Da Biffs, Attempted Moustache and any number of other Liverpool groups. Codman works part time at the Liverpool Institute of Arts and has been a professional actor since 1983. "I still drum occasionally on stage and screen. My last band, while still at college, was on keyboards for Egypt For Now, alongside Mick Head (Pale Fountains, Shack) on vocals and Yorkie (Space) on bass."

DISCOGRAPHY:

Boss Man/Back Yard Boys 7-inch (Rox ROX 002 November 1977) (the A-side announced "From the possibly forthcoming LP Mutants 20 Gold Hits." No such record exists)
Hard Time/School Teacher/Lady 7-inch (Rox ROX 005 1978) (issued in red vinyl)

Muvver's Pride

Sue 'Suby' Barnes (vocals), Dee Marsh (aka Dee Hurley; guitar), Lynne 'Pearl' Easton (bass), Nina 'Cuddles' Spencer (drums)

MUVVER'S PRIDE were one of the few all-female groups on the punk circuit during 1978, but seem to have largely disappeared from the history books. Yet all four members at various points were fixtures on the King's Road scene, several working at Boy. Lynne Easton had run away from her conservative boarding school to study make-up at Joan Price's Face Place. She was given the nickname Pearl by her boyfriend, Adam Ant. Drummer Nina Spencer had already had some stage experience, playing Magenta in the Rocky Horror Show when it was staged at the King's Road Theatre. Muvver's Pride quickly acquired their own following – including a male contingent who were rather obviously, but according to several reports quite accurately, nicknamed the Muvva Fuckers. Among them was Chips Chapman, who would write the band's best-known song, 'Brighton Rock'. As Nick Medlin, his later band-mate in Fourth Reich, subsequently told me, "He later admitted that it was a rip-off of 'Monster Mash'."

Muvver's Pride never did get a record out, though they certainly gigged quite prodigiously, with support slots to the Police and Menace, among others. However, the band folded when Barnes fell pregnant. Easton and Dee Hurley (who had replaced namesake Dee Marsh) subsequently formed the short-lived Pearl Harbour, before becoming the Spiders, who released a version of 'Mony Mony' in 1980 for Red Shadow. Nina Spencer subsequently joined Fourth Reich, who eventually evolved into Manufactured Romance (both bands also featured Chips Chapman and another 'Muvva Fucker', Suby Barnes' boyfriend, John 'Abe' Lincoln).

Easton became an acclaimed make-up artist, working with George Michael, Bananarama, Culture Club (she did the make-up for Boy George for an episode of the A-Team), Elton John and Paul Weller as MTV began to flourish in the 80s. Indeed, she was briefly married to Jam biographer Paolo Hewitt and toured the world with the Pet Shop Boys and Terence Trent D'Arby among others, and sometimes offered backing vocals, before working on the Bond movie Golden Eye. Later she ran a pigeon rescue centre in North London and cared for retired racing greyhounds before dying suddenly in February 2006. Spencer is currently a DJ in America.

Nazis Against Fascism

Ben Brierley (instruments, vocals), Heathcote Williams (lyrics)

A concept single put together by Ben Brierley, who'd previously been associated with both the Vibrators and the Front, who provides all the music, with vocals and lyrics from Heathcote Williams. This was one of several singles that emerged in the immediate aftermath of Sidney Vicious's arrest, including cuts by the Surgeons and, most famously, the Cash Pussies. It goes for the jugular, too – "The white blood was squirting/And Nancy was hurting/But Sid did it/All the pistols of sex/Had blanks up their spout/Shit and piss and vomit/Was all they could get out."

Heathcote Williams, is, of course, a world-renowned playwright, poet, actor, painter, etc. So, how did this lark all come about? "I was walking down Kensington Park Road and noticed graffiti on the synagogue there. It had been defaced by a swastika and accompanying it was the statement: 'Sid is Innocent.' Given the time when this appeared, it was clearly a reference to one of the Sex Pistols, Sid Vicious, who'd just been arrested in New York and was awaiting trial on a murder charge. Anyway, I took that to be the case and that was the germ of it. The song was sung by Ben Brierley, formerly of the Vibrators and the Front, and we worked closely with a producer called Michael Zilkha, who put it out."

The song's tile came "as a direct response to the graffiti and as a reference, obviously, to Sid Vicious's heroin-fuelled murder of his girlfriend Nancy Spungen in the Chelsea Hotel." Why **NAZIS AGAINST FASCISM**? "I remember that there was something about the coverage of the Spungen murder at the time in the music press which made me gag – Nancy Spungen was being portrayed as almost deserving of her fate depicted, as she was a gold-digging junkie hooker. There was also the notion floating about in the punk fanzines and the music press that Sid Vicious's celebrity should somehow transcend his crime if not even exonerate him; it was suggested, in other words, that because he'd become a punk idol he could do what he wanted. (The murder seemed to be the reductio ad absurdam of punk's anti-heroism.)

Williams thought this was "kind of elitist, decadent and fascistic even – the idea that some people were more special than others – it was a twisted reprise of rock star mystification and all the same elitist (and emetic) feelings that whirl about them. The band's title, Nazis against Fascism, was also a dig at punk's fascination with Nazi regalia and the way in which Pistols' fans and others had adopted it as a kind of kitsch fashion statement. I could never work out what all that Belsen Bling meant. Probably nothing at all, and anyway with the wisdom of hindsight, I'd have to admit that the title for the band which we cooked up was confusingly obscure, if not even slightly offensive itself. What exactly was it saying? Punk fascists against punk fascism? I have to admit it didn't make a lot of sense. But essentially we did it as a lark – It was a spur of the moment agit-prop thing. Clock the graffiti – song – rehearsal – studio – record pressed – all in about a week."

The song came out on Zilkha's Ze Records, using the sobriquet Truth Records, especially invoked for the occasion. "No money ever changed hands. I don't remember how many 45s were produced or whether or not they sold any copies. Rough Trade stocked it, I think. Under English law I suppose we could have been done for being in breach of the sub judice rule – it would certainly have been regarded as prejudicing the outcome of any forthcoming trial had one ever taken place, of course, but Sid Vicious never came to trial and died beforehand."

Subsequently, Ben Brierley married Marianne Faithfull, contributing a track to her Broken English album, 'Brain Drain' (Williams also contributed lyrics to one song on that album, 'Why D'ya Do It?'). "Then I believe Ben ended up in New York. I've not heard from him since. Michael Zilkha used to produce Kid Creole And The Coconuts, then he went off to Texas and got involved in the oil business, and now I believe he builds wind farms with a company called the Wild Horse Wind Power Project."

DISCOGRAPHY:

Sid Did It (Intelligible)/Sid Did It (Radio Version) 7-inch (Stage STAGE 1 1979) (reissued later in 1979 by Truth, TRUTH 1)

The Negatives (1)

Principal members were Kevin Cummins and Paul Morley, with other contributors including Steve Shy, 'Merlin', Richard Boon and Dave Bentley, all playing various instruments

Before becoming one of the most opinionated and opinion-dividing writers to emerge from the punk era, Paul Morley was bass player and occasional guitarist in Manchester's NEGATIVES. Inspired by reading about the Sex Pistols in the NME, when he should have been minding the bookshop he worked at in Stockport, Morley launched the idea for a concept band in the back room of his house on Hawthorne Grove, alongside photographic conspirator Kevin Cummins.

Regular likeminded visitors and houseguests at Hawthorne Grove included Pete Shelley and Vini Reilly. Both Morley and Cummins were already producing a fanzine entitled Girl Trouble, although the first issue included pieces on Dylan and Ted Nugent and pre-dated his exposure to punk. Cummins: "Girl Trouble was my idea – we both produced it. The idea was to take a photo of someone with it on their person for the following issue. We gave one to Hugh Cornwell at a gig in Sheffield and he folded it and put it in his back pocket – I photographed him on stage with it poking out slightly and that was the picture in the next issue. I've also got a picture of Paul Weller with it on a table in front of him – during an interview Paul and I did at the Circus."

Were they serious? Cummins: "Not really. It started with Paul Morley and myself sitting up night after night when we were working on various things for the NME. We felt the London press was so lazy and London-centric that we could more or less tell them anything that was going on in Manchester and they'd believe it. Our first piece together was about Manchester, which the NME had sat on for a couple of months. In the end we told them that Giovanni Dadomo was coming up from Sounds to do a massive piece about Manchester. The NME thought, oh, we'd better get it there first. So my first piece for the NME was a double page spread. Then we thought we'd invent a band. Initially, all we did was send a press release out to the news pages at both the NME and Sounds, and a list of gigs. We just trawled the Yellow Pages in Stockport and South Manchester and came up with things like The Grey Parrot Club, Nantwich – just places that seemed funny to us at the time. Of course, they just ran with it in their gig guide. Sounds ran it as a news piece and put "legendary new wave venues every one". We just thought it was funny that they'd believe this was going on.

"We sent a press release to the news pages that said the Negatives EP 'Bringing Fiction Back To Music' was going to be released, but deleted the day before it came out. And they put that in. I think they thought this was some sort of avant garde band in Manchester. It never occurred to them to find out who was behind it or anything. We took photographs and wrote all this rubbish about ourselves, and they just kept printing it. Paul and I went to cover a tour by Sham 69 for the NME. We were telling Jimmy Pursey about this. 'That's brilliant, man, that's punk, that's real punk spirit. Do you want to support us?' We thought, that sounds funny, what a laugh! So we thought we'd support Sham 69 when they came to play the Oaks in Manchester. We didn't even have a band. We had three backing singers who were girls who used to go to the Electric Circus called the Negalettes. We hadn't rehearsed. Suddenly we thought, we'd better try to play something. We had one rehearsal, which just deteriorated into throwing beer cans at each other."

At the resultant Sham 69 show they were 'appalling', he confesses. "We'd knocked up a few songs the night before. One was 'Theme From Coronation Street', which was exactly what it says. We just played that slightly out of tune with a singer chanting 'Theme From Coronation Street' over it." The band used a variety of vocalists, including Dave Bentley, who would count from 1 to 350 to 'musical accompaniment'. "The avant garde idea was that we'd have a guest vocalist every time we played rather than keep the same line-up. And we all played instruments that none of us had ever touched before. Richard Boon (Buzzcocks' manager) played saxophone because he knew someone who had a saxophone. Paul played bass, and sometimes guitar with three strings. We had a guy called Merlin who would also play bass or guitar. Merlin was a mutual friend of mine and Paul's who used to run a lock-up garage in Stockport called Merlin Motors. Steve Shy (of Shy Talk fanzine) did a couple of things with us. I'd play drums sometimes, sometimes just sit there. Because Paul and I used to go to all the gigs, we used to get talked into doing it a bit. We thought it was funny. Various people in Manchester shared the joke, but the punters didn't really share the joke at all. People used to get quite irate if we turned up. We supported Wayne County and they pulled the plug on us after 10 minutes and tried to stop us even watching the gig, they were so appalled at the noise we were making. We did a song called 'Sick Of London' that we made badges for. London, the band, played Rafters shortly before we had the song. We got about 100 badges from them that we nicked backstage, and wrote 'Sick Of' in marker above their logo."

They played at the Stiff Test/Chiswick Challenge alongside Joy Division, with whom there was a 'handbags' backstage scuffle. A demo tape was handed to a bemused A&R man from London, or at least that was the story that circulated. It included Morley's 'My Kind Of Girl Pays Fourpence On The Bus'. Cummins: "That was a bit of an un-PC song that Paul wrote before PC was invented. Girls under 15 could pay fourpence on the bus in Manchester at the time."

The Negatives were the only band to play both nights at the Electric Circus's final hurrah. Cummins: "Pete Shelley did one night with us. The second night we had another guy, some old friend of Paul's. He was really annoyed at us. He joined thinking it was all going to be really serious, we were going to be like Gavin Bryars and some jazz collective. He didn't understand what the deal was. He started singing his vocals to some of the notes Paul had given him, and there was this cacophony of sound behind him. He was furious." Virgin recorded the shows for their Short Circuit compilation. Sadly, or fortuitously, the Negatives didn't make the final track selection. Cummins: "I've still got a tape of that. The bloke in the Electric Circus is saying over the tape, 'I hope you're getting all this. The audience is showering the band with cans of liquid refreshment. And the band are throwing them back.' There was this huge bun fight at the Circus."

Thereafter Morley headed south for a career with the NME, while Cummins became one of the same paper's foremost photographers. Shy returned to working on his fanzine. "I seem to remember the Negatives being rather good," Jon Savage later told Mick Middles, doubtless wishing to bolster the myth he'd helped to perpetuate. Cummins: "Obviously, Jon Savage, if we ever played he'd review us and talk us up and make out it was something serious that was happening. It now becomes part of Manchester folklore, I guess, so that people like Dave Haslam and various other people who write histories of that period, place us in there as if we were part of the whole Manchester scene. Really, it was never meant to be like that. It was just something we were doing for our own amusement really. Our big mistake, as we will always admit, is that we actually played. If we'd stayed as a band purely on paper, that would have been fine. We should have never exposed ourselves to public ridicule."

But someone, somewhere, still holds a copy of that original demo. Bentley, who was credited with being the chief mover behind the bootlegging of the Buzzcocks' Time's Up, was last sighted driving trams in Australia, according to Pete Shelley in 1991.

Negatives (2)

Pete Eason (aka William Bonny; vocals, drums), Brad Martini (bass), Fraser 'Fritz' Charlesworth (guitar, piano)

The Sheffield NEGATIVES, as opposed to the Blackburn or Manchester adopters of the same name, were the north's answer to the Jam. While other mod revivalists such as Secret Affair, the Chords and Purple Hearts ploughed a furrow that seemed more concerned with replicating the footsteps of their forebears, bands like the Negatives had bags of energy and commitment. They were tight, practised, purposeful and wrote great songs, many of which were the equal of anything on In The City. Whether they had anything in their locker capable of competing with All Mod Cons-era Jam we will never know. They didn't last long enough for us to find out.

Like many of the mod revival bands, the Negatives began life in 1978 as a punk pop band, influenced principally by the Buzzcocks and Stranglers. They made their vinyl debut by contributing two tracks, 'Don't Say Goodbye' and 'Metallic Thread Shirt' to the Planet Records compilation album New Wave From The Heart, before Steve Wilmot joined on drums to allow Eason to concentrate on singing.

Their debut single 'Electric Waltz' was recorded in Cambridge for their manager Marcus Featherby's Limited Edition label. It was made single of the week in the NME in January 1980, though it had actually been released six weeks earlier. And it was, indeed, excellent, readily surpassing and making irrelevant the debate over which genre should claim them. Though widely perceived as a mod band by the national media, the band themselves were a bit bemused by the image, and felt 'sick' when they were advertised by promoters as such.

In the end the single was never followed up. Tired of Featherby's antics, and equally galled by the pigeonholing, though they were at least partially responsible for it by dint of their shared stage uniform, the band split up. Pete Eason continued as a singer and formed Person To Person, who secured a record deal with CBS in 1984 but failed to build on the initial strong notices after releasing debut album Stronger Than Reason the following year.

DISCOGRAPHY:

Electric Waltz/Money Talks 7-inch (Limited Edition/Aardvark December 1979)

Negatives (3)

Pete Stobbs (lead guitar), Bob Robinson (bass), Tino Palmer (drums), Dave Wilcox (vocals)

Not Paul Morley's Mancunian mischief-makers, nor the mod-influenced Sheffield band, Bradford's NEGATIVES were formed by Pete Stobbs in 1978. After recruiting Palmer from a Melody Maker advert, the line-up was completed when Robinson and Wilcox were drafted in after chance meetings.

Gigs were arranged alongside practice sessions at local band haunt the Coda Rooms, culminating in a series of Rock Against Racism and CND rallies as well as a piece in local punk fanzine Wool City Rocker. A demo was prepared and played on local radio, although the masters were subsequently lost. Meanwhile, the band established itself as a formidable live act, taking in most of the popular Yorkshire venues, often as the headlining act. Notable supports included Aswad at a Rock Against Racism festival and Stiff Little Fingers at the Queen's Hall, though they were less than taken at Jake Burns' 'rock star antics' at the latter.

Palmer's boss was eventually persuaded to stump up the readies to cover the recording costs, which came in at less than £100 anyway, for the band's debut single. This featured 'Stake Out' and 'Love Is Not Real' (a third track they recorded, 'We're From Bradford', was finally released on Bored Teenagers Vol. 2 in 2001 alongside both sides of the single). The single sold out of its 500-strong pressing almost immediately with support from John Peel and a trickle of national press coverage.

N

But there was little fanfare afforded the West Yorkshire scene, unless you were an art student in Leeds, of course. Palmer: "There was a bit of stuff going on in Leeds, as more of a major city, and the Futurama festival was held there in 1980. We were a bit stupid and thought that we would get 'discovered' anyway, but Bradford was never on anyone's list – except perhaps worst place to be. But I wrote 'We're From Bradford' as a bit of a riposte to all the fashionable places/people bands around. It didn't make any difference, but it made me feel better! It's now a bit of an anthem when we play it live – now at least everyone who comes to a gig knows where we're from, as if we didn't remind them enough." Despite that, Palmer insists there was a healthy live scene during the period. "Looking through an old fanzine from the time – the Wool City Rocker – over August and September 1980 there were at least two gigs every day, and over 100 gigs in the first two weeks of August alone. There were loads of venues putting on all sorts of bands – blues, reggae, pop, new wave, punk, jazz, and pretty much every one of those venues has gone. We played with Aswad at an outdoor festival in Bradford, which was halted by the police after a bit of a ruck on stage. But there weren't many 'big' bands that stopped off here, and as we didn't get to play Leeds very often – like today, it's quite insular and difficult to get into if you're not local – we didn't get a lot of the good support slots. But as we had a decent following around Bradford/Keighley etc, we didn't bother."

According to Palmer, the band's most memorable shows were "probably the Christmas gigs, especially the one when we released the first single. It was packed out, flour bombs, a special version of 'Rudolph', free beer and goat curry from the reggae club it was held at. The support with Aswad followed from that. Also, the fact that I could walk down the street and it seemed that every other kid knew me; not really fame, but it was just cool to be around and part of a cool club." However, on 19 January 1980 the Negatives would play their final show at the Lord Mayor's Ball at Bradford University's Great Hall, alongside the Squids and Shadowfax, after Wilcox announced his decision to leave. Which is where it gets complicated.

Wilcox took the name Negativz for his new act, while his former band members put together Mysterious Footsteps. The Footsteps released one single, the double A-side 'White Dread'/'Like They Do In The Movies' and played alongside the likes of New Model Army and Southern Death Cult, while a five-song video was recorded for Pete Townshend's Eel Pie Studios. But that all went awry when Townshend fled the country for tax reasons, and the momentum slipped away.

Palmer, an ardent Bradford City football fan, made a living as a sweet-seller, while Robinson worked in tax. However, prompted by bids of up to £200 for their solitary single, and further inspired by the inclusion of three tracks on the Detour Records compilation Bored Teenagers, they reformed in 2000. Palmer attempted to interest his beloved Bradford City into taking the field to the tune of 'We're From Bradford', as opposed to the customary 'A-Team Theme'.

So what was it like second time round? It sounds like Spinal Tap with flattened vowels. "There seems to have been more ups and downs this time. The original line-up weren't interested in playing live, but the band that I put together seemed like it could take on the world. There were problems with the singer Mick – he left and was replaced by Kev in February 2003. There were problems with him after a few months too – he thought we were his backing band! So he left too. Then the bass player Mark took over on vocals, brought in Tony on bass and we got on with it. Dizzy (of Detour/Bored Teenagers) put together a great showcase for four bands in London, which we enjoyed immensely. But there were also problems with the new singer and the lead guitarist which led to us slimming down to a three-piece who are now getting down to it and playing as many gigs as we can manage. Then we got the news that we were in John Peel's top 100 favourite singles box with 'Love Is Not Real'. We've released three CDs and are still writing new songs for more releases. If we've got things to say, might as well say 'em! We ain't gonna get rich and famous, so we're gonna have a good time before we keel over, and if we keel over doing it, then that could be cool too!"

N

DISCOGRAPHY:

Stakeout/Love Is Not Real 7-inch (Look Records LK/SP 6478 1979) (500 copies, 100 with wraparound paper sleeve)
Brain Damage CD (Not From London NFL 001 2002) (First 100 in handmade cardboard cut-out sleeve, stamped and numbered)
Wood City Rockers CD (Not From London NFL 002 2004)
I Promise/Mobile Attack/1984/I'll Only Ever Love You/(Another) Stakeout/Control
The Negatives Say... CD single (Not From London NFL 003 2005)
Social Insecurity/Friday Night/Steal/Rat Race
COMPILATION:
Bored Teenagers Vol. 2 LP & CD (Bin Liner RUBBISHLP/CD 003 March 2001; 'Stakeout', 'Love Is Not Real', 'We're From Bradford')

Neon

Tim Jones (vocals, guitar), Mark Dunn (bass, guitar), Paddi Addison (drums)

County Durham band formed in 1978 from the remains of local attractions such as Hephalumps & the Woozels and Eyes To The Sky. The latter featured both Addison and Jones. Addison was also a member of Scottish rock band Dragon, while Dunn and Jones played together in Whippet, which featured future NEON manager Paul Taylor on drums.

When Addison returned from Scotland, after Dragon ground to a halt, Neon came together early in 1976. They practised in the latter's bedroom, experimenting with different time signatures, learning to play their instruments as fast as humanly possible and writing original material which they would eventually describe as 'progressive punk'. Listening back now, it sounds like nothing so much as jazz on speed. They were essentially an experimental band, but soon found themselves tagged as punks, it being the nearest convenient shorthand genre. And they grew into it.

I asked Tim Jones if he thought that the band would have sounded the way it did without the advent of punk. "Definitely not! The arrival of punk had a huge impact on our approach to both writing and performing songs. It felt like you really had to go out there and prove yourself as the competition was fierce! There were so many fantastic new bands and there was such a vibrant scene going on in the North East of England. The pubs were packed out with punters eager to see new bands, the crazier the better and everything was so loud and brash. You would never get away with that kind of volume in your local pub these days. We might have had bottles thrown at us if the audience didn't like us but I can't honestly remember us being told to turn it down. The idea was to be loud and full of energy. We pushed ourselves to the limit and sometimes you wondered if you were going to pass out before the next song. There was a kind of expectant air at some gigs where nobody was sure what to expect next. The emphasis was definitely on originality and we wanted to be unique, to express something new."

Early shows included regular supports to Penetration (Jones worked in the same council office as Gary Chaplin) and Punishment Of Luxury. Later came shows with Siouxsie And The Banshees at Durham University, the Pretenders at the Nashville and Steel Pulse in Edinburgh. The only really bad times were due to the rivalry between Sunderland and Newcastle fans. "There is a lot of rivalry. It could sometimes be quite hairy playing in Sunderland and we encountered a disproportionate amount of violence there, to be honest." However, on the whole Neon grew up in a very supportive and vibrant music scene. "During the punk era, we were lucky to have excellent music journalists like Phil Sutcliffe, Ian Penman and Dick Godfrey living in Newcastle. They worked in local radio and wrote articles for newspapers like Sounds. They also helped promote a lot of gigs and ran local magazines about regional bands. We also had the likes of Rick Walton who were great photographers going to gigs taking photos of all of the bands. They helped enormously in getting people noticed by the major labels in London. It is true to say that you had to go to London if you were serious about getting signed to a major label. They would need to see you at places like The Hope & Anchor, Nashville, Music Machine, Marquee Club etc, to see how you went down with those crowds and where A&R people could just get on a tube to see you perform rather than travel hundreds of miles. The problem was getting the gigs in London. Having said that, once we did get an agent, the itineraries were knackering, especially travelling up and down the motorways in an old transit van, sleeping on top of the PA. We were nearly written off a few times when everyone in the van fell asleep, including the driver!"

The lyrics were mainly written by Jones. "It was left up to me, for some reason. We used the voice more as an instrument to complement the bass, drums and guitar. The words were used as much for the way the sound of them could be manipulated. A great influence on the vocals was Captain Beefheart too. There was also that idea of 'No Future', where the hell are we going, what's it all for? Why do I have to work in a horrible, boring job for very little money when all I want to do is play my guitar and express myself? The lyrics were written from the point of view of the little guy struggling to make sense of the world. We were young, idealistic, anti-war, anti-establishment and saw anarchy as a positive alternative to the pyramid structure of society where those at the top get more than their fair share of the benefits."

Their first single was released on Lenny Love's Sensible Records (original home of the Rezillos). 'Bottles' was inspired by the missiles commonly lobbed at them while playing on stage and featured some typically wigged out instrumental breaks and the band's customary 'race to the finish line' pacing. 'Anytime Anyplace Anywhere', meanwhile, betrayed the aforementioned Teutonic influence of the Krautrock bands. It was followed by a John Peel session in March 1979. Former colleague Martin Holder had returned to the north east after playing with bands in London and was thereafter installed as second guitarist.

There was interest from United Artists after the single's success, where their colleagues Punishment Of Luxury were ensconced. But producer Martin Rushent ushered them towards his new venture Genetics, which had a distribution deal with Jake Riviera's Radar Records instead and, with the exception of Jones, they moved down to London. A further single resulted, but it was the final release of the band's career. All they had to show for the years of solid gigging were mounting debts. Jones was invited to audition for the Vibrators but was "too knackered" after the band's demise. He hooked up with Punishment Of Luxury's singer Brian Bond in Punching Holes in 1979 before joining his former compatriots in Punilux.

Later Jones set up the label Stone Premonitions with partner Terri B, specialising in psychedelic music. Addison became a sound technician with the likes of Pink Floyd. Mark Dunn joined the Poison Girls. Martin Holder would work with Jah Wobble and then join Dunn in Who Said Charge? The former members of Neon would regroup in 1985 and record a six-track mini-album as Somebody Famous and two CDs as Body Full Of Stars, released through Stone Premonitions. The latter also now houses the Neon canon, including two new CDs of unreleased/archive material that came out in 2005.

"We still employ a totally DIY attitude in the music we produce," says Jones. "A real revolution has taken place as regards music technology and communication. Studio equipment has become so much cheaper and easier to use. It has put digital quality recording into the hands of musicians at home, in their own environment. The major record companies with their big studios and high rates do not have a monopoly anymore. You can produce CDs of your own music at home and create all of your artwork on a PC. Thanks to the arrival of the Internet, you can sell your releases through websites and become part of a truly international, alternative music scene. It is breathtaking in its possibilities, and you're only limited by your own skills and imagination. We have met so many like-minded musicians and enthusiasts through the Internet in recent years, all working for a common cause, freedom of expression. It is truly liberating for people that are into it for the music rather than the money. Contrary to popular opinion, not all punk rockers sold out or sold their souls to mammon."

DISCOGRAPHY:

Bottles/I'm Only Little/Anytime Anyplace Anywhere 7-inch (Sensible FAB 3 1978)
Don't Eat Bricks/Hanging Off An O 7-inch (Radar ADA 27 1979)
Archive Material:
Neon CD (Stone Premonitions SPCD 0015 2002)
Sign Of The Time CD (Stone Premonitions SPCD 047 2005)

Nicky And The Dots

Nick Dwyer (vocals), Chris D'Ouseley (guitar), Dave 'Blotto' Williams (bass), Paul Clark (organ), Ken Hogg (drums)

N

Brighton's NICKY AND THE DOTS managed one excellent pop-orientated punk single towards the twilight of Small Wonder's reign in 1979, as well as contributing three tracks to the highly-regarded Vaultage 1978 compilation – not that Nick Dwyer has high regard for them. They were formed in November 1977 when Dwyer and D'Ouseley met at art college. By 1978 they'd picked up some national press from Sounds, there was a session for John Peel and gigs alongside Crass. It resulted in a contract with Small Wonder.

I asked Dwyer how the tie-up came about. "I sent him (Pete Stennet) a demo and he phoned back. No-one else did. We had to quickly record on a Sunday in someone's front room (no amps allowed, DI into the desk) three different songs for Vaultage. They sound shit to this day. Small Wonder hired the Beat's producer to beef us up for the single release, and it still sounds pretty good." It could all have been so different. "We gave a demo tape of 'Never Been So Stuck' to Sting when we were extras in Quadrophenia. It has a very repetitive vocal hook and a jerky riff. Sting released 'Don't Stand So Close To Me' a few months later. Coincidence? Probably! A similar thing happened with the Vapors and 'Turning Japanese', a song with a very repetitive vocal hook and a jerky riff. We had supported them at a pub in Brighton only weeks earlier. Coincidence? I hope so. Because 'Turning Japanese' was shit."

However, Small Wonder wasn't the happy home many might have thought. "Pete Stennet really didn't like me at all. When we first met, he played us the Cure's '10.15 Saturday Night', which was on the label, and said we could be a bit like them if we tried hard. He then said, 'Nick, some people go far, some people dream of going far' and fixed me with a gimlet stare. He was right about both of us as it happened."

I thought I'd run my Brighton punk theory past the big Dot man. The bands seemed more experimental than in other regions, but there also seemed to be a strong drug legacy, and an enormous number of acts who cut just one or two singles, appeared on the Vaultage compilations, then disappeared. Would that be a fair assessment? "How does yes and no sound? The Brighton punk scene was perhaps more 'music hall' than others. I feel, in retrospect, most of it was pretend punk. Most punk in Britain apart from the Pistols, Clash, Damned, Sham and Siouxsie was pretend. I wasn't aware of drug problems at the time apart from (cough cough, link to better known pop band who rose from the scene) Although, let's face it, the two main guys who were in (further coughing) are not in possession of their full faculties any more. One of them is lost. He walks around town staring into space. A lot of bands broke up very quickly because they were kids jumping on a bandwagon. Except Peter and the Test Tube Babies!"

Indeed, for a time future Peter And The Test Tube Babies' member Chris 'Trapper' Marchant joined the dots, so to speak. But no further records ensued, despite the band being a popular local draw. By 1980 they had broken up. Williams would join Peter And The Test Tube Babies (briefly), the Corvettes, Karen D'Ache, the Soul Survivors and Global Village Idiot as well as working as a sub-editor on the Morning Star. Nick Dwyer joined the Louder Animal Group and released a single on his own label, then formed busking sensations Pookiesnackenburger with Johnny Piranha and Luke Cresswell. He's also an artist. He's wrong about the Vapors though.

DISCOGRAPHY:

Never Been So Stuck/Linoleum Walk 7-inch (Small Wonder SMALL 12 1979)

COMPILATIONS:

Vaultage 1978 (Two Sides Of Brighton) LP (Attrix RB 03 1978; 'Girl Gets Nervous', 'I Find That Really Surprises Me', 'Wrong Street')

Small Wonder Punk Singles Collection CD Vol. 1 (Anagram CDPUNK 29 1994; 'Never Been So Stuck')

Small Wonder Punk Singles Collection CD Vol. 2 (Anagram CDPUNK 70 1996; 'Linoleum Walk')

Vaultage Punk Collection CD (Anagram CDPUNK 101 1997; Wrong Street', 'Girls Get Nervous')

999

Nick Cash (aka Keith Lucas; guitar, vocals), Guy Days (guitar, vocals), Jon Watson (bass), Pablo LaBritain (aka Paul Buck; drums)

999 were one of Britain's most popular punk bands – only not in Britain. Instead, they ranked just below the Pistols, Damned and Clash in international renown, especially in America, where they played more than just about any other member of the class of 1977. The music press back home never afforded them much respect, pointing to their pub rock backgrounds (although the similar roots of the more photogenic Joe Strummer were glossed over). But while occasionally patchy on album, 999 were a genuinely great singles act, and many of their best efforts are the equal of their better known peers. As Cash once admitted, "I like writing songs that the audience can sing along to," and if you consider that an aesthetic failing, you're not going to like 999.

999 was formed on Sunday, 5 December 1976 by Keith Lucas, a veteran of over 100 gigs with Ian Dury's Kilburn And The High Roads until June 1975, having met Essex's favourite son when Dury taught him at Canterbury College Of Art. The High Roads' manager, incidentally, was Tommy Roberts, a friend of Malcolm McLaren's, who ended up outfitting them in Teddy Boy zoot suits. Lucas had also spent time in numerous other bands, including C Scream, Pentagon, Graduate and the wonderfully titled Frosty Jodhpur, etc.

He adopted the name Gene Carsons, and subsequently Nick Cash, after he'd decided he wasn't prepared to play second fiddle to Dury any longer. Musicians who auditioned in reply to the Melody Maker ads he placed included Jon Moss, Chrissie Hynde and Tony James, who actually joined for a short time but never played a gig. The listed quartet finally coalesced after rehearsals in the basement of a bakery in Brixton Road, and played together for the first time on 22 January as support to Stretch at Northampton Cricket Club, as the Dials. They changed their name to 48 Hours in tribute to the Clash, then the Fanatics, and finally 999, which would later cause them a few problems – not least when American baggage handlers refused to let their equipment through (999 upside down is, of course, 666). The Clash homage is interesting given that LaBritain actually played in Joe Strummer's Burgher Masters while both were boarders at the City Of London Freemen's School. The band's early songs like 'I'm Alive' and 'Quite Disappointing' were leftovers from Cash's time in the High Roads.

N

999's second show came three days later at Reading's Target Club for a fee of £20. More skilled musicians than most, they established a solid reputation at venues such as the Nashville, Vortex and Roxy. It saw them attract a core of followers from Southall aka The Crew (other 'Crews' would spring up in Manchester, Birmingham and worldwide, each chapter rivalling the others for the tenacity of their support). An early support to the Jam at the Nashville saw them taken under the wing of Albion management, one of the most active agencies in the early punk milieu. The band was simply grateful for the opportunity. "We sent tapes to all the record companies. They went, 'this is bloody awful,' and turned it down. Then the punk explosion happened and all these people were going, 'Sign here!'" They also won some early critical support. Paul Rambali, reviewing their June 1977 show at the Nashville for the NME, compared them favourably with that night's headline act. "They possess the required urgency in their playing and embellish it with a streak of inventiveness, which meant that, as was not the case with the Saints, it was possible to distinguish one song from another."

Their first single was recorded in July 1977 with producer Andy Arthurs and released the following month. 'I'm Alive', a song Cash wrote about the frustration of holding down a nine-to-fiver, was housed on their drummer's own LaBritain Records and sold out of its 10,000-pressing within weeks. Afterwards there was a stampede to sign them by the majors. They chose to go with United Artists, who reissued the single, while they cemented their reputation as one of the capital's hardest working live bands, their distinctive stencilled logo, designed by Days, popping up everywhere. A run of five minor hit singles followed, displaying both variety and an innate pop suss, starting with 'Nasty Nasty' – portrayed in some parts of the media as pro-violence, but in effect exactly the opposite, the clue being in the vitriolic chorus, 'What the hell is wrong with you?' 'Emergency' was even better, distinguished by Cash's elasticated vocals over a song with rapid-fire verses, backed by LaBritain's subsonic percussion, and a great one-word chorus. Their self-titled debut album, again produced by Andy Arthurs, didn't disappoint. It opened with 'Me And My Desire', a brusque, Stonesy punk blues that was also extracted as a single, though the prior singles (with the exception of 'Nasty Nasty', which was absent) and B-sides 'Titanic (My Over Reaction)' and 'Crazy' were other highlights. The band promoted it with their first headlining UK tour, and they were now a top-line live draw. "I used to like 999 a lot," London's Riff Regan told me. "We played a lot of gigs together at the Hope 'n' Anchor and the Nashville and they were similar in the fact that they had a huge stage presence and a great live show. When you came out to see London and 999 on the same bill you really got a great night's entertainment! Some of their songs like 'Emergency' were classics."

Prior to a follow-up album only six months later, the group excerpted 'Feeling Alright With The Crew' as their fifth single, a tribute to their growing fanbase, written following a North East London Polytechnic show on 11 February 1978, and played live for the first time a week later. Separates, produced by Martin Rushent, demonstrated a depth and flexibility to their songwriting that belied their status as punk also-rans, especially on cuts like the singles, 'High Energy Plan' and 'Let's Face It' (with its knowing tag line, 'Let's face it, the boy can't make it with girls'). Further extensive UK touring followed, extending to dates in Scandinavia, with United Artists throwing pots of money at the band. Taken from the album, 'Homicide', Cash's attempt to set Raymond Chandler to music, was an obvious choice for the next single. Again, it distilled the essence of the group's rhythmic muscle – which always counteracted the fact they operated at much slower tempos than the punk norm. It reached the Top 40, just, but events meant the band were unable to capitalise on the breakthrough.

LaBritain was hospitalised on his return from the Scandinavian tour. After completing a show and a little the worse for wear, he got out of the band's Volkswagen van, before reaching back inside to grasp his jumper. Unfortunately the door was then closed, and the van drove off with Pablo still attached. Down the road his free hand smashed against a Morris Oxford, smashing his left arm between the shoulder and elbow. His misfortunes increased when a subsequent operation left him with a severed radial nerve. For a short time it was considered he may be permanently disabled. Up stepped Southall crew member Ed Case, a van driver, aged just 17. He should have made his debut on Top Of The Pops promoting 'Homicide', but a BBC technicians' strike cut short the programme's duration and 999 were axed.

He was readied for his first shows in Germany with just two days notice, and he did get to appear on the Old Grey Whistle Test, where 999 were screened playing 'Homicide' and 'Let's

Face It'. The first of their American treks commenced in March 1979, starting with a show at the Hot Club in Philadelphia on the 16 March. They immediately connected with American audiences, perhaps willing to embrace their more musical stature in contrast with some of the rough and ready UK punk acts, and after returning to play three dates at the Marquee, they immediately set out on a further series of 50 North American shows.

On their return they booked time at Alaska studios, playing a show at the Wellington pub nearby, which saw Pablo return to the fold in August. By September they had signed a new deal with Radar Records, releasing a preview of their third album in the form of 'Found Out Too Late'. While there was still occasional sniping about the band's decision to spend so much time in the US, they proved their domestic popularity with five consecutive nights at the Marquee, with Ed Case and LaBritain alternating on the shows.

However, record company politics slightly delayed the album's release, and The Biggest Prize In Sport eventually emerged on Polydor Records. Produced by Vic Maile, with Ed Case making his 'swan song' appearance on a few of the tracks, it was a further move towards mature rock'n'roll, though a handful of the cuts retained the intensity of old. 'Trouble', sung by guitarist Guy Days, proved they could incorporate reggae and ska influences, though the title-track itself, with its harmonies, owed more to the straight pop tradition 999 were moving inexorably towards. Cash once claimed the song was used, without irony, as the theme to the international Windsurf World championships, though the lyrics were actually about 'morning stiffies'. There was also a rare song by Watson, 'Made A Fool Of You', an 'ode to transexual shemales in Detroit' entitled 'Boiler', and a denunciation of the falsehoods they'd encountered in America, 'Hollywood'. A further single, 'Boys In The Gang', the first song Ed Case played on, and a continuation of the 'Feelin' Alright With The Crew' aesthetic, was released in Germany only, backed by the band's traditional stage opener, 'Brent Cross'.

In the meantime 999 found themselves embroiled in an unlikely tabloid story following a knife attack on an audience member at a show in Palo Alto, California. "All I remember is that gig was a cracker," LaBritain recalled to Punk Lives. "We didn't know anything about the knifing at the time. Still, some ol chap in my local said it was good that we got some press at last."

Their American label tried to capitalise by issuing a live mini-album, The Biggest Tour In Sport, taken from their 56-date 1980 tour of the US and Canada. Thereafter they signed with Albion in the UK, making their debut with 'Obsession' in April 1980 (Australian and German copies carried a different version of the song, originally titled 'Sex'). Concrete continued the group's 'progression' away from punk. It was recorded at Jackson's Studios in Rickmansworth with Vic Maile as producer, with sessions taking place between heavy touring commitments. The inclusion of covers of 'Fortune Teller' and Sam The Sham And The Pharoahs' 'Lil' Red Riding Hood', also released as a single, led to rumblings that the group were running short of ideas. But the album actually housed some of 999's better work, notably 'Don't You Know I Need You' with its chanted, though vaguely nonsensical, chorus. 'Obsessed' sounds like Adam And The Ants jamming on a Sergio Leone score. Although their next release was another cover, it was at least stylish, a thudding reawakening of Paul Revere And The Raiders' 'Indian Reservation'.

A few months passed, interspersed by shows in Portugal, before 999 returned with a new song, an original this time, and one of their best. But despite Albion putting money into all sorts of formats for 'Wild Sun', a spaghetti punk meltdown very much in the vein of 'Obsessed', it didn't do the business. The band's only date of 1982 came at the Lyceum, and the portents were not good. 13th Floor Madness arrived and was righteously shouted down by the press for both its production and the confused mix of genres (even the word disco raised its ugly head). 999's problem was that, given the tempos at which they played, if the songs lacked inherent tension, they just sounded dreary (though they could have been so much better realised – check out the retrospective Cellblock Tapes for evidence of how they sounded at rehearsal stage). In contrast to the ferocious pace of their live engagements previously, there were only a smattering of American and Canadian dates in 1983. In fact, this most active of bands ducked out of view until early 1985, when they valiantly tried to put the previous album behind them with the release of Face To Face. It was a partial return to form which boasted invention as well as conviction, especially on the multi-layered '20 Years' and 'This Is Just A Lie', which tackled the expectation that Britain's poor pay for their own funerals. It was followed by extensive tours of England, Scotland, and then a return to the States and Canada.

By 1985 Watson had had enough, playing his final show on 28 December at the Clarendon Hotel, effectively leaving the band on hold. When they got back together again in 1987 Danny Palmer took over on bass, playing his first show at Brighton's Richmond Hotel in April 1987. Thereafter they released Lust, Power And Money, a live album featuring three unreleased songs, the title-track, 'White Trash' and 'On The Line'. From then on their studio output has been much more sporadic, though they've hardly relented in terms of touring. Since 1991 Arturo Bassick has fulfilled Palmer's role, while concurrently leading the reformed Lurkers. Both 1993's You, Us, It! and, especially, 1998's Takeover, are worth a listen, though their audience continues to contract. Sadly the label behind the latter went belly up shortly after its release, which hardly helped the cause.

By the end of the 20th century they'd totted up 26 UK tours, 13 of the US, 20 European tours as well as dates in Japan, Argentina, Brazil. Ladies and gentlemen – the hardest working men in punk rock?

Discography:

(Buyer's Guide: I'd propose the following purchase order – Separates, 999, Concrete then The Biggest Prize In Sport in that order. Hard to split the myriad live albums, but both Nashville – on which the sound quality is as rough as a badger's – and English Wipeout are historically appealing. Later studio albums You Us It and Takeover are respectable efforts. The best single-disc introduction is Captain Oi!'s Punk Singles Collection)

I'm Alive/Quite Disappointing 7-inch (Labritain LAB-999 August 1977) (reissued on United Artists, UP 36519, in October 1977)

Nasty Nasty/No Pity 7-inch (United Artists UAG 36299 October 1977) (green vinyl; also Nasty Nasty/No Pity promo; 78 rpm 7-inch; United Artists FREE-7 1977)

Emergency/My Street Stinks 7-inch (Untied Artists UP 36399 January 1978)

999 LP (United Artists UAG 30199 March 1978) (reissued on CD in June 1987 by Fan Club, FC026, then by Dojo, DOJO CD 145 in 1993, then by Captain Oi!, AHOY CD 147, in 2000. Bonus tracks 'Quite Disappointing', 'Nasty Nasty', 'My Street Stinks' on Dojo/Captain Oi! reissues)

Me And My Desire/Crazy 7-inch (United Artists UP 36376 April 1978)

Feelin' Alright With The Crew/Titanic Reaction/You Can't Buy Me 7-inch (United Artists UP 36435 August 1978)

Separates LP (United Artists UAG 30209 September 1978) (10.000 copies contained a voucher for 'You Get Action' maxi-single: Action/Waiting 12-inch EP, Labritain 12-FREE-1978. Reissued on CD by Fan Club, FC 027, in June 1987, then by Dojo, DOJO CD 150, in 1993, then by Captain Oi!, AHOY CD 148, in 2000. Bonus tracks 'You Can't Buy Me', 'Soldier', 'Waiting', 'Action' on Dojo/Captain Oi! re-releases)

Homicide/Soldier 7-inch (United Artists UP 36467 1978) (some in green vinyl)

High Energy Plan LP (PVC/Radar PVC 7999 (USA) June 1979) (American edition of Separates with two tracks changed – 'Action' and 'Waiting' added with 'Crime Part 2' and 'Tulse Hill Night' withdrawn)

Found Out Too Late/Lie, Lie, Lie 7-inch (Radar ADA 46 September 1979)

Trouble/Made A Fool Of You 7-inch (Polydor POSP 99 January 1980)

The Biggest Prize in Sport LP (Polydor POLS 1013 January 1980) (reissued on CD by Anagram, CD PUNK 67, November 1995, with bonus tracks 'Made A Fool Of You', 'Found Out Too Late', 'Lie Lie Lie')

Boys in the Gang/Brent Cross/Ain't Gonna Tell You 7-inch (Liberty-United March 1980; Germany)

The Biggest Tour in Sport mini-LP (Polydor PD-1 6307 (USA) 1980)

Obsessed/Change/ Lie, Lie, Lie (live) 7-inch (Albion ION 1011 April 1980) (first 10,000 with embossed sleeve and patch)

Obsessed (mono)/Obsessed (stereo) 7-inch promo (Polydor PD 2172-DJ (USA) 1980)

Concrete LP (Albion ITS 99 March 1981) (cassette version included the six live tracks from The Biggest Tour In Sport. Reissued on CD by Link in May 1991. Reissued again by Captain Oi!, AHOY CD 232, in 2003 with bonus tracks 'Change', 'Lie Lie Lie (live)', 'Wait For Your Number', 'I Ain't Gonna Tell Ya (live)', 'Indian Reservation', 'So Greedy (remix)', 'Wild Sun' and 'Scandal In The City'. Which, alongside the Nick Cash sleevenote, makes it a top package)

Li'l Red Riding Hood/Wait For Your Number to be Called/I Ain't Gonna Tell You (live) 7-inch (Albion ION-1017 June 1981) (with shrink-wrapped template sleeve)

Indian Reservation/So Greedy (remix)/Taboo (remix) 7-inch (Albion ION-1023 November 1981) (clear vinyl, with free sticker)

Wild Sun/Scandal in the City (Albion ION-1033 June 1982) (red and yellow vinyl; also available as 12-inch, in red and yellow, 12-ION-1033. Also available as a cassette single with bonus track 'You Know I Need You')

13th Floor/Madness/Nightshift 7-inch (Albion ION-155 October 1983) (also available as 12-inch with 'Arabesque', 12-ION-155)

13th Floor Madness LP (Albion AS-8502 November 1983) (cassette version featured four extra tracks, 'Indian Reservation', 'Wild Sun', plus the unreleased 'How The West Was Won' and 'How Can I Tell You'. They also featured on the reissue, ALCD 9 00073, in May 1991)

Face to Face LP (Labritain LAB-LP-1000-03 March 1985) (initial copies carried a free stencil. Should have been a sickbag. Reissued on CD by Obsession, OBSESSCD 003, June 1993)

Lust, Power & Money (live) LP (ABC ABC LP/K/D 11 May 1987) (reissued on CD June 1993 by Dojo DOJOCD 129 with two extra tracks. Also became Greatest Hits Live in October 1992 on Streetlink STRCD 026)

You, Us, It! CD (Anagram CDGRAM-71 November 1993)

Takeover CD (Abstract 1998)

ARCHIVE RELEASES:

The 999 Singles Album LP (Liberty-United SOS 999 June 1980)

Identity Parade LP (Albion ALB 118 March 1984) (unremarkable compilation, aside from the fact that it features the unavailable elsewhere 'Blaze Of Moon')

In Case of Emergency LP (Dojo DOJO LP 31 November 1986)

Live and Loud! LP (Link LINK LP 107 November 1989) (reissued on CD by Link, LINK CD 107, in January 1991. Recorded sometime in 1979, though no exact date is furnished on the packaging when 999 were pretty much at their peak, with the selections spanning their first three studio albums. Excellent sound quality too)

The Cellblock Tapes LP (Link LINK LP 125 1990) (early demos and live tracks, including far better versions of tracks that would later appear in more insipid form on 13th Floor Madness as well as then unreleased material such as 'Dead Or Alive')

The Cellblock Tapes/The Slaughterhouse Tapes CD (Step 1 STEP CD 045 December 1994) (combined reissue of Cellblock tapes as well as Slaughter And The Dogs' The Slaughterhouse Tapes)

Live And Loud! CD (STEP 1 CD 053 December 1995) (reissue of Live and Loud! With similarly titled volume by Sham 69)

The Albion Punk Years (The Independent Punk Collection) CD (Anagram Records CD PUNK 78 1996) (above average odds and ends/kitchen sink compilation. 'Lie Lie Lie' and 'I Ain't Gonna Tell You' recorded live at the Nashville, an earlier version of 'Obsessed' under its original title, 'Sex', and various remixes and B-sides)

Live At The Nashville 1979 (Anagram CD PUNK 93 April 1997) (the Nashville was the venue for 999's first ever London show, and their performance then got them secured their management deal. This show dates from 1979, just over a month prior to the release of The Biggest Prize In Sport, meaning the band is able to draw on the best of its repertoire. A decent memento)

Scandal In The City CD (Line CD 901326 February 1997) (pointless compilation)

Emergency CD (Receiver CD 245 1997) (though John Watson features on the cover, these are re-recordings of some of the band's standards featuring Arturo Bassick on bass)

Homicide: The Best Of 999 CD (Cleopatra 178 1999) (compilation for the American market)

Dancing In The Wrong Shoes CD (Receiver June 1999) (tracks 1-12 are from Face To Face, 'Heart To Heart' is a non-album track, and there are three live versions of songs from 13th Floor Madness LP from the tour to promote it)

Slam CD (Overground OVER 84CD 1999) (collection of early-80s demos of songs that would end up on Concrete and The Biggest Prize In Sport. 'Heart To Heart', 'Raindance', 'Christmas Cards', 'Cruel World', 'VGC', 'Investigation' and the semi-legendary 'Slam', which both Albion and Polydor refused to put out, are released here for the first time)

The Punk Singles 1977-1980 CD (Captain Oi! AHOY CD 176 2000)

English Wipeout CD (Overground OVER 90 VP CD 2001) (live album featuring shows from Leicester 1979 and the Electric Circus)

The Biggest Tour In Sport/The Biggest Prize In Sport CD (Captain Oi! AHOY CD 207 2002) (handy repackaging of both albums – well, one album and one mini-album – with sleevenotes by Nick Cash recounting tall tales of America from near plane crashes to shark wrestling. Very Ernest Hemingway, Nick)

Nipple Erectors/Nips

Shane MacGowan (vocals), Shanne Bradley (aka Shanne Hasler; bass), Jerry 'Arcane Vendetta' (drums), Roger Towndrow (guitar)

The NIPPLE ERECTORS were formed in 1977 by MacGowan and fellow Pistols' devotee Bradley, nicknamed Dragonella to avoid confusion with her near-namesake Shane, who himself would be reborn as Shane O'Hooligan. Shanne had been taught the bass by Captain Sensible, having briefly sung alongside Chrissie Hynde as backing singers for the Johnny Moped band, and was part of kitchen-sink punks the Launderettes. She was still reeling from her parents splitting up when she was 13, and was trying to focus her "seething resentment" she felt at the hypocrisy of middle class life in Hertfordshire. "When I was 16, the Pill had just come out, so I became quite promiscuous," she subsequently told the Mirror. "I got into art school early and I shaved all my hair off, pierced my ears and nose, cut up my clothes and wore big boots – anything not to be 'nice girl-next-door'."

She first encountered the Sex Pistols when they played St Albans, and Malcolm McLaren "approached me because I looked like them" (she'd just had an accident with peroxide that left her hair tangerine). She was briefly, for about an afternoon maybe, John Lydon's girlfriend (he legendarily wrote 'Satellite' about her, unflatteringly picturing her as "a big fat pink baked bean"). "I vividly remember wearing a bin liner walking hand-in-hand round St Albans with him." MacGowan had spent an unlikely year at Westminster private school after his early aptitude for poetry was noticed, but otherwise came from solid working class Irish stock, despite being born in Kent. He'd developed a taste for old soul records and formed his first band, Hot Dogs With Everything, while pursuing an abortive college course. He was working as a barman at the Griffin Tavern in Charing Cross while spending much of his free time attending Hope 'n' Anchor gigs by pub rock gods Dr Feelgood and the Count Bishops. On one such night, after watching Joe Strummer's 101ers, he fell off the back of his friend's motorbike on the Hammersmith Road. It is to this evening's frivolities that his famed crazy pavement dental arrangement can be attributed.

At a subsequent 101ers gig, on 15 June 1976, he happened upon the Sex Pistols for the first time. "They were all our age and had dyed hair and wore brothel creepers," he recalled, "and it was just a question of, 'Yeah, Fuck it. I hate everything and they're actually doing it.' I thought they were brilliant; the best group I've ever seen." He subsequently became one of their most vociferous camp followers and one of the emergent punk scene's "faces", having appeared pogo-ing in the opening footage of Don Letts' Punk Rock Movie and on the cover of Sounds above the caption 'The Face Of 1976'. He'd also been depicted as the willing victim of punk cannibalism in both the Evening Standard and Miles's November 1976 review of the Clash's show at the ICA. "My God, they're eating each other. These people are cannibals! The young man howls with pain as his blood-spattered young lady (actually Jane Crockford of the Modettes) is dragged away, all the while trying to slash her own wrists. But for the dudes in the audience, it's just a regular Saturday gig." Thereafter MacGowan was "the punk that got his ear bitten off", though anyone who has seen a subsequent profile of MacGowan in his Pogues' vintage will attest to the fact that his King Lears remained in rude health.

As if that wasn't enough, he got so carried away by a Jam performance at Ronnie Scott's that he single-handedly smashed up all their speakers. Prior to the Nips he'd shown his commitment to the punk movement by founding Bondage, a hand-written ("I haven't got a typewriter"), sloganeering fanzine, albeit for one, highly profitable, issue only. Shane met Shanne at the bar of the Royal College of Art, around the time Shanne started booking the Pistols and the Damned for shows in St Albans, until she was kicked off campus for non-attendance. MacGowan had originally tried to join the Launderettes, but only Bradley was interested in having him aboard, and decided to form a band with him instead after he auditioned, doing his best Iggy Pop impersonation, in her bedsit. They also had a personal connection, which Shanne claims was her "first serious relationship", though their propensity for walking to punk venues tied to each other by a dog chain signified a singular sort of romanticism.

After Shane briefly flirted with offers to be an A&R representative for various labels bewildered by the advent of punk, the duo set about auditioning new members. These included ZigZag's Adrian Thrills, who tried his hand at versions of 'Anarchy In The UK' but failed to get the gig, though he would remain a notable supporter. He also appears on the group's first demo, 'My Degeneration' – "a blistering effort", he later noted, "recorded in Shanne's bedroom." Rick Collett was the original drummer and played the Roxy with the band before he returned to Leamington Spa and worked with bands including Everyone Else and the Rails. Eventually Roger Towndrow and Jerry Arcane, a renowned contributor to Sounds' Gasbag column, were recruited, and they made their debut on audition night at the Roxy, though Arcane was subsequently dropped in favour of former Tools' drummer Gerry Mackleduff. It was to be the first of many such switches.

Though supported in the press by Sounds writer Jane Suck, the Nipple Erectors were far from universally popular – for every supporter who'd spotted MacGowan's diamond in the rough appeal, there were others who found him an irritating, uppity little prick. Their first single, 'King Of The Bop', betrayed a raucous rockabilly influence – its two-minute lyrical minimalism made them sound Ramones-esque, and has been cited as a precursor to Britain's psychobilly movement. That would probably horrify them – although the Pogues' later made their early live reputation as support to a roster of psychobilly bands including King Kurt, the Milkshakes and the Sting-rays. MacGowan's idolisation of 50s' rockers made the Nipple Erectors the first punk band to hold hands with their sworn enemies, the Teds. Indeed, the term 'rockapunky' was coined to describe one early performance. MacGowan was particularly proud of his quiff, and professed to "hating art students", which actually encompassed much of the punk circle at the time, and, of course, even his current beau and collaborator.

'King Of The Bop' was released on Stan Brennan (who produced most of the band's early material and managed them) and Phil Gaston's Soho Records. They'd taken over the Rock On record stall, where Shane worked on Saturdays, after its founders moved on to Chiswick, leading to the Nips' later connection to that label. Sounds gave the record a positive review ("perhaps the first record that will genuinely appeal to Teds and punks alike"), while noting that the B-side, 'Nervous Wreck', had harmonies which reminded writer Alan Lewis of Gilbert & Sullivan. "'King Of The Bop' was meant to be a rock'n'roll number," MacGowan later recalled to Dave McCullough of Sounds, "but we weren't that good at playing. Basically, we hadn't got it together properly and we just did it in a couple of nights. It came out like a mixture of punk and rock'n'roll... I don't think it's that good now." Some considered the marriage to be contrived – an accusation more pertinently levelled at the two other tracks recorded at the session, 'So Pissed Off' and 'Stavordale Rd, N5', which referred to MacGowan's old flat he rented for six quid a week next to Arsenal's Highbury stadium. But MacGowan was unmoved, arguing that he could dance to rock'n'roll, but not to 999 records.

Truncating their name to the Nips, they lost Towndrow to a job at the National Gallery and Mackleduff to a slot in the original version of the Pretenders. Larry Hinrichs, ex-Profettes and an occasional substitute vocalist for the Damned when Dave Vanian didn't show one night, came in on guitar while various drummers filled in at gigs – including Mark Harrison from Bernie Tormé's band and Eater's Phil Rowland. 'All The Time In The World', though, fared little better than their debut – though its masturbation-themed lyric raised a few eyebrows ('So lie on your back and think of England, and I'll put my hands on you/I've been dreaming of your picture, baby, creaming over you'). The back cover queried Uncle John Peel's lack of foresight in not offering them a session (he never would, though he was quick to sponsor the Pogues).

The rhythm section finally achieved some stability with the recruitment of John 'Grinny' Grinton, ex-Skrewdriver. Grinton maded his debut on the sessions that produced 'Gabrielle', arguably the Nips' finest moment, thought its debt to 'Louie Louie' did not pass undetected. It concerned one of MacGowan's former girlfriends, who formerly hung out at after-hours punk club Louise's. "She used to have blonde hair and tight leather-look plastic trousers and she used to model for Strawberry Studios," he told Adrian Thrills. "She was my first real love, but she wouldn't ever go to bed with me. She just used to take me back to her bedsit in Streatham and jerk me off! She had a bit of a hang-up about sex." It became Paul Weller's favourite single of the punk era. MacGowan was less generous about his own creation, calling it "a cynical move to dupe dumb Americans into buying it because all they like is dumb, stupid love songs, you know? So, we thought everybody else is making money out of dumb, stupid, love songs, so why shouldn't we?"

Heinrichs was now jettisoned in favour of Gavin 'Blondie' Douglas, aka Fritz, formerly of Bitch (Fritz from Bitch – hmmm). Douglas would also contribute original material to contrast with MacGowan's efforts, authoring 'Ghostown'. Mark Harrison, having previously filled in on live shows, stepped in to replace temporary drummer Roger, who joined the Smart. He had in turn replaced Grinton, bound for a career with the Post Office.

As the 70s ended, MacGowan became increasingly frustrated with the way punk's energy had dissipated into new wave, or "prats with synthesizers and a university education", to use his own words. "I got into the turgid debasement of punk rock in its bad days," he admitted to ZigZag in 1979. "I was snorting sulphate, spending money on drinks which were over expensive and missing the bands I was supposed to be watching. It was a load of crap in the end. The only bands I ever really liked were the original four; the Pistols, Clash, Jam and especially, the Damned. They summed up the true punk attitude. The only ones I've seen since that I like are the Members and Sham 69." However, it's important to note that MacGowan later changed his take on the post-punk movement after savaging the likes of Gang Of Four in print, professing his affection for both the Pop Group and Lydon's Public Image Limited. He was also bowled over by the early Spandau Ballet shows, so it's not like his radar was ever especially reliable.

The Nips subsequently became embroiled in the mod revival scene, touring with the Purple Hearts and even Dexy's Midnight Runners. MacGowan also talked about relaunching the band as a garage R&B act in the tradition of the Seeds and Electric Prunes and recording some "disturbing dance stuff". But then, as Shanne so eloquently pointed out at the time, "Shane changes his mind every six months." The mod connection was doubtless cemented by the influence of longstanding fan Paul Weller. MacGowan had profiled the Jam in his Bondage fanzine and declared them "fucking important". Weller, for his part, once stated that MacGowan was "the only real star to come out of the new wave". Weller certainly saw some value in the group – lifting the refrain of 'Gabrielle' for 'Strange Town'.

The Nips finally splintered in March 1980, releasing the following statement. "Basically, this is a situation where the record company are a bunch of old tossers" (Shanne had alluded to tensions with Chiswick's Roy Carroll in previous interviews). However, the truth was they'd just fallen out with each other one time too many. "We were just sick of each other and I hated the music The Nips were playing," Shanne told the NME. "Shane and I just weren't communicating. We were just beating each other up all the time." Their last 'official' gig came at Camden's Music Machine, supporting the Purple Hearts on 14 March 1980. But they did play again, with later Pogue James Fearnley on guitar and Jon Moss on drums. These dates included further supports to the Jam, including a date at the Music Machine where Shanne, eight months pregnant, dressed up the band in her mum's frilly nylon nighties while she wore a yashmak.

Weller produced the Nips' final single, the posthumous 'Happy Song', which mocked Secret Affair's Ian Page. The B-side was to feature the Jefferson Airplane-baiting 'I Don't Want Nobody To Love' ('Gonna go to the disco club/I'm gonna try and pull some fat old slob/Who won't say nothing smart/Just lie there with her legs apart'). Typical of punk's anti-romanticism, but hardly the sharpest lyric from a man who, as we all now know, was capable of a little more depth. Before forming the Pogues, MacGowan briefly played with the Millwall Chainsaws, an on-off group based around Burton Street in King's Cross, while Shanne joined the Men They Couldn't Hang before concentrating on bringing up her two daughters. She also completed a fine art degree – an impressive 20 years after punk first diverted her – from Central St Martin's School of Art. For her graduation project she used film of the Nipple Erectors practising in her bedsit. "I like the irony of the fact I finally graduated using material that had me kicked out in the first place." She was in turn faced with a teenage daughter, who framed her own rebellion by becoming a devoted Christian. She has also been immortalised by Shane in the waltz he wrote in her honour, entitled simply 'Shanne Bradley'. Fritz was rumoured to have taken up sheep farming, though this was a scandalous act of deliberate misinformation. Indeed, Fritz later wrote in to Sounds' Barry Lazell to set the record straight, requesting a picture of him in the band that featured him prominently "because I'm sick of being hidden behind Shane's ears".

DISCOGRAPHY

King Of The Bop/Nervous Wreck 7-inch (Soho SH1/2 June 1978) (Note: only 500 copies had 'glossy' p/s, later versions matt finish)

As the Nips:

All The Time In The World/Private Eye 7-inch (Soho SH4 August 1978)

Gabrielle/Vengeance 7-inch (Chiswick CHIS 119 October 1979) (Note: A second version of this single was issued on Soho Records – SH9 – and given away while on tour supporting the Purple Hearts).

Happy Song/Nobody To Love 7-inch (Burning Rome/Test Pressing, October 1981)

Only At The Beginning LP (Soho HO HO 001 October 1980) (recording of a March 1980 set in Wolverhampton)

ARCHIVE RELEASES:

Bops, Babes, Booze & Bovver LP (Big Beat WIKM 66 December 1987) (compilation album, credited to Nips 'n' Nipple Erectors. Reissued on CD by Big Beat, CDWIKM 66 September 2003, with the addition of regular set highlights 'Venus In Bother Boots' and 'Fuss & Bother'. Shame it couldn't have been expanded with some of the widely circulated live material though)

The Tits Of Soho LP (Bovver Boot Company BB-ST-8247 2000) (compilation album, featuring all ten known studio recordings, plus six tracks from the Only At The Beginning live album)

The Tits Of Soho/Only The End Of The Beginning (Bootleg SD CD 004) (The band's first appearance on CD, compiling both LP releases)

No Sweat

Clive Culbertson (bass, vocals), Adrian Culbertson (guitar, vocals), Paddy Scanlon (drums)

NO SWEAT, nothing to do with the later Irish rock band who frequently supported Little Angels in the UK, were led by songwriter Clive Culbertson and recorded briefly for Belfast's Rip Off Records. They signed in 1978 to release 'Start All Over Again', which really is worth searching out. In addition to the Culbertson brothers, it featured Martin Hughes on drums and Denis Forbes on second guitar, both of Pretty Boy Floyd And The Gems. Both sides of the single were reprised on the same label's 'Belfast Rock' compilation EP. "No Sweat were in fact quite 'punk', notes Clive Culbertson. "We recorded a lot of original stuff that was very fast and in yer face. When the band folded, Rip Off records put all that stuff in the store and refused to release it."

N

By 1980 various original members had left and the name was changed simply to The Sweat after the threat of legal action from Pete Townshend's Eel Pie Records, who had a band of the same title on their books. In the meantime they switched to Double Dee Records (owned by Dave Dee, of Dave Dee, Dozy, Beaky, Mick and Tich) and released the singles 'Why'd Ya Have To Lie' and 'I Must Be Crazy' in 1980. Culbertson: "'Why'd Ya Have To Lie' was for several weeks at the top of the British airplay charts in the summer of 1980. The DJs loved it in the UK and Ireland. Double Dee had serious distribution problems that affected not only The Sweat but every band on their label. I lived off the radio royalties of 'Why'd Ya' for several years."

They toured the UK, lost thousands in doing so, and eventually broke up. Culbertson pursued a solo career (he'd already cut a solo single for Rip Off in 1979, 'Busy Signal', backed by 'Time To Kill') with Mint Records. Culbertson: "Strangely enough, 1977 Records in Japan told me the reason they bought this material (that label is due to issue both the unreleased No Sweat album, the Sweat album and a collection of unreleased Culbertson solo tracks) was because of my two solo hits in Japan. Apparently 'Time to Kill'/'Busy Signal' charted in Japan in 1979, as did my solo single after leaving The Sweat, 'Kiss Me' in 1981. Always nice to know I was successful somewhere!"

Clive Culbertson went on to play with everyone from Van Morrison to Cliff Richard, as well as working as a record producer. He has his own studio in Coleraine and later started country rock band New Moon. He is also the founder of the Order of Druids in Ulster – eat your heart our Julian Cope – and is putting together a band to tour Japan at the end of 2006 to promote the reissues of his output there.

DISCOGRAPHY:

Start All Over Again/You Should Be So Lucky 7-inch (Rip-Off RIP 4 1978)
Compilations:
Belfast Rock 7-inch EP (Rip-Off RIP 101 1978; 'Start All Over Again', 'You Should Be So Lucky')

No Way

Paul Gardner (guitar), Paul Callan (bass), Marty 'Matey' Powell (vocals), Macca (drums; soon replaced by Pete Collins)

Stockton punk band who emerged in 1978 and played round local venues at the behest of local scene promoter, and Barbarians member, Dave Johns. He put them on bills at the Grand, the Zetland and various other venues that were opening up to the idea of punk in the Teesside area. They also picked up a series of supports to visiting 'star names' at the Middlesbrough Rock Garden, including the Skids, 999, the Lurkers, the Damned and even the Tourists.

The subsequently entered a local Battle Of The Bands competition, made it the grand final at the Fiesta Night Club and were amazed to find themselves the recipients of the winner's award. A small sum of money and champagne changed hands in tribute, despite their fans storming the stage for a sing-a-long. It seems the judges may well have been too intimidated by **NO WAY**'s strong local following (called, inevitably enough, the No Way Barmy Army) to consider giving the prize to anyone else – where now, Penelope Polaroid? They got a major write-up in the local press into the bargain. However, the substantive part of the reward was a day at the local Tees Radio studios. The recorded six tracks, two of which would later appear on the Bored Teenagers Volume 1 compilation.

Thereafter they continued to gig, including a support to the Undertones at Newcastle Rock City, before recording their debut single, 'Breaking Point'. Their manager was only able to finance a run of 500 copies, though the band believe that it could have sold many more than that. Blank Frank of local peers Blitzkrieg Bop agrees: "I was working as usual at the singles counter at HMV in Stockton when Matey, the singer from No Way, came in with a tape of their session at Impulse Studios. The main track, 'Breaking Point', blasted from the speakers, an impressive slice of power punk. I knew at that moment that when the single was released, No Way would certainly overtake Bop in the hearts of the local punks."

John Peel played the record three times, but the recognition wasn't enough to keep the wolf from the door. The members then forgot about their punk pasts until Dizzy of Detour Records approached them about including material on a compilation album, Bored Teenagers. Its success precipitated a reunion. Though Collins and Gardner couldn't make the show at the Middlesbrough Cornerhouse, replacements were found for what was judged a 'roaring success'.

DISCOGRAPHY:

Breaking Point/TV Pox/30 Seconds 7-inch EP (Our Own Records IS/NW 1035 1978) (500 copies)
COMPILATION:
Bored Teenagers Vol. 1 LP & CD (Bin Liner RUBBISHLP/CD 002 February 1999; 'Crazy Carol Carter', 'Destiny')

Noise Toys

Martin Stevens (vocals), Rupert (guitar), Mike (bass), Brian (drums)

NOISE TOYS grew out of the same Anti-Pop Monday night shows hosted at the Gosforth Hotel in Newcastle that gave the world Arthur 2 Stroke. Indeed, as well as regularly sharing headline status they would also share their debut vinyl release with the group in 1979. Other live staples such as 'Walkin' Down The Road In My Second Hand Raincoat' have never been released, sadly.

Rupert subsequently formed a band called Roland La Beat. There were dark mutterings about his future activities, none of which we'll repeat here in case he knows any solicitors or any of his progeny are reading and he's leading a double life as a consultant petrochemical salesman. Old friend Steve Nash remembers the Noise Toys well, having befriended them before joining Arthur 2 Stroke. "Martin and Rupert were very into a very specific look – second hand raincoats, trilby hats, baggy trousers (very un-punk), smoking loads of Woodbines and writing songs about all of these things. I shared a flat with them for a while but it was horrible. I was serious about my studies and they were serious about inviting everyone in the pub back for some late night rowdiness pretty much every night."

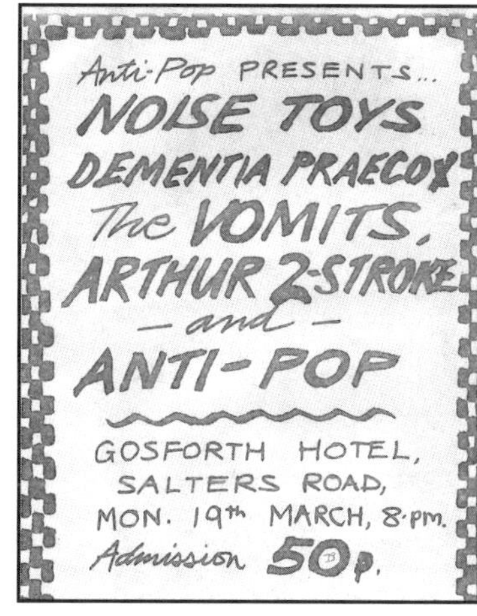

Anti-Pop PRESENTS...
NOISE TOYS
DEMENTIA PRAECOX
The VOMITS,
ARTHUR 2-STROKE
– and –
ANTI-POP
GOSFORTH HOTEL,
SALTERS ROAD,
MON. 19th MARCH, 8pm.
Admission 50p.

DISCOGRAPHY:

Pocket Money 7-inch (Anti-Pop Entertainmentarama AP 1 1979) (split single with Arthur 2 Stroke)

Notsensibles

Haggis (aka Michael Hargreaves; vocals), Sage (aka Stephen Hartley; guitar), Ploppy (aka Kevin Hemmingway; drums), Roger C Rawlinson (keyboards)

Inspired by the first wave of British punk bands, the NOTSENSIBLES formed in Burnley at the end of 1978. They stuck safety pins in their school uniforms, bless, and tried to play along to Slaughter And The Dogs, despite lacking a bass player or much in the way of aptitude. The inspiration for their name arose when Sage's dad took one look at their appearance and spluttered: "You're not... sensible."

"Our first gig was at our local youth club," recalls Rawlinson, "which we thought at the time would be the pinnacle of our career. After we phoned up all the working men's clubs in the area one eventually gave us a gig. We couldn't believe it, even though we only lasted one song." The band's first 'big break' came with a booking at the Band On The Wall, on a Manchester Musician's Collective night. "Mick Hucknall's band the Frantic Elevators were on the bill and unbeknown to us, Mick Middles from Sounds was there. The following week we received a rave review, while Mr Hucknall and co received a slagging (wonder where he ended up?) We played regularly around Manchester from then on, supporting the Undertones at the Factory, etc."

By then they had already released their debut single, 'Death To Disco'. They were still a quartet at this juncture, forcing Rawlinson to swap his keyboards for bass during live shows, until they 'poached' Gary Brown from local rivals the Pathetix towards the end of 1979. They were still having trouble finding gigs, though. They would routinely play nice, subdued sets as auditions for working men's clubs before going on the rampage when showtime proper came round. "We did get banned from quite a few venues around 1980 onwards, as we started using stage props such as shaving foam, pies and stage blood, and encouraging audience participation, making a general mess, usually pissing of the soundman or the promoter."

The follow-up single, '(I'm In Love With) Margaret Thatcher', got them a fair chunk of press. After all, punk musicians didn't usually respond with admiration towards their political leaders, and certainly not Thatcher, who was more normally embraced with scorn if not outright hatred (though she only came to power in May 1979 and the avalanche of 'Fuck Thatcher' songs would come later). It was neutral in regard to the old witch, as it happens, but was written because the Notsensibles "don't believe in sacred cows". "It brought us to national attention, landing us a John Peel session, and although banned from daytime Radio One, it could have charted if there hadn't been a delay in distribution after the first thousand pressed on Redball Records sold out."

Certainly they could never have been accused of taking themselves too seriously, as their stock in trade remained songs about their mates, local characters, relayed with affection and sarcasm in equal parts. Songs were committed to vinyl about the beauty of doing absolutely nothing with your life ('Lying On The Sofa'), Olympian-level ineptness ('I Make A Balls Of Everything I Do'), rubbish TV ('Coronation Street Shuffle') and luckless love affairs ('Girl With Scruffy Hair'). Much of this was shambolic, ramshackle stuff, studiously non-musical –

to the extent that it sounds like everything is being played through home-made fuzzboxes even when it isn't.

The Notsensibles didn't actually last all that long. It was pretty much all over soon after they released 'I Am The Bishop' in 1981 – the B-side of which, 'The Telephone Rings Again', was recently covered by America's Zodiac Killers. It was actually their finest moment, not unlike a junior league Damned. Rawlinson concurs, although he maintains the Damned were never that strong an influence. "Some of our unreleased demo stuff recorded towards the end would have been interesting if produced properly too," he notes. Sage left in 1981, to be replaced by Paul Wright, but by the following year the band had folded. They reformed again, minus Sage, for the 1996 Holidays In The Sun festival in Blackpool. "We're now back with the classic 1980 line up, hoping to complete unfinished business."

DISCOGRAPHY:

Death To Disco/Coronation Street Hustle/Lying On The Sofa 7-inch (Bent SMALL BENT 5 March 1979) (I'm In Love With) Margaret Thatcher/Concerto No. 2/Little Boxes/Gary Bushell's Band Of The Week 7-inch (Redball RR021 January 1980) (1,000 copies. Reissued on Snotty Snail NELCOL 1 1980)

I Thought You Were Dead/I Make A Balls Of Everything I Do/Teenage Revolution 7-inch (Snotty Snail NELCOL 3 August 1980)

Instant Classic LP (Bent BIG BENT 6 March 1980) (re-released in June 1980 on Snotty Snail, SSLP1, with different tracklisting)

I Am The Bishop/The Telephone Rings Again 7-inch (Snotty Snail NELCOL 6 March 1981)
(I've Just Had Enough) Brother CDS (Snotty Snail NELCOL 7 August 2005)
(I've Just Had Enough) Brother/Billy Jacobs (At The King George's Hall)/(The Battle Of) Barlick)/(I'm In Love With) Margaret Thatcher (contains some of the band's latter period demos – issued to commemorate the band's reunion to celebrate 25 years of the Railway Workers – "a venue that was the centre of the East Lancs punk movement from 79-81")
ARCHIVE RELEASES:
Instant Punk Classics CD (Anagram CD PUNK 38 1994)
Live At The Hop CDR Tuesday 27 March 1979 (Eli Records 2004) (Rawlinson: "Poor quality bootleg recording that was released on Sage's own label Eli Records, but probably sums up what an early Sensies gig was like)

The Now

Steve Rolls (guitar), Joe MacColl (drums), Mike McGuire (vocals), Paul 'Faz' Farrow (bass)

Peterborough's best-known first wave punk band, in common with similar aspirants, THE NOW were extant before punk's year zero rallying call, but found the new movement lent them a ready identity. As Joe MacColl told me: "I turned 18 in 1977, punk rock totally changed me, my life, my aspirations, the way I interact with other people, everything. And my experiences then have shaped my life to this day. I'm still playing drums, something I didn't do at the beginning of 1977. By the end of that year, I was on a single that reached number four in Sounds new wave chart, my hero John Peel had played us loads of times, and I'd gigged all over the country. It was fuckin' jaw-dropping. To cap it all, I spent Christmas Eve watching the Sex Pistols play in Cromer's West Runton Pavilion, as a guest of Sid Vicious!"

Several of the Now's gigs were conducted for the umbrella P.A.G.A.R organisation (Peterborough Action Group Against Racism), often on joint bills organised with the local West Indian Association. They played frequently with local reggae act the Legions, who later became Masai, and booked other acts including Kevin Rowland's Killjoys – though these events were often sabotaged by attacks from the far right.

'Development Corporations' was a scrappy, urgent slap of regional-agenda punk, entirely ignored by a media fixated on metropolitan expressions of dissent. Nowadays copies change hands for up to £100, much to the wide-eyed surprise of its former members. Peel's patronage helped get the band noticed, and the group started playing the London punk circuit, including the Vortex, the Marquee and the Roxy.

A second single, 'Nine O'Clock', backed by 'Into The Eighties', was finally released at the end of 1979 on Raw Records, over two years after it was recorded in September 1977 at Spaceward in Cambridge. But by the end of 1979 the Now were no more. "No musical differences here," reckoned Rolls. "In the punk spirit, boredom took hold." Rolls and McGuire formed Peel favourites Sudden Sway. Drummer Joe MacColl, together with partner Brenda Woods, befriended Billy Bragg's Riff Raff while they were ensconced in nearby Oundle, then formed The Name, with former members of The Dole and the Gobblinz. They released a single on Virgin subsidiary DinDisc at the height of the early-80s mod revival, and supported the Chords, Lambrettas and Purple Hearts. "I remember not being too interested in 'Nine O'Clock' at the time," MacColl told me, "as I was in the Name, and had just signed to DinDisc, with our own single nearing release. I couldn't be arsed with something I'd done almost two years previously." Later Joe, Steve and Faz joined Martin Stansfield as members of the Dead Sellers. Joe would also go on to the Pleasureheads, which allowed him to satisfy two of his remaining personal ambitions by recording a John Peel session, and in doing so, working with Dale Griffin of childhood heroes Mott The Hoople.

MacColl was also among those to follow through on punk's much-mythologised link with reggae. "I had the pleasure of playing in various locally based reggae bands throughout the 80s, and Phillip (of the Legions/Masai) was in all of them. This was all purely through the punk/rasta axis, and I developed a love of reggae, purely from going to see punk bands, as it was what they played in between. I loved the music so much, I started going to local blues nights. Peterborough's West Indian population at that time was insular and militant, and, thinking back, walking up to the door and blagging/talking/bribing my way in to find myself the only white face in this throbbing, weed-fugged, totally dark (save a torch over the decks) crowded environment took some bollocks. But I had that 'don't give a fuck, youth bravado' bullshit thing. Plus I wanted to learn. And some of the wiser dreads were aware of that punk/rasta thing. They knew we were getting shit from the National Front, as, obviously they were. So we were regarded as brothers in arms. Through that I started playing congos and bongos. I just love that Rasta heartbeat rhythm, and I ended up getting asked to play with whatever was hot locally reggae-wise, as well as rock'n'roll wise. It was cool, and through that I met people who have become life-long friends."

These days Joe also runs a mobile chip shop with Brenda. But as a result of the sustained bootlegging interest in the Now, at the end of 2002, Joe, Steve and Faz met up at a rehearsal studio and played songs together for the first time in 23 years. The week after, Mike was invited to lay down some vocal tracks. During this process, Joe informed me: "So far, they sound, well, like raw punk fuckin' rock really, so unless Mike messes up big time, I think we're gonna have a release we're all proud of. Which will be nice." The results, entitled Fuzztone Fizzadelic, were finally released in 2005. At which point I received the following hugely amusing email from Faz.

"One of my fondest memories – Christ, I've had a crap life – is when all four of us had jobs (yes we had jobs) for Thomas Cook. Peterborough was a development town, and three of us were on the train every day at 07.00 going to London to work prior to being 'relocated' to Peterborough, where we lived. Is it surprising that this seemed somewhat silly to our young minds? Call me slow, but I reckon it inspired the name of our first single. Mike sat in one carriage and I sat with Joe (same school, same estate, always friendly, god knows why). And we'd sit anywhere away from Mike – you'd never know Joe and Mike were in the same band. I was not in the band then; I was in a £20 crap suit and tie, and one January morning at 07.40 Joe drummed out 'Development Corporations' on the BR table in front of me, to the agitated interest of normal commuters. It wouldn't surprise me if BR/Network Rail claimed it as their own – it's always sounded like a train beat to me, written by kid commuters from and living in a crap boom town. I hated life back then. But I have to say those early morning train rides, the winter of 76 and especially the company I had to keep on the train were the worst moments ever. Err, that's it. No wonder punk took hold."

Faz continues, in epic form. "I didn't like growing up. Punk for me was incredibly uplifting; I wanted to be part of the fun of being in something shocking and new but clearly not daft, really without changing myself one little bit. I was only ever using negative words to describe my world and myself; punk was using the same vocabulary to scribe a really positive scene. It was not political to me – I have nothing to say about black and white, left and right. I remember a lot of vanity but that's youth; and for the first time in my life learning what I wanted to learn. Punk made me a happy person for the first time since I'd turned teen. Being in The Now was a great part of that."

DISCOGRAPHY:

Development Corporations/Why (Ultimate Records ULT 401 November 1977) (later reissued in March 1979 in blue vinyl in a limited edition of 1,000, although only 200 were actually sold. Reissued again in 2002 by Last Year's Youth, LAST 11, limited edition of 500)

Nine O'Clock/Into The Eighties (Raw RAW 31 November 1979) (originally scheduled for March 1979 release until Raw hit money problems. Eventually released in a batch of 800 later in the year. At least half of those were destroyed in a fire at Raw's warehouse. Hmm, Mr Wood! I hope you were insured. Oh, of course you were. Later reissued in 2000 by Last Year's Youth Records, LAST 1)

ARCHIVE RELEASES:

Into The Eighties/Nine O'Clock (rough mix)/Into The Eighties (rough mix) 7-inch (Last Year's Youth 12, 2000) (limited edition of 500, including eight-page booklet with photos, etc)

Here Come The Now LP (Last Year's Youth LAST BIG 4) (500 copies, red vinyl)

Fuzztone Fizzadelic (Damaged Goods 2005)

COMPILATIONS

All This And More Cassette (Solo Records 1982; 'Room At The Top', 'Don't You Believe Me?')

Open Sore

Bob Kyley (vocals), Sean Burke (guitar), Barry O'Connor (bass), Dave Arnold (drums), Holly Channer aka Jenny Rate (backing vocals)

Formed around September 1977 in Slough, OPEN SORE played regularly around London, but are mainly remembered for 'Vertigo', their contribution to the Farewell To The Roxy compilation. It was arguably the best track on there. Brian Sheklian of reissue label Grand Theft Audio considers it one of the finest punk songs ever recorded (it's subsequently been covered by both the Walking Abortions and Twisted Nerve).

Guitarist Sean Burke takes up the story. "I was in a band with Bob Kyley called Paradox. They were like a Genesis-type band. I just joined them because they were better players than I was. I thought I could learn from them. We used to do a cover of Van Morrison/Patti Smith's 'Gloria'. Of course, when I started to play it, I punked it up a bit." It was their version of 'Gloria' with which they passed an audition at the Roxy in Harlesden. Burke didn't know it at the time, but also auditioning that day were Gary Numan's Tubeway Army, whom he would subsequently join. "I just made a comment to Bob Kyley – I think we should be a punk band. Because it was happening then, and that's what I really liked. I listened to the Stooges at school and loved all that sort of music, the Dolls, Velvet Underground. All that Max's Kansas City stuff with Wayne County and so on."

"We got the gig at the Roxy before we had any songs. I was a bit wild at that point. I just went up there and said, 'I'm in a punk band, can you book us?' 'You'll have to do audition night.' 'That's OK. How long?' 'I can't book you for six weeks.' 'Oh, that's good.' So we had six weeks to find a bass player and drummer and put a set together." Open Sore had lift-off. "We did the clubs and all that, and we used to play in a lot of gay bars. That was the only place you could get a gig, unless you went into London, which we used to do. But the only places out of London were the gay bars. Because of the Pistols swearing on the TV and that, you know? If you tried to get a booking they'd say no. Bob Kyley wrote 'Vertigo' with me. The bass player was Barry O'Connor. And the first drummer was Dave Arnold. But he wasn't on the Roxy album." By the time that was recorded, Barry Benn had replaced him. "That was his first gig! That's why the drums sound like that. He carried on drumming after we finished the tune. If you listen to it, he keeps going, he fakes it."

The gig was booked through Roxy manager Kevin St John. "And he ripped us off over a show we did at the Richmond Rugby Club. He got £65 and he paid us a tenner for the gig. I found out when they tried to re-book us. Anyway, I wanted to box him out, but Bob didn't like it. 'No, we can't behave like that!' "Aw, I'm sticking up for the band! We ARE a punk band!" So I joined Tubeway Army after I saw an audition and that was the end of Open Sore. Then we got together for a party, which was a one-off sort of thing. They released the album and put a tour together. It was a different drummer and guitarist, but it wasn't the same band." Wasn't Burke tempted to rejoin? "Well, he asked me, but I was with Numan. I was better off doing that. And Barry Benn, the drummer from Open Sore, he joined Numan as well. He followed after me. So we were doing that. We would do the odd thing for fun. It would have been good, because Open Sore had some good songs. The thing with Bob, he had a voice. He really could sing. It was a really powerful voice. He used to like to use it. It was a good band, but it didn't last very long. Maybe if it had have done, we might have done something more."

The second version of Open Sore gave up the ghost in 1978 after both they and Blitz had their equipment stolen in Edinburgh on the Farewell To The Roxy tour. After Open Sore split Burke would continue with Tubeway Army before joining Jayne County's band, as did Barry O'Connor, and he also later worked with Invasion Of Privacy, Menace In Mono and Robert And The Remoulds. Menace in Mono actually reinterpreted the original Open Sore riff for 'Eyes On You' to come up with 'Perfect Fit', which got some attention on XFM. Burke also auditioned for the post-Mick Jones Clash and post-Derwood Generation X, and turned down a chance to play for the pre-Marco Pirroni Adam And The Ants. However, he was most upset by failing to get the gig with Brighton's Depressions, whom he loved. Bob Kyley would join The Company. Both principal songwriters are still in touch and contemplating putting something together musically.

COMPILATION:
Farewell To The Roxy (Lightning LIP 2 1978; 'Vertigo')

Ordinarys

Steve Phelps (lead vocals), Steve Phypers (drums), Jim Lewis (lead guitar), Steve Richmond (rhythm guitar), Neil Broadbank (bass)

O

Formed in the winter of 1976, the ORDINARYS were put together by former members of two local Hertfordshire bands. Phelps left Waltham Cross's Sonovabitch to join a quartet of musicians who had been performing in their hometown of Hoddesdon as Granite. They were alerted to the burgeoning punk movement by the antics of the Pistols and Clash, and had their faith in the 'new music' confirmed by watching a show by the New Hearts (Ian Page's pre-Secret Affair group) at Cheshunt's Wolsey Hall. They took their name from that band's song 'Here Comes The Ordinaires' and members of the group would follow Page and co from show to show. "To us, the New Hearts had something different to all the other bands, they had a bit of class," Steve Phypers told me. "They were carving their own way through, which is what initially inspired us along with a whole lot of bands around at that time."

Although they weren't balls-out punk rockers, their hard-firing pop sound was directly inspired by the energy of the movement, more in keeping with Generation X and the Jam (right down to the suits, accompanied by striped school ties). "It was our singer Steve Phelps who liked the idea of uniformity. Like early 60s bands, we contrived to make a holistic fashion statement! The Jam got in first, so our college boy image looked like a copy. We were gutted, but stuck with it anyway." Their set list contained a series of hyped-up R&B covers by Chuck Berry and Dr Feelgood, as they built a local following. These shows were frequent, thanks to the efforts of Phelps and his brother-in-law, Oliver 'Oli' Scarrott, and included residencies at venues such as the Bell, King's Head and the Hop Poles in Enfield, and the Cock in Ponder's End.

The band secured a slot on ATV's 70s abomination New Faces through the auspices of friend Les Cozens. Manager Monty Babson booked time at Morgan Studios in Willesden, while ATV

arranged for them to travel to Porcupine Studios in Mottingham. The sessions at Porcupine were engineered by the late Ted Taylor, a renowned jazz producer, whose son Nick still runs the studio. They cut three tracks, 'I Wanna Be An Ordinary', 'I Never Knew' and 'Get Me Up'. "We actually auditioned at a pub in the Elephant and Castle. We played for half an hour and the ATV scouts jumped at us. We then went to Porcupine some weeks later and recorded the demo, which was sent on to the producer of New Faces. Then we got the call to say we were booked to appear on it."

'I Wanna Be An Ordinary' was aired before seven million viewers in February 1978. It was great exposure in many ways, and Mickie Most loved them. "Mickie Most was the most positive because he understood what it took for us to stick our necks out to get chopped. We took 89 points, whatever that meant!" Michael Aspel conceded they had "bags of attack", but in the end the prize went to a bald bloke called Kenny Day. History does not record whether or not they finished above the ventriloquist and his Bassett hound. The whole thing makes for hilarious viewing now, the shock of the old meeting the new, the frankly bemused audience, etc. But their appearance would become something of an albatross around their necks. They also appeared, playing three original compositions on Malcolm Laycock's Radio London show, which included an interview segment with Phelps in which he bemoaned the band's inability to secure a recording contract, despite being able to sell out London venues like the Lyceum, in March 1978. This was a situation that was never resolved, despite some interest from managers of bands including the Killjoys and Suburban Studs. "After the TV appearance, there seemed to be a lot of pressure on us and everyone associated with us to make something happen. The timing was just slightly out, and the band very quickly became disillusioned with everything it was doing."

Ultimately, no-one would let them forget the fact that they were the punk band who had appeared on New Faces. Phypers: "The Jam auditioned for New Faces but didn't get through. Lucky them, eh?" The group persevered until the end of 1979 with a fluctuating line-up. Paul Hilder joined on lead guitar and vocals in May 1978, as did former New Hearts bassist John Harty. Paul Doyle replaced him on bass in 1979. Their last recording session came in the summer of 1978 in Epsom, at a studio owned by Rob Davis and Ray Stiles of Mud. Again, these efforts were shelved until they were unearthed by Detour Records for release on their compilation album Bored Teenagers Vol. 4 – Great British Punk Originals 1977-82. As a direct result of this, the band reunited for a series of shows, including one at Hertford's Marquee Club in October 2004.

Phypers, subsequently played with the Action, who cut demos with Eric Radcliffe of Yazoo and Assembly fame and who also won £300, presented by Annie Lennox, for coming fourth in the Melody Maker's 1980 Battle Of The Bands competition. He reflects fondly of his time in the punk trenches. "Lots of good memories, some not so good. Happily, though, I eventually met one of my heroes, Alan Lee Shaw (Rings, Maniacs). I became his drummer in '83 in a band called Hush Hush. Brian James of the Damned and Lords of the New Church was a good mate of Alan's and he came to a few of our shows." They've also found themselves drawn back into action – they supported Spizz at the 30th anniversary of the 100 Club Punk Festival and have other shows booked, while by the time you read this, they should have finalised the release of a live album.

Phypers continues to play in a 60s covers band, the Overtures (www.theovertures.com). "I've been with them for 17 years. We played at Elvis Costello's wedding to Diana Krall in Christmas 2003 at Elton John's house in front of Macca etc." Which was ironic, given that in 1997, his former lead singer in the Ordinarys, Steve Phelps, had appeared as Elvis Costello (singing 'Oliver's Army') on Stars In Their Eyes. "We also were invited by Sir Elton and David Furnish to perform at their wedding reception on 21 December 2005 in Windsor. We play anywhere and everywhere. QE2 to New York, London Palladium." And Cheshunt Wolsey Hall too, probably, which is still standing (£56 per hour for the main room, if you're interested).

COMPILATION:

Bored Teenagers Vol. 4 – Great British Punk Originals 1977-82' (Detour 2006)

The Out

Jo Roberts (vocals), Dave Bassnet (keyboards), George Borowski (guitar), Chris Daniels (bass), Brian Adamson (guitar)

THE OUT featured the punkish manifestation of one of Britain's great unsung guitar heroes, George Borowski, their principal songwriter. Surely no English speaker can have failed to come across the Dire Straits' lyric, "Check out guitar George, he knows all the chords" from 'Sultans Of Swing'? Few will have known to whom those lyrics referred.

As George later admitted to Q magazine in 1996: "We (The Out) had the job of opening for the bands at a place called Rafter's. When Dire Straits played, Mark Knopfler came over to me and said, 'That's a great guitar sound you've got. How come you don't play solos?' The thing is, I can't really play solos. I just play chords. He had a go on my guitar; it was a piece of plywood with two pick-ups and a reject neck, but it sounded terrific. I said 'You can have it if you want, it's only worth eighteen quid.' And he was like, 'Oh no, no, I can't take it.' That was about the long and short of it, really." Borowski, one of the most unassuming musicians I have ever spoken to, has long since become amused by the mythology. "I was over in America, and I said to them – 'Look, I don't actually think it's true. I don't think Mark Knopfler used me as the example in that song. I don't want you to be paying for the gig under false pretences. And they just roared back, "'No! You are Guitar George!'" It's a bit like the scene in Monty Python. The more Borowski tries to distance himself from it, the more people assume that it must be true.

So how did the Out get to grips with punk rock? "To me, it was the second biggest jump in English music since rock 'n roll. Me and Jo (Roberts) started working out a set. I'd been to the Lesser Free Trade Hall and seen the Buzzcocks and Slaughter And The Dogs. I loved fast music. So I loved punk rock by default." He found the emphasis on rhythm guitar perfectly suited his own predisposition. "I wasn't a good player at the start, so I started chugging, and became famous for that. Locally, it was kind of playing in a way that people hadn't played. You didn't have the secondary finger movement interchange that you do in rock'n'roll, but basically it was very much the same. And I've always just loved performing. I'm quite a shy person and it's a way of keeping out of fights in dodgy clubs."

I also asked about the TJ Davidson rehearsal facility, which was the birthing pool for so much of the Mancunian punk generation. "Anyone who was anyone rehearsed there, but it was good. There was a café there just next door. I did the painting and decorating for some ready cash. Everyone would play then meet up in the café. It was inspiring listening to the other bands. That's always a good environment, because if you'd had a bad session, you'd hear something good coming from somewhere else in the building and you'd want to go back and compete, and be better."

Afterwards they signed to Tosh Ryan's Rabid Records. The result was 'Who Is Innocent?' A real lost treasure, it was later dramatically covered by the Backsliders in 1987 and was one of John Peel's favourite singles of that year. It was also much admired by the likes of Pete Townshend and even Black Francis of the Pixies. "Martin Hannett wanted to produce it at one stage. Then it wasn't going to be released because the other two members of Rabid, Hannett and (Lawrence) Beadle, were resistant to us as a band. Tosh was convinced it was going to be a hit. And he forced it through. Off it went, and it was on radio and everything. It's kind of a lost classic. Tosh never forgave himself that it wasn't a hit. He said to me much later that that's the one he regrets most not doing as well as it could have done." It was later re-released on Virgin. "Chas Banks, the manager, and Tosh went to meet Virgin, and themselves and Chrysalis were interested in putting the single out. Because Rabid was celebrating a big hit single with 'Jilted John', they dug their heels in and said if you want the single, take the album, and Virgin said, no."

Lyndsey Frost drummed on the session, though thereafter David Alexander replaced him. There was a further single for Cargo at the turn of the decade, but by now Borowski had moved on to the Fabulous Wonderfuls. Yet another drummer, Kim Turner, had auditioned for the Outs, and Borowski, who was thinking about leaving anyway, advised the prospective drummer that they ought to hook up in their own band. The remaining Outs continued touring Manchester and remained relatively popular while Borowski joined first Sad Café and then later toured with Meat Loaf. Thereafter Borowski concentrated on a solo career, which has achieved massive acclaim (fans include Norman Blake of Teenage Fanclub and the aforementioned Frank Black, both of whom he has collaborated with, in inverse proportion to commercial visibility.

DISCOGRAPHY:

Who Is Innocent?/Linda's Just A Statue 7-inch (Rabid TOSH 113 1979) (reissued on Virgin, VS 308, also in 1979)

Better The Devil/It's Not Enough 7-inch (Cargo CRS 14 1980)

COMPILATIONS:

Rabid/TJM Punk Singles Collection CD (Receiver RRCD 227 1996; 'Who Is Innocent', 'Linda's Just A Statue')

Outcasts

Greg Cowan (vocals, bass), Colin Cowan (drums), Martin Cowan (guitar), Colin 'Getty' Getgood (guitar)

Formed in Belfast in January 1977, the OUTCASTS were often perceived to be more of a street gang than a band, by dint of their blunt, working class rock'n'roll aesthetic. They were also the only band of the province's big four – also comprising the Undertones, Stiff Little Fingers and Rudi – to remain permanently in Northern Ireland. Martin, the chief songwriter, was a former teacher, while his other brothers (real brothers too, eat your heart out, Ramones) worked for their father's painting and decorating business. All the band members maintained these jobs during the group's initial stages. Vocalist Blair Hamilton didn't last the summer, and was sacked after three rehearsals.

O

After Getgood, an employee of Terri Hooley's Good Vibrations shop, joined the brothers Cowan, they played their first show at Paddy Lambe's bar on the Upper Newtownards Road in Belfast in August. It promptly ended in a mini-riot when locals took exception to the Outcasts' audience, which included both Jake Burns and Henry Cluney of Stiff Little Fingers. "I liked the Outcasts," Cluney later confessed, "but the tough guy image was so stupid. Knew them all quite well and it really was just all talk." That gig was followed by shows at the Trident in Bangor, a support to the Radiators From Space at Jordanstown Polytechnic and the first of several appearances at early Belfast punk venue, The Pound Club. Most were, by the band's own admission, disasters. Meanwhile Getty devised his own unique manner of promoting the band at major gigs. This involved running on to the stage, grabbing the microphone, announcing the next Outcasts show, then disappearing under a carpet of vengeful bouncers and aggrieved rock stars.

Their first demo tape was cut at Wizzard Studios and produced a one-off deal with Portadown's IT Records, who'd unsuccessfully attempted to sign SLF. The resulting three tacks lacked studio polish; the band were so inept they took 30 takes to get everything right. But the spark was self-evident, particularly on 'You're A Disease', an attack on organised religion and its blighting effect on the province. Or 'You're A Decease', as some berk mis-spelt it on the label. Though it sold well in Northern Ireland, the band later claimed they were "ripped off" by IT. For their second single they moved to Good Vibrations, Terri Hooley having first seen them play at the Pound Bar alongside Rudi in January 1978. He remembered 'hating' them. Now won over, he set up a release on Good Vibrations, the third release in the upstart label's history, recorded in the summer of 1978, and released later that year. 'Justa Nother Teenage Rebel' employed no little cynicism about their kindred musical revolutionaries, while the B-side, 'Love Is For Sops', half-jokingly amplified their macho credentials ("I just want to get into your bed, nothing more"). Before its release they also had the honour of supporting the Clash at the Ulster Hall in October 1978, receiving the princely sum of £10 in recompense.

By now managed by Hooley, a full album was prepared for release by Good Vibrations at the end of 1979, the first on the label. There were eleven originals on offer, sadly not including the jokey stage favourite 'Johnny's A Wanker'. Good Vibrations also lifted the title-track, 'Self Conscious Over You', an affecting nod to the power of teenage hormones, if not harmonies, as a single. They were then profiled in John Davis's Northern Ireland punk documentary, Shell Shock Rock, using film of a show at the Ulster Hall. Davis would also later collaborate with the band on their video for 'Winter'.

When Greg was hurt in a motorcycle accident near Portrush, the band temporarily persevered with Gordon Blair (ex-SLF, Rudi) as their live bassist to promote the album. But after contributing 'Cyborg' to the 'Room To The Move' EP (released by Good Vibrations in conjunction with Energy Records) they were dropped from Good Vibrations – essentially for being bloody troublemakers.

Blair remained in place for the B-side of their next single, 'Magnum Force', which also saw them expand the line-up with a second drummer, 16-year-old Raymond Falls. The effect on the band's sound was dramatic – where they had always been the rawest of the Northern Irish punks, now their songs were buffeted by a compelling rhythmic punch. This was in evidence on their first John Peel session, broadcast in May 1981 (they would record a second in September 1982, as well as two for the Janice Long show and several for Northern Ireland's Downtown Radio). Meanwhile they also played five shows at the Gibus Club in Paris and signed, much to their eventual regret, with Marc Boullier for European distribution.

They took a residency at the Magnet in Dublin, but a couple of shows were marred by sectarian violence. The fate of 'Magnum Force', which was given a big push from John Peel, typified the band's problems. Though it topped the Irish alternative charts, it failed to sell more than a few thousand copies on the mainland. Having left Good Vibrations they also cut their management ties with Hooley and signed with Ross Graham. He'd produced 'Magnum Force' and helped Colin set up a new label, Outcasts Only, distributed through Spartan. The first release was a four-track EP, 'Programme Love', which was heralded by an appearance at the Christmas On Earth show at Leeds' Queen's Hall in December 1981. It seemed at last that they'd cracked the mainland, following a rapturously received end of tour show at the Lyceum.

But it never happened. Colin, the prime motivating force behind the band, was killed in a car accident in May 1982, which knocked the stuffing out of his brothers and bandmates. At first it seemed as if they would break up there and then. In the end, they elected to persevere, after a band meeting in a shed in Barnet's Park. They dedicated their next single, a cover of the Glitter Band's 'Angel Face', to his memory. The B-side, 'Gangland Warfare', was a new version of the 'Magnum Force' B-side, documenting a violent denouement to a night out at the Harp Bar witnessed by the brothers. This was a far better version, the original having been copied from a tape of a tape after the master was lost at the pressing plant. They played their first post-Colin show at the Harp Bar, an emotional moment for all concerned, and also toured as a trio while Getgood was hospitalised with food poisoning.

They moved to Abstract to record their second album, Blood And Thunder, released in France by New Rose. The key track here was 'Winter'. Effects-laden, atmospheric and claustrophobic, it used Shakespeare's Richard III speech as its central metaphor. Arguably the best song the band ever recorded, it was a long way from their original scratch-punk aesthetic. Some critics carped at the repetition of earlier material – though the versions here were far superior, and the band touted it in the press as their first album proper. By now the Outcasts were pretty much a straight-ahead rock band, albeit an adept and powerful unit, as Sounds recounted: "It's breathlessly loud, invincibly proud, and very much alive".

Abstract then issued a 12-inch, 'Nowhere Left To Run', which built on the sound of Blood And Thunder, pushing them further towards a style that mirrored the UK's psychobilly movement – raw, 50s rock'n'roll shot through with punk attitude and irreverence. After touring with the Meteors they again supported the Clash in Dublin during 1984. Seven Deadly Sins, a mini-album, featured an uninspired cover of Bowie's 'Five Years', though the title-track was a fantastic distillation of the Outcasts' key components – ferocious percussion and swampy rock'n'roll hell-raising – unlike many of their peers, this was a band you could dance to. The irony was that they'd peaked musically at exactly the point at which they'd lost heart in the project. A 1985 cover of the Stooges' '1969' rounded out their career.

The Cowan brothers, alongside Getty, formed Time To Pray for a while, playing in priest garb, before concentrating on the family's painting and decorating business. Falls joined the army. Greg Cowan also briefly set up the glam cover band Hades Whores. There are no plans for any reformation, though Greg is also a member of Shame Academy, the Ulster punk supergroup, alongside Petesy Burns of Stalag 17 and Brian Young of Rudi, who released Punk Rock For Dummies for Combat Rock in 2004.

DISCOGRAPHY:

(Buyer's Guide; The two Captain Oi! CDs, AHOY CD 68 (the two-for-one Blood and Thunder compilation) and AHOY CD 239 (the expanded Self Conscious Over You) are all you really need here)

Frustration/Don't Want To Be No Adult/You're A Disease 7-inch (It 4 March 1978)

Justa Nother Teenage Rebel/Love Is For Sops 7-inch (Good Vibrations GOT 3 November 1978) (later repressed in a different cover to coincide with the Good Vibrations package tour in April 1979)

Self Conscious Over You/Love You For Never 7-inch (Good Vibrations GOT 17 November 1979)

Self Conscious Over You LP (Good Vibrations BIG 1 December 1979) (the version of 'The Cops Are Comin'' is different to that on the 'Battle Of The Bands' EP. Reissued on CD on Dojo, DOJO CD 182, February 1994, adding 'Justa Nother Teenage Rebel' as a bonus track. Reissued again on Captain Oi!, AHOY CD 239 in 2004, with bonus tracks 'Frustration', 'Don't Wanna Be No Adult', 'You're A Disease (single version)', 'Just Another Teenage Rebel (single version)', 'Love Is For Sops (single version)', 'The Cops Are Coming (single version)')

Magnum Force/Gangland Warfare 7-inch (GBH 001 August 1981)

From Programme Love To Mania Via Beating And Screaming, Parts 1 & 2 7-inch EP (Outcasts Only OO 001 November 1981)

Programme Love/Beating And Screaming (Parts 1 & 2)/Mania

Angel Face/Gangland Warfare 7-inch (Outcasts Only OO 200 June 1982)

Blood And Thunder LP (Abstract ABT 004 January 1983) (reissued on CD by New Rose, ROSE 16 CD, 1984)

Nowhere Left To Run/The Running's Over Time To Pray 7-inch (Abstract ABS 017 June 1983) (12-inch version, 12ABS 017, adds 'Nowhere Left To Run (instrumental)', 'Ruby'. French version on New Rose includes 'The Cops Are Comin'' (live))

Seven Deadly Sins/Swamp Fever 7-inch (New Rose NEW 38 August 1984)

Seven Deadly Sins mini-LP (New Rose NEW 40 August 1984)

1969 (extended)/Psychotic Shakedown/Blue Murder 12-inch (New Rose NEW 52 July 1985)

ARCHIVE RELEASES:

Punk Singles Collection CD (Anagram CD PUNK 62 September 1995)

Frustration/Don't Want To Be No Adult/You're A Disease 7-inch (Combat Rock reissue; CRO 20; 1996)

Blood And Thunder/Seven Deadly Sins CD (Captain Oi! AHOY CD 68 1997) (compilation of the band's second and third albums. Features bonus tracks 'Nowhere Left To Run', '1969', 'The Running's Over Time To Pray (instrumental)')

Outpatients

Tom Newton (bass), Nick Burt (guitar), Paddy Carroll (guitar), Jents Olsen (drums), Tex Axile (aka Anthony Doughty; vocals)

The **OUTPATIENTS**' history is one of extended genesis followed by a solitary single and then the sound of everything going 'phut'. Formed in west London, variations of the band were active from as early as 1976. By 1978, when Tex Axile, a veteran of stints with Peroxide Romance and others joined, they had developed a more theatrical live show. They were managed by Nicky Tesco of the Members, who also co-produced their only single with John Brand, famed for his work with the Ruts, XTC and Holly And The Italians.

O

Tex Axile liked to start the shows by arriving on stage inside a coffin (an idea which Screaming Lord Sutch should have patented). Other props included inflatable dolphins, swords, masks, etc. They were fixtures at the Marquee, Lyceum, Music Machine etc, toured with the Members and supported the Police at the 100 Club. They also played regularly as support to the Psychedelic Furs (whose John Ashton regularly kipped on Tex's floor and whose girlfriend got the Outpatients' their subsequent residency at the Windsor Castle).

The Outpatients' sole release was the 'New Japanese Hairstyles' single for Albion in 1981. Which meant other cornerstones of their set, 'Siren', 'Natural Victim', 'Jacques Cousteau', 'Hiding', 'News' and 'Time Has Taken' lie in an unmarked grave. Possibly the biggest loss to posterity was 'Nailing Down', the band's trademark set opener which would accompany Tex's coffin trick ("Someone once nicked the coffin at a gig we had in Shepherd's Bush. We left it outside by our van to load it up, went back for the amps and when we returned it had gone!")

"The Outpatients were awesome," Nicky Tesco told me. "I loved them and produced a single and various other tracks. We came very close to securing a major deal for them but unfortunately their Danish drummer, Jens, buckled under the pressure, got very drunk before the gig (at the Portland Arms) and spectacularly blew it in front of most of the A&R community in London at that time."

Tex would go on to sundry further bands, tasting some mainstream success with Transvision Vamp, before settling on a solo career. Was it a relief to finally taste the limelight after so many also-ran ventures? "No, because all the other bands were successful in their own right. But it was nice all the same to be making a better living than ever before, and I think that the Vamps were a perfect pop/punk band. We played some fantastic gigs." Other members of the band included Rudi Thompson and BP Hurding on a break between gigs with X-Ray Spex and Classix Nouveaux. Meanwhile Newton, Burt and Tex still socialise and recently began recording together again. Check out xj5000.com for details.

DISCOGRAPHY:

New Japanese Hairstyles/Children 7-inch (Albion ION 1014 1981)

The Panik

Ian Nance (vocals, guitar), Paul Dale-Hilton (bass), Steve Brotherdale (drums)

On the lower rungs of the Manchester punk ladder, THE PANIK nevertheless released one excellent 7-inch, the 'It Won't Sell' EP, before their drummer, Brotherdale, moved on to the pre-Joy Division Warsaw. But the story goes back much further than that. "I'd met Ian Nance way back in 1975," Brotherdale told me, "and we copied the Heavy Metal Kids. We idolised them and Gary Holton was really good to us. I loved Keith Boyce, the drummer, and that was who I tried to emulate. We called the band Mental, a three-piece. Ian sang and played bass, which was actually a plank of wood with some nails in it, there was a guitarist called Scotch and me, and we were rehearsing around 1975, before any of the other bands that came up. Ian Nance used to walk down Deansgate in Manchester with bright orange hair one week, bright purple the next, and people just stared at him. That was the summer of 1975, he had ripped jeans, winklepickers, and 'Bollocks to You' and 'Shit' written on his shirts. Miles ahead of his time."

Brotherdale, meanwhile, is cited by writer Mick Middles as being a kind of mascara-heavy rock'n'roll Billy Liar, who fantasised about having played support slots to Kiss in America. He dismisses this, but says the author may have been confused by his friendship with Gary Holton, whose band did indeed support the greasepaint rockers as well as Alice Cooper.

'It Won't Sell' was one of the first genuine Manchester punk artefacts, but the history surrounding it has become somewhat obscured. In particular, the guitar playing is widely credited to someone called Random – this was actually not a person at all. Nance played most of the guitar and bass on the single – he'd been trying to teach Paul Dale-Hilton elementary bass but wasn't having much success, as Brotherdale asserts: "He simply couldn't play." So Nance performed those duties as well, while another acquaintance, Clive Robinson, later of Sister Ray, also contributed. "If you look at the Panik single, there's a picture of Ian Nance's head on the back, which says 'Random Guitars'. He basically did the guitar playing on that. The bass playing on it, which is a joke – 'Damnation' sounds like a jew's harp – it's supposed to be the bass, but it's only four strings on the guitar. Clive Robinson, a local guitarist, he was in the recording studio and did some guitar on it, but Ian didn't want to put his name down. Most of it was Ian."

Co-produced by band manager Rob Gretton, the bold red front cover featured pictures of "a parade of strutting gays", taken from a 1964 Life magazine article. The label included the regionalist dig: "We're so bored of London." But the single was never followed up. Brotherdale moved on to Warsaw, though he actually tried to encourage Ian Curtis to become the Panik's singer, while a counter rumour suggests Nance had once actually auditioned for the Stiff Kittens/Warsaw. "The Panik were recording a single entitled 'It Won't Sell', and although the title later proved sadly prophetic, they seemed to have a lot going for them at the time, especially in having Rob Gretton as their manager," Claude Flowers wrote in Dreams Never End. "During a party that summer, he tried to get Ian Curtis to jump camps as well. Ian attempted to sing along to a copy of 'It Won't Sell', but his voice was incompatible with the music. Thanking Steve for the offer, Ian shrugged, 'Well, I might as well go back to Warsaw.'"

Brotherdale confirms that Flowers is pretty much correct. "The problem was that the music was too fast for him. (He recites some of the lyrics from 'Urban Damnation' – £12.10 for drainpipe jeans, bosh bosh bosh, etc') Think of Ian Curtis singing like that! He agreed and went back to Warsaw. That was it." A wise move given that the Panik would only last a couple of live shows before splintering, with Brotherdale moving on to V2, where he would later be joined by Nance.

Nance had joined V2 by late 1978, in time for their second single, 'Man In The Box', released on TJM Records (Nance wrote the B-side, 'When The World Isn't There'). When V2 ground to a halt in 1980, Brotherdale helped out with Fast Cars, who'd supported V2. He then reunited with his former friends from V2, alongside Toby Tolman of the Nosebleeds and guitarist turned bass player Hugh O'Boyle, formerly of Victim, as the Earwigs, this time as singer. The Earwigs were heavily involved in the turn of the 80s psychedelic revival scene, appearing on the Warners' compilation A Splash Of Colour, alongside a pre-Doctor And The

P

Medics Clive Jackson, who often performed as a live compere. Brotherdale's other engagements as a drummer came in Beat The Square, a Wham! parody band featuring a salesman from French Connection as Andrew Ridgeley, and as replacement to former Wayne Fontana and the Mindbender's drummer Tony Bookbinder in the cabaret band Park Avenue. He has since joined the telecoms industry with NTL and currently trains people in fibre optics installation.

Discography:

It Won't Sell 7-inch EP (Rainy City Records SHOT 1 November 1977)
Modern Politics/Urban Damnation/Murder
COMPILATION:
Punk Rock Rarities Vol 1 CD (Anagram CD PUNK 63 1995; 'Modern Politics', 'Urban Damnation', 'Murder')

Pathetix

Knickers (aka Andrew Nicholson; vocals), Phil Image (aka Philip Husband; guitar), Jack Frost (aka Gary Brown; bass), Pete Hectic (aka Pete Rowlands; lead guitar), Star (aka Terry Sanders; drums)

Nelson, Lancashire band, formed as early as 1976, initially by Nicholson and Husband. Nicholson, now a producer for the BBC, first chanced upon punk while doing his paper round. "I was a 15-year-old paperboy delivering someone's NME when I noticed a photo of some bloke called Johnny Rotten sporting a bondage suit. It thrilled and frightened me. I wasn't sure what to think. I'd grown out of Slade and had been desperately looking for something to like. I bought shit album after shit album in a forlorn hope that this might be the one – it never was. I still hadn't heard the Pistols but even the way they looked was enough to hook my attention."

"Then sitting at home one night watching So It Goes on Granada Television, there they were – it was a seismic moment and although it sounds corny, things really would never be the same again. When 'Anarchy In The UK' came out, I went to the local record shop to buy it. The shop owner wouldn't even say the band's name. He called them the SP's. Already this was more exciting than anything else that had ever happened to me, and I hadn't even listened to the record yet. At home I had one of those record players that if you left the arm up, it would keep on playing the same record time after time. I put on my headphones and as my mum and dad watched Nationwide, I listened to it 15 times. It was and still is the most powerful manifesto any band has ever managed to put down on to

seven inches of vinyl. I went straight over to my friend Philip across the road, who I'd been writing songs with, and played it to him. It was obvious that this is what we'd been waiting for. That record redefined everything."

Thus enthused, Husband and Nicholson set about putting a set together. "We wrote lots of songs, and approached a time when we needed to play them to someone, but there was just the two of us. My brother told me he knew another punk called Star (Terry Sanders) who lived in Nelson. So we asked him through my brother if he wanted to be in a band, not knowing whether he could actually play anything. As it turns out, he couldn't, but somehow it didn't seem to matter. We were booked to do a gig at Bold Street Working Men's Club in Accrington, where we'd seen a local skinhead/punk band called Schoolgirl Bitch support Eater the week before. Star was going to play bass but was so bad he changed to drums two days before the gig. He bought his kit for the princely sum of a pint of mild – I kid you not."

So how did their debut gig go? "The soundcheck for the gig was really good, I think we surprised ourselves. Unfortunately, that was as good as it got. Philip and Terry got very nervous and drank far too much. We went on stage and Philip turned everything up and to appalling feedback, we announced the birth of the **PATHETIX**. After two songs I said to Philip: 'This is shit, let's get off.' Philip ripped all the strings off his guitar, Terry kicked his kit all over the stage and we walked off, feedback still reverberating around the room to huge cheers. Everyone thought it was some kind of stage act and wanted us back on. But Philip didn't have any more strings so that was that. To cut this interminable story slightly short, we added Gary Brown to the band, got a lot better then added Pete Rowlands on lead guitar and Peter Leeper on saxophone."

The band played a lot of gigs during the summer of 1978, until eventually "we thought it was time to make a record". However, the major labels were not beating a path to their door. "As no-one showed the slightest interest in signing us, we embraced the DIY ethic and went into Smile Studios in Liverpool. The track we chose for the A-side was a song that had been written one boring evening after the band and a bunch of friends had taken out a ouija board and attempted to contact the spirit world. To this day I still don't know who around that table knew who Aleister Crowley was, but I sure as hell didn't. Who knows – perhaps it really was the man himself. After a sleepless night waiting to die, myself Philip and a friend called Quentin wrote 'Aleister Crowley'.

The EP was duly released on their own No Records label, and its drunken séance diorama seemed to hit a chord, which was more than some of their peers were capable of at this stage. "These six sprightly young sprogs deserve encouragement for going it alone," stated Max Bell in the NME. "A good idea brilliantly realised." Both Giovanni Dadomo at Sounds and Mark Perry of Sniffin' Glue were impressed. The good press saw them reach the Top Ten of the (then unofficial) Independent Charts after the single was picked up for distribution by Rough Trade (ie they took 500 copies off their hands).

After a further batch of gigs they signed with Manchester's TJM label, which was "without a doubt the worst thing the band ever did. We thought it was going to change everything and sure enough it did – we never really recovered from the experience. We'd have been better looking after ourselves, what momentum we'd built up was lost over a period where Tony (Davidson) played at being Richard Branson with his dad's money." A further single emerged, by which time Leeper had left to join the theatre (he would appear as Malcolm Parrot on Grange Hill) and Brown had switched to the Notsensibles – he'd been practising with them and received an ultimatum from the band over his loyalties. "'Love In Decay' should have been great but Tony wouldn't pay for a producer, and just when we should have been sounding better and getting a push, there was a big nothing. At a time when every single had a picture sleeve, ours didn't."

TJM did at least organise a package tour for them. "It included a band called the Frantic Elevators with a flame-haired eejit as vocalist. He used to go bright red whenever he sang. They did lots of covers and I remember watching him singing 'Don't Let Me Down' thinking his head was going to explode. His name was Mick Hucknall. Imagine my surprise years later etc." Hucknall was a big fan of the Pathetix's 'Don't Let The Bastards Grind You Down', and once sang it back to its co-author verbatim in a drunken moment while doing an interview for Music Box. "The tour was a real Tony event. No hotels for us, we used to do the gig, jump on the coach and drive all the way back to Manchester. Then next morning meet up again and drive off to wherever we were playing that night for the whole routine to repeat itself." By now, their set had expanded to include the aforementioned 'Don't Let The Bastards Grind You Down', 'What Do You Expect From Me', 'Teenage Idol', 'Pressure Drop' (not the reggae staple) and 'My Friend's A Moron'. Nicholson's favourite, though, was 'Soldier Tommy', about Northern Ireland. "It's one of the first songs Philip and I wrote and it's a song I regret never recording."

But the band weren't satisfied that TJM were delivering on their promises and promoting their single nationally. So instead they signed a deal with French independent (with Mancunian connections) Sordide Sentimental. They ground to a halt soon after, though they were joined for a while by keyboard player John Finch. "It was 1979 by now. We all felt that punk was a moment in time, a moment that had gone. Bands like Discharge, the Angelic Upstarts and Crass were about as far away from what punk had meant to us as it was possible to be. To me punk was about limitless possibilities and not accepting your lot in life. The interesting bands were trying to articulate themselves in new ways and so did we – it didn't last long and maybe we were wrong. We made one last record for Sordide Sentimental (as Citizen UK, by which time Pete Rowlands had left and John Finch had joined permanently on keyboards) and that was that. By 1981 it was all over."

There was a further cassette release, as Citizen UK, while Husband and Nicholson were also involved in the punk-hip-hop hybrid Trash Culture. And as the man says, that was that. All over. But not quite. Nicholson: "In 1998 I was working as a director at the BBC. Noel's House Party needed a last-minute replacement for the NTV section of the show (in which viewers are unknowingly filmed in their own living room). By this time, Peter Leeper was an actor and pretty well known as Malcolm Parrot, a teacher on Grange Hill, so it was arranged for Peter to be the 'guest' on NTV that week. Noel clicked his fingers to reveal Peter apparently sitting at home utterly shocked. But once Noel mentioned the Pathetix, Peter dismantled the hidden camera by his TV set, and with the words 'I'm not up for this, Noel', put it in a cup of tea he was drinking."

DISCOGRAPHY:

Aleister Crowley/Don't Touch My Machine/Snuffed It 7-inch EP (No Records No 001 1978)
("When I say DIY single, I mean it in every sense. We even glued the sleeves together ourselves. Have you ever cut out and glued a thousand record sleeves? It takes fucking ages.")
Love In Decay/Nil Carborundum 7-inch (TJM TJM 12 1979)
As Citizen UK:
Apocalypse In 7 Notes/Leave Me Alone/Dining On Expenses 7-inch (Sordide Sentimental 1981)

Penetration

Pauline Murray (vocals), Gary Chaplin (guitar), Robert Blamire (bass), Gary Smallman (drums)

PENETRATION sprang to life in the mining village of Ferryhill, County Durham, where Pauline Murray moved at the age of 10. Murray: "They were moving people from the pit villages when the pits closed to places like Nottingham and Wales, or nearby places. But the coal mines in those places closed as well. It was that time in the 70s when the government was breaking down the NCB, more or less, and all the mines were closing." She moved from another pit village about seven miles away. "I've always wanted to escape wherever I've been, so I was quite pleased to move but it was very different to where I'd already lived. That was quite an innocent place. I started at the senior school and then I met someone older than me. In the second year of senior school I was going to see bands, and that really did get me off the hook."

She became obsessed with music, going to see anyone who would visit the north-east as well as heading down to London, her preferences being Bowie, Roxy and Patti Smith. Eagerly devouring the music press, she became fascinated by the Sex Pistols phenomenon. On a day trip to London with then boyfriend Peter Lloyd, she happened to spy John Lydon on a train, and gallantly trailed him back to Seditionaries, where Lloyd spoke to Malcolm McLaren. Ever the opportunist, McLaren remembered the pair and rang Lloyd a few months later about setting up shows in the north. Glen Matlock: "At a gig in North Allerton, Derbyshire, to our surprise there were two punk rockers in the audience. They turned out to be Pauline Murray and her boyfriend... Their appetite has been whetted by early reports in the music papers. This was their first opportunity to take a look-see and they certainly dressed for the occasion, sticking right out from all the other chicken-in-the-basket cases." The pair became unofficial ambassadors for the Pistols, dubbed "the Durham contingent" in a review of the Pistols' Screen On The Green show.

The next stage was to set up their own band. While Lloyd, soon to become Murray's husband, became a kind of informal manager, Murray hooked up with local guitarist Gary Chaplin after meeting him on a coach trip to see Roxy Music. They began practising together, eventually drafting bass player Robert Blamire and 15-year-old drummer Gary Smallman. They were all local kids drawn from working class families of miners, printers and roofers, which gave them a bond and enthusiasm distinct from their more jaded London-based contemporaries. The name Penetration was taken from the Iggy Pop song, but also served as a nice tryst on the Pistols' sexually charged moniker.

They played their first show at Middlesbrough's Rock Garden in October 1976, while their London debut came as support to Generation X and the Adverts at the Roxy Club on 9 April 1977, which Murray later recalled to the NME. "We all got in the back of a furniture van with all the gear. We spent a fortune in getting down there. We thought it was great. Then when we got there it was such a dump. I don't know what we were expecting, but it wasn't quite that. But we did get our first real publicity from doing it so it wasn't that bad." Reflecting on that Roxy debut in 2005, Murray remembers the venue as being "very dark, very black, but there were lots of punk rock celebrities there. We were very young, I was about 17 at the time. But yeah, it was exciting. We just went off and did stuff. We didn't think twice."

That 'stuff' comprised an initial set featuring covers of 'Road Runner' and various Stooges songs, as well as embryonic originals 'Destroy', 'Don't Spoil My Fun' and 'Nobody'. Further shows were secured by Lloyd with the Buzzcocks via Richard Boon, as well as supports around the Durham area to the Vibrators, Stranglers and Cherry Vanilla. Murray: "Gary Chaplin and I would ring up for gigs. But we'd sort of become known because we were the only punk band up here. So we'd get phone calls from, say, the Stranglers, to support them at the City Hall very early on, or the Vibrators, to ask us to do a residency with them at the Marquee. We were very isolated up here, I have to say, but we did get ourselves out and about. And other bands knew of us." Eventually they secured their own transport. "We had a Ford Transit that we put seats into. The main claim to fame for that van was that we gave Sid and Nancy a lift home one night in it. We'd been supporting the Heartbreakers at the Vortex, and Sid and Nancy asked for a lift home. So they piled into the back of our van, and Sid gobbed on to the ceiling. They'd thrown a bottle out in Marble Arch all over the road. And they got out and Sid's gob was immortalised on the roof of the van."

A demo cassette had been recorded at their local youth club – soundproofed by shifting the billiard tables around – and mailed out. After Warm Records had initially offered the group a show at a Portuguese wedding reception alongside the Adverts, which caused a bit of a stink when an audience member wiped their hands on the national flag, Virgin gave them the first sympathetic hearing. "They thought it (the demo) sounded promising," Murray later told Mark Paytress, "though of course it was dreadful, and they invited us to do a proper demo. So we did nine songs in a couple of days at Virtual Earth in London." At this stage, the group's sound was still evolving. Murray: "We'd never written songs before, so it was very new to us, to be honest. Whatever came out was what turned out. We were very, very young, 17 or 18. Hadn't even written songs before. So we weren't really thinking, let's be clever and write hit singles. The songs just came out as they came out, probably because of where we lived. Usually Gary Chaplin would come up with some riff or whatever, the band would rehearse it through, and then I would maybe take it away and write the lyrics and take it back the next week and sing on it. That really was how Penetration worked. Even with later guitarists, it was usually a bass line or a guitar riff, or a mixture of two people's riffs, and we would come together and I would write in the framework of what was there."

The sessions led to a one-off single deal with Virgin, before which they supported the

Vibrators at the Marquee for three nights during August. When 'Don't Dictate' emerged in November 1977 it was obvious that this was one of punk's most eloquent, not to mention melodic, early statements. Its tone was vogueishly anti-authoritarian but it wasn't, as many supposed, a retort to their parents, to whom this most homespun of bands remained fiercely loyal. Virgin had brought in Mike Howlett, bass player for Gong, to look after production, alongside engineer Mick Glossop, a more fortuitous partnership than it sounded on paper. Though it didn't chart 'Don't Dictate' did well enough to convince Virgin to persevere with the band. They also signed to Quarry management, who looked after Status Quo and Rory Gallagher. This would have implications for the band down the road, but in the meantime, it did give them some promotional muscle (check out the glossy programme they produced for the band's later UK tour).

It was also immediately apparent that Murray was a true talent. Indeed, Julie Burchill and Tony Parsons noted in The Boy Looked At Johnny that: "Pauline's best bet would be to take her musicians out of circulation for a year or two until punk is nothing more than nostalgia-music, and then display that extraordinary soaring, searing voice to the public afresh." Yet Murray would remain as reluctant to embrace any selling of herself as female icon or commodity as her old friend Gaye Advert. Offstage she was never more uncomfortable than when some damn fool NME/Sounds/Melody Maker reporter was thrusting a microphone in front of her face. Yet she was increasingly writing lyrics that, though often opaque, were sharply observed and, occasionally, remarkably prescient. Throughout their career there was also an extraordinary, exquisite sincerity to Penetration's songs.

By the start of 1978 they'd begun to amass more material including 'V.I.P', 'Firing Squad' and 'Silent Community'. However, Chaplin, up until that point their main songwriter, quit the band due to the "pressure" following a tour of France with Rory Gallagher where they were routinely bottled off the stage. "I wanted to go in a different direction and it was pretty plain that the band would go another," he later told Q. Murray: "I still know Gary and see Gary and I've spoken to him about this recently and asked him, why did he leave? We'd all packed our jobs in and made our commitment. When we signed to Quarry, I think Gary got cold feet. They were old school management. They managed Status Quo. It was the wrong type of thing, I suppose. I suppose he got cold feet at the time. I don't know, but I think he may have thought that it might all have collapsed without him, but actually we had to carry on. We hadn't chosen to leave, so we had to carry on. It was difficult, because we were actually busy doing stuff, and we had one week to get Neale in. I found a diary recently, and your memory plays tricks. I looked at this, and we had one week from Gary leaving to Neale doing his first gig. So at the time we weren't too happy with Gary, we were really pissed off with it at the time, but we had to carry on and see it through."

Blamire stepped into Chaplin's boots as Murray's principal musical collaborator, his first composition being the quietly adventurous 'Movement', distinguished by its spidery walking bass line. The aforementioned Neale Floyd, a long-time fan of the band, came in on guitar, and helped them complete further dates with the Buzzcocks (a clip of their Manchester Electric Circus show was shown on Tony Wilson's 'So It Goes'). Meanwhile Murray and Lloyd married in March. The group's second single, 'Firing Squad', followed in May 1978, another indication of abilities, and ambitions, beyond established punk rock rhetoric.

A second guitarist, Fred Purser, was added in June. While his affection for heavy metal licks alarmed some would-be punk purists, it gave the band a healthy dose of sonic invention beyond the more rigid rhythmic guitar stylings of their peers. As Tim Jones of frequent support act Neon noted to punk77, "We thought that Penetration were especially amazing after Fred Purser joined on guitar. We did quite a few gigs with them and Punilux. You listen to them now and they're both still amazing to hear. They haven't dated at all because they were real innovators. I used to work in a crap job for the council with Gary Chaplin, the original guitarist for Penetration and he invited me down to Saint Margaret's church hall in Durham to watch them rehearse. Pauline Murray was always an electrifying live performer."

Purser made his debut at a Marquee show with Virgin's top brass in attendance to decide on whether or not to extend the band's contract. As soon as they got the nod, Penetration took a break to prepare material for their debut album. Glossop and Howlett were retained for October 1978's Moving Targets, which confirmed that the new line-up had gelled quickly. Murray: "Mick Glossop was a very good engineer. With the two of them, it gave us confidence. Also, I think they did look for the best way of doing it. They were right into it, and they did explore different ways of doing things. Two heads are better than one, I think."

The album featured covers of the Buzzcocks' 'Nostalgia' (which even Pete Shelley approved of, whilst noting that Pauline couldn't quite sing as high as he could) and Patti Simth's 'Free Money'. "I'd always liked Patti Smith and I liked 'Free Money'. We used to mess about with it in rehearsal, then put it into the set. Then it just stayed in the set. When we came to do the album, all the stuff that was in the set was recorded." The second side of the album was equally notable for the inclusion of 'Too Many Friends' and the desolate relationship fable 'Reunion'.

However, the copies of the album that were pressed in gimmicky luminous vinyl buried what was actually one of the better-produced records of the era. This produced something of a backlash, one partly anticipated and partly instigated by Neale Floyd's letter to Sounds' Fair Deal column. It began, 'Dear anyone who bought our shitty luminous disc..." He'd acted under his own initiative and fair set the cat among the pigeons. The letter instructed fans to return the vinyl to Virgin if they felt unhappy, and many did. Virgin were not best pleased. But his actions were a testament to the straightforward honesty that Penetration stood for. "I knew once I'd written that letter the gimmicks would stop," Floyd told Phil Sutcliffe. "I'd rather sell the records on the music. You know, I wrote that people should send them back and get them replaced with black ones? Well, when I went in the office there was a stack of them returned, so I was really pleased. A bit after that I was sat next to some well-heeled Virgin executive at a dinner for the band and he virtually admitted that his hope was that people would keep the luminous ones for novelty and then buy another one for the music." Murray: "Record companies don't care at the end of the day. They're not interested in what it's like, as long as it sells. They don't care about the band at the end of the day, they just have to sell units."

Among the highlights on Moving Targets were 'Life's A Gamble', one of the band's earliest songs, about "how you can be optimistic and then people let you down, and not knowing where you're going with your life, which is a classic teenage thing. Which is probably what a lot of those early ones are about." 'Lovers Of Outrage' was about Murray travelling to see bands. "I've always been into fashion and art and that side of things, before I was even in a band. With the punk thing, when people did start to dress up – and we used to dress up before the punk scene – you would get chased down the street. It's just saying that it's that sort of age where you live at home with your parents, you have no responsibilities, you can spend all afternoon standing in front of the mirror if you wanted, dressing up. It's that young thing of saying, let people express themselves, let them look outrageous if they want. The freedom of being able to step out looking like whatever you want." Similar sentiments were expressed in 'Silent Community'. "That's a really early one. It's written from the viewpoint of a 17-year-old living in this place, Ferryhill, a mining community, where people don't get out of there or do anything. They live there and die there. They have no opinions. If anything's different they want to stamp on it, and how that breeds violence, because people aren't expressing themselves or being creative in any way."

To promote the album the label issued 'Life's A Gamble' alongside non-album track 'V.I.P', while the group embarked on major tours of the Europe and the US. A spring tour of the UK ensued in 1979, at which time their new single, 'Danger Signs', was released. It was further evidence, particularly in the form of Murray's elasticated, oscillating vocal, that Penetration were worthy of the high regard in which many held them. This was again intended to be a Glossop/Howlett production, but in the end the group elected to re-record it themselves after they'd cut a superior version for a John Peel session at Maida Vale studios (the rejected version would later appear on Race Against Time). This time Virgin were persuaded to give the band their head.

At their finest Penetration managed to observe the strictures of normality and domesticity without losing the idea that, behind the sofa and the saucepans, lay lives as intricate and rich, and occasionally as desperate, as those the media sought to celebrate. It's probably no coincidence that after the band's split, a rumour did the rounds that Murray had retreated to the role of housewife. She hadn't, but it was a lifestyle she'd depicted so keenly it seemed entirely feasible it had become self-fulfilling prophecy, especially in 'She Is The Slave': Lost with her thoughts/There's no one to confide in/The baby is crying/But she doesn't want to hear it." And the sentiment of escape, of moving on, was key to so many of her lyrics – 'Lifeline' ('So take all you need and move on'); 'Shout Above The Noise' ('Discontentment fills the air as everyone looks for some escape'; 'Challenge' ('So go back where you came from'); 'Come Into The Open' ('Maybe I should go or should I stay?') All of which made Murray's state of mind crystal clear.

The group returned to America for 34 dates in May 1978, where Sylvie Simmons watched them play LA's Whisky A Go Go. "The thing that hits me more than anything else... was seeing five people really working together, feeding off each other, making a web rather than a wall of sound." It was an exhausting trek, for Murray in particular, who wasn't exactly bowled over by the rock'n'roll lifestyle. It concluded with a premature return to the studio to record new material for a second album. However, the results couldn't mask the group's internal disharmony – despite Simmons' observations, Purser and Floyd weren't even on speaking terms, though they later claimed that this was exaggerated by the press. Coming Up For Air, produced by Steve Lillywhite, was less immediately engrossing than its predecessor, and certainly less focused, with many of the songs written in the studio, as the band began to unravel. Murray: "We had half of it written before we went into the studio, but half of it wasn't. So the band were in the studio doing backing tracks and sending them over to me. I hadn't been there when they did them, and I had to write words for them and go and sing them. That was really high pressure. But that's the way we usually worked. But after Penetration I worked in a different way, I started to do things myself. I could write the words first, or the tune first, or I was working with Rob. That was a different way of working. I think the thing about Penetration is that way of working. We're doing stuff again now, and we're sort of working in that way again, and what you get from that sounds like Penetration."

By the end of 1979, shortly after recording a BBC session for Mike Read in October, they called time on the whole affair, playing a farewell set at Newcastle City Hall (tracks were recorded and appeared on the compilation Race Against Time). They were left with a huge recording debt for the second album, the kind of thing which seemed to happen to every punk or new wave act Virgin came into contact with. So the label, prompted by the band's decision to release their own 'aftermath record', extracted various leftovers for the Race Against Time 'semi-official' bootleg.

Floyd worked as a building inspector for a housing association before moving to London and taking over as manager of the Jazz Café, Chaplin put together a band called Soul On Ice, who released two singles, then did a degree in communications and taught broadcast editing. He's also done various bits and pieces of soundtrack work including a film on Californian gold prospectors for the BBC. Smallman, who turned down an invitation to join Marillion, kept playing drums with a variety of north east bands, including covers band Project, in addition to a day job as a warehouse supervisor for an insulation company. He also produced Patrik Fitzgerald and recorded an unreleased album with Robert King of the Scars. Purser moved on to the Tygers Of Pan Tang before setting up his own successful studio, Trinity Heights in Denton, and producing the Whiskey Priests, Blyth Power, Jez Lowe and others, including the mighty Leatherface. Murray, alongside Blamire, who produced Send No Flowers and the Scars' riveting Author! Author!, continued to make music after Murray's brief appearance duetting with Pete Perrett on the Only Ones' 'Fools' single. They then hooked up with Martin Hannett, via a licensing deal with RSO, to record a well-received album billed as Pauline Murray And The Invisible Girls. However, "Martin did my head in," Murray confessed to Mark Paytress. "He was pretty off-the-wall to work with. I listen to that album now and it's his thing; I don't know where half those sounds came from. Martin and the band did all the music and the sound: I had no control over it at all." That doesn't mean it's a bad album; in fact, it's actually splendid, and proof that Murray was more than merely a product of punk rock who belonged solely within that idiom. Released in October 1980, it brought Murray and Blamire their first chart single with 'Dream Sequences'.

The Invisible Girls toured with John Cooper Clarke, sharing the same backing band. But it all went pair shaped, so to speak, when Murray and Blamire hooked up on a romantic as well as professional level and effectively eloped – to Liverpool. Bad choice, with the Toxteth riots just round the corner. There were a few demo sessions that amounted to nothing before they took the decision to move back to Newcastle.

When they got round to recording demos, through the auspices of Murray's publishing contract with RSO, there was little interest. So the pair decided to self-release material on their own Polestar label, credited variously to Pauline Murray and the Storm, Pauline Murray and the Saint, etc. Resultant singles included an excellent cover of Alex Chilton's 'Holocaust', 'New Age' and the 'Hong Kong' EP (featuring a version of John Cale's 'Close Watch'). However, there was no major putsch until 1989 when Murray et al recorded the Storm Clouds album for Abbo of UK Decay's Big Cat Records, before he promptly left the company. This saw re-workings of previous solo efforts 'Holocaust', 'Close Watch' and 'New Age'.

Discouraged by their travails with the industry, in the early 90s Murray and Blamire established the Polestar Rehearsal Studios in Newcastle as a kind of art space come studio. A reflective Murray told Paytress in 1993 that "Being in the music business has nothing to do with talent. It's to do with what record company you've got, and how much money they're putting in. I don't like to play games that I can't win, and you can't really win. We had a damn good shot at trying. In a way, we did change certain things, but the business is still there." However, with the interest generated in the band, not least by their truly excellent web presence, Lovers Of Outrage, in the millennium Penetration got back together for gigs and with plans for a new album. And if Pauline's teenage son and his mates are a bit tardy in tidying up after themselves, they can always regale Pauline with that old maxim. "Don't dictate, Mum."

For a last word though, who better than the writer who championed them from the get-go, Phil Sutcliffe. "Inspiration from metropolitan punk reaching out into a small pit village and grabbing hold of four bright kids who immediately connected the snarly Brit urban fashion with the intelligent, subtle New York sounds they already liked – Patti Smith and Velvet Underground – to come up with something all their own. It was fiery but still pop, sophisticated and innocent too. Which was a nice combo of opposite force. And Pauline was just as lovely and straightforward and unpretentious a person as you could ever wish to meet – Robert, more quietly, much the same. And Gary Chaplin was an ace likely lad but I thought they were even better when he left and prog guitarist Fred Purser joined to go with Bill Bruford fan Gary Smallman's brilliance. Harmonics! In punk!"

DISCOGRAPHY:

Don't Dictate/Money Talks 7-inch (Virgin Vs 192 November 1977)
Firing Squad/Never 7-inch (Virgin Vs 213 May 1978)
Life's A Gamble/V.I P. 7-inch (Virgin Vs 226 October 1978)

P

Moving Targets LP (Virgin V 2109 October 1978) (first 15,000 copies on, practically unplayable, luminous vinyl. Reissued by Virgin in 1990, CDV2109, and on CD in December 1999, CDV 203. Reissued by Captain Oi!, AHOYCD 270 October 2005 with bonus tracks 'Don't Dictate', 'Money Talks', 'Firing Squad', 'Never' and 'V.I.P.' Liner notes by yours truly)

Danger Signs/Stone Heroes (live) 7-inch (Virgin Vs 257 April 1979) (also released as a 12-inch, VS 257-12 also featuring 'Vision (live)'. How many disasters can attach themselves to one piece of vinyl? Note that a mistake on both the 7-inch and 12-inch sleeves advertised a 6.42 version of 'Vision', which didn't even feature on the 7-inch at all, and was only available in truncated form on the 12-inch. 15,000 copies were pressed with the wrong information. On top of which, the band was disgusted with the £1.49 rrp for the 12-inch)

Come Into The Open/Lifeline 7-inch (Virgin Vs 268 August 1979)

Coming Up For Air LP (Virgin V 2131 September 1979) (reissued in March 1984 by Virgin, OVED 40. Reissued on CD by Captain Oi!, AHOY CD 134, with three bonus tracks, 'Danger Signs', 'Stone Heroes (live)', 'Vision (live)', and liner notes and a fold-out poster booklet)

ARCHIVE RELEASES:

Race Against Time LP (Virgin/Clifdayn PEN 1 October 1979) (the farewell Newcastle City Hall gig, along with tracks from an earlier show from December 1978, as well as early demos featuring Gary Chaplin. The band was originally going to put it out themselves until Virgin got wind of it and arranged a compromise. Reissued in 1993 under the new title Penetration on Burning Airlines PLOT 1, along with a 12-page band history written by Phil Sutcliffe. There was also an Italian import version, Get Back GET13, which additionally featured the John Peel session tracks. It's this tracklisting, as detailed above, that CD punters should now acquire)

Don't Dictate/Free Money/Life's A Gamble/Danger Signs 12-inch (Virgin Vs 593-12 May 1983)

BBC Radio 1 Live In Concert CD (Windsong WINCD 009) (good concert recording of two fine bands who had little in common apart from a record label)

Don't Dictate – The Best Of Penetration CD (Virgin CDOVD 450 February 1995) (an agreeable-ish cash-in)

The Best Of Penetration CD (EMI Gold 5607622 January 2005) (useful principally for the release of demo tracks, though the photos and liner notes are drawn from the excellent Lovers Of Outrage site and are therefore worth a look)

Perfectors

Paul Robins (guitar, vocals), John 'Jango' Ford (vocals, bass), Michael Morgan (vocals), Martin Ford (drums), Ian Dumayne (guitar)

The Perfectors were South Wales' answer to the Rezillos – kind of. Three of the Newport-based band's roots can be traced back to an R&B combo that toured local clubs and pubs while they were still at school. Already influenced by the harder R&B acts such as Dr Feelgood, it didn't prove too much of a leap of faith to commit themselves to the emergent generational surge when the first punk singles started to reach Wales.

P

"The embryonic Perfectors were skinny teenagers who played the pubs and clubs in the late-70s in a band called Shalalee during the healthy (or unhealthy) R&B/pub rock boom," Gary Robins, who wrote many of the band's lyrics, told me. "They played stuff by the likes of Chuck Berry, the Pirates, Dr Feelgood, Eddie and the Hot Rods and a sprinkling of rockabilly. With spiky hair, drainpipe jeans and cap-sleeve t-shirts, they were an antidote to the fat, bearded, pony-tailed blues and heavy rock boozers that usually filled South Wales' stages. They played like demons and shocked and excited audiences as Paul aimed his Telecaster at them like a machine gun, while Jango leered and grinned and sneered. These lads did not become punk rockers, they were true punks."

Paul Robins met the Ford brothers in a church hall and ran through the songs he'd first written with his brother, including 'The Man With The X-Ray Eyes', 'Princes Of Darkness' and 'Journey To Mars'. "Unfortunately," continues Gary Robins, "the Fords had different ideas to Paul and without consultation they drafted in a singer, Mike Morgan. Paul pulled out, and the Fords got a new guitarist, a guy called Andy (who eventually left to be replaced by Ian Dumayne). Paul eventually compromised, and on returning found that Mike had written about four songs. These were eventually dropped."

Gary Robins' lyrics betrayed his childhood fascination with pulp science fiction and comic books. But it wasn't all flying saucers and children's TV themes – songs such as 'New Wave News' attacked the music press's myopia and 'When You're Young' was a rallying cry for

The Perfectors spot a five-pence coin on the pavement.

youth close in theme to Paul Weller's song of the same title. "I'd like to stress that Gary and I wrote that song a long time before the Jam did theirs," he points out. "I remember feeling a bit pissed off that they'd 'pinched' our title when I heard their song on the radio." However, their trump card was 'YT50295ID', which was hardly the catchiest of titles, but was written by Gary Robins to help him memorise his National Insurance number, because he would constantly forget it while signing on.

The Perfectors finally got their breakthrough when a four-song demo tape reached Kingsley Ward. Gary Robins: "According to Dave Charles (Rockpile and Perfectors producer), Kingsley played it one day on the M4 and nearly crashed because he was leaping about singing along to 'Journey To Mars' and 'YT50', and shouting things like 'this is what we need!' The Perfectors were invited to the first demo session at Chapel Lane studios in Hereford. Kingsley took a personal interest in the band, and through Chris Charlesworth, got RCA on board, who were launching a new label – Active Records. The Perfectors laid down quite a few tracks, mostly lost now unfortunately, and the studio staff were very impressed. A single was launched – 'YT502951D' b/w 'Tiny Radios'. The band was heavily involved in the whole process, including finding a suitable 'tiny radio' and the use of my dole card for the picture sleeve. Promotional gigs were arranged, firstly in Hereford with London types coming down and the band rocking up a storm, and then around the South Wales circuit."

The single was well received, particularly the a-side, which has gone on to become something of a punk anthem throughout South Wales. But the band was not flattered by the production, and they have since regretted not having more time to hone their material before being ushered into the studio. Unfortunately, as Gary Robins recounts, "All was not sweetness and light in the Perfectors. There was constant tension between the Ford and Robins camps. Mike nearly left (or was nearly ousted) a few times. Other singers were even auditioned – including a girl from the punk scene who failed the audition but went on to become Gary's wife! Andy left, Ian joined. What the band needed – as was pointed out by the producers at Rockfield – was leadership and hard decision making, but this was never established. The Perfectors never had a manager. The conflict never went away and was one of the factors in the band eventually splitting up."

A subsequent session was organised to record the 'Mysterons' demos, cut over a weekend at the house of a BBC sound engineer. The intention was to prove to their record label via these four songs that, given their head, they could get a much better sound for any future releases. Unfortunately Active were losing interest and by the summer of 1980 the band had broken up. The sessions were never released until over 20 years later. Still, at least Robins got to present a tape of 'Mysterons' to his hero, Gerry Anderson, supermarionation legend and Captain Scarlet creator, in 1997.

People do still remember the Perfectors with some small fondness, not least the 60 Foot Dolls, whose Richard Parfitt was a big fan of 'YT502951D'. Meanwhile several former Perfectors continue to gig and record. Martin Ford has played "almost continuously" according to Paul Robins, including stints with Dub War, Skin Dred and presently Raw Bud. Dumayne is in a band called Runt. "Gary and I are still writing and I'm still playing guitar, singing and recording with XL5 (another Gerry Anderson connection, incidentally). XL5, based in France, still occasionally dust down an old Perfectors' song, 'The Man With The X-Ray Eyes', in their set.

DISCOGRAPHY:

YT502951D/Tiny Radios 7-inch (Active Records ACT 4 1980) (1,000 copies)

COMPILATION:

Bored Teenagers Vol. 3 LP & CD (Bin Liner RUBBISHLP/CD 004 April 2004; 'YT502951D', 'Mysterons', 'New Wave News')

Peroxide Romance

Lenny (vocals), Dave Martin (guitar), Neil (guitar), Steve 'Rudi' Thompson (saxophone), Anthony 'Tex' Doughty (bass), Robbie 'Captain Birdseye' (drums)

Though their career, straddling the years 1977 and 1978, passed by unrecorded, PEROXIDE ROMANCE helped instigate almost as many punk bands as the London SS. They played around 80 gigs in the capital, taking in the Nashville, Marquee, Red Cow, Roxy and 100 Club. But their main bread and butter gig was the Vortex, principally because their manager, Barbara, helped run the venue. Tex Doughty shared a little of their history with me.

"I met Lenny down the Vortex in July 1977, I had just moved to London and went down there one Monday night with a big sign hung around my neck which said 'I am an excellent bass player'. I auditioned the next day, got the gig and went to live in the squat that we all lived in, at 14 Fairholme Road in West Kensington. Lenny and Dave had come from Leicester, Neil lived up the road. Rudi was from Australia. We all sort of came together through the Vortex, really. We did record some tracks at the Vortex for a live album on a mobile parked outside. Our manager at the time was a weird guy (ex-public school) who had followed us around and begged us for weeks to manage us. Lenny was relentless in torturing the guy, but he had meagre money that we could buy fags and booze with, so he was designated 'the manager'. His name was Hugh Stanley Clarke, and he went on to great heights in the A&R departments of various record companies. But at that time he was all for not signing the contract that the Vortex was providing, which I think was £100, and that's it. I do not know what happened to the recordings, but I would absolutely love to hear them. Lenny finally humiliated Hugh after one gig at the Marquee by making him walk back to Barons Court in the rain, and not giving him a share of the £35 we got for the gig. I think that we were the first band that Hugh ever managed. Shame we didn't put him off."

"Where we lived there was a guy called Michael Beal (album designer for the Only Ones) who lived round the corner in Vereker Road, with a couple of girls, Effie and Angie (Effie later hooked up with Dave Treganna of Sham 69 for a long time). It was a real 'scene' round there. Pretty much anyone who was anyone scored round there. Steve Lillywhite lived 50 yards away in a flat with David Philp, who had a band called the Automatics, and Steve was on his first production job, working on the Ultravox! album Ha, Ha, Ha over at Island Studios. BP Hurding (X-Ray Spex drummer) was always around and JC from the Members was a regular, as he and Steve both came from Camberley. There were always a lot of punk musos in and out of Vereker Road. Johnny Thunders was always there when he was in England, nodding out on the sofa most of the time. All the circles started and ended at Vereker Road, and at our squat round the corner."

Tax admits to having taken a fair amount of amphetamines at the time so his memories of the Peroxide Romance set list are hazy, though he does remember one song called 'Betty Was An M1 Waitress'. However, before they could secure a recording contract, they splintered. Dave Martin joined Chelsea. Thompson joined first X-Ray Spex, then the Members and Lords Of The New Church, while drummer Bob was lost to HM Prisons after a botched armed robbery. On his release he took up with the Unwanted. Tex, meanwhile, could boast of subsequent shifts in the Moors Murderers, Agent Orange (post-X-Ray Spex) and the Outpatients, before washing up alongside fellow punk wars veteran Nick Sayer (a veteran of countless Brighton bands) in Transvision Vamp.

Pete The Meat And The Boys

Pete Meat (aka Pete Brown; vocals), Richard Holgarth (guitar), Terry Hardy (drums), Martin 'O.D.' Holden (bass)

Formed in 1977, PETE THE MEAT AND THE BOYS were one of Harlow's first punk bands, though hardly the most serious. Live, they largely specialised in profanity and risqué humour, much of it directed at themselves and their fans, accompanied by blistering guitar solos from Holgarth. "They did things like Monkees covers, 'Stepping Stone' and 'I'm A Believer'," Richard Smith remembers, "and Richard Holgarth, who had really long hair, would play long guitar solos and dive into the audience. They supported the Banshees and all the punks who'd come from all over started to scream abuse at them for being hippies. But they played on regardless"

Pete Brown, incidentally, was elder brother of Dave Brown of the Spelling Missteaks, another local punk attraction. They were already veterans of the local gig circuit when Attila The Stockbroker, then a student at Kent University, was persuaded by Brown and Holgarth to put them on at one of his Rock Against Racism shows in Canterbury. They just about got away with it, and Attila, impressed by their chutzpah and scratch punk amateurism, agreed to become their manager and sort out some gigs.

Sadly, they never got a record out, despite a solid hell-raising reputation, and they dispersed to other pursuits, in most cases, marred by ill fate. Terry Hardy died in a motorbike crash, Holden died of organ failure, and Pete Meat died from cancer in 2004. Holgarth, however, is still active in music, being a regular accompanist to John Otway and the reformed Eddie And The Hot Rods. The Meat Boys finally reached the digital age with the release of the highly recommended 2-CD set Stortbeat: A Musical Collective. 'Superman', in particular, is superb, a song the Members would have been proud of. Holgarth went on to play with 80s Harlow punk/ska band The Internationalists, who released an album.

COMPILATIONS:

Stortbeat: A Musical Collective double CD (Handsignal Recordings Handy 2 and Handy 2A 2004; 'Look What She's Doing', 'Superman', 'Why Should I Care?')

Physicals

Alan Lee Shaw (guitar, vocals), Steve Schmidt (guitar), Christer Sol (bass), Steve Bye (ex-Starship, Jetz; drums)

One of Alan Lee Shaw's innumerable punk creations, alongside the Rings and the Maniacs, who like the PHYSICALS were managed by Sounds photographer Ian Dickson. They began in 1978, playing regularly at London venues such as the Nashville and Music Machine and built up a fair following. Their self-released debut EP, which sold 5,000 copies, was recorded live without overdubs on a two-track Revox, and released in September 1978. The Independent Broadcasting Authority banned it, solely due to its title. Former Sex Pistols Paul Cook and Steve Jones came on board to produce their next single, 'Pain In Love', having heard demo versions. Jones eventually pulled out, but Cook persevered with the project, and also contributed drums to the recording, although its release was delayed until 1980.

In the interim the Physicals supported Thin Lizzy and completed a tour of Ireland. Then Shaw accepted an invitation from Brian James of the Damned to join his backing band, the Brains. However, when James briefly joined Iggy Pop's band, Shaw, alongside fellow Brains members Alvin Gibbs (ex-Users, later UK Subs) and John Towe (ex-Chelsea and Generation X), resurrected the name Physicals to record five new songs, which remained unreleased until Overground issued the comprehensive retrospective CD Skullduggery in 1999. Shaw would work with Brian James again as a member of the Hellions before joining the Damned in 1993. His new band is called Mischief, formed with fellow Damned evictee Paul Gray. He would not let it lie. The Mischief album is shortly to be repackaged and re-released as Wicked Gravity, which is also the name the band now travels under.

DISCOGRAPHY:

All Sexed Up 7-inch 33rpm EP (Physical PR 001 September 1978)

All Sexed Up/Breakdown On Stage/No Life In The City/You Do Me In

Be Like Me/Pain In Love 7-inch (Big Beat NS 58 1980) (Shaw: "It took three days. One day rehearsing at the Sex Pistols rehearsal room in Denmark Street, Paul on drums and us using the rest of the Pistols gear, including Sid and Steve's amps. Which seemed a bit surreal at the time. One day at Wessex Studios doing the recording with Bill Price and one day for overdubs and mixing, again with Bill Price, the engineer on Never Mind The Bollocks.")

ARCHIVE RELEASE:

Skullduggery CD (Overground OVER 80CD 1999)

Piranhas

Dick Slexia (drums), Reginald Frederick Hornsbury (bass), John Helmer (vocals, lead guitar), Bob Grover (vocals, guitar), Zoot Alors (saxophone)

BRIGHTON ROCK
PRESENTS
PIRANHAS
+ The Dodgems
SUNDAY 8TH JUNE 7·30pm
JENKINSONS
KINGSWEST, SEAFRONT, BRIGHTON
TICKETS £1.60 in advance, £1.80 on door (if available)
From Jenkinsons,
Virgin Records, Fine Records (Worthing)
Over 18's only
MANAGEMENT RESERVE THE RIGHT TO REFUSE ADMISSION

Though most will remember the PIRANHAS as the chart-bound ska-influenced authors of 'Tom Hark' (recently revived as a benefit for Brighton & Hove Albion Football Club), they played a pivotal role in the development of Brighton's early punk scene. Look at some of those nicknames. Add the fact that they played their debut gig supporting the Flys as part of an 'anti-Jubilee' festival in 1977, and early songs such as 'I Don't Want My Body', 'Hilary Bites', 'Tell The Truth' and 'Maniac', and the Piranhas really were legitimate card-carrying punk rockers at their outset. Albeit ones that never took things too earnestly.

For further evidence see 'Jilly', 'Virginity', 'Tension' and 'Happy Families', all available on the Vaultage CD issued in 1997, all of which could have sounded like some of the post-punk bands coming out of Rough Trade were it not for the omnipresent humour. "We started playing punk in June 1977," Grover later confessed to Closed Groove fanzine. "We were pretty awful." Not necessarily true, actually.

The songs for their 1980 debut album had originally been recorded for a projected full-length release on Attrix a year earlier. "We re-recorded the rather rough-sounding original album following the success of 'Tom Hark' with the new production team, which included Pete Waterman," notes John Helmer. "None of us were that happy with the result, as it sounded a bit too cleaned-up to our ears. We were always better live, in my view, than in the studio." Of course, by the time of its release they were beginning to outgrow the punk scene. However, their subsequent recordings maintained the sense of adventure and light-heartedness that imbued those original shows.

Bob Grover has a new band together, entitled Dates.

SELECT DISCOGRAPHY:

Jilly/Coloured Music 7-inch (Attrix RB 4 1980)

Yap Yap Yap/Happy Families 7-inch (Attrix RB 6 1980)

Vaultage Punk Collection CD (Anagram CDPUNK 101 1997; 'Jilly', 'Virginity', 'Tension', Happy Families') (check this out first for the Piranhas' punky roots and take it from there)

Plague (1)

Greg Horton (drums), Marcus Jeffries (lead guitar, vocals), Graham Robinson (bass), Gareth Martin (rhythm guitar, vocals)

Despite the fact that they had the distinction of playing the Roxy Club more times than any other band, South London's PLAGUE all but disappeared off the radar until Detour Records announced that they were working on a round-up of the band's discography in 2005. They became the latest example of 77-era punk bands getting back together to reminisce over the good times and the gobbing, playing at the Cartoon in Croydon for a show on 9 January 2005. It was their first show together in 25 years.

The group originally formed in 1976 and cut early demos including 'On The Dole', 'Again And Again' and 'Nightmares'. Thereafter Jeffries took over the reigns as lead vocalist from Gareth Martin as they toured heavily, both in and outside of London. Five hundred copies of their debut single were released on Psycho in 1979, but after that batch sold out, the band repressed it, in new packaging, for Evolution. There was also a second single for the same label, 'Out With Me All Night'. Greg Horton: "The first single was re-pressed because the original pressing was self-financed. The distribution was terrible, because Evolution was a subsidiary of RCA Records. At the time we started getting a lot of Radio 1 airplay. Unfortunately, RCA's warehouse staff went on strike, so that was the end of that."

That blow meant that the band would flounder. When Martin left in 1981 they recruited a female singer, Sue Slack (wife of Steve Slack of the UK Subs) and cut three further demo tracks, but these would be the band's last recordings. Horton: "By the time Sue Slack came on board, punk had run its course. There were only three of us left (Marc, Graham and myself) so we thought we'd move in a different direction, and without compromising ourselves, we thought something more commercial would be a way forward. Sue was very good and had an edge we really liked – we also knew her husband from the days of playing with the UK Subs." Again, however, it was not to be.

DISCOGRAPHY:

In Love/Wimpy Bar Song 7-inch (Psycho P2615 1979) (first pressing of 500 copies on black vinyl. It was later reissued on Evolution Records on pink vinyl).
Out With Me All Night/Er?/I Don't Want To Be Like Jimmy 7-inch (Evolution EV4 1980)
COMPILATION:
The X Tapes LP (Bin Liner 2005) (500 copies on coloured vinyl. The latter three tracks are from the Plague's first ever recordings)

P

Plague (2)

Andy Suggett (guitar, lead vocals), Si Hill (guitar), Luke Cresswell (drums), Ezri Carlebach (bass)

The second version of the PLAGUE were "a Brighton teenage post-punk outfit that never played beyond a few south coast towns in 1978 and 1979," according to Ezri Carlebach. They became aware of the existence of the other Plague in London after they received a letter asking them to desist from the name's use and get a new identity, sharpish.

But as Carlebach points out, "We didn't last long enough to bother." Drummer Luke Cresswell went on to found Pookiesnackenburger, alongside Carlebach, before writing the hit show Stomp. This won an Edinburgh fringe award in 1995, then an Olivier, eventually spawning five spin-off companies across the globe and an eight-year and counting run on Broadway. Carlebach was also later a member of jazz-punk fusionists Betrayed.

Sadly, the group's originals, including 'Pogo On A Nazi', 'I Don't Really Care About You', 'Catch The Plague' and 'Tory Party Blues' (Carlebach: "in which I predicted, but I hasten to add did not welcome, Thatcher's general election victory of 1979") lie in an unmarked grave.

Plastix

Huggy Leaver (vocals), Nick Sayer (guitar), Mark Wilmhurst (bass), Mark 'Ogs' Hoggins (drums)

Though they never released anything other than a single track on the Farewell To The Roxy compilation, Hastings' PLASTIX are interesting in so much that its personnel went on to many and varied destinations. After a few shows at the Roxy and a support to the Crabs at the Marquee, the group disbanded, leaving other regulars in their set – 'Nothing 2 Do', 'Fleet Street', 'Terminal TV', Cheap Copy', '9 Till 5' and 'Politics', unrecorded. However, '9 Till 5', taped live when they supported Subway Sect in Brighton, was used in a documentary on punk filmed by Southern TV.

Sayer and Wilmshurst subsequently worked together as part of Fan Club. Indeed, Sayer demonstrated his persistence by working with a variety of bands, including the Kempton Rockers and Midnight & The Lemon Boys before ending up as guitarist with those pouty wastrels Transvision Vamp. Leaver, who unsuccessfully auditioned to join the Rivals in 1978, subsequently formed the mod band Teenbeats, who released a couple of singles on Safari Records ('I Can't Control Myself' and 'Strength Of The Nation') and made an appearance on the Uppers On The South Downs compilation. They bizarrely also enjoyed a Top 10 hit in Canada with the aforementioned 'I Can't Control Myself' for Gamma Records. Hoggins, meanwhile, became a pillar of Brighton's third wave piss-take punks Peter And The Test Tube Babies and currently roadies for Placebo. Post-unlikely Canadian success, Huggy became an actor, staring in Lock Stock And Two Smoking Barrels as well as Birds Of A Feather (THE punk rock sitcom). He then joined EastEnders as the character Clint Miller (thanks to Dizzy of Detour Records for this tantalising titbit). Wonder if he and The Shend (of the Cravats) ever nestle into the snug at the Queen Vic and reminisce about their punk rock pasts?

COMPILATION:

Farewell To The Roxy (Lightning LIP 2 1978; 'Tough On You')

Plummet Airlines

Harry Stephenson (vocals, 12-string guitar), Richard Booth (guitar, vocals), Duncan Kerr (guitar, vocals), Darryl Hunt (bass, vocals), Keith Gotheridge (drums)

PLUMMET AIRLINES were Stiff Records' great underachievers, harshly viewed by some as chancers who happened upon the punk bandwagon. Keith Gotheridge had previously been playing with 70s Derby longhairs The Pugma Ho Rock Band. Fisherman's son Darryl Hunt formed the group while studying fine art at Nottingham University.

In 1976 they caught the punk bug and headed south to London. They were subsequently spotted at the Hope 'n' Anchor by Stiff boss Dave Robinson, who paired them with Sean Tyla of Ducks Deluxe fame, and invited them to record 'Silver Shirt' for his label. They were also managed by Hope And Anchor promoters John Eichler and Fred Grainger, and actually lived at the venue at the time of the "punk explosion". In return, they would help out behind the bar and cellar when bands played.

The DIY nature of Stiff at the time meant they'd all troop down the office to help put records in sleeves, which led to them making friends with label mates the Damned. "They were really funny as people, with a great if somewhat destructive sense of humour." Gotheridge also remembers Stephenson offering Captain Sensible his first 'cigarette'. "'Harry: 'Ere, do you want some of this then? Captain: "It won't make me go mad, will it?" Harry (with his Captain Beefheart laugh): "I hope so!'"

Afterwards Plummet Airlines moved to State Records, releasing a further single to little avail. They broke up early in 1978, leaving behind a posthumous album, finally released in 1981, that again attracted little fanfare. Hunt and Kerr subsequently formed the Favourites before Hunt tour-managed the Modettes. He then dabbled again in live performance with the Lemons, a punk-flavoured doo wop band, and Baby Lotion, with Dave Scott (of Bank Of Dresden, Spizz Energi and Athletico Spizz '80). With Scott he formed Pride of the Cross with

Plummet Airlines choose the literally bleeding obvious for their promo shot concept.

Pogues' bassist Caitlin O'Riordan singing, between them releasing one (quite remarkable) single, 'Tommy's Blue Valentine'. Hunt then began work with the Pogues as their tour manager, taking over from O'Riordan on bass when she bunked off with Elvis Costello. Booth worked with Brainiac 5 and Donovan's Brain before taking up photography. Kerr is general manager of Reckless Records. There has recently been a spate of Plummets reunion shows, though these have stalled, according to Kerr, "for logistical and geographical reasons".

DISCOGRAPHY:

Silver Shirt/This Is The World 7-inch (Stiff Buy 8 1976)
It's Hard/My Time In A While (State STAT 66 October 1977)
On Stoney Ground dbl LP (Hedonics HEDON 1/2 1981)
COMPILATION:
Hits Greatest Stiffs (Stiff Fist 1 September 1977; 'This Is The World')

Pop Group

Bruce Smith (drums), Mark Stewart (vocals), John Waddington (guitar), Gareth Sager (guitar, keyboards, horns, strings), Simon Underwood (bass)

If punk was a blank canvas, many were content to stay with figurative caricatures. Not so Bristol's POP GROUP, who decided that, if the rulebook had truly been ripped up, there was no point in espousing a new orthodoxy in its stead. In the process, they released some of the most genuinely radical records, both musically and lyrically, of the late-70s and early-80s.

The group formed in 1977 and chose the ironic name Pop Group after an outing to London by Stewart, Smith and Sager. They'd checked out McLaren's Sex shop, and were immediately drawn to clothes that could shock and delineate difference. Later, local musician Alan Jones of Amen Corner would make the pilgrimage to the King's Road and bring back McLaren and Westwood designs to sell in his shop, Paradise Garage. He would subsequently manage the band.

They Pop Group principals attended several early London punk gigs. Indeed, in photographs of the legendary Clash show where Shane MacGowan 'lost his ear', Mark Stewart (and Jeremy Valentine of the Cortinas) can be seen standing alongside the fine young cannibals. Stewart and Underwood also appeared in photos of the Sex Pistols' show in Caerphilly, which ended up in the Sunday Times. Stewart even persuaded Patti Smith to accompany him to watch the Clash play at the ICA after travelling to London to watch her at the Roundhouse.

But while they soaked up punk's declamatory influence, the Pop Group looked elsewhere for sonic inspiration. The most obvious touchstones were reggae and funk, Stockhausen and Coltrane. A similar hybrid was, of course, being pioneered by James Chance And The Contortions in New York. But Sager is unsure of the comparison. "We had no idea about James Chance – well, I didn't! – And I played the sax!" The truth was that the Pop Group essentially drew on the music that sound-tracked Bristol as a city.

They earned their first press notice in local fanzine Loaded. Their debut performance at Tiffany's was reviewed by another local fanzine, Mrs O'Reilly's Dog, predicting that they "would go a long way". Nevertheless, the band fumed at the critical content of the review, and tried to convince the editors to withdraw it. Loaded, meanwhile, offered a similarly positive opinion: "This band will not be dictated to by current trends, they set their own."

Steve Walsh, who, it's important to note, was touring alongside them with his band Manicured Noise, watched their show at the ICA in April 1978. He had the temerity to ask them for further explanation of their mantra of 'anti-notes' in a feature for ZigZag. "White light is a combination of all the colours of the spectrum, white noise is a spectrum of 'all known sound'. Then say, for example, if you were to remove the note frequency of F Sharp from the spectrum, you would be able to write tunes with the notes that aren't there. The thing is, some guy tried this and found that if he'd written a tune in this manner, then the effect on a subject would be to reply that he had heard no tune. On the other hand, when asked to hum or sing any tune that came into his head, he would reply with the tune that he had just heard 'subconsciously'... hidden music."

Their first interview with the national music press came long before they'd released any musical 'commodity'. Andy Gill, writing for Sounds in July 1978, quoted Eliot's Waste Land at the start of his article, which is never a good idea. More usefully, however, he did a fine job in pinpointing the group's appeal. "The Pop Group's tactics involve primitivism and/or innocence. Gleaning the instructions for basic operation of their instruments, they just play – no styles or schools of performance, just personal expression/exploration of the instrument. But they're not another teeny punk band or Portsmouth Sinfonia. Their songs are rhythmic, memorable and, most importantly, accessible." Years later, interviewed in Uncut magazine, Stewart would reflect on the group's perceived dogma. "I was never 'taking a line' with those songs, never being dogmatic. Now, I think those titles should all have been issued with question marks. It wasn't about stating 'I'm right, you're wrong'. It was about questioning things. Questioning everything."

They embarked on a short tour promoting Amnesty International – the first band of their generation to do so – culminating in a major show at the Electric Ballroom with support from Nico, Linton Kwesi Johnston and Cabaret Voltaire on 12 October 1978. A full 18 months was spent honing their live sound, including December 1977 shows with Elvis Costello. Their rehearsal studios were subsidised by the Stranglers, whose Hugh Cornwell produced their first demos, while Stranglers tour manager Dick O'Dell, impressed by their ability to placate punk's most irascible audience, took over their management.

They were again featured in a December 1978 issue of Sounds, in which they seized the agenda and left the journalist to report a series of statements of intent. "Our main thing is to help people escape themselves. To try and trigger ideas in people that they didn't even know about. We're catalysts, so many people don't know what they've got – they don't even know who they are. We only use about one per cent of our minds. If we were taught in schools to find out who we were instead of what we're supposed to do, then people wouldn't do all those dumb jobs, the system would collapse." There was, undeniably, a strong element of adolescent pretension about this, but it was conversely heartfelt. "It's not just music. Music is really unimportant. It's the whole attitude, music is just the way we channel it. The big thing is not 'it' but what goes into it and what comes out. When we come off stage we feel empty, weightless."

Eventually they signed with Radar. Andrew Lauder was impressed by their ambition, as he told Sounds in March 1979. "The Pop Group are not content with being quite successful. They want enormous success. They're so convinced and certain of what they're doing that I actually find them awe-inspiring." The resultant 'She Is Beyond Good And Evil' said so much more about the incoming Conservative government than a million sloganeering punk singles. "'She is Beyond Good and Evil' is rightly regarded as the ultimate Punk Rock record," wrote Kevin Pearce in Something About O. "They never matched it. Who could?" It was produced by reggae legend Dennis 'Blackbeard' Bovell, in the absence of John Cale, who proved unavailable.

Bovell would also assist on their debut album. Y was, well, all over the place, that hoary old concept of difficult but rewarding listening – analogous to modern readings of 'post-punk' – encapsulated. The cover depicted the mud people of Papua New Guinea, and came with a photomontage poster of abject human misery. The contents were hardly bristling with bonhomie either. The NME's Paul Rambali subjected it more to sociological essay than review. "It actually sounds like it was made in a cave. The instruments swell and ring in the cavernous, reverberating mix; they pursue, like the folk devils depicted on the album's striking cover, their own impenetrable rhyme and reason. The words scream out with the weight of conviction but, again, their language is self-contained, inscrutable – like the primitive hieroglyphics painstakingly carved onto the cave wall."

Other critics mooted Beefheart, which is not that far from the mark, though as Sagers notes, "Bruce was the only one that had heard Beefheart. Strange as it seems, we didn't hear him for years." However, their financial condition remained precarious, and they even had to organise a Bankruptcy Benefit gig to keep themselves afloat. The truth was that, although they were reluctant to sign a formal contract, Radar had spent upwards of £40,000 on the band already, and the Pop Group were therefore a significant footnote in Radar's eventual collapse. So much for eating away at capitalism from the inside. By the end of 1979, they'd severed links with the label.

Thereafter they found a more sympathetic home at Rough Trade, though in the process they lost Simon Underwood to Pigbag, to be replaced by Dan Katsis of the Glaxo Babies. Cellist Tristan Honsinger also contributed to the sessions that produced 'We Are All Prostitutes', the second quintessential Pop Group moment, fitfully bracing in its refutation of Thatcherism, rather than an exercise in the retrenchment of ready clichés. "We are all prostitutes/Everyone has their price/And you too will learn to live the lie." Even though the song's focus was the self, it made for a hell of a t-shirt slogan. It was followed by a joint single with the Slits, 'Where There's A Will There's A Way', with Bruce Smith now dividing his time with that band in addition to the Pop Group.

Second album For How Much Longer Do We Tolerate Mass Murder was punctuated by angry tirades against conformity and consumerism. If anything, it was even more sonically challenging than previous releases. Incredibly, it actually topped the independent charts, despite a savage review from Paul Morley in the NME that utterly deflated the band. More appreciative was the excellent Sheffield publication NMX. "You don't remember tunes as such – there's no real songs to compare with 'She's Beyond Good And Evil' or even 'We Are All Prostitutes', but it's stirring, stimulating stuff nonetheless. Ordered drumming and pure funk bass lines mingle and merge with discordant guitar, freeform saxophone and hissing sounds of uncertain origin." After that they embarked on a well-received tour of the US. In particular, it's worth noting Slash magazine's appraisal of the band. "When we met the Pop Group it was obvious that once again we were the victims of media bullshit and slander. They were not at all the pompous, righteous and humorless bunch of militant politicos the British press has described. No party line, no dogma, no slogans."

We Are Time dovetailed their career, but was little more than an outtakes selection. "Although We Are Time storms off like the Pop Group at their best with 'Trap', an early demo," Andy Gill observed, "by side two it all begins to sound very forced, contrived, and overly histrionic for its own sake, rather than for the sake of the lyrics or any internal dynamics in the music. By the time the title-track at the end of the album is reached, the prospect of a gagged Mark Stewart has become highly desirable." The truth was that it was released primarily due to mounting bills and doesn't represent the Pop Group as the cutting edge force they once were.

Shortly after its release the group splintered, largely due to tensions between Stewart and Sager (Sager: "We split because I wanted to do something different – that's my side of it"). Stewart embarked on a long-term recording career with the Mafia, working with the On-U-Sound system and collaborating with the likes of Keith LeBlanc and Doug Wimbish of the Sugarhill Gang. Sager hooked up with Bruce Smith again to form Rip, Rig And Panic, then Float Up CP. Waddington joined Maximum Joy.

DISCOGRAPHY:

She Is Beyond Good And Evil/3.38 7-inch (Radar ADA 29 March 1979) (also released as a 12-inch, Radar ADA 1229)

Y LP (Radar RAD 20 April 1979) (came with large fold-out poster. Reissued in 1996 by Radar, SCAN LP 14, in gatefold sleeve with additional track 'She Is Beyond Good And Evil'.

P

Also available on CD, SCAN CD 14)
We Are All Prostitutes/Amnesty International Report On British Army Torture Of Prisoners 7-inch (Rough Trade RT 023 1979)
Where There's A Will There's A Way 7-inch (Rough Trade RT 039/YY1 1980) (B-side by the Slits)
For How Much Longer Do We Tolerate Mass Murder? LP (Rough Trade ROUGH 9/Y Y2 1980) (reissued on CD in 1996 by TDK Records TDCN-5575 but without 'One Out Of Many (Last Poets arrangement)' and Rough Trade Japan, TDCN-5153)
ARCHIVE RECORDINGS:
We Are Time LP (Rough Trade ROUGH 12/Y Y5 1980)
We Are All Prostitutes LP/CD (Radar SCAN 31 1998)

Pop Rivets

Billy Childish (aka Gus Claudius; vocals), Valentine Lax (aka Little Russ: drums), Bruce Brand (aka Will Power, aka Morris Minor: guitar, vocals), Big Russ (aka Russel Square: bass, vocals)

Note: "Russ Lax was replaced by someone who wanted to be called 'Cecil Batte' and whose real name was something like Pat MacLoughlin. He only did the John Peel session, and one or two gigs. The original bass player was Romas Foord (aka Romas O'Cool), due to his faint resemblance to Nick Lowe – 'Jesus of Cool', you see? He co-wrote some of the songs on the first album."

Introducing the maverick genius of Billy Childish, an undiagnosed dyslexic who was bullied at school, mucked up an apprenticeship in stonemasonry and then got himself chucked out of art school. Perfect qualifications for punk, in short, and Chatham's **POP RIVETS** were his first band. They were fired by punk's insouciance, Billy couldn't play (at this stage Childish had yet to pick up a guitar in anger) but they instinctively maintained a direct connection to the 60s through tracks such as 'Dream of '63' and 'Beatle Boot'. Of course, this would be more fully explored in subsequent Childish ventures such as the Milkshakes, but the Pop Rivets left behind plenty of charming material over two EPs and two albums (there was also a subsequent collection of demos and live material issued by Damaged Goods).

The Pop Rivets, also briefly known as TV 21, played their first show at Detling Village Hall in Kent in 1977. A year later they started recording what some consider the first truly independent punk LP, having borrowed the sum of £300 from a friend (Aka, of Aka and the Nice Boys, who died in 2005). He didn't actually like the band, but had just been given a year's social security back pay. The Pop Rivets' Greatest Hits was recorded in the front room of a bungalow in Herne Bay. It was a blissfully domestic setting, to the extent that they had to interrupt recordings so that their recording engineer's mum could watch the news. "The future of rock'n'roll", trumpeted the NME, which was prescient of them. Thereafter they recorded a second LP after entirely self-supported tours of Switzerland and Germany. There were two further singles in between and a John Peel session, and plans for a double album of rock'n'roll covers. But it never happened, and Childish moved on.

Describing his immersion in punk – well, he got halfway in the bathtub at least – Childish had this to say to MOJO in 2003. "As soon as they said I could be a singer in a group – and for someone who was told they couldn't sing and that I wasn't allowed to do music at school it was a big deal – I said, can we do 'Hippy Hippy Shake'? Johnny Moped and Joe Strummer, people like that, knew that punk rock was rock'n'roll all along. But a lot of people didn't understand that punk rock wasn't the beginning of now, it was the end of then... punk rock came along and it was the end of rock'n'roll. Not as a force, but as an era. Our generation have got more in common with World War II than the crap we've got now. By its nature, punk is glued into blues music. For me, I was waiting to have real music again, not David Bowie. I'm from out of town, you know, Chatham. I knew nothing about what was going on. Then I saw the Jam at London University and I'd heard the Sex Pistols, and I thought, this is exactly what I've been waiting for. At home I was listening to Buddy Holly, Bill Haley, the first Rolling Stones' records, early Jimi Hendrix, the Andrews Sisters, the soundtrack to Bugsy Malone."

Think that Bugsy Malone link might be a tad tangential, Billy.

DISCOGRAPHY:

The Pop Rivets Greatest Hits LP (Hipocrite HIP 007 January 1979) (reissued by Hangman as The Original First Album, HANG-27 UP, in 1989. Reissued on CD and LP by Damaged Goods, DAMGOOD 217, in 2003)

Empty Sounds From Anarchy Ranch LP (Hypocrite HIP-0 December 1979) (reissued on LP & CD by Damaged Goods, DAMGOOD 218, in 2003)

Double EP: Going Nowhere/When I Came Back 7-inch (Hipocrite HEP 001)

Souveniers/I'm So Happy Tonight 7-inch Hipocrite HEP 002 1980) (split with Medway group Sulphate)

First Two Singles double 7-inch (MT Sounds/Hipocrite HEP 001/002 1980) (100 copies pressed for Germany and Switzerland tour)

ARCHIVE RELEASES:

Live In Germany 1979 LP (Hangman HANG 35 1990)

Fun In The UK LP (Jim's 1 1987) (reissued on LP and CD by Get Hip GH-1024LP/CD 1995)

Chatham's Burning – Live 1977 and 1978 Demos LP (Damaged Goods DAMGOOD 142LP)

Pork Dukes

Original line-up: Vilos Styles (aka Colin Goldring; vocals), Ron Dodge aka Horendus Styles (aka Stewart Goldring; guitar), Scabs (bass), Bonk (aka Nicky Forbes; drums); Vince Santini (bass, from 2003)

The PORK DUKES were unseemly punk gross-out merchants who managed to orchestrate an impressive rumour mill concerning its participants' true identities. At times it felt like Porky's II – The Musical. It was even thought that they were members of Steeleye Span and the Baron Knights in disguise, sending up punk rock. Then it transpired that they WERE members of Steeleye Span in disguise – sort of.

They made their recorded debut in August 1977 with 'Bend And Flush'. And therein lie the origins of the band. They were put together by Caroline International after the head of the

The Pork Dukes' follicle envy has been a major driving force in the band's resurgence.

P

label circulated notice of a single to be titled thus, and was impressed by the size of pre-orders that rolled in. He passed the idea to producer Germun LePig, who rounded up a motley aspirant punk band from Witham in Essex, the Street Kings, and offered them studio time (he would also periodically drum for them). The guilty parties elected to set up Wood Records to protect Caroline's good name, while many of the group's sleeves had to be manufactured in Holland as no printer in the UK would handle them. Speaking of which, it's difficult to decide whether the first single's cover is more offensive than the A-side, or the B-side is more offensive than both ('Throbbing Gristle' even included a pre-Jonathan Ross sexual reference to Margaret Thatcher). Whatever, it sold over 20,000 copies and proved that the formula might just work.

"The Street Kings did some stuff that became Pork Dukes' numbers," drummer Bonk recalled for the Pork Dukes' website (yep, one actually exists, www.porkdukes.com) "and the 'filth' aspect was developed especially for the first singles and first album." Probably their definitive single, 'Making Bacon', again incorporated a cover featuring a porcine sexual predator. For it Ron Dodge had changed identity to Horendus Styles, while drummer Bonk had become Nikon Bonk. Though the sleeve suggests that Bonk and Scabs had been replaced by Mack E Valley (keyboards; by legend a famous American musician) and LePig (drums) for 'Telephone Masturbator', that duo remained active in the band as it operated on a "pick up and play basis", given that all members were involved with other musical projects. The female voice announcing the number at the start of 'Telephone Masturbator', which provided no respite from their blunt exploration of sexual geography, belonged to the secretary of the studio where it was recorded. They also intended to record her response when the song was played back to her – but she screamed so loud they couldn't get a decent recording level.

They were, however, winning some unlikely fans in the music industry, including Elton John, who famously recorded his advocacy in Sounds. The B-side, 'Melody Makers', did at least vary the subject matter, condemning journalists from said parish as "parasites" and, in its memorable chorus, "just a bunch of wankers". Former Melody Maker journalists have been heard to wax lyrical about the single to this day. The band also toured sporadically, with Vilos usually appearing in a pig mask, backed by Scab and Bonk, though his main songwriting collaborator Horendus usually passed on these engagements.

The Pork Dukes released their debut album as late as December 1979. Appropriately enough given their pornographic songwriting, it arrived in plain white wrapper with warning sticker. The music too was an X-rated affair. Throughout the recordings there was an unwritten rule that each musician would try to outdo the other by committing the most awful solo to posterity. Two of the most competitive efforts were Horendus playing saxophone on 'Penicillin Princess' and Mack E. Valley's keyboard fanfare on 'Dirty Boys'. Said keyboard player recalled how this spirit of one-upmanship carried over into the lyrics. "My favourite memory from the Pink Sessions was of us all sitting in the control room, working on the spoken bridge of 'Stuck' – it was crazy! We were all egging each other on to come up with more outrageous lines, absolutely killing ourselves laughing. And then came the take! We hadn't expected that cod upper class accent – there wasn't a dry pair of trousers in the place when THAT came over the monitors! Magic!"

Later, however, the whole Pork Dukes joke began to wear a little thin. Pig Out Of Hell boasted an impressive Meatloaf-parodying cover, though its purchasers were a little thin on the ground. The Beatles and Stones covers, meanwhile, were the result of the band "running out of filth", according to Horendus. "Some of the regular stuff the Street Kings did eventually made it onto the second album, including those bizarre cover songs, which I never approved of," reckoned Bonk. Typical of the Pork Dukes' wind 'em up and let 'em spin attitude was 'Marxist Leninist Feminist'. In case you couldn't guess the group's stance, it was introduced with the statement: "This song is taking the piss out of all those army fatigue-wearing left-wing lesbians at college!" It was a shame that they didn't proceed with their alternative concept – a Beatles' parody entitled Abbey Mills, named after the main junction for North London sewers. There was a photo taken of the band crossing the road in front of the sewage works, dressed as the Fab Four, but wearing pigs' heads with a coffin with "Paul Is Dead" sprayed on the outside. A second keyboard player Guardian Angel helped out on five tracks on Pig Out Of Hell, and is said to be another well-known industry figure (though Bonk is refusing to name and shame).

The band "withered away" in 1979 rather than splitting as such, and for a time Vilos continued with a new line-up that never recorded, while Bonk joined the Revillos as Rocky Rhythm. The first reunion gigs came in 1993, and at their first date back together they organised a raffle. The prize was a blow job supplied backstage by "an obliging local prostitute". Bonk: "The lucky winner was presented, by the band onstage, with one of those massive cheques, saying 'I promise to give the bearer on demand one blow job.'" Bonk also confirms that said raffle raised considerably more than they managed on door takings.

In 2002 they completed their first US tour, with Max Styles on drums, while a live album (featuring the return of Bonk) was recorded in Croydon. 2003 brought another line-up change, with Vince Santini (an old friend of Bonk's from the Revillos) coming in on bass. The Styles boys began writing new material again, resulting in the 'Pop Stars' EP and 7-inch single, expertly produced by another Revillos alumnus, the late Kid Krupa – his final piece of work.

The Pork Dukes continue to sporadically gig to original and new fans across the UK and Europe, and there is an established annual US tour. With most of the band having gigged together since 1976, they have come up with a slogan that neatly salutes both their established musical character and their longevity – "We were punk when you were spunk".

Discography:

Bend And Flush/Throbbing Gristle 7-inch (Wood Records Wood 9 August 1977)

Making Bacon/Tight Pussy 12-inch (Wood Records Branch 9 December 1977)

(45rpm - in lovely 'puke' yellow vinyl)

Telephone Masturbator/Melody Makers 7-inch (Wood Records Standard Wood 56 April 1978)

Pink Pork LP (Wood Records Pork 001 December 1979)

Dirty Boys/Stuck Up/Bend And Flush/Melody Makers/Telephone Masturbator/Sick For Sex/Untitled/Down Down Down/Soho Girls/Tight Pussy/Big Tits/Penicillin Princess/Loser

(released, naturally enough, on pink vinyl. The original sticker stated: "For a good time when in London, phone the Pork Dukes fan club on 01-203-1250 and ask for Suzi!" Those who did ring that number would be connected to John Pringle House, the largest venereal disease clinic in London)

Pig Out Of Hell LP (Possible Bootleg)

Devil Driver/Three Men In An Army Truck/House Of The Rising Sun/My Mother/Gin Sin/Let's Spend The Night Together/I'm A Guitar/Day Tripper/Do You Love Me?/Marxist Leninist Feminist/Stop/Around And Around

The Filthy Nasty EP (Damaged Goods FNARR 8 1994)

Telephone Masturbator/Bend And Flush/Down Down Down/Throbbing Gristle

(This archive release was accompanied by a badge stating: "I hate Melody Maker: A Pork Duke philosophy")

All The Filth LP (Vinyl Japan ASKLP 98 (December 1999)

Bend & Flush/Throbbing Gristle/Making Bacon/Melody Maker, You're Just A Bunch Of Wankers/Telephone Masturbator/Cocksucker Blues/I Like Your Big Tits – Let's See If It Fits/My Mother Gave Me A Gun For Xmas/Dirty Boys – You Dirty Cunts/Penicillin Princess/Stuck Up You/Soho Girls/Sick For Sex/Tight Pussy/Around & Around/Lady Diana

Telephone Masturbator 12-inch EP (Vinyl Japan TASK66 December 1999)

Telephone Masturbator/Melody Maker, You're A Bunch Of Wankers/Bend & Flush/Throbbing Gristle

All The Filth CD (Vinyl Japan ASKCD 98 December 1999)

Bend & Flush/My Mother Gave Me A Gun For Xmas/Melody Maker, You're Just a Bunch of Wankers/Telephone Masturbator/Throbbing Gristle/Making Bacon/I Like Your Big Tits - Let's See If It Fits/Around & Around/Dirty Boys - You Dirty Cunts/Soho Girls/Tight Pussy/Sick For Sex/Powers/Devil Driver/Cocksucker Blues/Banana Man/Penicillin Princess/Chat Line/Stuck Up You/Marxist Leninist Feminist/Lady Diana/Bend & Flush/I Wanna Fuck (not listed on CD)

(Note alternate titles on these two releases. 'Powers', 'Cocksucker Blues', 'Banana Man', 'Chat Line', 'Lady Diana', 'I Wanna Fuck' previously unreleased. 'Bend And Flush' is the different mix from Streets compilation).

Squeal Meat Again CD (Snails Records 2002)

Bend & Flush/Melody Makers/Telephone Masturbator/Chat Line/Tight Pussy/When I Fall In Love/Dirty Boys/Soho Girls/Makin' Bacon/I Like Your Tits, Let's See If It Fits/Throbbing Gristle/Fuck The Taliban/My Mother Gave Me A Gun For Xmas/Bin Liner/Fuck The Taliban (reprise) – "BONUS TRACKS" - Let's Spend The Night Together/Save The Pigs, Burn The Fucking Farmers

(Live CD recorded on 20 May 2002 at the Cartoon Club in Croydon)
Kum Kleen! CD (Damaged Goods DAMGOOD229CD November 2003)
I'm A Guitar/House Of The Rising Sun/Loser/The City Sleeps/Major Clive/Down Down Down/Gin Sin/Let's Spend The Night Together/Time Waits For No Man/Soho Girls (clean version)/My Mother Gave Me A Gun For Christmas (Waltz Version)/Telephone Masturbator/Bend & Flush/Down Down Down/Throbbing Gristle
(the superb artwork – a bit of a change that for the Pork Dukes – is by Vince Ray)
Pop Stars/Save The Pigs 7-inch (Bin Liner/Detour RUBBISH7003 May 2005)
(500 copies in coloured vinyl)
Pop Stars EP (Snails Records 2004/2005)
Crack Cocaine/Pop Stars/Lottery/Here I Come
IMPORTANT COMPILATION:
Streets: Select Highlights From Independent British Labels (Beggars Banquet BEGA 1 1977; 'Bend And Flush")

Prats

Paul McLaughlin (guitar, vocals), Greg Maguire (lead vocals, guitar), Jeff Maguire (bass), Dave Maguire (drums)

Formed at St Augustine's Roman Catholic Comprehensive in Edinburgh at the end of 1977, the PRATS mooted the Slits and the Mekons as their formative influences. Their ages ranged from just 12 to 15. Yet they managed to put out more vinyl than most of their peers, starting with three tracks on Fast Product's first Earcom sampler. They also cut a Peel session in September 1979, featuring 'Jesus Had A PA', ' Prats 2', 'Stranger Interlude', 'A Day In The Life Of Me', 'Poxy Pop Groups', 'Nothing', 'You're Nobody' and 'Prats 1', on which Tom Robinson played bass.

The idea, Paul McLaughlin told me, was that, rather than play a track every 30 minutes as was the norm on Peel's show, the band would record eight tracks and thus force him to play them every 15 minutes. In fact, good old Peely once offered the fee from one of his Edinburgh sets to help the Prats finance a single. Thereafter they signed with Rough Trade for two further releases. The band prepared its own fliers and promotional materials and managed to get a gig at Manchester's Factory. However, Paul McLaughlin was too scared to tell his mother he was in a punk band. He got round this by pretending to be attending tennis lessons.

They broke up in 1981, Elspeth McLeod having replaced Greg Maguire the previous September, and that would have seemed to have been that. However, interest in the band was revived when Jonathon Demme used 'General Davis' in his remake of The Manchurian Candidate in 2004. As a consequence the band ended up making an appearance on Channel 4 News, on which Paul McLaughlin was happy to spell out further details of the band's brief career. "We were considering different names. Violent Cats was one we thought of – and somebody said, 'Violent Cats – Prats!' And that's how the Prats came about, and we were Prats from then on I should say."

The band actually broke up after they'd left school, Paul going on to be a senior official with the National Union Of Journalists. Then Jonathan Demme rang him. "I was on a train going back to my home, here in Chelmsford, the mobile rang, and it's a guy from America, from LA, saying are you Paul McLaughlin of the Prats? And if you are, I am calling from Paramount Pictures and there's a guy called Jonathan Demme, who's directed Silence of the Lambs, and wants to put your music in a film with Denzel Washington and Meryl Streep." Naturally, he thought it was a wind-up. It wasn't, as Demme confirmed to Channel 4 News. "Back in the 1980s, before I became a parent, all I did was listen to music and like many of us, I was turned on by imports, and by independent bands like the Desperate Bicycles, They Must Be Russians. Then the Prats showed up and I would grab them and take them home and I loved that music. My fantasy is that one day, one of the Prats will go and see Manchurian Candidate and go 'Good God, listen, there we are doing 'General Davis'!" This did, of course, come to pass, with Paul McLaughlin attending the premiere.

DISCOGRAPHY:
1990's Pop EP (Rough Trade RT042 1980)
Disco Pope/TV Set/Nobody Noticed/Nothing
General Davis/The Alliance 7-inch (Rough Trade RT080 1981)

Die Todten Reyten Schnell/Jesus Had A PA (DADA Germany 1980) (translates as 'The Dead Travel Fast')
COMPILATION:
Earcom 1 12-inch EP (Fast 9a 1979; 'Bored', 'Prats 2', 'Inverness') (other tracks by Blank Students, Graph, Flowers)
ARCHIVE RELEASE:
Now That's What I Call Prats Music CD (One Little Indian TPLP490CD August 2005)
COMPILATION:
Earcom 12-inch (Fast Products 1979; 'Inverness', 'Bored', 'Prats 2')

Prefects

Robert Lloyd (vocals), Graham Blunt (bass), Paul Apperley (drums), Alan Apperley (guitar); later members Joe Crow (guitar), Graham Blunt (bass), Eamonn Duffy (bass)

The PREFECTS were founded in 1976 by (Hendrix fan) Alan Apperley and his (Hawkwind fan) brother Paul when they were augmented by Krautrock fan Robert Lloyd after he answered an advertisement in the Birmingham Evening Mail. "Punk bassist and singer wanted." Applicants included Nikki Sudden and Chris Collins, later the stand-up comic Frank Skinner, who "boasts about being in the Prefects in the early days," according to Alan Apperley, "but this can't be so because the name came from Robert. Even then he was a better comedian than a singer."

Lloyd also brought his friend Graham Blunt on board, his partner in Cannock, Staffordshire band the Church Of England (Lloyd had also rehearsed with a Cannock band consisting of local bikers, but left when he was informed that they would be taking the name Witchhazel). Both Lloyd and Blunt had made the pilgrimage to London to catch the Ramones supporting the Flamin' Groovies at the Roundhouse, and ended up being put up in the band's hotel by manager Danny Fields before the following night's show at Dingwalls. But Lloyd would decline Fields' offer of setting up a UK Ramones fan club in favour of starting his own band. Later, Lloyd bumped into the Pistols' bookers Endale Associates at a Ted Nugent show, of all places. They ended up driving him to Pistols' shows at the Cleethorpes Winter Gardens and the Electric Circus in Manchester. In the meantime he started experimenting with a 'pretend' band (featuring latter day Prefect Joe Crow) which made its debut in a friend's living room. Hanging out on the Anarchy tour, various ideas were put forward for potential names. Johnny Thunders liked Lloyd's suggestion of The Gestapo, the Clash preferred the Blackshirts and Lydon put forward the Nasty Party. None of which, in the end, were used.

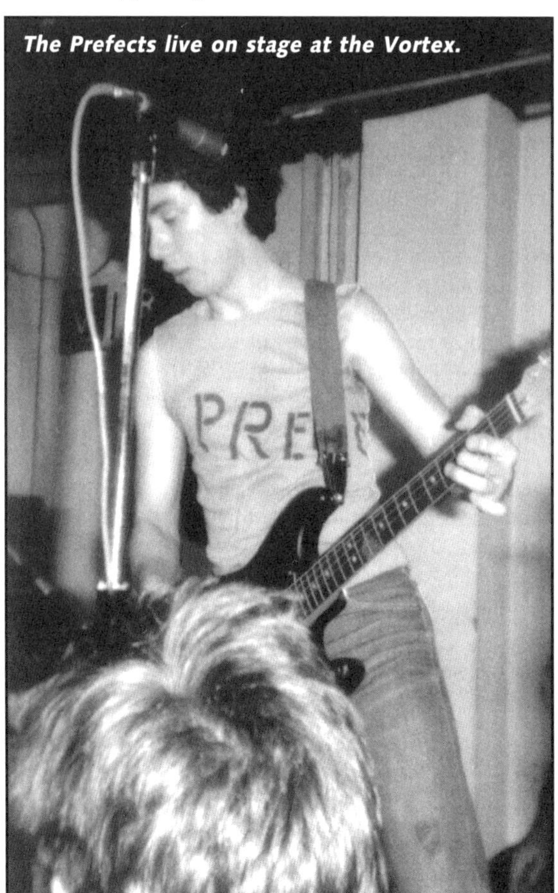
The Prefects live on stage at the Vortex.

The all-new Prefects made their debut on 12 March 1977 at a private party in Birmingham, which ended with a police raid. The first show 'proper' was at Rebecca's at the end of that month, supporting Model Mania. At which time they unveiled their new song 'Birmingham's A Shithole'. They were bottled from the stage, until the aggrieved punters (later UB40) realised they were actually locals and rationalised that the statement was, indeed, fair comment. Further supports followed at Barbarella's and Rebecca's, first with "ageing glam rockers" the Suburban Studs, and then the Buzzcocks.

According to Lloyd in a Trakmarx interview, Barbarella's was "a splendid mix of being great and shit. It was certainly the place to go to see groups, steal or blag drinks, find places to sleep, etc." And then the 'big time', as Apperley confirmed on the Nightingales website. "Robert was undoubtedly the mover and shaker of the group. He knew Mike Barnett and Dave 'Corky' Corke of Endale Associates, who put together the Clash's White Riot tour, and who added us to four dates. We got to travel on the tour bus with the Clash, the Slits, and Subway Sect, and we opened the famous Rainbow concert with our seven-second opus 'V.D', which John Peel still raves about." The Prefects had actually played a support to the Buzzcocks at Rebecca's on 5 May before the Rainbow show – Lloyd had rung up Richard Boon and convinced him to let the band perform, so worried was he that the Prefects would blow their big moment due to under-rehearsal. They were only originally due to play the one show at the Rainbow, but were then asked to deputise for the Buzzcocks, who had just dispensed with the services of bass player Garth Smith, for the last few shows of the tour. One phone call later, they were booked to play at Chelmsford the following evening.

Their first headlining show back home was at Barbarella's in June. Further supports came with the Adverts and Damned at Manchester's Electric Circus, and Wayne County at Barbarella's. They played the Vortex as support to the Slits on the night Elvis died, and the last night of the Electric Circus in Manchester – though they refused permission for Virgin to include them on the subsequent live album, Short Circuit. Paul Apperley left the band in February 1978, to be temporarily replaced by the surname-less Stephanie (of Manchester's Manicured Noise), then Adrian Moran. Joe Crow (who had supported the Prefects as part of the Motivators at the June Barbarella's gig and was another alumnus of the 'Cannock talent pool') joined the band in time for their support to Wire at Huddersfield Polytechnic in March 1978.

John Peel would book them for two sessions, the first in August 1978, their first time in the studio, the second in May 1979. The latter, released by Strange Fruit on 12-inch in 2001, is distinguished by a clarinet solo on 'Total Luck' and a tribute to local venue 'Barbarella's. The former included a truncated version of 'Bristol Road Leads To Dachau', Lloyd's extended account of a Birmingham pub bombing. Despite starting out as a bunch of hard-drinking troublemakers, the Prefects were bright enough individuals. In between the sessions there were wholesale line-up changes with only Lloyd and Alan Apperley surviving. But by now gigs were thinning out. They played a couple more shows in early 1979 but after that the band sundered as Lloyd went on to form the Nightingales (with other former Prefects Crow, Duffy and Paul Apperley). The Prefects' 7-inch for Rough Trade was released posthumously after they got a telegram from Geoff Travis and Mayo Thompson asking if they wanted to do a single. They had no interest in releasing even a posthumous record, according to Lloyd, but agreed to do so if Rough Trade would record the Nightingales. The tracks were taken one from each Peel session – 'Motions' from the second; 'Things' from the first.

The Prefects reformed for a few gigs in 2001 in Wolverhampton and Birmingham, for a night of Prefects and Nightingale songs, with the line-up featuring both Apperley brothers, Lloyd and Eamonn Duffy, who played on the second Peel session.

DISCOGRAPHY:

Going Through The Motions/Things In General 7-inch (Rough Trade/Vindaloo RT 040/UGH-2 November 1979)

ARCHIVE RELEASES:

Peel Session 12-inch (Strange Fruit SFPS025 2001)

Faults/Motions/Barabarella's/Total Luck

Amateur Wankers CD (Acute 007 November 2004) (the Prefects were always one of the most hermetic and confrontational groups," noted Jon Savage in his MOJO review. "They spared no one, least of all the public.")

Live 1978 – The Co-Op Suite Birmingham (Caroline True Records CTRUE 2 February 2006) (500 copies only. Sleevenotes by Jon Savage)

Private Dicks

Huw 'Shugs' Davies (bass), Paul Guiver (guitar), Mark 'Sybs' Seabright (drums), Gavin King (vocals)

Long-lost pop punk from Bristol, as featured on Heartbeat's epochal Avon Calling compilation. Reviewing 'Green Is In The Red' from the album for the NME, Rick Joseph praised the band's ability to marry the "unique vocal timbre of the Hollies (it's so uncanny) to a gloriously Buzzcockian nursery rhyme, complete with scattered nonsense lyrics and a teasingly impatient backbeat." "Actually," notes King, "the song was about being skint – think about it." The PRIVATE DICKS were a decent band, and there's plenty to like about the five-song repertoire that emerged on Heartbeat, swift tempos spiced with fetchingly arch vocals and a panoply of deft rhythmic twists.

Gavin King had spent a few years playing in pub rock bands in London, including a formative version of the Wasps, before moving to Bristol. The Private Dicks came about after he left Uncle Po in 1978. King's head had been turned by punk after watching a young fan – and later Stranglers manager Sil Wilcox – play at 90mph in his Bath punk band the Rejects. A band which, incidentally, featured a bass player who was the other half of the notorious GBH case involving ex-England rugby international Jeremy Guscott. "I couldn't believe it – this kid is totally out-doing me! Sod this, I thought, I really want to get involved in this. And that was the change."

In the summer of 1978 he attended a gig by the Wild Beasts, whose bass player Andy Franks became Robbie Williams and then Coldplay's tour manager, while the drummer, Kenny Wheeler, owned Sound Conception Studios. "I was watching them and a couple of guys I knew carried this bloke over to me – he was drooling and couldn't stand up. And they asked if I was still looking for someone to write with. 'This guy's brilliant'. They said he would come over to see me next week. Sure enough, next week I saw this bloke with a guitar outside my flat. I thought, I'm not letting him in, he'll soon go away. But he didn't. And I let

Bristol's Private Dicks model their 1979 autumn collection.

him in and he stayed till about three in the morning, and we wrote half a dozen songs that night, including 'She Said Go'. That was Paul Guiver."

They needed some collaborators though. Uncle Po's ex-drummer, Jimmer Hill, ended up playing in Sneak Preview. The main man behind that band, who also appeared on Avon Calling, was Neil Taylor, now Robbie William's lead guitarist. "Neil often played with the Dicks live, and on a few recordings. Jimmer's girlfriend cautiously mentioned that her young brother was in a band called the X-Purtz, and that they had parted company with their singer. They were very much a three-chord punk band, 15 or 16 years old. Guivey and I drove down to see them in Somerset but weren't particularly optimistic. However, the rhythm section blew us away. They were shit hot. Sybs – the drummer – was stunning, even though he was only 16. And Shugs played a Gibson Grabber with the treble turned incredibly high, like Jean-Jacques of the Stranglers. The guitarist was a bit arty, and he was more into Siouxsie And The Banshees – which was ironic because later on, one of the guitarists who used to jam with us a lot was Jon Klein. Anyway, we rehearsed down at The Docklands in St Paul's, and the other guitarist decided to move to London. The rest of us were sat in the bar and Guivey said, 'Look, we've been trying to accommodate this guy, but Gav and I have a ton of material. Do you want to give that a try?' We finished our pints and went downstairs and gave 'She Said Go' a shot. Twenty minutes later we all went, 'Fuck, this is shit hot'."

Their early gigs were at the Crown pub in the centre of Bristol, which Paul Guiver remembers as a dank, 'Cavern-esque' cellar bar "run by an old German lady who greeted us as her 'little darlinks'. The deal was that we would only receive payment if the bar showed a profit of something like £100. After three or four gigs we packed the place and we got paid! The Private Dicks were at that time a hard-hitting punk band, although we had more success after this short episode, I personally think this was our happiest time."

They booked into Sound Conception Studios with their three most likely songs. "I made them all go to bed the night before and got them up for breakfast in the morning, and in eight hours we laid down 'She Said Go', 'Forget The Night' and 'Green Is In The Red'. Then we went back on Tuesday and mixed for four hours, and that was the demo. I rang up Simon Edwards at Heartbeat and gave him a tape. He rang back and said I'm doing this album, Avon Calling, can I put 'She Said Go' on there. About two or three days later, the guys were round at my flat when the phone went. It was Simon – 'I've been listening to it, it's far too good to waste on the album, I want to put it out as a single.' Everyone went crazy."

The band drank regularly at the infamous Dug Out. "It was great. We used to get laid all the time. You could say to a girl there, where do you work? 'Oh, I'm at the BRI, I'm a nurse.' 'Do you want to fuck now or later?' That was exactly what it was like. It just went totally to our heads." But the Bristol music scene was still sharply divided. "There were a lot of bands in Clifton – the Clifton Trendies we called them. Big fringes flopping down. We used to take the piss out of them. We once had a band called Cliff Ton And The Trendies. There really was quite a rivalry."

P

The Private Dicks were playing the Music Machine in 1979 when the single came out. "We'd done the soundcheck and went across the road to a kebab house, and as we were waiting, Mike Read played the single. We went apeshit. It was one of those fabulous moments." Shortly thereafter, the played another show. "Simon Edwards was putting out our follow-up single, and he introduced us to one Mark Dean. He invited us to the Holiday Inn at ten o'clock the next day. He started talking about a management contract with his boss, Brian Morrison, who orchestrated the mod revival. He was saying, 'I'll get you a deal with the majors.' They were handed a sample contract to take away with them. Guiver: "We took a taxi, admittedly pissed as usual, and as we reached (notorious local squat) Elmgrove in the pouring rain, the contract fell out of the taxi door, into the rain soaked gutter. I accidentally trod on it, adding insult to injury, leaving my dirty size nine footprint on the front. There was a certain irony to this, as we never did sign it anyway."

Dean organised a date in the studio with a producer coming up from London. Unfortunately, the band weren't so sensible this time round, and King's orders to get a good night's sleep fell on deaf ears. "I went round to pick one of them up – speeding out of his skull, hadn't been to bed. 'You stupid bastard! Where's the rest of them?' 'Erm. I don't know.'" King finally traced the remaining duo to Elmgrove. "Paul didn't have his amp. The other one was upstairs, in flagrante with someone he shouldn't have been. I had to drag him out of there and the rest of them to the studio. So Mark Dean and the producer turn up and the band was completely out of it. It was a disastrous session." Guiver remembers Elmgrove well. "Jon Klein fell from the third floor at one our parties at Elmgrove. I think at the time that he thought he was Superman. He unfortunately broke his back, ankles and jawbone in the fall. He couldn't be anaesthetised for two days due to the amount of alcohol in his blood."

The relationship was patched up, but then Dean started putting them on bills with mod bands like the Purple Hearts, which was anathema. "We played with the Purple Hearts in Exeter and we turned up, having borrowed money for petrol, and he made us borrow money to get home. There were all those scooters outside. We went on stage and played to total silence. They didn't even throw things at us. They didn't do anything. We ended up mooning at them. And they STILL did nothing. We kept telling Mark Dean we couldn't do this any more. After the gig he said he wanted us to sign this contract. The contract was shite. The other guys were giving me grief about it, but it didn't feel right. So we were dropped. And he went off with a band called the Scars." The Private Dicks fulfilled an engagement to do the Mike Read session they'd been offered – Guiver remembers wheelbarrow races up and down BBC corridors, flicking peas at Kate Bush in the BBC canteen and being pissed for the whole experience "as usual", but that was that.

Over two decades later, the Private Dicks reformed to headline at the October 2005 show to celebrate the re-release of Avon Calling. "We'd stayed in touch with Simon over the years, and the four of us are still close mates. I knew the other guys would be up for it, and it seemed a shame not to have something to celebrate it." Was there a mass of Private Dicks' offspring in the auditorium? "Yeah, all my kids were there. The offspring of us all, quite scary! We're all godparents to each other's kids. It was a nice bit of 'closure'. The most difficult thing about re-learning the set was the pace. You came off stage thinking, Jesus, how did we do this night after night? Otherwise, it was just like getting on a bike again. Very enjoyable."

DISCOGRAPHY:

She Said Go/Private Dicks 7-inch (Heartbeat PULSE 6 November 1979) (reissued by 1977 Records, SO27, in Japan in 2002)

Don't Follow My Lead/You Want It You Got It 7-inch (Heartbeat PULSE 9 1980) (planned but never actually released).

COMPILATIONS:

Avon Calling – The Bristol Compilation LP (Heartbeat HB1 1979; 'Green Is In The Red'. Reissued in October 2005 on Cherry Red, CDMRED292, along with bonus track 'Don't Follow My Lead', and 'She Said Go' and 'Private Dicks' from the accompanying Heartbeat Singles Collection)

ARCHIVE RELEASES:

Homelife CD (77 Records A005CD; Japan 2003 (apparently this has sold out. Gavin would like to point out to Nobu, if he's listening, that the band stands ready to tour Japan to support any re-release. He only has to ask)

Live At The Marquee 79 CD (77 Records A007CD; Japan 2004 (King: "When Nobu of 77 Records re-released the studio album, he asked if we had any live stuff. The only thing we knew about was a video that was recorded by our friend Willie Westlake, who knew all the Bristol bands. He filmed us at the Docklands Settlement in St Paul's. We rehearsed in the basement right next to door to a very heavy dub sound system, often frequented by later members of Massive Attack. Willie shot a good video. We got in touch and asked for a copy. 'I would do,' he said, 'but I had my place broken into and the tapes nicked.' Now, Willie was a renowned ladies man, who used to like to use his video machine with his ladies. Some husband found out he had these tapes, broke in and took the whole collection out. The bastard!" If you're out there reading this, Gavin points out that he would be indebted for the return of the somewhat less salacious 'dicks' footage – so to speak)

Proles

John Black (vocals, bass, harmonica), Peter Short (guitar, vocals), Kevin Willis (guitar), Kevin Wilson (drums)

Gateshead punk act, not to be confused with a separate entity of the same name who recorded but never released the 'Proles Go To The Seaside' EP at almost exactly the same time. Black, Short and Willis were all in the same year at school. "I was three years younger than the others," remembers Kevin Wilson, "and I knocked

P

about with Peter's brother. When the drummer from a covers band left (because he could not play fast songs and was fat, hence his nickname Fat Bob) Peter found out that I had just started playing the drums through his brother. I was actually held hostage in Peter's parents' house until I agreed to rehearse that night with the band. That was on a Monday evening. After the rehearsal, I was told I was playing a gig on Friday night. I'd only picked up a drumstick for the first time five weeks earlier."

As for engagements, they took what they could find. "Our first gigs in the north-east were in gay clubs, as they held punk nights, whereas nowhere else catered for the punk scene. That didn't last very long, as some idiot pulled the water pipes off the wall and flooded the toilets." They also picked up supports to visiting bands like Siouxsie And The Banshees. "We turned up at the venue before they did and set out gear up. When they turned up they moved all our gear away to the sides. I reckon it was because we all had new gear, the three guitarists all had brand new HH amps and I had a brand new Pearl drum kit, and it showed their gear up somewhat. That night some laddo squirted Siouxsie with a soda syphon. She jumped off the stage and the band stopped playing while she chased him around the venue." Earlier in the evening the **PROLES** had played a set mullered by alcohol consumption. "While we were playing Peter lay on the floor with his legs up on the drum riser." That image later became the inspiration behind the cover for their Grand Theft Audio CD release.

After initially releasing 'Stereo Love' as a joint release alongside the Condemned on the Tyneside Rock Against Racism imprint, it became their debut single proper on their own label. "We used to get involved with the Tyneside branch of Rock Against Racism (TRAR) and meet in their office on a Saturday afternoon. It was on the third floor in a building on the seedier side of Newcastle. Malcolm (Peter's brother) and myself went into a joke shop and bought some 'snappers'. Snappers were a white piece of paper which, if you dropped them and they hit the ground, went bang. We bought boxes of the things. Malcolm and myself arrived early for the usual Saturday meeting and we decided to hold a few in our hands before the meeting started. Everyone arrived and sat down. I had my back to the window and part way through the meeting, I threw the snappers at the wall in front of me, which was behind everyone's back. What a noise – BANG! Everyone was jumping about. The TRAR mob were diving about, shouting we've been bombed. When they realised it was me they started shouting at me saying that they had been threatened by someone saying that they were going to blow up the building. The next week we went through to the office as usual and when we walked up the street we noticed there were no windows in the building and black soot was everywhere. Someone had petrol bombed the office during the week. Don't know how they did it, but they managed to lob a petrol bomb up three storeys and managed to get it through the office window."

P

Thereafter they signed to Walthamstow's Small Wonder Records in 1978. One further single emerged, 'Soft Ground', and very good it is too. Like their debut it was much admired by John Peel and eventually made the top ten of the independent charts. There was even some interest from the national press. "I always remember when Phil Sutcliffe of Sounds turned up at one of our gigs in Newcastle upon Tyne. We used to do an anti-royalist song called 'Where's The John', which was a total piss-take, and in the middle of the song we used to slow it down and get that audience to clap and chant 'we hate Philip'. John saw Phil in the front row and shouted 'not you', but I think we got a crap review from him anyway."

But their progress stalled. Wilson: "Our type of music had gone out of favour in the north and the punks in the area had now become weekend mods, weekend Two-Toners, weekend whatever was around at the time. That was the thing up north, whatever came around didn't last long. We did think about doing cover versions but our hearts just weren't in it, so we packed it in." They briefly reformed again in 1994 after enjoying some glowing on-air endorsements from Steve Lamacq. "I was listening to the radio and there was 'SMK' playing away on Radio 1 as the background music while he read out the gig guide four nights a week." The Proles' archive was subsequently compiled on two CDs. The first was on Overground Records, following a recommendation by Jello Biafra of the Dead Kennedys after he'd got in touch with Wilson. The second issue came on US label Grand Theft Audio, whose label head Brian remembers: "The Proles were one of the first groups to approach my label rather than having me approach them first. I found the guys in the band to be really quite sharp, though down to earth. They wrote some fantastic tunes and weren't trying to pose. I robbed them blind and bought a cheese sandwich." Wilson: "After the comp CDs came out, we resurfaced briefly, then disappeared again, only to come out for Christmas, birthdays and bar mitzvahs."

They went on to play Holidays In The Sun (a snapshot of their performance is available on the accompanying Cherry Red DVD). As a result of this Black, Short and Wilson decided to record together again, taking the name All The Madmen, in an attempt to write a suite of new songs. An album was recorded with Fred Purser, formerly of Penetration, but, unable to attract the attention of a suitable label, it was eventually released on Peoplesound.com, though a single was issued in Germany.

DISCOGRAPHY:

Stereo Love/Thought Crime 7-inch split EP (Rock Against Racism T.RAR 1 1978) (+ two tracks by the Condemned)
Soft Ground/SMK 7-inch (Small Wonder SMALL 23 1978)
COMPILATIONS:
Small Wonder Punk Singles Collection Vol. 1 CD (Anagram CDPUNK 29 1994; 'Soft Ground')
Small Wonder Punk Singles Collection Vol. 2 CD (Anagram CDPUNK 70 1996; 'SMK')
ARCHIVE RECORDINGS:
Thought Crime CD (Grand Theft Audio GTA 023 September 1996) (basically everything they ever put on tape, just about, plus some brand spanking new recordings – the first four tracks – from 1994. Usual GTA detailed liner note treatment, etc)

Protex

Aidan Murtagh (vocals), Paul Maxwell (bass), Owen McFadden (drums), David McMaster (guitar)

Originally formed as PROTEX Blue (the condom brand celebrated by the Clash, though the band had no idea of the term's provenance at the time) in January 1978, these Belfast punks had origins in the Incredibly Boring Band (Murtagh and McFadden), whose specialities were Thin Lizzy and Dr Feelgood covers. Thereafter exposure to local punks Rudi galvanised them and convinced them to change style.

Their first show as Protex Blue came in July 1978 at Knock Methodist Church Hall. Soon afterwards they shortened their name simply to Protex, and recorded a session for Downtown Radio. Shows at the Harp Bar, Northern Irish punk's spiritual home, gave them a foothold in the new movement. "Rudi gave Protex a nice break by letting us open for them at the Harp Bar in the summer of 1978," McMaster told me, "and I remember the encouragement they gave us. That night, from the (tiny) stage, Ronnie Matthews described Protex as a great pop band and that was great for us, as it gave us a bit of cred with the Harp Bar audience at that time."

A subsequent date at the Glenmachen Hotel persuaded Terri Hooley to offer them a single through Good Vibrations. There have been rumblings that he was on a mission to sign anything that moved at this point, but McMaster denies that. "Terri's enthusiasm for the whole 'punk' thing was derived from his love of music of all kinds. Coming from a generation before us, he had a great knowledge of music and I particularly remember he loved the Phil Spector stuff, the Ronettes, the Crystals, etc and I'm sure he wouldn't mind being noted for trying to create a stable of acts that made great two-minute pop

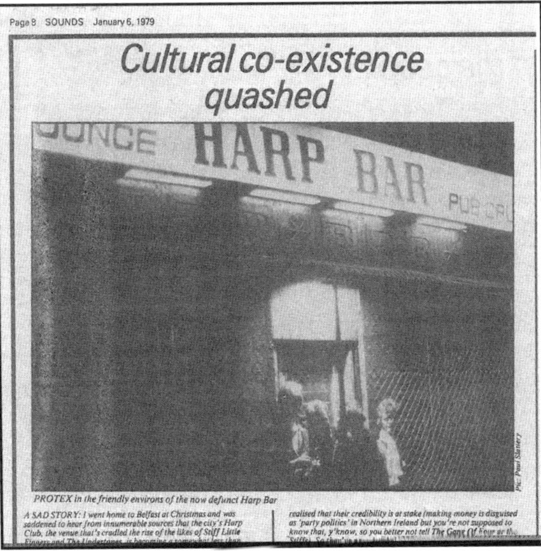

Page 8 SOUNDS January 6, 1979

Cultural co-existence quashed

Pic: Paul Slattery

PROTEX in the friendly environs of the now defunct Harp Bar

A SAD STORY: I went home to Belfast at Christmas and was saddened to hear from innumerable sources that the city's Harp Club, the venue that's cradled the rise of the likes of Stiff Little

realised that their credibility is at stake (making money is disguised as 'party politics' in Northern Ireland but you're not supposed to know that, y'know, so you better not tell The Gang Of Four or the singles." The subsequent EP, encased in typically basic Good Vibrations sleeve design, announced their "Everly Brothers of punk" melodicism. "I would take that as a compliment, and I know Aidan would," McMaster tells me. "Melody was important to us!"

The EP did well enough to secure a Kid Jensen session, arranged by Hooley. Afterwards several A&R execs flew over to catch them sharing a bill with the X-Dreamysts in Portrush – though the band were concurrently still studying for their A-levels. A deal with both bands was cut by A&R exec Alan Black, who'd previously signed Siouxsie And The Banshees, though neither Protex nor the X-Dreamysts could understand why they were scooped up in this fashion. There were obvious regrets about leaving all they'd known behind. McMaster: "The Good Vibes 'deals' were significant in that there were no legalities, just a verbal agreement that he would try to get his bands some exposure and let them run from there. That's what he did for the Undertones and that's what he did for Protex... Terri was great to work with. He was/is just a great music fan, and that's what drove him. He deserves to be noted as the driver behind the Belfast punk thing."

'I Can't Cope' was the first single to result from the Polydor deal, recorded in their Easter holidays. They then supported Adam And The Ants on a UK tour, "a disaster," according to McMaster. "The first date ended in violence and we got the feeling from the audience that our presence wasn't required. We decided that discretion was the better part of valour and bowed out. On hindsight we were lucky not to be shot by the dandy highwayman." Their own headlining shows at the Hope And Anchor followed in August. By which time they'd abandoned their studies in favour of moving to London full time.

A second single, 'I Can Only Dream', was produced by former Animals' bass player, and Slade producer, Chas Chandler, but again sank without trace. "The Chas Chandler sessions are not a happy memory for me," McMaster notes. "I got the feeling that he wasn't into the band at all (an understatement?) The RAK (Mickie Most's studio) sessions were far superior, but were rejected by Polydor because they sounded 'too produced'. I could believe it at the time, but maybe Polydor had another agenda." Nevertheless, Protex were beginning to build a good mainland live following, with support slots to the Boomtown Rats, who were just arriving as a commercial force. "The Rats tour was brilliant, they were very friendly and we struck up a great relationship with them and their road crew – very happy times for us. Some great laughs. At the last night of the tour, Geldof rode onto the stage on a bike while we were on stage. That's the only printable incident!" Afterwards came a brief tour of Scotland, and they also toured America and Canada in 1980 – "the best time we ever had." By coincidence, John T Davis, director of Shellshock Rock, was in New York for their debut show at the Hurrah Club and shot some footage of the band. Despite receptive audiences, they weren't able to capitalise by cementing a US deal.

P

They returned home to play at the Pound on 2 January, before the scheduled release of their debut album, again produced by Chandler. Polydor eventually canned it (it was rumoured to have appeared in Holland, but no-one seems able to confirm this) because neither they nor the band were happy with the results. The major's lack of faith was confirmed when they dropped Protex after a third and final single, 'A Place In Your Heart'. On reflection, McMaster believes they may have jumped into the 'big pond' too soon. "The Polydor thing was of no benefit to the band," he confirms. "There was minimal promotion from them and yes, it might have been better to build up a following on a smaller label, but there wasn't a strategy and the record deal looked very attractive. We were convinced Polydor would do it for us."

Subsequently McMaster, who is now a producer for the BBC, formed Cage in 2000, although he still collaborates, on and off, with Murtagh. All the other former members are "as happy as Larry".

DISCOGRAPHY:

Don't Ring Me Up/(Just Want) Your Attention/Listening In 7-inch (Good Vibrations GOT 6 1978) (reissued on Rough Trade, RT GOT 6, in 1979)

I Can't Cope/Popularity 7-inch (Polydor 2059 124 1979)

I Can Only Dream/Heartache 7-inch (Polydor 2059 167 November 1979)

Strange Obsessions LP (Polydor 1980; unreleased)

A Place In Your Heart/Jeepster 7-inch (Polydor 2059 245 1980)

Pseudo Existors

Paul Steel (vocals), Nick Armstrong (guitar), John Loonam (bass), Mark Siddy (drums)

One of the Lincoln bands documented by the Dead Good label, see also XS-Energy, Cigarettes, Whizz Kids, etc. The PSEUDO EXISTORS, formed in 1978, were based around the school friendship of Steel, Armstrong and Siddy, with Loonam completing the line-up. Dead Good Records sought the band out and attended a couple of rehearsals before they'd even made their live debut, and offered them a recording session. In fact, they managed only a dozen or so gigs in their entire pseudo-existence, including two shows with the Angelic Upstarts and one with Punishment Of Luxury, while a scheduled appearance with the Ruts was cancelled due to Malcolm Owen's sore throat.

They managed one EP for the label, recorded in February 1979, before disappearing, but all four tracks have bags of punch and energy. The reviews were not kind, though, for the 'Stamp Out Normality' EP. Regular punk supporter Giovanni Dadomo dismissed the EP as "hatefully dumb". The band were so outraged by this review they sent him a missive, cautioning him for being a "snivelling little shit", which, of course, he was.

Still, the EP did extremely well, and three of the tracks were played repeatedly by John Peel. However, Dead Good's cash flow problems impeded any potential further progress, as Siddy told Jean Encoule: "We made the second recording with the money from the EP, fully expecting Dead Good to want to release it, since the first had sold so well. First they had to release XS Energy's second single 'Use You' – which stiffed big time and lost them a lot of money. Martin Patton pressed the panic button and decided punk was over – refused to do a third pressing of the EP, and told us they were not interested in a second release." Patton instead bought out the B-Movie rights before moving on to Some Bizzare, while his partner Andy Stephenson joined Pinnacle distribution.

Disillusioned, the band continued for a while, until Armstrong, who would audition for the Banshees after John McKay's departure, threw in the towel. They tried out some replacement guitarists, but nothing was happening, so the band members either threw in their lot with other bands or went to college. Siddy is still playing with the Felicity Kicks. His best memories of his time with Pseudo Existors "relate to the crowd we used to go around with who also followed the band. All as mad as hatters and would do anything for a good time. Drag racing bikes in an Agricultural College car park while the others chased the peacocks around the grounds was always going to get us banned from that establishment."

DISCOGRAPHY:

Stamp Out Normality 7-inch EP (Dead Good DEAD 2 1979)

Pseudo Existence/Coming Up For Air/Now/Modern Warfare (stamped and folded picture sleeve with a pink/white label, while later copies had a white/black label and came in a stamped white sleeve)

Stamp Out Normality LP (Hibachi Records 2003) (the EP tracks reissued plus several archive recordings. These include four songs recorded at the same session plus live tracks. Limited edition of 500 copies. With a free button badge! Overground is due to release this on CD in 2006)

COMPILATIONS:

East LP (Dead Good GOOD 1 1980; 'Poison', 'Beyond The Zone')

Psychopaths

Andy Cooper (vocals), Andi Schurer (bass), Pete 'Peat' Melling (drums), Mark Cooper (guitar)

Formed in 1978 in Southend, the PSYCHOPATHS, aka the Psychos, began by playing their local Eastwood High School For Boys, which attracted an audience of 500, albeit a captive one. There was a second show at the school before the band appeared at the Southend Rock Contest at Shrimpers in 1978, where a mini-riot ensued when they lost. Thereafter they became regulars at local venues Focus, the Esplanade and Scamps. They also played a benefit gig for Southend fanzine Strange Stories.

Andy Cooper

The group's sole demo was recorded at Rock Star Studios in 1979, produced by the Glitter Band's bass player. 'Drugs' and 'Fake' were the two songs selected. The session was jointly convened with the Deciballs, featuring both John Dee (Machines) and Paul 'Blue' Dunn (Speedball). Several other original titles included 'Thalidomide', 'Daydream', 'Pull My Hood' and 'Speed', none of which were ever recorded.

They were due to support both the Ruts and Adam And The Ants through the auspices of Tonight's manager, who looked after them briefly, but when he dismissed Melling from the line-up, the band broke up. Thereafter Schurer and Melling formed the Decibels (no relation) in 1979. Their paths would cross again briefly as part of the Convicted, and then for a more stable time in the Prey in 1984. Melling would spend a long time with the Shakers thereafter. Andy Cooper, who sadly died in a car accident on London Road, also briefly played alongside his brother Mark in the Systems in 1980. Andi Schurer is still active on the music scene, most recently with local punk band Retrospex.

Psykik Volts

Victor Vendetta (aka Paul Metcalf; guitar, vocals), Nathan Teen (bass), Mick 'MJ' Reed (drums)

P

Formed by a trio of teenagers in 1978 in Dewsbury, West Yorkshire, the PSYKIK VOLTS were inspired by the giants of the period, namely the Clash, Pistols, Buzzcocks and Damned. They left behind one classic, John Peel-approved DIY single before disappearing from view, as well as one costume change in terms of nomenclature. Metcalf: "Nathan was previously known to us as Norman Hormone – I like that name better – and I changed my name to Slick Vinex, as in Vick's Sinex nasal spray, before we split up."

'Totally Useless' was the result of their first studio session, which retained fluffed notes and the feedback hum, with a lurid green handmade sleeve designed by bassist Nathan. The cover boasts the legend – "A-side recorded in a sock, B-side recorded in a morgue", which nicely covers its production values. Ellie Jay Records, incidentally, is now Ellie Jay Productions, a theatre/film production company based at Elstree Studios, who also released records by the Fenzyz, Wasteland and Bashful Alley before their warehouse burned down. Metcalf: "Ellie Jay was simply a pressing plant, not a record label, you paid them some cash and sent them your tape and they pressed the singles. Really, we could have called the record label anything we liked, so I don't know why we let them stamp 'Ellie Jay' on it. It was probably cheaper, knowing us!"

The spirit of reckless amateurism that pervades the entire enterprise doubtless impressed old man Peel. His patronage led to the single, having sold out of its initial 1,000 print run, being repressed on MHG Records (though without the sleeve). Another 1,000 copies emerged in this guise. Thereafter they signed a deal with Graduate Records (later famous for

UB40), but the three or four songs they recorded for them were never released. Metcalf: "Bastards! I've only got copies of two tracks, but I think we recorded three including 'Wooden Heart'." Instead Metcalf and Reed formed Poptones (named after the Public Image song) and released 'Wooden Heart' for Rockburgh Records in 1981. Metcalf then moved to Sheffield, cutting singles under various guises along the way, including The Toy Shop duo (who released a single for Towerbell Records) and Club X (the 'WAM RIP' CD EP in 1993). Meanwhile 'Totally Useless' has become a collector's item, at £40 plus, after its inclusion on the Killed By Death #6 bootleg.

Victor is now resident of Western Australia, where, as a Yorkshireman, he doubtless enjoyed the 2005 Ashes series as much as anyone.

DISCOGRAPHY:

Totally Useless/Horror Stories #5 7-inch (Ellie Jay Records EJSP 9262 1979). (double A-side, 1,000 copies. Also re-released on MHG Records GHM 109, 1,000 copies)

PVC2

Russell Webb (bass), Kenny Hyslop (drums) Billy McIsaac (keyboards), Midge Ure (vocals, guitar)

Hardly a band, certainly not a punk band, PVC2 were instead a testament to single-minded determination. After a promising start, Slik, themselves formed from the ashes of the similarly configured Salvation, failed to set the charts alight. So the remaining members put together PVC2. By the time of their only single, 'Put You In The Picture', they'd recruited future Skids member Russell Webb. The single itself is a cracker, oddly enough, demonstrating the group's musical grooming, but afterwards Midge Ure went straight to London to join the Rich Kids. Alex Harvey's cousin Willie Gardner replaced him as PVC2 blurred into the more enduring Zones.

Though the link between Slik and PVC2 is now well established, Billy McIsaac confirmed to me that: "We basically agreed (with Zoom's Bruce Findlay) prior to the Zones starting to do the PVC2 single. That was kept quiet. There was no official secrets act, and we knew it would filter out eventually. It didn't do us any harm; it sold pretty well. It's a good single." Indeed it is. Russell Webb: "'Put You In The Picture' was the first song I ever wrote. Not only did it get recorded, but it actually ended up on the A-side of a single. I was gob-smacked. But not as gob-smacked as I was a few weeks ago when I found out (I was stupidly naïve back when I was in Slik – still am) that Midge Ure actually claimed the writing credit for the song and subsequently re-recorded it to appear on the Rich Kids album. Never saw a penny from it."

P

DISCOGRAPHY:

Put You In The Picture/Pain/Deranged, Demented And Free 7-inch (Zoom ZUM 2 August 1977)

Rabbits

Roger Milton (vocals), Declan Barron (guitar), Lorcan Devine (bass), Stephane McGuire (saxophone) (No permanent drummer, but those sitting in included Mickey Howard (Sods), Clive Richardson (Pressure Stops), Terry Hardy, Allan Meadows (both Gangsters), Ken Shillingford, Dermot Donovan and Brian Wren)

They sounded very much as if they'd beamed in straight from the Manchester post-punk scene, but the dramatic dissonance of the RABBITS, who formed in the summer of 1978, was birthed in Harlow. At their early gigs they used a distorted drum machine (borrowed from Mickey Howard's dad and featuring saloon bar beat samba/bossa nova buttons) and ended their set with a 15-minute jam called 'Charlie Manson'.

They never got the kudos that fellow travellers such as Joy Division or Artery received, but then they probably weren't helped by a name that was more redolent of bucolic frippery than inner city dystopia. On the other hand, "maybe nobody got the joke," Declan Barron told me. Richard Smith remembers them as being sonic precursors to Blurt, whose namesake Ted Milton was, incidentally, no relation. But then, as Gordon Wilkins, who put together the Stortbeat compilation, points out: "They actually pre-dated bands like Joy Division. They were more of a progressive/psychedelic group than a punk band." Milton wrote the lyrics while the music was the preserve of Barron, whose main influences were Zappa, Beefheart, Patto and Planxty. Shane Roe (Sods) would lend them a good deal of support, recording the band at their regular sessions at Parndon Mill.

Their sole single was directly inspired by the advice given on the cover of Scritti Politti's 'Skank Bloc Bologna', which detailed the costs and logistics of putting out your own single. The sleeves were silk-screened, and in keeping with the Scrit script, recording took place at Spaceward Studios in Cambridge with mastering at Pye in London. They distributed the single themselves, though they claimed that Small Wonder refused to take any stock because there was a saxophone break on it. They were regulars at Hertfordshire and Essex venues including the Willow Beauty and the Triad. Milton would also perform his poetry to accompany the shows, and subsequently recorded the legendary privately circulated Vodka Tapes in 1982.

DISCOGRAPHY:

Kitchen Parties/Tonight 7-inch (Stortbeat Beat 4 March 1979) (1,000 individually numbered copies, all hand-screened by the band)

COMPILATIONS:

Airplay Cassette (compilation cassette. There were at least three other mail-order only cassettes)

Stortbeat: A Musical Collective double CD (Handsignal Recordings Handy 2 and Handy 2A 2004; 'Kitchen Parties', 'Tonight', 'Romantic Old Sod', 'Grab The Haddock'. Also features one of Roger Milton's poems, 'My Old Man')

Radiators From Space

Pete Holidai (guitar, vocals), Philip Chevron (guitar), Steve Rapid (aka Steve Averill; vocals), James Crashe (drums), Mark Megaray (bass, keyboards)

Dublin's RADIATORS FROM SPACE evolved out of trash-glam bands Bent Fairy And The Punks and, from January 1975, Greta Garbage & The Trash Cans, formed by Rapid after four years of thinking about doing something musical finally resulted in action. Several line-up changes then occurred, as well as dalliances with names such as Rockette, Hell Razors and even Rough Trade, before finally arriving at Radiators From Space in August 1976.

They subsequently became Ireland's first punk export via the auspices of Chiswick Records, whose Ted Carroll signed them on the advice of Eamon Carr, the Horslips drummer, for whom the band had cut its first studio session (an acetate of which emerged). All this happened before the band had even made its live debut, which eventually followed in November, when they supported Eddie And The Hot Rods in Dublin. Carroll had long since come to the conclusion that the dregs had been drained as far as London was concerned, as he explained to Music Week. "There are more major record company A&R men than punters in the Roxy Club these days, and the general vibe is, if it moves and has a guitar round its neck – sign it!"

Debut single 'Television Screen' reached number 17 in the Irish national charts, and number one in the UK indie chart, though Chevron still believed its lyric was both of its time and out of kilter. "It was less nihilistic than a lot of punk tracks," he told MOJO in 2001. 'Don't call me blank generation/I'm doing the best that I can.' I still think it's absolutely fucking marvellous!" The opening section was hewn from B Bumble & The Stingers' 'Nut Rocker' – according to Chevron, used in order that all the musicians came in at the right moment. But it wasn't Chevron's first recorded moment in music. No sir, for that you will have to track down Sonologue's St Patrick's Day In Dublin LP (SL 106, 1968), a quite disturbing slab of Celtic cliché which includes the O'Connell School Boys Choir, of whom Chevron was a member, backed by the No. 1 Irish Army Band.

After 'Television Screen' the band organised a punk festival in June 1977 at University College Dublin, with likeminded acts the Vipers, Revolver, the Undertones and the Gamblers. However, a fan was stabbed at the event, suffering a punctured lung and dying during the ambulance ride to hospital (the Undertones were actually quizzed by the RUC on their return home in case they'd had anything to do with it). With the band's regular venue Moran's closed for financial reasons and the Baggot Inn scared off from punk acts, the Radiators found their options limited just as their fanbase was expanding. Yet they remained the 'cool' epicentre of the Dublin scene. As Bill Graham recalled in his book on U2's early days, the Radiators drew their support from those "who prided themselves on being the most hip. Mostly from the Navan Road district in north-west Dublin, they claimed the pedigree of having bought the touchstone American punk albums by the Stooges, New York Dolls and MC5 as far back as 1975. They shunned the Boomtown Rats – Bob Geldof's courtship of publicity was suspect."

"I went to Dublin and cut 'Television Screen' in a very funky studio (Trend Studios)," notes Roger Armstrong at Chiswick, "brought it back and mixed it over here and it still sounds great. The rest of the album (TV Tube Heart) was done in the same way (actually at Lombard Studios, Dublin), though I have never really been happy with the mix." But things didn't go to plan, as Chevron told Get On The Right Track: "While we shared many of the characteristics of the UK punk bands – the energy and the attitudes – we had nothing to say about tower blocks or anarchy. Our best songs came from our experience of growing up in an Ireland still paralysed by political and religious hypocrisies but which, we believed, was in its heart youthful and forward-thinking. We were the first Irish band to grapple with these contradictions but first and foremost we were a pop group and we could readily identify with the UK's 'No Fun' slogan."

A follow-up single, 'Enemies' was flipped with their version of the Count Five standard, 'Psychotic Reaction'. It was the last recording to feature Rapid, who wanted to stay in Dublin rather than move to London, where the band had settled. He formed a new band the Modern Heirs (thereafter also known as Zed, Various Artists and Tell Tale Heart). In addition to encouraging The Hype to change their name to U2, he also designed their 'U2-3' EP sleeve and continues to collaborate with the band on design.

Chevron took over lead vocals as the sessions for their debut album were finalised, and it is his songwriting that dominated the band's output from then on (though the cover featured the full five-man line-up). The reviews were universally strong. Pete Silverton of Sounds, Barry Cain at Record Mirror, Phil McNeil of the NME and Niall Stokes of Hot Press all sang its praises. 'Roxy Girl', incidentally, is not, as some imagined, about Siouxsie Sioux. Chevron: "It's Pete's song, and he says no specific reference to Siouxsie. But there were hundreds of Siouxsie look-a-likes on the punk scene, all declaring their uniqueness and individuality. And that was just the fellas." A subsequent major UK tour with Thin Lizzy through November and December was interspersed with their first meeting with Tony Visconti, who provisionally agreed to schedule forthcoming studio sessions for their next single, with an album option. Their own headlining tour followed in January and February 1978.

The closest the band came to a hit single came at tour's end with February 1978's 'Million Dollar Hero' (sometimes referred to by its full title 'Million Dollar Hero (In A 5 & 10c Store)'). It entered the charts just outside the all-important Top 75. Had it advanced the week after, the Radiators, as they had now truncated their name, were booked for their debut Top Of The Pops appearance. Chiswick tried to capitalise on the strong reviews by re-releasing a new radio version and then, in September, a new mix, meaning a proposed follow-up, 'Walking Home

Again', was cancelled. But still the hit would not come. Chevron: "It's always a pisser when people don't like your records enough to buy them in their millions. It removes the option of early retirement from your life. But yes, $1m Hero was, and is, obviously a natural hit single. Go figure."

Meanwhile the band took on extra guitarist Billy Morley (who had played in Greta Garbage in 1975), who made his debut at the end of October as the Radiators played support to Stiff Little Fingers at the Electric Ballroom. Yet they found it dispiriting that their new, more ambitious material, was so poorly received by die-hard punks, who weren't necessarily maturing at the same rate as they were (interestingly, of course, SLF would encounter exactly the same problem a couple of years later).

A second LP, Ghostown, with Tony Visconti again producing at Good Earth Studios, wasn't released for a year after it was recorded, with guests including Mary Hopkin, Ruan O'Lochlainn and a full string section. Many consider it a classic staging post in Irish rock music. Niall Stokes of Hot Press called it "a monumental achievement in rock, possibly the most significant Irish rock album ever". There were also testimonials from Dave McCullogh of Sounds ("Astonishing, immaculate") and Carol Clerk ("outrageously masterful stuff"). But by the time of its release, both Mark Megaray and Billy Morley had departed, due to the growing disenchantment with the way their new material was going across live. The first evidence of the forthcoming album, meanwhile, arrived in the form of June's 'Let's Talk About The Weather' single, which featured the indecipherable run-out messages 'Anomic Catholics Ltd' and 'Songs Our Fathers Loved' on either side. I asked Chevron about the meaning of these. "The Ghostown run-out has the equally pretentious 'Paralysis in Parentheses' and '(Boredom In Brackets)', by way of explanation. They're just silly wordplays, substituting for 'A Porky Prime Cut' – though 'Songs Our Fathers Loved' was the motto of an RTE-sponsored radio programme in the 1960s. The sponsor was Waltons Music Shop, who specialised in Irish musical instruments and sheet music and had their own label too, Glenside Records, which provided all the music on the programme. The presenter always ended the programme with the exhortation, 'If you feel like singing... do sing an Irish song.' We hated it."

Following the eventual release of Ghostown in August, the band continued to deflate. As Chevron told Pogues' biographer Ann Scanlon: "The whole thing was really soul-destroying. We couldn't even play live 'cos we couldn't afford to. So we were forced to just retreat into the studio (with later Lion King Oscar winner Hans Zimmer) and make ever more ludicrously over-produced records in an attempt to get played on radio. The last couple of singles were all production; studio rubbish. Our heart had gone out of it." By October 1980 they'd recruited Nick Hurt on keyboards and Neil Whiffen on bass to help prepare for a new Irish tour. There was a prescient comment by Joe Breen of the Irish Times who took in their show at the Project Arts Centre in November. "Before a packed audience in the Project, they played a fine set that made a mockery of their fruitless search for gold across the water." It was a perceptive comment, embodying a feeling shared by many. And the hint of Leprechaun myth in that statement, if intended, was genius.

By the start of 1981, and new demos in Kensington, Johnny Byrne (who was actually the engineer on debut album TV Tube Heart) had stepped in on bass for Whiffen. But by March the group conceded the inevitable. A statement was made to the press saying that the forthcoming Irish tour would not proceed and that the band was over. A farewell single, 'Song For The Faithful Departed', followed later that month.

Holidai subsequently worked as a manager of Engine Alley, as a producer (for Tom Pacheco and Definitely Blue among others) and as a BCFE (Ballyfermot College of Further Education) music industry lecturer. Chevron took a job at Rock On Records in Camden and produced an album for the Atrix, alongside Midge Ure and John Leckie. He convinced Elvis Costello, a Rock On customer, to produce a version of Brendan Behan's The Captains And The Kings for his IMP label. It was backed by 'Faithful Departed', one of the stand-out songs from the second Radiators album. Christy Moore has subsequently covered the song on his Moving Hearts, The Time Has Come and Live At The Point 2006 albums – the latter the number one album in Ireland at the time of writing. Chevron also produced the Men They Couldn't Hang's debut single 'Green Fields Of France' for Imp and another LP by Berlin cabaret singer Agnes Bernelle (with whom he'd cut a 12-song LP entitled Bernelle On Brecht And... prior to the Radiators).

Thereafter Chevron hooked up with that home for stray post-77 punks, the Pogues.

In 1995 Chevron was drafted in to oversee two Radiators' retrospectives – the greatest hits set Cockles And Mussels and the (largely) concert disc, Alive-Alive-O! Doubtless that helped prompt events a couple of years later. In September 1987 the Radiators reformed for one night for a benefit for the Dublin charity Aids To Fight AIDS. The original quintet was augmented for the occasion by several guests, including previous members Hurt and Morley, as well as Gavin Friday. The evening saw the debut of a new Chevron song, 'Under Clery's Clock'. It specifically tackled homosexuality, but was not, as some, including this author, surmised, about AIDS. "It doesn't refer to AIDS, it couldn't anyway, as it needed to be set in the 1970s to work with the Ghostown concept. It was intended to remedy a failure of candour in the original work, as I was closeted when we recorded Ghostown. However, although I still like the song and we still play it, I now feel it was a mistake to let so much light into Ghostown, one of whose strengths as an album is its very sense of claustrophobia and concealment. Hey ho! We dropped it from the 2005 re-release."

In 2004, Chevron, Holidai and Rapid joined up with former Pogues bass player Cait O'Riordan (subsequently replaced by Jesse Booth) and Johnny Bonnie (of Those Handsome Devils) to put together a revised line-up of the band, dubbed the Radiators (Plan 9). They made their debut in June and supported U2 at their homecoming show at Dublin's Croke Park. As this is written, they are finalising a new studio album. "We have decided to return to the name Radiators From Space," notes Chevron, "as everyone calls us that anyway."

DISCOGRAPHY:

As Radiators From Space:

Television Screen/Love Detective 7-inch (Chiswick S10 April 1977) (later re-pressings carry catalogue number NS10. The Irish release, in May 1977, was on CBS 5354)

TV Tube Heart LP (Chiswick WIK 4 August 1977) (re-released in March 2005 by Chiswick, CDWIKM 251 in limited edition 'card sleeve' LP replica)

Enemies/Psychotic Reaction 7-inch (Chiswick NS19 September 1977) (there was also a promo version of the single, NS19P, featuring both mono and stereo versions of the A-side)

Sunday World/Teenager In Love 7-inch (CBS 5572 September 1977) (Irish only release)

Prison Bars/Teenager In Love 7-inch (Chiswick NS24 November 1977) (unreleased, as was another intended single, 'Blitzin' At The Ritz' c/w 'Not Too Late', though in this case both labels and sleeves were pressed up, as well as a few test pressings. Chevron: "I actually forget why the release was abandoned. Perhaps Chiswick figured that there was not, after all, much advantage to releasing a single in November in support of a tour when our album was only a few weeks old?")

As the Radiators:

Million Dollar Hero/Blitzin' At The Ritz (live) 7-inch (Chiswick NS29 April 1978) (also available as a promo, Chiswick NS29P, featuring a radio edit version of the A-side. Later in the year this was re-released, in remixed form, as Chiswick CHIS 106, for distribution through EMI)

Walking Home Alone Again/The Hucklebuck/Try And Stop Me 7-inch (Chiswick NS45 July 1978) (unreleased)

Let's Talk About The Weather/The Hucklebuck/Try And Stop Me 7-inch (Chiswick NS45 & CHIS 113 June 1979) (Irish version released on Mulligan LUNS 722)

Ghostown LP (Chiswick CWK-3003 August 1979) (reissued on LP and CD in February 1989 by Chiswick, WIK 85, with different running order. CD also had a 16-page booklet. Re-released again in March 2005 by Chiswick, CDWIKM 252 in limited edition 'card sleeve' LP replica restating original sequencing/tracklisting)

Kitty Rickets/Ballad Of The Faithful Departed 7-inch (Chiswick 115 August 1979) (also released as a promo, CHIS 115DJ, featuring a radio edit of the A-side, and in Ireland on Mulligan LUNS 732)

Four On The Floor EP (Big Beat SW57 February 1980)

Television Screen/Psychotic Reaction/Enemies/Teenager In Love

Stranger Than Fiction/Prison Bars/Who Are The Strangers? 7-inch (Chiswick CHIS 126 July 1980) (also released as a one-sided promo, featuring a radio edit of the A-side. There was also an Irish release, Mulligan LUNS 741 in August, featuring 'Paddy 'Guitar' Paddy' instead of 'Prison Bars')

Dancing Years/Dancing Years (instrumental) 7-inch (Chiswick CHIS 133 September 1980) (also released as a promo, CHIS 133DJ, featuring a radio edit of the A-side)

The Dancing Years 7-inch EP (Mulligan LUNS 742 September 1980)

The Dancing Years/Electric Shares/Sunday World/Enemies (Irish-only released recorded live

R

at the Roundhouse in 1978)

Song Of The Faithful Departed/They're Looting In The Town 7-inch (Chiswick CHIS 144 March 1981)

The Television Screen 2004 CD EP (625 RADCDEP 001 October 2004)

Kitty Ricketts/Prison Bars/Enemies/Television Screen 2004 (live) (the band's first release in its reawakened state, produced by Paul Russell for RTE Radio 1)

The Summer Season CD EP (625 RADCDEP 002 June 2005)

Hinterland/The Girl With The Gun/Sunday World/Electric Shares (limited edition with card sleeve)

ARCHIVE RELEASES:

Under Clery's Clock 7-inch (Chiswick NST 128 January 1989)

Under Clery's Clock/Take My Heart And Run (also available as a 12-inch, Chiswick NST128, with bonus track 'Strangers In Fiction')

Cockles & Mussels – The Best Of CD (Chiswick CDWIKD 156 November 1995) (comes with a 16-page booklet and is comfortably the best starting point for the uninitiated)

Alive-Alive-O! CD (Chiswick CHF164 June 1996) (not just a live album, as there are various demo tracks too, plus an eight-page booklet)

The Midnite Demo 7-inch EP (Rejected 1,000,038 October 2004)

Television Screen/Psychotic Reaction/Mistreater/The Hucklebuck (this EP, in "five-colour" vinyl, features the tracks the band recorded at Trend Studios in Dublin with Jackie Hayden and Horslips' drummer Eamon Carr producing, which led to the band signing with Chiswick. It includes the first version of 'Television Screen' with different lyrics)

Live At The Kursaal, Southend, December 1977 LP (Rejected 1,000,039 October 2004) (vinyl-only limited edition recording of the final show on the Radiators From Space's 1977 tour with Thin Lizzy. Pressed in yellow and with free poster. "Hmmm," thinks Chevron, on reflection. "More shite coloured, really!")

Radio Stars

Andy Ellison (vocals), Martin Gordon (bass), Ian McLeod (guitar), Steve Parry (drums)

Video did not, as it happens, kill the RADIO STARS. But egos and infighting eventually did. Still, for a while this happy band of post-hippy chancers rattled along on the back of the punk bandwagon and produced a few smiles with their zippy, smart new wave. So we forgive them – not least because they themselves weren't exactly taking it seriously. "I don't think I could sit down and write a song about a subject that didn't have any kind of humour in it," principal songwriter Gordon would tell the NME, "because I don't work like that. My songs are about trivial situations and things of no consequence because that's what interests me. Sometimes the themes in my songs are the usual themes people write about, which in themselves aren't particularly funny, but generally I find other people's approach to it – the humourless approach – rather boring. Ours is the opposite of that."

The origins go back to 1966 when Ellison, who would later cut three solo singles, had sung with Leatherhead's Silence, who later evolved into John's Children, who included a young Marc Bolan on backing vocals and guitar. However, Ellison and his on-stage acrobatics were the main attraction, and during their short life John's Children could boast of sparking riots in continental Europe. Ellison, who studied mime, would also earn a crust by jumping in front of cars as a stunt man for the Avengers. Martin Gordon, too, had enjoyed a brief flirtation with the mainstream, playing on Sparks' 1974 classic Kimono My House. After that ended, at the instigation of the truculent Mael brothers, Gordon and Ellison put together Jet, recruiting Davey O'List, formerly of the Nice and Roxy Music, and Chris Townson of Jook. But they were dumped after a solitary album for CBS. Apparently CBS objected to Gordon's visionary idea of recording an entire second album as one track.

The two main participants, Ellison and Gordon, shopped what were essentially second album Jet demos around London, eventually interesting Ted Carroll of Chiswick in 'Dirty Pictures' after 13 other labels had rejected them. The two songs that would make up their debut single were remixed by Gary Lyons and Gordon, at Island Studios in Basing Street. The Radio Stars duly made their debut in April 1977 with 'Dirty Pictures', backed by 'Sail Away'. The model featured on the cover, with attendant grubby finger marks, was actually Gordon's girlfriend which caused some embarrassment, as Gordon confirmed to me. "On tour, the road crew would very wittily stick pictures of her exploits on Page Three of the Sun all over my breakfast table. It was enough to put you right off your fried tomatoes with baked beans...."

'Dirty Pictures' was awarded the NME's single of the week accolade. The band then set off for a tour of Germany with UFO, making their live debut on 30 April 1977 with Gary Thompson coming in on drums. On their return the first of three John Peel sessions was recorded on 20 May 1977, comprising 'Horrible Breath', 'Dirty Pictures', 'Dear Prudence' and band standard 'No Russians In Russia', a song inspired by President Ford's Cold War statement that he disputed that Communists controlled Eastern Europe.

A four-track EP, 'Stop It', followed in August, notable for the recorded debut of 'No Russians' and another old Jet song, 'Johnny Mekon'. Then Ellison bumped into old sparring partner Marc Bolan in West London, who'd been checking out his old friend's progress, and promptly invited the band to appear on his Granada TV series, giving rise to a feisty performance of 'No Russians'. The Radio Stars then saw their first and only sniff of chart action when 'Nervous Wreck' breached the Top 40. Just, hitting number 39 during three weeks in the charts. The B-side, 'Horrible Breath', was actually a jingle for Amplex tablets which Marc Bolan, its author, recorded as 'You Scare Me To Death'.

The group's debut album followed in November 1977, appropriating a classic Frank Sinatra album title, Songs For Swinging Lovers, by which time Canadian Steve Parry had replaced Thompson. Naturally enough, the sleeve featured a pair of swinging lovers – albeit from gallows (it also came with a free single, featuring 'No Russians In Russia' and 'Dirty Pictures', as a kind of greatest hits bonus). Incidentally, Ellison is pictured on the cover wearing protective kneepads due to his legendary capacity for self-injury on stage. Chiswick had nixed the proposed album title, Bowels Stuffed With Spleen. The album's contents derived some of their humour from Monty Python, notably in the advertorial of 'Buy Chiswick Records', which must have pleased the Armstrong and Carroll firm no end. 'Beast Of Barnsley' concerned media folk devil Reg Chapman – and brought them some tabloid headlines after a hack door-stepped one of his victims' mothers and played her the song. More amusingly 'Elvis Is Dead Boring' had its title changed to 'Arthur Is Dead Boring' after an engineer at Olympic Studios refused to work on it. Monty Smith in the NME was especially frothing in his review, though his alliteration was gruesome. "Certainly preferable to the puerile proliferation of Pro-plus punks pathetically bleating their po-faced political naivety at self-pitying emotional retards who take all that guff about Ulster and the price of sulphate seriously, for Chrissakes."

Extracted from the album came 'From A Rabbit' in April 1978. The B-side was an updated version of the album's 'Beast Of Barnsley', re-titled 'Beast No.2', while the A-side concerned the new bodybuilding craze. This was also issued in a six-inch pocket version. Regardless, it didn't galvanise sales one iota. Strong reviews again greeted the release of second long player the Holiday Album in September 1978. By this time Steve Parry had been replaced by Jamie Crompton, concurrently of the New Hearts. Trevor White, formerly of Sparks and a co-producer of 'Dirty Pictures', provided additional guitar. The manager of New Hearts insisted Crompton not be identified on the cover, as Gordon told me: "I thought it would be a cunning ruse to get him to wear a mouse head, which he duly did, along with a T-shirt which said 'I am Jamie Crompton', just to provide a balanced view. He did hide behind a plant, though, we weren't that stupid."

This time the Python influences were even more candid – Graham Chapman providing a voiceover for the song 'Sex In Chains Blues', which referenced a recent court case involving Mormons. And there was also a cover of perennial Beatles' favourite 'Norwegian Wood'. "We usually come up with the titles in the first place," Ellison told Hot Press magazine about the songwriting, "a line that you see somewhere, like in a newspaper – I mean, newspapers are great sources of lines – and it comes from there. Then the lyrics are next, and the band will take it from there, playing around." Erm, I don't think chief songwriter Mr Gordon saw it like that. He gave the following introduction to the quote, sourced on his website. "Here Herr Elephant describes how he composes the songs for Radio Stars. Next week he tells us how he invented penicillin, discovered the Niagara Falls and eradicated communicable diseases from the civilised world." Titter titter.

John Mackie of the Stukas stood in for Crompton for promotional gigs, while the latter fulfilled his duties with the New Hearts ("he wore a T-shirt stating 'I am not Jamie Crompton', just for conceptual continuity"). They also appeared at the 1978 Reading Festival and completed two radio sessions in October, the first for Peel ('Boy Meets Girl', 'Radio Stars', 'Sex In Chains' and 'Sitting In The Rain'), the second for Jensen ('Radio Stars', 'Baffin Island', 'Norwegian Wood' and 'Rock'n'roll For The Time Being').

Chiswick then issued a full version of the album's opening track, 'Radio Stars', which had served as a one-minute intro on the LP, as a single. There were two versions of this, the first simply being two play-throughs of the original, back to back, spliced by Ellison's impersonation of a DJ saying, 'Well, there we are, the fabulous new single from Radio Stars, let's hear it again.' "The record company said that it was too short, so I suggested they put it on the record twice. We later re-recorded it with an extra bridge but, as time was pressing, we only recorded the bridge part, which was why the sound changed radically at that point." The B-side, 'Accountancy Blues', was based on the old Palin/Cleese sketch where the former visits the latter to pursue his career objective of becoming a lion tamer.

A final single, a new version of 'The Real Me', was released at the start of 1979, with Gordon kicked out and Trevor White reverting to bass while Parry rejoined. They toured in February but had split up by the summer. "After I was chucked out, the band embarked upon another huge tour of the UK to capitalise upon the generally glowing reviews of the recently released Holiday album and received equally glowing reviews," Gordon told me, diplomatically. However, a series of demos for a projected third album, written by Ellison, were rejected by Chiswick as sub-standard. Meanwhile Martin Gordon tried to get the Blue Meanies off the ground and get his wisdom teeth fixed. When they were dropped by Mercury, he put the Radio Stars back together in 1982. The result was a single for Moonlight Records accompanying a compilation album. They moved on to Snat Records for their second attempt at a swan song, 'My Mother Said' in 1983. In 1988 a few shows were played in Brighton under the Radio Stars banner, though Gordon was not involved, featuring new material.

There have been periodic revivals since, notably in 1997 when the band appeared at the Holidays In The Sun festival ('Blame It On The Youth' was included on the accompanying CD). In the meantime Martin Gordon, who was not involved in the reunions, worked with everyone from Kylie Minogue to Boy George to George Michael to Blur, and continues to release solo records. Check out 'Her Daddy Was A Dalek, Her Mother Was A Non-Stick Frying Pan' and 'Daddy Lost His Head In A Coup', an amusing twist on those begging e-mails from deposed African generals, on 2004's The Joy Of More Hogwash. The third solo release in the Mammal Trilogy, God's On His Lunchbreak (Please Call Back), followed in September 2005. About which I was inclined to say some nice things in a website review, remarking upon "the salty delivery of unwelcome home truths", which will serve as my capsule review here.

DISCOGRAPHY:

R

Dirty Pictures/Sail Away 7-inch (Chiswick S9 April 1977)
Stop It 7-inch EP (Chiswick SW17 August 1977)
No Russians In Russia/Box 29/Johnny Mekon/Sorry I'm Tied Up
Nervous Wreck/Horrible Breath 7-inch (Chiswick NS 23 October 1977) (also available as a 12-inch)
Songs For Swinging Lovers LP (Chiswick WIK5 November 1977) (initial copies came with free 7-inch, Dirty Pictures/No Russians In Russia, Chiswick PROMO 2. A cassette version, released later, included both extra tracks)
From A Rabbit/The Beast No. 2 7-inch (Chiswick NS 36 April 1978)
Radio Stars' Holiday Album (Chiswick CWK 3001 September 1978)
Radio Stars/Accountancy Blues 7-inch (Chiswick CHIS 102 September 1978)
The Real Me/Good Personality 7-inch (Chiswick CHIS 109 February 1979)
My Mother Said/2 Minutes Mr Smith 7-inch (SNAT ECG 001 October 1982)
Good Personality/Talking 'Bout You 7-inch (Moonlight MINS 001) (this is occasionally listed as Pronk 1, with the B-side 'My Other Hat Is A Balaclava', but this doesn't actually exist)
ARCHIVE RELEASES:
Two Minutes Mr Smith LP (Moonlight MNA 001 April 1982)
Somewhere There's A Place For Us CD (Chiswick CDWIKD 107 October 1992) (29-track round-up, including several unreleased tracks such as an alternative edit of 'It's All Over' from their second album, which was intended as a single but never issued).
Music For The Herd Of Herring Live CD (Radiant Future RFVP001CD 2001)

Martin Gordon Solo:
The Baboon in the Basement CD (Radiant Future RFVP005CD 2003)
The Joy of More Hogwash CD (Radiant Future RFVP006CD 2004)
God's On His Lunchbreak (Please Call Back) CD (Radiant Future RFVP007CD September 2005)

Raincoats

Ana Da Silva (guitar, vocals), Gina Birch (bass, vocals), Ross Crighton (guitar), Nick Turner (drums)

Beloved of Kurt Cobain and a whole host of US opinion leaders, the RAINCOATS started out in October 1977 when Da Silva, who'd arrived from Portugal to study, and Birch, both based at Hornsey Art College, decided to put a band together. Two months later they made their live debut supporting Doll By Doll at the Tabernacle in West London. After Crighton decided to concentrate on his day job at Rough Trade, he was replaced first by Kate Korus (original guitarist for the Slits), then Jeremie Frank. Nick Turner, later to join the Barracudas and Lords Of The New Church, subsequently made way for Richard Dudanski, formerly of the 101ers and Bank Of Dresden.

However, this line-up only proved temporary, and by the end of 1978 principals Da Silva and Birch had been joined, via a music press advert, by York University music graduate Vicky Aspinall (ex-Jam Today) and Palmolive, former drummer of the Slits, who was actually Dudanski's sister-in-law. Personnel shifts were a feature of the band, who would admit later that their fluid line-up would sometimes inhibit their ability to perform live, as there was always someone new to introduce to the material.

Immediately their sound was distinct from, but allied to, punk, as Birch later admitted to Richie Unterberger. "Neither of us (Birch and Da Silva) would have dreamt in a million years that we would be doing anything like that if it hadn't been for punk. So I think the major kind of focus and kind of landscape in which we operated was really to do with punk. By the time we went to record, I was really into what the Slits were doing. And in a way, one gets secondary influences from that. Ana was totally into what Patti Smith was doing. And I really liked what ATV were doing. I suppose I liked the punk bands that actually had that influence from dub stuff, maybe because I was playing the bass – I was really into the bass carrying the melody." Their sound was indeed a beautiful chaos. As one NME journalist suggested, the Raincoats sounded "so bad... that every time a waiter drops a tray, we all get up and dance."

The new line-up debuted as support to the Passions at Acklam Hall in January 1979 and in the same month recorded their first John Peel session. This included 'Fairytale In The Supermarket', which became their first single in April. "But Honey, don't worry/This is just a fairytale" observed Da Silva's oscillating lead vocal, and the allegory was clear – accept lukewarm contentedness rather than embrace change or challenge. Which was the exact opposite of what the Raincoats were reaching for. Theirs was, after all, "a specific, participatory feminist project" noted academic Caroline O'Meara. It sold 25,000 copies, probably a good batch of them to academics, and is unarguably one of the jewels in Rough Trade's canon of obdurate late-70s 7-inchers.

The fabled Raincoats debut album followed in November 1979. Recorded in two weeks, its marriage of offbeat rhythms, sharp lyrics and shrill harmonies won over a huge contingent of converts, although it was a gradual process, aided by the fulsome praise of Americans like Cobain, Sonic Youth, etc. This was music that made a virtue of its inherent lack of cohesion, the time signatures are all over the place, the drums and bass rarely read from the same hymn sheet and the vocals are... untutored. And yet, for all those frailties, it is immensely likeable and life-affirming, bristling with attitude and can-do kineticism that owes as much to Nico-era Velvet Underground as it does to the Pistols, due largely to Aspinall's violin (Lora Logic would also provide saxophone). The inclusion of 'Lola' added another layer of sexual confusion to Ray Davies' original, while other lyrics, such as Birch's 'In Love', are wickedly cynical. It was one of possibly two albums that made the brand name Rough Trade stand for something, as Geoff Travis later conceded. "That period, which Rough Trade is most famous for, was the post-punk period. It's very gratifying to read interviews with American musicians who say the

Young Marble Giants' and Raincoats' records were very important to them. The whole post-punk era was an attitude – a sort of a psychological attitude towards how you lived in the world." Even John Lydon would pay homage to them in 1980. "It's all over now... rock'n'roll is shit. It's dismal. Granddad danced to it. I'm not interested in it... I think music has reached an all-time low – except for the Raincoats."

Palmolive would leave the group for Spain shortly after the album's release. "I was only six months with the Raincoats because I realised it wasn't the personalities," she later reflected to punk77, comparing her new group with the Slits, "it was a problem with the music scene that I thought was very corrupt... We were destroying something rather than building something. I was just sick of the whole music scene."

New drummer Ingrid Weiss was recruited in January 1980, making her debut a month later at a show in Portsmouth. However, there were no further recordings for 18 months and only sporadic live appearances. These included a tour of Europe and the east coast of America in the spring alongside the Slits (one of the performances in New York was recorded for release as The Kitchen Tapes by Reach Out International) and a benefit for the Communist Party at Alexandra Palace in June. They also produced a 32-page publication, The Raincoats Booklet, which incorporated photos and lyrics to several unrecorded songs that would appear on their second album. It announced a deliberate attempt to distance themselves from the concept of the band as a purely feminist construct. They also recorded a second and final Peel session in December, though there would be a further session for Radio One via David Jensen the following August.

Their second album finally appeared in June 1981, by which time Weiss had left. Odyshape featured contributions from both Robert Wyatt and Charles Hayward of This Heat and a returning Richard Dudanski, and is less immediately strident than its predecessor. There's an impressive layering of the sound that sees various instruments emerge and recede from the mix, even if the rhythm section still sounds delightfully, indignantly undisciplined. There was still tempered aggression ('Go Away' is self-explanatory) while 'Only Loved At Night' is both radiant and devastatingly sad, and 'Dancing In My Head' simply joyous.

Afterwards Birch joined Mayo Thompson's Red Crayola and Aspinall contributed violin to the New Age Steppers' debut album. The Raincoats reconvened at the end of the year for further European dates, and issued only their second single, 'No One's Little Girl' ("I never shall be/In your family tree"), backed by their cover of Sly And The Family Stone's 'Running Away'.

The group expanded again for their third album, the more mannered Moving, which is pretty close to traditional English folk in places. Dudanski was again in situ as well as percussionist Derek Godard and saxophone player Paddy O'Connell. CP Lee of the Albertos also added trumpet. It doesn't get the plaudits reserved for Odyshape or their debut, but in the sumptuous ballad 'Rainstorm', it contains arguably the Raincoats' finest recording. It was released in February 1984, but the band had broken up before it reached the shelves, having agreed to do so even before recording it. It was only the intervention of close friend and band manager Shirley O'Loughlin that ensured the record came out. "We actually already had four songs recorded and Shirley just thought it was a shame that we had all these songs and they weren't going to be on a record," Da Silva stated in 1995. "She's good at thinking laterally, how to go about something so it can happen. So she thought the way to do it was to let each of us have the last say in our own songs. As it happened, in the end I don't think people were very unhappy with what other people were doing or deciding. It ended up being quite a good solution."

Birch and Aspinall would play together again in the late-80s as the duo Dorothy, recording an album produced by Phil Legg, the former guitarist with Essential Logic, that remains unreleased. They did, however, issue three singles, working on one in collaboration with Smith and Mighty ("We were big fans," notes Birch). 'Still Waiting' was B-listed at Radio One and went on to be a minor hit.

Birch subsequently went to the Royal College of Art to study film, where she made various dramas and music videos, notably for Daisy Chainsaw and various other Rough Trade bands. She has recently directed videos for bands including the Long Blondes, the Libertines, Beth Orton, and a while back, New Order and the Pogues, as well as the Raincoats. Da Silva worked in an antique store, which is where Kurt Cobain discovered her. The Raincoats reformed briefly in 1994 after Cobain's homage had whipped up interest in the back catalogue. After narrating the story of tracking the group down in England in order to obtain a copy of their album, recounted on the sleeve of Nirvana's Incesticide, he contributed liner notes to the re-release of their debut album and invited them to support Nirvana on their European tour). Birch and Da Silva were joined by violinist Annie Wood and Sonic Youth's Steve Shelley for an EP (Extended Play documented a new John Peel session they cut) and an album, before they again rested the Raincoats name.

1996's Looking In The Shadows veered wildly from the discordant 'Forgotten Worlds', which could have easily fitted on their debut album, to the hypnotic, My Bloody Valentine-esque '57 Ways To End It'. Many of the lyrics concerned themselves with motherhood. And it was a shame that PJ Harvey turned down their request to help with production, the group working with Ed Buller (Psychedelic Furs, Suede) instead. Thereafter Birch would form the Hangovers who recorded an album for Kill Rock Stars in 1994. She is in the process of finishing a new album, while Da Silva has just released a solo record for Chicks On Speed.

DISCOGRAPHY:

Fairytale In The Supermarket/In Love/Adventures Close To Home 7-inch (Rough Trade RT 013 April 1979)

The Raincoats LP (Rough Trade ROUGH 3 November 1979) (reissued on CD, Rough Trade R 3022, 1993, with bonus track 'Fairytale In The Supermarket)

Odyshape LP (Rough Trade ROUGH 13 June 1981) (reissued on CD, Rough Trade R 3042, 1994)

No-One's Little Girl/Running Away 7-inch (Rough Trade RT 093 May 1982)

Animal Rhapsody/No-One's Little Girl/Honey Mad Woman 12-inch (Rough Trade RT 153 November 1983)

The Kitchen Tapes cassette (ROIR A 120 1983) (Recorded in New York in December 1982. reissued on CD, ROIR RUSCD 8238, 1998. Sleevenotes by Greil Marcus)

Moving LP (Rough Trade ROUGH 66 February 1984) (reissued on CD, Rough Trade R 3062, 1994, with additional track 'No One's Little Girl')

Extended Play 10-inch EP/CD EP (Blast First June BFFP 99 June 1994)

Don't Be Mean/We Smile/No One's Little Girl/Shouting Out Loud

Looking In The Shadows LP/CD (Rough Trade R 403/2/1 June 1996)

ARCHIVE RELEASES:

Best Of CD (Tim/Kerr 1995) (US compilation of first three albums)

Raped

Paddy Fields (drums), Tony Baggett (bass), Faebhean Kwest (guitar), Sean Purcell (vocals)

With a name like that, you know you can expect trouble, which is exactly what happened to a band who combined showmanship with lashings of internationally-flavoured ego, sexual ambivalence and glam trimmings. All of this they hyped up, spreading rumours of bisexuality, Olympic-standard bitchiness and being the descendants of Aleister Crowley.

RAPED were there right at the start of the punk explosion. Faebhean Kwest had moved to London from his native Liverpool in 1971 with the intention of forming a band. "I was living near King's Road, Southwell Gardens, just round the corner from Gloucester Road. I worked for the Great Gear Trading Company, and a lot of people from the King's Road went there. I knew Soo Catwoman, Demelza, Jak Airport and Marianne from X-Ray Spex, Jordan – all those people. I lived in a flat with two guys called Simon and Ross, where Ross ran the Marc Bolan fan club. Simon was a friend of Boy George, Philip Salon and a lot of what would later become the New Romantic scene. I'd bought a Telecaster for £100, it was Joe Brown's old one, from money I'd earned working on building sites. Everyone could sense change in the air. The school of thought at the time was that music was in the most terrible doldrums. If you wanted to be in a band and get a record deal, you had to have a white suit, Marshall stacks, a Gibson Les Paul, all the pedals. The Moody Blues and Pete Frampton needed hanging, and Pink Floyd too. I actually went to see Deep Purple recently and they were a good band, no holds-barred English rock-blues band. Before they came on Peter Frampton was the support – what a boring fart still, he looks like Victor Meldrew. He was one of the reasons we all became punks in 1976. We watched things like Bob Harris on the Old Grey Whistle Test, Emerson, Lake &

R

Palmer, Wakeman, Pink Floyd etc. They'd come on and it would be – this is a song off our really cool, really nice new album with some groovy sounds, man... Oh, fuck off! We wanted something like our own version of the Who or T-Rex, and we weren't impressed by apologists who tried to make rock music respectable and turn it into quasi-classical mush. We wanted people who didn't look like our dads or the man next door. Music was very dull, fashion was dull. Everyone looked like Kevin Keegan or Karen Carpenter, it was tedious. The only places of excitement were Chagarama's, which later became the Roxy, the Sundown and Louise's, the gay clubs."

Kwest had played in rockabilly bands, and early garage and thrash groups, including a stint at a Soho strip club with a keyboard player. He was allowed any food he wanted, and could have sex with any of the girls, as long as he wasn't seen chewing gum on stage ("which was thought to be common"). He was then asked to try out for the Sex Pistols, alongside Steve New (later of the Rich Kids). Their 'failed' audition has led to two sharply contrasting stories. Malcolm McLaren suggested to Jon Savage that Kwest was 'hopeless', while Kwest maintains they were convinced that the whole project was rubbish and McLaren simply sulked. He's also intimated that Jon Savage's account of events was twisted because "me and a couple of other kids wouldn't sleep with him – tired old poof." Charming. He gave me this full account in order to set the record straight.

"I knew a lot of the people down the Kings' Road. And someone said, Sparks have an audition for a guitarist, I thought, that's a good idea. It happened just like when Noel Redding went into the wrong room for a Monkees audition and ended up playing with Jimi Hendrix. I went up to Denmark Street and went in through this great stable door. 'I've come for the audition.' They sent me upstairs. Malcolm McLaren was there, in his leather trousers and winklepickers, and mohair jumper. He told me to come up. He had the New York Dolls and Ramones albums there. 'Do you know who these are?' 'Yeah, I know the Dolls. And 'Beat On The Brat', I love that.' I remember saying that. I had cropped bleached white hair, an American crew cut, with a red streak in it. I had a Marc Bolan top, with two big green buttons on it. I had a pair of red drainpipe trousers, and white brothel creepers, and a battered 1950s Telecaster guitar. So I didn't look like an old glam queen (as other versions have suggested). McLaren said, 'You look exactly right, if you can play anything – you're in. We're definitely going to have two guitarists and possibly two drummers, so come down and audition.' Steve New of the Rich Kids was down there, and he seemed pissed off with the whole thing. I asked if I should tune up. (Steve) Jones said we'll do 'All Or Nothing', the Small Faces number. 'Tune up? Fuck off! Should be in tune already, etc'. Then they launched into 'All Or Nothing' by the Small Faces. 'What key is it in?' I asked. Then they started playing faster and louder. I was making noises, then McLaren said, 'Let's play him a blues number.' I said I don't do blues numbers. I said, let's do an MC5 number, cos they were my heroes too. And they started farting about being louts. I thought, this is going nowhere, this isn't a proper audition. They didn't seem interested. I walked out. McLaren said wait and give it another chance. I said no and walked down Denmark Street with Steve New, who thought they were a complete joke, and we agreed. McLaren ran after us asking us to come back. Nope. I don't mind a bit of piss taking, but I've never been to anything like that in my life. 'Let's have a coffee. Do you want me to buy you a drink?' Nope. He got in touch through a friend, asking if I wanted to come back. I said no and that was that."

Kwest subsequently went with old friend Jak Stafford (aka Jak Airport) to his audition with X-Ray Spex at Falcon Stuart's house in Fulham. While there he was asked to join Swank with singer/actor Gary Grant (later Gary Olsen, who played father Ben in the British sitcom 2 Point 4 Children) and Dave 'Baby' Rolf. That lasted for a few months and they opened for Adam And The Ants at The Man in the Moon in Chelsea.

Kwest then put together an unnamed group at the end of 1976, recruiting Sean Purcell from a Melody Maker advert before opting for the most offensive name they could think of. Further Melody Maker adverts saw Baggett and Fields added to the line-up. Rehearsals took place in Acklam Road in Notting Hill, next to Rillington Place, made infamous by John Christie, but not at 'a lunatic asylum' as has been suggested. "We were looking for a place to rehearse and Sean had found a bloke called Mike who ran a place called COPE, a halfway house for people with mental health problems, and we used that. We did a film in there with Michael Winner when London Weekend Television came down. Chelsea were there, watching. Gene October was as jealous as fuck. A couple of days later we saw Sid Vicious, and he'd heard we've been interviewed. He was as jealous as fuck too. 'Who with? LWT? I'd like to punch that lot out.'"

Kwest was never taken with the Pistols' resident fire-starter. "He wasn't much of a fighter. The best one was at Dingwalls. We were playing with the Slits. He had a thing about one of the Slits at the time. He was picking on this little lad with long blonde hair in the audience, him and his mate – calling him a hippy and weed-head and pushing into him. This lad just turned round and knocked Sid out and then took on his mate. The bouncer had to pull him off Sid, he was trying to rip his ears off. Backstage, Sid was going, "There were five of them...' By the time it had reached the press, he'd been jumped by 15 fellas and fought them all off. I thought he was a complete waste of space and I can't believe the industry that's grown round a total bum like him! He had a go at me for having my hair longer and bleached white. I was growing it out, but he said, 'You look like a hippy.' I told him, at least I'm not a rent boy who likes being handcuffed to beds and 'used'. Then he ended up hanging round with Nancy the Sponger – as we ended up calling her."

The band began to play regularly around London, attracting hostile reactions from more mundane punk contemporaries who were disturbed as much by their use of mascara as their name. However, they did receive the support of fanzines such as In The City and Ripped And Torn as well as lots of American and Japanese fans and magazines. They were filmed for TV shows in countries including Spain, Portugal, and even Russia. Ripped and Torn gave the band their first interview. They responded by whisking fresh-faced editor Tony D to the Colherne, a renowned sado-masochist gay bar in Earl's Court.

One of their detractors was Jimmy Pursey of Sham 69, who got the sharp side of Kwest's tongue for his troubles. "We were at a show and a member of Sham 69 told us off for having too many notes in our songs and Pursey had a go at Sean for wearing silver lame trousers and the way we dressed – saying we weren't 'punks'. We never said we were punks. Even in 1976, I never said I was a punk! We let everyone say we were punk. We were influenced by the same people as the Damned and Adam And The Ants – T-Rex, Lou Reed, the Faces, the Dolls, Richard Hell. That's how punk was originally. The idea that everyone looked like they worked in a garage with regulation black jacket, blue jeans and spiky black hair – that came later. Pursey says we're not punk rock because of the way we dressed. We didn't look working class. Pursey lived in an eight-bedroom house in Surrey. Surrey! His parents had three cars and one of those was a Bentley. What are you going on about, working class!"

Eventually their manager, Alan Hauser, decided to put together his own label to further their ambitions. 'Pretty Paedophiles' was the result, the name coined by Alan Hauser, prompting predictable outrage. It was banned by noted libertarians Rough Trade and copies burned. The Daily Mirror feigned moral umbrage. And a story in the late, unlamented Reveille announced that Kwest was Aleister Crowley's illegitimate grandson. And the music press were no more supportive. "Worthless... sewer sentiments throughout" ranted Melody Maker. "Devoid of any musical integrity, ideas or subtlety" pointed out Sounds. These were among the kinder comments. The band whooped it up for all they were worth by convincing a cinema to allow them to play a Saturday morning's children's show until they realised what was going on and pulled the plug.

Of course, this all meant that the EP sold better than it may otherwise have done. A follow-up, 'Cheap Night Out' included a competition to win exactly that with the band. But they weren't about to leave their low-rent credentials entirely alone. This time the B-side boasted 'Foreplay Playground', with a jolly sing-along chorus about having an erection. However, Kwest points out that there was no "Michael Jackson feel to those old records. Anyway, it was Alan Hauser who called the EP 'Pretty Paedophiles'. We didn't find out until the day of release. We were going to call the EP 'Wolfling'. I lay the blame firmly at Alan Hauser's feet."

Despite the controversies, they found like-minded souls in Generation X, Rudi (who played with them extensively) and the Damned – indeed Purcell would end up dating Dave Vanian's ex, Josie Munns. However, Raped were getting nowhere. There were some final gigs in Belfast during Christmas 1978, where Paddy managed to get lost post-gig, and was picked up by British Paras wandering the streets dressed in high heels and tights, leading to his arrest for his own protection. They then transmuted into the Cuddly Toys – the name suggested by John

Peel, a friend of their manager, in which incarnation they become almost famous. They were due to be managed by Marc Bolan before he died in a car crash. Bolan had handed Kwest a tape of songs he'd been messing about with, alongside David Bowie, and asked him to help himself (from whence came the Cuddly Toys' single 'Madman'). Bolan loved the name Cuddly Toys and wanted to found a production company with them and a number of other similar bands on the label. He also wanted to write songs with them to hoist them into the charts. But his premature death crushed those ambitions.

Nowadays, Kwest is in a guitar-based duo with Dave Ahmed. "We play a lot of 1930s/1940s stuff, like Django Reinhardt, Ray Noble, and gypsy jazz music, big band stuff. It's really challenging technically. A while ago I was jamming on some of these old songs with Hank Marvin, showing him the chords." Cripes, did the Shadows' foremost twanger, the late accomplice of Cliff Richard and born again Christian, know he was sharing a stage with the former guitarist of 1970s folk devils Raped? "Erm, no. I didn't mention it, actually."

DISCOGRAPHY:

Pretty Paedophiles 7-inch EP (Parole KNIT 1 January 1978)
Moving Target/Raped/Escalator Hater/Normal
Cheap Night Out/Foreplay Playground 7-inch (Parole PURL 1 November 1978)
ARCHIVE RELEASES:
The Complete Raped CD (Anagram CDPUNK 35 1994) (re-released as The Complete Raped Punk Collection, with same catalogue number, in May 2006)

Rats

Pete Lewis (bass, vocals), Julian Lobb (guitar), Paddy McCready (drums)

Formed in 1976, after 18-year old Pete Lewis disbanded his Truro School rock combo, X-Ray, the RATS were arguably Cornwall's first punk rock band. Taking their inspiration from the likes of the New York Dolls, the Sex Pistols, Generation X and the Ramones, they played a mix of punk covers and original material penned by Lewis.

Their regular haunt was Truro's William IV pub, sometimes playing under various aliases (such as the Lazy Bastards) "to keep the regulars on their toes". In 1977 the Rats recorded two songs at Roche Studios, with 'First Mistake' chosen to appear on the Double Booked album (a compilation LP featuring acts that appeared at the William IV). It resulted in airplay on John Peel's Radio 1 show.

Pete Lewis went on to study medicine at Nottingham University, reuniting the Rats when he returned to Cornwall during his holidays. He also played in a number of university bands including Make Up (featuring the BBC's Matthew Bannister on vocals). Whilst working as a doctor at Torbay hospital, Pete Lewis also fronted local act Heat Treatment. He now practices in Sydney, Australia.

COMPILATION:
Doubled Booked LP (W4 W4001 October 1977; 'First Mistake')

Reacta

John Bennett (drums), Gerard Bennett (bass, lead vocals), Mark Denn (guitar, vocals), Adrian Uwalaka (lead guitar, vocals)

Formed in Chelsea, West London in 1977, REACTA comprised the Bennett brothers alongside two friends from the London Oratory School in Fulham. The Bennetts had previously been founder members of the Television Personalities and O'Level, alongside fellow Oratory graduates Dan Treacy, Ed Ball and Joe Foster, and appeared on two classic singles – the former's 'Part Time Punks' and the latter's 'Malcolm'.

So what was in the water at the London Oratory School? John Bennett: "It was a God-fearing school, and strict! Myself, Ed Ball and my brother Gerard had come from an idyllic primary school into this nightmare with kids from all over London. We weren't part of any gangs, we just loved music and Chelsea Football Club! When we were streamed in the fourth year, I met Dan Treacy and Joe Foster. Ed was a big influence, always talking to people, always looking for musicians, bringing us together with his ideas and enthusiasm. We were just oddballs who didn't quite fit in anywhere else, apart from with each other. We spent most of our time talking about music, or attempting to write and play our first songs. There wasn't any real creative environment at the school, unless you were interested in choirs or religion! I guess we were reacting against the school, and what was happening around us, mainly in music."

Not only was their debut performance at the Servite Hall in Fulham attended by the TVPs posse, but one of their former Oratory teachers turned up, got extremely drunk, and embarked on a striptease mid-set. When they put Reacta together, Dan Treacy of the TVPs helped them to release their debut single, 'Sus', backed by 'Stop The World (I Want To Get Off)', on Battery Operated Records. The label was a forerunner to Treacy and Ed Ball's Whaam! imprint. The financial backing, meanwhile, came from Rough Trade. John Bennett: "To be honest, I didn't get involved too much with Rough Trade, I left that to Dan and Ed! I did buy records from the shop, and occasionally went to the warehouse. I remember loads of hairy blokes in Wishbone Ash and Pink Floyd T-shirts wandering around surrounded by boxes of records. I always wanted to leave quickly in case they handed back boxes of the first Reacta single!"

Reacta's songs were a little more direct than had been the case with the TVPs. John Bennett wrote both sides of their debut single, the A-side attacking the UK's 'Suspicion' laws. Thereafter both Gerard Bennett and Mark Denn would contribute more to the songwriting. John Bennett: "I had co-written some songs with Ed when we were in O'Level, so when that band broke up, and me and Gerard decided to form Reacta, I just fell into being the main songwriter. I wrote 'Stop The World', the band liked it, so I just carried on! I was being influenced by the political climate in 1977-78, and the growth of far-right organisations like the NF and Combat 18. We got involved with ANL and Rock against Racism. Also, I loved the first Clash album and was listening to Marley and other reggae acts like Steel Pulse."

As John Bennett confirmed to me, "Nothing further was released after 'Sus', although a number of tracks were recorded in two sessions. I still have the master tapes, and have been discussing the possibility of releasing these tracks with a couple of labels." After Reacta, the Bennetts would briefly form the Air Raids with Ed Ball before giving up the ghost (full details at www.reacta.net). John Bennett is currently working on his memoirs, and alongside his brother Gerard, will appear on a new TVPs album scheduled for 2006.

DISCOGRAPHY:

Sus/Stop The World (I Wanna Get Off) 7-inch (Battery Operated WAC 1 1978)
COMPILATION:
Messthetics #1 (Hyped2Death; 'Sus')

Red Beat/Jones Boys

Roy Jones (lead vocals, keyboards), Paul 'Drumologist' Jones (drums, backing vocals), Martin Jones (guitar), Kevin Man (guitar), plus sundry bass players; Majid Ahmed, Chris Thompson. Roy and Martin Jones also played bass on some recordings

RED BEAT formed in 1978 in High Wycombe and signed to Malicious Damage Records, the Rough Trade-distributed label that also gave the world Killing Joke. In many ways Red Beat anticipated Killing Joke's sound, or at least ran parallel to it, fusing elements of dub, militant funk and acerbic guitar playing.

Roy Jones: "I was at school with Paul Ferguson and used to play in the same band as him (initially titled Beowulf) back in High Wycombe. Red Beat's reggae-dub influence came from a Jamaican connection in High Wycombe, quite separate from Killing Joke. We used to go to a pub called The Red Cross Knight, where there were real Jamaican dub plates and live toasting. The band pre-dating Red Beat were called the Jones Boys and played at High Wycombe's Nag's Head pub as well as whatever small venues they could get in Reading, Amersham, Oxford etc. CBS came to a gig at the Nag's Head but didn't sign us, even though the music was more commercial and power-pop in nature, with an XTC influence. Then we were booked to play alongside Joy Division, Killing Joke, A Certain Ratio, and Section 27 at High Wycombe Town Hall. The time we were asked to play was so early, we felt it was pointless. So we tried to go on stage before Killing Joke and after A Certain Ratio as many people in the audience had come especially to see us. However, the Factory band didn't like this and got tough with us. Rather than get into a fight we backed off and didn't play at all. This was the reason we left Wycombe for the bright lights, as we felt we would never be taken seriously if we stayed."

It was at this stage that the Jones Boys transformed into Red Beat. "We financed our own recording of 'Machines In Motion'/'Red Beat' and played it to Malicious Damage. They loved it and agreed to release it. Then Killing Joke got signed to EG and Malicious Damage turned more into their management company, making it difficult for us and Ski Patrol, the label's other signing. That's why we formed our own label, Manic Machine, for our next releases."

Their debut 12-inch was recorded in 1979 at Gooseberry Studios in Gerrard Street, London. It led to a session for John Peel broadcast in February 1980 featuring 'See', 'The Wheel', 'Tribe' and 'Child'. The first of these was released as the A-side of their second single in 1981, followed by a second 12-inch, 'Dream'. "Gooseberry was tremendous fun. It was like a party. We'd only ever used a four-track before so we were in heaven. The Peel session was done more or less in one take. We were a live band and knew our stuff." By this time they had played alongside everyone from U2 to Joy Division to the Thompson Twins, as well as backing their brother, Howard Jones. The latter was never a member of the Jones Boys, contrary to some published accounts. "We did invite him to join us once," states his brother, Roy. "But he declined. But he ended up getting a great team of people working with him and was more level-headed than us."

Between 1981 and 1984 the group continued to persevere as a live act, but only released one single, a double a-side, in Germany, Austria and Switzerland. "We released 'Power Reflex' in 1984 hoping to ignite a new phase for the band. We had hours of songs and material which we'd recorded for majors but never released." These included two sessions as auditions for record labels; the first for Miles Copeland at IRS in 1982, and another one a year later for Stiff Records.

In 2004 the group announced it was back playing together ("we had so much creativity left to reveal") while drummer Paul Jones embarked on reissuing the group's discography, starting with the very pleasing Missing Album, which rounded up most everything they did during their peak years of 1979 to 1981.

DISCOGRAPHY:

Machines In Motion/Red Beat/More Or Less Cut/Cut Dub 12-inch (Malicious Damage MD 4940 1979)
See/Survival 7-inch (Manic Machine Products RB 002 1981)
Dream/Dream Dub 12-inch (Manic Machine Products RB 003 1981)
ARCHIVE RECORDINGS:
The Missing Album CD (Manic Machine 2004) (includes all the band's 1979-81 material, aside from 'Dream Dub', including their John Peel session plus unreleased track 'Shadow Boxing'. Digitally remastered with extensive liner notes)

R

Red Lights

Ian Russell (vocals, guitar), Ashley Cadell (guitar), Andrew Howell (bass), Dave McMullen (drums).

Formed in mid-1977 in Deptford, the RED LIGHTS, originally known as the Rats until Bob Geldof's success persuaded them to change to avoid confusion, made their debut as support to Menace on 12 November 1977 at the Roxy. "The Roxy was brilliant as far as I can remember," states Cadell. "I don't think we ever got paid for anything, but it was a place to play. I remember we were sitting in a pub in east Greenwich bored out of our minds and someone said: 'Let's go and play at the Roxy.' We rang them up, and they said, 'Yeah, whatever'. Two hours later we were playing. Not many venues would let you do that."

The Red Lights were typically modest in their ambitions. "The main thing I remember about the Red Lights was that we knew nothing about the music industry and we didn't know what the fuck we were doing," Cadell admitted to me. They would also record a track for the venue's farewell compilation. Their final live performance came as support to the Specials at London's Moonlight Club in May 1979, by which time Steve Townsend had become their drummer – their other drummers included Steve Tate and Nigel Preston, who later joined Theatre Of Hate and the Cult. McMullen died in the early-80s, Preston in the 1990s – "Seems we were killing off drummers before Spinal Tap thought of it," reckons Cadell. This was also the line-up that recorded their 'Never Wanna Leave' single, a catchy pop-punk effort that actually stands the test of time. According to Cadell, Townsend is current living in Enrith, having left the band to pursue a "normal career" and "to keep his girlfriend". Since the band's demise Cadell has been working as a writer and producer in Australia, and played keyboards on David Byrne's Uh Oh album. He also was a key session musician behind teen pop sensation and tabloid-fodder Peter Andre on his first (pre-Jordan) tilt at the pop charts. Sheesh!

DISCOGRAPHY:

Never Wanna Leave/Seventeen 7-inch (Free Range PF5 November 1978)
COMPILATION:
Farewell To The Roxy (Lightning LIP 2 1978; 'Never Wanna Leave')

Reducers

Graham 'Raggy' Holden (vocals), Graham Barstow (drums), Roy Tynan (guitar, vocals), Doug Hoyles (bass)

Bury's REDUCERS issued two excellent singles in their short lifetime before petering out when a third, for EMI, caused a final rupture in the band. Formed in September 1977, three months later they performed their first gig at Bury School of Art. Soon thereafter Tynan was offered Martin Bramah's role as guitarist in the Fall. The answer was an emphatic no. As Tynan rationalised, Smith was "a control freak" and "way too serious".

'Things Go Wrong', the band's first recording, was released in February 1978, financed by Bury retailer Vibes Records, though the band wanted the far superior 'We Are Normal' as the A-side. After Stuart Lyons replaced Hoyles on bass in April, they embarked on a succession of live dates. Though there were only two London gigs, they did support the Ramones at a brace of shows in Holland, before Jon Mather stepped in for Barstow on drums early in 1979.

The band were again unhappy with the choice of 'Man With A Gun' as their second single, leading to further internal friction. Eventually Lyons elected to leave to pursue his academic ambitions. "Bless him, we missed him," notes Tynan. He replacement was Steve Rutter. Ian X replaced Mather on drums.

The reconstituted band secured a one-off contract with EMI at the end of 1979 and early the following year released 'Airways'. Yet, once again, it wasn't the track they'd hoped to release. "I was so upset at the choice of single," Tynan remembers, "that I refused to play on the release. By this time, Raggy had gone totally electric with his synths and drum machines. The B-side was a couple of older demo recordings that should have been 'not for release' as well." In disgust, at both Raggy and EMI, Tynan quit the band. And that was it for the Reducers, who disbanded shortly thereafter, though there are inklings of a possible retrospective release coming soon.

Isn't it a bit odd that the band managed three releases, all of which were chosen against Tynan's wishes? "As a band we much preferred 'We are Normal' and a couple of other tunes we had to 'Things Go Wrong', but Tony Andrews (then the owner of Vibes) said he'd pay, so long as 'Things Go Wrong' was the a-side. The second single, I was out-voted in a democratic process. In my opinion we had stronger songs than 'Man With A Gun'. But it was not really a big issue. However, the EMI ditty was! Friction between Raggy and the other members was getting intense at times, nearly came to blows once. We sent four songs to EMI. 'Airways' was then a guitar song with a bit of synth in it, not bad actually, a bit Joy Division in style. EMI asked for a more electric version, so we went in the studio. Raggy took over the session, none of the other members played on it. EMI went with this new 'Raggy' version. EMI then used one other song from the demo on the B-side. I hated that single, and still do! However I got some royalties a couple of years later, as I wrote it. The instrumental bits were used in a Brazilian documentary, can you believe?"

Where are they now? Tynan fills me in. Hoyles was last sighted in Bury circa 1980. Lyons got his degree in English and ended up working for the council at some elevated level. Barstow followed his father into the Greater Manchester Police. Raggy emigrated to South Africa in 1987 and died in a road traffic accident there in 1998. As for the Reducers' multitudinous rhythm section; "Jon Mather, mad to start with, probably even madder now, Steve Rutter became a hippy and went to Wales to live off the land in 1982 and Ian X is an artist of some sort." Tynan himself went on to design professional recording equipment for 12 years before founding his own software company in 1996. At the time of writing, he was planning to travel the world on his motorbike. And Vibes Records is, apparently, still around.

DISCOGRAPHY:

Things Go Wrong/We Are Normal 7-inch (Vibes XP1/VR 001 February 1978).
Man With A Gun/Vengeance/Can't Stop Now (Vibes VR 002 1979)
Airways 7-inch (EMI 1980)

Rejects

Bruno Wizard (vocals), Ian (guitar), Howard (drums), "unidentified Paranoid Rasta bloke with an axe" (bass)

The REJECTS predated infamous London art punks the Homosexuals by a few brief months, before the principal figure, Bruno, who was present at the original recording of 'Stairway To Heaven', decided he'd outgrown the new conformity of the punk rock community. Like many though, he was an initial beneficiary of the have a go policy at the Roxy.

Bruno: "In January 1977, I'd heard about this new club for punk bands, where bands that couldn't get gigs anywhere else could play, called the Roxy. It was one night a week in a gay club called Chagaramas in Neale Street. This was before Covent Garden was gentrified. I went up there and introduced myself to Andrew Czezowski. 'I hear you put new bands on?' 'Yeah, what's your band called?' I didn't have a band, I'd always wanted one. I said, the Rejects. 'That's a great name, come back next Tuesday. You're supporting the Damned, the Adverts and the Vibrators.' I said, 'OK, cool.' So I had to scoot off and get a band together. I was living in South London at the time. I went straight to Goldsmith's College and got this crazy guy called Ian, he was a dishwasher there. He had this kooky haircut, going in one direction, and his trousers were so tight they were going in another direction, but he played piano and guitar. I went down to his place in Lewisham and he started playing me some songs on guitar. OK, I said, we'll use the music, but I'll write new words. So I wrote about 14 one-minute and two-minute songs with him. I got this drummer called Howard who was a young jazz drummer. His technique was really good, but we couldn't really have a jazz drummer playing in a punk club. So I said, imagine you're a woman and play as if you were a woman. What I meant was get in touch with the female side of your nature. It was enough to throw him off his stroke. When he was sitting playing, I could see him thinking, Oh, my God, do I look like a woman? It broke up his playing enough to make it sound a bit crazy."

The Rejects were nearly there. "Then I got this 6'2" bogus Rasta on bass. He was really paranoid that people were after him, he used to carry an axe in his inside pocket. So I said, you're not paranoid, they really are after you, and the only way to keep them away from you is to come and play bass with my band. He couldn't actually play, so we used to plug him in but not turn his amp on. Seeing as how all the kids at the Roxy were white, that played up to their preconceived notions – he's black and he's a Rasta, he's got a bass, so it must be great. Then I got this chainsaw guitarist from Sunderland, my home town. That was it. That was the band complete. We played the first gig in January 1977. I'd written this song about Gary Gilmore, this killer in America. All the liberal do-gooders were marching outside the jail. He was saying, no, I want to die, blah blah blah. So I wrote a song about Gary Gilmore. I was in the middle of singing this really serious song. And Captain Sensible of the Damned got up on stage, wearing a pink tutu singing doo wop backing vocals. At the end of this first gig, this American girl with 'Fuck Off' written on her T-shirt came up to me and said, hey, man that was really good. That was DIFFERENT. I had long hair at the time. I refused to cut my hair so I could play in a so-called punk club. I was already getting pissed off with the conformity with punk, how everyone was just imitating the Sex Pistols."

The Rejects were fixtures of that early Roxy scene. "We supported Sham 69 about three times, we did the Damned about three times. Went on a mini-tour of England and did a couple of gigs in Birmingham supporting Generation X. We also supported them at the Roxy as well, as well as the Jam. But the first night I supported the Adverts I had the lyrics to 'Gary Gilmore' in my bag, as well as my brand new microphone. When I got back to the dressing room the bag was gone, with the microphone and the lyrics. Then the Adverts started doing a song, 'Gary Gilmore's Eyes'. It may have been coincidence, but it was nothing like my song."

However, Bruno is not claiming ownership. In fact, he suggests it is just an example "of how incestuous that scene was. Nobody was well known. The Damned were starting to get well known. They'd brought out 'New Rose'. That got played about 20 times at the Roxy. There weren't any punk records to be played. It was all reggae played by Don Letts, then he'd play the odd bit of Iggy or the Ramones or the Stooges, stuff like that. Imported stuff from America. Within a very short time, bands were coming from all over England to play there. Slaughter & The Dogs and bands from Manchester, people were coming up from Plymouth, from Scotland. It was very, very exciting for about six months. Then we got a review from the dreaded Tony Parsons. He was actually living in Crouch End with Julie Burchill, and they were both complete fucking speed freaks."

You can't say that about such noted literary figures. Oh, go on then. "They were living in a house with a friend of mine, Alan Harrison, an art lecturer, not only at Goldsmiths, but in Coventry too. He was a good friend of Jerry Dammers in Coventry. And he brought Jerry down with the Specials to do their first gigs down here. Harrison was an amazing character, a real facilitator, he was really good at spotting people's potential even quicker than they actually knew it themselves. He was creative as well, he brought the best out of people. Alan was also a very good friend of Dave Stewart, from the Tourists at the time. So he was living with Tony Parsons and Julie Burchill. I'd met Alan at Goldsmiths, we'd got on really well together. I'd always talked a good visionary tale. He really liked the Rejects and said, I'll get Tony Parsons, this young writer, to come down and review you. Fantastic! Tony Parsons wasn't known at all then. He was just starting to get a little bit of a reputation on this small scene. Julie Burchill was better known. Tony Parsons came down on our guest list and did a review. I went running out to get the NME, and the band was waiting in rehearsals to see what the review was like. I get it and go back and read it out. 'The singer sounds like a braying donkey run over by a truckload of Librium whilst behind him the band play artlessly away on their cheapo Gibson Les Paul imitations…' It went on and on, it was fucking hilarious. I was cracking up. I looked, and the drummer was sliding down the wall, devastated. They couldn't believe it. I knew at that point that this wasn't the band for me. They just don't fucking understand. They want to be this year's version of Led Zeppelin or whoever their favourite band was." Outside the Speakeasy that evening, Bruno was smashed across the face with a whisky glass by his distraught guitarist, Ian. Joe Strummer helped him patch up the cuts and bought him a Scotch to console him. It was the last time he ever saw Ian.

That prompted Bruno, who was disappointed to note that his fellow band members didn't share his enthusiasm to use the review as a flyer for forthcoming gigs, to start anew. That band would become the Homosexuals, though they did play a couple of gigs as the Rejects before deciding on the new name.

COMPILATION:

Messthetics Greatest Hits: The Sound Of UK DIY 1977-80 (Hyped 2 Death Messthetics #100; 'Vision Smashed', 'Technique Street')

Revenge

Lol Hammond (vocals, guitar) Ian Strange (bass), Dave Edgar (drums)

Two great singles for Loony Records in 1978, then nada, but Cheshunt's REVENGE did provide the foundations for the career of one Lol Hammond, one of the capital's best known DJs. A regular at the Big Chill, etc, he has also recorded widely as Drum Club (notably the club smash 'U Make Me Feel So Good') and Girl Eats Boy. He's also remixed material by Jah Wobble's Invaders Of The Heart, Curve, Chapterhouse, the Fall, the Creatures and Killing Joke and collaborated with Roger Eno. Prior to gravitating to the DJ booth, Hammond also worked as ad hoc guitarist with one of

the many incarnations of Spizz. Most recently he was the musical director of hit film The Football Factory, managing to sneak a couple of tunes by the Buzzcocks and the Jam on to the soundtrack.

Hammond told me how Revenge came about: "Loony Records was basically our own little label. Somehow we cobbled the money together to do a run of 500 and it went on from there. I actually went out and bought 'We're Not Gonna Take It' myself from Rough Trade just off the Porterbello Road. It cost me a fiver! Still, well chuffed there's still interest. I was 16 when we recorded the two Revenge singles. We played the Roxy once, which was a real blast. Supported the Surburban Studs at the Rochester Castle in Stoke Newington, which was well cool. I also remember playing on the back of a truck at our local carnival." What about the cherubic faces looking out from the picture sleeve of 'Our Generation'? "I did have rather a lot of hair then! Hacked it off weeks later and had a jet black spiky crop."

Dance music of the late-80s/early-90s was punk rock for a new generation. Those who helped to mobilise the punk movement (i.e. left field liberals and hippies) played a similar role to the ex-punks in helping foster the new dance movement. Discuss. "The Drum Club were signed to ex-Killing Joke bassist Youth's label Butterfly Records, based in Brixton. It was great having all these wicked ex-punks around. Alex Patterson (who roadied for the Joke), Kris Needs (former editor of ZigZag), Jah Wobble, and of course Youth himself. Acid House had a very similar vibe to punk, in that it was DIY, anyone could have a go. Like punk, it also flicked two fingers to the establishment."

DISCOGRAPHY:

Our Generation/I Love Her Way 7-inch (Loony LOO 1 1978) (250 copies)
We're Not Going To Take It/Pornography 7-inch (Loony LOO 2 1978) (500 copies)
Note: both singles have been counterfeited.

Rezillos

Alan 'Eugene Reynolds' Forbes (drums, vocals), Dave 'Dr DK' Smythe (bass), John 'Luke Warm' Callis (lead guitar, vocals), Mark 'Hi-Fi' Harris (rhythm guitar, vocals), Sheilagh 'Fay Fife' Hynde (vocals), Alistair 'Angel' Paterson (drums), Alistair 'William Mysterious' Donaldson (saxophone), Gail Warning (vocals)

The REZILLOS were Scotland's first punk band, and by some way the classiest. Their musical horizons encompassed rockabilly, surf and bubblegum rock'n'roll, while their subject matter, similarly, couldn't have diverged further from the tower block rebellion of punks further south. Not only did their lyrical obsessions with space travel, TV, pop culture, cult comics, B-movies and gaudy 60s kitsch set them apart, musically they were both sophisticated and ambitious, playing around with studio effects, treated guitar and breathless girl-boy vocals.

R

It all began in 1975 with the Knutsford Dominators, who formed from a pool of friends at Edinburgh Art School. The prime movers were Callis and Forbes. At this stage they were a rock'n'roll revival outfit featuring two drummers, including Forbes, who played mainly at parties. About 7 times. It seemed to be going nowhere, so they embarked on a grander design. "It was our idea of the ultimate rock'n'roll group," Reynolds told Brian Hogg in The History Of Scottish Rock and Pop, "When we were at art college we made up these posters with 'Beware – the Rezillos are Coming', even before it existed. We got members by going up to people and saying: 'You look like a candidate for the Rezillos'. They would either look at us sideways or say, 'Yeah. I know what you mean'." The idea for the name came from a drawing of an insalubrious hostelry in a Marvel comic that displayed the sign "Playing tonight, the Revilos." Forbes changed it to Rezillos to ensure no-one else would replicate the name ("ironic, given that years later he would end up with pretty much the original name again," points out Gareth Holder of the Shapes, a long-term fan of the band).

The Rezillos took shape with the recruitment of Alistair Paterson on drums and Harris on rhythm guitar. The bass position was filled when Reynolds knocked on Dave Smythe's door in March 1976 and asked if he was interested. "I disappeared for a moment," recalled Smythe, "and re-emerged wearing a teddy boy fancy dress outfit, plus my guitar. 'You mean like this?' I said. I was in – Alan clearly perceived that I would fit in with the band's unpretentious self-parodying ethos."

The new line-up allowed Forbes to step from behind the drum kit. He also persuaded two fashion design students to attend rehearsals, Sheilagh Hynde and Gail Warning. Their backing vocals immediately offered a better sonic blend. Hynde briefly toyed with the name Candy Floss before becoming Fay Fife (as in – "where are you from?" Answer, delivered in broad Scottish accent: "I'm Fay Fife"). The line-up had expanded further by August 1976 with the addition of saxophone player Ali Donaldson, formerly of Edinburgh folk band Silly Wizzard. Yet it was a full four months before they made their live debut at the Edinburgh Teviot Row Student Union on 5 November 1976. That was because, alongside their enormous line-up and collective ambition, they were also disciplined about their intentions. "In contrast to the laid-back, casual, self-indulgent ethos of rock bands in that era." reckons Smythe. "We were slick, highly professional, well-rehearsed, and offered 60 minutes or so of frantic, non-stop fun rock looking back to the late-1950s."

The Rezillos are GO!

The set featured a series of well-travelled standards, including 'Batman Theme', 'Twist And Shout', 'Johnny B Goode' and 'You Really Got Me', alongside Gerry & The Pacemakers' cheesy 'I Like It' and Jeremy Spencer's Fleetwood Mac/Earl Vince And the Valiants oddity, 'Someone's Gonna Get Their Head Kicked In Tonight'. The latter was note and sentiment perfect for the punk era. The group was an immediate success, and with so many fervent supporters in the arts faculties across Edinburgh, several parties chipped in with promotion and photocopying. Outside student circles, there was some classic town/gown resentment directed at the group by its peers (Smythe recalls one set where their support band were so jealous of the reaction they were getting, they pulled the power mid-set). Soon they were playing regularly, travelling round in Smythe's Volvo saloon and Transit van, notching up some 200 gigs in their first year of existence. They became an enormously popular live draw, numbering among their fans the mother of Billy MacKenzie of the Associates. "I was 20, she was 40," he later recalled. "Yet she thought Fay Fife was brilliant. She used to be at the back of the hall pinching glasses of snakebite."

But their growing stature and the attendant demands wrought changes. Gail Warning drifted out of the band, mainly because Eugene thought the two female singers and one male vocalist set-up made their position look "subservient". While Fay and Eugene, the visual axis of the band, became romantically linked, Callis started to submit original compositions to augment the covers. To his credit, it blended perfectly with their revivalist instincts, drawing on 60s beat and girl group dynamics, with a punk wallop courtesy of the rhythm section and Callis's own gnarly guitar technique. The lyrics were esoteric and sharp-witted without being arch, taking in encounters with aliens, sculptors and the opposite sex. It was punk, captain, but not as we know it. "We may have been (slightly) anti-establishment," Smythe tells me, "and in common with punk we were certainly against the rock music establishment of the time, as being too self-regarding and complacent. However, I think we put musicianship and professionalism high up the agenda, whereas some punk rebellion deliberately downgraded these two aspects of band life and performance."

Another local, Lennie Love, moonlighting for Island Records while working as ad-hoc Rezillos manager, decided to put his own label together. He signed the Rezillos to Sensible, named in honour of the Damned's good captain, as his first act. (Reynolds later offered Love the chance to sign the Cramps, at that stage barely known, after seeing them play while in New York recording their debut album. He handed over the master tapes to 'Human Fly' and 'Domino', but Love "just couldn't see it"). 'I Can't Stand My Baby', backed by the Beatles' 'I Wanna Be Your Man', was in local shops in August 1977. That meant it was regarded as Scotland's first punk record, beating the Valves by a month (earlier singles by the Drive and Exile were considered by many to betray obvious pub-rock leanings). A sojourn to London's punk venues ensued. September saw them supporting the Stranglers in front of their biggest audience yet, 3,500 at the Glasgow Apollo. At which point Sire Records stepped in and made them their first UK-based signing. All of which meant that they were going to be a proper, professional band now, and would have to suspend their college careers. That prospect saw the departure of Harris and Smythe. The latter, having turned 30 as a well paid research geophysicist, opted for financial security and pastures academic. But there were no regrets. "I was just delighted that they were doing so well. Nor did I mind the fact that I had not made any money personally, because all earnings had been ploughed back into the band. I've recently discovered an old folder 'Rezillos contract' dated 1979-80, when I got my lawyer to try (in vain) to extract the £5,000 or so that Lennie Love owed us in royalties."

Ali Donaldson moved over to bass, leaving the quintet of Forbes, Hynde, Donaldson, Paterson and Callis for the big push. Sire reissued their debut single, and also prepared a new one, 'Flying Saucer Attack', backed by one of their signature tunes, '(My Baby) Does Good Sculptures'. It had originally been intended as their second effort for Sensible, which would only release one further single, Neon's 'Bottles', before disappearing.

A short UK tour with the Ramones (the Rocket To Russia tour, on which they recorded It's Alive) was scheduled and completed, but it was not the happy occasion it should have been. Though the camaraderie between bands was good, the brudders' management quickly grew cautious about the strength of the support act. "They didn't have too good a time once the Ramones management realised how good they were," confirms Gareth Holder. "They resorted to messing up their sound, putting them on before the doors opened, and putting Generation X on the bill in between them, so that the audience had a bit of light shite in between the two acts. It was their treatment on this tour that started to precipitate poor old William's problems, though it's fair to say that he was obviously fragile to start with." Still, by the time the tour arrived at the Rainbow, Elton John could be seen pogo-ing along to the Rezillos at the side of the stage.

Legend has it that the title of their ensuing debut album was suggested by Bobby Gillespie – no-one is sure if it was THE Bobby Gillespie – in a competition run by Bruce's Record chain in Scotland. Other suggestions included Tents On Fire, Look Skyscrapers! and Baby Stink On Ice. But Can't Stand The Rezillos it was.

There was talk of Nick Lowe, Roy Wood or Chris Spedding producing the album, but instead Sire sent them to a snow-swept New York to record their debut album alongside Tony Bongiovi. Jon Bon Jovi's cousin, he'd also worked as co-producer on the Ramones' albums Leave Home and Rocket To Russia as well as with Talking Heads, so there were plenty of cool reference points. As Eugene recalled to Big Takeover's Martin Percival: "When we recorded 'Good Sculptures' and got to the foot-stomping and hand-clapping part, he said, 'I know what to do here. I've done this with the Shangri-Las,' and brought out various paraphernalia and recorded the foot stomping and hand clapping. The second take he said, 'Great. When you get to the foot stomping bit, it sounded great, but it went out of time, and we don't have time to record anymore. But the first version is in time.' So he went to the big 24-track master tape and he ran it, listened to it, cut out the right part, and spliced it in to the overall better version. Amazing! He also showed us buzzsaw guitar a la the Ramones. The guitar was plugged in, you'd start playing it and he'd start recording five to ten seconds after you'd started playing, and then they'd hit record and edit it straight in, so the guitar was really loud and punchy as you'd been strumming for a while already." However, Bongiovi was ill much of the time, so, as Callis recalled: "(engineer) Bob Clearmountain really produced the album and helped create the Rezillos sound. He was fantastic... Stereo guitars on each side of the stereo field. He'd double everything up. Made it sound much bigger." And he did a great job, bolstering the inherent colour and drama of the group's quicksilver sound with flattering stereo separation – witness the improved re-recordings of both 'Sculptures' and 'Flying Saucer Attack'.

"We did most of that album at night during cheap recording time," Reynolds later told Brian Hogg. "We'd hang around CBGB's and Max's, waiting for a telephone call, then rush over to the studio, sometimes only for four hours. Most of it was done in one take." While in New York they played a well-received set at CBGB's, which for two decades looked like it would be their only stateside engagement. Oh, and Fay did nothing for their long-term career prospects when she threw a cream cake at Seymour Stein's wife Linda during a reception. (Famously, in 1980 Seymour would call the Dead Boys into his office and tell them: "I bet a whole lotta money on punk... and I lost.")

To promote the album, whose release date had slipped to July 1978 due to Sire's distribution difficulties, the label issued 'Top Of The Pops', backed by '20,000 Leagues Under The Sea'. The latter featured a partial theft of the 'Lone Ranger' theme, and included the use of a kazoo. It was to be their biggest hit, reaching number 17 in the UK charts. By the time of its release, Mysterious had disappeared ('in a flying saucer attack,' according to the band. The truth was the Ramones' experience had done for him). Simon Templar (Simon Bloomfield) became the new bass player. Press statements asserted he'd "left the TV series The Saint because he was 'pulling too many birds. It was too much of a strain.'" Another blistering sci-fi-themed single followed in November, 'Destination Venus', backed by 'Mystery Action'. Meanwhile the Rezillos, who had always been more Napoleon Solo than Napoleon Hill (the 'self-help' guru who is the base of the pyramid that inspired so many rubbish books) took to taking a Dalek on stage with them.

They should have been in the ascendant, but the Rezillos then collapsed into two bickering camps during a disastrous 40-date tour, supported by fellow Sire act the Undertones in December. "All groups have factions," Reynolds told Brian Hogg, "and, as Fay was my girlfriend, we were on one side while the others formed their own unit. We found it difficult to communicate at that time. Fay and I didn't want it to slip into 'just another group', but lacked the experience to articulate how we should do it. It just ended up as friction and little splits became great gashes." Despite the ill feeling, the real killing blow came when Fife's voice gave out midway through the tour, leaving the group in financial penury after a succession of promoters sued. Communal sourness enveloped the participants, and the divide grew wider. In one camp, Reynolds and Fife, always considered the visual focus of the band but not the songwriters. In the other Callis, the group's musical engine room, and in musical comradeship, Paterson and Templar. "They wanted to be competent musicians first and foremost," Fife complained to the New York Rocker in 1979, "and we wanted to be adventurous... They're not – they're still playing old Rezillos numbers for Chrissakes (a reference to Shake's live set, which featured a number of the songs that Callis originally wrote for the Rezillos). Secondly... there was a great deal of disrespect from the other three towards us because we were singers – not really musicians. Third was attitudes towards the music business. They were satisfied with Sire, prepared to take any shit given them, whereas we have always wanted total control of everything... who wants to get into the Top 20 with a record that's not your own work? 'Top Of The Pops' was recorded by some guy in a 24-track studio who we didn't want in the first place, and the artwork was awful." Once an art student...

Their old friend Professor Smythe offers an interesting view on the singer/musician fault line: "This is a well-known phenomenon which has long existed in the classical musical world as well. It's because there is something mysterious about the singer, whose 'instrument' is hidden from view within their body. Also, singers have a reputation for being bad readers of scores (which doesn't mean that they are unmusical – it just means that they can't read scores!) Pavarotti, for example, is coached through his parts to learn them, whereas any classical instrumental musician is expected to simply read it off the paper without assistance."

Sire attempted to recoup their losses by releasing live album Mission Accomplished... But The Beat Goes On, much to Reynold's and Fife's dismay, as they'd tried valiantly to block its release, unhappy with the sound quality. It attracted indifferent reviews, but is actually a scintillating testament to their live power. The songs were taken from the final of their three farewell gigs, in Glasgow on 23 December 1978. Gail Warning and William Mysterious had rejoined just for the occasion. Among the standouts are 'Someone's Gonna Get Their Head Kicked In Tonight', delivered in thuggish splendour, the Sweet's 'Ballroom Blitz' and a new song, 'Culture Shock', that Callis would later reprise for Shake.

Reynolds and Fife continued as the Revillos, because the other warring faction, and Sire, denied them the right to the name. They were joined by former Rezillo Hi-Fi Harris and released several affecting singles and two albums up to 1985, when both their professional and romantic partnership ended. Though they never replicated the sheer panache of the old Rezillos, there's much to cherish in their output during the period, in which they totally indulged themselves in their private obsessions. Reynolds then got involved in classic motorcycles while Fife appeared on stage and wrote screenplays before completing a post-graduate degree, having worked extensively with independent Scottish filmmaker Mark Bender. She co-wrote Blood Relations, a film about Scottish cannibals, and appeared as a lesbian witch in a production of Beware Women at the Edinburgh Festival. She's also been seen in episodes of Taggart and The Bill. Reynolds also founded Planet Pop. Callis, Paterson and Templar formed Shake, who cut a 10-inch EP in March 1979, released in July, and a single, 'Invasion Of The Gamma Men'.

Callis then joined the Human League – with whom the Rezillos had once shared management. He co-wrote a number of their most famous songs, notably 'Don't You Want Me'. When that ended he cut a faux-glam rock EP with S.W.A.L.K., who also featured Angel Paterson, and wrote 'Loving You' for Feargal Sharkey's solo career – that old Undertones connection again. Paterson worked with the under-rated TV21 and Troy Tate of the Teardrop Explodes before moving to the small village of Hilgermissen in Germany and working as an architect, playing part-time with his side-band, Angie & The Toasters. Templar, post-Shake, joined the Flowers and Peel favourites Boots For Dancing, who also fleetingly numbered Callis and Paterson among their personnel. Sadly, Ali Donaldson had a breakdown from which he has never fully recovered. However, he did release one single, under the name William Mysterious And Alistair Donaldson, entitled 'Security Of Noise'. Smythe continues to prosper as an emeritus professor and director of GeoLogica Ltd, which specialised in exploration geophysics.

The Rezillos' good name was kept alive by tributes from their many celebrity fans, including Dinosaur Jr's J. Mascis. Writer Garry Mulholland titled his 2002 book of the 500 greatest singles ever released, This Is Uncool, after a line in 'I Can't Stand My Baby'. Scots author Iain Banks namechecks them twice in his novel The Bridge, including an explanation of the origin of the name Fay Fife.

R

In October 2001 the band finally put its differences asunder as they were prised out of retirement. The idea was put forward by Stuart Nisbet of the Proclaimers, whose wife, Charlotte, was studying psychology with Fay Fife. She rang Eugene, who in turn rang Jo Callis, and all three declared themselves amenable to the idea. By the end of December they were rehearsing together, with the addition of Mekon (of the Revillos) on bass for that one-off Hogmanay show. It had been assumed that Angel Paterson was still domiciled in Germany and would be uninterested in getting back behind the drum kit. But in fact he was only too happy to take a break from his architect's business when the call came through from Eugene.

Dates in both Scotland and America were well-attended and rapturously received. Though their debut album had been recorded in New York, it was the first time they'd toured in the US with the exception of a sole CBGB's show 24 years previously. With Mekon unable to make the trip due to a new baby, Johnny Terminator played bass.

They also got some cheap publicity from the Sun: a page-long article headed by the legend: "Punk's back and we're going to kick karaoke Darius right into touch." There was something touching about the reunion too – in that, unlike some of their peers, none of the band members actually needed the money (Jo Callis, in particular, will have to empty a lot of very expensive wine bottles before he uses up his 'Don't You Want Me' royalties). They've even started to write new songs together, such as 'Crash My Car' and 'Pressure Cooker'. One new song, 'Number One Boy', was ready for the very first reunion performance, having been written in previous years when Eugene and Fay had contemplated putting the band back together, but not quite managed it. It's grand to have them back.

DISCOGRAPHY:

I Can't Stand My Baby/I Wanna Be Your Man 7-inch (Sensible Records FAB-1 August 1977)

I Can't Stand My Baby/(My Baby Does) Good Sculptures (demo) 7-inch (Sensible Records FAB-1 (MARK2) July 1979) (reissue: first pressing of 4,000 copies with different B-side, though the sleeve still refers to 'I Wanna Be Your Man'. Other copies restore stated B-side. The only visual clue to the difference is the matrix message De-Sire-able-Product, later replaced with 'Come Back John Lennon' on the standard version)

(My Baby Does) Good Sculptures/Flying Saucer Attack 7-inch (Sire 6078.612 November 1977)

Cold Wars/William Mysterious Overture (Sire 6198.215 1978) (Something of a rarity, as the single was recalled due to the termination of the distribution agreement between Sire and Phonogram)

Can't Stand the Rezillos LP (Sire K-5630 1978)

Top Of The Pops/20.000 Rezillos Under the Sea 7-inch (Sire SIR-4001 August 1978)

Destination Venus/Mystery Action 7-inch (Sire SIR-4008 November 1978)

Cold Wars (live)/Flying Saucer Attack (live)/Twist And Shout (live) EP (Sire SIR-4014)

Mission Accomplished... But The Beat Goes On (live) LP (Sire SRK-6069 1979)

Top Of The Pops/Destination Venus cassette single (Sire SPC3 April 1981)

Can't Stand The Rezillos: The Almost Complete Rezillos (Sire/Warner Bros 755-26942-2 1993) (One-stop shop option for Rezillos' archivists; in addition to the debut album it features the non-LP single tracks 'Destination Venus' and 'Mystery Action', plus all the tracks from Mission Accomplished aside from, criminally, set closer 'Destination Venus' and the Thunderbirds spoof intro, and extensive liner notes by Ira Robbins. IGNORE the 2005 Rhino/WEA re-release – no bonus tracks! HUH?)

Right Hand Lovers

Charlie 'Switch' Higson (vocals), Paul Whitehouse (guitar, vocals), Dave Cummings (guitar, vocals), Chris Barter (bass), Duncan Beaumont (drums) "and a long-haired greasy biker called Kevin on saxophone"

We all have to start somewhere in the entertainment business. It's well known that Charlie Higson was, well, a Higson during the early-80s. And a damned fine band they were too. I remember a gig at the Brixton Fridge where a couple of very scary girls of my acquaintance turned up. They've been following the Higsons around just because, whenever they looked at Charlie Higson, he did this very frightened look which they thought was affectation, but in retrospect may well have been terror. Unlike your common or garden lead singer, he seemed poorly equipped to deal with adulation, never mind stalking. I'm going to forward this piece to be my friends Georgina and Josephine, and I'm sure they'll be in touch. "I don't remember being scared in the Higsons," deflects Charlie. "I used to rather like the attention of female fans. Though I was always a gentleman..." But we digress.

R

Fast Show maestros Whitehouse, engaged on a splendidly titled Development Studies degree, and literature and film student Higson, started the **RIGHT HAND LOVERS** while studying at UEA in Norwich. "We formed at UEA in late 1977, mainly instigated by me and Paul Whitehouse. We both had punk leanings and I had renamed myself Switch in an effort to shed my middle class past and become truly with it. The music we played was actually just very fast R&B – with titles like 'Hampstead Girl', 'Get Lost' and 'Wrist Job' (ah, those were the days), plus the ubiquitous Velvet Underground covers – 'White Light White Heat' and 'Waiting For The Man'."

They didn't actually do much, though they did support Norwich's first punk band, the Toads, at their final show on 6 December 1977 at People's nightclub. As Higson would later tell the Observer, punk "came very much at the right time". The Pistols had been banned from UEA only a few months prior to his arrival there. "What people don't know about Paul is that he's a great guitarist and a very good singer," Higson would elaborate in the same piece.

"I can't remember supporting the Toads," he now recalls, "but then I can't remember anything from those days (large amounts of scrumpy and speed will see to that). We did play a lot of gigs in Norwich in clubs whose names I can't remember – the chief one being situated behind a burger bar. We never played outside Norwich, but did record some stuff at the UEA music department. I have a cassette tape somewhere. We kick-started a nascent Norwich punk scene, which later mutated into the Norwich scene, with bands like Serious Drinking, the Farmers Boys and the Higsons."

Whitehouse, who left college after a year ("Dropping out is BRILLIANT" – no, he didn't actually say that) would reminisce about pogo-ing to the Motors alongside long-term friend and Right Hand Lovers band-mate Dave Cummings. Cummings went on to play with Del Amitri, Lloyd Cole and others. He was an early member of the Higsons and has contributed to The Fast Show down the years (including creating the Taff Lad and Roger Nouveau 'middle class football fan' characters) as well as co-scripting Kevin And Perry Go Large etc.

"After Paul and Chris Barter were thrown out of UEA, the band fell apart. Punk was pretty well over by then anyway – and I went on to form the Higsons with Dave. Harry (Enfield) was a school friend of Dave Cummings' brother, which is how we knew him. We didn't meet him at a gig (as has previously been suggested), though he did roadie for the Higsons in the early days. I have no idea what happened to Duncan and Kevin. Chris Barter later went on to form Bonsai Forest in London with Paul and Dave. They were championed by Adrian Thrills and had a track on an NME tape. Chris also went on to play in Hackney 5-0 with some other ex-UEA friends. They were part of the country/punk/hillbilly movement that included bands like the Boot Hill Foot Tappers and the Blubbery Hellbillies, and most famously, the Pogues."

The Higson-Enfield-Whitehouse triumvirate is now part of comedy history, as Smashie and Nicey might say. I mean, I've always thought that whole sketch was a perfect send-up of bobbins mid-70s airwave complacency and inanity, but I had no idea that it was informed by ye olde year zero punk mentality. Possession of such knowledge doesn't make Smashie and Nicey any more or less funny, but context is always good.

Rikki And The Last Days Of Earth

Rikki Sylvan (aka Nicholas Condron; vocals), Valac Van Der Veene (guitar), Nik Weiss (keyboards), Hugh Inge Innes Lillingstone (drums), Andy Prince (bass)

RIKKI AND THE LAST DAYS ON EARTH, the consensus states, were posh toffs hitching a ride to the punk bandwagon, burdened further by a gloriously incongruous name. The group was formed when Sylvan, already immersed in studio technology and production, started singing along to records at a disco. The band featured fellow public school renegades Weiss and the triple-barrelled Lillingstone, who'd actually been to Eton. They were said to be able to boast 32 O-levels and six A-levels between them. This, of course, caused much sniggering among the punk community, when they weren't attempting to bury their own art school pasts.

They self-released their debut single, 'Oundle 29/5/1977', titled after the day of its recording, before a contract was offered with DJM, who would also attempt to sign Satan's Rats in an attempt to capture the punk buzz. The late Rikki Sylvan was always the main man of the quintet, being the lyricist and principal songwriter, and produced their singles (and also those of Satan's Rats too, much to their chagrin). The singles aren't too bad, but their debut album was lambasted for its 'overblown' production values. However, it has its fans, including the generally footsure Dave Thompson, who reckons it was a vital precursor to later synth-poppers like the Human League and Ultravox. The songs mined Rikki's key influences – Bowie and Roxy Music – and married them to something of an apocalyptic fervour.

With song titles like 'For The Last Days' and 'City Of The Dead', the album's opening salvo, Rikki really did believe these were the last days of earth. Lyrically, he was openly influenced by the work of Aleister Crowley (see the song 'Aleister Crowley' for incontrovertible evidence). In fact, in the press he claimed to take part in 'rituals' in order to make his records 'influential'. "Not successful, mind," he told Sheila Prophet, "influential." Legendarily Jane Suck loved the band and was poised to award their album five stars. Then she heard it and thought better of it.

DJM, meanwhile, set them off on tour with Satan's Rats, who by now loathed the sight of Rikki and his bandmates, as guitarist Steve Eagles recalled to me: "They were a bunch of ex-public school boys. Rikki with his low quavering voice, a guitarist called Valac Van der Veene and a keyboard player addicted to Benylin. They were a strange crew that, with their brand of what sounded like progressive rock, curiously, went down badly every gig." I put that to the band's Andy Prince, who definitively was not an ex-public schoolboy. "I'd like to say that although it wasn't always easy working with Rikki, I respected him greatly as a musician and feel that he never fulfilled his potential. He also had a great sense of humour. There was a tongue-in-cheek element to Rikki And The Last Days Of Earth (at least in private!) In my view, the band was irrevocably tainted by the ill-thought out Daily Mail article which was compounded by Sheila Prophet's piece."

Ah, the Daily Mail article, not exactly fertile territory for punk rockers. It was headlined 'Top Drawer Punks'. As Prince remembers, "it made much of Old Etonian Hugh's triple-barrel surname and featured such 'quotes' as 'the audiences misbehave more than we do' and 'the fans come across as totally ignorant' – both attributed to Hugh, whose father was a Crown Estate Commissioner. It also stated that three of the band were privately educated, while the 'other two' (Val and I) did 'rather well at grammar school'." Prince then pointed me in the way of a Tony Parsons quote from the Daily Mirror in 2005. "The great mass of the British public will forgive a man anything but going to Eton."

Afterwards Sylvan shortened the name to Rikki And The Last Days, released a single, 'Tokyo', then attempted to continue with a solo career, cutting the widely overlooked solo album The Silent Hours (Kaleidoscope 1981). In between he produced the Room's debut single 'Motion' at Pete Townshend's Eel Pie studios in exactly three hours – simply because someone had bet him he couldn't do it, and also helped out in Gary Numan's early career as mixing engineer on Replicas and The Pleasure Principle. He subsequently worked with Lords Of The New Church and Crown Of Thorns, alongside William Orbit, and briefly formed 3AM with former members of Random Hold (whom he'd also produced). At one point he also ran a studio underneath Miles Copeland's offices in Portobello Road. Prince would go on to work with Toyah and The Profile, who recorded an unreleased album for Polydor (see Masterswitch entry), as well as Random Hold, and spent seven years with Sham 69. Valac Van Der Veene also wrote extensively for Sounds. He once gave Tygers Of Pan Tang a single of the week award, the doofus.

DISCOGRAPHY:

Oundle 29/5/77 1-sided 33rpm 7-inch (Oundle Rocsoc May 1977) (song titles not listed, but tracks are early versions of 'City Of The Damned' and 'Picture Of Dorian Gray')
City Of The Damned/Victimised 7-inch (DJM DJS 10814 November 1977)
Loaded/Street Fighting Man 7-inch (DJM DJS 10822 1978)
Four Minute Warning LP (DJM DJF 20526 1978)
Twilight Jack/No Wave 7-inch (DJM DJS 10860 1978)

The Rings

Twink (aka John Alder; vocals), Alan Lee Shaw (guitar), Rod Latter (drums), Dennis Stow (bass)

THE RINGS weren't in their first flush of youth when punk started, and taking a name inspired by Tolkein hardly punctured suspicions about their authenticity. Indeed, Twink had been a journeyman contributor to a whole host of psychedelic pop bands, notably Tomorrow, the Pretty Things and the Pink Fairies. However, the Rings gave him the chance to emerge from behind the drum stool. The material drew on old Pink Fairies songs as well as a clutch of originals penned by Shaw ("I use the name Alan Lee Shaw because when I joined the PRS, there was already an Alan Shaw, so I used my middle name Lee to register").

A one-off deal with Chiswick resulted in the single 'I Wanna Be Free', backed by 'Automobile', in May 1977, produced by Radio Stars bass player Martin Gordon. They played a series of shows around London punk haunts the 100 Club, Roxy, Marquee and Music Machine, supporting the Heartbreakers, where Jane Suck caught them in June 1977: "Twink and his band juggle superb old Fairies numbers with transparent new songs: 'Chelsea 77', 'Teenage Rebel'... Are the boys surprised the audience scream for a bucket when they round off the set with 'I Wanna Get High'? Which bus to Woodstock, mate." Others were slightly more charitable, including Dick Tracy in the NME. "I watched Rings for a good ten minutes before grokking on the fact that the lead singer was none other than Twink, ex-Fairies drummer, who has undergone a severe restyling job. Gone are the waist-length curls and velvet suits of yesteryear, to be replaced by a close crop, ragged denim and heavy shades. The band rock out in style, running through a mixture of originals plus old MC5 numbers, but Twink's Iggy impersonation comes over more like the Notre Dame hunchback."

However, after the release of the single the band sundered, Twink announcing he was tired of being used as gobbing target practice after a particularly phlegm-filled evening supporting the Damned in July at the Marquee. Which was just as well, as the Rings' new bass player Robert Crash, later a producer for the Eurythmics, had concurrently decided that Twink was a hippy, and he hated hippies. The other members elected to form the Maniacs instead in August 1977. Twink kept the Rings going with former members of the Fairies and played at the Mont De Marsan Punk Festival. As did the Maniacs. Shaw: "The Rings were billed on the poster (which I still have) to perform at Mont de Marsan. The Maniacs were not on the bill until Marc Zermati asked us to be included at the festival as the Rings had folded. Twink threatened to sue Marc as he said the Rings were on the poster. So Marc relented and Twink put a makeshift Rings together to perform. It was all a bit of a storm in a tea cup."

A new Rings line-up including Sandy Sanderson and Chris Chesney completed the engagement. There were rumours of a further single, 'Psychedelic Punkaroo', and an album, but neither actually materialised. Afterwards there were also brief rumours of a band involving Chrissie Hynde before Twink worked with Elton Motello and then started turning up in TV staples like Allo Allo and Chocky's Challenge.

DISCOGRAPHY:

I Wanna Be Free/Automobile 7-inch (Chiswick S14 May 1977)

COMPILATIONS:

Long Shots, Dead Certs And Odds On Favourites LP (Chiswick CH 5 1978; 'I Wanna Be Free')

The Chiswick Story 2-CD box set (CDWIK2 100 March 1992; 'I Wanna Be Free')

Ripchords

Sean Dromgoole (vocals), Morris Gould (aka Maurice Gold, bass), Johnathan Jetlag (guitar), Michael Trei (drums)

South west punk band the RIPCHORDS released one solid EP in 1979, featuring some excellent lyrics, as part of the deluge of indie punk records of that era. The lead-track from the EP has been anthologised on at least two semi-legal compilations. Sean Dromgoole, now working in marketing ("which would have Vic Godard turning in his grave if he was dead") offered some bon mots.

"What to say? We didn't bump into other bands much because we were all secluded in darkest Somerset. Our sound wasn't instantly embraced either – I remember being booed off on a couple of occasions. We just loved what we did. It was Ramones covers to begin with and then I remember getting really into things when we covered Iggy Pop's 'Sick Of You'. Then we started writing our own stuff. They did some of my songs to begin with but slowly – and with a lot of biting cynicism – Maurice's talent began to emerge. His songs were more cynicism proof and therefore qualified – they were better too. One highlight was phoning up the Clash road manager – Johnny Green – and talking him into letting us be roadies for the Clash. For free of course. They were genuine democrats, especially Headon and Strummer – tried to get us to kip on the floor of their rooms but we said no, we're fine in the van – loving it! Three days later and with severe lumbago we bailed. I then went to Afghanistan and came back to find that, at the age of 18 we had a record deal – of sorts. We recorded the EP. John Peel liked it. We were off. Except we weren't. Maurice left school and the whole thing petered out."

Maurice Gould would go on to play with the Rhythm Method before becoming Mixmaster Morris, the famed rave, techno and ambient DJ noted for his collaborations with the Shamen alongside a plethora of solo releases, often under the title Rising Force. "Maurice and I stayed in touch – he DJs at a big party I do each August. The other guys I don't know – I'd like to see them – all those sweaty Sundays in band rehearsals should mean something!"

DISCOGRAPHY:

The Ripchords 7-inch EP (Cells Sell 1 October 1978)
Ringing In The Streets/Music's/Peace Artist/Television Television

Rivals

Mark Edwards (guitar, vocals), Marc Hebden (drums), Paul Leinster (bass, vocals)

Margate, Kent pop-punk band who are fondly remembered for two mustard-cutting recordings for Ace Records, particularly their cover of Them's 'Here Comes The Night', which is deftly executed, albeit in riotous fashion. This lot could certainly play, so it seems odd that they've sank into total obscurity. Ah, let's rescue them.

Leinster and Edwards had started messing about in the latter's mother's house in the mid-70s, when she was at bingo, pretending to be Bowie or Bolan, as the mood took them. Their first rehearsal as the **RIVALS** took place on Boxing Day 1977, after the participants had seen the Sex Pistols giving it plenty on So It Goes. The line-up was completed with the addition of drummer Marc Hebden, who was able to offer rehearsal space at his parents' home. Eventually the trio scrounged together enough money for a single, 'Future Rights', backed by 'Flowers'. Partially financed by Leinster's girlfriend's mum, it was glued together by the band and sold via mail order. It was also distributed to local record shops "and the usual bunking of the Ramsgate to Victoria train to ensure copies were delivered to Beggars Banquet, Rough Trade and other outlets". Thereafter school friend Paul Daley became their new drummer, as the band adopted a pub in Herne Bay as their permanent rehearsal space.

They recorded two further studio sessions, but these failed to elicit a response. However, the studio owner was quite smitten with the group's version of 'Here Comes The Night', which they'd discovered via David Bowie. Much to the band's surprise, the song became a radio hit when released as a single, played by the usually conservative Mike Read, no less. They were, of course, expectant of a John Peel play, and sure enough, he did indeed play their version, after first offering up Them's original (the first time that the band had heard it) and noting that "the next version will blow this one away".

All well and good, but the band simply didn't possess the logistics to press copies to satisfy demand. Manager Terry Noon told them that, following a single of the week accolade in Record Mirror, there were offers on the table from the majors for distribution. These were declined. It still pisses them off to this day.

Thereafter Daley left the group due to that standby excuse, musical differences. Leinster informed him that he'd never make it "with that attitude". Daley, of course, then went on to sell millions of records with Leftfield. The group's third drummer was Stan Gretsch, who also played with the Ignerents, but died in a police car chase after stealing a BMW in 1980. That persuaded Edwards to quit the band and he duly formed Naughty Thoughts and later the Gems. He went on to play with the Last Resort (alongside old pal Roi Pearce, who was one of the Rivals' biggest fans), the Heavy Metal Outlaws and eventually a later incarnation of the Anti-Nowhere League. Leinster worked with Theatre Of Hate spin-off band Under 2 Flags.

R

DISCOGRAPHY:

Future Rights/Flowers 7-inch (Ace ACE 007 1979)
Here Comes The Night/Both Sides 7-inch (Oakwood/Ace ACE 011 1980)
COMPILATION:
Punk Rock Rarities Vol. 1 CD (Anagram CDPUNK 63 1995; 'Here Comes The Night', 'Both Sides')
ARCHIVE RELEASE:
If Only... LP and CD (Detour RUBBISHLP007/RUBBISHCD007 2005) (vinyl version features different track-listing: 'Here Comes The Night', 'American Faces', 'Future Rights', 'Rose Of England', 'Women Of The East', 'Weekdays', 'Bastard Blues', 'Mine All Mine', 'Both Sides (demo version)', 'Good Times', 'Flowers', 'Can't Help It At All)'. "Only 25 years too late, but well worth the wait," states the PR).

Rockets

Andy Colquhoun (guitar), Jimmy Coull (vocals), Val Haller (aka Adrian Osbourne, the 'Anadin Kid'; bass), Dave Rochelle (drums)

The ROCKETS were active on the London scene in 1976, often to be found supporting friends the Clash. Their revolving cast of drummers included Stewart Copeland, who played for the band when they supported the (subsequently banned) Damned at the Nashville, towards the end of their brief career. "In 1975 we were all heavily into Dr Feelgood, who had a residency at the Kensington Pub round the corner," Colquhoun recalled to Punk77. Lyrics were provided by manager Frank Day, a friend of Dave Rochelle who had started the band via an advertisement in Melody Maker. Day worked for the London council by day, and by night, when he wasn't promoting shows for the Rockets, as a croupier.

The Rockets became attuned to the new punk spirit via imported Ramones and Patti Smith records. They also cut a six-track demo in 1976, featuring covers of 'Walking The Dog' and the Animals' 'Baby Let Me Take You Home'. Originals on the tape included the heavily Feelgood-indebted 'A Shot Of Rhythm 'n' Blues' and 'Speeding'. However, the arrival of punk, and the musical acceleration this engendered, saw the band unsure of its strengths. The result was a schism with Rochelle and Frank Day drifting away, the former to join the Pleasers. Colquhoun: "An NME reviewer stated that 'we couldn't make up our minds as to whether we were the Ramones or the Pretty Things'. I think that was fair enough, really. We were both. With the drummer and replacements gone, we decided to go further out and planned Warsaw Pakt."

Warsaw Pakt (see separate entry) recorded and released an album in a day, but were then dropped by their record label. As Colquhoun told me via email in 2005, "Clearly the Rockets were a big deal to me. When I joined the Rockets in 1975 the music scene was gentle and stale. The Eagles plagued the radios and jukeboxes of the nation. 'Musicians' were everywhere and they were skilled, but it was all so damned boring. The Rockets reached back into the abundant pool of great R&B songs and learned a set of high-energy cover versions. After a while they developed another bunch of original tunes, which formed the basis of the Warsaw Pakt set." Colquhoun subsequently joined Brian James's Tanz Der Youth, later playing with the Pink Fairies and Wayne Kramer of MC5.

Rowdies

Alan Emms (vocals), Robert Emms (rhythm guitar), Steve Sharpe (lead guitar), Kevin 'Elly' Ellison (bass), Paul Cooke (drums)

R

The ROWDIES formed in Evesham, Worcestershire, in November 1976, with a line-up initially featuring Alan Emms (vocals), Robert Emms (bass), Steve Sharpe (guitar) and Paul Cooke (drums). The name arose directly from Robert Emms' involvement in terrace violence at Worcester's St George's Lane football ground during an FA Cup tie, which resulted in injuries to 70 fans and four police officers. The resultant local headlines screamed, variously, "Football rowdies hit the city" and "Five Football Rowdies Fined". The latter headline accompanied a picture of Robert Emms and his co-accused leaving court after paying their fines.

By Christmas Kevin 'Elly' Ellison had taken over on bass, allowing Robert Emms to move to rhythm and Sharpe to lead guitar. Their debut show came in March 1977 at Evesham Town Hall, though Cooke managed to get so inebriated he fell off his drum stool during the performance. Well, it's one way of keeping time. He was replaced by Richard Kershaw as the band played regular gigs in a 60-mile radius of Evesham, appearing with the Police and Lurkers in Birmingham and X-Ray Spex in Redditch (which ended in a dust-up outside between 'punks' and 'straights'). There were also shows in Coventry and with young bucks the Spunes, whom the Rowdies all but adopted, in Worcester. Again, another mini-riot ensued.

The Rowdies entered the studio for the first time in August 1977. As Robert Emms recalls: "A member of a heavy metal band who were there waiting to record was so impressed by what he heard that he phoned up the studio's owner Muff, who soon offered us a recording deal." Muff's first move to was give the band a sack containing £15 in 50p pieces. Off they went to Worcester, where they fed the pieces into a cramped photo both and took the pictures that adorn the sleeve of 'A.C.A.B.'. Robert: "I am not going to pass comment about whether or not some of the money Muff gave us might have been spent at a Worcester pub." The single's title, which was of course an acronym for the popular (though not within the constabulary) saying 'All Coppers Are Bastards', predictably stirred up further local controversy. The band, meanwhile, informed Muff that it actually stood for 'All Coppers Are Beautiful'.

In May 1978 Alan left after a disagreement, and Robert tried to keep the band afloat until August 1978. Robert "My vocal style was just too different. Alan has a real depth and soul to his voice and to see him perform live is really incredible. We had played about 50 to 60 gigs in our existence and without Alan it was time to put it to rest." Robert had a break from band life but eventually got the itch again and put together mod/power pop group RPM, with fellow former Rowdies Steve Sharpe and Richard Kershaw, which lasted until September 1979.

By January 1980 brothers Alan and Robert had reunited with Ellison to form the skinhead punk band Spoils Of War (Robert: "I'd been a skinhead back in the late 60s"). It's been reported that Steve Sharpe subsequently joined mod revivalists Steve Sharp and the Cleancuts (who released 'We Are The Mods' for Happy Face in 1980, one of that movement's most collectable singles), but 'tis all porkies, according to Robert.

As Brian of Grand Theft Audio Records points out: "The Rowdies were one of the great unsung, anthemic, hard-as-nails proto street punk bands, and Spoils Of War could compete with Shock Troops-era Cock Sparrer, they were that good. That duo of brothers, Alan and Robert Emms, produced pure punk rock magic, no doubt about it."

DISCOGRAPHY:

A.C.A.B./Negative Malfunction/Freeze Out 7-inch (Birds Nest BN 109 1978)

Rudi

Brian Young (guitar, vocals), Ronnie Matthews (guitar), Leigh Carson (bass), Drew Brown (drums)

RUDI are often perceived to be the bridesmaids to Stiff Little Fingers and the Undertones in the Northern Irish punk scene, but, alongside the Outcasts, deserve merit for being the real instigators and pathfinders of that movement. Although they produced a series of fine singles, they never did achieve the breakthrough they long seemed destined for. And while punk's history has largely been annotated from London, and chiefly concerns those that made their impression there, it's important to remember that in Northern Ireland, Rudi had the largest fanbase of any of their peers.

Among those who have acknowledged their influence are Tuam's Saw Doctors and Therapy? – both of whom have recorded covers of Rudi's touchstone debut single, 'Big Time'. And Guy Trelford and Sean O'Neill's excellent It Makes You Want To Spit tome finally puts the band's importance into context. Rudi, effectively, was the jumping off point for everything that followed in the province.

Formed in East Belfast by a bunch of school friends in thrall to glam rock, their name was taken from the 1973 single 'Oo Oo Rudi' issued by obscure John's Children offshoots the Jook. Significantly, the song included the lyrics "All we hear and all we see/And everything we learn from/Is planned by the older generation." Main man Brian Young's world had been turned around completely by catching the New York Dolls on The Old Grey Whistle Test – when Bob Harris dismissed them as 'mock rock'. From then on, he'd become a man on a mission.

They began covering rock classics and the glam standards of the era, with Johnny Stewart brought in on bass and Graham 'Grimmy' Marshall switched to drums after the departure of Carson and Brown, the former because of his affection for heavy metal. Grimmy would nick boiler suits from his workplace which were then customised to become the band 'uniform'. "The first stuff Rudi played was old rock'n'roll and glam, which to me are the same thing anyways," Young confirmed to me. "I learned the guitar playing along to a Chuck Berry LP, as the Dolls and T-Rex stuff was too complicated for me to figure out... sad but true!" Writer

Guy Trelford also credits both Eddie And The Hot Rods and Dr Feelgood as primal influences. "Their gigs took place long before the Clash or any big name punk bands visited these shores, and at a time when Belfast was well and truly erased from the map as far as touring bands were concerned. Feelgood and the Hot Rods were, in my opinion, just as influential to the fledgling NI punk scene as the Clash and Pistols were."

By 1976 Rudi had begun to play private parties in the absence of proper gigs, such as Glenmachen and the Girton Lodge, though their set, still predominantly covers, remained an amalgam of influences – the 60s, mod, glam, pub rock and punk. They were then initiated into the cult of the Ramones. But their final conversion was borne out of the Clash's pulled gig at the Belfast Ulster Hall in October 1977 due to insurance cover being withdrawn. The outraged punks responded by blockading Bedford Street in pitched battles with the RUC. The Rudi song 'Cops' was written as a direct response to this incident.

Stewart then left to be replaced by original Stiff Little Fingers bass player Gordon Blair, after he'd answered an advert in Rocky Mungo's record shop for a "young, pretty, bass guitarist – no hippies". They first came to the attention of Terri Hooley, of the Good Vibrations shop at Great Victoria Street and later record label, when playing alongside the Outcasts at the Pound in January 1978. "I felt I was back in the 60s again when Belfast had a lot of clubs and a lot of good bands," Hooley enthused. They also picked up a support to the Buzzcocks, who had to cancel when their van broke down, leaving Rudi as headliners, then a show with Stiff Little Fingers and the Adverts at Queen's University. The Buzzcocks slot, incidentally, came about via Morrissey, whom Young knew threw their shared membership of the New York Dolls fan club.

They made their debut with 'Big Time' c/w 'No. 1', originally envisioned as a flexidisc to be given away with a fanzine (mirroring Stiff Little Fingers' experience with 'Alternative Ulster' – there are also those who allege that SLF's '78RPM' is based directly on 'Big Time'). They abandoned the idea when advised by Terri Hooley that they could issue their own single for the same cost. It was recorded with George Doherty and then manager Kyle Leitch of Caroline Music in two hours at Templepatrick Studios in February. It was the first release on Good Vibrations, in April 1977, and immediately attracted critical support. "This band almost remind you of what it was that was so appealing about the punks when it first started," reckoned Bob Edmands in the NME. Garry Bushell at Sounds went so far as to list the address for Good Vibrations' A&R department (like they really had an A&R department) to encourage major labels to seek them out. "I was surprised at the time (as everyone was) that their Good Vibes single 'Big Time' didn't do more for them, because they certainly deserved it," reckons Protex's Dave McMaster. "Rudi were the inspiration for a lot of local bands and their influence cannot be underestimated. Remember the scene in Belfast at the time? Nothing going on but fear – bands like Rudi were instrumental in creating the possibility of something more."

On the back of the single, the group temporarily relocated to London, which was "hopelessly naïve", according to Hooley. After siphoning enough fuel to make the trip, on which they were accompanied by Gavin Martin of Alternative Ulster fanzine, they found themselves sleeping in the van until old friend Dennis Forbes, whose band Pretty Boy Floyd had made a similarly reckless journey across the water, found them a squat in Clapham. They managed to secure a support slot to the Doomed (aka the reformed Damned) at the Electric Circus, and also supported Stiff Little Fingers there too, as well as playing regularly with close friends Raped.

But despite tentative talks with both Malcolm McLaren and Bernie Rhodes, as well as Polydor, they failed to pick up a management or label deal. Matthews and Marshall were jailed for a week by the SPG after the Clapham squats were busted, before they high-tailed it back to Belfast under threat of a six-month jail sentence. In the interim they starred on a second Good Vibrations release, contributing 'Overcome By Fumes' to Battle Of The Bands, a four-track double single additionally featuring the Outcasts, Idiots (who featured Brian's younger brother Barry) and the Spiders.

1979 began with an appearance in the Northern Ireland punk movie Shell Shock Rock and the Dark Space Festival in Dublin, alongside U2. They went down so well at the latter they were asked to play the second night also, at which they were joined by Terri Hooley for their encore, who delighted onlookers by removing his glass eye and waving it to the crowd. At this stage a deal was offered with Polydor, on the proviso they sacked Grimmy as drummer. It was impolitely declined. Instead the group set off on the Good Vibrations' package tour with the Outcasts and Tearjerkers.

Their second own-name release, the 'I Spy' EP, preceded another foray into England, by which time Gordy, somewhat unstable due to his drinking, was considered surplus to requirements. He eventually joined the Outcasts, while Matthews switched to bass. They appeared alongside the Undertones on the BBC2 youth programme Something Else in early 1980 – the source of much bickering between the two bands. The Undertones claimed they were heckled by Rudi fans, though Rudi denied any involvement, and insisted that their performance be re-recorded in an empty studio. The two songs Rudi recorded, 'Who You' and 'The Pressure's On', although only the former was screened, were due to have been issued as a single for Good Vibrations, but when that failed to materialise, they split from the label due to their frustration with Hooley's chaotic business methods. The tracks were bootlegged by fans anyway.

They returned to London for the first time in a year to undertake a headlining show at the Action Space in February followed by a March appearance at the Sense Of Ireland festival, sandwiching another TV appearance, this time on Good Evening Ulster, hosted by Gloria Hunniford. After recording their first BBC Session for Mike Read there was a talk of a projected new deal with Target Records, but the label collapsed before it got off the runway. Things seemed to get back on track with an offer from Pete Waterman to sign them to Ariola in Germany, but in the end they signed a recording contract with Jamming! – the label formed by Paul Weller in consort with magazine editor Tony Fletcher. 'When I Was Dead' followed, produced by Jam sidekick Pete Wilson, featuring the punk-reggae tinged 'Bewarewolf!' and the reclaimed 'The Pressure's On' on the B-side. Paul Weller, who kept his name off the record so as not to arouse suspicion, kept the studio budget to zero by sneaking them into Polydor's studios under a false name. It was followed by 'Crimson', single of the week in Sounds, by which time they'd added keyboard player Paul Martin of Pretty Boy Floyd And The Gems (who appeared on their third and final BBC session, for Kid Jensen, following on from another for John Peel during 1981).

They then supported the Jam on their Transglobal Unity Express tour, playing in front of packed audiences with the headlining act at the peak of their powers. Paul Weller and father John helped them set up their own tour in April and May. Another highlight was a blistering set at the 1982 Lady Of The Lake festival in Fermanagh, as the band readied their next release, 'Love Is Electric', with studio time booked at Abbey Road. But it was no fun for anyone when the Jam split up, including Rudi, who found themselves without a label after Jamming! folded, shelving plans to issue the single. It was one setback too many, and the band broke up, with Matthews, Young and Marshall re-emerging as Station Superheaven, specialising in Detroit-flavoured guitar rock (although some songs were more keyboard-textured). They were apparently almost signed by Tamla Motown at one point. Brian Young subsequently formed first the Tigersharks then the Roughnecks and finally the still extant Sabrejets, playing rockabilly around Belfast. Blair, who went on to spells with the Outcasts, Ruefrex and Big Self, moved to London to run Brixton's Ritz cinema. He was last heard of playing with cult Australians Dave Graney And The Coral Snakes, having moved permanently to Melbourne, though he is now involved in multi-media projects. Matthews and Marshall threw in the towel.

The prolific Young, still as faithful to the cause of rock'n'roll and he ever was, is currently behind the Ulster punk supergroup Shame Academy, alongside Greg Cowan of the Outcasts and Petesy Burns of Stalag 17. Shame Academy played their debut show at the launch party for It Makes You Want To Spit in November 2003 after being convinced to do so by the book's authors. They have kept going on and off ever since, and at the end of 2004 released Punk Rock For Dummies for Combat Rock.

As an epilogue to the Rudi story, Big Time was used as the title of the 2002 biopic of Terri Hooley's life. Which was fitting, as Henry McDonald noted in the Observer, because the single "is still one of the most perfect pop songs to come out of this island".

Discography:

Big Time/Number One 7-inch (Good Vibrations GOT 1 April 1978) (this was reissued in October 1979 with a completely different sleeve – which was a shame, as the original Boris Karloff in lipstick design looked great)

I Spy 7-inch EP (Good Vibrations GOT 12 July 1979)
I Spy/Genuine Reply/Sometimes/Ripped In Two
When I Was Dead/Bewarewolf!/The Pressure's On 7-inch EP (Jamming! CREATE 1 August 1981)
Crimson/14 Steps 7-inch (Jamming! CREATE 3 February 1982)
ARCHIVE RELEASES:
Big Time (The Best Of Rudi) CD (Anagram CD Punk 77 September 1996) (compiled by Brian Young, who wrote the sleevenotes, because he was fed up with other people reissuing the band's material without permission)
The Pressure's On/Who? You 7-inch (Bad Vibrations – Last Year's Youth Records LAST 2 1990) (the second GV single finally sees the light of day. 500 copies. Check the sarky label title)
14 Steps To Death 7-inch EP (Last Year's Youth LAST 5 2001)
14 Steps To Death/Crimson/Radio On/The Prince Of Pleasure (another vinyl release by the German label, containing unreleased 1981 tracks. 500 copies)
Yummy Yummy 7-inch EP (Last Year's Youth LAST 9 2002)
Yummy Yummy/Without You/Time To Be Proud/The Pressure's On (another 500 pressings with two different picture sleeves)
The Band That Time Forgot LP (Last Year's Youth LAST BIG 1 2002) (comes with a free booklet and coloured vinyl, limited edition of 900)
The Complete Rudi Singles Collection LP (Last Year's Youth Records LAST BIG 3 2002) (limited edition, with free 7-inch EP)

Ruefrex

Allan Clarke (vocals), Tom Coulter (bass), Jackie Forgie (guitar), Paul Burgess (drums)

Belfast's RUEFREX were born into the Protestant working class stronghold of the Shankill Road. Pupils at the Boys Model School on Ballysillan Road, Burgess and Coulter formed Roofwrecks at the end of 1977, rehearsing after school at Coulter's parents' house in Deerpark Road. Coulter initially tried out as singer, but was quickly replaced by Ivan Kelly. They started out with two guitarists but eventually recruited Forgie instead, rehearsing at the Glenbryn Community Centre, which hosted most of their early gigs.

They were completely immersed in music from the age of 13 onwards, and became obsessive about Bowie, Lou Reed and Alice Cooper, Roxy Music and Mott The Hoople. Burgess: "I was lucky to have a very motivated music teacher at primary school. The less said about my efforts on violin and recorder the better. Anyhow, he knew I was mad on drums and taught me to read music for percussion (not always necessary in the case of Ruefrex!) It since stood me in good stead. I was also a side drummer for an Orange band (wince!). Closest thing to being a local rock star before punk!" Those weren't the only skeletons in the closet, however. "We were incredibly possessive and draconian about what should be listened to and what not. We would have our own Maoist cultural persecutions! However, we were also very perverse about joining anything and subsequently refused to comply with any fashion. In this regard I think we were culturally more like the Fall. We kinda hated everyone and didn't wish to belong to any gang but our own. This partly explains why we were roundly hated by our peers. That and the simmering threat of physical violence! But yes, we did have our skeletons that were only whispered about – Black Sabbath, Gabriel era Genesis, King Crimson, Hawkwind!"

But it was the arrival of punk with its energy and immediacy that acted as the catalyst to make music on their own terms. Pretty quickly they were adding covers of punk staples such as the Adverts' 'Gary Gilmore's Eyes', the Hot Rods' 'Do Anything You Wanna Do' and Sham 69's 'Ulster Boy' to their set, alongside three separate Wire covers and the Monkees' 'Last Train To Clarksville'. Meanwhile, Burgess was beginning to shape his poems into lyrics.

Roofwrecks' most notable early show was as support to Stiff Little Fingers at the Trident in Bangor, whose Brian Falloon helped them out with the loan of a bass drum. From here on, the two bands, primarily drawn from the same Protestant community, saw their fates intertwine on several levels. Ironically, of course, SLF became known as Northern Ireland's de facto 'political punk band'. Ruefrex were never as well known on the mainland, but they were always far more explicit and dealt in political specifics. Where SLF stated their religion and background was unimportant, Ruefrex never shied away from stating what they were and where they came from, whilst all the time attempting to overcome those barriers and suspicions. The name Ruefrex was adopted simply as a "nonsense word to head-fuck journalists with". It meant nothing more than that, though that didn't stop writers theorising about it.

In April 1979 Ivan Kelly left the band to take up an invitation to replace Ian Lowery in the Wall. He was swiftly replaced by Allan Clarke, another Shankill local who "knew how to take care of himself". As did all the band, for that matter. Thereafter local maverick businessman cum music enthusiast Terri Hooley offered them the chance to record a debut EP. It actually took a bit of prodding to get Hooley to get his act together. But there were certainly no other offers on the table at that stage.

The EP's opening track was 'One By One', alongside 'The Ruah' (Hebrew for Holy Ghost) one of the earliest originals the band had written, partially inspired by James Plunkett's novel Strumpet City. You could see the connection Burgess was making with a novel that is one of the greats of Irish realism, depicting the misery of the tenement slums of Dublin and the injustice of trade union lock-outs. The clergy emerge as self-serving villains (the "Bibles clutched in bloody hands" in Burgess's lyric) while the middle classes are murderously unconcerned with the plight of their workers. 'Cross The Line' was a protest against contemporary sectarian in-fighting. They had already made clear their policy of playing to mixed audiences (in Northern Ireland, that meant Protestants and Catholics rather than black and white).

Later they would play benefits for the integrated secondary school Lagan College. Their opposition to sectarianism brought them enemies in both camps. "We evoked the wrath of both communities, although it was probably more politically incorrect and damaging to be portrayed as the 'Prod' band as opposed, say, to That Petrol Emotion as the 'oppressed' RC one. You'll still find – in regard to arts and cultural undertakings – that the Ulster Protestant community must overcome these initial prejudicial comparisons with the perceived cultural oppression of South Africa, Israel and the like. You can only sing with credibility about your own experience and culture. Or, of course, reject it and adopt some bogus stance. On the personal endangerment front, there are plenty of stories that I won't recount here. But they involved a gig in the killing grounds of the Shankill Butchers; being chased at gunpoint from the Harp after playing Sham 69's 'Ulster Boy' and having a succession of police and ambulances sent to my parents' house on the pretext of my murder! This followed a volley of pool balls through their windows after interviews I gave legitimising (in theory) a conditional United Ireland. I guess we must have been getting to the right people!"

They played three more support shows to Stiff Little Fingers at Cork City Hall, Mansion House, Dublin, and the Ulster Hall, Belfast, during September 1980. But by the Mansion House gig their relationship with Stiff Little Fingers was beginning to unravel. Ruefrex were targeted by some of the less progressive local Catholics, who attempted to stub out cigarettes on Clarke's bare torso. Clarke responded by undoing his belt and coshing the nearest troublemaker. That incident and others saw Stiff Little Fingers distance themselves from their increasingly troublesome and violence-prone support band. There was another, more significant moment of division, too. Burgess: "We had a close friend who died in a confused incident in West Belfast. This guy lived close to Burnsy but – as he hung with us – he derided their musical pretensions as we did. We were very pissed then, when his story appeared as 'Wasted Life', an SLF anthem. In a nutshell, we didn't believe that they ever had the cojones to occupy or deliver on their claims. There was a credibility gap that was fuelled by some careful management to make sure that they remained on the fence. Of course we were jealous as fuck when they were on Top Of The Pops and swore we would never do it!"

However, when Hooley's financial difficulties cut down Good Vibrations, Ruefrex's career was seemingly taken down with it. Coulter and Forgie messed around with various musical projects that didn't come to fruition. Clarke left to get married and Burgess, having previously worked at Short Brothers aircraft manufacturers, took up teaching and started his degree.

It was four years before they recorded again, prompted by an old friend from Dublin, Gareth Ryan, who had set up Kabuki Records in London. In the interim Forgie had left to form Colenso Parade, though he was still featured on the subsequent release, drawn from a Downtown Radio live session in March 1980. 'Capital Letters', a cryptic anti-nuclear protest, was a fantastic effort, building incrementally from Burgess's Scabies-like Armageddon percussion to a roaring crescendo. Yet absolutely no-one, seemingly, bought it. Gary Ferris was recruited as the new guitarist in time for the follow-up, 'Paid In Kind', released on One To One Records, a label set up by Keith McCormack in tribute to the band's first EP. The B-side, 'The Perfect Crime', came from the same Downtown radio session that produced 'Capital Letters'.

But their big break came with 'The Wild Colonial Boy', an attack on Americans donating blindly to terrorist organisations without reckoning on the consequences, specifically NORAID. Written in 1980 by Burgess, the studio time was paid for by a London friend. "We recorded 'Wild Colonial Boy' off our own bat, with our own money, and said fuck it, we're not going to compromise at all," Burgess told Tony McGartland. "So we stuck the Armalite on the cover, put the lyrics on the back and didn't expect any BBC play because it was too hot to handle. It was going to be our last shot. This was the song we felt had to be done, for every reason. Because of what we were trying to say."

Strangely, it all came together. Janice Long began playing the single, gave the band a session, and that led to performances of 'Capital Letters' and 'Paid In Kind' on the BBC's Channel One programme, and 'The Wild Colonial Boy' and 'The Ruah' on Channel 4's The Tube. The success of 'Wild Colonial Boy' resulted in a new deal with Kasper Records via Stiff's Dave Robinson, who licensed the label. Flowers For All Occasions was released in 1986, its title-track denouncing the then prevalent sectarian murders from a studiously neutral position ("Orange lilies, Shamrock greens/Bloody scarlet, Poppy Red"). The other standout was 'Even In The Dark Hours', demonstrating that the band could also write perfectly formed contemporary rock songs dwelling on subjects outside of the troubles.

However, their progress was disrupted with the departure of Coulter, with the well-travelled Gordon Blair (ex-SLF, Rudi, Outcasts) replacing him, while Burgess persuaded Forgie to rejoin. 'The Wild Colonial Boy', with production credited to Mick Glossop, was reissued on a 12-inch with a new cover (a wee drummer boy accompanied by the stars and stripes). The mainstream beckoned, with cover features in the Melody Maker (who asked: "Are they the most important band in Britain?" while again playing up Clarke's 'macho' image in a piece that verged on the homo-erotic) and a full roster of support slots to the Pogues and SLF.

But the projected second album, Political Wings, was never going to happen, principally because the band's core creative partnership, between Burgess and Coulter, was over. Although a mini-album did eventually emerge, the live studio snapshot Political Wings (sometimes referred to as Playing Cards With Dead Men), Burgess decided to pull the plug. He has since gone on to study at Oxford and Cork Universities, where he now lectures, and completed his PhD. He has published two books – A Crisis of Conscience: – moral ambivalence and education in Northern Ireland and The Reconciliation Industry: – Community relations, community identity & social policy in Northern Ireland. His latest poetry book is titled after an old Ruefrex song, 'Correct Your Fireside Manner'.

Forgie, who is a community worker in Belfast, formed a new band, the Black Taxi Ballads, in 2002, cutting a song, 'Shadows Over Windsor Park', which dealt with the Neil Lennon incident (awarded the Northern Irish football captaincy, he was subjected to death threats from loyalists because he was a Catholic). Coulter and Kelly work for the Northern Ireland Housing Executive. Clarke is a taxi driver. Ruefrex reformed in 2003, their most high profile shows coming at the benefit for Terri Hooley at the Empire Music Hall, Belfast, in September 2003. Stiff Little Fingers' drummer Brian Falloon filled the drum stool for the absent Burgess, who was in America. They also appeared at the launch party for Guy Trelford and Sean O'Neill's wonderful celebration of the Belfast punk scene, It Makes You Want To Spit. At both events, they were overwhelmed by the residual affection they were able to tap into. And, as a direct result, they've started to put together some new material with the hope of recording it in the near future.

DISCOGRAPHY:

One By One 7-inch EP (Good Vibrations GOT 8 1979)
One By One/Cross The Line/Don't Panic
Capital Letters/April Fool 7-inch (Kabuki KAR 7 April 1983)
Paid In Kind/The Perfect Crime 7-inch (One By One 1x1 1984)
Flowers For All Occasions LP (Kasper KATLP 1 1985) (though never officially re-released,

the band did issue a 1,000 copy CD-ROM version of the album).

The Wild Colonial Boy (Parts 1 & 2)/Even In The Dark Hours 7-inch (Kasper KAS 2 1986) (12-inch version, 12 KAS 2, adds 'The Wild Colonial Boy (extended version)')

In The Traps/Leaders Of The Last Resort 7-inch (Kasper KAS 3 1986) (also available as a 12-inch, 12 KAS 3)

Political Wings mini-LP (Flicknife BLUNT 041 1987) (recorded live at the Chocolate Factory Studio, London. Other songs cut at this session, 'Fightin' 36th', 'April Fool', 'Between Having And Wanting', 'Middle Ground', remained unreleased until the 2005 Cherry Red CD)

ARCHIVE RELEASE:

Capital Letters – The Best Of Ruefrex CD (Cherry Red CDMRED 290 September 2005) (this is one I put together with the help of the band, who produced lots of original artwork and photos, etc, to produce a decent package. We had to trim the songs to fit it all on to one CD – so, for example, 'Cross the Line' got cropped from the first Good Vibrations release, but at least you can find that elsewhere on the Good Vibrations compilation. The sleevenotes were written alongside Paul Burgess, using some of the material you'll read here, with a few nips and tucks)

COMPILATIONS:

Good Vibrations – The Punk Singles Collection CD (Anagram CD PUNK 36 1994; 'Cross The Line')

Ruts

Malcolm Owen (vocals), Paul Fox (guitar), Dave Ruffy (bass), Paul Mattocks (drums)

Was there ever a more musically taut group in punk's early history? Did anybody ever match the RUTS' sequence of white hot singles, 'In A Rut', 'Babylon's Burning', 'Staring At The Rude Boys', 'Something That I Said' and '(West One) Shine On Me?' Not for me the Pistols – play 'Babylon's Burning' back to back with the released version of 'Anarchy In The UK' and tell me which one sounds urgent and contemporary rather than merely declamatory and stolid.

The Clash might have been the more consistent album act, but compared to the sumptuous production and juggernaut rhythms of the Ruts they occasionally sound tinny on 45. And while the Clash are justifiably saluted for their eclectic exhumation of classic rock'n'roll, the members of the Ruts drew from their own unique tapestry of influences, being fans of funk, soul, jazz and reggae. Only the Damned and Buzzcocks, who enjoyed much greater longevity, can hold a candle to their single releases. If the brevity of their career and personal instabilities undermined any possibility of their rivalling the Pistols or the Clash, that doesn't mean the Ruts don't belong in that kind of elevated company.

The band was formed around the school friendships of Malcolm Owen and Paul Fox, who grew up together in Hayes, Middlesex. They first dabbled in music while living on a commune on the Isle of Anglesey in Wales, where drummer Paul Mattocks was also domiciled. The trio formed Aslan together, melding rock, Celtic and folk sounds in keeping with the prevailing hippy ethos. When the commune collapsed in 1975, Owen returned to London. As did Fox, who put together commercial funk band Hit And Run with Mattocks, who also included saxophone player and later Ruts DC member Gary Barnacle, as well as singer J.D. Nicholas, who would work with Heatwave and the Commodores. They recruited jazz-funk store owner Dave Ruffy as drummer and brought Owen in as their warm-up DJ. But eventually Fox and Ruffy started working concurrently with Owen's new band, the Ruts. Owen got the idea of starting a punk band after seeing the Sex Pistols play live. Where other bands were fawning in their assessment of the Pistols' impact, he was simply convinced he and his mates could do it better.

Owen (vocals), Fox (guitar), Ruffy (bass) and Mattocks (drums) played their first rehearsal on 18 August 1977. They hit the ground running – their formative experiences across a range of musical genres (they were all fans of reggae and funk, and Owen was big on jazz) made them uniquely capable of injecting subtlety and cadence into punk's three-chord bluster. That first practice also saw them write their first songs together, 'Lobotomy' and 'Go Go Go' (later to be re-titled 'Stepping Bondage'). They had enough songs to make their stage debut in September, supporting Paul Fox's other band, Mr Softy. The reaction was strong enough to ensure that they'd take this punk lark seriously from then on. Bandwagon jumpers? While they were not the most authentic 'one chord wonders' on the block, they were genuinely

R

impressed by the movement's spontaneity and attitude. "I was really delighted when punk happened," Owen told the NME in 1979. "I was into a lot of jazz... George Duke, Weather Report, Stanley Clarke... I never play them at all now. I was a regular at The Vortex. I used to be tied up in all sorts of (bondage gear). I just totally went along with it. And it turned me on so much 'cause it was so energetic." Having a wider vocabulary of riffs and rhythms with which to tweak their sound was simply a big advantage. And in Owen, whose performances ranged from raging conviction to throwaway self-mockery, often forgetting the words to songs and improvising them on the spot, or barking away like a rabid dog, they had one of the movement's most pivotal human forces.

They cut four songs at Free Range Studios in October 1977, 'Rich Bitch', 'Lobotomy', 'I Ain't Sofisticated' and 'Out Of Order', which was posthumously released as the 'Stepping Bondage' EP, and made their debut at the Roxy in November. It was followed by another show at the Target pub in Northolt. "The Target was a big pub with loads of bars and they were all busy," Ruffy recalled for Hometown Atrocities. "When we played everyone came flooding in to watch. It was a good vibe and sound. Then we did another gig at someone's wedding! There was a bit of a vibe in the area about the Ruts then and the Hit And Run band were getting pissed off about it. Paul and I then discovered there was a rehearsal. So we went down to this rehearsal and it was quiet when we got there. Then we saw there was another drummer there, and another guitarist. They said they'd been offered a one-off single deal with Ariola to do a disco version of 'Greensleeves'. They were really serious and said you're either in the band or out of the band. So we said OK. See ya. Paul Mattocks decided to carry on with Hit And Run, I moved onto drums and Segs (long-standing friend and roadie John Jennings) joined us on bass after a couple of weeks. Then that was it. We had our band then. There was something about it when we all got together. How can I put it? It was really exciting. Things clicked." Segs was inducted into the band on the understandable provision that he got his hair cut. He and Ruffy had become friends when the former, scouting for Parliament imports, noted the latter's Ramones T-shirt as he stood behind the counter of his record shop.

Further demos were recorded on a cheap Philips tape recorder in the band's New Cross squat but elicited little interest. Phil Lynott of Thin Lizzy did give them one of his songs, 'Eat Your Heart Out', but this was never recorded. The new line-up, meanwhile, made its debut supporting Wayne County and the Electric Chairs at High Wycombe Town Hall on 25 January 1978. In the meantime friend Lizzy Cook introduced them to Clarence Baker of the reggae act Misty In Roots, whose rhythm section they would study at close range. After playing a Rock Against Racism benefit with Misty In Roots at Southall Community Centre, their first single was released via Misty's People Unite record label. Recorded at the eight-track Fair Deal Studios in Gladwood Driver Hayes, owned by Stuart Johnson, 'In A Rut' showed how quickly they had advanced. It featured a jaw-dropping vocal effort from Owen, as well as strikingly spacious and loose acoustics – where the keynote of other punk bands was compression and claustrophobia. And Owen's lyric was brutally effective – "I can't concentrate, I'm in a state, I don't feel straight, I can't love or hate." In its own way, it's wonderfully reminiscent of Pushkin's 'Buggered Up' ("I've lived too long, I'm in the ruck, I've drunk too deeply of the cup, I cannot spend, I cannot fuck, I'm down and out, I'm buggered up").

The B-side was 'H-Eyes', a tragic prophecy of Owen's eventual destruction by heroin ("Don't want you back now, well, not just yet"). The initial pressing of 1,000 copies sold out quickly thanks to the support of Misty In Roots' biggest fan, John Peel, and the single went on to sell 20,000 copies. The two bands subsequently toured together on Rock Against Racism and Anti-Nazi packages. The Ruts began to incorporate reggae rhythms into rock structures, increasingly writing songs wholly within that idiom. The proficiency and dexterity they exhibited in the pursuit of this cultural and musical holy grail (as it was then considered) was equalled only by the Clash.

Virgin signed the band in the spring of 1979, which was something they'd come to regret. Jennings: "At the beginning me and Dave wanted to stay independent because that's where we were at. That's where we came out of. Malcolm and Paul both had wives, and didn't basically. It's as simple as that. They wanted to sign a deal. They said 'All the marketing will be taken care of and we'll just be able to concentrate on playing. We'll get the money up front.' So we said all right in the end. We didn't know. We'd just been gigging for about two years before that, and then 'In A Rut' came out and everyone went mad about us. So we ended up signing for Virgin. We're now in debt to about £23,000. It's taken ten years to get down to this level (because of Virgin's dubious policy of cross-collateralising their publishing). But I still do maintain now that it was better to have had a really bad deal, but had fun and released some great records than not at all. I don't have any regrets about it. I can't really afford to feel too bitter about it but I'd like justice. The point I think is wrong is that Virgin didn't misinform us but they didn't fully inform us either. They knew what they were doing. All record companies do and that's what I hate."

The Ruts were in prime form on the May and June 1979 tour with the Damned, in which each attempted to out-do the other. "We really learned everything about rock'n'roll off them, in a way," Jennings later recalled to The Big Takeover. "They thought they were the Who. They thought they could smash up everything, and I said, 'Yeah, this is the way it's done.' So we started doing it too, and we did it much, much better than them, really. And we used to follow each other around, and we'd find out where their hotel was, and we'd go and let fire extinguishers off and say, 'Right, see ya' and they never found out where we were staying, and it went on and on and on. Captain's going, 'Yeah, we'll fix you,' and Rat Scabies is going, 'Yeah,' all these tricks they were going to do. And we'd be on stage playing, and they used to come on stage. Captain would come on and read the paper as if we weren't in the middle of a gig up there. And we were getting bigger and bigger in England at the time, so they were getting a bit jealous." Other pranks included piping Led Zeppelin through their monitors while they were on stage. The bands got on so well that Ruffy would regularly man the drum kit to allow Scabies to sing 'Burglar'. And the Ruts definitely won the end of tour mischief stakes. Their manager, Andy, came up with the idea of stopping off at a farm, where they persuaded the owner to let them have several bin liners of horse manure. This was duly pelted at the Damned by Ruffy while they ran through 'Burglar'. This, incidentally, is where the famed photo of Captain Sensible, covered in not a stitch apart from said animal effluent, comes from.

The Ruts opened their major label account with the simmering 'Babylon's Burning', a compelling, apocalyptic lyric (which came from a dream Fox had) matched to a scintillating guitar coda that he'd previously used as a warm-up exercise. Even in an especially good year for punk singles, this was peerless stuff. I must have heard it 1,000 times over a 20-year period and I still can't sit still to it. They'd actually attempted to record it before on an eight-track prior to signing to Virgin, but this was by far the superior version, even if Segs maintains that it's "too clean". The B-side, 'Society', meanwhile, came about after producer Mick Glossop asked Fox to play as fast and as hard as he could. 'Something That I Said', this time a showcase for Owen's tungsten larynx, was another superb effort, backed this time by the John Peel session version of 'Give Youth A Chance' on the B-side.

The group then completed its debut album The Crack, recorded in three weeks again with Mick Glossop. The band members were unhappy with the final mix, yet it remains a timeless collection; heartfelt, skilful and intuitive where others were formulaic and rhetorical. Particularly impressive were the seven epic minutes of 'Jah Wars', written in the aftermath of National Front-organised violence at their Rock Against Racism performances and featuring members of Misty as well as Owen's wife Rocky. It was released on single as the truncated 'Jah War', though the BBC decided not to play-list it due to its lyrical content. But there was hardly a duff track on display, with the rhythm section in particular shining as they provided a lockjaw-tight but surprisingly intricate bottom line. For evidence see Jennings' astonishing star turn on 'Savage Circle', a song influenced by Captain Beefheart. Even Paul Fox's one-note solo on 'Out Of Order' seemed entirely fitting. Incidentally, the sleeve credit to Oh Pew Pah is a reference to Ruffy's dog, also featured on John Howard's cover art.

The feeling that the Ruts were something genuinely special was confirmed when 'Staring At The Rude Boys' arrived, bringing another appearance on Top Of The Pops. It was another majestic effort, incorporating several tightly orchestrated musical scene changes, lyrical wit and ferocious performances. The sleeve featured a crossword puzzle, with Virgin offering a dinner with the Ruts to anyone who could solve it. John Peel was also wheeled out for the resulting evening, as he later recalled to Jack Rabid. "We went to this restaurant on King's Road in Chelsea, and Malcolm was so out of his head that he just collapsed in his meal. He'd gone out and tried to sell his girlfriend's stereo in the afternoon to try to get money so he could get heroin. And the bloke he tried to sell it to hit him in the face with a tape deck. So he had this huge swollen face that looked like something out of a cartoon, and then he collapsed into his meal. Eventually I asked them to give me his parents' number and somebody did. So I phoned his mum and dad and I said, 'Listen, I've got Malcolm here and he's in a terrible state, can I get a minicab and put him in it and send him back to you?' And they said, 'Of course, do.' So I did, but two weeks later he was dead."

By the time of 'Babylon's' recording Owen's heroin intake had escalated beyond anyone's comfort levels. As Jennings recalled to Mark Wyeth in Record Collector, "We were recording 'Rude Boys'. I was in the hallway at the Townhouse with him. I was saying, 'You're still doing it, you've got to stop.' He put his face up to mine and shouted that he'd kicked it. It was a front. I said, 'Look at your eyes, just look at your eyes.'"

As a side effect of his heroin use, Owen had developed nodes on his throat, resulting in the cancellation of part of their Back To Blighty tour. For the sake of his own health, the rest of the band pleaded with him to leave while they backed Kevin Coyne on his Sanity Stomp LP and played live with reggae great Laurel Aitken.

For a while it seemed Owen might straighten himself out, with a reconciliation broached. Dave Ruffy takes up the story: "Malcolm's heroin problem lasted for about nine months to a year. It was a slow thing. Before he died we actually decided to split the band up. It was the only thing we could do. Heroin affects everything. He was just lying all the time and he wouldn't turn up for things. He was really trying to kick it but his life was in a mess. His woman had left him and all that. In order to try and get him off it, we split the band. It was the last resort really. There was a lot of grief at the time. I mean we were all special friends. What happened was he went in for a clean-up at the clinic for a couple of weeks and then came out. He'd gone through the physical thing. He hadn't had any for a fortnight. It all happened over one weekend. We'd already arranged with Virgin to record some songs in the studio as a three-piece. We had to carry on being positive.

"On the Friday night we all went to the 101 club in Clapham with Malcolm. He was really quiet cos he wasn't very well. He was a bit strung out. Then we went back to my house and Malcolm said, 'I'm going to do a single and I want you to play on it Dave.' He asked all of us individually and we sort of agreed. So then on the Saturday and Sunday the three of us went into the studio and did this three-track demo. That was really good. And Malcolm was back, so that was great. Then on the Monday morning the phone rings and it's a friend of Malcolm's. He'd phoned to say that he was going to break the news that Malcolm had been found dead in his bath. Malcolm had arranged to have a drink with him that lunchtime. So Malcolm had gone up for his bath and being the naughty boy that he was, he bought himself a little bag of heroin. I suppose to give himself a bit of a lift or whatever, and this is my interpretation of how he died. Because his resistance to it had gone right down and he had a hot bath, I think that he passed out and drowned. Technically, he had an overdose. So from then on all the things we did were kind of tainted by this."

On 14 July 1980 Owen was pulled lifeless from his bath, aged just 26. People often talk blithely of unfulfilled potential. In Owen's case, it is entirely justified. What could have been? As their one-time advocate John Peel mused to the NME in 1989 when asked about his sponsorship of 'In A Rut': "They then started making money and having successful records and Malcolm Owen got into heroin and died. And you sometimes think, if you hadn't played the record, if Virgin hadn't signed them, would he have had a brief but frustrating career and ended up a brickie but alive? But then, if you thought about those things, you'd never do anything."

The Ruts' final recording, 'West One (Shine On Me)' was released a month after his death – a song he'd written while he'd been in hospital undergoing an operation on nodules that had developed on his throat. The band refused to appear on Top Of The Pops to promote 'West One' as it would have required them to lip-synch to Owen's vocals. It was followed in short order by the budget-priced compilation Grin & Bear It. This featured both sides of the 'In A Rut' single plus Peel session tracks and three scintillating live cuts from French TV show Chorus, mixed live to two-track without overdubs. Despite its tragic birth, and the odds and ends nature of the contents, the whole collection shines. This has recently been paired back to back with The Crack, and minute for minute there's no better single-disc collection of UK punk rock out there (although that shouldn't stop you from buying the extended Captain Oi! reissues, which include worthwhile bonus tracks).

The Ruts became Ruts DC (Da Capo) after Owen's death and continued with Segs handling most of the vocals and old friend Gary Barnacle joining on keyboards and saxophone, having already distinguished himself on 'West One'. Prior to this, they played a single show at the Vortex with roadie Mannah (who had enjoyed his five minutes of fame by serving as backing vocalist on their final John Peel session in May 1979) and Max Splodge helping out on vocals. The decision to continue as Ruts DC was entirely down to Virgin, who threatened to drop the band unless they retained some connection with their former selves and nixed the idea of the remaining trio adopting a wholly new name.

They managed their first US gigs, in December 1980 at New York's Hurrah's Club, before returning to record a couple of terrific records – Animal Now and their collaboration with reggae dubmeister the Mad Professor, Rhythm Collision. Notable on the former was their explosive venting of frustration with Virgin Records, 'Parasites', and the single, 'Different View'. Rhythm Collision was released following Virgin's decision to drop the band (which was not exactly bad news given the way their relationship had deteriorated) who then set up their own Bohemian imprint. This was a more straight-ahead dub effort, largely concocted by Jennings and Ruffy. Though a critical success, it sold only 7,000 copies. This time the artwork came from Ruffy's girlfriend Rachel Howard, daughter of John Howard, who'd designed The Crack's sleeve, and had included his daughter's head in the assemblage. They played a few small scale UK shows to promote it (having once again played New York alongside the Gas after Animal Now, though their show at the Peppermint Lounge descended into a fist-fight between Segs and Fox) but then slowly fizzled out.

They finally walked away from it all in 1983. Paul Fox has had his own problems with drugs, while working with his own bands Dirty Strangers and then the Fluffy Kittens, as well as producing. Ruffy has made his name as a session player with Joe Strummer, Aztec Camera (from 1983 to 1986), the Lucy Show, Everything But The Girl, the Waterboys and Kirsty MacColl, among others. Jennings formed a band, Vendetta Palace, later Fat City, with his French girlfriend, who released one single, and toured the US with the Wolfgang Press, before hooking up with old sparring partner Ruffy to back Kirsty MacColl. Ruffy and Jennings also recorded an acid house single together, as well as backing French singer William Sheller (Les Objets). The rumours are that Foxy was keen to see some form of reunion in the late-90s, but his former rhythm section were not swayed by the idea.

But, oh, what could have been. Watch out for a new biography of the band written by Neil Brooks, slated for a 2007 release.

DISCOGRAPHY:

In a Rut/H-Eyes 7-inch (People Unite SJP 795 May 1979) (1,000 copies only, reissued on People Unite RUT 1 in June 1979)

Babylon's Burning/Society 7-inch (Virgin VS 271 July 1979) (also released on 12-inch, VS 271-12)

Something That I Said/Give Youth a Chance 7-inch (Virgin VS 285 V79 August 1979)

Jah War/I Ain't Sofisticated (Virgin VS-298 November 1979)

The Crack LP (Virgin V-2132 September 1979) (reissued by Virgin at mid-price, OVED 80, in August 1988. Later reissued on CD in July 1990 by Virgin, CD CDV 2132, with three B-side tracks. Note, US edition has different running order, omitting the excellent live version of 'Human Punk' that closes the UK issue)

Staring at the Rude Boys/Love in Vain 7-inch (Virgin VS 327 April 1980) (initial quantities in gatefold sleeve with competition)

West One (Shine on Me)/The Crack (Virgin VS 370 September 1980)

Grin & Bear It LP (Virgin V 2188 November 1980) (with £3.99 pay no more sticker. Reissued at mid-price in March 1984, Virgin OVED 57. Note: US issue has different track listing. Reissued on CD by Captain Oi!, AHOYCD 261, in August 2005, with bonus tracks 'West One (single version)', 'The Crack', 'Denial', 'Stepping Bondage', 'Lobotomy' and 'Rich Bitch'. Amazingly, this is the first time that the original single version of 'West One' has appeared on CD. Other bonuses include 'Denial', their contribution to the Bustin' Out compilation that preceded their emergence as Ruts DC. The last three tracks are the finest commercially available versions of the much bootlegged 'Stepping Bondage' demo. The original vinyl album liner notes are retained, with contemporary notes from the band discussing the bonus tracks.)

ARCHIVE RELEASES:

Babylon's Burning/XTC: Take This Town 7-inch (RSO RSO 71 1980)

Stepping Bondage/Lobotomy/Rich Bitch 7-inch Bohemian BO 4 March 1983)

Babylon's Burning 12-inch EP (Virgin VS 583-12 April 1983)

Babylon's Burning/Something That I Said/Staring At The Rude Boys/West One (Shine On Me)

Peel Session 14.5.79 12-inch (Strange Fruit SFPS 011 June 1987)

Sus/Society/You're Just A... /It Was Cold/Something That I Said (also issued on cassette, SFPSC 011)

You Gotta Get Out of It CD (Virgin COM CD 7 1987) (an absolute horror show. The tracks are titled incorrectly ('West On?'), wrongly sourced, badly sequenced, and the whole things reeks of 'let's knock one out before we go to the wine bar' music industry chutzpah)

Live: Ruts LP (Dojo DOJO LP 52 March 1987) (disappointing muddy sound, hardly representative of the Ruts' live power)

Live and Loud!! LP (Link LP 013 December 1987) (reissued on CD in October 1992 by Street Link, LINK CD 013, and later as part of a 2 for 1 package with the Adverts, Step 1, STEPCD 044, July 2002. Ditto the above comments. Surely there are better tapes around than this? Having said that, it's still worth hearing for Owen's between-song patter – trying to calm an obviously violent audience and suggesting, at the end of 'H-Eyes', that he'll "fuck the brain" of whoever chucked the can at him)

The Peel Sessions – Complete Sessions 1979-1981 LP (Strange Fruit SFRLP 109 June 1990) (also issued on CD as Strange Fruit SFR-CD-109)

BBC Live In Concert 1977 CD (with Penetration) (Windsong WIN CD 009 1991)

The Skids Versus The Ruts CD EP (Virgin VSCDT 1992)

Choice Cuts (Best of the Ruts) CD (Virgin CDOVD 454 1995)

Demolition Dancing CD (Receiver RRCD 182 April 1994)

Something That I Said (Best Of) CD (Virgin CDOVD 454 1995) (and the point of this compilation would be...)

Criminal Minds double CD (Snapper SMDCD 332 May 2001) (Guess who wrote the sleevenotes for this odds and ends selection, making use of several Link live tracks. Apologies for any sense of déjà vu... First CD is demos pre-first album and live, the second live tracks drawing heavily on Live And Loud!)

Bustin' Out – The Essential Ruts Collection CD (EMI 5335902 July 2001) (Scrappy compilation featuring alternate takes (often discarded for a good reason), Peel sessions cuts and interviews. Hardly 'essential', but the odd nugget to unearth, including the previously unreleased 'Denial')

In A Rut CD (Harry May MAYOCD 523 September 2002) (aka In A Can due to its packaging when released by the Cancan label (CAN 009), and drawing on the same pool as Bustin' Out, this features all the band's pre-Virgin recordings alongside the band's own sleevenotes and annotation. Do you really need four versions of 'Babylon's Burning', however titanic the song is? Still, at least you can trace the versions, with the sessions from Underhill and Fair Deal alongside the 'Mystery' sessions)

The Crack/Grin And Bear It (Punk 2 on 1) (EMI 584122 May 2003) (all of both albums on one CD. Uninspiring sleevenotes, but arguably the most explosive single CD of late-70s punk you could ever wish to hear, and available for only a few quid).

Salford Jets

Mike Sweeney (vocals), Diccon Hubbard, (bass, vocals), 'Shakey' Dave Morris (drums, vocals), Geoff 'Bubbs' Kerry (keyboards, vocals), Rod Gerrard (guitar, vocals)

The SALFORD JETS' origins date back to the late 60s when Sweeney became active on the local music scene. He was a member of Stackwaddy by 1973 and put together the Salford Jets three years later. They were initially influenced by the R&B of Canned Heat and the glam bands of the day, but with the arrival of the Ramones, things took a different course. The original line-up featured Don McKintyre on guitar before Gerrard and Kerry joined the band. They played dozens of gigs and secured a succession of singles deals with a variety of major labels, including EMI, Polydor, RCA and WEA. It was like a Pistols smash and grab raid, only they left the money behind.

"Manchester was an exciting place to be during the early punk/indie scene," Diccon Hubbard told me. "It gave people like me and Mike Sweeney a chance to express ourselves in a way previously denied to us – fantastic! We used to rehearse in an old school hall, then due to noise levels and complaints, moved to Tony Davidson's rehearsal rooms based in a Victorian warehouse behind Deansgate Station, Manchester. At that time it was full of aspiring new bands. The first day we were there we saw a guy playing guitar, working out some indecipherable song – which seemed to be total crap. It turned out to be Pete Shelley! Funnily enough, I came to quite like the Buzzcocks stuff, and some of them would come to watch our gigs. From there we moved to Mike Howell of the Drones place near Mount Street to practise. Most memories of that are at best rather hazy! The first time I met Peter Hook (in Joy Division at that time) he turned up at my house in a huge elderly Jaguar in order to buy a bass cabinet I had for sale."

The Salford Jets made their debut for WEA in 1978 with 'Looking At The Squares'. "Then they wanted us to do a 'rock'n'roll' single. We told them to fuck off." It was followed by 'Manchester Boys', this time on EMI. "When we signed to EMI International, they were in the process, unbeknown to us, of flogging that division to Paramount, who promptly closed the label down! I think you will find that ours was the last release on the label." The singles were peppy enough, power pop with just enough garnishing of punk attitude to sound contemporary. Their chart hit, 'Who You Looking At?', came via RCA. Peaking at number 72, there was talk of a Top Of The Pops appearance before they learned that all the Beeb's technicians were on strike that week. However, they did secure two Mike Read sessions. But it never quite came together due to further record label problems. "RCA were about to renew our contract, and we'd recorded what would have been our fourth single for them, 'I Don't Believe You', which had reached acetate stage. The new contract included an album clause, plus more singles. Unfortunately the UK boss at the label was sacked one week before it was due to be signed and the new guy got rid of our band along with various others in order to bring his own people in."

Instead they moved on to the independent Lunar Records for 'City Youth' and then Polydor for 'Soldiers Of Fortune'. Neither did the trick. "We signed a one-year, three-single deal with Polydor, with the usual options on completion. The first single, 'Soldiers Of Fortune', was spectacularly unsuccessful, and received what the majority of the band felt was poor support. The result was a group vote, which led to Polydor being told in no uncertain manner that we no longer wished to be associated with them. Polydor couldn't wait to get out, so maybe that was a mistake on our part."

There was a final single in 1983, 'Pain In My Heart', but that was it. "As to our live performances compared to the records – I must admit we always felt it was really difficult to put on disc the energy, rawness and edge that usually came with playing live. Recording studios nearly always felt too clinical, I always thought our best stuff was recorded in the early days using cheap, local demo studios, which were the best we could afford. The majors invariably put us in posh, expensive ones in London, e.g. George Martin's Air Studio in Oxford Street. Not what Salford boys were used to!"

After the group broke up in late 1984, original members Mike Sweeney, Diccon Hubbard, Dave Morris and Geoff Kerry formed the Thunderbyrds, with Geoff Foot and later Mike

Amatt. Under this guise they returned to their 60s roots, recording a number of tracks for Imaginary Records.

The first Salford Jets reunion show came in 1986, and ten years later they appeared at the Holidays In The Sun Festival in 1996, where they were joined on stage by Eric Faulkner from the Bay City Rollers on guitar. They then re-recorded 'Who You Looking At' with members of the Troggs (Chris Britton) and Inspiral Carpets (Clint Boon). In 2003 they supported Cheap Trick at the Royal Albert Hall and continue to play sporadically. These ventures are necessarily sidelines, however. Mike Sweeney is a DJ for Capital Radio and Diccon Hubbard runs his own talent agency. He also helped to put together the Adventures In Lo-Fi series of archive recordings of the band, issued in 2003.

DISCOGRAPHY:

Looking at the Squares/Dancing School 7-inch (WEA K18088 May 1978)
Manchester Boys/Last Bus 7-inch (EMI INT 590 July 1979)
Gina 7-inch EP (RCA PE 5210 November 1979)
Gina/Steady with You/I Want You/Hey (Can I fall In Love With You?) (there was also a promo 7-inch featuring 'Gina' on either side)
Who You Looking At?/Don't Start Trouble 7-inch (RCA PB 5239 May 1980)
I Don't Believe You 7-inch (RCA 1980) (two acetate copies only)
She's Gonna Break Your Heart/Bright City Lights 7-inch (RCA PB 5271 August 1980)
City Youth/Keep Away From My Baby 7-inch (Lunar Sal 1 November 1980)
Soldiers of Fortune/Young Bucks 7-inch (Polydor POSP 248 1981)
Cops 'n' Robbers 7-inch (Polydor) (one sided promo)
Pain In My Heart 7-inch (Single Records S0001) (limited release prior to moving to Ka Records, featuring a different mix)
Pain In My Heart/Pain In My Heart (alt version) 7-inch (Ka KA 17 March 1983) (also issued as a 12-inch with extra track 'Watch That Girl')
ARCHIVE RELEASES
Adventures In Lo-Fi 3-CD set (BM 102/103/104 July 2003)
COMPILATIONS
Manc Attitude CD EP (Exotica Pele 11CD 1996; 'Who You Looking At?') (re-recorded version featuring Sweeney and Hubbard plus Chris Britton of the Troggs, Clint Boon of the Inspiral Carpets and Phil Watts of the Out on drums)
Holidays In The Sun Volume 2 dbl CD (Anagram HITS 2 1997; 'Who You Looking At? (live))

Satan's Rats

Paul Rencher (vocals), Steve Eagles (guitar), Sharpie (bass), Clint Driftwood (drums)

S

SATAN'S RATS were formed at college by 17-year-olds Rencher and Eagles in Evesham in 1977. "We read about punk in the music press and quickly became obsessed," Eagles told me. "We had little idea of what it sounded like, but the attitude it expressed was definitely for us. We formed a band immediately. The 'name' took ten seconds to come up with. Something you could put on the back of a leather jacket, like local biker gang, Gypsy Warlords."

They set themselves up above a garage and ran through Led Zeppelin's 'Communication Breakdown', before Rencher began to pen new material. 'You Make Me Sick' was the first such concoction, and was targeted at "anyone who upset me in those days at Evesham College," according to Rencher's fascinating document of the times. They made their live debut at Bretforton Village Hall on 4 March 1977, a set kicking off with the Damned's 'New Rose'. After which Sharpie decided that he really didn't like this new punk rock jape, though his mate Roy Wilkes was more than happy to step in on bass. The new line-up was subsequently featured in the local press under the headline: "At last – punk without filth." Which was rank even by regional news sub-editor standards.

Afterwards it was decided, a little to Zep fan Wilkes's discomfort, that they needed more 'new' songs and less 'boring old fart' songs. Wilkes responded admirably, offering up 'The Year Of The Rats', which was aired at their next show at Bidford-On-Avon Village Hall. Eagles: "Out in the sticks there was nowhere to play so we did a tour of the village halls, thus galvanising a local youth movement." A day later they travelled to Muff Murfin's studio in Worcester to record their first demo, cutting six tracks in four hours.

Meanwhile Eagles had booked them to play at the Birmingham Punk Festival at Barbarella's. Only Driftwood's father had banned him from playing with punk rockers. It didn't really matter, as by the next day they'd found a new recruit, Ollie Harrison. He made his debut at Pershore College Of Horticulture on 17 June where the set was still a mix of originals and covers. "As far as songwriting goes," Eagles told me, "Paul and sometimes Roy would chuck lyrics at me and I would supply the chords, that was our method." From there to Barbarella's, alongside the Killjoys and Suburban Studs and sundry others, a night on which the Brummie punks rioted, as if to cement tabloid notions of what punk was really all about and confirm Driftwood Senior's misgivings.

They now had their own demo, which was sold at the Evesham Record & Tape Centre by shop owners Mick Butler and Duncan Hands. When the duo, who became the band's managers, mailed copies to major record labels, the only respondent was Dick James Music, whose A&R man Les Tomlinson came to see them play at local venue Tracy's. A few weeks later they signed a contract in Denmark Street and hopes were high. After all, this punk malarkey seemed to be making lots of money. But DJM wasn't really attuned to the ethos. Eagles: "When he introduced us to his sales team he had us jump into the conference room via a window, like real punks. Mortally embarrassing for everyone concerned." DJM's other main 'new wave' act was the reviled Rikki And The Last Days Of Earth. And who should the band find sat by the mixing desk on their entry to the studio but Rikki Sylvan himself. He'd agreed to do the production for nothing apart from a huge credit on the sleeve. The band felt even that constituted overcharging. Eagles: "He didn't like us from the off and we didn't like him and then after one aborted take Rencher said, 'I think Rikki's a cunt'. Mr Sylvan heard him loud and clear in the control room, and things took a nose dive." Their dread anticipation was confirmed when they heard the results of his production. "I don't think his production was THAT bad, actually," Eagles reflects. "It was more to do with the fact that he was a pretentious – like his music – twit. He wanted at one stage to replace Ollie with a session drummer. A move that was vigorously resisted."

DJM, meanwhile, had started to promote them via the legend 'Never Mind the Sex Pistols – Here's Satan's Rats'. It wasn't very clever, though it was inspired by barracking the band had received at the Roxy about their rustic inadequacies. By a bizarre-ish twist of fate, Satan's Rats would go on to support the Pistols at their Wolverhampton Lafayette show. They were entertained and suitably awe-struck by the prelims to the gig, which involved fetching John Lydon some cod roe from the chippy and failing to convince Sid Vicious to let them borrow his bass stack. Eagles: "A Midlands promoter felt he owed us a favour after a Rats gig the week before had been cancelled. What a great favour! It was a secret gig and we were told to get there early in the afternoon, as we would be locked in with the Pistols and their road crew. Paul Cook was quiet, Steve Jones swaggered, Johnny Lydon looned and a stoned Sid chatted with us, very amusingly, for what seemed like hours. We played and got an encore. The Pistols played and were awesome, with court jester Johnny imploring the crowd to 'Give me your clooothesah', and looking like the Michelin Man after pulling on dozens of mohair jumpers."

Further gigs with Slaughter And The Dogs and XTC ensued before the release of their debut single, 'In My Love For You', which managed to miss the prevailing ethos of despising boy meets girl lyrics by an impressive margin. Both that and the following 'Year Of The Rats', which was much better, failed to trouble the charts. John Peel did play the latter, after Eagles pestered him when he found himself stood next to him in the toilets of a gig at Leamington Spa. Meanwhile their shows at Barbarella's were doing well, until manager John Fewtrell took exception to Rencher's microphone antics one night. There was controversy in the ranks over his demonstrable lack of professionalism. Rencher, for his part, was vehement that professionalism had no place in punk rock. And so were sewn the seeds for inter-band disharmony which would gradually mount over coming months.

A third single was slated with recording taking place in Rickmansworth with Vic Maile. Eagles: "Vic was a lovely chap who made us a good sounding record and when we gathered in the dark car park, to thank him, he genuinely thought we were going to beat him up!" The entertainingly snotty 'You Make Me Sick' should have been their first single, rather than their last. DJM still hadn't quite lost all interest in their charges, and set up a tour for them.

Unfortunately, this again paired them with Rikki And The Last Days Of Earth. "To be reunited with Rikki et al for a tour round Britain was a cruel act," Eagles laments. "Blowing them off stage became tedious." Shows included one at Long Lartin Prison, where they bumped into John McVicar – not that they had a clue who he was.

By now Rencher had resolved to leave the band, having tired of the feuding. Before he did he discovered he would need surgery on his left testicle. When he and it had recovered, a band meeting was convened where he introduced four new songs. None of the others were interested. Or at least that's his version of events. Eagles sees it differently. "DJM began to lose whatever interest they ever had, Bob Geldof nicked our name, and some promoters refused to book us because of our name. One night after a group meeting we changed it to Dennis. Roy had argued that because it was on the front of every fire engine and dustcart, it would become instantly popular. The next day we changed it back to Satan's Rats. A period of group disharmony followed, well actually it was always there. All arguments stemmed from Roy and Roy was duly sacked (though Rencher would insist it was because he was "too square"). Sorry Roy. Dave Sparrow joined us (from a Melody Maker advert, playing his first show at the Marquee after a couple of stand-ins helped out) and a healthy period of songwriting ensued. More gigs were played but no records. Dave and Paul decided they didn't like each other and that really was it." Alas, Eagles is unable to vouch for the veracity of the testicle story.

The core of Satan's Rats (Eagles, Sparrow and Harrison) elected to recruit a new singer, Wendy Wu, and became the Photos, a moderately successful unit. Satan's Rats did later reconvene for one show in their hometown of Evesham, which was meant to be a Photos' gig until Wu pulled out sick. "It was all very cool, it must be said," remembers Gareth Holder of the Shapes, who were sharing the bill that night. After the Photos dissolved Eagles became the songwriter with Bang Bang Machine, of 'Geek Love' fame. Venerated old school label Overground, meanwhile, began to reissue Satan's Rats' singles in the late-80s. "They were my favourite band but nobody knew anything about them," John Esplen told Record Collector. "We did straight reissues of the original singles but in different packaging. At the end of their career, they advertised a fan club cassette for £2 in the back of the music press, with lots of unreleased stuff." This formed the basis of the eventual Overground CD What A Bunch Of Rodents...

DISCOGRAPHY:

In My Love For You/Façade 7-inch (DJM DJS 10819 November 1977)

Year Of The Rats/Louise 7-inch (DJM DJS 10821 January 1978)

You Make Me Sick/Louise 7-inch (DJM DJS 10840 1978) (Steve Eagles: "the B-side was another version of 'Louise'. Even though this was the B-side of the previous single, it was nevertheless the only other song that producer Vic Maile actually liked! So we did it twice!")

ARCHIVE RELEASES:

Year Of The Rats/Louise 7-inch (Overground OVER 01 March 1989) (600 copies in yellow, 400 in white, 25 in gold...)

In My Love For You/Façade 7-inch (Overground OVER 02 March 1989) (as above...)

You Make Me Sick 7-inch (Overground OVER 14 April 1991) (clear vinyl, 567 copies only)

What A Bunch Of Rodents CD (Overground OVER 46 February 1996)

COMPILATIONS:

Punk Rock Rarities Vol. 2 (Anagram CDPUNK 83 1996; 'You Make Me Sick', 'Louise')

S

Scabs

James Young (vocals), John Salmons (guitar, organ), Patrick Cunningham (drums), Steve Pardoe (bass), Simon 'Marcus' Grant (saxophone)

Formed at Exeter University in the late-70s, the SCABS wrote ultra-basic, biscuit-tin punk with snotty lyrics and vocals courtesy of James Young, the principal songwriter. The lead track from their sole EP, 'Amory Building', written about the site that housed most of the university's humanities faculties, features a saxophone break that makes Lora Logic sound like a virtuoso. Cunningham: "'Amory Building' was more of a put-down than a tribute. James wrote the song because it was a

building he, and I, had to spend a lot of time in. But it wasn't one you could ever grow to love – very functional and utilitarian – built long before the term ergonomic design was invented!"

Recorded at Fair Deal studios in January 1979, they drove up for the day but were stuck in snowdrifts in Somerset on their return and had to spend the night in the minibus freezing their collective rocks off. The single was released two months later on the studio's own Clubland label, as part of a 'package deal' including studio time and mastering. Two pressings, each of 1,000 copies, were distributed through Virgin and Rough Trade. Cunningham: "Fair Deal/Clubland had the studio and arranged the mastering and pressing. I then took delivery of all the records and handled all the postal orders and shop distribution but the majority of the records were sold locally and at gigs."

Melody Maker lambasted them for being 'college punks' as, in truth, did some of Exeter's local music fans. "We weren't taken seriously by anyone, which was probably just as well! We didn't really mix with other local punk bands, but I think it's fair to say that we weren't highly regarded." The band toured the UK in the summer of 1979 to support the single, but broke up soon after the completion of their courses. Pardoe and Cunningham continued as part of the M5s. Cunningham remained a lynchpin of the Exeter music scene, promoting and running the Cavern Club and running listings magazine Event South West and alternative newspaper The Flying Post.

DISCOGRAPHY:

The Scabs 7-inch EP (Clubland SJP 799 March 1979)

Amory Building/Leave Me Alone/Don't Just Sit There/U.R.E. (first 1,000 copies in blue and red sleeve, second 1,000 in black and red. Sleeve folds out into a 'star' shape. With inserts, all folded by hand, etc. Very fetching)

COMPILATION:

Year Zero: The Exeter Punk Scene 1977-2000 CD (Boss Tuneage/Hometown Atrocities Home 08/Bostage 508 2003; 'Amory Building')

Scars

Bobby King (aka Bobby Charm; vocals), Calumn Mackay (aka Plastic Mac; drums), John Mackie (aka John Doctor; bass), Paul Research (aka Paul Responsible; guitar)

Formed in Edinburgh by brothers John and Paul Mackie, the SCARS were a different kettle of spittle to most of the Ramones copyists who sprang up in the wake of punk. Their musicianship, derived partially from the glam period and particularly from Bowie and Mott The Hoople, distinguished them for a start. So too their wider reading, ranging from the beat poets to the existentialists, and their desire to look the part on stage, rather than just donning combat boots and regulation black. This, of course, could easily have been a disaster. But as the Americans say, the Scars had the chops, not least in the shape of Paul Research's extensive range as guitarist. He'd been classically trained and it showed. Indeed, it was not unknown for moments of on-stage improvisation to break out, which was about as anti-fashion in the prevailing climate as their use of make-up. King's lyrics encompassed a real sense of fatality and melodrama, and theatrical elements defined their shows, which maintained a sense of spectacle and spontaneity. Their ambition, and the haircuts, may account for the frequent occasions on which disgruntled punk fans canned them off stage.

S

After six weeks of rehearsal they took their bow at the Balerno Village Hall in October 1977, witnessed by Hanging Around fanzine. "They're fired with the enthusiasm that can overcome bad equipment and technical problems; the enthusiasm that tells them they're as good, if not better, than anyone else; the enthusiasm that turns a good gig into a great one and without which rock'n'roll becomes just another sanitised branch of the entertainment industry." The performance featured covers of 'You Really Got Me', 'Chinese Rocks', 'I Wanna Be Me', 'Rebel Rebel', 'Suffragette City', 'Blitzkrieg Bop' and 'Substitute', alongside originals 'Hard Luck Story', 'Problems' and 'Unbecoming', the latter said to be about John Lydon becoming 'part of the establishment'. Other songs to be written but never recorded included 'The Victim', about a road rage incident discovered by Mackie's father in a newspaper, 'White

Rockers', 'Bedsit Boredom', 'Chicks' and 'Shoplifter'. I asked Paul Research what happened to these mainly unrecorded songs. "I think we always had that Bowie-inspired notion that you had to keep moving on. There are tons of demos and bootlegs of 'The Victim' etc, but we had to stop playing some of the more frenetic stuff after Mac left (prior to Author! Author!), because no-one else could play like that."

At the start of 1978 the group took its place for the Stiff/Chiswick Challenge at Clouds in Glasgow, alongside Freeze, Cuban Heels and Skids. The latter band would become firm friends, inviting the Scars to join them in Liverpool for two shows at Eric's (Stuart Adamson later considered 'Mac' for a job in Big Country). In 1979 Fast Products issued the Scars' debut single, 'Adult/ery', backed by 'Horrorshow', the latter inspired by A Clockwork Orange. It made them the fifth band on Bob Last's fast-rising and revered indie after the Gang Of Four, Mekons, Human League and 2,3. "We never consciously went out for Scottish material," Last told Brian Hogg, "and the Scars simply evolved out of the scene. They were kids who hung around at our flat during the early days and signing them seemed the logical thing to do." Recorded at Rochdale's Cargo studio with engineer John Brierly, the sessions were completed in about eight hours. The overdubs and mixing were polished off the following day and the single was eventually released in March.

They played shows in London as support to Fast affiliates the Human League (during February 1979), Gang Of Four and the Mekons, and in March 1980 recorded the first of two sessions for John Peel. In June they appeared at the Anti-Nazi League Festival in Craigmillar. Due to perform in the middle of the afternoon, their set was introduced in French by Mac's penpal as Les Cicatreuses. It was like a red rag to a bull. A volley of missiles was sent arcing towards them from the openly hostile crowd, King even managing to catch one beer can mid-flight and drink its contents. Sounds wrote a piece about the crowd reaction while there were letters to the weeklies about the inhospitable welcome afforded its Edinburgh neighbours by Glaswegian punks, who were held largely responsible.

They gained their first major national press showing in their own right when Garry Bushell turned up to scout out local bands at the Edinburgh Astoria in August 1980. Research, also in the audience, persuaded him to attend their rehearsal the following day. As he recalled for the Scars website, "When I went to the bog, Guy, who had been peeking over his shoulder, followed me excitedly. 'You should see what he's writing – fantastic, brilliant – it's unbelievable!' Two weeks later our wee faces were centre-spread in Sounds, and we were picked out as Edinburgh's most likely to. We had got more publicity just for hanging out together than the record company had managed to buy in a year. My confidence at that time was unassailable."

With the subsequent release of Author! Author!, by which time Steve McLaughlin (brother of Paul, lead singer of the Prats) had replaced Mackay on drums, the Scars emphatically delivered on their promise. Of all the albums not readily available on CD in the last 20 years, this is one of the most missed, its re-release subject to all sorts of shenanigans ill-befitting its status. Which is strange, given that it was such a hit with the critics. How about this for a load of utter bollocks from Paul Morley in the NME. "The Scars epitomise the post-punk new seriousness that has radically re-activated pop music, destroying the dichotomy between intelligence and emotion and confronting a whole range of different fears and desires. New pop that treats the transient thrill seriously. New pop, the matter-realism that is today's heroic retaliation, has imagination and conviction."

Please don't let this nonsense put you off. Author! Author!, produced by Penetration's Robert Blamire, is a concise, hugely appealing pop album, its surface optimism counterbalanced by the dark recesses explored by King's bleak reflections on human relationships and Research's irresistible patchwork of Ian Hunter/John McGeoch-styled trebly hooks. The quasi-poetry reading of 'Your Attention Please' is probably the most effective anti-nuclear statement I've ever heard (and being a fan of punk, I've heard thousands). 'Leave Me In The Autumn' is an exquisite pop drama, so too the single 'All About You', which they got to play on The Old Grey Whistle Test.

The Scars were suddenly, though very fleetingly, hot news. They had moved to London and were splattered across the pages of not just the inkies, but also the pop press proper. Spreads for Record Mirror, International Musician and Smash Hits followed. For the latter they were photographed in Sheila Rock's apartment for a full-page colour spread, wearing clothes designed by Glen Matlock's wife Celia. The problem was that the band was now lodged somewhere between the post-punk and new romantic movements, yet they were too pop-inclined for the former and way too cutting and acerbic for the latter.

However, the impetus was lost and a tour of America failed to cement a breakthrough there, despite the release of an EP. "After 'All About You' I was really troubled by how to follow it up," Research confirms. "We remixed 'Everywhere I Go' but the label didn't want to release it because there was no chorus. We had a great song called 'Bone Orchard', which we recorded at Good Earth intending to release it as a single. But I insisted on a harder guitar sound, and the recording did not have the same yearning quality as the demo, so it was not released... It's a pity we didn't have the confidence to hold out for a better deal. We can't get Author! Author! released on CD because we basically gave away the rights. At the time people said we could renegotiate once we had sold a few, and we believed it. In a way, it's amazing that we made a good album at all. After 'Horrorshow' died down, we had such bad results from the sessions for 'They Came And Took Her' and 'Love Song', that I was really dreading going into the studio to do our album – I was pretty sure it would turn out to be rubbish again. The studio had seemed to suck out all of our energy. Some guy with a beard wanting you to put the chorus at the beginning etc. The 'Love Song' single seemed so brittle and weak to me. But Author! Author! tuned out great. Then 'Bone Orchard' was supposed to build on it, to be a great electric blaze, but turned into a quagmire. Damn it."

They continued to play in London but despite the critical reverence, interest was dwindling. After a headlining show at the Venue proved a disaster, the seeds were sewn for the eventual break-up of the band. That was confirmed when Charisma dropped them. "We continued to tour as a three-piece until 1982 but although musically we were still strong, the lack of a record deal meant it was impossible to continue." Both Bobby King (who temporarily stayed with their Charisma subsidiary Pre for his 'Paper Heart' single) and Paul Research continued to record solo. Research's recent releases include the 'Echo City', 'Golden Gate Bridge' and 'Bass Rock Dilemma' EPs. And he still plays 'Horrorshow' live.

All the other former members remain active in music, with the exception of King, notably Steve McLaughlin, who won a Grammy for his work on Tom Petty's Wallflowers in 1995. His other credits include soundtrack work on Robin Hood: Prince Of Thieves, Lethal Weapon 3, Interview With The Vampire: The Vampire Chronicles and Michael Collins. King now lectures on ancient languages.

DISCOGRAPHY:

Horrorshow/Adult/ery 7-inch (Fast Products FAST 8 March 1979)

They Came And Took Her/Romance By Mail 7-inch (Pre-Charisma PRE2 February 1980)

Love Song/Psychomodo 7-inch (Pre-Charisma PRE5 1980)

All About You/Author! Author! 7-inch (Pre-Charisma PRE 14 March 1981)

Author! Author! LP (Pre/Charisma PREX 5 1981) (this was apparently re-released on CD at some point with bonus tracks 'Horrorshow', 'Adult/ery', 'Author! Author!', 'She's Alive', 'They Came And Took Her', 'Romance By Mail', 'Love Song', 'Psychomodo' and both sides of the Robert King solo single 'Paper Heart' c/w 'Theme For Love'. However, I've never seen it, and I damn well want a copy)

Your Attention Please 1-sided flexidisc (I-D, ID1, with ID magazine issue 3, 1981)

Screen Gemz

Karl Hyde (vocals, rhythm guitar), Gary Bond (piano, synthesizer), Stuart Keeling (lead guitar, vocals), Alfie Thomas (bass, vocals), Steve Irwin (drums)

Cardiff punk band formed in the late-70s which featured Karl Hyde and later Rick Smith, who went on to moderate success with Freur and then joined the global dance music hierarchy as Underworld. At the time of the Screen Gemz, Karl, studying art at Cardiff University, was a chef in a café where Smith, who joined the band after their one and only single, washed the dishes (while studying electronics, also at Cardiff). Between them they took pity on starving musicians who visited and would feed them with leftovers at the back door.

The **SCREEN GEMZ** gigged regularly, often alongside another Cardiff University based band, Non Doctor. But it was to be a slightly disillusioning experience, as Smith later recalled to the Underworld website. "I genuinely thought that when I joined the Screen Gemz that they were the best band in the area; they had a single played on the John Peel show. I thought, 'It's all going to happen now.' And I think, within two months of joining the band that, reality just kicked in so serious. I had never schlepped up and down the motorway in a transit van and done all the gruelling (touring). It was so grim; twelve months after that I left the band because I thought it was so crazy."

DISCOGRAPHY:

I Don't Like Cars/Teenage Teenage 7-inch (Inflatable Records 1979) (screen-printed sleeve)

Scrotum Poles

Craig Methven (vocals), Colin Smith (guitar, vocals), Steve Grimmond (bass), Glen Connell (drums)

Scottish punk band, SCROTUM POLES, whose sole vinyl release was the 'Revelation' EP in 1980. They formed at Dundee College Of Education in 1978. They managed to gig through the Tayside area between 1978 and 1980, when they split. They are, naturally enough, absolutely nothing to do with the 90s Utah band of the same name, or the 80s Scrotum Poles from England, or the Northern Ireland Scrotum Poles. Sure is a dang load of Scrotes out there.

Prior to 'Revelation' came the cassette-only Auchtmithie collection, headed by the delightfully titled 'It Just Ain't Fuckin' Funny'. So what was getting their goat? Methven: "One of the early things about the band was that we veered between pop songs like 'Helicopter Honeymoon' and message songs like 'Blair Peach is Dead' and 'Victims Of Vietnam'. 'Funny' was an angry song about inequality and quotes Norman Mailer. Not an important song in the SP canon." Ah, but do you think that's where Lloyd Cole might have got the idea of quoting old Norm from, though?

S

'Revelation' was released as a 33rpm EP, in a cheap xeroxed sleeve bearing the legend, "DIY! We love the TV Personalities", because "none of us could agree what songs we should include," according to Methven. It was recorded at a four-track studio at (later Wet Wet Wet collaborator) Wilf Smartie's Edinburgh studios. However, having played for the last two years with an out of tune guitar loaned from 'Dave The Barman', they had to adjust all the other instruments to fit its tuning. As Methven pointed out on his website, "I remember on 'Radio Tay' that Wilf said there was no way he thought I could reproduce the energy I gave during the guide vocal, but, as the rest of the group were out having a curry, I gave it my best. Wilf thought that (Beach Boys and Sunday Post-inspired song) 'Helicopter Honeymoon' was the stupidest start to any song he had ever heard, but he loved it."

As Ugly Things magazine later wrote, recalling the 100 best DIY singles, "'Helicopter Honeymoon' is going to be played at at least three record collector funerals I know of, not including mine." Wow. That must be pleasing. Methven: "Yes, of course. The song was written after seeing a headline in the Sunday Post. I was always trying to get the band to do stupid surf songs/pop songs and this one worked well particularly when Steve began to put the backing vocals on. We did a version of the Scooby Doo theme tune too – really fast – a real gig favourite." The lyrics to 'Pick The Cat's Eyes Out', incidentally, came from a scribble on the back of a set list by local Dundee punk forerunners Bread Poultice And The Running Sores.

"The name of the band always gave us problems," Methven admits. "Everybody expected stupid meatheads and our gigging 'highlight' was supporting The Exploited and being showered by gob." Former members formed Pigs Are Cute, Aaga, and other bands, all of whom misfired. Methven went on to work for Amnesty International, Connell ran the El Bar in Edinburgh and Grimmond became an arts director for Dundee Council. Colin Smith works in the oil industry in Asia.

DISCOGRAPHY:

Auchmithie Calling cassette (One Tone Records 1979) (100 copies only. "Very poor quality copying, we got a bloke to do it for nothing. I think we might have bought him a pint").

Revelation 33rpm EP (One Tone Records 1980)

Why Don't You Come Out Tonight/Night Train/Pick The Cat's Eyes Out/Helicopter Honeymoon/Radio Tay (first 700 copies had the 'photocopied' sleeve, the next 300, sold to a dealer by their former bass player, came with a new sleeve. The single was later reissued as a CD single in 1999, with 'archive' material)

COMPILATION:

Messthetics #1 (Hyped2Death 'Pick The Cat's Eyes Out', 'Helicopter Honeymoon')

Sema 4

David 'Jock' Marston (vocals, bass), Steve Gibson (guitar, vocals), Geoff Hardaker (drums)

SEMA 4 were formed in York in 1978 after Marston had left the Cyanide fold and hooked up with his old friend from Nunthorpe Grammar School in York, Steve Gibson. They'd once had a sixth form band there, called Stratford Canning, with Dave 'Fawlty' Sollitt and Mick Gregg. Gibson: "This was the epitome of being bored and we practised and played anywhere and everywhere during our sixth form years, never achieving anything – original punks, I guess."

Thereafter the local York scene took off, led by bands like Cyanide and the Jermz. However, Marston found the constant touring with Cyanide too much and eventually quit. He got in touch with Gibson shortly thereafter and asked him if he wanted to form a new band that would just gig locally. With the addition of an appropriate drummer in the form of Geoff Hardaker, Sema 4 was born – the name a tribute to the duo's on-stage musical empathy, made explicit in the lyrics to the group's song cum mission statement, 'Sema 4 Messages'.

They rehearsed at Gibson's flat in Acomb, York, which resulted in several threats of arrest by the local constabulary, and the Lowther Hotel near the River Ouse. Gibson: "Jock used to turn up with a sheaf of lyrics and say Gibbo, see what you can do with these. It was then a case of using an old tape recorder to do a demo and then play it to Geoff who quickly picked up the idea." The key influence was the Jam, with short, catchy riffs the order of the day.

A succession of dates in and around York followed at venues like the Oval Ball, the Revolution, the Assembly Rooms and the Winning Post, while the furthest they ventured out of town were shows at the Marquis of Granby and the F Club in Leeds. As well as headlining in their own right, they also supported the Skids, Chelsea, Radiators From Space and the reconstituted Cyanide. Both of their EPs were released in limited editions with each copy numbered and signed, and sold through local independent Red Rhino Records. The releases brought comparisons with the mod revival bands, but in truth there was more in common with the Television Personalities and other lo-fi, pop-inspired punk bands.

Sema 4 split up due to "a number of different issues, but mainly musical differences." Marston formed the Pullovers with Dave Astley – "the singing taxidermist" – and from thence Our 15 Minutes. Tragically, after the band split, Marston was involved in a car accident in which he and his wife and young baby daughter all died. Hence the 'In Memory Of' title given the recent retrospective of Sema 4 released by Detour Records on both vinyl and CD, including all their recorded material, two unreleased studio tracks and live excerpts.

DISCOGRAPHY:

Untitled 7-inch EP (Master Room 1978)

Sema 4 Messages/Keep On Running/Be Aware (Gibson: "The 'Master Room' EP was only a demo/promo which we hawked around, but then decided to go back and do some different

tracks for the first EP. There were approximately six copies, of which I have one. Been offered loads of dosh for it – I don't know why!")

4 From Sema 4 7-inch EP (Pollen Records PMB 022 1979)

Even If I Know/Sema 4 Messages/Actors All/Do You Know Your Friends (500 copies)

Up Down Around 7-inch EP (Pollen Records PMB 024 1980)

Capital City/Talking/Dynamite (On The Night)/Up Down Around (1,000 copies)

ARCHIVE RELEASE:

In Memory Of... LP and CD (Detour DRLP/CD015 February 1997) (that's it for Sema 4, as everything is included in this one handy, thoroughly annotated package. However, it's not quite the end of the story. Steve's son's band Ratio 3, very much in the best traditions of Sema 4, are currently active and even feature some of pater's songs in their set. Their website is at www.ratio3.co.uk. Postscript: Just two months after this piece was completed, Steve Gibson died suddenly. In our brief acquaintance I knew him as a kind, courteous and helpful man, who maintained his enthusiasm for music right up to the end)

Seventeen

Mike Peters (vocals, bass), Eddie MacDonald (guitar), Nigel 'Twist' Buckle (drums), Dave Sharp (aka Dave Kitchingman; bass)

SEVENTEEN formed at the end of 1977 following the dissolution of Peters and Buckle's previous band, the Toilets. The idea was to step away from the conformity of protest punk and try something more akin to the power pop of the Rich Kids, whom Peters had seen on a trek to Eric's in Liverpool and been greatly impressed by. However, their link to punk remained embodied in their name, which was taken directly from the Sex Pistols' song. Sharp would provide a second guitar at various points between his studies and obligations with the Merchant Marine. Early shows came as support to Secret Affair (Hastings Pier), the Killermeters (Huddersfield), Squire (Rhyl) and Dexy's Midnight Runners (Cardiff). There were also headlining shows at the Albion in Chester and the Queen's Hotel in Rhyl. An early live review in the Melody Maker cited them as "a flashing blur of stripped down excitement".

In 1978 Seventeen produced demos of two songs, 'Don't Go' and, oddly, a cover of Tom Jones's 'It's Not Unusual'. This was taken to London in the vain hope of attracting some record company interest. They received the same short shrift that the Toilets had suffered a year previously. However, they found an advert for unsigned bands in the back pages of the Maker and the result was a one-off deal to release 1,500 copies of 'Don't Let Go' for Vendetta Records.

Eric Gavin, Vendetta's A&R director, took up the story for the Detour website. "They were well behaved and professional. We managed to pick up airplay on John Peel's show but couldn't get it playlisted and consequently it didn't sell many copies. To get airplay (I) invented a secretary, Mandy Enytime, who wrote to the radio stations and had inadvertently left her shopping list in the letter, on it many personal feminine items and a copy of the Seventeen single. The record code was VD001 and the catch phrase we used was 'Get A Dose Of This'. Their manager, however, called us up to complain about how we had besmirched the clean characters of his boys and was up in arms about it. However, it caught John Peel's attention and he even quoted the catch phrase when introducing the record on his show. The manager actually called us up and apologised. About 2,500 singles were sold to fans and friends of the band."

Seventeen continued to tour through 1979 and produced a demo of 12 songs at WSRS studios in Wirral (see A Flashing Blur Of Stripped Down Excitement CD) before a badly promoted tour of London in 1980. Their set list had expanded to include songs such as 'Destiny' and 'Street Of 1,000 Faces', and by 1981 'Alarm Alarm' (from whence Peters would take his new band's name, eventually shortened to just the Alarm) and '68 Guns'. The transition was completed with a final Seventeen show at the Half Moon in Dulwich in January 1981.

DISCOGRAPHY:

Bank Holiday Weekend/Don't Let Go First 7-inch (Vendetta VD001 1978)

A Flashing Blur Of Stripped Down Excitement CD (Vinyl Japan ASKCD 135) (CD round-up effectively culled from the demo tapes they sent out after the single's release to try to secure an album deal. The tracks were recorded on four-track at Wallasey Sound Recording Studios in the Wirral in 1979 and essentially document the band's live set at the time)

Sex, Hitler And The Hormones

This wonderfully titled London band had none other than Formula One driver Damon Hll among its ranks. This is, apparently, true. Rumours that Michael Schumacher was in a German Oi! band are not. In fact, I just started them. Later on the Hillster would be invited by Def Leppard to contribute guitar to their Euphoria album, thereby blowing whatever cool this fact might have lent him.

This information might actually be deeply suspect. But I'm a sucker for sports-related punk trivia.

Sex Pistols

Johnny Rotten (aka John Lydon; vocals), Steve Jones (guitar), Paul Cook (drums), Glen Matlock (bass)

The SEX PISTOLS started it all, of course – this punk rock thing. By accident or design, more likely a little of both, they set the snotball rolling. Not that they took much responsibility for the maladjusted child. "We set our own direction, and we don't follow anyone," railed Mr Rotten to Allan Jones in May 1977. "Not like the rest of those fuckin' bands, like the Clash and the Damned and the Stranglers. They're all bollocks. They're just doing what every other band has done. It's the same big fat hippie trip. They make me cringe."

And yet, the Pistols were a product of their times. The optimism of the 60s had been gainsayed by the grim reality of the mid-70s. Pop music, a weathercock of the national identity, had retreated from the succinct three-minute pop single to the languorous rock epic. It's all cliché now, but the idea of making music on any kind of intimate level had been usurped by the excesses of rock spectacle. Bloated wanksmithery on an epic scale had rid music of its ability to communicate anything other than self-importance. Everybody wanted to be from California. There was absolutely no voice reflecting the ground level experience of British kids.

The festering resentment of a generation watching the post-war dream of plenty retreat to the reality of the birth, school, work, death continuum, produced punk. Britain was sliding into decay amid systematic economic mismanagement. Combined with the musical complacency, those conditions conspired to create, initially, pub rock. Pub rock was a grassroots, back to basics music that enveloped the pubs of London and the south east from the mid-70s onward. It was about sweat and fury. It was earnest and honest, but it lacked the spark of difference. Glam had added a little flash of sex and sensuality but was lyrically escapist and purged of meaning. And rock music had become the preserve of the career musician, deified for their technique and accomplishment. Punk had to happen.

Between 1971 and 1973 Paul Cook and Steve Jones had been rehearsing in Acton with guitarist Warwick 'Wally' Nightingale, their friend from the Christopher Wren school in Shepherd's Bush, and bass player Del Noone. Their heroes were the Faces. They wanted to emulate them and get some pub gigs, and thereby secure some free beer and access to women. Initially called the Strand, and subsequently the Swankers, they were patrons, or shoplifters, of Malcolm McLaren's clothes emporia, first under the name Let It Rock and later Sex. McLaren, a veteran of the LSE sit-ins of 1968 and, according to his wife Vivienne Westwood, someone who had been thrown out of every art school in London, would finally find a vehicle fit for his purpose in the unlikely shape of the Faces wannabes from West London. According to many, including Nils Stevenson, he initially envisaged the band as 'the next Bay City Rollers'. Throughout the band's career he would constantly agitate for more outrageous stunts, most of them informed by the Paris revolts of 1968, including an unfulfilled plan to get the band to break into Madame Tussauds and burn effigies of the Beatles.

McLaren recommended his Saturday shop assistant and former grammar school boy Glen Matlock join on bass to replace the disinterested Des Noone. Matlock would later claim he'd previously played five-a-side football against Paul Cook and knew him anyway. He turned up with a battered £25 Hofner bass and was quickly supplied with a brand new, purloined Fender Precision. After he'd been persuaded to watch them rehearse at Riverside Studios in Hammersmith, McLaren encouraged them to oust Nightingale, who had started the band, though they were reluctant initially to do so, bringing in Nick Kent as prospective second guitarist. Kent was kicked out shortly afterwards when he recorded a demo of 'Ease Your Mind' without McLaren's knowledge. Legendarily, the group's displeasure at Kent was subsequently recorded in the lyric to 'I Wanna Be Me'. Matlock gave the band some songwriting impetus and injected a sense of melody into proceedings, but he was not initially popular with either of the 'tight' former school friends Cook and Jones. As Jones would later admit, with typical diplomacy, "He had this pompous face you wanted to slap."

Another important contributor to the project was McLaren's friend Bernie Rhodes, as Matlock later recalled in I Was A Teenage Sex Pistol. "Bernie did one very important thing for the Pistols. He made us focus our thoughts. In the early days of the band, before John arrived, he'd beaver away at us in the pub, making us think through our attitudes. We'd be sitting there talking about music, and he'd dive in... Bernie would go on and on at you like that, making you define and redefine your attitudes." McLaren's old art school friend Jamie Reid would also add suggestions and later, provide the group with its distinctive artwork. In the meantime there would be a lull through the summer of 1975 while Jones was ensconced at Ashford Remand Centre. McLaren, meanwhile, would travel to New York in his abortive attempt to relaunch the New York Dolls' career. Before he did so, he'd suggested a list of new names that the Swankers could relaunch themselves with. These included the Damned, Crème De La Crème and Kid Gladlove. The one they settled on was QT And The Sex Pistols, with the prefix quickly dropped.

At this stage Steve Jones was still singing and playing guitar, but McLaren, on his return from America, knew they needed a front man. He was furious that they had yet to sever the link with Nightingale, after an ultimatum that he would abandon the band unless he followed the dictum. They did as told.

McLaren initially tried to get Richard Hell over from America but was unable to do so – Hell actually wrote to the band saying he was up for the idea, but the nature of visas and financial restrictions ruled it out. Midge Ure, whom McLaren met while trying to sell some of Steve Jones' liberated musical equipment on a trip north to Glasgow, where they were searching for cloth for Sex's Zoot Suits, was also considered. In fact, he was invited to London to try out, but had just got Slik off the ground so declined. However, it was McLaren's assistant, Bernie Rhodes, who spotted John Lydon first, via his infamous 'I Hate Pink Floyd' T-shirt. After an initial meeting in the Roebuck pub he was then asked to audition for the group back at McLaren's shop, where he mimed to Alice Cooper's 'Eighteen', a McLaren favourite. "I just gyrated like a belly dancer," he recalled. Matlock described his audition thus: "He stood there, shouting along and flapping his arms round like an over-excited seagull. He looked just like he did when we played real gigs. He was John Rotten from that very first moment." According to Lydon, Cook was personable while Jones raged that "I can't work with that fucking cunt! All he does is take the piss and moan." They clashed immediately, but McLaren detected a little spark of respect for Lydon's refusal to adopt his vision of a Small Faces/Rod Stewart-styled band. Lydon's high-camp persona, a mix of Kenneth Williams and Laurence Olivier's Richard III, would give the band their entire visual signature. The boy from an Irish-North London family had by this time already been expelled from school, and would later boast of pissing on teacher Mr Prentiss's grave. According to McLaren, he also attempted to persuade him to shorten the band's name simply to 'Sex'. But then Malcolm is not the world's most credible witness, as subsequent run-ins with Lydon would prove.

The next meeting together was at a pub in Chiswick. Lydon had turned up to a proposed meeting at the Crunchy Frog in Rotherhithe but none of the others did – prompting the furious Lydon to offer to kill Matlock when he rang up to apologise. They began to rehearse regularly thereafter at the Rose And Crown in Wandsworth. It was pretty hit and miss, with cheap equipment and a mass of arguments, particularly between Lydon and Jones, who would nickname the singer Johnny Rotten due to his green teeth. Yet, as the latter was beginning to write lyrics, it seemed worth persevering with.

Eventually sessions moved to Badfinger's old studio in Tin Pan Alley, Denmark Street, after Matlock spotted an advert for cheap premises in the Melody Maker. McLaren did a deal with its owner Bill Collins, former Beatles roadie and father of the Professionals' Lewis Collins (he would attend the Pistols' first gig at St Martin's College). There was no working toilet. Jones and Matlock would sleep in the upstairs room. At an early stage Lydon, who was co-habiting a squat in Hampstead with his friend Sid Vicious, got Chrissie Hynde to try to teach him guitar, but he had no discernible talent for the instrument. He also agreed to marry Hynde for £2 to allow her to stay in the country, but then delegated the task to Vicious, who was, of course, too out of it to make it to the registry office.

The Sex Pistols played their first gig supporting Bazooka Joe, featuring future Adam Ant Stuart Goddard, at St Martin's College on 6 November 1975 – a plaque now commemorates the event. It was Matlock's former art college where he'd temporarily been social events secretary. The power was cut after five songs. Five further shows followed at colleges in London during November and December 1975. Matlock had also talked them into a show at the Central School of Art via joint entertainment secretaries Sebastian Conran, son of Terence and Al McDowell, who would later launch ID magazine, where they co-headlined with Roogalator.

Their first non-college date came at the Marquee on 12 February 1976, supporting an uninspired Eddie And The Hot Rods, whom Lydon would describe as "everything that was wrong with live music". During the Pistols set, Lydon attacked the PA, because he didn't like the sound of his voice. The gig was enough to convince Nils Stevenson to take up unofficial assistant management of the group. It also won over Vic Godard, who was walking round the West End with friends when the fracas encouraged them to check out what was happening inside. It was this show that attracted the infamous 'Don't look over your shoulder, but the Sex Pistols are coming' piece written by Neil Spencer for the NME. And the equally famous Steve Jones' rejoinder at the end of the ensuing interview, that "Actually, we're not into music, we're into chaos", which proved, the form franked by the subsequent Grundy interview, that at times he could out-Rotten Rotten.

The Marquee show was followed two days later by Andrew Logan's Valentine's party at Butler's Wharf. Logan, who had designed for Biba, had gone to the trouble of preparing a stage to resemble the court scene from Derek Jarman's Sebastiane. But Steve Severin recalls the band looking bored and playing the same set twice – though that impression might have been given by an interminable version of 'No Fun'. Again, the whole show ended in uproar when Lydon, who was tripping, took exception to the musical equipment, resulting in a stand-off with the PA company. Among those in the audience were Mick Jones, Tony James and Brian James of London SS, shipped in by Bernie Rhodes.

On 20 February they supported Screaming Lord Sutch at High Wycombe's Technical College. Again, as notable as the performance was the audience it attracted – future Buzzcocks Shelley and Devoto, as well as promoter Ron Watts. As Watts recounted to Dave Woodhall in Hundred Watts, "I had to see the social secretary about a stripper I was getting them for a show, and Screaming Lord Sutch was headlining a gig so I popped in to see him. My thought was that I might watch a decent gig. I didn't think that the evening would change my life. What could best be described as a bunch of London scruffs were on the stage. There seemed to be a lot of distraction amongst the audience, which I later found out was some of their friends fighting with the PA guys, but I liked what they were playing. They didn't bowl me over with obvious star potential, but I did like their attitude and I found out that they were called the Sex Pistols. I thought that I might find a use for them in the future, although I couldn't imagine at that point how they could pull a decent crowd."

Their debut appearance at the 100 Club came on 30 March. Later, Lydon had a bust-up with Matlock and had left the gig and was waiting for a bus home when McLaren all but physically dragged him back to the venue. Although the audience only numbered around 60, according to Watts, for which McLaren apparently apologised, he thought they'd played a "blistering" set. They then supported the 101ers at the Nashville on 3 April 1976, the show that convinced Joe Strummer to leave for the Clash. Strummer: "They played 'Steppin' Stone', which we also did, but they were light years ahead of us. The difference between us and them? When we played 'Route 66' to the drunks at the bar, we were going, 'Please like us'. But here was this quartet who were standing there going, 'We don't give a toss what you think, you pricks, this is what we like to play and this is the way we're going to play it.' As soon as I saw them, I just knew."

The early shows, alongside art colleges, were at London overspill/satellite towns like

Daily Mirror

TV's Bill Grundy in rock outrage

?!*!

THE FILTH AND THE FURY!

Judge in 'murder' pardon shocker

Uproar as viewers jam phones

When the air turned blue...

WHO ARE THESE PUNKS?

Welwyn Garden City, St Albans and Milton Keynes. These were organised, according to Paul Cook, because "we thought we'd be so awful, we didn't want to play and just be comfortable in a band. It was a chance for us to get away from the bullshit of London." These shows directly informed the lyric to 'Satellite', while others suggest that its subject was future Nipple Erectors member Shanne Bradley, with whom Lydon had enjoyed a very brief, and innocent, liaison, when she booked them for the St Albans show.

Thereafter Nils Stevenson was delegated to find venues and came up with the strip club El Paradise in Brewer Street, where they began a residency in March 1976. The venue was in such a state that the band felt compelled to wash the floors with disinfectant. Billy Idol: "They were getting better and better… Week by week we saw them get better and better, take out the 60s numbers and add new songs." There was a further press notice in Sounds, in which Lydon stated "I hate hippies and what they stand for. I hate long hair. I hate pub bands… I want people to see us and start something, or else I'm just wasting my time."

A second date at the Nashville on 23 April ended in violence. Someone had decided to take Vivienne Westwood's seat while she got herself a drink. When the man concerned refused to give it up, she attacked him and was joined by Steve Jones, McLaren, Sid Vicious, Lydon's sidekick and accident waiting to happen, and others. Later Pet Shop Boy Neil Tennant sent in a letter to the NME lamenting the group's lacklustre performance. "So how else do the Pistols create the atmosphere when their music has failed? By beating up a member of the audience. How else?" An alternative theory for the night's violence was ventured by Jonh Ingham. "Vivienne said afterwards that she was bored, the Sex Pistols were boring, she decided to liven things up. So she slapped this girl for no reason, just did it." As Matlock conceded, "A fight is always more interesting to watch than the band."

For a while they discussed taking on a second guitarist. Auditions were held, but by now Steve Jones was maturing rapidly as a guitarist and there was no real need for additional personnel. Besides, the idea was largely Paul Cook's, which Matlock would claim was a diversionary tactic to stop the rest of the band ragging on him for keeping up his apprenticeship at Watney's.

They were also building up the repertoire, beginning with Dave Berry's 'Don't Gimme No Lip Child' (originally the B-side to his debut hit 'The Crying Game') and proceeding to 'Pretty Vacant', Matlock's concoction. Inspired by Richard Hell's 'Blank Generation' schtick, Lydon switched one of the lines to 'Forget your cheap comments, we know we're for real' while Matlock used the riff from Abba's 'SOS' to fit the chord pattern, which itself was a Small Faces' lift.

Lydon also began to reveal himself as a lyricist and, contrary to legend and popular belief, he worked diligently at his craft. Among the first seismic sonnets he penned was 'God Save The Queen', which didn't amuse Matlock at all. He thought it would get them killed. He wasn't that far wrong. As he recalled in his autobiography, Lydon thrilled at his band's unease. "I couldn't have enjoyed myself much more if I had sat down and thought, 'How can I annoy them today?' What a pain in the arse I must have been. I wish I had done it deliberately." Despite this, Matlock came up with some music for the piece, partly inspired by watching bass player Paul Riley of Roogalator. After a while the group were able to leave aside standards like 'Substitute', 'Road Runner' and 'Steppin' Stone'. New originals included 'Submission', Lydon's sly dig at McLaren. It was actually written in a drunken get together by Lydon and Matlock when McLaren had given them £20 with the instruction to get pissed and sort out their differences.

There was a residency at the 100 Club during May, at which time they recorded their first sessions for Chris Spedding. Eventually released as part of the posthumous This Is Crap, they cut three songs at Majestic Studios in Clapham; 'Pretty Vacant', 'Problems' and 'No Feelings'. Unbeknown to the band, the sessions were financed by RAK's Mickie Most. But that didn't stop McLaren telling them it was coming out of his pocket and he'd need to recoup from their gig money. Spedding, for his part, recalls the band turning up at his Wimbledon home with a copy of the first Ramones album under their arms saying they wanted to sound just like that.

On 4 June 1976 they played their near mythical first show at the Lesser Free Trade Hall in Manchester, organised by Howard Devoto and Pete Shelley, as they would soon become known. Their band, the Buzzcocks, were due to support, but in the end they couldn't get a rhythm section together in time. So many future band members and media personalities attended – including Morrissey ("I liked them, but they seemed like a clued-in singer and three patched musicians"), Mick Hucknall, Alan Hempsall of Crispy Ambulance, Paul Morley and various future members of Joy Division – that the evening became the subject of a book, David Nolan's I Swear I Was There. Also spellbound was TV presenter and later Factory head Tony Wilson, specifically invited by Devoto. "I went back to Granada and told my producer, Chris Pye, that we absolutely had to have them on the show (So It Goes)."

Exactly a month later they offered the Clash their first live exposure at their gig at the Black Swan in Sheffield, before returning for a second tilt at the Lesser Free Trade Hall on 20 July. This time the Buzzcocks actually made the show, which also witnessed the first live performance of 'Anarchy In The UK'. Based on a Matlock riff, the bass player was, not for the first or last time, horrified when he read the lyrics Lydon had applied to it. Thereafter Tony Wilson fulfilled his earlier promise and invited them to play 'Problems' and 'Anarchy' on So It Goes, aired three days later in early September, where they were interviewed by Clive James. "The audience was stunned," recalled Wilson. "When it was over, there was silence except for the sound of the producer's footsteps stamping down from the control booth. He was looking for someone to hit."

A second round of recording sessions was undertaken at the band's Denmark Street rehearsal space in July 1976 with Dave Goodman. Versions of 'Seventeen', 'Pretty Vacant', 'Satellite', 'No Feelings', 'I Wanna Be Me', 'Anarchy In The UK' and 'Submission' were cut, with Goodman mixing the tapes back at Hammersmith's Riverside Studios, where he double-tracked Jones' guitar. The demos would eventually form part of the Spunk bootleg. Meanwhile, Goodman had driven the band to sparsely attended May shows at places like Northallerton, Whitby, where the committee members held an emergency meeting and asked them to leave the stage after two numbers, and supporting the Doctors of Madness at Middlesbrough Rock Garden.

Arguably their most important coming out show was at the Screen On The Green on 29 August 1976, supported by the Clash and the Buzzcocks. The band were struggling to find London gigs due to their reputation, but Screen film booker Roger Austin was one of McLaren's old friends. Various first hand testimonies suggest that McLaren had a falling out with Bernie Rhodes when he insisted that all the support bands played on a turned-down PA to enhance the Pistols' impact. Lydon lost his front teeth when he was slammed in the face by the microphone. Nick Mobbs, A&R head of EMI was one of the few industry figures to take up McLaren's invitation, though several journalists, including Charles Shaar Murray, were in the audience.

At the start of September the Pistols played the first of two shows in Paris, at the newly opened Chalet Du Lac. They were accompanied by the Bromley Contingent, driven over in Idol's yellow GPO van for the occasion. The Bromley Contingent, comprising Idol, Siouxsie Sioux, Simone Thomas, Simon Barker, Debbie Wilson, Bert 'Berlin' Marshall and Steve Severin, had been hanging round McLaren's Sex shop. It was Barker who had first checked out

McLaren's pet project at Ravensbourne College Of Art in South London, and told everyone they were the nearest thing to the Stooges he'd seen in Britain. He and his friends were dubbed the Bromley Contingent after a journalist's remark following the Pistols' Orpington College show, due to their regional base. As Severin later recalled, "I can see how the role of the Bromley Contingent has been miscast and misunderstood, as there was such a short transition between the time we were a bunch of people on our own and seen as acolytes to the Pistols. When our path crossed the group's, it was more a meeting of the minds. It was never so much that we were fans as much as they just happened to be guys who played in a group. At that time, nobody knew what was going to happen with the band. The circus-like notoriety hadn't yet set in." They were chided in Burchill and Parsons' The Boy Looked At Johnny as "a posse of unrepentant poseurs, committed to attaining fame despite the paucity of talent other than being noticed; achieving their aim by displaying themselves in a manner meticulously calculated to kill." Others saw them as prescient, bespoke cheerleaders for the coming musical and cultural revolution. The truth probably rests somewhere between those two poles.

On 20 September the Sex Pistols headlined the 100 Club Punk Festival. Bernie Rhodes refused to allow the Banshees to use the Clash's PA due to her swastika armband. Sid Vicious managed to blind an audience member during the Damned's set on the second night, after being persuaded by Ron Watts not to attack Stinky Toys simply on the basis that they were French. Sid also, according to whom you speak to, invented the pogo that night, as well as the horrible tradition of 'gobbing' at punk gigs.

In October, with the record labels circling, McLaren opted to go with EMI, who offered a £40,000 advance. Up until this point, Polydor's Chris Parry had made all the running. He thought he'd got the band was reduced to tears and reciting "Malcolm's a cunt" when he found out they'd gone to EMI, despite Polydor having paid for demo sessions.

Two days after signing, on 10 October, they entered Lansdowne Studios with Dave Goodman. But when they couldn't get a perfect take of 'Anarchy', they moved on to Wessex Studios. As well as further versions of 'Anarchy' and 'No Fun', this is where covers such as 'Wat'cha Gonna Do About It', 'Steppin' Stone', 'Substitute', 'Roadrunner', 'Don't Gimme No Lip Child' and 'Johnny B Goode' were laid down for posterity, distinguished by Lydon's self-evident distaste for the material. Matlock: "Those songs, like 'Johnny B Goode', as far as the band were concerned, we weren't recording them. We were mucking about because we got fed up with going over 'Anarchy' again and again. But we got a great version of 'No Fun' out of that."

Tim Friese-Greene, a tape op on the first two Queen albums, served as the engineer on the sessions. "Johnny Rotten went out of his way to be as difficult as possible – spitting on the Hessian vocal booth floor. Yuk! I said, 'Lay off, you're not the cunt that has to clear it up.' Betty, the tea lady, took the piss out of them by bringing their tea into the control room wearing a bin-liner."

For whatever reason, the sessions were not judged a success. Despite dozens of takes, somehow 'Anarchy' didn't sound right. So they returned to the studios with Chris Thomas at his house in Ealing and then back at Wessex, at Cook's suggestion because he was such a big Roxy Music fan, to get a workable version. By now, according to Matlock, they were "sick to death" of the song. Bill Price engineered while Freddie Mercury, working next door, did his best to earwig the sessions. EMI staffer, and the band's A&R contact, Mike Thorne, was also asked to try his luck, and got the band to record 'No Future' (the initial title for 'God Save The Queen') and others over a Saturday afternoon for 'internal distribution'. Goodman: "Glen must have whinged to EMI, 'cause EMI lackey Mike Thorne sneaked down to the studios over the weekend and tried to remix it. He had no authority to do this I might add." That's debatable. Thorne, for his part, had convinced Mobbs to work with the band after taking him up to the band's show at the Outlook Club in Doncaster on 29 September after he'd first passed on them after seeing them play the Screen On The Green.

However, it was the Thomas recording of 'Anarchy' which eventually was considered the best candidate, aided by overdubs of Jones's guitar, after McLaren, according to Mobbs, rejected Mike Thorne's version. Chris Thomas: "It took a very long day to get a backing track down, and it was probably edited. The problem was the interplay between the bass and drums. So we got a backing track down, then we did a lot of guitar overdubs. Steve already had a few ideas, and then we added a few more – there were a lot of guitar parts on 'Anarchy In The UK', about sixteen, I think." It was eventually released on 19 November 1976 and was immediately awarded Sounds 'Single Of The Week' status.

The Sex Pistols, the originators of punk, had been beaten to the punch by the Damned's 'New Rose', almost a month previously. While many were blown away by the iconic force of the Pistols' debut, there were others for whom the incredible fuss had blown expectations, including the Damned's own Captain Sensible. "We sat down to listen to it with baited breath. What are our rivals up to? They were rough and ready on stage all right, but no-one knew what they'd sound like on record. When we heard it, we all pissed ourselves with laughter. It sounded like some redundant Bad Company out-take with like, old man Steptoe singing over the top." For many, it was true, 'Anarchy' was disappointing. You could not argue with the lyric, but the musicianship sounded strangely tame, especially when compared to the adrenaline junkies the Damned. By the end of the month the Pistols' attempted show at Lancaster University was aborted when the authorities decreed they "didn't want that sort of filth within the town limits". It was a portent of things to come.

Then came the Today incident on 1 December 1976, which made flesh the media's new folk devil. They were in rehearsal for their forthcoming 'Anarchy' tour at Harlesden and had just watched Johnny Thunders Heartbreakers play when the call came through from McLaren that they should get in the black Daimler outside and go to Thames TV's recording studios. They objected. McLaren said they wouldn't get their £25 that week if they refused. EMI press man Eric Hall had got them a spot on the Today show after Queen had pulled out, due to the fact that Freddie was still recovering from some dental work. The band then helped themselves to the liquor cupboard in the Green Room.

When they entered the studio, the Bromley Contingent was already there. By the time it came to their interview, they had all been drinking but were not, as some reports have stated, drunk. Grundy turned to camera. "They are punk rockers. The new craze, they tell me. Their heroes? Not the nice, clean Rolling Stones... you see they are as drunk as I am... they are clean by comparison." The opening tone of the conversation was relatively calm, with Grundy making light-hearted banter about the group's artistic merits. Until Lydon said 'shit' under his breath. Grundy challenged him. "Nothing! A rude word. Next question." But Grundy persists. So Lydon, in deliciously taciturn fashion, repeats the expletive. Grundy's attentions then turned to Siouxsie. "I always wanted to meet you," she coos. Grundy offers to meet her afterwards in an act of faux-lechery. At which point Steve Jones, let it not be forgotten the cock o' the walk when it came to sexual congress with punk ladies, did what nature and circumstance dictated to him, and responded in kind. "You dirty bastard. You dirty fucker." As you would, perhaps, with a full bottle of Blue Nun swilling inside you. An irate 47-year-old lorry driver from Waltham Forest, James Holmes, was so incensed by the swearing in front of his eight-year-old son, it caused him to kick his television set in. "It blew up and I was knocked backwards," he confirmed to the tabloids. The headlines flowed from this point, the Mirror's 'Filth and the Fury' being one that the band would hijack and make their own (others were '4-letter Words Rock TV' in the Telegraph and the surprisingly prescient 'Were The Pistols Loaded?' in the Sun).

By all accounts, that would-be revolutionary Malcolm McLaren absolutely cacked himself backstage. Grundy, the man who had first interviewed the Beatles on TV, and was apparently pushed into doing the interview against his will, saw his career disappear up the swanee as the Pistols' career shot upstream in the opposite direction. Lydon: "Grundy was a fat, sexist beer monster who knew nothing about us and shouldn't have been interviewing us in the first place. All we did was point that out. All he was interested in was the tits." McLaren and the band were summoned to a meeting at EMI the next day, where Leslie Hill warned them that his boss, Len Wood, was not impressed, and could he please keep his charges under stricter control in future? Steve Severin: "The Grundy show was absolutely the hinge. Before, the Pistols were just a group of annoying musical hacks."

The Pistols' proposed Anarchy In The UK tour of 1977 was subject to a series of cancellations. With support from the Clash, Damned and Johnny Thunders' Heartbreakers, it was scheduled to take in 24 venues. In the event, less than half a dozen were completed. Throughout the shires of England, hastily arranged council pow-wows saw the group banned from town after town. The show at Caerphilly was picketed by placard-wielding, hymn-chanting churchfolk. By now, the footage of Derby councillors and protesting Caerphilly carol singers is as familiar as anything in the band's iconography of outrage. However, it's best employed in Paul Tickell's 1995 documentary Punk And The Pistols – when he sublimely intersperses it with clips from the Brit sci-fi classic Quatermass – as the band progressed from Severin's "musical hacks" to scapegoats for a nation's insecurities. Meanwhile John Read, chairman of the December EMI annual general meeting, was forced to issue a statement: "We shall do everything we can to restrain their public behaviour." On 19 December a story appeared in the Daily Mirror where Paul Cook's mother was interviewed and told he was no longer welcome back home. Mrs Matlock's reaction was even funnier. "Glen, it's terrible what you've done. You used to be such a nice boy, now every time I go to work at the gas board they call me Mrs Sex Pistol."

In the meantime, a threatened strike at their pressing plants in the run-up to Christmas gave EMI little choice but to pull 'Anarchy In The UK'. On their return to London, GLC Councillor Bernard Brook-Partridge announced that most of the new generation of punk groups "would be vastly improved by sudden death" while he reserved special contempt for the Pistols as "the antithesis of humankind". Good man. If you're going to be stuffy and outraged, you might as well do it with a dash of style.

1977 began with more tabloid fury. A five-date Holland tour saw the group accused not only of swearing and spitting, but vomiting, in the Heathrow terminal. An air-hostess was quoted as stating: "These are the most revolting people I've ever seen. They called us filthy names and insulted everyone in sight. One of them was sick in a corridor." Matlock later conceded that either he or Steve Jones might have been sick through flight nerves and alcohol, it certainly wasn't intentional. However, it is interesting to note that McLaren had pulled off a remarkably similar press coup with the New York Dolls when they arrived at Heathrow. It's been alleged, however, that the coverage of the Heathrow departure was the final straw in convincing EMI that their charges were beyond redemption. In the meantime, Glen Matlock played his last show with the Pistols on 7 January 1977 at the Paradiso in Amsterdam. Staying in a brown café in Amsterdam, Matlock was told by the Daily Mirror that EMI had decided to cancel their contract. Reflecting on the decision, EMI chairman John Read told the BBC in 2004 that "Their records were quite unacceptable for the average person. They didn't behave, they didn't accept the common rules of decency, so it was important to take out the poison."

McLaren, who'd pocketed £40,000 out of the mess, was alive to what was going on, and on 9 January met up with Derek Green, MD of A&M, to discuss the possibilities of a quick transfer. He took along a demo of four songs, 'Pretty Vacant', 'No Future', 'No Feelings' and 'Submission', as well as three versions of 'Anarchy'. Chris Parry had again tried to sign the band to Polydor, on exactly the same terms offered prior to their move to EMI, but this time was stymied by Polydor's owners Philips vetoing the idea.

On 28 February Glen Matlock departed the band officially to be replaced by Sid Vicious, with McLaren sending a telegram to the music papers to let them know Matlock had departed because he loved the Beatles. Matlock's retrospective version is that he was sick of working with Lydon anyway, and had already started thinking, and acting, on setting up the Rich Kids with old friend Steve New. Lydon has been unguarded about the fact that he issued a 'him or me' ultimatum to McLaren, but admits that Matlock was right in thinking he wanted Sid Vicious. His most famous contribution to the punk movement thus far was drumming for that epochal Banshees show at the 100 Club, and inventing the pogo, apparently as a means of getting up the noses of the Bromley Contingent, whom he loathed.

He was now in the band as an ally to balance out the single-headed amoeba, as Lydon perceived it, that was Cook and Jones. He'd also suggested John Wardle aka Jah Wobble, but Cook and Jones considered him way too scary. Vicious was all front when it came to his violent image, whereas Wardle was the real deal. Matlock even offered to give his replacement, Sid, some bass lessons, and to help out on the sessions for A&M if the Pistols needed him. Sid never did take him up on his offer of bass lessons, but sometime later Matlock agreed, over a drink, to back Sid in the Vicious White Kids, featuring Steve New and Rat Scabies. But by then the Sex Pistols were a distant memory. Much later, Lydon would reflect that "Malcolm would tend to say one thing to one person and another to another, and you would believe the information you were being given. Glen's right when he says Malcolm set us off against each other. When you're young, you don't see the wood for the trees."

In the meantime, the post-Matlock Pistols recorded both their forthcoming singles, at this stage with no idea of where they would find a home, at Wessex Studios with Chris Thomas at the start of March. Both 'God Save The Queen' and 'Pretty Vacant' were cut at these sessions. Sid did his best, but had to have his parts covered by Steve Jones. And Lydon's belief that having him in the band helped quickly soured after he hooked up with notorious American junkie Nancy Spungen.

The deal with A&M was completed on 8 March 1977, but a mocked-up signing was staged two days later, outside Buckingham Palace, which was head of press Kit Buckler's idea. It worked beautifully. McLaren invited journalists via telegram. It was naturally assumed that the police would turn up to monitor events, which they duly did. It was followed by an official press conference back at the Regent Palace Hotel in Piccadilly – after an inter-band ruck in the limo – before a final fling back at A&M's office. There, Sid disgraced himself by destroying the toilet bowl in the ladies after attempting to wash his gashed foot, and Steve Jones nicked all the secretaries' handbags and rifled through them for cash.

Their relationship with A&M quickly soured. Two days later they were at the Speakeasy when John Wardle 'thumped' Old Grey Whistle Test host 'Whispering' Bob Harris, who later recalled that he was the perfect "coconut on the shy". Just as they had almost disrupted the trooping of the colour two days earlier, the band was signalling its intent with regard to the changing of the media guard. Sid also went for an OGWT engineer who had to be taken to hospital with 14 stitches. With the tensions building, McLaren sent his charges away for a holiday in Jersey. The Island of Jersey kindly requested they return whence they came. So they ended up taking their holidays in Berlin.

The Speakeasy was the central incident behind Derek Green deciding to drop the band, after consulting with A&M head Jerry Moss. He felt that he just couldn't deal with the personal behaviour issues. However, others would maintain that A&M was facing internal pressure from artists such as Richard Carpenter and Rick Wakeman – one of the most vocal opponents of punk. An Evening Standard story asserted that both had threatened to quit A&M over its endorsement of punk. Wakeman subsequently denied this to Toby Manning. "I went apeshit. It made no difference to me whether A&M wanted to sign Sooty or the Queen herself, as long as they kept putting my records out... I felt like I was made a scapegoat. A&M wanted out and I was perfect – I was a key figure in progressive rock. I was living a thousands miles away, literally and figuratively out of touch." The result was that 'God Save The Queen' was pulled from A&M's presses, making it the greatest rarity in punk rock history.

So the Sex Pistols finally washed up at Virgin, at the behest of Richard Branson, signing for £15,000 on 14 May 1977. McLaren had actually shook hands on a deal following the band's exit from EMI, but in typical fashion abandoned his suitor when A&M came in with a better offer. 'God Save The Queen', the band's epic denunciation of the industry of institution, saw the Sex Pistols put arsenic in the Jubilee punch bowl. It immediately wiped everything else off the front page as the gutter press, then still in snivelling pageantry mode, leapt to the defence of this assault on Olde England, which was actually crumbling in the wake of unemployment, IRA attacks and an ailing economy. It would enter the charts at number four and sell 100,000 copies in its first week of release, yet be prevented from reaching the top of the charts due to a blanket media ban. Of course, the timing of its release was actually a matter of serendipity. It would not have disrupted Jubilee week had not A&M got cold feet and pulled it, and it was definitely not written in reaction to the celebrations.

On 7 June the band sailed down the Thames to mock the week-long Silver Jubilee celebrations that had just started. A 175-seat pleasure cruiser, actually called The Queen Elizabeth in a wonderful feat of unintentional irony, was hired for the purpose. The band opened up their set with 'Anarchy In The UK' and then 'God Save The Queen', before John Wardle became involved in a scuffle during 'I Wanna Be Me' and the ship's captain decided enough was enough. He radioed for the police to come aboard and steered his vessel to Westminster Pier. The police and their Black Marias were waiting there in force. After a few scuffles and some bottle-throwing, McLaren was among the first to be thrown in the back of the van, after a valedictory chant of 'fascist bastards' at the opposition, to be followed by Vivienne Westwood, who was later charged with assault. Lydon's brother Jimmy was among those lifted, out of eleven partygoers arrested in total. They appeared at Bow Street magistrates the following day, charged with a variety of offences.

For many, the Jubilee boat trip was a turning point. A day later, Nils Stevenson would write in his diary that "The psychos are taking over and the camp element are abandoning ship," probably unconsciously continuing the nautical metaphor. Jon Savage also considered it a key moment. Much later, writer Alan Jones would concede the same. "I gave up, started wearing Village People leather outfits and moved on to roller disco."

By the end of June the band was back in Wessex Studios working alongside Chris Thomas and Bill Price, where they put together the single version of 'Holidays In The Sun', having begun sessions for what would become Never Mind The Bollocks at sessions in January and April. Most of the recording centred on getting Steve Jones' guitar overdubs right, which accounts for the colossal sound achieved on the album. Sid half-heartedly contributed to a couple of the songs, 'God Save The Queen' and 'Bodies', and a rejected version of 'Submission'. But Jones, in unspoken consort with Thomas and Price, managed to bury his contributions so deep in the mix so as to be virtually inaudible. Jones: "Sid wanted to come down and play on the album, and we tried as hard as possible not to let him anywhere near the studio. Luckily he had hepatitis at the time. He had to stay at the hospital, and that was really good."

But their notoriety meant there were repercussions for the band. Lydon, Paul Cook and designer Jamie Reid, who had his leg broken, were all attacked. There was a further major bust-up at the Speakeasy, and Lydon's injuries were so severe – in addition to being knifed in the knee he had a stiletto heel pushed straight through his hand – that he is still unable to clench his left fist. The backlash was egged on by both the media and the establishment. Among the spurious claims levelled against the band was one put forward by Labour Councillor Margaret Williams, who bemoaned the fact that the group "cut up animals onstage and cover themselves in blood".

In fact, so concerned was Sid Vicious with the escalating violence directed at the band that he made a midnight phone call to McLaren's secretary Sophie, and demanded he organise something to get out of the country. McLaren came up with Scandinavia at the middle of July. Wholly unbeknown to Lydon, his partner Nora would have a miscarriage while he was away after falling while changing a lightbulb. Which may explain why Giovanni Dadomo recollected him reading a book he'd been given on the development of the human foetus while trapped in a hotel room in Sweden. Or it may not.

Lydon loved the unbridled enthusiasm for the band in Scandinavia, as opposed to the detached social critique afforded them in places like Holland, where the hippie ideals still held sway. John 'Boogie' Tiberi had the job of marshalling this crazy event, with frequent stand-offs between punks, the local Raggare and the police, though the latter were hugely more tolerant of the Pistols' circus than their UK equivalents. In many ways the tour saw the band at the height of their powers, albeit with a practically non-existent bass player. But Jones' sheer riffing prowess carried the day. As Lydon would later concede to Tom Hibbert: "I found it absolutely thrilling to be next to him on a stage, the power that would come out of that poxy little amp with usually three strings, because that's all he could remember to hit at any one point."

When they returned to the UK, their August tour had to be completed in secrecy. The S.P.O.T.S. tour (Sex Pistols On Tour Secretly) began on 19 August at Lafayette in Wolverhampton for six shows before moving over to Holland for a further nine dates. The Pistols used various aliases, including the Tax Exiles and Acne Rabble, as well as the Spots.

Never Mind The Bollocks was finally made available on 28 October 1977, the only album to be released in the Sex Pistols' lifetime. Many would rather point you in the direction of the Spunk bootleg recorded with Dave Goodman, and those recordings certainly have merits in terms of the simplicity and ruggedness of approach. But the official studio album was the one that all but a healthy clique got to hear the Pistols on a long player. While it's a much more produced record, dominated by Jones' oceanic guitar sound and Lydon's haranguing lyrics, the songs still triumph. However, one of those who was unimpressed with the eventual production was Lydon himself. "Fatty (Jones) would lay down 21 guitar solos," Lydon later lamented in 1978, "that was nauseous. I didn't like the sound of that album. Well old-fashioned... I'd be there making sure Chris Thomas didn't fuck us up and make us sound like Roxy Music and then find out that was exactly how Steve and Paul wanted us to sound." By the time he wrote his autobiography he'd revised his opinion, however.

Other objections to the album were more theoretical than aesthetic. That old wag Bill Drummond once wrote a note to Seymour Stein indicating why he wouldn't let Echo And The Bunnymen sign to his label. He used an analogy incorporating both Sergeant Pepper and Bollocks: "The Pistols were supposed only to release singles that blistered the charts and split the nation in two, not albums that students could sit down and listen to and contemplate." When all and sundry take it upon themselves, without invitation, to ring-fence what you 'were supposed' to do, some measure of success has been attained. Think of it as the 'public property' concept that Lydon would hit upon with PiL.

The album debuted at number one in the chart, despite being banned by Woolworth's, Boots and WH Smith. All four singles were reprised, including 'Holidays In The Sun', written in Berlin in March and released alongside the album in October. The other seven tracks were mainly recorded at Wessex between January and April 1977, with finishing touches applied in September.

Many feel that 'Holidays In The Sun' is the greatest song the band ever recorded. From its marching feet intro to Jones' spiralling guitar breakdown – although parts of it were self-evidently lifted from the Jam's 'In The City' – to Lydon's hilarious marriage of British package holiday culture with consumer fascism, it doesn't get a goosestep wrong. John Peel, bless him, was so moved by the 'cheap holiday in other people's misery' couplet that he was wracked with liberal guilt on all his subsequent travels. When released on single it also came in Jamie Reid's most effective sleeve, a wonderful pastiche of a brochure published by the Belgian Travel Service.

'Bodies' was the most brutal song the band ever recorded, inspired by a mentally damaged young punk who would turn up at Sex Pistols' shows with her own aborted foteus in her handbag. And the Pauline of the song did, indeed, live in a treehouse, apparently, when she could escape the grasp of the mental facility security guards where she resided. Later, Lydon would also acknowledge the influence of his mother's miscarriage in informing the imagery. However, for Tory MP Norman St John Stevas, it was the profusion of 'fucks' that led him to surmise the song was "... the kind of music that is a symptom of the way society is declining. It could have a shocking effect on young people."

'No Feelings' was a direct extension of Lydon's own bleak worldview, famously captured in his dismissal of sex ("a series of squelching noises"). But like 'God Save The Queen', which it accompanied as a B-side, whose 'no future' motif was taken way too literally, it can be read in more life-affirming terms – rejection can be endorsement and vice versa. 'Liar' was a makeweight early Lydon/Matlock collaboration from 1976. Another early song was 'Problems', dating from a late 1975 rehearsal.

'Seventeen', often known by its chorus 'I'm A Lazy Sod', was presented in a different lyrical guise to the song recorded for the Goodman sessions, which had originally taken the template of the Small Faces' 'Lazy Sunday' as its inspiration. The reference to the age of 29, made even more barbed on the original lyric's "When your business dies, you will not return", was Lydon's unambiguous dig at Malcolm McLaren. 'Submission' was written at the request of McLaren to promote his SEX clothes range.

S

The familiar 'Pretty Vacant', the Pistols' generational call to arms, was followed in the running order by another slight on their manager, 'New York'. This was Lydon mocking McLaren's infatuation with the New York Dolls and the Max's Kansas City milieu. It also namechecks two Dolls' standards, 'Looking For A Kiss' and 'Pills' as well as Captain Beefheart's 'Japan In A Dishpan'. Of course, years later Johnny Thunders would write a sarcastic response, 'London Boys', a record featuring Cook and Jones as the rhythm section for added sarcasm. 'EMI (Unlimited Edition)' was the last song recorded with Glen Matlock on bass at Gooseberry Studios in January 1977, with Dave Goodman producing, but the new Chris Thomas production had been completed at Wessex in March. It was a nice final two-fingered salute to EMI: "Too many people have the suss/Too many people support us."

The Pistols, and Virgin, would wind up in court as a direct result of the album's title, leading to a farcical court case in which it was proved that 'bollocks' was legitimate Anglo-Saxon.

Quite wonderfully, it was Cliff Richard's 40 Golden Greats that it dislodged at the top of the charts, the man who would later claim that the Sex Pistols were "the worst thing ever to happen to rock'n'roll". Nope. That'd be you, Cliff.

By the time the band's UK tour resumed on the 16 December at Brunel University, it had been renamed the Never Mind The Bans tour and comprised seven more completed dates. The last, at Ivanhoes in Huddersfield, included a short afternoon show for children. But it would be the band's last appearance in the UK. America called.

The band was scheduled to tour the US in January 1978. The itinerary was interesting, with gigs centring mainly around the southern states, with the most northerly date being the final show of the tour in San Francisco. The rationale was that the Pistols' rebellious nature would appeal to those states that prided themselves on an outlaw image. It was undertaken against the wishes of their American label Warner Brothers.

It was a surreal journey. To keep Sidney in tether, and away from hard drugs, a bunch of Vietnam Vet security guards were hired, with Noel Monk appointed by Warners as the beleaguered tour manager. The first date was in Atlanta on 5 January, followed by shows in Memphis, Texas, Baton Rouge, Dallas, Tulsa and finally San Francisco. Meanwhile, by the time the tour hit Dallas, Sid had carved "Give Me A Fix" on his chest, which pretty much summed up what his mindset was. Lydon was growing tired of the whole shebang – though he loved America – after he showed his bandmates a first draft of his lyric for 'Religion' (aka 'Sod In Heaven') and they rejected it out of hand. In the end, Cook and Jones opted to travel by plane to the destinations alongside McLaren, with Lydon travelling with the crew and Sid. Festering seeds of disharmony just festered some more.

It all ended at San Francisco's Winterland with Lydon's exquisitely observed final words, "Ever get the feeling you've been cheated?" In its own way, the utterance was every bit as off-hand iconic as Steve Jones' profanities on Bill Grundy. Reflecting in his autobiography, Lydon pointed out that "the last moment on stage in San Francisco was the truth. I had felt cheated. I felt that my life had been stolen from me by lesser beings. Our inabilities ruined something truly excellent." He would reflect further on that passage of the book in a later Q interview with Tom Hibbert. "The Sex Pistols just became a publicity fiasco rather than something with actual content and purpose. All that was thrown by the wayside and we ended up as some sorry rock'n'roll sad, sad thing that I didn't want to be part of."

By the time the band had actually reached San Francisco, that also meant poor, dilapidated Sid could get hold of his drugs again. That in of itself prompted a bust-up when he demanded money to buy Mandrax and McLaren refused him, according to the testimony of NME journalist Joe Stevens. There are various reports of the band meetings held at the Miyako Hotel in San Francisco. Cook and Jones had been telling McLaren how brassed off they were, while McLaren schemed about a trip to Rio to hook up with train robber Ronnie Biggs. Lydon had not been informed of this, and only found out through Stevens – though again, other accounts differ, alluding to the fact that only the timing of the trip, so shortly after the American tour, was a surprise to him. McLaren also had a go at Lydon for turning into "Rod Stewart". Cook and Jones decided it was falling apart and approached Lydon, who had been frustrated in his attempts to speak to McLaren further, at breakfast in the hotel the next day. Lydon said that the way forward was to get rid of McLaren, but couldn't get them to agree. Lydon then went up to McLaren's room. The meeting was short and curt. And that was that. The next day, Vicious overdosed on a combination of drugs and fell through a plate glass window.

Back in London, Lydon worked with Richard Branson on signing reggae acts to Virgin, roping in his old friends Don Letts and photographer Dennis Morris. And on Sid's return, they briefly talked about working together. But then Sid brought Nancy to the meeting, who said that Sid was the star and that Lydon could play drums. Branson, knowing full well that his record company could not be seen to sue Glitterbest without losing all the accrued prestige for marketing the Sex Pistols in the process, allegedly encouraged Lydon to take a case against McLaren to court instead.

Cook and Jones did indeed jet off to Rio and record 'Cosh The Driver' with Ronnie Biggs on vocals, while McLaren busied himself with The Great Rock'n'roll Swindle film project, the original intended director, Russ Meyer, having long since departed. He also held auditions for a replacement singer for the Sex Pistols at the Astoria in London. Even Lydon's little brother Martin tried out. Others, including Paul Cook, attest to the fact that the auditions were never serious and were more to do with getting something together for the film. By April, Lydon had started putting together Public Image Limited, their formation officially announced in July, and Cook and Jones were backing Johnny Thunders at gigs at the Speakeasy. Vicious would also gig with Rat Scabies, Glen Matlock and Steve New as the Vicious White Kids.

After Lydon left the Sex Pistols, the received critical view is that McLaren then took up the reins and buried the band's legacy amid a welter of cynical, manipulative releases. That's not completely true, however. As Jon Savage picked up in his review of the sprawling Great Rock 'n 'Roll Swindle double album that accompanied the release of that most tortured of films, there was a huge amount to like about the post-Lydon Sex Pistols. Even if so much of it was focused around McLaren's attempt to preserve the Pistols' legacy as 'his idea'. Straight after the Bill Grundy incident in December 1976 he'd been moving towards the idea of a documentary to cash in on the band's notoriety. To that end a huge amount of footage had been stockpiled in readiness.

'No-one Is Innocent' (aka 'Cosh The Driver', 'God Save The Sex Pistols' and even 'The Biggest Blow' on the 12-inch version with dialogue inserted by Cook and Jones) was an aberration. But there's much to admire about the Cook/Jones' 'Silly Thing' (Cook singing on the album version, Jones on the single). Rotten's utter contempt for a run-through of 'Johnny B Goode', presumably included by McLaren in an attempt to legitimate his claims to 'authorship' of the Sex Pistols concept, is actually useful in arguing the opposite case. The much discussed 'Belsen Was A Gas', originally written by Sid as a member of the Flowers Of Romance and briefly considered as the band's fifth single, gets an airing in two versions. The truly coruscating live take at the band's final show in San Francisco, the first time they'd played it live, and in which Lydon concludes the song with the lines "Be someone, kill someone/Be a man, kill yourself", transcends its mean-spirited, tasteless origins. The studio version, featuring a vocal by Biggs, pales in comparison as the squalid showbizzy stunt it is.

But Tenpole Tudor is hilarious on 'Who Killed Bambi', on which Vivienne Westwood manages to bag a composer's credit, and Bernie Rhodes' Black Arabs very nearly steal the show with their disco-punk revivals. But that final honour goes to Sid. However difficult it actually was to keep him on track to record his version of 'My Way', it's still hopelessly funny, absolutely rubber-stamping the Pistols' mythology. McLaren had originally suggested he record Edith Piaf's 'Non, Je Ne Regrette Rien', but Sidney wasn't having it, until Jean Fernandez of Barclay Records suggested 'Comme D'Habitude', the original French version of 'My Way'. Elsewhere, McLaren finally got to play the artist himself, and is actually quite funny. The album is, of course, completely unthreatening and a betrayal of everything the Pistols stood for, but as a listening experience, a jokey afterthought or footnote, it's great, thanks.

McLaren's misbegotten celluloid adventure, which celebrated the Pistols' smash and grab raid on the major record labels but actually ended up squandering all their ill-gotten gains, was the straw that broke the hunchback's back, and saw the opposing Lydon and McLaren camps end up in court. It was originally a straight fight, with the action also pursued against Cook, Jones and Sid's estate as defendants, until Cook and Jones elected to switch horses mid-race to preserve their own interests. Lydon won, though at one time the case looked so shaky that his brief advised him to pull out. The legal action lasted from 1978 to 1986 and its resolution didn't assuage the bitterness between McLaren and Lydon one iota.

Meanwhile legends, however squalid, were being birthed. Sid was arrested over suspicion of involvement in the murder of Nancy Spungen at the Chelsea Hotel on 12 October 1978. During his four-day stay at Rikers Jail he tried to commit suicide twice, before McLaren borrowed $50,000 from Virgin to bail him out. Sid died on 2 February 1979, just over three months after the murder. Of course, the Sid And Nancy story subsequently became the subject of Alex Cox's 1986 biopic, which blurred facts to suit its cinematic function, and outraged Lydon. It's become quite clear, not least through The Filth And The Fury, how deeply Sid's death actually affected Lydon, and how much he blamed McLaren for what happened. Talking to Q in 2005, McLaren was unapologetic. "You can't ever repair that damage. He's right to feel pissed off. We did manipulate him. But hey, fair game, mate, you wanted to be in the band – you were press-ganged into it a bit, but it was a good ride. A terrific deal: 18 months,

S

and you are living off the royalties ever after. That's my position. Simple as that." Does that sound callous? What's not generally reported in the story is the fact that he and Vivienne Westwood had a son, Joseph, who would have been nearly 10 when the Sex Pistols kicked off (he now runs a successful lingerie company entitled Agent Provocateur). McLaren was also, in some ways, loco parentis for Sid. But Sid was a glove puppet and thoroughly expendable.

All this was a side-show to the real event. But there was money to be made, so Virgin rush-released some product while rumours abounded that Cook and Jones were going to team up with Jimmy Pursey to form the Sham Pistols. How awful an idea was that? Aside from a couple of appearances at Sham gigs, nothing came of it, leading the rhythm team to set themselves up as the Professionals.

That was that. Cook and Jones flitted in and out of the industry. Lydon made some incredible records with PiL and a couple of enfeebled ones, and Matlock became the most amenable media figure in the story. Then the Sex Pistols reunited in 1996 to play at Finsbury Park. They'd even made it up with their old punchbag Matlock. Kind of – the wisdom of age, hatchets buried, new haircuts, etc. That baguette business hushed over. Jones' girth as meaty as his riffs. 'Fat, forty and back'. They were never going to be apologetic. And of course, Lydon, in his pre-I'm A Celebrity, Get Me Out Of Here days, jetted in from LA with a succession of inimitable one-liners that made you realise what a missed presence he had been in British cultural life.

As for Celebrity – it was quite good fun to hear Rotten point out that seeing the cellulite on Jordan's thighs put him off having a wank. Long gone were the days when he could be seen playing lucky dip down the undergarments of that other, rather more palatable Jordan. He's got his teeth fixed too, he's been a grandad and there's due to be a film version of his autobiography No Irish, No Blacks, No Dogs. Meanwhile, Steve Jones seems to be settling into middle age quite happily, as listeners to his hugely amusing hit LA radio show Jonesy's Jukebox (Indie 103.1) can testify. There are frank discussions on Viagra and how difficult it is to get laid when you get old and fat. Bless him. Bless them.

DISCOGRAPHY:

(So few songs, so much product. Tread warily. There are a huge number of compilations of material with the odd variation. Many are of dubious quality, others of dubious legitimacy. If in doubt, start with Kiss This and the box set. You've pretty much got everything then. It's worth picking up a good version of the Burton-On-Trent gig, and the Winterland show is a great piece of history)

Anarchy in the UK/I Wanna Be Me 7-inch (EMI 2566 November 1976) (there are two versions of the original label. The first credits the B-side to Chris Thomas, the second amends this to Dave Goodman. Several copies of the original were sent out with a note correcting this mistake)

God Save The Queen/No Feelings 7-inch (A&M AMS 7284 March 1977) (withdrawn. If you own a copy, you can retire)

God Save The Queen/Did You No Wrong 7-inch (Virgin VS 181 May 1977)

Pretty Vacant/No Fun 7-inch (Virgin VS 184 July 1977)

Holidays in the Sun/Satellite 7-inch (Virgin VS 191 October 1977)

Never Mind The Bollocks, Here's The Sex Pistols LP (Virgin V 2086 November 1977) (originally issued with a free bonus 7-inch of 'Submission', VDJ 24. This track was added to the track listing for the numerous LP and CD reissues, the first occasion being October 1986. It was also available as a picture disc, VP 2086, released in January 1978)

Post-Lydon Releases:

No-One Is Innocent (A Punk Prayer By Ronald Biggs)/My Way 7-inch (Virgin VS 220 June 1978) (also available on 12-inch, VS 220-12 A1/2, featuring 'The Biggest Blow (A Punk Prayer By Ronald Biggs)' and 'My Way'. Second 12-inch, VS 220-12 A3, additionally included interview segment)

Something Else/Friggin' In The Riggin' 7-inch (Virgin VS 240 February 1979)

The Great Rock'n'roll Swindle dbl LP (Virgin VD 2510 February 1979) (originally a double LP with poster, reissued in various formats including as a single album. The first 50,000 included 'Watcha Gonna Do About It?')

Silly Thing/Who Killed Bambi? 7-inch (Virgin VS 245 April 1979) (B-side with Tenpole Tudor)

C'mon Everybody/God Save The Queen Symphony/Watcha Gonna Do About It? 7-inch (Virgin VS 282 June 1979)

Some Product – Carri On Sex Pistols LP (Virgin VR 2 July 1979) (not music at all, but a

selection of interviews. Including, of course, the Bill Grundy interview. It was compiled by John Varnom of Virgin in the wake of Sidney's headline-grabbing death, but despite the paucity of music and the all round crapness of the contents, it still made the UK Top 10)

The Great Rock'n'roll Swindle/Rock Around The Clock 7-inch (Virgin VS 290 October 1979) (originally in American Express sleeve, later withdrawn)

Flogging A Dead Horse LP (Virgin VS182 February 1980) (the original 'greatest hits' collection, complete with 70s Top Of The Pops pastiche cover)

(I'm Not Your) Stepping Stone/Pistols Propaganda 7-inch (Virgin VS 339 June 1980)

ARCHIVE RELEASES:

Pistols Pack 6x7-inch (Virgin SEX 1 December 1980) (six singles in plastic wallet)

Kiss This dbl CD (Virgin V 2702 October 1992) (features Never Mind The Bollocks in its entirety, plus singles and B-sides, and colour poster. Original issue came with a free CD, Live At Trondheim 21.7.77. The latter is not one of those live Pistols' shows to cherish. The source came from video footage, so the quality is poor, and the fact that Rotten shouts "Fucking hell, half you lot are dead out there" at one point gives some indication of the level of audience interaction. Three songs from the set, 'Satellite', 'Bodies' and 'Pretty Vacant' were AWOL)

This Is Crap (aka Never Mind The Bollocks/Spunk dbl CD (Virgin SPUNK 1 June 1996) (Bollocks again, with added Spunk, so to speak. The second disc is by far the most interesting, as tracks 1-12 is Dave Goodman's Spunk bootleg, including the original alternative titles ('Anarchy' was titled 'Nookie' on Spunk when originally issued on Blank Records – after Tony Parsons' 'Blank Nuggets In The UK' review of March 1977) The trio of tracks from 'Problems' and 'No Feelings' to 'Pretty Vacant' are the band's first demo, with Chris Spedding at the controls, originally bootlegged as the 'We Don't Care' 7-inch. Tracks 16 to 20 are Chris Thomas out-takes from the NMTB sessions, which themselves were originally bootlegged as part of the Party Till U Puke bootleg, issued on Disc De Luxe. The last track, another Goodman version of 'Anarchy In The UK', originally came from the No Future bootleg, alongside the Spunk tracks)

Filthy Lucre Live CD (Virgin CDVUS 116 July 1996) (taken from the 23 June 1996 comeback show at Finsbury Park. Some of the dialogue from the show was censored – notably Steve Jones asking if any member of the audience wanted a "good shag." More reprehensibly, Virgin extricated the version of 'No Fun' to release on the live version of 'Pretty Vacant'. The con goes on)

The Filth and the Fury CD (Virgin CDVD 2909 May 2000) (to accompany the 2000 documentary of the same name. Selection of Pistols tracks plus contributions from 'complementary' musical sources. Don't bother, but do buy the DVD as it's a cracking document)

Jubilee CD (Virgin CDV 2961 June 2002) (singles compilation to celebrate the band's 25th anniversary that also came with a CD of promo videos for 'God Save The Queen', 'Anarchy In The UK' and 'Pretty Vacant'. Apart from that, it's pointless, but hats off to the art director for a very funny sleeve)

Sex Pistols 3-CD Box Set (Virgin SEXBOX1 June 2002) (pretty much a definitive round-up, with excellent liner notes, though there are some tracks from the Dave Goodman sessions released on This Is Crap that are NOT duplicated here. 'Flowers', incidentally, is the band's intro music. Matlock: "We did that just to get everybody to come away from the bar to see what the horrible racket was").

A Selection Of Unofficial/Archive Recordings

The Heyday cassette (Factory FACT 30 October 1980) (a tape of original interviews conducted by Fred and Judy Vermorel for their 1978 book the Inside Story, all of which predate the actual official release of Bollocks. Anyone who can bear to hear Vicious prattle on incessantly about nothing at all more than once is a certifiable masochist, but the authors also tracked down Matlock and McLaren's nan. Eventually repressed on CD in extended form in 2004 by LTM/Boutique, BOUCD 6603, the bonus material including an inspired rant by the inimitable Bernard Brooke-Partridge)

The Mini Album LP (Chaos Mini 1 January 1985) (Six of the seven July 1976 Denmark Street demos. This was re-released on picture disc, Chaos AMPL 37 January 1986, then on CD – Dojo DOJO CD 205 – in 1996, but with 'Pretty Vacant' restored. Several 7-inch vinyl versions of 'Submission' were also culled for single release)

The Original Pistols Live LP (Receiver RRLP 101 February 1985) (subsequently reissued on the EMI budget label Fame, EMI FAME CD0FA 3149 1993, without 'Stepping Stone' from the original set. The Best Of And The Rest Of: Original Pistols Live, released by Action Replay, is more or less the same thing)

After The Storm mini-LP (Receiver RRLP 102 1985) (includes four NY Dolls cuts. Reissued on CD RRCD 102 July 1991)

Best Of The Sex Pistols Live LP (Bondage BOND 007 November 1985)

Where Were You In 1977? LP (Hippy HIPPY1 November 1985)

Last Concert On Earth LP (Konnexion KOMA 788025 February 1986)

No Future UK? LP/CD (Receiver RR/LP 117 December 1989) Some additions. Since This Is Crap came out, the only thing that is exclusive to this issue is the original seven-minute version of 'No Fun')

Pretty Vacant dbl LP/CD (Receiver RRLD/RRDCD 004 January 1991/July 1993) (combines the No Future UK? and Original Pistols Live albums)

Eary Daze: The Studio Collection (Dojo DOJO CD 119 October 1992) (at one point the best place to get decent sounding recordings of the Goodman sessions, but not any more)

Live At Chelmsford Prison CD (DOJO CD 66 1992) (recorded through Dave Goodman's soundboard on 17 September 1976. But note that various Japanese and American editions have had overdubs and fake dialogue inserted)

Better Live Than Dead CD (DOJO CD 73 1992) (probably the best way to hear the much abused Burton-On-Trent show at the 76 Club on 24 September 1976, which was originally released as the Indecent Exposure bootleg. 'Anarchy' is not an encore, just a reprise. 'Suburban Kid' is, of course, 'Satellite'. The full set can be found on the Japanese bootleg Truly Indecent Exposure)

Live At Winterland CD (When! WEN CD 008) (the band's final, 14 January 1978 appearance at San Francisco's Winterland. Sadly, the compilers decided to edit out some of Lydon's stage proclamations. For the complete, unadulterated set, you need the Japanese edition of the CD or the Gun Control bootleg)

Wanted: The Dave Goodman Tapes CD (DOJO CD 216 July 1995) (of interest because it contains the rough mixes, sans overdubs, of the band's 1976 demo, plus an early take on Cook 'n' Jones' 'Here We Go Again', which was eventually paired with 'Black Leather' as part of the 'unreleased' single on the original Pistols' six-pack singles collection. 'Revolution In The Classroom' has absolutely nothing to do with the Sex Pistols, and dates from the various schemes in which Goodman milked his Pistols connection – see all the Ex Pistols' releases)

Alive dbl CD (Castle ESD CD 321 October 1995) (more Goodman out-takes. The second disc, all live, is a mix of the Chelmsford Prison and Burton-On-Trent gigs)

Pirates Of Destiny CD (DOJO CD 222 January 1996) (another ragbag collection, notable for the band's half-hearted, but previously unavailable, shoddy run through of 'Through My Eyes', in which Lydon voices his disapproval – "It's a load of shit anyway." 'Woodstock Baby' is actually 'Anarchy In The UK' with a different intro. Much of the material has been overdubbed by Uncle Dave, rendering it of little interest)

Raw CD (Emporio EMPRCD 716 1997 June 1997) (more Goodman barrel scrapings, both live and studio. Burton-On-Trent-A-Go-Go)

Live Worldwide CD (Chaos/Konnexion 788017) (comically awful compilation, with live material from Burton-On-Trent, again, plus the PiL version of 'Anarchy' sung on the Tube in 1983)

Sham 69

Jimmy Pursey (vocals), Neil Harris (lead guitar), Johnny Goodfornothing (rhythm guitar), Albie Slider (aka Albie Maskell; bass), Billy Bostik (drums)

S

Depending on where you sit, Jimmy Pursey and SHAM 69 represent the ugly defrocking of punk's creative and aesthetic potential or the sainted voice of the disenfranchised working class. They are equally despised and cherished by the two camps, branded either as a sloganeering self-parodists or trailblazers and torchbearers for the downtrodden. Lumpen proles or class warriors. And this divide is neatly reflected in their output, which ranges from anthemic, cathartic urban hymns of solidarity and defiance, to some utter twaddle that should never have reached the gates of the pressing plant. And all points in between.

Pursey was an odd jobs man before punk arrived in his native Hersham in 1976, at which point he was working at Wimbledon dog track. He'd also hang around the legendary Walton Hop, dancing there every Tuesday, Friday and Saturday. "It's so hard to explain to people who see in black and white the colour that existed in this club," Pursey later told Jon Ronson of the Guardian. "The Playhouse was a theatre for fringe plays and amateur dramatics. But on Tuesdays, Fridays and Saturdays it would become paradise… It was inspirational. This wasn't table tennis. This was dancing. This was testing out your own sexuality. Normal people would become very unnormal. It was Welcome to the Pleasure Dome. It was everything." Of course, this interview was conducted after the story broke that Tam Paton, Jonathan King and others were using it as a means to procure sexual favours from underage boys. Pursey, however, insists he never went for a ride in King's white Rolls-Royce, with all that entailed, though King would come down to watch Pursey's band rehearse at a local pig farm, owned by later member Albie Slider's mum.

The Hop was the inspiration behind his desire to pursue a career in 'entertainment', as he told Top Ten. "It was just an incredible place and we felt a vibe that was going on anyway at the particular time, and I was miming as well. This guy was inviting me to get on the stage. Now, half the time I was just drunk, I just leapt around and I would be Gary Glitter or Mick Jagger or somebody. He said to me, 'You should form a band, you should get a band.' And I thought, oh well, that's going to be completely different to me imitating someone drunk, you know what I mean? Then I heard this Ramones stuff, early 1976. I would say that I started to really think that this was just the most outrageous stuff I could possibly be listening to." Jimmy Edwards remembers Jimmy And The Ferrets, as they were then known, as a Bay City Rollers tribute band. "Absolutely true. They used to mime it. Jimmy was like the local entrepreneur. He was the local boy that got everyone together, and they'd go out miming." Soon, however, there was a swift change of image. Edwards: "Sham, at the beginning, were really the true punk band. They really could not play. I was like a big brother. I was a few years older than them. I was born between the waves, really, not old enough to be a Rolling Stone, and not young enough to be a Sex Pistol. We met in Walton in a chip shop, and I said you look like you're in a group. I worked with them quite a lot, in the studio, and I had the same management, Tony Gordon."

Pursey came up with the name Sham 69 from some graffiti sprayed on a local wall, which had originally stated 'Hersham 69', the first syllable having faded. They gradually developed a harder edge as punk spread. "I was always in different tribes before," Pursey recalled to Q, "but finding punk rock was the first thing (where) I could actually say, 'This is really me'. I remember playing Guildford University. People were still listening to things like Ten Years After. We were playing songs like 'Borstal Breakout' and 'What Have We Got', and they were sitting on the floor going, 'Oh, my God, what's this?' It immediately came across to me that no matter what this dustbin-type, raw jumble sale music was, it was hard-hitting. You knew people would respond to it."

Pursey ensured there would never be any doubt as to whose band Sham 69 were, and as vocalist and initially manager, he would sack Bostik, Harris and Goodfornothing when he deemed that they lacked commitment. "I don't think they understood what punk was, and I think that's why there were thousands and thousands of bands out there. But the essence of what it was, was to give your soul, to give everything of you to this thing, and the energy and the buzz you would get back would be rewarding, because you would have to give your soul to the people that you were playing to. So you have to have those four people believing in the basis of what you're believing and then when they go on stage musically they can actually give every single thing of what they're doing at that particular time in that hour, on stage."

Dave Parsons: "Jimmy was known by nearly everyone in the area – he was that sort of personality. The strange thing was, I'd never heard of him. Even stranger was that, as kids, I'd played with a friend who lived on a local farm from the age of six to fifteen, and I learnt later that Jimmy had been playing with his older brother at almost the same time. How we didn't bump into each other is still a mystery to me now. A concert was organised at the local Hop, which my band were playing on, and also Jimmy's band (now called Sham 69), A meeting was held in a function room at a local pub. The guys in my band were all very straight and middle class and when Jimmy and his band walked in, the presence and attitude almost knocked me off my chair. I felt like I was in the wrong band. My band was called Excalibur, which we later changed to Babalois at Jimmy's suggestion. We played local pubs and working men's clubs, playing mainly Kinks, Stones, Who and Beatles songs, with a few of mine thrown in. Anyway, at the Walton Hop gig I became good friends with Jimmy and Albert, and the three of us felt more at home together than we did with our own respective bands. It wasn't long before we bumped into Mark Cain (a local drummer) and decided to form the new Sham 69." He and Pursey became the engine room for Sham 69's subsequent songwriting. Pursey: "Dave Parsons was the only musician that had turned up, that really understood what this was all about. He had the same arm movements as Townshend from the Who. He could play riffs that sounded like the Rolling Stones."

A batch of originals was readied and the band played their London debut at the Roxy as support to Generation X on 12 August 1977. Tony Parsons offered them an enthusiastic write-up in the NME, and they were on their way. "Jimmy Pursey of Sham 69 is a star. Hardly anyone has heard of him or his band, he doesn't get interviewed by Vogue or Sunday Times magazine, and he probably don't pull any more birds than you do. Nevertheless, Jimmy Pursey of Sham 69 is a star... Sham 69 are ex-skinheads who don't have the cash or the inclination to dazzle you with the mandatory sartorial elegance of corporate sponsored urban guerrillas. They're content to use their performance to provoke REACTION! God, I wish you could have been there. Sham 69 are a band who do everything except lie." His partner in vile ink, Julie Burchill, had earlier managed to capture their aesthetic by noting: "Sham 69 play rock'n'roll in the manner that American negroes fight, not for fun but for existence." Dave Parsons: "We played quite a few gigs at the Roxy and after all this time it's hard to differentiate between them. I loved all the gigs there, There was just such a great atmosphere and a real feeling that you were involved in something happening. I remember Jimmy, with a broom, sweeping the place out to earn us enough money to go over the road for a Wimpey burger. Tony Parsons came backstage after the set, begging us to go out and play 'Hey Little Rich Boy' again. It was my introduction to a lifelong passion for dub music, my first joint, and a lot of sweat."

The group were also championed by Mark Perry ("God, in my eyes," Pursey later noted) and Danny Baker in Sniffin' Glue. They released their debut single on Perry's Step Forward label, set up with the backing of Miles Copeland. The cover featured a photo from the Lewisham clashes between the National Front and anti-fascist demonstrators – which would prove quite prophetic in terms of Sham's subsequent career. In fact, the band often slept in their record company premises. I asked Dave Parsons if he had any memories of Miles 'The Wallet' Copeland. "His office was a no-go area. We'd hang out in the other bit with Mark Perry and Danny Baker etc. I do remember we never got paid for anything. One memory I have was when we were at his dad's house (ex-head of the CIA). It was Sham, Miles and his brother Stewart. The next thing we know, his dad bursts in and proceeds to give both Miles and Stewart a huge bollocking. I'm not sure who was more embarrassed – them or us."

They hit the headlines at the opening night of the Vortex on 23 September 1977, playing from a rooftop that overlooked the venue. Naturally the police were called in to stop the performance, and naturally Sham 69 benefited from the publicity that ensued. Parsons: "The main problem here was that we ended up on the wrong roof. It was the opening of the Vortex café, just off of Oxford Street, and by the time we carried all the equipment up to the roof, we somehow managed to set up on the roof of the building next door. It brought Oxford Street to a standstill and made the mid-day news. When the police burst onto the scene we didn't know what was going on and because Jimmy was the singer and playing up to the crowd they just grabbed him and carried him off. The only concern we had was that he would be released in time for a gig later that night up in Leicester, I think. We weren't worried by Jimmy's actions, we felt we were unstoppable." Pursey was fined £30 for breach of the peace, though Sham did manage to complete three songs, 'I Don't Wanna' (making sure they got to promote the new single), 'George Davis Is Innocent' and 'Ulster'.

S

They continued to play at the Roxy, moving up the pecking order by dint of their growing profile but also by rubbing out others' names on the chalkboard outside the club, Andy Czezowski having by now moved on to be replaced by a taxi controller. "He never wanted to pay anybody anything. There was crap and cans all over the floor from the night before, and we didn't have any money to buy any food, and we were starving – not starving Biafran starving, just hungry. I said I'd sweep it all up if he gave us a fiver to go and get some food. So he said, 'Oh, go on and get on with it then.' So I'm sweeping up the Roxy floor, all the cans. And the support band to us walked in and they've got leather jackets, leather trousers. They're absolutely the part. They couldn't be the part more. And they say to me, 'What time is the main band getting here?' And I went, 'They're here.'"

In October 1977 the Inner London Education Authority asked the band to appear in a TV documentary about this new punk farrago. The show, entitled Confessions Of A Music Lover, included two Sham songs, and was shown around London schools, accompanying an interview with Mark Perry. Having been immortalised on vinyl, Albie Slider took his cue to leave, though he did remain a roadie with the band, with Dave 'Kermit' Treganna coming in on bass. Sham 69's most enduring line-up was now in place.

Meanwhile Polydor pounced. The deal was set up after the band acquired the management services of Tony Gordon. He introduced them to Jim Cook at the label, bringing him down to see the band play the Roxy. Cook was impressed – Sham's audience was queuing around the block to get in, and they turned in a good set. That resulted in an immediate offer, and Polydor bought out their Step Forward contract, which had one single remaining.

The group's major label debut was live favourite 'Borstal Breakout'. Released in January 1978, and written about real-life Feltham Borstal, it reinforced Pursey's identification with the outsider and the juvenile criminal – though the lyric actually pre-dated Sham 69. John Cale had been earmarked to oversee production, but in the end Pursey himself took control. "I got all the levels and pushed 'em into the red," Pursey later recalled to MOJO. "All I wanted was that blistering wall of sound behind me singing a 50s rock'n'roll song about running away from prison." It's still Pursey's favourite record from the Sham canon, though he is wont to change his mind on this subject as well as many others. "We were the dustmen of punk. We'd write about things that nobody else wanted to write about basically, because they were the things that really were going on in everyday life." In the meantime he'd philosophise to the NME in November: "I know I'm not going to change the world. If I ever believed I was gonna change the world I'd be a complete nutcase. All I can do is get out on that stage, sing about it, and make people enjoy it at the same time. I'm not a politician, I'm not a leader, all I am is a bloke who gets on stage and sings rock'n'roll."

'Borstal Breakout' was included on their debut LP, Tell Us The Truth, in February, featuring one side of live material and a companion selection of studio recordings. Not to mention 'backs to the wall' cover art that almost broke the cliché bank. As well as 'Borstal Breakout', tracks like 'Family Life' played on the more readily familiar reality of teenage rebellion – getting your mum to let you stay out late. The voice crying out "You bloody get upstairs and have a wash", incidentally, is popularly believed to have belonged to Wendy Richard or Pauline Quirke. Parsons: "The voice was done by the telephone operator in Polydor's Stratford Place studios. I forget her name now." The clash of generations was a theme returned to on the comical 'Sunday Morning Nightmare'. 'George Davis Is Innocent', meanwhile, was rather neutered as a protest song when its subject, though indeed innocent of the charge levelled at him, got banged up for a robbery he was responsible for. Dave Parsons, for one, doesn't think it was a mistake to go for the half-live/half-studio option. "Not at all, because we were predominantly a live band, and had such a lively audience. Don't forget that however naive it may sound now, punk was about breaking down the barriers between band and audience."

In the same month Pete Silverton of Sounds had a look at the Sham phenomenon in Sounds. "Jimmy's a striding ragbag of paradoxes and half-thoughts. He says he doesn't want to be a leader but insists that he can help to educate his audience. He passionately believes in the democracy of the crowd yet still feels (not unnaturally) cheated when his supporters decide to occupy the stage themselves. At least one person I know is convinced that Jimmy is in fact an utter con man, spouting rebel punk words in such furious bouts they conceal his real, less savoury beliefs. I find that totally improbable but understand perfectly how someone could think that – in a world of dishonesty disguised as good manners, Jimmy's passionate, naïve honesty sounds false. He comes over like a china seller at a market and who'd believe one of them?" Silverton then nails the essence of Sham better than anything else I've read. "Jimmy can't help it, of course. He's just the inevitable end result of poor white South London trash clambering its way up on to the stage in the day of the musical social comment. Crude, unsubtle, simplistic and all those things but with an inescapable gut-level power of delivery."

Their breakthrough was confirmed when 'Angels With Dirty Faces' reached the Top 20 in April. Dave Lee Travis was forced to play it, and did a typically moronic impersonation of 'Cockney geezers' to accompany it. They weren't varying the formula much, and B-side 'The Cockney Kids Are Innocent' announced a similar perspective. Jimmy wasn't going to thumb his nose at a Top Of The Pops appearance. "Hello, Mum, look who's on Top Of The Pops then! I always wanted to see whether they were miming or singing live, and I particularly said 'I want to sing live tonight' and I don't think they knew the reason why, and it was more to say hello to my mum on the television. And it was just a funny thing to do. I'd always wanted to do it, I'd always wanted to just get up there and carry on being anarchic on television." Of course, there were those, notably the Clash, who didn't want to skip to the establishment's tune, and playing the show was considered anathema by many. But that didn't concern Pursey. "Basically, just going on Top Of The Pops gave everybody a chance to get more into punk. If they weren't seeing us, how could we deliver the message to a wider audience? But that didn't mean you had to end up being Martin Luther King or John Lennon or whatever, do you understand, in the way of like 'I want to talk to the world'." Of course, Pursey is underplaying his hand here. He quite evidently had a far greater impact on the world than either of those also-rans.

The only blot on the landscape was the type of audience these terrace wobblers were attracting. With the bootboy anthems arrived the bootboys, and part of the skinhead element thus drawn didn't bother to hide their far right convictions (in either sense). Pursey stoically attempted to distance the band from this element, commendably trying to talk to them about why their antics were unwelcome. A boiling point arrived with a Rock Against Racism show alongside Elvis Costello which was all but wrecked by the National Front. "It was the most disturbing thing ever," Pursey related to Q. "Like being in a trench in the First World War, then having to live with it for years and years afterwards. It was a battle I could only win by carrying on. Sometimes I didn't want to, but thank God I did." More successful was another RAR set at Victoria Park where Pursey sang alongside the Clash to emphasise the pro-unity message. That didn't stop their audiences behaving like morons, however, notably booing Jamaica's Cimmarons while on tour.

'If The Kids Are United', based on the old trade union boast (substitute 'workers' for 'kids'), and featuring some colossal drumming, managed to crack the Top Ten. The B-side, 'Sunday Morning Nightmare', complete with retching sounds, is quintessential Sham, as our hero gropes his way towards daylight after a night on the beer. However, gigs scheduled for New York and Philadelphia had to be pulled when Pursey was refused a work permit for having committed a criminal offence in the preceding 12 months – that rooftop set to open the Vortex coming home to roost.

'If The Kids Are United' was followed into the Top Ten three months later by arguably Sham's definitive song, the beer and skittles sing-a-long 'Hurry Up Harry', or to be more phonetically correct, 'Urry Up Arry'. In the face of the systematic oppression of the proletariat by the bourgeois capitalist system, Pursey advanced the genius response "Weer goin' dahn tha' pub." "That's one of the reasons why I wrote 'Hurry Up Harry' and all those songs and let them come out as singles or whatever, cos it was to break up the monotony of 'If The Kids Are United' or 'Borstal Breakout' or whatever. To show what a human being was about, that he takes on emotional problems, he takes on a thinking stance to the life he leads." The titular Harry was actually Pursey's beloved hound, while the keyboard parts were performed by producer Peter Wilson. Meanwhile, rumours that Pursey was being considered for the role of Jimmy in Quadrophenia came to naught.

The band's second album, and first all-studio recording, That's Life, followed in the autumn. It was one of punk's first concept albums. The central story concerned a guy who loses his job for turning up late, wins a packet at the pony shop and blows it all on beer and women. Before its release the group played their biggest gig at the Reading Festival. Pursey: "We were living in John Lennon's house. There was 'John Loves Yoko' carved on the bed that I'm going to sleep in. It's the most mind-blowing time of my life, driving a mile and a half down the road from the house that we're recording in and making That's Life, and we're top of the bill with the Jam and they're just screaming for Sham. There's 40,000 people and I can't believe what I'm looking at. You felt like you could march on London."

Tot Taylor, formerly of Advertising, joined on keyboards for a few gigs at the end of January 1979, but his was a baptism of fire. Despite reasonable commercial success, the band were still being dragged down by elements of their audience, and Pursey was becoming vocal about his objections to audiences intent on wrecking gigs. The worst example came at a show at Middlesex Polytechnic on 26 January 1979, filmed by the BBC for an episode of Arena. Midway through third song 'Cockney Kids Are Innocent', the violence started, and later intensified to such an extent that Pursey was forced to call a halt to proceedings after 30 minutes. He was in tears as he brayed at the crowd to stop hitting innocents. It was actually the most moving spectacle of Sham's career, and there was no doubting his sincerity on this occasion. "That was enough, just a fucking mess of people running round, kicking the crap out of each other, going absolutely ballistic and it was horrible, just horrible, and that's enough." Some pointed the finger at Pursey for being naïve – why complain about violence when you open the show with the soundtrack to A Clockwork Orange and use Land Of Hope And Glory as an intro?

But then, as Dave Parsons remembers: "Yeah, it was upsetting. The violence at our gigs was getting worse and we were all well aware that if it continued it would eventually lead to the break-up of the band. Unfortunately, as always, it's a relatively small number of people who ruin it all for everyone else. We prided ourselves on the fact that we preached to the unconverted which is never an easy task, especially when you end up with people believing you're a right wing band, because of all the headlines they'd read. One of the most rewarding times would be when you'd get an odd fan who'd come back stage after a show, and say that due to where he'd been bought up etc, he's been a member of the NF or BNP. But due to Sham, he'd now left all that behind him. Even if it was on a very small scale, it was good to know that we were actually making a difference."

On the final day of January 1979, Sham played Aylesbury's Friars venue after which Pursey announced the end of the band, despite that particular show being almost completely trouble free. "A lot of people over the last months have slagged us, blaming us for everything," Pursey announced from the stage. "Because of those people, this is the last gig that Sham 69 are ever gonna play." They were two songs into the set, and the lyrics to 'Cockney Kids Are Innocent' were changed, as was now their custom, to 'Sham 69 Are Innocent'.

Pursey left for the Caribbean to relax and assess his future. On his return, he quashed rumours that the band was all over – rumours that he, of course, had started. In March Sham 69 released 'Questions And Answers'. "The music was secondary in every single way. This was the most beautiful time in English history where people like me who were eighteen and nineteen and the rest of us could all get up and say, this is bullshit and we're not having this cack. We're getting on with our life to say to as many people as possible – you can have a life, and you can say no and you can say yes to the things you really believe in, questions and answers, honesty, lies. That's what it is. That's what you have to deal with in life every day. So dealing with life as a teenager is the easiest thing because you can bounce off of walls. It's only when you get older that you don't bounce any more and they hit you harder."

By June 1979 rumours were rife of a further split, though apparently Polydor wanted the band to see out their contract – whatever troubles Sham were having as a live act, they were actually a commercial hot property in terms of record sales. News that Pursey and Treganna were practising with ex-Pistols' Cook and Jones also shook the grapevine. The group played another 'farewell' show, a hastily arranged date at the Glasgow Apollo, 'Sham's Last Stand', with the UK Subs and Valves on 29 June, featuring Sham's 'classic' line-up. Both Cook and Jones came on for the encores of 'Pretty Vacant', 'White Riot', 'If The Kids Are United' and 'What Have We Got'. The four-song encore was released by Link in 1989 before, in 2001, Sanctuary released the entire concert as Sham Pistols Live.

The 'farewell' was followed by their biggest hit, 'Hersham Boys', released in July. Did I say 'Hurry Up Harry' was Sham's definitive moment? 'Hersham Boys' certainly covets its mantelpiece status. The lyrics, according to a friend of Neil Harris's, were "based on a local folk/lad-culture song which had been around since time immemorial". But it seems that nearly everybody who has a connection to Hersham claims to have an uncle who wrote it. "They probably remember their uncles singing it, as did their uncles' fathers and grandfathers before them," Dave Parsons elaborated to me. "It was Gypsy families that were the first to live in Hersham, and Jimmy's family goes back to those times. In fact, his parents were still living in a caravan just before he was born. And yes, the Hersham Boys chorus was loosely based on an old chant from way back."

The 12-inch version was well worth hearing for the B-side tracks taken from the disastrous Middlesex Poly show. It captured a real moment of (tragic) history. However, by the time of its release, Sham 69 were officially defunct. It was over. Well, for a week or two anyway. On 28 July, Pursey having just appeared on Juke Box Jury, decided it was time for a third farewell show in seven months, this time at the Rainbow. Guess what? The nutters were out in force to trash it once again. The set was abruptly terminated, restarted, only for the violence to begin again and Pursey to walk off once more. Frustrated to his marrow,

Pursey confirmed that he'd be continuing to work with Cook and Jones, with whom songs had now been recorded, including 'Cold Blue In The Night', 'Money', both originally intended for the Quadrophenia soundtrack, and a version of 'Day Tripper' that was a regular Sham live favourite.

After a suitable period of dignified mourning, Pursey announced that Sham 69 would reform to promote new album Adventures Of The Hersham Boys. This neatly compiled previous singles 'Questions And Answers' and 'Hersham Boys' and some other less auspicious material, though the road-tested 'What Have We Got?' was the other standout. Bedecked in a cod-Spaghetti Western cartoon cover, a huge improvement on the band's previous artwork, it came with a free 12-inch single featuring longer edits of 'Borstal Breakout' and 'If The Kids Are United'. Pursey managed to put his foot squarely in his mouth in conversation with the NME around the time of its release: "Sham gives the punters their money's worth. Who else has given away 23,000 records?... It don't matter if people think the record's crap. The fact that we're giving it away is what counts, right?" Erm, that would be a no, Jim. The resulting tours of the UK and US saw audiences behave better, and the whole shebang seemed to be back on schedule.

Some confused fare followed. A cover of the Yardbirds' 'You're A Better Man Than I' was incongruous with prevailing notions of what Sham were, but actually fitted the band well. 'Give A Dog A Bone', on the flip, was the best song they'd written for some time. However, the punters had moved on, and the single peaked at 49 after a run of far more successful singles. Meanwhile Pursey busied himself with producing other bands, including the Angelic Upstarts and Cockney Rejects, the latter effectively seizing their mantle as the bootboy connoisseur's choice. If in doubt, play another farewell gig seemed to be the motto, so for the fourth time in 1979, on 19 October, Sham 69 said adieu, geezer, again at the Glasgow Apollo, this time with Rick Goldstein serving as drummer.

The Game was to be Sham's last 'proper' release, but it fared poorly. There's some merit in tracks like 'Run Wild Run Free', albeit the UK Subs were doing such stuff at least as well, but the low point had to be Pursey's attempt at an empathetic ballad. Entitled 'Poor Cow', Gawd bless him. Lots of British venues were too worried about their audience to book the band. Even for a farewell gig.

By July 1980 Pursey had split the band once again. Later, in an amusing article by Charles Shaar Murray, in which Pursey was confronted by one-time ally Mensi, who accused him of being pretentious, it was noted that: "Pursey can't keep anything in focus for more than ten minutes". Evidence is supplied for this in relation to his grand designs to document English working class folk music in a book and TV project, which is quickly forgotten as another idea pops into his head. In October 1979 he also stood in for BBC disc jockey Mike Read. He was interviewed by Nick Kent and asked for his reaction to events in the Pistols' camp. Some of what he said actually made sense. "Look at the way they exploited poor old Sid Vicious! People reckon I'm a bleedin' wally, and that the Pistols are so cool, but Christ, I'd rather be a wally who's alive and healthy, instead of some so-called rock'n'roll hero who's dead."

Pursey subsequently pursued a mixed-bag solo career. "I'd lost the plot of who I was. I didn't know who I was any more. I got a house, lived in a house, lost the house cos nobody would ever pay the bills, because my lovely manager Tony Gordon left me in a bit of a pickle, but I was in my own pickle anyway. He was moving on to Boy George in the 80s and I was going 'What the fuck is the 80s about?' It scared the crap out me." It's easy to scoff at Imagination Camouflage (recorded with Derwood and Mark Laff of Generation X) but the album itself is OK. However, Alien Orphan and Revenge Is Not The Password, his subsequent solo ventures, were widely ignored, aside from those journalists who thought it an excuse to give Pursey a good kicking.

With Pursey otherwise engaged, former bandmates Treganna, Parsons and Goldstein teamed up with ex-Dead Boys vocalist Stiv Bators to form the Wanderers (their debut, Only Lovers Left Alive, included material Parsons and Treganna had written for a fourth Sham album). Dave Parsons has rather less rosy memories of this period. "The Wanderers did the dirty on me. All the time Stiv was staying at my house in Walton On Thames, Brian James was continually calling up trying to poach him for his band. After a US tour where I returned home only to be admitted into Frimley Park Hospital's isolation ward with hepatitis, I had not one visit or call from the band. When I got out I found out through a friend that Stiv and Dave Treganna had gone off and formed Lords Of The New Church. They didn't even bother to tell me!"

The inevitable reformation came in 1986. Parsons was back on board, alongside a new rhythm section of Andy Prince (bass; ex-Rikki And The Last Days Of Earth, much later replaced by Matt Sergeant) and Andy Whitehead (drums), plus keyboard player Patricia Krugerman and saxophonist Linda Paganelli. According to Pursey, Parsons was "lost without me and I was lost without him musically, so if I was going to do anything musically, I could only do it with him and he could only do it with me. Cos we could feel safe on stage as we could still portray these two characters." Or, as Parsons admitted to Q, "We'd written some new songs and thought we had something to say. But it's been so hard here because of all the bad vibes towards us, and towards Jimmy. But I don't think he's any worse than any other front man with a big mouth." They cut 'Rip And Tear' in August 1987, preceding a studio album, Volunteer, in March 1988. It was hard to be generous. Volunteer seems to want to be, at various points, a rap album, an R&B album, and a hard rock record. They played one show to promote it and, tragically, this too ended in violence. 1992's Information Libertaire was an improvement, notably the Big Audio Dynamite-esque 'Planet Trash'. Soapy Water And Mr Marmalade (1995) was notable for its eponymous tribute to Otis Redding, with Parsons releasing his solo album Reconcile that year also (he is currently working on a new solo album alongside Jimmy Edwards, see daveparsons69.co.uk). 1997's A Files was, thankfully, better still. In fact, the latter is not bad at all. Not that anyone bought it. Not than anyone would believe me for saying so.

I made my reservations about the post-reformation albums known to Dave Parsons. "When we reformed in 1986, the easiest thing for us to have done, and what most people were telling us to do, would have been to go out on the road, like some cabaret band, playing all the old hits. The reason we got back together was that Jimmy and I started writing together again and we still had something to say. Punk was an attitude, not a fashion. We were living in a different time, hip hop was happening etc. We made an album (Volunteer) that reflected what was happening around us – not some backward-looking piece of nostalgia. Some tracks on the album I'm still very happy with, others don't stand up so well now. Since Volunteer we've put out at least four new albums – all of which contain tracks that I'm very proud of."

Good ole Jim is still out there, ranting away on any two-bit telly prog that will put a camera in front of him. Ask him about the infamous ballet dancing to the Stranglers' 'Meninblack' on BBC2's Riverside and he will offer no apology. "Don't forget I catwalked for Alexander McQueen, of Katharine Hamnett, you know. I've worked with Gap and got four grand for twenty minutes work with the best photographers in the world. I've done a recent Campari video. I don't drink Campari, but do you understand, to sit with Frankie Fraser and Rodney Marsh and all these different people and play the music to Get Carter in the background, it's the best CV you can have, as far as like, Jimmy's an actor."

Yep, he does talk about 'Jimmy' in the third person. Probably even to himself. He also paints in his spare time, so he's the punk renaissance man that appeals to blokes with tattoos. How does Jimmy view his career in retrospect? "It's like when Stanley Kubrick makes Eyes Wide Shut, the difference to Clockwork Orange, completely different films. One's a man making a film and one's a 'Wow, look, I'm being able to make Clockwork Orange as a youthful budding director.' And another one's a film of, do you understand, this is a film, I'm making a film. And that's how I felt at the end of what I've just done, in fact I feel now that I am from, I am Eyes Wide Shut. I feel that I introduced myself as Clockwork Orange and went out as Eyes Wide Shut."

OK, Jim! Well, that was that, until some advisor to Tony Blair thought it would be a good idea to trail the 2005 Labour Party conference with 'If The Kids Are United'. Jimmy reformed the band to appear on Newsnight. The lyrics were re-interpreted to suggest to Tony that the boys in Iraq should come home and he dedicated the song to 'Wolfgang and Walter', the two aged Labour Party members ejected from the building for daring to question the veracity of Jack Straw's speech. Dave Parsons: "I'd love to know myself whose idea it was. It was a shock for me when it happened, and then to be invited on to play Newsnight the next evening was stranger still. If anyone wants to use that song as a vehicle for bringing people together then I'm all for it. I don't believe in all of Blair's policies, but overall I think he's the best, most consistent Prime Minister we've had for many years."

Discography:

(Sham's discography was a right mess until Captain Oi! recently did the decent thing and repackaged them properly. I would guide you firmly in the direction of those reissues, and the A-Files of their most recent studio releases. If you fancy a live album, the original Live And Loud is recommended)

I Don't Wanna/Ulster/Red London 7-inch (Step Forward SF 4 September 1977) (reissued in 1979 as 12-inch with same tracks, SF 412)

Song Of The Streets 1-sided 7-inch (Polydor SHAM 69 1977)

What Have We Got (live)/Fanx (gig freebie)

Borstal Breakout/Hey Little Rich Boy 7-inch (Polydor 2058 966 January 1978)

Tell Us The Truth LP (Polydor 2383 491 February 1978) (reissued on CD by Dojo, DOJOCD 256, in 1996, with additional track 'What Have We Got'. Reissued again in 2005 in digipak CD by Captain Oi!, AHOY DPX 611, with bonus tracks 'What Have We Got', 'I Don't Wanna', 'Red London', 'Ulster (single version)', Borstal Breakout (single version)', 'George Davis Is Innocent (demo)', 'They Don't Understand (demo)', 'Borstal Breakout (demo)'. Features lyrics as well as the band's original 1977 demos)

Angels With Dirty Faces/The Cockney Kids Are Innocent 7-inch (Polydor 2059 023 1978)

If The Kids Are United/Sunday Morning Nightmare 7-inch (Polydor 2059 050 July 1978)

That's Life LP (Polydor POLD 5010 November 1978) (reissued on CD in 1996 by Dojo, DOJOCD 257. Reissued on digipak CD in 2005 by Captain Oi!, AHOY DPX 612, with bonus tracks 'The Cockney Kids Are Innocent', 'If The Kids Are United', 'No Entry', with lyrics and liner notes)

Hurry Up Harry/No Entry 7-inch (Polydor POSP 7 1979)

Questions And Answers/I Gotta Survive/With A Little Help From My Friends 7-inch (Polydor POSP 27 1979)

Hersham Boys/I Don't Wanna (live)/Tell Us The Truth (live) 7-Inch (Polydor POSP 64 1979) (also released on 12-inch, POSPX 64, with two extra tracks, 'Rip Off (live)' and 'I'm A Man, I'm A Boy (live)

The Adventures Of The Hersham Boys LP (Polydor POLD 5025 September 1979) (issued with free 12-inch featuring Borstal Breakout (Extended)/If The Kids Are United'. Reissued on CD in 1996 by Dojo, DOJOCD 258, with additional track 'Borstal Breakout (extended)'. Reissued in digipak CD in 2005 by Captain Oi!, AHOY DPX 613, with bonus tracks 'Questions And Answers (single version)', 'I Gotta Survive', 'With A Little Help From My Friends', 'Hersham Boys (single version)', 'I Don't Wanna (live)', 'Rip Off (live)', 'I'm A Man I'm A Boy (live)', 'Tell Us The Truth (live)', 'Borstal Breakout (12-inch version)', 'If The Kids Are United (12-inch version)')

You're A Better Man Than I/Give A Dog A Bone 7-inch (Polydor POSP 82 1979)

Tell The Children/Jack 7-inch (Polydor POSP 136 1980)

The Game LP (Polydor POLD 5033 May 1980) (reissued on CD in 1996 by Dojo, DOJOCD 259, and in 1997 by Essential, ESMCD 516. Both feature extra tracks 'United And Win' and 'Day Tripper'. Reissued on digipak CD in 2005 by Captain Oi!, AHOY DPX 614, with bonus tracks 'Jack', 'Unite And Win', 'I'm A Man', 'Daytripper', 'Voices (live)', 'Money (live)', Who Gives A Damn (live)', 'That's Life (live)'.)

Unite And Win/I'm A Man 7-inch (Polydor 2059 259 1980)

Rip And Tear/The Great American Slowdown 7-inch (Legacy LGY 69 1987) (also issued as a 12-inch single, LGYT 69, with additional track 'Rip And Tear (extended)' as well as 7-inch version)

Outside The Warehouse/How The West Was Won 7-Inch (Legacy LGY 71 1988) (also issued as a 12-inch single, LGYT 71, with additional track 'Outside The Warehouse (extended)' as well as 7-inch version)

Volunteer LP Legacy LLP 117 1988) (also issued on CD, Legacy LLCD 117. Reissued on Castle, CLACD 274 1992)

That's Live 12-Inch EP (Skunx SHAM XI 1988)

Hersham Boys/Angels With Dirty Faces/Hurry Up Harry/If The Kids Are United/Borstal Breakout

The Early Years live 12-inch (Receiver REPLAY 316 1991)

Rip Off/Borstal Breakout/Angels With Dirty Faces/If The Kids Are United

M25/Caroline's Suitcase/Information Libertaire 12-inch (Rotate ROTST 03 1992)

Uptown/Borstal breakout/Flowers/Wild and wonderful 12-inch (CMP Discs CMP 1T 1992)

Information Libertaire CD (Rotate ROTCD 6 1992) (reissued in 1996 on Dojo, DOJOCD 236. Japanese version includes 'M25', American version includes 'Flowers')

Action Time Vision/Bosnia/Hey Little Rich Boy/Reggae Giro CD single (Creative Man CMCDS 002 1993)

Girlfriend/25 years/Rainbow Warrior CD single (Plus Eye AISCD 001 1995)

Soapy Water And Mr Marmalade CD (Plus Eye AICD 001 1995)

Listen Up/Girlfriend/Little Bit Of This/Otis Redding/Junkie/The Doctor's Song/ Alice/Stevie/Chasing The Moon/Spunky Candy

Punk Fiction CD single (Scratch AICD 005 1997)

Swampy/Geoffrey Thomas/Studenthead/Windowstare

The A Files CD (Scratch Acid 004 1997)

ARCHIVE RELEASES:

The First, The Best And The Last LP (Polydor 2816 028 November 1980) (came with free 7-inch EP, Riot 1/2816 028) (reissued on CD in 1992, Polydor 513 429-2, with additional tracks Who Gives A Damn (live)/That's Life (live))

Angels With Dirty Faces/Borstal Breakout/Hurry Up Harry/If The Kids Are United 12-inch (Polydor POSPX 601 1982)

The Complete Sham 69 live LP (Castle CLALP 153 1983)

Angels With Dirty Faces LP (Receiver RRLP 104 1985)

Live And Loud LP (Link LINK LP 025 1988) (reissued on CD in 1987 by Link, LINK CD 04, with additional tracks Voices (live)/Give a dog a bone(live)/Lost on Highway 46 (live)/Day tripper(live)/The Stockholm kids are innocent (live). The same bonus tracks appear on the 2005 Harry May reissue, MAYO CD 559. If you want a Sham 69 live album, this is the place to start. The ever reliable Trouser Press reckons this actually outshines their studio output, and it's hard to disagree)

Live And Loud 2 LP (Link LINK LP 025 1988) (reissued on CD in 1991 by Link, LINKCD 025, and in 1998 by E2 as ETDCD 029, retitled Sham 69 live – this is a show from the 1987 reformation line-up)

The Best Of And The Rest Of Sham 69 live LP (Receiver RRLP 122 1989) (reissued on CD in 1980 by Receiver RRCD 112 and in 1990 by Action Replay CDAR 1011. (Incidentally, is this the worst title for an album ever? Why not just call it 'Some Of This Is Rubbish But We Were Hoping You're A Reckless Consumer And Wastrel'? It's actually from a gig in Oslo. 'From A Gig In Oslo' would have been preferable)

Sham's Last Stand LP (Link LINKMLP 075 1989) (reissued on CD in 1993 by Dojo, DOJOCD 95, and in 1999 by Snapper, SMMCD 540)

(this is an OK-ish live recording of the band's farewell show at the Rainbow in 1979)

Live At The Roxy LP (Receiver RRLP 133) (reissued on CD in 1990 by Receiver, RRCD 133. live at the Roxy? Erm, half of this material wasn't even written when Sham were playing the Roxy. And the sound is dreadful)

The Complete Sham 69 live LP (Castle CLACD 153 1989)

Rare And Unreleased CD (Limited Edition LTDEDTCD 5 1991) (fascinating early document of the band which is interesting because the vast majority of the contents were never subsequently released until Captain Oi! compiled Rarities 1977-1980)

Live At CBGB's 1988 CD (Dojo DOJOCD 62 1991) (recorded live during November 1988. Reissued by Harry May, MAYO CD 519, in 2003)

Live In Japan CD (Dojo DOJOCD 105 1993) (note: also issued in 1994 by Creative Man with slightly different running order; 'Us And Them' replaces 'Money')

BBC Radio 1 live In Concert CD (Windsong WINCD 049 1993)

Kings And Queens CD (Creative Man CMCD 69 1993) (reissued in 1995 by Dojo, DOJOCD 235)

Live And Loud CD (Step-1 STEPCD 053 1995) (this is a reissue of the vinyl version of live and Loud, not featuring the CD bonus tracks, paired with 12 tracks by 999)

The Best Of Sham 69 double CD (Essential ESCD 350 1995) (also issued as a single CD, Essential ESMCD 512, minus live tracks)

Sham 69 Live (Emporio EMPRCD 582 1995)

Tell Us The Truth CD (Dojo DOJOCD 256)

United – live CD (Hallmark 304462 1996)

The Very Best Of The Hersham Boys CD (Castle Select SELCD 504)

The Punk Singles Collection 1977-1980 CD (Cleopatra US CLP 0221-2 1998) (the same running order was used for the 2005 Captain Oi! CD release in the UK, AHOY CD 251).

Rarities 1977-1980 CD (Captain Oi! AHOY CD 139 1998) (a collection of studio demos and out-takes dating between 1977 and 1980, which includes four songs, including two versions of 'I'm On The Run', written specifically for the Quadrophenia movie, but never used. 'I'm On The Run' is the nearest Sham came to rockabilly. Six tracks are early versions of later songs from The Game. 'Freeman' is an early version of 'Simon', 'So Long To Find Out' became 'In And Out', 'Money Don't Make It Right' became 'Human Zoo' and 'Everything's Alright' evolved into 'Tell The Children'. 'Poor Cow' and 'The Game' retained their titles. Similarly the three tracks from Hersham Boys – 'TV Times' became 'Lost On Highway 46', 'Johnny's On The Street Again' became 'Joey's On The Street' while 'Broken Dreams' became 'Fly Dark Angel'. The first three tracks are demos hawked around the majors after their Step Forward debut. 'Borstal Breakout' sounds like a skiffle version.)

Borstal Breakout double CD (Snapper SMDCD 141 1998)

Sham 69 – The Masters CD (Eagle EDMCD 030 1998)
Live In Italy CD (Essential ESMCD 733 1999) (actually recorded in 1997, not 1996, as the cover states)
Green Eggs And Sham CD (Big Ear US EAZ 4023 1999)
Greatest Hits Live CD (Anagram CD PUNK 123 2001) (recorded live at Club Citta Kawasaki, Japan, March 1991. Sleevenotes are perfunctory and lacking in the use of a spellchecker, but there is some good live photography)
The Punk Singles Collection 1977-1980 CD (Captain Oi! AHOY CD 251 January 2005) (same as earlier Cleopatra release)

Shapes

Seymour Bybuss (aka Ben Browton; vocals), Brian Helicopter (aka Gareth Holder; bass), Nigel Greenway (guitar), Nick Hadley (guitar), Charlie Pullen (drums)

From Leamington Spa, the SHAPES were formed in the wake of the Billy Grundy incident by two ex-public schoolboys who'd been kicked out "for painting the school ocelot orange". They stockpiled armaments for the coming punk wars by appointing suitable pseudonyms. Browton's new tag was informed by the legend "See more by bus" that was emblazoned on local vehicles, though most people didn't get it and assumed he was French. Brian Helicopter was chosen because... well, it's a long story. Part of the reason for the subterfuge was, in typical punk fashion, they wanted to be able to sign on using their real names. However, Holder eventually got a job as a clerical officer in local government. He did frighten his fellow corridor-shufflers with green hair, mind. At the same time, employed in similar drudgery in the dole office nearby, was Browton. A plot was hatched over lunchtime pints to get in on the action.

Browton's parents' garage was employed as a makeshift rehearsal space while they pondered the chances of finding someone else to share their ascent to stardom. Guitarists Nigel Greenway and Nick Hadley, plus 15-year-old drummer Charlie Pullen, were found from Leamington's limited talent pool. Within weeks a debut show was booked at Warwick University, headlined by the Killjoys. Semi-legendary local music figure John Rivers allowed them the use of his Woodbine four-track mobile recording studio, and at a cost of £27, four songs were recorded. However, the new guitarists weren't ideal. They wanted to be in a group that sounded, variously, like Thin Lizzy or Wishbone Ash, and their compatriots wanted to be in a group that sounded anything but. It came to a head at the Ming Kee takeaway when our errant punk rockers were set upon by local 'casuals'. Browton was duly hammered to a state of unconsciousness while other members of the band ran for their lives and abandoned him to his fate.

By the time Browton had recovered, the Shapes had acquired a manager, Rob Atkins, who persuaded EMI to take a look. The man from EMI gave them some funny white stuff and put them in the studio. Such was his generosity, he also told them to change name to The Racket and offered them a "shite" song, 'My Hero' to record. "Then we are told that this is actually the finished product," Holder recalled, "and that all we are required to do is to mime it on Top Of The Pops and other TV appearances. We are to be a front band it appears, for a scam by some old hippies on EMI's roster to cash in. We will sacrifice our dignity for some small consideration." Hadley was particularly unamused and left the band, eventually going on to work alongside his heroes, Wishbone Ash.

EMI, in their wisdom, eventually decided to drop the 'My Hero' project, without publicly acknowledging how idiotic it was, so the quartet carried on as the Shapes. EMI's next big idea was to pair them with songwriter Nick Brind of Joe Public. And what did he come up with? A song called 'Truck Drivin' Man'. A quarter of a decade after the event, you can hear the sound of jaws hitting the floor echo down the years. Brind also offered another atrocity, 'Stick It PSU', his best effort at this new punk rock lark, which was even worse, while the band were allowed to record one original, 'Chatterbox'. But only if Mr Brind got to sing on it.

After the sessions Charlie Pullen was ousted in favour of Dave Gee, presumably so he could finish his homework, before they embarked on a new round of local gigs. These included famed rock'n'roll haunts such as the Crown Hotel, the Spa Centre (at which their manager got them banned after he started a baked-bean fight during 'Wot's For Lunch Mum?'), the Pump Rooms and the Free Floating Festival, whatever that was. Oh, and Sarah Jane Morris's 21st birthday party. At these salubrious events and others the band members would supplement their march to the top by, a la Steve Jones, nicking whatever bits of stray gear they could find from unsuspecting fellow travellers.

A couple of originals were written and recorded, again at Woodbine, including Holder's 'College Girls'. Brind unexpectedly turned up at the sessions and, after consulting with guitarist Greenway, decided to 'lift' the song for his own uses. Brind quickly made his exit, taking the Shapes' guitarist with him. Yet Greenway's tale ended in woe. Having moved to London and spent some time working for his father's business, he committed suicide in Southampton. His departure was enough to see off manager Atkins, leaving Holder and Browton, along with Gee, standing alone again.

An advert was placed an advert in the New Musical Express. Steve Richards from Andover was the only respondent worth considering, and fellow guitarist Tim Jee, a friend of Dave Gee, was also enlisted (though they overlooked the potential of a duo entitled the Jee Gees). Four songs were cut at Woodbine, '(I Saw) Batman (In The Launderette)', 'College Girls', 'Wot's For Lunch Mum (Not Beans Again)' and 'Chatterbox'. These were released as their debut EP on their own Sofa Records imprint, the band hand-stuffing the inserts, and mailed out to the 'industry'. Enter Uncle John Peel on his white charger, who played the tracks 'incessantly'. As a result the single was repressed at least twice as they drove round London vendors including Rough Trade and Small Wonder to satisfy demand, in the evenings playing support slots leading up to the Part Of The Furniture tour of 1979. The EP would eventually sell 10,000 copies. Nowadays copies on e-bay go for more than the entire original recording budget.

Support slots included the Fall ("miserable" in Nottingham), the Cure ("haughty" to such an extent that one member of the band beat up the drummer) in Sheffield, the Reaction (soon to be Talk Talk) in London. Then there was the bizarre coupling with 14-piece disco band Gonzalez at the Music Machine, booked by their new agency, Cowbell. This earned them the London Evening Standard's award for Worst Mix of Bands on a London Stage in 1979. "So after years of false starts," Holder remembered, "life is suddenly a blur of gigs, interviews, vans, chips, motorways, and social relaxants."

After more alarmingly badly organised gigs in the north and west of England, they were gratified to receive a phone call from John Peel offering them a session. Producer Trevor Dann, incidentally, would use one of the songs as the theme tune to his radio show. A break in the never-ending touring saw them return to Woodbine to record a second single, 'Airline Disaster', backed by 'Blast Off'. Deciding that they required the backing of a 'proper' label, they entered the topsy-turvy world of Good Vibrations' Terri Hooley, whom they'd been recommended to by Virgin distribution's Willie Richardson. Hooley schlepped over to Leamington, did his 'glass eye' trick in the pub (don't ask) and that was that. This neatly tied up with an appearance at the Royal Ulster Hall in Belfast headlined by the Saints, also featuring Good Vibrations' stalwarts Protex and Rudi. Much of their time in Northern Ireland was spent inspecting stationary vehicles for evidence of car bombs, as paranoid visiting English bands were wont to do at this time. Before this exciting trip, however, they dispensed with the services of Steve Richards, for no good reason really, except, perhaps, that Browton's girlfriend didn't like him.

On their return from Northern Ireland, they set out to support the Photos on tour, while recording a third single, 'Let's Go (To Planet Skaro)', a tribute to Davros's home turf in Doctor Who. But the dawning realisation that the leather jacket and mohawk set had begun to colonise punk deflated spirits. The prospect of touring even more toilets to face even more phlegm and missiles was too much. Terri Hooley did invite them back for one more gig in Belfast, though Holder had joined another band concurrently. Which left the Shapes to slowly fizzle out, the third single remaining unreleased.

That was until 2000. While living in California and working as a professional skydiver (I'm not making this up) Holder received a phone call from Browton enquiring as to the whereabouts of the Shapes' master tapes. John Esplen at Overground was interested in releasing a CD of Shapes' material, and thus did the Shapes' legacy finally acquire permanency. Songs For Sensible People is fantastic, actually, proving that punk could encompass flights of fantasy, domestic dogfights, celebrations of failure and sexual desperation without descending into gimmickry. The material, as the band would later confirm, was rooted in truth. They really weren't getting shagged, or paid, very much at all. In the meantime Browton had gone on to fame, of sorts, as the transvestite art critic nun Sister Bendy on Eurotrash, and also had a new musical collective, the Ambassadors Of Plush. Tim Gee was last sighted in Herne Bay, while Steve Richards breeds horses in Andover. Dave Gee ran the Greyhound recruitment agency in Northampton. And Holder writes very funny chronicles of his time as a punk rocker which are routinely plagiarised by lesser authors.

In a desperate search for a suitable "original" quote, I asked Mr Holder for some tortured analogy between punk rock and skydiving. He rose to the occasion manfully. "Er, there's no money in either of them really, and both can be dangerous to your health. I have actually met up with quite a few other musicians in the skydiving world. Dave Mustaine from Megadeth jumps, or at least used to, the keyboard player from King, and a few others. You'd be surprised who turns up in the oddest of places. One of the drummers from the successful period of Adam And The Ants is a plumber out here. It's fun to call him up and get him to come and unblock your loo. Dave Gee still drums and is in two bands as far as I know right now, Motherlode, and one that is a kind of Pink Floyd tribute band. Bloody hippy." And dare we mention reunion concerts? " I mean, if there is a market for people wanting to watch old fat bald guys play 'College Girls', who am I to say no? Brian fucking Helicopter apparently, that's who."

DISCOGRAPHY:

Part Of The Furniture 7-inch EP (Sofa SEAT 1/FRR 004 1979)
(I Saw) Batman (In The Launderette)/College Girls/Wot's For Lunch Mum (Not Beans Again)/Chatterbox
Blast Off/Airline Disaster 7-inch (Good Vibrations GOT 13 1979)
ARCHIVE RELEASES:
Songs For Sensible People CD (Overground OVER 81 CD 2000)

Shock Treatment

Barry McIlheney (vocals), Davy McLarnon (guitar), Basil McCausland (bass), Tim Kerr (guitar), Chris Loughridge (drums)

When Howard Ingram left mid-70s Belfast rock band Essence to form first the Detonators and then the Tearjerkers, the remaining members recruited Basil McCausland to become the North Belfast Boogie Band. From whence came Shock Treatment, formed in 1978, when it became obvious that their current appellation hardly reflected the cut and thrust of the new music sweeping through Northern Ireland – that and the Ramones debut album. From the original line-up, Niall McKay was quickly replaced by Tim Kerr, and Chris Loughbridge by Paul Kelly. They became regulars at the Harp Bar but also frequently took out of town bookings in Portstewart's Spuds bar and at Kelly's in Portrush where, conveniently, McLarnon's family owned a caravan.

They made their debut on the 'Room To Move' compilation EP in 1980, contributing signature song 'Belfast Telegraph'. From further sessions at Downtown Radio came their debut single, 1981's 'Big Check Shirts', backed by 'Mr Mystery Man'. Released on their own DAB imprint, it failed to garner much attention, despite support shows with the Skids and U2.

The band ended in 1981 when day job commitments got in the way. McIlheney, ironically, started writing for the Belfast Telegraph, then moved to London and began writing for the Melody Maker, eventually going on to edit Smash Hits before becoming Editor In Chief at EMAP Elan. McCausland worked as a taxi driver before becoming a counsellor in Manchester. Loughridge is a dentist, and McLarnon a chiropodist, after a brief spell with a band called Peacefrog.

DISCOGRAPHY:

Big Check Shirts/Mr Mystery Man 7-inch (DAB DAB 001 1981)

SELECTED COMPILATIONS:
Room To Move 7-inch EP (Energy NRG1 1980; 'Belfast Telegraph')
Good Vibrations – The Punk Singles Collection CD (Anagram CDPUNK 36 1994; 'Belfast Telegraph')

Sick Things

Unrelated to the later Melbourne punkers of the same name, though presumably also named after the Alice Cooper song, female quartet the SICK THINGS never released a single in their lifetime, though they did place two songs on the original Raw Deal compilation, 'Street Kids' and 'Bondage Boy'. With the latter spanning all manner of sexual perversity, including necrophillia and sadomasochism, the tracks were meant to form part of a four-track EP due for release in 1979 as Raw 28. It never happened. The recordings finally emerged in 1983 on Chaos Records, a label that we have strong suspicions also involved Raw's Lee Wood.

As Wood told punk77, "After the Killjoys record was released in July 1977, demo tapes started to arrive. I put an advert in the classifieds of Music Maker (in those days the main paper for musicians), and the telephone never stopped ringing. One of the phone calls came from a girl who called herself Charlie. She worked for a record pressing plant in the West London area (actually Battersea). In a call that probably lasted 45 minutes her personality was so sparkling that I agreed to record her band without ever seeing or hearing them. They were called The Sick Things!"

But that was it, at least until French band the No-Talents started covering 'Bondage Boy' and announcing their influence to the wider world. As Shredding Paper wrote about the Damaged Goods reissue of the single: "Now THIS is what I call punk: primal sounds from 1977 with appropriately (and stellarly) snotty female vocals. 'Bondage Boy' is a stone-cold classic and the other three tunes ain't nothing to sneeze at either! The better of today's punk bands probably sleep with a copy of this under their pillows, and if they don't they should." My old friend Steve Smith (of Spiral Scratch) thought them like the Crystals on amphetamines, and that's a pretty good description also.

DISCOGRAPHY:

The Legendary Sick Things 7-inch EP (Chaos CH3 1983)
Anti-Social Disease/Sleeping With The Dead/Street Kids/Bondage Boy
The Sick Things 7-inch EP (DAMGOOD 184 2000) (reissue of above, first 1,000 in yellow vinyl)
COMPILATIONS:
Raw Deal LP (Raw RAW LP1 1977; 'Sleeping With The Dead, 'Bondage Boy') (reissued in 1979)
Spiral Scratch EP (Spiral Scratch 201, August 1990; 'Bondage Boy') (free with magazine)

Siouxsie And The Banshees

Siouxsie Sioux (vocals), Steven Severin (aka Steven Havoc; bass), Marco Pirroni (guitar), Sid Vicious (drums)

S

Suburbia: Cosy, comfortable, reassuring, decent, respectable, cosseted, bland, soul-sucking, soporific suburbia. Away from the inner cities of Britain in the mid-70s was a parallel universe where Marks & Spencer were king, where minor promotions in middle management were the anvils on which life's ambitions were hammered out. And where any trace of individuality, flare or difference was stripped away in the guileless pursuit of conformity. You can hear the false gods of consumption and normality overthrown in punk staples like the Members' 'Sound Of The Suburbs', Gang Of Four's 'At Home He's A Tourist' or XTC's 'Making Plans For Nigel'. But you can hear it most acutely, and over an entire career, in SIOUXSIE AND THE BANSHEES.

Susan Ballion was a disaffected loner, her youth blighted by illness and an alcoholic father, who first met Steven Bailey, her future romantic and musical partner, at a Roxy Music show at Wembley Arena in late 1975. Bailey had a job in accounts at RCA, until the tedium got to him. Ballion, meanwhile, was already reacting against the stultifying Bromley environment by dressing as outlandishly as she could, hiding her shyness behind armadillo quantities of glamour and otherness. A gang formed around them, notably Simon Barker, Berlin, Simone and William Broad, aka Billy Idol. In some ways Ballion was, conversely, the most worldly of this emerging group, regularly travelling to London to visit gay clubs and woitressing at the Valbonne in Carnaby Street, where her sister was a go-go dancer. But it was Bailey who first clocked the Sex Pistols, supporting Fogg at the Ravensbourne College of Art on 9 December 1975. Suddenly they had, in his words, "a mission".

And so the adventure began. A knot of appreciative punters developed around the Sex Pistols, a coterie that would meet regularly at places like Louise's, preferring gay nightclubs where they could mingle without provocation. Their colourful parade of skin and cloth, each member of the fraternity trying to outdo each other, certainly shocked the good burghers of Bromley as they waited on suburban train platforms and bus stops, looking like the overspill from a Rocky Horror convention.

The Pistols turned up at 'Berlin's Bondage Party' in May 1976, which turned into a 'sex Olympics' according to Siouxsie's account. Lydon destroyed Berlin's stereo while blasting the Cabaret soundtrack through open windows. When a neighbour inevitably complained, Siouxsie answered the door in a see-through apron, naked underneath, and heels. "We thought," Glen Matlock later recalled, "this looks quite interesting." I'm sure it did. When the alarmed complainant called her a slut, Siouxsie decked her. Her new name, incidentally, was adapted from a postcard she'd received from Barker signed 'Si' with an 'x' after it, rather than any reference to the ancient Native American culture.

McLaren was keen to cultivate a glamorous following for his charges, and would ring up and alert them to forthcoming Pistols' shows. Such evenings usually concluded at 'Trashby Ashby's place (lesbian prostitute Linda Ashby's flat), where McLaren and Vivienne Westwood were frequent visitors. They were there at the Pistols' Screen On The Green gig, and travelled to Paris to watch their first overseas show at the Club Du Chalet Du Lac, in the back of Billy Idol's van. There were a few objections to Siouxsie's swastika in Paris, which she always treated as "high camp, not death camp". But not everyone saw it that way, and the Paris show ended in a pitched battle after Siouxsie was socked in the face. The enraged Algerians who visited this affront upon her were evidently not versed in the layered meanings shock culture entailed. It was after this show that Caroline Coon, covering events for the Melody Maker, coined the term 'Bromley Contingent' for the first time.

The Bromley Contingent were present en masse in December 1976 when the Sex Pistols turned up on Bill Grundy's Thames TV Today show. McLaren rang Simon Barker as soon as it was clear the Pistols had got the slot in place of Queen, offering to pay their train fares if they'd come to the studio. Both Siouxsie and Severin helpfully manned the telephones in the Green Room after the phones melted down under a barrage of complaints. And told them to piss off. And then they went home on the train, unaware of the fireball that was about to engulf the entire Pistols' entourage. "The Bill Grundy incident is written about like it was a landmark event," Siouxsie told Jon Wilde, "We were all just having a laugh."

S

Billy Idol was the first of their party to discuss getting a band together. Siouxsie, who had been to a few auditions but found her potential employers all to be dull pub rock bands, thought this might be a good idea. Indeed, Idol and Siouxsie even played about making tape recordings of the Velvet Underground's 'What Goes On'. There are various versions of events that led to the Banshees' subsequent appearance at the 100 Club. Severin assures me that the idea was first put forward by Idol at the Sex Pistols Screen On The Green show.

Within a few days Sid Vicious had been roped in on drums, and Marco Pirroni on guitar, at the suggestion of Idol, who'd defected to form Chelsea with Tony James, who had informed him that he should not split his loyalties. As Severin would later tell John Robb, "He reckoned it would really damage Billy's reputation if he was seen with us trendies!" Nils Stevenson, Malcolm McLaren's assistant, was at one point proposed as a potential guitarist, though there are disagreements about where the vital first 'band meeting' was convened (either at Louise's or at Billy Idol's folks' place). Severin: "My version is that Nils suggested both Sid and Marco one Saturday at Louise's followed by a 'meeting' at Nils's house in Finchley."

With three days notice, Sid scrounged some rehearsal time at the Clash's studios in Chalk Farm via Bernie Rhodes. This lasted for up to ten minutes before he got bored and wandered off, apparently declaring 'We don't want to actually learn anything, do we?' Severin didn't know one end of his bass from the other, and Pirroni, the only one with a modicum of musical know-how, realised that he'd have to procure enough screaming feedback to cover the deficiencies. They took the name Banshees after Severin's suggestion, before he quickly revised it to Suzi & The Banshees.

They turned up for the soundcheck kitted out in, variously, pinstripe jacket and swastika armband (Siouxsie), a customised 'Belsen Babies' T-shirt (Vicious), paint-splattered T-shirt with Union Jack motif (Severin) and 'Anarchy' T-shirt with Luftwaffe insignia (Pironni). All of which alarmed Bernie Rhodes, who cancelled a previous understanding that they could use the Clash's backline. As Bernie Rhodes later recounted to Johnny Black, "I felt she wasn't aware of what she was letting herself in for. If she used it, we too would be associated with the swastika. I felt she was mucking about with a loaded gun and we didn't want to have anything to do with it." Siouxsie would later protest that it was not a political but a fashion statement. And Joe Strummer would point out that the stand-off re-ignited a previous disagreement between Bernie Rhodes and Malcolm McLaren about a controversial swastika-based clothes design that Rhodes had objected to. John Lydon's later wife, Nora, was more shocked than most, given her background in post-war Germany. But she does give Siouxsie credit for innovation. "I was shocked when I saw Siouxsie at the (subsequent) Screen On The Green... she was walking around wearing some suspenders and a bra with her whole tits out. I was stunned. How could she have the nerve? I think she contributed a lot to the women's movement. Madonna got it all from Siouxsie, who was totally on her own then."

Carnage ensued at the 100 Club. Sid randomly hit the kit. Pirroni doused everything in feedback, moving from 'Sister Ray' through 'Captain Scarlet' and 'Smoke On The Water', while he kept entreating Severin to hit "the big thick string". Meanwhile Siouxsie sang 'The Lord's Prayer', ostensibly because she knew she could remember it, along with parts of 'Twist And Shout' and 'Deutschland Uber Alles'. "I guess we were just trying our luck at the 100 Club," Siouxsie later told Fiona Sturges of the Independent. "There was never any intention of doing it again, and there was certainly no thought of making a living out of it. That would have been absurd." At the time she was pleased with the performance, though "the ending was a mistake. We were going to play until we were thrown off stage, but we got bored before the audience did." Or, as she later told Nick Kent, "The point of that performance was simply that all the other bands were talking about not being able to really play, and being unrehearsed and into chaos, man, and we were simply doing what they were stating. Only they were really talking shit because they did rehearse and had worked up sets. We just wanted to take the whole thing to its logical extreme." Captain Sensible was not impressed. "Siouxsie was utterly useless. Appalling. They didn't deserve to be allowed anywhere near a stage. Most of the bands, even people like the Buzzcocks, knew three or four chords, but they didn't have a clue. As far as I could make out she was just this kid with loads of dosh from a well-to-do family. She was the only person I knew then who could afford to spend £200 a time on S&M outfits from Malcolm's shop in the King's Road." Severin: "Captain Sensible was, and always will be, a moron."

It was only ever meant to be a one-off, but the reaction was such that interest around the band was not going to dissipate any time soon. One audience member was Kenny Morris, who immediately offered his services as drummer. Nils Stevenson asked to become their manager. The latter, in particular, was convinced that Siouxsie definitely had 'something'. He tried to convince McLaren to join him in managing the band, but got short shrift. So Stevenson and McLaren parted company, Stevenson was paid off to the tune of £300 for something like a year's work on McLaren's behalf. But Stevenson did use his connections to get the Banshees use of the Pistols' rehearsal studio while they were away in Amsterdam.

Sid returned to the Flowers Of Romance and Marco to the Models. But Siouxsie and Severin did indeed persevere, first recruiting PT Fenton and a violinist named Simon who lasted just three rehearsals. They had no permanent drummer at this stage although Dixon, a surnameless individual who made his money by acquiring classic 50s clothes and selling them to ACME Attractions, sat in for a while. He didn't last, and eventually the group chose to take up Morris on his offer. Stevenson again blagged them rehearsal space, this time via Track Records, and they began to write together.

Their second show was as support to the Heartbreakers at the Red Deer in Croydon. They retained 'Captain Scarlet' for this, and introduced some new songs Severin had written, including 'Scrapheap' and 'Psychic'. In March further time at Track studios resulted in versions of 'The Lord's Prayer', 'Bad Shape', 'Scrapheap', 'Psychic', an early version of 'Love In A Void', as well as 'Captain Scarlet' and T-Rex's '20th Century Boy'. The sessions were widely bootlegged under the title 'Track Rehearsals'. At this stage the lyrics were Severin's, with the music composed by Fenton. This was also where the original version of 'Love In A Void', containing the infamous line, 'Too many Jews for my liking', can be found. A Jewish Sounds writer, Vivien Goldman, tackled them on this, only for Siouxsie to attempt to persuade her that "Too many Jews means, like, too many fat businessmen. That line was stupid, anyway. We knew what we meant, but..."

Later Goldman would admit that she'd rather let the band off the hook, because she so desperately wanted to like Siouxsie and everything else she stood for. Others have not been so kind. It's not just the swastikas. The most bizarre theory I came across as conclusive proof of their fascist cravings came via the fact that both Siouxsie Sue and Steven Severin had the initials 'SS'. Julie Burchill picked up on this when she reviewed their Nashville show and opened it with the line "You wish they all could be SS girls?" A statistical anomaly that was something like a 330,000-1 shot, given equal weighting to every letter of the alphabet? Tripe, really.

Fenton, who by now had attracted Siouxsie's ire for his rock star pretensions, played his final show with the band on 19 May at Dingwalls. In between they'd played the Roxy twice, Liverpool's Eric's, the Royal Oak in Manchester and the Music Machine, the latter show reviewed by Sounds' Jane Suck. She noted that they were "Polar rock that, sadly, soars over the heads of the Heartbreakers crowd tonight. Combining their best number ('Love In A Void') with 'The Lord's Prayer' and 'Twist And Shout' is a feat of manic inspiration not witnessed since Nico retched her way through 'Deutschlandied'." Fenton was eventually sacked on stage for playing an extended guitar solo, when Siouxsie pulled his jack out. There was a major barney backstage and the band had to be separated by the venue's bouncers.

His replacement would be John McKay, a friend of John Maybury, who was working as an assistant with Morris on Derek Jarman's Jubilee film. He'd been watching the Banshees for a while, and noticed their discomfort with Fenton. "When I first actually saw the group live, I immediately noticed that they seemed really uncomfortable with Peter Fenton on guitar – even to the point of looking awkwardly at each other all the time they were playing. It seemed incredibly unbalanced – mostly, I think, because the chord structures he was creating for the lyrics were almost too close to formal rock'n'roll structures."

The classic early Banshees line-up was now in place, and they now had some hope of converting their ideas – for pop music with an underlying edge of tension and fear – into reality. One of the earliest songs they wrote together was 'Suburban Relapse', which thematically at least, was based around the Psycho shower scene. McKay made his debut with the band on 11 July 1977 at the Vortex, where many, including reviewer Pete Silverton, presumed he was actually Fenton.

Gigs, especially those in out of town in places like Birmingham and Plymouth, were hugely confrontational affairs, rarely passing by without one or more members of the Banshees, often Siouxsie, being immersed in a ruck. As strange as it seems in retrospect, drunken young men would look up at Siouxsie and shout 'Get your tits out'. Which is as brave as it was foolish. In September they travelled to France for four performances at the Gibus Club in Paris, followed by a show in Amsterdam. On their return there were further dates in the north of England, with a show at the Music Machine where Marc Bolan, alerted to their cover of '20th Century Boy', was in attendance.

They made their debut at a 'proper' venue in October at the Rainbow as support to Johnny Thunders, and ended up in the cells over a confrontation outside the venue. It also became apparent that Nils Stevenson was starting to share some of Thunders' bad habits. Record companies remained unsure of them, though not so John Peel and his producer John Walters. They booked them for a session in December 1977. Both had been to see the band a couple of months previously at the Croydon Greyhound.

Given their later commercial stature, not to mention the amount of inept would-be punk bands being snapped up by the majors, it seems inconceivable that the Banshees were not immediately trawled. But the situation was such that their supporters mounted a graffiti campaign, scribbling or carving "Sign the Banshees now" on London record company exteriors in February 1978. Les Mills, who later discovered and managed the Psychedelic Furs, was the prime mover behind the campaign. The band actually considered signing to the BBC for a while. A week or so later their second Peel session aired, featuring the debut performance of 'Hong Kong Garden'.

That session and 'Hong Kong Garden' in particular finally pushed Polydor, via A&R man Alan Black, into a concrete offer. There had been discussions with Geoff Travis at Rough Trade, but Nils Stevenson, and the band, thought they deserved a wider audience. Prior to that, they had been all set to sign with Anchor before that label decided to go with the Adverts because the Banshees "weren't rock'n'roll enough". EMI's John Darnley was keen until the message came through from on high that they didn't want another Sex Pistols fracas on their hands. RCA came up with the excuse that the Banshees were not "compatible" with their roster. Chrysalis's Chris Briggs also backed out after expressing some interest. Dave Dee at Atlantic used the premise that "punk's finished" to bypass them. Decca made an offer, but it was so insulting (£5,000 advance and 5% royalties) that even in their desperation, it was chucked back. "We thought record companies were there to supply a demand," pointed out a frustrated Nils Stevenson to Pete Silverton. "We've been proved wrong. We draw more than any other unsigned band and more than 90% of the signed ones. But we've got this far and we're not giving up." Bootleggers, as they are wont to do, sought to make a quick buck on this growing gap in the supply and demand chain, notably via the Love In A Void album.

As Severin told Record Mirror: "No record company will ever agree to a contract stating the number of pages of advertising you're going to end up with – that was the last thing we argued about and we nearly didn't sign with Polydor because of that." And they came out, to their credit, with a contract that genuinely gave them the power of veto over the way their music was presented. If you compare the discography of the Banshees with their peers, it's remarkably concise.

'Hong Kong Garden' concerned Siouxsie's local Chinese takeaway in Chistlehurst, which had been the subject of continual raids by skinheads since it opened. Or at least that's the consensual view these days. The lyrics don't actually suggest that at all. Sessions for the single, recorded at Island Studios, were originally convened with soul producer Bruce Albertine. A strange choice, he didn't suit them and they certainly didn't suit him. The band were not amused at the results, so Nils Stevenson put them in touch with Steve Lillywhite, who was working with Johnny Thunders. They were knocked out by the results. As were the Banshees' public, who hoisted it to number seven in the national charts. This was, finally, confirmation of the absolute commercial potency of the Banshees. The B-side, 'Voices', was retained from the Albertine sessions.

Suddenly they were hot news. Everyone wanted to interview them, even Record Mirror with whom they would be at loggerheads for several months ("We hate Record Mirror, and the fact that they're interviewing us now after ignoring us for so long is really ironic"). It wasn't just Record Mirror journalists who got short shrift. The ever-amenable Pete Silverton was dumbfounded by their attitude and his Sounds feature called them 'The Most Elitist Band In The World', which the Banshees took as a compliment. "Any attempt to situate them in a musical context – with the one notable exception of Bowie – was met with assertions of their own supremacy. Ultimately, they think that there is only one worthwhile, intelligent, interesting, thoughtful, considered source of music in the world. That's right, you guessed it… Siouxsie And The Banshees."

The single's success gave them leverage with their record label, which decided that they wanted a whole album. So they booked time at RAK studios, again with Steve Lillywhite, who impressed everyone with his enthusiasm. In the meantime, they began a six-week tour of the UK, beginning at the Pavilion, Hemel Hempstead. The tour was almost completely sold out. Siouxsie was, of course, hugely photogenic, a cross between Cleopatra and Jean Marsh – haughty, superior, utterly in control. "Siouxsie reintroduced the figure of the witch," noted Joy Press, "with all its pagan power and majesty, into rock'n'roll. Her foreboding image – which evolved from no-frills dominatrix to exotic sorceress – made her a genuine icon. By the early 80s, Sioux had inspired thousands of girls all over the world to imitate her icy look, simultaneously inviting and repelling voyeurs." The only problem with that was that Siouxsie instinctively hated the idea of imitation. She saw it as a betrayal of everything the Banshees stood for. And it's important to note that it wasn't just the little girls who cared. Marc Almond, for one, was fired by the drama.

There was a secondary side to Siouxsie's projection of remoteness, the emphasis on distance between performer and audience, that so many other strands of punk were dedicated to dismantling. It was a facet that brought severe and direct criticism. "Our attitude to our fans was the complete opposite of the Clash's," Severin later recalled in the band's official biography. "We wanted as little contact as possible, whereas the Clash would invite fans back to sleep in their hotel rooms. I'm sure everyone thought we were completely snooty, but we really didn't care." In a Sounds interview with Vivien Goldman, Siouxsie went even further. "So many bands want to be liked by the audience, they want to be the same as the audience. That's so false." The support for the tour was Nico, a real coup for the confirmed Velvet Underground fans in the band, but she got booed off stage and quit after six shows. Midway through the tour, Severin's relationship with Siouxsie also ended.

The Scream, when finally released, benefited hugely from its extended gestation, though significantly 'Hong Kong Garden' was purged from the running order. The title was inspired not by the Edward Munch painting, but by the Burt Lancaster film The Swimmer. It was the latter's completely irrational dedication to vision, to the idea, that fascinated Siouxsie. The sleeve, like the songs it housed, was deliberately stark and colourless. There were at least three outstanding tracks. The first was 'Carcass', in which a butcher professed his love for his work before chopping off his own limbs and impaling himself on a meat hook. It was obviously comical, but as Nick Cave would discover, you can write the funniest little whiplash-noir nuggets and still never outgrow the perceived shroud of 'darkness'. 'Overground' was a taut, unsettling and beautifully staged travelogue into the nether regions of Siouxsie's psyche. 'Suburban Relapse' detailed the moment wherein the domestic tranquil finally melts into screaming madness.

Chris Westwood in Record Mirror gave it five out of five, and implored readers to "Buy it, nick it, borrow it, tape it, HEAR it." There was one dissenting voice, in the NME, where Julie Burchill was not about to let the 'too many Jews' line drop. "I am still particularly disgusted by the way the way Jewish writers (Viv Goldman) and otherwise extremely moral writers (Chris Brazier) have drooled over the silly cow, letting her get away with that line as long as she promises, 'Oh, it was an unwise choice. I'll change it as soon as I can think of something better!' Well, take your shocking song and stick it up your rude white ass, Sioux, because here's a review that don't believe in running with the pack. Oh daddy please, pretty please, won't you beat up that nasty girl and make her fade away? She hurts my ears and she bores me and the only reason she hasn't been written off yet as a corny 'art-rock' act is that she once used to hang around some, ah, punk band. Standing alone, the Banshee sound is a self-important threshing machine thrashing all stringed instruments down onto the same low level alongside that draggy sub-voice as it attempts futile eagle and dove swoops around the mono-beat." Severin: "Who cares what that obese, coke-head chav-lover thought? As you point out, she was the one dissenting voice concerning The Scream, and isn't it plain to see she was grand-standing for effect? She was the poseur."

After the album, conflicts began to creep in. Morris, in particular, was impressed by tour support the Human League, and wanted to incorporate more visuals into their presentation. Both he and McKay were growing suspicious of manager Nils Stevenson, and in particular his drug intake, but also his involvement of an engineer, Mike Stavrou, so that he could claim co-production royalties.

They entered Air Studios in Oxford Street in May with these simmering tensions hardly alleviated by the fact that insufficient time had passed between their albums. The time had mainly been taken up by extensive tour commitments.. Join Hands was readied for release by July. The divide between Siouxsie and Severin, alongside Stevenson, on one side, against McKay and Morris on the other, deepened. The latter faction were concerned that they were being rushed, that their music was being compromised. They were particularly unimpressed with efforts to re-record 'The Lord's Prayer' (for obvious reasons, it was absolutely nothing to do with them). It was Nil's idea to include the latter, owing to the paucity of material the band had to draw from.

McKay and Morris were unhappy with the sleeve for second single 'Staircase Mystery', but they were more particularly aggrieved about the cover of Join Hands, its WWI imagery reflecting the dour contents of songs such as 'Poppy Day'. Severin: "They were annoyed that John Maybury's original sleeve design was rejected because it was based on a bizarre brother/sister communion card from Utah. Polydor refused to use it, because they couldn't get copyright clearance. Siouxsie and I were really pissed off too (it was GREAT). The difference was, we believed Nils had done his utmost to push it through – they didn't, because Nils designed the soldier sleeve with Polydor's art department at the last minute. It was a shock to all of us but Siouxsie and I let it ride. To us it was paramount that the album came out the first week of the tour, not after it was over, which is what would have happened if we had not met the dreaded DEADLINE. I guess that's pressure... "

The contents of Join Hands were sterile, lacking the life force of The Scream. As Jon Savage noted in his review, "With the ensuing and final 'The Lord's Prayer' the alarm bells burst into a cacophony of sirens as the shortcomings come home to roost. Over 13 minutes, Siouxsie methodically pulls the wings off the Lord's Prayer over a Banshees' boogie which, when it shifts, provides the only moments of interest. It's not art, not proper noise, the Banshees aren't, respectively, good enough artists or incompetent enough musicians. The 100 Club one liner (and myth), taken out of context, is made absurd'. Agreed, though Severin, in particular, would later defend its inclusion. It was part of his legacy with the band, who were about to break up, and one of the central accusations flung at the 'engineers' of its downfall subsequently was that they were not part of the original creative vision that fuelled the Banshees.

It's a patchy album, though still pretty visionary in comparison to much of their peer group. In retrospect, it's doubtful whether Siouxsie has ever sounded quite so vengeful, or insightful, as she does on the matricidal 'Mother' ("The thing you grow to hate/The love you won't forget"). 'Regal Zone', like the Stranglers 'Shah Shah A Go Go', was written with recent events in Iran in mind. But 'Playground Twist' serves both to completely overshadow the album's other songs and remind listeners of the standards the Banshees had set themselves.

A disturbing account of schoolyard terror, 'Playground Twist' was unsurprisingly selected for release as a single. The sleeve depicted a painting by a mentally handicapped child from Kuwait, chosen at Siouxsie's suggestion. The atmosphere on the tour bus had turned rancorous. By the time they reached Aberdeen, they were told to do an in-store signing at the city's Other Record Shop. It was a disaster. McKay and Morris disapproved of the autograph ritual. McKay made his frustrations clear by removing Join Hands from the record player and playing the Slits album Cut instead (somewhat ironic, given that their drummer Budgie would later become such a stalwart of the Banshees). McKay and Morris started handing out, gratis, copies of the album, stamped 'promotional use' only. It later transpired that Polydor hadn't furnished the store with sufficient quantities and Stevenson had attempted to make up the shortfall with promotional copies at cost price. All of which annoyed Siouxsie, who gave McKay a shove. An altercation ensued. And that was it. They walked out.

S

Siouxsie and Severin fully expected their errant musicians to show up for the subsequent soundcheck. They never did. Nils Stevenson frantically took a taxi to the train station to find them. He attempted to intercept the Stonehaven-bound taxi they were departing in, but had his arm caught in the window as it was wound up, and the pair sped away. He was shouting something about the scale of the debts they were looking at, while the departing duo pointed out that "it was their money too". At the hotel they'd propped up two pillows and hung their tour passes round them as a symbolic act of farewell.

Back at the venue, the main support act was the Cure, who extended their set. Then Siouxsie and Severin came on stage to explain their predicament. It was Robert Smith who suggested that, rather than let the punters down, they perform a version of 'The Lord's Prayer' together. They proceeded to do so with some intensity. The punters were still entitled to a refund, if they desired one. And being practical to a man and a woman, the good citizens of Aberdeen did exactly that.

The repercussions of what happened were huge. The tour had not been underwritten by Polydor, which meant that the financial repercussions of cancelling shows would have to be borne by the Banshees. Siouxsie, and particularly Severin, made their views clear in the press.

It took two and a half months before they received any reply from McKay or Morris. It came from their lawyers, a bulletin full of veiled, but dignified, recriminations. It stated that the decision was reached because "the fundamental trust and communication within the group was missing". Only one charge was truly specific: McKay wanted his guitar back, which Stevenson had gleefully handed over to a fan outside the Aberdeen gig to express his disgust. A curt reply from Stevenson followed, emphasising the fact that Siouxsie and Severin were always the core of the group, and rubbishing the duo's claims that elements of Join Hands were a tilt at commercial acceptance.

Siouxsie made some very Siouxsie-like statements along the lines of, 'If you see them, kill them in my name'. The truth behind the absence of any statement on the departing duo's part was that they were literally in fear. They had good reason to be. A few months later, there was a party for Blondie at the Notre Dame Hall in London when Severin, Siouxsie and Stevenson spotted Morris. Severin was the first to reach him and smacked him from behind, before Stevenson and Siouxsie set upon him. Siouxsie, bizarrely, next bumped into John McKay in 1987. He was with his fiancée prior to his wedding day, in a bed and breakfast in the Lake District, where she was also staying with Budgie. Siouxsie would later talk gleefully of keeping them up drinking all night and wrecking the programme for their nuptials the next day. Which really wasn't very nice.

For their part McKay and Morris had decided that they couldn't stay at Polydor with all this ill feeling and moved on. McKay formed Zor Gabor in 1986 with vocalist Linda Clark, but managed just the one single. In the same week, by bizarre timing, Morris also released his 'La Main Morte' solo single. They seem to have done little since, though Morris, who later turned most of his attention to art, did turn down a chance to join Frankie Goes To Hollywood, and John McKay similarly refused an offer from Peter Gabriel. You can take McKay and Morris's subsequent low-level involvement in one of two ways. The first is to ridicule their non-achievements, which would buttress arguments made from the other side about them making the biggest mistake of their lives. The alternative view supports their contention at the time that the pressure was too much. Clearly, each had the chance to get involved in a working band again. Clearly, neither showed any real desire to do so.

Siouxsie and Severin, who were at pains throughout to emphasise the fact that the defections did not signal the end of the band, needed replacements as quickly as possible. They got old friend John Peel to appeal on air for aspirant guitarists to apply for auditions. Meanwhile in Liverpool, Budgie, who'd actually bred budgerigars to raise funds in his youth before attending art school, was embroiled in the local art school scene following the end of his first engagement with the Spitfire Boys. He'd then entered service with the Liverpool punk rock finishing school that was Big In Japan, and later the Planets. But when that ended he'd decided to make a go of it and headed to London, replacing Palmolive in the Slits after being tipped off about the vacancy by Clive Langer. Paul Cook of the Pistols subsequently told him about the Banshees' dilemma. Messages were exchanged. After a short rehearsal, Severin and Siouxsie decided he was perfect, and he immediately started to help them audition for a guitarist.

Nils rang Marco Pirroni to see if he'd be interested in rejoining. They rehearsed a couple of times, but the spark wasn't there. So the Banshees elected to take up Robert Smith on his offer to help out if a suitable replacement couldn't be found. This meant they could fulfil some of the remaining tour dates and help minimise the scale of the financial disaster that was looming. Even so, Siouxsie had to complete the rest of the tour suffering from hepatitis, another medical legacy of all the spitting that was taking place at punk gigs (thanks, in part, to the activities of her former drummer Sid). She was ordered to take a month out as soon as the tour was completed, which actually resulted in a useful writing sabbatical. She came up with the lyrics for 'Happy House', a name originally coined for the Banshees' fan club, during her convalescence.

John McGeoch of Magazine had already been moonlighting in Visage and Generation X and spending more time in London. Stevenson, again, made the call, which saw the two parties meet up in a pub in Notting Hill. He hit it off with Siouxsie and Severin immediately. Within two days, on 16 January 1980, they'd entered Polydor Studios and recorded an early version of 'Happy House' together. The B-side, 'Drop Dead', was quite obviously inspired by the

McKay/Morris departures. It opens with 'I hate you' repeated four times before the succinct announcement that "We don't care... if you vanish in thin air." However, Siouxsie maintained that people were overlooking the humour in the song. Or as she told Robbi Millar: "A lot of people think that 'Drop Dead' was written about them, but that's not true. It was, I suppose, inspired by them. But then you can look at a turd in the street and be inspired to write a song about it, can't you? Really, I don't want people to think that I'm going around all bitter saying 'fuck John and Kenny!', because I'm not. It doesn't matter." Right – and the turd analogy was just an accident?

The upside to the whole unsavoury affair was that Siouxsie and Severin were now writing prolifically, and Budgie and McGeoch were proving excellent foils. "We got bored with trying the old Banshees songs on people," Siouxsie later said of this period, "cos they just had to do their homework and maybe they could do it, but it wasn't good enough to say yes to. But we got bored with them anyway, there were a lot of boring guitarists, so we just started writing things on the spot in the rehearsal to see if they could join in and add something of their own." The songs she's discussing, such as 'Christine' and 'Happy House', were the best they'd composed so far, but others, like 'Trophy', which had been rejected for Join Hands, were also reactivated and reinvigorated. They'd booked studio time above a Co-op in Surrey. It was McGeoch's suggestion that they get in Police producer Nigel Gray. They also got the Pistols' Steve Jones in to guest on three tracks (apparently Jones, at a loose end, also jammed with the Banshees on 'Paradise Place' and 'Skin', though Severin discounts the rumour that they played the Pistols' 'Bodies' together). Both 'Happy House' and 'Christine', ultimately issued as singles, were cut at Phil Manzanera's studio.

Kaleidoscope, its title reflecting the dislocation and diffusion that had impacted on the Banshees camp and recorded at Surrey Sound, is for many their best album after The Scream. There were frequent claims in the press that the McKay/Morris departures had made the group immeasurably stronger, and, for once, the evidence of the record suggested this wasn't complete hubris. There was an encroachment of a pop sensibility not fully realised since 'Hong Kong Garden', but none of the Banshee's sharp edges were blunted in the process. 'Christine', in particular, was outstanding. It was inspired by Christine Sizemore, whom Siouxsie would also write about in 'Eve Black/Eve White', its B-side. There was a nice continuation of their debut album's obsessions with flesh and the corporeal, updating the butcher's love of his work in 'Carcass' with the cheap slash and dash plastic surgery merchants of 'Paradise Place'. Several of the songs had been written during sound-checks on the tour when roadies stood in for Robert Smith. This level of spontaneity informs the record, which is not uniformly successful ('Hybrid' drags its heels) but which is hugely engrossing. Yet Kaleidoscope was hammered by old enemies in the press, chief among them Dave McCullough in Sounds, who decried its inability to match the two overpowering singles it contained.

In November 1980 they travelled to America for their first shows there. On their return they decided to release 'Israel'. "I always wanted to do a Christmas song," Siouxsie told Dave Smeltzer, "so I wrote one!" 'Israel' was a chill meditation on the Jewish state, and the state of the Jewish, driven by Budgie's fecund tom tom work complete with a 30-piece choir, with prominent use of the star of David – perceived by some as 'atonement' for her prior misguided use of the swastika. Although Severin would confirm that there was also a separate agenda. Nils Stevenson thought that it might appeal to American record companies because so many of them were Jewish. He may have thought that, but in keeping with the Banshees' esprit de corps, it didn't actually require him to say it, but he did anyway.

Incessant touring continued, alongside Altered Images, whom Severin would produce. For a while Clare Grogan came across as Siouxsie's giggly little sister and, for a while, we loved her for it. The tracks for Kaleidoscope had been written and recorded in the studio. For JuJu, the idea was that the material should be road-tested first. Nigel Gray was again the producer, and he introduced the band to Roxy Music's Phil Manzanera, at whose studio they would also meet Kevin Godley and Lol Crème, with Sting apparently making the tea. JuJu was the Banshees' most self-consciously 'dark' album, underscored by the cover picture of an African statue from the Horniman Museum in Forest Hill. The songs were heavily indebted to Edgar Alan Poe and the term 'Gothic' was bandied around to describe it in the press. Which was ironic, since the Banshees had been self-describing elements of their music as such several years previously, long before the term (which Phil Sutcliffe had originally used in a Sounds piece around the time of Join Hands) acquired its pejorative slant. One of the touchstone influences were the Cramps, whom they'd caught on their American tour. Yet they were more interested in the building blocks of inner tension and psychological drama – Hitchcock was frequently cited as an influence – rather than corn horror elements. This was best realised on 'Monitor', which predicted the philosophical tug of war that would emerge in the wake of CCTV coverage, where the camera lens became a "sentinel of misery".

'Spellbound' again based itself on a childish sense of wonder and revelation, and while the subtext retained a sense of foreboding, there was something celebratory about the lyric. Fittingly, the video was filmed in the copse near Heathrow where the Hammer horror films were made. Severin was mortified because he wasn't able to watch Spurs play Manchester City in the cup final, a fact which rather undermined the band's perceived image as detached, ivory tower aesthetes. The second single from the album, 'Arabian Nights', was inspired by Siouxsie listening to the Doors, though that didn't necessarily come across in the finished song, which was an intoxicating piece of whimsical storyboarding drawing on childhood fable and fantasy. It was also possibly the only charting pop song to use the word 'orifices'.

The JuJu tour began in Brussels as part of a five-week European engagement before the band returned to the Woolwich Odeon in London in May. The second date of the European trek saw them become the first western act to play in Ljubljana in Slovenia. They would return there to play on the night that independence was declared. "They were ecstatic, people running around in the middle of the night, and car horns going and stuff," Budgie told me in 1995. "We had some kind of transaction to do, flogging some T-shirts or something, and they were counting out the money and they hadn't made a name for it, it had '100' but a blank, no denominations or rather, denominations of what? It was changing its value hour by hour because it was so new. It was incredible. And they gave us a little pennant and little enamel badges for the front of the bus so we could proudly bear the new flag. When we went to Prague from there we were one of the first Western acts to get in and play. The girls in the record station would tell us how they would have secret meetings in open fields to exchange records and stuff because they were banned. Ours weren't allowed in because they were too subversive."

During the JuJu tour they introduced a short duet, just Siouxsie and Budgie performing 'But Not Them'. It was indicative not only of their future in the Creatures, but also of a developing, and covert, personal relationship between drummer and singer. The manner of their relationship only became apparent when photographer Adrian Boot plied them with drink after a show in Newcastle. He got Siouxsie to disrobe in the bath with Budgie, with Siouxsie pictured in various Ophelia-esque poses. The rest of the band and management had no inkling of what was happening until they saw the contact sheet. Suddenly it was out in the open, and Budgie no longer had to traverse fire escapes half-naked in order to fulfil his nightly assignations.

S

Their second US tour began in October 1981, lasting seven gruelling weeks. All of which was something of an eye opener, especially the shows in the deep south and one of the first shows in Pasadena where McGeoch was thrown in jail for clobbering an audience member over the head with his acoustic guitar. Siouxsie loved America so much that after the tour finished, she took some time out to visit Disneyland. The band's relationship with Nigel Gray ended when they couldn't come up with a satisfying mix for 'Fireworks' between them. Instead they brought in Mike Hedges, whom they knew through his production of the Cure's 'Jumping Someone Else's Train'.

In the meantime, a gulf was growing between Siouxsie and Nils Stevenson when it was discovered that the latter had turned to heroin use again. Despite the fact that she'd recently been experimenting with LSD, narcotics were a big no-no for Siouxsie. So Nils was ousted in favour of long time booking associate Dave Woods, who'd been involved with the band for years. Little did they know that he would eventually head exactly the same way as Stevenson.

Their first collaboration with Mike Hedges, 'Fireworks', with full orchestra accompaniment, was imagined as an epic in the vein of Scott Walker, but is among the Banshees' few weak singles, despite sterling work from both McGeoch and Severin. The accompanying album, A Kiss In The Dreamhouse, was inspired jointly by listening to the Beatles' White Album and the idea of LA prostitutes impersonating film stars. Violinists Anne Stephenson and Gini Ball came along for the ride to expand the band's sound, which had left behind some of the darker infatuations of JuJu. The sessions were fun, but the long hours of partying took their toll, particularly on McGeoch. 'Circle' was disconcertingly intimate ("Pretty girl of 16 has fun and runs crazy"), but also accusatory ("If you wind up on the Circle line, hell, it's not from lack of options"). 'Obsession' was the most unsettling track, bordered by a soundtrack of coughing and wheezing. Absolutely terrifying lyrics, too. After all, you don't expect someone like Siouxsie to ask for forgiveness in any context, let alone so explicitly. 'Slowdive' was more ambivalent, and less succinct, but formidably atmospheric.

At a couple of low-key shows in Madrid in October 1982, McGeoch was all over the place. He was drinking so heavily he didn't know which song he was playing. Though his decline was masked by the PR machine, he effectively suffered a nervous breakdown. When the band returned to London, his wife booked him into rehab at Roehampton. When Severin and Dave Woods went down to visit, they found him out on day release, drinking to his heart's content in the nearest pub. They fired him on the spot and put in the call to Robert Smith to see if he was free for the upcoming tour. This time, if he was going to come on board, he wanted to record an album with the Banshees. It was a curt, unsympathetic and ultimately callous dismissal of someone who gave a great deal to the cause. But the Banshees – read Severin and Siouxsie – got on with it. McGeoch was history.

Siouxsie and Budgie flew to Hawaii to record a full Creatures album. In the meantime Severin and Smith were working on the Glove project and contributed a song, 'Torment', to Marc Almond's Torment And Toreros. However, the Glove sessions were taking much longer than expected – though they ultimately did result in a terrific album of multi-layered psychedelic pop exemplified by the singles 'Punish Me With Kisses' and 'Like An Animal', both sign-posting the sensual yet sexually brash contents. So in addition to Feast, the Creatures cut a brass-laden recording of Mel Tormé's 'Right Now'. It became Siouxsie's biggest hit since 'Hong Kong Garden'. And rightly so; it packed a terrific pop punch and was a showcase for Budgie's surround-sound tub-thumping.

There's some ambivalence within the Banshees' camp about what effect these diversions had on the core group. In any case, when they did reconvene to record Hyaena, it was the most difficult album to date – so much so that the sessions were interrupted by two full tours and a live album. 'Dazzle', written on a toy piano, was an instant success, but the rest of the sessions were strained by the fact that the Cure had just enjoyed their biggest hit with 'The Walk' and Smith was forced to divide his time between the two projects. A chink of light came from an unlikely source. Severin hit upon the idea of covering the Beatles' 'Dear Prudence', the second track from the White Album concerning Mia Farrow's sister Prudence, who'd travelled with the Beatles to meet Maharishi Mahesh Yogi, but became a recluse. "The Beatles got slated for it when it was released," Siouxsie later told the Independent. "It was unbelievable – but there's just something about that record." Severin picked up the thread. "One of the main reasons we chose (it) was that John Lennon's version sounds a bit unfinished. We recorded it in Sweden, and the idea came from touring round Scandinavia, listening to the Beatles." Robert Smith added guitar back in Islington, with his sister playing the harpsichord. Even though Budgie managed to break his foot filming the video in Venice, the single went top three – much to their annoyance, old London punk face Boy George stayed at number one with 'Karma Chameleon'.

They released the live album Nocturne in November 1983, a document of their first shows at the Albert Hall, with mixing completed at Pete Townshend's Eel Pie studios. But 'Dear Prudence' was still considered an artistic retreat by some, including Joe Strummer, talking to the NME in 1984. "Siouxsie? She's doing Beatles numbers. The Stravinsky Overture and the dry ice? Do we have to live through all that again?"

In the meantime, Smith's commitments were finally catching up on him, and he told the band that there was no way he could undertake the forthcoming British tour. Speaking to Mark Paytress for his authorised biography of the band, Siouxsie was still condemnatory about his decision, despite begrudgingly acknowledging that there was an unwritten agreement that he could return to the Cure whenever he chose to. "I never trusted Robert. I always thought he had another agenda, that he was using the situation. Look at the facts. In October, 'Dear

S

Prudence' made it to number three, thanks in part to the Creatures keeping the band's profile high. The Cure's first hit, 'Love Cats', came out just as 'Dear Prudence' was peaking. When he left, it felt a bit like, 'Thanks for the ride, I'm off'. All that bollocks about a sick note. That wounded sparrow act doesn't wash with me." Look at the facts? This has to be one of the most tenuous reconstructions of documented history ever. Ungrateful to a fault,. Siouxsie meanwhile took to referring to Smith as "Fat Bob". Nice.

Hyaena was finally unveiled on the 1st of June 1984, and exactly a week later John 'Valentine' Carruthers, formerly of Clock DVA, made his debut at the Brixton Academy, following a recommendation from Polydor. His first recordings with the band were made with Mike Hedges at a friend's studio in Bavaria, a reworking of two B-sides and two album tracks for 'The Thorn' EP.

Geffen, meanwhile, were preparing to get behind their first post-McGeoch/Smith album, Tinderbox. They booked Bob Ezrin, of Alice Cooper and Lou Reed (Berlin) fame for the sessions, but it was a disaster. Ezrin wanted to add a few bits and pieces in order to nail part of the publishing – one of the oldest producer's tricks in the book. The Banshees were a bit long in the tooth for that. He quickly retreated back to New York with a flea in his ear. Next up was Hugh Jones. When they'd worked out the songs with him they relocated to Hansa Studios in Berlin where Bowie had cut Low. The sessions were not fun, the setting was not glamorous, and very little of the studio's equipment actually worked. Including the band, with Budgie, in particular, going off the rails on a routine basis and being hospitalised at one point for alcohol poisoning. They sacked Hugh Jones on their return from Berlin on the basis that he'd let Polydor hear the sessions without their permission, which was siding with the enemy as far as they were concerned. Before the album's release they issued a new single, 'Cities In Dust', which actually dented the American charts, but is not one of their most memorable efforts, lacking the personal edge that hallmarks Siouxsie's better lyrics.

Dave Woods had booked them on their biggest tour to date, including three nights at the Hammersmith Odeon. Unfortunately, on the first of these, Siouxsie put her knee out. She was forced to complete the remainder of the tour in plaster. The album sessions were proceeding slowly. Severin would later ascribe the soporific pace to the fact that they were being entirely directional with their guitarist, Carruthers. They would instruct him as to what was required until he got it right. This was a huge contrast to their previous guitarists, McKay, Smith and McGeoch, each of whom contributed creatively even if they lacked the executive status enjoyed by Siouxsie and Severin. Tinderbox reveals the internal disharmony. It's listenable, and effective in passages, with Souxsie's vocals being particularly seductive on 'The Sweetest Chill', arguably as close as the Banshees had come to writing a straightforward romantic love song. And 'An Execution' is certainly profoundly grisly. But elsewhere the album does little to push the Banshees forward, serving as a holding pattern. The singles ('Cities In Dust', 'Candyman') traced predictable themes. Decay. Childhood. Haven't we been this way before?

In May 1986 they embarked on their first major US tour since 1981. On their return there was no appetite to repeat the exhaustive sessions that had produced Hyaena and Tinderbox. Instead they decided to put in action a prior plan to record an album of cover versions. They clearly enjoyed doing it, though it's doubtful whether it afforded their audiences as much fun. The choice of Disney classic 'Trust In Me', the album's highpoint, was imaginative and quixotically pleasing. Iggy Pop and Sparks all apparently approved of the versions of their songs, but refitting 'The Passenger' with a chirrupy horn section simply robs the original of its bite. Through The Looking Glass also featured the introduction of Martin McCarrick, a veteran of sessions with Marc Almond, whom Siouxsie had originally asked to provide a string arrangement for Billie Holliday's 'Strange Fruit'.

In November they embarked on a nine-date South American tour, becoming the first English band to play Argentina since the Falklands War. But thereafter there was a summit meeting about Carruthers' future. Severin was despatched to his flat to tell him he was out. The original intent was to use McCarrick's keyboards to cover the guitar parts, but in the end McCarrick decided that would be impossible. So in came Jon Klein, formerly of Specimen.

The first thing the new five-piece line-up was set to work on was the single 'Song From The Edge Of The World' in July 1987. Severin suggested using Mike Thorne, who had produced the first three Wire albums as well as various Pistols sessions. But it wasn't a good match. Such was the violent exception that Severin and Siouxsie took to Thorne, at least retrospectively, that they left the single off Twice Upon A Time so that he wouldn't get a credit on the album. In the authorised biography of the band, Siouxsie suggests they'd become frustrated with Thorne's inability to get a decent lead vocal mix and rang him up to issue an ultimatum. Thorne's own version was that he didn't take kindly to the hectoring demands Siouxsie issued in a late night phone call and responded with a curt, "Sorry, Mum." He also totally refutes the allegation that he resisted Klein's request to try some overdubs on the 12-inch version of the track by putting his head between the speakers and saying 'impress me'. But Thorne's most telling reflection on Paytress's book is that it's "a critical biography not so much of the group and its output as of the rest of the world". Now, ain't that the truth. One example; the Banshees are notoriously prickly about inaccuracies committed by journalists in discussion of their oeuvre. Yet they inaccurately disparage Mike Thorne for being an ex-public schoolboy.

A further jaunt to America saw the Banshees support Bowie on his Glass Spider tour, which even the designated support band felt impelled to take the piss out of. But there were simmering tensions with manager Woods, whom the band suspected of not being wholly transparent about their financial situation. They moved down to Ardingly in Sussex to begin work on the next album, Peepshow, again with Mike Hedges. The new boys were fitting in well. Except that Dave Woods' visage had taken on the familiar grey pallor of the heroin addict. So he walked out of their lives, leaving the small matter of an unpaid £100,000 tax bill. Just as she had done with the McKay and Morris 'betrayals', Siouxsie responded via the splenetic 'Are You Still Dying, Darling?', which seems like an open invitation to suicide.

Paul 'Suspect' O'Reilly was installed as their new manager. Instead of a heroin addict, he seemed to be big on coke – which was an improvement of sorts. At least the sessions seemed to be progressing. Via a combination of backward-masking of 'Gun', plus a hip hop beat and hints of drum and bass, they'd come up with 'Peek-A-Boo'. This was, by some distance, the band's most cheery single to date. It also brought them back to the charts. It was hardly indicative of the rest of the material on Peepshow. 'Rawhead And Bloodybones' is the lullaby well-intentioned parents are least likely to settle their children with, while closing track 'Rhapsody' addressed the murderous instincts of Stalin. But the rest is paint by numbers Banshees. In the meantime, a story circulated in the Mirror suggesting that Siouxsie had had a nose job. She won a subsequent libel case primarily on the basis that she'd already written a song ('Paradise Place' on Kaleidoscope) criticising plastic surgery.

Another tour began in September 1988, with an elaborate stage show that the band could ill afford. O'Reilly was completely out of his depth and the band realised he would need to be replaced. Meanwhile they were criss-crossing the US and playing sold out shows, although there was some friction when Severin decided to bring his girlfriend Lucy out on the tour. O'Reilly was fired and Tim Collins came in as manager. O'Reilly would go on to work with Sigue Sigue Sputnik before committing suicide, or overdosing, depending on which version you believe. New incumbent Collins discovered that the principals, Severin and Siouxsie, were at loggerheads and unable to bear being in the same room as each other.

After the Peepshow tour finished Siouxsie enjoyed a restorative break with Budgie to complete a new Creatures record. No-one was completely sure whether or not there would be another Banshees liaison, but with tempers cooled by geography and distance, the band decided to give it another go in 1990. They booked into a residential rehearsal studio in Wales. But Severin was becoming more immersed in computers, and experimenting with tape loops. He'd suggested Stephen Hague as prospective producer. Eventually they wound up back at RAK, where they'd recorded The Scream, though this process was disjointed with each member coming in to record their parts separately. It wasn't a particularly enjoyable process, lightened somewhat when Siouxsie and Budgie announced they were to marry.

Superstition was a more reflective effort. The songwriting was OK if occasionally formulaic, though the main problem was that both Siouxsie and Budgie loathed the way it was put together, feeling all the band's traditional strengths of spontaneity, the creative pinball that had characterised earlier albums, had been lost in the long grass. As a result they felt that it was Stephen Hague's record, not theirs. But both the elegant 'Kiss Them For Me' and to a lesser extent 'Shadowtime' are keepers.

In the summer of 1991 the band joined the Lollapalooza festival. They were specifically invited because Perry Farrell of Jane's Addiction was a huge fan. "It exposed the Banshees to a completely different audience to the one which has grown up with them over here," Budgie told me in 1995. "It's interesting, because you do get a wide mix of people – you'll look out at the back of the audience, and there's someone there with a T-shirt from your first tour. And there's always a younger element every time when we go back to the States, for instance... the good thing about Lollapalooza was having all these bands go through the same things and be in the same boat. We became very supportive of each other. As a band we're usually quite private, and there was no high kicking grand finales or anything. But, pretty much, some nights everyone wanted to get on that stage. On Lollapalooza we all had our allotted time, but that element crept back in, like, 'Can I, er, bang some drums like in that end song, the big one?' And Jane's Addiction asked me to go on and do an encore with them. It was this thing where everybody plays some percussion instrument. And it was nice, like a family bonding thing."

The experience was both artistically and financially restorative. It was followed by a tour of Europe in which they delighted in staying in the most prestigious hotels they could find. They returned to America at the end of 1991 to pick up where they'd left off, but they didn't find the warmth of welcome second time around.

Tim Burton had asked the band to write a song for the soundtrack to Batman Returns, alongside Danny Elfman, formerly of Oingo Boingo. The result was 'Face To Face', which certainly upped their profile, even if they didn't enjoy working with Elfman. Sadly, a forced rewrite of the film's ending meant that Tim Burton was no longer free to film the accompanying video. Which was a shame, as Burton confirmed to Entertainment Weekly. "I've always been a fan. Siouxsie is one of very few women who can create a realistic primal cat sound."

Siouxsie and Budgie had, in any case, decided to move to the south of France. Which was where sessions for The Rapture began. The idea was that, after the sterility of the Hague sessions, they'd all be in one room writing and recording again. The centrepiece of the album was the sweeping title-track, consisting of at least three movements. It was arguably the most beautiful, sonorous musical set-piece they'd ever recorded together. But again, the sessions were far from plain sailing. There were disagreements over a song Budgie had written, 'Hang Me High', which Severin loathed. At the end of the sessions, and for the first time, Polydor turned round and said they didn't think the album was complete. Before they could rectify the problem the Banshees had a series of European festival dates to fulfil, as well as shows in Australia. After these were completed, the decision was made to bring in an outside voice, and Siouxsie and Severin opted for John Cale. Polydor had suggested Scott Litt and Bob Clearmountain. They were told where to get off.

Cale has a reputation for his discipline and attention to detail in the studio, and he considered he was there to do a job. The Banshees thought he was there to do a job for the record company. In the meantime, the money was running out. Both Klein and McCarrick were on separate deals and were literally left without an income when these lapsed. Things came to a head on a night out in Soho when Klein, the worse for wear, threw a pint over a female friend of Pete Burns. They responded by viciously beating Klein, to the extent that he ended up in hospital. In the meantime, there were increasingly hostile arguments over publishing royalties. When Klein refused to back down over what he thought was the credit he was due on the album, he was curtly fired. The other side's take on this is that the band tired of him wishing to put his own royalties to the top of the agenda as the album sessions dragged on with the small matter of a world tour looming. One man's legitimate request to be financially rewarded for his efforts is another man's blackmail. In the meantime, Siouxsie's mother had died.

Despite the ill feeling, the band pressed ahead with the release of 'O Baby', a lovely, intoxicating slice of psychedelic whimsy. In the end Siouxsie flew to New York to oversee the final album mixes with Cale. Polydor were running out of patience. They'd just appointed a new MD and, when a Time Out feature reprinted Siouxsie's 1979 comment that she wouldn't "piss on Polydor if they were on fire", it was bad timing, as their option was up. They almost certainly would not have renewed anyway, but they were livid at what they thought was Siouxsie's ingratitude.

Behind The Rapture, Siouxsie was writing some of her most personal lyrics. Both 'The Lonely

One' and 'Falling Down' dealt with her childhood, as she later confirmed to William Shaw. "I grew up having no faith in adults as responsible people. And being the youngest in the family I was isolated – I had no-one to confide in. So I invented my own world, my own reality. It was my own way of defending myself – protecting myself from the outside world. The only way I could deal with how to survive was to get some strong armour." These songs saw her beginning to rationalise those formative events, her father's alcoholism, her personal isolation, and the sexual abuse earlier referenced in 'Candyman'.

I interviewed the band at the time of The Rapture's release, and found Budgie to be friendly and, while well versed in the band's traditionally terse rapport with reporters, accommodating and open. However, when I asked him if the generally upbeat nature of the recordings reflected the enviroment they were created in, he stumbled. "It wasn't all smiles. There were some very difficult moments during the course of making it. Mainly because we were producing yourselves – usually a producer comes in and mediates between two people over how this should go, or which chord, or which tempo it should be at or whatever. Whereas we had to sort this out ourselves, with no-one around to come in and wave a wand and put it all right. We believe in who we are, what we are and what we do. We're not fussed too much about the way we're written about, often it's just 'punk, goth, bleak, y'know? I don't think they take account of things like the humour we have. And people get things wrong because they use the things that have been written about us in the past, which are also usually wrong."

The atmosphere that surrounded The Rapture's release was one of indolence and apathy. Everyone bemoaned Polydor's lack of interest in them. Of all the complaints, this one from Severin takes some beating. "They simply saw us as something that was costing them a million quid or whatever." No shit! It's hard to think of any artists who have been allowed as much creative autonomy not to mention financial indulgence as Siouxsie And The Banshees. Severin: "The 'million quid or whatever' quote is taken out of context at the time. I was actually making the point that the accountants had taken over the game, and that the value of the band was equated by a line on the ledger. Yes, if they had exercised the option we would have been in debt to them for about £1 million. But they would have got another album for that and combined with the sales of the back catalogue, they were in no danger of not recouping. They have made millions out of the Banshees. I don't feel sorry for them, especially if they waste it all on Shed Seven!"

Nevertheless the tour continued, with Knox, an American guitarist, brought aboard to fill Klein's shoes. The behaviour of Budgie was again causing some concern, his demeanour being the most obvious outward signal of inner disharmony within the ranks. There was a further tour of the US, which was well attended, but the shows were played through grimaces. They recorded 'New Skin' for the Showgirls soundtrack at a dilapidated studio in Prague, but by the time the tour reached Belgium, where they played alongside Oasis, Simple Minds, Paul Weller and Faith No More at the Axion Beach Rock Festival, it was all over.

In the first week of April 1996, at the same time as the Pistols announced the support bill for their Finsbury Park reunion gig, the Banshees issued a press statement. "As the 'music industry' prepares to relive the heady days of 'punk' when confusing the opportunists with the protagonists, it proceeded to sign anything with a safety pin that could spit. Siouxsie And The Banshees would like to say thank you and goodbye." However, despite the press release being very specific, the message was still garbled, as Severin told me on the phone shortly thereafter. "Someone did a precis… for a wire service and loads of radio journalists have been ringing up saying 'are you splitting up because the Sex Pistols have reformed?' Which is ridiculous." I asked him who was the main motivator behind the decision. "Well, Siouxsie, I suppose. She always says, shall we do another one after we've finished doing an album. And I said no, probably not this time." I also asked him about the mention of McKay and Morris on the press release. "Well, how long should you bear a grudge?"

It took seven years before the Banshees would reconvene, appropriately enough, for the Seven Year Itch tour. They'd been getting various offers and the money was gradually ramped up. Having said repeatedly that they wanted nothing to do with the punk revival circuit, not surprising given that they'd always rejected the term punk, it must have been difficult for them to flog their wares on the road again. Yet with typical Banshees chutzpah, they figured they were somehow apart from those bands. "We always felt we were part of a heritage that went back to the Velvets and glam rock," Severin pointed out to Mark Paytress, "and kind of expected that someone would have picked up on what we did and taken it onwards. No one really has, though. I thought Nirvana had it for a while, but no-one else has come close to combining the drama, the subversion and the charisma of the Banshees at their best. Which is another reason why there was a validity in getting back and playing again." But even Severin can't top Siouxsie for peer disdain. "One of the things that annoyed me – the way everything was tagged with the same label. As though there was no difference between someone like Jimmy Pursey and me." Aloof, and magnificently arrogant, to the nth and to the last beat of their hearts.

But the Banshees are no more, we are repeatedly told, due to the fact that "bridges that should have been mended with the Seven Year Itch tour never were". Certainly the pressure has lifted from Siouxsie and Budgie. They're almost entirely self-sufficient. They've got their own studio built in their converted farmhouse between Toulouse and Bordeaux, from whence they run Sioux Records and continue as the Creatures (they released Anima Animus in 1999 and Hai! in 2003) as well as collaborations with Basement Jaxx and master drummer Leonard Eto. There was also a triumphant three-night return to the 100 Club for the first time since 1976, 'An evening with Siouxsie, the Banshees, and the Creatures'.

Steven Severin recorded his soundtrack to Nigel Wingrove's Visions Of Ecstasy in 1989, the only video to be denied a certificate on the grounds of blasphemy. He has also linked with Brazilian theatre company Os Satyros for Maldoror, as well as collaborating with Indo-Japanese avant-garde dancer Shakti and Vasanta Mala dance company. His third film soundtrack, Purifiers, was undertaken alongside old friend and flatmate Richard Jobson in 2004. He is just completing his fourth, again co-credited to wife Arban, for Paul Burrow's psychological thriller Nature Morte, due to be released in 2006.

Discography:

Hong Kong Garden/Voices 7-inch (Polydor 2059 052 August 1978) (also available in gatefold sleeve)

The Staircase (Mystery)/20th Century Boy 7-inch (Polydor POSP 9 March 1979)

Playground Twist/Pull To Bits 7-inch (Polydor POSP 59 July 1979)

The Scream LP (Polydor POLD 5009 October 1978) (reissued on CD, on Wonderland 839 008-2, in March 1989 and March 1995)

Join Hands LP (Polydor POLD 5024 August 1979) (reissued on CD, on Wonderland 839 004-2, in March 1989 and March 1995)

Mittageisen/Love In A Void 7-inch (Polydor 2059 September 1979) (Originally Germany only, before strong import sales led to a domestic release with the same catalogue number, with the A-side retitled 'Mittageisen (Metal Postcard)')

Happy House/Drop Dead – Celebration 7-inch (Polydor POSP 117 March 1980)

Christine/Eve White, Eve Black 7-inch (Poydor 2059 249 May 1980)

Kaleidoscope LP (Polydor 2442 177 August 1980) (reissued on CD, on Wonderland 839 0006-2, in March 1989 and March 1995)

Israel/Red Over White 7-inch (Polydor POSP 205 November 1980) (also issued as a 12-inch, POSPX 205, with extended mixes of both tracks)

S

Spellbound/Follow The Sun 7-inch (Polydor POSP 273 May 1981) (also issued as a 12-inch, POSPX 273, with extra track 'Slap Dash Snap')

JuJu (Polydor POLS 1034 June 1981) (reissued on CD, on Wonderland 839 0005-2, in March 1989 and March 1995)

Arabian Knights/Supernatural 7-inch (Poydor POSP 309 July 1981) (also issued as a 12-inch, POSPX 309, with extra track 'Congo Conga')

Fireworks/Coal Mind 7-inch (Polydor POSP 450 May 1982) (also issued in gatefold sleeve, POSPG 450, and as a 12-inch, POSPX 450, with additional track 'We Fall')

Slowdive/Cannibal Roses 7-inch (Polydor POSP 510 October 1982) (also issued as a 12-inch, POSPX 510, with extra track 'Obsession II')

A Kiss in the Dreamhouse LP (Polydor POLD 5064 October 1982) (reissued on Wonderland, 839007-2, in March 1989 and March 1995)

Melt/Il Est Ne Le Divin Enfant 7-inch (Polydor POSP 539 November 1982) (also issued as a 12-inch, POSPX 539, with additional track 'Sleeping Rain')

Dear Prudence/Tattoo 7-inch (Wonderland SHE 4 September 1983) (also issued in limited edition gatefold sleeve, SHEG 4, and as a 12-inch, SHEX 4, with additional track 'There's A Planet In My Kitchen')

Head Cut/Running Town 7-inch (FILE 1 December 1983) (fan club single)

Swimming Horses/Let Go 7-inch (Wonderland SHE 6 March 1984) (also issued as a 12-inch, SHEX 6, with extra track 'The Humming Wires', and as a limited edition 12-inch poster bag, SHEXG 6, also with 'The Humming Wires')

Dazzle/I Promise 7-inch (Wonderland SHE 7 May 1984) (also issued as a 12-inch, SHEX 7, with extra track 'Throw Them To The Ground' plus 'Dazzle (Glamour Mix)'

Overground/Placebo Effect 7-inch (Wonderland SHE 8 October 1983)

Nocturne double LP (Wonderland SHAH 1 November 1983) (reissued on CD, 839-0009-2, in March 1989 and March 1995. The intro, incidentally, is Stravinsky's Rite Of Spring)

Hyaena LP (Wonderland SHEHP 1 June 1984) (Also issued on CD, 821510-2. Reissued in March 1995)

The Thorn 7-inch EP (Wonderland SHEEP 8 (October 1984)

Overground/Voices/Placebo Effect/Red Over White

Cities In Dust/An Execution 7-inch (Wonderland SHE 9 October 1985) (also issued in a gatefold sleeve, SHEG 9, and 12-inch, SHEX 9, featuring 'Cities In Dust (Eruption Mix)' and 'Quarterdrawing Of The Dog')

Candyman/Lullaby 7-inch (Wonderland SHE 10 February 1986) (also issued in a limited edition of 2,000 as a double-pack 7-inch single, SHE DP 10, featuring 'Umbrella' and as a 12-inch, SHEX 10, with extra track 'Umbrella')

Tinderbox LP (Wonderland SHEHP 3 April 1986) (CD version, 829145-2, contains bonus tracks The Quarterdrawing of the Dog/An Execution/Lullaby/Umbrella/Cities in Dust (extended version). Reissued in Mach 1995)

This Wheel's On Fire/Shooting Sun 7-inch (Wonderland SHE 11 January 1987) (also issued in a limited edition as a double single, SHEG 11, with addition tracks 'Sleepwalking (On The High Wire)' and 'She Cracked'. Also issued as a 12-inch single, SHEX 11, featuring 'This Wheel's On Fire (Incendiary Mix)' and extra track 'Sleepwalking On The High Wire')

The Passenger/She's Cuckoo 7-inch (Wonderland SHE 12 March 1987) (also issued in a limited edition poster sleeve, SHEG 12, and 12-inch, SHEX 12, with extra tracks 'The Passenger (Lilliocomotion Mix)' and 'Something Blue')

Through the Looking Glass LP (Wonderland SHELP 4 March 1987) (limited edition cut-out sleeve available. CD version: 831472-2. Reissued March 1995)

Song From The Edge Of The World/The Whole Price Of Blood 7-inch (Wonderland SHE 13 July 1987) (also issued as a picture disc, SHEP 13, and cassette, SHEC 13, featuring extra tracks 'Mechanical Eyes' and 'Song From The Edge Of The World (Columbus Mix)', and as a 12-inch, SHELX 13, featuring 'Song From The Edge Of The World (Columbus Mix)' and 'Mechanical Eyes')

Peek-A-Boo/False Face 7-inch (Wonderland SHE 14 July 1988) (also released in a limited edition gatefold sleeve, SHEG 14, cassette single, SHECS 14 featuring extra tracks 'Catwalk' and 'Peek-A-Boo (Big Spender Mix)', 12-inch, SHEX 14, featuring extra tracks 'Peek-A-Boo (Big Spender Mix)' and 'Catwalk', and as a CD single, SHECD 14, featuring extra tracks 'Peek-A-Boo (Big Spender Mix)' and 'Catwalk')

Peepshow LP (Wonderland SHELP 5 September 1988) (CD version, 837240-2. Reissued in March 1995)

Killing Jar/Something Wicked (This Way Comes) 7-inch (Wonderland SHE 15 September 1988) (also issued as picture disc, SHEP 15, and 12-inch, featuring 'Killing Jar (Leipdopteristic Mix)' plus 'Are You Still Dying, Darling?', and CD single, SHECD 15, with same tracks as 12-inch, plus 7-inch version of 'Killing Jar')

The Last Beat Of My Heart/El Dia De Los Muertos 7-inch (Wonderland SHE 16 November 1988) (also issued in gatefold sleeve, SHEG 16, 12-inch, SHEX 16, with extra track 'Sunless', and in gatefold 12-inch, SHEXG 16, and CD single, featuring extra track 'Sunless' and 'El Dia De Los Muertos (Espiritu Mix)')

S

Kiss Them For Me/Staring Back 7-inch (Wonderland SHE 19 May 1991) (also issued as a 12-inch, SHEX 19, featuring 'Kiss Them For Me (Snapper Mix)' and extra track 'Return'. A limited edition 12-inch, SHEXR 19, featured 'Kathak', 'Loveappella' and 'Ambient' mixes of 'Kiss Them For Me'. CD single, SHECD 19, featured extra tracks 'Return' and 'Kiss Them For Me (Snapper Mix)'

Superstition LP (Polydor 847731 June 1991) (also issued on CD. Reissued in March 1995)

Shadowtime/Spiral Twist 7-inch (Wonderland SHE 20 July 1991) (also issued on 12-inch, SHEX 20, featuring 'Shadowtime (Eclipse Mix)' with extra track 'Sea Of Light'. CD single, SHECD 20, features same tracklisting as 12-inch plus 7-inch version of 'Shadowtime')

Face To Face/I Could Be Again 7-inch (Wonderland SHE 21 July 1992) (also issued on 12-inch, SHEX 21, featuring 'Face To Face (Catatonic Mix)' plus extra track 'Hothead'). CD single, SHECD 21, features same tracklisting as 12-inch plus 'Face To Face (7-inch remix)')

O Baby/B Side Ourselves 7-inch (Wonderland SHE 22 December 1994) (also issued on CD single, SHECD 22, with extra track 'O Baby (Manhattan Mix)', and on a second CD single, SHEDD 22, with additional tracks 'Swimming Horses' and 'All Tomorrow's Parties')

The Rapture LP (Polydor 523725 January 1995) (also issued on CD)

Stargazer/Hang Me High 7-inch (Wonderland SHE 23 February 1995) (also issued on 12-inch, SHEX 23, with additional track 'Black Sun', and as a remix CD single, SHEDD 23, with 'Mambo Sun', 'Planet Queen' and 'Mark Saunders' mixes of 'Stargazer')

ARCHIVE RELEASES:

Once Upon A Time – The Singles LP (Polydor POLS 1056 November 1981 1981) (limited edition with free print. Reissued on CD, Wonderland 831542-2, in March 1989)

The Peel Session 5.11.77 12-inch (Strange Fruit SFPS 012 February 1987)

Love In A Void/Mirage/Metal Postcard/Suburban Relapse (also issued on CD single)

The Peel Session 23.2.78 12-inch (Strange Fruit SFPS 066 February 1989)

Hong Kong Garden/Overground/Carcass/Helter Skelter (also issued on CD single. The two sessions were later combined on a single Peel Sessions LP by Dutch East India)

Twice Upon a Time – The Singles LP (Polydor 517160-1 October 1992) (also issued on CD. Reissued in March 1995)

The Best Of CD (Polydor 0651522 September 2002) (Pointless best of. Poor track selection. The ugly duckling in the Banshees' otherwise well-heeled discography)

Downside & Up – B-sides And Rarities 4-CD Box Set (Universal 9821823 November 2004) (tidy summary of the Banshees career on B-sides, many of which are excellent – 'Drop Dead', 'Eve White Eve Black', 'Are You Still Dying, Darling?' etc – as well as including 'The Thorn' EP tracks on CD for the first time. Excellent 72-page booklet too, with full contributions from Siouxsie, Severin and Budgie)

Skids

Richard Jobson (vocals), Stuart Adamson (guitar), Bill Simpson (bass), Tom Kellichan (drums)

The SKIDS, the most "unfortunately named band in history", according to Word magazine, managed to harness chest-beating Wermachtian guitar bravado with lyrics steeped in literary pretensions to sell an awful lot of records as one of the punk acts who were co-opted by Smash Hits and Top Of The Pops. The wonder was that they were all authentically working class kids from down at heel areas of Dunfermline.

With due respect to some other competent, occasionally inspired musicians, the story here is of two principals. Vocalist Richard Jobson was a man who could run Tony Wilson close for accusations of punk era pomposity. Stuart Adamson, seemingly a thoroughly grounded yet ultimately deeply troubled figure, was the guitarist whose playing was widely imitated and admired throughout the industry, and would later propel Big Country to global chart success.

Let's start with Jobson. Or Jobbieson, as some rather unkind fellow countrymen have described him. The youngest of five brothers, his father was a miner, while his mother worked on the docks. Of Irish Catholic descent, they nevertheless lived on a Protestant housing estate. He ran with the AV Toi, a gang named after the town's Abbeyview estate, while carving a name for himself as a talented footballer. "All my friends were die-hard Hearts supporters,' he later told Sean O'Hagan, "but I was never into that. I was always perfectly aware of who I was and where I was from. It was always Hibs or Celtic. But the sectarian thing was never an issue. It was music that united us – music and clothes.'

O'Hagan's article, published in the Observer in 2004, features the best description of Jobson's profound silliness I have come across. "One of my abiding memories of Richard Jobson is the first time I saw him on Top Of The Pops . It was 1978 and his post-punk group, the Skids, had entered the charts for the first time with 'Into the Valley'. It was a strange and effortlessly pretentious time in British pop culture and few bands were stranger or more effortlessly pretentious than the Skids. 'Into the valley/betrothed and divine,' sang Jobson, sounding like Robert the Bruce fired up by punk rock and speed on the eve of Bannockburn. What sticks in my mind is not his declamatory delivery, nor his odd skipping dance, nor even his knee-high tan leather boots, but the fact that he had his initials monogrammed on his Star Trek-style top. This suggested a man immune to accusations of pretension, someone so convinced of his singularity he had it imprinted on his chest for all to see."

Jobson would indeed have been irretrievably ridiculous, had it not been for the backing of a tremendously innovative and powerful musical unit. Adamson's guitar playing cramped echoed melodrama into the song textures, in a manner that the Edge would later recreate with U2. He has openly admitted the debt – play 'Out Of Town' back to back with 'Two Hearts Beat As One', or 'Another Emotion' and 'Where The Streets Have No Name', for evidence of this. Or for a more contemporary comparison, try Franz Ferdinand's 'Take Me Out' next to 'The Saints Are Coming'. The other, less celebrated but hugely important element of the Skids was their fearsome manager, Mike 'Pano' Douglas, who would routinely deputise as head bouncer and remonstrator on the band's behalf at their uproarious early gigs.

Skids bass player Bill Simpson had known Adamson from their days at Beath High School, rehearsing at the Adamson's family home in Crossgates. "When we started out, we were playing in Crossgates, at the Institute," Simpson later recalled. "We had a band called Tattoo, mucking about covering songs by Bowie, Roxy Music or Status Quo, just doing cover versions. We had some great laughs touring round, going to pubs and clubs all over Scotland, as far as Kinloss and Lossiemouth." Adamson had seemed set fair for a minor role in sewerage. "After I left school I started working as a student environmental health officer," Adamson later recalled, "doing a course in Sanitary Science – water sampling, shop and pub inspection, anything involved in pollution. The guy who was teaching me the job was great. He was a big mad drummer in a country and western group and he'd take me to see his band in his Ford Escort – you couldn't see the back seat for four years' worth of rubbish. He used to toss and twirl the sticks. He was a brilliant drummer."

Adamson's first exposure to punk came at age 16 when he saw the Damned play Edinburgh in 1976. Suitably inspired, he and Simpson posted an advert in the local paper. It read, succinctly, "New wave band looking for drummer. No hippies." "When the Skids evolved, punk kicked in at the right time," remembers Simpson, "and we were the first local punk band. We picked up a following and a name quickly." The group, completed by Jobson and Tom Kellichan on drums, supported the Stranglers and Buzzcocks. They made their debut with the self-financed 'Charles' EP, containing three tracks and credited to the regionally themed No Bad Records, financed by manager Sandy Muir. Charles' was Adamson's depiction of a metal drilling factory worker whose existence entwines with that of the machine he operates until they merge into a single entity. Both are subsequently sold off for scrap. Shortly after 'Charles', the Skids signed an eight-album deal with Virgin.

Their debut single for Virgin was 'Sweet Suburbia' in 1978, a snappy enough if inconsequential introduction to the band, but it was the B-side 'Open Sound' that announced Adamson's signature guitar style. It preceded the 'Saints Are Coming' EP, the first time the Skids truly gave notice of their potential, with some fantastic virtuoso playing by Adamson. Jobson's oblique lyric complements Adamson's fitful, restless guitar runs perfectly. It's also possibly Kellichan's finest hour, and one of the most perfect, succinct, explosive pop-punk tunes ever written.

There was similar anthemic material on their 1979 debut album Scared To Dance (1979; the US version featured a revised running order), its title derived from an NME article about pop music behind the Iron Curtain. However, the sessions were troubled, not for the last time in the group's history. Adamson was particularly unimpressed with producer David Batchelor's (Sensational Alex Harvey Band) 'tinkering', preferring the raw copy the band supplied, and had to be restrained from quitting.

Aside from a reprise of 'The Saints Are Coming', Scared To Dance also featured the stuttering 'Of One Skin', and their breakthrough hit, 'Into The Valley'. The latter featured such a confounding lyric that it was later featured in a television advert for blank cassettes. And those lyrics stand some pondering. "Prophesised, brainwashed/Tomorrow's demise/All systems failing/The placards unroll." But while Jobson's words read like he'd got a thesaurus stuck in his throat, the vocals and music, especially the echoed bass intro, produced a package that was blasted out like a terrace anthem, which in a way was exactly the nature of the beast. And mention must also be made of its B-side, a live rendering of stage favourite 'TV Stars'. In which Jobson handed the microphone to the audience for its singular chorus ('Albert Tatlock', shouted repeatedly), as he embarked on a long list of soap characters and other celebrities. Ena Sharples, Meg Mortimer, Kenny Dalglish, Stanley Ogden, John Peel, take a bow. I still, to this day, have no idea who Stanley Richardson is.

However, from here on the group's balance was marred by Jobson's increasingly grandiose designs. This did not please everyone in the band, not least drummer Tom Kellichan who was temporarily replaced by Rich Kids drummer Rusty Egan for the second album, which came just seven months after their debut. This was to be spearheaded by Be-Bop Deluxe head honcho Bill Nelson. "Much to my surprise, they approached me with the proposal that I should produce their records," he later recalled. "Initially, this was done in partnership with my old friend John Leckie, but I eventually did the job on my own. It turned out that Stuart Adamson and Richard Jobson had been long-time fans of my work, Stuart having learned how to play guitar from my recordings with Be-Bop-Deluxe and Red Noise. I remember being immensely flattered that I had inspired such passion in them and I was proud of Stuart's dedication and talent."

The album was criticised in some quarters, especially Sounds, for playing on Nazi themes, notably in the cover, which depicted a most Aryan-like Olympian crowned with laurel leaves. In defence of the album, Jobson informed the same publication that "We checked things out very carefully, even the Gothic script we used on the cover which supposedly has Nazi connections is actually Jewish."

Simpson decided he'd had enough on the tour that followed its release. Six months after the original, the album was re-released again in remixed form with Bruce Fairbairn overseeing it (with the exception of the single mix of 'Working For The Yankee Dollar', which was produced by Mick Glossop). The songs themselves are radically different, and hugely inferior, losing the nuances that Nelson weaved into the mix, the dissonant keyboards and compressed, multi-layered drums. Luckily, the first and only CD reissue, by Captain Oi!, reinstates Nelson's work.

The Skids relaunched themselves in 1980 with a new rhythm section featuring Russell Webb (bass; ex-Zones) and Mike Baillie (drums; ex-Insect Bites) for The Absolute Game. Mick Glossop's production made more sense of Jobson's increasingly expansive themes and it actually gelled impressively. Russell Webb: "The sound of the Skids was Adamson through and through, melodies etc, until I joined them for The Absolute Game. Stuart and I spent many weeks in Dunfermline together writing the new material. It was the first time Stuart had written with anyone else."

It was a top ten album, but only one of the extracted singles, 'Circus Games', made headway. This despite some extravagant marketing from Virgin (including the dreadfully conceited 'Woman In Winter' comic book issue, which no doubt was intended to parody the group's lofty assessment of themselves but actually came across as an exercise in rampant ego). Another extracted single, 'Goodbye Civilian', featured the obtuse 'Monkey McGuire meets Specky Potter Behind The Lochore Institute', a B-side instrumental, which was assumed to be a reference to characters in much loved Sunday Post cartoon strip Oor Wullie. But Russell Webb informs me that they were actually childhood acquaintances of Jobson, while the Lochore Institute was where the Skids played several of their first gigs.

The Absolute Game is a great record in any context. However, with Jobson spending more time on the London scene, and Adamson keen to return to Dunfermline, the tensions in the band saw it unravel and Adamson walked, in order to set up Big Country. Which left Jobson and his sole remaining bandmate, Webb, to work on the critically neglected Joy, an attempt at a Celtic concept album. JJ Johnson, formerly of the Electric Chairs, was among those who worked on the album, recorded between July and September 1981 at Britannia Row Studios.

"It was an attempt at reinventing the most ancient forms of musical expression (folk music, travelling storytellers) using the most advanced technology and production values available at the time," Webb later recalled, "coupled with basic acoustic instruments and sounds. We mixed hairy-arsed Scottish folk singers, with demure English classical musicettes, it brought out an underlying sexual tension, that, on reflection was vital in creating a new life, from this unlikely parentage, diverse background, and history." Others involved included Virginia Astley, like Jobson a fan of World War One poets, who contributed flute to the single 'Fields'.

Released in December 1981, it sank without trace. The Skids were all over shortly after its release. To be fair to Joy, I once published a piece on the band where I made some dismissive remarks about its value, and was then castigated by a sizeable number of correspondents who pointed out its inherent genius. While I can't concede that, nor do I like it as a piece of work, chiefly because I don't think the material suits Jobson's voice, it would be churlish to deny the fact that it embodied an admirable spirit of adventure.

Webb was, in any case, happy to redress the balance for me, pointing out that 'Iona' was made Simon Bates' record of the week on Radio 1 and got "masses of airplay". Bill Nelson started off as producer on 'Iona' (the recording was originally started in Inverness and has Kenny Hyslop on drums and Stuart Adamson – his last ever Skids session – on guitar). It didn't really work out with Bill so we moved to the Manor in Oxfordshire and continued with Mike Oldfield who – over a pint of Guinness in a local pub, told me I ought to take over the production reins, which I did. We moved back to the Townhouse studio in London and Virgin where I finished the recording and mixed the song. Virgin were happy enough with the result to allow me the privilege of producing Joy. It was a very hard record to compile as it was done to all intents and purposes without a proper guitarist to counter Jobson's vocal style – I think it probably shows. Incidentally, when the album was finished at Britannia Row, I took early mixes with me to Los Angeles (John McGeoch was a great friend of mine and he was playing at Perkins Palace in Pasadena with Siouxsie And The Banshees). For what it's worth, it made John cry (no, not laughing!) It touched something in him and that was good enough for me – John was one of my musical heroes."

Jobson and Webb subsequently formed the Armoury Show with the estimable McGeoch, alongside another Magazine alumnus, John Doyle, recording one album, Waiting For The Floods. Webb: "Jobson and I put The Armoury Show together – partly aided by the fact that I was working at the time as sound engineer for Pete Townshend in his Eel Pie studio in Soho and had access to unlimited studio time for personal purposes. Jobson and I used the time to re-start our writing partnership and John McGeoch, who was also at a loose end, came in to add his legendary guitar flourishes to our early compositions. The Armoury Show was born. John Doyle came in slightly later when the project started developing into a 'proper' group. We all had a bit of a laugh at the idea that was going around music business types that we were going to be a New Wave supergroup – Magazine and the Skids and all that bollocks. I enormously enjoyed writing with John McGeoch, more than I can say. I hated the depression that was killing him through the massive alcohol and drug abuse he fell into."

When the Armoury Show ended, McGeoch went on to join PiL. Webb toured Europe as support to Talking Heads' Chris Franz with his own band, the Ring (featuring Marty Williamson of the Psychedelic Furs and Sinead O'Connor's husband John Reynolds). He then hooked up with McGeoch again "for one last blowout", playing bass on PiL's farewell tour in North and South America. "John and I stayed firm friends until he died," Webb recalls.

Jobson subsequently released the solo album The Ballad of Etiquette in collaboration with Virginia Astley, McGeoch and Josephine Wells (Kissing The Pink) for Bill Nelson's Cocteau label. It saw him reading poetry over adaptations of Debussy, Britten and original material. The Bad Man double set was even more adventurous, or pretentious if you were among the growing lobby of Jobson detractors. Webb: "I was musical director of his first poetry reading in Leicester Square. Virginia Astley and I lived together for about three years. The Bad Man album was originally written and recorded as the second Armoury Show album for Parlophone (it had minor hits on it such as 'New York City' and 'Love In Anger'). I agreed for it to go out as a solo album, because I'm like that and Jobson really, really wanted to have a solo album on his CV!"

Then came the semi-autobiographical 16 Years Of Alcohol, which accompanied a book of the same name and was later the basis of Jobson's film breakthrough. He also acted, modelled, married Mariella Frostrup and went into film production (Tube Tales and Heartlands), presented TV shows such as As It Happens for Channel 4 and Men Talk (oh, how we laughed), as well as O-1 For London. He also wrote An Insider's Guide To London for Virgin (nice coincidence, that) and continued to indulge in performance poetry. I have particularly fond memories of an uber-absurd rendition of Sylvia Plath's 'Daddy' that had me in stitches. I kind of changed views on the fella after that. Yep, it was one of the most pretentious things I've ever heard. But boy, he had balls. Art deco balls, but balls all the same.

Following the good reception afforded 16 Years Of Alcohol, Jobson went on to direct the martial arts film, The Purifiers. Less well known is that Jobson is a diagnosed epileptic. Or the fact that he recently appeared in an episode of Neighbours From Hell after his Hertfordshire neighbour decided to build a pig farm next door to him.

Adamson, meanwhile, retreated to Dunfermline where his wife gave birth to their first child and he began writing songs with bassist Bruce Watson, formerly of the Delinquents and Eurosect, both of whom had supported the Skids on Scottish dates. Together they piloted Big Country to worldwide success, with The Crossing selling three million copies and earning two Grammy nominations.

Adamson was immensely popular and down to earth, and although he later settled in Nashville, he was a frequent visitor to Fife, where his two children from his first marriage remained and his parents resided. He was also often to be seen on the terraces of Dunfermline Athletic FC, where 'Into The Valley' is still played when Dunfermline Athletic take the field. Big Country's commercial zenith coincided with an appearance on the Live Aid bill. After that he announced his decision to quit alcohol, and stuck with it for twelve years, but it got him in the end. Nick Tesco of the Members: "I was surprised, actually. When the Skids were going, we were at their first gig. He always struck me as being the most sensible of the lot. I was surprised to find out he'd been treated for alcoholism, and then he goes and buys a pub! Then his marriage broke up – I think he just lost his rudder."

The Skids did reunite to play a memorial gig for Stuart Adamson following his suicide in Honolulu. At the tribute, held on 31 May 2002 at Glasgow Barrowlands, the rest of Big Country were in attendance, as well as Simpson, now an estate agent in Dunfermline, and Baillie, along with Midge Ure and Bill Nelson. Jobson had no idea that anyone still cared for the Skids. "I didn't realise that that band was so important to that generation of people. I'm quite awful about the past. I just dismiss it. Kind of blank the whole bloody thing out." He did, earlier, however, pay tribute to his old sparring partner. Adamson was "always the rock that made the Skids a credible and imaginative force. He was passionate and obstinate and an inspiring good friend." He also reflected that "I was very happy with the Skids. I tried my hardest to save that group but it was beyond saving."

DISCOGRAPHY:

(Buyer's Guide: In terms of the Skids' archive collections. Fanfare, the first compilation of singles and album tracks, was superceded by Dunfermline, which revisited the track selection, lost one track and added seven more. But you're best off going for the Captain Oi! reissues of the studio albums, which include my humble bumbles on the band's career, and are sufficiently well put together with bonuses and B-sides that you can almost overlook the car-crash prose)

Charles/Reasons/Test Tube Babies 7-inch (No Bad NB 1 March 1978)

Sweet Suburbia/Open Sound 7-inch (Virgin VS 227 September 1978)

The Saints Are Coming/Of One Skin 7-inch (Virgin VS VS 232 November 1978)

Wide Open 7-inch EP (Virgin VS 232 November 1978)

The Saints Are Coming/Of One Skin/Contusion/Night And Day (also available on 12-inch, VS 232-12)

Into The Valley/TV Stars 7-inch (Virgin VS 241 February 1979) (also available as a 12-inch, VS 241-12, with additional tracks 'Scared To Dance' and 'Working For The Yankee Dollar' 12-inch mix)

Scared To Dance LP (Virgin V 2116 February 1979) (reissued in April 1984, Virgin OVED 41, and on CD, Virgin CDV 2116 in June 1990 with bonus tracks 'Sweet Suburbia', 'Open Sound', 'TV Stars', 'Night And Day', 'Contusion', 'Reasons', 'Test Tube Babies'. Both of the latter two tracks had to be salvaged from single master tapes, which is why the sound quality drops. Reissued again in September 2005 by Captain Oi!, AHOYCD 262, with additional eighth bonus track 'Charles (single version)' and new sleevenotes by this writer)

Masquerade/Out Of Town 7-inch (Virgin VS 262 March 1979) (also available as a double single featuring 'Another Emotion' and 'Aftermath Dub')

Charade/Grey Parade 7-inch (Virgin VS 288 September 1979)

Days In Europa LP (Virgin V2116 November 1979) (Original copies featuring gothic lettering and 1936 Olympics picture were withdrawn. Reissued in March 1980 with additional track 'Animation'. Reissued on Virgin OVED 42 in 1984. CD reissue, AHOY CD 172 in 2001, on Captain Oi! restores the original Bill Nelson production and features bonus tracks Masquerade/Out of Town/Another Emotion/Aftermath Dub/Grey Parade/Working for the Yankee Dollar (Single Version)/Vanguards Crusade)

Working For The Yankee Dollar/Vanguard's Crusade 7-inch (Virgin VS 306 November 1979) (also available as a double single featuring 'All The Young Dudes', 'Hymns From A Haunted Ballroom')

The Olympian/10 Feet Tall (by XTC) flexidisc (Smash Hits HIT 002 1979) (free red vinyl flexidisc with Smash Hits)

Animation/Pros And Cons 7-inch (Virgin VS 323 February 1980)

Circus Games/One Decree 7-inch (Virgin VS 359 July 1980)

The Absolute Game LP (Virgin V 2174 September 1980) (first 20,000 copies issued with free album Strength Through Joy of studio out-takes, Virgin VDJ 33. Reissued in 1984, Virgin OVED 200, in 1988, and again on CD in 2001 by Track, TRK006CD, which rather pointlessly includes the reduced single edit of 'Woman In Winter', but is bereft of bonus tracks or any of the Strength Through Joy material. As of writing, this situation should be redressed by the release of a more comprehensive Captain Oi! reissue, which I was working on as this book hit deadline. One fantastic quote from an interview with Russell Webb for the latter project helps put the Skids in context: "Richard liked to put forward an impression of himself (call it a caricature) as a person of cultured learning and he would almost always walk about with a book – like Sartre or Sylvia Plath etc. – hanging out of his pocket. Mostly the book in his pocket betrayed its unopened pages and hid a well-thumbed thesaurus behind it. I must give Richard his due, he tried ever so hard to kill the idea he carried around inside that he was an ignorant son of a miner. He literally pulled himself up by his (football) bootstraps and tried to make himself better than he believed he was. He didn't always succeed mind you – actually I'll rephrase that – he often failed but he tried his bollocks off and that's worth something by any standards. Most of his lyrics are impenetrable only because he didn't use his thesaurus well. If you disassemble his words and backwards thesaurusize them (sorry!) I think they would show quite a bit of honest pain and poetic depth. Unfortunately those attributes terrified Jobson to a pulp, his thesaurus was the only weapon he used to try to destroy his enemy.")

Goodbye Civilian/Monkey McGuire Meets Specky Potter Behind The Lochore Institute 7-inch (Virgin VS 373 October 1980) (picture disc version, VSP 373, also available)

A Woman In Winter/Working For The Yankee Dollar (live) 7-inch Virgin VSK 101 November 1980) (with free comic book)

Fields/Brave Man 7-inch (Virgin VS 401 August 1981)

Iona/Blood And Soul 7-inch (Virgin VS 449 October 1981)

Joy LP (Virgin V 2217 November 1981) (reissued in 1988, Virgin OVED 200)

ARCHIVE RELEASES

The Skids Versus The Ruts CD EP (Virgin VSCDT 1411 1982) (the Ruts win. But only on points.)

Fanfare LP (Virgin VM2 May 1982) (from John Peel's sleevenotes: "Thus it was that when No Bad NB1 'Reasons', 'Test Tube Babies' and 'Charles' reached the sink-pits and stews of London, the Skids already enjoyed the first murmurings of a reputation, and when the band followed the record south, they must have hoped for an enthusiastic reception... when they clambered on stage in a Stoke Newington pub they must have been disappointed at the mute, incurious glances of the few regulars which greeted them. Happily, my old brave ones, this performance was enough to win the Skids an outing on Radio 1 and a subsequent approach from Virgin Records.")

Into The Valley/Masquerade/Scared To Death/Working For The Yankee Dollar 12-inch EP (Virgin May 1983)

Dunfermline – A Collection Of The Skids' Finest Moments LP (Virgin 1987) (reissued on CD, Virgin V 9022, in 1993)

BBC Radio 1 Live In Concert CD (Windsong WIN 008 1987) (excellent show dating from March 10 1979)

Sweet Suburbia (the Best Of the Skids) CD (Virgin CDOVD 457 1995)

The Greatest Hits Of Big Country and The Skids double CD (Mercury 5869892 May 2002) (What a bloody pointless concept. Does, however, contain three tracks from Adamson's alt-country group the Raphaels, if you're interested. Some sleevenotes might have helped)

The Best Of The Skids CD (EMI 5906582 July 2003)

Into The Valley – The Best Of The Skids CD (EMI Gold 5602142 January 2005) (a somewhat pointless exercise in duplication – this is essentially the same CD as 'Sweet

Suburbia' – and it's annoying that the whole thing is chronological with the exception of the title-track being lifted to the top of the running order. But it's cheap, and the sleevenotes by old fan Adrian Thrills are worth reading)

Skrewdriver

Yes, I did write something about SKREWDRIVER. But then I thought, hang on, I don't want any letter bombs, do I?

Skunks

Colin Ward (vocals), Gerry Lambe (aka Jerry Ram; rhythm guitar), Franco Cornelli (lead guitar), Hugh Ashton (ex-Danto and Oso; bass), Pete Sturgeon (drums)

The SKUNKS drew their membership from Dole Q (see separate entry), the name change hastened by some withering comments by Severin of Siouxsie And The Banshees, suggesting Dole Q, purely in their choice of name, symbolised the singular lack of imagination that had taken hold of the punk scene.

The band subsequently played a series of shows in the capital as support to XTC at the 100 Club, the Police at the Vortex and the Buzzcocks at Manchester's Free Trade Hall, which was recorded for Piccadilly radio, and also toured alongside the Killjoys. They had started to daub silver stripes in their hair, as well as wearing top hat and tails, so the choice of name became obvious. At which point Ashton came on board as their permanent bass player and their sound became more expansive and less rote 1-2-3-4 punk. Songs such as 'Take It Or Leave it', 'Smash And Grabber' (drafted from Ashton's time as a member of Specta), 'Heart Attack', 'Lucy', 'Bad From Good', 'Back Street Fighting' etc date from this period.

They were regulars at the Roxy, and Pete Townshend, Keith Moon and Alex Harvey watched them supporting Generation X at the Vortex. Cornelli recalled this memorable evening to punk77. After some mutual name-calling from the stage, and Cornelli's subsequent, laboured denial of any knowledge of Pete Townshend's identity, Moon responded by smashing up the dressing room and impersonating Long John Silver. Townshend, taking pity on the battered wreck that was Cornelli's guitar, eventually replaced it with a gleaming new Rickenbacker, and signed them to Eel Pie and put them in the studio.

The result of Townshend's sponsorship was 'Good From The Bad', written by Cornelli, backed by 'Back Street Fighting'. Lambe: "Pete Sturgeon drummed on 'Good From The Bad'. Pete was given a kit by Moonie (Keith Moon) after the Vortex, but then left to retire to Milton Keynes. JJ Johnson, as a mate of Hugh Ashton's, filled in for the Skunks whilst they tried to find a replacement. They supported Wayne County on tour (whom Johnson would subsequently join). Johnson was a great mate who once beat me to a pulp when I inadvertently threw one of his symbols at him, nearly decapitating the poor chap. Clive Pierce (probably the best drummer I have ever heard "technically") joined the band in 1979/80. Clive went on to be a great session musician in own right." Johnson has a slightly different recollection. "Gerry's claim that 'I beat him to a pulp' is grossly exaggerated, probably for dramatic effect. It was only a minor fracas, more like 'a good shaking' after Gerry got over excited and out of control during a 'jam' session and decided to try to smash up my drum kit. But yes, it's true, he did accidentally nearly decapitate me with a cymbal. In retrospect it was all ridiculous and fairly humorous so, I don't bear any grudges about it."

Townshend, in a letter to the band dated 23 May 1979, was enthusiastic about their work: "The new stuff is great, I like 'Lucy' and feel it could make a good single but then the instrumentals are incredible too. The organ sound is amazing. God help us if you ever get a synthesiser." It managed to sell out of its print run of 2,000 copies, and was spun by John Peel (who compared it to an "educated Beatles track"), though it was always intended as a promotional device in order to alert record companies to their presence. It worked – after that they joined EMI subsidiary Cobra Records, renaming themselves Craze, releasing 'Motions (Going Through The)' and 'Lucy'. 'Motions' was actually a major hit in Australia, reaching number twelve in the charts. An album of more Kraftwerk-influenced material was prepared, provisionally entitled Spartans, of which demo recordings were made, but never released. It was to have included several tracks drawn from the group's time as Dole Q/Skunks. "The band split up when Thorn took over EMI and the band were red-ringed by the accountants in 1981," Lambe told me. "Publishing deals with EMI are still in situ, so you never know Spartans may just released one day. I still have the early demos though and they are real class!"

Hugh Ashton and Skunks' producer Robert Doran (now an established name in TV and commercial work) later played in Beasts in Cages. Lambe: "The guys in the band still meet up as part of Clapham Collage 5th Veterans. Clive and Gerry play in goal with Cornelli still convinced he can play as an Italian defender type. Gerry is a logistics manager with BAA at Gatwick, married, three kids, mortgaged to the hilt and living in Purley. Clive lives in Kingston, self-employed, Franco lives in Dorking in a ten-bed detached house (so that's what happened to the royalties!). Hugh still lives in Brixton Hill, and Rob lives in the Oval. Our manager, John Boyle, who used to do great trade showing porno movies on a 6mm cine projector in Fulham Broadway, has since moved to Blenchingly in leafy Surrey. I could never work out how comes so many members of Parliament could attend a midweek afternoon showing in Fulham, when they should have been in Westminster! Anyway, John did good business on the door!"

And the best times? "Supporting the Buzzcocks at Manchester Free Trade Hall for Piccadilly Radio. On the same tour we shared the bill with the Killjoys and a great band called the Spitfire Boys from Liverpool. The piano at Bradford University (another story and much too rude); meeting Pete Townshend and Keith Moon and rehearsing at Twickenham Sound stage a week after Wings had been there. Plus the 1950 Fender Telecaster loaned to me by Pete Townshend for a Twickenham College gig, which I duly smashed up (by accident!) and which he kindly allowed me to get away with. His accountant wasn't very happy. Still, his accountant did get slammed up for fraud about ten years later! 1976 to 1982 were probably the greatest years for me personally – and that we were lucky enough to have been involved in the music business and so much fantastic radical change for the better."

DISCOGRAPHY:

Good From The Bad/Back Street Fighter 7-inch (Eel Pie EPS 001 June 1978)

Slaughter And The Dogs

Wayne Barrett (vocals), Mick Rossi (guitar), Mike Day (guitar), Brian 'Mad Muffet' Grantham (drums), Howard 'Zip' Bates (bass)

SLAUGHTER AND THE DOGS provided conclusive evidence that not everyone took heed of the year zero ethos of punk. Or if there was a year zero, it was not 1976 but 1972, when David Bowie released Ziggy Stardust. Based in the forbidding, forlorn council estates of Wythenshawe, a tough district of Manchester that doubled as a skinhead mecca, the band were formed around childhood friends Mick Rossi and Wayne Barrett, who met aged 14 and 15 respectively. They hit it off over their mutual admiration for Bowie – Rossi being a huge fan of his Ziggy-era guitarist Mick Ronson. "Wythenshawe was – and still is, unfortunately, one of the biggest housing estates in Europe," Barrett later told Big Takeover. "A lot of crime there. You had few choices: football, music, prison, being on the dole, or the end of a needle."

S

While at Sharston High School they decided to form a band, initially using the name Wayne Barrett & His Mime Troupe, partially due to their singer's other main interest; the mime work of Marcel Marceau and Lindsay Kemp. He'd also appeared in a stage production of Jesus Christ Superstar – as Jesus. Desirous of a name more befitting their gang mentality, Barrett, while lying on his bed one day, combined elements from posters of his two favourite albums – Mick Ronson's Slaughter On 10th Avenue and Bowie's Diamond Dogs. Slaughter and the Dogs was a "shit" name, he later conceded, but there – he was stuck with it. The rhythm section was established as Howard Zip Bates and Brian 'Muffet' Grantham.

Managed by Mick's brother Ray Rossi, who had "a great way of extorting money out of people", they started playing local clubs during 1975. "We would come on between the Frank Sinatra impersonator and the bingo," Rossi recalls. These gigs led to a self-promoted show at the Wythenshawe Forum that drew an audience of 300, close to the venue's 500 capacity. "I can't tell you how important it was for a band to come from Wythenshawe," Rossi told me, "to be up and running and creating gigs. It really did open it up for a lot of other bands." The

first song they wrote together was entitled 'Love, Speed And Beer'. Iain Grey relates a great story about Rossi in Granada documentary I Swear I Was There. "I used to go to school with Mick Rossi. There was one time, going to a music store in Manchester. He hadn't warned me, but he had a guitar case with him – which I thought had a guitar in. So in we go, he picks up this Fender Stratocaster, puts it in the case, and walks out. The woman had seen what he done and he just said to me, run! I get home, the police are at my house, Mick's buried it in his garden. He left it there for six or seven months till he thought it was safe to dig up. That's the way they were. Wythenshawe scallies."

They were still playing working men's drinking dens and bingo halls, often mistakenly introduced as Slaughtered Dog, when the Sex Pistols first stopped off at Manchester. As Rossi would later admit, apart from a Caroline Coon article and a couple of mentions by their soon-come producer Martin Hannett, they had no idea what the punk thing was all about. But they were smart enough to deduce that something was in the wind, and Ray Rossi pestered Malcolm McLaren with promises of the local crowd they could draw for an upcoming, Howard Devoto-promoted return. They shared the bill with the Pistols and the Buzzcocks, who were making their live debut, at the second Lesser Free Trade Hall show on July 20 1976. Steve Shy recalls events. "I'm a glazer by trade. There was this apprentice painter who didn't fit in at the company. They put him with me because I didn't get on very well with anybody either. At the time, I used to go to the Ranch, which was Bowie/Roxy then. And this lad kept saying, 'I'm in a band, come and see us.' He mithered us that much, I went. And it was the second night at the Lesser Free Trade Hall. My apprentice was Wayne Barrett. That's how I saw the Pistols and Buzzcocks. Everything clicked. I knew it was what I was waiting for and my life changed overnight."

S

Taking the stage with long hair, dressed in satin and throwing practised rock star shapes to covers of Roxy Music's 'Both Ends Burning' – at exactly the moment the Sex Pistols were about to play their new creation 'Anarchy In The UK' – Slaughter And The Dogs were wholly out of step. But then so was everyone else. There was serious friction between the Buzzcocks and Slaughter camps on the night. Paul Morley inflamed the situation by flicking peanuts at Barrett, who actually changed his stage costume twice on the night because "that was what Bowie used to do". John Cooper Clarke, meanwhile, was transfixed. "Slaughter were fantastic, sensational. They were the only real punk band there, they were like glam rockers. It was before the punk uniform was established. Wayne had one green satin pyjama pants and matching hair."

It was Day's last show with the band as they reconsidered their direction. Rossi remembers

Lydon had a bad cold that night, and was walking around with the lyrics to 'Anarchy In The UK' on a rough sheet of paper that looked like a used handkerchief. But as soon as he heard it, it sounded "completely awesome". Lydon was also impressed with the Dogs, noting "They had a very young guitarist who was astounding. He looked like he could have been a star, but egos got in the way."

That night re-wired Manchester's entire musical circuitry for anyone younger than Sad Café. That included Slaughter And The Dogs, who believed their brand of glammy, driving R&B wasn't that far removed from the Pistols that it couldn't be adapted. "We didn't know what punk was," Rossi told me. "We were playing high-energy, street rock'n'roll, but we found our calling through the Pistols." The transformation was instant. "As soon as we saw that, we had to regroup and look at ourselves again. You're enlightened, but then you have to find your own style." They immediately dropped the silks to wear their own street clothes – which were authentically ripped and torn. Aside from Barrett, of course, who was still something of a luvvie at heart and liked to incorporate capes and an excess of talcum powder into their live shows. Prior to their debut single, the band recorded two sessions for Piccadilly Radio, including versions of 'Boston Babies' and 'Runaway'. "That was the first time we'd been in a proper studio," Rossi told me. "Ray got us that with the help of Paul Young from Sad Café." The tapes are still in his mother's loft.

Ray Rossi followed McLaren's advice to get down to London, which tallied nicely with the band's own ambitions to get out of Wythenshawe at all costs. As far as Barrett was concerned, all the local bands, the Nosebleeds, Drones, Buzzcocks, V2 and Warsaw/Joy Division, were just as desperate to "get out of Dodge".

Slaughter And The Dogs picked up a support to the Pistols at the 100 Club, then shows with the Damned. They made their first appearances at the Roxy after Ray Rossi talked Andy Czezowski into regular bookings. They also played the Vortex, Marquee and Nashville on a regular basis, building up to larger venues like the Roundhouse. Yet the snobbery of the London scene persisted, especially when it came to northern interlopers, and disputes often spilled over into fights. Not that the band ever fitted in with the more arty punk types back back home in Manchester. "Slaughter And The Dogs never had much credibility with the tastemakers in Manchester during the punk era," Dave Haslam reflected. "The purists resented them for jumping on the punk bandwagon, and Buzzcocks fans, in particular, failed to mix well with the rough-hewn Wythenshawe types who followed Slaughter round the circuit." Pete Shelley later recorded the origins of the dispute in Granada documentary I Swear I Was There. "They always used to think they were the best. We knew that thinking that you're the best doesn't necessarily mean you are the best. So we were more philosophical about the dispute. As a result, they saw us as being rivals, and as a result lost the plot completely."

The bandwagon issue is one which irritated Mick Rossi aplenty when I talked to him. "Bandwagon jumpers? We were the bandwagon. We were there before 90% of the bands in Manchester, up and running. We were just four street kids with dreams, but we were there at the beginning." It was something Barrett also countered in a September 1977 interview with Sounds. "When we first started it was actual punk we were playing. We were doing numbers like 'Blood, Speed And Beer', about the different kicks you can get. People sing about politics but we sing about street things, these were things that were actually happening."

Rossi is particularly persuasive when he talks about Slaughter being airbrushed out of history – see the brilliant but not entirely literal Mancunian travelogue 24 Hour Party People for evidence. You can trace a direct link between Slaughter and almost everything that followed – Wilson, Hannett, Morrissey, etc were all closely linked with the band, and Johnny Marr and the Stone Roses were among their fans. Another fellow Manchester City fan and Wythenshawe native, Rob Gretton, worked for Slaughter as a roadie, headed their fan club (publishing the fanzine Manchester Rains) and co-managed them when Ray Rossi was sent to prison for motoring offences. According to Rick Goldstraw of the Ferrets, this was due not to the fact that he drove a big converted sports car with attention-seeking polycarbonate fins, but rather to the occasion on which he'd 'slapped' a copper, but got away with it in court. That meant "he would get pulled by the police every time he went 100 yards down the road". Goldstraw also told me of the time when he and partner Alan Wise decided to invite Ray Rossi to share an office with them. Pretty soon Rossi was shunted into a side office, to which Wise still had a key. So when he had a phone installed, Wise would sneak in at night and make dozens of international phone calls. Only when the bill arrived did they realise that Ray Rossi was one step ahead of them. He'd had the phone installed on an extension line back to their office.

They were certainly no press darlings, though they did attract a degree of critical support. Neil Spencer (then the editor of the NME), Caroline Coon (Melody Maker) and Garry Bushell (Sounds) all had nice things to say about Slaughter And The Dogs. Factory head honcho and So It Goes presenter Tony Wilson, who'd first seen the band at Portwood's Garage club, was even-handed in his assessment. He compered their pre-punk show at the Wythenshawe Forum. "They probably had a little bit too much Bowie and a little too much Mick Ronson, but nevertheless, they were good." Wilson was "strangely charmed". However, Slaughter weren't initially endeared to him. "Fuck off, Wilson," Barrett once offered, "A punk is supposed to be a pauper, so fuck off, you posh git, you mean nothing to us."

Their debut came on Manchester indie Rabid, set up by local legend Tosh Ryan. Ryan, quoted in his first feature article in the NME by Paul Morley, defended the group against its many detractors, calling them "working-class kids from Wythenshawe, the true embodiment of what punk was about; raucous, challenging and shouting at the establishment." 'Cranked Up Really High' c/w 'The Bitch', produced by the Mancunian legend Martin Hannett, with vocals recorded in the studio's kitchen in a single take with a budget of £300, had sufficient bravado and energy to qualify as a genuine punk artefact. But it would have sounded just as good in 1973 as 1977. "We got on like a house on fire with Martin," Barrett later told the Big Takeover. "He was a great guy. And Tosh as well. Even though the cunt has never paid me the royalty money that I'm due!"

As Hannett recalled in an interview with Jon Savage reprinted in his testimonial, And Here Is The Young Man, "I got Slaughter into the studio, I was straight into the weird stuff; right, let's have a tape loop! Looped guitar notes on 'Bitch'. They didn't mind, they went out for a walk with Rob (Gretton), president of their fan club at the time, and bumped into Tommy Cooper, they were made up." 'Cranked Up Really High' has gone on to sell over 80,000 copies (they gave royalties from the CD to Hannett's widow). But what was Hannett like to work with? "He was lovely," Rossi says. "He was always eating cheese all the time. We knew him through Alberto Y Lost Trios Paranoias, because we rented their van off them to do gigs. I always thought he was a little 'out there', but a lovely guy. I'm very proud of that single and what he did for us."

Shortly after their debut, 'Boston Babies' and 'Runaway' were appended to the Roxy's live album, and they appeared in Don Letts' film documenting the venue, The Punk Rock Movie. In August Decca Records stepped in for them, desperate to sign a punk rock act having rested on its laurels since signing Thin Lizzy. The signing ceremony took place outside Wythenshawe dole office in a parody of the Pistols' Buck House stunt. Barrett took great delight in signing off from the employment exchange by writing "new job: rock star!" in the appropriate box, and for a while the major treated them like princes. They were flown to gigs and pampered, and like working class lads tasting the high life for the first time, they inevitably and irrevocably blew it. Sessions for Do It Dog Style, recorded immediately after they'd signed, featured Rossi's hero Mick Ronson. "It was fascinating to watch," he told me, "I'd bought a Marshall stack, because I thought that was what you had to do. In five minutes, he (Ronson) changed the settings, and started playing through it. Suddenly I was listening to Ziggy Stardust. Awesome."

Given the band's long pre-punk career, most of the songs were ready to go, with only 'Keep On Trying' written in the studio. Before its release Decca pushed out three quick singles from the sessions, and all were arresting in their own ways. 'Where Have All The Bootboys Gone' ensured that they would be deified by the later Oi! generation who were taken with its allusions to unfettered machismo. Of course, it was misconstrued, notably at a Music Machine show when Barrett caught the audience sieg-heiling. "I couldn't take that," he later told Q. "I believe in the Jewish religion, and I came out on stage in my tallis (prayer shroud) and did the Kaddish (prayer for the dead). I said, 'If you want to kill someone, kill me.' They thought, 'You're Nazi, because you did bootboys.' It's just a song about when we used to go beating up Manchester City fans or Liverpool fans when we were kids. There's nothing in it saying,

'We kill all the Jews and hate blacks.' It's pathetic. This is why we never did anything political. Mick and I believed music is there to have a good time." 'Dame To Blame' featured the non-album B-side 'Johnny T', widely perceived to be a Johnny Thunders tribute, whom the band had met in Leeds in 1977. It was actually a pop at Barrett's old headmaster, John Tickett, who'd told him he'd never amount to anything. 'Quick Joey Small' was a cover of the bubblegum classic by the Kasenetz-Katz Singing Orchestra Circus, again featuring Ronson.

The album, which also included a cover of the Velvet Underground's 'Waiting For The Man' and the New York Dolls' 'Who Are The Mystery Girls', was eventually released in May 1978, in a lurid green cover that the band hated, designed by Kevin Cummins. By now tensions were rising and Barrett, in particular, was growing apart from all but Mick Rossi. And then love played a hand and broke up the band. Barrett decided he'd had enough, and ran off to France for eight months with his girlfriend Lola. "I think it became a little bit too commercial," he later told David Nolan. "I mean we were in it for the money as well, but we were in it for having a good time firstly. If we make money out of it then that's the reward of fame. We wanted to do just 'local famous'. When it became kind of national, people came in from the outside and started distorting it. And that's why I buggered off to France." Barrett admitted to being "incredibly hurt" by his decision, but decided to persevere.

In the interim DJM issued a four-track 12-inch of 'pre-punk' studio tracks cut in May 1976 and Rabid released a live album recorded at Belle Vue on 9 July 1977 – though the perfunctory sleeve actually gave the impression it was a bootleg. Thereafter a couple of rehearsals were staged with Billy Duffy (ex-Nosebleeds, later the Cult) on guitar, Bates on bass, Muffet on drums and one Steven Patrick Morrissey on vocals. "Billy was always an advocate of Morrissey pre- and post-Slaughter," Rossi told me. "He actually put Marr and Morrissey together. At the time, he said he knew this singer who loved the New York Dolls and introduced us. I still have four or five songs on tape, in my mother's house, that no-one's heard. He was an incredible lyric writer, but very introverted and very shy. Nothing like he is today." So why didn't it work out? "I just didn't think it gelled. It was hard, because I'm coming from Wayne, a really in-your-face front man, to this very subdued person. It just stopped and we didn't carry through with it." Thereafter Muffet left, though Ray Rossi apparently wasn't amenable to his defection, in a "nobody leaves the family" type stand-off, meaning the poor fellow had to go into hiding for a brief period until the ruckus died down.

Bates, Phil Rowland (ex-Eater) and Rossi briefly reunited with Duffy as the Studio Sweethearts, who released a solitary single, 'I Believe' c/w 'It Isn't Me' for DJM, which attracted caustic reviews. "Shit name," reckons Rossi, "given to us by Ken Pitt." Pitt was a music business legend, a 'gentleman manager' who had previously worked with Frank Sinatra and David Bowie. Having read his name on the sleeves of some of their favourite Bowie albums, Rossi was advised by a friend at EMI that he was still active in the business and gave him a call. "But it was a great experience, as we got to work with (Brinsley Schwarz and Dr Feelgood producer) Vic Maile again, who produced 'You're Ready Now'. It was also good to work with (Billy) Duffy, who's a great guitarist."

Pitt, as well as Rowland, was kept on when Slaughter And The Dogs reformed to release 'You're Ready Now', a terrific version of the Frankie Valli hit written by Bob Gaudio and Bob Crewe, and a kind of Mancunian route marker for the Stone Roses' 'This Is The One'. How did it feel for Slaughter to be managed by the man who once looked after such industry heavyweights? "It was chalk and cheese compared to Ray (Rossi). Ray, to get us our first demo money, told us to nick sewer grids and then sold them to scrap metal companies. He was very free enterprise, and whatever it took to get to the next stage, he'd do it. With Ken, he was very old school. We'd sit in his office, and he'd say – 'David (Bowie) used to live on £25 a week...' We'd say, 'Yeah. That was in 1969, Ken.' But a very nice man, and smart too."

But then Barrett left for France once more, to marry Lola, bring up his child and work as a greengrocer in the family business. He was replaced by Eddie 'Ed Banger' Garrity (ex-Nosebleeds), who had to be roped in to complete the vocals on 'East Side Of Town' and Bite Back, produced by Dale Griffin of Mott The Hoople. Griffin was another band hero. "I just rang him up," Rossi told me. "I said, if you want to do this, it would be great, but if you don't, that's fine." Griffin was only too happy to help out. So too, Garrity, as he confirmed in I Swear I Was There. "I got a phone call and joined them within two days, because I already knew the songs from way back. Just a matter of stepping in at two days' notice and straight into the tour. We did the album and a couple of singles, but we split up again."

By now the group had truncated its name to Slaughter, but that, and a relatively disappointing album, were not about to change their fortunes. The band duly collapsed in 1981. Rossi would later collaborate with Gary Holton, One The Juggler, the Duelists and Boy George's brother. Barrett issued a single credited to Wayne Barrett And The Lovers, and later got a call from Ritchie Blackmore's management and played a stadium tour to support him as Scum. Garrity has a cabaret act on the Isle Of Wight, the last he was heard from. Rowland went to LA with the London Cowboys among other projects.

Throughout these activities, Rossi and Barrett remained in touch. In 1991 they cut a new album for Receiver, with some pretty awful sub-heavy metal artwork that might have convinced many that this was the hard rock band Slaughter rather than the punk originals, and it hardly showed up on the radar. "God's honest truth," Rossi told me, "there's probably, for me, four or five good songs on it. The rest isn't good. We rushed into it and didn't think about it." Afterwards he produced Martin Degville's solo album, and, as part of the Swingers with Glen Matlock, covered the Ronettes' 'Be My Baby' for Magnet. He also played live with Pete Wylie and Talk Talk, and worked on Michael Aston (of Gene Loves Jezebel)'s solo album. Occasionally he could also be found hammering out 'Suffragette City' as part of pick-up band the Usual Suspects, alongside Steve Jones of the Sex Pistols ("the only person who can play a power chord in that magical way").

When the subject of the 1996 Holidays In The Sun punk festival in Blackpool came up, both Barrett and Rossi were keen to give it a go. Though the other original members were interested, Barrett was keen to use the drummer he'd been working with, Noel Kay, and Rossi brought aboard bass player Nigel Mead, with whom he'd played in the Duelists. The event was a rousing success, and eventually resulted in the permanent recruitment of bass player JP Thollett. Further dates followed in Europe and Japan, and, eventually, a new studio album arrived, after Mark Brennan stumped up the readies. Beware Of... can be filed among a limited number of post-reformation punk albums, like the Damned's Grave Disorder and Buzzcocks' Trade Test Transmissions, that was genuinely worthwhile rather than a mere pension top-up.

However, it was not an easy album to co-ordinate. Barrett was still living in Lyon, while Rossi had decamped to Los Angeles. So they rented a house in Manchester to soak up the local vibe again. As Rossi elaborated to Holly Day: "There's this very repressed, pent-up energy that just builds and builds when you're there (Manchester). And when you finally let go, you know, all this anger just comes rushing out. But it's a good anger. I don't think it's a negative thing. It's the only place we really are Slaughter And The Dogs."

Slaughter And The Dogs are still going strong. They packed out shows on the east coast of America in 2002, and undertook a similar jaunt in 2003. Rossi tells me the gigs now are more fun than they have ever been. "We enjoy it more. There's no agenda, and it's kind of a cult thing in a way. But it's definitely more fun now."

DISCOGRAPHY:

Cracked Up Really High/The Bitch 7-inch (Rabid TOSH-101 May 1977) (four different label designs)

Where Have All the Boot Boys Gone/You're A Bore 7-inch (Decca F-13723 September 1977 (initial pressings didn't have a sleeve, but this was rectified with the March 1981 reissue. Also released on 12-inch in a limited pressing of 10,000 copies, LF-13723, which states 'disco version' on the labels, but the songs are identical versions to the 7-inch)

Dame to Blame/Johnny T 7-inch (Decca F-13743 November 1977)

Quick Joey Small/Come on Back 7-inch (Decca F-13758 February 1978)

Do It Dog Style LP (Decca SKL-5292 May 1978) (reissued in 1989 on Damaged Goods FNARR2, and on CD by Captain Oi! AHOY CD 131, in 2000, with bonus tracks 'Johnny T' and 'Come On Back')

Live Slaughter Rabid Dogs LP (Rabid HAT 23 December 1978) (recorded live at Manchester Belle Vue 9/7/77. Released in plain white sleeve. Reissued in March 1989 on Receiver, RRLP 109, as Rabid Dogs)

Build Up Not Down 12-inch aka The Slaughter & The Dogs EP (DJM TJM3May 1979)

It's Alright/Edgar Allen Poe/Twist & Turn/UFO (the band's earliest known recordings from May 1976 – i.e pre-punked. "We did it for TJ Davidson," Rossi told me, "who ran our

rehearsal space. There was us there, the Buzzcocks, Frantic Elevators (including Mick Hucknall) in another room. A bunch of bands. He approached us to ask if we could be the first release on his new label." The tracks were actually recorded in May 1976)

You're Ready Now/Runaway 7-inch (DJM DJS-10927 November 1979)

As Slaughter:

East Side of Town/One by One 7-inch (DJM DJS-10936 February 1980)

Bite Back LP (DJM DJF-20566 1980) (reissued on CD by Captain Oi! AHOY CD 142 1998, with bonus tracks 'I'm The One', 'One By One' and 'What's Wrong Boy (live)')

I'm the One/What's Wrong Boy (live)/Hell in New York 7-inch (DJM DJS-10945 June 1980)

As Slaughter And The Dogs:

Shocking CD (Receiver RR CD/LP 151 May 1999)

Beware Of... CD (Captain Oi! AHOY CD 175 2001) (first 1,000 copies came with a free Live In Japan CD)

ARCHIVE RELEASES:

Half-Alive 12-inch EP (Thrush Thrush 1 February 1983)

Twist And Turn/Cranked Up Really High (live)/Where Have All The Boot Boys Gone (live)

Live At The Factory LP (Thrush THRUSH-1 June 1983) (Recorded December 1979. Reissued May 1989 on Receiver; RRLP-114. Features a show with Barrett on vocals, as well as four tracks from LP that would become Bite Back, though poor sound quality mars both these songs and the first album material).

Where Have All The Boot Boys Gone/You're A Bore/Johnny T 7-inch (Damaged Goods August 1988) (available in red and green vinyl, 500 of each. Damaged Goods only put it out as a one-off, but its success led to the record label continuing and prospering to this day)

The Slaughterhouse Tapes LP (Link LP 092 June 1989) (out-takes, demos, live, interview. First hearing for studio versions of 'Twist And Turn' and the Velvet Underground's 'White Light White Heat', plus the 'Half-Alive' tracks. Reissued on CD in 2002, Step 1, along with 999's The Cellblock Tapes)

Where Have All The Boot Boys Gone CD (Receiver RRCD 183 March 1994) (this is basically a two-for-one package featuring the live albums Rabid Dogs and Live At The Factory)

Cranked Up Really High CD (Captain Oi! AHOY CD 50 1995) (reprises some of the previously issued Link material, as well as their early Rabid workouts, as well as both tracks from Live At The Roxy. Also released on vinyl)

Barking Up The Right Tree CD (Amsterdamned AMD 102 May 1998) (Recorded live in London in 1996 with Noel Kay on drums – the title may have related to a previous comment by Hannett, that the glam model SATD were "barking up the wrong tree")

Punk Singles Collection CD (Captain Oi! AHOY CD 154 2000)

(the complete singles, including both Studio Sweethearts songs, plus four bonus acoustic tracks recorded by Barrett and Rossi in July 2000 just before their headline appearance at the Morecambe Holidays In The Sun Festival. Includes a detailed breakdown of the band's history on 45)

We Don't Care: Anthology 2-CD (Sanctuary/Castle March 2002)

A Dog Day's Afternoon: Live In The USA CD (TKO 113 2003) (titled after the 28-date US tour of 2003 it was released to promote, the material comes via the preceding year's dates in New York and San Francisco. Excellent sound quality and pretty strong all-round performances. Also released on vinyl in 2004)

Slight Seconds

Kevin Eden (vocals, guitar), Peter Hibbert (drums, vocals), Mike Shaw (bass)

SLIGHT SECONDS evolved out of the Elite, who'd been formed in Stockport in 1977 by school friends Mick Coates, (vocals), Kevin Eden (guitar, vocals) and Peter Hibbert (drums, vocals). Taking their inspiration from near-neighbours the Buzzcocks' 'Spiral Scratch' EP, they were lured into punk from an existing preference for glam, prog and the singer-songwriter school. Eden and Hibbert wrote most of the material, which was recorded in the latter's parents' kitchen on a basic cassette recorder, with plastic container and knitting needles serving as a drum kit. A series of cassette recordings were circulated among friends. Eden "worries" that he might still have them somewhere.

The Elite joined the Manchester Musicians Collective in 1978 and performed at their King Street basement using borrowed equipment – including the first drum kit Hibbert had ever used. Augmented by bass player Mick Church – an unrepentant Deep Purple fan and another school colleague – they began to pick up gigs in the Manchester area. But by 1978 tensions between Church and Coates led to the latter walking out during a rehearsal. Eden took over lead vocals as they continued as a three-piece, but soon Church too had moved on, although he did agree to play at their final show at the Band On The Wall.

After recruiting a replacement bass player, yet another school friend, Mike Shaw, the central duo decided a name change would be appropriate and became Slight Seconds. Eden: "Around this time the Spherical Object leader and Object Music label founder, Steve Solomar, had contacted the Manchester Music Collective about recording a compilation of some of the groups in the collective. Slight Seconds were chosen to record two tracks."

Recordings took place at Revolution Studio in Cheadle Hulme. Eden: "We were not happy with the way our two tracks were mixed and disowned them immediately." Object Music subsequently offered the band a chance to record one side of a three-group project entitled Waiting Room. So Slight Seconds convened in Cargo Studios in Rochdale in June 1979 and over two days cut their side of the record. Eden co-wrote 'Building Bridges' with former Magazine keyboard player Bob Dickinson and attempted to get him to join the band, but he'd already committed to continue his studies at Keele University.

The album was well reviewed and Slight Seconds continued to play around the north west and Lancashire, supporting the Passage and Joy Division among others, as well as further Manchester Music Collective-organised shows at the Band On The Wall. However, enthusiasm dipped towards the end of 1980 and plans to record a self-financed mini-album were aborted.

The group was falling apart, but before Eden had the chance to announce his departure, Hibbert took his own life. Eden continued to record in the 'open-ended' musical project 41 Degrees, who also cut a track for Object Music ('Just My Crazy Mind' on Do The Maru) as well as their own full-length album, Open Heart, on the 41 label. Eden published his biography of Wire, Everybody Loves A History, through SAF in 1991. He has also written about Brian Eno's video installations and Laraaji and is currently co-writing a biography of Eno with Sid Smith.

COMPILATIONS:

The Waiting Room LP (Object Music OBJ 007 1980; 'And...', 'Puppet On A String', 'Building Bridges', 'Where Were You?', 'Slight Seconds', 'Lost Love', 'Fallen (Again?)', 'Chameleon Lens', 'Further Down The Line')

A Manchester Collection LP (Object OBJ 003 1979; 'Double Face', 'New Me')

Messthetics #2 CD (Hyped2Death; 'Where Were You')

Slits

Ari Up (aka Arianna Foster; vocals), Suzy Gutsy (bass), Kate Korus (guitar; later replaced by Viv Albertine), Palmolive (aka Paloma McCardy; drums)

S

The SLITS were, according to whichever account you choose to accept, an embarrassing, utterly non-musical abomination, or visionary feminists who did more than anyone to build something substantive out of punk's confusing and contradictory rhetoric. The cliché would be to state that the truth lies somewhere between the two poles, but I'm inclined to favour the latter theory over the former, for reasons I'll attempt to explain without boring myself, and everyone else, senseless. And without mentioning Derrida or Focault, which would be a novelty.

Or even, as academic Rob Horning cites in his piece on the band, semiology. Take it away Robster. "Ari Up's singing illustrates Kristevan semiosis: yelping pre-lingual nonsense noises from outside the oppressive paradigms of comprehensible language (aka the Symbolic). The guitar playing is unconventional: "angular" or "jagged" in rock critic terminology. The songs evince an untutored "purity" that's supposed to ensure that this is tapping into some sort of pre-rational spontaneity. The idea is that training means automatically training into a phallologicentric musical heritage/hegemony." He's a right one to talk about the 'oppressive paradigms of comprehensible language', isn't he?

For a start, let's shred those objections to the gals' musicianship. Since when was that important to a punk band? It seems odd that the much-cited mantra about musical proficiency being a barrier to creativity is applied so selectively. As Judy Nylon is fond of saying, she'd rather hear a good idea played badly than a bad idea played well, and that cuts to the essence of the Slits. There are several male musicians of the genre I've corresponded with during the course of this book who almost spit at the mention of the Slits. But that just makes them that little bit more punk rock to me (ie the Slits, not the foaming, resentful male punk rockers). There were a number of great musicians in the early punk movement, but ideas and attitude were the driving force. And just occasionally the Slits managed spectacular results, and put out records, in the process, that endure, particularly Cut. Or, as the cuddly News Of The World would have it in their January 1977 'Here come the Punkesses' feature on the Slits (and the Castrators), "Fasten your seatbelts! The all-girl rock shockers who make those Sex Pistols look like choir boys are ready to land."

The band's origins go back to 1976 when Viv Albertine, who was Mick Jones's boyfriend, was studying at Hornsey Art College. Together with Spanish drummer Palmolive, named thus by Paul Simonon because he couldn't get his tongue round the pronunciation, they'd rehearsed with Sid Vicious and Keith Levene as part of embryonic children of the Pistols, the Flowers Of Romance. Paloma and her sister, Esperanza, who would marry the 101ers drummer Richard Dudanski, ended up at the band's squat at 101 Walterton Road where she eventually became Joe Strummer's girlfriend. Sid, the world-renowned virtuoso musician, sacked them for 'lack of talent' (or alternatively because they refused to sleep with him), though Viv would continue to work with Vicious for a short time.

They added guitarist Kate Korus and bass player Suzy Gutsy to the line-up, as well as precocious, some would say bratty, 14-year-old singer Arianna Foster. Ari Up, as she became known, was the daughter of Nora Forster, descended from a marriage between a wealthy German publisher and a gypsy dancer. Nora, who promoted Jimi Hendrix shows in Germany in the 60s, would handle the band's early management, and later marry John Lydon in 1979. But it was Arianna's conversion to the Sex Pistols' cult that led to Nora becoming an intimate of that circle, after they'd initially met when the Sex Pistols recorded demos with her then partner Chris Spedding. Arianna was such a fan of the band that she jumped on stage at an early gig and kissed Lydon, and would take Nora's television for Sid to watch when he was hospitalised with hepatitis. "My first exposure (to punk)," Ari later told Big Takeover, "was with everyone hanging around my house. Joe Strummer taught me how to play guitar. Paul Simonon used to come around. Steve Jones, Vic Godard, Paul Cook, John Lydon after a while – everybody just came around Nora's house. She threw parties or whatever – not official parties, but punk parties. Everyone just showed up for no reason, all hours of the day."

As to the beginning of the Slits 'proper': "I met Ari at a (Patti Smith) gig and asked her if she wanted to play with me," Palmolive later recalled to Mike Appelstein, "and then together we decided we're gonna be a band. She was gonna sing, and I was gonna play the drums. I knew I wanted to play the drums. So then we looked for a guitarist and a bass, and we were just gonna do it, you know?" Ari: "Palmolive was really out there. Totally crazed. The epitome of what you would consider punk. She would have scared the shit out of anyone. But not me. Cause I'm really scary myself!"

The initial line-up lasted for just a few shambolic rehearsals, jamming around with a version of 'Blitzkrieg Bop', before Gutsy was kicked out for being "out of it all the time" and left to form a new band, the Flicks, who never progressed beyond practice sessions. The Slits, the name suggested by Kate Korus and accepted because it sounded 'provocative', recruited Tessa Pollitt, formerly of the Castrators, on bass. She had two weeks to practice her new instrument before her live debut on 11 March 1977 at Harlesden, supporting the Clash. "I was terrified," Pollitt recalled to the 3am website, "but you know I was just 17, and at that age you have so much energy and excitement in you, it carries you." "It was very natural for me to be on stage," Ari later recalled of that first show to Big Takeover. "It was something I was born to do. It was like an explosion for me. Made that stage my living room. We were musically so fucked up and untogether. And we were just so amazing in our time-bombing up there, we just went up there totally fucking up every single note, ever single beat! And we were just great. We were brilliant at it."

Sniffin' Glue reviewed them thus: "Their set was mad, noisy, chaotic, brilliant... They were inspired but totally unrehearsed..." Or, as Palmolive recalled, "I didn't know how to fix the drums and the drums were moving. I would try to grab the drums and bring them back, and Ari was just screaming...you couldn't hear nothing. I mean, it's very different to practice in the studio and then get there. And we hadn't done much anyway. So we started a fight on the stage. She started telling me I was off beat and I started throwing the sticks at her. People thought it was a show and we were for real. We wouldn't care, you know, and that was part of the attraction."

Kate Korus stuck it out for a total of three shows before being asked to leave because "her image wasn't right". She later formed the Modettes as Viv Albertine took up the guitar. One of the three shows was as support to the Sex Pistols at their Screen On The Green showcase on 4 April 1977, at which Ari was the victim of an attempted knifing by an anonymous punter who shouted "So you're the Slits? Well, here's a slit for you!" Luckily her clothing largely protected her buttocks, but the incident was symptomatic of some of the hostility aimed at the band. Ari, the walking mouthpiece who was often at the eye of the storm, was also wont to show her bosoms to passing journalists.

Keith Levene, who later did their sound for them, and also incidentally claims to be the one who gave Palmolive her name, was fundamental to the Slits' project. "I used to live in a squat with Vivienne (Albertine, who subsequently replaced Korus) and a friend named Q," he told Perfect Sound Forever. "All these magical moments. I really liked her. But we weren't having a scene or anything. I really fucking liked her and she really liked me. She'd come to me for this and come to me for that. She's talking about how fucking interesting Johnny is and 'I wonder what it would be like to meet him.' And 'oh, by the way Keith, could you teach me how to play guitar.' And the next thing is that she's got a Les Paul Jnr and she can't play. A real punk rocker. So I taught her how to play."

The most enduring line-up of the group in place, they went on the road as support to the Clash for the White Riot tour, beginning in April 1977, alongside the Buzzcocks and Subway Sect. The tour was filmed by Roxy DJ Don Letts for The Punk Rock Movie, and Letts would informally take over the band's management before deciding that actually they were completely unmanageable, while Ari's mum Nora was always helping out too. The tour went well, with a shared sense of adventure that contrasted with the backbiting of the Pistols' Anarchy tour, though the bus driver might not agree – the mere sight of Ari's visage enough to drive him to the edge of a nervous breakdown. Ari also persuaded her school, Holland Park Comprehensive, to host a Slits performance that summer. And invited along the Moors Murderers to play back up. Later the Slits also appeared, in typically mischievous form, in Derek Jarman's Jubilee film, as a kind of post-apocalypse girl gang. It wasn't that far from the truth. Flyers from July 1977 would advertise the band as "The All-Girl Controversial/Infamous/Rude/Exciting/Stimulating New Wave Band," so they were aware of the power of their own image. And they were beginning to amass a repertoire of songs, with all the band members contributing. Palmolive was the most prolific writer at this stage, contributing 'Shoplifting', 'FM', 'Number One Enemy', 'New Town ' and 'Adventures Close To Home', while Albertine's compositions included 'Typical Girls' and 'Love & Romance'. Ari wrote 'Slime' and Pollitt 'Vaseline'.

The Slits recorded their first session for John Peel in September 1977, comprising 'Love And Romance, 'Vindictive' (aka 'Let's Do The Split'), 'New Town' and 'Shoplifting'. "That was the first time we'd ever been in a studio," Albertine later recalled for Ken Garner's In Session Tonight. "Lots of people thought the result better than the album. It was absolutely raw, more raw than any boys' band. I almost can't believe we had that much energy. Ari was 14, I think, and the rest of us were all under 20." The studio engineer Nick Gomm was taken aback too. "It was everyone hitting anything as loudly as possible; vaguely in time, there was a sort of rhythm there, and this maniac shrieking on top. On stage, at that time, it probably sounded quite good, when it was loud, but, when it came out over little speakers, fairly quietly, it just sounded painful. The tuning of the guitars was all over the place. We couldn't stand listening to these guitars, they were so badly out of tune. So myself and the other engineer, both guitarists to a certain degree, had to go out and tune them ourselves. Every now and then we'd have to go back in and re-tune them, because they didn't have a clue how to. I wonder if we did the right thing." Presumably yes, as Peel rated this as the finest session ever released on Strange Fruit, and placed both Slits performances in his top ten sessions of all time.

Meanwhile, with no record contract looming (they were widely perceived to be 'trouble') a bootleg circulated of a show from Dingwalls. However, they drifted away from Letts as Malcolm McLaren began to express an interest in them, taking over their management for a

short time. He wanted to sign them to Hansa as a 'disco' act and get them to take part in a leery film about a girl band being chased from Paris to Mexico. Though dubious about the merits of this project, the Slits did record sessions in January 1978 on a mobile recording unit during a five-night residency at Paris's Gibus Club. As part of the set they deconstructed 'Femme Fatale' in honour of Nico, who was attending, but she failed to recognise the resultant mutation. The master tapes of these shows were given to Dave Goodman as payment for money owed by McLaren, and remained at his house in Gypsy Hill before being unearthed in the early 21st century.

In the summer of 1978 they supported the Rich Kids on tour. However, in October Palmolive was axed from the band, ostensibly because McLaren wanted a more professional player. "They kicked me out. In a way, I provoked it in the sense that, as I say, I started losing interest. But there were issues that, as a group, you have to deal with – OK, let's do a record. What are we gonna put on the cover? I didn't want to do that cover (she is referring to the infamous 'topless' sleeve for Cut) I mean, I wasn't a saint or anything, I just didn't want to do it. They wanted to go with Malcolm, I didn't want to go with Malcolm McLaren. I had talked to the guy, and I could see that I just didn't agree. We talked to him, he said, 'I want to work with you because you're girls and you play music. I hate music and I hate girls. I thrive on hate. I wanna work with you.' I said, 'No thank you.'" Palmolive elaborated on this in an email to me in 2006. "After playing with the Raincoats (whom she subsequently joined after 'temping' with Spizz Oil), I realised that I had more of a problem with the values behind the punk music scene than the people themselves. As far as I was concerned, I had no answer for my life, but the people around me were as clueless as I was."

In came Budgie, formerly of Liverpool bands the Spitfire Boys and Big In Japan, who joined in time for support duties on the Clash's Sort It Out tour of November 1978. By April 1979 they had finally secured a recording contract, with Island, though some wondered why they'd never bothered to link with some of the independent institutions which were now offering a viable alternative, notably Rough Trade. Certainly Palmolive had preferred the independent route, but was outvoted and eventually ejected. In 1979 Albertine told ZigZag that Island "were interested at the start (1977) but we didn't think we were ready." Sessions on their debut album began in spring 1979 at Ridge Farm Studios. The group's debut single, 'Typical Girls', announced their smart-ass approach to female empowerment. "Don't create, don't rebel... worry about unnatural smells." It was backed by a searing version of Marvin Gaye's 'I Heard It Through The Grapevine', one of Ari's most arresting vocal performances. The single reached number 60 in the charts, their only 'hit'.

Debut album Cut also appeared in September 1979, the band's sound honed by reggae producer Dennis Bovell. "I was asked to do some production for the Slits, it was like three girls trying to thrash out some of the punk era. And I listened to some of their material and thought, 'Yeah, I'll have a go at this'." It's a fantastic effort, Bovell adding a gloss to the group's urchin wares that benefits the songs enormously, accenting Pollitt's bass lines, which were distinctively married to the melody lines in keeping with the reggae dynamic. While some considered this to be a dilution of the Slits' original aesthetic, the loping dub rhythms carry the tunes to new planes. The result is a messy amalgam of space, rhythm and melody that gels better than it has any right to, and is arguably, though it doesn't sound punk, one of the most influential records in the entire genre. For others, however, like Mick Mercer, some of the magical chaos had been lost. "The Slits were fantastic live for a couple of years. It was raw, it was inspired, and on some nights was bloody awful, but when they got it right, they were doing something no-one else was, because they had their own undulating rhythm from which true dementia could pour at certain moments. When they started to get serious they lost that spark of originality and had to include others who were better musicians, which robbed them of that special intensity. I saw them about ten times and at least half of the gigs were as good as any of the other bands, as a real experience. Short though! They could be gone in 15 minutes."

The sleeve, featuring the three female members bare-breasted and covered in earth, like Amazonian warriors, or maybe mud wrestlers, was considered by some to be an uncomfortable concession to marketing and a demonstration of a confused ideology. "Nuder than the average Oui model," wrote academic Carola Dibbell, "the image stakes out the female body as female territory... solid, varied, flawed, defiant, and irreverent." Not everyone agreed, notably Palmolive, though upfront sexuality was always a large part of the Slits' antics, Ari Up routinely wearing white underwear outside of her stage clothes. However, their relationship with feminism was more complex. "We're just not interested in questions about Women's Liberation," they told Caroline Coon earlier in their career. "You either think chauvinism is shit or you don't. We think it's shit."

Most interviews with the band saw them distance themselves from the (popular 70s terminology alert) women's libbers. As Palmolive stated to Lucy Toothpaste in the Jolt fanzine in 1977, they was a pragmatism and sense of humour to the Slits that was more important to them than ideology. "We are feminists in a way. We don't want to tell anyone how to act, we just want to show them what we're doing, what girls can do." Ari, who was both the most verbose though not necessarily articulate member of the group, occasionally hit the nail on the head. "Most girls don't push themselves enough. The world is changing, It'll leave us all behind if we don't change with it. One way to change things is for us to get on the stage."

Going back to the Cut album cover, there was a very funny story concerning a driver threatening to take the group to court after crashing his car while being distracted by a large Cut promotional poster. And this in the days before Claims-R-Us and the ambulance chasing industry. Ari has gone on record to say that the whole idea was hers, as a reflection of the band's "natural, jungly, artistic nakedness" rather than resulting from an outside source, though she does admit that Island head Chris Blackwell was "thrilled" when he saw it.

After the album's release Budgie replaced Kenny Morris in Siouxsie And The Banshees, and the Pop Group's Bruce Smith filled in. "I always loved what they (the Slits) were doing," Budgie later told Q, " but felt I'd done all I could with them." They played a short tour to promote the album, on which jazz trumpeter Don Cherry was drafted in alongside a keyboard player, Penny. Support came from the On-U-Sound posse (Adrian Sherwood, Creation Rebel, Prince Hammer), deepening the band's links with reggae which would eventually see Ari record with On-U-Sound as the New Age Steppers (appearing on New Age Steppers in 1980 and Action Battlefield in 1981), and later move to Jamaica.

Dropped by Island, 'In The Beginning There Was Rhythm' saw the musical approach shift to funk, no doubt partially inspired by their increasingly close links to Bristol's specialists in subsonic rebel noise, the Pop Group. Indeed, they formed the Rough Trade distributed Y label with the latter, whose 'Where There's A Will There's A Way' filled the B-side. The single retailed at 70p Another budget release, officially untitled but widely known as Retrospective – Official Bootleg, appeared in a plain white sleeve with the song titles scrawled on the label. I remember picking this up and believing it really was a bootleg. It might as well have been, the half-formed demo tracks and live takes were barely listenable. Their next single was a cover of John Holt's 'Man Next Door', followed by 'Animal Space', on which Flying Lizards' keyboard player Steve Beresford guested.

They returned to a major label by signing with CBS in June 1981, which resulted in their swan song, Return Of The Giant Slits. "Rough Trade are slimy," blurted Ari to Kris Needs of ZigZag. "These people (CBS) are in the business and they know their thing and we can work with them. With Rough Trade, it's like they're on a throne." They'd shifted musical shapes again, this time using rhythms inspired by the African continent, Albertine being a big fan of Nigerian Afrobeat founder Fela Kuti. Dennis Bovell was again aboard as producer, and fitted well with the band's erratic nature ("He works a lot off instinct," confirmed Albertine, "and his moods"). One single emerged, the album's mission statement 'Earthbeat', but it attracted little attention, the media's fascination with the Slits having long since expired.

The announcement of their split came in December 1981, Viv Albertine electing to spend more time in the fields of dance and film, becoming an independent film producer, currently with the BBC. Bruce Smith joined Rip, Rig And Panic while Albertine revisited the Slits' legacy by producing a 1990 Channel 4 documentary on female musicians. After a debilitating dalliance with heroin, Pollitt had a daughter with Rip, Rig And Panic bass player Sean Oliver, exhibited her art in Bristol, and backed Brion Gysin at Genesis P. Orridge's Final Academy concerts. She now has a black belt in martial arts. Ari Up spent time in Jamaica, working on production with reggae titans Sugar Minott and the Roots Radics while running her own labels, and recording dancehall material under the name Medusa. Now based in New York, she is again performing solo and revisiting that old Slits' songbook, and released a new solo album, Dread More Than Dead, in 2005.

As of 1997, Palmolive was playing drums alongside her husband in a Christian rock band in Massachusetts, Hi-Fi, who cover the Slits' 'F.M.' as well as other Slits and Raincoats selections. She remained unconvinced of the Slits legacy being a positive one when I spoke to her in 2006. "I have this vivid memory, like it was today. We had been playing in a church. It was a church building but it wasn't a church any more. I was on my way out – something inside me was saying something is really wrong here. I was trying to figure out where I was going. But I was very observant of everything. I had earplugs because it was really loud! But for some reason, I was detached, and I was able to observe myself. It was a period of three or four weeks and I remembered people coming out of there. Honest to God, everybody was so wasted, they were so bummed out. I remembered thinking – I am helping to do that to them. It wasn't morbid or a guilty feeling, it was just the reality. I am part of this. Not only a part, I am carrying the banner for it."

I tired to persuade her that this was an unnecessarily negative view of the band's impact. She did acknowledge the special alchemy behind the band, but she continues to have grave concerns about the trajectory of the music industry. "There was something in the abandoment we had. The "throwing ourselves into it, no matter what." That was a unique quality. We were young women and we had that. And it just happened, like a flash. I really thought I was doing the best I could. I thought I was helping society, we were being honest by being uninhibited. And I have to say, if I had stayed in Spain, and gone along with what everyone was doing, my older brother and sisters, you know, I might never have discovered things that I totally value today. I totally give you that. But it doesn't mean that I cannot look back, and when I talk to younger people, or people that are interested, I think there is some positive and negative stuff. But I do think in the music business as a whole – listen to what they're saying. And when your kid is 15, and they're listening to a song – and I remember how I was when I liked someone! I would lock myself in my room and listen to them for hours – they're listening, and you're looking at the words. And the words are saying, life stinks, shoot yourself, shoot someone. Look at the lyrics of so many groups."

DISCOGRAPHY:

Typical Girls/I Heard It Through The Grapevine 7-inch (Island WIP 6505 September 1979) (also released as a 12-inch single, Island 12WIP 6505, with bonus track 'Liebe And

S

Romanze' plus the 'Brink Style' version of 'Typical Girls')

Cut LP (Island ILPS 9573 September 1979) (limited quantities were signed by the band in mauve marker pen. Reissued on CD by Island, IMCD 89, in 1990 – but gremlins got into the remastering process. The October 2000 reissue, IMCD 275, added two bonus tracks, 'I Heard It Through The Grapevine' and 'Liebe Romanze (Slow version)', with detailed sleevenotes by Mark Paytress)

In The Beginning There Was Rhythm 7-inch (Rough Trade/Y RT 039/Y-1 March 1980) (B-side by the Pop Group, 'Where There's A Will There's A Way'. Demo copies featured both songs on separate one-sided singles, plus a promo version came with promotional photos)

Untitled aka Bootleg – Retrospective LP (Rough Trade YY-3 May 1980)

Man Next Door/Man Next Door (dub) 7-inch (Rough Trade/Y RT 044/Y-4 June 1980)

Animal Space/Animal Spacier 7-inch (Human HUM 4 November 1980)

Earthbeat/Begin Again Rhythm 7-inch (CBS A 1498 August 1981) (also released as a 12-inch single, CBS A 131498, with bonus track 'Earthdub')

Return Of The Giant Slits LP (CBS 85269 October 1981) (came with free 7-inch single, XPS 125, comprising a US radio interview, 'American Radio Interviewer', and a dub version of 'Face Place'. Seemingly, this has only been reissued on CD in Japan, and not in either Britain or America)

ARCHIVE RECORDINGS:

The Peel Session 19.9.77 12-inch EP (Strange Fruit SFPS 021 January 1987)

Vindictive/Love And Romance/Newtown/Shoplifting

The Peel Sessions mini-LP (Strange Fruit SFPMA 207 November 1988) (also issued as a CD, SFPMACD 207, and again as SFRSCD 052, in 1998, with additional tracks 'Difficult Fun', 'In The Beginning', 'Earthbeat/Wedding Song', these tracks again featuring Neneh Cherry on backing vocals)

In The Beginning (A Live Anthology) CD (Jungle FREUDCD 057 October 1997) (features a show from London Dingwalls in September 1977 as well as a version of 'In The Beginning' featuring Don Cherry's daughter, Neneh Cherry. Released in the US on Cleopatra)

Live: At The Gibus Club CD (Castle February 2005 CMQCD 1058) (also available on vinyl, Earmark September 2005. Recorded 26 January 1978. Sleevenotes by Don Letts. Musically 'interesting', you might say, but definitely spirited)

Smeggy And The Cheesybits

Smeggy (aka Gary Cayton; vocals), Neville (bass), Dave Cheesybits (guitar)

SMEGGY AND THE CHEESYBITS were the anarchic underbelly of the Brighton punk scene, never taking themselves seriously, but packing them in at chaotic Alhambra shows. Song titles such as 'Pratt', 'Glue', 'The Noisy Song' and 'You Hate Us, Don't You', and lyrics such as "I wanna be your hunchback, baby", somewhat informed by their leader's lack of posture, delineated their charm. It was no surprise that they ended up supporting the Damned, as they were, to a man, in thrall to Captain Sensible's life view, while their internal dynamic was not that far removed from his old friends Johnny Moped. Smeggy who, like Sensible, had a penchant for undressing on stage, could trace his musical heritage back to Bexhill Downs' school band Hospital Treatment.

S

Thence the Cheesybits. The trio listed above had come together after their second show as Dave, who'd been in the audience, recounts: "A strange sneering hunchback wearing a beret came onto the stage with a bass player and started throwing insults at the audience. I watched in amazement as everybody in the room moved to the front of the stage, and then realised that I was doing the same thing. What mystical power had this tuneless mutant exerted over me? Was he some kind of wizard or necromancer? No, it was Smeggy and Neville doing their second gig. It was spellbindingly awful. I seem to remember that they only had one song, which they did three times. It got worse and worse with each rendition. It was the most astounding thing I had ever seen. I suddenly realised what punk had to offer (what you could get away with anyway). As soon as they had finished I went and offered my services as a guitarist."

Several of their early shows came as support to Fan Club. "We followed them to some truly bizarre gigs including Ronnie Scott's in London, where we met Tom Baker in a pub and tried to get him to come to our gig. The gig lasted for about two songs, as I recall, before the big black dudes that ran the place came and muscled us off stage. This was not unusual at all. We billed ourselves as the worst band in Brighton at the time and got most of our gigs by turning up on the night and blagging our way onto stage. Of course, when Dick Damage and the Survivors came along, we couldn't compete for the title of worst band any more. We were simply outclassed. I can't remember how this line-up broke up it was clear we were going nowhere but there was a definite break for a few months."

But an awesome musical chemistry twitched and then sparked into life once more. "Line-up two started with Smeggy turning up on my doorstep one day with a new bass player, another Dave, in tow, and announcing that we were going to support the Damned that night, which we did. We just turned up with our guitars and were waved through the door. I remember that as being a good gig. We ended up mostly supporting the Molesters in this line-up. We may have had a drummer occasionally. I think we got Mark Oggins from Fan Club to drum for us when we recorded 'Baby Don't Boogie with Me' but I don't know if he ever did any gigs with us. I do remember hiring a van and driving all the way to Deal in Kent to do a gig only to find that it was cancelled when we got there, and also doing a gig in Gosport which I seem to remember went quite well. I can't remember what happened to this line-up. I know Dave (he was known as Wanky Dave to distinguish him from all the other Daves in Brighton) disappeared for a while and was rumoured to have something to do with the Piranhas getting all their gear nicked from the Vault. But I don't remember if anything came of this."

Line-up three, our original Dave believes, was "the longest-running and best." It consisted of Smeggy, Dave, Bernie Richards (drums), Chris Anderson (saxophone) and Bruv (bass). "Bruv was the brother of Helen McCookerybook from the Chefs, Bernie had recently escaped from touring with The Elvis Show and Chris was moonlighting in Midnight and the Lemon Boys. I don't remember how long we played together but we had some major experiences (a lot of them pretty miserable but all exciting)."

After the demise of the Cheesybits, Smeggy went on to replace Jef Harvey in King Kurt, while other former Cheesybits and Hospital Treatment members put together the Clockwork Criminals, who put out a single in 1982 and appeared on Crass's Bullshit Detector compilation. There's a couple of tracks, 'Baby Don't Boogie With Me' and 'Steven Was A Mod', originally recorded at Wings studio in Bexhill for a projected EP or one of the Vaultage compilations, no-one can remember, that remain unreleased. They can be downloaded Dave's somewhat disorientating but ultimately alluring Cheesybits website at www.cheesybits.com.

Snivelling Shits

Giovanni Dadomo (vocals), Pete Makowski (guitar), Dave Fudger (bass), Steve Nicol (drums)

The Snivelling Shits were that most despised of institutions, a band formed by journalists, in this case punk-era Sounds scribes Giovanni Dadomo and Dave Fudger, using Eddie And The Hot Rods drummer Steve Nicol. They'd originally used the name Arthur Comics? for their one-off appearance on the Streets compilation, offering 'Isgodaman?' ("Does he get up in the morning and go for a piss?/Does he shave and strap a digital watch on his wrist?"). Beggars had insisted they operate under a different guise because they were frightened of using the word 'shit' on the cover. The Snivelling Shits, however, more readily defined their musical rationale, to cause as much fuss as possible while poking a stick at punk's self-conscious rebellious posture. And they did it very well.

Their debut single, 'Terminal Stupid' was backed by 'I Can't Come', the latter a paean to erectile dysfunction. The A-side tackled the stupidity of waking up next to someone you can't remember meeting the morning after the night before. Both were charming in their grubby demeanour. The sleeve, incidentally, featured a Brian Randle photo of a woman watching the Stranglers in Manchester that was captioned 'Punk Rock Jubilee Shocker' and graced the cover of the Sunday Mirror in June 1977.

But that was it. The late and much missed Dadomo was also responsible for co-writing two of the Damned's finest songs, 'I Just Can't Be Happy Today' and 'There Ain't No Sanity Clause'. Other musicians who were involved in the group's activities at various points included Steve Lillywhite, his brother Ade Lillywhite, Barry Myers, Lou Salvoni and Nick Ratbite – which we presume was not his real name.

In 1989 Damaged Goods re-released the single, with the added bonus of Arthur Comics? 'Isgodaman?', and also assembled demos and outtakes for a CD collection. The highlights included 'Bring Me The Head Of Yukio Mishima', about the Japanese writer who ritually disembowelled himself in 1970, 'I Wanna Be Your Biro', aimed at John Cooper Clarke, and a version of 'Waiting For The Man' themed on the Crossroads TV series. Ian Ballard at Damaged Goods takes up the story. "I always loved their single 'Terminal Stupid' that came out on Ghetto Rockers Records in late 77, but I knew nothing about them. So when I started Damaged Goods it was something I wanted to unearth and possibly reissue. I asked around and eventually someone mentioned that the main person behind the band was Giovanni Dadomo and that he worked in Record & Tape Exchange at Notting Hill. So I headed down there and eventually met him. We arranged to meet for a beer after he finished work and that's how the album came about. I showed him the Slaughter album and said I wanted to reissue the 7-inch, and he said did I want any other tracks? We met up at his parents' house and searched through old boxes and dug up a whole load of cassettes and even an acetate or two. We then went over to Dave Goodman's house and cleaned everything up and eventually put the album together. Photos were found at Ray Stevenson's house and we had a cover. Gio put together a mock review of the album and we were away."

DISCOGRAPHY:

Terminal Stupid/I Can't Come 7-inch (Ghetto Rockers PRE 2 August 1977)

ARCHIVE RELEASES:

Isgodaman?/Terminal Stupid/I Can't Come 7-inch (Damaged Goods FNARR 4 1989) (also issued as a box set with badge and inserts on pink vinyl, Damaged Goods FNARR 48. This is the original 'demo' recording rather than the version that appeared on the 'Streets' compilation)

I Can't Come LP (Damaged Goods FNARR LP 3 1989) (later released on CD, DAMGOOD205CD, in September 2002, with four extra tracks, including Dadomo singing 'There Ain't No Sanity Clause' backed by the Damned, plus demo versions of 'Terminal Stupid', 'I Can't Come' and 'Isgodaman?' The sleevenotes are a riot. But then so was the band.)

Sods

Steve Horton (keyboards), Chris Wood (bass), Mickey Howard (drums), Shane Roe (lead guitar, backing vocals), Kevin Jones (vocals)

From Harlow in Essex, the SODS also travelled under the name the Rage for a brief time. Responsible for two bona fide collectors' items in the shape of a brace of rather nifty 7-inchers, they supported Wire at Harlow College, where Jones and Roe were students, and the Banshees at the Triad in Stortford. They were, by

repute, one of the finest and most irreverent bands you could ever hope to catch live. Which, having seen them play in 2005, I can confirm to be the case. Kevin Jones, in particular, looked and sounded like a particularly vicious night-club bouncer, though we are told he has subsequently found gainful employment as a social worker.

Howard left the band in May 1978, but did return to play on both of the singles. A talented multi-instrumentalist, he subsequently played guitar for the Bobby Henry Band, who toured with the Police and Cramps, and for Chelsea on an American tour. Ralph Collins replaced him. Declan Barron from the Rabbits played bass on the first single after Chris Wood left, Scott Barker from the Fatal Microbes joined in time to play bass on the second. Steve Horton also contributed to the debut album by Harlow pop-punk band the Gangsters while Micky Howard contributed to numerous Stortbeat-era bands, including the Rabbits, Urban Decay and Verticle Strokers.

The Sods' first 7-inch, recorded for Stortbeat in 1979, is a throwback to the garage punk of 60s American bands like the Shadows Of Knight, though Horton's billowing church organ scales brought inevitable comparisons to the Stranglers and Doors. 'No Pictures Of Us', which featured an empty frame for a sleeve so the band could decorate it by hand, is driven by Horton's keyboard embellishments, as well as Jones's brusque vocal (especially the point at which he invites listeners to "stroll on"). The main impression though is of the stunning energy levels that underpin the record. It's a relentless effort, much beloved of John Peel, who played it four times, and it was later lifted for inclusion on both the Killed By Death and Messthetics series. The lyric attacked punk uniformity, while the conceptually consistent absence of pictures on the cover was a consequence not just of budget constraints. Shane Roe: "When the Harlow Citizen asked us 'to get into our outfits' for a publicity shot to promote the first punk gig in Harlow we were miffed as hell. In 1977 there was no uniform. The middle eight was straight out of the Velvet Underground songbook."

A second single followed in 1979, 'Mopy Grope', backed by 'Negative Positive', but it never received the same attention as their debut, and it is almost always misspelled as 'Moby Grape'. "Chris and I deliberately wrote this as the second single," Shane Roe recalls. "I thought I'd come up with a perfect arrangement of ye olde rock'n'roll chords." He also points out, in relation to the B-side, that "It was the Sods versus the world until Scott Barker joined. A great bassist, fab songwriter, and most importantly, totally great bloke." After they broke up Roe formed Mirror Co while taking a business studies degree in London.

They band did reunite in 2004 for a gig to promote the release of the Stortbeat compilation CD. It was good fun, by all accounts, and led to the same label planning a Sods retrospective. A second reunion took place in September 2005 as support on the Newtown Neurotics at their Harlow Square homecoming show. The show neatly book-ended both bands' careers. Back in the day, as Steve Drewett of the Neurotics confirmed to the Harlow Star, "They (The Sods) just said, 'come on, Steve, form a band. You can support us.'" Kevin Jones remained a pretty intimidating sight when he returned the compliment that evening. Punters who thought the band under-prepared because Jones was reading the lyrics from a sheet of paper should be aware, as Gordon Wilkins observes, that "Kevin always read the lyrics from a piece of paper, as far as I can remember."

DISCOGRAPHY:

No Pictures Of Us/Plaything 7-inch (Stortbeat BEAT 5 1979)
Mopy Grope/Negative Positive 7-inch (Tap 1 1979)
Compilations:
Stortbeat: A Musical Collective double CD (Handsignal Recordings Handy 2 and Handy 2A 2004; 'No Picture', 'Plaything', 'Snakes', 'Work')
Messthetics #2 ('No Picture')
ARCHIVE RELEASE:
The Sods Album CD (expected 2006)
No Picture/Plaything/Mopey Grope/Negative-Positive/Them/Makes Me Sick/Work/I Don't Care/Snakes/I Don't Like You/Hit Single/Little Miss Friday/No Luck/No Pictures (alt version)/Local News/Pillow/Suffocation/Work/Pile Of Shit (Look A Like)/Kevin... (I asked Shane for a few bon mots to describe the songs on this upcoming album. Here's what he remembers of the songs not discussed above. "'Plaything' was musically a Doors type thing. Lyrically, I think I can say we've all been there. 'Them' was the second song we

wrote – one chord for most of the song. I thought it would be easy for everybody – wrong. It hardly ever worked live, though we always dug the Jim Morrison-style lyrics. The final 2005 session was a chance to nail this down. Steve's keyboards are a real treat, having mulled over in his mind for 28 years. If I ruled the world 'Makes Me Sick' would be a hit single. Chris wrote the words as a response to the straight politicians playing the race card. He put the words to a collage of Nazi and other racists. I felt we needed a marching song – but for a liberal army with a fondness for psychedelic keyboards. 'Work' – one chord, that lovely E-major/E-major 7th suspend serving the rock'n'roll public since Chuck Berry in the 50s. Everyone else had a song called 'I Don't Care', so we felt obliged. 'Snakes' was us trying to be flash. 'I Don't Like You' was us doing all we could at our fourth rehearsal. We gave 'Hit Single' that title because the keyboard was a deliberate – to us – attempt to write a Stranglers-style song. 'No Luck' was a great song but we never seemed to get it right. 'Pillow' was us being funky sods and 'Suffocation' was Chris's crie de cour, and a song we always thought was our best at the time. 'Pile Of Shit' was a more direct 'No Pictures', and sadly too true of the whole scene by then.")

Some Chicken

Ivor Badcock (vocals), Terry Bull (bass), Jess Chicken (guitar), Galway Kinnell (drums)

SOME CHICKEN tend to get overlooked as non-entities behind the Users and Killjoys when people assess the impact of Lee Wood's Raw Records. But they're actually pretty good, in a scratchy, primitive vein. Certainly both sides of their raucous debut single are well worth investigating. John Peel was certainly a fan – he included 'New Religion' in his posthumously famous box of treasured 7-inch singles "that he couldn't live without". The Melody Maker was less taken with their efforts. "Landlocked punk. Dull, thudding, nothing new." By the advent of 'Arabian Daze' they'd opted for a much poppier sound, which is not unappealing but the production is terrible. And the band keep falling in and out of time.

Galways Kinhell was Bob Fawcett, who later worked with groups including Skin Patrol, while Mark Askwith was Ivor Badcock, who later left the music industry to work as a housing officer before drowning on holiday in Spain in 2006. But there was no stable line-up, as Keith Gotheridge told me. "It was all a pool of people at that time from the local music community, who used to do things like use Trent Polytechnic's repro department to make posters and put on shows, etc. I actually played in Some Chicken for a while, but everything was very fluid in those days."

DISCOGRAPHY:

New Religion/Blood On The Wall 7-inch (Raw RAW 7 October 1977) (re-released by Damaged Goods, DAMGOOD 185, first 1,000 copies on red vinyl)

Arabian Daze/No. 7 7-inch (Raw RAW 13 1978) (also available on 12-inch, RAWT13. Later reissued on Raw RAWT 17 for people who were "suspicious about buying a record with the catalogue number 13")

COMPILATION:

The Raw Records Punk Collection CD (Anagram CDPUNK 14 1993; 'New Religion', 'Blood On The Wall', 'Arabian Daze', 'No. 7')

Spasms

Glen Broadhurst (vocals, guitar), Pete Monk (guitar), Dr Cheng (bass), Brian Slater (drums)

From Tupton in Chesterfield, the SPASMS formed at Tunton Hall Comprehensive and swiftly became one of the area's most popular live acts, though not necessarily with local landlords. They were banned from both their local pub and from a venue in Alfreton where they allegedly upset the country and western singer trying to perform downstairs.

They got some more positive local press, however, when an anonymous 'near pensioner' wrote in to tell the newspapers how exciting the band's set was, and compared singer Glen Broadhurst to a "young Joe Cocker".

They were one of the many bands to use the Ellie Jay service to get their single out. However, it was never followed up and the band disappeared. These days Pete Monk runs a well-established guitar shop and mail order company in the north of England.

DISCOGRAPHY:

Never Happens Like It Does On The Telly/Monday Morning 7-inch (Ellie Jay SPA-001 1980)

Speedball

Robin Buelo (aka Rob Paveley; vocals, guitar), Guy Pratt (bass), Dave Dyke (drums)

Another of those bands, like Amber Squad and the Scoop, who fell uncomfortably between the stools of second wave punk and the mod revival, SPEEDBALL formed in 1979 after Idiot, one of Southend's first punk groups, folded. Bass player Guy Pratt, incidentally, is the son of songwriter and actor Mike Pratt, best known for playing Jeff Randall in Randall & Hopkirk (Deceased). He was also the writer of Tommy Steele's kitsch classic 'The Little White Bull'.

Managed by Roger Allen, editor of Surrey Vomet fanzine, Speedball incorporated a number of unreleased Idiot songs in their repertoire, including 'Ging Gang Gooly', that band's sole vinyl appearance (on the Southend Rock compilation). There was a cover of 'First Time', Honest John Plain's Boys' classic, while band originals included set opener 'Don't You Know Love By Now?', 'Is Somebody There?', '60s Girl' and 'Billy Gets What Billy Wants'.

The material was located somewhere between punk bristle and mod pop dynamics, as Southend musician and writer Steve Pegrum told me. "I remember seeing quite a lot of mods with Speedall written on the backs of their Parkas, and funnily enough, a year earlier in 1978, seeing a couple of punks with Idiot stencilled on their safety pin-festooned blazers – quite a barometer of the times!" The fact that Speedball was a three-piece and not averse to wearing the odd 'target' emblem, led to comparisons with the Jam. They were duly interviewed by that band's house magazine, Jamming!, in 1979. The feature accompanied the release of one very good single, 'No Survivors', a song about media hypocrisy and intrusion, backed by 'Is Somebody There?' – an existentialist inquiry into the existence of God. It was issued on No Pap Records, set up by local shop Record World. The band was horrified, however, when they saw the picture sleeve and labels credit the record to 'Speedballs'.

The single got nowhere, and the band immediately jacked it in. Guy Pratt, who initially joined Icehouse in Australia, continues to work in the industry as a session musician, having collaborated with Pink Floyd, Madonna, Michael Jackson and Bryan Ferry, among others. He has also become an in-demand composer, writing scores for Channel 4's Spaced, Linda Green and Jimmy Nail's Crocodile Shoes (you bastard!). He tells a great anecdote about being approached by a punk rocker in some dingy club at the end of the 70s. 'So what's your name?' 'Erm, Guy Pratt.' Punk rocker muses this over. 'Wow, what a fantastic name!' Pratt, in addition to that great name, now has a Grammy Award and two Ivor Novello nominations to his credit. Buelo is thought to be in Australia, and Dyke in Sweden.

DISCOGRAPHY:

No Survivors/Is Somebody There? 7-inch (No Pap Records DD 1 1979) (1,000 copies, most with striped sleeve and band's name spelt wrongly)

Spelling Missteaks

Dave Brown (vocals), Ben Evans (guitar), Allan Meadows (drums), Paul Harper (bass)

Harlow punk band who managed to release one EP, produced by Steve Drewett of the Newtown Neurotics, and play some sporadic and shambolic gigs around Essex. The EP got some airplay from John Peel, which was encouraging, and instigated a night of sustained celebration in one of the band member's kitchens. Of such modest triumphs are career highlights made. It's good stuff, actually; roustabout, doughty, splenetic punk rock of the old school.

The tracks were later compiled on Gordon Wilkins's excellent Stortbeat compilation, in which Ben Evans, at some length, failed to remember anything useful about the band other than the fact that their guitarist has a sieve-like memory. Evans being said guitarist. Still, the songs will suffice; deliciously snotty stuff, which don't overstay their welcome even if their attempts to be humorous (they were all big Ian Dury fans) are a little laboured – see 'Rubber Duck'.

The EP, unusually, was the only thing ever recorded by the **SPELLING MISSTEAKS**, and unfortunately the master tapes have disintegrated. When it was originally recorded the equipment out of phase, which is why the tracks rescued for the Stortbeat compilation sound as if they're taken from a warped record. Ben Evans would go on to play lead guitar with the Pharaohs. Dave Brown was brother of Pete Brown of Pete the Meat and the Boys.

DISCOGRAPHY:

Spelling Missteaks 7-inch EP (Stortbeat BEAT 7 1979)
Popstar/Mirrors/Rubber Duck/Urge
COMPILATION:
Stortbeat: A Musical Collective double CD (Handsignal Recordings Handy 2 and Handy 2A 2004; 'Popstar', 'Mirrors', 'Rubber Duck', 'Urge')

Spitfire Boys

Mike Rigby (vocals), Paul Rutherford (aka Maggot; vocals), Dave Littler (aka Jones; guitar), Peter Griffiths (aka Zero; bass), Budgie (aka Peter Clarke, aka Blister; drums)

Liverpool's best kept punk secret, the SPITFIRE BOYS, who actually hailed from St Helen's, were formed on 14 May 1977, just six weeks after bumping into the Heartbreakers who needed a support band for an upcoming show at Parr Hall in Warrington, with Slaughter And The Dogs and the Buzzcocks. Littler and friend Griffiths used the name Blackmailers but changed to the Spitfire Boys after it was suggested to Littler by Wayne County one evening at Eric's. Budgie, who had

S

previously played in the (pre-Yachts) Albert Dock and the Codfish Warriors after an apprenticeship in St Helen's working men's clubs, was persuaded to join after being played a tape of the Parr Hall show.

After a couple of gigs, including a booking to support Siouxsie and the Banshees at Eric's that they arrived too late for, original singer Mike Rigby was sacked. "He was completely crap," Budgie reminisced to Mark Paytress, "he wore safety pins and stuff." They built a set around Ramones' covers and originals such as 'Mary Whitehouse', 'Spitfire Girl', 'TV Stare', 'Straight Hate' and 'Ridicule'. Paul Rutherford was the final recruit. "The first thing the Spitfire Boys did was get Paul Rutherford on stage with us... at that time he was this young kid we'd seen dancing in the audience. He was one of the first people in Liverpool to wear bondage trousers."

They picked up numerous shows at Eric's supporting visiting London and American acts, and subsequently made the trek to London to play venues like the Vortex as support to the Slits, with Holly Johnson and Julian Cope making the trip with them in their van. As Littler would tell punk77.com: "We played at the Wigan Casino on one of their 'rock nights' and Peter Griffiths was approached by the club's manager. He wanted to manage us and arranged for us to do a demo in some small studio in Wigan. Shortly after we signed a record deal with RKO Records (run by publisher Robert Kingston). We were impressed at the time because they had 'You Really Got Me' by the Kinks on their books."

'British Refugee', the tale of a survivor of the Troubles in Northern Ireland leaving for the mainland, suffered from a poor production. Budgie subsequently disowned it to Rhythm in October 2002. "It was pretty bloody awful and nobody wanted to buy it, so we used to throw it out from the stage." Indeed, they did exactly that at their final gig at Eric's. Littler: "I was not happy with the production of the single. I wanted a much bigger sound and because of youth and naivety, I didn't understand what went wrong. Some few years later I was talking with Steve Jones and Paul Cook and asked them how they got the powerful sound on the 'Anarchy' single. Paul Cook's reply was 'I don't know, but we used all 24 tracks.' This means about ten guitar tracks layered. I think we had two guitar tracks, and we recorded in a 16-track studio with plenty to spare!"

Pete Wylie would join in December 1977 for a few rehearsals, but by the end of the month the band had collapsed. There was also a track recorded for an Eric's compilation that was never released due to the profanities involved, or, as Littler suggests, because RKO wanted too much money for its inclusion.

The final straw was Rutherford's failure to turn up for a recording session (for 'Nice Words Pretty Story') which infuriated RKO's Barry Kingston. However, Littler, alongside Pete Millman (guitar), Kurt Prasser (bass) and Chris Brazier (drums) did record another Spitfire Boys single almost by accident. "The second single came about with a totally different line-up. I wrote, sang and recorded 'Funtime' whilst in Wales in 1979 with a scratch band. I did not want to use the Spitfire Boys name on it, but was persuaded by the guy who financed it to use the name because he thought it would sell better. It only had a short run of a thousand copies. The original band was well finished at that point and I sort of owned the name as it was all my own making."

Wylie would go on to Wah!, Rutherford to the Opium Eaters and then Frankie Goes To Hollywood, Griffiths to Nova Mob and Budgie to Nova Mob, Big In Japan, the Opium Eaters, the Secrets, Planets, Slits, Siouxsie And The Banshees and the Creatures. Littler joined the Photons and would co-write later Visage hits 'Mind Of A Toy' and 'Tar' with Steve Strange. He joined the White Brothers, a kind of poetry collective that featured writers Kevin Evans and Glenn Carmichael and was managed by Nils Stevenson. Thereafter his main interest became electronic music.

The Spitfire Boys' importance to the development of both Liverpool's indigenous punk movement and the flowering of art pop that followed (the early-80s' holy trinity of Bunnymen, Teardrops and Wah!) has too often been overlooked. As well as Wylie actually playing with the Spitfires, and Julian Cope and Holly Johnson undertaking the aforementioned trip to London with them, Ian McCulloch was also a huge early fan. That whole exquisite Liverpudlian pop renaissance, as many have noted, was rooted in Love's Forever Changes and the Velvet Underground. But maybe there was also a measure of Spitfire Boys in the cocktail as a kicker, at least as a practical if not sonic inspiration. Certainly they were much, much more than the "false start" to the Liverpool punk scene they have been characterised as by Paul Morley in articles accompanying his compilation North By North West – though it was nevertheless good to see them represented in more elevated company.

DISCOGRAPHY:

British Refugee/Mein Kampf 7-inch (RK RK 1001 October 1977) (originally issued in plain sleeve, then reissued in picture sleeve in the early-80s)
Funtime/Transcendental Changing 7-inch (SRT SRTS 948 1979)
COMPILATIONS:
Unearthed Liverpool Cult Classics Volume 3 CD (Viper July 2004; 'British Refugee')
North By North West dbl CD (Korova KODE1001L June 2006; 'British Refugee')

Spizz

SPIZZ came into being after Kenneth Spiers, a Warhol fan who'd trained in fine art, made his live debut as a solo performer at the punk festival staged at Birmingham's Barbarella's in August 1977. Just Kenneth, soon to be known as Spizz, and his acoustic guitar, with a bit of improvisation and a lot of heckling. "It was my first performance to a paying public, about 1,000 people," Spizz told me. "I was excited but more anxious that the promoter wouldn't let me perform – I wasn't billed, he didn't know me from Adam." The new age had been delivered to him via the pages of the music inkies. "I was an avid reader of all the music weeklies. I regularly bought NME, Melody Maker, Record Mirror and Disc and Music Monthly. I heard stuff on Peel, then I bought 'Anarchy' when it came out. Wow! I thought. But my mates thought it was crap."

He then began working with Pete Petrol (Pete Dowd) as Spizz 77. They'd mutated into Spizz Oil by the following year, with the addition of drummer Frank Guest (Frank Wolstenholme). "He came down with a view to playing spanners as an industrial percussionist," notes Spizz, "but played two notes repeatedly on piano on 'Pure Noise'." I asked Spizz what the motivation behind the constant name changes was. It turns out it wasn't conceptual. "I was called Spizz 77 which would not look so good as Spizz 78. Also, by November Pete (Dowd) was playing alongside me, so it was a duo now. Then I saw a TV programme about the new North Sea oil rigs being 'the biggest man made structures ever to have moved across the surface of the earth'. Therefore, Spizz Oil, the biggest… etc."

Spizz Oil supported Siouxsie And The Banshees at the Roundhouse prompting an invitation to record a John Peel session. That, in turn, brought them to the attention of Geoff Travis at Rough Trade, for whom they would release two singles, including the oddly mesmeric '6,000 Crazy'. They got a fair amount of press, and headlined a series of gigs around the Midlands, at one of which they were supported by the Shapes. Gareth Holder: "Last on the bill is Spizz, who goes on to fame as, well, Spizz. He is notable for two things: getting picked up after the gig by his mum, and receiving a punch up the bracket in the course of the evening courtesy of the Shapes' Nick Hadley Esq. I'm not sure what that was all about, but I'm sure he deserved it." Spizz has no recall of this. "There was only one gig where a family member, my eldest brother, picked me up, and that was when we were supporting Punishment of Luxury and the Human League in Coventry in 1979 where we ran away from the mates of a bricklayer I had beaten up." Back to Gareth Holder. "I'm pretty certain that it happened as described, but who knows? Someone from the Shapes always seemed to be punching someone all the time. It seemed all the rage back then for some reason. The only departure from this was me and the singer. People used to punch us, as I remember."

When Petrol left the band in 1979 Spizz recruited a new team of collaborators including Mark Coalfield (keyboards), Pete Hyde (guitar), Brian Benzine (drums) and Jim Solar (bass) and the Spizz project was rebirthed as Spizzenergi. "After a year of almost constant gigging Petrol and I fell out. I was introduced to new musicians, talented but up for anything, so I felt it was a new band. Therefore it needs a new name as it was so different. Oil produces energy or oil turns into energy." Hence Spizzenergi.

Sticking with Rough Trade, they joined the label's package tour with the Raincoats and

Kleenex. "We replaced Cabaret Voltaire who dropped out days before the tour was due to start. Subway Sect were added to boost the end of the tour show (Sat 2nd June). However, they pulled out too and were replaced by Dexy's Midnight Runners, which I think was their first London gig." I asked Kleenex's Marlene Marder how mad Spizz actually was. "Spizz became mad... because he toured with us." But I don't think she can take all the credit.

Their debut release as Spizzenergi was 'Soldier, Soldier', their first claim to greatness. Featuring a dense rhythmic mix accented by keyboards, an occasionally lopsided vocal and a series of great, atmospheric ebbs and swells, it sounded quite unearthly. As did its follow-up, 'Where's Captain Kirk?', a meditation on the whereabouts of the Starship Enterprise's big fella, which belted along and managed to combine reverence with playfulness, notably in the vocals ("Where's captain Kir-ee-er-ee-urk?", strained his Spizzness).

"Back in 1979, after rehearsals, me and Jim would have a few beers and we had been running through one of Mark's tunes which had a very obscure lyric, except for the line 'Oh, but it's true – you are a nobody's who'. So on the bus home this metamorphosed into the first two verses and choruses. I had no pen or paper, so for the entire journey I repeated those in my head until I walked in the house wrote them down and within a few minutes the third verse came to me. Next rehearsal, I said I had written some new words. We went through it and we thought it was so funny we played it over and over. That's when I added the Star Trek theme tune because Jim had a WEM Copycat echo unit. We knew then that this was more catchy than 'Soldier Soldier'." It became the first single to top the newly created Independent Chart in 1980 and stayed there for seven weeks. As Melody Maker noted, "Spizz has... taken the great leap forward from new wave mascot to fully fledged participant with humour and senses intact."

In fact, at one time Spizz held five separate independent chart entries for his Rough Trade singles, using three separate band names. 'Soldier Soldier' had been single of the week in the NME, and 'Captain Kirk' secured the same prestige billing with Melody Maker. Which meant that Spizz were a hot property, though typically and defiantly, he insisted on another change of name, this time to Athletico Spizz. "During the preceding twelve months we got through four drummers and seven guitarists so, as we stabilised near December 1979, we started toying with the idea of a new name for the settled line-up. The three smokers in the band were all considering quitting smoking and the Olympics were coming in 1980. Then NME's Paul Morley rang me up on Boxing Day and asked what we were going to be called in the new year. So I said Athletico Spizz 80. This name also had a limited shelf life." A sell-out five-night stand at the Marquee followed during August 1980, including a non-drinking matinee for the young u's.

Another single for Rough Trade ensued, 'No Room', with the line-up now featuring Dave Scott (ex-Bank Of Dresden) on guitar and another pseudonymous drummer, C.P. Snare (aka Clive Parker, who would later join Big Country for a short time). A&M offered the group a contract and Spizz accepted, leading to 'Hot Deserts' and 'Central Park'. Both were lost in the confusion over the name change. And remain lost, given that it's harder to licence from a major, neither single ended up on subsequent compilations. A&M also offered the band a chance to record its first album. Do A Runner was judged uneven by critics, but it does contain one of the greatest ever anti-nuke rhymes in the course of 'Energy Crisis' ("Nuclear scientist producing plutonium/Nasty little substance that we can't controlleum"). The album climaxes in two contrasting sides to the Spizz story, the nonsensical but highly diverting 'Clocks Are Big' and the mini-space opera, 'Airships'. The album broke the Top 30 and the group briefly toured America, but failed to impress critically. Even if it had, you suspect that their leader was due a new name change anyway, so behold the Spizzles.

Spizzles featured Lu Edmonds on guitar and piano as replacement for Dave Scott and in this guise they cut two further singles and an album for A&M after they'd been advised by their management that they could be bigger than the Beatles (hence Spizzles). I asked Spizz if he thought signing with A&M was a mistake. "No, it was that the musical climate had changed and the Sounds assassination did help. Nicky Horne announced our signing on Capital before we managed to tell Rough Trade. Our deal with Rough Trade was not even written down – we recorded, they released. No contract, just figures and costs, etc. There must have been some bad mouthing, which fuelled the music press backlash. Thatcher's policies began to hit

S

our fanbase – we would have more people trying to see our soundcheck than could pay to get in on the night." I asked how A&M had treated the band. "Very well, until our increasingly flawed manager fell out over video payments."

Spizzmania did not ensnare the populace as planned and the band were dropped and returned to Rough Trade. Where, it has to be said, they staged something of a revival. Both 'Mega City 3', in particular, and 'Jungle Fever', recorded as Spizzenergi 2 with Petrol and Benzine back aboard, arguably surpassed any of their recordings for the major. "Rough Trade seemed a natural fit. "Geoff (Travis) was great. Scott Piering was very professional. Nearly all the others were very cool and considered us uncool. Largely due to the fact that we were from Birmingham, ambitious, wore clean clothes and our socks matched."

1983 brought a one-off performance as Spizzorwell (using backing tapes produced with Ian Page), before he put together the theatrical venture The Last Future show, which featured half a dozen female vocalists. A cult hit, it got him a bit of notoriety but not enough to pay the bills. Thence came Spizzsexual, featuring former members of Friends Of Gavin, who toured for a while.

There was a solo Spizz effort in 1987, a reprise of 'Where's Captain Kirk' featuring Mark Ferda on guitar, as well as the single 'Love Me Like A Rocket', which was co-written with future house DJ Lol Hammond, who appeared with the band at several Marquee shows. "Spizz is a top geezer," he told me. "A real larger than life character. Always great fun and up for anything. I do recall a Roly Poly Gram jumping up on stage mid-number and thrusting Spizz's head (whilst still singing) in between her huge breasts. It was Spizz's birthday and some rascals had booked her for the night." There were a couple of other odds and ends, including a festive version of Lennon's 'Happy Xmas (War Is Over)', but the recording career was superceded by other pursuits. Spizz concentrated more on his pop art doodles. Hunt 'em down on eBay.

However, the band has continued in various formations and can still be caught live, after they originally reunited for the Holidays In the Sun festival in 1996. He still loves performing with the 'modern' Spizzenergi given the office, and the line-up, featuring Matt Broughton on bass, Simon Kinder on guitar and Jeff Walker on drums, has been unchanged for a decade. "We laugh till it hurts. Especially between soundcheck and encore."

Discography:

As Spizz Oil:
6,000 Crazy/1989/Fibre 7-inch (Rough Trade RTS 01 October 1978)
Cold City 7-inch EP (Rough Trade RTSO 2 December 1978)
Cold City/Red And Black/Solarisation (Shun)/Platform 3
As Spizzenergi:
Soldier Soldier/Virginia Plain 7-inch (Rough Trade RTS 03 September 1979)
Where' Captain Kirk?/Amnesia 7-inch (Rough Trade RTS 04 December 1979)
As Athletico Spizz:
No Room/Spock's Missing 7-inch (Rough Trade RTS O5 June 1980)
As Athletico Spizz 80:
Hot Deserts/Legal Proceedings 7-inch (A&M AMS 7550 July 1980)
Do A Runner LP (A&M AMLE 68514 July 1980)
Central Park/Central Park (Dr & Nurses dub version) 7-inch (A&M AMS 7566 October 1980)
As Spizzles:
Risk/Melancholy 7-inch (A&M AMS 8107 February 1981)
Danger Of Living/Scared 7-inch (A&M AMS 8124 April 1981)
Spikey Dream Flowers LP (A&M AMLE 68523 April 1981)
As Spizzenergi 2:
Mega City 3/Work 7-inch (Rough Trade RT 096 February 1982)
Jungle Fever/The Meaning 7-inch (Rough Trade RT 108 June 1982)
As Spizz:
Where's Captain Kirk?/Living Is Better With Freedom 7-inch (Hobo Railways HOBO 01 September 1987) (also issued on 12-inch)
As Spizz Orbit:
Love Me Like A Rocket 12-inch (Plastic Head PLASPOP 1 1988) (split single)
As Spizzmas:
Happy Xmas (War Is Over) 7-inch (Damaged Goods DAMPUD 57 1994)

ARCHIVE RECORDINGS:
Spizzhistory LP (Rough Trade SO 1 1981) (compilation of all their Rough Trade singles)
Spizz Oil: The Peel Session 12-inch EP (Strange Fruit SFPS 022 1987)
Pure Noise/Alien Language/Protect From Heat/Platform 3/Switched On
Unhinged LP (Damaged Goods DAMGOOD 36 1994)
Spizz Not Dead Shock! CD (Cherry Red CDM RED 130 1996) ('On My Own' is unreleased and 'Three Lions' is Spizz's attempt to write a theme tune for Euro 96)
Where's Captain Kirk? The Very Best Of Spizz (Cherry Red CDM RED 212 May 2002) (features Spizz's eulogy to his beloved Aston Villa as well as video footage of 'Kirk' at the Holidays In The Sun punk festival)

Squad

Terry Hall (vocals), Danny Cunningham (guitar), Sam McNulty (bass), Marc Hatwood (drums)

"If you're talking Coventry and punk then you're talking SQUAD," wrote Pete Chambers in the Coventry Evening News in 2005. "They were without doubt the finest punk band to ever come from this beloved city of ours. They were lunatic, loud and loveable – nothing malicious, just out for a good time as their audiences inevitably were."

Although the Automatics are generally regarded as Coventry's punk forefathers, given their links to the Specials, the Squad also contributed personnel – and musical apprenticeships – to the 2-Tone figureheads. Terry Hall made his first appearances with Squad, before moving on to the Automatics after Jerry Dammers spotted him singing with the band. But Squad never did enjoy a stable line-up. As Carolyn Spence noted in Sounds in 1981, "Considering the number of people who are supposed to have begun their musical careers in the Squad, it's amazing they ever found time to play between line-up changes." Squad emerged at the end of 1977 out of the punk clique that would drink at the Rose and Crown, a gay pub in Coventry, and released two highly affecting, and highly-wrought, singles, both of which came after Hall's departure and featured instead ebullient vocalist Gus Chambers.

Pete Chambers rescued the following anecdote from his brother for a local news report in 2005. "We were sitting in this club (after a show by the Boomtown Rats) with a couple of band members, when in burst a guy with a huge kitchen knife screaming all punks must die because they had killed Elvis Presley. No-one was hurt but it shows what a negative role the media played in its portrayal of punks. But there were some positives in that time. The race barriers were smashed down during this period and there was nothing stronger than a united front."

Squad made their debut with 'Red Alert' on their own label in 1978 (the B-side, '£8-a-week', was later covered by Oi! band the Last Resort). The sleeve actually credited Terry Hall, though drummer Hatwood's face was blotted out on the rear because he'd left the band after they turned down an offer from EMI to distribute the single, choosing instead to move to Bristol to work with the Stereo Models. From here the line-up changes came thick and fast. Hatwood was replaced by Billy Little, who subsequently joined Urge, then Rob Hill. McNulty was replaced by Nigel Mulvey, who was in place for the recording of their contribution to the Sent From Coventry compilation. By that time the line-up was Mulvey (bass), Chambers (vocals), Steve Young (drums) and Johnny Adams (guitar), the latter two both ex-members of RU12. Cunningham went on to join the Ramrods, and later Major 5 and Gdansk. Mulvey would join the Giraffes.

The Squad were enormously popular in Coventry for a time, with their own devoted fan base, as Simon Frith recalled for the Melody Maker. "Squad have become too authentic for their own good. Their fans are so committed that the group is excluded from every local venue (fan loyalty = fan fights) and don't fare much better elsewhere – their supporters got duffed up by Brummies at Barbarella's, by Cockneys at the Marquee. Squad gigs stopped being fun and then stopped altogether, and the band, meanwhile, just want to make a living, want to move and change and challenge their increasingly hidebound audiences. Squad are desperate, for all the right reasons, to be stars."

Gus Chambers went on to play with metal acts 21 Guns (who recorded new versions of 'Millionaire' and 'The Flasher' and appeared on Neville Staples' label) and Grip, Inc, who featured Slayer founder Vince Lombardi. But Chambers was back working with a new line-up of Squad in 2002. In a letter to Punk77 he stated: "The Squad is not a reunion of old band members but is a serious, hard working band that has the spirit of '76 and are really fed up with corporate bubble gum Punk Rock." Grip Inc, meanwhile, released their fourth album in 2004.

I tried on several occasions to interview Gus for this book. He did eventually get back to me, pointing out that he was sorry not to have replied, but he'd been away in prison. Then he disappeared again.

DISCOGRAPHY:

Red Alert/£8-A-Week 7-inch (Squad SQS 1 1978)
Millionaire/Brockhill Boys 7-inch (Squad SQS 3 1979)
COMPILATIONS:
Sent To Coventry LP (Kathedral KATH 1 1980; 'The Flasher')
Punk Rock Rarities Vol. 2 CD (Anagram CD Punk 83 1996; 'Red Alert')

Starjets

Terry Sharpe (vocals, guitar), Sean Martin (bass), Paul Bowen (vocals, guitar), Liam L'Estrange (drums)

The STARJETS, formed in 1976 in West Belfast, were as influenced by classic pop as they were by classic punk. Their early shows relied largely on cover versions of pop nuggets, from the Beatles to the Archies' 'Sugar Sugar'. A glimpse of their commercial premise can be grasped by the fact they even got the nod to support the Bay City Rollers at the Tonic Cinema in Bangor and the Glitter Band in Enniskillen.

Sharpe was concurrently an employee at local record shop Harrison Records in Castle Street, which meant he was alerted to the arrival of punk. The band immediately took the decision to relocate to London in November 1977 to write the next chapter in their story, thinking their original material might get a fairer hearing on the mainland. They immediately got their heads down to playing any gig that was offered, appearing alongside punk luminaries, and the not so luminous, including the Rezillos, the Late Show, the Fabulous Poodles, Brakes and the Banned.

They made a good impression, too. Although they are often written out of punk for the pop quotient of their work, and they were conversant in both harmony and melody, their songs maintained both the energy and enthusiasm of the day. The lyrics, too, were occasionally more caustic than a surface appraisal suggested. And while they weren't up there with the Boys in terms of songwriting ability, the approach wasn't a million miles different.

They were the first signing by the legendary Muff Winwood after he saw them at the Hope And Anchor. They cut their first demos shortly thereafter, before making their recorded debut for Epic with 'Here She Comes Again' in December 1978. However, though some copies of the single emerged, it was then shelved in favour of January 1979's 'It Really Doesn't Matter', produced by Pip Williams of Status Quo infamy. In March came 'Run With The Pack', along with lots of probably unwelcome press coverage in the likes of Jackie magazine, where the band were described as the "Bay City Rollers of punk". And they were said to be 'close' to various members of Bananarama. But then who wasn't.

Prior to major tours with the Tubes and Stiff Little Fingers, the band released their third single proper, 'Ten Years', in the summer of 1979. The Starjets seemed to be getting the nod in all the right places, and their best single, 'War Stories', stalled just outside the Top 50 and produced a Top Of The Pops appearance, as well as slots on Roundabout and even Crackerjack.

Sadly, sales for debut album, God Bless The Starjets, were disappointing, despite the band being installed in the hugely expensive Manor Studios in Oxfordshire, while recording radio sessions for both Mike Read and Kid Jensen. The poor performance of the album dampened spirits, and the band's fortunes began to wane. Two further singles, 'Schooldays' (a tougher, re-recorded version of the 'It Really Doesn't Matter' B-side) and 'Shiraleo' failed to arrest the decline. Bowen was replaced by Pat Gribben (ex-Jets) and the band elected to change their name to Tango Brigade. They managed one further single, the quietly impressive 'Donegal', before folding the band, which was by then up to its eyes in hock to CBS.

After the band Sean Martin joined Jake Burns of SLF in the Big Wheel while Terry Sharpe put together the Adventures, along with Starjets roadie 'Spud' Murphy and Gribben, who enjoyed significant success in the mid-80s, having also contributed to a couple of Angelic Upstarts albums. Sharpe also recently played with Jim Reilly of SLF in the Dead Handsomes. Bowen is still involved in music in Dublin. Sean Martin works for the Inland Revenue and L'Estrange defied his nom de plume by becoming a computer analyst.

DISCOGRAPHY:

Here She Comes Again/Watch Out 7-inch (Epic EPC 6902 December 1978) (withdrawn)
It Really Doesn't Matter/Schooldays 7-inch (Epic EPC 6968 January 1978)
Run With The Pack/Watch Out 7-inch (Epic EPC 7123 March 1979)
Ten Years/One More Word 7-inch (Epic EPC 7417 1979)
Ten Years/Any Danger Love/One More Word 7-inch (free single 1979) (given away at shows with the appropriate venue stamped on the label)
God Bless The Starjets LP (Epic EPC 83534 1979) (re-released on CD by Captain Oi!, AHOY CD 99, as God Bless The Starjets – The Punk Collection, in 1999. It featured these bonus tracks; Here She Comes Again/Watch Out/It Really Doesn't Matter/Schooldays (B-side version)/One More Word/Do The Push/Shiraleo/Standby 19/Donegal (as Tango Brigade)/In Vain (as Tango Brigade)
War Stories/Do The Push 7-inch (Epic EPC 7770 1979)
School Days/One More Word 7-inch (Portrait 2-700036 1979)
School Days/What A Life 7-inch (Epic EPC 7986 1979)
Shiraleo/Standby 19 7-inch (Epic EPC 8276 1980)
It Really Doesn't Matter/School Days/Run With The Pack/Watch Out dbl 7-inch (promo)

Stiff Kittens/Warsaw

Ian Curtis (vocals), Pete Hook (bass), Bernie Dicken (aka Barney Sumner, aka Bernard Albrecht; guitar), Terry Mason (drums)

The legend of Joy Division and New Order traces its origins to these two earlier, and far more punk-derived, Manchester bands, although in truth they were more or less a single entity. And for once the myth is true – they were indeed inaugurated the day after Pete Hook and Barney Sumner saw the Pistols play at the Lesser Free Trade Hall, Hook purchasing his bass (Sumner already had a guitar) from Mazel's music shop the day after. He'd never played an instrument before. They also invited Pete Shelley of the Buzzcocks to a pub in Broughton to ask his advice on forming a band.

Hook and Sumner originally met at Salford Grammar, and would start rehearsing, in shambolic fashion, on Friday nights after school. Schoolpal Martin Gresty was offered the vacant singing position, but turned it down as soon as he got a job at a local factory. Terry Mason, who'd also attended the Lesser Free Trade Hall show, was encouraged to learn drums. They met Curtis, from Macclesfield, at a subsequent Pistols show at the Electric Circus, and moved rehearsals to the Black Swan in Salford. Their transformation was complete on hearing the Buzzcocks' 'Spiral Scratch' EP. Indeed, it was Pete Shelley (some histories credit Richard Boon) who suggested the name Stiff Kittens, though they soon decided they hated it. It was changed to Warsaw, inspired by the David Bowie Low track 'Warszawa', in time for their debut performance, supporting Penetration and the Buzzcocks, on 29 May 1977. However, the name **STIFF KITTENS** was employed on the original poster, which didn't please Curtis, while other promotional materials cited Birmingham's Prefects as the support. By this time they'd enlisted Tony Tabac as drummer, Mason taking over management duties.

The show was reviewed by Sounds stringer, and tax inspector by day, Ian Wood. Paul Morley in the NME noted that they reminded him of the Faces, but was substantially more impressed. More significantly, maverick producer Martin Hannett was in the audience, and put them on the books of Music Force, which he ran with Susannah O'Hara from Oxford Road, with the New Manchester Review produced downstairs – for whom Howard Devoto compiled the rock listings. New Hormones was also based at the same building for a spell. They then played three 'squat' gigs, one of which was watched by Gail Egan. "Even then, I thought they were very intense and rather haunting and I was transfixed." There were also shows at Rafters, including the infamous occasion where Curtis cut himself on stage, in a crude imitation of his hero, Iggy Pop.

Steve Brotherdale debuted behind the drums for a show at Rafters on 30 June as Tabac left for the retail trade. He'd jumped ship from local punks Panik, who were managed by Rob Gretton, and knew Warsaw through his DJ sets at Rafters. According to Manchester musician and Rabid Records affiliate Rick Goldstraw, Warsaw were initially considered "the runt of the litter", and nobody, aside from Gretton, was convinced they would get anywhere.

"The first time I saw Warsaw play was at a college gig," Brotherdale recalls. "Tabac was drumming. I thought, they're awful, these. And the drummer's really pedestrian. I talked to the other three of them afterwards. I said, it's all right, but Tabac is shite. 'Do you fancy having a go?' So I said I would. They invited me down to some pub in Salford, the Black Swan. That was it. Me and Ian spent a lot of time together. Barney and Pete, they both had good jobs. Ian didn't, and neither did I. Ian was in Macclesfield, which was nearer to me. He'd come to Didsbury and go for a few beers. He liked a drink and smoked for England, always Marlboro cigarettes. He wasn't a miserable bastard like they make him out to be. He was a really good laugh. They gave him some laxative chocolate or gum one time, and he ended up singing on the toilet." He also remembers a night chez Curtis where, after a particularly heavy drinking session, a semi-naked prostitute threw up over Mike Drone's head, who'd brought her back from the local pub. Drone slammed the door, got in his car and drove off. Then Ian Nance tried his chances, only for the girl to head to the bathroom. When she came out of the toilet, she fell straight into the wholly innocent arms of Ian Curtis, on his way to bed, at the same time as Mrs Curtis opened the bedroom door to enquire as to what was going on, before kicking everyone out. Quite right, too.

Brotherdale played on the band's first demos, cut on 18 July 1977 at Pennine Sound Studios, "I've never heard those sessions since," Brotherdale concedes, despite them being routinely bootlegged for the last 25 years. "I always liked Ian's voice, but he was more suited to what Joy Division did. With the old Warsaw stuff, it was more punky, faster." He encountered the same problem when he got Curtis to audition for the Panik – anything above mid-tempo sounded wrong. Brotherdale subsequently joined V2 and was replaced by Stephen Morris, after he responded to an advert in Jones' music store in Macclesfield.

Warsaw played on the last night of the Electric Circus, where Jon Savage first encountered them, and added 'At A Later Date' to the 10-inch live album of the occasion – with Barney screaming 'Do you remember Rudolf Hess?' at the song's close, which hardly diluted the brewing 'Nazi' accusations. This is the only legitimate recording made by Warsaw, though a widely circulated bootleg, The Ideal Beginning, documents five songs: 'Inside The Line', 'Gutz', 'At A Later Date', 'The Kill' and 'You're No Good For Me'. These were drawn from the Pennine sessions back in July 1977, and have been bootlegged in sundry formats since. Their final date as Warsaw came on the last day of 1977 at the Swinging Apple in Liverpool.

Earlier that month, while still named Warsaw, the band recorded the tracks for 'An Ideal For Living', though on release it would be credited to Joy Division, after they'd heard of London band Warsaw Pakt. Curtis took the single to Derek Brandwood, who headed RCA's Manchester promotions unit. He didn't like it, but his 10-year-old son Howard did (who always had good taste, he once tried to nick this writer's girlfriend at college in Liverpool). With his support he agreed to help put them in the studio. Although the "RCA sessions" were something of a misadventure, they soon ended up clutched to the bosom of Tony Wilson's Factory Records, the two entities, band and label, eventually becoming synonymous. The rest is, indeed, history.

COMPILATION:

Short Circuit: Live At The Electric Circus 10-inch LP (Virgin VCL5003 June 1978; 'At A Later Date') (listed as Joy Division on the sleeve, though they performed on the night as Warsaw. Sadly, it seems the rest of the tape documenting the show has disappeared)

Bootlegs:

The Ideal Beginning 12-inch EP (Enigma PSS 138 May 1981)

Inside The Line/Gutz/At A Later Date/The Kill/You're No Good For Me (just one of dozens of variations of the same tracks, collecting demos from July 1977. It was put out by Manchester's Chaos Cassettes, whose John West confirmed that he had released it partially at the behest of the band. "We only had 2,000 pressed so it would remain collectable. It was done with the approval of the band's management. They did it just to show people what early Joy Division were like." It was released on May 18 1981, exactly one year after Ian Curtis's death).

Stiff Little Fingers

Jake Burns (vocals, guitar), Henry Cluney (guitar), Gordon Blair (bass), Brian Faloon (drums)

While London punks fantasised about armed conflict on the streets of their capital, their Northern Irish counterparts lived in close proximity to the real thing. Yet the province's two biggest and most enduring exports, STIFF LITTLE FINGERS and the Undertones, took different tacks entirely. The Undertones, though plenty politicised as individuals, fantasised about the girls on the streets of their town. Stiff Little Fingers, grounded in the social realism of the Clash, addressed 'the troubles' with occasional naiveté but also humane, first-hand insight. They seldom receive the plaudits customarily afforded their peers as a first-tier punk band, but Stiff Little Fingers' two-decade plus kinship with their fans is forged on commitment to old fashioned entertainment principles without the attendant rock star bull, and no little musical as well as personal fortitude. That they were a coach ride away from the cutting edge and two shuttle flights removed from cool was always part of their appeal.

Prior to punk's year zero Burns, who boasted the disposition of a choirboy but a larynx that could splinter gargoyles, had got the A-level grades to get him to polytechnic, but only lasted four months. Afterwards he spent a few months on the dole and two painful weeks as an accounts clerk in an engineering firm (doubly painful considering he failed his Maths O-level four times) while putting together a group. Highway Star, a covers band, were happy to play whatever, whenever, wherever. Cluney took the gig to get off the dole himself, while Faloon moonlighted as a telex operator. It was Cluney who instigated the musical turnaround when he turned up at Burns's house one day with a batch of punk singles. Burns was smitten.

But it wasn't until the first imports of the Clash's debut album reached the province that the band felt empowered to move away from Irish-Americana retro. "There was nothing for us in Belfast," Burns told Top Ten. "It was sheer tedium. Up till then I'd been in cover bands singing 'Sweet Home Alabama' when I hadn't been further west than Donegal." Emerging with a new set of punk covers – 'White Riot', 'Complete Control', 'God Save The Queen' – they took the name Stiff Little Fingers from a Vibrators' album track. It was chosen in a hurry to satisfy a gig they'd signed up. Burns had toyed around with the name The Fast only to find it was taken. Asked by the promoter what he should bill them as, Jake scanned an album cover and chose their new title, thinking they could change it later. But the show got a good review and he decided they couldn't waste the publicity.

Before the transition from Highway Star to SLF, ex-student Ali McMordie was recruited in April 1977 in place of Blair, who departed to join Rudi, a band who vociferously criticised SLF for their lack of punk 'authenticity'. "The fact is that SLF were really looked on as a complete joke over here until they went off to England and fooled the gullible Brit media," Rudi's Brian Young later concluded. "Don't get me wrong, they were great live (they oughta been as they had been around for years) but they were about as punk as the Wombles." That may be true, but all the major punk protagonists had patchy CVs when it came down to it. And its most enduring players were, to a large extent, those transformed by the experience of punk – custodians rather than conceptualists. Stiff Little Fingers were no different. And, in a later e-mail to me, Young conceded "I don't wanna slag 'em over much in print, as Henry is still one of the all-time good guys."

It only became clear just how resentful elements of the Northern Ireland punk community were towards Stiff Little Fingers on the publication of the superb It Makes You Want To Spit anthology. Here's a typical comment from P. Checkoff, who later recorded with the Hit Parade for Crass Records. "They never attempted to tackle any real issues in the North, whilst being heralded as the representatives of Northern Irish youth. Indeed their highly ambiguous lyrics argued for a 'normality' under which they could progress as a rock band, that the only thing wrong in the North was the fact that they hadn't anywhere to play." More than one person, beyond their fiercest critic Brian Young, has criticised some of the 'rock star' attitudes that, according to them, attended SLF's success. Others in the Northern Ireland punk community, such as Spit author Guy Trelford, supports Young's view that Burns sometimes employs a "selective" memory.

Fair enough. But SLF meant so much to so many people and I've met dozens of fans who have met the band and have been impressed by Jake's openness and humility, whilst he has always admitted to the "naked ambition" that drove the band. I myself attended a Stiff Little Fingers' video shoot way back in the day. When Jake realised I wasn't getting paid for coming along, he tried to blag my train fare from his manager for me, despite me protesting that this wasn't necessary. In following the dictum take as you find, I found Jake Burns to be a good guy.

The other tangible charge relating to the band's authenticity arose from their connection with an outside hand, that of Daily Express journalist Gordon Ogilvie, a man who, by Cluney's admission, "knows more about words than we ever will". On 14 November 1977, Ogilvie, along with fellow stringer Colin McClelland, whom Burns had first contacted with the hope of obtaining some press, saw the band play at the Glenmachen Stables. They encouraged Burns to steer the group away from their diet of Clash/Damned/Vibrators covers, suggesting he write songs which reflected his own environment – though the only one he'd written at that point, 'State Of Emergency', embarrassed him. Within a fortnight, Burns came back with 'Suspect Device' and 'Wasted Life'. "There was such an incredible outpouring of anger and meaning and so forth about what it was like to be a teenager in Belfast at that time," Ogilvie, who later became Burns's flatmate, recalled. He helped them set up their own Rigid Digits imprint and started working on lyrics with Burns.

They cut 'Suspect Device', the opening riff cleaved from, of all things, Montrose's 'Space Station Number 9', and 'Wasted Life', written about a friend who'd been killed after he succumbed to the local pressures of joining a paramilitary organisation, at Downtown Radio's jingle studio. "We did it in two runs, all live," Jake later told Chris Bryans. "We didn't have a clue. And the guy who was engineering it was just glad he wasn't doing another ad for Kerrygold butter or something."

The subject matter pinpointed their locale. "We did play on the Northern Irish thing," Jake admitted to MOJO in 2001. "We mocked up the demo tape for 'Suspect Device' as a fire bomb. One record company threw it in a bucket of water." Burns later elaborated that the friend depicted in 'Wasted Life' had been recruited while the two of them played in the street, and later died under the wheels of a bus he was trying to rob to raise funds for the paramilitary. The opening line, 'I could be a soldier', stemmed directly from this friend's words. Others later claimed that the friend concerned had actually left the 'organisation' by the time his death occurred, but that hardly robs the song of its emotive legacy.

They could only afford an initial press run of 350 copies, folded and glued by the band themselves, and its was symbolically released on St Patrick's Day 1978. One was sent to John Peel by Ogilvie, along with a letter, later reprinted on the inner sleeve of All The Best. "Understand a couple of weeks ago you read out a letter about the new Northern Ireland bands and said you would be interested if any had a record out...." Burns and Ogilvie would have been delighted with a single spin. Instead, Peel played it every night for a week, causing the band and Ogilvie to frantically repress the single.

S

The group was invited to record a flexidisc for local fanzine Alternative Ulster, edited by later Sounds writer Dave McCullough and later NME journalist Gavin Martin. "We were certainly indebted to Alternative Ulster when we started," Burns told So What magazine, "but having said that, you'd read one copy of it and you'd read them all. Every time it came out, which was quite regular, there were reviews of Rudi, the Outcasts and us and that was it. Occasionally there was a bit about a bunch of idiots from way up north called the Undertones who we'd never heard of and that was it." Later, talking to the Guardian in 2003 about the song's inclusion on the compilation Belfast Songs, Burns noted: "It was a song written in the classic punk mode about having nothing to do, because that was the over-riding reality of life in Belfast for a teenager in the mid-70s. Not the fear of riots, or bombs, or whatever. It was the sheer tedium of having nowhere to go and nothing to do when you got there."

When it was realised that the economics of the situation would prevent the flexidisc's release, the band used the song they'd written in the fanzine's honour to make their debut proper with Rough Trade. Years later, following the release of Nobody's Heroes, Alternative Ulster's editor Gavin Martin wrote a piece for the NME challenging SLF's authenticity which still rankles to this day.

Between singles they'd experienced some confidence-sapping record company shenanigans. Island had spent several months setting up a deal that they subsequently reneged on. Matters had progressed to the recording of demos in London with Ed Hollis of Eddie And The Hot Rods producing (including 'Alternative Ulster'). Eventually Chris Blackwell, on his return from Jamaica, stymied the deal. The band, having given up their jobs and moved to England, were devastated, the betrayal later lambasted in song on their debut album. In tribute to their new independent label, they called this riposte 'Rough Trade', which featured a slight lift from the Clash's 'Clash City Rockers'. Later, when Burns found out that Bono, once a big SLF fan, had signed his band to the same despised record company, he was mortified.

Rough Trade, who would also repress copies of 'Suspect Device', were more than pleased to offer the band a temporary home, having seen first hand the healthy sales Peel's patronage of the band had engendered. 'Alternative Ulster' attacked inertia and complacency. Burns would introduce it live as "a song about having nothing to do", and for many it became Stiff Little Fingers' most celebrated song. The sleeve, too, is one of the most impressive of the era, featuring a carefree, laughing scamp perched a few feet above the head of a seemingly oblivious, armed British soldier. They followed it up with a 28-date UK tour supporting the Tom Robinson Band in the autumn of 1978. "They gave us a big break when we really needed it," Burns later recalled."

Inflammable Material, produced by Geoff Travis of Rough Trade and Mayo Thompson (Red Crayola), was one of the great debut albums of the punk era, entering the charts at 14. "Inflammable Material is the classic punk record," trumpeted Paul Morley in the NME. "A crushing, contemporary record brutally inspired by blatant, bitter rebellion and frustration, that supplies neither questions or answers but consistently explodes: 'Fuck Off: Leave Me Alone' in the most scalding, dirty way since the set slogans, Anarchy In The UK and White Riot, were laid to rest." Chris Westwood in ZigZag was even more effusive. "In terms of pure, sustained, venomous rock'n'roll assault, Inflammable Material will snap up just about any record you care to name-check, and devour it for luncheon."

The two singles were standouts, so too 'Wasted Life'. It's arguable whether or not the insularity of the concerns expressed actually strengthened the overall impact or detracted. Burns, for one, would later object to being painted into a corner marked "political songwriter", which he somewhat encouraged by spouting "If we can stop a kid from picking up a gun and shooting somebody we'll have achieved something worthwhile" as a partial doctrine. But for now the conviction was unmistakable. 'White Noise' parodied racist stereotypes, though the line 'Ahmed Is A Paki' was distasteful to some, including Newcastle's Community Relations Officer who thought the song might cause "bitterness and hatred" without ever looking at the lyric as a whole. 'Barbed Wire Love' was throwaway teen romance schlock making use of paramilitary vernacular, while 'Breakout' was inspired by Burns' time as an accounts clerk. And while the inclusion of a version of Bob Marley's 'Johnny Was' was undoubtedly influenced by the Clash's similar ventures into Jamaicana, it offered a brilliant distillation of reggae's hypnotic backbeat with punk's tenacity via Burns's growling, wracked vocal. Nowadays Burns is a little embarrassed by the playing and production, but he has no need to be.

Afterwards Faloon decided he wanted to return to Ireland and 'settle down' (a decision Burns would lament in 'Wait And See'). Jim Reilly, an ex-pat Belfast man currently working for his uncle in Sheffield, and the band's first Catholic member, was installed in his stead after ringing the band up and convincing them of his merits. Beforehand, Ogilvie had talked of the band containing both Protestants and Catholics, and an equal division in the band. Again, Brian Young of Rudi disputes this. "The 'two plus two' was a publicity stunt dreamed up by Gordon Ogilvie. The press release he handed out at their first UK gig in the Electric Ballroom was sickening, clichéd rubbish about bombs and bullets and hands across the barricades etc - designed cynically to wring the approval of guilt-ridden English liberal twats. We laughed, cos we thought it was so dumb that no-one with a brain or a mental age of more than six would fall for it, but we wuz wrong!"

Reilly would add a certain level of anarchy to all matters Stiff Little Fingers, variously appearing naked, or dressed as a chicken or gorilla, as the occasion demanded. He was in place in time for 'Gotta Getaway', a self-explanatory but irresistible rejection of the suffocating dearth of possibility that attended a young man's life in working class Northern Ireland –

written in the realisation that London was calling. Its construction was flawless, a staccato intro led by Burns' vocal eventually giving way into a plunging, overlapping bass and guitar run. It was also their final single with Rough Trade.

Their breakthrough was cemented by a busy touring schedule. The band were interviewed by Radio Metro in Newcastle, which was all going swimmingly until Jake let slip the word 'crap' off air. "He played the Sky record," he recalled to Dissident magazine, "and faded us out and actually leaned across and said, 'You can't say that. I said, you can't say what? He said, 'You can't say crap, the station manager's listening. If he hears you say crap, he'll be down here, I'll lose my job.' So, I said right, fair enough, OK. So it came to the end of the record and he went, 'Right, those were Sky and with me I've got Jake Burns and Ali McMordie of Stiff Little Fingers. Ali, what do you think of Sky?' Ali said, 'I think they're fucking shite.' That was it, he threw us out, and Ali said: 'I didn't say crap!'" Hardly a Bill Grundy moment, but their hosts were mortified and refused to play SLF from that point. However, Burns would at least get a song out of it – 'You Can't Say Crap On The Radio', which collapsed into a version of the Clash's 'Capitol Radio' at its close.

After joining Tom Robinson for a Rock Against Racism show at Alexandra Palace, they negotiated a new contract with Chrysalis for a reported advance of £30,000 – though Burns claimed Pye had offered £100,000 and their own label, but weren't prepared to grant total artistic control to the band. Aware of the cries of sell-out that had already accompanied their decision to relocate from Belfast, their first effort for a major, an attack on international mercenaries entitled 'Straw Dogs', was the least commercial song they could come up with. It was backed by the Metro-inspired 'You Can't Say Crap On The Radio'. Nobody's Heroes followed in short order, produced between November 1979 and January 1980 by Doug Bennett, reaching the UK Top Ten. Though most would nominate their debut as SLF's finest moment, the better-realised songs here, while still channelled through Burns's scorched, emphatic vocals, were beginning to stretch the band and its audience. Only 'I Don't Like You' fails to hit the spot, and while critics at the time challenged the group over its cover of Jerry Dammers' 'Doesn't Make It Alright', it sounds solid enough twenty years down the line. So too 'Bloody Dub', a version of 'Gotta Getaway's B-side 'Bloody Sunday'. Whether or not they'd pinched the idea from the Clash, SLF actually had developed a marvellous way of embracing reggae without making it seems like cheap tourism or pale imitation.

The keynote title-track, inspired by fan letters, sought to demystify the group as a rock'n'roll band, whilst pushing self-reliance, sentiments that were antithetical to accepted wisdom concerning fan-band relationships. 'At The Edge', released as a single, was based around the clichés Jake would hear fall from his father's mouth, whilst attacking the vision of selfish personal advancement that underscored this bleak vision – lessons in "How to kick someone and run away". Their only A-side written without Ogilvie's involvement, it completed a fantastic trilogy, following 'Wasted Life' and 'Gotta Getaway', of compelling essays on the need to escape a suffocating domestic environment, wherein notions of difference were treated with hostility. But the lyrical focus was no longer simply the Troubles, but the eternal negotiations that take part between generations. The anti-jingoism of 'Fly The Flag', complete with a guitar-led approximation of 'Rule Britannia' that echoed Hendrix's reclamation of 'The Star Spangled Banner', was another highlight (though the John Peel session version is preferable). Burns's songwriting was not just rooted in rejection and despondency, but the more optimistic premise that a life existed outside these narrow confines – nowhere better expressed than in the Faloon-inspired 'Wait And See'.

'At The Edge' was the band's most successful single, reaching 15 in the charts, while the B-side boasted an example of their traditional 'Silly Encores'. The versions of 'Running Bear' and 'White Christmas' confirmed that Stiff Little Fingers were incapable of piety. Indeed, they took the Silly Encores principle to its logical conclusion at Aylesbury Friar's on their Go For It tour by playing a 20-minute set in Halloween masks as the Wingnuts, before they were pelted off stage. Years later, Q magazine took the band to task for their version of 'White Christmas' and dubbed it 'hopeless'. "I recall at the time of recording the members of the band describing it as 'hopeless' and the producer leaving the studio with his head in his hands muttering: 'You can't seriously put this out,' Burns responded. 'Coupled with the fact we rehearsed this number for at least ten minutes during a soundcheck, you could at least stretch to 'absolutely hopeless'."

A double A-side, 'Tin Soldiers' and 'Nobody's Hero', followed. 'Tin Soldiers' was again written from personal experience, this time of a friend who had joined the armed forces as his post-school options narrowed. At the time, young recruits were sold on the premise that they were signing up for "just three years", without being told that the first two of these, while they were training, didn't count. As such, it neatly bookends 'Wasted Life' by depicting the 'legitimate' soldier's options as no more rewarding than the paramilitary volunteer's. Building songs around the experiences of friends and acquaintances was a trademark lyrical device. They also made their American debut playing at Trax in New York on 1 October 1980 to a packed house.

'Back To Front', inspired by the fresh waves of skinhead seaside violence, saw them drop the ball for the first time. The far more effective B-side, 'Mr Fire Coal Man', was a version of the Wailing Souls' oldie Jake had discovered on a reggae compilation. In the meantime Burns also made his first and only acting appearance in the BBC Play For Today Iris In The Traffic, which also featured 'Alternative Ulster'. He was said to be so embarrassed on watching the result he vowed never to be so foolish again.

By Go For It in 1981, Burns' was moderating his vocal bluster and allowing the music more space to breathe. Pop hooks were breaking out like it was springtime on the Garvaghy Road. The lyrics, too, were again progressively less specific, though still intensely personal, as Burns attempted to divest himself of the "albatross" of being a political rocker and, one suspects, a political punk rocker. Amusingly, this transformation came at almost exactly the same point as the Undertones, tarred with the reverse side of that brush, were beginning to explore issues that they'd traditionally steered clear of. "When we started writing the Go For It album," Burns later recalled in the sleevenotes to its reissue, "our rough ambition was to write eleven singles. That was the idea. To get back to what an 'album' originally was... It didn't quite pan out like that. In fact, we were in the studio recording, without a title cut even written. And it only got written because Henry physically stopped me from going down the pub with the others, to write the thing!"

Certainly there were elements of the album bound to startle existing fans – Q-Tips guested on 'Silver Lining', which Ogilvie wanted released as the first single in preference to 'Just Fade Away', Jake's touching memoir about ending a relationship with a girlfriend who was becoming too clingy. According to Reilly in an interview with Barricade fanzine, "We'd just put down the backing track. It sounded a bit 'ampy' and we were wondering what we could put on it and then we thought about some brass, so we tried it and it sounded all right. Bit of a change." 'Hits And Misses' was the first of a number of pro-feminist songs the band would record, berating the wifebeater next door. 'Gate 49', sung by Cluney, was titled after the departure point for Ireland at Heathrow airport. For many, however, the album's keynote was 'Piccadilly Circus', wherein Burns related the tale of his friend's stabbing in London – after he'd arrived from Northern Ireland to escape the Troubles. Reilly left after the accompanying tour took them to France, later to drum with Red Rockers and Rain Dogs, before returning home to Belfast and hooking up with former members of the Starjets in the Dead Handsomes. He was replaced by former TRB drummer and 'token Brit', Dolphin Taylor. The irascible Reilly kindly offered to sell him his drum kit, but Dolphin was already sorted, thank you.

Taylor was on board for the '£1.10 Or Less' EP, titled after its budgetary concession to fans, which actually included some of the finest songs the band would record – and some awful artwork. By now they really had shed their punk skins. The material, however, was no less heartfelt or impassioned, particularly 'Listen', another song written by Burns following the thread of a first-hand conversation, while 'Two Guitars Clash' was Cluney's Clash tribute, paraphrasing Culture's reggae hit of the punk period. 'That's When Your Blood Bumps' was Ogilvie's concept about the excitement of encountering a new idea or person.

1982's Now Then, despite its many qualities, effectively killed off Stiff Little Fingers. Its attempts to broaden the band's musical reference points were rejected outright by long-term supporters, and no new audience was endeared by its clean, contemporary sound. There was some good and some exceptional songwriting on offer, not least the single 'Bits Of Kids', which Jake wrote after talking to Ogilvie's girlfriend about the kids she taught. Dolphin's 'Stands To Reason', questioning accepted truths printed in the newspapers, was impressive too. Their cover of Nicky Thomas's 'Love Of The Common People', which inspired Paul Young to record a hit version, continued their dalliance with reggae. 'The Price Of Admission', the band's first acoustic ballad, even featured Dolphin on the mellotron. 'Is That What You Fought The War For?' was the most popular song with fans – at least those prepared to listen, of which there were now a diminishing number.

Despite the album reaching 24 in the UK charts, it was obvious the group were stalling. If they were in any doubt, half-filled venues reiterated the fact. Stiff Little Fingers, in essence, wanted to be a rock'n'roll band, and their audience didn't want a rock'n'roll band, as Jake told me in 1991. "Even on the first album we were pointing towards it. We've always owned up to what we are, and what made us. We were caught in a quandary by being too honest. We tried to progress and our audience followed us so far, then just said: 'no, we can't follow you any more' and gave up." As well as 'Suspect Device' fatigue, he'd had just about enough of violent audiences. And some of the punk rituals were getting him down. "If I see the person who's gobbing on me after this gig," he announced on tour in Dundee, "I'm gonna boot his face through his head." At the same gig Dolphin kicked his drum aside in order to assault a member of the audience. "He must have had a good reason for it," surmised his singer, before discovering that the miscreant had been flicking cigarette butts at McMordie. By the time 'The Price Of Admission', coupled with Cluney's 'Touch And Go' emerged as a single, Stiff Little Fingers were no more.

Burns sent out a letter to the fan club explaining the decision. "There was nothing wrong with the material the band was writing… except it lacked ambition. There was no sense of adventure and experiment about it any more. In other words, we had become safe and boring. The things I hoped we would never become." Though Burns and the others talked of new horizons, there was some acrimony over the decision. For a while Cluney and McMordie toyed with the idea of keeping the band together without Burns, with Ogilvie's assistance. "Obviously Jake's departure means the end of Stiff Little Fingers as we know it," he told Melody Maker. "I hope to continue writing songs with Jake and will back him in what he is going to do. And, if what Henry, Ali and I are working on pans out as well as we expect, we hope to produce records, probably with an official change of name to simply SLF." But the others quickly realised this would be futile. "Apart from the fact that we hated each other," McMordie recalled to Ink Disease, "we were living out of each other's pockets while we were on tour. We were four guys thrown together, the only thing we had in common was a desire to get out of Belfast, and to make noise, and get away with it. Get away from the shit called life."

Burns formed the Big Wheel, which allowed him to indulge his Elvis Costello and Who fixations, and secretly played guitar on a few Bananarama records, before working for 'Hairy Cornflake' Dave Lee Travis and his fellow Radio 1 DJ Bruno Brookes. "I found myself drifting more and more towards the mainstream and when I sat in a pub one night defending a Jason Donovan single, I realised that was the day I had to get out." McMordie joined Friction Groove and wrote the song 'Jerusalem' for Sinead O'Connor, while Dolphin toured and recorded with Spear Of Destiny.

In 1987 McMordie phoned Burns to see if he wanted to see a TRB reunion gig and hook up with Dolphin again – it was the first time the former band members had spoken in five years. Although he couldn't make that, they did arrange to meet up for a drink. Over a few jars they bemoaned their current impoverishment. Bereft of the funds to make it back to Ireland to see their parents for Christmas, they thought a few reunion gigs might provide sufficient funds. McMordie posited that they should call it "the legend returns" tour. The others fell about laughing.

The size, and enthusiasm, of the audiences they attracted genuinely shocked them. "I've got no explanation for it," Burns shrugged to Andy Peart. "I was talking to Eddie from the Alarm and he asked how we'd become legends, and I just said it's easy, take five years off and don't do anything." Attendances were greatly in excess of those they had previously experienced. Over two nights at the Brixton Academy in 1988 more than 10,000 attended. Which rather naturally prompted the thought of permanently reforming the band. Especially as Burns was finding it impossible to fulfil his contractual obligations to the BBC while touring, and having just married, wanted some kind of permanence to his life. He only had a six-month revolving contract with the BBC in any case.

Since the early 1990s Stiff Little Fingers have tried to establish themselves as a going concern rather than bait for forty-something punk nostalgics. They were just about to execute plans to return to the studio when McMordie decided he couldn't dedicate himself to an album and tour. He elected instead to concentrate on his Ghostwood management company, building on his experiences tour-managing Simply Red, before working extensively with Moby. With about a week to go before a scheduled tour of Japan, Burns went to see Bruce Foxton of the Jam in his new band the Rhythm Sisters. Foxton, Burns and Dolphin had previously worked on unreleased demos as Go West back in 1983, which were only aborted because Arista waved a solo contract under Foxton's nose. Six years later, he became the obvious candidate to replace McMordie. He had to withstand barbs along the lines of 'Alternative Woking' or 'Suspect Device (In Surrey)', but he remained with the band for close on 15 years. One additional quality he brought with him, according to Jake, was enthusiasm and discipline – being a great one for "cracking the whip" in the studio alongside the self-confessed old lags.

The first glimpse of new material, recorded over six weeks during June and July 1991, came with 'Beirut Moon', an attempt to persuade the British government to move their carcasses in order to help free John McCarthy, held hostage in the Lebanon. The song was inspired by Jake watching an interview with American Frank Reid on the news after his release from captivity, prompted by his country's diplomatic intervention, in which he confirmed that both McCarthy and Keenan were alive. Asked if there was any chance they would be released, he replied "not until your government does something about it". I was there to interview the band at the video shoot. When I got back home, the news had broken of McCarthy's release. It didn't help that the IBA claimed that it contravened section three of the broadcasting act, stating that any political statement has to be 'impartial' in its treatment of the government. Given that royalties from the single were being donated to the Friends Of John McCarthy, this seemed a little myopic.

Flags And Emblems, though lacking the punch of their earlier albums, touched on similar concerns. "We didn't have to go looking for the subjects on the album," Burns told Andy Peart. "They are all products of the mismanagement of this country over the last twelve years. If anything, the world seems slightly worse than it was when Stiff Little Fingers started and the Tories had just come into power. The subjects are all easy targets and someone said to me, how can you still find things to be angry about, but how can you not?" However, perhaps he'd unconsciously highlighted the album's weaknesses by invoking the phrase easy targets – alongside a completely unconvincing production. 'Each Dollar A Bullet' raged against the funding of terrorist organisations from America. 'It's A Long Way To Paradise (From Here)' competently documented the grind of everyday life, while Cluney's 'Johnny 7', named after the toy gun, expressed his desire to return to the innocence of childhood. But 'Stand Up And Shout' and 'No Surrender' were SLF by numbers, and nowadays Burns will admit it's "not the shining light of my career".

Stiff Little Fingers continued to gig sporadically over the next four years, sometimes featuring Dave Sharp and Ian McCallum as additional live guitarists following the acrimonious departure of Cluney. He complained to the press of being "stabbed in the back" and that Burns had lacked the courage to tell him personally. Burns reasoned his style "had become too thrash metal to suit our material". Get A Life followed in 1994, with the thirteen songs drawn down from twenty-one written for the purpose. Despite the rigorous selection procedure and greater conviction than Flags And Emblems, it again failed to match the group's late-70s/early-80s peak, despite a couple of co-writing credits for Foxton on 'Forensic Evidence' and 'When The Stars Fall From The Sky'. The single excerpted was 'Can't Believe In You', its lyric inspired by a tour of Germany shortly after the Berlin Wall collapsed. "The kids that had grown up under the Communist regime in the east had suddenly been given, if you like, their freedom," Burns told Dissident, "and the first thing they did was shave their heads and start setting fire to Jewish premises again. It was just astonishing to watch how they had come from one totalitarian regime and instantly embraced the exact opposite, the mirror image." 'Baby Blue' addressed politics closer to home – effectively the notion that a child born when Stiff Little Fingers' first album came out would have known nothing but Tory governments. 'Harp' was based on a derogatory term used in Boston to describe Irish immigrants.

By 1996 Steve Grantley, formerly of Jake's Big Wheel project, was the latest incumbent as drummer, with Dolphin concentrating on business and family concerns, while McCallum also become a permanent member. Their third post-reformation studio album, Tinderbox, followed in 1997. The oddball extra here was a version of Grandmaster Flash's 'The Message'. "A lot of people will be surprised at SLF attempting a rap tune," Jake admitted, "but I think we've added enough of ourselves to make it blend with the main body of what we do. Certainly the themes of disenfranchisement, disillusionment and a desire to better yourself are central to everything we've tried to do since day one." The track that picked up most press was the perceived Paul Weller dig 'My Ever Changing Moral Stance'. Parodying the Style Council song of similar title, the lyric clearly related to the bad blood between Weller and his former bandmates in the Jam. 'Hurricane' and 'You Can Move Mountains' were worthy additions to the canon. But most of the songs documented relationships and not all rang true, possibly due to the limited amount of studio time the band could afford.

Hope Street, packaged with a Greatest Hits selection in the UK, followed in 1999. At this point, it was the most worthwhile of their post-break up records. 'The Last Train From Wasteland' is a good effort at celebrating the partial cessation of hostilities in Northern Ireland which inspired their original songbook. 'Half A Life' and the title-track are equally strong. Against expectations, it seemed the reformed SLF were finally beginning to hit their stride. Not that many outside the fanbase were interested, but that camp entails a fairly substantial and loyal core, one swelled by numerous appreciative comments from upstart American punkers, which is seemingly sufficient to keep the band in business. The US issue instead featured a live CD, taken from a King Biscuit radio broadcast of their Newcastle Riverside concert in September 1998. Perhaps SLF live CDs are still a novelty in America. They ain't over here.

2003's Guitar And Drum was better still, opting for a more mature, and graceful, accommodation of energy and pop hooks which harked directly back to the unfairly overlooked Now Then. The key track was the Joe Strummer tribute, 'Strummerville', in which Burns acknowledged his chief inspiration. Burns had just left Tribeca in New York when the planes struck the twin towers. He was subsequently asked by the girlfriend of an English SLF fan who had lost his life to write something for his funeral. That experience informed 'Achilles Heel', while the 'new punk' generation raised his ire on the title-track, in which Burns confessed to being a "cynical old bastard" – which is actually the last thing he ever was.

At the start of 2006 news filtered through that Bruce Foxton was amicably ending his tenure with the band, with Ali McMordie rejoining. Which means they've doubled their (almost) original member quotient, but one can imagine the set list will no longer include 'Smithers-Jones'. Meanwhile another original member, Jim Reilly, cropped up in 2004 with his chip off the old block band Jimmy Reilly's Little Fingers. They played their debut show at the West Belfast Festival in 2004.

In summary? Jake seems a stand-up guy to me. SLF have made some duff albums, but at the moment are probably doing their best work since the late-70s. To begrudge them their right to continue as working musicians is to take those original punk values at face and fake value. They may never write another song that will touch people's hearts in the manner that 'Gotta Getaway', 'At The Edge' or 'Piccadilly Circus' did, but with 'Strummerville', for one, they're getting closer again.

S

DISCOGRAPHY:

(BUYER'S GUIDE: With the exception of the Pistols, Stiff Little Fingers' discography is punk rock's most daunting minefield. The surfeit of live albums was bad enough, but then the flood of concert CDs cannibalising tracks from previously issued albums just got silly. If you think the following list is a testing read, just imagine what it felt like to compile. However, a purchasing plan is simplicity itself. Stick with the four studio albums – I especially recommend Nobody's Heroes, though nine out of ten Fingers' fans will point you towards Inflammable Material as base camp. If you fancy a live album avoid Hanx! and Live And Loud! or any of its numerous variations. The later-period St Patrix or Fly The Flags are both better, so too See You Up There, if you can find a copy (it's currently part of the Anthology package). Guitar And Drum is the best of their reformation efforts and is well worth a listen – though it's not very fashionable to say so. Hope Street is pretty good too. All The Best remains a great compilation, although there are several excellent album tracks you'll be missing out on if you rely on it to the exclusion of everything else – and Stiff Little Fingers were never, by their own admission, a singles band)

Suspect Device/Wasted Life 7-inch (Rigid Digits SRD-1 March 78)

Alternative Ulster/78 R.P.M. 7-inch (Rigid Digits/Rough Trade RT-004 October 1978)

Inflammable Material LP (Rigid Digits/Rough Trade ROUGH-1 February 1979) (reissued on CD in March 1989 by EMI, CDP 792105-2. 2001 reissue, EMI 535884, adds 'Suspect Device' (single version; i.e. thereby reinstating the album version) plus 1978 R.P.M.' and a Jake interview with Alan Parker)

Gotta Getaway/Bloody Sunday 7-inch (Rigid Digits/Rough Trade RT015 May 1979)

Straw Dogs/You Can't Say Crap On The Radio 7-inch (Chrysalis CHS-2368 September 1979)

At The Edge/Silly Encores 7-inch (Chrysalis CHS-2406 February 1980)

Nobody's Heroes LP (Chrysalis CHR-1270 March 1980) (reissued on CD in March 1989 by EMI, CDP792106-2. 2001 reissue on EMI adds 'Bloody Sunday', 'Straw Dogs', 'You Can't Say Crap On The Radio' and the second part of Alan Parker's interview with Burns)

Nobody's Hero/Tin Soldier 7-inch (Chrysalis CHS-2424 May 1980)

Back To Front/Mr. Fire Coal Man 7-inch (Chrysalis CHS-2447 July 1980)

Hanx! LP (Chrysalis CHR-1300 September 1980) (tracks taken from shows at Rainbow, London, July 20 1980, and Friar's, Aylesbury July 25 1980. Still the SLF live album by which all the many others are judged, although it draws on only two albums' worth of material and everyone involved with the band hated it at the time. Reissued on CD in February 1989 on Fame-EMI FACD-3215, then again in 2001 with the addition of the Silly Encores versions of 'Running Bear' and 'White Christmas', and the third part of Alan Parker's interview with Jake)

Just Fade Away/Go For It/Doesn't Make It Alright (live) 7-inch (Chrysalis CHS-2510 March 1981)

Go For It LP (Chrysalis CHR-1339 April 1981) (reissued on CD in February 1989 on Fame-EMI, FACD-3216, plus 'Back To Front' as a bonus track. 2002 Captain Oi! reissue, AHOY CD 151, additionally adds 'Mr Fire Coal Man' and 'Doesn't Make It Alright (live)' and features Jake Burns' memories plus a liner note from Mark Brennan.)

Silver Lining/Safe As Houses 7-inch (Chrysalis CHS-2517 May 1981)

R.E.P. £1-10 Or Less 7-inch EP (Chrysalis CHS-2580 January 1982)

Listen/Sad-Eyed People/That's When Your Blood Bumps/Two Guitars Clash

Talkback/Good For Nothing 7-inch (Chrysalis CHS-2501 April 1982)

Bits Of Kids/Stands To Reason 7-inch (Chrysalis CHS-2637 August 1982) (also issued as a 12-inch, CHS-12-2637)

Now Then... LP (Chrysalis CHR-1400 September 1982) (early copies came with free poster. Reissued on CD in December 1994 by EMI Fame, CDFA 3306, then again by EMI Gold, CDGOLD 1090, in April 1997. Far more worthwhile than either, however, is the repackaging by Captain Oi! in 2002, AHOY CD 152, adding 'Listen', 'Sad-Eyed People', 'That's When Your Blood Bumps', 'Two Guitars Clash' from the R.E.P £1-10 Or Less EP, plus 'Good For Nothing'. Mark B and Jake again handle the sleevenotes)

The Price Of Admission/Touch And Go 7-inch (Chrysalis CHS-2671 April 1983)

Beirut Moon/Stand Up And Shout/Interview CD EP (Essential ESSX 2035 November 1991)

Flags And Emblems LP (Essential ESSLP-171 November 1991) (also available as CD, ESSCD-171. Reissued at low-price, Dojo DOJO CD 243 in July 1995)

Can't Believe In You 12-inch EP (Essential ESS-T-2035 January 1994)

Can't Believe In You/Silver Lining (unplugged)/Listen (unplugged)/Wasted Life (unplugged) (also released as CD, ESS-X-2035 with different tracks: Can't Believe In You/Can't Believe In You (extended version)/Alternative Ulster (live)/Smithers-Jones (live) (live tracks from Pure Fingers Live – St Patrix CD)

Get A Life CD (Essential ESSCD 210 February 1994) (the US CD version, Taang! 100, features 'unplugged' versions of 'Silver Lining', 'Listen' and 'Wasted Life'. Reissued April 1997 as ESMCD 488)

Harp/Shake It Off/Not What We Were (Pro Patria Mori) 12-inch (Essential ESS T 2040 June 1994) (also released as a CD-EP, ESS X 2040. 'Shake It Off' and 'Not What We Were' taken from April 1993 "Go West" demos)

Tinderbox CD (Spitfire SLF 100 July 1997) ('No Barriers' is uncredited on the sleeve. In 2003 EMI re-released the album, featuring a new sleeve and notes by Alan Parker. It additionally included five extra tracks from the Live At Newcastle Riverside CD, available to fans at the Hope Street premiere, and included as a bonus package on the US release of Hope Street).

And Best Of All... Hope Street CD (EMI 1999) (includes bonus Best Of CD. Americans got a bonus live CD of tracks recorded in 1998 and 1999)

Guitar And Drum CD (EMI 5914802 August 2003)

ARCHIVE RELEASES:

All The Best (Singles A's and B's) dbl LP (Chrysalis CTY-1414 January 1983) (reissued in September 1991 on EMI Fame CD EM 1428. Still a great collection, despite the sniffy NME swipe: "Let's hear it for the Bill Oddie of Airfix Kit punk. Only in a diseased economic

S

situation could people make a living out of such utterly useless product")

The Peel Sessions 12-inch EP (Strange Fruit SFPS004 September 1986)

Johnny Was/Law And Order/Barbed Wire Love/Suspect Device (recorded 12 September 1978, broadcast 18 September 1978. Reissued on cassette in May 1987, and on CD, SFPSCD004, July 1988)

Live And Loud dbl LP (Link LINK-LP-026 April 1988) (recorded at the National Ballroom, Kilburn, 17 December 1987. Reissued on CD September 1989. An OK album, but the pacing of the songs is totally amiss. It sounds like they've been recorded at half-speed)

No Sleep Til Belfast CD (Kaz KAZ CD 6 June 1988) (exactly same tracklisting as Live And Loud)

No Sleep Til Belfast 12-inch (Skunx SLFX-1 June 1988)

Suspect Device (live)/Alternative Ulster (live)/Nobody's Hero (live) (live tracks from Live And Loud/No Sleep Til Belfast)

St Patrix 12-inch (Virgin SLF-1 March 1989)

The Wild Rover/Johnny Was/Love Of The Common People (also available as 3-inch CD; SLFCD-1. Tracks from See You Up There!)

See You Up There! Dbl LP (Virgin VGD 3515 April 1989) (CD version available as double CD VGDCD 3515, and double cassette, VGDC 3515. Recorded live at Brixton Academy, 17 March 1988. The vocals on 'The Wild Rover' are by Cluney. Incidentally, this was released as a direct effort to spike the sales of Live And Loud on Link as a document of their '88 comeback shows)

The Last Time 12-inch (Link LINK-1203 October 1989)

The Last Time/Mr Fire Coal Man/Two Guitars Clash (recorded live at Brixton Academy 1989, featuring three songs left off their Live And Loud LP)

Live In Sweden LP (Limited Edition LTD-EDT-3-LP October 1989) (also available on CD, LTD-ED T-3 CD. Recorded live in Stockholm, Sweden, 1979. Originally released as the bootleg, Christmas Album/Live In Sweden)

The Peel Sessions (1978-1980) LP (Strange Fruit SFPS 106 November 1989) (also available as a CD, SFR-CD 106. Sessions date from 12 September 1978, 3 September 1979 and 12 February 1980. 'Nobody's Hero' has slightly different lyrics, and it's the second session featuring more raw, less produced versions of the band's second album material that will be of most interest here. It's been suggested that the versions of 'At The Edge' and 'Fly The Flag' are vastly superior, but I'm not sure I'd agree with vastly. Dave Cavanagh provides stoical sleevenotes.)

Greatest Hits Live CD (Dojo DOJO CD 110 May 1991) (same tracks as Live And Loud, except for 'The Only One', which is missing. Reissued no Snapper SMMCD 538 1999)

Alternative Chartbusters CD (Link AOK 103 October 1991) (recorded live at Brixton Academy on 1 October 1988)

Fly The Flags CD (Dojo DOJO-CD-75 December 1992) (live at the Brixton Academy, 27 October 1991. Reissued on Snapper Recall SMMCD 537 1998, and featuring sleevenotes from Jake, and Alan Parker's 'Each Dollar A Bullet' tattoo story)

BBC Radio 1 Live In Concert CD (Windsong WINCD-037 August 1993) (recorded live at the Paris Theatre, London, 8 April 1981, and featuring a Go For It!-dominated set. The bass is mixed a little low, but otherwise, good quality)

Pure Fingers Live – St Patrix 1993 (Dojo DOJO-CD-224 1995) (recorded live at Glasgow Barrowlands on 17 March 1993, with Ricky Warwick of the Almighty guesting on 'Tin Soldiers' and 'Alternative Ulster'. Henry Cluney gets to sing Val Doonican's 'Walk Tall'. The album also included a voucher entitling the redeemer to B's, Live, Unplugged And Demos, below. Reissued by Snapper in 1998 with new sleevenotes by yours truly)

B's, Live, Unplugged, And Demos dbl CD (Dojo DOSLF CD 1 1995) (several demos from the Flags And Enblems period, a rejected potential single, 'The Cosh', 'Johnny Was' from St Patrix that was left off the CD due to time restrictions. 'Shake It Off', 'Not What We Were' comprise the "Go West" demos, then live tracks recorded at Nottingham Rock City on the Get A Life tour, featuring Dave Sharp on guitar. 'The Last Time', 'Mr Fire Coal man' and 'Two Guitars Clash' live at the Brixton Academy 1989, originally released as Link 12-inch LINK-1203. 'Alternative Ulster' also taken from St Patrix show)

Live CD (Music Collection E2 ETDCD 015 1988) (odd live album – old stuff for the first eleven tracks, then a clutch of Flags And Emblems-era songs. 'At The Edge' has what I can only describe as a Sergio Leone via the Glitter Band intro. OK sound quality but no indication of source.)

Tin Soldiers CD (Harry May MAYO CD 105 1999) (inessential odds and ends. It does include the original versions of 'Long Way To Paradise' and 'Stand Up And Shout' from Flags And Emblems, the original version of 'The Cosh' and acoustic versions of 'Listen' and 'Silver Lining', 'Johnny Was', which was omitted from the original Pure Fingers live album, and various live selections from Greatest Hits Live and Fly The Flags)

Live Inspiration dbl CD (Snapper/Recall SMDCD276 March 2000) (Mixed bag of live tracks drawn from Greatest Hits Live aka Live And Loud!, Fly The Flags and St Patrix live albums. Sleevenotes are a work of genius, I tell myself)

Back Against The Wall CD (EMI 5324692 2001) (a collection of non-single album tracks. The cupboard is getting bare)

Anthology 3-CD Box Set (EMI International March 2002) (For an anthology this is pretty uninspiring – basically this is All The Best plus See You Up There, the live disc three, plus a few odds and ends from the early 90s on the second disc, including an interview with Jake around the time of Beirut Moon. As for the packaging – disappointing. We are reliably informed Henry Cluney is now living in some place called Minasotta)

Handheld And Rigidly Digital CD (March 2003) (sold via the website and gigs, much of the material was recorded at the Hope Street premiere in London. Also available as a DVD, which features an uncredited 'Johnny Was' at the end)

Song By Song CD (EMI Gold 5715032 June 2004) (tie-in with the book, subtitled 'a selection of Jake Burns' personal favourites. Somehow I can't see 'Suspect Device' being one of his choices ahead of, say, 'Piccadilly Circus', but there you go)

Stiffs

Ian 'Strang' Barnes (guitar, vocals), Phil Hendriks (vocals, guitar), Tommy O'Kane (drums), Mark Young (bass)

Blackburn's first and finest punk band, the STIFFS formed in 1976 when Barnes and Hendriks were 14-year-old school friends. The initial line-up was assembled in time for a live debut in late 1977. By 1978, Young had been replaced by 'Big' John McVittie on bass – he had the advantage of being able to offer his parents' back garden as a rehearsal space. Gigs at the time were principally built around stock punk covers; the Vibrators, Saints and Ramones etc.

In July 1978 they'd gained sufficient confidence to enter a recording studio, though not necessarily the budget. They cut early versions of originals 'Inside Out' and 'Volume Control' at Pennine Sound in Oldham, but didn't have enough money to purchase the master tape, and had to content themselves with a cassette recording (engineer Paul Adshead retrieved the original tapes 22 years later).

They subsequently cut a second seven-song demo in December 1978 and January 1979 at

a small studio in Great Harwood in Lancashire. From these nerve-affected sessions – the eldest member of the band was still only 17 – they selected the three strongest songs for release as the 'Brookside Riot Squad' EP. Pressed in a batch of 1,000 copies financed by Hendriks' father, these featured self-assembled sleeves for the first 200 copies. But the band was disappointed with the record and ended up hiding them under a bed as soon as they'd sold enough to repay the loan. At this stage the sound was equal parts Thin Lizzy to the Skids.

They had developed exponentially by the advent of their second single, 'Inside Out', backed by 'Kids On The Street'. This time they'd returned to Pennine Sounds in July 1979, and, not wishing to repeat earlier mistakes, were in two minds about releasing the results in case it again failed to capture their live sound – leading to the five-month lag before its release. Despite the first 1,000 copies featuring the labels printed the wrong way, the single sold out of its print run of 5,000 and was played frequently by John Peel, who declared it the "... greatest record in the entire history of the universe", though this may have been a small exaggeration. He booked them for the first of two sessions on 14 February 1980, at which they recorded four songs, 'Let's Activate', a much-improved 'Brookside Riot Squad', 'Best Place In Town' and 'Innocent Bystander'. In attendance was a representative from EMI, who invited them to a meeting with A&R head Chris Biggs the following day.

They dropped anchor with EMI subsidiary Zonophone in 1980, a five-year deal for two singles and an album a year, with Hedley Leyton (brother of 60s pop star John Leyton) becoming their manager. However, in time-honoured fashion, Briggs left the label shortly after signing the band. EMI re-released 'Inside Out' but passed on several new recordings the band submitted. In the meantime they recorded a session for Mike Read which led them to former Mott The Hoople drummer turned BBC producer Dale Griffin, who introduced his former Mott associate Overend Watts as their producer. Three tracks were cut in July, 'Innocent Bystander', 'Volume Control' and 'Best Place In Town', but EMI passed on these and subsequent remixes. They also withheld financial backing during the impasse. By October EMI had relented in so far as they had booked the band into Rockfield Studios under the tutelage of engineer Pat Moran and Rockpile bass player John David.

The results were finally judged acceptable by EMI, and 'Volume Control' was released in November, backed by a September demo version of 'Nothing To Lose'. Although it received good airplay and reviews, it failed to breach the Top 40 and thereafter Leyton went head to head both with the band and EMI, insisting on a new version of 'Innocent Bystander' as the follow-up single, whilst objecting to its hookline. The rows continued through 1981, as did discussions over the scheduling of the band's debut album, though they did return to Pennine in January to record 'Love Is Last Year's Thing' and 'Over The Balcony', the latter a jokey waltz dedicated to Leyton. 'Hogjowls' also originates from this session, a document of studio hi-jinks featuring a variety of musicians, including keyboard player Neil Summersgill. On hearing the tape, Leyton legendarily recalled: "I see you cunts had a good laugh in the studio, then, at someone else's fucking expense." There was a silence. "Don't you like it, then?" asked one impertinent Stiff.

EMI were due to release 'Innocent Bystander', but it was subsequently withdrawn from their release schedule on the grounds that it was "not commercially viable". Sensing the way the wind was blowing, Leyton freed them from their EMI contract and secured a one-off deal with Stiff, a natural home, at least in titular terms. It led to a cover of the Glitter Band's 'Goodbye My Love', recorded and released in February 1981 – "pop with steel toe-caps", according to Carol Clerk at the Melody Maker. They toured with the UK Subs but still failed to make any kind of breakthrough. They prepared for one last shot by recording 'Crazy Mixed Up Emotion' at Pennine Sound in April, produced by Leyton and his assistant Tommy Sanderson. But no-one was interested in releasing it, and Leyton's Marksmen Music offices were destroyed by fire shortly before the liquidators moved in. By July 1981 the Stiffs were bereft of management, record label, master tapes and rhythm section, O'Kane and McVittie having decided enough was enough.

Not giving up the ghost just yet, Hendriks and Barnes attempted to change tack, and made use of free studio time they were entitled to as part of their publishing deal with Marla Music. Complemented by bass player Mark Hurlbutt (of the Strides) and drummer John 'Juice' Mayor they recorded 'Your Passenger' and 'Standing Ovation', but these efforts weren't judged successful (engineer Paul Adshead dismissed them as "shit"). Hurlbutt returned to the Strides as the band drafted Nick Alderson as bass player to play intermittent shows at venues including Dingwalls, their touring curtailed somewhat by the demands of day jobs.

They completed another John Peel session after a cancellation in February 1982. However, as 'Juice' couldn't make the quick turnaround producer Dale Griffin was enticed out of retirement to pound the skins, under the pseudonym Bloody Rich. But the band then split again, Hendriks and 'Juice' reviving the Dork label in 1984 in order to release two singles as Idol Rich, 'Blaze Of Love' and 'Skye Boat Song', the latter backed by a new version of unrecorded Stiffs number 'Stand Up'. However, they achieved little outside of Lancashire (Idol Rich's principal songwriters John Wade and Neil Summersgill would later form the Miracle Birds).

A second Stiffs reformation followed in January 1985, with Mayor and bass player Mark Hurlbutt drafted in as the rhythm section. The sessions resulted in 'The Young Guitars' (credited to Stiffs '85). Former Idol Rich guitarist John Wade also featured on the B-side, 'Yer Under Attack'. Another incarnation of the band developed in mid-1986 after the departure of McVittie and Mayor. Yet another new rhythm section, this time featuring Mark Coleridge (drums; ex-Gary Glitter's touring band, Afraid Of Mice, Glass Torpedoes) and Steve Fielding (bass; the author of a series of crime books) was in place by late 1986. There were over 250 shows between then and the end of 1988. But by Christmas the band was again on hold, having failed to arouse any interest after recording a cover of Keith Marshall's 'Tonight We Dance'. Hendriks: "We'd covered 'Star Studded Sham', a Russ Ballard song recorded by Keith Marshall's former band Hello, in 1987. That led to Hello manager David Blaylock pitching 'Tonight We Dance' at us."

Captain Oi! collated the band's singles and odds and ends for a retrospective in 1999, and there was a live album from bargain booty label Receiver featuring the (almost) original line-up (i.e. McVittie instead of Mark Young). This was digitally recorded at the Stiffs' reunion concert on 31 July 1999, which the participants enjoyed so much they figured they'd give it another go. A year later they took in the Holidays In The Sun Festival in Blackpool. In 2002 Tokyo label 1977 Records released the Stiffs' first single since 1985, 'Four Winds'. They followed this with a four-date tour of Japan. The reaction? "Unbelievable. I didn't expect any of the audiences to know ANY of the songs, but they knew every word to every song and came along with all the old records for signing. After the first bar of the first song there were Japanese kids flying through the air. It was like 1977 again – small, packed clubs, hot and sweaty, just how it should be. The weirdest thing was that by 10pm the gigs were finished and the fans had politely collected their autographs and disappeared off into the night whilst we stood in an empty club wondering where the hell our after show party was gonna be. The biggest culture shock was not having to endure one single drunken pillock falling over or bellowing into our ears and never experiencing even the merest hint of impending violence."

Meanwhile, alongside Hendriks' collaborations with Dave Philp of the Automatics, Overend Watts of Mott, Alan Merrill of the Arrows and Saxon guitarist Graham Oliver, the Stiffs have continued to gig. After another hometown reunion in November 2005, there are plans for new recordings. So, 25 years down the line, is the band still informed by the same spirit? "Exactly the same. It's just the spare time that's harder to find nowadays. We tried (and still try) to make records that we'd like to buy ourselves. There's still no finer noise to me than a couple of filthy guitars chugging away or blasting out some power chords behind a good tune."

Discography:

Brookside Riot Squad 7-inch EP (Dork UR1 April 1979)
Standard English/D.C. Rip/Brookside Riot Squad
Inside Out/Kids On The Street 7-inch (Dork UR2 December 1979) (reissued on Zonophone Z 3 1980)
Volume Control/Nothing To Lose 7-inch (Zonophone Z 14 November 1981)
Goodbye My Love/Magic Roundabout 7-inch (Stiff BUY 86 February 1981)
The Young Guitars/Yer Under Attack 12-inch (Dork UR 7 1985)
Volume Control – Live CD (Receiver RRCD 289 2 June 2000) (recorded 31 July 1999 by Paul Adshead)
Four Winds/Everlasting 7-inch (1977 Records SO41 October 2002; Japan only)

ARCHIVE RELEASES:
The Punk Collection CD (Captain Oi! AHOY CD 102 March 1999)
Stiffology 1981-1988 CD (Angel Air SJPCD 062 2001) (features the 82 Peel session plus demos, alternative takes, the Vicious Rumours single and sleevenotes from their producer Dale Griffin)
Innocent Bystanders CD (EMI 7243 5 32468 2 April 2001)
JAPANESE REISSUES:
Volume Control/Nothing To Lose 7-inch (1977 Records SO39 October 2002)
Goodbye My Love/Magic Roundabout 7-inch (1977 Records SO40 October 2002)

Stinky Toys

Bruno Carone (guitar), Albin Deriat (bass), Jacno (guitar), Elli Medeiros (vocals), Herve Zenouda (drums)

Although they were chronologically the first French punk band, the STINKY TOYS, discovered by Malcolm McLaren, made their initial impression in London. Their diminutive blonde vocalist Elli, who was actually born in Uruguay, takes up the story. "We used to hang out near the Trou Des Halles (in Paris), after they pulled down the central market Les Halles, before they rebuilt the hideous shopping mall, at a T-shirt shop owned by a guy who also produced some records. And Malcolm was there. I was wearing safety pins all over my pants because they were torn and falling apart (nobody was wearing safety pins yet). I also had a fake slice of hard-boiled egg glued to by coat, and Malcolm loved that, so we started talking. I told him we were a band, blah blah blah, and he said he was organising a punk rock festival sometime soon in London. 'Do you guys want to come over?' And we said, sure, yes."

They did indeed play at the 100 Club Punk Festival at Malcy's invitation, but Elli was reportedly upset when a curfew on the first night ensured their performance was held over to the second evening. "We went to London by train and boat. The guys just carried their guitars and drumsticks, so when we got to the 100 Club we had nothing. The Sex Pistols didn't want us to play on their stuff, but the Clash said sure, no problem... We were very drunk. We were drunk most of the time. I remember Siouxsie and the Clash and Subway Sect playing, but I liked the Clash best because they were really politically concerned and musically interesting. The Sex Pistols were more like a boys' band, a group put together by a manager. We couldn't play the first night because there was some kind of curfew. We were there the second night and played. I remember a journalist called Caroline Coon (who wrote that Elli had walked out into the night, kicking tables in her frustration). I never remembered being upset or angry for not playing, but it could be. I remember somebody writing that I tried to kill myself, tried to throw myself under a bus or something, and Johnny Rotten saved me. Quite unlikely..."

The group stayed for a few days and "never stopped drinking". Someone subsequently set up a tour of pubs and small clubs of which Elli has little memory. "People in London are very passionate; they love getting into trends or stuff. The punk scene was super-intense. The gig at the 100 Club got us a lot of press coverage, and although mainly to say they hated us, we had big pictures of us all over the rock press, including a picture of myself on the cover of the Melody Maker. So when we came back to Paris and the Melody Maker came out, everybody freaked out, and all the record companies wanted to sign us." It was Polydor who won the day. Their debut was hardly 'punk', essentially comprising mid-tempo rock tunes. "The first album we recorded at a Parisian studio called Ferber. It took five days. We recorded two songs a day and mixed them. It seemed cool to us. It's really live, old school, like the jazz bands used to record. We didn't give it much thought. I recorded the voice as a guide track, and we just kept those tracks. Of course, we were probably drunk by the end of the day." French websites are fond of describing Stinky Toys as "urban dandies" rather than a punk band, and they may have a point. But certainly the attitude, especially as embodied in Elli, was perfect for the time. "I remember they (Polydor) were really unhappy with the record cover. They stopped the release of the album, trying to make us change it, but we wouldn't. It seemed that nobody had seen a grey cover in those days and were appalled by its ugliness. We thought it was pretty cool. Plus they refused to pay what the photographer asked for our pictures, so we took our pictures in a photomaton (photo booth) and that was beyond what they could take."

Polydor released the band, but any chances of a further deal with a major went up in a plume of smoke, or more accurately, puke, when the band returned to France from London. "I vomited at Kraftwerk's Trans Europe Express party. Kraftwerk's record company wanted to sign us, and they invited us to the party, but after the vomiting and our friend, journalist Alain Pacadis, setting fire to the curtains, they didn't want us anymore."

There was a second album, which wasn't widely distributed outside of France, recorded at Vogue Studios in Paris. "I played the guiro on one song because nobody knew how to do it, and I wanted that sound on a song I sang in Spanish. The music was quite experimental on certain songs, cause all the guys were (good) musicians actually, and some, like the bass player, had crazy ideas that I thought were exciting."

After the group's demise, Jacno enjoyed a big hit with his instrumental track 'Rectangle', from the score to Olivier Assayas's (Irma Vepp, Demonlover, Clean) first short film, which starred Elli. and is where the 'Anne Cherchait L'Amour' song originated from. She also sang on the B-side to 'Rectangle', which was later revived as an advert for children's drink 'Nesquik'. After the split Elli & Jacno, under that billing, released several albums together, most recently Les Nuits De La Pleine Lune, the score to Eric Rohmer's film of the same name. Jacno would also produce Lio and Etienne Daho, who were both fans of the Stinky Toys. Thereafter Medeiros embarked on a solo career, enjoying several hits in France, the biggest of which was 1986's 'Toi Mon Toit'. She acted too, appearing in films including Mamirolle (2000), Jet Set (2000) and the title role in Lulu (2002). She was romantically linked with director Brian De Palma, whom she met in 2000 at a film festival in Cognac, contributing 'Altar' to the soundtrack of his 2002 film Femme Fatale.

So, does Elli's punk upbringing still play a part in her craft? "Well, I think what you really are finally comes out, whatever you do or did. Back then I would say no, I'm not punk, because I wanted to follow my own thing. When everybody started wearing safety pins, I stopped. It never occurred to me to buy torn clothes or shapeless sweaters at Sex for a zillion pounds. My clothes were naturally torn and I kept them together with safety pins, then I moved to something else. I thought "no future" was crap and insincere. Everybody wants some kind of future. But we rejected the kind of future we were offered. A lot of us just didn't make it and it's a shame. But when you're (even in a very personal way) very ambitious about what kind of future you want, and you just won't be OK with the usual thing, and you want to go the whole way whenever you do something, you take risks. I started singing because I started writing, and I started writing to survive, to be relieved of the pain. It's turning the pain into something creative, turning the self destructive energy into something that can come out of you as energy that can connect to others... even if it lasts for the five minutes of a song."

Elli is currently finalising her new solo album. "I've done all kinds of things in my life, but I feel that I'm the same person I was, I've changed and had a lot of experiences, but I have not become a different person. And that's how I make choices, and the choices you make define you as a person. I would like to make choices that wouldn't embarrass the person I was when I was 17 or 18, cause that person is not a foreigner... each time I start walking away from certain things, I walk away, and I walk away and then I realise, I'm back where it's really me."

DISCOGRAPHY:

Boozy Creed/Driver Blues 7-inch (Polydor 2056 630 1977)
Stinky Toys LP (Polydor 2393 174 1977) (aka the 'grey' album)
Stinky Toys LP (Fr. Vogue June 1979) (this is a different collection to their eponymous debut, only issued in France. There it's known as the 'yellow' album)

The Stoat

Richard Wall (bass, vocals), John Waters (guitar, vocals), George Decsy (drums)

THE STOAT came from south west London and were the first band to sign to City Records, which later gave the UK Subs their break, as well as releasing Girlschool's first single. John Waters: "Richard Wall and myself were at school with the founder of City Records, Phil Scott. He had been in the band at school when it consisted of five guitarists and nothing else. After leaving school, George answered a drummer wanted ad in Melody Maker and completed the three-piece line-up. We had done a

few small local gigs, but the release of the singles led to much more work and the Peel session, which added to the 'snowball' effect. Most of our work came through Nigel Morton, who was running Nimoco, a kind of sister agency to City Records from the back of the record shop in Kingston, where it was all based in the beginning."

Their debut single was 'Office Girls'. "I worked in an office at the time, but it wasn't about anyone in particular. It was about the first half-decent song I had written by then, influenced by The Jam, whom we had seen on the pub circuit. And they were in turn influenced by the early Who – which suited Richard and myself, as we were both big Who fans. We'd got into them when Who's Next was released. Their Rainbow, Finsbury Park gig in 1971 was a pivotal point in my life, after which all I wanted to do was be in a working band."

A second single followed, the B-side, 'Loving A Killer', dedicated to Mary Bell, the 11-year-old child murderer. "The Mary Bell thing was just something in the media at that time, and I thought a song about 'loving a killer' kinda fit with the punk thing that was popular then. I don't rate the song highly myself either as a piece of music or a performance." Their Peel session aired on 17 October 1978, comprising 'Tears Run Dry', 'No Way To Say Goodbye', 'Don't Say Nothing' and 'Escorts'. "The Peel session was great fun, but due to our undeveloped musicianship and time pressures, the performance was a little scrappy in places. We didn't get to meet him, but the experience of working in a big BBC studio with a house producer made me want it all the more. We were also paid Musicians Union rates – which was nice!"

'Up To You' was to be their last release, but they remained a popular live attraction. "We played a lot of bigger support gigs and smaller headline venues to a wide spectrum and size of audience in that period (from three to 3,000 punters). There were lots of shows at the Music Machine in Camden. I recall one blues bill where all the musos got back on stage at the end for a jam. But I wasn't quick enough to plug into an amp, so I stuck the guitar lead in my back pocket, which made things interesting when the singer signalled it was my turn to solo. I just posed silently, no-one seemed to notice! We played Dingwalls, the Rock Garden, lots of colleges and universities, pubs, clubs, anywhere really. We expanded to a four-piece and changed the name several times. Got into a running battle with local skinheads in Canterbury one night, nearly lynched by headbangers in a Welsh mining town ("Be 'eavy" was the growled advice before we went on). We were gobbed at by punks on one or two UK Subs supports we did. Played for a crowd consisting of mock Pearley Kings and Queens at a 'Cockney's Night Out' in Clapham. I think George played a 25-minute drum solo for them to 'Do The Lambeth Walk' that night. I can laugh about it now!"

However, much to Waters' regret, they were never able to give up their day jobs. "I completed 25 years in my current job yesterday as it happens," he told me in 2005. "You trade off boredom and disinterest for security in my opinion. I miss being in a band. Still, I'm luckier than some of the characters in this story." That doesn't include George Decsy, incidentally. He is now director of business development for The World Headquarters Of International Yachtmaster Training. No, really.

DISCOGRAPHY:

Office Girl/Little Jenny 7-inch (City NIK 1 November 1977)
Up To You/Loving A Killer 7-inch (City NIK 3 1978)
COMPILATION:
Punk Rock Rarities Vol. 1 CD (Anagram CDPUNK 63 1995; 'Office Girl')

Stormtrooper

Nigel Hutchings (vocals), Jeffery Piccinini (bass), John Pilka (guitar), Mike Lee (drums)

STORMTROOPER's 'I'm A Mess' was briefly the toast of the Soho punks in 1977 – despite the fact that they were a pre-punk Isle of Wight band who had broken up two years previously. Yet the single, with its debauched lyrics about loading up and crashing out in London's West End, fitted the zeitgeist perfectly. So much so that Sid Vicious was regularly seen bearing a "I'm A Mess' button badge, as was Wreckless Eric.

John Waterman of the Isle of Wight's Solent Records described the record's origins thus. "Jeff Piccinini, who was an American living in Havenstreet, came to me with a tape. He said:

'I'm a bit worried about the quality of the tape.' The tape was a bit raunchy, but it was an archetypal punk, or post-punk song." That tape had been recorded in September 1975 and met with complete indifference when mailed to a number of record companies. So they gave up the ghost, playing their last show at the Bath Pavillion on 1 October 1975. But eventually they decided to try to get a single released, enlisting the help of local label Solent. It fit snugly with the emergent punk scene – "And the man from down the 'dilly/Sells me bombers and hash/And I'm always found in Wardour Street/Where the junkies all crash." Solent put out a press release calling it the first punk record and saw it sell 3,000 copies, mainly in the London area, although 500 were exported to New York. Jon Savage called it "grungy but charming", the NME's Tony Parsons decried it for being "as musical as the sound of a commuter getting shoved under a tube train during the rush hour" while Melody Maker considered it "a howling confusion". The 'Mess' badge which accompanied the single "was created by Nigel and myself," notes Piccinini.

Piccinini, under the name Jeff Myles, went on to join Gene October's Chelsea, bringing with him an old Stormtrooper song, 'I'm On Fire'. Stormtrooper had actually reformed in 1978 and cut a version of the song, "but I joined Chelsea after the session and then Chelsea recorded it, which was incidentally their debut US single," notes Piccinini. In 2003 Stormtrooper seemed finally set to get an official CD release, mastered by East Bay Ray of the Dead Kennedys, collating the group's far from prolific output. But then the intended label went under. Piccinini is currently working for a Californian visual and film company and his current band is Revanant, and intends to self-release the Stormtrooper CD at some point in 2006 on his own Purple Raven label.

Discography:

I'm A Mess/It's Not Me 7-inch (Solent SS047 October 1977) (note: 'Harbour Lights' by Stormtrooper on Heartbeat Records is a different band)

ARCHIVE RELEASES:

In 2003 a CD retrospective, I'm A Mess, was announced on Muck Records. This was never released. Instead, there's due to be a limited vinyl release in June 2006 on Italian label Rave Up. This will feature the original four songs cut at the 1975 sessions, plus 'I'm On Fire', recorded in 1978. There will also be a new recording of 'I'm A Mess' from 2003, featuring Nicky Garratt of the UK Subs on guitar and Guns N' Roses drummer Brian, as well as previously unrecorded live songs. A full Stormtrooper retrospective CD will eventually be released in 2006 on Piccinini's own Purple Raven Music label.

Stranglers

Hugh Cornwell (vocals, guitar), Jean-Jacques Burnel (bass, vocals), Dave Greenfield (keyboards), Jet Black (aka Brian Duffy; drums)

Ah, the STRANGLERS. Punk rock's ugly sisters, trying to cram their mildewed feet into year zero's glass slipper. Biographer David Buckley called them "the most despised group in British popular music," and it's not much of an exaggeration. They were truculent, they'd been around the block. They wrote rude songs about the fairer sex. And when they weren't knocking up women, they were knocking out journalists who remained unconvinced of their genius. They didn't look right, either. Dave Greenfield had the worst rock'n'roll haircut since Slade's Dave Hill was at his peak – this at a time when hair and trouser length, famously, was suddenly deemed equivalent to intellectual standing. People were a little suspicious of, but more especially intimidated by, the Stranglers. Yet they enjoyed the greatest sustained success of any of the original punk bands. And yes, they were punk, at least to those who were buying those records, usually against the advice of critics.

It's understandable that ugly people get complexes.

Jet Black, the Old Father Time of punk, who ironically had once attended an institution in Kent entitled The Holy Cross Convent School For Delicate Boys, was in his late 30s when the Stranglers began to make progress. He'd lived through skiffle, never mind the rock'n'roll boom, and once played drums for Julie Andrews' mother. But by the mid-60s music took a back seat as he set up several enterprises, including one of the first home breweries, before buying an ice cream business and accompanying flotilla of vans. But then he suddenly

remembered his ambition to be a drummer and in 1972, after advertising in the Melody Maker, he held auditions in his home-made studio above his off licence. But nothing really happened until he himself responded to a drummer wanted notice in the Melody Maker and ended up speaking to Hugh Cornwell.

Cornwell had dropped out of his research studies in biochemistry to launch a rock band. He'd already been in school group Emile And The Detectives, later the Germs, which included Richard Thompson of Fairport Convention and jazz critic Max Jones' son Nick on drums. They managed a support slot to Helen Shapiro in the 60s before fizzling out. Later, while scraping a third in biochemistry at Bristol University, he would play solo guitar at friend Keith Floyd's chain of restaurants. He then started a PhD, on amino acids and the development of schizophrenia, while studying in Lund, Sweden. There he joined Johnny Sox with singer Gyrth Godwin. Gyrth, like the band's drummer, 'Chicago' Mike, was over from the States to dodge the draft. Johnny Sox also featured guitarist Hans Wärmling and bass player Jan Knutsson. After Cornwell jacked in his doctorate, they ended up moving back to England, though Wärmling declined to make the trip.

Johnny Sox ("very rockabilly, very fast" according to Cornwell) soon became Wanderlust and posted the advert that Jet Black responded to, after the threat of the draft had lifted and their original drummer returned to Chicago. Black invited them to move back to his off licence to rehearse. The third part of the puzzle fell into place when Gyrth Godwin hitched a lift back to Guildford with delivery driver Jean-Jacques Burnel, who was subsequently invited to check the band out at the off licence.

Burnel had grown up the son of French restaurateur parents who'd settled in England. It was an affluent background, though he rebelled at school, conscious that schoolboys didn't necessarily embrace the credo of 'Viva La Difference'. He played classical guitar before becoming infatuated with motorbikes and karate, and there was also a small flirtation with right wing ideologies. By now he'd dropped out of his economics studies at Bradford University. He joined the embryonic Stranglers at Hugh's invitation after Godwin and Jan Knutsson had decided to move on. Cornwell went over to his flat and Guildford and coaxed him into joining over a bottle of wine.

They worked on songs together, Black subsidising the operation by slowly selling off his fleet of ice cream vans, while his two younger charges would help out at the off licence or man the ice cream vans. Hans Wärmling also hooked up with the band after he came to England to look up old friend Cornwell. They were pooling their songwriting resources, and already had the rudiments of 'Go Buddy Go', which Burnel had first written on his guitar in 1967, as well as old Johnny Sox songs 'Country Girl' and a Wärmling/Cornwell collaboration, 'Strange Little Girl'.

Black eventually sold his remaining business interests, including the off licence, and found the band a rehearsal place and living accommodation in a house in the picturesque village of Chiddingfold. They were now playing regular local club dates under a variety of aliases, including Oil And The Slicks, until Burnel was overheard complaining that "The Stranglers have done it again" after one misbegotten performance. It stuck, though they would sometimes play under the extended title Guildford Stranglers. But it was all hand to mouth stuff, their staple diet being tomatoes that Burnel would harvest from the local sewerage works.

From 1974 onwards Black was routinely petitioning record companies without a sniff of an opening, apart from an invitation to record three demos for Reg McLean's Safari Records with Alan Winstanley ('Strange Little Girl', 'My Young Dreams' and 'Wasted'). But it came to naught. All of which was frustrating Wärmling, who was desperate to see the band move ahead and didn't enjoy being in a 'covers' band. The final straw came en route to a wedding reception when it was announced they'd have to cover 'Tie A Yellow Ribbon'. Wärmling, who drowned in 1995, promptly told the band he was leaving. The ice cream van they'd retained as group conveyance pulled over, and out he got.

Cue another Melody Maker advert, in May 1975, looking for a saxophone and keyboard player for a 'soft rock' band. The saxophonist who replied didn't work out. But keyboard player Dave Greenfield, a musical prodigy who'd served his apprenticeship playing airforce and army bases in Germany, did. He'd also been a member of several working bands including Credo and the Initials.

Gigs only improved when they hooked up with Albion management, headed by Derek Savage and Dai Davies. Cornwell hit on the idea of petitioning them with a weekly comic, The Adventures Of Dai And Derek. Suitably flattered, they offered the Stranglers management, alongside their new recruit Ian Grant, a former member of the Angry Brigade who'd already booked Greenfield when he was a member of Brighton-based band, Rusty Butler. The Stranglers began to play better, more receptive venues, such as the Nashville and Red Cow, and subsequently The Hope And Anchor.

Bell Records stumped up £1,000 to Albion Management to record demos in July 1976 at Pebble Beach, Worthing. 'Go Buddy Go' and 'Bitchin'' were the selections. Further sessions at Riverside saw them record 'Grip' and 'Peasant In The Big Shitty'. They then secured further prestigious supports, this time to the Ramones and Flamin' Groovies in July, the first at the Roundhouse, the second at Dingwalls. Which was when the famed set-to occurred between the Clash/Sex Pistols camp and the Stranglers. It's easy to make too much of what happened in the ensuing skirmish. Burnel, not a hardened drinker, had consumed two bottles of red wine and was certainly the instigator. There are various conflicting reports, but it would seem any potential violence proper was averted by the actions of the Stranglers' biggest, and toughest, early fan, Dagenham Dave, who threw John Lydon into a wall. But it meant the Stranglers were, even within a subculture they'd helped to create, further isolated. "We were totally ostracised," Cornwell confirmed to William Church. "Suddenly it wasn't hip to be seen talking to us. It was just because we had keyboards and our keyboard-player had a moustache. And we didn't wear the punk uniform, the safety pins and shredded clothes. Everyone was so super-aware of how they were being seen. It was handbags, basically."

The band had by now acquired its famous, and feared, following. The Finchley Boys, modelling themselves on Burnel's machismo, were honoured in song in the lyrics of 'Burning Up Time'. Which didn't please Dagenham Dave one iota. He ended up challenging a half dozen of them to a fight at the 100 Club, resulting in a fractured skull for him and sundry injuries to the Finchley Boys. A while later, he would be excised from the studio by producer Martin Rushent while the group recorded their debut album, and, with girlfriend Brenda leaving him, took his own life by jumping off Tower Bridge. He was, of course, immortalised in song himself by the band with the eponymous 'Dagenham Dave'.

Meantime, they were still unsigned. Fascinatingly, CBS had made them the subject of a market research exercise, before concluding they were too old and grizzled to be successfully taken to market. Assistance came in the form of Andrew Lauder at United Artists, whom Dai Davies had tapped up. He came to see them, again supporting Patti Smith on her return to the UK in October 1976. He subsequently checked them out in December at a specially convened live rehearsal. Convinced, he tabled a £40,000 advance. What he didn't know was that a few minutes earlier, Cornwell and Burnel had been rolling round the floor wrestling with each other, after Burnel turned up late.

UA wanted to get product out quickly. A live show was recorded at the Nashville in December 1976, but the tapes weren't good enough. It was decided to record a conventional, studio-based album first. UA's in-house producer Martin Rushent, at that point best known for his work with Shirley Bassey, was despatched to work on their debut single, to be recorded at TW Studios in Fulham, with Alan Winstanley as engineer. '(Get A) Grip (On Yourself)' was Cornwell's account, written in Chiddingfold, of the band's life and tribulations to date. The saxophone break came at the suggestion of Dai Davies, who dragged in his friend Eric Clarke, a coal miner from Wales fresh from his shift down the pit. It reached number 44 in the UK charts despite a week's sales being unaccounted for due to a clerical error.

An album, tentatively titled Dead On Arrival, was scheduled for April 1977, but United Artists brought the date forward by a month due to the 'buzz' surrounding the band. The album title switched to Rattus Norvegicus after Paul Henry, UA's art director, stumbled upon the rat by moonlight image, making the thematic link with the group's early standard 'Down In The Sewer'. The band also elected to dump some of their older, more melodic material, including songs like 'Strange Little Girl', 'Promises', Charlie Boy', 'I Know It' etc. There was a conscious decision to go with the new climate and stick with the harder songs that were going down well live. In keeping with that, Rushent pushed Burnel's 'barracuda' bass sound to the fore. It was already a huge sonic characteristic due to his employment of a creaking cabinet and the way his classical training allowed him to effectively play it as a lead instrument.

The reviews were generally good, though NME's Phil McNeill, who'd had his runs in with the band before, decried the band for their sexism, setting up something of a template for media-band relations. 'Peaches', actually written about Burnel and Cornwell's adventures running a PA in Peckham for reggae bands, and intended to reflect the voyeuristic feeling of being the only white faces in the crowd, came in for most criticism. But there's something deeply comic and overblown about the peeping tom lyric, arguably the first in the syntax of popular music to include the word 'clitoris'. 'Sometimes', which unbeknownst to critics was a song Cornwell wrote after physically striking his girlfriend when he'd found out she'd been unfaithful, also came in for censure. Julie Burchill later laid into the band for its public pillorying of writer Caroline Coon in 'London Lady', following a sexual encounter with Burnel, who wrote the song. The lines about a 'Mersey tunnel' were certainly less than gallant.

The leering 'Peaches' eventually became the Stranglers second single, though its lyrics were amended slightly for airplay, including the bizarrely enunciated 'clitoris'. Cornwell would later admit he didn't actually know how to pronounce it, which makes a change from not knowing where to find it. It was actually a double A-side with 'Go Buddy Go', a popular encore and a song Burnel had originally written prior to joining the band. However, it was left off the album because it wasn't considered 'dark' enough to match the rest of the material.

But it's astounding, in retrospect, that the one song yearning for single stature, 'Hanging Around', wasn't released. Black's patient, somnambulant hi-hat intro builds the mood before Burnel's bass crashes down like a piano falling through the ceiling. Whereas the Stranglers were often criticised for the literal nature of some of their lyrics, 'Hanging Around', even when its various component parts have been explained, retains its otherworldliness and sense of myth and portent. The lyric was a joint Cornwell/Burnel collaboration. Burnel's namechecking of the Colherne pub in Earl's Court related to an evening Burnel spent there decoding the use of the handkerchief as a kind of sexual semiology. Jesus was invoked by Cornwell in reference to the old 'hanging around this Easter' joke.

The album's other truly pivotal song, 'Down In The Sewer', was another collaboration between Cornwell and Burnel. There was something about the naked Darwinism of the sentiments that transposed the band's status within the punk fraternity, while Cornwell would later admit that the sewer of the title was, in fact, London. A kind of bleak, survivalist communiqué, Cornwell wrote the words while most of the musical sections to the four 'movements' were brought in by Burnel. However, the real triumph of the song is Greenfield's sweeping organ motif towards the song's crescendo, alongside a hugely powerful arrangement that drew on the classical tradition. It became a natural choice as set closer. It climaxed the album with the sound of a toilet chain being flushed, just to show that the band's sense of humour remained intact.

It was also impossible to ignore 'Ugly', Burnel's Ozymandias-inspired requiem for life's less fortunates, boasting one of the most vicious vocals in the history of rock. It included the line 'It's different for Jews somehow'. Hell, you were a punk band, you had to fuck with that stuff. Or did you? It's actually about the least offensive line in the entire song. To quote the lyric, "It was a futile gesture, anyway."

The album eventually reached number two in the charts and stayed on the listing for a year. 'Peaches' too, became a major hit, reaching number eight. For their resulting Top Of The Pops appearance, Cornwell mimed bass and Burnel lead guitar as a joke. Unlike the Clash and the Pistols, they were more than happy to appear on the show, which was considered a tired and discredited promotional vehicle by the punk community. In fact, they delighted in breaking ranks.

After the album's release the Stranglers pitched in to back Celia Gollin (see Celia And The Mutations) while Burnel travelled to Japan to train under Master Oyama, the doyen of kyokushin karate. He also had the small matter of deferring his national service with the French army. While he was away, the flat he shared with Wilko Johnson and occasionally Billy Idol was broken into. The female tenant, Suzie, was raped at knifepoint, with her attackers threatening to slit her cat's throat, leading to the lyric for '5 Minutes'.

In the meantime A&M had signed the band to America, and their first dates were completed in New York, Los Angeles, San Francisco and Boston. A sell-out national tour ensued before they returned to TW Studios to record a second album in June, just four months after the release of Rattus. Unlike their punk peers, notably the Clash, they'd stockpiled a huge amount of original material during their wilderness years. This time they'd get fourteen days to record, rather than the six allocated their debut.

'School Mam', a long-time live highlight in which Cornwell routinely 'masturbated' his neck before discharging a volley of gob, became the album's multi-tiered centrepiece, akin to 'Sewer' on their debut and later, 'Toiler On The Sea' on Black And White. The countdown at the end revealed Cornwell's love of mathematics (and prefigured The Raven's 'Genetix'). The lyric was inspired by Cornwell's time as a supply teacher at Mary Hobbs Tutorial College near Guildford, but equally by the Velvet Underground's 'The Gift'.

'Dead Ringer', as well as 'Peasant In The Big Shitty', was sung by Greenfield, with a Cornwell lyric attacking double standards within the punk movement. But the fade out lines, "Productivity, credibility, impossibility", actually addressed Cornwell's personal dilemma that the band was advancing too quickly and sacrificing quality for a constant product line. 'Peasant' was also the album's most obviously 'acid' influenced song, deliberately evoking the feel of a bad trip. 'Burning Up Time', conversely, was more amphetamine-themed, name-checking the Finchley Boys and partially inspired by Burnel travelling by train to Brighton to see his girlfriend.

'Bitchin'' also re-emerged from their first demo sessions. In the wake of the accusations of sexism, Cornwell penned the provocatively literal 'Bring On The Nubiles', inspired by Nabokov's 'Lolita', to up the ante. It's a suitably libidinous, albeit attention-seeking song. In some ways more offensive is 'English Towns', in which Cornwell, via Burnel's lyrics, declares he has found "no love in a thousand girls". Presumably they'd slept with them all between them, though.

The other attention grabber was opening track 'I Feel Like A Wog'. David Buckley compared this to the Clash's 'White Riot' in terms of its sentiments, and there are clear similarities. But the Stranglers, typically, used the most base and revolting nomenclature to make their point. The Clash empathised with the black situation. The Stranglers did too, but drew a parallel with their own isolation within the punk community. Unlike the Clash, the Stranglers were opposed to the Rock Against Racism movement, being ideologically reluctant to nail their flag to any mast. Many of the lines were drawn from the Stranglers' first foreign dates in Hamburg, when a local pimp did, indeed, invite them down to 'Sao Paulo', part of the red light district, and failed to laugh at Cornwell's attempts to ingratiate himself for some 'freebies' with a surrealist joke.

No More Heroes is generally looked upon as the poorer half of a twin set with Rattus. But the album is, if anything, more focused, its mantra of misanthropy more sustained. 'Dagenham Dave' and the single 'No More Heroes' are equally vibrant. The former was their tribute to their one-time talisman. The spoken reference at the end refers to the meeting between Dai Davies and Malcolm McLaren at the 100 Club in 1976 when it was suggested that the Stranglers might participate in the Anarchy In The UK tour. McLaren apparently withdrew any offer after Dagenham Dave decided to take on the Finchley Boys, his usurpers, single-handed.

'No More Heroes' itself name-checked counter-culture rebels from Trotsky to Sancho Panza, and also forger The Great Elmyra. It was great, overblown, heavy-duty pop music with a real rhythmic kick riding a powerful, punk-rooted sentiment. The Stranglers, in keeping with that ethos, initially refused to sign autographs on tour. It spoke also of the loss of the concept of the Victorian gentleman explorer. The lyric was inspired by the deaths of Grouch Marx and Elvis Presley while the Stranglers played their first four American dates, at which time Cornwell had taken the chance to check out Trotsky's house in Mexico City, where he'd been assassinated.

The sleeve for No More Heroes caused some inner disquiet when John Pasche at UA came up with the idea of a cover shot of Burnel, the pretty boy, albeit the pretty vicious boy in the Stranglers' ranks, lying on a mock-up of the tomb of Trotsky. And the album did not receive universally good reviews. Jon Savage in Sounds wrote that "having your face rubbed in a cess-pit can, on certain occasions, be salutary (shock/emetic). Beyond a point, reached on this album, it seems more redundant, self-indulgent... the Stranglers offer nothing positive, not even in their music... what comes off this album, with its deliberate unrelenting wallowing, is the chill of death." Burnel didn't take this lightly, and went around town trying to hunt Savage down. He eventually found him at the Red Cow, and duly administered a 'kicking'. Burnel was, of course, a prick for so doing. But this incident would have grave repercussions down the line for the Stranglers as they became routinely edited out of the punk archive. 25 years later, Savage was still calling them "ghastly, retro rubbish". But 1977 was a year that the Stranglers can claim to have dominated more than any punk band.

The driving, brutish '5 Minutes' was released in February 1978, backed by Cornwell's Devo tribute 'Rok It To The Moon', at which time the group engaged in a round of back to basics pub gigs, each of which were sold out. It indicated the group's willingness to eschew the traditional approach to touring. Such idiosyncrasies were amplified by a press junket to Iceland. Iceland's geographical harshness suited the band, and they simply looked perfect, frozen in black and white against the monochrome backdrop of Reykjavik, somehow emphasising their inherent malice. The journey included many bouts of journalist-baiting that resulted in one member of the profession allegedly permanently losing his sanity.

Work on Black And White began in November 1977 at the Bear Shank Lodge in Oundle, Northampton, under the ownership of Ruan O'Lochlainn, who also took the striking front cover photograph. His friend Billy Bragg, also in residence with his punk band Riff Raff remembers the band being allocated their pocket money by Jet Black each morning. This time they were writing from scratch, having previously been able to draw on three years' worth of performance-honed material. A concept album, it was originally envisaged that one side (the black side) would feature Burnel's lyrics and Cornwell's music, while the white side would feature the reverse combination.

The predominantly Burnel-written dark side featured his meditation on the Japanese Samurai Yukio Mishima, 'Death And Night And Blood (Yukio), which cross-faded from 'Do You Wanna' and featured a huge keyboard surge halfway through just when it seemed the album was beginning to sink under the weight of the concept. The conjoined tracks were preceded by 'In The Shadows', the Stranglers at their most moribund, and Pink Floyd-influenced, led by a Greenfield melody line that sounded like a belching donkey, and the tremendously funny 'Threatened'. The latter was memorable for its punchy couplet "Bring me a piece of my Mummy, she was quite close to me". Burnel had quite an Oedipal thing going at one point, observing that "I just wanna fuck my mother basically. Always have done. Not so much now because she's getting a bit older, she's losing her grip on her looks. She's a cute little French girl." Doubtless shock tactics, but still. The most conventional of the 'dark side' songs was the opening 'Curfew', ostensibly one of the Stranglers' most explicitly political lyrics – a fantasy predicting the imminent collapse of the socio-political system, its depiction of Scotland as a separate nation state again linked to Burnel's Europhile tendencies. The line 'Maybe I'll find love when there's nothing to do' said something, too, about Burnel's state of mind.

On the white side of the record there was the military fetish of 'Tank', Cornwell depicting the soldier's life as akin to that of the touring of a professional musician. Whereas other punk bands were writing about the folly of joining the army, the Stranglers were attempting to simulate the visceral buzz of being in charge of all that scrumptious hardware. The quixotic 'Outside Tokyo' furthered the band's tradition of waltzes. 'Sweden (All Quiet On The Eastern Front)' reflected on Cornwell's time in Scandinavia and its slow pace, and is undoubtedly the only song in the rock canon to fit 'Cumulus Nimbus' into a lyric. 'Hey! (Rise Of The Robots)' was inspired by Isaac Asimov and the Wizard Of Oz and featured Lora Logic of X-Ray Spex, at Burnel's suggestion. 'Toiler On The Sea' was the album's 'Sewer' or 'School Mam', inspired by Cornwell's adoration of the Shadows' 'Apache', made obvious by the twang of the opening guitar parts. The title was taken from the Victor Hugo novel. Cornwell's lyric, written while on holiday in Morocco, embraces some of the same romantic language ("We didn't use cruel words/to navigate cruel seas"). Another part of the lyric, of course, gave Mike Score's abysmal synth-pop band A Flock Of Seagulls their name.

The first single from the album was 'Nice 'n' Sleazy', themed on events in Amsterdam the previous autumn when the Stranglers had enjoyed a quiet night in with the local hell's angels, amid scenes of outrageous Bacchanalian bedlam, including gangbanging and a machine gun, later recalled in a Sun story. The song, its title a play on Sinatra's 'Nice 'n' Easy', utilised a reggae undertow with a highly religiose, Biblical storyline. It was an excellent example of the way in which Cornwell's odd vocal technique, rhythmically enunciated, added a distinctive edge to the mix. Meanwhile they used their old gig poster – featuring a strangled woman on the sleeve – just to make sure they were still getting up everyone's noses.

It was then decided to release 'Walk On By' as the band's next single proper, though doubtless its sales profile suffered due to the fact that at least 75,000 copies were already in circulation through the freebie that came with the album. By now the song had been refined into a multi-layered improvisational showcase, with Cornwell's voice again proving strangely appropriate. It was a nice contrast, one of pop's most heartbreaking songs sung in the same trenchant style that had delineated punk's hardest group. The shades of submissiveness in the original were thus rendered defiant.

Black And White peaked at number two in the UK charts. The reviews were hugely positive, though Melody Maker's Harry Doherty reserved judgement on some attributes of the record. That was enough for Burnel to issue a proclamation suggesting he would "go the same way as Jon Savage – tell him to stay out of town." A little later, Burnel would go even further. Ronnie Gurr of Record Mirror would write a hostile review of one of his solo shows. He was duly abducted and taken to the next Stranglers show with the express intention of being lowered, naked, into the audience while trussed up like a pig. Later, of course, Burnel would strap one Phillippe Manoeuvre to the Eiffel Tower with gaffer tape. How to win friends and influence people? The Stranglers were storing up hostility that would drip-feed through the media in the ensuing 20 years.

The continued to tour the UK, but had problems finding London shows because of their previous run-ins with the GLC over Cornwell's 'Fuck' T-shirt. So they arranged an open-air show at Battersea. One of the women who shared Burnel's lodgings was a stripper, and suggested she and some of her friends make an appearance. They were joined by a rather enthusiastic Finchley Boy. Cue repeated dismissals of the band as dyed in the wool sexists (much to Burnel's delight, having found a niche for himself as the band's liberal-baiter) and an eventually dropped prosecution for lewd behaviour.

Misfortune was also waiting for them in America. A show in Lansing, Michigan in April 1978 saw them greeted by an army of female protesters, the Housewives Movement, with placards and a leaflet entitled 'Punk Rock/Dooley's – Partners In Sexism' (Dooley's was the venue). Burnel responded, in typical fashion, by trying to kidnap one of the protesters. Cornwell fuelled the fire with his declaration on stage that evening that "The Stranglers have always loved women and their movements, and will continue to do so."

Burnel, in particular, didn't enjoy the American tour, having already developed a geopolitical philosophy which he would explore fully on his April 1979 solo work, Euroman Cometh (recorded with accompaniment from John Ellis among others). In an interview with Chris Brazier of the Melody Maker, he crystallised his distrust not only of American culture, but also Americans. "Everyone knows that Americans have smaller brains. Fact of life, you know – they're just inferior specimens." A&M were beginning to realise that breaking the Stranglers in America was not going to be easy. Matters escalated when they tried to put together a sampler album drawn from the first two Stranglers albums. A telex to A&M America on which was written, "Get fucked, love, the Stranglers" ended their association. Which is a nice parallel to the way the Clash were prepared to put up with their label's dicing and slicing of their early records. Ian Grant was horrified. "So A&M put all their money and energy into the Police and Joe Jackson instead, and made them very successful in America. I went to the American offices about three years later. The Stranglers' telex had been blown up into a big poster in reception."

The 1979 album Live X Certs, drawn from shows in 1977 (the Roundhouse) and 1978 (Battersea), bought the group some time. It's a good live album, recorded faithfully without overdubs. It also features Cornwell's amusing put-downs of audience gobbers and hecklers: "Someone say wanker?." On the Japanese lyric sheet, always a good source of inadvertent humour, this was translated as 'Anyone seen Sir Winker?' There was also a prophetic announcement about a forthcoming benefit for the 'preservation of the rights of prisoners'. Reviews were unkind, with most critics considering it a water-treading exercise, though it did reach the Top Ten.

The group then set out on tours of Japan and Australia. While they were warmly embraced in the former territory, in Australia they faced problems. At one date a female journalist was bound and gagged before being lowered into the audience. Which led to more feminist protests at Adelaide, while they gained nation-wide exposure by aping the Sex Pistols' Grundy appearance on Channel 7's Willesee At Seven, in which they told the interviewer that "drugs are great". Drugs are great, but they can be very destructive, and by now everyone was doing rather too many of them.

Alan Winstanley was promoted to producer status for The Raven after Rushent decided he couldn't live with the group's change in direction. He'd walked after attempting to record 'Two Sunspots' as a single, only to despair when the band chopped its speed in half and presented it to him as 'Meninblack'. Despite his reservations, the songs on The Raven rarely hit a duff note. 'Longships' was a briefly dazzling waltz-like intro, running into Burnel's mysterious, evocative title-track, an accompaniment to 'Toiler On The Sea' again touching on themes of isolation and community, but with the scriptures switched from Judea-Christianity to Nordic runes and legends.

It was an album with a global perspective. The contents veered from the fall of the shah in Iran ('Shah-Shah-A-Go-Go') to their tremendously harsh, but funny, put down of plastic Americana ('Dead Loss Angeles') as well as Australian gerrymandering ('Nuclear Device'). 'Shah-Shah-A-Go-Go' served as both journalistic document and further evidence of the band's growing infatuation with Nostradamus. 'Dead Loss Angeles' referenced the preserved Mastodon discovered in the La Brea Pits, and featured Cornwell playing second bass. 'Nuclear Device (The Wizard Of Aus)' was inspired by the corrupt, draconian policymaker and right wing poster boy Joh Bjelke Petersen, catchphrase – 'Don't You Worry About That'.

'Ice' was a more successful distillation of Burnel's interest in Mishima, directly quoting the writer in lines like 'die like cherry blossom'. The odd time signatures of 'Baroque Bordello', and its interweaving bass and overlaid keyboard parts, is one of the album's huge successes, a melodic patchwork that works beautifully. 'Meninblack' was comfortably the oddest track, an examination of the UFO phenomenon, introduced to the group by skywatcher Jet Black, and in particular the 'security' forces used to erase memories of encounters. By now the group were playing around with studio effects, lowering the snare drum by an octave and thus removing the need for any bass on the track, treating the vocals via a harmoniser, etc. It was all profound silliness, but at this stage not as wearisome as the concept would become when played out as the source of a whole album. There was a rare Dave Greenfield vocal on 'Genetix', on which Cornwell returned to the subject of his degree and explored the possibilities of expanding biological science. 'Don't Bring Harry' signalled how large a feature in the lives of Burnel and Cornwell heroin had become, abetted by a suitably narcotic musical accompaniment that echoed Lou Reed's 'Waiting For My Man', dragged, or drugged, down to a funereal pace.

The single that promoted the album, 'Duchess', was the band's finest commercial pop song to date. The lyric was hilarious, taking pot shots at the disintegrating upper class and its parade of Henry's and Rodney's, inspired by one of Cornwell's seemingly innumerable girlfriends. But the video, in which the Stranglers performed as choirboys, was banned by the BBC for fear of causing offence, despite the cleric at the church, one Fr R A Coogan, testifying to their all-round decency and gentlemanly conduct (we can assume that JJ was on a good day).

The second single was 'Nuclear Device (Wizard Of Aus)', the video shot in Portugal where Deanne Pearson was covering the story. The Stranglers, the charmers, decided they would dump her in the middle of nowhere with no money and see how she managed to get back on her own. The single failed to breach the Top 30 for the first time since their debut single.

The Stranglers carried on touring, but before the last show on 1 November at the Roundhouse, on the way back from the previous night's engagement in Cardiff, Cornwell, along with three French girls and tour promoter Paul Loasby, were stopped in Hammersmith. Police eventually found small quantities of heroin, cocaine, cannabis resin, grass and magic mushrooms in his bag in the boot (presumably he'd left the acid tabs and sulphates somewhere else). Comically, the copper who nicked Cornwell was a Stranglers fan and requested his autograph.

Everyone was surprised by the sentence handed down for a first offence. But Cornwell was high profile, and something of an apologist for drug use, as well as a habitual user. His appeal was quashed and he was sent to Pentonville for an eight-week stretch, which rather messed up the Stranglers' plans for two forthcoming dates at the Rainbow that had already sold out, as well as a proposed tour of India. So Ian Grant organised a benefit show with John Ellis, then with Peter Gabriel, playing Cornwell's guitar parts, and a variety of guest singers. He later admitted to David Buckley that he managed to get the guests on the promise of £1,000's worth of free cocaine. Prisoner F48 444 Cornwell served five weeks of his sentence and recorded his experiences in a pamphlet written with Smash Hits journalist Barry Cain. Despite a statement of contrition on his release, he continued with his drug use, having become something of a connoisseur. But his, and the band's troubles, were far from over.

Two singles sandwiched his incarceration. In March 1980 their first new recording after the Raven sessions, 'Bear Cage', was released. It suffered from an insipid chorus, sadly, and its attempt to approximate the techno revolution of Giorgio Moroder and Kraftwerk was misplaced. It only reached 36 in the charts. 'Who Wants The World', released in May shortly after Cornwell's release, another song themed on alien incursions on earth, was an improvement, but it still failed to sell in large quantities.

In the summer of 1980 they were touring Europe when a proposed show at Cannes had to be rescheduled to Nice University. Various teething problems ensued, but the real problem was that the university couldn't provide enough electricity. After various shortages, the power finally gave out after 30 minutes. Hugely frustrated, Burnel made a statement in French from the stage. Black also spoke, as did Cornwell. Whatever was said (and this was the cause of a great deal of later dispute), the crowd simply rioted and began to tear the venue to pieces.

The band were arrested later that evening and charged with inciting a riot under Article 314 of the French Criminal Code and holed up for 48 hours in squalid police cells. Greenfield was released first, having not spoken at the show, while the other three were shunted to the Maison D'Arete, Nice's main prison. This proved much more comfortable until Ian Grant could arrive with the 30,000 Francs bail money necessary to spring them. They were eventually given fines and suspended sentences, but had to wait until January 1981 to discover whether or not they'd have to return to France to serve time.

In October 1980 the Stranglers set off on another US tour. About a third of the way through, at their fourth show at the Ritz in Manhattan, New York, they had all their equipment stolen while one of the drivers nipped into his flat to get a shower. Jack Rabid of The Big

S

Takeover remembered the band directing their anger and frustration at New York audiences in subsequent shows, thus further alienating the American media. They discussed quitting the tour, only to decide to play each town with borrowed equipment. It was only later that they discovered, in the shuffle of managers following Ian Grant's departure, that their insurance had gone unpaid.

The Stranglers were at a low ebb. Reeling from prison sentences, in hock to the record company and bereft of chart success. The first single from the new album, 'Thrown Away', failed to break the Top 40. A subsequent single, 'Who Wants The World', also disappointed commercially. The resultant album, which had been expensively produced around a series of top European studios, only reached number eight in the charts.

The Gospel According To The Meninblack is now widely regarded as the band's first de facto turkey, a sprawling, ostensibly single-issue UFO conspiracy theory. Several songs suffused the religious idea of a 'second coming' with the equivalent War Of The Worlds type visitation/reclamation. The Stranglers had become utterly obsessed with this self-created new mythology, and the songs suffered badly. The music affected a more futuristic, high-tech tone, with various experiments with drum and tape loops. An ambitious album that predicted the decade's later fixation with technology, it nevertheless meant that the material lost much of the musical punch evident on all previous releases.

There are small salvations. 'Waltzinblack', much beloved of Keith Floyd who would use it as theme music for his cookery programme, is wonderful. Combined with the be bop meets township jive syntax employed on 'Just Like Nothing On Earth' and the uncharacteristic poppiness of 'Second Coming' and 'Waiting For The Meninblack', it made for a good opening. But the second side was moribund. 'Two Sunspots', the same song that had mutated into the original 'Meninblack', had earlier been rejected as a single for good reason. 'Four Horsemen' has some interesting instrumental syncopation, but not enough to save it as a song. 'Thrown Away' tried to marry synthesised percussion and backing to a lyric of stately grandeur. Burnel would achieve the latter much more effectively on 'Northwinds' later, but the song plodded. 'Manna Machine' is simply indulgent. 'Hallow To Our Men' is only partially saved by Greenfield's keyboard intrusion about two-thirds of the way through. It feels like a long wait.

It didn't sell, the critics hated it, and the fans weren't too chuffed either. Cornwell still thinks it's the best Stranglers album. He's in a minority.

The theme for the next album was to be love. Which was interesting, as Jet Black, whose house hosted the pre-album sessions, had previously written, at length, about love as the 'universal myth' in previous issues of fan magazine Strangled. One of the ideas was that 'love' was actually not about romance but instead a heightened affection for anything from sports to cars or even stamps. Sessions began in August 1981 at the Manor, Richard Branson's Oxfordshire studio. Steve Churchyard (who'd worked with Cornwell on his solo album) was the engineer, with the Stranglers producing themselves. Tony Visconti, the most noted producer of the Bowie/glam years, was brought in to mix the results.

What emerged was a collection of fairly straight pop songs, appetising and fulfilling, with a great variety of subject matter. Burnel's 'The Man They Love To Hate' was an obvious standout, alluding in many ways to the band's own status. 'Non-Stop' was fanciful and as profoundly silly as anything mentioning nuns should be. 'Everybody Loves You When You're Dead', inspired by John Lennon's death, is both mawkishly funny and catchy while 'Let Me Introduce You To The Family' was Cornwell's paean to the close family life he'd never enjoyed. 'Ain't Nothing To It' was based directly on the expressions developed by Milton Mezzrow, the American jive-talker. 'Pin-Up' was again throwaway, while the Beach Boys-esque harmonies on 'Two To Tango' are faintly diverting. And has anyone else noticed how much 'How To Find True Love And Happiness' sounds like 'Last Living Souls' from the Gorillaz Demon Dayz album?

Of course, the cornerstone of La Folie, and the song that revived what was a flagging career ('Let Me Introduce You To The Family' had once again failed to dent the Top 40 when released as a single) was 'Golden Brown'. The song grew from an original idea by Greenfield, which Black then extemporised, before Greenfield worked up the idea on the harpsichord. When Cornwell heard it in this form, he spent 15 minutes writing one of the most discussed lyrics in popular music. Its subject was both women (Cornwell was dating a brown-skinned woman at the time) and heroin. Or 'toast', as Jet Black was wont to tell anyone later on. Tellingly, Burnel hated it and didn't want it on the album.

Suddenly the Stranglers were given all the radio exposure previously denied them (fogey David Hamilton made it his single of the week on Radio 2) as it rose to number two in the charts, just behind first, Tight Fit's 'The Lion Sleeps Tonight', then the Jam's 'A Town Called Malice'. The band was keen to follow up this breakthrough, and 'Tramp' seemed to be the obvious pick from the album. Unfortunately, Burnel was digging his heels in and insisting that his 'La Folie', with its spoken French verses, was the right candidate. It was, in retrospect, the more interesting song, both mysterious and intoxicating. Its subject matter concerned Issei Sagawa, who lured Parisian student Renee Hartman to tea, then had her for tea. Burnel was fascinated by cannibalism, and the subject had been addressed on several previous Stranglers songs including 'Straighten Out', 'Death And Night And Blood (Yukio)' and 'Who Wants The World'. All of which was fine. But as a single it was an absolute non-starter. It stalled at 47 in the charts.

The band had been trying to escape their EMI/Liberty contract for some time. EMI finally agreed to their departure on the assurance that they would release one further single for the label and a greatest hits album (featuring the 'keep fit' girl on the cover, much to the band's eternal embarrassment). Virgin were interested in the band, but the Stranglers eventually struck a deal with CBS when they came up with a higher advance. They also transferred management from Eddie Kleinman to former tour manager Bill Tuckey. The single they gave EMI as a parting gift was none other than one of the oldest songs in their repertoire, 'Strange Little Girl', demoed in 1974 (at which time, EMI were among the labels who'd rejected it). Tony Visconti remixed it and it raced into the Top Ten.

Churchyard was retained for their first CBS album, with the Stranglers themselves confident enough to produce, with Visconti again coming in for the remix. Feline saw the group adopt a more acoustic approach to material, in a premeditated attempt to marry the music of northern and southern Europe – a style that was actually a signpost to Cornwell's subsequent solo work. With a new contract with CBS the pressure should have been off. But tensions were mounting.

At one point, Cornwell walked out of the sessions and flew home, after music he and Black had worked on was dumped in an envelope with 'This is shit' written on it. Things were patched up when both Burnel and Greenfield apologised. They'd been out on the lash and thought it would be a laugh. It was the first of several incrementally more damaging spats leading to Cornwell's eventual departure.

The lead single from Feline was 'European Female', its arch, cosmopolitan lyric written by Burnel about his girlfriend Anna Von Stern, a dancer at the Paris Opera. She would also contribute backing vocals to 'Paradise'. But a similar soft focus approach to composition also led to the nadir of 'Blue Sister', which everyone hated. As a sister album to La Folie it fails to scale the same heights while working with similar textures. There are at least three charming songs in addition to the single – 'Midsummer Night's Dream', written by Cornwell about an old gentleman who lived in a flat above Jet's off licence, is hugely evocative, and both 'Last Tango In Paris' and 'All Roads Lead To Rome' deserve a hearing. So too 'Never Say Goodbye', which again mentioned Dagenham Dave and fallen tour manager Charlie Pile. However, Jet Black had largely forsaken live drums for synthesised ones, and that lack of feel defeats some of the other songs. Several of the songs were rooted in drug use, and by now the drug of choice for the two principal songwriters was heroin.

Much of the material for Aural Sculpture was written via correspondence, with Burnel and Greenfield in Cambridgeshire, and Black and Cornwell based in Bath. Despite the band drifting apart, particularly Cornwell and Burnel, the tone of the album is by far the Stranglers' most upbeat, emphasised by the glossy colour of the cover. Saturated in strings and brass, the production by Laurie Latham (of Paul Young fame) is highly commercial, and the songs traded edge and menace for a clean, unapologetic pop dynamic. Cornwell was now singing rather than grunting, and there was a more traditional distribution of musical space, instead of the songs being led by Burnel's bass. 'Ice Queen', like Midnight Summer Dream' and 'Punch And Judy' written about Cornwell's American girlfriend, with whom he'd just split up, and 'Skin Deep', which featured the backing singers who would form Londonbeat, are stellar pop songs.

Burnel's 'North Winds Blowing' was exquisitely resigned. Cornwell wrote 'Let Me Down Easy' for Burnel about the loss of his father, and while it's one of the Stranglers' most gentle efforts, it has sumptuous depth.

Sessions began for the band's ninth studio album, Dreamtime, themed on the Aboriginal journey of self-discovery. Laurie Latham was again drafted as producer for sessions in Brussels. It was immediately problematic, with a schism opening up between Cornwell and Latham on one side, and the rest of the band on the other. Latham thought the demo material wasn't strong enough, and rejected it, insisting the band go back and write stronger material. The other party's version of events is that they thought Latham wasn't working out, and the songs were fine, so he was fired. Mike Hedges was brought in to finish off the sessions back at Spaceward Studios in England. Burnel brought in four songs, as did Cornwell, and three were joint collaborations. The best of Burnel's efforts were 'Was It You?' and 'You'll Always Reap What You Sow', which featured BJ Cole on pedal steel guitar, while Cornwell's 'Ghost Train' was his despondent summary of the band's situation, while the most interesting instrumental work came on 'Mayan Skies'.

The first single was 'Nice In Nice', ostensibly a reflection on their troubles in France. However, great things were expected of 'Always The Sun', Cornwell's Everly Brothers-esque pop song. But that too only peaked at number 30. Two further singles, 'Big In America' and 'Shakin' Like A Leaf' were nothing more than adequate. Dreamtime thus became the band's worst performing album to date. They sounded like a tired unit. "Knackered", in fact, as reviewer Mat Smith put it.

An uninspired, though largely faithful cover of the Kinks 'All Day And All Of The Night' gave them a surprise Top Ten hit in January 1988 and helped shift a few copies of the similarly titled live album – on which it was untidily included in studio form. Even though the album was in parts excellent, that just reinforced the impression that they'd taken their eye off the ball and sacrificed quality assurance (just check the cover) for a quick buck.

10 was recorded at Burnel's new Cambridgeshire studio, constructed in a couple of weeks from Black's designs. It was readied early in 1989 with Owen Morris engineering, but Muff Winwood at CBS was unhappy with the sound and demanded the band remix it. In came Roy Thomas Baker, a veteran of Queen sessions including 'Bohemian Rhapsody', as sessions were relocated to Holland. The results sounded flat, and completely bereft of any edge the band once had. Some say the Owen Morris versions were better, but the quality of the songs was so painfully lacking that it's doubtful if any producer could have rescued them. It had been written with the express intention of having another crack at America, which was a fatal mistake. The single 'Sweet Smell Of Success' and 'Someone Like You' were just about passable.

Still, the Stranglers did manage to pull one further hit single out of the wreckage, a cover of ? And The Mysterions' garage classic '96 Tears'. But their last two hits had been cover versions. The once prolific songwriting partnership of Cornwell and Burnel was at loggerheads. The writing was on the wall.

S

The accompanying tour saw John Ellis added to the line-up, according to Burnel, because Cornwell was losing interest in playing a full hand musically. Cornwell was ready to jump ship anyway. He made the decision on the afternoon of the Alexandra Palace finale of the tour, while watching England's hapless quickie Devon Malcolm try to fend off the West Indian pacemen. In frustration, big Dev heaved away, miraculously connected, and the ball disappeared over the boundary. Cornwell took this as an omen.

After the gig Cornwell first rang Jet Black, then Greenfield, and finally, Burnel. It was apparently a long conversation, with tears on both sides. There was suspicion, probably unfounded, that Cornwell had planned his solo career in advance. He'd already been working with Roger Cook (ex-of Blue Mink) on new material. Apparently neither manager Colin Johnson (who'd taken over in the late 80s, having previously worked with Status Quo) nor Jet Black could persuade him to remain, even for a farewell tour. By the time he was questioned about this, several years into his solo career by Jack Rabid, Cornwell had perfected his soundbite on the issue. "We weren't communicating anymore, musically and otherwise. And I was bored. It's like getting to the end of the life in a pair of trousers; the ass has gone, the knees have gone and you need a belt and you feel you need to go out and buy a new pair of trousers."

Much to Cornwell's surprise, the remaining Stranglers eventually decided they would continue. There was some discussion as to whether or not the name should be changed, but they decided there were sound commercial reasons not to. John Ellis was immediately recruited full-time, in the knowledge that he was also a capable songwriter and already familiar with the material. Talk of a new front man included consideration of both Dave Vanian of the Damned and Ian McNabb (Icicle Works). They eventually auditioned four aspirants, Boo Hewerdine (ex-Bible and solo), Sil Wilcox, the band's production manager and formerly a member of Bath punk band the Rejects, and Medicine Head's John Fiddler. The latter was nearly as old as Jet Black. The fourth applicant, then aged 30, was the relatively unknown Paul Roberts. A former teenage drug addict, having failed to make it as a footballer he'd worked with various misfiring musical units including songwriter Nick Graham (Cheap Trick, etc), and Then Jerico. The link came via Colin Johnson and his appointment was confirmed in January 1991.

He made his debut with the band on 22 February 1991 in Greece, followed by a UK club tour. I caught the band playing at the Brixton Academy in June, and they sounded good. But, as one reviewer pointed out, it was obvious Roberts, whom I'd interviewed a few months previously, really was trying a little too hard. His presence diffused the traditional menace of the band. The Stranglers were never, ever, ever, eager to please. The points had shifted. Sony gleefully dropped them, leaving them without a record label. Rumours crept out that there was widespread rejoicing throughout the major's offices at finally relinquishing the 'problematic' band.

The new line-up made its debut with the Mike Kemp-produced Stranglers In The Night – an absolutely shocking title – in 1992. Highlights included 'Wet Afternoon' and 'Heaven Or Hell'. Most notable, though, was 'This Town', a song about gay rights. The rest of the material was not nearly as compulsive or entertaining, but it was surely better than 10, which had set the band a particularly low benchmark.

It was the band's least successful album to date. Cornwell's departure hadn't sat well with fans (Roberts was heckled at several shows) and they weren't about to appraise any new product on its merits. This was understandable in many ways. Every other band of their generation had experienced innumerable personnel changes. The Stranglers had lasted 15 years with a very enduring template.

The Stranglers began work on their next album About Time at Southwark Studios, in early 1995, with Alan Winstanley returning as producer. Although better than its predecessor, the songwriting still lacked the edge that Cornwell had given the songs, though John Ellis's 'Face', which featured Nigel Kennedy on violin, and 'Still Life', which saw Roberts outgrowing Cornwell's shadow, were the highlights. Jet Black contributed his first song ever, 'Lies And Deception'.

Written In Red fared even worse. It seemed that the remaining original members of the band were all too busy with their personal lives, indulged by good-ish royalty cheques, to get their heads behind the project. Explicitly, the sessions, produced by former Gang Of Four man Andy Gill, were piloted by Roberts and Ellis with the rest of the band putting in only cursory appearances. The result was dispirited, dispiriting performances. The band disliked the original mixes so these were handed over to engineer Cenzo Townshend to improve. There was an attempt at getting another hit single by covering the Lovin' Spoonful's MOR standard 'Summer In The City'. This time, it did not do the trick. Partly because they'd already used up their goodwill. Partly because the track itself was an abomination, a signalling of the inherent lack of effort being put in. There were a couple of decent tracks, especially Roberts' 'In Heaven She Walks' and 'Valley Of The Birds', about the only track where Dave Greenfield put in a showing of note. They arranged a press launch at the end of 1997 in EuroDisney. The press turned up, drank whatever free beer there was, and pissed off.

The band was now, without any hint of a doubt, scratching around for its survival. Perhaps JJ may even have contemplated the old hagakure mantra – "a timely, dignified end is important in all things." Certainly there was nothing dignified about the situation the band found itself in. Worse, they'd lost every hint of their own identity. The subsequent album, Coup De Grace, could easily have been entitled Fall From Grace. At least this time there was a bit more commitment from the old guard, with Burnel singing on four of the ten tracks. Much of the writing drew on the band's journeys entertaining British troops in places like Bosnia. The highlight was the ballad 'In The End', and an honourable mention too for the title-track, but that aside…

John Ellis left the band in March 2000 after ten years service. Baz Warne, formerly of Smalltown Heroes, stepped into his shoes. The Stranglers were, to all intents and purposes, buried. Burnel was told to go off to a remote Norfolk retreat to write new material on his own for five months. Nobody was expecting much. So it was to everyone's surprise that their 2004 return, Norfolk Coast, turned out to be such a stunningly good effort. The title-track was driven by the grittiest bass line Burnel had come up with in many a long year. Greenfield's keyboard arpeggios were back, 'Tucker's Grave' was fantastic, and 'Long Black Veil' the type of song the Stranglers Mark II had been trying to pull off for a decade. 'Sanfte Kuss', inspired by Django Rheinhardt, saw them tackle gypsy jazz without embarrassing themselves. Five years in the making, there's still some dispute as to whether it reaches the high points of the group's original studio albums, but there's absolutely no doubt that it completely obliterates the other records released by the post-Cornwell Stranglers.

Paul Roberts left the band after over a decade's service in 2006, leaving Burnel and Baz Warne to share vocal duties. Do they still have something left in the locker? Will Hugh bury the hatchet and return to the fold? Too much water under the bridge (or effluent through the sewer, if you prefer).

DISCOGRAPHY:

(BUYER'S GUIDE: Rattus, The Raven, No More Heroes, Black And White, all essential, and in no particular order. After that go for Aural Sculpture and La Folie. The only studio album worth owning by the MKII Stranglers is Norfolk Coast. Of the rest, Live X-Certs is still a pretty impressive live album. Singles (The UA Years) is the best single-disc introduction, but The Old Testament, if you can find it for a reasonable price, will provide you with pretty much everything you need – and spare you the expense of the original studio albums)

(Get A) Grip (On Yourself)/London Lady 7-inch (UA UP 36211 January 1977)

Stranglers IV – Rattus Norvegicus LP (UA UAG 30045 April 1977) (Initial copies came with free 7-inch, 'Choosey Suzie'/'Peasant In The Big Shitty (live)'. Re-issued on Fame, FA 3001 May 1982, and on CD, CDFA 3001, in 1988. Re-released in 2001 with bonus tracks 'Choosey Suzie', 'Go Buddy Go' and 'Peasant In The Big Shitty (live)')

Peaches/Go Buddy Go 7-inch (UA UP 36248 May 1977) (initial cover withdrawn)

Something Better Change/Straighten Out 7-inch (UA UP 36277 July 1977)

No More Heroes/In The Shadows 7-inch (UA UP 36300 September 1977)

No More Heroes LP (UA UAG 30200 October 1977) (reissued in 1985 on Fame, ATAK 32, reissued on CD in 1987 on Fame, FA3190, with bonus track 'In The Shadows', and on EMI CDP 746613-2. Re-released in 2001 with bonus tracks 'Straighten Out', 'Five Minutes' and 'Rok It To The Moon')

Five Minutes/Rok It To The Moon 7-inch (UA UP 36350 January 1978)

Nice 'n' Sleazy/Shut Up 7-inch (UA UP 36379 April 1978)

Black And White LP (UA UAK 30222 May 1978)

Tank/Nice 'n' Sleazy/Outside Tokyo/Hey! (Rise of the Robots)/Sweden (All Quiet on the (first 75,000 copies issued with free EP, FREE 9, featuring 'Walk On By', 'Tits' and 'Mean To Me'. Reissued in January 1986 on Epic, EPC 40 26439, reissued on CD in July 1988 on EMI CZ 109 with bonus tracks 'Mean To Me' and 'Walk On By'. Re-released in 2001 with bonus tracks 'Mean To Men', 'Walk On By', 'Sverige', 'Old Codger' and 'Tits')

S

Walk On By/Old Codger/Tank 7-inch (UA UP 36429 July 1978)

Live (X-Cert) LP (UA UAG 30224 March 1979) (reissued in 1985 on ATAK 33. Reissued on CD in July 1988, EMI CZ 110, with bonus tracks 'Peasant In The Big Shitty' and 'In The Shadows'. Re-released in 2001 with bonus tracks 'Peasant In The Big Shitty', 'In The Shadows', 'Sometimes', 'Mean To Me', 'London Lady', 'Goodbye Toulouse', 'Hanging Around (different version)')

Duchess/Fools Rush Out 7-inch (UA BP 308 August 1979)

The Raven LP (UA UAG 30262 September 1979) (20,000 copies in 3D sleeve. Reissued in September 1985 on Fame, AF 3131, reissued on CD in August 1988, CDFA 3131, and in October 1987 on EMI CZ 20 with additional track 'Bear Cage'. Re-released in 2001 with bonus tracks 'Bear Cage', 'Fools Rush Out', 'N'emmenes Pas Harry' and 'Yellowcake UF6')

Nuclear Device (The Wizard Of Aus)/Yellowcake UF6 7-inch (Liberty BP 318 October 1979)

Don't Bring Harry 7-inch EP (Liberty STR1 November 1979)

Don't Bring Harry/Wired/Crabs (live)/In The Shadows (live) ('Wired' by Hugh Cornwell, 'Crabs' by JJ Burnel)

Bear Cage/Shah Shah A Go Go 7-inch (Liberty BP 344 March 1980) (also released as a 12-inch, 12BP 344, with extended versions of both tracks)

Who Wants The World/Meninblack 7-inch (Liberty BP 355 May 1980)

Thrown Away/Top Secret 7-inch (Liberty BP 383 January 1981)

The Gospel According To The Meninblack LP (Liberty LBG 30313 February 1981) (reissued in 1985 on Fame FA ATAK 34, and on CD in September 1988, FAME CDFA 3298, with bonus tracks 'Top Secret' and 'Maninwhite'. Re-released in 2001 with bonus tracks 'Top Secret', 'Maninwhite' and 'Tomorrow Was The Hereafter')

Just Like Nothing On Earth/Maninwhite 7-inch (Liberty BP 393 March 1981)

Let Me Introduce You To The Family/Vietnamerica 7-inch (Liberty BP 405 November 1981)

La Folie LP (Liberty LBG 30342 November 1981) (reissued in November 1983 on Fame. Reissued on CD, CDFA 3083, in August 1988, and on EMI, CZ 86, in February 1988, with bonus track 'Cruel Garden'. Re-released in 2001 with bonus tracks 'Cruel Garden', 'Cocktail Nubiles', 'Vietnamerica', 'Love 30', 'You Hold The Key', 'Love In Your Hands' and 'Strange Little Girl')

Golden Brown/Love 30 7-inch (Liberty BP 407 January 1982)

La Folie/Waltzinblack 7-inch (Liberty BP 410 April 1982)

Strange Little Girl/Cruel Garden (Liberty BP 412 July 1982)

The European Female/Savage Breast 7-inch (Epic EPCA 2893) (also released as a picture disc, EPCA11 2893)

Feline LP (Epic EPC40 25237 January 1983) (came with one-sided 7-inch single, 'Aural Sculpture Manifesto'. Reissued in April 1986 on Epic 32711. Note, the US issue of the LP came with 'Golden Brown'. Re-released in 2001 with bonus tracks 'Savage Breast', 'Pawsher', 'Permission', 'Midnight Summer Dream/European Female (Live)', 'Vladimir and Olga', 'Aural Sculpture Manifesto')

Midnight Summer Dream (edit)/Vladimir And Olga 7-inch (Epic 3167 February 1983) (also released on 12-inch, Epic 13 3167, with extended version of a-side)

Paradise/Pawsher 7-inch (Epic 3387 July 1983) (also released on 12-inch, Epic 13 3387, with bonus track 'Permission')

Skin Deep/Here And Now 7-inch (Epic 4738 September 1984) (also released on 12-inch, Epic TA 4738, with bonus track 'Vladimir And The Beast')

Aural Sculpture LP (Epic EPC 26220 November 1984) (reissued in May 1987, 450488, and on CD in September 1993 on Sony Collector's, 474676. Re-released in 2001 with bonus tracks 'Here and There', 'In One Door', 'Head on the Line', 'Achilles Heel', 'Hot Club (Riot Mix)', 'Place de Victoires', 'Vladimir and the Beast (part 3)', 'Vladimir Goes to Havana')

No Mercy/In One Door 7-inch (Epic 4921 November 1984) (also released on 12-inch, TA 4921, with bonus track 'Hot Club' and 'No Mercy (Cement Mix)', and 7-inch EP, GA 4921, with bonus tracks 'Hot Club (Instrumental Riot Mix)' and 'Head On The Line')

Let Me Down Easy/Achilles Heel 7-inch (Epic 6045 February 1985) (also released on 12-inch, TA 6045, with bonus track 'Places De Victoires' and extended version of a-side, and as limited edition 12-inch, QTA 6045, with bonus tracks 'Vladimir Goes To Havana', 'Aural Sculpture Manifesto' and 'Let Me Down Easy (extended version)')

Nice In Nice/Since You Went Away 7-inch (Epic 650055 August 1986) (also released on 12-inch, Epic 650055-6, with 'Nice In Nice (Porridge Mix)', plus Midnight Summer Dream/European Female (In Celebration Of) (live)')

Always The Sun/Norman Normal 7-inch (Epic SOLAR 1 October 1986) (also released as 12-inch, SOLART 1, with 'Hot Mix' of a-side, and bonus track 'Souls (live)')

Dreamtime LP (Epic EPC 26648 October 1986) (reissued on CD in February 1989, 463361. Reissued in 2001 with bonus tracks 'Since You Went Away', 'Norman Normal', 'Dry Day', 'Hitman', 'Was it You? (7" version)', 'Burnham Beeches')

Big In America/Dry Day 7-inch (Epic HUGE 1 December 1986) (also released as a 12-inch, HUGET1, with bonus track 'Uptown (live)' and 'Texas Mix' of a-side)

Shakin' Like A Leaf/Hit Man 7-inch (Epic SHEIK 1 February 1987) (also released as a 12-inch, SHEIKQ1, with bonus track 'Was It You? (live)' plus 'Jelly' mix of a-side, and as 'Official Bootleg' live 12-inch, SHEIKB 1, featuring live version of A-side plus 'An Evening With Hugh Cornwell')

All Day And All Of The Night/Viva Vlad! 7-inch (Epic VICE 1 December 1987) (also released on 12-inch, VICET1, with bonus track 'Who Wants The World (live)', plus 'Jeff' remix of a-side, and CD single, CDVICE 1, with bonus track 'Strange Little Girl (live)')

All Live And All Of The Night LP/CD (Epic 460259 February 1988) (Recorded live at Le Zénith in Paris on April 29th 1985, at the Hammersmith Odeon in London on March 31st 1987 and at the Reading Festival on August 30th 1987. Re-released in 2001 with bonus tracks 'Souls', 'Uptown', 'Shakin' Like A Leaf', 'Who Wants The World', 'Peaches', 'Straighten Out', 'Nuclear Device', 'All Day And All Of The Night' and 'Punch And Judy')

96 Tears/Instead Of This 7-inch (Epic TEARS 1 February 1990) (also released on 12-inch, TEARST 1, and CD, TEARSC 1, with 'Tearaway Mix' of a-side, plus bonus track 'Poisonality')

10 LP (Epic 466483 March 1990) (reissued on CD in December 1992. Re-released in 2001

S

with bonus tracks: 'Instead of This', 'Poisonality', 'Motorbike', 'Something', 'You', '!Viva Vlad!', 'All Day and All of the Night (Studio Version)', 'Always the Sun (Sunny-Side Up Mix)')

The Sweet Smell Of Success/Motorbike 7-inch (TEARS 2 April 1990) (also released as a 12-inch and CD single, TEARS T/C 2, with bonus track 'Something'. Also issued as a limited edition remix 12-inch featuring 'Indie-Pendence', 'Strangled House' and 'Strangled House Dub' versions of a-side)

Heaven Or Hell/Vicious Circles/Brainbox (live) 7-inch (China WOK 2025 August 1992) (also released on 12-inch, WOKT 2025, with bonus tracks 'Hanging Around (live)' plus extended version of a-side)

Stranglers In The Night LP/CD (China WOL 8007 September 1992)

Sugar Bullets/So Uncool 7-inch (Psycho 002 October 1992) (also released as a CD single, PSYCD 002, with bonus track 'Sugar Bullets (Extended version)')

About Time LP/CD (When! May 1995 WEN 001 May 1995)

Lies And Deception/Swim/Danny Cool 12-inch (When! WENT 1007 June 1995) (also released on CDS, WENX 1008, featuring A-side plus bonus tracks 'Kiss The World Goodbye' and Bed of Nails')

Written In Red CD (When! 009 January 1997)

In Heaven She Walks/Golden Brown (live)/In Heaven She Walks (extended) CDS/cassette single (When! WEN N 108 February 1997) (CD single features alternative B-sides 'Grip (live)' and 'Something Better Change (live)')

Coupe De Grace CD (Eagle EAGCD 042 October 1998)

Norfolk Coast CD (EMI 5969512 February 2004)

Big Thing Coming CD single (EMI 5480690 February 2004)

Long Black Veil CD single (EMI 5489062 April 2004)

Long Black Veil (radio edit)/Life's Too Short/Waltzinblack/Long Black Veil (extended album version)

ARCHIVE RELEASES

The Collection 1977-1982 LP (Liberty LBG 304353 September 1982) (reissued in 1985 on CD, CDP 746066-2. The very first Stranglers compilation, it wouldn't be the last. Shite cover)

Off the Beaten Track LP (Liberty LBG 5001 September 1986) (like it says on the tin. Useful at the time, but now rather overtaken by CD compilations of the same material)

Rarities LP (Liberty EMS 1306 November 1988) (reissued on CD with bonus tracks: Rok It to the Moon/Shut Up/Old Codger/Yellowcake UF6/Vietnamerica/Love 30)

Singles (The UA Years) LP/CD (EMI 1314 February 1989) (not a bad starting point. Still in print)

Greatest Hits 1977-1990 (Epic 47801 November 1990) (inferior track selection to above compilation)

All Twelve Inches CD (Epic 471462 March 1992) (the remixes of 'Skin Deep' and 'Let Me Down Easy' are worth hearing. The rest are not)

The Early Years 1974, 1975, 1976 Rare Live and Unreleased CD (Newsspeak, SPEAK CD 101 1992) (fascinating selection of the band's earliest demo recordings and some very early live cuts. It was also released as a coloured vinyl double LP. The album was later re-released with a new cover as 'Rare, Live & Unreleased' by Castle Music, ESM CD 715, in 1999 on CD only)

The Old Testament 5-CD Box Set (EMI CD STRANG 1 1992) (nice package if you don't have the original UA studio albums. Good sleevenotes)

S

Live at the Hope 'n' Anchor CD (EMI CDP 7987892 1992) (the documentary record of the band's much-discussed Hope 'n' Anchor show from 22 November 1977, excerpts from which had previously appeared on the Front Row Festival compilation)

Saturday Night, Sunday Morning CD (Essential ESSLP 194 June 1993) (the final chapter in Hugh's residency with the band, taken from their Alexandra Palace show. If you listen carefully you can hear Devon Malcolm about to uncoil. Still a great gig)

Strangled From Birth And Beyond CD (SIS SIS CD001 1993) (some early and mid-period oddities – 'Tomorrow Was The Hereafter' was one of the Stranglers Information Service's original vinyl releases – plus some solo cuts by JJ. Marriage Of Convenience was Jet on drums and Stranglers fan Chris Twomey on vocals re-recording one of the songs on the Stranglers' first 1974 demo. 'The Beast' was an instrumental version of a 1984 track, which would also form the basis of Burnel's solo record 'Un Jour Parfait'. Some interesting moments, but these were rejects for a reason)

Death And Night And Blood CD (Receiver RRCD 187 1994) (typically un-sourced Receiver effort of the period. 'She Was Quite Close To Me' is, of course, 'Threatened'. This is the same live recording that also produced Rialto's 1997 Live In London – Rialto Archive RMCD 220 – which manages to lose four tracks and rejigs the running order. They still manage to misnomer 'Threatened'. And to top it all off, the on-mic mention of being stopped at the Italian border would make it seem somewhat improbable that this really was recorded in London. To confuse matters even further, this same set came back to haunt Stranglers fans as 'The Stranglers Live: Death And Night And Blood on Castle Music, CMRCD 455, in 2002. This time the show was credited to the band's show at The Volkhaus in Zurich on 14 April 1985. 'European Female' appears twice on this re-release, once on its own, and also as a the familiar live segue as part of 'Midnight Summer Dream')

The Sessions CD (Essential ESSCD 283 1995) (a very worthwhile release combining three BBC sessions. The first session for John Peel features four songs recorded prior to Rattus early in 1977, and they're noticeably slower. 'Bring On The Nubiles', with additional Greenfield 'squelch', is notably less offensive than the released version on No More Heroes on the second. The third session for Kid Jensen in 1982 features a cracking version of 'Nuclear Device' – in which Cornwell extemporises by shouting 'Bruce' and 'Sheila' between verses – plus a worth-hearing recreation of 'Down In The Sewer')

Access All Areas CD (SIS CD003 1995) (issued by the fan club. Later reissued on Voiceprint in July 1998. Tracks compiled from the band's 1995 tour)

The Stranglers And Friends: Live In Concert CD (Receiver RRCD 195 1995) (aka The Stranglers Play While Hugh's away. An interesting historical document, as various guests take over the lead vocal spot to cover for the imprisoned Hugh. Re-released in 2002 by Castle, CMRCD 459, with vastly improved packaging and new sleevenotes. Which makes it doubly sensible to avoid the 1997 issue of the same concert – as Hallmark 302902 – as it loses four of the tracks and shuffles the running order for no apparent reason. However, if you're really interested you should find the Italian bootleg double CD And Then There Were Three, released in 1993, which is far more comprehensive than the official releases)

The Hit Men – The Complete Singles 1997-1990 CD (EMI 3759 February 1997)

The Collection CD (EMI Gold 56239 2 1997) (great music, shite sleevenotes. Apparently the Stranglers chalked up three hit singles in 1973. Go figure.)

The Best of the Epic Years CD (Epic 487997 2 1997)

Friday The Thirteenth CD (Eagle EA GCD006 1997) (recorded live on 13th June 1997 to mark the band's 21st anniversary of their signing to United Artists, and taken from their show at the Royal Albert Hall. The band are backed by the Electra Strings 18-piece orchestra, though several songs that featured on the accompanying video release didn't make this CD. The contents of which later became disc one of the Snapper release Lies And Deception (see elsewhere) and later Live 'n' Sleazy)

The Masters CD (Eagle BAB CD 111 1998) (combines tracks from About Time and Written In Red plus three live tracks lifted from Friday The Thirteenth. To what end? Haven't the foggiest)

Collection CD (Disky Communications CD 881872 1998) (a completely pointless effort)

Exclusive Fan Club CD 1998 (SIS SOF 003CD 1998) (live selection from MkII line-up put together by the fan club)

BBC In Concert: Live At The Hammersmith Odeon '81 CD (EMI 724349777323 1998) (part of the BBC Archive series of reissues, the concert actually dates from the band's show at the Odeon on 8 February 1982, despite the title. The show was recorded for the BBC's In Concert series but never aired)

Hits Collection CD (EMI 7243 4 98749 2 3 1999) (let's milk those UA tracks again. Someone will buy it)

Hits And Heroes dbl CD (EMI 5 210892 – single version EMI 5 232180 1999) (Released to celebrate the band's 25th anniversary, Hits And Heroes comprised one CD of established hits, plus a second CD of out-takes and rarities. This was initially most interesting because of the previously unreleased 'You Hold The Key To Love In Your Hands', a rejected La Folie demo. Rejected for good reason, mind)

The UA Singles 77-79 CD singles box set (EMI 8891722 2001) (the first ten UA singles packaged with original artwork on individual CDs in a flip-top box)

Always the Sun CD (February 2000) (any Stranglers compilation that includes 'Blue Sister' should be avoided at all costs)

The Stranglers CD (Armoury ARMCD053 2001) (horrible. A variety of post-Hugh studio tracks plus feeble live versions. Without Hugh).

5 Live dbl CD (SPV Recordings 085-71052 DCD 2001) (the first recordings featuring John Ellis's replacement Baz Warne, with tracks taken from various shows during 2000)

Rattus Brittanicus & Forgotten Heroes CDs (2001) (two former bootlegs given an 'official' release in 2001. Forgotten Heroes was recorded in Cleveland and officially released on Triangle, PYCD064. Rattus Britannicus is the old London Ladies bootleg, officially released on Lust For Live, LFL071)

Laid Black CD (AMD CGTSM001CD August 2002) (well, this is an amusing concept. The Stranglers – none so mellow! – Re-record some older tunes in a quasi-Unplugged fashion. The results are interesting. OK, I'm being generous)

Lies and Deception dbl CD (Snapper SMDCD 373 2002) (Snapper regularly commission the author so I won't have a bad word said against them. No sirree)

Peaches: The Very Best of The Stranglers CD (Liberty 724354020223 2002) (TV advertised as the "perfect father's day gift". Christ, I feel old)

UA Singles, 79-82 CD single box set (EMI 5516722 2003) (the next ten UA singles, again in a flip-top box with original artwork)

The Rarities CD (EMI Germany 5410792 October 2002) (this stuff is available elsewhere already, and some of it ain't so good anyway. Additionally, it's got a completely different tracklisting to the 'Liberty' version of Rarities)

Out of the Black CD (Delta 4 006 408 471035 2002) (more Stranglers Mark II studio and live)

Sweet Smell of Success: Best of the Epic Years CD (Sony Music Intl 5 099750 982624 2003) (Why?)

Live 'n' Sleazy dbl CD (Music Club MCCD533 October 2003) (It's Friday the Thirteenth time again! Then why not lump in a collection of Mk II tracks for the second disc? Genius. Would any self-respecting record collector ever buy an album from a label with the title Music Club? Is this what we fought the punk wars for?)

Miss You CD (Nobel Price 220779 2003) (Nobel Price? Great label name. Budget comp and it shows)

Gold dbl CD (Déjà vu/Retro Gold R2CD42-57 2003) (officially a German release, but was also distributed in the UK. Features the Cornwell-era Stranglers on the pictures. But, of course, it's actually the Roberts-era Stranglers on view. Pants)

Live At The Apollo CD (SIS 2003; internet only) (recorded 23/11/81, originally for Radio Clyde. Also released as 'Apollo Revisited', Burning Airlines/Alchemy PILOT 177, which includes additional tracks 'Who Wants The World?', 'Nuclear Device', 'Genetix' and 'The Raven'. Also issued as PILOT 160 on the same label)

Coast To Coast CD (SIS 2005; internet only) (live souvenir of the band's Norfolk Coast Tour in 2004 – note the domination of material from that album, which at least points to the band's confidence in it)

Suburban Studs

Paul Morton (bass), Keith Owen (guitar), Steve Pool (drums), Eddie Zipps (aka Arthur Edward Hunt; vocals, guitar), Steve Heart (saxophone)

Birmingham's SUBURBAN STUDS formed in 1976, and quickly picked up a recording contract with WEA's appallingly-titled Pogo subsidiary, later culpable for Julie & Gordon 'Gordon's Not A Moron' novelty hit cash-in. They picked up an early support to the Sex Pistols and Clash at the 100 Club on 31 August 1976 – a performance that was savagely reviewed by Jonh Ingham in Sounds as "a laughable mixture of tacky jumpsuits, tacky make-up, tacky props and tacky music". There was also a further date supporting the Clash at Barbarella's in October 1976 before they joined AC/DC on tour.

Their debut single, 'No Faith' backed by 'Questions', was pretty rudimentary, but the band decided to recut it to remove the saxophone. "Punk bands don't have sax players" came the message from on high. That decision led to Steve Heart disappearing to join the Neon Hearts. The Studs made a few treks to London and appeared on the Hope 'n' Anchor Front Row Festival album, presenting their signature song 'I Hate School'. They also cut a John Peel session on 21 December 1977 comprising 'Suburban Studs', 'I Hate School', 'Necro' and 'No Faith'. But otherwise the critics and media all but passed on them.

Their debut album, in truth, had little to recommend it. There's testosterone-a-go-go on cuts such as 'Throbbing Lust' and 'Bondage', and a serviceable cover version of 'My Generation'. The singles sound OK, but that's about it. Probably the most interesting feature of the album was its cover. As they couldn't find the straitjackets they required to deliver on the concept, they had to have them tailor-made. Which was not very punk rock.

No-one seemed to take the band seriously and they died a quiet death in 1979. They did, however, reunite in 1996 to appear at the Holidays In The Sun festival. One of the band was rumoured to have become a teacher – ironic given that their best remembered song was the acidic 'I Hate School'. Keith Owen would eventually return in Ramones tribute band Havana A Go Go, who toured with the Rezillos in 2004.

Discography:

Questions/No Faith 7-inch (Pogo POG 001/LYN 44845 June 1977) (first 500 copies feature the 'sax' versions of the songs, and no picture sleeve, two further editions feature the revised versions, plus picture sleeves, with two different label designs. The subsequent two versions also credit 'No Faith' with A-side status)

I Hate School/Young Power 7-inch (Pogo POG 002 1978)

Slam LP (Pogo POW 001 1978) (reissued on CD, Slam (The Complete Suburban Studs Punk Collection), by Anagram, CD PUNK 21, 1993, with bonus tracks: Snipper/Hit And Run/I Hate School (live)/Sinkin Down/Hudini Charms/Savier Of Love/White Light/All That Jazz/Supernatural/Questions (Sax version)/No Faith (Sax version))

Subway Sect

Vic Godard (vocals), Robert Symmons (guitar), Paul Myers (bass), various drummers, beginning with schoolfriend Ray Price, but most permanently Bob Ward

Publicity shy and unflinchingly individualistic, there are many who believe that SUBWAY SECT were the great 'lost' band of the punk years. Certainly their cast of influences ranged far beyond the nouveau orthodoxy of Stooges, Ramones and Dolls, while Godard never overcame his childhood affection for Dean Martin and Cole Porter.

Godard and Symmons began in music by playing at college in south London, busking around tube stations for keep money. The name Numb Hearts was considered before, with old school friends from Sheen Secondary School aboard, they elected to adapt their name from the Hammersmith subway they frequented. At this stage Godard didn't have a musical role in the band, but when original vocalist Price decided he was the only one fit to staff the drum stool, Godard took over. After one abortive show at a friend's party, at which the audience walked out, Paul Packham replaced the disinterested Price on drums. They started playing music "... about the time of Doctor Feelgood and all that lot. If we'd had technique, that would've been what we would've done if we could've done, but that was way beyond what we could do. So we did stuff like the Velvet Underground – we had one of those early tape recorders with a mic which you could get good feedback noises out of. That was the way we approached it because we couldn't play at all. The only one who had a guitar was Rob and he only knew about three chords and even then he had trouble playing them."

Godard chanced upon the Sex Pistols playing at the Marquee. He'd been walking past when he observed Malcolm McLaren having an argument with the club owner. "That looks interesting," he recalled to Q. "So I went inside. I'd never seen anything like it before. It was total chaos. The manager hated the Pistols and in between each song was trying to drag them off the stage. What appealed most to me were the lyrics Johnny Rotten was singing. They were just completely overpowering."

Godard had seen the light, though he remained ambivalent to the aesthetic qualities of the music. "I thought the Pistols were the end of rock'n'roll..." Godard later told Jon Savage, "but they weren't. Nor were the Clash... We never used ordinary guitars, a Gibson or a Strat: we used Fender Mustangs because they have a trebly, scratchy sound. We became quite purist. Our guitarist refused to allow any macho, rock'n'roll attitude on stage." Still, with the Pistols there was at least a kindred spirit at work, and Subway Sect set about rehearsing, at the behest of Malcolm McLaren, for 12 hours a day at Mano's in Chelsea, in preparation for their live debut. McLaren had seen the band members hanging around at Pistols shows and discovered they were a group, which was something of an exaggeration at that point. After making a direct approach to Godard at the Ramones' Roundhouse show on 4 July 1976, he added them to the bill for the 100 Club Punk Festival on 29 September 1976 – though they would actually make their live debut at a friend's party in Ealing.

McLaren paid for a cheap rehearsal space and gave them enough for a deposit on a drum kit. "I remember listening to him through the door,' Symmons recalled to Enclave fanzine, "(he was) going 'This group are going to be really big, you've got to do them a big favour – they can't afford to pay for a rehearsal place. What time do you open in the morning?' The bloke said 11 o'clock. He said, 'I want you to come in and open at seven and they're going to be there all day.' He just talked this guy into opening really early and doing it really cheaply – he was selling us to him, convincing him it'd be worth his while. So it was a couple of days, first thing in the morning till late in the evening. We had four songs, and we came in and rehearsed solidly."

They duly made their appearance at the 100 Club decked out in uniform grey, Godard in a raincoat he'd found at Oxfam. The band ran through five songs, 'No Love Now', 'Nobody's Scared', 'Don't Split It' (Symmons' only writing contribution to Subway Sect), 'Parallel Lines',

Godard's attempt to rewrite 'Love Comes In Spurts', and 'Out Of Touch'. 'No Love Now' was lost to history until it was unearthed in the late 90s. "We started off with 'No Love Now', Godard later recalled, "and when they printed the words in the music press they got totally the wrong end of the stick. That's what made me laugh. It went "Now we're part of the new creed/Love is not what we need." In the Melody Maker write-up they quoted it as "We're part of the U.K." That symbolised everything about punk to me — the fact that everyone got the wrong end of the stick all the time."

It was an auspicious debut according to the music weekly headlines, but that wasn't the initial impression on the band, as Symmons recalled: "I remember arriving and it was an empty hall. The Pistols were there, and The Clash, and Steve Jones was really nice to us, helped us tune up cos we just sounded a racket. The Clash were just sort of laughing at us, and I remember Rotten was really nice – he came over and said, 'Don't take any notice of them, you're really good, don't worry about them.' They helped us a lot. Then I remember when we were playing, just thinking this was what I wanted to do – it was what we wanted to do." That night did, indeed, change everything, as Godard later recalled. "Before the festival, it was a secret society. All the people who went to see the Sex Pistols were different from everyone else — at least to look at. Afterwards, it broke out of the tiny cult thing, and got hijacked by a load of 'dockers', as we used to call them. It was sad in a way."

They'd made a good impression. "Subway Sect had really interesting songs, gave off a good vibe," soundman Dave Goodman recalled. "They were quite fragile — things would go wrong quite easily and they weren't very confident. But they had some good songs." Bernie Rhodes was at the gig and later that week rang to offer them management, though they would probably have gone with McLaren had not the Bill Grundy farrago forced him to devote all his time to the Pistols. They were paid a weekly wage of £15 each and given time at Rehearsal Rehearsals, the Clash's playpen in Chalk Farm.

Mark Laff replaced Smith in March 1977, who'd taken a job loading trucks for the brewery, Watney's. "He nicked the drum kit and sold it," Symmons recalled. "He was instrumental in getting a lot of our equipment, and getting rid of it as well." The new unit hooked up with the Clash. "The first phase was when we played the 100 Club, the Royal College of Art, the ICA and the Lacey Lady," Symmons told Blackmarket Clash, "all with the Clash and with no-one there. That was with the Clash there, in London, and there was literally no-one there. Then we stopped for a bit that winter, rehearsed loads, wrote loads of songs, did Harlesden, and then stripped it down more for the White Riot tour. Before the UK dates for that, we started off going over to France. There was supposed to be a lot (of shows) but they all got cancelled. We did about three – there was Rouen and another place in the outskirts of France. We played this cinema in Paris, which was supposed to be this famous place where Johnny Halliday played, and the Rolling Stones in about 1963. It was all seated with lots of older people there, so that was quite strange."

S

The Harlesden show was reviewed by Caroline Coon. "Subway Sect — teenagers from Mortlake — the blankest of all the New Wave bands... (they) pose in choreographed tableaux of studied seriousness. Deadpan and ice cold in black-and-white attire, they play what they themselves aptly describe as 'complete noise'. It's an acquired taste. Their exit is suitably nihilistic. Vic flings himself off stage, landing flat on his face in the wings. The Buzzcocks move in over the top of him."

As Godard told punk77, the Clash tour offered a stiff learning curve. "We were bottled in Le Mans by Hells Angels, but still carried on through the set with no nut holding the strings in place on the bass. I think one of the Clash even jumped up and tried to hold it there while we played. We were spat at incessantly in England and the Scots went wild. Most audiences were there for the Clash and barely tolerated us, but on some nights it all gelled and we went down really good. Every time we played through something different or unexpected happened because of our total inexperience and naivety."

Among those they impressed on the White Riot tour was a young Edwyn Collins. "We thought they were brilliant. The Clash were more like a traditional rock group, but Subway Sect made a glorious racket. We found it all very inspiring." When Alan Horne's Postcard Records went on to document 'the sound of young Scotland', it was not the Clash but Subway Sect that bands such as Collins's Orange Juice, Josef K and the Fire Engines aspired to emulate.

Davey Henderson of the latter later recalled that the Sect "were one of the scariest things I'd ever seen". Much later, Collins would invite Godard to sing backing vocals, and write a small section, on his international hit 'A Girl Like You'.

Laff's tenure proved temporary, however, and he took the vacant drummer's position with Generation X when it came up in May. Bob Ward stepped in to replace him. The fact that he had long hair and hated this new-fangled punk rock music immediately endeared him to the other members. That and the fact that he wasn't overly intimidated by Rhodes. "When Bernie started to manage us he would lock us in the room until we came up with something," Godard told John Robb in 1992. "Rob Ward would sneak out down the drainpipe and try to escape, but we wouldn't because we were cowards."

They subsequently undertook their own tour alongside French band the Lou's, playing three supports to Patti Smith, alongside Tapper Zukie, at the Rainbow, and in October recorded their first Peel session. It would be repeated several times by Alan 'Fluff' Freeman. When the tour was complete they turned to sessions for their debut single, 'Nobody's Scared', backed by 'Don't Split It', released on Bernie Rhodes' Braik label in March 1978. The A-side featured one of Godard's most acute lyrics: "Media teach me what to speak/Take my decisions/It's how to find your inner self time/On the television." In an interview with Jon Savage in July 1978, he laid bare his growing unease with the direction punk had taken. "Most of the punk things that get into the charts are mere rock things that have just taken the place of the occasional rock'n'roll tiling that used to get into the charts. It seems so funny: when it first started, I couldn't believe that was going to happen. I didn't think anybody was interested in that sort of thing any more. I think, when it first started, a lot of people were hiding what they were really after."

The B-side was as strong as the flip. "When we did 'Don't Split It'," recalled Symmons, "apart from the organ and piano we did it live with Vic singing and everything, and that was the first time Bob Ward ever played the song. It was just looking at each other, nodding heads, and that was what came out on the single. It was also the first time Vic had sung it with new lyrics – I remember giving them to him in the car on the way there and he sung it live, still reading off that bit of paper." Thereafter they hooked up with the Buzzcocks for a national tour.

By the time 'Nobody's Scared' was released work had been underway for some time on their debut album at Gooseberry studios. However, Bernie Rhodes decided to abandon the project with only six tracks mixed, sacking the band in its entirety apart from Godard. Rhodes, serving as producer alongside Mickey Foote, stated that the musicianship was inferior, despite the subsequent success of 'Ambition'. But a degree of mystery still surrounds events. The band never saw any written contracts and a large advance was seemingly paid. So what happened to the original tapes? "Well, he never showed them to me," Godard told the Motion Records website. "I always assumed he had them but I just had to go on his word. I'd like to see the evidence of it. You never know with him. He's such a double-dealer you could never really know what was going on. Bernie always used to give us big lectures about all the people he worked with in the 60s. Rob Symmons might've been impressed because he was into all that but it never really did anything for me. I never liked any of those people but obviously there was some truth in it all. I've never been interested in rock biographies – it bores me rigid. He always claimed he was involved with Hendrix and the Who. I don't know in what capacity because he never really went any deeper than that he used to share a flat with Donovan. Donovan's his son's godfather."

Godard would subsequently state that he regretted trusting Rhodes, who kept him on as a songwriter and paid him £100 to write 10 songs a week, instead of leaving with the rest of the band. They, in turn, found out about his defection almost by default, though Symmons and Godard remained friends. Symmons joined the library service and Myers would later work with the Professionals. But Godard also acknowledges that he was frustrated by the constraints of the original musicians: "The drummer was OK," he told 3am, "but the bass player and the lead guitarist were never interested in learning really. My big thing then was about getting better. The way I thought we could get better was learning more chords. So when melodies went to different places you could actually write songs around it. Whereas when you've got a guitarist who can do C major, D major, and E major, it's really restrictive. Once you've done punk style it's really hard breaking out of that without learning new chords.

And already, early on, you had the Buzzcocks who were using minor chords. Out of all the English groups, they were the ones we felt closest to. I was already writing songs, and couldn't work out really how to do them with the musicians that we had."

'Ambition', probably the band's best remembered single, previewed by the Austrian Punk In London documentary where they played it at rehearsals, was their debut for Rough Trade. The remnants of the band's Who fixation are clear in the opening Townshendsian power chords, but the feel is closer to the Buzzcocks' 'Spiral Scratch', especially the vocals. Godard hated the cheesy toytown organ Rhodes insisted on adding to the mix, which co-existed alongside the sound of table tennis balls from an arcade machine, once again, an idea Rhodes incorporated without asking the band (in a move which preceded his tampering on the Clash's Cut The Crap fiasco).

Even though Subway Sect's abilities were rudimentary, their influences, ranging from French pop, swing jazz and northern soul to the Voidoids and Television, immediately set them aside from their peers. "We were very anti-rock," Symmons noted. "We wanted to see the end of the rock thing, whereas lots of other people just seemed to want to carry it on. We were at music college by then, and listening to a lot of strange experimental stuff. We used to do experimental music in college, with everyone playing instruments they couldn't play, banging things, and we used to record it all. The lecturer, Christopher Small, might have the tapes. We'd been learning about people like Erik Satie, Debussy, people I'd never heard of before."

Despite 'Ambition' auguring well for the album, Rhodes dragged in the Black Arabs for the album sessions, for whom Godard would write their unreleased single, 'The Devil's In League With You', alongside Terry Chimes and his brother John (later of the BBC Philharmonic Orchestra). They were billed as Vic Godard And Subway Sect. Thereafter a new line-up featuring Ward, plus Steve Atkinson (keyboards), Johnny Britton (guitar) and Colin Scott (bass) was assembled for a second Peel session, recorded in December 1978.

The much-delayed debut album What's The Matter Boy? was finally released in April 1980. Although the budget was minuscule and shows, and Bernie Rhodes' production leaves a lot to be desired, the songwriting, always Godard's strong suit, still impresses, encompassing classy French-styled vocal pop and plaintive jazz and soul. But the lyrics had lost none of their bite. Check out in particular 'Stool Pigeon' – "I remember money wrapped in dishonesty/Feeling part of a page in a book/Now I rummage among the debris/Me and my shadow ill at ease." Or try 'Vertical Integration' or 'Enclave', great songs all. Subway Sect promoted it during a support slot to the Banshees at the Music Machine with the band, dressed in tweeds, wheeling out a Hammond organ to underscore their reputation for contrariness.

Extracted from the album, Rough Trade issued 'Stop That Girl' as a 45 in January 1981, included on the soundtrack to Clare Kilner's Janice Beard 45wpm film. Rhodes continued to keep the faith with Godard, promoting him as a solo artist. The first results of this were the jazz-inflected 'Stamp Of A Vamp' 45 on Rhodes's imprint Club Left (named after the venue run by Rhodes and Sean McLuskey, formerly of the Stingrays), before Godard transferred to Island. The resultant album, Songs For Sale, saw him reborn as a 40s crooner, singing mainly originals with his central inspiration the works of Cole Porter. 'Hey Now (I'm In Love)' was extracted as a single, with Godard backed by guitarist Rob Marche, keyboard player Dave Collard, bassist Chris Bostock (formerly of the X-Certs as well as the Stingrays) and drummer Sean McLuskey. Occasionally the embryonic Bananarama would help out on backing vocals.

"We teamed up, playing swing and wearing silly sparkly suits with bow-ties," Godard recalled for the sleevenotes to 20 Odd Years. "Before long we had our first gig at Heaven and, eventually, Sean (McLuskey) got us a residency at the Whisky-A-Go-Go in Wardour Street, which became Club Left every Thursday night. Here, any fool could play (and regularly did)... This swing-style set soon built up a small repertoire of swing classics and the band could play backing for anyone who cared to get up and sing. Next came a nationwide Club Left tour, where Tom Cat, Lady Blue and me were joined by our regular DJ, Johnny Britten. We toured with all sorts of teen-bop, goth and heavy metal bands, such as Bauhaus, John Cale, The Dead Boys, The Damned and Altered Images, most notably being bottled off stage in Liverpool when supporting Bauhaus. We were wedged between them and The Birthday Party on that tour, wearing our tuxedos and smiles in a sea of gothic black leather and mascara. This was the most satisfying rebellion I have ever been a part of." It's worth noting that when Bernie

Rhodes saw the tuxedos prior to their Heaven show, he tried to prevent the band going on. But Godard has stated that the band had always collectively loved Frank Sinatra and Tony Bennett, and during 1977, "it was the only music that all four of us could agree we liked".

Songs For Sale, recorded in 1981, disappointed the participants by failing to translate the immediacy of their stage shows. So Godard's band upped and left to find chart success as JoBoxers, alongside one of the guest vocalists who appeared at Club Left, Dig Wayne.

Godard continued to plough his own furrow, working with Simon Booth (later of Working Week) on another jazz swing album, T.R.O.U.B.L.E., for Geoff Travis and Mike Always' blanco y negro label. This featured Pete Thomas's Jump And Jive, who were also Joe Jackson's backing band on his swing album. However, this was never released after the roster of musicians and studio time escalated to such a stage that it frightened the accountants half to death. A single, 'Holiday Hymn', was belatedly lifted from the sessions for release in Benelux countries. In 1986 Rough Trade elected to issue the T.R.O.U.B.L.E. album after it had lain on the shelves for three years. Godard was appalled that the final version resulted from unmixed tapes and quit the music business to join the Post Office. Many discerning critics mourned the loss of a unique talent to the sorting office, but somehow Godard's career path, very much like that of Howard Devoto, only underlined his status as someone entirely removed from the attention-seeking egotism endemic in the industry.

He eventually turned back to music as a part-time activity. While reading an obituary on Johnny Thunders by Chris Salewicz in the Independent he decided to write a tribute song on a guitar his wife had bought him for Christmas. This was recorded in tandem with fellow postie Paul 'The Wizard' Baker at the latter's house in Whitton, which was jammed full of musical nick-nacks. An eight-track recorder was borrowed from Geoff Travis at Rough Trade to finalise the recordings. However, when Rough Trade got into financial trouble, Travis was unable to support the release of an album, so Edwyn Collins took over the project, and it was released on Alan Horne's revived Postcard label in 1993.

End Of The Surrey People's title-track was based around a dream Godard had about the Balkans conflict being relocated to the hamlets of south England, but like the subsequent Long-Term Side-Effect LP, despite their collective merits, it sold only a couple of thousand copies. Edwyn Collins also produced much of Long-Term Side Effect, and contributed guitar and vocals. The latter project had started with Godard collaborating with former Bow Wow Wow guitarist Matthew Ashman, and got as far as finished versions of 'Outrageous Things' and 'Place We Used To Live'. However, Ashman died before the sessions were complete and instead Godard found other collaborators in the shape of Roddy Frame of Aztec Camera, Claire Kenny of Shakespear's Sister, percussionist Martin Pines and Dexy's Midnight Runners' keyboard player Pete Saunders. Paul Cook of the Pistols and Dave Morgan played drums. Godard also revisited the unrecorded 'No Love Now', originally played as an opening salvo at the 100 Club Festival and never subsequently recorded, for Pat Gilbert's singles label Garcia.

There were a variety of reissues over subsequent years, including an Overground repackaging of 'Ambition' with unreleased versions of 'Chain Smoking' and a version of the a-side, albeit with annoying hiss, from the 'lost' debut album. Demon reissued What's The Matter, Boy? on CD (Universal subsequently repackaged it) and finally, in 1998 Godard got the chance to recut the vocals and oversee new mixes of the T.R.O.U.B.L.E. material.

In 2002 Godard switched tack again for Sansend, utilising beats and samples after being heavily influenced by contemporary hip hop. He'd been enlightened by a trip to Japan in company with superfan Edwyn Collins. Assisted by his best man Nick Brown, who had just built his own studio in Sand's End in Fulham, it was recorded over two years on Sunday afternoons and weekday evenings. Featured guests included vocalist Chantelle Lamond and Simon Rivers, who also provided lyrics for his sections, and Paul 'The Wizard' Baker, part of Godard's sometime backing band, the Bitter Springs. Reggae singer Larry Marshall also contributed vocals to 'Heavy Heavy Heavy' while general encouragement was proffered by longstanding friend Paul Cook.

Godard also collaborated on a musical with Irvine Welsh, entitled Blackpool. His solo work is now backed by "the very hip young band Wet Dog, who have given him a new lease of life," according to James Dutton. "They are recording the 'lost' punk album. As Vic says, they sound more like Subway Sect than Subway Sect ever did." Meanwhile, Godard has finally managed to secure a proper postie round which allowed him to work in the mornings and spend the afternoons working on music. He had, he told MOJO, been 'christened' by a dog. "It comes with the territory. There's one in particular looks like he's been experimented on by the Huntingdon Life Science project. He sees my uniform and goes for me. I stand there; I figure, he's welcome to bite me."

Discography:

As Subway Sect:

Nobody's Scared/Don't Split It 7-inch (Braik BRS 01 March 1978)

Ambition/Different Story 7-inch (Rough Trade RT 007 December 1978)

As Vic Godard And The Subway Sect:

Split Up The Money/Out Of Touch (Oddball/MCA April 1980)

What's The Matter Boy? LP (Oddball/MCA MCF 3070 April 1980) (reissued on CD by Demon, MAUCD 645, April 1996. Reissued again in August 2000 by Universal, 844-973-2, with four bonus tracks, the Peel session featuring 'Watching The Devil', 'Stool Pigeon', 'Double Negative', 'Head Held High'. It's worth noting that the album in this form never sounded as it was intended, as Bernie Rhodes hit on the bright idea of speeding up the tapes to make it sound more authentically punky. That's why the bottom end in the recording is all but non-existent. It was only years later, too, that Rhodes informed him he'd got the studio engineer to go in and re-record all the guitar parts...)

Stop That Girl/Instrumentally Scared/Vertical Integration 7-inch (Rough Trade RT 068 January 1981)

Stamp Of A Vamp/Hey Now (I'm In Love) 7-inch (Club Left CLUB 1 November 1981)

Hey Now (I'm In Love)/Just In Time 7-inch (London LON 005 May 1982) (also available as 10-inch and 12-inch single with extra track 'Mr Bennett', LONX 005 and LONT 005)

Songs For Sale LP (London SH 8549 June 1982)

as Vic Godard:

Holiday Hymn/Nice On The Ice 7-inch (El Benelux EL 4 July 1985) (also available as a 12-inch single, with extra tracks 'Stop That Girl', 'Ice On A Volcano' and 'T.R.O.U.B.L.E.', El Benelux EL 45)

T.R.O.U.B.L.E. LP (Rough Trade ROUGH 86 May 1986)

Johnny Thunders/Imbalance 7-inch (Rough Trade 45 REV12 September 1993)

Won't Turn Back/Won't Turn Back Dub 7-inch (Postcard DUBH 937 May 1993) (also available as a CD single, features A-side plus 'The Water Was Bad', 'Conscience Be Your Guide' and 'Same Mistakes', DUBH 937CD)

End Of The Surrey People LP and CD (Postcard DUBH 936 June 1993)

No Love Now/She's My Best Friend 7-inch (Garcia POUM 003 September 1996)

In T.R.O.U.B.L.E. Again CD (Tugboat TUG 001 May 1998) (reissue of T.R.O.U.B.L.E. featuring remixed tracks)

Long-Term Side-Effect CD (Tugboat TUG 003 November 1998)

As Subway Sect featuring Vic Godard:

Sansend CD (Motion PACE CD011 September 2002)

ARCHIVE RECORDINGS:

A Retrospective (1977-1981) LP (Rough Trade ROUGH 56 January 1985) (the two Peel sessions plus both sides of 'Nobody's Scared', a cut from their debut album and a B-side)

S

We Oppose All Rock'n'roll CD (Overground 1996) (remastered version of debut album, came with free bonus CD of unissued tracks, 'Exit No Return', 'Parallel Lines (alternative version)' and 'Staying Out Of View'.

Ambition/Different Story/Chain Smoking/Ambition 7-inch (Overground OVER-45 April 1996) (also released as a CD single, OVER-45CD)

20 Odd Years – The Story Of... dbl CD (Motion PACE CD010 October 1999) (Vic's personal selection of his career highlights to date. Includes all surviving six songs from the 'lost' debut album, new songs 'Wayward Biro' and 'Nasty Man' plus 'The Place We Used To Live', co-written with late Bow Wow Wow guitarist Matthew Ashman. Also, the first album is revisited and remastered at the correct speed)

Singles Anthology CD (Motion PACE CD013 March 2005) (all the singles, 'A's and 'B's)

Sussed

Kevin Law (guitar), Dave Bass (aka Dave Powell; bass), Roger Boden (drums), Kevin Singer (aka Kevin Inman; vocals)

One of a smattering of punk bands who took up the challenge in Britain's 'second city', Birmingham's SUSSED began life in 1977 as the Worms. Their origins can be traced to school music sessions involving Powell and Law. It was the former who

introduced his schoolmates to the glory of the Sex Pistols' 'Anarchy In The UK', but only Law was interested. After a temporary sojourn in Eastbourne they began to put a new band together after they'd returned to Birmingham and found a flat in Edgbaston.

The Worms, still without a drummer, made their live debut at Barbarella's on 29 August 1977 as part of the venue's all-day punk festival, alongside other such johnny-come-lately aspirants as Spizz. By the time they took the stage at the Stone House in Brum in January 1978, they'd evolved into the Sussed, though Kevin Inman was shortly to be replaced by new vocalist Oscar. Balding and bespectacled, Oscar was later dubbed "a likeable ninny" in the national music press. The line-up eventually solidified with the addition of a rhythm guitarist, Mal R Joey (Malcolm Ball) as the Stone House dates evolved into a residency.

The Sussed were early on the scene, and were supported by the better known Killjoys, whose Kevin Rowland they befriended, Misspent Youth and, legendarily, an early incarnation of Duran Duran. They were regulars at Birmingham's premier punk stomping ground Barbarella's, where they supported visiting headliners including the Damned, Clash and Generation X.

The band's friendship with the Killjoys led to Bob Peach and Keith Rimell helping them secure studio time at Outlaw Studios at the start of 1978, but their recording debut proper came in the summer, with a single for the local Shoestring Records, run by Dansette Damage. As Oscar told the local press's musicians' page Soundwave: "A friend of ours saw a piece in Soundwaves in which Smethwick band Dansette Damage were asking groups to join them on their own record label. At first we thought we couldn't afford it, but we went along and had a chat, and a few weeks later we were in the studio." The sessions didn't begin in auspicious style. Oscar was arrested on the way to the studio and detained, meaning the recordings had to be finalised a few days later. I'd heard that this was because of illicit substances found in his vehicle. But sadly, as Kevin Law informed me, the truth was a little less Hello magazine, and a little more Exchange And Mart. "Oscar was actually arrested for driving a knackered old van with no MOT, road tax or insurance. I know this sounds very boring, and a bit "anti-punk", but I don't ever remember any drugs (other than cigs) during my time in the Sussed. I don't think we could have afforded any even if we had wanted them!"

Later the Sussed and Dansette Damage would jointly headline a landmark show at the California Inn in Harbourne, which was actually Dansette Damage's first live appearance. The Sussed's subsequent appearance at Barbarella's was reviewed by Stephen Gordon. "A shambles," he noted, before concluding that "every town should have at least one band like the Sussed. Any town with two is in dead trouble."

Sadly, the single was where everything began to go wrong. It didn't sell, initial interest from a major label cooled and there were disputes with their management (recruited following the statement on the single's cover that they were rudderless). The result was the band breaking into two factions – both of whom adopted the name Sussed, which is pretty ironic, in retrospect. Eventually, however, the Sussed Mk II got their act together, dropping vocalist Oscar ("he couldn't sing" was the blunt press statement. "They couldn't play" came his reply) and guitarist Joey and bringing in Nigel Dolman as singer. As a result the band also moved away from the rote punk of their previous incarnation, and managed to sustain themselves by playing the college circuit as a support band. They progressed to the national final of the Melody Maker Battle Of The Bands competition in 1979, but it led nowhere. Eventually they changed name to Pop Art, but by 1980 had broken up permanently. Oscar And The Sussed, meanwhile, signed to UB40's label Graduate and released the single 'I Got Me Parka', a kind of punk/mod revival novelty record after the fact. Sample lyric: "I used to be a punk/But now punk's unc-cool/I Got Me Parka." Oscar described his Sussed as "Heavier Than New Wave Funk Rock", while the single described the joys of a young punk spending all his cash on bondage gear and ripped T-shirts just as the mod revival hit town.

Joey formed the Troops and later collaborated with Jon Buxton of Misspent Youth and Kevin Law in the Jet Set. Dolman formed Michelangelo's David before becoming an actor (numerous roles including Boon) while his 'High Sex Drive' single, released as a solo effort credited to 'Dolmann', actually topped the Mexican charts. He now presents for local radio. Law runs a video production company and plays with the punk tribute band Punkd – The Spirit of 77. Dave Powell is also in that band and, rather more incongruously, Bee Gees Fever.

DISCOGRAPHY:

I Like You/Tango/The Perv triple-A-side 7-inch (Shoestring LACE-002 July 1978) (Kevin Law: "The confusion over the release date of the single is due to Lightning Records picking it up for distribution early in 1979. They sold their entire back catalogue to Hansa Productions (I think) in 1980, so sometimes the single was dated as late as 1981. It was officially released in July 1978." (Garden Records is preparing a CD anthology of Sussed recordings during 2006)

Swell Maps

Dave Barrington (aka Phones Sportsman; vocals), Paul Godfrey (aka Epic Soundtracks; drums, vocals), Nicholas Godfrey (aka Nikki Sudden, aka Nikki Mattress; vocals, guitar, piano)

The existence of SWELL MAPS stretches back to 1972 when the band was put together by brothers Epic and Nikki Sudden, alongside friend Dave Barrington. They'd formed in Solihull, taking their chief inspiration from Marc Bolan and recorded a number of tapes with members drifting in and out, the core trio augmented by Richard Earl (aka Dikki Mint, aka Biggles Books; guitar), John 'Golden' Cockrill (guitar, bass) and Jowe Head (bass, vocals). Some of these bedroom sessions, which vary wildly in both quality and conception, were later released on the Whatever Happens Next... compilation. The name Swell Maps, incidentally, was taken from charts surfers employed to gauge wave intensity.

"I first saw the Pistols at the Nashville Rooms on 23 April 1976," Sudden later stated in a 2003 interview. "My reaction was that they sounded the same as what we were doing. The only reason that those early Maps' tracks (home recordings) will never be released is because my vocals are so out of tune – musically they sound very strong. 'Forest Fire' was one of my earlier T-Rex numbers. Mind you, I was also listening to the Dolls from 1974 on and they would have been influencing my writing to some extent. The trouble with punk was that it made most everyone speed up/play their songs too fast – and we were no exception. So if it hadn't been for 'punk', Swell Maps would probably have been better – but then, how long would it have taken us to realise that anyone could book a studio? We thought that only 'real' bands on 'real' labels could do that."

In September 1977, still some months before they'd made their live debut, the band entered Spaceward in Cambridge to record 'Read About Seymour', though its release would be delayed until February 1978, when they pressed an initial 2,000 copies on their own Rather Records. Rough Trade picked up the distribution. Written by Sudden and clocking in at just under 90 seconds, it fizzled, faltered, and then collapsed in on itself. John Peel, who was later described as "old and smelly" during a snatched conversation recorded on Trip To Marineville, was spellbound, and Sounds gave it a single of the week award. They finally took to the stage on Boxing Day 1978 at Birmingham's Barbarella's.

S

The first of three sessions for John Peel was recorded in October 1978. 'International Rescue' was envisaged as the follow-up single but finances scuppered this. By December they'd chosen to go instead with another Sudden composition, written back in 1976, 'Dresden Style', aka 'City Boys'. Featuring delightfully tuneless, almost disinterested vocals, apocalyptic sheet guitar and a lyric that was impenetrable, many regard this as the Swell Maps' finest moment, and a landmark in post-punk. With finance provided by Rough Trade, this time they could afford to press up 14,000 copies, though the 1980 reissue, on which the A-side was remixed, removed the original 'Mystery Track'.

From the same sessions came their July 1979 debut album, A Trip To Marineville, released with a bonus 4-track EP of instrumentals. One of the great lost albums of the 70s, while the Clash were closing out the decade with a sound built squarely on the foundations of rock'n'roll, the Swell Maps were quietly unearthing them, throwing fag ends in the toilets and running amok through any kind of pre-conceived notions of what music should be. Unlike other wanton noise terrorists, for instance Throbbing Gristle, they still managed to make such a conceptual tryst sound fun. The impression persists that music was a big romper room they would redecorate with Day-Glo crayons while throwing the toys around. While their brothers in arms (Jowe Head was in both bands) the Television Personalities expressed the childlike joy of discovery, the Swell Maps trawled the growing pains between infant and adult worlds. Perfect example, 'Midget Submarines', an exhilarating, perfect anti-pop song, rising above the Maps' chaotic hum before collapsing straight back into it. 'Full Moon In My Pocket', like many tracks, betrays an ear for Faust and Neu!, while 'Adventuring Into Basketry' is essentially freeform improvisation. Elsewhere there are moments of rhapsodic keyboard playing, insouciant instrumentals and raging art-noise doused in reverb. Had the Fall covered 'See Emily Play' it might sound similar.

The group's third 45, 'Real Shocks', was released in September 1979. This pivoted on one of Epic's soon to be familiar piano interludes, shades of Erik Satie garnishing the rumbledethump, scattershot rhythms. The B-side featured the brothers' bedroom-recorded monologues. 'Let's Build A Car' followed in January 1980. "The first Swell Maps single I bought ('Let's Build A Car')," wrote Thurston Moore of Sonic Youth, "still to this day gives me a soul scorched buzz 'n' rush. As soon as Nikki Sudden's guitar comes slicing, slabbing and all out fuzzifying off that crackling vinyl groove you know yr gonna rock. The Swell Maps had a lot to do with my upbringing… I wish I saw them." As others pointed out, the single is founded on but a single note of (actually Biggles') guitar. As well as Sonic Youth, lo-fi pioneers Pavement and Sebadoh were also listening in, alongside others such as Pussy Galore ("I don't really like their music," Sudden later noted, "but I do appreciate their good taste"). Meanwhile group members collaborated with a wide array of friends and accomplices. Notable among these was an appearance as the AFV's on the Steve Treatment EP and as part of the Cult Figures' 'Zip Nolan' single. Sudden contributed to two Metrophase singles and each of the core trio would cut solo singles.

Second album Jane From Occupied Europe followed in July 1980. This comprised more conventional pop-rock textures as well as a series of piano-led instrumentals that veered towards jazz improvisation, such as 'Collision With A Frogman Vs The Mangrove Delta Plan'. The slightly more conventional songs, 'Secret Island' and 'Whatever Happens Next…' are the most readily digestible, and while it lacks some of the sonic scale of the debut album, and the minor compromises with tonality actually defeat some of the material, it still stands as an admirable achievement. And few albums, certainly, have been recorded with the assistance of both an eiderdown and a cement mixer as musical instruments.

However, inter-band bickering that had started during their Italian tour in the spring of 1980 derailed the band thereafter. It was intended that they tour the US in 1980, but the shows were abandoned. They'd played exactly 50 times in their brief existence. "The Swell Maps 'split up' because we never were a 'proper' band in the first place," Jowe Head informed Groovy Black Shades fanzine in 1983. "We only existed as a group in that, usually, four of us would make live appearances. Even that was fluid; it was often necessary to operate as a trio or add a few people. I'm hedging, aren't I? Basically we got sick to death of each other on our first ever tour – in Italy of all places… " Sudden's view: "The others, Richard and Epic, thought I wanted to become to 'rock' n roll' while they wanted to become more experimental. Jowe was out to lunch at the time – literally. Since then Epic told me that the stuff he was proudest of doing during the 1980s was the Jacobites' albums and 'Texas'. And both of us ended up doing music based on the same roots. As Epic put it, 'We grew up together but grew apart.' At the time I think the band should have stayed together. In retrospect we'd probably achieved a lot of what we were meant to achieve."

Talking to Zip Code magazine in the mid-90s, Sudden was reflective. "We made two singles and an album and suddenly we were flavour of the month, except we were flavour of the month for about a year. We just thought, this is what happens when you make a record. You sell loads of records, get written about in the paper, it's easy! When the band broke up we found it didn't work like that all the time. I'm really proud of what we did with Swell Maps. I can't understand why the English music weekly press has had such a thing against me ever since then. It's like some people feel I've betrayed the spirit of new wave or something, by going back to listening to Jerry Lewis or Johnny Cash. It's just music. Lots of people seem to think music started in 1977."

In May 1981 Rough Trade put together a double compilation album, Whatever Happens Next, but the inspiration was spread far too wide on this, and much of the contents are indulgent and pointless. Far more rewarding listening was provided with Collision Time, a year later, another compilation featuring the singles and choice album tracks. Epic Soundtracks would play with These Immortal Souls and Crime & The City Solution before turning solo. His brother Nikki also pursued a solo career, backed by the Jacobites, who sometimes included Epic on drums, collaborating with the likes of R.E.M. and Wilco.

There was no more news of Swell Maps until April 1987 when Antar released Train Out Of It, another compilation featuring a smattering of unreleased material. However, the king of the odds and ends compilations was Mute US's Collision Time Revisited, which was comprehensive rather than discerning. Sadly, Epic Soundtracks died in 1997 after a long fight with depression, on the same day that Michael Hutchence passed away. The Swell Maps reformed to play a tribute concert, and Sudden would dedicate the Jacobites' album God Save Us Poor Sinners to his brother. In March 2006 Sudden himself passed away after completing work on his latest album, The Truth Doesn't Matter, shortly after playing a show at New York's Knitting Factory. He had nearly completed his autobiography, The Last Bandit.

DISCOGRAPHY:

Read about Seymour/Ripped and Torn/Black Velvet 7-inch (Rather GEAR 1 December 1977) (reissued by Rough Trade, Rather/Rough Trade GEAR 1 (Mkt2) RT 010 1977)

Dresden Style/Mystery Track/Ammunition Train/Full Moon (dub) 7-inch (Rather/Rough Trade GEAR 3/RT 012 1979) (reissued by Rough Trade, Rather/Rough Trade GEAR 3/RT 012 1980, minus 'Mystery Track')

Real Shocks/English Verse/Monologues 7-inch (Rather GEAR 5/Rough Trade 021 1979)

A Trip to Marineville LP (Big Rather/Rough Trade TROY 1/ROUGH 2 July 1979) (Issued with free EP – Loin of the Surf/Doctor at Cake/Seven Does/Bronze & Baby Shoes, Rather/Rough Trade GEAR 5-TROY-1/ROUGH-TWO 1979. Reissued by Mute, MAPS 1, in 1990, and on CD by Mute, CD MAPS 1, in 1990 with eight extra tracks – Read About Seymour/Ripped And Torn/Black Velvet/Dresden Style/Nothing Much – Mystery Track/Ammunition Train/Full Moon/Midget Submarines)

Let's Build a Car/Big Maz In The Country/...Then Poland 7-inch (Rather/Rough Trade GEAR 7/RT 036 1980)

Jane from Occupied Europe LP (Rough Trade ROUGH 15 1980) (reissued by Mute, MAPS 2, in 1990, and on CD by Mute, CD MAPS 2, in 1990 with eight extra tracks – Let's Build A Car/Epic's Trip/Uh/Secret Island (2)/Amphitheatres/Big Empty Field (2)/Stairs Are Like An Avalanche/Then Poland

ARCHIVE RELEASES:

Whatever Happens Next double LP (Y/Rough Trade ROUGH 21 1981)

Swell Maps In Collision Time LP (Rough Trade ROUGH 41 1982) (reissued by Mute, MAPS 3, in 1991, and on CD by Mute, CD MAPS 3, in 1991 with eight extra tracks)

Train Out Of It LP (Antar ANTAR 4 1987) (reissued on CD by Mute, Mute CD MAPS 3 1991 with four extra tracks – Blues Number 1: Garden Of Medals/Pop In Packets/Tokyo Airport/Bridge-Ghost Train)

Collision Time Revisited double LP (Mute/Restless US 7 71421-1 1989) (also available on CD, Mute 7 71321-2)

International Rescue CD (Alive 0035 1999) (arguably the most appropriate introduction to the band, as it includes much of their best work plus some undiscovered stuff that was actually worthwhile discovering)

Sweep The Desert CD (Alive Records Alive 0041 2000)

Wastrels And Whippersnappers CD (Overground March 2006) (sadly this release, featuring early versions of established SM classics such as 'Dresden Style' to wholly unheard stuff, came out almost exactly as Nikki's death was announced).

The Table

Russell Young (vocals, guitar, keyboards, bass), Tony Barnes (guitar, bass), Len Lewis (drums), Mickey O'Connor (guitar)

THE TABLE came from nowhere and rapidly returned there over a short career that promised much, but in the end delivered just two superb singles. Their debut for Virgin, the epic 'Do The Standing Still', ostensibly introduced a new dance craze, but the acerbic punch of the A-side was shocking even in an environment that was adapting to punk. It was Virgin who insisted on naming the band thus, rejecting their original title, Do You Want This Table? – which came from an overheard remark.

They had actually formed in Cardiff in 1974, and played a single show at the Windsor Free Festival that year, at which time they were augmented by bass player Alan Hughes. Previously Young and Barnes had been members of Cardiff avant-rock band John Stabber, the name taken from the nickname one of the band members gave to his flick-knife.

The NME described 'Do The Standing Still', which was first recorded as a demo in 1975, as "a seething turmoil of furious punk rhythms, multi-tracked psychedelic guitars and bizarre comic book lyrics". Indeed, those surreal lyrics were essentially a list of Marvel Comic titles. Although it didn't make NME's Top 30 of 1977 singles (topped by 'Pretty Vacant'), it did get an 'honourable mention'. They played a handful of gigs through the summer of 1977 on which the single was accompanied by an animated film (both Young and Barnes worked as professional cartoonists). They had actually intended that the band be a studio venture before succumbing to record company pressure to tour behind the record. In this role they supported XTC, Siouxsie And The Banshees, Wire, the Radio Stars and the Police.

And then they disappeared, complaining of promotional pressure put on them by Virgin, only to return 14 months later with a second single on Chiswick, with Barnes and Young accompanied by guitarist Kevin Bannon. 'Sex Cells' was as forthright as its predecessor, but despite its boisterous claim that "I'm obsessed with a mad desire for sex with schoolgirls", it sank without trace. Despite talking to the press about a forthcoming album that would feature a shopping list set to music, and a song about rape ('Love Or Love?'), no further records were issued. However, in 1979 Barnes and Young had revised the line-up to include Richard Rae on drums and Tim Cox on guitar. Cox then made way for Tony Lowe, while Barnes was replaced in 1980 by Rod Fogg. Later in the same year, Dave Regan from Local Operator stepped in for Rae.

The line-up changes are partly attributable to the group's onstage volatility, and their habit of deliberately inciting their audiences wherever possible via the use of disagreeable art-noise, or 'anti-music'. The band finally ended in 1982 after Young and Regan cut a single, 'Yes', which was shelved before release. Young, Lowe and Regan also recorded a single under the name Flying Colours, 'Abstract Art', on No Records in 1981, at the invitation of label boss Andrzej Sojka, the dance producer who 'discovered' Level 42.

They're all but forgotten now, but they definitely left an impression, Dave Thompson rating them as his "band of the decade". Possibly because, although they only recorded four tracks, they didn't hang around long enough to ruin their legacy.

DISCOGRAPHY:

Do The Standing Still (Classics Illustrated)/Magical Melon Of The Tropics 7-inch (Virgin VS 176 April 1977)
Sex Cells/The Road Of Lyfe 7-inch (Chiswick NS 31 June 1978)

Take It

Igor (aka Steven Wright; keybaords), Simon Pearce (vocals, guitar, bass),

A duo formed in Hornsey, London, in 1978, the founder members of TAKE IT grew out of the ashes of Blue Screaming, one of the original experimental DIY punk bands. Their debut three-track EP features a deliberately brutal keyboard riff deconstruction on 'Taking Sides'. As band intimate and 'memory aid' Adrian Taylor recalls, "I really liked that single and wildly enthused over it at the time to John

Peel. So there!" Following the release of the EP, Pearce left and Else Watt, who would later work with 49 Americans and the Avocados, joined on violin and drums. Igor also worked with Collective Horizontal, a side project, between 1979 and 1980.

There was a much later incarnation of Take It which featured Alan Tyler on guitar, Dave Morgan on drums, Igor on piano, Etta Saunders on vocals, Liduina on saxophone and Barbara Snow on trumpet. Igor: "We actually played a jazz set downstairs at Ronnie Scott's, when Bernie Rhodes commandeered it for one of his Club Left nights. We supported Dig Wayne and the Subway Sect, who later became the horrible JoBoxers." Morgan later played in the Loft, Weather Prophets, the Rockingbirds and Sun Dial while Tyler put together Alan Tyler's Lost Sons Of Littlefield.

DISCOGRAPHY:

Man Made World 7-inch EP (Fresh Hold Releases TR1 1979)
Man Made World/Taking Sides/How It Is
COMPILATION:
Messthetics #2 (Hyped2Death; 'Taking Sides', 'How It Is')

Tanya Hyde And The Tormentors

Tanya Hyde (vocals), Ronnie (bass), Pete Sutton (guitar), Mr Wilcox (drums)

Formed in St Albans in Hertfordshire, the Tormentors, managed by local promoter Barry Clarke, came about after Hyde, formerly of Words, and Ronnie, ex-Crossfire, put together a new band with local musician Pete Sutton and recruited Wilcox through a Melody Maker advert. By January 1977 they had played their first show and embarked on their first demo sessions immediately thereafter.

Currying favour by mixing a whole batch of rock'n'roll classics ('The Kids Are Alright', 'Let's Spend The Night Together') alongside their original material, they were courted by several record labels including Virgin, but it came to nothing.

Tanya Hyde did eventually release a solo single, 'Herr Wunderbar' (Waldo's 1979), but it sank quicker than a Zeppelin in ze quickzand, although it is enjoying a bit of a renaissance through the patronage of Euro-dance DJ Casey Jones.

Tax Exiles

John Evans (vocals), Wayne Jones (guitar), Kevin Evans (bass), Carlos de Freitas (drums)

South Wales' TAX EXILES were formed at the end of 1976, taking their influences from across the Atlantic as much as the new domestic punk bands. "All the members of the Tax Exiles were heavily influenced by American garage bands like MC5, Stooges, Pere Ubu, Seeds, Velvet Underground, etc," Evans told me. "We were a group of working class kids who couldn't relate to the music being churned out in the UK at that time, especially the prog rock from bands like Yes, Pink Floyd, Barclay James Harvest etc. We felt the harsh, abrasive industrial music of those American bands suited our lives and our landscape. And we'd all evolved our own distinctive style of dress – a mix of early American punk, and with a touch of style influence from the only bands we could relate to here, like Bowie and Roxy Music."

They caught the Pistols playing at Caerphilly on their Anarchy tour on 14th December 1976 and later the Clash, having met Joe Strummer before a show in Cardiff. "On the first Clash tour they headlined (the White Riot tour) I bumped into Joe Strummer in Cardiff and took him for a drink in one of the only pubs I was allowed in at the time (dyed hair and ripped clothes weren't popular around town). It was a very rough pub called The Greyhound, whose patrons consisted entirely of meth-drinkers, alcoholics and residents of the local Salvation Army hostel. I remember the uncomfortable look on Joe's face when we first walked in, but he soon warmed to what was actually a very friendly atmosphere – the people didn't give a shit about how you dressed. After I saw him backstage after the gig, he thanked me for taking him to that pub, because he said it reminded him of 'what it was all about'. I met most of the punk big names around in 1976 and 1977, but without doubt Strummer was one of the most genuine, down to earth and intelligent of the lot. There was no pose, the man was the embodiment of what punk proclaimed itself to be."

He was less enamoured of the way the Pistols conducted themselves. "After going to see Iggy Pop at the Rainbow, Finsbury Park, in 1977, I called in at the Roxy. There were very, very few people there – myself and two friends, two hippies, a few girls – but Lydon, Steve Jones, Sid Vicious and a couple more people I didn't recognise were gathered in the corner (I later learned they'd come from the studio where I think they'd been working on Never Mind the Bollocks). Lydon was up to his usual antics – being intimidating to the two hippies etc. Anyway, later I was upstairs in the club, and one of the hippies came up holding his head with blood gushing down his neck and face. I guessed what had happened. It was confirmed when Lydon later came upstairs, looking for further trouble. He seemed to be looking for the hippie and was wandering around with that mad stare in his eyes. My friends and myself watched slightly bemused, that first one of their crowd had bothered to pick a fight with a rather pathetic looking hippie, but why they were pursuing the guy further? Now, having grown up in the mining valleys of South Wales, both myself and my two friends weren't strangers to a bit of trouble, and we weren't known to back down to anyone or anything, but given the fact that Lydon was one of our heroes, we just watched."

"Later, when we left the Roxy, we found Lydon and his crowd all gathered around two girls sitting on a car outside the club. Lydon said to one of the girls, 'If it wasn't for me you'd still be into Roxy Music.' To which the girl replied, 'I still am!' Then, for some strange reason, Sid Vicious decided to pull out the chain he'd been wearing as a belt around his jeans, and began to swing it around his head, presumably intending to attack the girls. 'Heroes' or not, for us Valleys boys, our good old fashioned working class conditioning clicked in. Hitting a hippie was one thing, but hitting a woman was a definite no-no, and we started mouthing at Vicious and Lydon and co, who to be fair, had now also all started to try to restrain Sid. Anyway, they didn't seem to want to fight three fairly fit guys of the same age and they all headed up the street, with the sounds of our offers of a fight following them up the road. A strange night, indeed. I never had much time for Sid. He seemed to believe the hype. Whenever I encountered him he was always mouthy (mainly towards tourists) and I actually think he believed he was 'vicious'."

The Tax Exiles' live debut came at the Roxy audition night on 23rd August 1977, alongside the Speedometers and Crabs. Parts of the show were filmed by a visiting Canadian TV crew. They went on to put in appearances at Dingwalls, returning to the Roxy to support Adam and the Ants and the Zips. They were also stalwarts of local venues like the Top Rank in Cardiff, often as support to visiting bands including X-Ray Spex, 999, Sham 69 and the Rich Kids. They were exceptionally popular throughout South Wales, and boasted strong travelling support. "Although the Tax Exiles were definitely much lesser known," Evans says, "we were actually quite good. And at the time we played to big audiences in Wales – most punk bands touring here would ask us to support because they were guaranteed a big crowd. I remember we completely outplayed EMI's 'hot new act', the Rich Kids. In the early days of punk the Tax Exiles' audiences were often hostile to the way we looked, and our music, and much to our audience's surprise, often we'd actually end up fighting with them midway through our set. We gradually evolved an image of being a band worth going to see because something unexpected would happen, often a fight. We became so infamous that before we were allowed to play with the Rich Kids, EMI rang our manager to promise we'd behave and presumably to check we wouldn't do anything to them. We also played most of the London

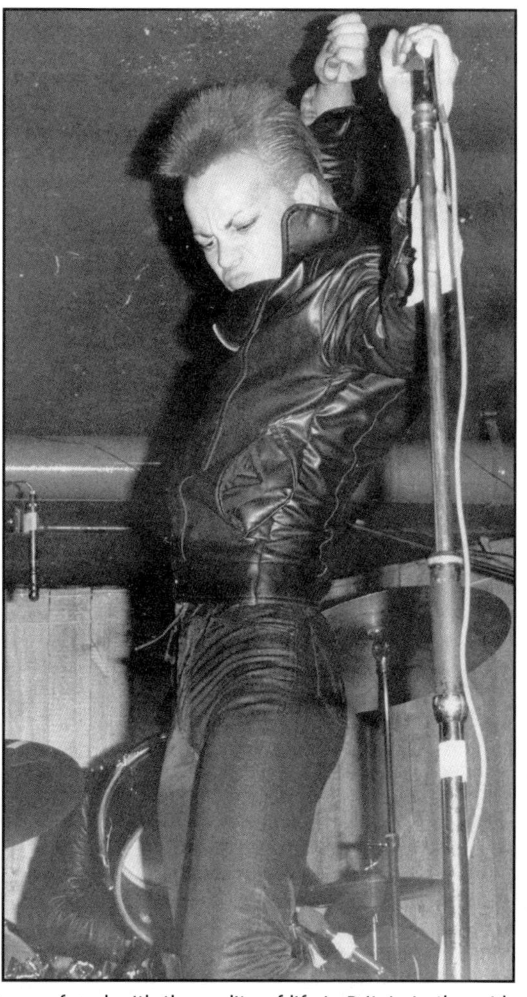

venues at that time. I was around the early-pre-punk London scene and got to know most of that crowd. I remember watching Generation X's very first gig at the Roxy in the company of Malcolm McLaren and Vivienne Westwood. Both were very nice people. There was often a spirit of bonding back in those early days, a feeling of us against them."

Their early repertoire encompassed versions of the Velvets 'Waiting For The Man' and 'Violence' by Mott The Hoople, alongside originals such as 'Rough In The Valley' (a kind of Welsh punk national anthem), 'Attack And Destroy' and 'Miracles'. These songs and others were issued on home-made cassettes for sale to fans. "Two of the most popular Tax Exiles' songs both reflected a particularly South Wales Valleys message and content, although they were equally relevant to other post-industrial areas in the UK. 'Rough in the Valley' basically said there was nothing here – no prospect of employment except down the mine, nothing to do accept go to a pub or working men's club and wait to get old, and so we wanted out. The other song, 'Miracles', was about how we were all brought up with religion and were forced to attend strict chapels when we were kids. And now, faced with the reality of life in Britain in the mid-70s, we could no longer relate to the stories we were told there – 'I don't believe in miracles, or stories with a happy end/life... is... no-one's friend'."

They featured on a BBC Wales documentary in 1978 playing two live songs, while interviews with the band and their fans were also taped and broadcast. Sadly, this never translated into any kind of recording contract and the band broke up in 1978, having come close to securing a support tour with Talking Heads in America.

On his return to Cardiff Evans formed a new band, including Phillip and Stuart Moxham, who would later form the much-loved Young Marble Giants. When this didn't work out he elected to record solo under the name John Marlon. The backing band for his solo ventures included former Tax Exile Carlos de Freitas on percussion. The group's guitarist, Nigel Buckland, later achieved some notoriety as the presenter of the Vids TV show for Channel Four. Signed to Beggars Banquet's Situation 2 in 1981, he subsequently released the single 'Sister Soul'.

However, since the early 90s Evans has worked as a full-time writer and filmmaker, a "post-punk type of art, an apocalyptic vision, an orgy of disgust,' according to his website. He is the editor of books including Black Harvest – Contemporary Poetry from the South Wales Valleys, Out of the Coalhouse – New Writing From the South Wales Valleys, and Mogg Williams - Selected Works. His films include the 1996 short Industria (also the title of a book) and the graphic novel G.B.H. (1996) and How Real Is My Valley – Postmodernism and the South Wales Valleys (1994). That's not to mention his contribution to birdwatching – The Red Kite In Wales (1991).

"I was a punk, and I still am a punk. My ideas haven't changed at all. As a writer today, I'm proud when anyone describes my work as punk, or post-punk, or any of those related terms. And I still feel most empathy with people who still embody that spirit – and often they are people who were also a part of that punk rock movement, like Lydia Lunch. I still much prefer to do things myself – like set up my own publishing company. It's the only way you get to make sure your work doesn't get watered down, and you don't have to compromise for the money men, the men in suits."

ARCHIVE RELEASE:
Miracles 7-inch (Low Down Kids LDK 45-3 March 2005) (one-sided)

Tearjerkers

Nigel Hamilton (drums), Paul MacIlwaine (guitar), Paul Maxwell (vocals), Howard Ingram (bass), Brian Rawson (guitar)

By the time Portadown's TEARJERKERS came into being in December 1978, its component personnel were weathered hands. Both MacIlwaine and Ingram were former members of the Detonators. Hamilton had been a member of Cobra and Maxwell of Speed, judged by many to be Northern Ireland's first 'new wave' band to hit vinyl. Their debut show was played at the Rockin' Chair in Derry in February 1979. Soon after they handed a demo to Terri Hooley and were duly signed to Good Vibrations, in that casual manner that Hooley signed bands. A month later they were ensconced in Keystone Studios in Dublin to record their debut single, 'Love Affair', backed by 'Bus Stop'.

Their debut at the Harp Bar was not a happy one. Convinced that the Tearjerkers were bandwagon jumpers trying to catch the punk wave, the evening erupted into violence, a pint glass bouncing off Howard's bass. "From there, all hell kicked off," Ingram later told the Tearjerkers website. "It's all a blur for a while. More glasses might have been thrown, but it was obvious that we'd have to stop and get the gear out. It was getting dangerous. For ourselves, obviously, but also for anyone caught in the crossfire. Anyone who was there will remember the stage was in the far corner of the Harp, and getting gear out meant running the gauntlet and getting it down the stairs. On one of my trips out to the van I spotted a UDR foot patrol at the end of Hill Street, told them what was kicking off inside and asked if they could call the cops. They did, and I went back in to get more gear out. Things were really ugly by this point. My first concern was to get our hard-earned gear out safely, which meant not getting into a full-scale fight too quickly. But by the time I went back in Paul Mac, Paul Maxwell and Brian appeared to have abandoned that in favour of getting stuck in. So I joined them. What's recorded is that Paul Mac received a 'hand wound'. What's not been previously recorded is that he got that lamping some gangly tit who went down like a sack of potatoes squealing 'you split my lip!' Maxwell, who also needed stitches, was whacked from behind with a glass from some hero lacking the balls to challenge him face on. The cavalry arrived into the middle of this wild west scene, truncheons drawn and giving no quarter. We got the rest of the gear out and headed for the City Hospital, where both Pauls were patched up. Then back to Maxwell's flat, I think. Someone's house, anyway, where a discussion on the evening's events began."

Despite this unwelcoming experience, they subsequently joined the Outcasts and Rudi on the Good Vibes spring tour of 1979, principally set up by Hamilton. And, contrary to assertions elsewhere, Ingram points out that they did, indeed, play Belfast again. He does not share the belief that the Harp fracas was instigated by a jealous band, as some speculated. Meanwhile, they were proving themselves as a live act and playing throughout the province as well as Eire. 'Love Affair' was performed on Gloria Hunniford's Good Evening Ulster show before they entered Downtown Studios to record a session for the eponymous station on June 1979, which was also broadcast by John Peel.

Further touring ensued backing Thin Lizzy, some of the shows recorded for a live album that only came out posthumously, while they themselves were supported by U2 on a couple of expeditions south of the border. After signing with Phonogram subsidiary Back Door Records, they shelved plans to release a second single with Good Vibrations, 'Don't Blame Me', and instead returned to Downtown to re-record 'Murder Mystery' and 'Heart On The Line' as their next single, released early in 1980. Thereafter they set up their first tour of England and recorded a second session for John Peel. They also recorded their next single with Chris 'Merrick' Hughes (of Adam And The Ants) at Parkgate Studios in Sussex. 'Comic Book Heroes' c/w 'Fingers' was scheduled for release by Mercury, but it never happened. It was a sign of trouble to come.

When they returned to Downtown in June 1980 Gregg Lindsay had temporarily replaced Hamilton, before handing the sticks to John Lee, formerly of Blue Steam. A projected single was again nixed through litigation, though the intended tracks, 'Where's Julie' and 'Lip Gloss', did eventually see release in 1982, credited to Paul West & His Mood (some white label copies of the single in its original incarnation did sneak out). As if the catalogue of disappointments wasn't long, or confusing, enough, a third effort at releasing a single, I'm Sorry' c/w 'True Love Stories', back on Mercury, was again foiled.

I asked Howard Ingram if he had any explanation for the series of botched releases. "I've no idea. Some of the stuff was released in the US on Mercury and also Phonogram in the Benelux countries and France, but not in the UK or Ireland. Record company politics, I think. Our A&R man moved on and the whole label was just allowed to drift (and then close). So there was something of an ad hoc release policy. I spoke to the A&R man some years later on a trip to London (we just met up for a drink) and he told me that there was no vision, despite us having had 'a hit' in Belgium. One of the tracks, allegedly, apparently, got to 46 or 56 or something in Belgium. I've never been able to check that story (nor had much interest in even trying to) but I found it amusing to have been, sort of, nearly but not quite, bona fide chart contenders in Belgium, without anyone saying 'do some gigs in Brussels'."

The band returned to Belfast but had already fallen apart. MacIlwaine and Maxwell formed a new band, ETC ETC, while the remaining members recruited Dave Huntley, of P45, to supply vocals for a last session for Downtown. Ingram and Maxwell subsequently set up their own Blue Rhythm Audio label. Hamilton and Rawson flew the Tearjerkers flag again in 1982 to release a final single, 'Fool' c/w 'Comic Book Heroes', which featured Janine Mullawley on vocals. Maxwell still records as part of the Blue Strings, alongside Lindsay, and is involved in youth drama. Ingram has his own UBC studio, and MacIlwaine still plays solo guitar.

Ingram picks up the band's recent history. "Guy (Trelford) and Sean (O'Neill) asked us to play at the Spit book launch, so Paul MacIlwaine, Paul Maxwell and I talked to Nigel Hamilton about it, but it was clear that we couldn't really do it with him because he had health problems. We then contacted Johnny Lee, who agreed to do it and loved the idea, but the poor man went and had a heart attack and died a few days later. We'd lost contact with Gregg (Lindsay) but by one of those quirks, he rang me a couple of months later, was having a birthday party and fancied doing a live gig thing. So we did that (the two Pauls, Gregg and myself) in April last year and we repeated it for Paul Maxwell's birthday this year (2005) on Easter Monday. The chances are that that line-up will gig again, but we seem to have evolved something more funk than punk, by doing a whole bunch of obscure northern soul songs."

And interest in the Tearjerkers continues to surprise the founders. "Paul MacIlwaine compiled a CD that sold in Japan last year in curiously large numbers, a reissue of Everybody Wants To Shag. One bloke wanted us – the original band – to go out to Japan for some gigs, which is seriously weird. And he still persists with this notion, but no-one seems particularly keen on rehearsing our old songs when there's another Dr John track to mash up in our own way! There was also the offer of some festival in Morecambe last year, but none of us fancied that much either."

DISCOGRAPHY:

Love Affair/Bus Stop 7-inch (Good Vibrations GOT 9 1979)
Don't Blame Me/Chit-Chat 7-inch (Good Vibrations, unreleased 1979)
Murder Mystery/Heart On The Line 7-inch (Back Door DOOR 1 1980)
Fool/Comic Book Heroes 7-inch (Vixen FM 003 1982)
COMPILATIONS:
Thru The Back Door LP (Mercury US 1980; 'Comic Book Heroes', 'Fingers', 'Murder Mystery', 'Heart On The Line')

ARCHIVE RELEASES:
The Tearjerkers LP (Gray Records GRC-1 1983) (this is a bootleg of the band's unreleased 1980 LP The Grey Album)
Everybody Wants To Shag... The Tearjerkers Live April 1980 LP (NHM 01 1989)
A's And B's Collection CD (NHM TJ01 2002)
Good Evening Sligo CD (NHMT 305 2002) (live at the Baymount Ballroom, 6/4/80)

Television Personalities

Dan Treacy (vocals), Ed Ball (guitar, vocals), John Bennett (drums), Gerard Bennett (bass)

Amid the assembled masses of Pistols and Clash wannabes who sought to imitate their elders in the immediate aftermath of punk, most chose to produce xeroxes of the original template, resulting in smudged, monochrome duplicates without any of the romance, danger or innovation. The TELEVISION PERSONALITIES, however, working with similarly limited resources, found the colour button on the photocopier, producing charming, wry pop songs that were witty, self-effacing mini-milks concerning love and life in the slow lane of contemporary British life. They have also given us, over a 20+ year career, probably the most impressive list of song titles in outsider art/pop music, enough to make even Morrissey weep with envy.

The band was formed by a quintet of school friends in Chelsea in 1976, initially playing raggedy sets of Who and Pink Floyd covers. "I lived around the corner from Dan Treacy," Ed Ball told Spiral Scratch magazine, "and even though we both went to the same God-fearing Catholic grammar school, London Oratory in Fulham, we'd never really spoken to each other. That is until we'd got put in the same classes at fourth form. Although we were quite different, we did discover that we had common interests in music and that we both had guitars. I introduced Dan to some of my pals, John and Gerard Bennett, who I'd known since primary school. They had a drum kit and various amps in their basement. Another was Joe Foster, proud owner of a Rickenbacker copy and a bloody-minded nature that endeared him to us all. The four of us would get together at weekends and play Who, Beatles and Pink Floyd numbers, or rather Dan would want to be Pete Townshend. I would teach them all Beatles songs and Joe would play a lot of rubbish and say it was 'Interstellar Overdrive'!"

However, their heads were turned by the arrival of punk. "Punk was just happening..." Treacy related in the first edition of the TVPs fan club magazine. "I lived across the road from Beaufort Street market where it all seemed to spring from. I remember when Malcolm McLaren opened his shop. I think it was just called SEX. It had a huge pink bow tie above the name. My mother was manageress of the dry cleaning shop opposite and she did all their cleaning, including the Sex Pistols. It was great fun then, there seemed to be cameramen in the shop all the time. Jordan was totally outrageous, nobody caused a fuss like she could. She travelled from Brighton every day to work. We often chatted in the laundry."

The inspiration came later. "There was a gang of us who wanted to do something but we didn't know what," Treacy told Sounds. "The punk scene hadn't come then and we were sitting waiting for something to happen. Then we had the idea of making our own single 'cos I'd read this thing about the Desperate Bicycles in Melody Maker." Meanwhile, Ball and the Bennett brothers (who would later form Reacta) had put together O-Level and played a couple of school dances. Treacy, for his part, started writing letters to those early DIY pioneers such as the Desperate Bicycles (who sent them a 'how to' leaflet) and Robert Rental. He also became a close pal of Scritti Politti. "They helped with information (about getting a record out) and roadied for us. Ed had suggested that O-Level were going to make a single, but it did not look like they ever would. By this time I had been working and saving money. I figured out that if Eddie would come and play drums in the studio, I could record a single. He agreed he would."

So they entered Shepherd's Bush recording studios, where Treacy was a tad suspicious about the presence of the rest of the O-Level band. "I went away with the tape feeling very pleased. It took four hours recording and cost the huge amount of £18 plus the bus fares. This was August 1977. I was quickly disheartened to find that my original costing was wrong (the pressing plant had upped the prices) and I had not enough money to release the record." Disgusted at this turn of events, he returned home. "It was terrible. I come home and just bunged the tapes in a cupboard. A couple of months later I thought, well, I might as well get one copy done and we brought it out as a single."

Their original name was Teen 78, but Treacy arrived at Television Personalities entirely by accident. He was hand-writing the song titles onto one of the two white label copies, preparing one to send to John Peel, when he decided to identify the line-up as Hughie Green, Bob Monkhouse and Bruce Forsyth. Peel did indeed play the record regularly. Encouraged, his parents offered to lend him some money (John Peel had also offered a loan) to press up more copies, as long as he agreed to go back to work, which he duly did, at Led Zeppelin's label Swansong. In fact, Treacy and Jimmy Page would sometimes organise impromptu 'office jams'. Initial copies of the single, released in a picture sleeve featuring a young Dan Treacy sat on Santa's lap, sold out. Later versions had a written sleeve and a third with a picture of Cilla Black – 867 copies sold the final tally.

However, it was their second single, recorded on 26 August 1978 for the sum of £22, that built the TVPs' reputation. "It was all first takes of songs the night before. How I marvelled at his (Treacy's) lyrics on the way to the studio!" Ball recalled for Spiral Scratch. The 'Where's Bill Grundy' EP, released in the wake of the Pistols appearance on London Weekend TV that prompted national indignation, politely inquired as to the whereabouts of the show's host, the lewd lush who pushed Lydon, Jones and co to profanity before retreating into obscurity. But the keynote address was 'Part-Time Punks', a wonderful and affectionate snapshot of the absurdity creeping into the movement, a shopping list of the good and great. There was a blatant plug for Ed Ball's first side project, O-Level, as well as likeminded fellow travellers the Swell Maps, who would reply in kind in 'Dresden Style'. And, somewhat more dismissively, the Lurkers. Its unrefined amateurism, and some of the worst 'la la la la la las' ever heard in popular music, endeared it to thousands. 'Happy Families' also gives a nod to both X-Ray Spex and 'Mr and Mrs Strummer', while the Billy in 'Posing At The Roundhouse' is undoubtedly one William Broad.

The EP was released on the King's Road label set up by Treacy and Ball for the purpose and released in November 1978. This time the first 2,000 copies featured a picture of Reginald Maudling (Conservative MP for Barnet who was frequently also the butt of Monty Python sketches) on the cover, before alternating sleeve designs, including one with a letter from Garry Bushell of Sounds on the rear. Bushell would grant it single of the week status and describe the band as Gang Of Four meets the Barron Knights.

Having made their statement, and a few sovereigns from the 20,000-odd sales, the group retired from the scene until January 1980, when Geoff Travis of Rough Trade persuaded them to go back into the studio (in the meantime Treacy helped out on Ball's next project, the Teenage Filmstars). When they emerged with 'Smashing Time', a kind of London travelogue which was dismissed by one critic as "self-conscious naivete", it was apparent that their punk days were behind them, the group now steering a course through straight 60s-inspired pop.

Their sole John Peel session (there was a much later one for Andy Kershaw) came in the summer of 1980, when they came in at two hours' notice after the Skids cancelled. Producer Dale Griffin was terrified when bass player Joe Foster attempted to 'decapitate' drummer Mark 'Empire' Sheppard, and had to be locked in a separate room while Treacy talked him out of it. "It's such a shame that children have to grow up", Peel reckoned, but one can only imagine he was talking about the session, which he repeated several times, rather than the recording of it. They set out on their first European tour in November, playing a residency in Berlin. Foster again played bass, and also recorded a solo single for Rough Trade under the name Missing Scientists (featuring Mute's Daniel Miller), but afterwards flew the coop.

The TVP's debut album,...And Don't The Kids Just Love It, followed in January 1981, comprising a series of evocative, sterling pop workouts. Naturally enough, 'I Know Where Syd Barrett Lives', released as a single at the height of conjecture about the wellbeing of the former Pink Floyd star, was attention-grabbing. It even made the Dutch national charts, but it's actually one of the lesser songs – though years later it would inspire an answer song by America's Mr T Experience: 'I Don't Know Where Dan Treacy Lives'. The swinging London references were made explicit by the album's cover, featuring both Patrick Macnee (of Avengers fame) and model Twiggy. The Kinks' influences were self-evident in tracks such as 'A Family Affair' and, especially, 'The Angry Silence', its title lifted from the 'kitchen sink drama' of 1960. 'Look Back In Anger' drew from a similar if better known source, John Osbourne's play of the same title, Richard Burton having immortalised the concept of the 'angry young man' in the accompanying film version. 'Geoffrey Ingram', meanwhile, was a character from Sheilagh Delaney's play A Taste Of Honey. "In my personal opinion this LP contains one of the best love songs ever in 'Silly Girl'," wrote Alan McGee in Communication Blur fanzine. "The album is an absolute pop classic. Even by Daniel's standards, it will be hard to match."

Thereafter the group established its own imprint, Whaam! Records, named after a painting by Roy Litchenstein. "We had problems at Rough Trade over the Dutch tour," Treacy told Slow Dazzle fanzine. "They put it together at the last minute just to keep us happy, and it was an absolute disaster. They didn't book hotels or anything and I got ill and came home and they took £600 out of my royalties for gigs that we didn't do which was totally wrong, so I just went, 'Oh, I've had enough'. So me and Edward set up Whaam!" They marked its investiture with a single by the Times (Ed Ball's sideline) and the Gifted Children, the Television Personalities under a pseudonym (more accurately, Treacy with Empire and bass player Bernie Cooper). "We didn't have any money, we just went and recorded a single each. We didn't make anything on those first two records, then the Marine Girls record that we put out (Beach Party LP) sold so many and made so much money it funded the label." Other artists who recorded for the label would include the Pastels and Doctor And The Medics. Cooper, also the TVPs new bass player, then succumbed to a nervous breakdown, leaving Ed Ball to fill in for the spring 1981 Times/TVP UK tour.

Mummy, Your Not Watching Me (or checking my spelling, either, presumably) was released in January 1982. It saw them immersed in 60s psych and pop art, utilising songs they'd recorded in sessions for the Gifted Children project (at which time the future of the TVPs was in some doubt) and later material to which Ed Ball was a contributor. The period detail of songs such as 'David Hockney's Diaries' left listeners with few doubts about the group's obsessions (it was the title of a 1973 documentary about the artist). However, the finest song, 'If I Could Write Poetry' would have shone in any genre (OK, perhaps not death metal), though it cried out for a more strident production. Extracted from the album, 'Three Wishes' served as a good introduction to their contemporary craft. Meanwhile, forsaking the bombast of rock performance as we have known it, the TVPs reinvented their live show as a mobile café. Alan McGee reckoned it was the best thing he'd seen since the Clash at Glasgow Apollo in 1977.

A year later the compilation, They Could Have Been Bigger Than The Beatles, included their debut 45 plus a series of demos and outtakes, as well as covers of the Creation's 'Painter Man' and 'Making Time'. "I had this great title which I thought sounded like a retrospective album from a band that had split up," Treacy recalled to John Reed of Record Collector, "so we played at the London Musicians Collective in Camden and billed it as the last TVPs gig ever. We fooled everyone into believing it was going to be filmed by Channel

Four and I even dragged some friends along with video cameras to pretend to be the TV crew. The music papers, who had virtually ignored me since 'Part-Time Punks', all churned out misty-eyed obituaries. It worked so well I thought that it should end there. But to my surprise the 'Beatles' LP received some really good press in Europe." However, they were unable to capitalise on this due to Treacy's nervous breakdown, while Ball left to concentrate on the Times.

Bass player Mark Flunder joined them for live engagements alongside Mark Sheppard (later of Robyn Hitchcock's Egyptians), though he had departed by spring 1983. Treacy then added organist Dave Musker to the line-up, with Joe Foster contributing 12-string guitar. Still without a drummer, they recorded The Painted Word, a much darker affair than previous TVPs albums, notably the harrowing 'Back To Vietnam' (though it's worth noting that this was, again, a 60s reference, albeit from the dark side of that decade). 'You'll Have To Scream Louder' (seemingly influenced by the chilling text about domestic abuse, Scream Quietly Or The Neighbours Will Hear) was also uneasy listening, though the mood was lightened somewhat with pastoral throwbacks like 'Stop And Smell The Roses'. In the meantime, Treacy was sectioned as his personal problems began to escalate.

At the end of 1983 the TVPs were ready to record again, with Foster back on board, for an album provisionally entitled And God Snaps His Fingers. After Geoff Travis heard the sessions, Rough Trade stepped in to offer a single deal, which resulted in 'A Sense Of Belonging', an anti-nuke protest song dressed in thrift store pop chic. However, there was a fuss over the picture sleeve, which featured a battered child. Some saw this as exploitative (the TVPs were attempting to make the link between personal and global violence), and Rough Trade released the single but left it to die on the vine, finally severing the group's link with the label. The album then transferred to Illuminated after an 18-month hiatus after Treacy experienced legal problems with the pressing plant (i.e. he hadn't paid them for previous releases) when he tried to issue it on Whaam! Ostensibly comprising subdued, melancholic psychedelia, The Painted Word, as it was now titled, was again immensely likeable, though some critics still railed against the acquired taste that is Treacy's voice. Illuminated went into receivership almost immediately after its release, scuppering its chances.

Thereafter Jeff Bloom joined the band on drums and Flunder was replaced by former Swell Maps bass player Jowe Head. They toured Europe as a quintet in 1984 but at the end of the tour, Musker and Joe Foster both departed to work on Alan McGee's Creation label (Foster having released two early singles for Creation as Slaughter Joe, while Musker was part of the Jasmine Minks). Foster's later labels included Kaleidoscope Sound (My Bloody Valentine et al) and the Cherry Red-distributed Revola.

The TVPs continued as a trio comprising Treacy, Head and drummer Jeff Bloom, their longest-serving settled line-up. By 1985 they had set up another label, Dreamworld, as Whaam! was too readily associated with the chart endeavours of Messrs Ridgeley and Michael, and they were threatening writs. Dreamworld revived several out of print recordings. However, in the CD age much of the band's catalogue would subsequently be lovingly restored by Overground. Dreamworld would also house material by bands including the Mighty Lemon Drops and Hangman's Beautiful Daughter. In 1986 Dreamworld issued the TVPs' 'How I Learned To Love The Bomb', though this was a rare own-name vinyl excursion, as the band gigged intermittently and contributed tracks to a series of compilation albums.

Treacy spent much of his time thereafter promoting shows, alongside his girlfriend, at The Room At The Top club, upstairs at the Enterprise pub in Chalk Farm, while the TVPs worked on a new album, Privilege. A move to Fire Records saw this issued in 1990 as their first original album in six years. The extracted single, 'Salvador Dali's Garden Party', was a return to the affectionate art-rock of yesteryear. 'Conscience Tells Me No' seemed to be a dig at Thatcher (whom they also attacked in 'Grocer's Daughter') and boasted the arresting image of the old witch being embalmed, Wicker Man-style. In the meantime Nirvana selected them as their opening act for their 1991 London Astoria show, as Kurt Cobain embarrassed the indigenous population about their neglect of several great bands that only American anglophiles seemingly remembered.

1992's Closer To God was more ambitious and varied, the tone being intimate and personal, especially on the painfully autobiographical 'My Very First Nervous Breakdown'. 'Goodnight Mr Spaceman' was a line lifted from later Altered Images' star Clare Grogan in Bill Forsyth's Gregory's Girl film, but its optimism contrasted with the likes of 'You're Younger Than You Know', which offered another bleak contemplation on mental instability.

Jeff Bloom left in 1993, a year after their first tour of America, with Lenny Helsing of the Thanes standing in for a repeat engagement in July 1993. They would also tour Japan in 1994, but Jowe Head would also bow out on their return. That left Treacy to record intermittently through 1994 and 1995 at Toe Rag studios, often accompanied by bass player Liam Watson. Over two albums' worth of material was amassed. After two singles for Vinyl Japan they cut their first album for Overground in 1995. I Was A Mod Before You Was A Mod featured a cover of Pink Floyd's 'Bike' (the closing track on Piper At The Gates Of Dawn), a rewrite of 'Me And My Desire' ('Meanwhile In A Luxury Dockland Home') and nods to alt-rock US gods Michael Stipe ('John Belushi Said') and Evan Dando ('Evan Doesn't Ring Me Anymore'). Watson and drummer Sexton Ming contributed, but essentially this was a Treacy solo project.

A new version of the TVPs was assembled in the summer of 1995, featuring Treacy, Ming and Watson, for dates in Germany, with a repeat engagement the following year. Amid all the reissues and compilations, new studio material was unveiled in October 1998 by Damaged Goods. Don't Cry Baby, It's Only A Movie had been delayed by two years, and consisted mainly of cover versions, drawing on the unreleased Toe Rag sessions of 1994 and 1995. Among the more successful efforts was a cover of Jonathon Richman and the Modern Lovers' 'Pablo Picasso' (cementing obvious parallels between the pair, both sonically and lyrically), while the least likely was a version of Psychic TV's Brian Jones tribute, 'Godstar'. There was also a single released, 'When I Grow Up I Want To Be...' in 1999, but this again was an old recording. From 1996 onwards Treacy retired the TVPs, amid rumours that he was variously suffering from depression and heroin addiction.

On his release from Dorset prison ship HMS Weare, his fourth incarceration for minor offences related to drugs, he spoke to MOJO. "I'm struggling at the moment," he confirmed. "I should have got treatment years ago but I refused. But it will get better, because I want it to." He was said to be engaged in new sessions, partially sponsored by fans the Scissor Sisters, utilising material written in prison. He made his live comeback in London on December 10 2004, with a line-up featuring his stalwart friend Ed Ball on bass, plus drummer Matthew Sawyer and backing vocalist Victoria Yeulet. An album is due for release at the time of writing.

DISCOGRAPHY:

(Buyer's Guide: For a single-disc introduction, including 'bloke's a genius' sleevenotes from Alan McGee, the best starting point is Part-Time Punks, Cherry Red's best of released in 1999. Of the studio albums you won't go wrong with And Don't The Kids Just Love It and Painted Word. I Was A Mod Before You Was A Mod is actually so personal and distraught it's heartbreaking to listen to, but if you can bear the misery, it's an exceptional, if disturbing, work of self-portrait)

14th Floor/Oxford Street W1 7-inch (Teen 78 SRTS/CUS 77089 January 1978) (available in three different sleeves)

Where's Bill Grundy Now? 7-inch EP (Kings Road LYN 5976/7 November 1978) Part-Time Punks/Where's Bill Grundy Now?/Happy Families/Posing At The Roundhouse (reissued in December 1979 by Rough Trade, RT033)

Smashing Time/King & Country 7-inch (Rough Trade RT 051 July 1980)

I Know Where Syd Barrett Lives/Arthur The Gardener 7-inch (Rough Trade RT 063 January 1981)

...And Don't The Kids Just Love It LP (Rough Trade ROUGH 24 January 1981) (reissued on Fire, REFIRE 7, in 1991, and on CD on March 2002 on Fire, SFIRE002CD)

Painting By Numbers/Lichtenstein Girl 7-inch (Whaam! WHAAM 001 May 1981) (credited to The Gifted Children)

Mummy Your Not Watching Me LP (Whaam! WHAAM 3 January 1982) (reissued in June 1986 on Dreamworld BIG DREAM 4 June 1986, and on Fire, REFIRE 8 in 1991, and on CD, SFIRE007CD, April 2002)

I Know Where Syd Barrett Lives/Magnificent Dreams 7-inch (Rough Trade Japan RT 08 1982)

Three Wishes/Geoffrey Ingram/And Don't The Kids Just Love It 7-inch (Whaam! WHAAM 4 June 1982)

Biff Bang Pow/A Picture Of Dorian Gray (Live) (flexidisc, Creation Records, 1982, given away with Communication Blur fanzine)

T

A Sense Of Belonging/Paradise Estate 7-inch (Rough Trade RT 109 December 1983)

The Painted Word LP (Illuminated JAMS 37 March 1984) (reissued in 1991 on Fire, REFIRE 10, and on CD in May 2002, SFIRE029CD)

Chocolat Art (A Tribute To James Last) LP (Pastell POW 2 1985) (recorded live at the Forum, Enger, 20 September 1984. Reissued, same cat., in 1991))

How I Learned To Love The Bomb 7-inch EP (Dreamworld DREAM 10 November 1986)

How I Learned To Love The Bomb (longer version)/The Grocer's Daughter/A Girl Called Charity (also released as a 12-inch with different tracks)

Salvador Dali's Garden Party/The Room At The Top Of The Stairs 7-inch (Fire BLAZE 37S October 1989) (also available as a 12-inch, also featuring This Time There's No Happy Ending/Part One: Fulfilling The Contractual Obligations, Fire BLAZE 37T)

I Still Believe In Magic/Respectable 7-inch (Caff Corporation CAFF 5 December 1989)

Privilege LP (Fire FIRE 21 February 1990) (reissued on CD in January 2003, SFIRE026CD, with bonus tracks: The Room At The Top Of The Stairs/This Time There's No Happy Ending/Part One: Fulfilling The Contractual Obligations)

The Strangely Beautiful 12-inch EP and CD EP (Fire Blaze 48T August 1991) Strangely Beautiful (7-inch mix)/Reaching For The Stars/Not Even A Maybe/Strangely Beautiful (Chill Out Reprise)

She's Never Read My Poems 12-inch and CD EP (Fire Blaze 44049 55049 February 1992)

She's Never Read My Poems (7-inch mix)/The Day The Dolphins Leave The Sea/Christ Knows I Have Tried/She's Never Read My Poems (12-inch mix)

Favourite Films/The Dream Inspires/Happy All The Time (version) 7-inch (Overground OVER 27 1992)

We Will Be Your Gurus/An Exhibition By Joan Miro/Love Is Better Than War 7-inch and CD single (Seminal Twang TWANG 15 July 1992)

Closer To God LP Fire LP (Fire FIRE 32 October 1992) (reissued on CD in September 2003, SFIRE018CD)

How I Learned To Love The Bomb mini-LP/CD (Overground OVER 30 December 1992)

Goodnight Mr Spaceman/If I Was Your Girlfriend 7-inch (Fire Blaze 65 May 1993) (also released as 12-inch and CD single with bonus tracks She Loves It When He Sings Like Elvis and Goodnight Mr Spaceman (Lost In Space mix)

You, Me And Lou Reed 12-inch EP (Fantastic Plastic FP003 1993)

You, Me And Lou Reed/My Imaginary Friend/I Remember Bridget Riley/I Wish You Could Love Me For What I Am

Far Away And Lost In Joy 12-inch EP and CD EP (Vinyl Japan TASK 28 April 1994)

I Don't Want To Live This Life/Far Away And Lost In Joy/Do You Know What They're Saying About Me Now?/I Get Frightened

A Sense Of Belonging/Baby's Turning Blue 7-inch (Overground OVER 34 January 1994)

The Prettiest Girl In The World 7-inch EP (Overground OVER 38 November 1994)

The Prettiest Girl In The World/Miracles Take Longer/If That's What Love Is/Apples And Oranges

Not Like Everybody Else 7-inch EP (Little Teddy LiTe 709 1994)

I'm Not Like Everybody Else/I Hear A New World/I've Been Down So Long It Looks Like Up To Me/Whatever Gets You Through The Night

Do You Think If You Were Beautiful You'd Be Happy? 12-inch EP and CD EP (Vinyl Japan TASK 48 1995)

He Used To Paint In Colours/Who Will Be Your Prince?/Do You Think If You Were Beautiful You'd Be Happy?/I Suppose You Think It's Funny

Time Goes Slowly When You're Drowning/Meanwhile In A Luxury Dockland Home 7-inch (Little Teddy LiTe 716 1995)

I Was A Mod Before You Was A Mod LP (Overground OVER41 July 1995)

I Was A Mod Before You Was A Mod 7-inch and CD single (Overground OVER50 September 1996)

I Was A Mod Before You Was A Mod (easy mix)/She Lives For The Moment/None Of This Will Matter When You're Dead/I Was A Mod Before You Was A Mod (instrumental)

The Happening 7-inch (Little Teddy LiTe 739 1996) Jennifer, Julie & Josephine (B-side – The Bartlebees 'Why Don't You Smile Now?')

Where's Jowe Head Now? EP 7-inch (Perfect Pop POP 25 1996)

Constantinople/White Light, White Heat/Part Time Punks/The Man Who Paints The Rainbows (live, Oslo 1990)

Made In Japan LP (Little Teddy BiTe017 1996) (recorded live in Tokyo, 10 April 1994. First 500 copies came with free 7-inch featuring live versions of 'If I Was Your Girlfriend' and 'Salvador Dali's Garden Party' – LiTe 729)

Now That I'm A Junkie!/How Does It Feel To Be Loved? 7-inch (Little Teddy LiTe 741 1997)
Seasons In The Sun/Bike/No One's Little Girl 7-inch (Twist TWIS 20 1997)
Don't Cry Baby.... It's Only A Movie CD (Damaged Goods DAMGOOD64 October 1998)
The Boy Who Couldn't Stop Dreaming/When I Grow Up I Want To Be... 7-inch (Damaged Goods DAMGOOD 170 May 1999)
ARCHIVE RELEASES:
They Could Have Been Bigger Than The Beatles LP (Whaam! BIG 5 August 1982) (reissued in June 1986 on Dreamworld, BIG DREAM 2 June 1986, and on Fire, REFIRE 9 1991, and on CD in July 2002, SFIRE014CD)
14th Floor/Oxford Street W1 7-inch (Overground OVER 003 March 1989) (reissue)
I Know Where Syd Barrett Lives/Arthur The Gardener/Mystery Track 7-inch Overground OVER 013 October 1990) (reissue)
Three Wishes/Geoffrey Ingram/And Don't The Kids Just Love It 7-inch (Overground OVER 020 July 1991) (reissue)
Camping in France LP (Overground OVER21 August 1991) (recorded live In France on 12 December 1985. Bonus tracks on CD version, OVERCD21: Happy All The Tim/Girl On A Motorcycle/Just Call Me Jack)
Smashing Time/King & Country/Three Cheers For Simon 7-inch (Overground OVER 23 February 1992) (reissue)
Where's Bill Grundy? 7-inch EP (Overground OVER 25 1992) (reissue)
Yes Darling, But Is It Art? (Early Singles & Rarities) LP (Fire FLIPCD001 January 1995) (reissued on CD in February 2003, SFIRE024CD)
Top Gear LP (Overground OVER48 March 1996) (recorded live in Osaka, Japan, 6 April 1994, though sleeve states 1995)
Paisley Shirts & Mini Skirts LP (Overground OVER52 October 1996) (recorded live at Hammersmith Clarendon, 22 May 1980)
Mod Is Dead LP (Teenage Kicks Kick LP-14 1996) (recorded live at Circus Gammelsdorf, Germany, 13th December 1991. 30 copies only, apparently)
You, Me And Lou Reed 7-inch EP (Little Teddy LiTe 740 1997) (reissue)
Prime Time Television Personalities 1981 – 1992 CD (Nectar Masters NTMCD563 September 1997)
Part-Time Punks – The Very Best of Television Personalities CD (Cherry Red CDMRED 152 March 1999) (features glowing sleevenotes from Alan McGee)
The Boy Who Couldn't Stop Dreaming CD (Vinyl Japan CD ASKCD112 March 2000)
Fashion Conscious CD (Little Teddy CD BiTe026CD December 2001)
And They All Lived Happily Ever After CD (Damaged Goods DAMGOOD 245 August 2005) (ragbag but appealing collection of unreleased material, live cuts, spoken word performances, and testimonials from the likes of Peel and Morrissey. Among the revelations are a cover of Abba's 'The Visitors' and a version of 'Girl At The Bus Stop' which Treacy originally gave to the BMX Bandits)

Terry And The Idiots

Terry Sylvester (vocals), Malcolm Joseph (bass), Stephen 'Gibbsy' Gibbs (guitar), Versa Manus (drums)

They have their place in history, via Lech Kowalski's D.O.A. – A Rite Of Passage, in which their shambolic efforts are recorded in an effort to depict the hopelessness of British youth. Kowalski – who would later film Ramones' documentary 'Hey, Is Dee Dee Home?' – couldn't have stumbled upon better subject matter than Terry, who wanders around council estates and complains of his lot with all the innate charm of fence post. As Peter Hardy of This Is Not TV noted: "To be fair though, it looks like he has a lot to moan about, as Kowalski does a wonderful job of making late-70s Britain look like the grottiest place in the universe."

The band's 'performance' (wherein he seems to be singing 'Anarchy In The UK', though the band is playing 'God Save The Queen') to a disinterested London pub audience is so rank it will stink out the rest of your DVD collection. You secretly cheer when he gets doused in beer. God knows where Kowalski found them, but be grateful no-one else did, let alone a record label.

Ian Canty of Part Time Punk fanzine eventually tracked down the wrongdoers, or at least bass player Malcolm Joseph. "The story of DOA was that the director was in a cab and asked the cab to go to the King's Road, but instead the cabby took him down to Kingsmead Estate,

Hackney. And then he met Terry. He asked if there was a punk band here gigging at the time. Terry didn't have a band and so he arranged with the director that he had a band and would play for him that evening at the Golden Shoe pub." Malcolm never got to see DOA because he was 15 at the time and the film came out with an 18 certificate. All he remembers of the band was that they also had a song called 'Ma Sylvester's Apple Crumble Pie'. However, he later persevered in music as part of 7th Heaven, who had a small hit in 1980 and collaborated with Massive Attack and Neneh Cherry. He also toured with Womack and Womack, Kool And The Gang, etc. Now, who'd have thought that?

They Must Be Russians

Guy Rope (aka Guy Wigmore; vocals), Spotty Dick (aka Mike Clarke; guitar), Lance Boil (aka Adrian; bass), Reggie Mental (aka Mark Breton; drums)

One of the first generation of Windsor punk bands alongside Open Sore – a dodgy spot to peddle punk considering the town's royal connections, THEY MUST BE RUSSIANS were the first band to feature Mike Clarke, head of Inflammable Material distribution and record label and the founder of Defiant Pose fanzine.

Clarke had started in his first band at school, which included the Humberstone twins, Klive and Nigel, who went on to form In The Nursery, playing covers of the Cortinas and Chelsea, alongside a smattering of originals. They played one school gig, supporting a local John Cooper Clarke-styled poet, alongside the first incarnation of They Must Be Russians (Clarke and Wigmore on guitar and vocals). However, their attempts to stage a show a Jubilee party in Windsor were predictably rejected by officialdom. Thereafter the two entities joined forces. They Must Be Russians were, of course, titled after a letter sent in by Irene Harris to a London newspaper protesting at Jamie Reid's safety-pinned desecration of the monarch. This headline also inspired the industrial/avant garde group of the same name in Sheffield, though, bizarrely, their guitarist, who later joined Clock DVA and the Box, would date Clarke's sister.

Their sole release came in 1979, a split-single with Joe 9T and the Thunderbirds, recorded in late 1978. "Joe 9T were two Scots guys who paid for the whole thing," Clarke recalls. "We met them whilst dossing for a summer on a beach in Antibes (near Nice, South of France). Lots of English punks drinking cheap wine, splitting up with our girlfriends and fighting with locals, etc." Shows followed at the Chippenham in Maida Vale alongside the Modettes, Passengers, Tesco Bombers (who included members of the Homosexuals) and Bank of Dresden. Though Peel played the single a couple of times, by the summer of 1979 the group had fizzled out.

From there Clarke took a break from bands before joining Bracknell punks Disease and helping promote shows at Slough's Studio One club (now a car park) with Windsor groups Void and Revolt, Farnborough's Black Easter, Slough's Death Pop and others. He then formed Bastards Of God before joining Youth In Asia, and finally Decadent Few in 1984, who played their first show at Studio One with the Sears. He's a bit bemused by the sudden rush of interest in his older bands, though. "It's only the last couple of years that anyone's actually asked me about it, mainly since Chuck Warner did a CD of old obscure UK 7-inches on his Hyped to Death label in the US." In the meantime he continues to run Inflammable Material distribution and the venerable Defiant Pose fanzine.

DISCOGRAPHY:

'Psycho Analysis' 7-inch (B-side by Joe 9T and the Thunderbirds; Gemme Joe 9T/LYN 6526 1979)
COMPILATION:
Messthetics # 3 CDR (Hyped2Death; 'Psycho Analysis')

Those Helicopters

Alan Robinson (vocals), Stephen John Maughan (bass), Andrew Barnden (drums), Harlan Cockburn (saxophone, guitar), Vincent Whitlock (keyboards), Andy Wood (guitar)

THOSE HELICOPTERS originally formed at the Maidstone College of Art in Kent, where the members were all students with the exception of Cockburn, who was a tutor in the film, video and sound department. Robinson was the principal lyricist, and named the band from the opening scene of Apocalypse Now, but the

songwriting remained essentially collaborative. Nowadays they are chiefly remembered for their inclusion on a popular MFP budget sampler of punk bands, We Do 'Em Our Way (alongside the likes of the Slits, Stranglers etc). Their version of Lennon and McCartney's 'World Without Love' was taken from their debut EP for Bonaparte Records in 1979.

"From the start there was a great deal of anarchy and creativity among band members," Cockburn told me. "It was not unknown to find Andy Barnden and Steve Maughan playing two different songs at the same time, and then having a punch-up onstage to decide who was right. I also demolished a guitar over Steve's head at one recording session. Andy said recently, 'We were great at starting songs, and great at doing the middle bits, we just often forgot to have an ending'."

Punk was just "in the air", he notes. "The previous year at Maidstone Art College, there'd been a casual band of staff and students called Vic Damone. We had a rule that as soon as anyone got halfway good at an instrument, they had to swap for something else. We recorded several times a week, and it was these tapes that formed the basis for student David Cunningham's hit singles as The Flying Lizards – 'Money' and 'Summertime Blues' (that's my home-made guitar that you hear on the intro bars to Money)."

I asked him about the nature of the songs. "Alan was particularly interested in madness and the work of RD Laing, also the work of Arthur Janov and primal screaming. A lot of the lyrics were quirky. The first single 'South Coast Towns' was a list of some of the out of the way towns on the south coast. 'Shark' was about paranoia, 'Eskimo' about alienation and so on. We didn't really do lurve songs."

Presumably because of their college connections, there was little dalliance with the local scene in Guildford. "Almost none. We did play Guildford and Reigate and Redhill. There was a time after guitarist David Ives had stopped playing with the band, and he was managing a centre for people with Down's Syndrome and other learning difficulties. He brought several coachloads of people to a gig in Reigate or Redhill, and they went crazy, dancing and bopping about from the first bar of our set. David had told them that we were very, very famous. All the other punters cleared out of the bar, and we played one of our best-ever gigs to about 50 people who were off their heads with excitement and arhythmic dancing."

So why did the band not conquer the world. "No idea. Too much fighting? Too much booze? Alan got married, went legit. Andy Barnden went crazy. I can't really recall... It was a great time to play music – all the walls had been knocked down. I'd previously played in some 'art rock' bands that were careful to get everything 'right'. In Those Helicopters we never got anything right. We were messy, chaotic, and very creative."

Cockburn was good enough to fill me in on the activities of the band's former members. He co-produced an album of songs with Steve Maughan, Singing Brains. "At about this time Steve was living in astonishing poverty in Tottenham, eating baked beans out of the can, heated over a candle. I think he was involved with Vic Reeves and Bob Mortimer at an early stage of their careers. Sometime later he was invited to a wedding, had nothing to wear, and decided to make himself a suit (I think out of old blankets). The suit was so admired at the wedding that Steve was commissioned to make several more, and he started doing very well as an art tailor. He says it was because of his training in sculpture that he could see how to cut and shape cloth. This went well for a while, but it was taking too much time to make each suit, so Steve turned his attention to hats, and became very successful, with factories in London and Europe." However, after a heart attack a couple of years ago, he moved away from the millinery business and started studying bricklaying. "When I saw him about a month ago, in a busy pub, he spent most of the time flicking through a book of designs for brick walls. Steve doesn't listen to music now, because he says it sounds better in his memory."

Barnden moved to Newcastle where he played in a series of bands before moving to Splott in Wales. He still drums and does voiceovers for TV and has his own storyboard company, having recently worked on Tomb Raider and Troy. He has also written a film script, set in Newcastle, called Pie. Original guitarist Andy Wood was last spotted in the Medway area. David Ives, who occasionally played additional guitar, went on to run a care home in Liverpool. Robinson worked with Cockburn on Dansing Curtains "and did some pretty wonderful stuff", according to the latter. They re-established contact together in 2005. In the intervening period

Robinson had worked as a producer and director for Television South in Maidstone, before going on to be a producer for RTE in Dublin. Whitlock demonstrated keyboards for a manufacturer and designed fonts for Letraset.

Cockburn, in addition to the aforementioned projects, engineered and co-produced albums with Jim 'Foetus' Thirlwell and became house engineer at Lavender Sounds, working with artists including Tenpole Tudor, the Mekons, Wreckless Eric and several reggae names. Thereafter he became a corporate video director, but also made music with Blah Blah Blah. He's collaborated with artists including Adrienne Thomas and a spoken word concept album with Roger Hillier, Ship Without Rudder, on ex-Bonzo Dog Band bassist Dave Clague's DJC Records. He also published his first novel in 2004, The Halcyon Way, on Via Books, and has recently moved back to the UK after several years in the States. And he's threatening to unleash his Those Helicopters tape archive on the world to see if they consent to show a little more interest second time around.

DISCOGRAPHY:

South Coast Towns/World Without Love/Flash Bernadette 7-inch EP (Bonaparte BONE 4 1979)
Shark/Eskimo 7-inch (State of the Art STATE 0000001 1980)
Dr Janov/Technical Smack 7-inch (Lavender Sound LAVENDER 001 1981)

Those Naughty Lumps

Martin 'Armadillo' Cooper (bass), Pete 'PM' Hart (vocals), Tony 'Max Factor' Mitchell (guitar), Kevin Wilkinson (drums), Peter 'Kid' Younger (guitar).

Formed in Liverpool in the summer of 1977, the NAUGHTY LUMPS secured a residency at the Havana Club and were fixtures on the early Liverpool punk scene. "While I was in my final year at Liverpool University in 1976/77," Wilkinson told me, "I got to know a first-year student called Pete Wylie through the university and Eric's. He didn't continue his degree and the rest is history. I was with Pete around the time of the first Clash gig at Eric's. It was in front of the stage that night that Wylie introduced me to (Ian) McCulloch (it was common in that 'scene' to refer to people by their surname; especially short names; Eagle, Cope, Drummond, Hart, McCulloch, Burns, Casey, etc). I can't imagine that I was referred to as the slightly unwieldy 'Wilkinson', although I do remember being hailed and referred to as 'Kevin Naughty Lump'. Anyway, that was the night that Julian Cope writes about in his OTT, misty-eyed way in Head On as the time that the Crucial Three were formed, although I don't remember Julian actually being around that early on. I remember him being around Eric's vaunting his abstinence from drugs (something of a tiresome Cope leitmotiv; all he seemed to do was criticise the rest of us for being into pharmaceuticals, although to be fair, drugs were not such a prominent phenomenon in the Eric's scene at that time). The Lumps were referred to in Merseybeat, the punk zine, as the grandfathers of the scene. Wylie fondly referred to me as the first real punk in Liverpool, although I would bow to the wonderful Spitfire Boys and perhaps the Accelerators as the seminal Liverpool punk bands, and people like Pete Burns and Holly Johnson as seminal scene punks, i.e. not in bands, till later, anyway."

Despite having something of a chronological head start, the Lumps didn't make their vinyl debut until 1979, when they became the second release on Bill Drummond's Zoo Records. He also placed 'Iggy Pop's Jacket', one of the era's more unlikely punk anthems, on Zoo's To The Shores Of Lake Placid sampler. It's a flight of fantasy in which the Ig's jacket is imbued with all sorts of mystical rock star properties, and is thus deemed the passport to, among other things, sports cars and cult success. It's very Liverpudlian and very funny, especially in its pay-off (the jacket doesn't fit, either figuratively or thematically).

There was a second EP for another Liverpool independent, Open Eye, in 1980, by which time Wilkinson, Hart and Cooper had been joined by guitarists Bobbie Carr and Gordon 'Beam' Anderson. Other members at various points included three additional bass players; Dave Dadwallader, Tony Bayliss and Steve Nelson, while both Bill Drummond and Julian Cope joined the band on stage for two shows. "I was present in the basement of the Open Eye Studios in Whitechapel at one of the first Teardrops rehearsals," Wilkinson remembers, "and was asked to join them on drums. I declined as the Lumps were more established, gigging regularly with residencies in the Havana Club and regular bookings at places like the Masonic and Wirral clubs and pubs. We were touring and managed by the formidable Frances Crook, girlfriend of singer Pete Hart (now famous as head of the Howard League for Penal Reform). We also had our first single ('Iggy Pop's Jacket') under our belt, and I got on well with my band. But I remained friendly with the Teardrops (and all the

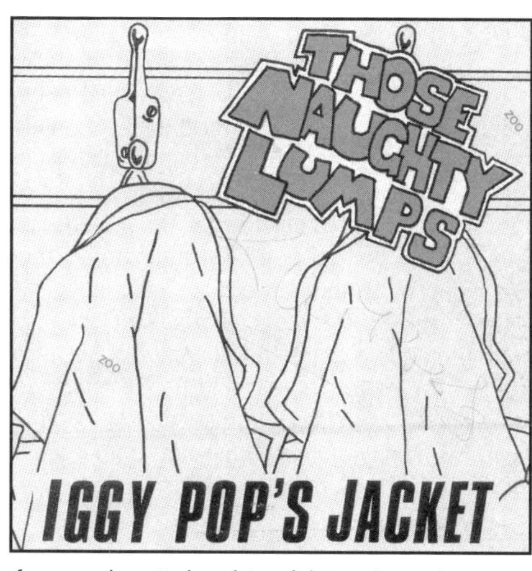

bands of the time, really), feeling very sorry for an exhausted and tearful Teardrops drummer, Gary Dwyer. This was during one of the early Teardrops recording sessions at the Open Eye Studio (aka Zoo Records), while he was having to do a backing track over and over again, take after take. Being a penniless job creation person having finished my degree, I was a little jealous of the local young Scouser punks who got their mummies and daddies to buy their equipment for them. We, the Lumps, were far from our non-Scouse homes and living hand to mouth in two communal households in Jubilee Drive."

After Those Naughty Lumps, Carr later joined the Moderates, Ton Trix (alongside Mike Score of A Flock Of Seagulls) and Surreal Estate. Younger went on to join Pete Wylie's Wah! Heat and Wilkinson, who once held John Lydon's pint when he played at Eric's, joined China Crisis and is currently a member of Norfolk's Melanie's Red Fleece as well as a lecturer.

Meanwhile 'Iggy Pop's Jacket' has become a cult item, not least in parts of North America, where Henry Rollins is among many to sing its praises. And there's a whole heap of unrecorded originals that never saw the light of day, for example 'Monosodium Glutamate', 'Disco', 'Tape Loop Life', 'Maybe It's Because I'm Gong Mad', etc.

DISCOGRAPHY:

Iggy Pop's Jacket/Pure And Innocent 7-inch (Zoo CAGE 002 1979)
Down At The Zoo 7-inch EP (Open Eye OP-EP 1002 1980)
Ice Cream/Down At The Zoo/I'm Gonna Die/Love Is A Reflex

Thrust

Pete Simpson (vocals), Mick Griffiths (guitar), plus six different drummers and three bass players

The THRUST, formed in Pontefract, Yorkshire in 1977, enjoyed a three-year existence, culminating in the release of their debut EP in February 1980. The group, which always featured Simpson and Griffiths but never a consistent rhythm section, played its debut gig on Christmas Eve 1977. The lack of permanence in the ranks undoubtedly impeded their progress, though they did make an impression, not least at an Anti-Nazi League benefit at Knottingly's Big K miner's social club, alongside Gang Of Four.

T

The most permanent of several different line-ups crystallised around the debut EP, which featured bass player Ifan Thomas and drummer Richard Battye. Only 100 of these arrived in picture sleeves because, in their own words, the band got bored of gluing them together. Despite developing a new set of songs ready to take on the world with, the band was put into mothballs when Griffiths took up a job as a hospital porter in Wakefield. They played their final show in December 1980 at Pontefract Town Hall and broke up shortly thereafter.

Battye subsequently became a successful Midlands-based photographer, spending three years compiling his acclaimed This England exhibition and specialising in performance photography, including many bands. "The Thrust was an odd time for me," Battye told me. "I was into the whole punk thing, but was still at school at this point. Pontefract was well placed for 'the movement' – sandwiched between Castleford and Featherstone. Pits were closing and punk was there for 'bored teenagers'. It was liberating and gave people a voice. We were the typical DIY band, but it mainly hung around Mick as he was the songwriter and was the only member who had a tiny bit of money. We could have been big, but needed a manager or at least some money. We played a youth club in Carleton and my drums got there half on a bus and the rest by skateboard! At the gig I was shot in the knee by an airgun. We got support slots that never quite happened, promised by John Keenan of the F club in Leeds – the Cure then The Monochrome Set (I was a huge fan of both). These fell through, but we were promised a slot with Generation X, we turned up, they didn't! We played anyway."

After the band, Thomas and Battye remained close friends. "We were both best men at each other's weddings. He has gone on to great things – tour manager with Blur for eight years, worked with many huge acts, from Black Sabbath to Erasure. He's now in Tasmania and works with The Bloodhound Gang."

DISCOGRAPHY:

The Thrust 7-inch EP (Ellie Jay EJSP 9341 February 1980)
Society/Northern Town/Fed Up/Reality (500 copies only, 100 in sleeves)
COMPILATIONS:
Bored Teenagers Vol. 2 CD (Bin Liner CD003 March 2001; 'Society', 'Fed Up')

Tights

Malcolm Orgee (vocals), Robert Banks (guitar), Barry Island (bass), Rick Mayhew (drums)

Worcester's TIGHTS can boast a couple of firsts – their excellent 'Bad Hearts' single being the debut release on Cherry Red Records, while their second effort, 'Howard Hughes', was one of the very first cassette singles. I asked Rob Banks if the Tights would have existed outside of the punk timeframe and schematic. "(It was) totally punk, with the feeling that anyone could get up and make some noise. God bless the Pistols for that. I remember Barry Island striding down my road, bass guitar in hand, looking like a man on a mission. The next thing I know 'we're a punk band'. By the end of the day we'd written a couple of tunes. We needed a singer and a drummer. Malcolm Orgee was the only punk in Worcester at the time. He looked great. 'Can you sing?' we asked him. Rick Mayhew joined the gang because he could play fast. I personally hated the 'new wave' bands at the time – they seemed like a watered down version of what was going on."

He has, as you might expect, fond memories of the time. "We all headed up to Barbarella's in Birmingham for an all-dayer. It was probably the first time we'd seen more than four punks at one time. The bands we can remember playing were the Killjoys, the Banshees (before they were signed), Johnny Thunders, and the Worst – they were great two-chorders! We came up with the name at that gig, inspired by a girl who wore stink bombs for perfume and had ripped up fishnet tights. Gigs were really hard to find in the area. People were nervous about putting punk bands on. After all, it was the sticks. However we got to play to bigger crowds as support to bands like Dr Feelgood at the Malvern Winter Gardens, where Cherry Red were promoters. Playing with Wire was great; they liked the band. Besides which, they bought a great PA system with them."

Richard Jones and Iain McNay had been promoting shows in Malvern under the auspices of Cherry Red Promotions. Iain McNay: "It was Richard again who persuaded me in the Malvern wine bar, on New Year's Eve 1977, that we should start a record label to release a Tights record." After cutting their first demo in a builder's lock-up they spent a weekend at Millstream Studios in Cheltenham, with John Acock producing. McNay: "On 2 June 1978, the Tights' first single was released. The following week it was record of the week in the now defunct Record Mirror. The week after that John Peel played it, and before we knew where we were, we had sold our initial pressing of 2,000 records. Meanwhile I had secured proper distribution for the single as a friend, David Thomas, had just started the first proper distribution service for independent records; Spartan Records." Indeed, almost all of the reviews of 'Bad Hearts' were favourable. Banks: "Making records for us, while we were still teenagers in a proper studio, was a big thrill, we thought our 'Bad Hearts' had cracked it! It felt odd at the time having such good reviews, we really just wanted to be hated by the old school hacks."

'Howard Hughes', which featured a picture of Charlie Watts' limousine on the cover, was again recorded at Millstream with John Acock. "The second Tights single ended up selling over 4,000 copies," McNay remembers, "but the band broke up soon after. They were all young and somehow not really prepared to commit themselves to gigging regularly." Does Banks agree with that appraisal? "No. Try to think of our situation, we were on the dole with no money, the drummer left and with him his van. Prior to that we played headline at the old Marquee in Wardour Street, so where's the lack of dedication there? So what could we do but move down to London where there was at least a music industry. We were very frustrated, having had two singles in the alternative charts, and all those reviews, and no support, so we went looking for it... Finally we ended up living in a brothel in Earls Court for five months, doing bum jobs and rehearsing on days off. Did we grow up quick! The first time I was shown to my room, the girl in charge smashed the door down with a hammer to let me in.

Youth from Killing Joke lived there for a while. I remember him telling us that his band had just been signed that day. A transvestite called Dennis also lived there and was in the process of having the 'chop and tuck'. He was known as Denise by the time we left. The Clash used to rehearse at the same studio as us. They liked to play music in between playing football in the kids' playground. We were taking a break when suddenly a plastic football came flying over some bushes and landed at our feet. The drummer picked it up and booted it as high as he could towards the playground. There was no sound from it landing on the concrete... shit. As we walked around the corner there it was – impaled on the railings. Topper was the only one to see the funny side in the pub later."

The Tights have since got back together and played a reunion show in December 2004 at Drummond's in Worcester, and recording a new EP. "We feel there's a lot of 'unusual business' still to finish," Banks adds.

DISCOGRAPHY:

Bad Hearts/It/Cracked 7-inch (Cherry Red CHERRY 1 June 1978)
Howard Hughes/China's Eternal (Cherry Red CHERRY 2 September 1978) (also issued on cassette)

Toads

Dave Smith (vocals, rhythm guitar), David Viner (vocals, rhythm guitar), Paul Cheetham (vocals, bass), Alan 'Polo' Pollard (drums)

The TOADS were Norwich's first punk band, formed in February 1977 after Smith placed an advert in the shop window of Cooke's Band Instruments. Though none of the members had much in the way of experience, Smith could boast of having played one show with a group who called themselves Dick Dangler And The Testicles. Just a few months later, in either May or June 1977, the Toads attempted to make a studio recording at Touchstone Studios, off Duke Street in Norwich. Three songs were recorded, 'Blood On My Wheels', 'Eyes' and 'I Don't Care About You', with Viner contributing two songs and Smith the third of those listed.

"The early gigs were interesting," Viner later noted on his website, "as we had very little equipment and sometimes two guitars had to share the same amp. The first (awful) gig (at the now-demolished Kingsway Pub in Norwich, stopped by the landlord when he realised it was being turned into a 'punk party') also had the vocals going through a guitar amp as well. All members except Polo wrote songs and the composer of each song always sung lead on it. This caused problems as both Dave Smith and Paul preferred to play rhythm guitar while singing lead vocals and therefore swapped over guitars if the lead changed. I didn't play bass and so stuck to rhythm." Another notable gig came when they played alongside the Stains at a Jubilee party in Cambridge Street in Norwich.

Cheetham would leave in the autumn due to 'musical differences', forcing Smith to take over on bass. Though auditions were held for a replacement, the group eventually decided to continue as a three-piece. Further tape recordings were made of practice sessions at Ranworth Village Hall, resulting in a demo tape that was circulated to London record companies, none of whom expressed any interest. A gig at Wymondham College was also the subject of a rather primitive recording. But after deciding to take a long hard look at their material (the Toads penned over a dozen original compositions, as well as live covers such as Bowie's 'Heroes'), by early 1978 they'd taken the decision to split up.

Dave Smith was subsequently behind Peel favourites Silent Noise (of 'I've Been Hurt (So Many Times Before)' fame). He also continued to work with Viner on bedroom tapes (songs were credited to various bands, some fictional, including the Toads, the Broadside Outcasts, Turkey Molesters, Dead Dogs Fly In Space, etc, on a cassette entitled Kilamadgargoyle). Despite getting a favourable review in the local paper, it never managed to sell a single copy.

Cheetham went on to a succession of bands including Ebonyset, the Blue Warthogs and the Ruskinsons, and then worked solo as a singer songwriter under the name Jean Paul Dionysis. He returned to Norwich to form The Time Machine and became involved in theatre before moving to Brighton and launching Club Space Toad, and his most long-running project, the Doctor Spacetoad Experience, a band which would occasionally feature Captain Sensible on guitar.

ARCHIVE RELEASE:
In The Subway 7-inch (Low Down Kids LDK 45-9 2005) (one-sided)

Toilets

Mike Peters (aka WC Smith; guitar), Glyn Crossley (aka Steve Shock; bass), Nigel Buckle (aka Des Troy; drums), Richard 'O'Malley' Jones (aka Beau Locks; vocals)

The story of Rhyl's first punk band, formed in 1977, is illustrative of the struggles young groups had to endure to get themselves a hearing. The idea was planted when Mike Peters saw the Sex Pistols play at a club called Quaintways in Chester in 1976. His conversion was immediate, and he decided to form his own band, though he elicited little interest initially from local musicians.

Instead he deepened his interest in the emerging punk movement by attending a Manchester show by the Clash in May 1977 on the White Riot tour. On his return he persuaded bass player Glyn Crossley and singer Gaz Hughes to join, with a rehearsal set for the following Saturday at Rhyl's Bee hotel. Peters, meanwhile, took the name from this new venture from a sign at the Victoria hotel in Prestatyn – though what was so special about the facilities there is a mystery lost to time. Hughes didn't bother to show at the ensuing rehearsal and so old school friend O'Malley was drafted. The drummer was recruited from a local paper advert. Together they played through covers of the Pistols, Buzzcocks and Ramones – which was enough to get them banned by the bar's owner. The nameless drummer was similarly unimpressed and vanished.

A local pro musician, Mogga, helped them out by allowing them to rehearse in his converted garage come practice room in Elwy Street, as Peters began to write his own songs – 'Alarm Alarm', 'Office Jobs', 'Social Security', etc. Meanwhile Nigel Buckle had come on board as drummer (Crossley, Buckle and Dave Kitchingman, who would later become Dave Sharp of the Alarm, had all previously played, alongside Kurt Wallinger of World Party, in the band Quasimodo). Kitchingman secured the group a show at the Palace hotel, for which the band re-christened themselves with their new silly punk names. The show was a success, and picked up excellent reviews. It led directly to a support slot to the Slits at the Stables in St Asaph, where by all accounts they upstaged the headliners.

Further gigs at the Palace followed as the group added songs such as 'Ice Cream And Rock' and 'James Bond' to their set. A Prestatyn punk, John Sox, was in the audience and told Peters he could hook him up with Roger Eagle, proprietor of Liverpool's Eric's club. The **TOILETS** appeared there on 22 October for a lunchtime show alongside the Shattered Dolls. Among the audience was Bob Geldof, who'd played Liverpool the previous evening with the Boomtown Rats. He was impressed, as was Eagle, who offered the Toilets a support slot to the Clash, booked to play later that evening. Peters described the ensuing 20 minute set (plus two encores) as the band's "finest moment".

It was downhill from there. They took on a manager, Chris Harrap, the Eric's DJ, but a trip to London went seriously awry when they found no record industry interest and were unable to secure a venue to play. There was another support slot at Eric's, this time to the Buzzcocks. But Buckle, who had never been particularly happy in the group because it wasn't providing any sort of wage, and had to be persuaded to make the trips to Eric's, was increasingly disillusioned, while O'Malley was wary of the more pop-orientated material Peters was now writing. With the band in turmoil, Peters and Sox took the opportunity to establish an alternative disco night at the 1520 Club in Rhyl, inviting local punks like the Cellophane Boys, Fractures and Amsterdam to play there.

Amsterdam featured Eddie MacDonald, an old school friend, on guitar. Frustrated with his current band's unwillingness to play his songs, and fired by the same kind of pop-punk vision as Peters, he asked if there was a position open within the Toilets – so to speak. Before that could happen Glyn Crossley hastened the band's demise by announcing he was moving back to London. That led Peters to conclude that the Toilets had run their course, and an announcement was made to the local press that the group's show on 27 January 1978 at the 1520 club would bring the curtain down on their career. MacDonald played with the band for the first time that night and Peters made his debut as a vocalist. They would work together again as part of Seventeen, before Peters moved on to form the Alarm.

The Toilets were resurrected in 1992 by Peters for a one-off performance at the first MPO (Mike Peters Organisation) Gathering weekend, as Pete Cole remembers. "The Toilets reunion was at an after show party of a home town gig for Mike Peters, at the Swan pub in Rhyl in January 1992, which is/was a pub run by Mike Peters' brother Steve. The place was heaving and the band was literally rubbing noses with the audience. The Toilets soared through a half-hour set of punk classics, culminating in a rip-roaring version of the Ramones' 'Sheena Is A Punk Rocker'.

Sadly, there will likely be no more such reunions. On 26 September 2001 Richard 'O'Malley' Jones died in Rhyl, aged 42.

Trash

Simon Wright (vocals), Mick Brophy (guitar, harmonica), Keith Oswald Jeyes (aka Steptoe; bass), Steve Pearce (drums)

The mythical properties of the Sex Pistols in igniting the music scenes of London and Manchester are well documented, but when they did get to play, their Mercury-like reach also extended to less celebrated suburban communities, as Mick Brophy recalled to me in 2005. "In Spring 1976 the Sex Pistols played support to Andy Ellison's Jet at the National College of Food Technology in Weybridge, Surrey. Of the 100 or so of the local crowd at the start of the gig, apart from the social committee, only nine were keeping Malcolm McLaren's imported punk-art-rock entourage company at the end. As with the legendary Free Trade Hall gigs in Manchester, all these folk went on to form or manage bands.

So it was that a bunch of broke Food Technology students adopted Sniffin' Glue's 'here's three chords, now form a band' mantra, locked themselves in the assembly hall and three months later had a set."

They were briefly a five-piece, featuring shared lead vocals from Jane 'Weasel' Wimble, before they settled on the above line-up. "Tony Bellekom – now Antony Bellekom, conceptor-in-chief of the BBC Radio Station 6 Music – took on management duties, helped by Pete Hawkins, who ran a sideline job with the Albion Agency while pretending to study, throwing what breaks he could at the act. For those that keep score that's seven of the nine at the Pistols gig. The remaining two people were the mysterious French lady Marie Claire Gauthier, who became the fan club secretary and Jordan-esque inspiration, the other was Linda Allen, now Linda Bellakom."

Weybridge didn't know what was about to hit it, or much care either. "Weybridge is dull if you have no money, and pretty dull even then. This is true for all of the Surrey towns on the Guildford train line, each of which spawned its own band at the time. Woking had the Jam, Hersham had Sham 69 (briefly and concurrently managed by Brophy) and Walton-on-Thames had the sadly under-rated Lurkers. However, luckily for **TRASH**, what Weybridge did have was an abundance of music industry movers and shakers. At one time St George's Hill housed John Lennon, but by 1977 Weybridge was home to Gordon Mills, manager of Tom Jones, Engelbert Humperdink and Gilbert O'Sullivan, Tim Rice and most importantly for Trash, Clive Selwood, the former UK label manager of Elektra Records. Clive, like his friend Chas Chandler, had a small label deal funded by Polydor and was looking for bands; again, luckily for Trash, his daughter Bee (the label was called SaraBee after his two girls) caught Trash playing in the college canteen, told her dad and the rest was history. Bee Selwood now has her own successful label but Trash can claim no credit for that."

The band cut their debut single, 'Priorities' backed by 'Look', shortly thereafter, with Steve Pearce replaced by Reading's Brian Devoille, later to join Twelfth Night, on drums. "Keith and I graduated, Simon dropped out and Trash moved to Reading, where we had a band house and were adopted by Danny and Vic, old-school managers of Bones Club. Danny and Vic took a shine to Trash, partly because they lived over the road and would turn up at the drop of a hat when bands pulled out. And partly because Marie Claire Gauthier (now presciently calling herself MC) wore next to nothing as she danced enthusiastically to Trash's punky-r'n'b-powerpop." At Bones Club, and other gigs in London and the south, Trash supported the Slits ("who nicknamed us the Pinta Boys when we were in our all-white clothes phase"), the Lurkers ("a great band"), Wire, 999, Johnny Curious And The Strangers as well as Burlesque ("truly odd and fab").

The garnered some media support, but it was not enough. "Despite the promo stunt of playing on the back of a flatbed truck through the centre of London en route to the Polydor offices, and Mike Read, then at Thames Valley Radio, plugging the song as far as he could, 'Priorities' was never a priority for the discerning listener. It didn't make the second pressing. However, the band thought they'd really made it when their poster was used as a backdrop for a bed-sit scene in a Coronation Street episode and in the film Jubilee." They failed, however, to win a role in the Quadrophenia movie. "Simon was very good at blagging using Trash demos under various band pseudonyms. This is how Trash got to the final in a competition, judged by Roger Daltrey and John Entwistle, to be a band in Quadrophenia. The winner was Cross Section performing an authentic version of 'High Heel Sneakers', rather than Trash performing an out of tune 'Can't Explain'."

Clive Selwood persevered with the idea for another single, however, employing the services of Shel Talmy, the US producer now based in London who had worked with the Who, Kinks et al. "Shel had a flat in Knightsbridge with what looked like wardrobes converted into speaker cabinets. Clive took Mick to meet him. In my naivety, I had misheard a rumour and was worried that Shel was deaf. In fact, Shel was nearly blind and smoked like a trooper. His dimps missed ashtrays as he moved around, so the white carpet in his flat actually looked polka dot." 'Nervous', backed by 'Dumb Blondes', was recorded at Roundhouse Studios with new drummer Simon Butler-Smith ("three in 18 months; This IS Spinal Tap"). "Despite sounding great, it did naff all." Live work started to fall off as the pay to play ethos took hold. "In the spring of 1978, Simon called it a day and everyone went their separate ways."

Brophy moved to Manchester and answered an advert in the NME for a singer. "The pub scene was healthy, even paid the acts, and Idiot Rouge's singer/writer Nick Simpson had left to go to college (later to form 23 Jewels) and the drummer had left to form Magazine, and later Swing Out Sister." Bass player John Martin and guitarist Neil Cossar (Coss the Boss) had gigs lined up, many with buddies Any Trouble with whom they shared a small van and a PA. So they became the Cheaters with the addition of drummer Mike Juckes, the first of innumerable line-up changes. Thanks to a brief resurgence of interest in roots music overall – R&B, rockabilly and soul, the Cheaters got a deal with EMI, cutting one single for Parlophone, 'Nothing Ever Happens On Saturday'." There was also an album for Revo Records, Sweat It Out and an 'airplay hit', 'Confidante'.

The Cheaters broke up in the summer of 1986. Cossar and Brophy went on to play in Cosmic (sic), "the world's only two-man one-man band." Brophy is now the sales director for a loudspeaker company, Neil Cassar ran a local radio station before becoming a record plugger and recently wrote the book This Day In Music based on his website. Antony Bellekom is "big at Radio 2", Pete Hawkins manages Neil Brockbank, now a producer, among others. Marie Claire Gauthier got an MBA and is a financial controller for a French corporation. Simon Wright is a major authority on organic food and Fair Trade. Steve Pierce is a teacher, Keith Oswald Jeyes rejoined the food industry. Digger Barnes directs pop promos.

DISCOGRAPHY:

Priorities/Look 7-inch (Polydor 2058-939 October 1977)
'N-N-E-R-V-O-U-S'/Page 3 (Dumb Blondes) 7-inch (Polydor 2059-013 April 1978)

Trax

Willie Adamson (vocals), Neill 'Nobby' Martin (keyboards), Derek Armstrong (bass), Dougie Ross (guitar), Neil Thompson (drums)

The band that eventually became TRAX was formed early in 1978 as the Straits, though they were also known as the Zips for three gigs. Oft-likened to fellow Dunfermline punks the Skids, whom they would frequently support, they would struggle to avoid comparisons. "This perception (that they laboured under the shadow of the Skids) was never particularly accurate anyway," notes long-term band friend and roadie Colin Gourlay, "and stemmed from their shared hometown and press laziness when describing them, preferring to pigeonhole rather than write original, imaginative text."

While supporting the Skids on a foray down south, at the Marquee in London in February 1979, the Straits were informed of the existence of another band of that name, an all-female quintet from York. They took the immediate decision to adopt the name Trax instead. That year, with new drummer Tony Taylor on board, they completed some 70 shows.

Trax merited a small national write-up in Garry Bushell's Scotland Uber Alles November 1979 feature for Sounds, in which he described a live set he caught in Edinburgh: "Sinewy modern rock is the aptest description for their driving, impressive, bursting, bruiser of a sound." Gourlay later recalled a show at the Kinema Ballroom on 29 March 1979. The audience demanded a Trax encore at the expense of the Skids – and the fact that Stuart Adamson was generous to offer them the stage so to do, though the band had enough humility about them to decline.

The band recorded just the one single, on their own Lonely Records imprint in September 1979, recorded at Cargo Studios in Rochdale. John Peel played the record three times, and there was also local support from Radio Forth (who made it their record of the week). The original 1,000-copy pressing sold out, and a similar amount were repressed, though there were problems over the late arrival of the picture sleeve (recounted in an article in Sounds 'Fair Deal' column). As well as the Skids, Trax also frequently appeared alongside the Delinquents (aka the Delinx, featuring future Big Country guitarist Bruce Watson), the Freeze, Cuban Heels and the Subject (whose Peter Wishart would later join Runrig).

The band stuttered to a halt in January 1980 when Taylor left due to personal differences. Tony Whelan took over on drums but there was little further progress, and by July 1980 they were no more (though there was an ill-starred attempt at a reformation featuring Bruce Watson in place of Armstrong). Martin, Adamson and Taylor, along with Willie Gardner of the Zones, subsequently worked on the short-lived Geneva. Martin then joined the Baby Knives and the Happy Family before collaborating with Momus. He is now a lecturer in Celtic and Scottish Studies at the University of Edinburgh. Adamson remained in Fife and continued to make music with 7 West. Armstrong teaches English in Thailand. Colin Gourlay, meanwhile, reckons there are up to 30 Trax songs still in his personal vault, mostly originals, alongside covers of the Buzzcocks, Stranglers, Dr Feelgood and the Motors, as well as the live favourite, 'One Track Mind' by the Heartbreakers.

DISCOGRAPHY:

Trax 7-inch EP (Lonely LONESOME ONE September 1979)
Home/Losing Out/Late Nite Call Out (1,000 copies, then 1,000 more re-pressed)
(More details about Trax can be found at Colin Gourlay's website, www.kinemagigz.com)

Tunnelrunners

Madoc Roberts (vocals, guitar), Graham Jones (guitar), Jeff Burton (drums)

Neath trio formed by Roberts and Jones in 1977 who played around the Swansea area between 1978 and 1982. "We started the band because we were young!" Roberts told me. "Punk came at just the right time for our rebellious teens. The main thing was the attitude – music had become stale and self-indulgent. Even we could play punk. The reason we only lasted a few years was because we all went off to college. We played a few gigs when we all came home for holidays but our gigs were once described as being 'as rare as manners in Penclawdd'."

T

"The venue in Swansea was the Circles Club. The changing room walls were signed by all the bands, and the carpet in the club was sticky. In later years they found a dead body there! This was the first place we played. We had been practising for weeks with a drummer who pulled out on the night. We told our last minute replacement that we would hold the first note of the song until he got the beat. The PA was set up so that all the vocals were on one side and the guitars on the other. At the start of the night a bloke at the bar was shouting for us to get off and booing. By the end he was pleading with us to get off, claiming we were ruining his night out! When we got off stage our one fan told us not to worry and to go back on and do 'Do You Wanna Dance' (our one and only cover). We told him we had just done – it was so bad he didn't even recognise it. Next gig was at the Heathcliff (a local community centre). Gary Glitter was playing in town so they weren't expecting many people. We were due to be

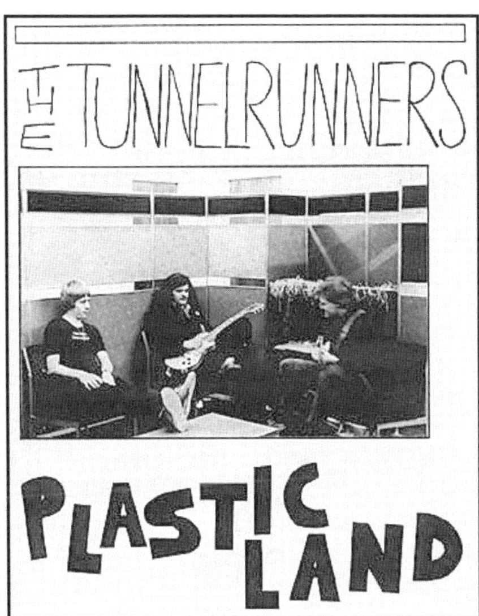

on first but due to the lack of audience, the other bands pulled rank in order to get it out of the way. By the time we got on Glitter had finished and the place had filled up. I finished the gig with one string – still forming the full chords or I wouldn't know where to put my fingers – the place was in uproar and after that things took off."

They issued an EP for Steve Mitchell's Sonic International Records in 1980, but to little impact. "We loved playing live but always had a feeling of not overdoing it and it becoming ordinary. The single wasn't that important to us at the time, probably more so to Steve as that was all he did." A follow-up EP shared its fate. Mitchell narrated the story thus: "I had the tapes, and had released the 'Plastic Land' EP. The band had told me I could do whatever I wanted with the extra tracks so, when I decided I wanted to press up a second 7-inch, I went ahead despite not being able to contact the band members who had by then moved away. I thought I'd find them at some point. I only pressed 100 copies – all white labels, no sleeve – just for sale locally. However, just at this time our local Virgin shop closed. The singer of the Pseudo Sadists allowed his goat to piss in the shop during a visit from the area manager, who was already contemplating closing the shop as it barely made any money. I then had nowhere to sell the record. I estimate that maybe 20 copies were actually sold. The remaining copies were destroyed by accident sometime in the 80s when I was throwing out some other white label single I'd made but had too many of (the Crash Action Winners single). Now I don't have one, though my mother does! I have never been able to find anyone in Swansea who actually has the record."

I asked Roberts about his impressions of the punk scene at that time, particularly in relation to Wales. "When punk first started there was very little in the press or on the radio so there wasn't a uniform like the Sid Vicious clones all in black that came along a bit later. This meant that everyone wore what they wanted and interpreted it as it suited them. This led to what was actually a very colourful scene both in terms of the look and the music. I went to see bands nearly every week including the Clash, the Damned, the Buzzcocks, etc also lesser known bands like the Lurkers who I loved and saw many times. I also saw a very early Adam and the Ants in their tartan gear and the Coventry Specials. My favourite band were the Ramones."

After the band's split Jones became a projectionist at an arts cinema, Burton is "something big in computers and travels around Europe". "I am a TV producer/editor," Roberts tells me. "When I am not making programmes about Hitler's relatives or chasing him up the Andes, I still work on youth music shows, which I have always done. I have edited shows and videos with a lot of the Welsh bands that have emerged over the recent years such as Catatonia, Super Furry Animals, Gorkys, Stereophonics etc. So music is still there and the punk attitude definitely helps – both with sorting out the crap and with my freelance lifestyle. I think the best thing I got from the punk era was a healthy suspicion of people in authority."

Your best chance of tracking down any recorded instances of the **TUNNELRUNNERS** is via the tracks included on the Powerpearls and Teenage Treats compilations. They subsequently reformed in the wake of the interest and were playing live as recently as 1999. "Yes, we did reform a couple of times. We made a film in the mid-80s, it was a musical about unemployment. The arty types at the local art centre hated it. Then we had a more serious go in the 90s, which lasted until a few years ago. We had a very good drummer, Guy Lawrence and a very musical bass player, Neil Sinclair. The stuff we did was still pretty raw – we never polished it up and right at the very end we were doing some stuff that sounded pretty much like our early stuff. We quit when the venues dried up and the waistlines expanded beyond acceptable limits."

T

DISCOGRAPHY:

Plastic Land 7-inch EP (Sonic International SI 4282 1980)
Plastic Land/Forever Crying At Love Songs/Average/Words/I Can, You Can (only 250 copies, later re-released with a 'live' picture sleeve in 1981)
100MPH 7-inch EP (Sonic Sound International 1982; no catalogue number, white label)
Colours/Candy/Blue Peter/I Hate Love (only 100 copies)
COMPILATIONS:
Powerpearls Vol. 4 ('Words')
Teenage Treats Vol. 10 (Xerox 2000, 'Colours')

TV Product

Simon Hinkler (vocals, guitar), Tony Perrin (bass, vocals), Paul 'Jess' Jesperson (drums)

Sheffield punk band which featured Simon Hinkler before he moved on first to Artery and subsequently Pulp and then the Mission. I tracked him down over the net. "I thought I'd managed to keep that band quiet all these years! TV PRODUCT really were the first band I was in. The single we did was my first time in a studio, and it sounds nothing like the band we actually were. I recently dug out the one and only existing copy of a cassette we put together over several rehearsals, and in retrospect we were totally acceptable, and generally quite punky."

Hinkler filled me in on the background to the band. "It all started with just me and my neighbour, Tony Perrin (later to be manager of Artery and the Mission). I taught him to play bass. We were both into stuff like the Pistols, Stranglers, Buzzcocks, etc. Tony was a student over from Manchester. He looked around the Polytechnic to find other people who could play, and came up with a drummer, another guitarist, and a singer who couldn't sing at all. He just looked the part. None of us had ever written a song before, but the other guitarist, Glyn Thomas, came up with about three or four songs ranging from one to three minutes long. We probably rehearsed less than half a dozen times, and put together about ten songs, each of us having a go at writing."

"The songs had no major thread or message, just new wave, punk-ish stuff about being different and anti-establishment etc. The music was sometimes a bit like the Buzzcocks, at other times more experimental (depending who wrote the initial idea). Our first gig was in someone's bedroom at a party. I did the singing. The second one was supporting Artery at Sheffield Polytechnic. Tony arranged that gig so we could get to play in front of a crowd."

"After that, I think we only played twice more. By this time the singer and the other guitarist had finished college and buggered off out of Sheffield. So we became a three-piece, with me singing and playing guitar. It was with this line-up that we went into Cabaret Voltaire's studio to record that awful single." Perrin had approached Stephen Mallinder after noting that Cabaret Voltaire had recorded other local bands at their Western Works studio and badgered him for some free studio time, which was willingly granted. The record would be issued on Product via Marcus Featherby's Limited Edition Records. "Tony and I had become big-time aficionados of the Sheffield scene, going out to all the gigs and generally being into it. So as it turned out, we tried to make the two songs on the single a bit more experimental instead of 'punky'. It was also my first time in a studio, and it all just turned out crap. In retrospect we should have recorded them straight, as we would have played them live." Incidentally, the other band on the split single, the Prams, featured another future Artery member, Neil Mackenzie.

Perrin then left Sheffield. "I tried to keep TV Product going with just the drummer (Jess Jesperson) and a new bass player called Paddy Shaw. I tried to lead it in a more experimental direction, quite honestly to be more like Artery, and maybe Joy Division, who were my faves then. At that time, I was regularly driving Artery to gigs in my van, and I thought they were the best thing ever. One night I was asked to join the band on keyboards, and I had no hesitation in saying yes, and leaving TV Product. Jess, Paddy and Glyn Thomas, who'd returned to Sheffield, recruited a new singer, Ian Cutler, and carried on briefly as TVP but then folded." Jespersen would go on to join Springsteen tribute band Glory Days.

I asked Simon for a general overview of the Sheffield punk scene at that time. "They were wonderful times. I was aged from 18 to 25. I'd left school and grown up at exactly the right time to see it all develop, unfold, and to be a part of it. There were never many punk bands in Sheffield. You'd see students from out of town dressed punky in 1977 for a year or so, but very soon Sheffield became something very different. It was thanks largely to Cabaret Voltaire, who had been pioneering originality since before punk. Then with the late-70s spawning bands like Human League, Artery, They Must Be Russians, etc there was a slew of people getting up on stage and doing whatever they wanted. Being original was a major factor. I don't think there could possibly have been a more free, creative period anywhere in the history of British music. I often look back and think they were the best days of my life."

DISCOGRAPHY:

Nowhere's Safe/Jumping Off Walls 7-inch EP (Limited Edition Take/24 1979) (B-side tracks by the Prams; 'Me', 'Modern Men')

Twisted Nervez

Dave 'Stena' Stinson (vocals, guitar), Paul Allen (bass, vocals), Nigel Spears (bass), Peter Fitzmaurice (drums)

The origins of TWISTED NERVEZ can be traced to main man Stinson bumping into a youthful Pete Wylie, then a member of the Glass Torpedoes. Wylie's initial interest was in the zipped jacket that Stinson had acquired in Amsterdam, which he wanted to buy, but it led to a friendship. Wylie would help Stinson purchase his first guitar and introduced him to a prospective bass player.

Twisted Nervez made their debut at St Saviours Church in early 1978. "We were invited to play after we told the priest we were a nice local band! Little did he know what we were about, as over 100 punks descended on the church and caused a near riot. The priests were shouting at us to stop and saying we were sinners!" The first song they wrote together was 'Test Tube Babies', "as we thought the idea was lunacy at the time, and still do". They gigged regularly both in Liverpool and elsewhere, including shows at the Warehouse, Liverpool University, Eric's and Brady's, with bands including the Damned and pragVEC (their first show at Eric's in April 1979). "We rehearsed in a place called Olly's at the top of Renshaw Street, a punk clothes shop. They later called the shop Nervez. Every time a band pulled out of a gig in the local pub around the corner, The Masonic, we played."

They thus got a bit of a reputation, not least for the amount of graffiti they generated. "One thing we did do a lot was get drunk," confirms Stinson, "and go all around Liverpool with spraypaint, spraying the name everywhere and we even got a viewing in the Open Eye art gallery under a section called graffiti, which was pleasing."

There were several recordings made, but these were all issued on cassettes that were given away free, or at nominal cost. "We thought at the time the peeps should have everything for free and we didn't want to know about labels, etc." A single did finally emerge on the local Troubador label. Which is a story in of itself. "The Troubador label was originally set up in the 60s for the Beatles, but they turned it down and Gerry and the Pacemakers were the label's first artist. And then years later we came along, Liverpool's other favourite sons (of bitches) and said yes, and got ripped off big time!"

By this time the line-up featured Stinson and Allen plus Mark Nunnen on vocals and drummer Steve Corrigan.

Twisted Nervez got a fair amount of local press, including radio interviews and the like, and had a solid following, but they were never considered an essential act by the scenesters. "We were never the most hip band around for all the so called in-crowd, but we rocked like a mother and played it like it should be." These days Stinson is still playing live with A Thousand Fake Heroes (previously 0898). Paul Allen played with Ministry Of Love II. "Hey," Stinson points out, "I was just told that the Twisted Nervez single is worth 10 quid now. I may sell the 50 copies I have left!"

DISCOGRAPHY:

Return Of Faith, Hope And Charity 7-inch EP (Troubador 1980)
Youth/Opportunity Knocks/Always Alone

T

UK Subs

Charlie Harper (aka David Charles Perez; vocals), Richard Anderson (guitar), Robbie Harper (drums), Steve Slack (bass)

It's easy to berate the Subs. After all, they've given their critics plenty of ammunition. If you lie down with dogs, you get fleas. And if you lie down in fleapits, where many of the Subs' endless latter day gigs took place, and you've got a singer who was born sometime during the Norman conquests, you're gonna get hammered by the music press. Especially when you veer into karaoke punk rock albums, when it seemed Charlie Harper was seeking to redefine pointlessness as an art form, and swap drummers and bass players like schoolkids exchange Pokemon cards.

But for all that... the early **UK SUBS** albums especially, despite what the punk fashion police would have you believe, are engaging, entertaining, and musically literate. Few who do not know these records would associate the UK Subs with the level of finesse and aural bite they often displayed. It didn't exactly help that they got caught up in the second wave of punk and were bracketed alongside one-trick ponies like the Exploited. But their first four studio albums contain some of the most searing musicianship of the punk era. And the band that produced them was smart, funny and personable. There are also a few treasures to be found on their later output, particularly anything that their genuinely innovative guitarist Nicky Garratt was associated with, but the gems are spread a good deal thinner.

Charlie Harper, as everyone knows, was knocking on a bit when punk kicked in. In fact, he was old enough to be a part of London's last big generational upheaval, the swinging 60s. He'd busked around Europe with a harmonica and an acoustic guitar, hung out with the Rolling Stones (he was at one time nicknamed 'Charlie Stones') and taught Rod Stewart how to play blues harp. Thereafter he set up several pay-the-bills R&B ventures, the first being Charlie Harper's Free Press Band, titled in tribute to Muddy Waters' song 'Albert Harper's Free Press'. They split when his fellow band members showed no interest in turning professional, so instead he led the Charlie Harper band and also moonlighted with a group called Bandana. By the mid-70s he was playing countless pub and club engagements alongside Scott Gorham, before he joined Thin Lizzy, as Fast Buck (later Gorham would also record with the Pistols' Cook and Jones as part of the Greedy Bastards). These nocturnal activities were largely subsidised by his hairdressing business in Tooting.

The fourth or fifth incarnation of his various R&B combos were the Marauders. He decided to switch tack after a few nights at the Roxy watching bands like the Damned. "To me," reckoned Harper, "punk was an excuse for fanatics to have their say, people like me who never had a chance before, people who have just been laughed at. Blokes like me who've just been through life being sneered at, fingers pointing, saying, 'That's the local nutcase'. When punk came along it was the best thing that ever happened to me. I was accepted." The Damned would remain a particular influence, as he recalled to Phaze One fanzine. "The Damned are one of the bands that actually changed my whole life. I was going to Damned gigs, jumping around and then playing completely different music the next day." A new name was evidently required so he opted for the Subversives, later trimmed to the Subs, and finally the UK Subs when he learned of the presence of a Scottish band of that name on Stiff Records.

Of course, Harper was in a unique position to compare the impact of the swinging 60s with the somnambulant 70s, as he confirmed to me in 2005. "The punk explosion was almost an exact parallel to the 60s R&B scene. In fact, early punks adopted all the 60s style, buying up all the old clobber. 'My suit only cost a quid,' someone would say. Then someone would announce, 'Mine was 50p!'. 'Yeah, but it's held together with safety pins.' Every band played a cover version like 'Wooly Bully', a big hit in the 60s, every band has a 60s song on plastic, so the similarities were there."

The line-up quoted at the start of this entry, essentially the Marauders in punk garb, was soon shuffled, shortly after Harper suffered his 'first' heart attack, largely as a result of prolonged sulphate use. Rehearsals at the Furniture Cave on the King's Road saw Harper's flatmate Greg Brown replace Anderson, who joined the Pentecostal Church, while Steve Jones took over on drums and a saxophone player, Dave Collins, was added. Of much greater import was the recruitment of guitarist Nicky Garratt, Harper's soon to be longstanding co-

Charlie Harper, head in hands, and his Subs.

writer. Classically trained but principally self-taught, he moved to London from Leicestershire on 1 January 1977. Previously he's enjoyed a minor career in a local blues band with Honey Boy Hickling and Big Al Taylor, then a band with Geoff 'J.B.' Blythe, later of Dexy's Midnight Runners.

In London he formed the Specimens, a short-lived punk band, though their song 'Ronnie Biggs' did transfer to the Subs' set, where it became 'B.I.C.'. He'd been advised to check out Harper's group, who had "loads of gigs booked", but had mistakenly presumed they were called the US Jets. "I first met Charlie at his apartment, where I was waiting for him to return from his salon," Garratt told me in a letter in 1991. "Charlie was a hairdresser with a small business at the rear of a clothes store where the band would meet before gigs to load the ancient Marshall PA into the van. The UK Subs, as they turned out to be called, had been playing since the end of 1976 with a variety of personnel fronted by Charlie. They played a mix of punk and R&B with, at that point, a temporary guitarist and even a sax player filled in on covers like 'Woolly Bully' and 'Talking Book'."

Garratt made his debut at the Western Counties pub on 15 October 1977, three days after that first meeting, and without an audition. "He was dressed in black and looked like a young Wilko Johnson," Harper later recalled. "I played the early demos that we did and he liked them and that was it." "Although we kept the extra guitarist and sax player for another week," Garratt told me, "Charlie and I put together a core of punk songs for the set in those two days before the first show. The songs included some that Charlie had written like 'I Couldn't Be You' that Charlie had reworked while in the Marauders and 'Stranglehold', along with new (more punk style) songs we wrote together like 'Telephone Numbers' and 'Illegal 15'. Suddenly the Subs were a 100% punk band." Albeit one with a musical pedigree, as Garratt notes. "Charlie had a 'street' background as far as live performances, while I had five years' training on classical guitar, as well as earlier bands. Charlie's 'get up and play' spirit certainly taught me a great deal, but I think our musical DNA was fully loaded before that."

With the line-up now settling down to Harper, Garratt, Slack returning on bass and Jones on drums, they secured residencies at the Western Counties and Tooting's Castle pub. Jones was replaced by Rory Lyons in November 1977 as the group, whose HQ remained Harper's Tooting salon, where he coiffeured punk hairstyles for the likes of Adam Ant, further honed the new material. A show at Brighton's Buccaneer venue on the 18th was filmed by Southern TV and transmitted in January 1978 – a photograph from the same show later appeared on the cover of the American release A.W.O.L. On 21 November they cut their first demo as the

UK Subs, featuring 'Stranglehold', 'Tomorrow's Girls' and 'Disease', at YMC studios. "Our first attempts at recording were not good," Harper told me. "We all recorded together in the studio to get a more 'live' sound, but it was hard to capture the live energy and attack." Two days later they played Croydon Scamps to a crowd of absolutely no-one – the manager being required by his licence to put music on, receiving £35 for their efforts before the doors were even opened. Later that month they made their debuts at London's most prominent punk venues, the Roxy and Marquee.

Steve Slack was losing interest, but agreed to remain while the band made their recorded debut as part of the Farewell to the Roxy compilation album (the UK Subs' set, recorded on 28 December 1977, was later released as Live Kicks). His elder brother Paul took over immediately this was completed, and was given three days to prepare for his debut show at Liverpool's Eric's. In attendance that night were representatives from Stiff and Chiswick, both of whom passed on the group, though Stiff would later issue Live Kicks, much to the band's consternation, shortly after debut album Another Kind Of Blues had charted. But then Charlie had sold off the publishing rights to the Roxy set in exchange for a crate of beer while down the Vortex one night.

The group, with Robbie Bardock stepping in for Lyons, who later moved on to King Kurt, continued to gig extensively throughout London, at the Vortex, Bridge House, Music Machine and 100 Club. Their 10 January show at the latter saw Paul Weller and Joe Strummer among the audience. "We were supporting a reggae band," Lyons recalled, "We'd finish a song and Charlie would say, 'We're just waiting for the drummer to catch up.' I ended up tying him to a table in the bar by the end of his scarf after the gig. He didn't even notice and the table and drinks toppled over when he got up to walk away." At the end of January they'd secured a five-week residency at the Mitre in Tooting, which unfortunately fell through when the landlord was hit on the head with a pool ball.

On 3 February 1978 they entered the studio for the second time to record 'Tomorrow's Girls' at Barry studios in London, but were unable to get the right drum sound. Despite the failure of these sessions, they continued to pull good audiences at venues including the Mitre and Forrester's Arms in Tooting, Battersea Arts Centre, Putney's White Lion, the Moonlight Club, Music Machine and Canning Town Bridge House. In so doing they established a reputation as the hardest gigging band of their generation and Harper as the James Brown, or indeed, Peter Pan, of punk music. However, getting gigs was becoming increasingly difficult as the group faced bans from at least five pubs, as their volatile audience swelled and proved a little boisterous. At one point Wayne County accused them of having a 'fascist' following, which was unequivocally denied by the band, who also played a couple of Rock Against Racism shows to emphasise the point.

They picked up yet another new drummer, Pete Davies, in April. He was aboard for the group's debut John Peel session, recorded on 23 May. Such was Peel's enthusiasm for the band that he offered to finance their debut single, after sympathising over the lack of record company interest. (Two further Peel sessions followed, on 6 September 1978 and 17 June 1979). Their first national tour came as a support to the Farewell To The Roxy album, an ill-fated Scottish haul alongside Blitz, Acme Sewage Co and the Jets. Funding was non-existent and the group subsisted by undertaking washing up duties. They were forced to hire a car, on Nicky Garratt's girlfriend's credit card, in order to get back to London. Garratt: "By the time the tour happened, the UK Subs were by far the biggest band on it. Really, the attempt to do the tour was puzzling, as none of the other bands were really doing much. It was like the UK Subs and a ton of opening bands. I think the organisers were trying in vain to promote a couple of bands they were managing." A series of supports to Sham 69, Girlschool, Tubeway Army and the Ramones, who would later cancel, at the Plymouth Metro, on 6 September, lifted their spirits somewhat.

Prior to that, on 11 July 1978, the UK Subs entered Spaceward Studios in Cambridge and cut three tracks; 'C.I.D.', 'I Live In A Car' and 'B.I.C.'. These would comprise their debut single, released as part of a one-off deal with City Records, the only label thus far to express any interest. Garratt: "We most likely met Phil Scott of City through Girlschool, who were close friends of the Subs at the time. He was a good guy and did his best for us, as far as I can remember." The single was released in eight different colours, establishing the Subs' reputation for rainbow vinyl. The A-side was informed by the old bill constantly sniffing around their shows at the Castle in Tooting. 'I Live In A Car', always one of the band's most enduring tunes, was "just about living in a tour van and not seeing much of anything else. The basic idea was that when the taxman or anyone's after you you're never there, you're in the van, you're away somewhere else. That's the kind of basic message, whenever anyone's trying to get money off you, you're not in. Which was very, very convenient. Most of the time." A second TV appearance followed as part of a BBC2 Omnibus documentary on independent record labels.

Following the single's release the Subs signed to Alistair Primrose's Ramkup management team, including manager Mike Phillips, on 16 May, over a couple of beers at the Prince William Henry in Blackfriars. He negotiated a deal with RCA subsidiary Gem later that month. The group were now 'proper' punk recording artists, though, interviewed by Garry Bushell for Sounds in August, Pete Davies insisted: "I don't consider us to be a punk band, because punk when it started was young kids who didn't really know how to play. We've all been playing for years apart from Paul, the bassist, who started from scratch. He learnt the bass in about one week before we played Eric's." In the same interview, Harper pointed out how the band had changed. "When UK Subs started we were really political. We did a couple of numbers like 'No Rules' and 'World War,' which was about the Baader-Meinhof gang, and was about 24 seconds long. We had to slow it down to 30 seconds so you could hear the words. We've dropped the heavy political angle now because when we get on stage we just wanna forget reality and create our own escapism."

Sessions for the band's debut album began on 29 May 1979 at Kingsway Studios in London's Strand, owned by ex-Deep Purple singer Ian Gillan, whose bass player John McCoy would serve as producer, mainly because he'd previously worked with Samson, who shared the Subs' management. Sessions were preceded two days earlier by an appearance at the Loch Lomond festival alongside the Buzzcocks, Stranglers and Skids. They also became tabloid fodder on the intervening day when they ran a story about fan Phil Sick bumping into Prince Charles in Windsor and inviting him to a subsequent Subs' show at the Music Machine. Other versions of this story have Subs' fans writing to old jug ears and receiving a personal reply stating he had a prior engagement. Either way, it sounds like a record company scam to me. "Actually the original incident was purely a fluke," Nicky Garratt told me in 2005, "as some of our fans walked across the side of a polo field where Prince Charles was playing. The press actually brought them together – it made the front page of the Daily Express and the Sun. It was our management who tried to make a meal of it by inviting the prince to the Music Machine."

The UK Subs' first release for Gem, 'Stranglehold', gave them their strongest ever chart showing in June, peaking at number 26, selling 75,000 copies and bringing an appearance on Top Of The Pops. The 'Stranglehold' tour began soon thereafter, though the group decided to pull out of a planned appearance at the Glastonbury festival (which brought them a front cover story for Sounds). However, their final show at the Lyceum was also filmed for Punk Can Take It, and four of the tracks were recorded and issued as the 'For Export Only' 12-inch, later given away free with copies of the Crash Course album. They actually had more punch than the parent album, too. A third single, 'Tomorrow's Girls', was readied, the cover featuring Joanne Slack, Paul's sister, who also briefly ran the group's fan club. It sold almost as well as its predecessor and brought another Top Of The Pops appearance.

Riding the momentum, Another Kind Of Blues, initially released in blue vinyl, reached number 21 in the national album charts on release in September, as Pinnacle re-released 'C.I.D.'. Garry Bushell gave the album a five-star review in Sounds, noting the songs were "Short, sharp, fast with great hooks, nifty, simple guitar" and that the album was a "near perfect slice of good time high energy punk". Certainly, none of the songs outstay their welcome. 'Young Criminals' was originally written to be played as the fadeout to the film Scum. 'Rockers' was not, according to Charlie, a challenge to the new mod movement, but an adaptation of an old song called 'Totters' – totters being gypsies, and the name of a pub the group used to play. A strong blues influence, courtesy of Harper and Garratt's previous bands, could be detected, alluded to in the album title. Producer John McCoy actually co-wrote and played on a rough version of 'Crash Course' with Nicky Garratt while the rest of the band were on a lunch break. Another Kind Of Blues also started the tradition of Subs' albums being issued in alphabetical order.

A 35-date national tour, including three successive nights at the Marquee, also began in September. By this time 'Tomorrow's Girls' was resident in the Top 30. Booked to appear on Top Of The Pops, the band refused to pull at show at Exeter and insisted their record company fly them down after they'd recorded their clip. And to make sure the fridge was full. For their next single they elected to record their cover of the Zombies' 'She's Not There', which again hit the top 40 and brought them to Top Of The Pops. Because Harper couldn't hit the right range, Paul Slack handled the vocals after they'd toyed around with it during sound checks. Later Charlie would slate it as "awful", though its rama-lama haste is actually quite endearing. The year was rounded out by their first, 12-date tour of America and Canada, beginning on 20 November 1979, and including two shows as support to the Police.

Brand New Age, this time produced by Harper and Garratt at Underhill Studios with engineer Laurie Dipple, was released in January 1980, and reached 18 in the charts. Many of the lyrics were written in the studio by Harper at the mixing stage, while the more esoteric musical inspirations included Syd Barrett's 'No Man's Land' (on 'Rat Race'). Once again Garry Bushell gave it five stars in Sounds, though the band might as well have not existed for all the attention trendier publications like the NME would afford them. The highlights included the nugget-tough 'Emotional Blackmail' as well as opener 'You Don't Belong' and a brace of fine singles. These comprised 'Warhead', soon to become the Subs' signature tune, constructed over a thumping bassline Paul Slack used to play at sound checks, which Charlie wrote the words to one day in a chip shop, and 'Teenage'. The latter was a bit of rabble-rousing aimed at the mod revival scene (and a song Mr Harper routinely dedicates to himself on set, despite now being well past 60). While 'Warhead' was probably Harper's finest lyric, the sort of prophetic Nostradamus text that Jaz Coleman would later make Killing Joke's speciality, the B-side was also worth checking out for Harper's harmonica-driven instrumental 'The Harper' and a cover of Lou Reed's 'Waiting For The Man'. 'Teenage' was also backed by two of the band's strongest songs of the period, 'Left For Dead', which could have been Motorhead, and the sterling 'New York State Police' ('Keep your mouth shut or we'll break your nose')

In February they embarked on a major European tour as support to the Ramones (a bootleg from this period, Dance And Travel in The Robot Age, recorded at the Palilido in Milan, offers an effective souvenir of these happy times). On their return they were back to Top Of The Pops to perform 'Warhead', which had reached number 29 in the charts, and they returned again for 'Teenage'. We're at a crossroads now," Charlie confessed to Garry Bushell, "the temptations are coming up, the big houses, the holidays abroad, and we'll either split through it, or see it through to a real brand new age."

Shows in Scotland followed, though Paul Slack had to be temporarily replaced by brother Steve when he caught pneumonia. At the same time Charlie recorded his solo single 'Barmy London Army', rejected by the rest of the band, with Chelsea's guitarist, dedicated to Jimmy Pursey, whom he felt was getting a hard time. Blow me if Pursey's legal representatives didn't then pursue him for half the royalties for using the 'Kids Are United' chant – which must have amounted to about 30p when all's said and done. Charlie went on to record another solo single, 'Freaked', most notable for its excellent B-side, 'Jo'. There was also an album of covers, Stolen Property. It's not unlistenable, surprisingly.

A 21-date full UK tour to promote Brand New Age culminated in a May 30th show at the Rainbow, but inter-band tensions had begun to surface. According to Harper's comments at the time, Slack and Davies had become a little star-struck with the group's new found popularity. It ended in a fist-fight one night after a Dutch TV show, and the two factions parted company after their management's attempts at mediation failed. Slack and Davies briefly formed the reggae-influenced Allies to pursue a direction they'd forlornly attempted to push on the Subs.

Harper and Garratt immediately drafted in Steve Roberts from perennial UK Subs support act Cyanide as drummer, and then held auditions for a new bass player, which ex-Users and Brian James And The Brains' man Alvin Gibbs successfully attended after a recommendation by John Towe. As the line-up gelled, making their debut at a show at the Music Machine, they worked on new material, including 'The User' and 'Isn't It A Pity', Gibbs taking some of the pressure off Harper and Garratt as songwriters by submitting his own material. They were undecided who to use as a producer, however, and Gibbs suggested his friend Guy Stevens, with whom he socialised frequently and who had just been lauded for his work on London's Calling. But by the time the rest of the group met him, Stevens' decline was even more pronounced, and they weren't impressed with his idea to make the band sound "like Jerry Lee Lewis". Instead they opted for Mike Leander, best known for his work with Gary Glitter in the early-70s. However, they were entirely displeased with the finished results, and Garratt remixed several of the tracks prior to release. "He (Leander) barely showed up," Garratt remembered, "and managed to get a kind of hollow sound throughout the whole thing. I remixed as best I could, but for the most part the damage was done. For myself, I wanted to expand our sound to simply make better and more lasting recordings. Of course, the other major difference is that Alvin co-wrote a number of songs on the album."

The new line-up's first release was the effervescent, even poppy, 'Party In Paris', featuring Captain Sensible on keyboards. The album that housed it, Diminished Responsibility, followed, as did a tour of Europe, climaxing with a run of four headlining shows at the Marquee. Steve Keaton interviewed them on tour in Europe, once again for Sounds magazine. Garratt was asked about his new rhythm section. "Well, I'd never put a slur on the old members of the group, they were really good – they still are, but new blood in a band always injects something else. There's no way we've gotten any worse, we think we've got a lot better. Alvin writes a lot of the material now whereas the old stuff was just me and Charlie, so we've added another songwriter to the band and Steve can handle faster rhythms without losing time as well." Meanwhile the old line-up had secured the Subs' biggest chart success, for Crash Course, a live document of the Rainbow gig that had concluded their previous UK tour (this arrived with a free 12-inch featuring an additional four tracks recorded at the Lyceum, the aforementioned 'For Export Only'). It reached number eight in the UK charts and brought the band a gold disc.

The UK Subs were now, if not pop stars, certainly highly visible, as colour pictures appeared in Smash Hits and other teen pop magazines. However, an appearance on Top Of The Pops for 'Party In Paris' was never screened due to the 'pitch invasion' staged by their fans. 300 hardcore Subs fans had been following them on tour from town to town. They hitch-hiked to the BBC studios en masse, only about half being allowed in. Captain Sensible also turned up for the mimed performance, and gleefully performed a stage dive at the conclusion of the song. But also appearing on the bill was Adam Ant, at that time subject to a tidal wave of criticism from once-admiring punks for his conversion to the cult of pop. He, Marco Pirroni and Adam's girlfriend, actress Amanda Donohoe, were subsequently set upon by a couple of Subs fans in the corridors. "A knife was produced," remembers Gibbs, "and if it wasn't for Donohoe's swift punch to the blade-wielding assailant's jaw, the incident could have had a much more serious outcome." However, Adam did receive a serious facial injury in the incident, resulting in a prominent white stripe across the bridge of his nose, which some mistakenly took as a fashion statement. Maybe. The UK Subs were blamed for the attack and banned from Top Of The Pops (though the ban was revoked a year later for Keep On Running) "All this may or may not be true," notes Garratt, "I didn't know the inside details. But the so-called ban could merely have been the normal Top Of The Pops practice of recording an additional 'standby' song. The former is a more interesting story though."

Diminished Responsibility, which this time received four stars in perennial advocate Garry Bushell's Sounds review, albeit announcing his consternation as to where all the songs about schoolgirls had gone, got a typically sneering NME write-up via Gavin Martin. "The UK Subs are the missing link in an existence which helplessly and needlessly goes from torturing animals and bullying younger kids to beery wife-beating evenings by the fireside." Or try "The UK Subs are a reactionary cesspit." A bit harsh. They found a more sympathetic ear in Melody Maker's Carol Clerk, who at one point was considering writing a biography of the band. "Not that there's been a total change of direction. It's just that the band have taken several steps away from the battering punk of their reputation, while retaining the aggression that is their trademark." It's actually a fine album with some far more expansive songwriting. Songs like 'Time And Matter', later covered by the Fastbacks, caught them branching out without falling off their perch. Although Glitter Band associate Mike Leander was provisionally the producer, most of his mixes were eventually rejected.

The next single was 'Keep On Running', a ho-hum effort with notable similarities to the Police's 'Message In A Bottle'. It was produced by pop maestro Pete Collins (the Beat, etc) but stalled at 41 in the charts. The controversy here surrounded the record's cover and the band's subsequent appearance on Top Of The Pops. Gem decided that the UK Subs' 'look' of basic black leather needed a bit of tweaking. And that new romantic thing seemed to be big. Hence they were sent out shopping for a makeover. And behold, frilly dress shirts, Chelsea boots and silk scarves. Photographer Sheila Rock had funded the wardrobe outrage to the tune of £100. "We thought we could tap into Duran Duran's pool of groupies," Garratt maintains. You could hear a nation of punk diehards whispering to themselves, "What the **** is Charlie wearing?" Gibbs would claim the new look was partially influenced by their Scandinavian tours with Hanoi Rocks. No-one believes him.

The record label, in an effort to push the single higher and keep the band's momentum rolling, issued a subsequent EP version (including a demo of the forthcoming 'Ice Age' and the French version of 'Party In Paris' that had originally been recorded as a one-sided fan club single). That didn't work, and a short time later Gem went bankrupt when they backed a failed Eurovision entry (they should have pushed 'Party In Paris', surely?) Their American backers pulled the plug and the Subs were left without a label and without management, whom they sacked at the end of 1981, preferring to chart their own course for a while.

As the band regrouped, signing a new contract with NEMS, a new single and album were prepared while they played 'secret' dates at Gossip's in the West End, at which future members Captain Scarlet and James Moncur were audience members. The semi-legal bootleg by Chaos Tapes would be recorded at these shows. They then entered Jacob's Studios in Farnham, Surrey. It had a swimming pool, no less, where Harper would write the lyrics to one of the album's less immediately distinctive songs, 'Down On The Farm'. "Blue skies and swimming pools have so much charm/But I'd rather be back in Soho than down on the farm".

'Countdown', the first single from these sessions, a song similar in some aspects to 'Warhead', failed to chart. "I knew it wasn't commercial," Charlie told Flipside. "I wanted to put out something beefy and heavy, something we can believe in rather than something that could be the most commercial thing we had." Endangered Species was promoted on another UK and European tour starting in October 1981. The album, which had been held up over legal hassles regarding their new contract thereby allowing the band to build up their reservoir of material, was something of a composite effort. One side featured songs designed to appeal to existing fans, the second was more experimental, in keeping with Garratt and Gibbs' future vision. "Well, everyone thinks we're morons and we can't play intelligently," Gibbs told Sounds. "We've developed, we're proud we can play well and that we've got the expertise. We don't want to lose old fans, but the band has to progress, and the way we've planned it we hope they'll follow through with us." The highlights included the title-track and 'Living Dead' (written and sung by Gibbs) on the 'conservative' side and the atmospheric 'Ice Age' and poppy 'Sensitive Boys' (originally intended as a single) on the 'progressive' half of the record. Strangely, it all seemed to hang together, even Harper's bluesy 'Ambition', on which he got to wheel out his harmonica (and also, alas, some pretty appalling lyrics).

1982 began without a label and bereft of management. Eventually they signed with the New York-based Wartoke Concern agency and former Patti Smith manager Jane Friedman, in a bid to set up their second American tour. However, Harper and Garratt had come to a decision over the increasingly unreliable Steve Roberts, who was drinking heavily, and thus considered too unstable for such a long tour. Against Gibbs's wishes – though he could see their point – ex-Chelsea drummer Mal Aisling (aka Sol Mintz) was drafted in his stead. He was on board for their subsequent US tour, which saw them criss-cross America, making some 30 domestic flights in the process. Nick Garratt recalled the sadness the decision engendered within the band to Maximum Rock'n'roll. "There was tension in the band. The drummer dropped by the wayside about six months beforehand because of his drinking problem. And although punk rock is an alternative, there's still a lot of work involved. We came to the conclusion, the three of us, that there's no way we can do a major US tour with this guy in the band. You know, he's going to get us thrown off planes... So we had a temporary drummer, and I don't think the spirit of the band after Steve had gone was ever quite the same."

NEMS were strapped for cash and the group lacked the promotion they had enjoyed at Gem. It was no surprise to anyone when the label went belly up shortly after Endangered Species' release, which was a great shame, as arguably the UK Subs' finest album was lost in the confusion. The year ended with a second on the bill performance in front of 7,000 at the Leeds' Christmas On Earth punk festival.

'Shake Up The City' was their first release for new label Abstract in October 1982, but failed to ignite much interest. A third US jaunt was timed for November, following a European tour, at which time the lucky extra passenger (i.e. drummer) was John Towe, operating under the guise of Kim Wylie, for reasons best known to himself. But the US dates failed to yield a much-desired American recording contract, and so the band returned home, with Towe, Garratt and Gibbs murmuring about their intention to quit.

Harper and Gibbs put together a side venture, the Urban Dogs, featuring Knox from the Vibrators and old friend Andy McCoy of Hanoi Rocks, along with Matthew 'Turkey' Best on drums. It was an effort to reinvigorate some old New York Dolls and Stooges numbers, as well as some originals, for fun and quick cash, which helped take their minds off the fate of the Subs.

Reluctantly, the mother group set off on another trek of Britain and Europe, but the fun was gone. A split was obviously close, but was averted when they found that a tour of Poland had been scheduled. The opportunity of becoming the first western punk band to tour Communist Poland, still under General Jaruzelski – who wanted to do some last-ditch teenage crowd-pleasing to appease the growing Solidarity movement – was too great to refuse. So they didn't.

However, the split had been delayed rather than averted. Garratt and Gibbs wanted to take the band to a higher level, and were bored with playing small English pubs and repeating material that was now several years old. The fact that there was no longer a recording deal, and therefore no regular income, exacerbated matters. "We quit the UK Subs and formed a new band," Garratt remembers. "John Towe dropped out very quickly but Alvin and I recruited Mal Wesson from TV Smith's Explorers and the Scott brothers, Andy and Ken, from Wasted Youth. Ken was the former guitar player and second vocalist in the Tickets who were on the Farewell to the Roxy album. We got some backing from EMI, but ultimately the Scotts' drug use destroyed the fledgling band. We were called Target Generation by half the band (after the story by Clifford Simack) and The Soft Pulse by the other. Two sets of the EMI demos do exist."

So Garratt bunked off to New York, where he would eventually form the label New Red Archives (its first release being 'lost' UK Subs album A.W.O.L.) and also played with The Rebekka Frame and Ten Bright Spikes. He subsequently lived in New York City, Los Angles, San Francisco, Hanover in Germany and again in San Francisco, but continued to help out the band with American dates through the second half of the 90s.

The end of the Subs? Nope. Charlie being Charlie, he elected to persevere, recruiting the first of what would be a steady stream of musicians to become, for a few gigs at least, the Original UK Subs, in March 1983. The new line-up featured two returning members, Steve Slack (bass) and Steve Jones (drums), with new boy Captain Scarlet (aka Dave Lloyd) on guitar. Together, they set out to play the nation's toilets again, supported by New York's exhilarating Bad Brains, with the final show the Punk and Disorderly festival at the Lyceum.

In August the group recorded new album Flood Of Lies and single 'Another Typical City' at Alaska, between shows in Scandinavia. The album was notable for its lithe title-track, which was originally titled 'Money For Guns', 'Dress Code', whose elongated intro was reminiscent of what Captain Sensible would do with 'Smash It Up Part 2', and 'Seas', which one critic noted was pretty similar to Amon Duul II. The cover was also arresting – a picture of Madame Thatcher as a diseased leper. 'Another Typical City' was, as a rather hostile critic pointed out, another typical UK Subs song: "Listening to this is like watching Jimmy Greaves try out for West Ham Youth", they pointed out, unhelpfully.

On their return from Scandinavia the Subs embarked on their biggest UK tour to date, taking in a massive 42 venues. The tour eventually finished in January 1984. The 12-inch, 'Magic', which was awful, was rush-recorded in a day before setting off for Norway. Harper maintained that part of the reason for the poor sound was that Captain Scarlet spent too long in the studio completing overdubs and left him only a couple of hours to do the vocal takes. The line-up shifted again for the next American tour, booked by LA punk music biz legend Gary Tovar. Terry 'Tezz' Roberts (ex-Discharge, Broken Bones) came in on bass and Pete Davies rejoined on drums, with Captain Scarlet still present and correct.

Steve Roberts was lined up (yet again) to take over the drum stool on their return, but in the event could not commit the time necessary. Captain Scarlet was then abducted by the Mysterons (presumably) just before a Spanish tour with Chelsea and the Anti-Nowhere League. Actually he more prosaically missed the ferry, though he would later return to roadie for the band in 1986. The tour was completed with Tim Briffa on guitar (who had to be taught the chords on the ferry), 'Deptford John' Armitage on bass and Matthew 'Turkey' Beat on drums. On their return Steve Roberts played a few London shows before Tezz returned on guitar. Armitage was joined in the rhythm section by Rab Fae Beith, formerly of the Pack and the Wall.

Gross Out USA was a clock-punching exercise recorded on a four-track studio by Sandra Bruce while on tour at Chicago McGeevies and released in January 1985. The Harper/Armitage/Beith/(Tezz) Roberts line-up then toured the UK alongside the Exploited, and made their vinyl bow with 'This Gun Says'. When it failed to sell even out of its first pressing of 1,000, the Subs hit the live trail again, once more returning to America. Tezz was replaced mid-tour, due to his erratic behaviour, by the Subs' guitar tech James Moncur, formerly of Combat 84 (Tezz had, fittingly, been pictured on the cover of Gross Out USA vomiting).

Ricky McGuire (aka Plonker Magoo), formerly of the Fits, became the replacement bass player when Deptford John was dismissed and elected for life as a tour manager. The new line-up set to work on Huntington Beach, a set distinguished by Moncur's 'Rock'n'roll Savage' and the Moncur/Beith composition 'Sk8 Tough'. A double live album to celebrate the group's 10th anniversary was also planned. In Action was meant to draw on shows at Telford Oakingates Hall and Aberdeen, but in the event the tapes weren't suitable so the songs were run through 'live' in the studio. And its impact was scuppered further by Dojo issuing the Subs Standards compilation at almost exactly the same time.

Another US tour followed in April 1986, lasting until June, and, invariably, they managed to lose their drummer. Though this time it was because Fae Beith met the love of his life in America, Monique ('She lost her love to a UK Sub', to paraphrase an old Gonads' song title). He decided to return stateside once he'd completed a final show at the 100 Club. Pete Davies once again stood in before former Chelsea man Geoff Sewell took the post, and in August Doncaster native Mark Barrett replaced McGuire, who joined the Men They Couldn't Hang. The year was rounded out with a short British mini-tour following a filmed appearance in Belgrade.

Japan Today, originally destined to be called Jungle Blue, until some clever interloper noted the potential of the Far East market, was recorded at Alaska between 24 September and 7 October. However, by the time sessions were scheduled, Steve Roberts had, almost inevitably, returned to the drum stool, with Dave 'Flea' Farrelly on bass (he was handed a copy of In Action and ordered to learn 40 songs in just over a week). Alan Lee joined on guitar on a temporary basis from Sic Boy Federation alongside Bath. The new line-up made its debut with the 'Hey Santa!' 12-inch, which included 'Street Legal' as well as the title-track, a version of Australian comedian Kevin 'Bloody' Wilson's original, and a burn through of 'Captain Scarlet', the old Gerry Anderson theme. Knox of the Vibrators added additional guitar, and Charlie's girlfriend provided backing vocals on 'Japan Today'. However, despite the massed ranks of contributors, few involved were happy with the finished result, Knox declaring it "unfinished".

So how long did Steve Roberts last this time? Oh, just a few months. Next up, Duncan Smith (ex-Icon) warmed the drum stool for a European tour. By the start of 1988 Roberts was back again, Charlie clearly making a mint on his UK Subs drum stool timeshare scam. More UK shows followed before another 30-plus dates were undertaken in America, including a support to Iggy Pop at the Starlight Amphitheatre in June.

After that there was a hiatus, during which Harper, and old pals Garratt, who had guested on the previous tour for their CBGB's date, and Gibbs found themselves in New York. Borrowing a drummer, not for the first time, in the shape of Belvy K of Demolition Boy, they decided to have a crack at the studio. It was some studio, too; Sonic Edge was state of the art and they only got access to it by pretending they were working for advertising giants Saatchi and Saatchi. The result was Killing Time, which Garratt released on his own label, New Red Archives. It was the Subs' finest album for some time, notable for the inclusion of Gibbs's 'Drag Me Down', which featured his friend from Iggy Pop's band (with whom Gibbs had been playing), Andy McCoy, and the sweeping 'Lower East Side'.

On his return to England, Harper put together UK Subs Mark CVIIXXII, with Matt McCoy, son of Another Kind Of Blues producer John McCoy, taking over from Steve Roberts. Lee returned to play guitar only after he won a horse bet to pay for the flight back from the States. A successful UK tour ensued as the group signed to Vince Mortell's Released Emotions. A 12-inch, led off by 'Motivator', again, one of the best things they'd recorded for some time (an outtake version of this had been included on Killing Time) followed in December. The sessions were produced by Dave Goodman and included his anti-Apartheid song 'Fascist Regime', which he confessed he'd originally written for 1977 band the Front – members of whom later became the Vibrators. They also offered a seasonal punk variation on 'Auld Lang Syne', which featured a tramp that Goodman had found in the park playing the accordion. He gave him a fiver for his troubles and told him to buy a new suit. The sessions had one other repercussion – Goodman was impressed by Lee's guitar sound and used him to record his Ex-Pistols' scam, 'Schools Are Prisons'.

By January 1990 Bath had been replaced by Karl Morris, formerly of the Exploited, while Released Emotions pushed out a couple of live albums (Live In Paris and Europe Calling, the latter featuring a smattering of studio tracks recorded during the time Alan Lee was with the band). Meanwhile Leo Mortimer deputised for McCoy, who ran off to America with his girlfriend, for Finnish and Spanish dates, and Darrell Barth rejoined to help complete sessions for the upcoming Mad Cow Fever album, once again helmed by Dave Goodman. It was preceded by the release of the seasonal 'Hey! Santa!, a punk cover of Australian comedian Kevin 'Bloody' Wilson's novelty hit. In the meantime Harper received a phone call from LA to tell him that Guns N' Roses had played 'Down On The Farm' at the Farm Aid Festival on 5 April 1990. The group also set up a new management company, the ill-starred Rocksparrow, while demo-ing new songs 'Back To Maryland' and 'Summertime' with Urban Dogs' bass player Laura.

Released in January 1991, Mad Cow Fever was the band's absolute nadir, an unlistenable coupling of so-so new tunes with bar room blues on the other side. It was promoted via a six-week tour of Europe, though absolutely no-one was shouting for the likes of 'Ecology Blues' during the encores. During a British tour in April, Flea departed to be replaced by Brian Barnes, who handled bass for subsequent US dates in July. In the meantime Charlie got married to a girl about a third of his age (conservative estimate), and his bandmates cheekily sent in a photo of the poor thing to Spiral Scratch, which I was editing at the time. "All I wanna know," I thought about replying, but didn't, "is does she drum?" Well, that would have been useful.

Sporadic gigging continued in the early 90s without any studio albums to support. By 1993 they were playing the former eastern bloc again, their show in Zagreb broadcast live on radio and released as a bonus CD on their next studio album, Normal Service Resumed. This featured a line-up of Harper, Alan Campbell (guitar), Brian Barnes (bass) and Pete Davies (drums). The standouts this time round were 'Jodie Foster' – not the first time she's been immortalised in a punk song – 'Mohawk Radio' and 'Here Comes Alex'. But their attempt at reggae, 'Squat The World', is horrid. McCoy was back on drums for the subsequent American tour, while concurrently playing with support act Johnny Bravo.

In the meantime the long-rumoured inclusion of a UK Subs song, 'Down On The Farm', on Guns N' Roses' The Spaghetti Incident album of punk covers, finally happened. The LA decadents had picked up a copy of Endangered Species alongside a Black Flag LP some years previously, as a result of Barth hosting Guns N' Roses in his Stockwell flat when they first came to Britain in 1987, when they also jammed together. Duff McKagan, an old punk rocker himself, selected the track. It brought an influx of much needed mullah, but not quite as much as some assumed. "The Guns N' Roses thing is a very sad thing," Harper later recalled to No Pictures, "because... the NME wrote we were gonna get £100,000 from it. The initial money, our money from the song, was around £100,000, but by the time it got through our publisher, who was screwing us at the time, we had to have a court case against them. It came to about, taxed and through all these agencies, it was down to £30,000, and this was shared between three people... So we each stood to get ten grand. The thing is that our court case cost us 27 grand. So we had to pay that and we ended up getting a grand each. So it was a very sad affair but we did win the case and our money started coming through to us from way back, and then we did get a whole bunch of money, like five grand, in a lump sum. It put us on the road and we could buy lots of T-shirts and do all the things we wanted to do, like get a new van."

New van or no, the transatlantic touring continued apace. 1994's US dates featured George Kramer on bass and Karl Morris on guitar. They also issued a one-off single, 'Betrayal', for New Red Archives, featuring Garratt and Tezz playing the guitars alongside Harper, McCoy and Kramer.

It's the start of 1996, so we must be in Germany, right? Or Austria, Slovenia, Poland, Sweden or Finland, perhaps. The new album is called Occupied and the line-up is a return to the Harper/Davies/Campbell/Barnes formation. A return to form? It's not bad, the better tracks still crunch, like 'Darkness'. And 'Let's Get Drunk' does what it says on the, er, tin. They also appeared at the inaugural Holidays In The Sun festival in Morecambe, where rumour had it that one of the attendees was older than Charlie, but this turned out merely to be a sighting of an OAP's coach party from Ludlow.

Harper, Garratt and Gibbs spent the tail end of the year in the US, working with Samiam drummer Dave Ayer, recording enough material for three singles and two albums over a three-week period. These were released in a burst of 20th anniversary celebrations at the beginning of 1997, Quintessentials in January followed by Riot in March. The three singles were 'War On The Pentagon' (a bit pre-9/11 that one), 'The Day Of The Dead' and 'Cyberjunk', with B-sides featuring the City Records' versions of the original tracks from their first single (i.e. 'C.I.D.', 'I Live In A Car' and 'B.I.C.') plus new tracks. "We were going to do one album," Garratt told Maximum Rock'n'roll, "but I called them a bunch of sissies. I said let's do TEN albums! But we settled on two. But to me, songs are like a reservoir, and when we were doing two albums a year, all that water was being siphoned off. But since I haven't been doing this for thirteen years, or actually since '88 when we did Killing Time, I've got all this anger inside me, and all these fast riffs. In fact, if you listen to these albums, most of my parts are fast riffs almost like the first album." Which discomforted Charlie a little. "In fact we had to tell Nicky, look, we can't get off on all this fast stuff anymore, so we told him actually to slow down. But the albums are still pretty fierce." They were, with Quintessentials being the marginal pick. The themes remained constant, the titles of anti-authority tracks such as 'Killer Cops', 'Power Corrupts' and 'Human Rights' pointing pretty accurately in the direction of their content. While a song like 'Flat Earth Society', from Riot, was too much of a penalty kick for some critics, it was glorious to hear the Harper/Garratt/Gibbs line-up in unison again.

The same line-up toured in February, though due to Gibbs's sickness the final dates featured a female bass player by the name of Carly. Then it was a second tilt at Holidays in the Sun, some European dates and finally a British tour, with newbies Gary Frantic on bass, Gary Baldy on drums and a succession of different guitar players. By now, as Harper admitted to Maximum Rock'n'roll, there was effectively a UK and a US version of the band. "Yeah. A European version and an American version. There has been ever since Pete Davies told the band never to play in the US 'cos they can't earn any money, which is basically true, you know. You don't earn any money. It's a shame, you have to get a work permit to work here but you don't earn anything. It's criminal, what a con! So one by one the band just stopped coming over. The whole band were over one year, then it was just like three of us, the next year it was two of us, and the last time I came over I came completely by myself. But there's easily enough former UK Subs in the US to not bother about getting new musicians." It should be noted that having separate line-ups for two continents is an achievement that even the Beatles or Rolling Stones, or anyone else for that matter, could not rival. An entirely worthless achievement, but an achievement nevertheless.

For January 1999's European tour the line-up featured old stagers Alvin Gibbs on bass and Darrell Bath on guitar, plus Gary Baldy refusing to relinquish the drum stool and thereby totally dishonouring a proud Subs' tradition. It was soon Holidays In The Sun time, before Harper was reunited with Gibbs and Garratt, plus new drummer Gizz 'Lazlo' Navarro of Dead Lazlo's

Place, for their Social Chaos tour of America. This lasted from July to August, though by the end of the month they were back gigging in Britain.

The new millennium began very much like the last ended with more touring, this time of Europe, with Couch confirmed as the band's new permanent drummer (permanent drummer? In the UK Subs?) Naturally enough he'd gone by June, with Vice Squad's Pumpy getting the most temporary of temporary jobs in punk history. They managed another British tour, an appearance at the second Punk Aid and some more American and Canadian shows, as well as releasing a mini-album, The Revolution's Here.

The group's most recent studio album was 2003's Universal for Captain Oi!, now the home of most of their (quality) re-released material. This saw Charlie backed by Alan Campbell on guitar, Simon Rankin on bass and Jason 'Dulldrums' on percussion. The release was preceded by a reworking of the traditional 'What Shall We Do With The Drunken Sailor'. A couple of the songs are actually keepers, especially the schizophrenic blues of 'Last Man Standing', and the chopping rhythms of 'The Dark', though 'Don't Blame Islam' is more ambiguous than it sounds. Harper: "Universal came out better than expected. The then new bassist Simon Rankin was actually the guitarist from Zero Tolerance. He wrote some very good stuff. As a guitarist, he was very 'Subs influenced', a la Nicky Garratt. The finished package was very well received. I'd rank it easily in the top five. Or maybe sixth…" So will the Subs ever fulfil their prophecy of an album for every letter of the alphabet? "V is done! W will be the hardest, 'cos I've kind of got X worked out. But it will take us the best part of five years to finish." It seems rumours of Harper's impending retirement are premature.

In the autumn of 2003 they launched their biggest US tour so far, with 48 shows through October and November, with Harper and Gibbs joined by John Towe on drums and Soho Steve on guitar, with Nicky Garratt then returning for the early 2004 European dates. Over Christmas Charlie would contribute to the Punk Aid Christmas single featuring Captain Sensible and TV Smith.

In 2004 they announced the forthcoming American dates would be the last by the band. Hmmm. The new line-up was, basically, impenetrable, comprising anyone they found in the parking lot. Another contributor was Jay of the Short Bus Window Lickers – a band whose three drummers at various times have all played with the UK Subs. I once bumped into Noel Martin of Menace at a show in East London where the Subs headlined. "I'll probably end up playing the drums for the Subs too," he pointed out. He did, too.

That's your lot. If you want to know more about the line-up changes, or spot any holes in the discography, please make an urgent appointment with a counsellor. The UK Subs are an institution, of sorts. The fact that I like them, despite being as fashionable as asbestos, doubtless disqualifies me from polite society. But I still play (mostly) Diminished Responsibility and Endangered Species from time to time, and I'm yet to be convinced by anyone that these aren't fine albums.

DISCOGRAPHY:

C.I.D./I Live In A Car/B.I.C. 7-inch (City Records NIK5 September 1977) (issued in six different shades of coloured vinyl as well as black. Reissued in 1979 by Pinnacle Records, PIN22)

Stranglehold/World War/Rockers 7-inch (GEM GEMS 5 June 1979)

Tomorrow's Girls/Scum Of The Earth/Telephone Numbers 7-inch GEM GEM 10 August 1979)

Another Kind Of Blues LP (Gem GEM LP 100 September 1979) (Issued in blue vinyl with insert. Reissued on CD by Abstract, AAB CD 801, 1991, and in red vinyl, AAB LP 801. It was then reissued by Dojo DOJO CD 226 July 1995 with bonus tracks, and by Diablo, DIAB 86-2, July 1998, with bonus tracks 'Scum Of The Earth' and 'Telephone Numbers'. It was then given a more fitting reissue by Captain Oi!, AHOY CD 134 in 2000, with bonus tracks 'C.I.D. (single version)', 'I Live In A Car (single version)', 'B.I.C. (single version)', 'Stranglehold (single version)', 'World War (single version)', 'Rockers (single version)', 'Tomorrow's Girls (single version)', 'Scum Of The Earth', 'Telephone Numbers')

Warhead/The Harper/I'm Waiting For The Man 7-inch (Gem GEM 23 March 1980) (brown vinyl)

Brand New Age LP (Gem GEMLP 106 April 1980) AABT 802, in red vinyl in 1989, and later on CD, AABT 802CD. Reissued again by Dojo, DOJO CD 228 in 1995, with bonus tracks, and finally on Captain Oi! AHOY CD 136 in 2000, with bonus tracks: She's Not There/Kicks (Single Version)/Victim/Same Thing/Warhead (Single Version)/The Harper/Waiting For The

Man/Teenage (Single Version)/Left For Dead/New York State Police)

Teenage/Left For Dead/New York State Police 7-inch (Gem GEM 30 May 1980) (pink vinyl)

Crash Course LP (Gem GEMLP 111 1980) (live at the Rainbow Theatre, London, 30 May 1980. There are overdubs on some tracks, allegedly due to the fact that Charlie was a bit intoxicated at the actual gig. Came with free 12-inch single, For Export Only, GEM EP1 featuring 'I.O.D.', 'Lady Esquire', 'Blues', 'Young Criminals', from a Lyceum show in 1979. Reissued on CD by DOJO, DOJO CD229, in 1995, with 'Export Only' tracks included, then on Captain Oi! AHOY CD140 in 2000, again with the 'For Export Only' tracks).

Party In Paris/Fall Of The Empire 7-inch (Gem GEM 42 October 1980) (orange vinyl. Also issued with a French vocal as a one-sided single by UK Subs fan club, RAMKUP CAC002, 1981)

Diminished Responsibility LP (Gem GEMLP 112 1981) (originally issued in red vinyl. Reissued in red vinyl and on CD by Abstract AABT 804 LP/CD in 1991, and again by Line Records Germany, TCCD 9 00546, in a different sleeve. Re-released on CD in 1995 by Dojo, DOJO CD232, with six bonus tracks, and again by Captain Oi! in 2000, AHOY CD 143, with bonus tracks: Party In Paris (Single Version)/Fall Of The Empire/Keep On Running ('Til You Burn)/Perfect Girl/Ice Age/Party In Paris (French Version)/Barmy London Army (Charlie Harper)/Talk Is Cheap (Charlie Harper)

Keep On Runnin' ('Til You Burn)/Perfect Girl 7-inch (Gem GEM 45 April 1981)

Keep On Runnin' ('Til You Burn) 7-inch EP (Gem GEMEP 45 1981)

Keep On Runnin' ('Til You Burn)/Ice Age/Perfect Girl/Party In Paris (French version)

Countdown/Plan Of Action 7-inch (NEMS NES 304 January 1982)

Endangered Species LP (NEMS NEL 6021 1982) (originally issued with full lyric insert. Reissued in 1990 in limited edition of 1,500 copies in red vinyl by Link Classics, CLINK 4, with an out-take version of 'I Don't Need Your Love'. Reissued on CD by Line Records Germany, TCCD 9 00546, with different sleeve, and again by Captain Oi! in 2000, AHOY CD 143, with bonus tracks: Plan Of Action/I Don't Need Your Love/Keep On Runnin' (demo)/Limo Life (demo))

Shake Up The City EP (Abstract ABS 012 October 1982)

Self Destruct/Police State/War Of The Roses

Another Typical City/Still Life 7-inch (Scarlet/Fall Out FALL 017 August 1983) (also issued as a 12-inch, FALL 12 017, with additional tracks 'Veronique' and an extended version of 'Another Typical City'. Featured Knox from the Vibrators' artwork on the sleeve, a pastiche of the Sex Pistols' 'Holiday In The Sun')

Flood Of Lies LP (Scarlet/Fall Out FALL 018/SIG 3 October 1983)

(re-released, again as FALL 018, in 1987, then issued on CD by Fallout in 1995, FALLCD 018, as Flood Of Lies + Singles 1982-1985, with different sleeve and 12 bonus tracks drawn from various permutations of the band. Reissued by Captain Oi! AHOY CD 166, with bonus tracks: Another Typical City (7-inch version)/Still Life/The Spell/Private Army/Multiple Minds/Primary Strength/Another Typical City (12-inch Version). The Captain Oi! version restores the original 'Thatcher' artwork and contains everything released by the Harper/Scarlet/Jones/Slack version of the band)

Magic 12-inch EP (Fall Out FALL 12 024 September 1984)

The Spell/Private Army/Multiple Minds/Primary Strength

Gross Out USA LP (Fall Out FALL 031 January 1985) (live album recorded at McGeevies, Chicago, 1984. Reissued on CD, FALLCD 031, in 1995)

This Gun Says/Speak For Myself/Wanted 7-inch (Fall Out FALL 36 May 1985)

Huntington Beach LP (RFB RFBLP 01 1986) (reissued on CD, CDRND 001, in 1999, and on Captain Oi! AHOY CD 114, in 2000 with bonus tracks: This Gun Says/Stranglehold (Live)/New Barbarians (Live)/Tomorrow's Girls (Live)/Between The Eyes (Live). Rreissued by FM Revolver Records, RECCD/LP 150, June 1990, then by Captain Oi! AHOY CD 114 1999, with bonus tracks 'This Gun Says', 'Stranglehold (live)', 'New Barbarians (live)', 'Tomorrow's Girls (live)', Between The Eyes (live)')

In Action double live LP (RFB RFBLP 02 1986) (reissued on CD, CDRND 002, in 1999)

Live In Holland EP (RFB RFB SIN1 March 1986)

Stranglehold/New Barbarians/Tomorrow's Girls/Between The Eyes (lifted from the ROIR album Left For Dead – Alive In Holland)

A.W.O.L. mini-LP (New Red Archives NRA 05 1987; USA) (the versions of 'Runnin'' and 'Police State (part 2)' are new, and this was the first airing of 'New Barbarians'. Also available on CD)

Hey! Santa 12-inch (Fall Out FALL 12044 1988)

Hey! Santa/Captain Scarlet/Thunderbird Wine/Street Legal

Japan Today LP (Fall Out LP 045 1988) (reissued on CD, Fall Out CD0045, in 1993, with a different sleeve, and by Captain Oi!, AHOYCD 167, in 2000, with five bonus tracks from the 'Motivator' 12-inch – 'Motivator', 'Combat Zone', 'Fascist Regime', 'Auld Lang

Syne', 'Cycle Sluts From Hell')
Motivator 12-inch (Released Emotions REM 004 1988)
Motivator/Combat Zone/Fascist Regime/Auld Lang Syne/Cycle Sluts From Hell
Killing Time LP (Fall Out FALLLP 048 1989) (also released on CD, FALLCD 048)
Live In Paris (Greatest Hits) LP (Released Emotions REM 005 March 1990) (show recorded from French Radio Bienvenue, Strasbourg, on 11 February 1989, with additional mixing on 1 September 1989 by Nick Head. The band were a bit embarrassed about their 'blues jam' at the end, but label head Vince convinced them it would add to the record's desirability to fans... if not necessarily music fans. This has now been reissued as Live And Loud! by Harry Mary, MAYO CD 561, in 2005. It was originally licensed by Link from Released Emotions for a Link release but it never came to pass. The Harry May reissue includes the original planned cover for the Link release)
Europe Calling LP (Released Emotions REM 012 1989) (five studio tracks, the rest drawn from live shows in Vienna and Paris. Reissued on CD, REM 012CD, in 1997, and again in 2000, Pinhead Productions PINCD 101)
Mad Cow Fever LP (Fall out FALL LP 048 1991) (also issued on CD, FALL CD 048)
Normal Service Resumed LP (Fall Out FALL LP 050 1993) (also issued on CD, FALL CD 050, first 5,000 copies with free bonus CD – Live In Croatia CD (Fall Out FALL CD 049 1993), taken from a Radio 1, Zagreb broadcast in February 1993)
The Road Is Hard The Road Is Long 7-inch EP (Fall Out FALL 051 1993)
The Road Is Hard The Road Is Long/Jodie Foster/Here Comes Alex/Another Cuba (also issued on CD, FALL CD051)
Split Vision Vol. 1 split 7-inch single (New Red Archives NRA 44 1994)
Postcard From LA plus Swinging Utters' 'Teenage Genocide'
Betrayal/Nobody Move 7-inch (New Red Archives NRA 49 1994)
Occupied LP (Fall Out FALL LP 052 1996) (also released on CD, FALL CD 052)
Quintessentials LP (Fall Out FALL LP 053 March 1997) (also released on CD, FALL CD 053)
Riot CD (Anagram CDMGRAM 113 1997)
War On The Pentagon/Rebel Radio/Live In A Car 7-inch (New Red Archives NRA 46 1997)
Day Of The Dead/Chemical War/C.I.D. 7-inch (New Red Archives NRA 47 1997)
Cyberpunk/Quintessentials/B.I.C. 7-inch (New Red Archives NRA 48 1997)
Riot 98 7-inch EP (Fall Out FALL 056 1998)
Riot/It's A Scam/Bathroom Messiah/UK Subversives
The Revolution's Here CD (Combat Rock CR050 2000)
Universal CD (Captain Oi! AHOY CD 204 2002) (first 1,500 copies came with a free CD, Live At The Borderline (AHOY CD 204B)
Drunken Sailor/Reclaim The Streets 7-inch (Captain Oi! AHOY 701 July 2002)
ARCHIVE RELEASES:
Live Kicks LP (Stiff Mail 1 1980) (unofficial live album available by mail order only and recorded at the Roxy on 31 December 1977, featuring the Lyons/Steve Slack/Harper/Garrett line-up. "We fought against it all along," Harper told a Cambridge fanzine. "As you know, two of the tracks, 'I Live In A Car' and 'Telephone Numbers', were taken off the original recording for inclusion on the Roxy album. Those two were the only two that were good enough, the rest was to me reject stuff. It just wasn't good enough to put out, which was true. The whole affair was an embarrassment.")
Danger: UK Subs Live cassette (Chaos cassettes LIVE 009 1982) (4,000 copies, live recording from Gossip's, London, 28 September 1981 of 'unofficial' status, and pretty poor sound quality)
Recorded 1979 – '81 LP (Abstract AABT 300 1982)
Demonstration Tapes LP (Konnexion 1982; Belgium) (Out-takes collection, including a version of 'I Don't Need Your Love' featuring Gibbs on vocals, demos from Brand New Age, a version of 'Sensitive Boys' from an early 1981 session and live recordings from New York in 1982, 'Cocaine' and 'Limo Life', plus snippets from Crash Course. The cover featured the band's drawing of Charlie on the cover. It was originally released as a cassette through the Tuck Shop fan club. Would be re-released as Raw Material)
Subs Standards LP (Dojo DOJOLP 28 1986)
Left For Dead cassette (ROIR ROIR A42) (recorded live in Holland, featuring Harper/Moncur/Plonker Magoo/Rab Fae Beith line-up. Reissued on CD in 1999 by ROIR, RUSCD8256. Sleevenotes by the amazing Jack Rabid!)
Raw Material LP (Killerwatt KILL LP 2001 1986) (vinyl reissue of Demonstration Tapes with same track-listing)
Flood Of Lies – Singles 1982-1985 CD (Fall Out FALL CD 018 1991)
Mad Cow Fever/Japan Today CD (Fall Out FALL CO48)

The Singles 1978-1982 LP (Abstract AABT 800 1991) (released on CD by Get Back, GBR001CD, 1991, with bonus tracks 'Ice Age', 'Self Destruct', 'Police State', 'War Of The Roses' and 'Anti Warfare')

Live At The Roxy LP (Receiver RRLP 146 1991) (a reissue of the Live Kicks set, sadly without the encore of 'Strangleholdʼ. Also issued on CD, Receiver RRCD 146, with sleevenotes by John Tobler. Reissued again by Going For A Song, GFS 621 2004, but sadly once again without the encore version of 'Stranglehold')

Endangered Species/Huntington Beach CD (Dojo LOMA CD 7 1992)

Down On The Farm – A Collection Of The Less Obvious CD (Dojo DOJO CD 117 1993)

Another Kind Of Blues/Crash Course CD (Get Back GBR 002 CD 1993)

Brand New Age/Diminished Responsibility CD (Get Back GBR 003 CD 1993)

Greatest Hits Live CD (Dojo DOJO CD130 1993)

Punk Singles Collection CD (Anagram CDPUNK 66 1993) (includes Harper's solo A-sides, 'Barmy London Army' and 'Freaked', but sadly not the excellent B-side 'Jo' from the latter)

Scum Of The Earth – Best Of CD (Music Collection International MCCD 120 1993)

Peel Sessions 1978-1979 LP (Fall Out FALL LP 053) (tracks 1-5 23/5/78, tracks 6-10 6/9/78, tracks 11-15 16/6/79. 'Totters' is actually an embryonic 'Rockers'. Also issued on CD, FALL CD 053, with sleevenotes by Nicky Garratt)

Punk Rock Rarities CD (Captain Oi! AHOY CD 93 1998) (rarities collection with detailed liner notes and an extensive discography)

Warhead CD (Harry May MAYO CD 107 1998)

Sub Mission – Best Of The UK Subs 1982-1998 double CD (Fall Out FALL 055 1999) (Charlie Harper's personal selection of the best of the band's work from 'f' to 'r' in the album sequence, plus a live show from Bristol)

Time Warp: Greatest Hits CD (CD PUNK 120 2000) (re-recordings of all the old hits)

Countdown/Europe Calling CD (Snapper Recall RECALSMD331 2000)

Staffordshire Bull CD (Invisible Hands IHCD 28 2003) (recorded live at Lichfield Festival 8 August 2002)

Before You Were Punk CD (Anarchy Records March 2004)

Complete Riot CD (New Red Archives NRA99CD 2006) (Quintessentials and Riot on one CD)

Undertones

Feargal Sharkey (vocals), Damian O'Neill (guitar), John O'Neill (guitar), Billy Doherty (drums), Mickey Bradley (bass)

In November 1975 in Derry, Northern Ireland, a bunch of working class Catholic lads decided they want to put a band together around the nucleus of the O'Neill brothers – John and Vincent, who were Saturday boys at their dad's fruit and veg shop. John was the family's musical obsessive, his young life revolving around the weekly purchase of the NME. Billy Doherty was recruited principally because he lived in the same street. And Vincent knew Mickey Bradley from St Peter's Secondary school so he got the call as well a few months later. Initially, they had no musical equipment, were bereft of songs, and didn't rehearse beyond fiddling around with some acoustic guitars. If anything at all was going to happen, they needed a singer.

That paved the way for Feargal Sharkey, a member of Billy Doherty's class and also his second cousin, renowned throughout his peer group for his incongruous clothes and for the singing trophies that were piled high in the Sharkey family home.

They collectively leaned on their parents to secure a loan from the Provident and saved hard to build up an arsenal of musical equipment, paying the loan back at £2 a week. Sharkey was a Boy Scout, which meant the group transferred from the overcrowded bedrooms of the O'Neill homestead to practice facilities at an outhouse next door to the Scout Hall in nearby Creggan. After four months of practice, they were ready for their first appearance – playing blues covers in front of an audience of Creggan Scouts in February 1976, but not before Vinny had decided to opt out to concentrate on his O-levels. That left the second guitarist's berth free for younger brother Damian, who was already showing promise. In fact, he was so good that elder brother John has jokingly claimed he started to write songs to make sure he didn't end up getting chucked out of the band. At this stage, everything was still "a bit of a giggle". Their second show came a month later, at St Joseph's

Secondary School as part of their variety concert. Asked by the teacher how they should be introduced, Sharkey came up with the name the Hot Rods. His bandmates were not best pleased. For the next show, at the Waterside Youth Club, Sharkey managed to come up with the even less imaginative Little Feat.

At their outset, the band had been wrapped up in the giddy excitement of the glam rock era of T-Rex and the Glitter Band, as well as hardy perennials the Who and Rolling Stones. But soon they were in thrall to imported New York Dolls albums. And then the Ramones, in particular, would galvanise the band. Friend Domhnall MacDermott, leader of local legends Dick Tracey & The Green Disaster, with whom it is rumoured both Bradley and Doherty would enjoy stints, introduced the band to these imported delights, and in his own way lit the path to punk rock righteousness. As a result, they eventually settled on the name **UNDERTONES** because it sounded a bit like the Ramones.

Their early adventures at various youth clubs around Derry were greeted with appalled indifference, apathy and, often, open hostility. At some concerts they would slip in a version of 'Anarchy In The UK' to raised eyebrows. By April 1977 they were playing regularly at the Casbah, "Derry's Cavern", immortalised in the fade-out 'song' at the end of their debut album, 'Casbah Rock'. Gradually, they found an audience, doing so by introducing a new band original on each successive date as they built up their repertoire and dropped the covers. This 18-month period helped them pay off their equipment as the receipts of £40 a week were divvied up. Meantime, a new rehearsal space was found, The Shed, a converted stable at the back of a relative's house near the Bogside, the nationalist area just outside Derry's city walls. Which meant that the O'Neill family might at last have some peace.

On the back of their Casbah apprenticeship, the Undertones were offered a chance to appear at Dublin University's Belfield Festival in June 1977, at the invitation of locals Radiators From Space, with whom they'd shared a stage in Derry. But the gig ended in chaos when audience member Patrick Coultry was stabbed to death. The Undertones concluded their set, having witnessed what they thought was a scuffle in the audience during an earlier act's performance. Doherty was wrongly identified by an audience member as the potential assailant, and interrogated by the police over the incident. Rumours emerged that the band faced parental pressure to withdraw from their rock'n'roll careers as a direct result.

Undeterred, they elected to record a demo tape at a local studio to send round the UK-based independents such as Radar, Stiff and Chiswick. No-one was interested. The cassette contained five rough cuts; 'Teenage Kicks', 'Get Over You', 'Gotta Getta', 'Girls Don't Like It' and 'Emergency Cases'. A copy was despatched to John Peel, who didn't get to hear it for two months due to the size of his tape mountain.

The most important early intervention came from local music biz maverick and Good Vibrations proprietor Terri Hooley. The ensuing release was intended more as a swan song to their travails and a historical document – they wanted to leave a memento before they disappeared back into the 'ordinary' world. A friend of the band, Bernard McAnnany, whose brother worked with Sharkey at Radio Rentals, served as the intermediary, badgering Hooley and telling him that if he didn't sign the band they'd split up and the opportunity would be lost. Actually, they had already split up. There had been one row too many and Sharkey had walked out.

Good Vibrations, which had already released records by Protex and the X-Dreamysts, offered the band a four-track EP. Which was enough to cajole Sharkey to return to the fold. Hooley also set Damian and Sharkey up with their first interview, with Belfast's No Fun fanzine, conducted above his shop. 2,000 copies of the EP, recording budget £100, were initially pressed up, which in its own way seemed pretty optimistic. The sessions were taped at Wizard, a 16-track studio in Belfast, in a single hour, with mixing taking place the next day. The only overdubs were the hand claps on the title-track.

In the event, John O'Neill's 'Teenage Kicks' had been chosen as the lead track and the title of the EP. Then Peel, reminded about the band by either a phone call from Billy Doherty or Terri Hooley leaving him a copy of the single at Radio 1 on a trip to England to try to get the band signed, or via Sharkey sending him a copy – take your pick – gave it a spin. He was stunned and humbled by the perfection of its encapsulation of adolescent romantic angst. There's also the story that wife Sheila popped her head round the door and pointed out that

Revised first album cover.

it was the best thing he'd played all day. On Tuesday, 12 September 1978 he played all four songs from the EP and pondered: "Isn't that the most wonderful record you've ever heard?" He quickly declared it his favourite single of all time and in all the intervening years until his death, and in the face of a landslide of vinyl, he never rescinded or withdrew the accolade.

'Teenage Kicks' was utterly contagious, the O'Neills' sheet barre chords drilled home by Sharkey's oscillating, trebly vocals, screaming in incontrovertible unison about the indignity of not getting any. Of course, recently the song has become subject to the revisionist slant that it was an ode to masturbation. This contention has been flatly and fiercely denied by author John O'Neill, who really ought to know.

U

There's little doubt that John Peel thought that, in some ways, he had tripped over the elixir of youth resulting in some kind of psychosomatic emotional convulsion. Yet it's an essentially straightforward three-chord pop song, with lyrics that don't embellish or glad-hand the sentiments. They are just deliciously true to the marrow of the emotional yearning that afflicts all adolescents. Yet everyone in the band was convinced that 'True Confessions' was their stronger suit.

Suddenly, via Peel's patronage, the Undertones were a hot property. Peel himself was still their biggest fan, and wrote a letter acknowledging their earlier submission to the programme: "Dear Undertones, I've behaved like a typical music business arsehole over your tape, and I'm genuinely sorry about this. Really liked the tape. I think you should record a session for us. I can't afford (for) you to come over to London to do a session, but I'd like to actually pay for it myself for you to do it in Northern Ireland if you can."

The previously disinterested music industry conducted a swift about turn. Sire was first on the case, Seymour Stein having heard Peel playing 'Teenage Kicks' while driving his car through London. He subsequently despatched Paul McNally to the scene. Approaches were also received from Virgin, Polydor and Island. But the band, still without management, was happy to stick with their first suitor, Sire. Kind of. After getting a local solicitor who had never seen a music contract before to confirm that, well, it seemed OK, the O'Neills and Doherty signed to the tune of a £20,000 advance. Sharkey and Bradley were sent over to London to conclude negotiations. They talked Stein into doubling the advance, then rang the O'Neill household to see if that was OK with them. With considerable pluck, the negotiating duo were asked if Seymour could not make it £60,000? After all, that's what the Rich Kids got. Stein was furious. This was no way to treat a mogul who should have been running rings around these callow youths. But he eventually caved in.

As the band were all fans of the Ramones and Talking Heads, the deal seemed a marriage made in heaven, not least because they figured they'd be able to get some cool free records out of it. It also introduced them to later manager Andy Ferguson, a Warners promotions man whose advocacy would be a long-term plus for the band, right up to the present day.

Within a month of 'Teenage Kicks' being released on Good Vibrations, it was repackaged in a new, but ultimately less charming sleeve, and issued by Sire on 13 October. It's worth noting that, on the back of Peel's support, Peter Powell later made the EP his record of the week. "I was driving up to see Liverpool play," Peel later recalled, "and was in a traffic jam around Stoke-On-Trent and I heard Peter Powell play 'Teenage Kicks', which I'd been playing for months. To hear it played by someone else was a stupendous thing and I actually burst into a flood of tears in the traffic jam."

Before the deal was signed, the band indeed cut that first Peel session, the great man putting up £70 of his own money so they could record at Downtown Radio 1 with Stephen Nelson as engineer. It was a three-hour 'private session'. As Nelson later recalled to Ken Garner, "The first number they played, I thought, ah, that's a hit record. Then they did another, and I thought, ah, now that's a hit record; and every song was like that." Four tracks were cut, 'Get Over You', 'Top 20', 'She Can Only Say No' and 'Male Model', broadcast on 16 October. These tapes were never part of the original Peel Sessions releases as they were lost until 1992, when Peel found a copy in his attic.

Given Peel's protracted and impassioned endorsement, 'Teenage Kicks' eventually rose to 31 in the charts and resulted in a Top Of The Pops booking. This necessitated some urgent strategic rethinks. Feargal Sharkey negotiated a three-day pass from his work as a TV repairman – even though his boss was sceptical that he would be appearing on idiot boxes rather than repairing them. Two days after that debut Top Of The Pops appearance, they played a pre-arranged show on a flatbed truck at a local youth club on Halloween night and were pelted with eggs – so much for conquering heroes.

Their mainland UK debut at the Marquee served as a precursor to a UK tour with Sire's other great white hopes, the Rezillos. The schedule was 37 dates over 43 days. But the Rezillos were in turmoil, and split after just six dates, after Fay Fife came down with laryngitis. The Undertones were also carrying their own 'emergency case', with Doherty becoming seriously unwell. That meant that subsequent Irish dates were lost, while the NME helpfully printed a story suggesting that the drummer had passed on to the other side. Which was, actually, a direct result of Bradley phoning up said paper and planting the rumour that he'd been run over by a bus.

U

'Get Over You', rescued and revitalised from the band's original demo tape, was issued as the second single in January 1979, as the band's debut proper for Sire. It was the first time they'd worked with producer Roger Bechirian, who would shepherd their efforts on their first three studio albums. It was, again, superb, another eloquent eulogy to the hard facts of love unrequited. The Undertones, determinedly unpretentious in their media profile to the extent that frustrated journalists would press them about their 'image' – a bewilderingly misconceived approach to the subject – were depicted in hugely patronising tones. Their clothes weren't contrived. In those days "you wore what your ma bought you".

The 'Tones finally nailed their debut Top 20 hit with 'Jimmy Jimmy', which reached number

16 and saw them return to the Top Of The Pops stage. It was, of course, pure colloquial Undertones, concisely rounded out with a thumping and insistent chorus. It was also their first third-person single. Mickey Bradley has suggested in the past that the lyric referred to Prime Minister Jim Callaghan's visit to Derry, a city divided by name as well as population, in the 70s. Sounds writer Garry Bushell decided that the Undertones were hiding something beneath the pop veneer, noting the suggestion that the titular Jimmy might be a fallen paramilitary type. By this juncture, the contrast with rivals Stiff Little Fingers had become clear. The Undertones wrote pop songs. Despite having personal political convictions with regard to the Troubles, they and their audiences lived directly in the middle of it and the last thing they wanted to do with their limited and oft-blighted leisure time was talk about it.

Part of that life-affirming joy was encapsulated in the 'Jimmy Jimmy's B-side, 'Mars Bars', a straightforward, unrepentant eulogy to the energy-giving properties of the popular chocolate bar. Budgets dictated that it was actually part of their staple diet at the time. Their debut album followed a month later to universally fawning reviews. That was understandable. It would have been churlish to object to a suite of majestic pop songs about girls and girl trouble rendered with an energy quotient that pretty much outstripped anything up to, and at times including, the Buzzcocks. Dave McCullough, bless him, almost expired with enthusiasm in his Sounds review. The songs were awesome. '(She's A) Runaround' was a rare but wholly affectionate put-down of a member of the opposite sex, who were largely quantified on the album as an impossibly alien species and the epitome of human mystery. The protagonist of 'Girls Don't Like It', the crestfallen and loveless Eddie, new car owner or no, fitted that same adolescent schematic perfectly. 'Male Model' was brilliant escapist fantasy, its catwalk nomenclature a superb contrast with the band's ma-approved standard attire of Parkas and jeans. 'I Know A Girl' was actually inspired by John O'Neill's chivalrous efforts at exchanging a pair of jeans his girlfriend and later wife had purchased. Indeed, yes, the Undertones had discovered, rather than merely theorised about, the joys of the opposite sex.

Eventually the album was repackaged in a more colourful sleeve, inspired by the Who's My Generation. That meant that the original iconic black and white shot of the boys with their legs draped over a brick wall in Derry was lost, at least until the CD reissues. There was also an amended tracklisting, with 'Teenage Kicks' and 'Get Over You' added to seduce the punters. The second issue also included the remixed version of 'Here Comes The Summer' that emerged as the band's fourth single. It would be the last time that the Undertones would appear so in hock to the Ramones, but it was still an absolute thumper of a single, a frenetic tune that recalled the Beach Boys at warp speed. When issued on single, it came complete with an authentic Derry postcard image.

In the meantime Joe Strummer had declared himself a fan and invited the 'Tones to join the Clash's Take The Fifth tour of the States. Much fun was had by all, with the star-struck Derrymen unable to believe their luck, as third support behind soul legends Sam And Dave. But they quickly grew homesick. After all, what was the point of having your love requited, finally, if you then traipsed across to the other side of the world? Apparently, Strummer told the band to "get an image". If this is true, it's about as far wide of the mark as he ever got. The band's enduring appeal was that they were totally unversed in the mechanics of fashion, to the point where they could happily take on the role of catwalk anti-matter. And they were so homesick, they also turned down the offer of continuing as support on the west coast leg of the tour.

Although the Undertones will forever be associated with 'Teenage Kicks', for many their finest song was delivered at the end of 1979. John O'Neill's "You've Got My Number' was monstrously and indisputably wonderful, as crunching a pop creation as the punk wars ever produced. Deliciously simple, brutally effective, with an arrangement that was surely engineered in the heavens, its three minutes of compulsive riffery sizzled on the turntable. But it also spoke of encroaching adulthood and self-empowerment – "if you wanna wanna wanna have someone to talk to… " The 'Tones were no longer merely pleading for attention. The world had shifted, a bit, and there was the implicit recognition that they had something to bring to the table with regard to the sex wars. Ah, bollocks. It was just a great pop song.

Meantime the Undertones were becoming unlikely but wholly welcomed fixtures in the pop press. The Smash Hits Department Of Gritty Realism (their joke) profiled them on their 1979 tour. They had previously been stereotyped as homesick greenhorns without an ounce of sense about the world. That wasn't the case. Nor did they play on that image, but it did make for good copy. The tour was interrupted by an appearance on Top Of The Pops to promote 'You've Got My Number'. In the meantime, their new-found popularity was routinely dismissed with protestations that they were undeserving of the plaudits chucked their way. "The Jam and the Buzzcocks are a lot better than we are, really" was a not too untypical example. But they were growing wiser, as Mickey Bradley confessed to Trouser Press: "The first thing we used to say was no, and then maybe. Now we ask, how much?"

The band's most commercially successful single was to follow in 1980. 'My Perfect Cousin', based on a real-life relative of Mickey Bradley's family who did actually appear on Mastermind and reached the finals answering questions on the subject of Steve McQueen, soared to number nine and became their sole Top Ten hit. Its sublime name-dropping of fellow chart residents the Human League could not have been bettered had they employed Oscar Wilde as chief lyricist. One of the reviews, understandably, queried whether the band had been taking Open University courses on the sly. And the Subbuteo-themed cover, with the players' legs snapped off on the reverse of the sleeve, ought to be hung in an art gallery somewhere. But it didn't end there. The Julien Temple-directed video, complete with inane band dancing, was largely filmed right in the garden of the O'Neill family home. As Mickey Bradley later recalled in his genuinely amusing "extended childhood" recollections on the Undertones website, that was all very well. But the O'Neills' house was metered and a technician had to be despatched to the local shop to supply them with enough 50ps to complete the job.

The band's second album, Hypnotised, was subtitled '15 Rockin' Humdingers'. Maturity would be about the last charge you could level at the contents, but there was a clear development in the realisation of the band's innate gifts as songwriters. Irony is generally the last refuge of the grossly untalented, yet the Undertones sent themselves up savagely whilst running for cover at any hint of press-generated accolades. Nowhere was this more clearly the case than on 'More Songs About Chocolate And Girls', an exquisite rebuttal of the group's press image, citing full ownership of their own brand of 'dumb entertainment', while also slyly name-checking Talking Heads' More Songs About Buildings And Food. It was, and is, one of the best jokes in pop music.

'What's With Terry', apparently a reference to Damian's eyesight, saw the band's signature rhapsodic double guitars entwine beautifully. 'Tearproof' was achingly precise in its depiction of boyish lust tempered by realism. The cover of the Drifters' 'Under The Boardwalk' saw Feargal in croon-tastic form. 'Hard Luck' was part of their 'Gary Glitter day' – each day of the sessions being dedicated to a favoured musical influence. That influence can also be traced to the title-track, which returned to the Undertones' favoured lyrical perch – viewing women from afar, worshipping them from afar, and failing to understand them from afar.

The band toured with TV21 and friends the Moondogs while 'Wednesday Week', their first de facto ballad, was released. Written during a break between sessions for the album, it served as a heart-stopping depiction of the colossal import of classroom romance in a young man's life. Apparently, it was the first Undertones song that Feargal's mum and dad approved of.

1981 began with the "See No More" tour, which transpired as shorthand for their displeasure with Seymour Stein and Sire. They were annoyed at the lack of backing they were being given in America, among other matters. So Andy Ferguson exploited some loopholes in their contract to spirit the band away, with their rights to their catalogue intact. It was a neat trick, and it wouldn't be the last time he pulled it off for the band.

The intention now was to form their own label and take a greater hand in the whole process, while still linking with a major to afford them sufficient visibility. "Cutting out the middle man," as Sharkey explained to the press. The band invoked their own label, Ardeck (as in "A Record Deck") and EMI agreed to act as licensees. The new label was inaugurated with the release of 'It's Going To Happen', alongside third album Positive Touch. This was effectively the second phase of the Undertones' existence. An altogether more complex group emerged. While their audience struggled with the transition, the music succeeded admirably on the whole. This was a lush recording, befitting the tightly layered melodrama of the songs. It was no longer enough for the band to ride the buzzsaw bandwagon. 'It's Going To Happen', which was more EMI's idea of a single than the band's, featured a rudely parping brass section.

If that wasn't enough of a signal that times were changing, the lyrics ("The best story I ever heard, the truth about Fat Mr X and the young girl") were far more oblique and less literal. It only later transpired that they were written in direct response to the IRA hunger strikes. The band promoted it on Top Of The Pops on the evening after Bobby Sands died – Damian wore a black armband.

Positive Touch was recorded in January 1981 at Wisseloord Studios in Holland. It was the band's most sophisticated production to date, with the Rolling Stones' Beggars Banquet and Between The Buttons being key cited influences, most notably on 'When Saturday Comes', which unashamedly appropriated the 'Paint It Black' riff. One of the dominant musical strains was the harmonies. Always a key element of the band's sound, where once these had been gruff imitations of the lead vocal line or chorus, now they veered across the songs, notably on 'Crisis Of Mine', which was later revealed by John O'Neill to be another indirect response to the Troubles. Other songs, like 'When Saturday Comes', 'Boy Wonder' and 'His Goodlooking Girlfriend', bridged the gap between the band's earlier incarnation and its current, more expansive musical horizons. 'You're Welcome' was one of the most successful post-transition songs, a precious, cowed lullaby that sounded utterly brittle. Similar in tone was 'Sigh And Explode', featuring a keyboard break that was hugely reminiscent of the Doors circa 'People Are Strange'. As on the next single to be released from the album, 'Julie Ocean', it saw Sharkey's voice retreat to a crumbling whisper amid subtle shifts of rhythm and emphasis. Again written by John O'Neill, it was directly influenced by touring partners Orange Juice and the new school of Scottish pop. 'I Don't Know', introduced by flamenco guitar, saw its delicious melody neutered somewhat by an over-reliance on studio effects, a criticism that could also be levelled at 'Hannah Doot'. Producer Roger Bechirian drew flak in some quarters over the perceived over-production, and this would be the last time he worked with the band.

The critics, who'd showered praise on the band from the outset, were restrained in their enthusiasm. "Every note on this album's in the right place," noted Dave McCullough, "but the Undertones' hearts aren't." But as with everything else with the Undertones, the decision to remodel their sound stemmed not from caprice or planning, but from instinct. They went from small trousers to big trousers, not from grand design, but from necessity. And in retrospect they did both brilliantly. They were great as whippersnappers, but they were almost as convincing as young adults on the threshold.

However, though the accompanying tour was a sell-out, the album only reached 17 in the UK charts. 'Julie Ocean' was extracted from it – featuring a more abrasive chorus – in July 1981. However, the fact that the single didn't break the Top 40, despite yet another Top Of The Pops appearance, signalled a slide in the band's popularity. There was a feeling abroad that in pushing forward they had left many of their original fans behind. 'Beautiful Friend' built on the sound of 'Julie Ocean'. It was the first time they'd recorded a single without playing it live first. It was impossibly melancholic, beautifully observed and melodically intriguing. But it was still not the most obvious commercial single to promote the album and in relative terms, died a death.

The group took a break for the rest of 1982, although EMI did thoughtfully restock the shelves with their original singles, while the band toured Europe and Scandinavia. On their return, they embarked on sessions for what would be their final studio album. This was introduced in January 1983 by the release of 'The Love Parade'. Featuring a swarthy, over-revved psychedelic groove, powered by swirling fairground organ, the single announced the band's impending lurch towards soul and R&B.

It was a fitting introduction to The Sin Of Pride, the sound of Derry youth playing Motown. Meticulously crafted and finely honed, over-involved and over-egged songwriting had replaced the two-minute pop-blasts of old. The chill black and white or colour-fuzzed Polaroids of Hypnotised were supplanted by a band image that was far more composed. Mike Hedges was brought in as co-producer, and it's interesting to know how similar the guitar parts sound on songs like 'Valentine's Treatment' to his subsequent work with the Stranglers circa Dreamtime.

The album kicked off with a version of the Isley Brothers' 'Got To Have You Back', complete with female backing vocals. It was the song that most keenly anticipated Sharkey's subsequent solo career, and announced John O'Neill's rediscovered Motown fixation. A lot of critics pointed to the fact that the lush environment defused the band's innate charms, and there's a fair amount of truth in that. But the songs are generally good, and wholly in keeping with the band's customary mastery of melody. 'Bye Bye Baby Blue', for example, could have been the theme tune to a 50s Ealing comedy. 'Conscious' is lovely, as is John O'Neill's 'Soul Seven', a worthy successor to 'Julie Ocean' and 'Beautiful Friend'. 'Chain Of Love', a breezy deliberation on romantic jealousy bolstered by harmonica and a thoroughly jaunty production, was the last in a long time of summer's day classics.

However, there were tensions backstage. While attempting to escape musical deadlock, they had pretty much lapsed as a commercial proposition. Mickey Bradley would later tell Jack Rabid that it was "the first and only Undertones record that was tampered with by record company people". Internal difficulties, largely due to conflicts over songwriting credits and clashes with Sharkey, had the unfortunate effect of pinning the blame for the band's imminent split on The Sin Of Pride, which wasn't the case. The tensions predated the album and its commercial failure compounded rather than instigated problems. The sessions were laboured, and In the end the tapes were completely remixed and the running order drastically revised. Three songs, John's 'Bittersweet' and 'I Can Only Dream' and Damian's 'You Stand So Close (But You're Never There)' missed the cut. The band approached song selection democratically, with one vote per member and one for manager Andy Ferguson, and these were simply voted off. However, they did appear on acetate, demonstrating how close they'd come to selection, and EMI mistakenly pressed a handful of copies of the album in this format. The songs have been restored to the running order on subsequent CD reissues. 'Bittersweet', the closest Sharkey came to Rat Pack croonersville, was a particularly glaring omission in retrospect.

Just weeks after the Sin Of Pride's release, it was officially announced that the Undertones were no more. There were final shows in the UK, Europe, and at Punchestown Racecourse in June. John O'Neill had decided that it was unfair to continue splitting songwriting royalties five ways when he was by far the most prolific writer in the group. Sharkey, who as a non-writer had most to lose, was having none of that, flying home to Derry without further comment. It was an impasse exacerbated by the fact that the guitarist was less than enamoured with some of Sharkey's 'melodramatic' vocal takes on the album. But it was Sharkey who told the band, on tour, that he'd have enough. His resolution was met with practically no resistance, so dispirited were his bandmates.

Sharkey hooked up with Vince Clarke from Yazoo to hit the Top Ten with the Assembly's 'Never Never'. He then went all the way to the top of the charts with the Maria McKee-penned 'A Good Heart'. Both 'Listen To Your Father' and 'You Little Thief' were far better songs but didn't catch the housewives vote. But when EMI announced their intention to release 'Save Me' from the Sin Of Pride with the billing 'The Undertones featuring Feargal Sharkey' you could hear the anguished screams carry all the way from Derry. Eventually Sharkey would join Polydor's A&R staff and is now forging government initiatives to encourage young people to get involved in music.

The O'Neill brothers turned the latter day direction of the Undertones on its head by forming That Petrol Emotion, who cut five albums of caustic guitar rock in the 80s on a succession of labels. For those who sorely missed the magnificent musical chemistry that existed between the O'Neill brothers circa Hypnotised, it was a wonderful return. Eventually John O'Neill, now reverting to the Irish form of his name Sean, would return to Derry to work on various community music projects, latterly Derry's Nerve Centre, as well as forming Rare. Mickey Bradley worked briefly with Damian in a band called Eleven before becoming a London bicycle courier and eventually a producer and DJ for BBC Radio Foyle – where he rejoiced in the nickname 'Grumpy'. Damian moved back to guitar from bass following his brother's defection from That Petrol Emotion and is the only member of the Undertones still based in London, where he's now a house husband. Billy Doherty joined the Carolines and the Hickeys and now works in computersville

The band agreed to reform for John Peel's 50th birthday party in September 1990. Sadly, John and Damian's father died during rehearsals, meaning they had to leave the festivities to the Buzzcocks, House Of Love and the Fall. Over the next few years, there were various attempts to coax the band out of retirement, notably in 1993, when Castle issued Teenage Kicks: The Best Of The Undertones, and they were offered "a lot of money" to tour Europe. But Sharkey was totally resistant, despite his former band mates meeting in London and agreeing in principle. So, eventually, the Undertones decided if they were going to do it, they really didn't need him. But it took a while. They were enticed into appearing at the 1999 Galway Festival, where long-term fan Davy Carlton of the Saw Doctors volunteered as stand-in.

"For some reason John and I said yes," Damian later told Q. "We had the lead singer of the Saw Doctors with us as we knew Feargal wouldn't do it – I don't know if we even bothered asking. We got offered a shitload of money – a quarter of a million or something – by the Mean Fiddler to play a few years ago and he wouldn't do it then, so there's no way he would now. I respect that. It's a shame though, because he doesn't know what he's missing." That led to an invitation to join the Saw Doctors on further dates, which meant the establishment of a new model Undertones in the 21st century, with Paul McLoone, a radio producer with Today FM in Dublin, who'd worked with Doherty in the Carolines, coming aboard as replacement singer. The Undertones were again a going concern, although the band decided that they should remain semi-pro this time round.

The Undertones were celebrated in celluloid in 2001 with the Teenage Kicks documentary. Perfectly filmed by the perfectly named My Perfect Cousin Productions by Vinny Cunningham and Tom Collins, it was narrated by John Peel himself. As well as archive footage it featured extensive interviews and contributions from both Seymour Stein and Terri Hooley. But it was the additional footage that gave so many insights to the band. Sharkey confesses to Peel, seemingly the only one in the Undertones story that he retains any great affection for, that the real reason he left came when his child returned from his front garden with a bloody nose, inflicted by another child simply on the basis of his parentage. There's also a strong indication that what the other band members considered slights and affectionate jokes, he considered ostracising and bullying. Feargal was never truly a part of this gang, and there are hints of how deeply that affected their one-time singer in his painfully candid interview at Peel Acres.

The reconstituted group's first new recording was 2003's 'Thrill Me', which Peel promptly played three nights in a row, as enthusiastic as ever – though as Bradley admitted to Jack Rabid, they were "very, very cautious about playing the new songs live," let alone committing them to the band's discography. "We wanted these new songs to be as good as the old songs. I remember what we did the first couple of times we did the new songs. We only did about three of them, and we pretended that they were cover versions, just to get away with it and to see. One of the songs, 'Oh Please' (written by Bradley), I said that it was a Saints' song." An album, Get What You Need, followed.

And it was great not only to have them back, but also to hear them serve up fizzing great wallops of pop again. It's actually a fine album and McLoone does a first-rate job at maintaining the tradition without sounding like a karaoke Sharkey, which was always a danger. If anything, he's closer to Steve Mack of That Petrol Emotion on several of the tracks, notably 'I Need Your Love The Way It Used To Be'. Albeit with a Derry accent, and without the vibrato. 'Shut Down' was a revelation, arguably heavier than anything the band had recorded to this point. 'Thrill Me' again bridged the musical generations between the Undertones and TPE. 'Everything But You' sounded as fresh-faced and eager as anything in the original Undertones' canon – and proof of the band's stated intention to recreate the aesthetic of those early Nuggets pop-psych compilations that had so informed their early catalogue. There was even a dash of rockabilly on' Touch'. It wasn't as if they'd divorced themselves entirely from the latter period version of the band, as the soul-infused 'You Can't Say That' demonstrated. The best song, however, was 'Oh Please', a more than passable attempt at Morrissey-like sarcasm that complained of pointless CDs headed for landfill sites. There was even a name-check for the Clash. So was it OK for a band who radiated youth more acutely than just about anyone else of their musical generation to return as forty-somethings? On the evidence it was just fine. Get What You Need was a cracking effort, whether or not the participants were now growing hairs out of their ears and between their toes.

It was, in short, a far better album than anyone had a right to expect. Of course, you're forced to overlook the fact that they've lost one of the most distinctive vocalists of the era. And it's worth acknowledging that, as wonderful musicians as the Undertones were, and as great a songwriter as John O'Neill, in particular, was and is, Sharkey's hugely distinctive pipes were a major component in their success. There was always an imbalance in the way that the band was perceived, granted, but the pendulum should not swing too far in the opposite direction. Sharkey was the perfect cipher for those songs and they would have sounded different, and inferior, without his presence.

Of course, now there are day jobs to be fitted in between touring engagements, but everyone seems to be having a fine time. Prior to the reformation, Mickey Bradley had analogised their career decline up to The Sin Of Pride in the sleevenotes to True Confessions. "The usual pattern for bands: they start off simple, things getta wee bit more complicated, then they make their big Sgt Pepper type thing, after which they make their back-to-basics White Album. We never got to our back-to-basics things!" Well, they have done now, and great it sounds too.

DISCOGRAPHY:

(Buyer's Guide: Basically the four original studio albums are all hugely recommended, as is the band's post-Sharkey effort Get What You Need. In terms of the original quartet of albums, the 2000 reissues on Castle are the ones to get, as they feature extensive sleevenotes and more thoughtful presentation. The original Dojo reissues, which I worked on, have effectively been made redundant. After that, True Confessions comprises all those wonderful 45s with their essential B-sides, and the recent Listenin' In finally does a good job of rounding up the various radio sessions. Everything else, in the perplexing absence of a good live recording of the band at their peak, is superfluous)

Teenage Kicks 7-inch EP (Good Vibrations GOT 4 September 1978)

Teenage Kicks/Smarter Than U/True Confessions/Emergency Cases (reissued in new sleeve on Sire Records SIR 4007 in October 1978)

Get Over You/Really Really/She Can Only Say No 7-inch (Sire SIR 4010 January 1979)

Jimmy Jimmy/Mars Bars 7-inch (Sire SIR 4015 April 1979) (initial quantities in green vinyl with PVC sleeve)

The Undertones LP (Sire SRK 6071 May 1979) (note: 'Casbah Rock' not listed on sleeve. Reissued in new cover, SRK 6088, in October 1979 with bonus tracks 'Get Over You' and 'Teenage Kicks', and a remixed 'Here Comes The Summer'. Reissued on Ardeck, ARDM 1647391 July 1983, and again on Fame, FA 3188, October 1987. Reissued on CD on Dojo, DOJO CD 191, in May 1994 with extra tracks 'Smarter Than U', 'Emergency Cases', 'Top Twenty', 'Really Really', 'Mars Bars', 'She Can Only Say No', 'One Way Love'. But 'Casbah Rock' got lost in the shuffle, and, at Damian's insistence, the original 'True Confessions' was substituted for the album version. Reissued in 2000 on Essential, ESMCD831, with Dojo extra tracks PLUS 'True Confessions (version 2)', 'You've Got My Number (Why Don't You Use It)' and 'Let's Talk About Girls' in a revised, and probably more appropriate, running order)

Here Comes The Summer/One Way Love/Top Twenty 7-inch (Sire SIR 4022 July 1979) (reissued on Ardeck ARDS 4 in April 1982)

You've Got My Number/Let's Talk About Girls 7-inch (Sire SIR 4024 October 1979) (reissued on Ardeck ARDS 5 in April 1982)

My Perfect Cousin/Hard Luck Again/I Don't Wanna See You Again 7-inch (Sire SIR 4038 March 1980) (reissued on Ardeck ARDS 6 in April 1982)

Hypnotised LP (Sire SRK 6088 April 1980) (initial copies with free cardboard mobile. Reissued on Ardeck, ARDM 1647421, July 1983, and again on Fame, FA 3145, October 1988. Reissued on CD on Dojo, DOJO CD 192, in May 1994 with extra tracks 'You've Got My Number (Why Don't You Use It?)', 'Hard Luck (Again)', 'Let's Talk About Girls', 'I Told You So' and 'I Don't Wanna See (You Again)'. Reissued in 2000 on Essential, ESMCD832. This time the original album was accompanied by three bonus tracks, 'Hard Luck (Again)', 'I Don't Wanna See (You Again)' and 'I Told You So')

Wednesday Week/Told You So 7-inch (Sire SIR 4042 June 1980) (reissued on Ardeck ARDS 7 in April 1982)

It's Going To Happen/Fairly In The Money Now 7-inch (Ardeck ARDS 8 May 1981)

The Positive Touch LP (Ardeck ARD 103 May 1981) (reissued on EMI Price Attack, ATAK 46 April 1984. Reissued on CD on Dojo, DOJO CD 193, in May 1994 with extra tracks 'Kiss In The Dark', 'Beautiful Friend', 'Life's Too Easy', 'Fairly In The Money Now'. Reissued in 2000 on Essential, ESMCD833. The time the original album was accompanied by three bonus tracks, 'Fairly In The Money Now', 'Julie Ocean (single version)', 'Kiss In The Dark', 'Beautiful Friend', 'Life's Too Easy')

Julie Ocean/Kiss In The Dark 7-inch (Ardeck ARDS 9 July 1981)

Beautiful Friend/Life's So Easy 7-inch (Ardeck ARDS 10 February 1982)

The Love Parade/Like That 7-inch (Ardeck ARDS 11 January 1983) (also issued on 12-inch, 12 ARDS 11, with additional tracks 'You're Welcome', 'Crisis Of Mine' and 'Family EntertaiNMEnt') Got To Have You Back/Turning Blue 7-inch (Ardeck ARDS 13 March 1983) (also issued on 12-inch, 12 ARDS 13, with additional track 'Bye Bye Baby Blue')

The Sin Of Pride LP (Ardeck ARD 104 March 1983) (some copies mis-pressed with extra tracks 'Bittersweet', 'You Stand So Close (But You're Never There)' and 'I Can Only Dream'. Reissued on EMI Price Attack, ATAK 47, August 1985. Reissued on CD on Dojo, DOJO CD 194, in May 1994 with extra tracks 'Turning Blue', 'Like That', 'Window Shopping For New Clothes', 'Bitter Sweet', 'You Stand So Close (But You're Never There)', 'I Can Only Dream'. Reissued in 2000 on Essential, ESMCD854. This time the original album was accompanied by bonus tracks 'The Love Parade (12-inch version)', 'Like That', 'You're Welcome', 'Crisis Of Mine', 'Family EntertaiNMEnt', 'Turning Blue', 'Window Shopping For New Clothes', 'Bitter Sweet', 'You Stand So Close (But You're Never There)', 'I Can Only Dream')

Chain Of Love/Window Shopping For New Clothes 7-inch (Ardeck ARDS 12 April 1983)

Save Me/Tearproof 7-inch (Ardeck ARDS 14 May 1986) (also issued on 12-inch, 12 ARDS 14, with additional track 'I Know A Girl')

Thrill Me/I'll Carry The Light 7-inch (For Us Records FU 028 May 2003) (2,000 copies)

Get What You Need CD (Sanctuary SANCD210 October 2003) (enhanced CD featuring additional demo versions, a photographic section and the video for 'Thrill Me')

ARCHIVE RELEASES:

Teenage Kicks/Emergency Cases 7-inch (Ardeck ARDS 1 June 1983) (two-track re-release of debut on green vinyl with original picture sleeve. Also available on 12-inch, 12 ARDS 1, with 'Smarter Than U' and 'True Confessions')

My Perfect Cousin/Hard Luck Again/I Don't Wanna See You Again 12-inch (Ardeck 12 ARDS 6 October 1983)

All Wrapped Up dbl LP (Ardeck ARD 1654283 November 1983) (also issued as a single album with a-sides only, ARD 1654281)

Cher O' Bowlies LP (Ardeck EMS 1172 May 1986) (re-released on CD, FAME CDP 746365-2 in 1987, then again on FAME CDFA 3226)

Peel Session 12-inch (Strange Fruit SFPS 015 November 1986) (also released as a CD single, SFPSCD 015 March 1988)

Double Peel Sessions 12-inch (Strange Fruit SFRLP/MC/CD 103 December 1989)

The Peel Sessions LP (Strange Fruit SFRLP 103 November 1989) (also issued on CD, SFRCD 103. A real must have for Undertones fans, as the first session – January 1979 – has great versions of their debut album material, and the second, recorded a year later, features radically different, grittier versions of songs that would appear on Hypnotised, plus their stage favourite Glitter Band cover 'Rock n' Roll'. The final session from November 1982 draws on The Sin Of Pride, which many fans rejected out of hand, but is still well worth a listen)

Teenage Kicks: Best Of The Undertones CD (Castle CTV CD 121 1993) (with sleevenotes by Lesley Wesley, aka Damian O'Neill)

Teenage Kicks CD EP (Dojo TONES CD 1 1994)

Teenage Kicks/Smarter Than You/True Confessions/Emergency Cases (CD reissue of the debut EP replicating original packaging and advertising original Dojo CD reissues)

True Confessions – Singles A's and B's CD (Essential ESDCD788 September 1999) (this time the sleevenotes go to Paul Lester of Uncut alongside Mickey Bradley)

The Singles 12-CD Box Set (Essential June 2000) (features all 12 'true' Undertones original singles – without the 'Undertones featuring Feargal Sharkey' 'Save Me'. Note, that the album version of 'Bye Bye Baby Blue' is featured. Reminds you once and for all what great artwork the band used).

The Best Of The Undertones CD (Sanctuary TV TVSAN005 September 2003) (also released in 2-disc format, TLSAN005, with an accompanying promo video for 'Teenage Kicks' and a trailer for the DVD)

Listenin' In – The Undertones BBC Sessions 1978-1982 CD (Sanctuary SANCD179 March 2004) (makes obsolete all previous Strange Fruit issues of the Peel sessions etc by combining all the band's radio sessions in their entirety. Most interesting of all is the presence of the very first, Peel-funded session which sounds magnificently primitive. 'Just Like Romeo And Juliet' was originally recorded by 'Tones side project the Wesleys)

Unwanted

Olli Wisdom (vocals), Mark Curzon (guitar), Paul 'Grotesque' Gardner (bass), Danny Destroy (drums)

The **UNWANTED** were formed in March 1977 when student Mark Curzon met Olli Wisdom, who ran a stall in the King's Road's Beaufort Market, close to that of Poly Styrene's legendary boutique. "I had a stall called Scabs," remembers Wisdom. "The Beaufort Market was very much the centre of attention of the punk clothing story. You could rent a 6x6ft stall for £30 a week, you didn't have to rent a whole shop. So people like us could get a foot in the door." The retail line was "really

The Unwanted of Raw Records fame.

freaky, punky gear", as an alternative to Sex and ACME up the road. "Every Saturday, the King's Road would be full of all the punks, and the Teddy Boys. It used to be a place where a lot of fighting happened. They would come and attack my shop every Saturday. But I had this little back room, and I'd keep a few people out back, ready for them. We'd cut the Teds' quiffs off and set fire to their brothel creepers in the middle of the King's Road, make them walk home in their socks with their quiffs cut off."

Wisdom had formerly been a shipping clerk before boredom forced him out. "It was a very creative period, it (punk) really gave people the chance to do whatever they felt like doing. The idea of actually getting in a band and playing music was almost impossible before that. To do almost anything of any interest was. It really blew the doors open." He was wearing a notice pinned to the back of his leopard skin t-shirt advertising the fact that he needed collaborators – "guitarist wanted, apply within". Curzon spotted it and that led to the formation of the Unwanted. In the spirit of the times, they ended up on the Live At The Roxy compilation completely by accident. "We only had one half hour rehearsal before the Roxy gig and we ended up on the album. We weren't even really a band when we got that gig. We got a van, had a half-hour rehearsal, turned up at the Roxy, told them that they'd booked us, managed to blag our way on to the gig with X-Ray Spex, etc. Then we found out afterwards it was being recorded by EMI and they were making an album out of it. So even before we knew it, even before we were really a band, we had people breathing down our necks offering us contracts." Their contribution, 'Freedom', was reviewed in the NME as "the ultimate pogo song".

As for the Roxy itself: "It was really good until it changed management. Then it went really downhill from there. But at the start, it was the one place where punks could go to. There wasn't anywhere else. If you look at where the Sex Pistols and the Clash were playing gigs, it was at weird places. There were only certain gigs, and the Roxy was the first centre where people could go and meet likeminded idiots. By April 1977, lots of punk records were beginning to come out, but before that, Don Letts played reggae and brought that whole thing across to the punk scene. When nothing's on record, what do you play? So he played reggae records."

Shortly thereafter the band were augmented by Robin Bad Habits, aka Robin Wills, on second guitar, whom Wisdom had met at Beaufort Market. He played with them as they undertook shows with Skrewdriver, X-Ray Spex et al. He also authored two songs, 'Factory Floor' and 'Destroy', before departing in the summer of 1977, later to form the Barracudas and Fortunate Sons, before going into production. He was replaced by Toby Topic, hired on the basis that he had a van. Danny Destroy "self-destructed pretty quickly," according to Wisdom. His replacement was Vince Ely, aka Vince Elite, who played briefly alongside Wills as RAF at the tail-end of 1977. His sole claim to fame was employing a toilet seat as a drum stool.

Dave 'Postman' Lynch, having spent a short period in Flowers Of Romance with Sid Vicious, also came in for Paul Gardner. And yes, he really was a postman. John Ashton would eventually replace Toby Topic as second guitarist.

The first of their brace of Raw singles, 'Withdrawal', was recorded on 22 August at Spaceward, and released in October. As a play on the band's name, but also an unintentionally ironic comment on the numerous personnel shifts, the rear cover featured question marks obscuring the faces of the personnel involved. The second single, 'Secret Police', was recorded on New Year's Day 1978, though a planned follow-up, 'Memory Man' c/w 'Guns Of Love', was shelved. Robbie 'Captain Birdseye' of Peroxide Romance also filled in for a short while on drums after Ely's departure to join the Psychedelic Furs, where Ashton had already berthed. Ely additionally spent his post-Unwanted days with the Photons and, allegedly, the Moors Murderers, joining the Furs after their debut John Peel session but before they had released vinyl. Paul Wilson, the Furs' original drummer, was also reported to be a member of the Unwanted (notably in Dave Thompson's Furs' biography Beautiful Chaos, in which the Unwanted's live shows are recounted as "seldom less than wonderful"). "Never heard of him," is Wisdom's reply. Others to have claimed membership of the Unwanted include John Dunn, who later played with American hardcore icons Iron Cross. Unless he happened to be the 'Mad Jerk' mentioned by some as their discarded, pre-Roxy bass player. "Never heard of him either," says Wisdom, emphatically.

As for Lee Wood's Raw Records roster: "It was probably a bad mistake, but it sounded good at the time. We were completely naïve. Someone giving us the chance to make records when we weren't even a proper band? We didn't say no, that's for sure." Wood later recalled to punk77 that the band was "Totally untogether. I should have passed on them..." Wisdom: "Totally untogether? We could say the same about him too!" Did they ever get paid? "No, never got paid a penny."

They left behind a posthumous retrospective, Secret Past, plus a live bootleg of one of their Vortex shows. Wisdom went on to become manager of the Batcave and singer for Specimen. "The Batcave was really the night-club meant to launch Specimen. But it ended up launching Goth instead." He was last sighted organising raves in Bali and now has his own Space Tribe musical/party outlet, run from his new base in Australia. "Space Tribe is my artist name, I play all over the world. It's psychedelic trance music, full power and kicking! Often we play outside in beauty spots around the planet, on beaches, deserts, etc, and at eclipses, more often outside than inside. Some of the parties draw up to 25,000 people. I played Greece last week, and I'm playing Portugal next week, then the solar eclipse party in Turkey." Nice work if you can get it. Does he still have the stamina? "I play live off a laptop and using synthesizers, so I don't have to cart a whole band around me with these days, it's much easier!" He's certainly surfed more musical waves than most. "Punk, Goth, Trance, they all evolved from one another," he reflects. "I wouldn't have arrived where I am today otherwise. I'm still quite a punk really, and it still shows in my music. It's amazing how many people I know from the punk and Batcave days who are in the psychedelic trance scene now."

DISCOGRAPHY:

Withdrawal/1984/Bleak Outlook 7-inch (Raw RAW 6 October 1977) (also issued on 12-inch as Raw RAWT 6 without picture sleeve. Reissued by Damaged Goods, DAMGOOD 183, on white vinyl but minus 'Withdrawal')

Secret Police/These Boots Are Made For Walking 7-inch (Raw RAW 15 February 1978)

Memory Man/Guns Of Love 7-inch (Raw RAW 30 1978) (scheduled but never recorded after the drummer broke his arm)

ARCHIVE RELEASES:

Secret Past LP (Delorean 1985) (all the studio tracks plus five unreleased demos from October 1977 on the other side)

COMPILATIONS:

Live At The Roxy LP (Harvest SHVL 4069 June 1977; 'Freedom') (reissued on CD by Receiver, RR 132, in 1991)

(Oh No It's) More From Raw LP (Raw RAWL 2 1978; 'Withdrawal', '1984')

Raw Records Punk Collection CD (Anagram CD PUNK 14 1993; 'Withdrawal', 'Bleak Outlook', '1984', 'Secret Police', 'These Boots Are Made For Walking', 'I'm Not Me', 'End Is Night')

Urban Decay

Steve 'Til' Timcke (guitar), David 'Maz' Marriot (bass), Dean Tisbury (vocals), Mickey Howard (drums)

One of Harlow's earliest punk bands, first formed in 1977, URBAN DECAY never made it to vinyl, but were later immortalised via the inclusion of two tracks on the 2004 Stortbeat compilation. Gordon Wilkins, who organised that release, had earlier collated a full CD of archive material in 2002. The original version of Urban Decay, formed at school, ran aground. In 1978 sole surviving member Timcke resurrected the band, along with songs such as 'Abuse' and 'Concrete Jungle', written in its earlier guise. Marriot came in on bass and, after a few months of searching, vocalist Tisbury joined with Mickey Howard of the Sods serving as makeshift drummer. The latter was a vacancy that was never properly filled throughout the band's career, or at least until it was almost over. They played regularly alongside Bishop Stortford's Epileptics, whose Kev Biscoe would occasionally provide second guitar, in Essex and Hertfordshire, and managed to secure a support to the Newtown Neurotics in Belgium. Stringy of the Eratiks also frequently appeared as guest vocalist at their shows. Tilbury would return the compliment.

By 1982, still without vinyl to their name, the line-up incorporated Olly Matthews serving as second vocalist, Ray Jones adding saxophone and, finally, a permanent drummer in the form of Nigel 'Rhino' Trotter. But it was all in vain as the band collapsed by year's end, leaving only a handful of live recordings and studio demos behind them. This led to Gordon Wilkins piecing together a full CD release, There Is No Escape, in 2002. The sound is reminiscent of their better known fellow travellers the Epileptics, a claustrophobic, dense production with bold, hectoring vocals, blending the original 1977 punk ethos with the more agit prop-inspired aesthetic of the early-80s. But it's obvious by the later tracks the band was pushing their personality a bit more, and by the early-80s there's a pop sensibility to the tracks that recalls Zounds or the more quirky anarcho bands of that period.

ARCHIVE RELEASES:
There Is No Escape CD (Hand Signal Handy 1 2002)
COMPILATIONS:
Stortbeat: A Musical Collective double CD (Handsignal Recordings Handy 2 and Handy 2A 2004; 'Severalls', 'Sex Assault')

Urge

Kevin Harrison (guitar, synthesizer), David Wankling (vocals, saxophone), John Westacott (bass), Lynda Wulf (vocals), Billy Little (drums)

The URGE formed in the summer of 1978, under the auspices of vocalist, saxophonist and lyric writer David Wankling, who'd spent a couple of years working as a croupier in Brighton. He founded the band on his return to his native Coventry, alongside flatmate John Shipley. Billy Little of the Squad was drafted on drums, before Harrison was recruited in January 1979.

Harrison had already spent time in elemental Coventry band Transposed Men, which also featured John Bradbury (Specials) and later Selecter musicians Desmond Brown and Neol Davies. "It was a good time." Harrison recalls. "The Sex Pistols proved you didn't have to be able to play like Segovia or Jimmy Page and also – despite some bands best efforts to disprove it – even play music of a specific style. It was also freedom from a tyranny of self-indulgent musical wankers well past their best and self-appointed style-makers who thought they were running the music business. Neither having anything to say of any interest."

Harrison's wife, Lynda Wulf was brought in as vocalist. "I was a fan, I got the chance to guest on a couple of numbers, and the first booking I did with them was at Hewell Grange Borstal, in July 1979." Shortly thereafter, in August, Shipley departed to join the Swinging Cats. The band was now called Urge, losing the definite article. Harrison: "In the late 70s in Coventry, there was a feeling of optimism and a basic need for self-expression, for the first time perhaps since the late 60s, reflected by the number of bands that seemed to have sprung up from nowhere. Through word of mouth, or by friendly staff at Virgin Records letting bands advertise, there was suddenly a local grapevine, bolstered further by Alternative Sounds fanzine, which supported the scene in depth, plus any number of pub gigs available to play. Most of the musicians knew of each other, and many played in different bands over the period. The scene was competitive but friendly and regardless of the style of the music played, it didn't seem to deter a gradually growing audience for local bands and gigs."

During the autumn of 1979 they supported the UK Subs on their Another Kind Of Blues tour, which was a strange alliance. Their musical influences were far from structured 4/4 punk, and several dates were distinguished by bemused leather-jacketed hordes hurling pint glasses at them. Their debut single, 'Revolving Boy', recorded at Spaceward in Cambridge, was released early the next year on their own label, inspired by the DIY approach of the Desperate Bicycles, by which time the highlighted line-up had coalesced. John Peel and Kid Jensen were both appreciative, the latter making it his single of the week.

Thereafter further demos were recorded at Woodbine Studios in the hunt for a major deal. Arista clinched them after interest from CBS and Beggars Banquet was spurned, and agreed to licence their Consumer Disks imprint as a boutique label. After an abortive session with reggae legend Dennis Bovell, they recorded their debut for the major with Nigel Gray (Police, etc). The NME paid tribute to its combination of "the style of the Shangri-Las with the warmth of the Rezillos". A re-recorded version of 'Revolving Boy' was intended as a follow-up. It should have been the beginning of something glorious, of course. But it wasn't. Afterwards, interest shifted when Arista's MD and Head of A&R packed their cases and headed for Warner Brothers, Urge were left on the shelf.

By September 1980 Westacott had been replaced on bass by Nigel Mulvey, also formerly of Squad. Despite some strong TV and press coverage, notably from fan Chris Salewicz, by the time the already delayed single came out impetus had been lost. Their final tour came in 1981 as support to the Selecter, with Steve Teers joining on keyboards and trombone. Their last show was at the Marquee in April 1981. After the contract with Arista was torn up, there was acrimony within the band, and shortly thereafter they broke up. There was tentatively a new, Chic-influenced Urge line-up, which included Dave Gedney, Rick Medlock and Dennis Burns, which played several times. But as Harrison later admitted: "By this time we'd had too much shit kicked out of us, and despite tentative record company interest, we reluctantly decided to call it a day."

Following the band's demise, Kevin Harrison has continued to write and record, with several albums and collaborations under his belt. His website, www.dnastudio.freeserve.co.uk has full details, as well as access to the entire Urge recordings as well as his solo and collaborative work.

DISCOGRAPHY:

Revolving Boy/ 7-inch (Consumer Disks January 1980) (2,000 copies)
Bobby/Teach Yourself Dutch 7-inch (Consumer Disks/Arista November 1980)
COMPILATION:
Sent From Coventry LP (Kathedral KATH 1 March 1980; 'Nuclear Terrorist')

Users

U

Andrew Bor (drums), Chris 'Panic' Free (guitar), James Haight (vocals), Bob Kwok (bass)

Originally formed as a trio comprising Bor, Free and Haight in Cambridge in 1977, the USERS were inspired by American garage rockers MC5 and the New York Dolls, as well as the Rolling Stones and British Beat. These influences informed a set of originals that included 'Russian Roulette', 'Heart To Heart', 'Moving In A Fast Lane', 'Red Hot Rag' and 'Bad Decision'. There were also covers of 'Louie Louie' and the Flamin' Groovies' 'Slow Death'. They then lucked out by wandering into Lee Wood's Remember Those Oldies record shop in Cambridge. "Members of the Users, who had been in the record shop before, asked me if I could spare the time to come and hear them rehearse," Wood told punk77. "I can't remember the details, but somehow we decided to make a record together."

After christening the new venture Raw Records, informed by their mutual love of the

Stooges' Raw Power (the original, rejected idea for the label's name) they booked into Spaceward in Cambridge. The band were just two gigs into their career when they produced this first single for Raw, one of the most devastating early punk artefacts, 'Sick Of You', in May 1977, rated by many as one of the genre's finest. The botched earlier version of the single was replaced by a spanking new version, recalling the Stooges 'Search And Destroy' with Haight's incendiary "When we meet, you're like a bitch in heat" declamation. Adverts were placed in the music papers and fanzines, and the single was promoted by a show with Cherry Vanilla headlining, above the Police. This led to a college show in Bishops Stortford at which Wood remembers them being "totally fucking amazing, both musically and visually. There is no doubt that with the right backing they would have been mega."

John Peel played 'Sick Of You' a few times and they picked up reviews in the NME and Sounds ("promising... if a little humourless"). Jello Biafra of the Dead Kennedys told me in the early 90s that he was mightily impressed. "I even brought 'Sick Of You' into the studio to show the engineer the sort of sound I wanted when mixing 'California Uber Alles', but Ray's guitar setting was so different, we didn't have a chance." Opportunities to gig were limited due to the band's inability to acquire their own equipment (most of their money seemed to go on pot), though they did headline a Rock Against Racism gig at South Bank Polytechnic in February 1978, as Pete Bevington replaced Bob Kwok on bass.

By the summer they had switched labels to their own label, Warped, to release the similarly frenetic 'Kicks In Style', produced by Dave Goodman. Thereafter Alvin Gibbs, ex-Rage, replaced Bevington on bass. He'd followed up an advert, which didn't name names, for a punk bassist in Melody Maker. He was delighted to discover this was for the Users. Gibbs resigned from his day job the next morning. They began rehearsing together, often in Gibbs's south London home, and played a succession of college dates as well as the Marquee, Nashville Rooms and Music Machine. To better facilitate these London dates, the trio moved into a flat Gibbs rented off his girlfriend's parents.

They continued to play shows in London. However, things didn't work out when, according to Gibbs, he discovered that his co-workers ingestion of dope was rather impairing their work ethic. To the extent that they would go missing for days at a time when gigs were scheduled. An album's worth of material recorded with Dave Goodman was never released. Gibbs left, and the remainder unsuccessfully attempted to relaunch themselves. "After I left they became a mod band," he recalled to Phaze One fanzine. "That just about sums them up. They became the Persuasions or something. I saw them in this club and they were all wearing Fred Perry T-shirts and going round on Vespas – terrible!"

I asked Alvin about this again in 2005. He now thinks their adopted name may have been the Vespas. "The singer went on to manage bands and I saw Chris Free, the guitarist, in Camden a couple of years ago, and it seems he has a record store and is doing pretty good." Gibbs went on to play first with the Brains (with Brian James, before quitting when drummer John Towe was sacked), then the UK Subs and others.

DISCOGRAPHY:

Sick Of You/(I'm) In Love With Today 7-inch (Raw RAW 1 May 1977) (also released as a 12-inch, RAW T1 and reissued by Damaged Goods, DAMGOOD 139)
'Warped' 7-inch (Warped WARPED 1 1978)
Kicks In Style/Death On Arrival (limited edition of 5,000 copies)
COMPILATIONS:
Raw Deal LP (Raw RAW LP1 1977; '(I'm) In Love With Today') (reissued in 1979)
Oh! No, It's More From Raw LP (Raw RAW LP2 1978; 'Sick Of You', '(I'm) In Love With Today')

UXB

Col Bennett (guitar, bass, backing vocals), Mark Read (guitar, backing vocals), Mick Turner (drums, vocals)

Formed in Cannock, Staffordshire in 1978, UXB grew out of jam sessions at Furzebank Community Centre in Willenhall, though early guitarists John Stainthorpe and Steve Sankey didn't last the course. As a trio they played their first show in February 1978, doing their best to affect a presentable approximation of their heroes the Clash. Bennett: "I suppose it was their look, attitude and political

stance, combined with great songs. We found the Pistols a bit too contrived and shambolic." In keeping with Strummer's men, they were huge fans of reggae, whose rhythmic timbres were incorporated into their sound from the get-go. "We were aware of reggae from the original ska scene from the late 60s. I think John Peel originally made us aware of the cool dub reggae stuff. The Clash really made us realise that white boys could have a go too."

They got their break via local scenester Little Winston, a DJ and record label owner. "Little Winston was a mobile DJ doing dance halls and private parties etc. Winston's day job was at the same company as me. That's how I got to know him. I knew he had a record label and asked him to come and see us. Well, he didn't come for ages and it's a good thing, really, because initially we didn't have a proper lead singer and our bass player at that time was not very tight, so we did sound very sloppy and were just doing cover versions." At the end of 1978 they were joined by Tony Clamp on bass, but he departed early the following year to join Walsall's Bescot Sidings. His departure signalled a major overhaul of the band's personnel, with Dom Roche becoming their vocalist and Bennett switching to bass. "We had also written four or five original songs by now. So when Winston did turn up to see us, we were very tight."

He offered the band a session at his Ginger Recording Studio in Aldridge, which resulted in the release of the double A-side 'Crazy Today' and 'Mr Fixit'. It got a good reception, including plays on John Peel, Mike Read and Peter Powell. The A-side even featured some discernible singing rather than shouting. "It's the way it turned out in the studio really. At rehearsals and live, Dom used to have to strain his voice more. We were always aware that the studio stuff may have sounded a bit too nice!" However, a follow-up single was withdrawn when the band fell out with Crazy Plane Records, though promotional copies of '2 Steps' do exist.

Still, they still had a good reputation as a live act, and the support of a phalanx of Radio 1 DJs led to an offer from Knott Management. They paired the band with reggae producer Dennis Bovell, and sent them to work at his Studio 80 complex in South London. "Don Evitts, who ran Knott Management, knew Dennis as some of his other acts had recorded with him. It was a fug of ganja smoke and very laid back, but Dennis is a perfectionist and put us through the mill a bit to get everything tight and in tune. Lynton Kwesi Johnson turned up a few times, which was very cool." Three tracks were cut, 'Go!', 'Not Enough' and 'Imagination', but they failed to elicit any interest from record companies. They continued to play live but by the summer of 1981, Roche had departed, eventually to found Balaam And The Angel. Pete Higton became the band's new vocalist. Turner and Bennett would subsequently form Fire In Cairo.

Like many bands, the former members were given pause for thought by the resurgent interest in their original records among the collector's community, especially in Japan, where 'Crazy Today' was attracting silly money. It led to a series of reunions, including a joint show at the Garage with the Zips, Knife Edge and the Negatives, all of whom featured on Bored Teenagers Volume 2. "That night was brilliant. Seemed like we had never been away. What was most impressive is how the PA systems have improved over 20 years, the on-stage mix was perfect." And UXB continue as an ad hoc venture.

DISCOGRAPHY:

Crazy Today/Mr Fixit 7-inch (Crazy Plane SP002 June 1980) (reissued in Japan on 1977 Records, SO12, in October 2001)

48 Hours/2 Steps/In The Q 7-inch (Crazy Plane 1980) (promo copies only, no stock release. Reissued in Japan on 1977 Records, SO13, in October 2001)

ARCHIVE RELEASES:

Crazy Today 7-inch EP (Last Year's Youth LAST-15 June 2003)

Crazy Today/Imagination/Stop 'n' Stare/Rescue Me

COMPILATIONS:

Bored Teenagers Vol. 2 CD (Bin Liner CD003 March 2001; 'Crazy Today', 'Over The Wall')

Don't You Know, It's Last Year's Youth CD (Last Year's Youth WIV-039 January 2005; 'Crazy Today')

The Valves

Gordon 'Pada' Scott (bass), Ronnie MacKinnon (guitar), Dee Robot (aka Dave Robertson; vocals), Gordon 'G' Dair (drums)

THE VALVES were honoured with the first release on later Simple Minds' manager Bruce Findlay's pioneering Scottish indie, Zoom. They were also the first Edinburgh 'punks' to reach vinyl – "if punk is taken to mean DIY music" – notes Dair. The two Gordons had been members of Angel Easy when they invited Robertson to join them from his ailing pub duo. He agreed to do so, on the condition he could write his own lyrics and they learn the New York Dolls' back catalogue. Robertson was a huge David Johansen fan, check the vocal similarity.

Punk "happened at about the same time, with the result that we found an instant audience for our racket," notes Dair. They were slightly older than that new audience, particularly in the case of Robertson, while shoulder length hair betrayed their pasts. However, whatever accidents of timing and fate collided to produce the Valves, they produced a fine noise, which some likened to Edinburgh's take on Doctor Feelgood. Others dubbed them "Nazareth on speed". They didn't, however, take themselves too seriously or succumb to the revolutionary froth of some of their peers. "We were 'lads'," reckons Dair, and playful with it too, a fact attested to by song titles such as 'Everybody's Got Nipples'.

In 1977 the Valves had already supported the Saints at their first Scottish concert when a customer at Bruce's Records persuaded Findlay to see them live. He saw them in tandem with Rezillos' manager Lenny Love, who was initially also interested in signing them to Sensible. Their debut single 'For Adolfs Only', recorded in August at Edinburgh's REL Studios, was released in September. It sold 14,000 copies and Zoom hurried the band to arrange a follow-up. Two tracks were duly recorded and released in December. Dair: "A big mistake, as it disappeared in the Christmas rush and sales were poor. Zoom soon lost interest, especially after they managed to sign Simple Minds."

The Valves' sense of humour is readily apparent on the second Zoom single, 'Ain't No Surf In Portobello' – which envisaged surfers trying to catch a wave at the local sewage treatment works (rather than London's Portobello Road, as many assumed). If their debut, 'For Adolfs Only', borrowed from the Rezillos' 'I Can't Stand My Baby' riff, 'No Surf' was equally indebted to Jan and Dean's 'Little Old Lady From Pasadena'. Ironically, in 1978 there was an offer on the table from EMI to update Manfred Mann's '5-4-3-2-1', which had been a regular part of their live set. But it was rejected, with the band confident that its original material was strong enough to see them progress. Did Dair ever regret this? "I have no regrets. I can't speak for the others, but at the time it was the will of us all, arrogant as we were. In retrospect, if it had been a hit, we could have got on TV, gained wider exposure, got a possible career boost, etc. On the downside we could just as easily have become a one-hit wonder, and it wasn't representative of the band as we had dropped it by early 1978 to make way for new material. EMI owned the publishing and it was a one-off deal anyway."

They were now picking up good press, including a favourable notice in Sounds in 1978, citing the band as "vital and undiluted amid the rock'n'roll fallout". Their management, meanwhile, instigated a major London-based graffiti campaign, which resulted in a £400 fine. The graffiti outlived the band – check out the film McVicar, and the wall above Roger Daltrey as he emerges from Notting Hill tube station. During this time they also gigged regularly in London, and did a full tour with Joe Jackson.

Despite their heightened profile, including a set at the Edinburgh Anti-Nazi rally, gigs at the Glasgow Apollo with Sham 69 and The Stranglers, a support at the London Electric Ballroom to the Greedies and solo tours of Ireland and Sweden, record company interest did not solidify into a contract. "We signed to Albion on a publishing deal in 1979," remembers Dair, "and in a final attempt to attract the majors they decided to push out a single, which got a few radio plays." But many observers, including members of the band, felt that 'Linda Vindaloo' rather than 'It Don't Mean Anything At All' should have been pushed to the fore. They recorded two sessions for the BBC, including one for Kid Jensen, but split soon after.

Dee went on to form the Mudsharks with Pada, "a great live band" according to Dair, but they again failed to attract record company interest. Dee also performed a series of spoken word sets, which resulted in a tour supporting the Proclaimers. But, according to Dair, the material proved too near the knuckle for the twins, and he was asked to leave after a few dates. He went on to work for the Church of Scotland sending out mail-order Bibles before moving to Belgium and changing his name to Viking Dave Robertson. As you do. He also worked with dEUS off-shoot Kiss My Jazz, writing a major part of the album In A Service Station, before putting together his own band, Wall of Sweat (www.heavenhotel.be/wallofsweat), in 2000. MacKinnon returned to printing, after a brief spell with Fun City. Gordon Scott works for the government and Gordon Dair had an unsuccessful stab at management before moving to Spain to teach English.

DISCOGRAPHY:

For Adolfs Only/Robot Love 7-inch (Zoom ZUM 1 September 1977)

Tarzan Of The King's Road/Ain't No Surf In Portobello 7-inch (Zoom ZUM 3 December 1977)

It Don't Mean Nothing At All/Linda Vindaloo 7-inch (Albion June 1979) (issued without a picture sleeve, though the original plan was to have it issued in four separate sleeves, ala Generation X, and designs were drawn up, but Albion lost interest).

The Vandals

Peggy Mount (aka Alf, or Alison Moyet; vocals), Mirror Milk (aka Kim Forey; backing vocals), Emu (aka Sue Paget; bass), Rob Allen (guitar), Simon Kirk (drums)

THE VANDALS were legendarily formed because the central trio of Basildon gals (who would also appear on the one-off Pete Zear single) were pissed off with the local nightclubs in and around Essex, couldn't afford to get to London, and therefore decided "something had to happen".

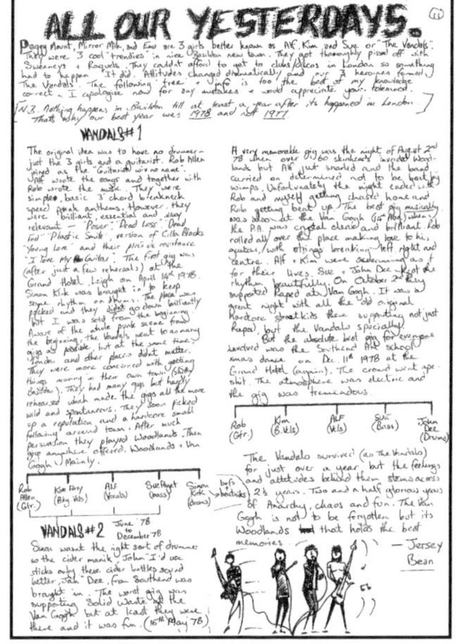

ALL OUR YESTERDAYS.

Peggy Mount, Mirror Milk, and Emu are 3 girls better known as Alf, Kim and Sue or "The Vandals". They were 3 cool "trendies" in nice Basildon new town. They got thoroughly pissed off with Sweeneys + Raquels. They couldnt afford to get to clubs/discos in London so something had to happen. It did. Attitudes changed dramatically and our 3 heroines formed The Vandals. The following tree + info is too the best of my knowledge correct. I apologise now for any mistakes + would appreciate your tolerance.

[N.B. Nothing happens in Basildon till at least a year after its happened in London. Thats why our best year was 1978 and not 1977.]

VANDALS #1

The original idea was to have no drummer – just the 3 girls and a guitarist. Rob Allen joined as the "Guitarist wiv no name". Alf wrote the songs and together with Rob wrote the music. They were simple, basic 3 chord breakneck speed punk anthems. However, they were brilliant, essential and very relevant – "Poser", "Dead Loss", "Dead End", "Plastic Smile", version of Cilla Blacks "Young Love" and their [illegible] "I Love My Guitar". The first gig was (after just a few rehearsals) at the Grand Hotel, Leigh on April 14th 1978. Simon Kirk was brought in to keep some rhythm on drums. The place was packed and they didnt go down brilliantly but I was sold from the beginning. Aware of the whole punk scene from the beginning, the Vandals went to as many gigs as possible, but at the same time, London and other places didnt matter. They were more concerned with getting things moving in their own town (shitty Basildon). They had many gigs but hardly rehearsed which made the gigs all the more wild and spontaneous. They soon picked up a reputation and a hardcore small following around town. After much persuasion they played Woodlands. Then gigs anywhere offered. Woodlands + Van Gogh mainly.

Rob Allen (Gtr.) – Kim Forey (Bkg. Vcls) – Alf (Vocals) – Sue Paget (bass) – Simon Kirk (drums) → bofs + beatniks

VANDALS #2 June 78 to December 78

Simon wasnt the right sort of drummer so the cider manik, John "I'd use sticks only these cider bottles sound better" Dee, from Southend was brought in. The worst gig was supporting Solid Waste at the Van Gogh but at least they were there and it was fun. (16th May 78)

A very memorable gig was the night of August 2nd 78 when over 60 skinheads invaded Woodlands but Alf just snarled and the band carried on determined not to be beat by wimps. Unfortunately the night ended with Rob and myself getting chased home and Rob getting beat up. The best gig musically was also at the Van Gogh (14th Aug) when the P.A. was crystal clear and brilliant. Rob rolled all over the place making love to his guitar, with strings breaking left right and centre. Alf + Kim were screaming as if for their lives. Sue + John Dee kept the rhythm beautifully. On October 2nd they supported Raped at Van Gogh. It was a great night with all the old original hardcore streetkids there supporting not just Raped, but the Vandals specially.

But the absolute best gig for everyone involved was the Southend Art school xmas dance on Dec. 11th 1978 at the Grand Hotel (again). The crowd went ape shit. The atmosphere was electric and the gig was tremendous.

Rob (Gtr.) – Kim (B. Vcls) – Alf (Vcls) – Sue (Bass) – John Dee (Drums)

The Vandals survived (as The Vandals) for just over a year, but the feelings and attitudes behind them stems across 2½ years. Two and a half glorious years of Anarchy, chaos and fun. The Van Gogh is not to be forgotten but its Woodlands that holds the best memories.

– Jersey Bean

The idea was to have no drummer and a guitarist, to which end Rob Allen was recruited, who wrote the music behind Alf's lyrics. 'Poser', 'Dead Loss', 'Dead End', 'Plastic Smile' and other basic three-chord punk rockers poured forward from this liaison, as well as their 'potential hit', 'I Love My Guitar'. There was also a version of Cilla Black's 'Young Love' in the mix too. After just a handful of rehearsals, they made their debut at the Grand Hotel in Leigh on 14 April 1978, by which time they'd rethought the 'no drummer' idea and brought in Simon Kirk.

From then on they would play around Basildon, especially the Woodlands and Van Gogh clubs, and neighbouring Essex towns, at the drop of a hat, and generally had a great time kicking up as much of a fuss as possible. However, Kirk didn't work out, so from June 1978 to the end of the year they picked up the services of John Dee (aka John Dearlove, ex-Machines). Subsequent shows included an October appearance with Raped. However, after a final triumphant show at Southend Art School's Christmas Dance in December 1978, recalled as "electric" by the editor of local fanzine Some Of That, Moyet would move on to put together the Vicars and the Screaming Ad-Dabs before joining Yazoo. Dee joined the Electric Shocks (later simply the Shocks) and subsequently reggae bands Bush Fire and Charas.

VDU's

Michelle Archer (vocals), Andy Bates (bass), Paul Dewey (guitar), Jef aka Julian Harvey (vocals), Steve Patterson (drums)

The VDU's were born out of the Gotham City Rockers. "That was a much better name in my view," reckons Julian Harvey. "I was a VDU operator at the time and hated it! Myself and Michelle fought for the limelight on lead vocals. 'Chopper'

Dewey on guitar was named after his footballing attributes rather than any appendages. Steve Patterson on drums was an interesting one because he suffered from memory loss on account of a close encounter with carbon monoxide after a (thankfully) failed suicide bid. It made for an erratic rhythm section! Andy Bates on bass was the youngest of the combo and arguably the coolest. I will always remember with envy his black corduroy bondage trousers (from Boy and not the de rigeur Seditionaries) but great nonetheless, very pucker! Tragically, Andy died in a car accident shortly before or after (I can't remember) the band split. A waste of a talented young life in any case."

The VDU's left just one single behind, though it's a bit of a cracker. Harvey: "I went on to form Beach Red (with Michelle), then separately King Kurt, The Shrew Kings (briefly joining with Michelle to do a fine rendition of 'Greensleeves' used by Andy Kotting in one of his films) and a short-lived but nonetheless NME-reviewed combo named Woman.Also, Nick Corker of Thin Sliced Records deserves a mention for putting out the single as the first on the label – before going on to work with King Kurt, Billy Jenkins, The Rain Gods, Lester Square and The Shrew Kings. A fine stable!"

Michelle, simultaneously a fashion designer (The Art Of Stealing) and face on the late-70s punk scene, having attended the 100 Club Festival, eventually led Brigandage into action. I asked her for any memories she might have of her time in the VDU's. "I've remembered a gig – it was at Chislehurst caves – our local prehistoric cave system. You know the sort of thing, guided tours, druidic sacrificial altars, a hospital and chapel from the Second World War. Anyway it was a fabulous idea – what could go wrong? It cost £22 to hire — hey that's a lot of money in 1979 and a large deposit. You could tell the guardians of the caves were unsure at allowing our punk rock presence. Anyway, they were right. We lost our deposit! The caves got trashed. To this day, I still don't know how you can wreck a cave!" Harvey: "Yes we played at Chislehurst caves (I remember the amps being emergency-repaired by foil from a cigarette box) and Ravensbourne College of Art. My main memories are the songs, the drug-influenced 'Little White Lines', cheesy pop song 'Holiday Romances' and Michelle's singing on 'Don't Cry'."

DISCOGRAPHY:

Don't Cry For Me/Little White Lines/Holiday Romances 7-inch (Thin Sliced TSR 1 1980)

Vermilion

Vermilion Sands (vocals), Pete Davies (drums), Fritz (bass), Kenny Alton (guitar)

VERMILION, who took her name from the JG Ballard novel, enjoyed the unique position of being right in the mix of both the early London and Californian punk scenes. She shared a flat with Steve Strange while working as London-based correspondent for Search & Destroy magazine (she was a former girlfriend of editor Vale), while also contributing to UK fanzine Ripped and Torn. She'd caught her first blast of the UK punk scene when the Damned played New York, and after befriending Rat Scabies, returned to Britain with them, from where she filed a series of reports. My favourite interview she conducted was with the Clash. "What do you think about Wilhelm Reich?" she enquired. Joe Strummer: "Who's he?" Presumably Bernie Rhodes was out of earshot.

Prior to that, she'd been a member of Mary Monday's Band, led by the eponymous glitter queen from Montreal who first rented the Mabuhay Gardens from Ness Aquino, thereby giving San Francisco punk its first home. They played just two shows, but made a big impression. "The bug-eyed audience could not believe the real-life trashing, slugging and ripping of flesh, BY WOMEN!" blazed Search & Destroy, albeit through a filter of well-intentioned nepotism. "People were standing on tables and chairs!" Mary Monday And Her Bitches would later record the one-off single 'I Gave My Punk Jacket To Rickie', which featured Vermilion on backing vocals.

In the UK she was part of the Notting Hill biker community that numbered among its passing membership Lemmy and Chrissie Hynde. Her first band was Dick Envy (aka Venus Envy), who played several supports around the capital, and featured later Adam And The Ants guitarist Johnny Bivouac (who would play on 'Angry Young Women'). She then released two singles under her own name, announcing a kind of feminist biker-punk schtick. Her second single, 'I Like Motorcycles', featured the Aces (Charlie Casey, bass; Noel Martin, drums; Steve Tannett, guitar). This was essentially Menace minus lead singer Morgan Webster, while the record was released on Illegal Records, which she helped run with Nick Jones. She was most proud of the publicity photo she hawked around at the time that showed her pissing in a sink.

Noel Martin told me about their brief liaison. "The Aces had their own identity anyway. But this was Vermilion's gig. Miles Copeland had put it all together for her." What was she like? "She was a gas. I used to lift her up with one hand above my head, which was kind of my party trick. And she wasn't light. We did a couple of nice gigs, and helped her write one of the songs on the record. Put some bones to it." However, their partnership ended after they played together at a Gary Glitter show. "After she'd done her thing and gone off, we stayed on and did 'GLC'. The place erupted. She wasn't too pleased. And that was that. It was a paying gig for us, only we didn't get paid. But it was more that we could keep playing together. Morgan (Webster) had had enough, so we kept going for a while doing the Aces, playing more mod-orientated stuff."

Later Vermilion would replace Ron Rouman (aka Lol Pryor) as manager of the Business. Her byline was last sighted as a contributor to a book of JG Ballard interviews edited by old friend Vale in 2005.

Discography:

Angry Young Women/Nymphomania/Wild Boys 7-inch (Illegal ILM 0010 1978)
The Letter/I Like Motorcycles 7-inch (Illegal ILM 0015 1979)

Verticle Strokers

Simon (vocals), Stephen Lake (bass), Jonathon Ingleby (guitar), Pete Gleadall (electric violin and guitar). Various drummers, including American Chris Carle and the Sods' Mickey Howard on their demo sessions, but none on a full-time basis

When Gordon Wilkins put together his excellent Stortbeat compilation in 2004, the only band he was unable to trace, despite adverts in the local press, were the VERTICLE STROKERS. Formed at Burnt Mill Secondary School, they'd played regularly around Bishops Stortford and Harlow in the late-70s, and had their demos produced by Shane Roe of the Sods. The results, including the two tracks included on the Stortbeat CD, can only be described as odd, featuring messy post-punk shouting with added violin, which actually sounds like a kazoo. Thereafter, however, the band seemingly disappeared off the radar. However, one-time near-neighbour Richard Smith was able to point to a link with later Pet Shop Boys' collaborator Pete Gleadall. He was good enough, despite his surprise at the enquiry, to answer my questions.

So how did he get involved in this punk rock malarkey? "Punk was the most vital and exciting thing to happen to this (then) teenager. Loved the look, attitude and music." So how did the band's determinedly non-conventional line-up and instrumentation go down live? "Often with much puzzlement from the audience! We did some gigs without a drummer and this made us stand out, then when you add an electric violin to the mix, this added to the puzzlement. The more effects I put on the violin, the more people seemed to like it. Simon, the vocalist, was very into the Velvets, so that was his image fix re the violin." They played regularly alongside other Harlow bands, Gleadall's favourite being the Newtown Neurotics. "They were always good to play with, they seemed better than most of the rest. I was surprised they didn't do better. I remember lots of not very good gigs, with lots of unresponsive audiences, who would later say they enjoyed it!"

Thereafter the band broke up and the former members drifted apart. "Simon started work as a gardener and started going to church, which I couldn't understand at all, not being religious. I went to university at Queen Mary College to do a geography degree (very useful, not) and started/joined other bands. Directly after the Strokers, I started the Klingons and we did one single, self-financed in the punk style. At college I met several other likeminded musicians and we formed a co-operative, Blue Ridge Productions. We won an inter-London college talent contest, and won a session in a studio that we all hated. There were nine of us with three bands with one floating drummer! We did one EP, which John Peel (RIP) played all of one night." Those three bands were the Anonymous Sisters, John and Those Virginia Mountain Boys.

"I eventually stumbled into the music business (via freelance journalism about music technology) and earn a living doing pop music (George Michael, Pet Shop Boys, Robbie Williams, Bowie etc) and have fun with dance music. I started doing sessions using the technology I wrote about for the magazines, and found myself working with the reggae scene, doing a lot with Aswad, and some with Maxi Priest. This led me to meeting George Michael's engineer (Chris Porter) and I somehow leapt from working with Aswad to programming his first tour (to promote his Faith album) doing production rehearsals in LA and finding myself onstage at the Budokan stadium in Japan for his first show!"

Any comparisons between then and now? "Dance music is like punk for me because the band/artist has the means of production in a way we could only dream about in the punk days. Technology allows us to make and master and distribute our own music. With other collaborators I've had five Billboard number ones in the dance charts, and many other reasonable successes. I currently (last ten years) have a studio in west London called Hoedown City."

But do those core punk values remain, several gold discs down the line? "I think my distrust of people in power has held me back in my career, as I still have a bit of a punk attitude towards authority. Actually, I sometimes play acoustic guitar live with Pet Shop Boys and Neil thinks I have a punk style of playing, which I suppose I must have. Just like my punk days, when I'd put my violin through lots of effects pedals to make a big racket, I still have a lot of fun making very dirty synth noises!"

COMPILATIONS:
Stortbeat: A Musical Collective double CD (Handsignal Recordings Handy 2 and Handy 2A 2004; 'Holidays', 'Saturday Girls')

Vibrators

Ian 'Knox' Carnochan (vocals/guitar), Pat Collier (bass), John Ellis (guitar), Eddie (John Edwards; drums)

Lots of people berate the VIBRATORS' contribution to the punk explosion on the basis that they were essentially old stagers given a new lease of life, the terms bandwagon and jumpers materialising like Mr Benn's shopkeeper in any introductory paragraph. Yet the vast majority of the architects of punk had antecedents in pub rock, R&B or even less creditable musical endeavours, from the Clash to the Damned, the Adverts to the Buzzcocks.

While the punk movement has been recognised for its social and political import as well as its musical achievements, some of its originators continue to be written out of its history. For want of being fashionable, the Vibrators have suffered more than most from this affliction. Yet the frenetic bubblegum punk of the Vibrators' best songs – 'Judy Says', 'Baby Baby', 'Automatic Lover', makes a nonsense of such flippant, po-faced dismissals.

Several factors conspired against the Vibrators, the first being that they were seasoned musicians. Knox, an art school escapee who also paints and exhibits, and the group's main songwriter, had been around the block. Indeed, he'd appeared in everything from Irish show bands to would-be Teddy Boy groups, notably the wonderfully titled Heavy Parrot, who, circa 1974, specialised in classic rock'n'roll covers. When Heavy Parrot became Rocking Pneumonia, quite reasonably, Knox threw in the towel. His next destination was Despair, who evolved into Lipstick, regulars on the pub rock circuit, often playing alongside the 101ers at the Elgin Arms and swapping personnel with Kilburn And The High Roads. He also appeared solo and as part of Stiletto, with whom he played later Vibrators' staples such as 'Sweet Sweet Heart' and 'Whips And Furs'. The latter contains a chord sequence familiar to anyone who has heard – and there can't be many that haven't – the Only Ones' 'Another Girl Another Planet'. However, as Knox points out, it was written in isolation from, and in advance of, Perrett's masterpiece.

Knox on stage in the mid 80s.

The idea for the Vibrators came about after discussions with Lipstick's regular van driver and roadie, Eddie, at the end of 1975. John Ellis and Pat Collier, for their part, had been members of Bazooka Joe (Ellis founded the band with Danny Kleinman), the original home of Adam Ant, and the band that gave the Sex Pistols their first support slot. Their average age in year zero was 28.

Other objections to the Vibrators included the fact that they signed to Mickie Most's RAK label, home to the critically despised plastic pop of Suzi Quatro and Mud. Third, the lyrics generally simply augmented the music rather than established some kind of agenda, which for their supporters made them lovably artless, but added fuel to the fire of their detractors. Finally, they didn't do 'obnoxious'. The Vibrators were regular Joes to a man. Mark Perry was among many to challenge their authenticity: "They were competent live but blew it all with their involvement with Chris Spedding and his stupid 'Pogo Dancing' single. The punk bandwagon seemed to have room for anyone and the Vibrators were one of the groups to take full advantage of the fact."

It's something that clearly still irks Knox. "We should have a bigger place in the punk thing... they occasionally still say we jumped on the punk bandwagon when, if these people really did their homework, they would know I was playing early Vibrators songs two or three years before the Vibrators started, in a band called Despair." John Ellis similarly disparaged punk's 'hall of mirrors' effect on perception with David Buckley. "One of the terrible things about punk was that we all threw the baby out with the bath water in a way. You weren't allowed to admit the fact that you liked Abba or Genesis. It wasn't a cool thing to say." For the Vibrators, it was all about the music and playing live. They came bearing gifts of melody and slamming power chords rather than manifestos. Take Knox's response to a question from Teenage Depression magazine in 1978. "Why did you do the RAR (Rock Against Racism) gig?

Because you believed in it?" Knox: "No, actually what most people don't realise is that bands do get paid for it. We just did it because it was a gig to do . ."

Formed in February 1976, the Vibrators made their debut supporting the Stranglers at Hornsey Art College on 7 March, receiving £5 for their troubles, and began a residency at the Lord Nelson. Thereafter they appeared at the 100 Club Punk Rock Festival. "When we turned up there," Eddie recalled to Q, "there was no PA system. Luckily we'd played a gig at the Lord Nelson up in Holloway Road the night before, so we agreed to let them use our PA system. It was meant for little pub gigs, so it was really useless, too small for the 100 Club. All these other bands kept complaining that it was a crap PA, but if it wasn't for us they'd have had nothing." In addition to playing their own set at the 100 Club, they also backed old school session man and ex-Nucleus guitarist Chris Spedding – then living with later Mrs Lydon Nora – as a prelude to performing the musical chores on his novelty punk single, 'Pogo Dancing'. The two parties had been introduced by venue owner Ron Watts, and only shown the songs in the dressing room beforehand. Watts: "Chris Spedding had been down the club to see a few punk bands play and he'd really enjoyed it. He sided with them, and asked me if he could be on the bill for the festival. He really wanted to be associated with it."

As Eddie remembers: "Spedding showed up in the afternoon and said, 'Alright, so what's this gig I'm supposed to be playing?' It was like he had seen an advert announcing he was playing, but no-one had told him anything about it. He was put together with us and we spent the rest of the afternoon and the evening in the dressing room learning the chords for his songs." Knox also saw his loaned-out guitar amp blown out by the volume of the Stinky Toys' guitarist. More seriously, the gig witnessed Sid's infamous glass-throwing stunt. "People started coming into the dressing room," Eddie remembered. "There was one guy with his forehead gashed open and pouring blood. All we could do was wrap towels around his head. Then a girl came in with blood coming out of her eye. I thought, Christ, if this is what punk's about, you can shove it."

The Vibrators' debut was recorded for Spedding's label, RAK, in November 1976. Pat Collier's 'We Vibrate', one of the earliest punk records, is a solid marriage of trad rock-pop hooks with the abandon and energy that was characterising the new movement, though the 'C'mon Everybody's' really anchor it to another era. "Chris Spedding got Mickie Most interested," Knox recalled to Q, "and asked if we wanted to do a single with him, so we said yes. But it was very difficult because he (Most) was a pop person and punk was very anti all that stuff. No other record company was interested, so we thought we'd just do it. So we went in and did two singles, 'Pogo Dancing' with Chris Spedding and 'We Vibrate'.

'We Vibrate' garnered single of the week status in the NME and National Rock Star, though this wasn't enough to see it chart. It was selected by Mickie Most, which raised some suspicion among the punk aesthetes, but the band, especially Eddie, were still cocksure: "We've brought back real rock'n'roll. For years the kids have been duped – they thought they were getting real music. They were just getting cabaret." The B-side was 'Whips And Furs', Knox's nod to his hero Lou Reed, a 1977 update on 'Venus And Furs'. A month prior to its release they recorded the first of three John Peel sessions ('Dance To The Music' – actually 'Whips And Furs' in a different guise, 'We Vibrate', 'Jenny Jenny', 'I'm Gonna Be Your Nazi Baby', 'Sweet Sweet Heart'). A second session followed in January 1977 where they again backed Spedding ('Pogo Dancing', 'Hurt By Love', 'Motorbikin'', 'Get Out Of My Pagoda' and 'Misunderstood'). At the same time, faux-punks or not, they were part of the Sex Pistols foray to Amsterdam for two nights at the Paradiso.

In May 1977, having supported Iggy Pop, whose keyboard player for the occasion was David Bowie, on a six-date UK tour, they moved to Epic Records at the instigation of manager Dave Wernham, Knox's cousin. A second single for RAK, 'Bad Time', was recorded but shelved. Part of the impetus was to escape RAK's ready identification with shallow pop in the minds of critics. Mickie Most was said to be 'displeased' at their decision to jump ship. But as Knox would later reason, "the money we were going to get wasn't very good". Then again, if they'd stayed with RAK, "Mickie Most would have produced the tracks, and he had an amazing hit rate, so who knows what might have happened?"

Their debut for Epic was 'Baby Baby', undoubtedly the world's first (sincere) punk ballad. Built around a dominant, drawling riff, it was pure Spector-lite bubble-gum punk with a reassuringly daft lyric. While everyone else on the punk scene was burning rubber and accelerating tempos, the Vibrators had seemingly slammed the brakes on.

'Baby Baby' was followed in short order by their long-playing debut, Pure Mania. As well as the single, and re-recordings of the RAK material, it included defining Vibrators cuts such as 'Bad Times', 'Wrecked On You' and 'Stiff Little Fingers', which a Belfast band subsequently purloined for their name. Recorded over ten days at CBS's Soho studios, the production by Robin Mayhew, who had previously overseen their live sound, was both rich and beautifully balanced, giving full vent to the band's innate love of melody. The musicianship is controlled, crisp and as spotless as the sentiments expressed in 'Keep It Clean'. The group mines its Ramones' influences with real gusto and humour – disastrous relationship entanglements a speciality – and the album peaked at number 49 in the charts. Even Rolling Stone was impressed. However, the record label were less sure that it was suitable for the American market, so Knox and Ellis spent a day remixing the album alongside Epic A&R man Lem Lubin for US consumption.

In the month of its release they recorded their second Peel session in their own right, comprising 'Petrol', 'Keep It Clean' (this time including far more appropriate sound effects to accompany the line about getting your legs broken), 'Baby Baby', 'London Girls' and 'She's Bringing You Down'. Thereafter they joined Ian Hunter (of Mott The Hoople) on tour as Pat Collier left for the Boyfriends and production work and was replaced by Gary Tibbs, formerly of Red. "Gary was known by our manager Dave (Wernham) and drafted in," Eddie later wrote in the reissued album sleevenotes. "At his audition he played the whole of Pure Mania note-perfect. He was young, he was keen, he was in!"

A second album, rather cutely entitled V2, was readied alongside producer Vic Maile in Berlin, where, bizarrely, they were raided by the local police on suspicion of involvement in the Scheler kidnapping. The band had been impressed with Maile's work with Dr Feelgood and Tom Robinson and thought he might be able to bring a little more studio polish to the table without sacrificing the band's vivacity. Everything generally fell to plan, especially on album closer 'Troops Of Tomorrow', which benefited from dozens of vocal overdubs as well as being among John Ellis's finest recorded moments. 'Nazi Baby' even features strings, though its centrepiece is actually a full-blown orchestra of over-driven guitars. Most interesting is 'Destroy', in which the protagonist sets out to blow up the world because his girlfriend has dumped him – a bleak romantic narrative offering a sharp contrast to the surface nihilism of the Pistols. Sometimes things became unnecessarily intricate, however, and 'Sulphates' approximation of a celestial choir to fit the lyric is the album's most corny moment. In keeping with the album title the opening track, confusingly titled 'Pure Mania', featured a simulated doodlebug expiring and exploding. Sounds called it "the album the new wave was made for," but others were less generous.

Following a Canadian tour, 'Automatic Lover', a typically incessant slice of cultivated pop-punk, became their most successful single. It reached 35 in the UK charts, and resulted in the group's sole appearance on Top Of The Pops. "I wrote it about a girl I met at a gig where Iggy Pop was playing," Knox later told Record Collector. "I went for a drink with her before the show and she had this gun with her, I think it was probably only a gas pistol. Anyway, we went to see Iggy Pop and I kept an eye on her as I thought, maybe she'd go crackers and get the gun out and try to shoot Iggy (my vivid imagination!) I wrote the words loosely around this on the boat the next day going back to England. I wrote the music and put the whole thing together on an electric piano my cousin lent me later, and I don't think I could have got the same idea on a guitar." However, Epic rejected the original version until a more 'rocky' sound was secured via Maile's intervention. He suggested the 'stabbing' up-down chords Knox uses at the song's climax. The finished track was chosen ahead of 'Pure Mania' and 'Fall In Love' as the single Epic would push. Yet its eventual chart position was a disappointment – possibly due to the fact that a wholly different song with the same title, by Dee D Jackson, had just hit the Top Ten.

John Ellis departed to join Rapid Eye Movement in the wake of V2's commercial failure, to be replaced by Dave Birch. Tibbs moved on too, initially to Roxy Music and then Adam And The Ants. Keyboard player and saxophonist Don Snow augmented the ranks for the fiery 'Judy Says (Knock You In The Head)', which gave the band their second and final chart hit. It also provided the UK's closest vinyl approximation to the Ramones outside of the Lurkers, albeit with a sax break. Further personnel changes ensued. Snow left for the Sinceros and Squeeze. Bassist Ben Brierley (Marianne Faithfull's husband and a collaborator on the Nazis Against Fascism project with playwright Heathcote Williams) and Jayne County guitarist Greg Van Cook joined briefly before the band fizzled out. Knox also left, putting his departure down to comments he made off the record to a CBS employee about being burned out by touring which were relayed to Muff Winwood and resulted in the label forestalling on a third album.

Eddie managed to revive the group, initially with Ian Woodcock of Eater on bass and vocalist Kip, formerly of Cane, in between stints drumming for the Inmates. With a line-up now featuring Phil Ram (aka Birdman; guitar) and Adrian Wyatt (guitar) they recorded two further singles for Rat Race in 1980; a version of the Spencer Davis Group's 'Gimme Some Lovin' and 'Disco In Mosco'. The latter was actually highly amusing chug-a-lug Vibrators featuring a quite ridiculous Hi-NRG disco-punk chorus. For about a year Eddie and Kip worked with Birdman as part of the Shots until the latter gave it all up to become a farmer. Kip joined the Chords. Knox worked with Charlie Harper's Urban Dogs before releasing a solo album for Razor in 1983, Plutonium Express, and then set up Fallen Angles with members of Hanoi Rocks.

The original Vibrators reformed the band in October 1982, at Collier's suggestion, recording a new version of 'Baby Baby' for Cherry Red's Burning Ambitions compilation, and releasing Guilty for Abstract later that year. "Pat and John decided to it would be a good idea when pissed one evening," Eddie recalled to Second Edition fanzine. "They phoned Knox who said yeah, and finally myself, and I thought – why not. It was always a good band. Plus we had time at Pat's studio and the idea of doing an album and making a bit of cash and going on the road again was too good to pass up, especially as we have all been friends for years." The resulting album, Guilty, saw each member provide three songs each, with a couple of covers.

With a fluctuating line-up (around the core of Knox and Eddie), they have recorded and gigged, as Eddie notes, "ever since". Further studio albums Alaska 127 (named after Collier's studio, and notable for 'Amphetamine Blue', effectively a rewrite of 'I Fought The Law', and the impeccably romantic 'Flying Home') and Fifth Amendment followed. There was also a live album for Revolver, by which time Collier had returned to production work, and was replaced by Noel Thomson. Knox and Eddie brought in Marc Duncan (ex-Doll By Doll; bass) and Mickie Owen (guitar) for the albums Recharged and Meltdown, before Nigel Bennett (ex-Members) replaced Owen for 1989's Vicious Circle.

In 1996 Knox and Eddie were joined by Darrell Bath (ex-UK Subs, Crybabies, Dogs D'amour) on guitar and Nick Peckham (ex-Big Boy Tomato) on bass, but Bath had left by June leaving them as a three-piece. In this format they recorded French Lessons With Correction (1997) and Buzzin' (1999), amid extensive touring. When Peckham left in September 1989 he was replaced by Robbie Tart (ex-Heartbreak Angels), who was in place in time for the 2002 studio album Energize on Track Records (the revived label of Jimi Hendrix). John Ellis returned to guest on two tracks. The standouts were the vegetarian-themed 'Animal' and 'Moonlight', a quasi-waltz. A year later Tart left to be replaced by Pete of Finnish band No Direction. As Knox confirmed to a San Diego journalist, only death will take them off the road. "Yeah, well if Eddie died or I died it might be rather difficult! But, no not really. I think, if you're a musician, it's not a big deal. You just carry on, like the old jazz musicians. I think what we do is probably quite a lot harder physically than what jazz people do. You don't really know how you'll be doing. You have to kind of train up for it, writing songs and touring, like an athlete – then it becomes like second nature, you see."

Meanwhile Knox completed his biography of the band, The Vibrators: 21 Years Of Pure Mania, and is writing a science fiction book. John Ellis later worked with Peter Gabriel and Jean-Jacques Burnel before becoming an established member of the Stranglers in the 90s, though he's since left to work solo. Pat Collier's credits as a producer include Robyn Hitchcock, Katrina And The Waves, the Men They Couldn't Hang, New Model Army, the Soup Dragons, the Wonderstuff and many others.

DISCOGRAPHY:

(Buyer's Guide: Get Pure Mania and V2, the Captain Oi! reissues, as your starting point. Then add the BBC Sessions. The band's later work is on offer via Anagram and Overground on good value two-for-ones. Guilty/Alaska is probably the best of these)

We Vibrate/Whips & Furs 7-inch (RAK RAK 245 November 1976)
Pogo Dancing/Pose 7-inch (RAK RAK 246 December 1976) (with Chris Spedding)
Bad Time/No Heart 7-inch (RAK RAK 253 March 1977) (not issued, though acetates exist)
Baby Baby/Into The Future 7-inch (Epic EPC 5302 May 1977)
Pure Mania LP (Epic EPC 82097 June 1977) (reissued by Repertoire on LP/CD in August 1991; REP 2001; American version has different versions of 'Sweet Sweet Heart' and 'Bad Time'. Reissued by Captain Oi!, AHOY CD 241, in 2004, with bonus tracks 'London Girls (live)', 'Stiff Little Fingers (live)', 'We Vibrate' and 'Whips & Furs (single version)'. Features sleevenotes from Eddie and full lyrics)
London Girls (live)/Stiff Little Fingers (live) 7-inch (Epic EPC 5565 August 1977) (promo version available featuring studio version of 'London Girls')
Automatic Lover/Destroy 7-inch (Epic EPC 6137 February 1978)
V2 LP (Epic EPC 82495 April 1978) (reissued on LP/CD by Repertoire, REP 2002, August 1993. Reissued by Captain Oi!, AHOY CD 242, in 2004, with bonus tracks 'Judy Says (Knock You In The Head)' and 'Pushing Too Hard', as well as, again, a sleevenote by Eddie and a full set of lyrics)
Judy Says (Knock You In The Head)/Pure Mania 7-inch (Epic EPC-6393 May 1978)
Gimme Some Lovin'/Power Cry (live) 7-inch (Rat Race RAT 2 February 1980)
Disco in Mosco/Take a Chance 7-inch (Rat Race RAT 4 January 1980)
Baby Baby (new version)/Dragnet 7-inch (Anagram ANA 4 November 1982)
Guilty LP (Anagram GRAM 002 January 1983)
Guilty/Hang Ten 7-inch (Anagram ANA 8 May 1983)
MX America/Shadow Love 7-inch (Ram RAM 7005 November 1983)
Flying Home/Flash Flash Flash 7-inch (Ram RAM 7007 March 1984) (also released as a 12-inch with bonus track 'MX America' RAM 7007T)
Alaska 127 LP (Ram RAM LP 001 March 1984) (also issued as Carrere CAL 205 and as Anagram GRAM-002)
Flying Home/Punish Me With Kisses 7-inch (Carrere CAR 329 May 1984) (also released as a 12-inch with bonus track "MX America' Carrere CART 329)
Baby Blue Eyes/Amphetamine Blue 7-inch (Carrere CAR 338 July 1984) (also as issued on 12-inch with bonus track 'Flying High', CART 338)
Fifth Amendment LP (Ram CHP LP 002 January 1985)
Blown Away Be Love/The Demolishers 7-inch (Ram CHP 7011 January 1985) (also as issued as 12-inch with bonus track 'Still Not Over You' RAM 12-CHP-7011)
Vibrators Live LP (Revolver REV LP 85 January 1986) (14 tracks recorded in concert in Germany in the early-80s. Decent sound quality. Reissued as Rip Up The City)
Recharged LP (Revolver REV LP 101 January 1988)
String Him Along/Disco in Mosco (live) 7-inch (Revolver REV 45 April 1988)
Meltdown LP (Revolver REV LP 121 November 1988) (also issued on CD as CD Rev XD 121 with bonus tracks 'Wasted Life' and 'Don't Trust Anyone')
Vicious Circle LP (Revolver REV-LP-135 October 1989 (also issued on CD as CD REV-XD-135)
Halfway To Paradise/Drive 7-inch (Revolver REV 52 January 1990) (also issued on CD, CD REV XD 52, with bonus tracks 'Rocket Ride To Heaven' and 'Fire')
Volume 10 LP (Revolver REV LP 159 October 1990) (also issued on CD, CD REV XD 159)
Hunting For You LP (Dojo DOJO CD 179 October 1994) (re-released on Cherry Red, CD PUNK 132, August 2003)
Unpunked CD (Vibrators VIBES 001 February 1996)
French Lessons with Correction CD (Anagram CDM GRAM 114 September 1997)
Energize CD (Track 1016CD August 2002) (the band's 15th studio album, no less. "Pretty good," notes Knox. "In our top five, I'd say!" There's also a DVD, Live Energize CBGB's 2004. Check Vibrators website for details)
ARCHIVE RELEASES:
Batteries Included LP (CBS CBS 31840 July 1980)
Yeah Yeah Yeah LP (Repertoire REP 4001WZ August 1991)
The Power Of Money (The Best Of The Vibrators) LP (Anagram GRAM 52 1992) (also available on CD, CD GRAM 52, this features the 1982 line-up running through re-recorded versions of older material)
Live at the Marquee 1977 CD (Released Emotions REM 018CD May 1993)
(reissued by GIG 10092 in June 1999. 1977 show from the Marquee which is well worth hearing, relying as it does on strong versions of Pure Mania-era material and some choice covers)
BBC Radio 1 Live in Concert (with the Boys) (Windsong WIND CD 036 October 1993) (recommended for the feedback-soaked 'Keep It Clean', one of the better live documents)

Guilty/Alaska CD (Anagram CD PUNK 16 November 1993)

Fifth Amendment/Recharged CD (Anagram CD PUNK 34 April 1994)

1976-77 The Demos CD (Dojo DOLE CD 179 October 1994) (first release of the 76-77 demos. Now long deleted but content is available elsewhere)

Best Of CD (Anagram CD PUNK 43 August 1995) (a repackaging of Power Of Money. The bonus tracks relate to the 1999 reissue only, which comes with a complete discography)

Meltdown/Vicious Circle CD (Anagram CD PUNK 58 September 1995)

Live at the Marquee 1977 CD (Dojo DOLE CD 110 January 1996)

The Independent Punk Singles Collection CD (Anagram Records CD PUNK 76 May 1996)

Public Enemy Number 1 CD (Harry May MAYO CD 106 1996) (a collection partially comprising eight demos for their Epic albums, many of which are substantially different to the finished versions, with eight songs from a 1977 Marquee gig originally released by Released Emotions in 1991. However, this is one of those CDs when the manufacturers were at home to Mr Cock Up. Instead of 'She's Bringing You Down', the CD plays 'Frenzied Beat' by Demented Are Go! Which is novel)

We Vibrate: The Best Of The Vibrators CD (Cleopatra August 1997) (absolutely not what it says on the tin – many of these tracks, due to licensing difficulties, are demo or live versions, or 1991 re-recordings. Avoid)

Unpunked/Volume 10 CD (Overground OVER73 CD June 1998)

The BBC Punk Sessions (Captain Oi! AHOY CD 135 2000) (the three Peel sessions plus nine tracks from a Radio 1 In Concert show at the Paris Theatre. Eddie once again provides the sleevenotes. The Vibrators were one of those bands who used Peel's patronage to significantly remould their material, which makes this a more interesting purchase than most in the series. So we get backwards masking on 'She's Bringing You Down', and a slightly less strident vocal take on 'Automatic Lover'. 'Dance To The Music' is an early incarnation of 'Whips And Furs')

Demos And Rarities CD (GIG 10112 2000; US) (first 22 tracks are 76/77 demos. Vocals are mixed low, but worth hearing, and there are a couple of totally unheard tracks – though 'Ready Stead Go' is not a cover of the Generation X single, as some have reported, but 'Day Tripper' is indeed a Beatles homage – via Syd Barrett. 'Dance To The Music', as noted above, is an early version of 'Whips And Furs')

Rip Up The City (Live) (Receiver RCD 263 February 1999) (reissue of Vibrators Live CD. Dodgy sleevenotes courtesy of this author)

Noise Boys CD (Receiver RCD 201 June 2000) (features 10 previously unreleased tracks recorded between 1977 and 1979 originally intended for V2, plus a shelved third album and further rarities)

Best Of: 25 Years Of Pure Mania CD (Epic 500631 2 February 2001) (combines Pure Mania and V2 with Live At The Marquee)

Punk Rock Rarities CD (Captain Oi! AHOY CD 181 December 2001) (a collection of demos from Knox's vaults covering the band's entire career, with sleevenotes by Knox and Eddie)

Live At CBGB's (Almaframe Victory 1 February 2002) (excellent recording of the band's Cinco De Mayo 2000 set at CBGB's featuring the trio of Knox, Eddie and bass player Robbie Tart. However, in this format, with only Knox playing guitar, you do miss some of the Vibrators' early muscle. Spliced with cries of "1977!" from the audience)

Pure Mania/V2 CD (Track 1013CD August 2002) (as well as both studio albums includes bonus tracks 'Judy Says', 'Automatic Lover (single version)' and 'London Girls (live)')

Live At The Nashville and 100 Club (Overground 2003) (another live album, the first 18 tracks recorded at the Nashville on 29 April 1977 via a recently discovered tape. The last six tracks document the 100 Club punk festival on 21 September 1976, recorded on a cheap cassette by a friend. As you'd expect, the quality is dubious, but this is a vital live document all the same, the only one released of the original line-up. And their versions of 'Saw Her Standing There' and '1969' are otherwise unrecorded)

Vicars

One of the great voices of 80s pop first took flight in this Southend punk band. Alison 'Alf' Moyet had previously been a Vandal, before replacing the VICARS' original vocalist, Mike Maynard. Boy, does he have a story to tell the locals down his pub. There's a good website on Southend's punk scene on the net written by Steve Pegrum that recalls "Alf's searing vocals (leading) this band through dozens of blitzkrieg concerts." These included appearances at Southend's Shrimpers Club and the local College Of Technology.

Moyet's first vinyl appearance had come as backing vocalist, alongside fellow Vandals members Kim Forey and Sue Paget, on 'Tomorrow's World', by Pete Zear of Southend band the Jukes. Featuring Ruffy and Segs of the Ruts and produced by Rat Scabies, 1,000 copies were pressed. Incidentally, Ruffy would later help out with Moyet's solo work. Although, as Moyet confirmed to the ExtraordinaryGirl website: "I never got a copy as I wasn't down the pub on the right night."

While the Southend region boasted the pub rock veterans Eddie And the Hot Rods, a thriving local punk scene developed. This included the Machines, who released the scene's first vinyl document, the Psychopaths, Nomads, the Spurts (from whence came Perry Bamonte, later of the Cure) and Idiot. The Vicars never released anything in their own name, but did contribute one track, 'I'm Going Mad', to the Southend Rock charity compilation, which trawled the musical talents of bands from Southend and Canvey Island in the late-70s. The nearest musical comparison would be X-Ray Spex. A review of the time called their track a "brave, but in the light of the growing Manchester scene, suicidal attempt at adventurous new wave". There was supposedly a video made by someone at a local college.

Moyet would subsequently form the Screaming Abdabs, a set list from the late-70s revealing titles such as 'Roaming Woman', 'Turtle Blues' and 'Shame Shame Shame'. Although the Abdabs started out in a punk/new wave vein, and indeed drew on much of the Vicars' set in their early shows, as the group developed they shifted to an R&B direction. An edition of Strange Stories reviewed an Abdabs' show in Basildon on 25 July 1979. "The Screaming Abdabs hit the stage with a rendition of 'River Deep Mountain High' infused by Alf's own super duper vocal delivery. Then straight into 'Shame Shame Shame' which was followed by the bands own 'Nobodies Diary', which is one of the most beautiful songs in the world."

Ah, but will we ever get to hear them?

Compilation:
Southend Rock LP (Sonnet SNTF 806 1979; 'I'm Going Mad')

Vice Creems

Kris Needs (vocals), Colin Keinch (guitar, backing vocals), Nigel Birchall (guitar), Chris Lugmayer (bass), Martin Godfrey (drums)

Kris Needs, the noted punk writer (especially through ZigZag) and former Mott the Hoople roadie, not to mention future dance music guru, has a CV that is not so much chequered as higgledy-piggledy panoramic. From pub rock beginnings, going on the lash with the Clash, teaching Sid Vicious some rudimentary bass lines, managing Department S, ending the ascent of Flexipop magazine by putting Aleister Crowley on the cover to recording as Secret Knowledge and DJing for Primal Scream and the Orb, Needs has been there, done it, and sold the T-shirt for a tidy profit on eBay.

The **VICE CREEMS** were based in Aylesbury, where Needs had started playing music in the late 60s, sometimes as bongo-playing companion to John Otway, growing out of an earlier incarnation known as the Aylesbury Ducks. His musical compatriot was Colin Keinch, and it was the guitarist that first caught the US punk bug. "I went to NYC in 1976 to try and find Bob Dylan – but instead I found the Ramones, Talking Heads, Television, the Dictators, and got myself a girlfriend!" he told Trakmarx website. Significantly, Needs' first engagement as a writer was interviewing the Ramones.

The Vice Creems first featured on their hometown compilation LP, Aylesbury Goes Flaccid, in 1978. By this time Needs had become noted for his stage performances while supporting acts such as the Lurkers and the Adverts, particularly his penchant for flapping his arms like a bird attempting to take flight. As he later admitted, "I'll never be Jim Morrison! I think I've always known that." Indeed, he was also advised by John Peel "not to give up the typewriter just yet".

In fairness, although the Vice Creems only released five tracks, they're all actually quite purposeful, gutsy R&B-punk. Their debut single, recorded during downtime at a Flaming Groovies album session, was OK, but bettered by the seething B-side, '01 01 212'. There was some territorial pissing from Sounds, who called Needs a "silly tit", while the Record Mirror made the factually irrefutable accusation that it was "Record journalists playing at being pop stars". For their second single, from their Olympic Studios session of March 1979, the Vice Creems retained only Needs and Keinch whilst recruiting, according to the sleeve credit, Michael Blair (lead guitar), Anthony Ross (bass), Nicholas Khan (drums) and Robin Banks (animal noises). Which is of interest to Clash fans as behind those pseudonyms lurk Topper Headon (Khan) and Mick Jones (Blair). And the bass player was actually Tony James. "A guy came in with money via ZigZag," Needs told Trakmarx, "and we were gonna launch ZigZag Records. Only problem – the band split up the week before – leaving just me and Colin. I phoned Mick Jones who'd already agreed to produce the record and told him I had Olympic Studios sorted but no band. Mick said he'd get a band and told me to be there. We showed up – first thing we see is Johnny Green and the Clash gear and flight cases. We realised our backing band was gonna be Topper, Mick and Tony James. We had a warm up jam. It was surreal."

The Vice Creems also got the third support slot on the Clash's 16 Tons tour when they stopped at Aylesbury in January 1980. Needs, who wrote his autobiography Needs Must in 1999, recently published his biography of Joe Strummer.

Discography:

Won't You Be My Girl /01 01 212 7-inch (Tiger Records Grrrr 1 1978)
Danger Love/Like A Tiger 7-inch (ZigZag Records ZZ22 001 1979)
Important Compilation Appearance:
Aylesbury Goes Flaccid LP (Flaccid Flac-1 1978, 'No Passion')

Victim

Wes Graham (bass, vocals), Colin Campbell (guitar, vocals), Jeff Beatty (drums)

VICTIM were formed in Belfast in the summer of 1977 by Graham and his cousin Campbell, and were initially nothing more than unapologetic Jam copyists, both in sound and vision (black suits, white shirts, black ties – which rather reminds me of an Ian Dury lyric). They got their break almost immediately when they were filmed playing a rudimentary version of 'In The City' at their second gig at the Pound for UTV's punk documentary It Makes You Want To Spit.

Shortly afterwards, and with the focus on writing original material, the line-up was expanded with the addition of rhythm guitarist Ken Matthews, younger brother of Ronnie Matthews of Rudi. They hooked up with Terri Hooley who released their debut, 'Strange Thing By Night', recorded at Wizard Studios for £90, on Good Vibrations. It was the label's second single.

Frustrated by the lack of local facilities, Graham and Campbell persuaded the proprietor of Belfast's Harp bar in Hill Street in Belfast's Docklands area, at that stage ostensibly a strip joint, to book them. In the process they established one of the city's major punk venues in one of its most intimidating locations – having been bombed previously, gaining entry to the bar meant traversing a steel security cage. The first show there saw them supported by the Androids on 21 April 1978. However, shortly thereafter both bands broke up. That led to Graham and Beatty recruiting Joe Zero (aka Joe Moody; guitar, vocals) and Aza Middleton (guitar) from the Androids to form a new band, Emergency. Middleton remembers, "I think

Joe and Wes Graham started to get friendly and when Victim split Joe and I decided we'd prefer to be in a band with Wes and Jeff Beatty, so we left and formed Emergency." They practised together, alongside Rudi and Stiff Little Fingers, at the local Lombard Street rehearsal rooms in the city centre. Several Belfast shows followed before Emergency supported the Fall in Manchester.

With Aza leaving, Graham, Beatty and Moody reverted to the name Victim and added keyboard player Davy Johnstone, in which format they supported the Monochrome Set on their visit to the Harp. A subsequent set at the Harp in November 1978 was also filmed and 'Trademark World' included in legendary Irish punk film Shellshock Rock, though it was wrongly credited as 'Trademark City'. When Johnstone left, the band was augmented first by John McGee, who was in place for their support slot to Penetration at Queen's University, and then by guitarist Hugh O'Boyle in early 1979. By this time they'd decided to accept a recording deal in England, the result of a modest offer from Manchester's TJM Records.

They settled into practice sessions at TJM's rehearsal rooms only to have their equipment stolen in their first week there, forcing them to borrow instruments from V2 to meet upcoming engagements. Their second single, and first for TJM, was 1979's 'Why Are Fire Engines Red?' The band had vetoed TJM's preference for a four-track EP based on earlier Belfast demos of 'I Need You', 'Junior Criminals', 'Based On Bluff' and 'Trademark World'. They'd originally invited Ludus's Linder Sterling, who designed the Buzzcocks' 'Orgasm Addict' and Magazine's 'Real Life', to come up with a sleeve, but rejected her design as "too arty" (what were they expecting?). In they event, while they dithered TJM simply knocked together a far less appealing alternative anyway. Meanwhile the band had no income, and no lodgings, being forced to sleep in a derelict shop in Oldham Street.

They then set off on an extensive UK tour of Britain, amid the usual on the road shenanigans you'd expect from headliners the Damned, including superglue and various efforts at setting each other's hair on fire. Not to mention cramped and subsequently wrecked hotel rooms, copious amounts of alcohol and being arrested by the police in Hull. Rat Scabies liked Beatty's drumming so much he would regularly allow him to take over the headline act's drum stool so he could perform lead vocals on 'Burglar'.

Prior to the tour Scabies produced their next release as part of the deal behind the package tour (which was originally to have included the Misfits and Slaughter And The Dogs too). It comprised three tracks recorded at Cargo Studios in Rochdale, headed by 'Teen Age', and released by Illuminated Records in 1980. Beatty confesses to the recording sessions flying by in a few hours, accompanied by some strange white powder that Scabies offered them. However, the release was delayed when TJM managed to mislay the master tapes and had to rely on a copy the band had sent to John Peel.

Beatty, who would later join Colenso Parade with Jackie Forgie of Ruefrex, elected to move back to Belfast on a ticket his parents forked out for. Weighing 7 stone 3lbs due to lack of food, he booked himself into 'mental institution'. Manager Ian Jamison left with him, while O'Boyle teamed up with members of V2 to form a new band. That left the songwriting core of Graham and Moody looking to fill the gaps. They used a nameless local drummer to record the projected double A-side 'Lady Lioness' and 'The Last Laugh' in March 1981, but couldn't find anyone willing to release it. They finally secured a drummer from Manchester punk band the Hoax, Mike Joyce (ironically, members of the Hoax also went on to form a band called Emergency, and both the Hoax and Victim would record versions of 'Hang On To Yourself'). The new line-up set about recording demos and in 1982 embarked on a short tour. They returned to the studio in an effort to record a new double a-side, 'Cause Or Consequence' and 'The Bluff Brigade', but once again a release was thwarted. Joyce then departed to take up the offer of work with the Smiths.

That was it for a while, as Graham returned to his former occupation as a journalist while Moody studied music and the history of art. Beatty formed Ultraviolet in 2005. Campbell, meanwhile, teamed up in the Zenn with former members of the Zipps before forming The Famous Five with Protex's Aiden Murtagh. The core duo reconvened again in the mid-80s, but instead of reviving the Victim name they chose to label themselves Beethoven's Kiss, using former Frantic Elevators' drummer Kev Williams (whom they knew from the TJM rehearsal studios). A projected single, 'The Strangest Stars', fell through due to financial strictures. After recruiting Toni Isaac (famed, if that is the appropriate term, for being the girl leaning on the lamp-post on Jilted John's single) on keyboards, they released 'The Wonder Of You', in 1988 on their own Akashic Records. Further tracks were recorded but they were unable to elicit any record label interest. Beethoven's Kiss was eventually shelved in 1990, though both Moody and Graham continue to work part-time on music and have their own studios in Chester from whence they record as Webcore. How about a reunion show? "Very unlikely... unless we renamed ourselves the Victims of Middle Age," came the wry reply on the band's website.

DISCOGRAPHY:

Strange Thing By Night/Mixed Up World 7-inch (Good Vibrations GOT 2 1978)
Why Are Fire Engines Red?/I Need You 7-inch (TJM TJM 14 1979)
The Teen Age/Junior Criminals/Hang On To Yourself 7-inch (Illuminated ILL 1 1980)
ARCHIVE RELEASES:
Everything CD (Overground April 2003) (all three singles and 15 unreleased studio recordings)

Victimize

Andy Johnson (guitar), Andy James (aka Keaton, vocals), Mike Rudman (drums), Bryn Merrick (bass)

Barry punk band, formed originally as Red Alert & the Rejects in 1977 at the Buttrills community hall, who are now chiefly famous for being a stopping off point for Merrick and Roman Jugg (pronounced 'Youg', incidentally; it's Yugoslavian in origin) before they joined the Damned. They were equally renowned in Wales, however, for the ferocity of their support, which comprised a fair contingent of Cardiff's infamous football hooligans.

Both singles were issued in limited quantities in 'outsize sleeves' and are now worth a mint on the collector's market. "Merrick and me were starting to play together in the summer of 1977," Andy Johnson told me. "Up to this point our music influences came from AC/DC, Hawkwind, Zeppelin and Bowie. My background included the glam rock scene too. Steve Alexander (known as 'Stiff') was a big influence on both of us.

His loyalty to the John Peel show meant he was getting the punk stuff first hand and passing it on to us. He attended the Pistols gig in Caerphilly and in 1978 he left for London and roadied for the Count Bishops before working at the Stuart Henry record shop, which was distributing all the good punk and reggae stuff. He lived in Ladbroke Grove. Every week he sent us a package of the latest punk sounds including Subway Sect, Buzzcocks, Slaughter, Lurkers, Chelsea and American stuff like the Ramones, Television, Voidoids and Dictators. Reggae included Prince Far I, Lynton Kwesi Johnson and Lee Perry. These new influences gave Merrick and me a new direction with our limited talent and we began writing short, sharp three-chorders."

"While this was happening one Andy James, who had been the one and only 'punk' in town, was attracting plenty of attention with his classic punk look. A small group from the Buttrills council estate began to follow suit, including me. The first look was the classic school blazer, Tesco drainpipes and bumper boots all decorated with badges, pins and paint spray. Most were listening to the Stranglers, Clash, Pistols, Dead Boys, Damned and the Jam."

"When me and Bryn coaxed James into the band, 15-year-old Rudman (who had previously played in a jazz band) was already a member. James was found to have a string of lyrics, about all manner of subjects (early song titles included 'Grunwick', 'Headlines', 'This Is The Age', 'Hi-Rising Failure', 'Where Did The Money Go' and 'Baby Buyer') ready to put to our hard edged three-chorders. Red Alert were formed at the local community hall. Bryn was married at the time with twins so he didn't venture out much apart from rehearsals. Me and James started to explore the Cardiff scene which was a bit posey! Everyone seemed to shop at Paradise Garage and drink at the Lexington. The bands of the time were the Nylons, Rudi and the Russians and Mad Dog, who were basically heavy metal."

Red Alert & the Rejects played their first show in February 1978, at the Barry Hotel. They'd been augmented on New Year's Eve 1977 by second guitarist Peter David Hopkin, though he left in the summer of 1978 and later committed suicide by taking cyanide after being arrested for drink driving after a police chase. He did, however, stay long enough to help arrange 'Baby Buyer' and contribute songs such as 'Commercial TV' and 'I'm So Bored'. His replacement was Tim Weaving, but only for a short period before they reverted to the quartet that would become the Victims, whose debut show was at the Lion's Den, Great Western Hotel, in September 1978, supporting Mad Dog, whose equipment they managed to wreck. Eventually confusion with the Scottish band of the same name forced them to lengthen the name to **VICTIMIZE** towards the end of the year.

"There was a growing number of hardcore punks starting to surface in Cardiff and Victimize soon became the band to be seen with. The Grassroots coffee bar became the centre of all punk activity throughout 1978 and 1979. Bands included the Riotous Bros, Addiction, Doc Savage and French Lettuce, to name a few. Grassroots was a home to punks, skins, blacks, early soul crews and anyone else who cared to join the cause. The 'cause' being the growing punk bandwagon. Top Rank in Queen Street were booking all the top acts. I saw the Clash, Damned, Buzzcocks, Subway Sect, Jam, Stranglers, Dictators, Suicide, Adverts and the Coventry Specials. All the 'names' (well known punk faces) were there every week. Sid and his mad brother Kevin who grew a beard to get past the bouncers; Pete Lawrence and his band Doc Savage; Socket and Fuzzy – the black punks; Pugsley and loads more!"

After they became Victimize their fans became "an army", according to Johnson. They were managed by Richard Haines of Grannies Nightclub, which ran at the former Prince of Wales cinema, where they played a series of shows between December 1978 and May 1979, in support of the likes of the Skids, John Cooper Clarke and the Damned. 'Baby Buyer' was recorded in early 1978 in Hayes, and released by Cardiff label I.M.E. Records, run from a dirty bookshop in the city's Mill Lane. John Peel was impressed but was forced to play the B-side due to the lyrical content of 'Baby Buyer'. Following the first single keyboard player Roman Jugg joined in 1978 from Ystrad Mynach, at the same time as new drummer Jeff Davies (ex-Bargoed), who introduced Jug to the band, came on board. This line-up played a series of dates at Grannies as well as Grassroots in Charles Street, introducing new songs such as 'One Of Our Aircraft Is Missing', 'The Day I Met God', 'Society's Child' etc. "Grannies didn't run for long," recalls Johnson. "I think it had serious structural problems. It was on two floors and the main bands played upstairs. I remember seeing the ceiling bowing about two feet up and down when SLF played." They broke up two years to the day after their inception on February 4 1980, supporting Gang Of Four in Cardiff, at which new drummer Trevor Rees played his one and only show with the band. "Victimize plodded on – Roman was writing crap power pop tunes and it just didn't have the energy that the original band had. I think it folded naturally after the Gang of Four gig."

A second single, 'Where Did The Money Go?', was released by Haines after the group split up with no involvement from the original band. The B-side, incidentally, was a reworking of John Cooper Clarke's 'Innocents'. "I suppose we were a little bit pissed off. However it was nice to see it released anyway. Haines claimed to be trying to make his money back because 'we'd let him down by splitting up!' There's some bollocks on the sleeve about losing his Rolls-Royce but not getting fooled again! He really thought he was the McLaren of South Wales, he always had a scam. He actually put a band together featuring a few Cardiff lads about 16 years old and called them Victimize and tried to promote the single by gigging them. They were shite and the scam never worked! I remember he came looking for me once, with an axe, because I changed my guitar to a Telecaster without telling him. He reckoned it changed the whole sound of the band and hated me for it. He was probably right, but what did I know at 18?"

Merrick, Johnson, Jugg and Rees continued in the Scanners and Carburettors, as well as the Missing Men (Merrick, Jugg, James, Johnson, plus ex-System drummer Don Sinclair), who played a Lyceum support to the Ruts and Damned. Merrick had a spell with heavy metal act Storm Queen before he and Jugg joined the Damned in 1981. Johnson and James formed the Warhead Sisters. Johnson and Sinclair then put together the Missing, who managed one single, 'Electricity Head', on their own I Futurist Records. Johnson is currently playing around Cardiff with the Fabulous 'Asbeens and has taken over a pub in Barry. Andy James works as a photographer in Cardiff. Rudman became a fireman, and Jeff Davies a policeman in Hengoed. Trevor Rees works for Barry's employment agency.

DISCOGRAPHY:

Baby Buyer/Hi Rising Failure 7-inch (I.M.E. IME 1 1979) (2,000 pressed)
Where Did The Money Go?/Innocence 7-inch (I.M.E. IME 1980) (1,000 pressed)
Victimize 7-inch EP (Last Year's Youth 2004)
Baby Buyer/Hi Rising Failure/Where Did The Money Go?/Innocence

Vincent Units/Tesco Bombers

Neal Brown (vocals), Inigo Batterham (saxophone) and a cast of thousands, namely: Tex Woodward, Nick Smith, Derek Goddard, Jane Woodgate (Modettes), Sera Furneaux, Palmolive (Slits), Gina Birch (Raincoats), Chris Gray (Milk from Cheltenham), Richard Dudanski (101'ers/PiL/Bank of Dresden), Smiler, King Kobra (Homosexuals, L Voag), Mole (101'ers), Sarah Fancy (Amos and Sara), Griz Johnson, Lucy Edkins, Latif Gardez, Roger Pomphrey, Glen Colson, Keith Allen, Ivor Cutler, Sean Cooke, Josephine Cooke, Kate Korus, Ramona, Nico Brown, Patrice Felix Tcicaya

Both the VINCENT UNITS and THE TESCO BOMBERS were started by Neal Brown when he was at Hornsey College of Art in the late-70s; Gina Birch from the Raincoats was also a student. Brown was part of West London's large squatting community, and had been following Joe Strummer's 101ers since their very early gigs (later writing sleevenotes for the original vinyl release of their Elgin Avenue Breakdown LP).

The Tesco Bombers specialised in absurdist covers and parody, whereas the Vincents (at their best) were more thoughtful. After a punk and (pre-2 Tone) ska beginning, they eventually favoured a poeticised, atonal 'punk jazz' chaos. Brown and saxophonist Inigo Batterham were the only constants in the two bands, whose members were so interchangeable as to defy record.

The Vincents performed all over West London, supporting bands like the Clash, the Slits and the Raincoats but, unlike those artists, they conspicuously lacked career commitment. The Tesco Bombers, in spite of the energy and gig-getting ability of Keith Allen (drummer, and only other composer in the two bands apart from Brown) were even less motivated. "I remember the Tesco Bombers!" recalls Dave Scott of Bank Of Dresden and Spizz. "One of THE best pop combos. They played in our street, Monmouth Road, and also the Chippenham and the Crypt, etc. Neil always had some interesting people playing with him." A glowing review of the Vincents by Ian Penman in the NME, and a highly flattering quote from the Pistol's Paul Cook (in one of a couple of features about them by Robin Banks in ZigZag), gave a rare outsider's insight to the band's activities. What was, at its best, a sophisticated eclecticism was, too often, confusion – sometimes left field avant gardist, sometimes mock-pop heroic, "but always too drunk and stoned". Singles by each band fell well short of expectations. "The Vincents' title song was chosen simply because it was the song with the most chords in it," Brown says, "so I thought it must be the best. Obviously it was not."

Brown recorded backing vocals for Viv Stanshall, and was a co-author of 'Naughty Christmas' by Keith Allen's Fat Les, which rose to number 22 in the UK charts. Ivor Cutler also recorded an (unreleased) track with the Vincents. This, and their superior, acoustic material (recorded under the kind financial patronage of Joe Strummer, Allen and others) has remained unreleased. However, some of these recordings – a collection of Brown's songs, Early English Recordings (including the Ivor Cutler collaboration) – are due out under Brown's own name in 2007.

DISCOGRAPHY:

Vincent Units:
The Vincent Units 7-inch EP (Y Records Y8 January 1981)
Carnival Song/Martini/Everything Is Going To Be All Wrong (produced by Dick O'Dell)
The Vincent Units cassette (Pro-Star Pro 1 1981)
Carnival Song/Martini/Everything Is Going To Be All Wrong (produced by Chris Gray and Neal Brown)
Tesco Bombers:
Hernando's Hideaway/Break The Ice At Parties/Girl From Ipanema 7-inch (Y Records Y 14 1982)

Vitamins

Addison Cresswell (vocals), Michael Wilkins (bass), David Turvey (guitar), Carl Rutter (drums)

The VITAMINS were the youngest of the Brighton-based bands featured on the second of the Vaultage compilations, with no member over the age of 18. Prior to their vinyl debut they'd been playing together for just over a year at school in Falmer, though by the time of the album's release Wilkins had joined the bank and Cresswell had signed on as an art student. "Their track on the album is about loneliness in the modern world," John Wellington told us in the Brighton & Hove Gazette's review of Vaultage 1978. Sadly, it was the only release by these peppy young upstarts.

Cresswell was subsequently replaced by Grant Boult for a short time before the band stalled. Boult went on to join mod band Chicane and following that the Techniques, who played supports to Martha And The Muffins, the Comsat Angels and others. "The Vitamins was short-lived as we were all at the same school, Falmer High," Boult told me, "and it fizzled out soon after we all left. Mike Wilkins is now a bank manager and the fact that this uncle was Steve Harley was certainly an inspiration at the time."

COMPILATION:

Vaultage 1978 (Two Sides Of Brighton) LP (Attrix RB 03 December 1978; 'New Town')

V2

David Wilks (aka Jonathon E, after the Rollerball character played by James Caan; vocals), Mark Standley (guitar), Stan the Man (bass), Steve Brotherdale (drums)

Slaughter And The Dogs weren't the only members of Manchester's punk vanguard to absorb both style and image from the glam rock era. Almost as raucous and showy were V2, formed in December 1976 by Standley, who'd just left the RAF, and Wilks, the latter having attended the second Sex Pistols' Lesser Free Trade Hall show in 1976. Both were school friends and veterans of Pips nightclub, where they'd bonded in the dedicated Bowie/Roxy room. They persuaded Stan to pick up the bass due to the fact that he was a fellow Bowie fan and had "good hair". Ex-Panik and Warsaw drummer Steve Brotherdale was invited to join after he met them on a bus, after asking him for directions to the Electric Circus.

They subsequently picked up supports to Slaughter, with whom Stan had struck up a long-standing friendship - their second ever show was at a Dogs concert at the Middleton Hall, alongside Fast Breeder. V2 would also support Slaughter at the Marquee when they ventured to London. However, by the time of the Dogs' homecoming gig at the Wythenshawe Forum in 1978, tensions between the two bands had emerged – encouraged on the night by the fact that visiting London band the Plague had their equipment 'misplaced' by the headliners and V2 got the blame.

V2's debut single, 'Speedfreak' ("It was more of a double a-side with 'Nothing To Do', which was really popular live," reckons Brotherdale) was the first song Standley ever wrote. It was released at the tail end of 1977 and immediately sold out of three separate pressings, despite a dismissive review from Tony Parsons in the NME ('packs the aural punch of a fart in a rust-corroded bean can'), although pretty much everyone else seemed to like it. The distinctive wailing on the single, incidentally, came from "a real World War II siren".

There was a recording hiatus until the end of 1978, by which time Brotherdale had convinced the others to bring in his former Panik colleague Ian Nance on lead guitar. "They needed a proper lead guitarist," he reckons, "and Nance was a great guitarist". By now they were a capable live attraction. There was some support in the media too, not least from the fickle pen of Paul Morley, writing in the NME in June 1978: "V2 think about presentation. Their music is stripped, effective, trebly punk – anachronistic if you will. They vigorously project this with garish musical homage to the ironical nursery surrealism of Alice Cooper, and the non-stop colour barrage of the Damned. Any irony is perhaps destroyed by the apparent seriousness of their intentions, but their show is very flash, and very imposing. Lots of smoke,

V2: Four pints of lager and a tub of mascara, please.

lights, make-up, glam(punk)rock, potentially extremely popular. Locally more popular than the Dogs and the Drones"

The combination of glam and punk didn't please all the purists, but it was an honest derivation of both Slaughter and V2's influences, and in many ways helped give Manchester punk a dash of colour and vitality. As Mick Middles recalled in From Joy Division to New Order, "The bands adhered to no universal dress code. On the contrary, the genres were disparate and often clashed quite strikingly. One remembers Gorton glam rockers V2, for instance, slumped menacingly in one corner, clad in figure-hugging flame-red or marine-blue plastic, bleached hair and make-up, while at the next table sat the darkly-clad Bohemian jazz outfit Ludus, whose inspiring and beautiful singer, Linder, would at all times be clad head to toe in regulation black."

Their stage show was certainly something to behold, even for the heady times. Flour would be thrown on audiences during encores, there were sporadic outbreaks of violence, a mock onstage electrocution (in order to diffuse said fights). Wilks was once set on fire by a cheap pyrotechnic thrown on stage by a drunk roadie. While at one show in some northern backwater, Steve Brotherdale recalls the purpose-made floor collapsing and Standley falling halfway through, leaving only his shoulders and head visible, and his leg badly gashed. Only for a girl in the audience to leap on the stage, take a run at him and try to pull him out by his hair. This was done because "she liked him", Brotherdale thinks. 12-inch 'Man In The Box' followed for TJM Records, recorded at Arrow's Studios (as 'Speedfreak' had been) on 25 October 1978, reaching the top of the alternative charts and selling 8,000 copies in three months.

Despite a strong live following, including many women, who occasionally proffered chocolates at gigs as well as assaulting them physically, the group fell apart mostly due to Standley's discovery of magic mushrooms and LSD and drifted in various directions, calling a close to operations in 1980. The core of the group became the Earwigs with the addition of

Toby Tolman of the Nosebleeds and later Primal Scream on drums and guitarist turned bass player Hugh O'Boyle of Victim. By a bizarre twist, V2's former drummer Steve Brotherdale became their singer. "They asked Dave Wilks of V2 to sing," Brotherdale told me, "but his voice didn't fit. I was having a pint with Mark and he asked me to listen. Mark was singing and I just said let me have a go, I was only joking, and we did one of their songs, 'Mr Greed'. We did that, and they wanted my voice. It was kind of a psychedelic thing. We played with Mood Six and the [WEA compilation album] Splash Of Colour bands at Gossips in London, where I also drummed because our drummer had hepatitis, despite having a broken leg myself." After the Earwigs, Ian Nance returned as lead vocalist, alongside Toby on drums, and they recorded an unreleased album, Enter The Reptile House, that never came out (from which some of the Overground V2 material is drawn). Brotherdale also recently unearthed further unreleased Earwigs recordings in his shed in 2002, which have now been cleaned up ready for release by Tosh Ryan.

V2 reformed first in 1988, the 'Man In The Box' line-up reappearing at the Boardwalk. "We didn't think anyone would turn up, but it was packed," Brotherdale recalls. And again in 1996 after Overground offered to release a compilation of the band's back pages. That year they returned to the stage at the Holidays In The Sun punk festival at Blackpool's Winter Gardens. However, during rehearsals Wilks was taken ill, and sadly died a few months later, while Phil Pope stepped in to anchor the vocals. They also played a second set on the Sunday featuring vocalist Eddie Mooney, an old friend of Standley's and another former veteran of TJM. Standley concurrently joined the reformed Drones on bass in 1997, playing a number of gigs in Britain and a three-week American tour in 1998. V2 issued their first single in 19 years on the Data label (featuring a song that was originally scheduled to have been their second single for TJM). When Pope left to concentrate on his Doors tribute band, the Doorz, Mooney became the group's new vocalist in 2001. He also sings with the Dakotas.

Standley is still musically active with Pleasuredome and has a film production company called Tib Street Films. The first release is Inside the Smiths, filmed over two years and starring Andy Rourke and Mike Joyce. "It's the first ever in-depth look at what it was like being in the Smiths," notes Standley. It's set for an autumn 2006 release on TV and DVD.

DISCOGRAPHY:

Speedfreak/Nothing To Do/That's It 7-inch (Bent SMALL BENT 1 1977)
(initial print run of 3,000 copies, subsequently issued in red and blue vinyl)
Man In The Box/When The World Isn't There 12-inch (TJM TJM1 1978)
Is Anyone Out There?/If You Could Only See/So Much Life 7-inch (DATA 002 June 1998)
(originally to have been their third single, but withdrawn. Featuring two new b-side songs)
ARCHIVE RELEASES:
Anthology CD (Overground OVER55 CD August 1996)

Warsaw Pakt

Jimmy Coull (vocals), Lucas Fox (drums), Andy Colquhoun (lead guitar), John Walker (aka John Manly; rhythm guitar), Chris Underhill (bass)

Nowadays chiefly remembered for the gimmick surrounding their debut album, with was stocked by local shops within 24 hours of it being recorded, WARSAW PAKT also housed some interesting personnel. Fox was the original Motorhead drummer and Colquhoun had been a member of R&B group the Rockets, who supported the Clash. The Rockets had also featured Val Haller and occasionally JJ Johnson, both later of Wayne County's Electric Chairs, and Stewart Copeland, later of the Police. Colquhoun was also approached by Miles Copeland about joining Chelsea, but elected to throw his hat into the ring of another band managed by Copeland, the Zips, before that too went phut.

Warsaw Pakt were formed in spring 1977 in Ladbroke Grove, West London, after Colquhoun decided he wanted to do his own thing. "John Manly, Wolf (their original German drummer) and I built a rehearsal room out of concrete blocks in the basement of Forbidden Fruit on Portobello Rd," he later told Punk77, "and called it The Bunker. And started Warsaw Pakt. Instrumentally we wanted to be the Who/MC5 of the scene. Ace up the sleeve was Mick Farren's lyrical output. Check out 'Nosebleed' on the CD. That's what passed for emotion in those days." Much of their repertoire was drawn from earlier Rockets material that Colquhoun had written with that band's principal lyricist, manager Frank Day, with some of the words reshaped by Manly. The most enduring example was 'Even Money', which was transformed from a pick-up song to a lyric about scoring heroin. Mick Farren also contributed lyrics for songs including 'Fast Eddie' (which he would reprise on his Vampires Stole My Lunch Money LP, which featured Colquhoun), 'Believe Me Honey' and 'Breastbeating', inspired by a dream Colquhoun had.

By the end of the year they had secured a deal with Island Records through the auspices of Mim Scala, the ice cream salesman turned gambler, agent and record producer, who recently wrote the highly regarded 60s travelogue A Memoir Of The Long Sixties. Island booked them a support slot with Siouxsie And The Banshees whilst hatching a plot to garner column inches for their debut album, while Lucas Fox was recruited to replace Wolf. Their debut single, 'Safe And Warm', was recorded in October 1977 and featured another Farren lyric.

Needle Time was recorded, mastered, packaged and distributed within 24 hours, starting at 10pm on Saturday 26 November, the process completed by 7pm the next day. "It was play side one, break, tune up, play side two," Colquhoun told Ugly Things. "This was done three times. The engineers were very concerned about us destroying the cutting lathe heads, which run to about five grand each. At first the sound in their control room at the top of the building was very restrained. By the third take of the two sides, it was OK, but not as good as the room sound. They used that take anyway."

Suitably, the packaging for the album featured a mailing envelope with rubber stamps, while the insert logged the entire 21-hour process. To the press they reiterated that this was a demonstration of the way new technology was opening up the world for musicians who wanted to communicate something. To the cynics it was a desperate marketing ploy. The overall feel is of a one-take set, opening with a version of the Who's 'It's Not True'. But the feeling remained of a rather polite punk record. "'Please allow me to introduce myself,' the opening line of 'Sympathy For The Devil', as my late friend Kevin Sparrow once remarked, is the prime example of 'polite rock'," noted Andy Colquhoun in an e-mail to me in 2005. "That's the only reason I ain't offended by your description of the Warsaw Pakt as polite!" Island then decided, in keeping with the spirit of the occasion, though without the band's consent, to cease pressing the record after the first week, in which 5,000 copies were sold. And that was it.

Colquhoun still stands by the record. "Nobody dumbed down for punk. We always played at the height of our perhaps limited abilities. We wanted to be another MC5/Who, though obviously at that time, that was simply a lofty goal. We figured that our sound was close enough to the emerging punk movement to be included in that wave. We didn't really make any musical reference to our contemporaries, favouring the 'Golden Age' of the 60s and our

Warsaw Pakt, whose album was recorded and released within 24 hours.

own interpretations of those riffs. Whereas the Ramones created something very fresh, which is now seen as pop music, the Pistols had attitude and made great sounding records, their live show was mostly about attitude, and for me at least, barely approximated the recordings. So we weren't exactly on the same page as the other bands, which may account for the 'mannered' impression we may have made. John Manly, Lucas Fox and me were all part of the Ladbroke Grove/Portobello Road alternative scene. Yes, the very drug-addled hippies the punks allegedly despised, although they weren't averse to the pharmacopia of illicit substances we enjoyed. Warsaw Pakt were signed to Island, whose only other band remotely in our category were the somewhat disdained, pre-hit Ultravox! By releasing an 'instant album' we were trying to achieve something honest. Some rumoured that this kind of recording was a dry run for the Who. I believe the Count Bishops also attempted a similar scenario, but it didn't work out for them. Needle Time remains labelled as a gimmick, but what the hell does that mean? As Chico Marx said, 'It's better to have lost and lost than to never have lost at all.'" And thereby may lay the distinction between punk rock and Warsaw Pakt. It all hinges on which Marx you choose to quote.

Without major label support, the band persevered for a few more months as the Pakt, and released a cassette of previous studio outtakes for an independent, then disbanded. By that time they'd racked up gigs at all the major London punk venues, including the Red Cow, Nashville and Dingwalls – their final gig as support to Ian Dury for a homeless benefit. There was talk of a deal with Miles Copeland's Illegal label, but that came to nothing. Colquhoun went on to Brian James's Tanz Der Youth, appearing on the single 'I'm Sorry I'm Sorry' and a John Peel session, and later played with the MC5's Wayne Kramer. Fox joined the Sisterhood. Coull formed Maidenhead's Argonauts. Sadly, John Manly committed suicide. "Since 1992 I've been living in Los Angeles," notes Colquhoun, "and I've recorded quite a few CDs with Mick Farren and the Deviants, most of which came out on Captain Trip Records."

Colquhoun recently released a CD for that label entitled Pick Up The Phone, America, featuring Mick Farren and assorted former members of Motorhead and the Pink Fairies. The same label has also released a live Pink Fairies CD drawn from 1987 shows on which he appears, entitled Chinese Cowboys.

DISCOGRAPHY:

Safe And Warm/Sick And Tired 7-inch (Island PAKT 1 November 1977)
Needle Time LP (Island ILPS 9515 1978) (reissued on CD in remixed form in 1999 by Captain Trip, CTCD 238, with both sides of the single, 'Safe And Warm' and 'Sick And Tired', plus three additional demo tracks; 'Lorraine', 'Even Money' and 'Cut Glass Jaw')
See You In Court cassette (Stuff Central 1979)

Wasps

Jesse Lynn-Dean (vocals), Del May (guitar), John Rich (drums), Steve Wollaston (bass)

There are plenty of hard luck stories from the London punk scene of the late-70s, but few can measure up to the fate of Walthamstow's WASPS. Such were the slings, arrows and flying gob of outrageous fortune they faced that, had they fallen into a bag of nipples, the band would have emerged sucking their thumbs.

They began in 1976 when singer-songwriter Lynn-Dean, from Islington, made the acquaintance of a trio of East London-based musicians. Rich had been playing in bands from the age of 15, notably in Trance, alongside Wollaston. He also played alongside May as part of Maud, later Blockade, between 1971 and 1972, and East London pub rock legends Remus Down Boulevard, who included later Iron Maiden guitarist Dennis Stratton in their ranks. Wollaston was part of uber hippychick Lady June's Elysium, whose fellow revellers included Brian Eno and Kevin Ayers. Lynn-Dean, for his part, had landed a deal with EMI in late 1975 when he'd talked his way into their offices in Charing Cross Road and convinced executive Dave Ambrose, formerly bass player with Brian Auger and Julie Driscoll, of his talents. Ambrose told him to come back when he had a band together. It was then that he came across May, Rich and Wollaston.

Rehearsals ensued at Rich's mother's house in Millais Road, Leytonstone. Luckily, Ma Rich had hearing problems so wasn't unduly disturbed by their activities. With a drum kit, a rare imported stainless steel Asba set-up, bought by Rich's uncle and May's Gibson SG partly strung with Ernie Ball banjo strings, the chemistry between the new quartet was immediate. Lynn-Dean's theatrical, high-pitched vocals could have sounded awful in isolation but syncopated beautifully with the band's rhythms, notable for the number of tempo changes employed. With a set comprising originals and covers of Tommy Tucker's 'High Heel Sneakers' and Bowie's 'Jean Genie', they were given their live debut by Bridge House proprietor Terry Murphy in Canning Town. This was reviewed, favourably, by Giovanni Dadomo for Sounds, who later did PR for the group. That led to Lynn-Dean approaching the London booking agency Evolution. Side-stepping the fact that they were a punk band, he persuaded later Wasps' manager Bob Herd to give them a shot.

The phone call brought immediate results – that night Herd rang back to ask the band if they could substitute at short notice for a Georgie Fame show at the Marquee. The shocked audience made a bee-line for the exits on witnessing the Wasps. The band picked up gigs at all of London's main punk haunts, including the Roxy and Rock Garden, where they supported Talking Heads. Most notorious was an out of town show at Shrewsbury Civic Centre which involved all sorts of bottle-throwing shenanigans, an on-stage fire and shocked newspaper headlines suggesting the concert had put intolerable strain on the local accident and

emergency department. At another show at the Roxy, Lynn-Dean's on stage demeanour, which was already causing the rest of the band concern, resulted in a stage dive sans catchers and a good kicking before he was rescued by soundman Gary Wellman and Joe Strummer, who lost a tooth in the melee.

May had taken enough, and resigned by letter (reprinted in the sleevenote to the subsequent Overground compilation). He was convinced that punk would not go anywhere. Although he continued with the band through August gigs with the Police and XTC at the Music Machine, he was replaced by former soundman Wellman at the same venue in September. They also found a new manager in the shape of journalist Myles Palmer, subsequently replaced by Adrian Miller.

The band finally made their debut with 'Teenage Treats', recorded at Pathway Studios for 4-Play in November 1977. The B-side was their ferocious set-closer 'She Made Magic', which eventually won inclusion over the third track they recorded, 'Free Country'. Bob Geldof described it as "a great single" as guest reviewer in the NME. Writer Kevin Pearce, who later quoted the lyrics to 'Can't Wait Till 1978' in his book Something Beginning With O, was among the many taken by it. "A definitive classic of manic melody which sounds as if their life depends upon it. The Wasps epitomise the urgency, which ultimately went nowhere fast, but was fun for a few minutes. Nasty little nobodies no doubt, but this is essential. This (one-off?) single was produced by Kim Turner, the master of tinny, canny pocket symphonies. He would later play on 'Action Time Vision', one of the ten best songs ever, and if you see any punk 7-inch produced by Turner, do not hesitate." The late Turner would, of course, subsequently work with the Police and Sting.

A month later the Wasps were featured on Live At The Vortex with 'Can't Wait Till 78' (and a live cover of 'Waiting For The Man'). Recorded in October 1977, it was also chosen as the lead track, alongside a cut by Mean Streets, on a promotional single for the compilation. It produced a string of letters in the music press after it was slated by Jon Savage. Afterwards they played shows in France and Sweden and recorded the first of two John Peel sessions, broadcast in February 1978. Alan 'Fluff' Freeman played the single, and also repeated the first Peel session on his 'Your Mother Wouldn't Like It' programme. As Lynn-Dean recalled to me, "In an unguarded moment in a well-known Mayfair 'watering hole', he confided in me that he found 'the French bit' in our song 'Jjjenny' 'a bit of a turn on'. Alan was a very likeable guy and, like John Peel, always had an open mind and enjoyed listening to new music."

However, more trouble followed their London shows. After refusing to allow Iggy Pop to perform with them at the Roxy, a fan at a show at the Bell, King's Cross, was attacked by bouncers and died from his injuries. The Roxy also provided the inspiration for their barnstorming 'Jjjenny', written about a punkette with a stutter who changed clothes from her mainstream life to come out at night, incorporating a punk parody of Serge Gainsbourg and Jane Birkin's 'Je T'aime'. "I think the Roxy club in its heyday was great," Lynn-Dean told Punk77, "it was a genuine punk venue, it was seedy, unpredictable and real and I loved it. Even though you sometimes had to threaten to beat the management to death with a mic stand to get paid for a gig."

Afterwards Lynn-Dean flew to America at the suggestion of his management, with a view to obtaining a US deal. This all occurred while the band was shoved into a studio for seven months "to write hit singles", given new suits and filmed for potential videos of 'Angelica', 'Jjjenny' and 'Something To Tell You'. While in America Lynn-Dean played with the Ramones at CBGB's and stayed at Sharon Osbourne's house in LA. But nothing was to come of the trip, despite interest from Jet and CBS, because manager Adrian Miller wasn't happy with the deal. So there was yet another change of management. Although it didn't work out, Lynn-Dean and Miller remain friends. "I had some amazing times with Adrian along the way, both in the UK and America, where Adrian seems to know just about everybody, from Dustin Hoffman to Sharon Osbourne. Adrian is one of those people who thinks it's better to travel than to arrive and we had quite a journey."

On his return the band, who had signed with RCA, had broken up. Lynn-Dean recruited a new line-up, Neil Fitch (guitar), David Owen (bass; though Steve Dominic played on their February 1978 Peel session) and Tim Grant (ex-Sam Apple Pie; drums). According to Lynn-Dean, the reason was simple: "I split from the manager of the band and the rest of the band unfortunately were still in his control and legally we were unable to get back together unless I went back to being managed by their manager. It would have been great to get back with John, Steve and Gary, because as musicians the chemistry was definitely right. The energy was there and we had a unique feeling for working together. The ironic thing about this is that it was me who got the band involved with the manager in question in the first place and for this I do feel responsible."

The new line-up provided overdubs of the original 'Rubber Cars' in order to gain sleeve credits, which became their debut single for RCA. It's actually superb, the martial drumming and OTT singing making it sound like the Clash meets Sparks. In fact, it's strangely reminiscent of both Steve Harley's 'Mr Soft' and, bizarrely, predictive of Radiohead's 'Airbag'. The other former members were not best pleased at having their contribution erased from history. It wasn't actually Lynn-Dean's choice of single, but someone at RCA had heard him strumming it and insisted on its release. The song concerned a friend who had died in a car crash. "I still think the best version of 'Rubber Cars' is the demo version (included on their posthumous Punkyronics CD) recorded with the original line-up," notes Lynn-Dean.

Such was the hubbub surrounding the single that it was rumoured an animated series based on the band was being considered. It even brought a TV appearance on kiddies show Runaround. However, its success also had a downside, with a series of writs from former managers that forced RCA to pull the single, despite it being the label's fastest seller of the week. With RCA now indifferent, the second line-up played a series of "dispiriting" showcases to other labels to no avail. In the face of this disappointment, the band broke up for the final time. The Wasps were officially over, though the final line-up, with the addition of Anna Chen, supported Tom Petty at the Venue, billed as The One.

The former members dispersed to various professions. Wollaston took a degree in religious studies as well as a graphics diploma, later co-writing the personal development guidebooks Tune In To Your Spiritual Potential and 21 Steps To Reach Your Spirit with Glyn Edwards. He also writes on mysticism and yoga under the name Santoshan and still records. He has another book, co-written with Swami Dharmananda, projected for release in 2007 through 'O' Books.

Rich joined No Dice, but turned down an offer to join Iron Maiden in favour of session work. Wellman pursued an unsuccessful solo career before becoming a businessman. Lynn-Dean also went solo and released the single 'Do It', backed by 'Boyfriend's Back In Town', for Creole, accompanied by Charlie Burchill and Michael McNeill of Simple Minds, as well as the Wasps' second drummer, Tiam Grant. Grant in turn would briefly play with X-Ray Spex, Modern Romance and Transvision Vamp. Lynn-Dean continues to write songs (the second version of the Wasps even recorded a demo of 'Boyfriend' for a proposed Eurovision entry after his EMI publisher suggested it) but then moved to Spain, where he manages a couple of bars as well as writes songs.

DISCOGRAPHY:

Teenage Treats/She Made Magic 7-inch (4-Play November 1977) (also reissued a month later with 'Illegal' labels)

Can't Wait Till 1978 split 7-inch (NEMS NES 115 December 1977) (promotional single for Live At The Vortex, B-side by Mean Street)

Rubber Cars/This Time 7-inch (RCA PB 5137 February 1978)

ARCHIVE RELEASE:

Punkyronics CD (Overground Over 100VPCD 2001) (this features the demo version of 'Rubber Cars', the debut single and ten unreleased studio recordings, with sleevenotes by Lynn-Dean. Shame the original version of 'Rubber Cars' isn't present, but we can blame that on licensing)

IMPORTANT COMPILATION:

Live At The Vortex (NEMS NEL 6013 December 1977; 'Can't Wait Till 1978', 'Waiting For The Man')

Wild Boys

Roddy Byers (guitar), Pete Davies (drums), Jett Boy (guitar), Roger (bass)

Formed in Coventry in 1975, the WILD BOYS are notable chiefly for being the first home of later Coventry Automatics and Special AKA guitarist Roddy Byers, aka Roddy Radiation. Their set list included Roddy originals such as '1980's Teddy Boy'

and 'Concrete Jungle', which later turned up on the Specials' debut album, as well as covers of 'No Fun' and 'I'm Not Your Stepping Stone'. "I formed the Wild Boys in 1975," he told Record Collector in 2004, "a pre-punk 'n' roll band. The influences were Lou Reed, Bowie, Iggy Pop, New York Dolls. We played covers and also my originals... We headlined loads of local punk gigs, and supported the Buzzcocks, but split up in 1977. Just as punk was kicking off!"

The Wild Boys were the first Coventry band to pick up the punk sound and look. They directly influenced others, such as Squad, who attended their first shows. Byers had been present at the Notting Hill riot of 1976, as had his friend, Wild Boys roadie and fellow day-tripper Ratty Roadent, aka Steve Connelly. Ratty, after being locked up by the police, befriended Joe Strummer and brought back an acetate of 'White Riot'. As Byers later told Richard Eddington, he felt compelled to check it out. "The Clash looked the way I wanted the Wild Boys to look, but with musicians in Coventry, you basically have to dress them and explain that you can't wear flares. When Peter Davies joined the Wild Boys, he had shoulder-length hair, a wax moustache like Salvador Dali and a big floppy hat." Subsequent line-up changes would see Dec McConkie come in on bass and Steve Young on drums while Pete Davies joined the UK Subs.

Byers elaborated on this to me in 2005. "There was a sort of punk thing already starting, from the Bowie-Roxy music fans, that was similar to the Bromley London crowd. We had all been listening to Iggy Pop and the Ramones and Doctor Feelgood and the pre-pub rock, back to basics thing. I guess that all over England there were likeminded people moving towards what would become British punk rock. The same thing happened later with Madness and the Beat doing the ska-reggae sound." The Buzzcocks' support slot came about via local friends and frequent Buzzcocks' support act the Flys. Their bass player, Joe Hughes, later worked with Byers in 1981 in his Tearjerkers project, established during a Specials' touring hiatus. There were also strong local connections with bands like the Urge. "It was a small scene and everyone hung out together."

After Roddy joined the Automatics, "My brother Marc Byers took over the name and some of my early songs," he told me. The Wild Boys Mark III featured on the epochal local compilation Sent From Coventry, playing two of Roddy's old songs, 'We're Only Monsters' and 'Lorraine'. In addition to Marc Byers on lead guitar and vocals, this line-up also featured Johnny 'Wild' Thompson on lead vocals and second guitar and Rob Lapworth, who was concurrently appearing on stage in the Coventry-based play Risky City, on bass and vocals. The 'original' Wild Boys "never recorded anything, as far as I can remember".

DISCOGRAPHY:

Last One Of The Boys/We're Only Monsters 7-inch (Ring Piece 1980)
COMPILATION:
Sent From Coventry LP (Kathedral KATH 1 1980; 'We're Only Monsters', 'Lorraine')

Wire

Colin Newman (guitar, vocals), Bruce Gilbert (guitar), Graham Lewis (bass, vocals), Robert Grey (aka Gotobed) (drums)

WIRE were the thinking man's punks – even if they themselves repeatedly queried any connection to the genre – for whom the new musical environment provided a conduit for taking artistic chances and the opening of intellectual and aesthetic space. In trying to establish a dialogue with their audience they were instantly more sophisticated than the new rock'n'roll orthodoxy, much of whom had simply dressed up in the new clothes.

W

The art school-reared Wire, significantly older than their peers (Gotobed was 25 before he even started to play drums, while Gilbert, in his 30s, was actually an audio-visual technician rather than a student at Watford Art College) were adopted by critics as totemic cerebral individualists. They also drew a constituency that was often otherwise disinterested in punk, or at least suspicious of its growing conformity and innate machismo. For example, as Roger Sabin noted in Punk Rock So What: "Being a bit of a weed, I felt relatively safe going to see them because they had a less 'heavy' following than Sham 69 or the Pistols." But for all that

Wire, live on stage in 1976.

they released a series of wonderfully involving, endlessly fascinating records that belied their 'experimental' status. As Ira Robbins memorably put it when reviewing Pink Flag, "Wire dredges up images of Kerouac and Ginsberg – beat poetry – short fragments of impressions set to music. In 1953 the accompanying instrument would be bongos. 1978 bongos have six strings and make lots of noise. They have volume. They have lots of loose ends and rough edges. They be Wire."

While the mark they left on British bands, notably My Bloody Valentine, Blur and Elastica, who had to go to the cashpoint big time over their use of 'Three Girl Rhumba', is well documented, they were hugely influential on the American punk and post-punk scene. Big Black, R.E.M (who recorded a memorable version of 'Strange'), Henry Rollins, Minor Threat, Firehose and Yo La Tengo are but a fraction of that nation's alt-rock hierarchy to have turned in cover versions of Wire songs. "The Banshees and Wire were the two bands I really admired," Robert Smith of the Cure once noted. "They meant something."

Wire was effectively formed by accident, as Newman recalled to The Big Takeover. "My girlfriend threw me out of her apartment the first year I was at art school, and I had to go and live somewhere else. Just in that process of trying to find a new place to live, and people to live with, I met the people who were in that nascent, original version of Wire." They were emancipated by punk's liberating DIY ethos, and the fact that musicianly expertise was an entirely arbitrary consideration. Based at Watford art school in October 1976, the initial line-up included John Good, son of film director Jack Good, on bass guitar, with Newman invited to sing, and fellow student George Gill and Bruce Gilbert providing the guitars.

With the addition of Lewis and Gotobed, the latter having already sung with the Snakes (and later with the Art Attacks), they made their debut in London on 2 December 1976 as support to the Derelicts. But there were immediately tensions with Gill. "The material was tedious, to be honest," Newman would later tell John Robb. "George fancied himself as a bit of a poet, he drank quite a lot and he had a temper – it was a weird combination. I thought his songs were very average, even though we were putting layers of sound over it." When Gill left the band in early 1977, his absence was famously attributed to "one blues solo too many". What had actually happened was that he'd fallen down some stairs and broken his leg. He would come back to play a couple of gigs with the band later before being deemed not so much surplus as antagonist to requirements, and going on to form the Bears.

Following his two tenures with the band, Wire were offered £35 to play two nights at the Roxy. The shows were to be recorded for a live compilation album, released in March 1977. Mike Thorne was in charge of the project. "No matter the audience size, Wire's set had an instant, imposing mood, and their sound was as good as anyone's over the two weekends, so good that rumours persist that I re-recorded them later because they were signing to EMI. They created a mood and it stayed." Their two tracks on Live At The Roxy, '12XU' and 'Lowdown', were widely judged to have stood head and shoulders above the rest of the ragbag contents.

Wire were the only act on the Roxy compilation to sign a deal with parent label Harvest, and were set to work with house producer Thorne, who would also provide keyboards as an unofficial fifth member on their second and third albums. "I thought Wire were great," Thorne later recalled. "Very strong, distinctive music with an attitude. It was music that I liked. And the criteria I stuck with for production was to make music I liked with people I liked. I don't make music that I like with people I don't like, and vice versa."

It was Thorne, also, who was largely responsible for securing their record deal. "Wire were an unopposed EMI signing from the time I played Nick Mobbs, my boss, the Roxy roughs on a car cassette. I had bent his ear about the Sex Pistols, and that seemed to deliver. Even live at the club, Wire's sound was good enough for a real record. We did some demos of further songs, including 'Mr Suit' and 'Pink Flag' in the eight-track recording studio that was a treasure in the basement of the company's Manchester Square offices. No further persuasion was necessary. The rank and file of the company had been very upset by the firing of the Sex Pistols by a senior management none of us had ever met, and the A&R department had become to all intents and purposes a welcoming punk hangout."

The sessions resulted in 'Mannequin', one of the definitive, and most jarring, 1977 punk singles. "That was a deliberate ploy on my part," Newman told ZigZag, "to make the lyrics the opposite to the tune. Before you realised what the words were you could hum the tune. In a way it appears to be tongue in cheek when I sing it on stage. I want to sing it with half a smile. Other times I want to sing it straight. It is ambiguous." It sounded like nothing else out there, as Lewis explained to The Onion: "The Pistols made some good singles, but musically it was always rock'n'roll. And the Clash subsequently proved that to be the case as well, very quickly. And the Damned produced probably one of the best punk singles, 'New Rose', and they got their album out first, but we were always separate from it. We never felt that we were part of that scene. We didn't socialise with those people. We were getting on with what we were doing, really. We were far more aware of what everybody was doing, but what interested us more was the experiments Eno was doing with Bowie, very much the work that was coming out of the States; Pere Ubu, early Talking Heads, very early Devo. Obviously, stuff coming out of Europe on the other side – Kraftwerk, stuff like that. That was what was informing us."

'Mannequin' heralded the much-loved Pink Flag album – 21 songs, none lasting more than three minutes, of wilful non-conformity. Within the space of its opening two tracks – Lewis's chilling, bullet-point travelogue 'Reuters' paired with the 28-second kindergarten cacophony that was 'Field Day For The Sundays' – Wire ran amok with conventions both modern and ancient. '12XU', which reappeared but was as brusquely compact as ever, was "about sexual exertion in any direction, really," reckoned Gilbert. "If you see your boyfriend kissing a man. If you see your girlfriend kissing a man. It could be a woman or a man. That was my line." Newman would add: "It was a joke about censoring. Lots of people were putting out records with 'fuck' on them and immediately getting banned." While alienation was a theme common to the point of compulsion for other punk groups, Wire's take was playful and nuanced, as on 'Ex-Lion Tamer' – "Next week will solve your problems/But now, fish fingers all in a line/The milk bottles stand empty/Stay glued to your TV set."

'Reuters' was just one example of the band's ability to escape punk literalism and the verse-chorus-verse ghetto. The musical influences here were not the Pistols and the Clash, but a mesh of the Velvet Underground, Can and Beefheart. Thorne remembers the sessions thus: "When we went in the first day I took in a jar of home-grown, just so they could settle into the studio. I didn't want them to get precious and put undue pressure on that first day. Everybody got completely ripped and the studio fear was completely gone after that." It was Thorne who provided the noises at the end of 'Strange' by hitting the fire escape with a drumstick, while his flute teacher Kate Lucas provided further sonic texture. The dynamic of the band, meanwhile, was beginning to take shape. "Basically, the way I viewed it, when there were four of us," Gilbert remembered in conversation with Thorne. "Colin was the most musically experienced. He was always viewed as kind of the bandmaster, but not in terms of the concept or where it was going musically. There's got to be somebody who says, 'we should do that again' or 'that's not quite right'. It's better if the singer did that because they have to be more secure about what's happening behind them."

Claustrophobic, tense and unfamiliar, Pink Flag's twitching rhythms and diffuse instrumentation confirmed that the Pistols' breakthrough would not merely result in a succession of copyists. As Newman recalled: "I remember at the end of Pink Flag saying, 'well, I don't know what this is,' and Graham said, 'they might get it in a few years' time.' I think we've always been conscious of the fact that, although the music has a kind of accessibility, for some reason it seems to be incredibly difficult for people to realise how direct and accessible it can be, because of the way we're presenting ourselves." As with all their Harvest studio albums, Gilbert and Lewis designed the distinctive sleeve.

They toured with the Tubes to promote it, before releasing a second fantastic single, 'I Am The Fly' at the start of 1978, its swelling rhythmic insistence a signpost to later work. The song featured a distortion box with a flanger "set on complete feedback", while the musical backing was a deliberate inversion of a 12-bar chord structure.

They toured heavily during the spring before starting work on Chairs Missing, again produced by Mike Thorne, who would join the band on stage to play keyboards allowing Newman to concentrate on guitar. Chairs Missing was released following a short US sojourn and promoted by a full UK tour in September. This time the sessions were more considered and involved. It housed two outstanding singles, the aforementioned 'I Am The Fly' and 'Outdoor Miner', their only 'hit' single despite controversy over chart hyping – EMI believed at just 105 seconds, the album version was too short, and had additional copies pressed up with a piano-based middle eight. "It was an idea of Mike Thorne's," Lewis later stated. "It got to the point when Wire were definitely going to be on Top Of The Pops, but I think that Donny and Marie Osmond came into town that week and they got the slot instead." Whatever Wire's intellectual deliberations over their art – and by now they were being widely earmarked as 'Punk Floyd', the idea of being popular on a mass scale was evidently appealing. "That was our big moment gone," Newman would later lament to John Robb, "when we could have been weird and pop at the same time."

For Thorne himself, "Chairs Missing has persisted as my personal favourite of the three Wire albums that I was involved with. It doesn't have the rough clarity of Pink Flag, or the polish and arrangement coherence of 154, but there's a spirit of newness and discovery about every moment which takes you on a journey, perhaps closely related to the one we made at the time. Courtesy of new, basic electronics, completely fresh sound effects units were making it to market…These sounds promised a whole new world for us, so off we went. A gesture could come from a simple chord, non-virtuoso playing, and an inspired setting of some mysteriously named knobs. For me too, that was liberation." Thorne had stumbled on a group that shared his appreciation of timbre and cadence, and his appetite for reinventing tiny fragments of sound to renew the whole. That those tweaks, in which each element was broken down and rearranged according to its sonic possibilities rather its conventional properties, rendered the album one of the most astonishing of the era. To illustrate – can you imagine a more imperiously minimalist song than 'Waiting For The Man'? If not, you haven't heard 'Heartbeat'. You want sonic menace? 'Mercy' provides the unforgiving route map to My Bloody Valentine or the Swans. You think Jonny Greenwood was the first guitarist to hit an end of the millennium non-chord, check out, well, the whole album.

The spring of 1979 was spent as support to Roxy Music on their European tour, but they were revolted at the sight of one-time innovators going through the motions. 'A Question Of Degree' followed. "Mike Thorne arrived at the 154 sessions," Newman recalled to MOJO, "with the idea that we would do a series of singles that would later get compiled as an album. 'A Question Of Degree' was the first one. It all got into a mess, however, as there were a lot of competing and conflicting interests in the band at that time. Ultimately, it didn't go on the album because it had already been released." For some commentators, the single marked the exact point at which the whole post-punk genre took shape. "Wire's concern, almost since conception," Newman continued, "had been to be rather 'not punk'. Well, as 'not punk' as

four blokes with spiky attitude and straight jeans could be. It was about being as different as possible within the general thrust of where it was all going. This was borne out of one simple truth of 1976 – the world didn't need another Sex Pistols, it needed the next thing and we were it!"

154 was released in September 1979. Titled after the number of gigs Wire had thus far completed, it had less immediacy than its predecessors, though 'Map Ref 41°N 93°W' (which if you look it up actually pinpoints Des Moines in Iowa) was superb. While Newman's 'The 15th' retains some of the pop zest that undercut early work, 'The Other Window' serves up grotesque, macabre imagery and deliberately skewed, off-kilter background rhythms in a tiny but unflinching morality play. Musically, however, it was atypical of the rest of the contents, in which the focus shifted to arrangement rather than component detail. There are those for whom 154 remains Wire's definitive statement, preferring its seasoned songwriting and aura of implied discord to either of its forerunners. Indeed, 'pick your favourite Wire' album is one of the great idle pursuits for devotees of the era. It remains stunning that one band, in the course of three years, could produce a similar number of albums of such staggeringly individual character.

Each member of the band would later attest to the fraught, intense nature of the 154 experience. The studio tensions certainly grew too strong for Thorne, who walked away. The album came with a free four-track EP which allowed each member to record a solo track, presaging the group's disparate activities during the 80s. By February 1980 Wire had announced the dissolution of their contract with EMI. A press statement read: "Due to internal and corporate problems currently besetting EMI, there has been a breakdown of communication between the company and Wire. In addition to this, the company's reticence to consolidate future plans and projects has led to Wire taking advantage of the fact that they are no longer under any contractual obligation to EMI."

Their final show came in July 1980 at the Electric Ballroom, recorded and later released as Document And Eyewitness. The shows were reviewed by Chris Bohn for the NME in 1981: "Where the spectators would have been satisfied with the cosy illusion of a greatest hits re-run, Wire demanded that they should participate with their imaginations by playing totally unfamiliar sets. Did that make them arrogant? On the contrary, they were crediting their followers with intelligence to grapple with the unknown. Their attempts weren't always successful but they were invariably provocative and the Electric Ballroom concert – featured here – caught them at their most extreme. With a battery of fringe theatre techniques they proceeded to alienate the punks still yelling for '12XU', even mocking them via an MC's request spot for the same – they obliged for about 30 seconds... Why did the group keep disappearing behind a sheet? Why is Graham Lewis hammering away at an old stove? What's the singer doing with that lit-up goose in his hand? Don't ask me – just laugh or throw something. If the sketches carried any deeper significance beyond their visual bluff, it passed me by."

Subsequent solo projects (notably Gilbert and Lewis's Dome) resulted in a welter of material throughout the early-80s, while Newman produced the Virgin Prunes and recorded songs originally intended for a fourth Wire album on his solo debut A-Z (parts of which were used extensively in Silence Of The Lambs).

The band reunited in June 1984 after Newman returned from India. He contacted Gilbert and Lewis, who had a show booked at Oxford's Museum of Modern Art. They rehearsed for three days and aired new songs such as 'A Serious Of Snakes' and 'Drill'. This was initially envisaged as a one-off, though the show's popularity persuaded them to press ahead with further gigs and Mute Records to release the 'Snakedrill' EP. "It's not like we did some records in the 70s, had a bit of a laugh, got drunk a lot and then went away and got proper jobs," Newman recalled to Chris Hollow. "We made an artistic statement in the 70s, the ramifications of which we've spent years dealing with – people coming up to us and saying what you did then inspired me to do this, this and this. And when you've made effective artistic statements there's no going back. You can't just say, 'Oh, I wasn't being serious, I'm really a plumber.'"

Simon Reynolds noted the group's innate ambivalence towards their 'consumers': "Wire despise the uses people subject music to, detest the currency of rock discourse; driven by the desire to avoid being reduced to a synopsis, they create a vivid, blank and quite inconsequential beauty. The aim: to dazzle, rather than enlighten; build edifices, rather than edify." Sadly, Wire Mark II's output would prove to be so wilfully obtuse that it managed to alienate even their fiercest and most longstanding advocates.

A new album, The Ideal Copy, emerged in 1987. This introduced the band's 'dugga' concept – specifically 'monophonic monorhythmic repetition'. Doesn't sound like something to get the pulses racing, does it? And it wasn't. 'The Point Of Collapse' is intriguing musically, but the vocals are so mis-matched, it's painful. That's an affliction that pervades the whole album, though 'Ahead' sounds complementary to the direction New Order were reaching for, particularly in its overdriven bass lines. Typically contrary, they would also tour the USA with a support act The Ex-Lion Tamers performing Pink Flag in its entirety to relieve them of the necessity to do so. A Bell Is A Cup Until It Is Struck followed in 1988, their second successive album recorded in Berlin, while 'Eardrum Buzz' restored them to the national charts. Then came It's Beginning To and Back Again in 1989, an album made up of live recordings overworked and overdubbed in the studio. By 1990 Wire had decided to abandon the 'beat-combo' concept in favour of using electronics and midi technology. This resulting change brought about Manscape in 1990, the group's most unappetising album – though it did include 'Torch It', a rewrite of Big Black's 'Kerosene'.

Following the recording and on the eve of a tour Robert Gotobed left and returned to farming. Given the group's current direction, there was little requirement for a human drummer. He even acknowledged that he had painted himself out of the picture by accepting the use of drum technology. The band would later concede that this period did not represent the pinnacle of their career. "80s Wire by common consent within the band was not the most stellar period," Newman admitted. "We had some great ideas, and on occasion some good results, but it was not a happy band. In the 70s obviously there was a level of innocence and naivety, which you can never go back to. But I like the idea of approaching music and art from a point of view of not really knowing what you are doing. Also in the 70s we had a manager who was fantastic at getting attention and not very good on the money side which is why it all went a bit pants. In the 80s we had precisely the opposite – we had a manager who was fantastic with money, runs to this day a hugely successful business, but didn't really understand that you need to have a more dynamic relationship with the band."

To pile confusion upon confusion Wire recorded The Drill LP. Containing eight versions of the title-track, it took the Wire theory of 'dugga', the monophonic, monorhythmic, repetition to sublime and ridiculous ends. Each track being a reinterpretation and reinvention of 'Drill'. Recorded prior to Gotobed's departure, it was used as a test bed for the use of sequencing and computer technology. It ultimately fell between the cracks and remains a forgotten facet of Wire's recorded output.

The remaining members shortened their name to Wir and cut The First Letter, created by the three members playing MIDI guitars into a computer and cutting and pasting, slicing and looping the results. Which sounded more interesting in theory than in practice, though 'It Continues', 'Tailor Made' and the morose but insistent 'Ticking Mouth' are all worth hearing. 'So And Slow (It Grows)', released as a single, saw them close to chart success, but by the end of the year the project had ground to a halt, though Wir did remix Erasure's 'Fingers And Thumbs' single. The members once again concentrated on solo projects.

Wire reformed for a US tour in the spring of 2000 as EMI reissued their back catalogue. "By the late 1990s things had moved on," Newman told Alexander Laurence. "Both Bruce and I (who are London residents) independently developed the sense that there could be a Wire construction for that period. A specific invite came to play a show at Daniel Miller's 'mini Meltdown' in 1998. In the end it came to nothing, but the seeds were sown."

The following year they were invited to curate an evening at the Royal Festival Hall, with "reasonably sized cheque attached". They headlined, performing before the largest audience of their lives, and selling out the 3,500-seat venue. Newman: "In order to do the show we had to tool up the band from a more or less cold start." Gotobed confirmed that the unifying purpose of Wire had returned. "During those three days, there were lots of anxieties about – was it a mistake to go back into the group, and would I end up being in the same position as when I left? I just thought it was worth trying. We played 'Drill' at Bruce's fiftieth birthday

party and that was after a period of about five years and I hadn't really spoken to anyone in Wire. Although I didn't feel close to the other people in the group, it just made me feel that there was this indefinable bond between the members in the group and having the four people which make up Wire on the stage seems to be the right place for it to be." The good news for fans was that the 2000 shows saw them draw on their classic first three albums, albeit in radically reshaped versions – selections from which had been noticeably absent on the 1986-1991 reunion tours.

They have continued to issue new product, often through their own website. The best of these comprised the 'Read And Burn' CDs, in which they returned to the textures of their Harvest albums, at least in spirit, with a sound akin to digital hardcore rock (check out 'In The Art Of Stopping' and 'Germ Ship' in particular). These tracks were collated, along with four new songs, on Send, which is essential listening for those who had written Wire off after their unloved 80s experiments with dance music and atonal minimalism.

While they always claimed they were not a punk band as such, there is an acknowledgement of the part the spirit of 77 played in allowing them an entry point, as Bruce Gilbert confirmed to Mike Thorne. "Well, for all its faults, I think the punk era solidified the notion of the crossover between the arts and music. Culture was something that could be explored and was worthy, whether the audience was big or small. The situation we are in at the moment could not have arrived, I'm fairly sure, without the punk period. The notion of the 'do it yourself' aspect to these things, and the fact that people came out of the closet with their artistic aspirations seems to be not as embarrassing as it was in previous times."

Discography:

Mannequin/Feeling Called Love/12XU 7-inch (Harvest HAR 5144 November 1977)

Pink Flag LP (Harvest SHSP 4076 November 1977) (issued on CD in July 1994 by Harvest, CDGO 2063, with extra tracks 'Dot-Dash' and 'Options R')

I Am The Fly/Ex-Lion Tamer 7-inch (Harvest HAR 5151 February 1978)

Dot-Dash/Options R 7-inch (Harvest HAR 5161 June 1978)

Chairs Missing LP (Harvest SHSP 4093 October 1978) (issued on CD in July 1994 by Harvest, CDGO 2065, with extra tracks 'Outdoor Miner (single version)', 'A Question Of Degree' and 'Former Airline')

Outdoor Miner/Practice Makes Perfect 7-inch (Harvest HAR 5172 January 1979) (limited edition white vinyl)

A Question Of Degree/Former Airline 7-inch (Harvest HAR 5187 June 1979)

154 LP (Harvest SHSP 4105 September 1979) (issued on CD in July 1994 by Harvest, CDGO 2064, with extra tracks 'Song 1', 'Get Down Parts 1 & 2', 'Let's Panic Later', 'Small Electric Piece', 'Go Ahead')

Map Ref 41°N 93°W/Go Ahead 7-inch (Harvest HAR 5192 November 1979)

Document & Eyewitness LP (Rough Trade ROUGH 29 July 1981) (recorded live at Electric Ballroom 29 February 1980, the group's final show, wherein they played behind a sheet with the spectacle provided by actors and an open mic) (released with free 12-inch LP, Rough 2912. This was recorded live at Notre Dame Hall on 19 July 1979 with the exception of 'Heartbeat', which was recorded at Montreaux on 9 March 1979. Reissued on CD in April 1991 by Mute, WIRE 80 CD, with extra tracks 'Our Swimmer' and 'Midnight Bahnhof Café'. Also issued as limited edition box set)

Our Swimmer/Midnight Bahnhof Café 7-inch (Rough Trade RTO 79 September 1981)

Crazy About Love/Second Length (Our Swimmer)/Catapult 30 12-inch (Rough Trade RT T123 March 1983) (taken from a John Peel session from September 1979)

Snakedrill EP 12-inch (Mute 12MUTE 53 November 1986) (A Serious Of Snakes/Drill/An Advantage In Height/Up To The Sun)

Ahead/Feed Me (live) 7-inch (Mute MUTE 57 March 1987) (also on 12-inch, Mute 12MUTE 57, with additional tracks 'Ambulance Chasers (live)' and 'A Vivid Riot Of Red (live)' plus different version of 'Ahead'. A US-only 12-inch, Enigma V-75503 in April 1987, comprised both versions of 'Ahead' plus the three live tracks)

The Ideal Copy LP (Mute STUMM 42 April 1987) (issued on CD by Mute, CDSTUMM 42, with extra tracks Ahead (alternative version)/A Serious Of Snakes/Drill/Advantage In Height/Up To the Sun/Ambulance Chasers (live)/Feed Me (live)/A Vivid Riot Of Red (live))

Kidney Bingos/Pieta 7-inch (Mute MUTE 67 February 1988) (12-inch version, 12 MUTE 67, adds Kidney Bingos/Over Theirs (live)/Drill (live)/Pieta (la piccolo) to a-side. A 3-inch CD version, CDMUTE 67, featured A-side plus Drill (live) and Pieta. American CDs, 12-inches and cassette versions also issued featuring various permutations of above)

A Bell Is A Cup... Until It Is Struck LP (Mute STUMM 54 May 1988) (issued on CD by

Mute, CDSTUMM 54, with extra tracks The Queen Of Ur & The King Of Um (alternative version)/Pieta/Over Theirs (live)/Drill (live)

Silk Skin Paws (7" remix)/German Shepherds 7-inch (Mute MUTE 84 June 1988) (12-inch version, 12MUTE 84, featured Silk Skin Paws (12-inch remix)/German Shepherds/Ambitious (remix)/Comeback In Two Halves (re-recorded)

Eardrum Buzz/The Offer 7-inch (Mute MUTE 87 April 1989) (12-inch version, 12MUTE 87, adds It's A Boy (instrumental). 3-inch CD, Mute CDMUTE 87, features A-side plus Silk Skin Paws (7-inch remix)/A Serious Of Snakes/Ahead (12-inch version). Limited edition 12-inch version, Buzz Buzz Buzz, LMUTE 87, April 1989, features Eardrum Buzz (live)/Ahead (live)/Kidney Bingos (live))

It's Beginning To And Back Again LP (Mute STUMM 66 May 1989) (issued on CD by Mute, CDSTUMM 66, with extra tracks 'Eardrum Buzz (12-inch version)', 'The Offer', 'In Vivo'. This is, in essence, a document of live shows in Chicago and Portugal, but the contents then underwent some serious studio reappraisal and remixes. But you're better off sticking to Document and Eyewitness)

In Vivo (7-inch mix)/Illuminated (7-inch mix) 7-inch (Mute MUTE 98 July 1989) (12-inch version, 12MUTE 98, features In Vivo (12" mix)/Illuminated (12" mix)/Finest Drops (live). Limited edition 7-inch, LMUTE 98, features In Vivo (7-inch mix) plus Stillbird (Excerpts from Drill). 3-inch CD version, CDMUTE 98, features In Vivo (7" mix)/In Vivo (12" mix)/Illuminated (12" mix)/Finest Drops (live). 12-inch US-only version, Enigma 75044-0, features In Vivo (dance remix)/In Vivo (dance remix instrumental)/In Vivo (dance remix edit)/Illuminated (remix)/Finest Drops (live)

Manscape LP (Mute STUMM 80 May 1990) (issued on CD by Mute, CDSTUMM 80, with extra tracks Life In The Manscape/Stampede/Children Of Groceries)

Life In The Manscape 5-inch CD single (Enigma 75553-2 June 1990, US)

Life In The Manscape (album version)/Life In The Manscape (7-inch remix)/Life In The Manscape (12-inch remix)/Gravity Worship/Who Has Nine?

The Drill LP (Mute/STUMM 74 April 1991)

(issued on CD by Mute, CDSTUMM 74, with extra track (A Chicago) Drill (Live))

Third Day CD (pinkflag pf1 February 2000)

Pink Flag (rh1)/Blessed State/Mercy/Art of Persistence (1st draft)/Pink Flag (rh2) (sold on tour and through Wire's website, 1,000 copies only. Recorded in rehearsal at the Ritz, London, 29 November 1999)

Side X: Twelve Times You/Side U: XU Version 7-inch (pinkflag vpf3 November 2000) (sold through Wire's website)

Read & Burn 01 EP (pinkflag PF4 June 2002)

In the Art of Stopping/I Don't Understand/Comet/Germ Ship/1st Fast/The Agfers of Kodack

Read & Burn 02 EP (Pinkflag PF5 October 2002)

Read & Burn/Spent/Trash/Treasure/Nice Streets Above/Raft Ants/99.9

Send CD (Pinkflag PF6 April 2003)

(mail order version came with extra CD, PF6L: Wire at the Metro, Chicago, 14 September 2002)

ARCHIVE RECORDINGS:

And Here It Is... Again LP (Sneaky Pete 334882 February 1985)

Wire Play Pop LP (Pink PINKY 7 March 1985)

In The Pink LP (Dojo DOJOLP 36 August 1986)

The Peel Sessions 12-inch (Strange Fruit SFPS 041 December 1987)

Practice Makes Perfect/I Am The Fly/Culture Vultures/106 Beats That (issued on CD by Strange Fruit, SFPS CD041, in January 1990)

It's Beginning To And Back Again LP (Mute STUMM 66 May 1989) (issued on CD by Mute, CDSTUMM 66, with extra tracks 'Eardrum Buzz (12-inch version)', 'The Offer', 'In Vivo'. This is, in essence, a document of live shows in Chicago and Portugal, but the contents then underwent some serious studio reappraisal and remixes. But you're better off sticking to Document and Eyewitness)

On Returning (1977-1979) LP (EMI SHSP 4127 July 1989) (issued on CD by EMI, CDP 7 92535 2, with extra tracks Straight Line/106 Beats That/Field Day For The Sundays/Champs/Dot Dash/Another The Letter/Men 2nd/Two People In A Room/Blessed State. reissued on CD by EMI in January 2000

The Peel Sessions Album LP (Strange Fruit SFR 108 January 1990) (issued on CD by Strange Fruit, SFRCD 108, in May 1996. Sessions recorded between January 1978 and September 1979. A must-have, if only for the primal version of 'The Other Window' and the raging Pink Flag tracks from January 1978, though the 15-minute version of 'Crazy About Love' should be marked enthusiasts only)

The A List (1985-1990) double LP (Mute STUMM 116 May 1993) (also issued on CD by Mute, CDSTUMM 116. The track selection was made by a panel of 35 friends and family members asked to choose their favourite tracks)

Behind The Curtain CD (EMI CDGO 2066 May 1995) (this is principally a collection of demo versions from the band's three albums for Harvest, with the first six tracks recorded live at the Roxy in April 1977)

Turns And Strokes CD (WMO WMO 4CD May 1996) (features live and demo material from July 1979 to May 1980)

Coatings double CD (WMO WMO 14CD October 1997) (more archive and demo material)

On The Box: 1979 CD/DVD (Pink Flag PF7TV September 2004) (Superb quality CD/DVD of live concert recorded between Chairs Missing and 154 on St Valentine's Day 1979 for German TV's Rockpalast. The first time the band has been captured in this time period outside of bootlegs. Stunning stuff, with the band at their most ferocious, wild-eyed and insistent, despite a seemingly non-plussed audience. The package comes with an audio CD of the gig as well as the DVD, and an interview in which Wire wind up a clueless journalist)

The Scottish Play: 2004 CD/DVD (Pink Flag PF8TV March 2005) (essentially a DVD release but includes accompanying CD of material recorded in Glasgow and Liverpool during 2004 drawing largely on the Send release, with bonus tracks from their Barbican show)

Miscellaneous:

A Houseguest's Wish: Translations Of Wire's Outdoor Miner CD (Words On Music WM10 November 2004) (I guess this artefact gives some indication of Wire's influence. It collects 19 different takes on perhaps the band's best song, with artists from five countries, including Swervedriver's Adam Franklin, Flying Saucer Attack and Mark Bandola of the Lucy Show, while the contributors shuffle genres from blues to folk to jazz to hardcore punk)

FOOTNOTE:

My immense gratitude to Kevin Eden, author of Everybody Loves A History, the definitive biography of Wire, for his assistance in checking and correcting this draft. I thought it only fair to incorporate some of his comments as a corollary to my own views.

"My own personal take on their stuff is that all the Harvest/EMI stuff is amazing. The 80s stuff I play less. The Ideal Copy has some great moments. A Bell Is A Cup, again, has some moments of brilliance. I think the lyric writing in the 80s was sublime and extremely funny – 'Kidney Bingos', 'Eardrum Buzz' and 'Boiling Boy' stand out. I love It's Beginning To And Back Again for its sheer perversity and trying to re-invent the wheel. Manscape and The First Letter have moments of greatness as well as some duff ones. The 00s Wire are another thing altogether. I never thought they could sustain that ferocity and speed and energy for long and this has proved the case with Bruce's departure from the fold."

The Worst

Ian Hodge (drums), Dave aka Woody (bass), Alan Deaves (lead guitar, vocals).

Musical illiterates on purpose, THE WORST, who did everything in their power to live up to their name, were "kind of" managed by Steve Shy, barman at Manchester punk gossip central, the Ranch bar, and editor of Shy Talk fanzine. They could not play, definitively, and in no way saw this as a drawback, evidenced by Hodge's use of a cheapo Chad Valley kit. Live, they always dressed head to toe in black leather and chains. "Fantastic Band!" recalls Pete Shelley's then girlfriend Gail Egan. "My friend Pam was going out with Ian at the time, and I remember he had Cadillac cars. That drum kit was superb! They never wanted the record deal bit from what I can remember. They just wanted to have a good time. They played the Ranch and were great. I remember Ian getting a tattoo and wearing the gauze that had been put over it, complete with blood and pus, as an earring!"

Jon Savage gave them a full-page feature in Sounds and called them "inspirational". "We didn't really start with the intention of getting anywhere, did we?" they told Savage. "It's only during the last few months that we've all seemed to be aiming for something – none of us had been so sure as to what it was. I think we've found out now." Or as Hodge summed it up: "Punk was like cries for help. You're much better on stage working out your aggression than, say, you are smashing phone-boxes, and that's the sort of urgency the music should have."

Hodge, who originated from Preston and was a former accounting student, was pictured on the cover of the Sex Pistols' Lesser Free Trade Hall bootleg, and featured in a 'new wave' piece in the Sunday People, titled King Of The Punks. He also appeared in a studio debate, alongside John Peel, Pete Shelley and Pastor John Cooper, who 'banned' punk in Caerphilly, about the merits of the nascent movement in a Granada TV Brass Tacks special. Julie G of the Shock remembered the Worst thus: "Ian and Alan were from Preston. They used to go down to London to the 100 Club and saw The Pistols early on. I got to know Ian and Alan around Autumn 1976, when they would go to The Lodestar in Ribchester. Saturday was Roxy and Bowie night but they played 'Anarchy' and 'New Rose' demos – which probably belonged to Ian and Alan. I used to go every other Saturday cos I had a mate who lived in Blackburn and I would stay over. The Lodestar never gets a mention when it comes to early punk venues but I think that place and Manchester's Ranch were the earliest venues outside London to air punk."

As Steve Shy told me: "I wasn't really a manager as such. To be honest, it was a clique. The clique was the Buzzcocks, the Fall, Joy Division to a certain extent – Barney and Hookey. The other ones we only really saw at concerts. Hookey and Barney were part of the Ranch crowd. We were the 'in crowd' sort of thing. It's elitist to say it, but we were. Believe it or not, they could make or break a band. There were probably some good bands that never got a look in. Because somebody in that elitist crowd said they were shit, or whatever."

As Mick Middles wrote in From Joy Division to New Order, "Unlike Buzzcocks or the Fall or Sad Café even, the Worst actually enjoyed languishing in a total lack of ambition." They were, to an extent, 'the real thing'. Their fans included John Cooper Clarke, the Buzzcocks, whom they supported at Birmingham's Barbarella's and later on their tour of Ireland, and Siouxsie Sue, and she's notoriously picky. Alan would also contribute to Pete Shelley's side project, the Tiller Boys. Pete Hook of Warsaw/Joy Division was another advocate. "Two of them, they couldn't play. One had the drum kit and one had the guitar and they just used to rant and rave. Oh, it was great. And he'd smash his kit up at the end. The second gig we did, the Worst played with us. Great days." John McGeoch, too, thought they were fabulous. The only dissenting voice seemed to come from the Sounds critic who dubbed them "colourless, humourless, relentless".

Steve Shy filled me in on their haphazard concerts. "I remember the time they were playing the Shrewsbury Ritz on a Sunday, supposedly supporting the Buzzcocks. And the van broke down with the PA. The Worst turned up, and the Prefects. So the concert was cancelled. We'd come all that way, so we got the bloke who was doing it, and said let us play, let us use the house PA. He wouldn't. But there were a few hundred people there. In the end we talked him into it, and the Worst and the Prefects played together with the house PA, then went round with a hat afterwards." Did they get away with it? "We did all right. We got about £30. We supported the Buzzcocks in Croydon, and went down really well. People got it. It was about a month later they played the Marquee with the Fall. There were three coachloads came from Croydon raving over it."

Savage would review them playing at the Electric Circus's last stand. "They look as though they've stepped right out of the industrial waste, totally uncompromising, blinking in the spotlight. No 'image'. They play not as though their life depends on it, but because it does. There's a hunger there. A three piece; the lead singer moves little, sings high – much is lost in the sound, and when his guitar breaks, they call it a day, with only one song, 'Fast Breeder', staying in the head. They're haunting, seeming to epitomise the evening's movie perfectly." Sadly, they were not included on the attendant concert recording, and nothing else has emerged in the interim. That's about all we know, apart from the fact that Woody once stayed at Ian Brown's house and managed to burn the curtains down after he fell asleep smoking a cigarette. His last gig was the Electric Circus show, after which Robin Utracik replaced him, making his debut as support to the Gang Of Four at Leeds Polytechnic. Utracik: "Therefore we had no bass player, and never found the need to replace Woody, which probably contributed to our unique sound!"

We should remember the Worst as true one-offs, as Steve Shy recalls: "The Worst, whenever they could, they'd charge a toy to get in or a donation. Anything left after taking petrol money out, they used to send that to the Pat Seed Scanner Fund at the hospital. It was only a few pounds at the time, but that was their idea of what punk was about. You're fighting for yourselves and looking after other people." Asked for her favourite record from Manchester by Q in 2006, Linder Sterling of Ludus didn't hesitate to mischievously frame the Worst. "There are no other candidates, regardless of whether or not the Worst actually made a record. Great poets, you know, often simply cannot write a line... too vulgar."

Discography:

The Worst LP (hmmm, details are sketchy on this one. Did it come out, on what label, and when? Answers on a postcard. Probably be out again by the time you read this, if they find the master tapes. Or maybe not)

Wrist Action

Tommy Maltby (vocals), Mark Passi (drums), Pete Smith (guitar), Tony Paine (bass; later replaced by Dave Turvey)

Seminal, in every sense, Brighton punk band, which brought together the talents of later members of Fan Club (Mark Passi) and the Vitamins (Dave Turvey). They played regularly at Brighton's punk haunts the Buccaneer and Alhambra, the highlight of their short sets being theme song 'Get Yourself Some Wrist Action'.

WRIST ACTION were formed in November 1976 by Passi and Paine after they'd heard 'Anarchy In The UK' for the first time. However, they had a bit of previous to hide. At the time of their conversion, they'd both been playing in a funk band, Tempus Fugit, alongside Bob Grover, later of the Piranhas. All three had also been members of So And So's Travelling Whatsits between 1973 and 1976, along with vocalist Trevor Jackman. With punk in its infancy Paine and Passi recruited Maltby and Smith to complete Wrist Action's line-up. Things moved quickly. After playing their debut show at a youth club in Hangleton in March 1977, they were headlining Brighton Art College by the following month.

Wrist Action were prime movers behind the Brighton Fuck The Jubilee show, alongside the Piranhas. They also appeared in a punk documentary, with the Molesters, shown on Southern TV. Their section focused on their offer of a contract by Lightning Records following a show at the Buccaneer. Legendarily, they refused to put ink to this when they found out that there was a stipulation whereby they would have to record songs that Elvis Costello had demo'd for Lightning. Maybe it would have been a good idea to have gone for it – by December 1977 the band was over. Which means the world never did get to hear their 'You Make Me Puke', which would doubtless have dwarfed Costello's offerings in a straight fight.

X-Certs

Clive Arnold (vocals, guitar), Simon Justice (guitar), Phil 'Taff' Lovering (bass), Neil Mackie (bass)

The X-CERTS were formed by Arnold and Justice, and anyone else they could find with access to an instrument, during their final year at school in Bristol in 1977-1978. Initially they took the name Psychos. Some presumed there was a connection with the band of the same name that recorded for Raw Records – there is not. The line-up had solidified by the end of the school year, an event that was celebrated by the customary end of term disco, at which the X-Certs played their first gig. Mackie, in true punk rock style and to the manor born, managed to upset the German exchange students by brandishing a swastika.

Simon Edwards of Heartbeat Records subsequently invited them to contribute a track to his 'Four Alternatives' EP. They cut 'Blue Movies' at Crescent Studios in Bath, which led to a subsequent invitation to contribute to Avon Calling, a document of the Bristol scene that remains one of the finest regional compilations of the era. The NME called their contribution "four-star garage raunch" and they weren't wrong, 'Anthem' is an excellent stab at rudimentary punk.

Thereafter the line-up shuffled, as Arnold and Mackie moved the band in a more dub/reggae direction, recruiting new contributors Kev Mills (guitar) and Chris Bostock (bass) to this end. They also built a solid live reputation, supporting the Only Ones at Bristol University Union and the Angelic Upstarts and Pere Ubu at Trinity Church, while headlining numerous shows around Avon and the West Country. The highlight would be supporting the Clash and Mikey Dread at Sophia Gardens in Cardiff in 1980.

Their next vinyl appearance came on the 1980 compilation The Recorder 2. Two songs were included, 'Queen & Country' and 'Visions Of Fate', though there was no room for their cover of Culture's reggae standard 'Fussing & Fighting' recorded at the same session, one of the highlights of their live shows. 'Queen & Country' was subsequently re-released on CD as part of the Western Stars – The Bands That Built Bristol Volume 1.

By this time, their local reputation established, the X-Certs opted for a belated own-name release. There was interest from Revolver Records, based in The Triangle at the top of Park Street in Bristol. They'd created a new label, Recreational Records, and the X-Certs would become their first release. John Peel played both sides of 'Together' several times, and it also got airplay via Kid Jensen. Great things looked possible. However Bostock, alongside other Bristolian musicians, was lured away to London by Bernie Rhodes to back Johnny Britton, before ending up as backing band to Vic Godard. Bostock and pals would subsequently ditch Godard to enjoy brief chart infamy as JoBoxers. Bostock's defection rather took the wind out of the X-Certs' sails. Clive Arnold: "We played one gig to promote the single with a stand-in bass player, but not being able to find anyone to replace Chris, we disbanded and went our separate ways."

Bostock would subsequently collaborate with Dave Stewart and the Spiritual Cowboys, while Mills worked with Jon Klein and Olli Wisdom in the Specimen. Mackie now runs a Taiko drum group Mugenkyo, based in Scotland, who regularly tour the country and, according to Arnold, are well worth seeing. Lovering, who had previously been a member of the Review, would later join Disorder, becoming one of the few constants in that band's erratic 20-year plus career. Arnold, for his part, is now a TV drama director.

DISCOGRAPHY:

Together/Untogether 7-inch (Recreational Play 1 January 1981)

COMPILATIONS:

Avon Calling – The Bristol Compilation LP (Heartbeat HB 1 1979; 'Anthem') (reissued on CD in October 2005 on Heartbeat/Cherry Red CDMRED 292 with additional track 'You Have Been Warned' plus 'Blue Movies' on bonus CD The Heartbeat Singles Collection)

Four Alternatives 7-inch EP (Heartbeat PULSE 4 1979; 'Blue Movies')

The Recorder 2 LP (1980; 'Queen & Country', 'Visions Of Fate')

ARCHIVE RELEASES:

Western Stars – The Bands That Built Bristol Vol. 1 CD (Bristol Archive Records ARC 001; 'Queen & Country')

Queen & Country/Visions Of Fate 7-inch (77 Records SO26 2003; Japan)

XL5

Bob Simmons (vocals, guitar), Bruce Maine (bass), Dick Simmons (drums)

Named in honour of the Gerry Anderson series Fireball XL5, this Brighton-based group contributed just one track to the Farewell To The Roxy compilation and then disappeared, leaving absolutely no trace. At least until Captain O!'s CD re-release of said compilation, which saw guitarist Bob Simmons contact Mark Brennan. And so the story can be told.

Bob Simmons: "In 1976 I was a good friend of Dave Greenfield's and asked him about starting a group. But he told me he'd joined a band called the Stranglers and they had a year's worth of gigs lined up. Because I couldn't get him as keyboard player, we basically formed a guitar band. First of all it was a fairly basic rock band, and the drummer in that band, Dick Slexia, would later join the Piranhas. All the local bands used to rehearse at the Resources Centre, aka the Crypt. The culture was that most Brighton punk bands rehearsed down there, including the Piranhas. **XL5** came out of another band, Easy Glider. My brother decided to come and join as drummer, and we inherited the bass player from that group in its early stages. Easy Glider in turn came out of another group, Swift, which played with the Troggs and Spencer Davis in 1972 and 1973. Bruce Maine left fairly quickly and then Martin Ayris came down from Canterbury and that became the XL5 line-up."

The band's first gig was at Canterbury Art College in 1976. XL5 started working around London and then played up and down the country. They had an extensive set of originals, including unrecorded and forgotten numbers like 'Sex Tax'. "We had quite a lot of long songs and quite a few short songs and very little in between! Lightning chose 'Here Comes The Knife' for the Roxy album. It was all recorded on the RAK mobile. Unfortunately the album didn't sell that well. We did a tour of Scotland with some other bands to promote it, but it didn't seem to push it a lot. We were up there with the UK Subs – I used to promote them in Brighton and we played a lot of gigs with them in London. Jimmy Pursey was a fan of ours. We used to do the 'XL5' theme as an encore and he leapt up on stage, off his head, and joined in. We had a lot of good fun."

The only tapes that may or may not exist, Simmons thinks, would belong to Martin's brother David Ayris, who recorded the Canterbury Arts College show. "After XL5 ended I got together with Dick Slexia of the Piranhas and the brass section from Dexy's Midnight Runners and we put together a reggae band, the Tribe, which lasted about a year." There was some interest from Pete Waterman, but it never came to anything. Bob Simmons continued to write, notably for Wishbone Ash, and has just completed his first play, set in Brighton.

COMPILATION:

Farewell To The Roxy (Lightning LIP 2 1978; 'Here Comes The Knife') (reissued on CD, Captain Oi! AHOY CD 86, 1996)

X-Ray Spex

Poly Styrene (aka Marianne Elliott; vocals), Jak Airport (aka Jack Stafford; guitar), Lora Logic (aka Susan Whitby; saxophone), B.P. Hurding (aka Chris Chrysler; drums), Paul Dean (bass)

The debate over whether punk truly created a public sphere where women could find their voice and compete with something approaching equality is well rehearsed. But for many, the Slits aside, the ideal metaphor for female emancipation came in the form of Poly Styrene's X-RAY SPEX, scourge of materialists and patriarchs everywhere. At the same time, they reclaimed punk as a rainbow movement – eschewing military black for day-glo and krazy kolor, while their music, not least through school friend Logic's shrill, jarring saxophone, recalled the excited and invigorated squeal of a child in rapture.

"Imagine the ensuing centuries of Judeo-Christian moral debate," Mark Sinker once wrote, "had Moses returned from the mountain carrying not two stone tablets inscribed with five commandments each, but the first Siouxsie and the Banshees LP." "I saw them at the Roxy," noted the aforementioned Siouxsie. "I mean, Poly certainly had a set of lungs. She had a great voice. I think that was the most important thing. But there was also Lora Logic on saxophone. It was just impressive, seeing people like that get up on stage, and spontaneous."

Elliott was born of mixed Somalian (father) and English (mother) parentage in Brixton. As a child she was encouraged to mime in her infant choir because her voice was deemed too loud. She was also present at parties attended by members of Led Zeppelin and Pink Floyd. She bored of school, however – despite having future Queen guitarist Brian May as a maths teacher – and ran away from home, aged 15. "When I was young I used to be so insecure, really full of complexes..." she told the NME in May 1978. "You think all sorts of stupid things about yourself, and of course, that's what's wrong." She'd subsequently become a paid-up member of the hippie movement, involving herself with the Bath Arts Workshop, attending readings by Allen Ginsberg and at one point she'd attempted to live off the land for a year.

In May 1976, as 'Mari Elliott', she cut her first single, 'Little Billy'. Released on GTO Records (GT58 1976), home to Gary Glitter, Billy Ocean and Donna Summer, the accompanying biography talked about her interest in tarot cards and fringe theatre. "I was in my late teens, and that was just before X-Ray Spex," she notes. "I was living in Brixton and I liked patois, and I was also at drama school. I was really into acting. So that's why I did it, it was kind of like acting for me. I didn't really intend to do music, I intended to do acting. I sang it one day to Falcon (Stuart; later X-Ray Spex manager), who was my first boyfriend. We were dating, and I happened to sing him that song. The next thing, I was in a recording studio, and then in some office at GTO, and it was released. It was very strange. Falcon was a film student at the London Film School, and I was at the Oval House Drama School, where I met him. He came in and I was on the stage in a little fringe production. But then I didn't get into RADA. But I ended up making that record. It wasn't particularly where I wanted to go, because I was working with session musicians, and I wanted to do my own kind of music and have a band."

By now he'd travelled widely and temped for dozens of companies including Woolworth's – two experiences that would help shape her worldview. However, it was never the case that she worked on Woolies' pick'n'mix counter. "That was Falcon's idea, the sweet counter thing. He had this idea that I'd be like a Sandie Shaw type girl, who had been reported as working on the floor of a lightbulb factory. But it was easy to get jobs in those days. I was a copy typist at Woolworth's head office, just a temp; I was with a recruitment agency. I did lots of different day jobs for various companies. I didn't have a lot of qualifications. My grandfather had built up his own business by the time he was in his 30s, and he hadn't had the money to attend school. So I always had that in my background, so I didn't really worry about things like qualifications."

The 'Mari' single comprised a reggae-tinged A-side addressing teenage pregnancy and calypso-influenced flip, 'What A Way'. Melody Maker actually gave the disc a mildly encouraging review. 'What A Way' was co-written with Stuart, who alongside Elliott attended a show by the Pistols, supporting Budgie, on her 19th birthday. As Elliott confirmed in England's Dreaming: "I liked the way they (Sex Pistols) were writing about their surroundings; it was definitely a change in consciousness. It was painting the world to be ugly, which it is from a certain point of view: there are some horrific things that are happening so why whitewash everything?" But it wasn't so much that she was impressed by the music, more it convinced her she could get up and do her thing. "Basically they were not that good," she'd later tell John Robb. "But I realised it didn't have to be so polished. It could be rawer."

It was Stuart who invented her new identity while she was running a stall at the Beaufort Market on the King's Road. "Poly Styrene was the name Falcon gave me," she told me in 2005. He said, 'I've got a good name for you' one day while I was doing the shop. It wasn't a name for me personally; it was a name for my fashion label, so it was my designer name. If anyone's got any original Poly Styrene clothes, they would know I used to have these labels I would hand sign. You know school labels you would sew into clothes? I would sew those in, with that little logo in indelible ink. I was selling things like skinny Day-Glo ties there. My friend worked with Zandra Rhodes, and I used to find fabrics and come up with designs and she'd actually physically hand sew them. I'd put these little Poly Styrene labels in, because that was actually my designer name."

Influenced by "the Artful Dodger, Johnny Rotten and my singing teacher," she placed an advert for fellow "Young punx who want to stick it together" in the pages of Melody Maker.

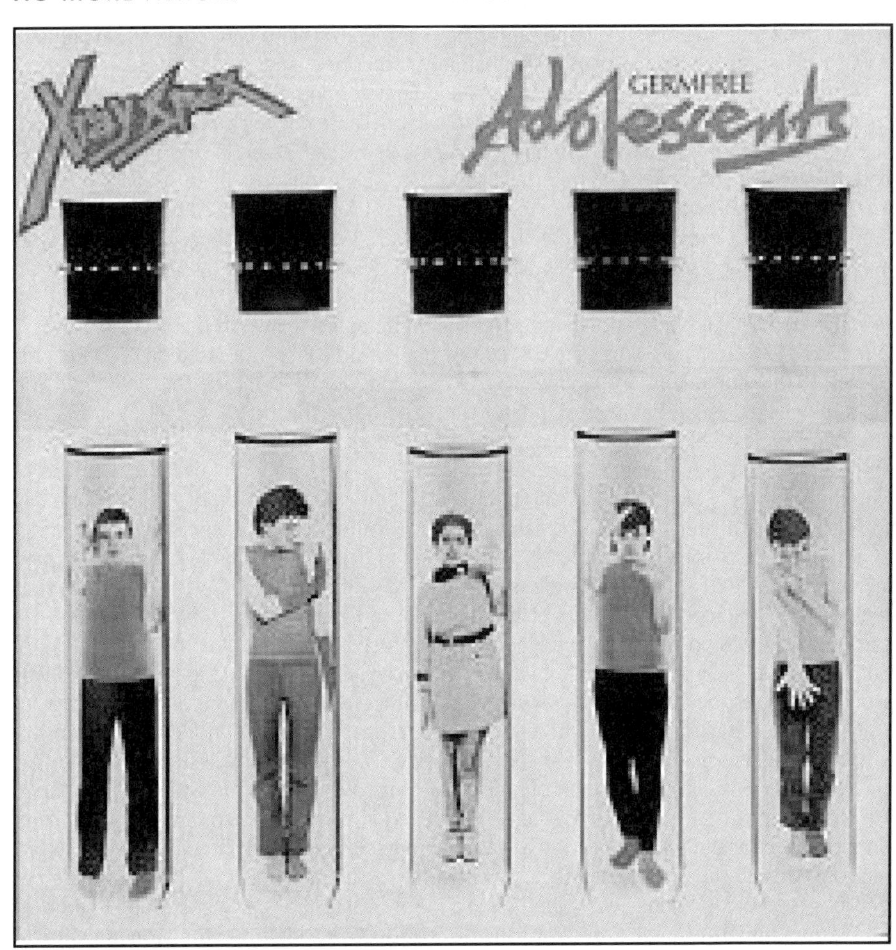

The sleeve of X-Ray Spex's debut album.

"I don't know how – I just did! It was just that time when anyone could form a band!" she told Julie Burchill and Tony Parsons in The Boy Looked At Johnny. Jak Airport and Paul Dean were quickly aboard, followed by Hurding, who had previously roadied for Skrewdriver, having formed his own youth club punk band, Shag Nasty. The final component would be Lora Logic, then only 16.

For Poly, X-Ray Spex remained indivisible from the Beaufort Market scene. "We had people like Olli from the Unwanted, he had a shop there. And Dave Vanian's wife was next door to me. Robot, they were there. They were selling brothel creepers, that whole 50s retro look. Robot went on to Covent Garden, but they started there. So lots of designers were there. It was an upmarket fleamarket, I suppose. It was a good location, just round the corner from Vivienne Westwood's shop. I had people coming over from New York to check my place out, all the buyers used to come around. It was like a little Mecca for alternative fashion – Joe Strummer, Sebastian Conran. There was a guy who used to come in and buy ties from me who was the manager of the Man in the Moon, or maybe the downstairs bar only. But the downstairs bar there at the time was very, very quiet, there was nothing happening. I had a whole entourage of people who would come into my shop and hang out."

"He just asked one day when he found out I also had a band if I'd like a residency. So we did a residency at the Man in the Moon every Wednesday night. We had Annie Lennox play there, before she was in the Eurythmics, Adam and the Ants, Bruno Wizard from the Rejects, etc. We had a very arty set for an audience, people like Andrew Logan, Zandra Rhodes, all those people who hung out on the King's Road fashion scene. Although it was a very small scene, it was very happening. We were like art punks. If it hadn't been for Beaufort Market, and me being there, doing all the fashion stuff, I wouldn't have started playing live half as fast. Although I had a band and I was rehearsing, it was that venue that gave us our identity; and separated us from the other punk bands. We had our own club nights, we ran it, looked after the door, and ran the whole thing ourselves, and let people play there from other parts of the country that we thought would be good."

Their ascent, even by punk standards, was vertical. They were filmed by a Youth TV show, and their third gig was recorded for the 1977 live album, The Roxy, London WC2. Among the audience were Jon Savage and Ari Up of the Slits, both of whom were instant converts, though Elliott would later claim the latter didn't fancy the competition and pulled her microphone wires out of the PA. A ramshackle version of 'Oh Bondage Up Yours' neatly defined Elliott's inability to accept her place in the world (the rest of the set would later be released on CD, revealing both the group's inherent energy and flair and their early musical failings).

'Bondage' was a spectacular call to arms. Playing on the old nursery adage, "Little girls should be seen and not heard," it was a savage rebuttal of submissiveness, acceptance and the dearth of female ambition – though it sounded, aesthetically, more like a celebration and affirmation of identity. However, while the lyrics addressed conformity and consumption rather than sexual dominion, the group was certainly skating around that interpretation. It was also not written about the punk scene, as many assumed – Elliott had actually made a demo of the song in 1975 with Gary Moore of Thin Lizzy playing guitar.

'Bondage' was released as a single shortly after they signed with Virgin Records, following a minor bidding war, backed by 'I Am A Cliché', which predicted some of punk's pratfalls. Elliott's toe-curling shriek wasn't for everyone – later she would reveal the warmth in her voice, but initially it was simply a weapon. But it was not untrained. "No, it was very, very, very trained singing. I didn't do it in the style I was traditionally trained in. Obviously my singing tutor would have liked me to go into opera, but I had different ideas. But I still use his techniques. But yes, the idea behind that style of singing is that you can throw your voice to the back of the room without having to strain it." The savagery of the vocal was "just something that the lyric of that song demands. Because I was more interested in acting initially, it's like playing a part. So you do what's required for the songs." I asked her if that was true of many of those early songs – that she was, in effect, acting? "Definitely. I wrote them specifically like that. It was an act. I would write songs around this character, Poly Styrene. It wasn't my own name."

'Bondage' was banned from radio, much to Richard Branson's pleasure, but failed to dent the charts, which was less pleasing. So the band passed to EMI. Somewhat ironically given Elliott's already strident outlook on the counterfeit culture of materialism, they pumped more money into advertising spend than the advance they gave the band. 'Poly Styrene' was widely acknowledged as one of the new movement's most eloquent lyricists, while her fashion sense – bin liners and braces – made her instantly recognisable and photogenic. Which was sometimes awkward given the band's lyrical focus. "If somebody said I was a sex symbol, I'd shave me 'ead tomorrer," she told Sounds in 1977. "'Oh Bondage Up Yours' ain't about sex particularly. In fact, I don't even think of myself as a girl when I'm on stage. I think I'm sexless. Girls that go and flaunt themselves are using the oldest trick in the book. I'm just me. I just do what I feel like. Do anything you wanna do. Individualism. That's what it's all about, isn't it?" And she wasn't really wearing a bin liner, incidentally. "It was actually a green foam-backed designer tank dress, by the young fashion student Sophia Horgan, thank you."

By the time of their second single, Logic had formed Essential Logic, to be replaced by Rudi Thompson. There were suggestions that she'd been 'persuaded' to leave because she was attracting too much attention. But given Poly's reluctance to embrace the limelight, this seems an odd observation. The truth, as Poly confirmed to Richie Unterberger, was rather more prosaic. "She couldn't really (tour), she had to finish her education. And when we used to play live, she used to play the saxophone over all my lyrics. I could never hear myself sing! I couldn't actually discipline her into playing in the spaces when I wasn't singing."

The group's four singles for EMI were, arguably, even better than the debut. 'The Day The World Turned Day-Glo' started the run with a stampede of frantic instruments, vituperative, elasticised vocals (a screech that could "disinfect the Roxy toilets", noted Greil Marcus) and a lyric that made the plastic landfill of the 70s sound like a new, unexplored planet. "ICI inventions like polystyrene and new science fabrics – everybody was wild about them in the 60s," Poly recalled for Top Ten. "And what would happen eventually if it gets recycled back into the earth? You'd end up having see-through fibre leaves from the rayon trees. It was about the sci-fi dream gone out of control." As the late Falcon Stuart once confirmed, "The brilliant thing about Spex's songs was that each song was a concept in its own right, which worked as both music and a message. The Pistols were about anarchy, The Clash revolution, and Spex offered a third option, exploring the delights and dangers of consumerism and the techno synthetic universe."

Those concepts, arising out of concerns about environmental responsibility, and pre-packaged culture, were incredibly prescient. "I came from the fashion industry so I could see the way things were going," Elliott told me. "Also, as a young post-war 60s child, I was very aware of changes that were taking place rapidly around me. I remember as a young girl going to an old style grocery store, where the cheese was still on a block and cut by hand with a wire cutter, and I would take this home for my mother in a brown paper bag. When I was a little older, the supermarket was being introduced on the high streets and slowly things were becoming more packaged and more consumer friendly. Reading Time magazine in my late teens and having attended an Earth fair in North Devon a few years prior to this, I was exposed to the re-cycling of organic and non-organic waste while at this festival. So on the one hand there was this counter culture of environmentalism and on the other there were very futuristic articles crossing the Atlantic about genetics and consumerism. I always felt that if you strayed too far away from Mother Nature human beings would screw up! I guess that affected my writing. 'Synthetic Fibre see-thru leaves fell from the rayon trees'. A nightmare scenario where consumer led passion for everything that is modern destroys the planet. In hindsight I do think that everything that is derived from the earth must break back down into earth matter eventually."

They made it over to CBGBs for a two-week stint in March 1978, although any progress in that 'market' was impeded by the fact that their subsequent debut album wasn't released there until Caroline did the decent thing in 1992. Second EMI single 'Identity', the video filmed at Andrew Logan's studio in Butler's Wharf, was another subject close to Poly's heart. Yes, it touches on fame, specifically mentioned in the lyric, but the heart of the song is about living with the hidden self – Poly Styrene, of course, being a separate entity from the author. Here she seems ambivalent, at best, about her creation, as if her very soul is in some way tainted by it.

But by the advent of 'Germ Free Adolescents', X-Ray Spex's biggest hit and most deeply moving song, the group was shedding its shrill, occasionally atonal approach and writing timeless pop songs. "'Germ Free Adolescents' came about through me and Jak messing about in the studio one day and experimenting with delayed echo. He came up with this great sound that hadn't really been heard before. At the time I wanted to write a love song, but all the love songs were really awful. So I tried to make it really clinical, to see if that would work." It's a wonderfully haunting melody and all, but there's something about the lyric that is so depersonalised, so ransacked of emotional attachment and feeling, that it just sounds utterly heartbreaking.

Elliott was already expressing concerns about being "totally exhausted" and subject to music industry machinations she wanted no part of to the NME, while touring in the summer of 1978. "It's strange because it's not real. I tried not to get involved in any of it, but up to a point you can't help it, because people try and get you sucked into it and pull you into their little games, and I don't want to get pulled into anybody's little games… nothing actually took me over, but I could see that it might, and I felt very vulnerable." By the time the tour reached Doncaster, she claimed to have seen a "bright disc of light" leave her body at three in the morning – reawakening her interest in finding a more spiritually nourishing lifestyle. Which is fine, but a bit of a downer for those who had adored what she'd done up to now. Naturally, the press ripped into her.

Germ Free Adolescence (aka Germ Free Adolescents depending on which part of the album sleeve you think takes precedence) was also the title of X-Ray Spex's sole album, which reached number 30 in the UK charts. It's rightfully considered a landmark in terms of both feminism and punk, though its appeal crossed gender and international frontiers. Among its many fans are Mike D of the Beastie Boys and Brody Dalle of the Distillers, while Kathleen Hanna of Bikini Kill and practically the entire Riot Grrrl movement have acknowledged their indebtedness. Hurding would later bump into Henry Rollins in the studio by accident. Rollins: "I was all over him like a cheap suit with questions. No memorabilia, no live tapes – nothing but the memories. I was crushed."

The singles were, as previously noted, outstanding, but 'Let's Submerge' is a perfect, vivacious snapshot of the real, aesthetically brutal London of the time and 'I Live Off You', with its kiddie-chorus, a bleak admission of co-dependency. 'Obsessed With You' returned to the lyrical terrain of 'Identity', but this time from an outsider's vantage point. "My mind is like a switchboard," Poly noted in the highly theatrical 'Plastic Bag', drawing, one assumes, on her temping experience, but also encapsulating the confusion and excitement of punk. Given that the majority of the lyrics had been written when she was 15, it was an extraordinarily coherent broadside of ideas, images and words.

'Highly Inflammable' was backed by the splendid 'Warrior In Woolworths' in April 1979, but the band's split, which came as no surprise given the evident strain Elliott was facing, was announced in August. Unhappy with their one-time leader's new 'acoustic' material and reluctance to tour, X-Ray Spex disbanded (although John Glin, formerly of Newcastle's the Young Bucks, temporarily replaced Thompson). For a while the remainder of the band contemplated advertising for a new singer as Classix Nouveaux – Hurding and Airport eventually recruiting Sal Solo, though Airport would leave before they cut their first single. Jak Airport and Paul Dean also worked as the inspiringly titled Airport & Dean. Glin formed the Living Legend. Poly Styrene, under that name, cut a solo album – the haunting and emotionally candid Translucence. And it was beautiful, if somewhat more serene and restrained than X-Ray Spex – a continuation and enhancement of the kind of nursery rhyme-ska she'd first reached towards on 'Highly Inflammable'.

Elliott's distrust of consumer society saw her link up with the Hare Krishnas, where she took the name Maharani. In tandem with being quoted as having seen a UFO in a magazine article, it saw her widely labelled as having gone cuckoo – indeed, an industry rumour that she was actually a schizophrenic, following a breakdown, persists to this day. However, she was coaxed back to the stage in September 1991 as part of a sell-out punk revival concert at the Brixton Academy. She also worked on Boy George's 'Bow Down Mister' and the Dream Academy's 'Love'. Rumours of her musical demise were exaggerated – she has continued to make music during these wilderness years, much of it stockpiled due to the lack of a record label.

X-Ray Spex finally returned to the studio in 1995, completing the self-produced Conscious Consumer, released by Receiver in October 1995. The cast list included Dean and Lora Logic, while the guitars were provided, under a pseudonym, by Crispian Mills of Kula Shaker, who had long been a family friend of Poly's through his mother's connection with the Hare Krishna movement. Kula Shaker's drummer Paul Winterhart was also involved. New product it may have been, but many of the songs had been written up to 15 years earlier for a projected follow-up to Germ Free Adolescents. Conscious Consumer was dismissed by the critics, but while the music lacked the urgency and verve of old, the lyrics were just as forthright. "Johnny's got an addiction," began 'Fast Food Junkies', "He's strung out without conviction/He was raised with a microwave/Sticky trashy fast food slave." 'Peace Meal' was defiantly pro-vegetarian, and far more accusatory and didactic than previous writing. 'Dog In Sweden' paraphrased and name-checked Iggy Pop while disparaging the rock'n'roll circus, while 'Good Time Girl' was the closest she came to revisiting the sentiments of 'Oh Bondage'.

Shows were planned for early the next year but were pulled when Elliott broke her hip after being hit by a fire engine. When she recovered, she fell out with the booking agent, who went ahead and set up gigs without her – which resulted in one scheduled show with a replacement singer, with the singer's absence marked by a note stating she was not present due to "circumstances beyond their control". Elliott had to issue legal proceedings to prevent the con. Or, as she told Ian Canty: "Everybody was a loser. Greed and the green eyed monster called envy really messed up that project and it was very unfortunate from my point of view, as I had worked so hard on it all. But it was a lesson for me to be more discerning when I employ

people and not to be fooled that everybody in the Hare Krishna movement has the same goals. There really are a lot of spiritual posers out there!"

Sadly, Jack Stafford died in August 2004 after a two-year fight against cancer. He had been working as part of the BBC corporate and public relations team. A family friend sent this report of his funeral to the X-Ray Spex website. "Amongst the guests were Bob Tyler, the very man who taught Madonna to play the guitar, who sang 'Perfect Day' accompanied by bass guitarist Paul Dean. For the last year of his life he turned to organic food. With his eco-friendly mind he requested to have a coffin made completely from recycled paper, a sight for the people, but typical of his loving nature."

In the meantime Marianne Elliott-Said finally released some new material. Much of the content of Flower Aeroplane had been written as the follow-up to Germ Free Adolescents, but was shelved in favour of Conscious Consumer when it became obvious that the music industry wouldn't stomach such a departure from X-Ray Spex's perceived sound and place. It revisited several songs first heard on Translucence, and is available online from her immaculately curated website. She is currently planning her memoirs.

Discography

Oh Bondage Up Yours!/I am A Cliché 7-inch (Virgin VS-189 October 1977) (also released on 12-inch, VS-189-12)

The Day The World Turned Day-Glo/I Am a Poseur 7-inch (EMI INT-553 March 1978) (released on orange and black vinyl)

Identity/Let's Submerge 7-inch (EMI INT-563 July 1978) (released on pink and black vinyl)

Germ Free Adolescents/Age 7-inch (EMI INT-573 October 1978)

Germ Free Adolescents LP (EMI INS-3023 November 1978) (CD reissue, Virgin/Artificial CDVM 9001 1991, adds 'Oh Bondage Up Yours!' Reissued again in 2005 on Art-I-Ficial/Sanctuary, with the addition of seven John Peel tracks)

Highly Inflammable/Warrior In Woolworths 7-inch (EMI INT-583 1979) (some in red vinyl)

Conscious Consumer CD (Receiver Records RR CD 205 November 1995)

ARCHIVE RELEASES:

Live At The Roxy LP (Receiver Records RRCD/MC/LP 140 March 1991) (Just 25 minutes long. Witness the bemused audience reaction. Completely ramshackle but a vital historical snapshot)

Anthology dbl CD (Sanctuary 81148 2002) (It seems a feat of archival overindulgence to eke out X-Ray Spex's output over two CDs. And indeed it is, but this is a well-packaged document, featuring Adolescents, some demos and instrumental versions, plus those Live At The Roxy tracks once again, a couple from Conscious Consumer, and some decent sleevenotes from Mark Paytress. Although it's something of a pity that the 'dayglo' reproduction renders them practically indecipherable...)

Xtraverts

Nigel Martin (vocals), Steve Westwood (guitar), Mark Chapman (bass), Andy Crawford (drums)

The XTRAVERTS were High Wycombe's premier punk band of the late-70s, alongside Zyklon B, Plastic People and the Jones Boys (later Red Beat). Their debut single, released on a label set up by Spike Jones (formerly of 70s Buckinghamshire band the Shucks) managed to secure them a few Peel plays. They started out with original drummer Dave Lee, before he decided there was more money to be made on the dinner and dance circuit backing a girl playing bagpipes.

Andy Crawford replaced him, while Glen Spicer joined the band from the Plastic People as lead guitarist. Spicer: "I was with the Plastic People and got kicked out by Gary Quelch, who wanted to take over as singer. They had a meeting and decided I wasn't part of the band any more. Steve Hylands, my friend in the Plastic People, put me in touch with the Xtraverts and they came round to see me. They'd just released the debut single." Spicer was a little more technically fluent than many in his immediate peer group. "I used to organise gigs down in Wycombe with the Plastic People. When the bands tuned their guitars before starting, I used to be the only one who knew how to do it properly."

The idea of a shared single with his former band Plastic People came about through local businessman Lloyd Walker. "He had a record stall in Wycombe Fayre, an indoor market. He wanted to be an entrepreneur and it was him who decided on the shared single. We had a competition between the bands to find out who was buying it for which side." The winners of that contest are lost to the mists of time and false accounting.

The band were tremendously popular in their local environs, their reputation lasting long after the graffiti extolling their virtues was scrubbed from Wycombe's civic spaces. The Xtraverts even appeared on a local TV show, Twentieth Century Box, hosted by Danny Baker. But events didn't run smoothly. "That was an interesting day. I had a Triumph motorbike and sidecar, which they were going to use in the segment. We were doing these shots in Saunderton, which is in the Chiltern Hills near Wycombe. They were just setting the camera up on the hill and we were moving into position, and we had a head on collision with a car. The driver had been watching the cameras and wasn't paying attention. I pulled into the side as she came past. The next thing I knew, she went straight into us. I had to break the car open to get her out after she slid into a ditch. Danny Baker said he'd sort us out with the insurance if there were any problems, but he never did. We had a 30-second segment, which got about 15 seconds air-time and got £50 for appearing."

The band ground to a halt when Martin was sent to prison, just after they'd recorded their debut album, primarily using drummer Richard, a 14-year-old ingenue borrowed from local band Patrol. These sessions were never released until years later. Spicer was left to pick up the studio bill. "Nigel Martin got into a fight at the Friars in Aylesbury, and the silly sod used a knife. I didn't go out with them that night. I didn't hear about it till the next rehearsal, when everyone was getting nervous. The victim's name was Spinsky, I think. Eventually one of Nigel's friends broke down under pressure from the police. Nigel was very capable of starting World War Three. That was his biggest problem." Part of the Xtraverts' tough image arose from the fact that the Windsor Hell's Angel chapter had adopted them and provided security for their shows.

Interest in the band was rekindled when Dizzy of Detour Records found out that the group had a whole album's worth of unreleased back catalogue, and put it out as the first release on his specialist new imprint, Bin Liner. To celebrate its release, on 4 April 1997, the band reunited for new shows. But Spicer couldn't get the rest of the band to maintain their enthusiasm for playing music, so the momentum gradually faded away. Among those who took part in the reunion were Mark Riley, the original 1977 guitarist with the Xtraverts, who'd gone on to play with Matt Bianco. The drummer was Steve McCormack, who'd played with the band at various points and would later go on to impersonate Billy Idol on Stars In Their Eyes. Andy Crawford's allegedly 'formidable' wife had banned him from returning to the drum stool.

Glen Spicer went on to form Cherry Black Dawn, who were operational until 1993 and released one single in 1984, 'Blue Baby Blue', coincidentally the name of the wartime jeep he's currently 'doing up'. Spicer is now Jacquie Blue and is a regular on daytime TV, where she openly discusses her gender reassignment. She sees her personal and musical development as separate, but does note that: "Punk brought me out cos I could portray what I was without the hassle. You could do whatever you wanted. You'd be happily wandering around in Wycombe, then you'd turn round and 50 people would be walking behind you, a small army of misfits. You never get people following you around like that at this age."

Discography:

Blank Generation/A-Lad-Insane 7-inch (Spike SP 001 1979) (250 copies)
Police State/B-side by Plastic People 7-inch (Rising Sun RS-2 1979)
Speed/1984 7-inch (Xtravert Records 1981)
So Much Hate LP/CD (Bin Liner Rubbish LP001, CD002 May 1997)

Yobs

Jack Black (aka Ebeneezer Polak; drums, vocals), Matt Dangerfield (aka Noddy Oldfield; vocals, guitar), Honest John Plain (aka H J Bedwetter; vocals, guitar), Kid Reid (aka Kid Vicious; vocals, bass, guitar), Casino Steel (aka Baron Von Bratboy; keyboards, vocals)

The YOBS were an offshoot of first-wave punk stalwarts the Boys, having a hearty ho ho ho at the expense of the Yuletide season. Happily, this meant they had both the instrumental muscle and the irreverence to pull it off. Their debut single in this format, a cover of Chuck Berry's 'Run Rudolph Run', featured a picture of Rudolph Hess on the cover (the Wehrmacht would feature heavily in subsequent covers too, which all helped to engender that commercially useful element of controversy). They kept up the gag with a version of 'Silent Night' the following year, released while main band the Boys were in dispute with record company NEMS (owned by RCA, who switched all their resources into promoting Elvis after he died). They then issued an entire album of festive follies on Safari in 1980.

The original cartoon which became the cover for The Worst Of The Yobs

"The main reason behind the Yobs," Matt Dangerfield told me, "was that we wanted to use a rehearsal studio and it was our favourite studio. They wouldn't let us book in because NEMS owed them money. This was normal at the time for NEMS. Everybody they used, they didn't pay their bills. They were working on the American principle that if you don't pay your bills, something like 60% of your creditors will drop it. Or you just pay up at the last minute if they really get heavy. A photographer friend of mine actually got a court order against NEMS for a photographic bill. And the bailiffs went round and they couldn't take anything away, because nothing was in their name. So we booked into this rehearsal studio as the Yobs. Then shortly after that, when we were on strike with NEMS, a bootlegger friend offered to bootleg us so we could make some money. So we bootlegged ourselves as the Yobs, and that's how it started. It started as a Christmas thing, then it became kind of a tradition." Jack Black: "The Yobs were a variation on B-O-Y-S. Everybody knew you couldn't have a hit without being a known band. We did the Yobs for a laugh, and they became very, very popular. It was just mucking about with Christmas carols. It was totally done for a laugh."

With Baron Von Bratboy aka Casino Steel ducking out, the Yobs' Christmas album was released in 1980, allowing his fellow travellers opportunity to adopt similarly silly pseudonyms – H J Bedwetter, Noddy Oldfield, Ebeneezer Polak and Kid Vicious. The songs were chosen, recorded and mixed at Pete Townshend's Eel Pie Studios in just two days. Their re-write of '12 Days Of Christmas' was fabulously lewd: "12 smelly cunts, 11 faggot rings, 10 turd burgers, nine ways of wanking," etc. There was also a further single, 'Yobs On 45', parodying the voguish Stars On 45 series.

That was it until 1991 when they released 'Xmas II'. This was followed by a live album, Leeds 3 Amps Utd 0. They also had plans for a best of, but with tracks stretched across three labels, they were unable to negotiate its release. So the five original members reconvened in September 2001 alongside a new drummer, Johnny Hosepipe (aka Vom Ritchie). Fourteen Yuletide classics were re-cut, alongside a new song, 'Who Had All The Christmas Cake?', to produce their tombstone effort, The Worst Of The Yobs.

DISCOGRAPHY:

Run Rudolph Run/The Worm Song 7-inch (NEMS NES 114 1977)

Silent Night/Stille Nacht 7-inch (Yob YOB 79 1978)

Christmas Album (Safari RUDE 1 1980) (reissued on CD in 1990 on Great Expectations PIPLP 006, and in 2000 by Captain Oi! AHOY CD 157, which additionally featured bonus tracks Run Rudolph Run/The Worm Song/Silent Night (Single Version)/Stille Nacht/Rub A Dum Dum (Single Version)/Another Christmas (Single Version)/Yobs On 45).

Rub A Dum Dum/Another Christmas 7-inch (Safari YULE 1 1981)

Yobs On 45/The Ballad Of Warrington 7-inch (Fresh FRESH 41 1982)

Xmas II LP/CD (Receiver RR LP/CD 153 1991)

Leeds 3 Amps United 0 LP (Revolution REX CD 12 1995) (live and unplugged, whatever that means)

The Worst Of The Yobs LP/CD (Captain Oi! AHOY CD 184 2002 and LP Knock-Out Records KOLP 149 2001) (note: because of the impossibility of getting three former record companies to agree with each other, the tracks were specially re-recorded for this CD, alongside a brand new composition, 'Who Had All The Christmas Cake'. Nice cartoon artwork!)

Zero Zero

Steve Jamison (guitar, vocals), Julia James (bass), Keith Shadwick (saxophone), Nick Sinclair (drums)

ZERO ZERO were authors of a little-known indie-punk single, which came in a great comic-strip cover, which would have probably dwelled in obscurity for ever had it not been compiled on Killed By Death #24. As is so often the case with these things, such exposure has pushed up its value with collectors. They are not to be confused with a later Zero Zero who recorded a session for John Peel in 1991.

Was their saxophonist the same Keith Shadwick who is now the famed jazz author? Yup. "In mid 1978 I came back to London after being away in Australia for more than 15 years. In early January 1979 I answered an ad in one of the music mags: Melody Maker or NME, I can't recall which. In fact, I answered two the same week – two very different bands looking for a sax player. One was a south London outfit doing modified blues, the other Zero Zero. I talked to Steve Jamison on the phone and he told me they were based in Highgate, were at that time a guitar-bass-drums trio and wanted a sax player. The original ad said they were recording a single. It turned out they were putting up the money to make their own single. They had no management or booking agency or anything of that sort. They had a gig booked in Jackson's Lane Community Centre for about a month later. The recording session was already booked, at a small Cambridge studio, for 5 February, according to my notebook. I took the tube up to Highgate and met Steve and his girlfriend Julia, who was also the bass player. They lived in a small terraced place on the 'wrong' side of Highgate – which amused them at the time. Steve was a well-spoken, well-educated guy, very talkative, ambitious, full of ideas, most of them to do with subjects for songs, if I remember accurately. Their friend Nick turned up for the next meeting. He was the drummer. Taciturn, like most drummers, but likeable enough. I have a feeling he might have been in more than one band at the time. By that time I certainly was, because I was also rehearsing with the south London band. I'm pretty sure I let both bands know this, but tried to be discreet about it."

"Steve's musical technique was pretty primitive, and his songwriting basic, but he had an urgency to his vocals and an enjoyment of sound that were attractive properties. He was also a decent lyricist. So we worked at the two songs he wanted to record – 'Chinese Boys' and 'Coupé de Ville Dawn' and also some cover versions that I no longer recall in order to do this gig. Steve had booked the studio but it became clear prior to the session that none of the three had been inside one before. I'd done quite a bit one way or the other, so I ended up co-producing and mixing the two sides with the studio engineer, a guy called Tony Durant."

And that was the story behind the single, almost. "When it came to sorting out a sleeve design, nobody had much of a clue until I remembered that a friend of mine, Michael Fitzjames, who was then doing financial and political cartoons for the Guardian, was a keen fan of the current scene. It was quickly arranged that Michael would do the whole design. As he was practised at working in black ink, he did a really great set of cartoon-like pictures for the back and front sleeve, worthy of much better paper than that chosen to print them on for the sleeve itself! He also did the record centre labels."

Sadly, very few people got to see either Michael's work, nor Zero Zero's. "The single vanished without trace as far as I can remember. I don't recall it being played even by John Peel (another single I ended up producing in 1981, for The Sadista Sisters, was by contrast a John Peel pick of the week at that time). So that was that. With no gigs, and Steve quite naturally wanting to command the songwriting, and with a very limited set of musical abilities to work with, I decided to go with the South London group, Lowdown. So I regretfully resigned from Zero Zero. I liked Steve, Julia and Nick and we parted on good terms. I have no idea what happened to the band after that. This would have been March-April 1979. That's about it! I have never come into contact with anyone from Zero Zero again but it was fun at the time and I have nothing but good feelings about it all."

DISCOGRAPHY:

Chinese Boys/Coupé de Ville Dawn 7-inch (Interference INT 001 1979)

Zips

John McNeill (vocals, guitar), Brian Jackson (lead guitar), Joe Jaconelli (drums, vocals), Phil Mullen (bass, vocals)

Formed in Glasgow in 1978 after McNeill and Jackson split from pub rockers Road Angel to try their hand at the burgeoning punk rock movement. "The original ZIPS were inspired with the energy and freedom of expression that the punk movement, in general, provided," McNeill told me, "and politicised by the Clash. We much preferred doing benefits for the likes of Rock Against Racism than standard pub gigs. Personally, I get a great kick out of using the music to draw attention to issues, and make people think about things they weren't aware of. I totally believe a punk band has almost an obligation to write politically charged songs. Let's face it, there are enough lightweight, pure-entertainment-for-the-now-people, songs out there."

"As far as gigs go, the Zips played all the so-called legendary local venues like the Mars Bar in Glasgow. Tiny wee bar, led to a backroom where the bands played, at floor level, as I remember. So, when you had about 100 punters packed into a space for 50, the people at the back had no chance of seeing the band – unless they pogoed! I'm sure the Skids played there. Simple Minds (known then as Johnny And The Self-Abusers) definitely did. And The Zones. They used to sell Mars bars behind the bar, 'cos they thought it would prevent Rowntree's/Nestle from suing them. It didn't work, and they had to change the name to Countdown. It's now a gravel-covered temporary car park. When I pass the site, at night, I could swear I hear the echoes of the music trapped in the rubble. The Bungalow Bar in Paisley was another tiny wee place, but terrific atmosphere. A guy called Loudon Temple used to book the bands, and there were some classic nights – Chelsea, Cockney Rejects (who we supported), Sham 69, and loads of others."

The two most popular venues the original Zips played were Custom House Quay and the Atlantis. "The Custom House Quay, which is the walkway beside the River Clyde, opposite Glasgow's Barfly, had, up until a couple of years ago, a bandstand, which was owned by the council. They used to put on mostly jazz and hoochter-choochter concerts in spring and summer, and we approached them to hire it for a gig. To our surprise, they not only let us use it, but also paid us a £25 performance fee! We put on fairly regular Saturday lunchtime gigs, and young bands used to turn up with no more than their guitars and blag their way into doing a 10 or 15 minute set. One of them, Raw Deal, later became The Bluebells. It was an ideal venue 'cos it was free entry in the city centre, on a Saturday, and open to all age groups."

The Zips drew a large crowd, mainly on the strength of word of mouth. "We also got mentions on Radio Clyde's token punk show, Streetsounds.. Eventually other bands began doing gigs there as well, and during 1979 there was a real 'scene' based around the place. It was demolished in 2003, after years of neglect, to make way for a future marina. Funny thing was, we were at the planning and storyboarding stage for a video to be shot there, for our last CD ('Hotwired'). The Atlantis, a pub in Kilbowie Road, Clydebank, which is still there, provided us with a residency every Thursday night and a steady income for over a year. We used to do covers in the first set and Zips' originals in the second set. Then, gradually, as we wrote more and more songs, we phased out the covers almost completely. Members of what was to become Wet Wet Wet were regulars, as was a guy called Arthur Haggerty, who managed Bruce's Record Shop by day, and was one of Glasgow's foremost promoters at night. He set up a gig in the Hardgate Halls, Duntocher, with The Zips supported by a band giving their debut performance. They were called Orange Juice."

For the most part, the Zips centred their activities in west Scotland, save a trip to Edinburgh to support Peel favourites the Flowers and to take part in the finals of a Battle of the Bands competition at the Venue in London. "We were fourth out of four, the token punk band. Even John Peel's presence on the judging panel wasn't enough to prevent Tina Charles, Biddu (her producer) and some other staid (deaf) industry types awarding first prize to some Midlands-based, soft-rockin', Fleetwood Mackin' retro-bates! Hey. I'm not bitter. Phil, disgusted, refused to come out and accept his runner-up tankard, and we extracted some sort of revenge by running up a champagne bar-tab on Tina's record company account. The following week our one and only 'live' review appeared in the Melody Maker. Reading between the lines of purple prose by Allan Jones, I think our performance was vindicated."

By the end of 1978 they had enough original material to consider recording. "We recorded all four songs on the Zips EP in a four-hour stint in the Burns' Howff pub in Glasgow, in 1978. We had to have the recording finished before 5pm, when they re-opened the bar. From memory we just made it! Backing vocals were done at Black Gold Studios in Kirkintilloch a couple of weeks later. The guy had the tape running in one room, and we had to listen through a door (no headphone facility) and try and shout in time with the track. Some of it worked, but the backing vocals on 'Don't Be Pushed Around' are ragged, to say the least. The master tape got sent away for pressing and the artwork for sleeves and labels went to separate printers – the whole thing took about six weeks to produce."

The four songs were finally released in April 1979. Black Gold Records, incidentally, was owned by a member of Middle Of The Road, of 'Chirpy Chirpy Cheep Cheep' fame. Local record shop owner Charlie 'Hannibal' Hayes provided the finance to press 500 copies, which brought plays from John Peel as well as regular airings on Radio Clyde. Instead of repressing it, they recorded a second single, the anti-nuke 'Radioactivity', at Sirocco Studios in Kilmarnock in January 1980, housed on their own Tenement Toons label in April 1980. This time the budget ran to 1,000 copies. The finance this time round came from Jackson's grandmother.

However, this time sales were disappointing with the media's gaze having shifted from punk, and the band found it tough to get gigs. When Jackson elected to emigrate to Australia that was the end of the Zips, who played their last show on 11 December 1980 at the Sandrianne Hotel in Kilmarnock.

And that was that. But not quite. Punk reissue specialists Detour Records contacted the band in 2002 with a tentative enquiry about including them on their Bored Teenagers Volume 2 compilation. The Zips reformed with guitarist John McMahon replacing Jackson for a special one-off gig for Detour Records at the Garage, London, in the spring of 2002, alongside the Negatives, Knife Edge and UXB. And they've kept at it ever since, playing the Wicker Man Festival etc, though McMahon was replaced by Brian Kerr (ex-Fire Exit). They also got round to recording two new CD EPs – 'Hotwired', in November 2002, and the 'Dumb Struck' EP in July 2004. A more contemporary affair, this tackled subjects including the Iraq War ('Not In Our Name') and the death of Marilyn Monroe ('Whodunnit?').

So, once a punk rocker, always a punk rocker? McNeill: "You only have to look at the charts any time in the last 25 years to see that there's always a need for punk. My taste in music hasn't changed in all those years – as Lou Reed said, 'If it's got any more than three chords, it's jazz'."

DISCOGRAPHY:

The Zips 7-inch EP (Black Gold Records April 1979)
I'm In Love/Over And Over/Take Me Down/Don't Be Pushed Around (500 copies)
Radioactivity/I'm Not Impressed 7-inch (Tenement Toons TEN01 January 1980) (1,000 copies)
Hotwired CD EP (Tenement Toons TEN05 November 2002)
King Money/Barbara Wire/Never Neverland/Sunburn/Drink To Forget
Dumb Struck CD EP (Tenement Toons July 2004) (Whoddunit/Not In Our Name/Govern Meant/Been There Too)
Compilations:
Bored Teenagers Volume 2 (Bin Liner Records Rubbish CD003 March 2001; 'Don't Be Pushed Around', 'I'm In Love')

Zones

Kenny Hyslop (drums), Russell Webb (bass), Billy McIsaac (keyboards), Willie Gardner (vocals, guitar)

The ZONES were formed in Glasgow by members of Slik and PVC2 after Midge Ure had flown the coop to join the Rich Kids, his place taken by former Hot Valves guitarist and vocalist Willie Gardner. They immediately signed with Bruce Findlay's Zoom Records (with whom they'd recorded the PVC2 single) and released the Webb composition 'Stuck With You'.

I asked Billy McIsaac how premeditated the switch to 'punk' status was. "It was a combination of factors. You've got to be influenced by what was happening at the time, there was a fairly monumental shift in music. It did rub off. It was a relief to get involved in something more 'credible', too. The other key issue was the fact that we'd got newer members in the band, particularly Willie Gardner, and he put his own stamp on things."

Findlay, remembered as being "tremendously enthusiastic" about the developing music scene, then took them to Arista as part of a distribution deal for Zoom. They gigged relentlessly during 1978, supporting Magazine on their Second Hand Daylight tour, cut two John Peel sessions and seemed set to make some kind of breakthrough. This mini-golden period climaxed in support slots with the Clash. "We supported them at the (Glasgow) Apollo. Paul Simonon approached us and said he'd enjoyed the set, and invited us down to the Rainbow. We headed down in a rickety old van. Ourselves, Sham 69 and the Clash were on the bill. We had a crap sound. Usual support band complaint, no soundcheck. We went on stage and sounded pretty dire. But these things happen. We still went down OK. It was just a great experience and a huge buzz."

But by now they were moving away from punk's musical strictures, increasingly highlighting McIsaac's synth. This was most notable on second single, the Graeme Douglas-produced 'Sign Of The Times', while 'Looking To The Future' employed reggae tempos. Neither clicked with record buyers, however. Nevertheless, Arista installed them at Manor Studios to record a debut album, which traced old glam influences such as Mott The Hoople as much as the energy of the new wave. "It was one of the first times when we were doing all our own material. (Future Talk Talk producer) Tim Friese-Green was producing. We were well psyched up, and we'd done plenty of rehearsals for the session. We went down and it was a great place to live and work. For 'Look Into The Future' we decided it would be great to have some saxophone on the track. The girl managing the studios said, 'My boyfriend plays sax, he's recording down the road.' It turned out she was talking about the guy who played the saxophone break on 'Baker Street' by Gerry Rafferty (top session player Raphael 'Raf' Ravenscroft, not, as the enduring urban myth would perpetuate, Bob Holness). Even to this day I remember the guy coming in and doing it in one take and putting down one incredible solo. That was a buzz."

After the album they toured with Iggy Pop, "which was a real... eye-opener," says McIsaac, resisting the temptation to divulge more than that. "We were young-ish men... " he says, before tailing off. The band broke up in November 1979. "It was down to ourselves pulling the plug, rather than Arista. The death knell was Willie having had enough. His girlfriend had taken very poorly. We were at the Music Machine in London. There were a few musical differences kicking about, but really the catalyst was his girlfriend's illness. He decided he was going back home, so we cancelled the Music Machine. And after that we just didn't want to carry it on any more."

That was it for the Zones, well, almost. Russell Webb: "When Willie went home to Glasgow to be with his girlfriend – who had meningitis – Midge, Kenny and I hastily arranged a gig at a rock café in Covent Garden – just to kill some time. It was a good gig and we played some old Slik songs as well as Zones, PVC2 and various covers."

I asked McIsaac if he had any regrets? "A lot of great things were expected of the band, and there was the possibility of building something quite substantial, but no regrets. You do the best you can at the time. I look back and I think of some things that I wrote that were performed in other bands, the lyrics were atrocious. But not necessarily with the Zones. But you're young and you do the best with what you have... We weren't an out and out punk band. We had a lot of energy, we put lots into it. I look back on it and I enjoyed the whole period. I was about 27 then, I was much older than the average punk, but I still felt I could relate to it, and I felt the energy of the time."

Hyslop and Webb joined the Skids before Hyslop went on to Simple Minds, whom Findlay would manage. Billy McIsaac now leads "Scotland's number one wedding band". The Billy McIsaac Band, natch. They'll probably play a version of 'Stuck With You' if you ask nicely.

DISCOGRAPHY:

Stuck With You/No Angels 7-inch (Zoom Zum 4 1978)
Sign Of The Times/Away From It All 7-inch (Arista ARIST 205 1978)
Looking To The Future/Do It All Again 7-inch (Arista ARIST 265 1979)

Under Influence LP (Arista SMART 1095 June 1979) (appeared in four different covers)
Mourning Star/Under Influence 7-inch (Arista ARIST 286 1979)

Zoot Alors

Kevin Thorpe (vocals), Alan Fearn (guitar), Pete Pearson (drums), Paul Sneap (bass, vocals)

Nottingham's ZOOT ALORS are noteworthy, aside from one distinguished single, for the fact that the band was one of the few of the punk era to grace children's TV. They appeared, as did Secret Affair, on the Get It Together show alongside presenter Roy North, famous for being Basil Brush's right-hand man, or possibly just right hand, if you prefer.

The group originally comprised bass player Paul Sneap and drummer Pete Pearson, who both appeared on the band's original demos. Fearn: "I sent off our original demo in response to an advert from a publishing company in Melody Maker. This was on a Tuesday afternoon. On the following Saturday morning, four days later, we were offered a publishing deal with Gas Songs/Heath Levy and a management deal with Ray Williams (also of Gas Songs) who had, in the early-70s, managed Elton John and was responsible for breaking him in the US. Our demo had been one of thousands sent in which had been thrown into a huge plastic dustbin. On their way home, staff at Gas would stick their hands in, lucky dip style, and listen on the tube home. Ray picked ours and immediately loved it. Tom McGuinness, ex-Manfred Mann etc, subsequently produced us. That's how I thought the music business worked – it had been the first tape I'd sent off!"

However, the rhythm section was subsequently axed from the band, much to Sneap's chagrin. Thorpe: "Ray Williams offered Alan and myself a publishing deal. Tom McGuinness bought the Gas back catalogue, so effectively became our publisher. We moved to London without Paul and Pete. It was hard to split, but it was the only way to keep the deal. Alan and myself worked in the clubs of Soho to keep the wolf at bay. But the wolf was a bastard. I lost my job at the Talk of the Town after going out on the piss with Cook and Jones of the Pistols. We were contracted to write three songs per month, not necessarily as Zoot Alors. Zoot Alors was signed to Decca for two singles and an album by Frank Rodgers – brother of Clodagh Rodgers – hence the FR prefix."

'Send Me A Postcard' was produced (or "over-produced", according to Thorpe) by Tom McGuinness and Lou Stonebridge, at Air No. 1 on Regent Street. "There are two mixes of 'Send Me A Postcard', both of which ended up being released. That was because the first was one was the wrong mix." It was given single of the week status by Mike Read, and the band were set to record a follow-up, 'Talk To Me' c/w 'OO Baby', the latter featuring the saxophone of Irish Earle, at Pye Studios in Marble Arch. However, Decca was then taken over by Polygram, and the single was never released.

There are tapes of several unrecorded compositions cut between 1977 and 1979 at St James's Studios in Nottingham, including 'Inside Out', 'Judy', 'Is It True?' and 'We're All Alone'. Thorpe also has demos cut at Heath Levy's Ariola Hansa Studios. After the abandoned second single, Zoot Alors broke up. Fearn re-emerged in Blue Train and scored a Billboard Top 100 single in the US, also playing with local act the Favourites. Thorpe continues to record and perform as a blues guitarist and singer, and it is not unknown for he and Fearn to collaborate together. Thorpe: "Where there's a song, there's a glimmer in the darkness... shit, sounds like another song comin' on... "

DISCOGRAPHY:

Send Me A Postcard/It's A Crime 7-inch (Decca FR13874 1979) (no picture sleeve, but issued as both a demo and stock copy featuring different versions. Thorpe: "I've seen copies of the single go for £150 – but I don't own one!")
Talk To Me/OO Baby 7-inch (Decca) (unreleased)

Zyklon B

Mark Ormrod (vocals), Kieron Palmer (bass), David Ross/Crabtree (guitar), Tony Ashworth (drums). Other members included Garry Evans (drums), Russell Moorhouse (keyboards) and Mark Frith (bass)

Blackpool's first punk band, ZYKLON B played their debut show at Poulton Library at the end of 1977, and were soon gigging around the area with forays into Manchester and Preston. Their leader was Mark Ormrod, and it was a textbook case of regional punk rock inspired by the Pistols' tabloid furore.

"Prior to 'year zero', I'd had no interest at all in any form of music – I would turn the TV over when TOTP was broadcast! Not for me, even though I had an elder brother whose definitive collection of prog rock I could trawl through to gain a foothold in the contemporary music scene. I liked football – and that was it. Having said that though, I did attend youth club discos where the 'big lads' danced to Northern Soul, and if I had to pin my colours to any mast, Northern would have been it. Onward, fevered discussions whilst reading articles in the Daily Mirror about outrageous bank clerks festooned with safety pins. Was this the 'end of days'? Our imaginations went into overdrive – let's form a band!"

That band was, initially, the Plastic Lizards – Ormrod on vocals, Dave Crabtree on guitar, Tony Ashworth on drums, Kieron Palmer on bass and Andrew Cross on guitar. Their only show was in Palmer's garage before a bemused collection of six school friends "covered in gob".That was enough for Cross, who promptly left. "At this point we'd moved from rank amateurs to obsessed collectors. We'd test each other's knowledge daily. "Who's the drummer in the Lurkers? What label are the Desperate Bicycles on?" etc. Punk Rock had now become THE most important driving force in all our tiny lives." Though not necessarily for Kieron Palmer, who promptly joined the armed forces. His replacement was Mark Frith, who brought a more 'chaotic' element to the band. "He once turned up at a gig bearing pig's heads as gifts." He also introduced the name Zyklon B. "We thought it looked great, the right combination of vowels and weird consonants. Germanic to boot, so any excuse to have a dig at the older generation! Only later were we to realise the connotations."

Their first recordings were made in January 1978 at Cargo Studios in Rochdale, with "John Peel/favourite uncle look-alike" John Brierley engineering. The six tracks were recorded in eight hours, "all sounding very 'tinny' with 'swirly' cymbal crashes and guide vocal tracks still audible at the final mix. We didn't care though (we didn't know, actually!) We'd got out of our pre-determined lives and managed to break free!" Among the tracks recorded at the session were 'School', 'Weapons', 'Prophet Said' and 'People In Glass Houses'.

Better gigs followed. "We regularly played at Poulton-le-Fylde Old Library building, a former Masonic meeting house with Tardis-type qualities with other rudimentary local bands like Section 25 and The Final Solution. There would always be a 'mass jam' at the end of every gig." Other shows were booked at the Bispham Community Centre with Speed, Male Models and Section 25, Blackpool Collegiate Sixth Form with the Membranes, Kirkham Palms Disco with the Membranes, Jalgo's Club in Preston, the Mardi Gras Night Club in Blackpool, and an all-day event at the Stanley Park Bandstand.

Despite being celebrated as "Blackpool's best punk band" by John Robb when he was MCing the 2005 Wasted festival, they never got a record out, though earlier tapes were scoured to produce their contribution to the 2005 regional compilation The Ugly Truth, 'Manic Depressive'. Roger Wikeley joined on bass towards the end of their brief career as Zyklon B. "As 78 moved toward 79 our musical horizons had leapt in quantum bounds. Punk rock had now officially been declared dead, and as four aspiring young gunslingers we too had moved on to post-punk-industrial-Factory type stuff, and more line-up changes." They'd become Syntax in 1978, who recorded one song on the 'Blackpool Rox' compilation EP. The name change was partially inspired by growing fears that their original name might attract Nazi accusations.

Syntax have now reformed, with various members of fellow local travellers Section 25 and Tunnel Vision.

COMPILATIONS:

Blackpool Rox 7-inch EP (Vinyl Drip 1 1980) (includes Syntax's 'Dot Dot', plus tracks from the Ken Turner Set, Section 25 and the Membranes)

The Ugly Truth Volume 1 CD (Just Say No To Government Music JSNTGM 018 August 2005; 'Manic Depressive') (also included is Syntax's 'Dot Dot')

Punk DVDs
FROM CHERRY RED RECORDS
CRDVD 001N Dead Kennedys - DMPO's On Broadway
CRDVD 003N Buzzcocks - Auf Weidersehen
CRDVD 005N Johnny Thunders - Dead Or Alive
CRDVD 006N Punk & Disorderly - The DVD, Various
CRDVD 008 The Exploited - Rock N Roll Outlaws / Sexual Favours
CRDVD 10 Toy Dolls - We're Mad / Idle Gossip
CRDVD 15 Peter & The Test Tube Babies - Cattle & Bum / Live In Manchester
CRDVD 16 Adicts - Joker In The Pack
CRDVD 17 Extreme Noise Terror - From One Extreme To Another
CRDVD 21 Slaughter & The Dogs - Cranked Up Really High
CRDVD 22 UK/DK & Holidays In The Sun - Various
CRDVD 26 One Way System - No Return / All Systems Go
CRDVD 27 GBH - Live At The Ace, Brixton
CRDVD 29 UK Subs - Live At The Retford Porterhouse
CRDVD 30 The Fall - Perverted By Language / Live At Leeds
CRDVD 41 GBH - Kawasaki Live / Brit Boys Attacked By Brats
CRDVD 43 Chelsea - Live At The Bier Keller
CRDVD 44 999 - Feelin' Alright With The Crew
CRDVD 49 The Exploited - 83-87 / Live At The Palm Cove
CRDVD 51 Vibrators - 1976-2004
CRDVD 54 The Lurkers - Bollurks, The European Tour
CRDVD 55 Young Marble Giants - Live At The Hurrah
CRDVD 62 Burning Britain - The DVD (The History of UK Punk 1980-1984)
CRDVD 65 Oi! Oi! Oi! - Highlights from over 2 decades of Oi!
CRDVD 68 Eater - Live - Outside View
CRDVD 69 Punk & Disorderly 2 - Further Charges - Various
CRDVD 72 The Business - Surburban Rebels - Live at Rio's
CRDVD 76 Menace - GLC
CRDVD 77 Eddie & The Hot Rods - Do Anything You Wanna Do
CRDVD 79 The Drones - Further Temptations
CRDVD 82 Holidays In The Sun - Various
CRDVD 88 Red Alert - Take No Prisoners
CRDVD 90 The Varukers - Live: Protest and Survive
CRDVD 94 GBH - Live in Los Angeles / Live at Victoria Hall
CRDVD 95 Angelic Upstarts - Solidarity
CRDVD 97 Vice Squad - Last Rockers: The Vice Squad Story
CRDVD 101 Germs - Media Blitz, The Germs Story
CRDVD 102 Subhumans - All Gone Live
CRDVD 105 Spizzenergi - Where's Captain Kirk?
CRDVD 106 Newtown Neurotics - The Long Goodbye
CRDVD 115 Nothin' But Trash - Various
CRDVD 120 Wendy O Williams - Bump 'n' Grind
CRDVD 125 D.O.A. - Live at the Assassination Club
CRDVD 126 The Boys - Sick On You
CRDVD 130 Goldblade - Testify!
CRDVD 131 The Exploited - Live in Japan / Live in Argentina
CRDVD 132 Punk On The Road - Various
CRDVD 134 English Dogs - Psycho Killer
CRDVD 140 New Bomb Turks - Reigning on Edinburgh: Live
VISDVD 003N Black Flag - Live
CHERRY RED FILMS
The above DVD's featured on this inlay are available in all good record stores, distributed by Pinnacle. Alternatively, they can be ordered directly from Cherry Red Records mail order department on 0208 740 4110 or via the website
www.cherryred.co.uk
CAN YOU HELP? Have you any suggestions for releases that would work as part of our DVD series or as a Cherry Red release? If so, please e-mail ideas@cherryred.co.uk or write to Cherry Red Records, Unit 3a, Long Island House, 1-4 Warple Way, London W3 0RG

downloads

analog baroque

SIDEWINDER SOUNDS

FiveFour

GIANT STEPS RECORDINGS

The Cherry Red Records download shop has arrived. We have thousands of tracks available from many of your favourite Cherry Red Records associated labels and artists, including some extremely rare material previously unreleased on CD. The tracks are available in MP3 format, so are compatible with the majority of digital players (including the ipod). Visit *www.cherryred.co.uk/downloads* to discover material from artists such as ***Dead Kennedys, Felt, Alien Sex Fiend, Marc Almond, Momus, Everything But The Girl, Sid Vicious, Cabaret Voltaire, Clifford T. Ward, Cockney Rejects, Graham Parker, Marc Bolan, Nico, Spencer Davis Group, The Runaways*** and many others.

ALSO AVAILABLE FROM CHERRY RED

Those Were The Days

Stefan Granados

An Unofficial History of the Beatles' Apple Organization 1967-2002

Paper covers, 300 pages including photographs £14.99 in UK

The Rolling Stones: Complete Recording Sessions 1962-2002

Martin Elliott

Paper covers, 576 pages plus 16 pages of photographs £14.99 in UK

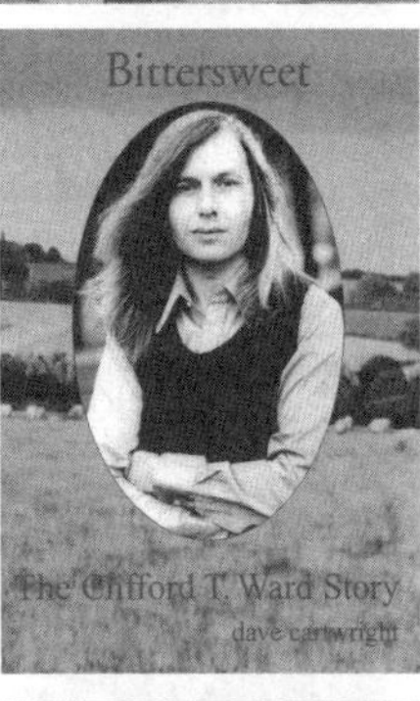

Goodnight Jim Bob – On The Road With Carter The Unstoppable Sex Machine

Jim Bob

Paper covers, 228 pages plus 16 pages of photographs £12.99 in UK

Our Music Is Red - With Purple Flashes: The Story Of The Creation

Sean Egan

Paper covers, 378 pages plus 8 pages of photographs £14.99 in UK

Bittersweet: The Clifford T Ward Story

David Cartwright

Paper covers, 352 pages plus 8 pages of photographs £14.99 in UK

The Secret Life of a Teenage Punk Rocker: The Andy Blade Chronicles

Andy Blade

Paper covers, 224 pages and photographs throughout. £12.99 in UK

Burning Britain

Ian Glasper

Paper covers, 410 pages and photographs throughout £14.99 in UK

Truth... Rod Stewart, Ron Wood And The Jeff Beck Group

Dave Thompson

Paper covers, 208 pages plus four pages of photographs. £14.99 in UK

www.cherryred.co.uk